THE OXFORD HANDB

THE FRENCH REVOLUTION

The Oxford Handbook of the French Revolution brings together a sweeping range of expert and innovative contributions to offer engaging and thought-provoking insights into the history and historiography of this epochal event. Each chapter presents the foremost summations of academic thinking on key topics, along with stimulating and provocative interpretations and suggestions for future research directions. Placing core dimensions of the history of the French Revolution in their transnational and global contexts, the contributors demonstrate that revolutionary times demand close analysis of sometimes tiny groups of key political actors—whether the king and his ministers or the besieged leaders of the Jacobin republic—and attention to the deeply local politics of both rural and urban populations. Identities of class, gender and ethnicity are interrogated, but so too are conceptions and practices linked to citizenship, community, order, security, and freedom: each in their way just as central to revolutionary experiences, and equally amenable to critical analysis and reflection.

This *Handbook* covers the structural and political contexts that build up to give new views on the classic question of the 'origins of revolution'; the different dimensions of personal and social experience that illuminate the political moment of 1789 itself; the goals and dilemmas of the period of constitutional monarchy; the processes of destabilisation and ongoing conflict that ended that experiment; the key issues surrounding the emergence and experience of 'terror'; and the short- and long-term legacies, for both good and ill, of the revolutionary trauma—for France, and for global politics.

David Andress received his DPhil from the University of York in 1995, and has worked at the University of Portsmouth for the last twenty-five years. He has published widely on the French Revolution, from micro-studies of Parisian responses in 1789–91 to introductory textbooks, and from monographs to major syntheses and works of comparative history.

Contributors

Micah Alpaugh, David Andress, Pierre-Yves Beaurepaire, Marc Belissa, David A. Bell, Howard G. Brown, Simon Burrows, Ambrogio Caiani, Kirsty Carpenter, Jean-Luc Chappey, Lauren R. Clay, Manuel Covo, Malcolm Crook, Philip Dwyer, Dan Edelstein, Joël Félix, Michael P. Fitzsimmons, Alan Forrest, Paul R. Hanson, John Hardman, Jennifer Ngaire Heuer, Jeff Horn, Annie Jourdan, Thomas E. Kaiser, Marisa Linton, Silvia Marzagalli, Laura Mason, Peter McPhee, Noelle Plack, Jeremy D. Popkin, Mike Rapport, Jay M. Smith, Ronen Steinberg, D. M. G. Sutherland, Charles Walton, Edward J. Woell, Isser Woloch.

THE OXFORD HANDBOOK OF

THE FRENCH

REVOLUTION

Edited by
DAVID ANDRESS

OXFORD
UNIVERSITY PRESS

OXFORD
UNIVERSITY PRESS

Great Clarendon Street, Oxford, OX2 6DP,
United Kingdom

Oxford University Press is a department of the University of Oxford.
It furthers the University's objective of excellence in research, scholarship,
and education by publishing worldwide. Oxford is a registered trade mark of
Oxford University Press in the UK and in certain other countries

© Oxford University Press 2015

The moral rights of the author have been asserted

First published 2015
First published in paperback 2019

Published in the United States of America by Oxford University Press
198 Madison Avenue, New York, NY 10016, United States of America

British Library Cataloguing in Publication Data
Data available

Library of Congress Cataloging in Publication Data
Data available

ISBN 978–0–19–963974–8 (Hbk.)
ISBN 978–0–19–884594–2 (Pbk.)

Cover illustration: Sketch by Jacques-Louis David of the
Tennis Court Oath 1789 © World History Archive/Alamy

Links to third party websites are provided by Oxford in good faith and
for information only. Oxford disclaims any responsibility for the materials
contained in any third party website referenced in this work.

FOREWORD

Although the demise of the French Revolution as a field of active study has sometimes been prophesied, and in recent years cautioned against if a new 'paradigm' is not
found to revive it, in practice it is an area prone to recall the biblical injunction that:
'Of the making of many books there is no end, and much study is a weariness of the
flesh' (Ecclesiastes 12:12). A recitation of the edited collections that have appeared in
French, English and other major languages devoted to the events and antecedents of
the 1790s, even limited to those after the flood of bicentennial celebrations of the 1990s,
would absorb more space than is available here.[1]

One of the challenges of producing a major collection on the French Revolution is
thus to avoid the thought 'Oh no, not again!' in the mind of the prospective, yet potentially already jaded, reader. This was particularly the case with this collection, as it began
construction when a volume under Peter McPhee's editorship, *A Companion to the
French Revolution*, was already underway, and a second text, *The Routledge Companion
to the French Revolution in World History*, was in formation.[2] As this editor is not alone
in having contributions to all of these volumes, the challenge is only redoubled.

This volume seeks to be an original, complementary, and engaging contribution by
looking both backwards and forwards in ways which are unlike the parallel offerings
mentioned. Global contexts and perspectives, for both the French Revolution and the
Age of Revolutions in general, are a significant and fruitful development in current historiography.[3] Understandings of the French Revolution as part of an 'Atlantic world',
and writings about events in the French Antilles, have flourished in recent decades.[4]
Indeed, while the first generation of scholars to write of the 'Atlantic Revolution' did so
without mentioning Haiti, the events which overtook people of all colours on French
Saint-Domingue now merit, quite rightly, treatment as one of the major revolutions of
the era.[5]

It is precisely for that reason—that the French Revolution in its Atlantic dimension
now represents an entire field of historiography in itself—that this collection chooses
to return its focus, thematically at least, on to new developments in historiogra-
phies of events within European France. This is not to say that wider perspectives are
neglected: our very first chapter on economic and demographic developments in the
eighteenth century points clearly to the significance of colonial trade in understanding the state of the nation in the years before 1789. The chapters immediately following, though, show that on very 'traditional' questions of the role of the bourgeoisie, the
nobility, and the monarchy itself in that situation, there are still important new debates,
and as-yet unanswered key questions to be posed.

In general, this is the pattern for the whole volume. Individual authors were asked to write about what made their particular area still an active field of debate, to review the 'state of the art' in current understanding, and to suggest ways forward for future research. Some chapters offer in themselves striking new interpretations—Lauren Clay on the pre-revolutionary bourgeoisie is one such, as is Simon Burrows on the extent to which the pre-revolutionary literary sphere was simply not what a previous generation of historians assumed it was. Contributions such as those of Ambrogio Caiani, Charles Walton, Marisa Linton, and Ronen Steinberg represent significant new work as well as opening spheres of exploration for the future. But to name those is only to give examples of one kind of valuable approach here.

Kirsty Carpenter, Marc Belissa, and Mike Rapport draw together strands of their own and others' work on still relatively neglected areas of the border-crossing impact of the Revolution. Manuel Covo demonstrates that we do not need to look to the Caribbean to see the direct impact of slavery and race, for it penetrated to the heart of debates in Versailles and Paris. Michael Fitzsimmons, Jeremy Popkin, and Peter McPhee are among those who take superficially straightforward topics and add an original and thought-provoking twist of chronology, setting or conclusion. And thus I have named only a third of what is on offer here. The rest is for the reader to discover.

In aiming to put a twist on existing debates, there may appear to be some surprising absences: contributors have, for example, tended to write around the question of actual violent conflict with counter-revolution, rather than zoom in on it as an issue. Perhaps even more disconcertingly, there is no 'gender chapter' in this collection.[6] Contributors were asked to consider the place of gender within the various topics they were discussing, and to treat it as a mode of analysis wherever appropriate. This is visible, for example, in Kirsty Carpenter's chapter on emigration, in Jean-Luc Chappey's discussion of elite reconstruction in the later 1790s, and as part of my own understanding of the sans-culotte phenomenon and crowd activity in general. Jeremy Popkin's treatment of revolutionary identities addresses what some women tried, and failed, to get from the determinedly masculine political sphere of the 1790s. Jennifer Heuer's wide overview of revolutionary legacies discusses gendered issues from contests over women's perceived 'place' in post-revolutionary society to the mutilated masculinity of injured war veterans. Marisa Linton's reading of the personal stakes of terrorist politics is a study, among other things, of the construction of a certain form of public and private masculinity. I hope readers will agree, ultimately, that the absence of gender from the contents page has produced an enhanced sense of the integration of such issues into the wider landscape of thematic debate.

Such continuing debate is the ultimate goal of this volume. We have, as contributors, set out to ask more questions than we answer, or at the very least, to reframe old answers and new understandings in a way that will point others to new and better questions of their own. We offer new opportunities for reflection on the revolutionary past, in a decade that has already seen more than its share of upheavals in the name of revolutionary futures. Many of those recent events have run out of the control of their more optimistic advocates in ways that might seem very familiar to a French *émigré* in 1794, or an exiled regicide a generation later. It is not the historian's job to preach solutions—and indeed the history of beliefs about revolution over the last 200 years illustrates the problem of trying to do so all too neatly.[7] But if history does have a role in the public sphere, it is surely to promote a more reflective approach to the kind of very vexed questions—of social justice, of power in its manifestations both subtle and violent, of freedom and its limits, and of the intersection of all these things with the two contemporary shibboleths of identities and rights—that the French Revolution allows us to discuss. If this volume makes a small contribution to such a large and urgent goal, we will be more than satisfied.

It remains only for me to thank all my fellow contributors, with a special mention for Manuel Covo, who stepped in as a very-close-to-last-minute replacement. Thanks also to Christine Baycroft for her translation work, to Christopher Wheeler for commissioning this volume originally, and to Cathryn Steele and Michael Dela Cruz for taking it forward through production. If I use my editorial privilege at this point to name my own family, Jessica, Emily and Natalie, as the ones that keep me going, I will also gladly note that they stand among a crowd of those who do the same for all of us who have written here.

David Andress

Notes

1. For a brief discussion of why I think alarm over lost paradigms is misplaced, see my 'Introduction: Revolutionary historiography, adrift or at large? The paradigmatic quest versus the exploration of experience', in David Andress (ed.), *Experiencing the French Revolution* (Oxford, 2013), 1–15.
2. Peter McPhee (ed.), *A Companion to the French Revolution* (Chichester, 2013); Alan Forrest and Matthias Middell (eds), *The Routledge Companion to the French Revolution in World History* (forthcoming in 2015).
3. Suzanne Desan, Lynn Hunt, and William Max Nelson (eds), *The French Revolution in Global Perspective* (Ithaca, NY, 2013); David Armitage and Sanjay Subrahmanyan (eds), *The Age of Revolutions in Global Context* (Basingstoke, 2010).
4. See Nicholas Canny and Philip Morgan (eds), *The Oxford Handbook of the Atlantic World 1450–1850* (Oxford, 2011), including chapters by Silvia Marzagalli and David Geggus on French/Haitian events and structures, and many other contributions that include comparative discussion of French engagement in social, economic, and political developments.
5. Jacques Godechot, *France and the Atlantic Revolution of the Eighteenth Century, 1770–1799* (New York, 1965), contains no reference to Saint-Domingue/Haiti. Slavery is noted simply as a form of agriculture in the Americas, and as an unresolved problem of the United States Constitution: 10–11, 37–9. More recent historiography that explodes this view is summarised in Jeremy D. Popkin, *A Concise History of the Haitian Revolution* (Malden, MA, 2012). For unequivocal discussion of Haiti as a revolution worthy of comparison with the canonical events of the period, see Wim Klooster, *Revolutions in the Atlantic World; a comparative history* (New York, 2009).

6. In keeping with the theme of complementarity, chapters on both topics can be found in McPhee (ed.), *Companion*: Anne Verjus, 'Gender, Sexuality and Political Culture', 196–211; Jean-Clément Martin, 'The Vendée, chouannerie, and the State, 1791–99', 246–59. There is also an excellent piece by Suzanne Desan, 'The French Revolution and the Family', 470–85, which could have found a home in the present volume, had she not already written it.

7. A subject on which I have blogged: www.historymatters.group.shef.ac.uk/return-revolutions/>

Contents

PART III REVOLUTION AND CONSTITUTION

PART IV COUNTER-REVOLUTION AND COLLAPSE

LIST OF CONTRIBUTORS

Micah Alpaugh is Assistant Professor of History at the University of Central Missouri, after teaching at the University of Pennsylvania, Mount Allison University and University of California-Irvine. His first book, *Nonviolence and the French Revolution: Political Demonstrations in Paris, 1787–1795* is being published by Cambridge University Press.

David Andress is Professor of Modern History at the University of Portsmouth, UK. His major publications include *The French Revolution and the People* (London, 2004), *The Terror: Civil War in the French Revolution* (London, 2005), and, as editor, *Experiencing the French Revolution*, SVEC 2013: 05 (Oxford, 2013).

Pierre-Yves Beaurepaire is Professor at the University of Nice, fellow of the Institut Universitaire de France. Chair of the international programme of research 'Communicating Europe: Circulations, netwoks and territories', he has published *La France des Lumieres 1715–1789* (Paris, 2011) and with Silvia Marzagalli, *Atlas de la Révolution française, circulation des hommes et des idées, 1770–1804* (Paris, 2010).

Marc Belissa is maître de conférences and directeur de recherche in Modern History at the University of Paris Ouest Nanterre – CHISCO. He has published numerous books on the eighteenth century, the Enlightenment and the French Revolution, including *Fraternité universelle et intérêt national. Les cosmopolitiques du droit des gens* (Paris, 1998), *Repenser l'ordre européen, 1795–1802* (Paris, 2006), and with Yannick Bosc *Robespierre. La Fabrication d'un mythe* (Paris, 2013).

David A. Bell is Sidney and Ruth Lapidus Professor in the Era of North Atlantic Revolutions at Princeton University. He is the author of *Lawyers and Citizens* (Oxford, 1994), *The Cult of the Nation in France* (Oxford, 2001), and *The First Total War: Napoleon's Europe and the Birth of Warfare As We Know It* (Boston, 2007).

Howard G. Brown is Professor of History at Binghamton University (State University of New York). He has published several books, most notably *Ending the French Revolution: Violence, Justice, and Repression from the Terror to Napoleon* (Charlottesville, 2006), as well as numerous essays on politics and violence in French history. His latest research examines the psychological and cultural impact of violence from the sixteenth to nineteenth centuries.

Simon Burrows is Professor of History at the University of Western Sydney, Australia. He has also worked at the universities of Waikato and Leeds. He is principal investigator of the ground-breaking 'French Book Trade in Enlightenment Europe' database project; author of three books; and co-editor of collections on the press and public sphere; cultural transfers; and the Chevalier d'Eon.

Ambrogio A. Caiani is Senior Lecturer in Modern European History at the University of Kent. His chief publication to date is *Louis XVI and the French Revolution* (Cambridge, 2012). He is in the process of preparing a second book tentatively entitled: *Napoleon versus the Pope*. Together with Michael Broers of Oxford University he has edited a two volume collection of essays, the *History of the European Restorations*, to be published by Bloomsbury in 2019.

Kirsty Carpenter is Associate Professor in History at Massey University, New Zealand. Her research concerns the émigrés and their connections to French Revolution politics and British and European literature. *Eugénie et Mathilde by Madame de Souza* has just been published by the MHRA (Critical Texts, Vol. 26). She is the author of: *Refugees of the French Revolution, Émigrés in London 1789–1802* (New York, 1999), and *The Novels of Madame de Souza in Social and Political Perspective* (Bern, 2007).

Jean-Luc Chappey is Professeur universités en histoire moderne at the Université de Paris 1 Panthéon-Sorbonne. He is a member of the Institut d'histoire moderne et contemporaine (UMR 8066 CNRS), and associated with the Institut d'histoire de la révolution française (UMS 622 CNRS). His most recent work is *Ordres et désordres biographiques. Listes de noms, dictionnaires et réputation entre Lumières et Wikipedia* (Seyssel, 2013).

Lauren R. Clay, Assistant Professor of History at Vanderbilt University, is the author of *Stagestruck: The Business of Theater in Eighteenth-Century France and Its Colonies* (Ithaca, NY, 2013), as well as articles on professional performance in early modern France. Her current research addresses the culture of commercial capitalism in France during the age of Revolution.

Manuel Covo is an Assistant Professor in the Department of History at the University of California, Santa Barbara. His research explores the transition from early modern to modern European colonialism in the long eighteenth century, specialising in French imperialism, political economy and Atlantic revolutions. He has published a number of articles and chapters, and is a 2018–19 Barbara Thom Postdoctoral Fellow at the Huntington Library.

Malcolm Crook is Emeritus Professor of French History at Keele University. Among his publications are *Elections in the French Revolution, An Apprenticeship in Democracy, 1789–1799* (Cambridge, 1996) and *Revolutionary France 1780–1880* (Oxford, 2002). He has just completed a book entitled *How the French Learned to Vote*.

Philip Dwyer is Director of the Centre for the History of Violence at the University of Newcastle, Australia. His primary research interest is eighteenth century Europe. He is the author of *Napoleon, 1769–1799: The Path to Power* (London and New Haven, 2007 and 2008), and *Citizen Emperor: Napoleon in Power, 1799–1815* (London and New Haven, 2013).

Dan Edelstein, Professor of French and (by courtesy) History, Stanford University, is the author of *The Terror of Natural Right: Republicanism, the Cult of Nature, and the French Revolution* (Chicago, 2009), and *The Enlightenment: A Genealogy* (Chicago, 2010). He is also the editor of *The Super-Enlightenment* (Oxford, 2010); and, with Keith Baker, of *Scripting Revolution* (Stanford University Press, forthcoming).

Joël Félix is Professor of History at the University of Reading. His research focuses on the transition from the old regime to the modern world, in particular, by exploring the impact of fiscal issues on domestic development and the international order. His main publications include *Finances et politique au siècle des Lumières. Le ministère L'Averdy, 1763–1768* (Paris, 1999), *Louis XVI et Marie-Antoinette. Un couple en politique* (Paris, 2006). He is currently completing a book on the Fiscal Origins of the French Revolution, 1688–1789.

Michael P. Fitzsimmons is Professor of History at Auburn University Montgomery. He is the author of *The Parisian Order of Barristers and the French Revolution* (Cambridge, MA, 1987), *The Remaking of France* (Cambridge, 1994), *The Night the Old Regime Ended* (University Park, PA, 2003), and *From Artisan to Worker* (Cambridge, 2010), as well as articles in the *American Historical Review, French History* and the *Historical Journal*.

Alan Forrest is Emeritus Professor of Modern History at the University of York. He has written widely on the history of Revolutionary and Napoleonic France and the history of modern warfare. Recent books include *The Legacy of the French Revolutionary Wars* (Cambridge, 2009), *Napoleon* (London, 2011), and (co-edited with Etienne François and Karen Hagemann), *War Memories: The Revolutionary and Napoleonic Wars in Modern European Culture* (Basingstoke, 2012).

Paul R. Hanson is Professor of History at Butler University. He is currently at work on a book comparing the French Terror to the Chinese Cultural Revolution.

John Hardman, formerly lecturer in history at the University of Edinburgh, has published widely on the history of the French monarchy in the later eighteenth century. Among his works are *Louis XVI: The Silent King* (London, 2000), and *Overture to Revolution: The 1787 Assembly of Notables and the Crisis of France's Old Regime* (Oxford, 2010).

Jennifer Ngaire Heuer is an Associate Professor at the University of Massachusetts Amherst. She is the author of *The Family and the Nation: Gender and Citizenship in Revolutionary France* (Ithaca, NY, 2007). Her essays have appeared in journals including *French History, History Compass, Annales historiques de la révolution française, Clio: histoire, femmes et sociétés,* and *Law and History*.

Jeff Horn, Professor of History at Manhattan College, is the author or editor of six books. He recently completed a biography tentatively entitled *The Making of Terrorist: Alexandre Rousselin and the French Revolution* currently under review and is writing a textbook, *A People's History of the World* for Oxford University Press that is slated to appear in 2022.

Annie Jourdan is research fellow at the University of Amsterdam, European Studies. Her publications include: *La Révolution, une exception française?* (Paris, 2004); *La Révolution batave entre la France et l'Amérique* (Rennes, 2008), *L'empire de Napoléon* (Paris, 2000); *Napoléon. Héros, Imperator, Mécène* (Paris, 1998). Her next book will be on the French Revolution in comparative perspective.

Thomas E. Kaiser, Professor of History, University of Arkansas at Little Rock, is a specialist in eighteenth century French politics and culture, has published more than thirty articles and book chapters and has co-edited two volumes of essays. His principal current interest lies in court and diplomatic history, and he is currently preparing a book entitled *Marie-Antoinette and the Austrian Plot, 1748–1794.*

Marisa Linton is reader in History at Kingston University, UK. She has written extensively on the French Revolution. She is the author of *Choosing Terror, Virtue, Friendship and Authenticity in the French Revolution* (Oxford, 2013), *The Politics of Virtue in Enlightenment France* (Basingstoke, 2001), and the co-editor of *Conspiracy in the French Revolution* (Manchester, 2007).

Silvia Marzagalli is full-time professor at the University of Nice and senior member of the Institut Universitaire de France. Her research focuses on merchant networks and warfare reorganization of maritime trade flows. Recent books dealing with the Revolutionary period include: (with M. Biard and P. Bourdin) *Révolution Consulat et Empire* (Paris, 2009), (with P.-Y. Beaurepaire)*Atlas de la Révolution française. Circulations des hommes et des idées, 1770–1804* (Paris, 2010), and *Bordeaux et les États-Unis, 1776–1815: politique et stratégies négociantes dans la genèse d'un réseau commercial* (Geneva, 2015).

Laura Mason, senior lecturer in History and the Program in Film & Media Studies at Johns Hopkins University, is the author of *Singing the French Revolution: Popular Culture and Revolutionary Politics* (Ithaca, NY, 1996) and numerous articles on French revolutionary political culture. She is completing a study of the Directory entitled *The Last Revolutionaries: The Conspiracy Trial of Gracchus Babeuf and the Equals.*

Peter McPhee is an Emeritus Professor at the University of Melbourne, where he was Provost until 2009. His most recent books are *Robespierre: a Revolutionary Life* (London and New Haven, 2012) and *Liberty or Death: the French Revolution, 1789–1799* (London and New Haven, 2016). He was awarded the Order of Australia in 2012 for services to education.

Noelle Plack is reader in French History at Newman University, Birmingham, UK. The author of numerous articles, chapters and *Common Land, Wine and the French Revolution; Rural Society and Economy in Southern France, c. 1789–1820* (Farnham, 2009), her current project explores the intersection of wine drinking, taxation, and popular rebellion in France from 1789 to 1848.

Jeremy D. Popkin is T. Marshall Hahn, Jr Professor of History at the University of Kentucky. His books on the French Revolution include *Revolutionary News: The Press* *in France, 1789–1799* (Durham, NC, 1990), *You Are All Free: The Haitian Revolution and the Abolition of Slavery* (Cambridge, 2010), and *A Short History of the French Revolution* (New York, 6th edn, 2015).

Mike Rapport is reader in Modern European History at the University of Glasgow. His publications include *The Napoleonic Wars: A Very Short Introduction* (Oxford, 2013), *1848: Year of Revolution* (London, 2009), *Nineteenth Century Europe* (Basingstoke, 2005), and *Nationality and Citizenship in Revolutionary France: the Treatment of Foreigners* (Oxford, 2000).

Jay M. Smith is Professor of History at the University of North Carolina, Chapel Hill. His major works include *Nobility Reimagined: The Patriotic Nation in Eighteenth-Century France* (Ithaca, NY, 2005), and *Monsters of the Gévaudan: The Making of a Beast* (Cambridge, MA, 2011).

Ronen Steinberg is Assistant Professor of History at Michigan State University. His research interests include transitional justice and trauma theory. His book, *The Afterlives of the Terror: Facing the Legacies of Mass Violence in Post-Revolutionary France*, is being published by Cornell University Press.

D. M. G. Sutherland teaches at the University of Maryland. The themes of his work include collective violence that destabilized the Revolution. An example would be the Catholic and counter-revolutionary peasants in the West of France: *The Chouans* (Oxford, 1982). Another would be the ferocity of both the White Terror and extreme Jacobinism in the Midi: *Murder in Aubagne: Lynching, Law, and Justice during the French Revolution* (Cambridge, 2009).

Charles Walton, reader in History at the University of Warwick, is author of *Policing Public Opinion in the French Revolution: The Culture of Calumny and the Problem of Free Speech* (New York, 2009). He is Director of the Eighteenth Century Centre at the University of Warwick and is currently writing a book on reciprocity and redistribution in the French Revolution.

Edward J. Woell is a Professor of History at Western Illinois University. He is the author of *Small-Town Martyrs and Murderers: Religious Revolution and Counterrevolution in Western France, 1774–1914* (Milwaukee, 2006) as well as several articles and book chapters. His current research and writing focuses on the confluence of religion and politics in small towns during the French Revolution.

Isser Woloch is the Moore Collegiate Professor of History Emeritus at Columbia University. His books include *Jacobin Legacy* (Princeton, 1970), *The New Regime: Transformations of the French Civic Order, 1789–1820s* (New York, 1994), and *Napoleon and his Collaborators: the Making of a Dictatorship* (New York, 2001). His most recent publication is *The Postwar Moment: Progressive Forces in Britain, France, and the United States After World War II* (New Haven and London, 2019).

PART I

ORIGINS

CHAPTER 1

....

ECONOMIC AND DEMOGRAPHIC DEVELOPMENTS

....

SILVIA MARZAGALLI

MANY of those who witnessed the events of 1789 were aware of the importance of the French Revolution, and debate over its causes began long before the radicalization that led Louis XVI to the guillotine. Whereas some authors pointed to the depravity of French morals as its major cause, others, like John Robinson, professor of philosophy at the University of Edinburgh and secretary of the Royal Society, privileged conspiracy theories, conceiving the Revolution as the result of a destructive alliance between Bavarian *Illuminati* and Freemasons.[1] Some contemporaries, however, conceived the Revolution as the consequence of long-lasting processes: while waiting to be guillotined in 1793, Barnave explained the outbreak of the Revolution as the result of eighteenth century economic changes and growing political opposition between the aristocracy and the monarchy.[2] In doing so, he initiated a historiographical tradition conceiving the Revolution as the ineluctable issue of a complex set of structural forces on the move.

Since the 1790s, the causes of the French Revolution, a founding moment of French political life as well as a seminal event for Europe and parts of other continents, have been widely, and often polemically, discussed. The debate on the origins of the Revolution and its driving forces is entangled in the even harsher controversies on the inner logics—or teleology—of the revolutionary process once it had started, on its alleged 'degeneration' into mass violence, and in the diverging evaluations of its consequences in terms of costs and benefits.[3]

More than other historiographical issues, the French Revolution is controversial. The general acknowledgement that it represented a crucial event (or process) leading to a society and a political system grounded on new principles increases the verve of those who prize or disdain the Revolution. If they undoubtedly offer an interesting glimpse into historians' age and culture, opposite interpretations make it difficult for readers to reach a coherent understanding of the revolutionary process itself: how it came into being, the respective importance of economic and demographic factors versus political and cultural explanations, the balance between structures and conjuncture.

Debates opposing conflicting interpretations of the origins of the French Revolution largely reflect the underlying *Weltanschauung* on the leading forces of historical development. It is obvious that for the three influential generations of French Marxist historians who considered economic forces and relations of production as the base determining the cultural, institutional, and power relations of society, any attempt to conceive this latter 'superstructure' as the commanding element of Revolution was misleading. When looking at the causes of the Revolution, influential historians like Alphonse Aulard, Albert Mathiez, Georges Lefebvre, and Albert Soboul, who dominated the historiography of the French Revolution from the end of the nineteenth century up to the 1960s, concentrated largely on the inner dialectic of the economic and social order of old regime France and its growing contradictions, leading allegedly to its final explosion. The Revolution was conceived as the ultimate consequence of the eighteenth century rise of a capitalistic bourgeoisie aiming at disrupting the existent feudal society: in introducing the French Revolution, Soboul wrote that it 'marks the advent of the bourgeois and capitalistic society [… and settles the problem] of the historical law of the transition from feudalism to capitalism.'[4] Economic growth was therefore conceived as a decisive element of the historical process leading ineluctably to the triumph of the bourgeois Revolution.

Controversies on the social and economic background of the Revolution became particularly acrimonious during the thirty years from the late 1950s, when the Marxist interpretation of its driving forces began to be seriously challenged. Alfred Cobban, George Taylor, Colin Lucas, and Guy Chaussinand-Nogaret among others contested the existence of opposition between a nobility attached to feudalism and a self-conscious bourgeoisie calling for a capitalist society. A wide range of researches has since insisted on the community of interests among pre-Revolutionary French elites belonging to the second and to the Third Estate, and on the inner divisions within each estate. Parallel to this revision, the goals of the urban and rural masses in the revolutionary process have been scrutinized anew. It is widely admitted that their action was crucial in 1789 for the consolidation of the political revolution that started with the opening of the General Estates, but the significance of their action has raised controversial issues, as revolutionary masses largely expressed anti-capitalistic views: a fact which increases the complexity of the interpretation of the French Revolution as a bourgeois and capitalistic process.

The acrimonious intellectual fights both among Marxist historians (on the anachronism of recourse to the notions of class struggle, class consciousness, or proletarian vanguard to interpret mass behaviour in the Revolution), and between Marxists and the revisionist school (the latter considering the Revolution as a political, as opposed to social, revolution and exploring its ideological origins while rejecting class labels), have slowly and steadily calmed down after the peak reached during the Bicentenary in 1989. Debate has not been vain, though, as it has contributed to promote a large number of inquiries and case studies, offering the opportunity today to look at these phenomena with a more distanced and possibly neutral eye—a result also of the evolution of global geopolitics after the end of the Cold War and the decreasing ideological dimension of historiographical debates.

One key point emerging from these debates was the breakdown of a dominant image of the Revolution as a long-lasting event, the phases of which were teleologically determined from its very beginnings, and to conceive it rather as a process capable of producing new and unpredictable outcomes, notably through accelerating processes of politicization among rural and urban populations under the influence of their new contexts.[5] If we admit this perspective, the question of the 'origins' of the French Revolution consists no longer in finding out the underlying forces leading inexorably to a decade-long revolution, the nature of which is judged through the lens of its long-lasting achievements, but in understanding which factors led contemporaries to question so radically in 1789 the principles on which French society had previously been based. We also need to understand what made them believe that collective action could efficiently lead to a change.

Refusing to conceive the Revolution as an intrinsic teleological necessity does not imply, however, that the eighteenth century evolution of existing structures did not play any role: 1789 can be conceived as the product of different groups' demands converging, at a moment of major financial difficulties for the state and under the pressure of a dramatic short-term economic crisis, to reverse a number of established social, political, and legal principles. The Revolution is not the result of a preconceived plan of an organized group sharing clearly identified interests. The men and women who made the Revolution did not, in fact, share common goals. It is precisely because they had divergent ideas of the regenerated society they sought and on the political priorities to be followed, that the revolutionary process lasted so long and experienced such dramatic turning points.

The aim of this chapter, thus, is to highlight the elements in eighteenth century French demography and economy, which help us to better understand the tensions that traversed French society in the late 1780s and pushed contemporaries to action. Few would claim today that demography and economics are the sole, perhaps even the main, underlying forces responsible for the Revolution. They cannot, however, be disqualified as irrelevant, and if they are embedded in a broader analysis taking social, cultural, and political aspects into account, they offer important keys in a highly complex puzzle. The outbreak of the Revolution—or rather of the three revolutions occurring in 1789, the political one led by the Third Estate with the support of parts of the two other estates, the popular Parisian one which saved this from repression, and the rural one, which appears as largely autonomous—is an extremely intricate, multi-causal event. Its understanding requires consideration of structural as well as short-term aspects, notably why a recurrent phenomenon like temporary grain shortage could, in 1789, be an essential ingredient in a new explosive blend.

DEMOGRAPHY

At the eve of the Revolution, France was the most populous country in Europe. The number of his subjects and the fertility of French soil contributed to make the French king one of the five sovereigns playing a decisive role in the international arena, although keeping this role had an extremely high cost for public finances, as it implied the involvement of France in all major conflicts.

The French population increased from 22 million inhabitants in 1715—a level already reached in a previous peak in 1550—to 28 million in 1789. This was part of the general demographic growth that Europe experienced in the eighteenth century, and the growth rate in France was actually weaker than elsewhere. This argument has been used to deny any significant contribution of demographic factors in explaining the French Revolution. Whereas the continent increased its population by 60 per cent, France had in 1789 only 30 per cent more inhabitants than a century before. However, overall French demographic growth was uneven, and whereas the population of the *généralité* of Rouen grew by only 10–20 per cent between 1700 and 1787, the number of inhabitants of Alsace doubled. In certain parts of France, thus, demographic pressure might have a more relevant impact than the national average suggests. Besides, the consequences of demographic growth depend on the capacity of a given economy to absorb it, an element which makes international comparisons of absolute demographic growth less straightforward.

The technical explanation of French demographic growth lies in mortality decrease. Fecundity (birth) rates (approx. 38–40 per thousand) remained stable or slightly decreased, either because young people postponed their marriage, or through a moderate deliberate family limitation (although this phenomenon was mostly confined to elites and the urban population). Age at marriage was relatively high (25–26 for women, 27–28 for men) and tended to increase, as many young people had difficulty finding the resources to start a household. Child mortality fell slowly—and unequally according to economic conditions—but enough to increase overall life expectancy. Even so, almost one child out of two did not survive until adulthood, and life thereafter was still fragile: a child who was still alive at his or her 15th birthday could expect to live approximately another 30 years.[6]

Beside the decrease in child mortality, a growing number of French people survived longer than former generations because of the decreasing frequency of previously regular 'mortality crises', defined as an increase of at least 100 per cent of ordinary mortality over a year or more. Contemporaries identified three major causes of demographic crises: epidemics, warfare, and harvest failures. They had learned to prevent widespread outbreaks of plague, the most dramatic cause of mortality: although Marseille and the surrounding region lost half of their inhabitants in the early 1720s, the epidemic was confined to this area through severe control on the circulation of goods and people. Thereafter, France was free from such disease.[7] Military campaigning affected French territory very little in the eighteenth century, as wars were largely fought abroad. Harvest failures became possibly less frequent, owing to climatic factors, and above all, when they occurred, their demographic consequences were less dramatic than in previous centuries.

Whereas this was not the first time that the country experienced intensive century-long demographic growth, the striking feature of eighteenth century growth is that no dramatic drop followed, as it had before as a consequence of increasing strain on resources, malnutrition, and consequent vulnerability to diseases. Contemporaries successfully faced the challenge of feeding approximately six million inhabitants more on substantially the same agricultural base—the overall increase of cultivated land being less than 2.5 per cent. We shall see how they managed to do so, but it is important to stress here that eighteenth century pressure on resources had demographic, cultural, social, and economic consequences. Demographically, it provoked rural migration flows to towns (defined as urban centres with more than 2,000 inhabitants). In 1789, approximately one person out of five lived in a town or city, many of them in highly precarious economic conditions. Culturally, the fact that the urban population was more spatially concentrated and more literate than the rural population—65 per cent of men versus 42 per cent, respectively, in 1780–89 could sign their name upon marriage—increased the potential impact of the circulation of ideas. Migration to the towns was in many instances seasonal or short term, so that migration flows also made possible a wider circulation of ideas back to villages and rural communities. Socially, it increased tensions, notably because agricultural prices grew faster than wages, producing differentiated effects on different social groups. Economically, it stimulated proto-industrial activities and research into techniques for increased agricultural productivity.

Surprisingly, contemporaries were hardly aware of this growth, and most of them actually believed that the country was experiencing depopulation, along with Europe in general, if not the planet as a whole. In the 113th *Persian letter*, Montesquieu wrote: 'After a calculation as exact as may be in the circumstances, I have found that there are upon the earth hardly one tenth part of the people which there were in ancient times. And the astonishing thing is, that the depopulation goes on daily: if it continues, in ten centuries the earth will be a desert.' This passage was quoted in the article 'Population' of Diderot and d'Alembert's *Encyclopedia*, without challenge. Perceptions of population decrease had actually being contested since the mid-eighteenth century by few proto-statisticians, known as the 'political arithmeticians', like the *intendant* of Auvergne La Michodière in 1757, or the abbé d'Expilly, member of the academies of Berlin, Stockholm, Madrid, and Copenhagen, in his unfinished *Dictionnaire géographique, historique et politiques des Gaules et de la France* (6 vols, 1762–70). The most radical challenge was produced in 1778 by a former secretary of the *intendant* of Provence (1773–76) and member of the bureau of the Secretary of War, Jean-Baptiste Moheau (*Recherches et considérations sur la population de la France*). Moreau demonstrated—through a path-breaking statistical method based on parish registers of birth that historians would refine in the 1950s—that the French population was indeed growing.

For Montesquieu—who discussed the topic in detail in his 1748 *Esprit des Lois* (book XXIII)—and for his contemporaries, debating the causes of depopulation was generally the starting point to discuss moral and political virtues of past and contemporary societies, to debate related topics such as divorce and religious vows of chastity, or to argue on the consequences of warfare, economic policies or colonization. Such considerations also produced immediate actions, for instance, through philanthropic associations working to improve conditions of childbirth or providing dowries to young poor girls. In this sense too, demography did matter, as it added a piece in the global puzzle that eighteenth century thinkers were conceiving to understand the world they lived in under all its possible facets, including politics, and in the connections they tested between the rational, open analysis of a phenomenon and the concrete collective actions they undertook towards whatever they considered as improvements.

Eighteenth century French demography does not explain the Revolution in a mechanical way, but offers a background for a better understanding of the social expectations and tensions in pre-revolutionary rural and urban France. Demographic pressure on resources exacerbated social tensions, and was a cause of concern and debate in itself, just as its effects increased the circulation of ideas across the country. It is therefore difficult to conceive the French Revolution as the pure result of political factors and to entirely dismiss the impact of the country's demographic evolution over the past decades. Demographic growth also brought to the forefront a generation of young men and women who had enjoyed greater chances to become adults, and who felt they deserved a better world to live in, although they certainly expressed different, if not opposite sensibilities about what this better world should be. In analysing popular rebellions in France from 1660 to 1789, Jean Nicolas observes a more consistent participation of young people in riots in the second half of the eighteenth century, and argues that juvenile turbulence took on a political content in 1787–89. Young people added a decisive, destabilizing element to the recurrent conflicts within French society by backing traditional popular demands for cheap bread, better job conditions, or the reduction of fiscal burdens.[8]

ECONOMY

Analysts of the eighteenth century French economy insist on the dynamism of its industry and trade and on the considerable enrichment of some entrepreneurs, helping to bind together a wealthy elite comprising both commoners and nobles. A part of the multi-confessional merchant elite in port cities, for instance, was noble, and if successful bourgeois still bought their way into the nobility, they were less inclined than in the previous century to abandon active business as a result. However, while some of the elite shared a common willingness to be more involved in policy-making, and others debated within the structures of eighteenth century sociability, economic interests within this group were far from homogeneous, and they did not act as a group, but rather promoted their own personal interests through their personal networks.[9]

In some instances, entrepreneurs required the intervention of the state in order to take advantage of specific economic opportunities, such as the slave and colonial trade, to be granted monopolistic rights, or to be protected from competition in domestic or external markets. In other instances, they wished the government to suppress existing traditional protective mechanisms that countered their own interests, such as collective rights on land, limitation in the circulation of cereals, and interdictions on specific industrial production or processes.[10] Some of them took advantage of the monarchy's massive need for naval and military supplies, especially in times of war. These economic elites did not contest the monarchy or the foundations of old regime society, which was solidly grounded on the principle of privileges, or 'private laws' applying to an individual or a group. Many of the well off, whether they belonged to the more dynamic economic elites or to the traditional landowners living from seigneurial rights, land leases and agriculture, had actually very strong interests in the continuation of the existing system, which among other benefits allowed the bulk of taxation to fall on the peasants. Economic elites also shared the benefits of the profitable credit system, drawing money toward the increasing insatiable needs of state expenditures.

This picture of a relatively prosperous French economy contrasts singularly with the increasingly dramatic condition of public finance. On the eve of the French Revolution, half of the state's income was being used to pay interest on the public debt. Failure of reiterated attempts to reform the fiscal system proved fatal to the absolute monarchy, leading to the convocation of the Estates-General and awakening hopes of a profound reformulation of the relation between the king and the country's economic elites.[11] The latter wished to take part in societal decision-making processes in a more decisive way. This followed the emergence of forms of sociability and writings which promoted a vast debate on reforms through the second half of the eighteenth century, affecting all fields. Economic change contributed, together with non-economic factors, to making such debate possible, but it produced at most a push toward political change, and not toward radical political upheaval.

The effects of eighteenth century economic dynamism and demographic growth, however, were not confined to elites. Price growth, notably for agricultural products, encouraged landowners to seek a share of rising incomes by raising rents. The latter doubled between 1730 and 1780.[12] This factor, combined with demographic pressure, increased pauperism among the significant part of the rural population who did not own the land they cultivated. Those who depended on wages to make ends meet were affected by the fact that agricultural prices tended to grow more rapidly than wages in agriculture. The eighteenth century decrease in real wages for urban workers was probably less significant than assumed, but they too were affected by rising food and lodging prices.[13]

The fact that the French economy was increasingly, but incompletely integrated—the price of wheat on local markets could vary by 300 per cent—and that some sectors were globalized and depended on international economic and geopolitical factors, complicates any attempt to present a coherent national picture, as almost any case-driven assertion can be countered by looking at a different area, city, or economic sector.[14] However, the relevant problem is to understand why, whereas neither demographic pressure nor rises in prices were new as such, they resulted in the 1780s in increasingly structured political demands, and mass participation.

AGRICULTURE

On the eve of the Revolution the French economy rested on agriculture, and the relation of individuals and groups to landed property and revenues largely determined the structure of society. Because of the low productivity of land (compared to today's stand-ards, and with the remarkable exceptions of north-east France) the vast majority of the population was engaged with the production of food for their own, and the wider soci-ety's, survival. Moreover, whether they lived from agricultural rents and incomes, from wages, or public charity, virtually all French people were sensitive to agricultural prices.

The centrality of agriculture ought to be stressed, as the dynamism of other sectors of the eighteenth century French economy which historians often point to—such as colonial trade and industry—tends to mask this basic reality. The distribution of rural profits and crops largely shaped French old regime society, and virtually all elites pos-sessed land. In fact, agricultural revenues were a more stable and substantial compo-nent of income for the urban bourgeoisie than those coming from trade and industry, with which this category is often identified.[15] A set of relevant contemporary debates were linked to agriculture: over the best basis for taxation, the legitimacy of feudal privi-leges on land and people, the role the state should play in facilitating the emergence of a national market for cereals, the right to access to bread at a fair price and the role of authorities in facilitating this right. Studying how different groups engaged with these crucial questions offers an insight into the positions they adopted once the Revolution had started.

Given the centrality of cereals in feeding the French—who ate up to two kilograms of bread daily when they could eat their fill—availability and affordability of flour was a major concern for governments and local authorities, although views on how to reach this goal, like the underlying economic interests, diverged widely.[16] Large parts of the French population were extremely vulnerable to price increases in food, and popular unrests in 1788–89 cannot be understood without noting the grain shortages and the high prices of bread since the poor harvest of 1787 and crop failure in 1788. Prices, how-ever, had increased just as dramatically between the late 1760s and early 1770s, provok-ing unrest, but no revolution. The fact that rural and urban unrest had a broader political meaning than previously is linked to the evolution of popular perceptions of responsi-bility for the 1789 situation, but also to the long-term effects of economic changes affect-ing the redistribution of income within society. Such tensions over the redistribution of the material and symbolic fruits of the land make the economy—both in terms of its long-term evolution and of its unforeseeable pre-revolutionary situation—an essential ingredient in understanding the French Revolution, although these economic factors acquired their political meaning only via the cultural and political lenses through which the French perceived them.

Since the 1720s and 1730s, French agriculture had been changing to meet increased demand stimulated by demographic pressure. Those who were able to produce sur-pluses benefited from increasing prices and growing economic integration with wider markets. The question of the transformations of eighteenth century French agriculture provoked a vivid scholarly debate opposing Jean-Marc Moriceau and Michel Morineau, among others, about the existence of an agricultural revolution in eighteenth-century France.[17] Globally, the absence of major demographic catastrophes despite a consistent increase in population proves that France was able to face the challenge of feeding more people. Historians suggested that better climate, wider diffusion of minor but cumulative technical advances, diversification of crops limiting the impact of climatic accidents, improved transport possibilities, increasing integration of French territories, and a more market-oriented management of large estates, all contributed to raise production without necessary provoking significant (or 'revolutionary') productivity changes. From the 1720s to the 1760s, France did not experience major crop failures on a nationwide basis. The overall growth process, however, did not prevent rising pressure on resources and consequent tensions in the distribution of agricultural revenues. When agricultural difficulties occurred in the mid-1760s, against a background of a more densely populated landscape and high rents, French peasants were less inclined than their forefathers to accept grain shortage and famine as an inevitable result.

Because land, rents, and agricultural incomes represented the crucial source of wealth, and abundant crops were the basis of the prosperity of the country and its king, agriculture was an object of public concern, intensive theoretical debate, and reformist efforts. Reformists believed that the government could and should favour economic development, and abolish what was perceived as a backward set of local traditions preventing an expansion of the market economy. Changes affecting the circulation of crops, taxation mechanisms, or the access to commons in the second half of the eighteenth century provoked fierce reactions from those who felt their positions were endangered. They had major political consequences too, as they undermined the traditional vision of a paternal king efficiently policing the grain markets in order to guarantee his subjects' subsistence. As Steven Kaplan has shown, the king's role was the counterpart of the subjects' acceptance of the duties imposed by the state on individuals and communities. Liberal reforms in the 1760s and 1770s, which occurred alongside bad harvests, generated the rumour that the government, and ultimately the court and the king, were responsible for the grain shortage, or at least that they were unable or unwilling to stop 'monopolists' speculating on grain prices.[18] In shaking this fundamental element of state legitimacy, the reforms paved the way for the politicization of traditional popular actions occurring whenever the prices of flour and bread went beyond what contemporary consumers perceived as the fair price.

The analysis of eighteenth century agriculture does not converge towards a uniform picture of a triumphant march toward capitalism, leading to a bourgeois revolution. Eighteenth century agriculture shows, instead, a complex web of conflicting interests and a diverging redistribution of revenues. While major landowners welcomed the possibility of integrating national and international markets and took advantage of rising agricultural prices, they opposed any attempt to tax land and incomes in a more substantial way, and defended their existing privileges. The Church, for instance, was not only exempt from all taxes on property—although it paid a negotiated sum yearly to the Crown (the *don gratuit* or 'free gift')—but benefited also from the right to collect the tithe on crops and livestock. It also benefited from the seigneurial system. The latter—while benefiting many commoners as well as nobles—worked by controlling peasants' communities and imposing taxes and duties in kind or cash on local inhabitants, besides other constraints. French provinces differed greatly as far as seigneurial rights were concerned: although they deprived peasants of approximately 15 per cent of their revenues in the region of Toulouse, they were consistently heavier in Bourgogne or Brittany. Before they paid taxes to the state and set aside the seeds for the next sowing—which might alone require 20–25 per cent of the harvest—peasants had delivered to the Church and the local seigneur up to a quarter of their crops. In abolishing these duties, the French Revolution undoubtedly contributed to improve the situation of the peasantry, but although the *cahiers de doléances* expressed grievances on these issues, they targeted what was perceived as an abuse or abnormality, and not their existence as such.[19]

Rising agricultural prices encouraged owners and those who enjoyed privileges allowing them to tap a part of the crops to augment their own production, their leases, and the shares they could obtain on other people's production. In order to do so, they could increase the area under cultivation (for much land remained wood and 'waste'), revive older privileges, increase existing ones, or annex parts of the village commons to their own profit. Historians studying this so-called 'feudal reaction' have found a considerable number of conflicts opposing seigneurs to peasant communities in the 1770s and 1780s, as well as a widespread perception among contemporary observers that peasants were more reluctant than before to comply with seigneurial rights. While it is clear that this conflict no longer set a purely noble 'class' against the peasantry, social tensions were undoubtedly high.

These tensions were due to both absolute and relative impoverishment: over the long term agricultural revenues were more and more unequally redistributed. As peasants only owned approximately one-third of the land, most were involved in paying rent for at least some of the fields they worked. From 1726–50 to 1781–87, rents increased at a greater rate than agricultural wages and more slowly than wheat prices.[20] Landowners were therefore the main winners from agricultural growth. Most rents went to a relatively narrow elite: the Church owned 10 per cent of French soil, the nobility slightly less than a third, and members of urban bourgeoisie approximately a quarter. As state taxation fell on peasants rather than landowners, the French state did not benefit from the enrichment of the latter, and in seeking to increase taxation to meet its rising financial needs it merely worsened peasants' living conditions.

National averages mask great differences: peasants' property, for instance, accounted for less than 10 per cent in the region surrounding Versailles, but 50 per cent in the Limousin. Their vulnerability to cereal prices or decreasing demand for agricultural work in case of crop failure was therefore extremely variable from one province to another, and sometimes from one village to the next, where, for example, much could depend on strongly fluctuating grape harvests. Peasants' interests, indeed, were not homogeneous. Only a minority of peasants possessed enough land to feed their family conveniently and were able, in a moderate year, to sell a part of their crop on the markets. The majority owned or rented farms which could hardly guarantee their survival, unless they obtained some revenues as agricultural or proto-industrial wage-earners. With cereal prices and rents rising more quickly than wages, they became increasingly indebted, and the most vulnerable among them had to sell their property. From the mid-1770s, different sectors of agriculture were hit by a series of accidents—livestock diseases (late 1770s–early 1780s), and hay failure (1785 and 1786)—while grape-harvests alternated with bad years, such as 1778, and overproduction, from the mid-1780s. Pauperism resulted in an increased number of beggars and vagabonds.

Under these circumstances, duties and taxes demanded by seigneurs, the Church, and the state were met with growing hostility. Peasants were increasingly inclined to believe that the Crown, the government and the rich in general were responsible for their situation, when not deliberately conspiring against them. On different occasions in the 1760s, 1770s, and 1780s, the government tried to favour the expansion of an integrated market economy by lifting existing constraints on the circulation of cereals.[21] These measures deprived local rural communities of a proportion of the crops that were sold at distant markets. Peasants' opposition to reform—and more generally, their overall attitude toward the emergence of a more market-oriented economy and the extension of larger, profit-oriented estates—was fundamentally anti-capitalistic in scope and aimed at protecting existing communitarian structures.

The amount of social unrest expressing economic and fiscal grievances augmented considerably in the period 1765–89 (3,350 events, 60 per cent in villages or small towns) and peaked in the months preceding the opening of the Estates-General.[22] The *Grande Peur* in the second half of July 1789 should be understood against a background of growing tensions. Although the rural revolution was largely separate from the events in Versailles and Paris since the opening of the Estates-General and from the implosion of old regime municipal institutions, it was not unrelated to the general context.[23] The mobilization of rural communities for the drafting of the *cahiers de doléances* played an essential role in increasing the conviction that existing difficulties were amenable to a political solution from a benevolent king listening to his people. Circulation of model *cahiers* by urban-based reformers and discussion through the drafting process among the representatives of different villages favoured increasing political consciousness. The convocation of the Estates-General created an immense hope of regeneration throughout France, and news of the political stalemate in May–June 1789 magnified the sense of frustration. But only the political void created by the collapse of the state allowed peasant aspirations to approach reality.

The intensity of the peasants' unrest in July 1789 pushed the National Assembly to abolish personal feudal rights on the night of 4 August 1789, and to foresee the repurchase of feudal rights based upon property. This was a decisive moment, as the representatives in Versailles eradicated by the same token the principle of privilege, on which old regime society relied.[24] Three months before, at the opening of the Estates-General, none of the representatives had ever thought this outcome was possible and only an insignificant number of their electors had ever wished it. The decision was not the result of a conscious political programme, but the product of a specific political and economic conjuncture in a socially explosive context. The further radicalization of the Revolution and the refusal of peasants to pay for the redemption of rights would result in the feudal system's eradication. This development ultimately accelerated the process of privatization of land ownership, which was not necessarily what the large majority of rural inhabitants had wished for. The dramatic financial situation of the state, increased by the reluctance of the king's subjects to pay taxes in the expectation of a major fiscal reform, led to nationalization of the properties of the Catholic Church and to the consequent, unplanned redistribution of land through the sale of the *biens nationaux*. This decision had hardly any benefits for the small peasantry—the number of landowners increased by only 10 per cent—and ultimately accelerated the emergence of a post-revolutionary society and a political system based on an elite of capitalist landowners.[25]

INDUSTRY AND TRADE

French industrial production experienced an impressive growth in the eighteenth century, with several distinct dimensions: a wide rural putting-out system, new centres of intensive development such as those at Anzin, Saint-Gobain, and Creusot, and an increase in national and international trade.[26] Setting aside the question of the emergence of a numerically increased elite and of its composition, discussed above, analysis of how these economic sectors might be related to the origins of the French Revolution leads us to question whether some of their structural or short-term features increased social tensions.

In analysing the state of French industry by the 1780s, French historians have been obsessed by comparisons with Great Britain, and the basic question of whether the Revolution was responsible for allowing the British to gain industrial primacy in the nineteenth century.[27] A similar debate exists with regard to the state of French external trade.[28] Fully assessing the comparative performance of French industry in the international context is beyond the scope of this chapter. More relevant for our purpose is the fact that French industry faced difficult conditions in the late 1780s. The Eden-Rayneval Treaty of 1786, which came into force in May 1787, opened French markets to cheap British manufactured goods. French imports of British cotton goods, for instance, increased fifteen fold between 1786 and 1788. This competition created major difficulties in northern and north-eastern France, both for proto-industrial and factory workers, reflected in the *cahiers de doléances* and in an increasing level of disorder.[29] In the Amiens-Abbeville region, the number of working looms dropped by a third between 1785 and 1789.

Unemployment or underemployment affected rural and urban workers at the very moment where the price of cereals was dramatically increasing. In late spring 1789, urban wage-earners spent 80 per cent of their wages on bread, compared to 50 per cent in a more normal year. Moreover, by obliging people to postpone all other expenses, the agricultural crisis accentuated the fall in demand for manufactured goods, and thus aggravated the difficulties of the industrial sector. The conjunction of unemployment and high bread prices considerably increased the number of food riots: Jean Nicolas counted 58 riots in 1788, and 231 during the four first months of 1789. Fifty-three per cent occurred in cities.[30] Although the army was generally able to repress popular riots swiftly, there was increasing concern about soldiers' willingness to do so. As is well known, bread prices reached a peak in Paris on 14 July 1789.

Whereas the industrial sector was affected by a temporary crisis at the eve of the French Revolution, with dramatic results, there is no visible sign of difficulties in trade, which had experienced considerable growth throughout the eighteenth century. This was the result of the expansion of national markets and increasing integration with swelling international and colonial markets. Eighteenth century growth in agricultural and industrial production led to an expansion of internal exchanges, which was accompanied by the authorities' efforts to facilitate trade. Within the country, an extremely dense network of regular local markets—2,500 according to Dominique Margairaz, 60 per cent of which were in towns and villages with fewer than 2,000 inhabitants—and seasonal fairs (4,200 places had at least one fair each year) contributed to knit together the different parts of the kingdom.[31] Besides providing an essential economic function, they also facilitated the circulation of information and created spaces for informal discussions.

External trade grew strongly throughout the eighteenth century. French ship-owners carried to Marseille half of the Ottoman Empire's exports to Western Europe, and French merchant houses were particularly successful in Cadiz, a gateway to the Spanish Empire. However, the most impressive growth occurred with regard to the French West Indies: the colonial and slave trades, and colonial re-export trade to northern Europe and the Levant (through Marseille), explain the considerable growth of Bordeaux, Nantes, and Le Havre, both demographically, and in terms of wealth, and the rapid recovery of Marseille after the dramatic plague in 1720. At the eve of the French Revolution, the French West Indies produced half of the sugar and the great majority of the coffee consumed in Europe. Sugar imports increased twentyfold between 1720 and 1789.[32]

Whilst attacking the Marxist interpretation according to which a triumphant commercial bourgeoisie was a major actor of the French Revolution, some historians have insisted on the catastrophic consequences of the Revolution on this group.[33] Questions have been raised, however, about the long-term viability of the eighteenth century structure of French foreign trade, and its real performance.[34] By 1789, colonial imports from the West Indies represented a third of total French imports, and an increasing part of French exports consisted of colonial goods, which were mostly re-exported without being transformed, together with other agricultural products, such as wine and oil. In other words, trade did not contribute to foster industrialization. Moreover, re-exports occurred mainly in foreign vessels, without contributing to a greater development of the maritime sector. The role of industrial products in the structure of French exports was far less significant than for Great Britain, although representing half of all exports to French colonies, they made up only 25 per cent of total exports. The whole colonial system relied on slavery, and an increase in colonial production and trade occurred through an intensification of the plantation system and slave exploitation—a factor which created an explosive situation in Saint-Domingue (today's Haiti)—and not through decisive technological changes in colonial production.[35]

Moreover, despite impressive growth rates in production, the plantation economy in the French West Indies suffered from a crisis after the Seven Years War, owing to rising production costs, while the price of colonial crops stagnated, or in the case of coffee declined. Planters owed increasing amounts of money to French merchants, and by 1788, colonial debt amounted to 148 million *livres*. French merchants frequently acquired plantations in repayment of debts, but were rarely able to run them as profitably as they hoped.[36] Michel Morineau has suggested that the enormous increase in colonial production might have been due to nothing else other than the attempt to pay off debts.[37]

Whereas these debates do not directly question the origins of the Revolution, the structure of French external trade is related to the difficulties that led to the Revolution. Morineau has further proposed that the logics of a colonial empire built to favour metropolitan interests created a set of imbalances that required complex international compensation mechanisms, of which warfare was a major component. Building on this idea, I have suggested that warfare was necessary to keep the eighteenth-century French colonial system viable.[38] Given the fact that war represented the main cause of the desperate financial situation of the French monarchy at the eve of the Revolution, and the reason that forced the king to accept the convocation of the Estates-General, the development of eighteenth century French trade and the political choice to favour colonial trade can be considered as an element leading to the outbreak of the Revolution.

Contemporary French elites clearly perceived the importance of colonies and were concerned with conceptualizing their role for France: Paul Cheney has recently shown how the growth of colonial trade affected contemporaries' thought on the relation between trade, politics, morality, and taxation. The evolution of discourses created the ideological background against which Barnave and Mirabeau, among others, faced the challenge of imagining the place of the colonies and of slavery in a post-revolutionary world.[39]

CONCLUSION

Ultimately, when analysing the economic origins of the French Revolution, it becomes evident that their understanding requires a consistent awareness of the interactions between politics and economic life, both of which are embedded in a complex web of social and cultural interactions among individuals and groups.

The reassessment of the composition of French elites at the eve of the Revolution, which has been undertaken in the past forty years, no longer supports the view of an emerging capitalistic bourgeoisie strengthened by long-term industrial and trade growth, fighting against a feudal nobility to access political rights. However, rejection of the traditional Marxist interpretation does not eliminate demography and economy from the picture of the origins of the Revolution. The French Revolution cannot be understood by only taking political and cultural factors into account. In stressing the escalation of social tensions provoked by an unequal redistribution of the resources created by sustained growth in agriculture, industry and trade, analysis of the demographic and economic developments of eighteenth century France helps us to understand the background against which the convergence of political and short-term subsistence crises pushed rural and urban masses to revolt in 1789. Without their actions, which cannot be explained without this background, the political revolution led by a majority of the representatives who met in Versailles would have been repressed.

It is much more questionable whether the political revolution itself had an economic origin. Like all historical processes, the French Revolution is the result of long-term tendencies and situational events, to which actors add their own perceptions and intentions. Looking at the causes of the Revolution by observing its consequences is therefore misleading, because in doing so, historians erase the uncertainty of the times in which actors lived, and which influenced their actions. Looking at the results, historians attribute a consciousness in the pursuit of goals which ought to be demonstrated instead of postulated. The French Revolution produced, indeed, a turn toward a capitalistic world in the sense that it freed property from collective rights and complex jurisdictional webs, and put the working classes under stricter control. The Revolution ultimately gave political rights to a new social category of landed proprietors, in which non-nobles were numerous. Assuming that the Revolution occurred because a capitalistic class-conscious bourgeoisie aimed to achieve these goals is simply contrary to historical evidence. But it could be said that the eighteenth century evolution of the French economy reinforced and shaped an elite of wealthy people, almost all of whom were landowners, with some investing in industry and trade, and that this elite, experiencing a long revolutionary process which brought the mass of the population to the fore time and again, might come to recognize its common interest in guaranteeing social control over them.

NOTES

1. John Robinson, *Proofs of a Conspiracy against all the Religions and Governments of Europe, carried on in the Secret Meetings of Free-Masons, Illuminati and Reading Societies, etc., collected from good authorities* (Edinburgh, 1797). For a different configuration of conspiracy, see Abbé Barruel, *Mémoires pour servir à l'histoire du jacobinisme*, 5 vols (Hamburg, 1798–99).

2. His 'Introduction to the French Revolution' was first published in *œuvres de Barnave* (Paris, 1843).

3. On the historiography of the Revolution and its causes, see Norman Hampson, 'The French Revolution and its Historians', in Geoffrey Best (ed.), *The Permanent Revolution. The French Revolution and its Legacy, 1789–1989* (London, 1988), 211–34.

4. Albert Soboul, *La Révolution française* ([1965] Paris, 2010), 5.

5. On this issue, see François Furet, *Penser la révolution* (Paris, 1978), 32–46.

6. On the demographic of old regime France, see Jack A. Goldstone, 'Demography', in William Doyle (ed.), *The Oxford Handbook of the Ancien Régime* (Oxford, 2012), 201–18; Jacques Dupaquier, *Histoire de la population française, vol. 2: De la Renaissance à 1789* (Paris, 1988).

7. On the reasons why the well-known prevention system proved inefficient in Marseille see Charles Carrière, Marcel Courdurie, and Ferréol Rebuffat, *Marseille, ville morte: la peste de 1720* (Marseille, 1968).

8. Jean Nicolas, *La rébellion française. Mouvements populaires et conscience sociale (1661–1789)* (Paris, 2002), 479–82. See also John R. Gillis, *Youth and History* (New York, 1974).

9. On the importance of eighteenth century sociability based on voluntary affiliations, see Pierre-Yves Beaurepaire, 'Sociability', in Doyle (ed.), *The Oxford Handbook of the Ancien Régime*, 375–87.

10. Jean-Pierre Hirsch and Philippe Minard, '"Laissez-nous faire et protégez-nous beaucoup": pour une histoire des pratiques institutionnelles dans l'industrie française', in Louis Bergeron and Patrice Bourdelais (eds), *La France n'est-elle pas douée pour l'industrie?* (Paris, 1998), 135–58; see also Jean-Pierre Hirsch, *Les deux rêves du commerce. Entreprise et institution dans la région lilloise (1780–1860)* (Paris, 1991).

11. John Francis Bosher, *The Single Duty Project. A Study of the Movement for a French Customs Union in the Eighteenth Century* (London, 1964).

12. David R. Weir, 'Les crises économiques et les origines de la révolution française', *Annales. Economies, Sociétés, Civilisations* 46, no. 4 (1991), 928.

13. Labrousse estimated that salaries increased by 25 per cent between 1726–41 and 1785–89, and wheat prices by 60 per cent. Camille-Ernest Labrousse, *Esquisse du mouvement des prix et des revenus en France au XVIIIe siècle* (Paris, 1932), but revised this pessimistic assumption in his later works. Weir, 'Les crises économiques', 930, suggests that salaries increased rather by 40 per cent, although with major differences between cities and job sectors. He also stresses that, compared to British workers, French real wages declined much less, although the overall level of salaries in Great Britain was higher (ibid., 919–21).

14. Weir, 'Les crises économiques', 926. In 1781–87, a hectolitre of wheat cost 7.93 *livres tournois* in Douai (Nord) and 23.37 *livres tournois* in Aix (Bouches-du-Rhône).

15. William Doyle, *Origins of the French Revolution* (Oxford, 1988), 129–30.

16. Steven L. Kaplan, *Provisioning Paris: Merchants and Millers in the Grain and Flour Trade during the Eighteenth Century* (Ithaca and London, 1984). Reynald Abad, *Le grand marché: l'approvisionnement alimentaire de Paris sois l'Ancien Régime* (Paris 2002).

17. Jean-Claude Toutain, 'Le produit de l'agriculture française de 1700 à 1958. 1. Estimation du produit au XVIIIe siècle', *Cahiers de l'Institut de Science économique appliquée* 115 (July 1961); Jean-Marc Moriceau, *Les fermiers de l'Île-de-France. L'ascension d'un patronat agricole (XVe–XVIIIe siècle)* (Paris, 1994); Jean-Marc Moriceau, 'Au rendez-vous de la "Révolution agricole" dans la France du XVIIIe siècle. À propos des régions de grande culture', *Annales. Histoire, Sciences Sociales* 49, no. 1 (1994), 27–63; Michel Morineau, *Les faux-semblants d'un démarrage économique: agriculture et démographie en France au XVIIIe siècle* (Paris, 1971). David R. Weir suggests the possibility of conciliating these different positions in stressing that productivity gains could be reached without increasing the production per surface, though increased integration: Weir, 'Les crises économiques', 919–22. For a critical review of the debate on the performance of eighteenth century French agriculture, see Christian Morrisson, 'La production française au XVIIIe siècle: stagnation ou croissance?', *Revue européenne des sciences sociales* [online], XLV-137 | 2007, online since 1 July 2010 (accessed 28 July 2013). URL: http://ress.revues.org/224; DOI: 10.4000/ress.224.

18. Steven L. Kaplan, *The Famine Plot Persuasion in Eighteenth-century France* (Philadelphia, 1982); Edward P. Thompson et al., *Guerre du blé au XVIIIe siècle: la critique populaire contre le libéralisme économique au XVIIIe siècle* (Montreuil, 1988).

19. Jean Gallet, *Seigneurs et paysans en France, 1600–1793* (Rennes, 1999).

20. Weir, 'Les crises économiques', 925, 934–5.

21. Steven L. Kaplan, *Bread, Politics and Political Economy in the Reign of Louis XV* (Den Haag, 1976).

22. Nicolas, *La rébellion française*, 34–5.

23. On the autonomy of the peasants' revolution, see the pioneer works of Georges Lefebvre, 'La Révolution française et les paysans (1932)', in *Etudes sur la Révolution française* (Paris, 1954); Georges Lefebvre, *La Grande Peur de 1789* (Paris, 1932); and Paul Bois, *Les paysans de l'Ouest. Des structures économiques et sociales aux options politiques depuis l'époque révolutionnaire dans la Sarthe* (Le Mans, 1960).

24. Anthony Crubaugh, 'Feudalism', in Doyle (ed.), *The Oxford Handbook of the Ancien Régime*, 219–35.

25. Bernard Bodinier and Éric Teyssier, *L'événement le plus important de la Révolution. La vente des biens nationaux* (Paris, 2000).

26. For an example of a proto-industrialized region and its links to the West Indies, see Claude Cailly, *Mutations d'un espace proto-industriel: la Perche aux XVIIIe–XIXe siècles* (Lille, 1993). Gérard Gayot, *Les draps de Sedan* (Paris, 1998); Jean-Pierre Hirsch, *Les deux rêves du commerce: entreprise et institution dans la région lilloise, 1780–1860* (Paris, 1991).

27. See for instance Pierre Chaunu, 'Préface', in François Crouzet, *De la supériorité de l'Angleterre sur la France. L'économie et l'imaginaire, XVIIIe–XXe siècle* (Paris, 1985), p. III: 'At the end of the Old Regime [...] nothing prevents us supposing that [...] France would ultimately gain. [...] In eight years, from 1792 to 1800, all chances were wasted.'

28. See for instance Jean-Pierre Poussou, 'Le dynamisme de l'économie française sous Louis XVI', *Revue économique* 40, no. 6 (1989), 965–84. For a divergent point of view, Michel Morineau, 'La vraie nature des choses et leur enchaînement entre la France, les Antilles et l'Europe (XVIIe–XIXe siècle)', *Revue française d'histoire d'Outre-mer* 84, no. 314 (1997), 3–24, and Silvia Marzagalli, 'Le négoce maritime et la rupture révolutionnaire: un ancien débat revisité', *Annales historiques de la Révolution française* 352, no. 2 (2008), 183–207.

29. Nicolas, *La rébellion française*, 291–3, records 63 conflicts in the 1770s and 99 in the 1780s.

30. Nicolas, *La rébellion française*, 260–1.

31. Dominique Margairaz, *Foires et marchés dans la France préindustrielle* (Paris, 1988).

32. Silvia Marzagalli, 'The French Atlantic World in the seventeenth and eighteenth centuries', in Nicholas Canny and Philip Morgan (eds), *The Oxford Handbook of the Atlantic World, c.1450–c.1820* (Oxford, 2011), 235–51.

33. François Crouzet, 'La ruine du grand commerce', in François-Georges Pariset (ed.), *Bordeaux au XVIIIe siècle* (Bordeaux, 1968), 485–510; Poussou, 'Le dynamisme de l'économie française sous Louis XVI'.

34. Louis Meignen, 'Le commerce extérieur de la France à la fin de l'Ancien Régime', *Revue historique du droit français et étranger* 56, 4 (1978), 583–614; Pierre Léon, 'Structure du commerce extérieur et évolution industrielle de la France à la fin du XVIIIe siècle', in *Conjoncture économique, structures sociales. Hommages à Ernest Labrousse* (Paris, 1974), 407–32.

35. The 1791 slave revolt in Saint-Domingue is both related to political developments in France and to local tensions provoked by the past decades of economic development on the island. However, while the colonies played a role in French revolutionary processes and political decision-making after 1789—see Yves Benot, *La Révolution française et la fin des colonies* (Paris, 1987)—their role in discussing the origins of the French Revolution is mainly confined to their contribution to the emergence of a rich merchant elite in French ports.

36. Françoise Thésée, *Négociants bordelais et colons de Saint-Domingue: Liaisons d'habitations, la maison Henry Romberg, Bapst et Cie, 1783–1793* (Paris, 1972).

37. Morineau, 'La vraie nature des choses', 13–14.

38. Morineau, 'La vraie nature des choses'; Silvia Marzagalli, 'Is warfare necessary to the functioning of eighteenth century colonial systems? Some reflections on the necessity

of cross-imperial and foreign trade in the French case', in Càtia Antunes and Amèlia Polònia (eds), *Beyond Empires: Self-Organizing Cross-Imperial Economic Networks versus Institutional Empires, 1500–1800* (forthcoming, 2014).

39. Paul Cheney, *Revolutionary Commerce. Globalization and the French Monarchy* (Cambridge, 2010).

SELECTED READING

Ado, Anatoli, *Paysans en Révolution. Terre, pouvoir et jacquerie, 1789–1804* (Paris, 1996).

Béaur, Gérard, *Histoire agraire de la France au XVIIIe siècle: inerties et changements dans les campagnes françaises entre 1715 et 1815* (Paris, 2000).

Braudel, Fernand and Labrousse, Ernest, *Histoire économique et sociale de la France* (Paris, 1970).

Daudin, Guillaume, *Commerce et prospérité. La France au XVIIIe siècle* (Paris, 2005).

Doyle, William, *Origins of the French Revolution* (Oxford, 1988).

Dupaquier, Jacques, *Histoire de la population française, vol. 2: De la Renaissance à 1789* (Paris, 1988).

Kaplan, Steven L., *Bread, Politics and Political Economy in the Reign of Louis XV* (Den Haag, 1976).

Labrousse, Camille-Ernest, *Esquisse du mouvement des prix et des revenus en France au XVIIIe siècle* (Paris, 1932).

Labrousse, Camille-Ernest, *La crise de l'économie française à la fin de l'Ancien Régime et au début de la Révolution* (Paris, 1944).

Lemarchand Guy, *L'économie en France de 1770 à 1830. De la crise de l'Ancien Régime à la révolution industrielle* (Paris, 2008).

Morineau, Michel, *Les faux-semblants d'un démarrage économique: agriculture et démographie en France au XVIIIe siècle* (Paris, 1971).

Nicolas, Jean, *La rébellion française. Mouvements populaires et conscience sociale (1661–1789)* (Paris, 2002).

Soboul, Albert, *La Révolution française* ([1965] Paris, 2010).

Weir, David R., 'Les crises économiques et les origines de la révolution française', *Annales. Economies, Sociétés, Civilisations* 46, no. 4 (1991), 917–47.

Woronoff, Denis, *Histoire de l'industrie en France: du XVe siècle à nos jours* (Paris, 1994).

CHAPTER 2

THE BOURGEOISIE, CAPITALISM, AND THE ORIGINS OF THE FRENCH REVOLUTION

LAUREN R. CLAY

IN the autumn of 1788, as France prepared for the first meeting of the Estates-General in nearly 175 years, the president and deputies of the Chamber of Commerce of Montpellier sent a striking proposal to their king.[1] Several months earlier, on 5 July, the royal government had invited the nation to offer recommendations concerning the forms that representation should take for this historic event, a proclamation that was widely seen as authorizing, for the first time, open political debate. Among the eight hundred or so political pamphlets that appeared between July 1788 and January 1789, the request sent by the merchants of Montpellier, along with similar demands presented by several dozen other commercial institutions located in cities throughout France, stands out.[2] Rather than joining the chorus calling for a doubling in the number of deputies representing the commoners of the Third Estate and for voting by head rather than by order, the 'patriotic reflections' that these business communities offered to Louis XVI and his ministers specifically addressed the role that the commercial bourgeoisie should play in the upcoming assembly. Following the lead of the Merchant Court of Nantes, a broad coalition of France's chambers of commerce and merchant courts asked that the category of business elites known as *le commerce* be granted special direct representation to the Estates-General. If *le commerce* elected its own deputies, separate from the general elections for the Third, they argued, this would ensure that those with hands-on knowledge of business practices would participate in crafting the policies that were necessary to pull France out of several years of painful economic recession, to reform taxation, and, ultimately, to save the nation from bankruptcy.[3]

Such representation by France's commercial *corps*, the Montpellier merchants acknowledged, was unprecedented: 'Our historical annals, it is true, do not offer any example of the admission of commercial deputies to the Estates-General.'[4] Indeed, from their perspective, this lack of participation by business elites was precisely the problem. Given the relatively low social status of even the most successful traders when compared with lawyers, city councillors, landowners, and other notables of the Third Estate, the leaders of the nascent commercial bourgeoisie feared that their community would fare poorly in elections and would thus be relegated to a marginal role, at best, in policy-making at the very moment when extensive political and economic reform was clearly on the horizon.

Daringly, French business leaders justified their campaign for political representation by arguing that economic structures in France had changed so significantly since the most recent meeting of the Estates-General that the traditional tripartite hierarchy of clergy, nobles, and an undifferentiated Third Estate no longer adequately represented France. A century and a half earlier, they explained, commerce had only been in its infancy, exercising little real influence on national prosperity. In the intervening decades, however, trade—and especially trade with the colonies—had taken off, with important consequences for all Frenchmen. 'Commerce, Sire', they wrote, 'is essentially tied to the prosperity of the state; it is through [commerce] that agriculture improves, that industry develops, that the population grows, and that the poorest class of your subjects, always the most numerous, finds sure means of subsistence.'[5] Both directly and indirectly, business leaders argued, the international wholesale merchants known as *négociants* provided a critical support to the state by generating the tax revenues that France relied upon to maintain its great power status. Could France's strategic geopolitical interests be served by maintaining an outmoded political structure that was itself the legacy of the 'feudal tyranny' that had marked 'unhappy centuries of trouble and ignorance'?[6] History and tradition, French commercial corps explicitly argued, should be discarded in favour of a system of representation that reflected the new bases of power in the contemporary world, one that weighed the contribution of various groups to French national interests.[7]

This little-known political campaign to gain recognition for France's commercial and manufacturing elites as a distinct socio-political category in the body politic has been all but forgotten by mainstream histories of the Revolution, most likely because it failed so miserably to achieve its objective. There would be no commercial 'fourth estate'—a term in fact used by their critics—at the meeting of the Estates-General in Versailles that opened in May of 1789.[8] Just as they had feared, *négociants*, bankers, and manufacturers fared relatively poorly in elections to the Third, and those who were elected did not feature prominently in revolutionary politics, at least not on the national stage.[9] Nonetheless, these early if ineffectual efforts at national political organization by business elites provide an intriguing opportunity to revisit what has been one of the most vexed questions in the past half century in the field of revolutionary history: what role did the bourgeoisie—and, more broadly, capitalism itself—play in the origins of the French Revolution?[10]

To many readers, it may seem foolhardy to return to the question of the bourgeoisie as revolutionary actors. The resounding defeat of the Marxist 'rise-of-the-bourgeoisie' paradigm in the scholarly battles of the 1960s and 1970s sparked a general retreat from economic and social analyses of the origins of the Revolution. Most scholars turned their energies to developing the rich fields of revolutionary politics and culture. For more than a generation, the capitalist bourgeoisie has been all but banished from most general accounts of the Revolution.

Yet, if the dynamic and transformative impact of commerce on contemporary France was self-evident to the *négociants* of cities such as Montpellier, who used this fact to justify unprecedented claims for political representation, perhaps we should not be so quick to dismiss their perspective. In fact, pre-revolutionary capitalism is emerging as a vital field of historical inquiry. The weight of new evidence concerning consumption and colonial trade, in particular, has inspired scholars to take a fresh look at the social, cultural, and political consequences of changing eighteenth century economic practices in inquiries that span from the intimate to the global. In 1789, when the French overthrew absolutist monarchy and set out to redefine their political and social world, could their understandings of liberty, equality, and individual rights have been shaped by everyday practices of consumerism? Given France's prominence as a global commercial power in the late eighteenth century, could capitalism—and perhaps even capitalists themselves— have had a role to play in the collapse of the old regime and in 'the unexpected invention of revolutionary politics', after all?[11]

THE CONTESTED QUESTION OF THE FRENCH BOURGEOISIE

Some fifty years ago, it would have been difficult to conceive how contested the question of a revolutionary bourgeoisie would become, for there was a time in the not-so-distant past when professors knew with some certainty why the French Revolution happened. They could confidently teach their students that it was a social revolution that was the product of class struggle.[12] According to this social or 'Marxist' interpretation of the Revolution, which dominated the scholarship through the 1970s, long-term structural changes in the French economy—namely, the foundations of capitalism—had created an ambitious yet politically and socially frustrated bourgeoisie. In 1789, this bourgeoisie seized the crisis of state finances as an opportunity to overthrow the absolutist monarchy and to triumph over the decadent, reactionary feudal aristocracy. Sweeping away France's privilege-bound society of orders, France's bourgeoisie established a liberal regime marked by civil equality, meritocracy, protection of private property, and laissez-faire economic practices—changes of which they themselves were the primary beneficiaries. In destroying the traditional feudal systems of production, they set the stage for liberal capitalism to emerge in full force in the nineteenth century. According to the last great proponent of the Marxist interpretation, Albert Soboul, the French Revolution 'forms the culmination of a long economic and social evolution which has made the bourgeoisie the master of the world'.[13]

For the first three-quarters of the twentieth century, this narrative provided a seductively clear framework with which to present the origins of the revolutionary decade, one, moreover, that situated the Revolution as a world historical event that marked the dawn of modernity. In the 1960s, however, cracks began to emerge in the Marxist edifice. 'Revisionist' scholars such as George V. Taylor, Alfred Cobban, and William Doyle proclaimed that the empirical evidence did not add up.[14] Rather than Marx's industrial capitalists, it was professionals, especially lawyers, and venal office-holders who predominated among deputies to the Third Estate, those who in June 1789 declared themselves, as representatives of the sovereign nation, to be the National Assembly. In their revolt against the 'tyranny' of absolute monarchy and the injustices of aristocratic privilege, they were joined by liberal nobles and clergy. Meanwhile, the minority of manufacturers, bankers, and international traders were relegated to the political sidelines.

Far from the bourgeoning industrialization that Marx envisioned, revisionists saw a French economy gripped in the vice of traditionalism. The vast majority of Frenchmen and women, some 80 per cent, were peasants, and from their perspective this expansive agricultural sector remained 'sluggish', especially compared to those of England and the Low Countries. Industrialization was only in its early stages of development and would not take off until the mid-nineteenth century. Manufacturing was still dominated by inefficient 'pre-capitalist' and 'anti-entrepreneurial' guilds.[15] Real wages failed to keep pace with rising prices. To many, when compared with rapidly industrializing Britain, France's economy on the eve of the Revolution appeared downright backwards.[16]

This lack of economic dynamism was attributed in no small part to specifically French cultural and social values, namely that status was acquired through the ownership of land, whereas trade and manufacturing were subject to widely held prejudices. Consequently, when French merchants and manufacturers had earned their fortune, they did not prudently reinvest the profits in their enterprises, accumulating capital to expand their operations like their Anglo-American counterparts. Instead, at the earliest opportunity, most took their money out of more lucrative, productive, and risky investments in production and trade in order to advance socially by acquiring land and annuities, by purchasing an office in the judicial system or in administration, or even by buying a noble title outright. Far from viewing nobles with hostility as their class enemies, France's ambitious lawyers, landlords, office-holders, and even business leaders aspired above all to *become* noble. Over the course of the century, an estimated six to seven thousand wealthy commoners acquired aristocratic status by purchasing an ennobling office. By 1789 these *anobli* families collectively accounted for as many as one-sixth of all nobles.[17] Wealthy elites of the Third Estate emulated noble lifestyles and culture, married their daughters into noble families, and socialized with aristocrats in salons and Masonic lodges. The two social groups, scholars argued, were in the process of merging into a single elite, a society of notables whose fault lines only became truly apparent in 1788 with the calling of the Estates-General.[18]

Even those who acknowledged that strong economic growth marked certain sectors during the pre-revolutionary era denied that this produced a coherent social or political identity among France's diverse non-noble elites. For some, France's economic development had been too little and too late to produce a politically self-aware capitalist class.[19] Others pointed out that even in the business sector itself 'class' boundaries blurred, with nobles playing a key role in the development of heavy industry such as coal mining and iron production, economic pursuits that they could pursue freely without fear of *dérogation*, or loss of noble status.[20] Nor were old regime merchants quite the enthusiastic proponents of 'laissez-faire' economics that the Marxists had proposed. The commercial corps called for both liberty *and* protection from the royal government—often in the same breath—and were not afraid to strategically leverage privileges such as local monopolies or free port status to protect and enhance their market share.[21] During the 1770s and 1780s, the impetus for economic liberalism came to a large degree from political economists known as Physiocrats and even from within the royal administration itself.[22] Finally, the corporate organization of commercial elites hampered the emergence of a national community of interest. Historically, France's commercial cities viewed one another as competitors for market share and rivals for the privileges bestowed by the Crown. Even on the local level, the economic elite was fractured. On the eve of the Revolution, Gail Bossenga argues, among business leaders of cities such as Lille there was no unified 'bourgeois' social community or political position to represent.[23]

By the late 1980s, the new consensus was clear: the French Revolution was a political rather than a social phenomenon. It was the Revolution that made the bourgeoisie as a social and political class, many argued, rather than vice versa.[24] The defeat of the Marxist paradigm was so complete that in 1991 the historian Colin Jones observed that 'the idea ... that the Revolution was a bourgeois revolution is now held up to ridicule'.[25] Even economic and social historians of the Revolution went so far as to explicitly renounce concepts such as bourgeoisie, class, and capitalism.[26]

Perhaps most devastating for the fate of the revolutionary bourgeoisie has been Sarah Maza's *The Myth of the French Bourgeoisie*. Posing the question why no group identifying itself as the bourgeoisie or middle class came forward during the revolutionary era to propose itself as an alternative to traditional noble leadership or to constitute an icon for representative politics as in the Anglo-American context, Maza turns to cultural representations of French society—what she terms the 'social imaginary'—to understand how contemporaries perceived the bourgeoisie. In the process she lays out the problems associated with the term 'bourgeoisie', often used by scholars as a catch-all category to include anyone who was neither an aristocrat nor a worker or servant. To accommodate such diversity, the bourgeoisie is frequently subdivided into categories such as a *rentier* bourgeoisie 'living nobly' off its investments; a professional bourgeoisie of lawyers, notaries, and doctors; and a petty bourgeoisie of artisans and shopkeepers, among others—groups that often seem to have had little in common. Such lack of analytic specificity, Maza points out, is hardly new. For contemporaries, too, 'bourgeois' was a polyvalent term, one that could be adopted with pride by legally privileged residents of a city, as in 'bourgeois de Paris', or deployed as a term of scorn, as was more frequently the case. Portrayed as self-interested and motivated by personal gain rather than the honour and patriotism that characterized the nobility, the upwardly mobile bourgeois occupied an unstable rung in the French social hierarchy; he was 'perceived as both despicable and dangerous'.[27]

Having uncovered no positive discourse celebrating bourgeois identity in the popular political culture of the revolutionary era, Maza provocatively concludes that the French bourgeoisie 'did not exist'—and would not constitute itself as a self-aware political and social class until the 1820s. In the field of social representation, however, she argues that the bourgeoisie did play a critical role in revolutionary politics because the construct of the much-reviled, divisive bourgeoisie came to constitute a negative 'other' against which the virtuous and unified nation could be constructed.[28] The revolutionary bourgeoisie, in other words, has been relegated to the status of a myth—and an unpopular, albeit consequential, one at that.

COMMERCIAL CAPITALISM AND THE CONSUMER REVOLUTION

In recent decades, France's eighteenth century economic performance has been subject to a thorough reassessment, and new research has decisively tipped the balance in favour of an economy that was in the midst of a robust if uneven expansion, although one rooted in commercial rather than industrial capitalism. Scholars now suggest that France forged its own distinctive—and not unsuccessful— path to economic modernity. Although large-scale mechanized industry did gain a foothold in pre-revolutionary France, textile production expanded primarily through dense manufacturing networks that penetrated the rural countryside. Rouen manufacturers, for example, employed an estimated 60,000 domestic workers who lived in the surrounding area. This putting-out work supplemented peasant incomes, providing cash that industrious households used to participate in the expanding consumer economy. France's agricultural sector, too, has been reappraised in a more favourable light. Farmers, after all, were able to feed a population that grew by about one-third between 1715 and 1789, from roughly 21.5 million to 28.6 million. Famine became a thing of the past. Although the experiences of peasants varied widely, in certain areas scholars describe communities embracing 'rural capitalism', pursuing opportunities for market specialization made possible by significant improvements in roads and canals.[29]

The once-moribund guilds have likewise been rehabilitated as 'flexible instruments that served mercantile interests in the competitive world of commercial capitalism'.[30] French manufacturers, scholars note, set the standard for luxury production, leveraging the prestige of the French court and aristocrats' desire to be fashionable to successfully dominate Europe's high-end markets. For those seeking capital, Paris's vast credit market, coordinated by notaries, engaged a diverse cross-section of society from aristocrats to artisans as both borrowers and lenders. On the whole, domestic commerce, bene-fiting from France's population surge, grew impressively during the eighteenth cen-tury. International and colonial trade, however, positively took off, multiplying over the course of the century by factors of four and ten, respectively.[31] It was this thriving external trade, Guillaume Daudin argues, that constituted the 'heart of growth' for the economy as a whole.[32] Colonial slavery, the labour regime that produced the tobacco, coffee, and sugar that growing numbers of consumers craved, came to be defined by 'unrestrained commercial calculation'. The number of African slaves toiling in French domains grew exponentially, from about 10,000 in the 1650s to an estimated 700,000 in 1789.[33]

Especially influential in reframing scholars' understanding of the pre-revolutionary economy has been the work of Daniel Roche, Cissie Fairchilds, and others who have analysed after-death inventories to reveal striking changes in what people owned—and consequently how they lived—that are known collectively as the consumer revolution. From courtly nobles to struggling journeymen, Parisians spent more money acquiring larger and more varied wardrobes, accessories such as umbrellas and fans, and special-ized furniture and home decor. Homes—even those of working-class Parisians—were increasingly warmed by stoves, decorated with tapestries and mirrors, and furnished with chests of drawers, writing tables, and bookshelves. Earthenware dishes replaced tin plates. By the 1780s, nearly half of working-class households owned coffee pots or tea-making accessories. Even as growing numbers of artisans splurged on genuine luxu-ries like gold watches, affordable 'populuxe' products such as papier-mâché snuffboxes, created for a mass market, sold widely. Although Paris led the way in these new con-sumer trends, provincial cities followed and even the countryside trailed along.[34]

Changes in clothing are particularly revealing because clothing constituted a form of social representation that was laden with symbolic meaning. Historically, clothing had announced an individual's status within the social hierarchy—one was what one wore. New consumption patterns that took shape during the century challenged this prin-ciple. The French acquired more items of clothing—twice as many or more—and the overall value of their wardrobes increased significantly across almost all social groups, with women outspending men. At the same time, the clothes themselves became lighter, more colourful, more comfortable, and more stylish. Perhaps most significant, the once-great distinctions between the clothing styles and fabrics worn by elites and com-moners began to erode. Gifts of clothes from masters to servants and brisk sales on the second-hand market placed items such as formal waistcoats and silk gowns within reach of even working-class men and women. As such acquisitions destabilized the semiotics of clothing, contemporaries took notice. Moralists, unsettled, lamented that the taste for luxury was undermining traditional society and its values.[35]

At the same time, the production and sales of books and periodicals rose quickly, while commercialization fuelled the success of the new advertising newssheets known as *affiches* that served as local newspapers in forty-four French cities. Customers desiring more shocking or titillating fare turned to the black market, where they pur-chased forbidden books including censored works by philosophes such as d'Holbach and Rousseau, pornographic texts, and libels that revealed in sordid detail the alleged depravity of the royal court. New commercialized forms of sociability and entertainment rose in popularity as well. In the capital, customers flocked to the 1,500 or more cafes that had opened by the late eighteenth century. Tens of thousands of spectators attended theatrical performances in public playhouses that opened in at least seventy-two metropolitan cities and eleven colonial cities. Among France's increasingly urbanized population, the rapid circulation of new commodities, texts, fashions, and cultural practices created important connections that helped to transform city dwellers into Frenchmen.[36]

In light of such research, it has become almost impossible to deny that economic growth, which peaked in the mid-1780s, significantly influenced everyday life for Parisians and provincials, elites and commoners, and even colonists and their slaves. Mining the juncture of economics and politics, historians are moving beyond the Marxist-revisionist impasse by bringing the methods and insights of political and cultural history to bear on the economic processes that transformed eighteenth century France and by disentangling the question of capitalism, as a complex set of phenomena that affected French society, broadly speaking, from the contested question of class. One set of studies focuses on the relationship of global capitalism to the precipitous collapse of the old regime. In the most immediate sense, almost all scholars agree, the Revolution was unleashed by a crisis in state finances. The royal government, confronting imminent bankruptcy, found itself unable to do either of the two things that might have forestalled catastrophe: convince historically tax-shielded nobles and clergy to accept a more equitable distribution of taxes, or borrow the money necessary to keep the government operational until such reform could be undertaken. The first failed on political grounds, when France's courts of law (*parlements*) and the Assembly of Notables refused to accept new taxes and demanded that the king convoke the Estates-General. The second, however, was a failure of credit. Why, Lynn Hunt asks, was the French state unable to manage debt levels that were, relatively speaking, lower than those of Britain?[37]

Lacking a national bank and burdened with a poor credit history, the French government was forced to seek high interest loans in international lending markets to finance the costs of fighting the Seven Years War and, later, the War of American Independence. Its very success in obtaining such loans only exacerbated the government's financial woes, however, by enabling the French, in Hunt's words, 'to borrow themselves into bankruptcy'.[38] By the 1780s, simply paying the interest on these loans consumed more than half of tax revenues. Growing annual deficits, in turn, necessitated even more loans. This cycle might have continued, however, had not a scandal that broke in 1787 over government-sponsored speculation on the Paris bourse destroyed confidence in the state's financial practices. Public opinion turned against scheming financiers and corrupt royal ministers, dangerously undermining the political capital of the monarchy at a time when it was sorely needed. As interest rates rose impossibly high and state default began to appear a genuine possibility, foreign lending dried up completely. By August 1788, the treasury had run out of money. Unable to master the situation, the king delegated responsibility for resolving the fiscal crisis to the Estates-General, which would meet in May 1789. The monarchy's declining financial credit and its declining political credit, scholars argue, were intimately linked.[39]

The fact that the debt crisis coincided with a painful economic recession that was compounded by back-to-back poor harvests in 1787 and 1788, driving the price of bread to record highs in the spring and summer of 1789, certainly did not help the monarchy's cause. Making matters worse, the Anglo-French Commercial Treaty of 1786 lowered trade barriers, allowing France to be flooded by inexpensive British manufactured goods. Greatly exacerbating the already difficult circumstances confronting French manufacturers in sectors such as textiles and glass making, the treaty resulted in unemployment levels that reached 50 per cent or more in areas stretching across the north of France. Angry commercial elites, who had opposed the treaty from the start, castigated the royal government for producing widespread destitution. The Crown's efforts to liberalize trade produced increasingly outspoken opposition and demands for reform.[40]

At the same time, the economic competition that characterized early modern globalization cannot be separated from the questions of empire—and of human rights—which came to the fore in 1789. Empire was at the heart of France's eighteenth century rivalry with Britain, and the wars that France fought to protect its status as a global economic and military power generated the debts that would become so troublesome.[41] During this era, educated elites became increasingly preoccupied by questions of political economy, publishing literally thousands of books and pamphlets on the topic; in these debates, empire assumed a place of prominence.[42] According to Jeremy Popkin, contests of authority in Saint-Domingue, where resentful colonists sought greater economic and political independence from the metropole, contributed to the destabilization of the royal government. Furthermore, contemporaries could no longer ignore the disturbing fact that some of the most profitable commodities circulating in the eighteenth century Atlantic economy were, in fact, human beings, the African slaves referred to by traders as pieces of 'ebony wood (*le bois d'ébène*).'[43] How would France reconcile the desire for greater liberty and equality, expressed widely in the lists of grievances compiled in 1789, with the troubling reality that their economy had significant interests in slavery? Among the earliest matters taken up by the National Assembly in June and early July of 1789, Popkin points out, were the contentious issues of colonial political representation, the status of people of colour, and even the legitimacy of slavery itself, conflicts that would stoke the flames of violent revolution in Saint-Domingue in 1791.[44]

A second theme in recent scholarship shifts the focus from the global to the intimate, addressing connections between new consumption practices and the 'cultural origins' of the Revolution, defined by Roger Chartier as those conditions that made the Revolution 'possible because it was conceivable'.[45] How and why did significant numbers of the French become willing—and even eager—to discard their traditional socio-political order and replace it with something new? Historians have highlighted ways that eighteenth century consumerism operated in tension with the legal inequalities, social hierarchies, and absolutist politics that still formally defined pre-revolutionary France, undermining their legitimacy while offering up different values and new social possibilities. The new material world that opened up to Frenchmen and women during the late old regime not only held out the promise of greater physical comfort, but also the opportunity for more expansive freedom of choice and individual self-expression. For Roche, the entry of the common people into consumerism constituted 'a fundamental silent revolution, as important in its way as the spread of literacy'.[46]

The old regime's traditional order has been famously described as a divinely sanctioned 'Great Chain of Being' with the king standing closest to God and the clergy, nobles, and commoners each assuming their natural rank along vertical links representing unequal relations of status and privilege. In an influential article, Colin Jones proposes that rising consumerism undermined this deeply hierarchical world view by forging a competing 'Great Chain of Buying', characterized by its 'horizontal' links connecting buyers and sellers in market-driven relationships of relative equality. Jones finds evidence of this emergent, egalitarian commercial world view in the pages of the personal advertisement-driven *affiches*. Because the identity of subscribers mattered less than their status as potential consumers, these newssheets addressed a 'unitary economic subject', one who assumed his or her place within 'a hierarchy of wealth and taste, not birth or privilege'.[47] Here and elsewhere, Jones seeks to restore the bourgeoisie in the broad sense of educated and market-oriented middling classes to a place of prominence in the Revolution.[48] He argues that this 'Great Chain of Buying', although inclusive, was created principally by, and for, an entrepreneurial bourgeoisie that included significant numbers of office-holders and professionals, precisely the individuals who would take up the mantle of political leadership in 1789.

Although the *affiches* were in the business of cultivating and satisfying personal needs and wants, editors also used their pages to propagate enlightened ideals and civic values among readers, effectively constructing a 'new community of citizen-consumers'.[49] In this way, Jones argues, the *affiches* and the commercial relationships they celebrated offered a new model for the social body and the body politic that anticipated revolutionary citizenship. Similarly, in current work, William Sewell suggests that consumerism played a critical role in preparing the way for widespread acceptance of civil equality in 1789. As everyday life during the late eighteenth century became 'interlaced with new capitalist forms of social relations', this enabled the French to make the imaginative leap to a society in which all citizens would enjoy equal opportunities and rights.[50]

Finally, commercialization has been linked to the politicization of the consumer. In France's playhouses, for example, when theatre directors or authorities refused to accommodate audience demands, spectators increasingly invoked a rhetoric of consumer rights to justify their cause. In a number of cities, aggrieved fans went so far as to stage boycotts of local stages until their demands were met, actions that escalated into high-visibility public protests that placed military authorities on alert.[51] Moreover, the state itself became a primary target of consumer hostility. Michael Kwass argues that the hefty indirect taxes that the monarchy levied on consumer goods generated smouldering resentment, driving frustrated customers to buy goods such as tobacco, salt, and calico on France's extensive black market. Smugglers openly and even violently flouted royal authority, with the most famous among them, Louis Mandrin, achieving legendary popularity as a 'Robin Hood' figure. At the same time, elites wrote tracts attacking the 'despotic' institution that collected such taxes on behalf of the Crown, known as the General Farm, and decrying the barbaric punishments meted out to smugglers, who received harsh sentences working in the galleys. In fact, the Farm was one of the earliest targets of popular revolutionary violence. In 1789, in a dozen cities including Paris, urban crowds attacked the customs booths that collected the *octrois, aides*, and other indirect taxes on consumer goods entering cities, taxes that hit struggling workers especially hard by significantly raising the cost of food, wine, and other necessities.[52]

THE PROBLEM OF THE CONSPICUOUSLY ABSENT BOURGEOISIE

As we consider the consequences of this eighteenth century economic expansion, we confront a seeming paradox. With France's commercial economy booming, the middling classes grew at a rapid pace, roughly tripling in size to about 2.3 million, or nearly 10 per cent of the population, by 1789.[53] Although *le commerce*—an exclusive elite comprised of international traders, manufacturers, and wealthy wholesale merchants—comprised only a fraction of this total, local studies suggest that it, too, experienced robust growth, especially in France's largest ports and commercial centres.[54] Even as the numbers of *négociants* grew substantially, they became, on the whole, wealthier, better educated, more cosmopolitan, better organized, and more prominent in urban public life.[55] Yet when the revolutionary crisis arrived, French businessmen would seem to be one of the only prominent social cohorts that lacked political initiative and a distinctive voice. Those who might most closely resemble Marx's long-lost capitalists have been rendered rather conspicuously absent from the history of the Revolution.

Just how much is known about the political culture of commercial capitalists? There is some irony in the fact that Soboul himself was forced to concede in the 1970s that 'we do not have a history of the French bourgeoisie in the Revolutionary period'—by which he meant a synthetic work of social and political history on the national scale.[56] What Marxists themselves did not undertake proved to be of little interest to revisionists.[57] If freed from the lingering Marxist assumption that the commercial bourgeoisie should have constituted (or failed to constitute) a politically *triumphant* force in 1789, what might scholars find?

All of which brings us back to the Chamber of Commerce of Montpellier and the failed campaign for special commercial representation to the Estates-General. Amalia Kessler, in her study of the Paris Merchant Court, draws welcome attention to the campaign by investigating the origins of this novel political alliance.[58] Why, she asks, did France's chambers of commerce and merchant courts, 'each with its own particular, local interests, come to see themselves as together constituting a unified *corps*, capable of, interested in, and entitled to a role in national governance?'[59] For Kessler, the campaign represents the culmination of decades of commercial legal unification under the leadership of the Parisian court, of collaboration among merchant courts on issues of common concern, and of tenacious self-promotion by merchant court justices, who proudly (and controversially) represented themselves as royal judges. At the same time, in their decisions, merchant court judges gave commerce a new definition that located it at the heart of political economy. Traditionally understood as the business dealings undertaken by merchants with other merchants, commerce came to be represented much more expansively as the circulation of goods and wealth, a natural and essential function that defined modern society.[60] When the calling of the Estates-General unleashed what Kessler describes as 'a massive, nationwide status dispute', chambers of commerce and merchant courts joined forces and built on traditions celebrating merchant honour and patriotism to present themselves as a national 'meta-corps' of commerce that merited social recognition and political representation.[61]

Such self-congratulatory assertions concerning the political and social importance of commerce—and of merchants themselves—for the French nation provide critical insight into the changing 'social imaginary' of the commercial bourgeoisie. At the same time, I suggest, they paint only half the picture. Even more revealing is the campaign's darker underside, which highlights the frustration and insecurity of France's wealthy and distinguished business elites. For the political mobilization of the business class was catalysed not by corporate pride or a sense of entitlement so much as by something even more potent: fear, specifically the fears of those who were faced with mounting evidence of their economic vulnerability and political impotence. What was at stake in 1788 was nothing less than control over economic policy and, consequently, over the riches produced by colonial trade.

Although couched in polite language, the memoirs that commercial corps sent to Versailles in 1788 convey sharp criticism of recent policy decisions along with anger at their exclusion from decision-making, with what they considered to be disastrous consequences. In just four short years, business communities had seen their privileged trading positions undermined by a series of government policies which had left them, in their words, 'groaning under the weight of a destructive regime'.[62] In 1784, the monarchy had relaxed the Exclusif (metropolitan merchants' monopoly on trade with the French colonies) by opening certain colonial ports to foreign trade, a move that many *négociants* feared was just a first step towards a broader liberalization of colonial trade. Just two years later, the devastating Anglo-French Trade Treaty revealed to the commercial bourgeoisie the extent to which their prosperity was exposed to politics. As key pillars of the manufacturing sector collapsed and royal ministers threatened to do away with the privileges of free ports such as Marseille, growing numbers of French business leaders felt themselves to be in crisis—economic, political, or both.[63]

To build support for a special commercial deputation, the Merchant Court of Nantes, which also acted as a chamber of commerce, leveraged its dual institutional networks by sending out circular letters in late July proposing that chambers of commerce and merchant courts join forces in demanding political representation.[64] The collapse of royal authority, these Nantes merchants recognized, marked the beginnings of a new kind of politics. To build the political authority in the Estates-General necessary to shape legislation regarding taxes, tariffs, and other key economic matters, they would need to rally a national community. By some measures, they succeeded wildly. According to Jean-Pierre Hirsch, the distinctive social, political, and economic frustrations confronting commercial elites were discussed and debated in some sixty cities in metropolitan France. Ultimately, fifty-six commercial corps petitioned the king, the royal ministers, and the Assembly of Notables.[65] This chorus of commercial voices carefully crafted a social and political identity for the commercial bourgeoisie that was deceptively coherent. Deliberately obscuring the conflicts and jealousies that divided them, their pamphlets strategically emphasized their common social and economic position and shared political outlook. In circular letters written to sister institutions, they repeatedly stressed themes of community and the importance of presenting a unanimous front.[66] The message they delivered, moreover, was radical. Months before the storming of the Bastille, French merchants brazenly announced to the king that a 'new order of things almost always requires a new [political] regime'.[67] As they called for political tradition to be disregarded so that they might secure representation, they seemed entirely unaware of the fact that, as David Bien has observed, 'within the existing framework reform was never a real alternative to revolution'.[68]

Despite its fervour and scope, the campaign failed to accomplish its goals. In late December 1788 an observer at Versailles explained the ministers' reaction: 'It does not seem that they want to isolate the interests of commerce from the general interest ... they seem to me persuaded that the great commercial cities, of which commerce is the main force, would understand their own interests well enough to deputize *négociants* in the order of the Third'.[69] The king never officially responded to their demands.[70] For better or for worse, however, the campaign's influence did not end there, for by setting themselves apart and seeking to enhance only their own political authority, commercial corps reinforced the already negative public perception of a self-serving bourgeoisie out for personal gain. In a rare dissenting pamphlet, the savvier commercial elites of Grenoble warned their colleagues that a movement to obtain special political consideration for business elites stood to harm social perceptions of *le commerce* by raising fears that *négociants* were conspiring to promote the interests of business at the expense of those of the nation as a whole.[71] Rather than deny the centrality of interest to their politics, however, commercial corps actively acknowledged and defended interest politics. It was precisely their specific knowledge of commercial practices and their commitment to prosperity for themselves but also for others, they argued, that made traders and manufacturers ideal legislators of commercial matters. If *le commerce* were able to participate in the Estates-General in adequate numbers, the merchants of Marseille argued in January of 1789, the commercial deputies 'will watch after one another; the interest of a single one would not be the interest of all'.[72] They suggested that France's merchant-deputies, by defending their own economic self-interest, would collectively arrive at policy decisions that would benefit the nation as a whole. Ultimately, they asked, who was better equipped than *commerçants*, 'independent by principle, free by honor', to defend 'the property of citizens and the activity of industry?'[73]

The critical fallout was ugly. One satiric pamphlet adopted the form of a secret letter from one *négociant* to another claiming to expose the 'real' motives behind the failed campaign to enhance the political authority of France's leading businessmen: 'In spite of our millions, we have to renounce ... the desire to erect a FOURTH ORDER ... O shame! O sadness! *We will continue to be part of the Third Estate. WE WILL REMAIN THE EQUALS of the [retail] merchants, the lawyers, the notaries, the doctors, the workers, the laborers, &c. &c.*'[74] In retrospect, the political strategy embraced by *le commerce* in 1788 proved a mistake that may well have helped to seal the fate of the commercial elite in national politics in the years to come. The problem was that these commercial elites had sought to garner for themselves the very political privileges that the abbé Sieyès castigated as early as November 1788 as 'unjust, odious, and contrary to the supreme end of every political society'.[75]

Yet neither the failure of the campaign for special representation nor the derision that it attracted marked the end of the political mobilization of the commercial bourgeoisie. In fact, these developments spurred it on even as they altered the forms that it took by pushing *le commerce* to pursue its political goals outside of the bounds of elected office. When the election results for the Estates-General began to come in, the predictably poor showing of commercial elites proved a powerful motivator for France's chambers of commerce to embrace more direct collective action. In April 1789, the Chamber of Commerce of La Rochelle, worried that 'the vast majority of the Third will be total strangers to commerce', urged its colleagues that to prepare for this 'misfortune, which would be perhaps irrevocable', they should join together to form 'a committee of 30 or 40 wholesale traders of different provinces' to send to the Estates-General to work collectively to influence the legislative process.[76] Before democracy was even out of the cradle, France's commercial bourgeoisie would embrace lobbying as the most effective means at their disposal to shape revolutionary politics. A substantial number of chambers of commerce paid to send one or even several 'Extraordinary Deputies of Commerce' to work collaboratively lobbying the official deputies of the National Constituent Assembly on matters of economic policy.[77] The first such lobbyists, those from Nantes, arrived in Versailles on 14 July 1789. By October they had succeeded in winning official access to the legislative bar, the right to review all materials that the revolutionary state received related to commerce, and even permission to attend the meetings of the official Committee on Agriculture and Commerce. Their behind-the-scenes actions would prove consequential in shaping the economic and political agenda of the early Revolution.[78]

This all-but-overlooked campaign for political representation for *le commerce* is just one small episode in the coming of the French Revolution. Yet, it suggests that Sarah Maza's assertion that the French bourgeoisie existed solely as a myth needs to be revisited. When commercial capitalists are approached not as the celebrated leaders that an earlier generation sought and failed to find, but rather as frustrated political actors struggling to find their footing in a rapidly changing political environment, it becomes clear that at a critical moment they did openly identify themselves as a distinct social and political community within the nation. Moreover, their political voice is worthy of

further study precisely because it clashed with the main currents of revolutionary politics. For, as scholars of political culture have shown, the revolutionaries would adopt an
increasingly strident refrain of national unity that denied legitimate differences of interest and worked to silence dissent. Interest rapidly became 'a code ... for betrayal of a
nation united'.[79] French business leaders nonetheless insisted upon conceiving of the
Estates-General and, later, of the National Constituent Assembly as representative bodies whose deputies promoted the necessarily competing hopes and needs of their constituents and ultimately balanced them to achieve a national 'union of interests'.[80] During
the first two years of the Revolution, until the chambers of commerce were abolished in
the fall of 1791, *le commerce* found ways to pursue a politics of interest, paying dozens of
merchant-lobbyists generous salaries to shape policies from behind closed doors.

Today, one is hard pressed to find historians who argue that capitalism and a rising
bourgeoisie 'caused' the French Revolution in the structurally determined way that
leading scholars once believed. Armed with more nuanced approaches to causation and
agency, however, a new wave of scholarship is revealing that there is still much to be
learned about the relationship between changing global economic practices and the fall
of the old regime, and between rising consumerism and the development of new conceptions of individuality, liberty, rights, and citizenship. In order to fully understand
the revolutionary reinvention of the social contract, such work suggests, we may first
need to give the humble commercial contract its due. Taking the business class seriously
as political actors, moreover, has become a necessary task. It may just be the case that
the much-despised commercial bourgeoisie and their embrace of an unpopular coun-
ter-discourse of interest provide an essential key to understanding the development of
French Revolutionary politics, after all.

Notes

1. Archives de la Chambre de commerce et d'industrie de Marseille Provence [CCM], A 25,
   Requête au roi (n.p., 1788).
2. On the 5 July declaration, see Raymond Birn, 'The Pamphlet Press and the Estates-General
   of 1789', *Studies on Voltaire and the Eighteenth Century* 287 (1991), 59–69. On trends in
   pre-Revolutionary politics, see Kenneth Margerison, *Pamphlets and Public Opinion: The
   Campaign for a Union of Orders in the Early French Revolution* (Lafayette, 1998) and Mitchell
   B. Garrett, *The Estates General of 1789: The Problems of Composition and Organization*
   (New York, 1935).
3. This analysis draws on pamphlets and correspondence authored by chambers of commerce and merchant courts in forty-two cities, located primarily in CCM 25 A and in the
   Archives de Paris [AP] D1 B6 1, n. 18–98.
4. CCM, A 25, *Requête au roi*, 3.
5. CCM, A 25, *Requête au roi*, 2–3.
6. CCM, A 25, *Requête au roi*, 3.
7. AP D1 B6 1, n. 65 (Montauban), 5; n. 51 (Dijon), 2; and n. 90 (Toulouse).
8. Newberry Library Case Folio FRC 9699 'Correspondance secrete, ou lettre d'un négociant
   en gros à un de ses pairs' (n.p., n.d.), 2; CCM B 214, 31 December 1788.

9. William Doyle, *Origins of the French Revolution* (Oxford, 1980), 100; and Timothy Tackett, *Becoming a Revolutionary: The Deputies of the French National Assembly and the Emergence of a Revolutionary Culture (1789–1790)* (Princeton, 1996), 20, 37–38. Commercial elites enjoyed greater success in municipal politics. Lynn Hunt, *Politics, Culture, and Class in the French Revolution* (Berkeley, 1984), 155–70.

10. On the continuing controversy concerning the bourgeoisie and the Revolution, see Jean-Pierre Jessenne (ed.), *Vers un ordre bourgeois? Révolution française et changement social* (Rennes, 2007).

11. Lynn Hunt, *Politics, Culture, and Class*, 3.

12. Colin Lucas, 'Nobles, Bourgeois, and the Origins of the French Revolution', *Past and Present* 60 (1973), 84–126, 84.

13. This interpretation is most closely associated with Georges Lefebvre's *The Coming of the French Revolution* (Princeton, 1989) originally published in 1939, and Albert Soboul, *The French Revolution, 1787–1799: From the Storming of the Bastille to Napoleon* (London, 1974), quote from 21.

14. See especially Alfred Cobban, *The Social Interpretation of the French Revolution*, 2nd ed., (Cambridge, 1999 [1964]); George V. Taylor, 'Noncapitalist Wealth and the Origins of the French Revolution', *American Historical Review* 72 (1967), 469–96; and Doyle, *Origins of the French Revolution*.

15. See, for example, William Doyle's *The Oxford History of the French Revolution* (Oxford, 1989), 9–21, 'sluggish' 14. Quotes on guilds from Jan de Vries and William Reddy, respectively, in Gail Bossenga, 'Protecting Merchants: Guilds and Commercial Capitalism in Eighteenth-Century France', *French Historical Studies* 15, no. 4 (1988), 693–703, 693.

16. For a traditionalist perspective, see Doyle, *Origins of the French Revolution*, esp. 30–4. On French 'backwardness', see David Landes, *The Unbound Prometheus: Technological Change and Industrial Development in Western Europe from 1750 to the Present* (Cambridge, 1975).

17. Lucas, 'Nobles, Bourgeois, and the Origins', 89–92; Colin Jones, *The Great Nation: France from Louis XV to Napoleon* (London, 2002), 326; Doyle, *The Oxford History of the French Revolution*, 26.

18. Guy Chaussinand-Nogaret, *The French Nobility in the Eighteenth Century: From Feudalism to Enlightenment* (Cambridge, 1985), 114; Daniel Roche, *France in the Enlightenment* (Cambridge, 1998), 390–419.

19. Liah Greenfeld, *The Spirit of Capitalism: Nationalism and Economic Growth* (Cambridge, 2001), 147–8; William H. Sewell, Jr, *A Rhetoric of Bourgeois Revolution: The Abbé Sieyes and What Is the Third Estate?* (Durham, NC, 1994), 39.

20. Chassinand-Nogaret, *The French Nobility*.

21. Jean-Pierre Hirsch, 'Les milieux du commerce, l'esprit de système, et le pouvoir à la veille de la Révolution', *Annales. Économies, Sociétés, Civilisations* 30, no. 6 (1975), 1337–70; Gail Bossenga, *The Politics of Privilege: Old Regime and Revolution in Lille* (Cambridge, 1991), 131–67.

22. Paul Cheney, *Revolutionary Commerce: Globalization and the French Monarchy* (Cambridge, 2010), 141–167; Arnault Skornicki, *L'économiste, la cour, et la patrie. L'économie politique dans la France des Lumières* (Paris, 2011); Charles Walton, 'The Fall from Eden: The Free-Trade Origins of the French Revolution', in Suzanne Desan, Lynn Hunt, and William Max Nelson (eds), *The French Revolution in Global Perspective* (Ithaca, 2013), 44–56.

23. Bossenga, *The Politics of Privilege*, 206.

24. Lucas, 'Nobles, Bourgeois, and the Origins', 126; and, more recently, David Garrioch, *The Formation of the Parisian Bourgeoisie, 1690–1830* (Cambridge, 1996), 1.

25. Colin Jones, 'Bourgeois Revolution Revivified: 1789 and Social Change', in Colin Lucas (ed.), *Rewriting the French Revolution* (Oxford, 1991), 69–118, 71.

26. For example, Jack Goldstone, 'The Social Origins of the French Revolution Revisited', in Thomas Kaiser and Dale Van Kley (eds), *From Deficit to Deluge: The Origins of the French Revolution* (Stanford, 2011), 67–103, 70; and Florian Aftalion, *The French Revolution: An Economic Interpretation* (Cambridge, 1990), 5–8.

27. Sarah Maza, *The Myth of the French Bourgeoisie: An Essay on the Social Imaginary, 1750–1850* (Cambridge, 2003), 5, 25.

28. Maza, *The Myth of the French Bourgeoisie*, 5, 13.

29. Jeff Horn, *The Path Not Taken: French Industrialization in the Age of Revolution, 1750–1830* (Cambridge, MA, 2006); Jan de Vries, *The Industrious Revolution: Consumer Behavior and the Household Economy, 1650 to the Present* (Cambridge, 2008), 71–72, 96-10; Jones, 'Bourgeois Revolution Revivified', 78–93; and *The Great Nation*, esp. 349–60; Jonathan Dewald, *Pont-St-Pierre, 1398–1789: Lordship, Community, and Capitalism in Early Modern France* (Berkeley, 1987).

30. Bossenga, 'Protecting Merchants', 703.

31. William Sewell, 'The Empire of Fashion and the Rise of Capitalism', *Past and Present* 206 (Feb. 2010), 81–120; Philip T. Hoffman, Gilles Postel-Vinay, and Jean-Laurent Rosenthal, *Priceless Markets: The Political Economy of Credit in Paris, 1660–1870* (Chicago, 2000); Jones, *The Great Nation*, 354.

32. Guillaume Daudin, *Commerce et prospérité: la France au XVIIIe siècle* (Paris, 2011), 8, 394.

33. Robin Blackburn, *The Making of New World Slavery: From the Baroque to the Modern, 1492–1800* (London, 1997), 10–11, 282, 379, quote on 589; Jeremy Popkin, 'Saint-Domingue, Slavery, and the Origins of the French Revolution', in Kaiser and Van Kley (eds), *From Deficit to Deluge*, 219–48, 221.

34. Daniel Roche, *The People of Paris: An Essay in Popular Culture in the 18th Century* (Berkeley, 1987), 118–19, 137–8, 151, and *The History of Everyday Things: The Birth of Consumption in France, 1600–1800* (Cambridge, 2000), 166–220; Cissie Fairchilds, 'The Production and Marketing of Populuxe Goods in Eighteenth-Century Paris', in John Brewer and Roy Porter (eds), *Consumption and the World of Goods* (London, 1993), 228–48.

35. Daniel Roche, *The Culture of Clothing: Dress and Fashion in the Ancien Régime* (Cambridge, 1996), 99, 106, 108, 110–11, 142, 168, 505; Roche, *People of Paris*, 160–94; Roche, *History of Everyday Things*, 213–20.

36. Colin Jones, 'The Great Chain of Buying: Medical Advertisement, the Bourgeois Public Sphere, and the Origins of the French Revolution', *The American Historical Review* 101, no. 1 (1996), 13–40, 18, 32; Robert Darnton, *The Forbidden Best-Sellers of Pre-Revolutionary France* (New York, 1996); Jones, *The Great Nation*, 181; Lauren R. Clay, *Stagestruck: The Business of Theater in Eighteenth-Century France and Its Colonies* (Ithaca, 2013), 2, 16, 7.

37. Lynn Hunt, 'The Global Financial Origins of 1789', in *The French Revolution in Global Perspective*, 32–43, 33.

38. Hunt, 'Global Financial Origins', 33.

39. Hunt, 'Global Financial Origins', 39–40; John Shovlin, *The Political Economy of Virtue: Luxury, Patriotism, and the Origins of the French Revolution* (Ithaca, 2006), 153–9.

40. Walton, 'The Fall from Eden', 49–54.

41. Suzanne Desan, Lynn Hunt, and William Max Nelson, 'Introduction', *The French Revolution in Global Perspective*, 1–11.

42. Shovlin, *The Political Economy of Virtue*, 2; Cheney, *Revolutionary Commerce*.

43. Pierre Pluchon, *La route des esclaves: négriers et bois d'ébène au XVIIIe siècle* (Paris, 1980).

44. Popkin, 'Saint-Domingue, Slavery, and the Origins of the French Revolution'.

45. Roger Chartier, *The Cultural Origins of the French Revolution* (Durham, 1991), 2.

46. Roche, *The Culture of Clothing*, 110.

47. Alfred O. Lovejoy, *The Great Chain of Being: A Study of the History of an Idea* (Cambridge, 1933); Jones, 'Great Chain of Buying', 19.

48. See also Jones, 'Bourgeois Revolution Revivified'.

49. Jones, 'Bourgeois Revolution Revivified', 24, 26.

50. My thanks to Professor Sewell for sharing his unpublished article manuscript, 'Connecting Capitalism to the French Revolution: The Parisian Promenade and the Origins of Civic Equality in Eighteenth-Century France'.

51. Clay, *Stagestruck*, 188–94, 208.

52. Michael Kwass, 'The Global Underground; Smuggling, Rebellion, and the Origins of the French Revolution', in *The French Revolution in Global Perspective*, 15–31; on such protests outside of Paris, see Bossenga, *Politics of Privilege*, 225 n. 59.

53. Jones, 'Bourgeois Revolution Revivified', 93–4.

54. Charles Carrière, *Négociants marseillais au XVIIIe siècle. Contribution à l'étude des économies maritimes*, 2 vols (Marseille, 1973), I: 260–3; Hirsch, 'Les milieux de commerce', 1338.

55. On merchant culture, see Roche, *France in the Enlightenment*, 140–73; Margaret Jacob, *Strangers Nowhere in the World: The Rise of Cosmopolitanism in Early Modern Europe* (Philadelphia, 2006), 66–94; Maurice Quénet, 'Un exemple de consultation dans l'administration monarchique au XVIIIe siècle: Les Nantais et leurs députés au Conseil de Commerce', *Annales de Bretagne et des pays de l'Ouest* 85, no. 3 (1978), 449–85; Clay, *Stagestruck*, 14–67, 163–94.

56. Soboul, *The French Revolution*, 24.

57. Philippe Minard, 'L'héritage historiographique', in *Vers un ordre bourgeois*, 21–35, 32.

58. Amalia Kessler, *A Revolution in Commerce: The Paris Merchant Court and the Rise of Commercial Society in Eighteenth-Century France* (New Haven, CT, 2007), 238–81, quote from 239.

59. Kessler, *A Revolution in Commerce*, 239.

60. Kessler, *A Revolution in Commerce*, 238–97.

61. Kessler, *A Revolution in Commerce*, quotes on 270, 240, see also 292.

62. Quoted in F. L. Nussbaum, 'The Deputies Extraordinary of Commerce and the French Monarchy', *Political Science Quarterly* 48, no. 4 (1933), 534–55.

63. Nussbaum, 'The Deputies Extraordinary of Commerce', 543–6, 551; Cheney, *Revolutionary Commerce*, 177–9; Walton, 'The Fall from Eden', 44–56; Horn, *The Path Not Taken*, 63–77; CCM, B 214, letter from Guillaume Rostagny, 3 May 1788.

64. CCM, A 25, letter from Merchant Court of Nantes, 23 July 1788.

65. Hirsch, 'Les milieux de commerce', 1337.

66. See, for example, CCM, A 25, letter from CC Montpellier, 18 October 1788.

67. AP D1 B6 1 98, n. 51 (Dijon).

68. David Bien quoted in Sarah Maza, 'Politics, Culture, and the Origins of the French Revolution', *Journal of Modern History* 61 (December 1989), 704–23, 720.

69. CCM, B 214, letter from Guillaume Rostagny, 31 December 1788.

70. Émile Garnault, *Le commerce rochelais au XVIIIe siècle: d'après les documents composant les anciennes archives de la Chambre de Commerce de La Rochelle* (La Rochelle, 1898), 331.

71. *Réponse des Négociants de la ville de Grenoble. A MM. les Juges-Consuls de Montauban, Clermont-Ferrand, Châlons, Orléans, Tours, Besançon, Dunkerque & Saint-Quentin, & à la Chambre de Commerce de Picardie, de Saint-Malo & de l'Isle en Flandre* (n.p., n.d.).

72. CCM, A 25, petition from the *négociants* of Marseille, 23 January 1789.

73. CCM, A 25, petition.

74. 'Correspondance secrette' (italics in original).

75. Emmanuel Joseph Sieyès, *Political Writings* (Indianapolis, 2003), 71.

76. Quoted in Garnault, *Le commerce rochelais au XVIIIe siècle*, 331.

77. J. Letaconnoux, 'Le Comité des députés extraordinaires des manufactures et du commerce de France et l'oeuvre économique de l'Assemblée constituante (1789–1791)', *Annales révolutionnaires* 6 (1913) 149–208, 154–7.

78. Letaconnoux, 'Le Comité des députés extraordinaires', 156–79, 196–200; Nussbaum, 'The Deputies Extraordinary of Commerce', 554.

79. On the problem of interest politics during the Revolution, see Hunt, *Politics, Culture, and Class*, 43–8, quote from 44; François Furet, *Interpreting the French Revolution* (Cambridge, 1981), 25–61, 77–8; and Keith Michael Baker, *Inventing the French Revolution: Essays on French Political Culture in the Eighteenth Century* (Cambridge, 1990), 5–6, 224–51.

80. I borrow this term from Cathy D. Matson and Peter S. Onuf, *A Union of Interests: Political and Economic Thought in Revolutionary America* (Lawrence, 1990).

SELECTED READING

Cheney, Paul, *Revolutionary Commerce: Globalization and the French Monarchy* (Cambridge, 2010).

Cobban, Alfred, *The Social Interpretation of the French Revolution,* second edition (Cambridge, 1999).

Desan, Suzanne, Lynn Hunt, and William Max Nelson (eds), *The French Revolution in Global Perspective* (Ithaca, 2013).

Doyle, William, *Origins of the French Revolution* (Oxford, 1980).

Hirsch, Jean-Pierre, *Les deux rêves du commerce. Entreprise et institution dans la région lilloise (1780–1860)* (Paris, 1991).

Jessenne, Jean-Pierre (ed.), *Vers un ordre bourgeois? Révolution française et changement social* (Rennes, 2007).

Jones, Colin, 'Bourgeois Revolution Revivified: 1789 and Social Change', in Colin Lucas (ed.), *Rewriting the French Revolution* (Oxford, 1991), 69–118.

Jones, Colin, 'The Great Chain of Buying: Medical Advertisement, the Bourgeois Public Sphere, and the Origins of the French Revolution', *The American Historical Review* 101, no. 1 (1996), 13–40.

Kessler, Amalia, *A Revolution in Commerce: The Paris Merchant Court and the Rise of Commercial Society in Eighteenth-Century France* (New Haven, 2007).

Lefebvre, Georges, *The Coming of the French Revolution* (Princeton, 1989).

Letaconnoux, J, 'Le Comité des députés extraordinaires des manufactures et du commerce de France et l'oeuvre économique de l'Assemblée constituante (1789–1791)', *Annales révolutionnaires* 6 (1913), 149–208.

Maza, Sarah, *The Myth of the French Bourgeoisie: An Essay on the Social Imaginary, 1750–1850* (Cambridge, 2003).

Roche, Daniel, *The Culture of Clothing: Dress and Fashion in the Ancien Régime* (Cambridge, 1996).

Roche, Daniel, *The History of Everyday Things: The Birth of Consumption in France, 1600–1800* (Cambridge, 2000).

Soboul, Albert, *The French Revolution, 1787–1799: From the Storming of the Bastille to Napoleon* (London, 1974).

CHAPTER 3

··

NOBILITY

··

JAY M. SMITH

ON the eve of the bicentennial, when David D. Bien was asked to write an essay on 'aristocracy' for François Furet and Mona Ozouf's *Critical Dictionary of the French Revolution*, he agreed to do so only with reservations. 'What are we to understand by aristocracy?' he asked. The term aristocracy, 'used loosely' under the *ancien régime*, 'was made looser in the Revolution'. The French *ancien régime* had lacked a true aristocracy in the Aristotelian sense, and the Revolution effectively made the word a floating signifier invariably applied to 'the defeated political enemy'—with Feuillants, Dantonists, and Robespierrists all joining the list of the defeated in rapid succession. Bien therefore made the reasonable decision to shift the focus of his essay to the subject of nobility, a category that at least seemed to retain some use for 'objective social description'.[1]

A generation later, the assignment to survey the state of the nobility on the eve of the French Revolution looks nearly as daunting as the subject of aristocracy appeared to be in the 1980s, and for many of the same reasons. One glance through the titles of recent work devoted to the subject of nobility shows an increasing emphasis on the theme of plurality: 'Nobility, nobilities', 'the nobilities of France', 'nobilities *obligent*', 'a divided nobility', 'plural strategies surrounding the model of nobility'.[2] Excellent original research continues to be dedicated to the second estate, especially in France—Michel Figeac and Josette Pontet suggest that nobility has inspired a new generation of scholarship precisely because it 'resists all unifying schemas'—but any attempt at generalization is bound to become empirically vulnerable to other renditions of 'objective social description'.[3]

The divisions within the nobility tell an important story, nonetheless. One could even say that the elusiveness of the social referent for the term 'nobility', and the word's availability for rhetorically divergent purposes, was precisely what made the term *noblesse* so powerful, so very full of meaning, at the outbreak of the Revolution. Nobility may have been a 'shadow' no longer worthy of the fear and trembling it had once excited, as the abbé Sieyès would contemptuously observe in 1789, but few other spectres ever had such a capacity to mobilize, to antagonize, to inspire, to incite.[4]

How had the famously fractured and politically disorganized second estate managed to retain, or acquire, the ability to inflame passions on the eve of the Revolutionary rupture? The divisions within the *noblesse* were certainly real, and widely recognized at the time. Since the seventeenth century, the state had provided legal titles to families whose nobility had been properly authenticated, and it thereby established official membership in the nobility, but beyond the state's legal assurances what else did nobles share? As David Bien himself showed in a series of path-breaking articles, nobles with longer genealogies tended to look with suspicion at those with shorter genealogies, and the movement to reform, purify or otherwise improve the second estate in the last decades of the eighteenth century often proceeded on the basis of an implicit goal of excluding the impostors (however defined). Bien further demonstrated that a newly professional orientation explained some of this rising genealogical consciousness—with army officers, in particular, making the assumption that long family traditions of sacrifice, service, and military glory decisively shaped childhood and the early stages of professional formation.[5] As army reformers understood it, the infamous Ségur ruling (1781) that excluded from the officer ranks those who came from deficient social milieux counted as an important step in a process of professionalization.

But profession was only one of many principles of division within the nobility. For example, the urban/rural fissure was not specific to the second estate, but nobles were hardly exempt from its effects. More than half the nobility in the eighteenth century still lived outside urban areas, but nobles had migrated to cities in large numbers over the course of the late seventeenth and eighteenth centuries, making urban centres such as Rennes and Aix-en-Provence 'cities of blue bloods' (as Emmanuel Le Roy Ladurie has memorably phrased it).[6] The legal dynasties (the nobles of *robe longue*) that dominated Aix, with their training in French and Roman law traditions, their civic attachment to their place of residence, and their fabulous *hôtels*, would have had little in common with the rural seigneur of modest means.[7] The comte d'Antraigues, relaying his experiences from the nearby Vivarais, evoked the 'gothic beauty' of dilapidated chateaux found 'amid abandoned ruins' and inhabited by 'simple men not rich enough to have ruined it all' by seeking to import a fashionable decor. But he also acknowledged that a confrontation with the 'long and dark halls' of such places made him feel 'as though I am leaving my century'.[8] Some seigneurs happily ensconced in the countryside were fully committed to modernity—including, for example, the astute estate managers of Burgundy studied recently by Robert Schwartz—but the poorer provincial *hobéreaux* lived in a cultural world very different from that of city dwellers.[9]

Many noble families managed to keep one foot in the rural seigneurie while they spent part of the year in Paris or the nearest provincial city. For many of the merchants and financiers who acquired noble status through purchase of an ennobling office, the establishment of a dual urban–rural identity seemed imperative, given the traditional association between the nobility and the land.[10] But the ability to move between town and country also established a stark line of division between noble families. 'Noble nomadism', as Roger Baury has labelled the phenomenon, was a habit especially characteristic of the *grands seigneurs* and others who controlled fiefs in multiple provinces. Feeling a need to maintain some presence on all of their most important estates, they made seasonal migrations that recalled the European grand tour of the Renaissance aristocrat. Such travel required both significant resources and a taste for worldliness, however, and the eighteenth century's increasingly navigable highways and byways thus created a clear division between those who, by necessity, stayed rooted in the familial *terroir* and those who had 'entered the age of cosmopolitanism' and travelled freely and often.[11]

Differing degrees of mobility reflected and reinforced differing degrees of access to wealth, resources, and power. Perhaps the most dramatic expression of this fundamental divide within the nobility was seen in the varying levels of access to, and familiarity with, the royal Court. Provincials of modest means often aspired to appear at Court, and some of long lineage proudly pursued the 'honours of the Court' to which their genealogical credentials entitled them. The experience of being introduced to the king, of riding in the royal carriage, or of taking a seat in the queen's presence usefully affirmed a family's social standing and provided indelible memories that could enter into family lore. (The scions of more than 900 families made the trek to Versailles to stake their claim to these honours in the eighteenth century.) Coming into contact with networks of court patronage could also, eventually, prove useful to the younger members of a family that lacked connections. But provincial nobles' contact with the splendour of Versailles not infrequently produced expressions of awe and humility, if not outright resentment. Marie de Cugnac could be 'presented' to the king only after leaning on the generosity of the comtesse de Noailles, who was willing to loan her own fine jewels for the occasion ('she had at least 50,000 écus in diamonds …'). François de Carbonnier worried so much about expenses while planning his second trip to the capital that he was moved to gallows humour: 'It is a quite fortunate thing to find oneself in this city [Paris] during a time of mourning; black attire then suits everyone equally.'[12]

Carbonnier's concern about the runaway costs of life in Paris (he advised one correspondent to 'spend as little as possible' if he wished to remain untroubled during his stay there) reflected the powerful impact of the Court on the consumption patterns of the capital. As Natacha Coquery has observed, it was largely the nearby presence of a lavish 'court society', one that concentrated many wealthy and highly competitive aristocrats in one place, that drove Parisian consumption to immoderate levels, 'multiplied needs endlessly', and made Paris the hub of 'a true luxury industry'.[13] Interior decorators, tapestry makers, sculptors, wood workers, chefs, coach makers, portrait painters, architects: all worked to meet the demands of a noble upper crust that sought to project its power, maintain an image, and find new marks of distinction that would further distance the elite from the common herd. (The duc de La Trémoille spent at least 25,000 livres on the purchase of fifteen separate coaches, including four berlines, in one ten-year period ending in 1787.)[14]

This is not to say that courtiers formed a homogeneous unit, or that all nobles at court inspired envy, jealousy, or admiration in the same way or in equal measure. As Norbert Elias emphasized long ago, the court was a cauldron of competition where status anxieties and the constant desire for affirmation and promotion created clear hierarchies within the elite of the elite. Whether competing for space at Versailles, asserting ceremonial rights, building their credit networks, positioning themselves for office, or exploiting the opportunities offered by 'court capitalism', court nobles remained acutely aware of the marks of standing and influence that separated them from others within their own milieu.[15] The elaborate facade of etiquette and order at Court masked 'a system of representation operating on the exclusion of this or that group', and on occasion all but the royal family had to endure, or anticipate enduring, the humbling experience of exclusion.[16]

Robe and military, town and country, provincial and cosmopolitan, mobile and immobile, rich and poor, well connected and not: the principles of division within the nobility were many. To these might be added geography (the sea ports of Brittany had little in common with the dark interior of the Massif Central); education (the world of the Parisian salons, thoroughly aristocratic in tone and composition, deliberately favoured the well read and the quick witted—'bon mots', Madame de Staël would write, 'count as events in Paris ... they can be the subject of conversation for days'); as well as attitudes toward the Enlightenment (the philosophes' supporters and their enemies both counted many nobles among their number).[17] Nobles, in short, had they ever had the chance to convene in one place, would have seen eye to eye on very little. Through their differing social formations, cultural orientations, intellectual dispositions, professional inclinations, and family ambitions, the nobility may have constituted the most diverse collectivity found anywhere on French soil under the *ancien régime*.

So diverse was this collectivity by the middle of the eighteenth century that some were already saying, in anticipation of Sieyès, that nobility was largely illusory. The sale of ennobling offices, introduced in the sixteenth century and fully institutionalized in the seventeenth, continued to bring many new nobles into the fold every year— William Doyle estimates that venality facilitated the creation of 50,000 nobles in the course of the eighteenth century.[18] The acquisition of nobility had become such a routine process that one mid-century commentator called it 'the most common form of larceny'.[19] To satisfy the seemingly universal desire for noble status, and to mitigate losses to the state treasury (the extension of tax exemptions being the most larcenous aspect of the creation of these new nobles), the writer proposed making 'nobility' a commodity sold on the open market, subject to stiff sales taxes, and treated like any heritable property. In the new system, 'a young *gentilhomme* wanting to make his entry into society, but finding himself without a sou and unable to buy a Company [in the army], will advertise with notaries, or in the papers, that he intends to sell fifteen or twenty years of his nobility at a good price; he'll find his money and his position'.[20] This advocate for 'ubiquitous' nobility hardly offered a serious plan of reform; he mocked a reality unfolding before his eyes.

The fracturing of the nobility along professional, cultural, and economic lines, and the ease with which noble status could be acquired and noble habits imitated, drew new critical attention to the gap between sign and signified. It was in part the loosening of the terms of definition surrounding nobility that inspired the abbé Coyer in 1756 to propose a controversial restructuring of the scale of values underlying the second estate. 'Today,' the abbé asserted with some exaggeration, 'the nobility is a dispersed corps, having no occasion to assemble, no representation, and no influence in public affairs.'[21] Given the crumbling of its traditional institutional supports, why should the nobility resist bringing its values up to date and entering the modern world? The honour of the nobility had always been associated particularly with military service and the ideal of selfless bravery. Self-interested mercantile pursuits were deemed so antithetical to proper aristocratic morality that formal involvement in retail trade caused the loss (*dérogeance*) of noble status. In light of both practical and philosophical considerations, Coyer believed that the time had come for nobles to embrace 'this other honor, less brilliant, that consists in the knowledge of needs, in the perfection of the arts, in application, frugality, probity, public credit, in the pursuit of enterprises that are peaceful but useful'.[22] The time had come, in other words, for nobles to become merchants and for merchants to become nobles.

Coyer's closing of the presumed cultural gap between noble and merchant would have had the effect of opening another path toward 'ubiquity'. The suggestion that French citizenship was rooted in a moral substance common to all—honour could be found anywhere, the abbé implied—was also a way of saying that all French citizens had the capacity to be noble. As his fiercest critic, the chevalier d'Arc, later put it, Coyer aspired to make Frenchmen 'a people of nobles'.[23] The economist Forbonnais, also writing in 1756, saw that possibility already coming over the horizon. 'We will all soon be nobles', he observed in another contemporary essay on the progress of commerce.[24] Changing economic conditions, and the cultural aspirations they enabled, seemed to promise the eventual removal of barriers that had long prevented common citizens from basking in the glory of public recognition. But those same conditions, by turning nobility into a more widely available social marker, also threatened to deprive the nobility of its meaning and purpose.

Or so it seemed to some. For others, the confusion that surrounded nobility—What was nobility's true source? To which occupations should it be connected? Should it be an open or closed elite? Were all nobles created equal? Were the privileges of nobility defensible or sustainable? Had the nobility been corrupted by modernity or renewed by it? Were luxury and conspicuous consumption expressions of nobility or causes of its demise?—inspired an earnest effort to establish clarity. Many hoped that a stronger, rejuvenated nobility would eventually step out of the fog of uncertainty that clouded the eighteenth century social hierarchy.

As the new attractions of the 'honours of the court' attest, genealogy stood out as one of the more obvious clarifying tools available to the second estate. Since the early years of the seventeenth century, proudly ancient families had enthusiastically used length of lineage to distinguish the securely established nobles from the newcomers. (Many of the newcomers invented or embellished their own genealogies in an effort to cloud the distinctions—like the minor robe Bragelongne family, whose history was found by the royal genealogist to have been filled with 'lies and extravagant claims'.)[25] French monarchs had reinforced the emphasis on family history. Louis XIV's *recherches de la noblesse*, initiated in the 1660s and carried out over decades, had investigated and verified the noble origins of each aristocratic family of the realm.

The king and his agents acted largely for fiscal reasons—a clear line of demarcation between the ins and the outs would also be a negotiable line, and many of the excluded could be expected to buy their way back into the ranks of the exalted—but by providing legal reinforcement to the principle of antiquity the state also set a precedent that would be followed again and again in the century before the Revolution. The honours of the Court, linked directly to antiquity at the time of their formalization in 1732, were joined by other genealogically-based honours from the late seventeenth century onwards. Rights of entry to the school for noble daughters at St Cyr, to the cadet companies of the army, to the Ecole Royale Militaire, and to various provincial bodies were denied those who lacked sufficient genealogical lustre. From a certain point of view, the 1781 Ségur ruling that blocked entrance to the officer corps to all but those boasting four generations of nobility merely continued a century-long trend toward genealogical exclusivity.

François-Joseph Ruggiu has rightly pointed out that even 'antiquity' could not serve as a fixed anchor for noble identity in the eighteenth century. How long was long enough? Four generations or four centuries? Through the male line or through both lines? For purposes of Court ceremonial or for claims to leadership in local political bodies? Antiquity was an unstable concept that corresponded to no 'universally recognized scale of values'.[26] Even so, the nobility's increasing attention to antiquity and lineage in the eighteenth century is unmistakable. The tendency to invoke the past as a support for current claims to pre-eminence marked thinkers as diverse as Saint-Simon, Boulainvilliers, Fénelon, Montesquieu, and Mirabeau, each working toward somewhat different ends but each convinced of the special legitimacy conferred by the passage of time.

The absolutist state provided intermittent support for the genealogical pride of the nobility. But the example of Boulainvilliers, who idealized a pre-monarchical nobility vested with powers and qualities allegedly drained away by a centralizing royal Court, shows that the appeal to the past could also work against or apart from the perceived interests of the state. The nobles of Brittany, for example, first resisted the *recherches de la noblesse* precisely because they resented the intrusion of the state into affairs left customarily in the hands of local elites. Yet in the wake of the *recherches*, with legal membership in the nobility more clearly defined and with status differences more visible, the second estate of Brittany ever more self-consciously used exclusivity as one of its chief identifiers. The assimilation of wealthy merchant families into the nobility, common enough until the mid-seventeenth century, became extremely rare in the eighteenth— even as overseas trade channelled great wealth into St Malo, Nantes, and Lorient. At the provincial Estates-General, where noble membership was policed with new rigour after the 1670s, leaders of the second estate came increasingly to associate nobility with the exclusive prerogative to participate in their Assembly. The proudly exclusive body became a staunch defender of provincial rights and a force of obstruction chronically bothersome to the monarchy. So rigid was the bond of identification between *noblesse* and the rights conferred by antiquity that the Breton nobles refused to send a delegation to the national Estates-General in 1789. The electoral procedures announced by the Crown, which would have denied the provincial Estates the exclusive right to select

Brittany's noble deputies, threatened a form of contamination that purebred nobles could not abide.[27]

The constitutional debates of the mid-eighteenth century became another arena in which antiquity came to be used as a vital tool against the state's claims to authority. What Boulainvilliers did for the nobility as a whole—he had claimed that the true nobility descended from the Franks who had conquered Gaul and thereby established the foundation for the French monarchy—Parisian jurists sought to do for the 'sovereign' court of *parlement*. By the 1750s the jurist Louis Adrien Le Paige and his colleagues in the magistracy claimed that *parlement*, too, traced its origins to the deliberative Assemblies of the Franks. Since time immemorial it had been recognized as the protector of 'the traditions and laws that constitute the common security of the prince and the peoples'.[28] Grounding the source of its own authority in practices ratified in the distant past, the *parlement* at mid-century became increasingly aggressive in contesting the seemingly arbitrary fiscal and legal measures of the Crown.

The rights of lineage thus came to be employed more self-consciously in the eighteenth century. The assertion of long-recognized rights and status provided a claim to legitimacy that could be used to resist unwanted innovations by the state—including its continuing practice of selling nobility through venal offices. The call to respect antiquity functioned as an assertion of authenticity in an environment where honours and titles continued to proliferate at an alarming rate. By brandishing their authentic proofs of nobility, families (and noble institutions) with long and illustrious histories could distinguish themselves from what one reformer called 'a crowd of newborns … raised on their piles of gold'.[29]

As the most obvious 'sign' of nobility, however, lineage could hardly escape the critical questioning that came to envelop the *noblesse* in the eighteenth century. Sieyès, in his *Essai sur les privilèges* of 1788, would mock the nobles who meditated before the 'portraits of their ancestors', their eyes 'fixed incessantly on the noble *past*'. (He also wryly noted that all people, no matter their status, shared the honour of 'descending from men who lived in the thirteenth and fourteenth centuries'.)[30] But such attacks on the nobility's genealogical pride predated the turmoil of the pre-Revolution, and nobles numbered among the harshest critics of noble self-satisfaction.

The baron d'Holbach denounced nobility itself as a 'frivolous and ridiculous distinction' in 1776, and he singled out the hereditary principle—the dependence on 'superannuated parchments'—as the feature of nobility that most offended him. Must the descendants of those long-dead medieval knights 'still think themselves, after so many centuries, entitled to ill-treat their vassals, oppress the tillers of the soil, exact from them harmful rights, cruel servitudes, and indeed throw onto laborious indigence taxes that wealth alone should bear?'[31] A few years later the comte de Mirabeau launched what Doyle calls a 'comprehensive onslaught on nobles and all they stood for'. In an adaptation of an earlier text devoted to the American founding of the Society of the Cincinnati, Mirabeau eviscerated the idea of 'honour by succession' and insisted that 'true nobility' was a quality of the soul unrelated to bloodlines. Countries afflicted with 'lineal nobility' found that it inevitably became the source of 'vanity and beggary, of meanness and pride, of slavery and tyranny', and of all that was incompatible with 'personal dignity'. He advised the Americans to steer clear of any distinction that would have the tendency to become hereditary, for the great promise of America stemmed from its innocence, its original freedom from Europe's 'barbarous feudal system', with its accompanying 'broods of tyrants'.[32]

The atheist d'Holbach and the notorious libertine Mirabeau were perhaps atypical because of their close affinity with the most radical currents of reformist thought in the late years of the *ancien régime*. But the impulse to question tradition was not confined to groups of radicals or outsiders. Nobles of a less iconoclastic disposition also expressed the desire to move beyond genealogy in the quest to define social superiority. At about the same time that the baron d'Holbach launched his attack on the hereditary principle, in the late 1770s, an obscure noble army captain composed a reform project for the Minister of War in which he asserted that nobility was on the verge of becoming 'a chimera founded on parchments that register the actions of others'.[33] The military, this captain Blangermont argued, should recommit itself to instilling in every young officer a respect for 'duty and patriotism'. If new entrants to the corps were properly conditioned by positive examples and a carefully constructed educational programme, they could revive the 'almost extinct' virtue of patriotism, thus recapturing the 'good spirit' and 'patriotic enthusiasm' that had once defined the nobility and all of France.

By simultaneously promoting and criticizing nobility, captain Blangermont conveyed the ambivalence of an age. His reform project betrayed impatience with the status quo and an eagerness to repair a social hierarchy that looked increasingly incoherent. But Blangermont still sought to restore nobility, not replace it or eliminate it. He took for granted, in fact, that the nobility would lead the way in implementing the moral reforms he desired. He imagined that specially chosen groups of 'gentlemen cadets' would be placed in charge of the schools that would need to be established in each regiment, and he insisted, despite his contempt for desiccated parchments, that all new officers would need to come from genuine noble stock suitably verified by the royal genealogists. Blangermont's response to the clouding of the social and moral hierarchies of his era was to point the nobility back toward the moral substance he assumed to be the underlying foundation and final justification for noble status. He sought to revive the 'good spirit' characteristic of the nobility's medieval forebears, a spirit that 'little by little, has been extinguished'.[34]

In pointing to the need for a patriotic renewal, Blangermont joined a long list of reformers in the wake of the Seven Years War who became convinced that France needed to rekindle selfless devotion to country. He was not alone in assuming that 'real' nobles were the natural carriers of this cherished moral disposition. In 1773 the noble diplomat and historian Louis-Gabriel Du Buat-Nançay composed 'patriotic reflections' in which he appropriated some of the language of Montesquieu's *Esprit des Lois* to assert that the nobility should serve as 'an intermediary corps in the realm of morals'. Since the noble citizen was the natural 'moral man', one whose vision could rise above material wants, physical labours, and petty local concerns, the state should take advantage of the noble's inclination to patriotism by initiating a national educational programme. New schools could train nobles for any of a dozen honourable vocations, while also reinforcing youthful lessons learned in the noble household, where 'the morals of our fathers' and the principles of monarchical government had been instilled through the power of example and precedent. Such a national educational programme would revive the 'spirit of chivalry', combine useful expertise with nobles' natural commitment to leadership, and put noble examples 'always within reach' of even 'the last citizen'. Commoners would then be inspired to emulate the behaviour of standard-setting superiors. By firmly re-establishing 'inequality of conditions', and reconstituting the nobility as 'the protector of national mores', the state would also lay the foundation for a national renewal.[35]

Blangermont and Buat-Nançay wanted nobles' titles of superiority to rest on more than mere parchment. They both regarded the spirit of chivalry as the likeliest source of a new and morally reinvigorated nobility. Other reformers found inspiration in other traditions. The marquis de Mirabeau (stern father of the libertine comte) and other critics of luxury encouraged their noble readers to avoid the corrupting influences of the city and to forge new connections with the countryside, that authentic source of their traditionally simple manners and their original claim to pre-eminence. Moral resistance to the blandishments of luxury, and a nostalgic craving for a simpler and pre-commercial past, found reinforcement in developing Physiocratic theories about economic productivity and in the broader reformist energies directed toward French agriculture after the middle of the eighteenth century. Amid the general sense of crisis precipitated by the Seven Years War (1756–63), some saw the prospect for agrarian reform and economic restructuring as an opportunity to reassert seigneurial stewardship over the land and to seize an actively patriotic role for a languishing nobility. The author of *Le gentilhomme cultivateur* (1761), for example, in a paean to Rome's past glories, stressed the organic connections between rustic mores, the vocation of the farmer, and military readiness. The 'harmful error' of luxury led inevitably to 'the fall of all Monarchies', he claimed, and the patriotic virtues of a Cato or a Cincinnatus could not be expected to emerge from subjects of a state where farming had given way to the 'luxury arts'.[36]

Such rhetoric appealed to nobles (and others) anxious over the moral health of the polity and worried about the shifting sands of the French social order. As John Shovlin has shown, the years following the Seven Years War saw a proliferation of royal agricultural societies across French territory—from Paris to Tours and Lyons, from Caen to Montauban and Aix-en-Provence. Established by royal intendants, these societies disseminated patriotic rhetoric, provided incentives for landowners making technical improvements on their land, and offered concrete advice for agrarian reformers. As Shovlin puts it, they also 'provided opportunities for an office-holding and landowning elite to dabble in agronomic experimentation and to converse with other amateurs of agricultural improvement'.[37] By throwing their energies into irrigation projects, experiments with new crops, and upgrades to their labourers' farming equipment, some nobles combined their traditional landowning identity with the new patriotic impulses coursing through the French public sphere during and after the conflict with the English and the Prussians. They found the basis of their superior status not in their genealogies but in their moral aspirations, their inclinations to leadership, and their dedication to the greater good.

These various new efforts to recapture a 'good spirit' seemingly 'extinguished' by forces associated with modernity—commercialism, royal despotism, luxury, physical and moral dissipation, artificiality—reflected a noble determination to counter positively the ills afflicting the second estate. But in their efforts to realign the 'signified' of moral excellence with the 'sign' of official noble status, noble reformers also acknowledged the nobility's drift from its traditional moorings. In the confusing fog that surrounded the terms noble and nobility, the rearrangement of the pieces that made up both appearance and reality had the potential to solidify and refurbish the nobility's traditional position of eminence—as men such as Blangermont and Buat-Nançay clearly hoped. Other possibilities, potentially more destabilizing, also emerged from within the nobility's fitful self-(re)fashioning after mid-century.

The move to reassert the moral qualities long considered the basis of noble status carried real rhetorical risks. By rooting the nobility's identity in idealized sentiments and qualities of the heart—patriotism, honour, magnanimity, sturdiness, selflessness, rural simplicity—reformers highlighted criteria of excellence that many embraced and to which many could aspire. Non-noble farmers could also bring a sense of civic duty to the project of agricultural renewal (and agronomic societies even awarded peasants prizes for their good efforts); common soldiers shared with commissioned officers the desire to have their honour recognized and affirmed (Blangermont and other officers even tried to capitalize on this seemingly universal French trait in their efforts to improve the military); merchants brought glory and prosperity to the *patrie* by representing French interests abroad, by honouring their contracts and working dutifully, and by increasing aggregate wealth and employment (an argument advanced by Coyer and many of his emulators—including the author of the 1779 *Le négociant patriote*). In a context where the rights of birth were mocked and questioned as frequently as they were respected and honoured, discussions about the patriotic essence of nobility had the effect of opening up 'noble' status to many new claimants. In 1784, when the playwright Beaumarchais had the servant Figaro taunt his haughty noble employer for his undeserved enjoyment of rank, position, and nobility—'You've gone to the trouble of being born, nothing more'—he did not merely lampoon noble pride. He reflected a generation's worth of encroachment on the territory of nobility by critics unimpressed by birthright and convinced that moral character formed the basis of 'true' *noblesse*.

The signifier of nobility ranged over many qualities, it had multiple sources, and it became available for appropriation by an array of different actors in the eighteenth century. In a brilliantly counter-intuitive study, Antoine Lilti has shown that poets, philosophes, and artists sought entry into aristocratic salons not in order to challenge their elitist assumptions but, on the contrary, to gain the imprimatur of nobility. They knew that their association with intellectual enclaves shaped by and encoded in the manners of the high aristocracy would help them to win patrons, acquire social polish, and gain access to the halls of power.[38] The attractions of the nobility's continuing cultural cachet, as much as the material reality of noble privileges, also explain why so many families on the fringes of the second estate continued to purchase expensive ennobling offices, to request official verifications of their questionable nobility, and to seek paths of assimilation into the world of the established elites. Throughout the eighteenth century *commissaires des guerres* at Versailles and colonial planters in Saint-Domingue—that is, individuals from the heart of the metropole to the periphery of the French Empire—continued to assert their membership in, or at least their fittingness for, the ranks of the second estate.[39]

Nobility retained its allure, but debates about and the continuing uncertainty around the component parts of *noblesse* meant that negative as well as positive connotations could also be freely applied to the symbols of noble status. Negative stereotypes of nobility—nobles had long been accused of being under-educated, idle, haughty, violent, contemptuous of others, self-interested, and morally undisciplined—had circulated for centuries, of course. Some of these older tropes survived and found new purchase in the years before the Revolution. The second half of the eighteenth century also saw the development of more concentrated forms of criticism of the nobility, however. The new critiques linked supposed (or imagined) characteristics of nobility to structural defects of the government, the economy, and the political culture—all of which attracted heightened attention in the wake of the Seven Years War.

In his analysis of the proliferating literature on political economy in the second half of the eighteenth century, Shovlin finds that the nobility ironically came to suffer from the effects of an anti-luxury discourse that its members had helped to invent and promote ever since the age of Fénelon. Their suspicions of trade, their open contempt for the upwardly mobile wealthy, and their loud condemnations of the moral ills associated with material self-indulgence came back to haunt the nobility in the 1770s and 1780s. Just as the monarchy's fiscal problems were multiplying and attracting greater public notice, a number of high-level financial scandals made the royal Court into the apparent seat of luxury and drew attention to some audacious self-dealing and political chicanery among prominent aristocrats. Having earlier inspired jealousy and bitterness on the part of modest provincial nobles resentful of the rich grandees who dominated positions of power and influence, the Court nobility attracted wide opprobrium in a period when the political stakes of such criticism were climbing ever higher. To an agitated and reform-minded populace, corrupt and extravagantly wealthy courtiers seemed a reasonable stand-in for the nobility as a whole. By late 1788, after important representatives of the nobility had insisted on the need to maintain the distinctions within the traditional society of orders, the Breton radical Volney was ready to accuse nobles of forgetting about their nobility as they indulged their craving for material splendour. 'Those French gentlemen, so jealous of honour, so free with their blood, we thought them avid for glory, [but] they were [avid] only for money; and for a little of that vile metal, they have set fire to their *patrie*, and preferred the loss of their Nation to the loss of their tyranny.'[40] The patriotism, simplicity, and moral leadership that so many nobles had tried to brandish as signs of nobility since the 1760s had become, by the eve of the Revolution, stark measures of noble failure.

Other recent developments also contributed to the tarnishing of the image of the second estate. As Sarah Maza noted in her classic study of the lawyers' trial briefs (*mémoires judiciaires*) that filled the public sphere in great numbers in the 1770s and 1780s, a series of notorious legal cases featuring misbehaving aristocrats helped to construct the social imagery on which contemporary political controversies were mapped.[41] Rhetorically skilled lawyers drew on the details of their cases to portray moral contests between cruel and exploitative nobles, on the one hand, and powerless, unjustly abused exemplars of virtue, on the other hand. These publicity-minded lawyers sought sympathy for their clients in the 'public tribunal' constituted by French readers. In at least some cases, they also argued implicitly for the reform of the social and legal systems that they and their clients had to navigate. The fact that most victims in these melodramatic narratives were commoners and that most perpetrators of wrongdoing were high and mighty elites meant that nobles, in the burgeoning world of legal literature, were frequently placed in an unflattering light in the twenty years that preceded the Revolution. The trial briefs provided new lenses for diagnosing the social ills of the late eighteenth century, and nobles and their privileges emerged time and again as regrettable sources of all that was wrong in the existing order.

By the 1780s, the nobility had acquired a set of associations that would create complications for its later political history. For reasons having as much to do with the cultural environment as with social reality, nobles had come to be widely impugned for an unhealthy love of luxury, greedy self-interest, the heedless oppression of innocents, and a blinding concern for genealogy. During the turmoil of 1787–8 Crown propagandists contributed to the bad publicity by accusing nobles (especially those of the *parlements*) of setting out to establish an 'aristocracy' mindful only of its own interests and tending toward an oligarchic 'despotism'. Many were predisposed to assume the worst about the nobility's goals and motivations.

One of the great ironies of the so-called 'pre-Revolutionary' crisis that proved so costly to the long-term prospects of the second estate is that nobles, too, mistrusted nobles—even as they continued to believe in nobility. The divisions that had characterized the nobility all across the eighteenth century had created conflicting visions of reform that almost invariably elevated certain segments of the corps at the expense of others. Mid-level army officers, convinced of their virtue, championed meritocracy because they resented the titled nobles who monopolized the highest ranks. Agrarian reformers ridiculed those nobles content to wallow in urban corruption. The oldest families refused to see newcomers as their equals. Military nobles expressed residual disdain for those in the magistracy (as would be shown in the 1789 elections to the Estates-General, which produced few representatives of the *robe longue*). The promoters of Enlightenment wanted no association with the retrograde nobles who resisted or opposed modernity. Almost everyone outside the high society of Paris and Versailles resented the nobles at Court.

All, nevertheless, would have agreed on the importance of nobility itself. Montesquieu had taught his readers that an honour-based hierarchy was so important to the French constitution that 'no nobility' effectively meant 'no monarchy'. But in the decades that followed publication of *L'Esprit des Lois* (1748), would-be reformers had discovered new value for the nobility, value that stretched beyond its supposed role as an intermediary body that could check monarchical despotism. After mid-century nobility was variously represented by its admirers as the basis of military professionalism, the patriotic corps par excellence, the restorer of virtue, the guardian of the French chivalric spirit, the embodiment of the national character, the defender of provincial liberties, the engine of economic renewal, the protector of French law, and Buat-Nançay's example-setting 'intermediary body in the realm of morals'. Many within the nobility would have happily reformed or even purged certain elements within the second estate, but few could imagine a society without a corps of nobility. For this reason nobles brought with them to the political and ideological battles of the late 1780s robust plans for reform, many of which presumed to save the nation by first saving the nobility.

Yet it was the defence of the formal constitutional and political existence of the nobility which finally unleashed the torrent of resentments that had accumulated since the days of Louis XIV. When the *parlement* of Paris decreed, in September 1788, that the coming Estates-General should convene in accordance with its traditional forms, with the first and second estates meeting in their own chambers and retaining veto power—a claim that would also be supported by an Assembly of Notables that met in December—nobles of all political persuasions were powerless to stop the subsequent degradation of the nobility's public image. Until September 1788, nobles had taken the lead in the fight against 'ministerial despotism' and had earned a certain amount of good will in the process. But the *parlement*'s sudden decision to hold the line against constitutional innovations that could curtail noble political influence created an opening, or a provocation, for those who had grown suspicious of Court nobles and all other beneficiaries of the established order.

The inclination to self-serving and secrecy that the *parlement*'s manoeuvre seemed to symbolize led critics to collapse all distinctions and to brand as unpatriotic the second estate as a whole. As Thomas Kaiser has noted, the apparent treachery of the nobility in the period of the pre-Revolution, judged in light of the embarrassing scandals of the 1780s, conjured another damaging stereotype that had been used intermittently since the days of Catilina: the noble-as-conspirator. Linked rhetorically to notorious noble traitors of the past and lumped with other presumed malefactors—scheming ministers, sycophantic favourites, unscrupulous speculators—the nobility and its leaders were stigmatized as a band of self-seeking plotters.[42] By the end of 1788, Sieyès was hardly the only observer inclined to see in the French nobility an 'aristocracy' run amok.

When the noble deputies who gathered at Versailles in May 1789 resisted invitations to collaborate with the Third Estate in a joint programme of fiscal and constitutional reform, the appearance of staunch corporate solidarity confirmed the darkest suspicions of the critics. By rejecting a proposed 'union of orders' in the spring of 1789, the noble deputies inadvertently sealed the fate of the society of orders itself. They ceded the initiative to common deputies who prized 'nation' over 'nobility' and who proceeded in the following year to dismantle the hierarchies of honour that had always buttressed noble privilege. Ironically, but perhaps predictably, the divided body that had been engaged in an unending process of refashioning for half a century or more, and to which a multitude of conflicting identities had been assigned, was in the end too fissiparous to resist the new label crafted for it in the cauldron of Revolutionary debate: enemy of the nation. In their various attempts to resist persecution, marginalization, and elimination, and in their desire to recover some of what had been lost, nobles in the generation after 1789 found a degree of unity that they had never enjoyed under the *ancien régime*.[43]

NOTES

1. David D. Bien, 'Aristocracy', in *A Critical Dictionary of the French Revolution*, ed. François Furet and Mona Ozouf, trans. Arthur Goldhammer (Cambridge, MA, 1989), 616–28.

2. Arlette Jouanna, 'Noblesse, Noblesses', in *Dictionnaire de l'Ancien Régime*, ed. Lucien Bély (Paris, 1996), 887–93; Philippe Bourdin (ed.), *Les Noblesses Françaises dans l'Europe de la Révolution* (Rennes, 2010); Philippe Bourdin, 'Introduction: Noblesses obligent', in *Les Noblesses Françaises*, 9–32; Gail Bossenga, 'A Divided Nobility: Status, Markets, and the Patrimonial State in the Old Regime', in *The French Nobility in the Eighteenth Century: Reassessments and New Approaches*, ed. Jay M. Smith (University Park, PA, 2006); 'plural strategies' was the title given to Part one, *La Noblesse de la fin du XVIe siècle au début du XXe Siècle: un modèle social?*, ed. Josette Pontet, Michel Figeac, and Marie Boisson, 2 vols (Anglet, 2002).

3. *La Noblesse de la fin du XVIe siècle*, 1: 5.

4. Emmanuel-Joseph Sieyès, *Qu'est-ce que le tiers état?* (Paris, 2002), 24.

5. David D. Bien, 'The Army in the French Enlightenment: Reform, Reaction, and Revolution', *Past & Present* 85 (1979), 68–98; but also 'La réaction aristocratique avant 1789: L'exemple de l'armée', *Annales: ESC* 29 (1974), 23–48, 505–34. Bien's classic *Annales* article is now available in English as *Caste, Class and Profession in Old Regime France: The French Army and the Ségur Reform of 1781*, ed. Guy Rowlands (St Andrews, 2010), available online at http://research-repository.st-andrews.ac.uk/handle/10023/967

6. Emmanuel Le Roy Ladurie, *Histoire de la France Urbaine*, 5 vols (Paris, 1980–1985), 3: 391.

7. On the distinctiveness of Aixois elite culture, see especially Monique Cubells, *La Provence des Lumières: Les parlementaires d'Aix au XVIIIe siècle* (Paris, 1984).

8. As cited in Roger Barny, *Le Comte d'Antraigues: un disciple aristocrate de J.-J. Rousseau* (Oxford, 1991), 72–3.

9. Robert M. Schwartz, 'The Noble Profession of Seigneur in Eighteenth-Century Burgundy', in *The French Nobility in the Eighteenth Century*, 77–109.

10. As in Bordeaux and other towns of the Aquitaine. See Michel Figeac, 'Noblesse urbaine et gentilhommerie rurale: deux modèles nobiliaires en Aquitaine', in *La Noblesse de la fin du XVIe siècle*, vol. 2, 127–42, esp. 133–4.

11. Roger Baury, 'L'ubiquité nobiliaire aux XVIIe et XVIIIe siècles', in *La Noblesse de la fin du XVIe siècle*, vol. 1, 133–55, esp. 152.

12. Both of these experiences are recounted in Olivier Royon, 'La noblesse de province face à la noblesse de Cour, entre admiration et rejet, de l'imitation à l'élaboration d'un contre-modèle social dans la dernière moitié du XVIIIe siècle', in *La Noblesse de la fin du XVIe siècle*, vol. 1, 217–31, esp. 221–2.

13. Natacha Coquery, *L'Hôtel Aristocratique: Le marché du luxe à Paris au XVIIIe siècle* (Paris, 1998), 21.

14. Ibid., 137.

15. Norbert Elias, *The Court Society*, trans. Edmund Jephcott (New York, 1983); on the space constraints and the tensions created, see William Ritchey Newton, *L'Espace du Roi: La cour de France au chateau de Versailles, 1682–1789* (Paris, 2000); on court capitalism see Gail Bossenga, 'The Financial Origins of the French Revolution', in *From Deficit to Deluge: The Origins of the French Revolution*, ed. Thomas E. Kaiser and Dale K. Van Kley (Stanford, 2011), 37–66.

16. Frédérique Leferme-Falguières, 'La Noblesse de Cour aux XVIIe et XVIIIe Siècles: De la définition à l'autoreprésentation d'une élite', *Hypothèses* (2000–1), 87–98, esp. 93.

17. Antoine Lilti, *Le Monde des Salons: sociabilité et mondanité à Paris au XVIIIe siècle* (Paris, 2005), esp. 275; Darrin McMahon, *Enemies of the Enlightenment: The French Counter-Enlightenment and the Making of Modernity* (Oxford, 2001).

18. William Doyle, *Venality: The Sale of Offices in Eighteenth-Century France* (Oxford, 1996), 165.

19. Jean H. Marchand, *La noblesse commerçable, ou ubiquiste* (Amsterdam, 1756), 46.

20. Ibid., 82.

21. Gabriel-François Coyer, *Développement et défense du système de la noblesse commerçante*, 2 vols (Amsterdam and Paris, 1757), 1: 92.

22. Ibid., 1: 139.

23. Philippe-Auguste de Sainte-Foy, chevalier d'Arc, *La noblesse militaire, opposée à La noblesse commerçante; Ou le patriote français* (Amsterdam, 1756), 48–9.

24. François Véron Duverger de Forbonnais, *Lettre à M. F., ou examen politique des prétendus inconvéniens de la faculté de commercer en gros, sans déroger à la noblesse* (n. p., 1765), 79.

25. Such was the harsh assessment of Charles d'Hozier, *juge d'armes de France* in 1699. See Martine Bennini, '"L'audace" de la généalogie des Bragelongne', in *Epreuves de la Noblesse: Les expériences nobiliaires de la haute robe parisienne (XVIe–XVIIIe siècle)*, ed. Robert Descimon and Elie Haddad (Paris, 2010), 161–89.

26. François-Joseph Ruggiu, 'Ancienneté familiale et construction de l'identité nobiliaire dans la France de la fin de l'Ancien Régime', in *La Noblesse de la fin du XVIe siècle*, vol. 1, 309–25, esp. 314.

27. Philippe Jarnoux, 'Des ambiguïtés d'un modèle idéalisé aux crispations identitaires: la noblesse bretonne au XVIIIe siècle', in *La Noblesse de la fin du XVIe siècle*, vol. 1, 89–107.

28. As cited in Keith Michael Baker, *Inventing the French Revolution: Essays on French Political Culture in the Eighteenth Century* (Cambridge, 1990), 37.

29. Pierre Augustin de Varennes, in *Réflexions Morales, Relative au Militaire François* (Paris, 1779). As cited in Jay M. Smith, *Nobility Reimagined: The Patriotic Nation in Eighteenth-Century France* (Ithaca, NY, 2005), 211.

30. Emmanuel-Joesph Sieyès, *Qu'est-ce que le tiers état, précédé de l'Essai sur les privilèges*, ed. Edme Champion (Paris, 1982), 10–11.

31. As cited in William Doyle, *Aristocracy and its Enemies in the Age of Revolution* (Oxford, 2009), 141.

32. Ibid., 125–6, 137.

33. Smith, *Nobility Reimagined*, 205.

34. Ibid., 205–7.

35. For a broader discussion of Buat-Nançay's *Eléments de la Politique*, see ibid., 214–16.

36. Jean-Baptiste Dupuy Demportes, *Le gentilhomme cultivateur, ou Corps complet d'agriculture, traduit de l'anglois de M. Hale* (Paris, 1761–4), as discussed in John Shovlin, *The Political*

Economy of Virtue: Luxury, Patriotism, and the Origins of the French Revolution (Ithaca, NY, 2006), 73.

37. Shovlin, *The Political Economy of Virtue*, 85–6.

38. Lilti, *Le Monde des Salons*, esp. 169–222.

39. François-Joseph Ruggiu, 'The Kingdom of France and its Overseas Nobilities', *French History* 25 (2011), 298–315; Samuel Gibiat, *Hiérarchies Sociales et Ennoblissement: Les commissaires des guerres de la Maison du Roi au XVIIIe siècle* (Paris, 2006). Gibiat explains that the *commissaires* wanted mainly to cross the 'social frontier' of nobility because they identified with its traditional values and craved acceptance in high society. See esp. 375–463.

40. As cited in Shovlin, *The Political Economy of Virtue*, 177.

41. Sarah Maza, *Private Lives and Public Affairs: The Causes Célèbres of Prerevolutionary France* (Berkeley, 1993).

42. Thomas E. Kaiser, 'Nobles into Aristocrats, or How an Order Became a Conspiracy', in *The French Nobility in the Eighteenth Century*, 189–224.

43. This discovery of unity mirrored the earlier experience of David Bien's non-noble professionals who, in 1789, 'created a unified nobility, at least in their minds, before they destroyed it'. See 'Manufacturing Nobles: The Chancelleries in France to 1789', *Journal of Modern History* 61 (1989), 445–486, esp. 486.

SELECTED READING

Bien, David, *Caste, Class and Profession in Old Regime France: The French Army and the Ségur Reform of 1781*, ed. Guy Rowlands (St Andrews, 2010).

Bourdin, Philippe (ed.), *Les Noblesses Françaises dans l'Europe de la Révolution* (Rennes, 2010).

Descimon, Robert and Elie Haddad (eds), *Epreuves de la Noblesse: Les expériences nobiliaires de la haute robe parisienne (XVIe–XVIIIe siècle)* (Paris, 2010).

Doyle, William, *Aristocracy and its Enemies in the Age of Revolution* (Oxford, 2009).

Lilti, Antoine, *Le Monde des Salons: sociabilité et mondanité à Paris au XVIIIe siècle* (Paris, 2005).

Pontet, Josette, Michel Figeac, and Marie Boisson (eds), *La Noblesse de la fin du XVIe siècle au début du XXe Siècle: un modèle social?*, 2 vols (Anglet, 2002).

Shovlin, John, *The Political Economy of Virtue: Luxury, Patriotism, and the Origins of the French Revolution* (Ithaca, NY, 2006).

Smith, Jay M., *Nobility Reimagined: The Patriotic Nation in Eighteenth-Century France* (Ithaca, NY, 2005).

Smith, Jay M. (ed.), *The French Nobility in the Eighteenth Century: Reassessments and New Approaches* (University Park, PA, 2006).

CHAPTER 4

....

MONARCHY

....

JOËL FÉLIX

> Representatives, we all bear in our hearts the hatred of *royauté*; but as we
> are to judge he who called himself the king of the French, we must not for-
> get that we are judging a man.
>
> (J. Barbaroux, *speech on the trial of the King*, 27 December 1792)

THE trial and sentencing of Louis XVI by the National Convention, followed by the king's public execution in January 1793, are certainly among the most striking in the series of remarkable events that make up the French Revolution. Beyond the personal torment that the renamed Louis Capet suffered in his perception of himself as a monarch and in his affections as a man, the fall of the Bourbon monarchy illustrates the difficulty—some might argue the sheer impossibility—of effecting a peaceful transition from old-regime society to modernity. That Louis XVI, hailed as the very ideal of a benevolent king, fell victim to the guillotine says a lot about the challenge historians face in interpreting this complex epoch. Alexis de Tocqueville perhaps expressed best the difficulty of making sense of an old regime and a revolution which can be considered both as a process and a failure, a rupture and an achievement: 'Philosophers and statesmen may learn a valuable lesson of modesty from the history of our Revolution, for there never were events greater, better prepared, longer matured, and yet so little foreseen.'[1]

The concepts of 'natural rights' and 'national sovereignty' sum up the tensions between the new-born regime and the monarchy whose popularity, building upon the idea of mutual 'affection' and 'interest' between the king and his people, remained firmly grounded in historical tradition and heredity, with a large pinch of coercive power and a dose of divine right. Once enshrined in the 1789 Declaration of the Rights of Man and the Citizen, the sovereignty of the Nation (article 1) and the principles of liberty, property, security, and resistance to oppression (article 2) opened up a new political landscape. In theory, harmony between the monarch, political representation, and the people was to derive from the rule of law, in particular the constitutional procedures that would set out the relationship between the legislative and executive power. A long historical tradition, however, has labelled the new regime a 'republican monarchy', an oxymoron which describes and implies, at the same time, the failure of the well-intentioned but inexperienced men of 1789 to establish a viable institutional framework. Based on criticisms of the Constitution of 1791 put forward at the time by supporters of the British model like Jacques Necker and Stanislas de Clermont-Tonnerre, this tradition has been recently challenged in a terse analysis which argues that the fall of the constitutional monarchy owed less to its legal framework than the ways in which men, in particular the king, used the terms of the Constitution to destroy it or change the nature of government.[2]

The purpose of this chapter is not to explore the conflicts which led to the storming of the Tuileries Palace and the birth of the republic. On the face of things, the fall of the monarchy was the least expected and yet the most likely result of the sequence of events that unfolded from the first deadlocked meetings of the Estates-General. The abortive 1791 flight of the king, in particular, called into question the initial promise of cooperation between the king and the Nation, while the critical memorandum signed by Louis XVI put the promise of a constitutional monarchy on a collision course.[3] To understand at a deeper level why these conflicts arose, this chapter focuses on the period prior to 1789 and examines some of the key issues which brought about, in the first instance, the downfall of the absolute monarchy.

Louis XIV and the Absolute Monarchy

It is impossible to discuss the problems of the Bourbon dynasty in the eighteenth century without looking at the discussions about Louis XIV's reign and his legacy. In the past decades, specialists of early modern France have devoted much work and energy to revisiting the conclusions of a historiographical tradition in France which saw Bourbon rule as an integral, and perhaps key, stage in a long-term historical process which replaced a traditional feudal society with the features of the modern state. Central to this new research is the extent to which the Bourbon kings, in particular Louis XIV, should be seen as absolute rulers who had effective power to overcome the restrictions that old regime social and economic structures imposed on the government of the kingdom.[4]

By and large, answers to this crucial line of inquiry depend on the observer's point of view and choices of chronology. Specialists of government are naturally more likely to emphasize the authority ministers enjoyed to mould France according to their views of the country's needs, even if it is commonly agreed that success also depended on effective use of familial bonds and networks of patronage.[5] By contrast, historians who look at the wider society insist on limits to the imposition of the royal will, and the level of bargaining that the Crown had to accept, in particular with powerful aristocratic families and corporate bodies of venal officers, to rule over one of the largest and most populated countries in Europe—suggesting more the model of a composite than an absolute monarchy.

In fact, both approaches are valid, and their apparent contradictions are subsumed by the inherent tensions between the discourse and practice of power in old regime France.

Louis XIV's famous *coup d'autorité* against the *parlements* in 1673 offers a good example. For about three centuries, historians have taken it for granted that the magistrates, twenty years after a threatening visit by the king to the Paris *Parlement*, in his hunting boots and whip in hand, were forced to bow to the royal will and, from that moment, registered the king's edicts without further ado. Recent research, however, has showed that the reality was more complex: the magistrates did not stop sending remonstrances against royal decisions, just as they had done before and would continue to do after Louis XIV's reign.[6] Beyond the display of absolute royal power, supported by legal treatises and a vocabulary of obedience to the king's will, the magistrates who registered the king's laws at first command did not stop submitting critical observations and making recommendations to ministers which were integrated through interpretative decisions. As such, the relationship was not only based on tension and submission but also on negotiation and cooperation.

In many respects, the Bourbon monarchy is probably best described as a polity which rested upon the king's claim to absolute power but whose effective operation depended on collaboration. Some would argue that it was a system of sharing of the spoils with traditional elites that had an interest in relaying, imposing, or facilitating the implementation of Versailles's policies. It is important to recognize, however, that the monarchy also had peaks of authoritarian rule, in particular in wartime, when the king and ministers stopped negotiating, curbed potential resistance, and encroached on individual rights.[7]

The three decades that followed Louis XIV's death were dominated by the need to restore the strengths of a kingdom which had suffered deeply from the impact of two very long wars that France fought almost alone, and with little respite, against powerful European coalitions. As the political and fiscal experiences of the Regency (1715–23) failed to produce viable solutions to endemic economic and social problems, the structures of power and government set out by Bourbon rulers, which had been much criticized in 1715, re-emerged by default. Louis XIV's interminable reign (1643–1715), and the almost unfailing support he showed to his ministers and their clients, had shaped a distinctive political culture. The appointment of cardinal de Fleury (1726) as prime minister abruptly put an end to the dreams of reformers. The reinstatement of the *parlements'* right to issue remonstrances before registration of royal legislation (1715) seemed to be all that remained of the expectation that peace and the close of Louis XIV's reign would be the dawn of a new age.[8]

While the soothing effect of time helped France slowly to recover from its hardships, the monarchy barely evolved and its structural problems remained deeply entrenched. The nickname neo-Colbertian used by historians to qualify governmental economic policy under Fleury aptly expresses common views at the time that the monarchy had reached its apogee in the second half of the seventeenth century, when Louis XIV's motto, *Nec pluribus impar* (Not inferior to anyone), and the image of the Sun King, were coined. In other words, the solution to current issues seemed to lie in the past. If one agrees with Peter Campbell that stability in the first part of Louis XV's reign relied on the king's unwavering support for cardinal de Fleury and the latter's ability to contain conflicts by careful management of institutions and men so as to avoid escalation and ideological conflict, then the three decades that followed his death were a watershed.[9]

LOUIS XV AND HIS *PARLEMENTS*

The publication in 1748 of Montesquieu's *L'Esprit des Loix* (*The Spirit of Laws*), one of the eighteenth century's most influential books, provided the French elites with a new and powerful tool to interpret the dynamics of power in the monarchy. Montesquieu argued, in particular, that the personal nature of sovereignty in the monarchy was the source of its potential degeneration as the king could abuse, or be incited to misuse, his absolute authority, which had to be limited by positive checks. 'For if there be only', wrote Montesquieu, 'the momentary and capricious will of a single person to govern the state, nothing can be fixed, and of course there is no fundamental law.'[10] At the same time, the critique of tradition by philosophers provided additional arguments which the king's subjects could use in order to voice their concerns on a number of current and divisive issues. Religious conflicts between Jesuits and Jansenists, resumption of warfare and fiscal burden fuelled a series of political crises in the 1750s and the 1760s which opposed the government, the clergy, and the *parlements* and which resulted in individual and collective exiles, ministerial instability, and even an assassination attempt on Louis XV (1757). Eventually, these accumulated tensions reached a new climax with abbé Terray's partial bankruptcy (1770) and the famous coup against the *parlements* (1771) by new chancellor Maupeou, who regarded compulsory registration of laws as a part of a wider programme of judicial reform: what the majority of his contemporaries called a revolution in the government of the monarchy.

In many respects, the history of Louis XV's reign (1715–74) can be understood and, indeed, has been read, through Montesquieu's conundrum. To most of his subjects, the reign of the king who had been nicknamed *Le Bien-Aimé* (Well-beloved) exemplified the extent to which the exercise of personal power might easily tip the monarchy over into despotism. The unstable nature of the regime seemed all the more obvious when set against the hesitancy of fiscal policy and economic legislation. For instance, in 1749, Louis XV backed Machault d'Arnouville's introduction of a new tax, the *vingtième*, a 5 per cent levy on all sources of revenue, including privileged landowners, calculated on the basis of a declaration of income submitted by taxpayers. The king, however, failed to fully support his minister's policy as the Assembly of the Clergy refused to submit to the tax and provincial estates obtained the privilege of paying a lump sum instead of the *vingtième*. Similarly, in 1763–64, Louis XV accepted that the trade in grain and other agricultural products should be a free activity but, in 1770, repealed the liberal legislation and restored the laws which prevented import and export between the provinces and with foreign countries.

The nature of the Bourbon monarchy seemed to have very little of fixity and stability about it, as Montesquieu anxiously noted. What remained from Louis XIV's strong rule was the principle of the king's absolute authority, which even the *Encyclopédie* dared not confuse with arbitrary and despotic power, at least as long as the fundamental laws were observed. In their letter of protest against Maupeou's policy towards the *Parlement* of Paris, the princes of the blood were adamant too that they did not wish to challenge Louis XV's power, but reminded him of the words couched in the preamble of the royal declaration of 21 November 1763 concerning the French finances, where he had solemnly declared he wanted to rule 'not by the sole impression of authority, but by love, justice and observation of regulations and forms wisely established in the kingdom'.

The hesitations of royal government over fiscal policy, which traditionally burdened the poor by favouring privileged groups, and economic legislation, which prevented growth and limited competition between protected markets, are ideal case studies to examine the capacity of the monarchy to address some of the old regime's most defining and hotly debated issues. While it would appear at first glance that Louis XV failed to provide the kind of leadership required to make progress on these vital questions, the evidence suggests that the king's policy reversals might also be interpreted as pragmatic responses to divisive problems in difficult and changing contexts. For if Louis XV had no doubt whatsoever about the legitimacy of his authority, old regime politics was not purely a game of words where language was used for the purpose of articulating, defending, and representing established and entrenched rights and privileges. Politics dealt also, and above all, with the formulation and implementation of sustainable answers to a variety of problems which dogged the established order and weakened France's international standing.

To be sure, most of the issues brought to the attention of government were straightforward and dealt with swiftly by means of administrative procedures or legal precedent. The concept of kingship being a business or craft, a 'métier', as Louis XIV called it in his *Memoirs*, was paramount in a monarchy where the king, as the source of all authority, was supposed to rule personally. The 'métier de roi' drew upon a well-established structure of government. At the top, ministers dealt with the matters of their respective portfolio of responsibilities (war, finances, navy, foreign affairs, etc.). They were advised and seconded by an administrative structure made up of individuals who, like them, were normally chosen for their prior experience, and selected from families traditionally attached to the service of the king, the so-called *noblesse de robe*. As a consequence, the contents of state affairs—which implied also the communication of information between Versailles and royal officers across France—were thoroughly examined before they were reported, discussed, and decided by the minister, with his advisers, or, by the king himself, either in the regular and ad hoc individual meetings he had with each minister, or in the more formal sessions of the King's Council.

The bureaucratic nature of royal government has been analysed in much detail by historians who have generally been very impressed by its effective organization and professionalism, as well as its ability to identify problems and propose solutions.[11] With this mechanism in hand, and the budget that accompanied it, ministers who had the ear of the king and his confidence—manifested through the distribution of rewards for them personally or for onward distribution to their family and clients—enjoyed considerable authority and leverage. Yet this system of administration was permeated by competition and conflicts. Structural tensions opposed the secretaries of state, who competed for resources, in particular the ministers in charge of the army and the navy, to the *contrôleurs généraux des finances* who struggled to fund the military establishment and sought to exert some level of control over their colleagues concerning the destination of the monies raised.

In theory it was the duty of the king (who was supposed to act as his own prime minister) to maintain cohesion in his government. In practice, and although they did a lot of work and were very well informed about affairs, the monarchs were far too busy, too unapproachable, and too accustomed to being served or relying on written reports, to take a proactive role in the management of the monarchy. This is the sense of Marie-Antoinette's sentence when she wrote in 1788 about Louis XVI that 'the man above me is not able'.[12] Julian Swann also contends that 'despite his intelligence and good intentions Louis XV never ruled' as 'his government was paralysed by internal feuds and dissensions'.[13] De facto, the king's true sovereignty rested on the power to appoint and advance his ministers when they were doing well, to back them when they faced resistance, and to change his advisers when the advantages of keeping them in office were superseded by drawbacks.

Another key problem was the dual nature of the monarchy, considered as a polity where the affairs of the state were not separate from the interests of the royal family. International relations, for instance, were intrinsically rooted in matrimonial politics. The dynastic element in the monarchy explains why, in addition to ministers, a number of persons had the privilege to communicate, directly or indirectly, with the king either by virtue of their blood or through personal friendship and service of the royal family. By contrast to the administrative monarchy, which organized the preservation of its working documents, the ways in which the court meddled with government remain largely uncharted. The historian can only rely on a limited amount of sources, in particular a few diaries from courtiers, like the duc de Saint-Simon and duc de Luynes, or personal memoirs of ministers to penetrate inside Versailles, which was home both to government and the court proper—that is the *Maison du Roi*, and the members of the royal family with their respective households of high-born aristocrats.[14]

To an extent, the court was domesticated by administrative power as well as by the famous *étiquette* which established codes of behaviour and represented hierarchies and fixed rules for access to the king and the royal family according to ranks. While men were dominant in government activities, women played a crucial role at court as intermediaries between the ministers and the members of the nobility who came to Versailles to claim favours. Each year hundreds of important positions and offices at court, in the army, the clergy, the administration, the magistracy—to which were attached revenues, privileges, or career prospects—were vacant. Although appointments complied with regulations—for instance the *ordre du tableau* in the case of promotion to military offices—there were always more candidates than posts to be filled and a word from a trusted or assertive person could be decisive. The queen was traditionally recognized as having an important power of patronage at court along with the other members of the royal family and, of course, the king's mistresses. For ministers, maintaining their authority over the court and the king's trust while, at the same time, keeping good relations with influential women who could find ways of communicating with the king, could be a real challenge and at times a test of power. In the cases of Maurepas and Choiseul, powerful ministers were exiled when they challenged the claim of the king's mistresses—or Marie-Antoinette, in the case of Louis XVI—to be allowed influence over their decisions. In effect, the administrative monarchy, with its centralising and rationalising ethos and bureaucratic practices, was mitigated by the Court's culture of hierarchy and privilege and the power of patronage.

Beyond the workings of royal administration, which remained secret, and of the Court, which was even more opaque, the monarchy offered very little space for public or informed discussion of state matters. Although censorship was relaxed from the mid-1750s and allowed philosophers to critically analyse their society and to propose reforms, a political press as such did not exist and foreign newspapers were under control or simply manipulated. Only a limited number of corporate bodies, like the clergy or provincial estates in some regions, had the privilege of administering some of their internal affairs and, like the *parlements* and other superior courts of justice, the right to discuss with ministers and issue remonstrances. As Marie-Laure Legay has argued in the case of the estates of the north of France, the freedom enjoyed by corporate bodies might be just an exercise in window-dressing around what was in fact an essential tool for the monarchy to implement royal policy. Louis XVI could not be more explicit about this when he told Loménie de Brienne, in 1787, that the provincial Assemblies that were to be established throughout France would not enjoy the 'simulated power' of the provincial estates over taxation.[15] Similarly, the support of *parlements*, whose magistrates judged the infractions to the laws they had registered within their respective jurisdiction, was paramount to maintain public order in the monarchy.

The problem is that king and ministers expected obedience in principle from all royal officers, in particular magistrates of the *parlements*, whereas the latter, literal owners of their offices purchased on the open market, naturally believed in an independence which they were jealous to maintain. Moreover, as members of a *compagnie*, they benefited from rights and privileges, in particular the right to participate in collective debates. They also benefited from corporate protection, as long as they submitted to internal rules of collective discipline. There is little doubt that *parlements*, in their conflicts with the ministers, defended their rights as magistrates and their interests as members of the aristocratic elite. Nonetheless, they had a very high opinion of their role in the monarchy and used their skills as legal experts to protect their margins for manoeuvre by relying on legal precedent. What is striking is the extent to which young and gifted magistrates in the eighteenth century were able to use their talents and acumen to challenge the traditional authority of the first president and his senior colleagues, who were usually in the pay of ministers. The conflicts over Jansenism gave these magistrates opportunities to advocate moral limits to obedience in religious affairs, arguments which were then transferred to discussions of fiscal issues. More importantly, in the absence of the Estates-General which had been convened for the last time in 1614, the magistracy was widely regarded by the king's subjects as the only body which could, by virtue of the right of remonstrance, voice their concerns to the king and defend their interest by appealing to the rule of law and royal justice.

It would certainly be excessive to seek to limit eighteenth century French history exclusively to the conflicts that opposed government to *parlements*. This would neglect the stresses on society exacerbated by international warfare, and the ways in which this made the issue of reform at home inevitable and the ideas of the Enlightenment appealing, by offering new concepts that helped articulate and unify critical discourses in the sphere of public opinion. Yet the quarrels between government and *parlements* dominated politics in the last two decades of Louis XV's reign, especially as remonstrances and the king's responses were published and cross-examined in pamphlets sponsored by all parties involved, including the government, in a bid to influence the public. At first glance, these rhetorical exchanges seem to have led nowhere. Indeed, the representation and the language of politics remained couched either in terms of submission and rebellion to the king's authority, or abuse of despotic rule by ministers against the spirit of the law. In practice, the magistrates sought to find ways of justifying their opposition to government's policy without being accused of challenging the king's authority.

To achieve this, legal experts in the *parlements* put forward a variety of claims. The theory of the *union des classes*, for instance, argued that *parlements* were all members of the same institution so as to justify and secure common action by magistrates when a specific court of justice was at odds with government. The assertion that the *Parlement* of Paris was the only court of justice involving peers of the kingdom (*Cour des Pairs*) and, as such, should be considered a national Plenary Court (*Cour Plénière*) above all other courts, is one of the more striking initiatives that came out of the game of judicial politics.[16] As the series of long royally commanded internal exiles and judicial strikes show, the debates opposing government and *parlements* made hardly any progress. The context of the Seven Years War (1756–63), which required more money to be raised, naturally hardened the ministerial line. However, the assassination attempt on Louis XV brought about the first important cabinet reshuffle since the death of cardinal Fleury: the king sacked both Machault d'Arnouville and the comte d'Argenson, who had been his most trusted and favourite servants.

On the face of things, this change of ministers did not alter the stalemate between government and *parlements*. In wartime, Louis XV's natural authoritarianism was unlikely to lessen and his rebukes of remonstrances remained very firm. However, for the first time since Louis XIV's reign, the political crisis of 1757 saw a significant change in the social background of the newly appointed ministers. Instead of selecting his new advisers from among the prominent dynasties of the *noblesse de robe*, Louis XV chose members of the *noblesse d'épée* for the posts of secretaries of state and picked candidates from outside the pool of provincial intendants to fill in the important post of *contrôleur général des finances*. Although there was no written rule for appointing ministers, the changes in their profile reflected the extent to which the structures of the administrative monarchy were seen as failing.[17] For their part, the *parlements*, which were clearly shocked by Damiens' attempt on the king, did not stop opposing government's policy. Scrutiny of the remonstrances of the *Parlement* of Paris show, however, that on fiscal issues the magistrates tried to avoid frontal attacks on the king's authority, and set themselves the task of devising legal constraints on government. In their criticisms of

Silhouette's (1760) and Bertin's (1763) fiscal policy, the *Parlement* of Paris argued, for instance, that the concept of necessity brandished by ministers to force through registration was not sufficient to command obedience and needed to be justified by positive laws such as accounting procedures to justify where the money went.[18]

One long-standing interpretation of the Terray-Maupeou crisis of 1770–71 has argued that royal authority was the last remedy for the monarchy to escape from the claws of selfish magistrates whose resistance to ministers was motivated by the defence of their fiscal immunities, and therefore to implement the reforms that would have saved France from the excesses of the Revolution. This thesis suffers from at least two major weaknesses. First, as William Doyle has pointed out, neither Bourbon kings nor their ministers ever contemplated the total abolition of *parlements*.[19] Therefore, political crises must be understood as adjustments in the policy towards the magistrates and their relationship with government, which could take various forms. Second, it must be remembered that Maupeou and Terray, before they were respectively appointed to the post of *chancelier de France* (1768) and *contrôleur général des finances* (1769), had served long years as *président* and *conseiller* in the Paris *Parlement*, and had been involved in all the disputes of the 1750s and 1760s. Such an overlap in their functions shows that the noise from the controversy was so deafening that it has long masked the profound disagreements among the magistrates over royal policies, which split the king's subjects and royal administrators alike.

As already mentioned, the princes of the blood, in their protest against Maupeou, reminded the king of the spirit of moderation which pervaded the royal declaration of November 1763, a text that was negotiated with the *Parlement* of Paris and which set out the basis for fruitful collaboration between government and magistracy. The symbol of this new policy, which had the support of Madame de Pompadour and the duc de Choiseul, was the appointment to the post of finance minister, for the first time ever, of a magistrate of the *Parlement* of Paris, in the person of L'Averdy, to facilitate the implementation of reforms and resolve the fiscal problems of the monarchy. In his comments, Voltaire expressed the views of almost everyone in France who had been convinced by the *Parlement*'s remonstrances that French finances would henceforth 'be governed according to the rules'.[20] In some respects, this policy was a success, as Louis XV obtained from the magistrates the prorogation of the taxes and support for the policy of freeing the grain trade. In exchange, the magistrates were directly involved in the management of the king's finances and involved in the discussion of reform.

Overall, this policy of appeasement proved a failure for three main reasons. First, the many disasters that France had experienced during the Seven Years War needed time to heal and solutions were not straightforward. Even the fiercest enemies of negotiations with the *parlements* recognized the difficulties. In a memorandum designed to warn his father against the effects of Choiseul's politics, the Dauphin wrote: 'I confess to you that deep in my soul I often take the liberty of making bold judgements about the ministers ... often also I excuse them for the difficulties they experience when they try to propose appropriate remedies for hardship and from which they can reasonably hope to achieve some success.'[21] Second, the tensions accumulated over the years had left profound scars which were difficult to hide. Supporters and opponents of the *parlements* quickly found reasons to clash. The hatred between La Chalotais, *procureur général* of the *Parlement* of Rennes, and the duc d'Aiguillon, former commander of Brittany and heir to the powerful Richelieu family, soon divided ministers, inflamed a whole province and spread to all *parlements*. Finally, the idea of involving the magistrates in the making of the laws failed because the *parlements* were far from united in their views when it came to debating key issues, such as the freedom of the grain trade. For magistrates were neither simply selfish *privilégiés* nor reformists. They were all of that: internal dynamics in the *parlements* and opinions varied according to the personality of their magistrates, power relations between the provinces and Versailles, and the evolution of the national context. Montesquieu's dream of an assertive royal policy moderated by negotiation with the magistracy faltered because there were as many voices as there were *parlements*—and superior courts of justice, which prevented the formation of a broad consensus to identify, implement, and enforce reforms against all kinds of oppositions.

Louis XVI and the Fall
of the Absolute Monarchy

On his deathbed, in May 1774, it seemed that Louis XV was handing over to his successor the annals of the monarchy in the state that he had inherited on his accession in 1715. Just as the Sun King's aura had faded at the end of his long reign, so animosities had mounted against the ageing Louis XV: as the monarch who bore responsibility for all the decisions, the erstwhile *Bien-Aimé* had ruled far too long not to be held fully or partly responsible by his subjects for their hardships and dissatisfactions. Montesquieu's predictions seemed to have come true: in 1771 the absolute monarchy had turned into despotism. The draconian rule reimposed by Maupeou meant that magistrates were compelled, once again, to register the king's law at first demand or be exiled and replaced by more compliant officers.

In his forbidden best-seller *L'An 2440* (1771), a work profoundly influenced by Montesquieu, Louis-Sébastien Mercier put in the mouth of his time-traveller the question that haunted the king's disaffected subjects as they reflected on their future:

- May I ask what is the present form of government? Is it monarchical, democratic, or aristocratic?
- It is neither of them; it is rational, and made for man. Monarchy is no more. Monarchical governments, as you knew [them], though to little purpose, lose themselves in despotism, as the rivers are lost in the bosom of the ocean; and despotism soon sinks under its own weight. This has been all literally accomplished, and never was there a more certain prophecy.[22]

Like his grandfather, the young Louis XVI was to inherit one of the largest, wealthiest, and most developed countries in Europe, with clear potential for growth like most countries involved in the booming Atlantic economy. Yet, the litany of the monarchy's problems had not reduced dramatically: with the exception of the religious issues solved by the expulsion of the Jesuits from France, the burdens of war still stood in the way of France's claim to great power status in Europe and the world. The question of fiscal privilege and economic policy, let alone the political institutions that could generate political consensus to implement an administrative, reformist agenda, remained unresolved. The failed attempt at involving magistrates in the royal administration had proved unsatisfactory and the Maupeou reform had left the *parlements* more divided than ever and, to an extent, weakened and discredited in the eyes of their sympathizers and enemies alike.

In such a dire context, and after sixty years of a reign that felt like an eternity to most, the unexpected death of the king again increased the sympathy of the French towards what had seemed at best a moribund monarchy. As Robert Darnton has rightly observed, Louis-Sébastien Mercier's utopian fantasy was a multi-layered text with multiple possible outcomes.[23] Like a dream, it juxtaposed confusing images: the disenchantment with the absolute monarchy coexisted with faith in the virtues of an enlightened monarch that would change their world for the better:

> We have experienced how contrary an absolute sovereignty is to the true interest of a nation. The art of raising refined tributes, all the powers of that terrible machine progressively multiplied; the embarrassment of the laws, one opposing another; chicanery devouring the possessions of individuals; the cities crowded by privileged tyrants; the venality of offices; ministers and intendants treating the different parts of the kingdom as conquered countries; a subtle hardness of heart that justifies inhumanity; royal officers, who are in no degree responsible to the people, and who insult them, [in]stead of listening to their complaints; such was the effect of that vigilant despotism [...] All these evils were known; but evident principles were avoided to embrace a system of dissipation, and the shadows that were raised, authorised the general depredation.
>
> Can you believe it? The revolution was effected without trouble, and by the heroism of one great man. A philosophic prince worthy of a throne, because he regarded it with indifference; more solicitous for the happiness of the mankind than for the phantom of power, offered to put the estates of the nation in possession of their ancient prerogatives ... Hence all lives, all flourishes.[24]

In these few pages published in 1771, Mercier summarized the evils of the old regime so familiar to historians of the Bourbon monarchy. For these problems had been clearly identified, in the 1750s and 1760s, if not long before, in manuscripts, memoranda, political pamphlets, and learned books written by progressive royal administrators, reforming magistrates and radical philosophers.

As Louis XVI came to the throne, expectations were overwhelming that this young man, who had been kept remote from power and its discontents and lived in the company of his wife and brothers, would be the longed-for philosopher king. Manifestations of happiness across France were vivid expressions that, if Louis XV had died, the power of monarchical feeling remained still very much alive in the body of his unstained successor. Popular love for the king, which mattered a lot to Louis XVI, was immediately capitalized on by his ministers for political purposes, inflating the image of the benevolent monarch to the point that the crisis of 1787–88, as well as the Revolution of 1789 and its republican developments, would appear contradictory and mysterious.

The capital of popular confidence and trust regained by the king was certainly a significant change of direction, as the *parlements* under Louis XV had drawn much of their strength from discontent with the government and support for their opposition, in particular from the lawyers and other judicial-related professions. Louis XVI's much awaited first political decision, recalling the magistrates exiled by Maupeou and restoring the *parlements'* right of remonstrances before registration (1774), gave him the popularity, and hence the moral and political advantage, to use his authority for the reform and betterment of society. The king was surfing the wave of European monarchies, like Sweden, Austria, and Spain, where enlightened despotism in the 1770s triumphed over aristocratic constitutionalism as the political method to implement the much needed reforms required to heal the ill-effects of the Seven Years War and to respond to public pressure in favour of increased liberties.

Louis XVI's favourable beginnings, the appointment of a liberal—if short-lived—ministry with Turgot (finances) and Malesherbes (*Maison du Roi*) who were both close to the Republic of Letters, the convocation of the Nation with the Estates-General, all these have traditionally been regarded by historians as evidence of the king's open mind and goodwill. In reality, the new reign soon showed that Louis XVI was a Bourbon monarch after all: policy at home was almost immediately dominated by war against Britain, first to prepare the French military establishment and seal international alliances, then to plan and oversee the operations of five long campaigns of war (1778–82), and to rescue the French finances exhausted by a ruinous naval conflict which cost above 1.2 billion *livres*, or about four years' worth of gross revenue in additional military expenditure. The war did not just increase the capital and debt service to levels unprecedented since Louis XIV's death. Having just turned 30, the victorious Louis XVI considered himself—or was invited by Vergennes, the true artisan of war and victory, to regard himself—as being far more successful than his grandfather, a situation which gave him strong legitimacy to govern and to embark upon the reform of the monarchy.[25]

In reality, Louis XVI had almost no experience of the challenges of rule without the political advantages of the wartime suppression of opposition. Although his ministers had been far from united during the conflict with Britain, the peace of 1783 increased their divisions and saw the royal family, including Marie-Antoinette, the king's brothers and their intimate circle, get more involved in matters of government. Tensions were useful inasmuch as the king was kept abreast of conflicts of interests opposing groups or factions while he retained the authority to act as arbiter. By far the most critical arbitrages he made concerned Calonne's appointment to the Ministry of Finances (1783) and, later in 1784, his decision to support Marie-Antoinette, who acted on behalf of her brother, the Holy Roman Emperor Joseph II, to save him from international humiliation after he had failed to impose free navigation of the river Scheldt upon the Dutch

Republic, also an important French ally. The unfortunate diamond necklace affair, which Marie-Antoinette had nothing to do with, and the decision of the Paris *Parlement* (1786) to set free cardinal de Rohan, also a victim of Madame de La Motte's successful swindle, sealed for good the perception that the Austrian queen, with her entourage at Court, acted against France's best interests, was responsible for the kingdom's financial hardships and abused the king's royal authority. Indeed, regardless of the *Parlement*'s fair decision in the most famous of the *causes célèbres*, Louis XVI ordered Rohan to exile.[26]

Of course, polemics about the Court and the king's wife or mistress were anything but new; since the building of Versailles by Louis XIV, if not before, it was common-place to associate excessive taxation with lavish expenditure at Court. Like many other criticisms, the accusation was partially true and came partly from within the Court. Its purpose was to find culprits, weaken ministers, and avoid considered examination of the true reasons for the general malaise which was rooted in the social and political structures of the Bourbon monarchy, which gave absolute power to the king and, at the same time, justified the privileges of the wealthy. Inevitably, the resurfacing of hostile discussions against the Court was problematic as Calonne, who had advocated public expenditure to stimulate the economy and sustain market confidence, realized in 1786 that the structural deficit had become so large that, unless something serious was done, and sooner rather than later, the monarchy would be once again contemplating bank-ruptcy. Once Calonne had revealed his concerns to the king, justified his administration and submitted his proposals for reforms, there was no escape route for Louis XVI, other than to try to patch up the problems or get rid of his minister, which in itself was not a solution since it would simply impose delay and increase instability.

Just as after each war, a crunch time of making vital decisions had arrived, which required government to decide who was to bear the costs of the conflict (in particu-lar how to service its accumulated debt), and find a way to implement policy. In 1749, Machault d'Arnouville managed to partly enforce the levy of a peacetime war tax by allo-cating its proceeds to the redemption of debts incurred during the War of the Austrian Succession. In 1763, Louis XV bought another fiscal lifeline by appointing L'Averdy, who was able to secure the *parlements*' agreement to maintain war taxes for a few years, with the proviso that discussions with the magistracy would bring rapid solutions to the monarchy's financial problems and political divisions. In 1786, Calonne persuaded Louis XVI that the convening of a small national consultative body, in the form of an Assembly of Notables, would be necessary to support his reforming agenda, in particu-lar his plan to tackle the deficit by levy of a new tax on landowners.

Calonne's suggestion was hardly new. Although the institution had remained dor-mant since 1626, the idea of calling an Assembly of Notables had been considered since the mid-1750s as one of the possible solutions, alongside the fuller national representa-tion of the Estates-General, in order to gain support for the government's reform plans. In one of the memoranda he was in the habit of submitting to his father Louis XV, the Dauphin (Louis XVI's father, 1729–65) floated the idea that disclosure of fiscal policy to an Assembly of Notables could facilitate registration of fiscal edicts by *parlements*, or even make them redundant.[27] Like his nemesis Necker, Calonne was well abreast of the post-1763 discussions between the government and *parlements*, as he had been personally involved in the settlement of the poisonous Brittany affair. Calonne's strategy in 1787 cannot be understood without reference to his prior experience and his understanding of the reasons why Choiseul's policy of appeasement had petered out in Terray's bankruptcy and Maupeou's coup. For instance, as William Doyle has pointed out, Calonne had reached the conclusion that 'the consent of the *parlement* would not be enough to win general confidence for his proposals'.[28]

CONCLUSION

It is easy nowadays to identify faults in ministers' programmes and complacency on the *parlements*' side which prevented, deferred, or diluted the monarchy's repeated attempts to bring about the transition from the old regime to the modern world. If pressure on government to introduce reforms seemed all the more pressing in times of hardship, the call of necessity did not make the task any easier. For the purpose of institutions is not to reform but to preserve the structure of societies. The Bourbon kings may have let Fénelon publish his *Télémaque* and condemn the excesses of personal power, Vauban to issue his *Dîme royale* to air the need to distribute taxes equally, and Diderot and d'Alembert to question tradition in the *Encyclopédie*, but sovereignty in the monarchy remained firmly based on the principle of the king's absolute authority and the practice of cooperation with privileged elites.

At this juncture, the question to be asked is, who were these privileged elites? The profile of the 144 Notables invited in February 1787 to meet in Versailles is telling: they were selected from among the ultra-privileged on the assumption that their position and rank in the monarchy would make these men more sympathetic and compliant to royal authority than magistrates. As under Louis XIV, Calonne and the king sought to exercise absolute power through the complicity of a few dominant families who had an interest in enforcing obedience. Clearly, this model no longer worked in the eighteenth century as younger generations, who grew up in a world challenged by the ideas of the Enlightenment, rejected the tradition of their fathers and the power of aristocracy. If one looks for the social origins to the Revolution, they lie as much in the possibility for the nobility, as Jay Smith has argued, to redefine its role within the monarchy as in the rise of a critical bourgeois public sphere.[29]

At first glance, the failure of the Notables and the sacking of Calonne fit well into the dual interpretative models of a reforming minister determined to fight abuses on behalf of the Nation but sacrificed to the interests of a selfish aristocracy or, alternatively, the victory of *privilégiés* using their corporate rights and moral authority to oppose ministerial despotism and wrong policies. In reality, the Notables were meant to circumvent these pitfalls by avoiding public discussion of government reforms. From the outset, Calonne's proposals had been kept secret and were examined by a small committee of three ministers, one of whom, Vergennes, died before the opening of the Notables, while the other, the keeper of the seals Miromesnil, was personally hostile but then surrendered. The two secretaries of state were excluded for a variety of reasons, the most important being suspicion that the maréchal de Castries might leak information to his friend Necker and allow Calonne's opponents, perhaps with the queen's support, to abort or rally opposition to the project before it was even disclosed. Needless to say, Castries was astonished when he learnt about the plans in a plenary meeting of the King's Council. He was even more surprised when, after his plea that the new tax, to be levied in kind, could not tackle the problems of fiscal inequality and the deficit, the king assured him that he was in the wrong.

The meeting of the Assembly of Notables was meant to bridge the obvious contradiction between the government's secrecy over its reform projects and the ultimate need to disclose them. Caught unaware by criticisms he had failed to recognize and found personally difficult to accept, Calonne had a moment of political lucidity when he told the Notables: 'The power to agree taxation is not the power to oppose it.' This observation justifies amply Malesherbes' conclusion in 1774, that 'Ministers and all the supporters of arbitrary authority claim that our right of remonstrance which is much valued in France is limited to this alone: the right to speak after which it is necessary to obey'; from which he argued the necessity to find where obedience must stop: 'Il faut se permettre de chercher où est le terme de l'obéissance.'[30] Needless to say, such reflections were bound to end up in a crisis as long as government, on the one hand, considered that taking advice—or *conseil*—required obedience in return, while *parlements*, on the other hand, were kept in an uncomfortable straitjacket which forced them to obey and oppose and, as such, prevented them from making any co-active and positive contribution to crucial debates.

In spite of these structural problems, it is quite remarkable that in the absence of legal ways to represent opposing interests and, more importantly, for independent institutions to be allowed to access information and discuss public policy, the French broadly agreed in 1789 over the reforms that needed to be introduced in the monarchy. On the eve of the meeting of the Estates-General, issues which had been (and would later prove again to be) profoundly divisive, such as the reform of economic policy and fiscal system, were not contentious problems any more. Only a few die-hards among the nobility still opposed the principle of equality of taxation. Progress had been slow but nonetheless real. In this process, political clashes and the way that all parties appealed to the tribunal of public opinion neutralized the capacity of the monarchy's institutions to resolve pressing problems. Calonne was first to break from the strategy of containing politics within Versailles' walls when he took it on himself to publish an *Avertissement* and call on the Nation to exercise moral pressure on the Notables. Calonne's *faux pas* and his dismissal by the king did not bring a remedy as the Notables were soon sent back home and the *Parlement* of Paris declined to register fiscal edicts (July 1787).

For his part, after a series of failed attempts by Loménie de Brienne to negotiate another lifeline with the magistrates (November 1787) and hand out registration of laws to a Plenary Court (May 1788), the king was left with the last political resource: a call on the Nation in the form of a meeting of the Estates-General. In effect, Louis XVI himself had also surrendered his power to levy taxes. It would take only a few months for the Nation to fill in the power vacuum and obtain what liberals in the *parlements* had claimed: positive laws in the form of a constitution to limit the absolute authority of the king by making ministers accountable, and a declaration of rights to settle the contentious debate about sovereignty and liberties. By that time, as Louis XVI's attitude had already indicated, the principle of the sovereignty of the Nation was unacceptable to a Bourbon king, and the nobility would quickly regroup in the defence of privileges and status, public order, and a loathing of equality.

Notes

1. Alexis de Tocqueville, *The Old Regime and the French Revolution* (New York, 1856), 13.
2. The classical legal interpretation is based on the work of constitutionalist Henri Carré de Malberg and developed by François Furet and Ran Halevi in their interesting book *La Monarchie Républicaine. La Constitution de 1791* (Paris, 1996). A professional jurist, Guillaume Glénard in *L'exécutif et la Constitution de 1791* (Paris, 2010) has challenged their approach and adopted Clermont-Tonnerre's concept of 'co-legislator powers' to argue that a legal reading of the constitutional debates shows the king had more effective power than has been assumed.
3. On the importance of the king's flight as a turning point see Timothy Tackett, *When the King Took Flight* (Cambridge, MA and London, 2003) and Mona Ozouf, *Varennes: la mort de la royauté, 21 juin 1791* (Paris, 2005). On the king's role in the Revolution see Joël Félix, *Louis XVI et Marie-Antoinette. Un couple en politique* (Paris, 2006) and Ambrogio A. Caiani, *Louis and the French Revolution, 1789–1792* (Cambridge, 2012).
4. For an overview of the debate and its evolution see Nicholas Henshall, *The Myth of Absolutism: Change & Continuity in Early Modern European Monarchy* (London, 1992), and Fanny Cosandey and Robert Descimon, *L'Absolutisme en France. Histoire et historiographie* (Paris, 2002).
5. This argument is particularly developed by Guy Rowlands, *The Dynastic State and the Army under Louis XIV: Royal Service And Private Interest, 1661–1701* (Cambridge, 2002).
6. Albert N. Hamscher, *The Conseil Privé and the Parlements in the Age of Louis XIV: A Study in French Absolutism* (Philadelphia, 1987); Michel Antoine, 'Les remontrances des cours supérieures sous le règne de Louis XIV (1673–1715)', *Bibliothèque de l'École des Chartes*, vol. 151 (1996), 87–122.
7. On cooperation and its limits see Darryl Dee, *Expansion and Crisis in Louis XIV's France: Franche-Comté and Absolute Monarchy, 1674–1715* (Rochester, 2009).
8. For a recent evaluation see Alexandre Dupilet, *la Régence absolue. Philippe d'Orléans et la polysynodie* (Paris, 2011) and Laurent Lemarchand: *Paris ou Versailles? La monarchie absolue entre deux capitales (1715–1723)* (Paris, 2014).
9. Peter Campbell, *Power and Politics in Old Regime France, 1720–1745* (London, 1996).
10. Montesquieu, *De l'esprit des loix*, Book II, chapter 4.
11. See in particular P. M. Jones, *Reform and Revolution in France: The Politics of Transition, 1774–1791* (Cambridge, 1995) and, in general, the research of Michel Antoine on 'la monarchie administrative', which is summarized in his biography of *Louis XV* (Paris, 1991).
12. Note, however, that most recent biographers of the king have accepted John Hardman's argument in *Louis XVI. The Silent King* (New Haven and London, 1993) of Marie-Antoinette's

letter to Count Mercy, the Austrian ambassador at Versailles, as evidence that Louis XVI was literally not able (i.e. he suffered depression from 1787) and was not capable any more of performing his duties.

13. Julian Swann, *Politics and the Parlement of Paris under Louis XV, 1754–1774* (Cambridge, 1995), 362.

14. On the court see Jeroen Duindam, *Vienna and Versailles: The Courts of Europe's Dynastic Rivals, 1550–1780* (Cambridge, 2003), Emmanuel Le Roy Ladurie, *Saint-Simon ou le système de la cour* (Paris, 1997) and Bernard Hours, *Louis XV et sa Cour. Le roi, l'étiquette et le courtisan* (Paris, 2002).

15. Marie-Laure Legay, *Les États provinciaux dans la construction de l'Etat moderne aux XVIIe et XVIIIe siècles* (Genève, 2001).

16. See in particular Julian Swann, *Politics and the Parlement*.

17. On the king and his ministers see Julian Swann, 'From Servant of the King to "Idol of the Nation": The Breakdown of Personal Monarchy in Louis XVI's France', in Julian Swann and Joel Félix (eds), *The Crisis of the Absolute Monarchy: From Old Regime to Revolution* (Oxford, 2013).

18. For this argument see Joël Félix, 'Nécessité et obéissance: Le Parlement de Paris et la critique de la raison d'Etat, 1741–1763', in Alain J. Lemaître, *Le monde parlementaire au XVIIIe siècle. L'invention d'un discours politique* (Rennes, 2008), 39–56.

19. William Doyle, 'The Parlements', in Keith Baker (ed.), *The French Revolution and the Creation of Modern Political Culture. Vol. 1: The Political Culture of the Old Regime* (Oxford, 1987), 157–167.

20. Joël Félix, *Finances et politique au siècle des Lumières. Le ministère L'Averdy, 1763–1768* (Paris, 1999), 153.

21. Bibliothèque municipale de Besançon, Ms 888, *Mémoire de feu M. le Dauphin* (no date, *ca.*1765), 361.

22. Mercier, *L'An 2440* (London, 1772), Chapter IX, 116–117.

23. Robert Darnton, *The Forbidden Best-Sellers of Pre-Revolutionary France* (New York, 1996).

24. Mercier, *L'An 2440*, 121–123.

25. Munro Price, *Preserving the Monarchy: the Comte de Vergennes, 1774–1787* (Cambridge, 1995).

26. Sarah Maza, *Private Lives and Public Affairs. The Causes Célébres of Prerevolutionary France* (Berkeley, LA, and London, 1993).

27. Bibliothèque municipale de Besançon, Ms 888, *Mémoire de feu M. le Dauphin* (no date, *ca.*1765), 362 vo, 370 vo.

28. Doyle, 'The Parlements', 165. For discussion of the motives behind Calonne's proposals see Olga Ilovaïsky, *La disgrâce de Calonne* (Paris, 2008) and Hardman, *Overture to Revolution*. The fundamental work remains, however, Hans Glagau, *Reformversuche und Struz des Absolutismus in Frankreich (1774–1788)* (München, 1908) which edited the series of memoranda submitted by Calonne. See also Felix, *Louis XVI et Marie-Antoinette*.

29. See Jay M. Smith, *Nobility Reimagined: The Patriotic Nation in Eighteenth-century France* (Ithaca, NY and London, 2005) and the volume of essays he edited on *The French Nobility in the Eighteenth Century. Reassessments and New Approaches* (The Pennsylvania State University Press, 2006), in particular the essay by Gail Bossenga, 'A Divided Nobility: Status, Markets, and the Patrimonial State in the Old Regime', 43–75. See also the work of Rafe Blaufarb, *The French Army, 1750–1820: Careers, Talent, Merit* (Manchester, 2002).

30. Archives nationales, 126Mi9. Archives du château de Rosanbo, fonds Lamoignon, dossier n. 4, *Premier éclaircissement sur l'usage ou sont les Rois de casser les arrêts du Conseil.*

Selected Reading

Campbell, Peter, *Power and Politics in Old Regime France, 1720–1745* (London, 1996).

Félix, Joël, *Finances et politique au siècle des Lumières. Le ministère L'Averdy, 1763–1768* (Paris, 1999).

Hardman, John, *Overture to Revolution: the 1787 Assembly of Notables and the Crisis of France's Old Regime* (Oxford, 2010).

Jones, Colin, *The Great Nation: France from Louis XV to Napoleon, 1715–1799* (London, 2002).

Jones, P. M., *Reform and Revolution in France: The Politics Of Transition, 1774–1791* (Cambridge, 1995).

Legay, Marie-Laure, *Les États provinciaux dans la construction de l'Etat moderne aux XVIIe et XVIIe siècles* (Genève, 2001).

Markoff, John, Shapiro, Gilbert, *Revolutionary Demands: A Content Analysis of the Cahiers de doléances of 1789* (Stanford University Press, 1998).

Swann, Julian, *Politics and the Parlement of Paris under Louis XV, 1754–1774* (Cambridge, 1995).

Swann, Julian, *Provincial Power and Absolute Monarchy. The Estates General of Burgundy, 1661–1790* (Cambridge, 2003).

Swann, Julian and Félix, Joël (eds), *The Crisis of the Absolute Monarchy: From Old Regime to Revolution* (Oxford, 2013).

CHAPTER 5

BOOKS, PHILOSOPHY, ENLIGHTENMENT

SIMON BURROWS

THOSE who experienced the trauma and exhilaration of revolution tended to attribute an explosive power to ideas, particularly those commonly associated with the Enlightenment philosophy of the eighteenth century. Even Jacques Mallet du Pan, one of the most sober and judicious of contemporary commentators, accused the *philosophes* of 'having shaken all that time, experience and wholesome philosophy had consecrated, and of having thus prepared public anarchy by the anarchy of the mind'.[1] Many historians have likewise attributed significant influence to enlightenment *philosophie*. Books—as the main vehicle by which enlightened ideas were communicated—therefore enjoy a privileged position in many understandings of the enlightenment and its links to revolutionary causation. However, when it comes to delineating those links in detail, historians have been considerably less successful. A number of theoretical models have been propounded, but they often struggle, faced with the accumulated evidence of empirical studies, including mine.[2] Conversely, those propounding empirically-based understanding have often been rightly criticized for the naivety of the mechanisms that they use to link texts and reading to the beliefs, practices, and actions of historical actors.[3] The bridge connecting enlightenment and revolution remains as elusive as ever. This chapter certainly cannot resolve every dilemma suggested by this preliminary analysis. What it will attempt is to establish a *juste milieu* between the theoretical models and empirical rigour, reviewing the historiographical possibilities in the light of the freshest evidence, to establish the place of the book in enlightenment and Revolutionary print culture and politics.

Such an analysis requires us to address numerous historical, methodological, and definitional dilemmas. What is a 'book'? What is the place of books in eighteenth century print culture? What was the enlightenment? By what media was it disseminated? How can we discern and measure the influence and reception of books in distant historical periods? What books were influential in the heavily censored and economically controlled print culture of the *ancien régime*? Which were the influential texts in the early Revolution? Who read them and how? How did they understand them? What are the links between reading and belief, belief and action? And in order to answer these questions, we need to establish how books were created, traded and disseminated across France, and to make comparisons between the reading tastes of the French and other Europeans.

Early explanations of the Revolution, which generally emerged from hostile, counter-revolutionary *milieux*, often privileged the ideas of the *philosophes*, whether the constitutional-democratic ideas of Jean-Jacques Rousseau; Voltaire's mocking attacks on *l'infâme*; or the militant atheism of d'Holbach. In their eyes, Rousseau's *Social Contract*, Voltaire's *Philosophical Dictionary*, and d'Holbach's *Système de la nature* were the unholy trinity of the enlightenment: three powerful books containing insidious ideas fatally toxic to political and religious stability. Moreover, *anti-philosophe* counter-revolutionary writers such as the abbés Barruel and Bergier were already demonizing the socially corrosive effects of these texts before the Revolution, even to the extent of predicting the cataclysm.[4] The reality of their phobia seemed to be confirmed by events, but also by the actions of the revolutionaries themselves, who solemnly enthroned Rousseau and Voltaire in the Pantheon. Although the dechristianization campaign during the winter of 1793–94 deeply divided the revolutionaries and fuelled their deadly factional warfare, to hostile eyes there seemed little difference between the dechristianizer, Joseph Fouché, placarding that 'Death is but an eternal sleep' over the cemetery gates at Nevers, and the deist, Maximilien Robespierre, presiding over the festival of the Supreme Being. It appeared self-evident that both men were avatars of the apocalypse foretold by Barruel and Bergier; incarnations of the evil genius of Voltaire and d'Holbach. The outcome of the philosophic conspiracy was plain for all to see.

The revolutionaries played into the hands of Barruel and Bergier in other ways, too. In searching for a legitimizing intellectual tradition to justify their displacement of *ancien régime* institutions, they rummaged through the ideological grab-bag of their enlightenment heritage for ideas and thinkers suited to their purposes. These were then elevated to canonical status. Thus Roger Chartier goes so far as to propose that perhaps the enlightenment was more an invention of the revolutionaries than vice versa, 'since it was the revolution that gave a premonitory and programmatic meaning to certain works'.[5] This seems untenable. Educated contemporaries habitually spoke of living in the age of enlightenment, and many sought to bask in the light of Voltaire and his minions. Others sought to establish that those with more conservative credentials, including Christian thinkers, could legitimately illuminate what was a veritable *siècle de lumières*. Moreover, as noted already, the idea of enlightenment as anti-Christian and socially destabilizing also predates the Revolution.

Nineteenth-century republican historians, like their clerical and legitimist opponents (the intellectual descendants of Barruel), also believed that the ideas of the *philosophes* were instrumental in shaping a Revolution whose main goal was, in their view, the establishment of a liberal-constitutional, and ultimately republican *régime*. Unashamedly Whiggish, this view blithely ignored the monarchic ideological and social predilections of many of the French enlightenment's leading thinkers. For example, it overlooks the incipient illiberalism of Rousseau's *Social Contract*, with its highly theorized system of intellectual intolerance; indoctrinating state education system; systematic enforcement of a state religion; and all-powerful foundational lawgiver. Nineteenth-century liberal-republican teleological preferences were carried into the mid-twentieth century, particularly by American historians, many of whom saw the origins of the sister revolutions in the United States and France in a modernizing, essentially republican enlightenment. This is still the view commonly peddled by textbooks and Western civilization primers—a progressive, liberal enlightenment engendering a benign revolution, albeit one that later judders off course.[6] This heroic, politically-driven enlightenment resurfaces in the work of Jonathan Israel, who makes the case for the spread of a radical enlightenment worldview from about 1760.[7] This represents a subtle shift of emphasis from his earlier work, which suggested that there was hardly a single important enlightenment idea that had not been expounded by the late seventeenth century. On this view, by the early 1700s it was all over bar the shouting.[8]

And yet, the shouting, as Professor Israel himself acknowledges, is surely what the enlightenment was all about. When Immanuel Kant formulated his celebrated definition of enlightenment in 1784, with its catchphrase 'dare to know', he stressed that the progress of enlightenment was dependent on discussion, debate, education, spreading the word.[9] His depiction of enlightenment was thus as much, or more, about process and media than about content or ideology, an approach that foreshadows the dominant thrust in enlightenment historiography over recent decades.[10] This historiographical trend has been strongly influenced by two main strands of thought. The first, championed by Rolf Engelsing, proposes that the eighteenth century witnessed a 'reading revolution'. The more ready availability of ever cheaper print products promoted more critical reading habits, as readers moved more fluidly through and between texts, and grew more private in their reading habits.[11]

In earlier centuries, this theory argues, most readers had access to only a few texts, and these usually bore the imprint of religious or political authority. Highly prized, expensive, and giving access to truths required for eternal salvation (and/or legal-political survival), these texts were considered authoritative, precious, and not open to question. They were read intensively, repeatedly, and frequently in public. In the eighteenth century, the more ready availability of texts, together with an increasing variety of forms and genres, allowed solitary readers to compare and contrast texts more critically. These habits of mind were eventually applied even to texts once considered authoritative. Following the path-breaking initiatives of Pierre Bayle and Voltaire, even Holy Scripture was treated by some readers as just another literary text. Hence, there developed a more critical and engaged reading public accustomed to questioning received authority and whose relationship with printed texts was not necessarily one of trust.

This leads us to the enormously influential ideas of Engelsing's compatriot, the German theorist, Jürgen Habermas, on the emergence of the public sphere.[12] Habermas argued that (alongside this reading revolution) there emerged in the eighteenth century an increasingly important rational-critical 'bourgeois' public, which, operating in a 'public sphere' autonomous of state control, both critiqued and shaped the political choices of government. On both an ideological level and—since governments needed public credit and support for their fiscal-military policies—in the realm of practical politics, the judgments of the rational-critical public came increasingly to be seen as definitive. Hence the youthful Louis XVI's assertion: 'I must always consult public opinion: it is never wrong.'[13] The institutions of this 'public sphere' took two main forms—printed products, first and foremost journalistic texts, and new sociable institutions, such as salons, debating societies, scientific academies, reading circles, subscription libraries, Masonic lodges, and coffee houses, where members of the public might discuss ideas and political news. These institutions were inter-related, since printed texts informed the debates in sociable institutions and those same institutions often stocked or published works pertaining to their discussions. Although aspects of this model have been heavily revised by historians, particularly Habermas's assertions that the public sphere was necessarily bourgeois, robustly autonomous, and inherently rational-critical, its central core remains widely accepted.[14] By the late eighteenth century, a growing public was becoming involved, and demanding a say, in public policy discussions.

Habermas's account of this public sphere privileges journalism, a relatively new form of print, over the book. For journalism offered readers a regular point of contact with news information and opinion, the possibility of regular feedback, repeated suggestion, and possibilities of interaction with the journalist that did not exist with books. This potentially turns on its head the assumption of many literary scholars and historians that the book is the more influential and important form, and returns us to the question of the book's place in eighteenth century French print culture. To explain that, we need to define what constitutes a book.

This question has long tied 'book historians' in knots. One way to answer it is to see how an eighteenth century bookseller dealt with their stock. The celebrated Swiss francophone publisher-wholesaler, the *Société typographique de Neuchâtel* (STN), whose much-studied records provide rich insight into the book trade, is a good starting point here.[15] The rolling stock inventories kept through the 1770s and 1780s include only certain types of printed merchandise: those items that they could inventory and sell through their *catalogues des livres* [book catalogues]. For practical business purposes, a book was a printed text that might generate one-off sales to the general public. They did not, therefore, include their own journalistic products in their inventories, a natural enough decision given the difficulty of keeping up-to-date subscription records. Nor did they include job printings of official documents, forms and notices; fliers, trade cards and other advertising material for local businesses; or miscellaneous small print jobs for individuals. These sorts of 'ephemera' were accounted for elsewhere. Nevertheless, the Swiss 'bookseller's' inventories include a variety of printed genres besides what we would think of as books.[16] Their *marchandises* included one-off single volumes of newspapers, scientific and literary periodicals; almanacs and yearbooks; political pamphlets; and trial briefs. They even include a four-side promotional brochure for Voltaire's *Questions sur l'Encyclopédie* (which the STN published in nine volumes), containing the article 'Dieu' [God].

From a professional bookseller's viewpoint, then, 'books' included a vast middle ground spanning periodicals, once-off printed ephemera and job-printings. They could include the shortest of pamphlets and large multi-volume works of literature, *philosophie* or history—anything, it appears, that might be sold to their trading partners or the local reading public. In particular, there was no obvious difference between a book and a pamphlet, except perhaps its shelf-life. Such works could, nevertheless, be lucrative. The Neuchâtelois booksellers seem to have done very well, for example, from the controversies stirred by the publication of their compatriot and French finance minister Jacques Necker's *Compte rendu des finances* in 1781. Pamphlets related to this controversy account for their five 'best-selling' works in 1781. The *Compte rendu* itself also appears—but only in tenth place.[17] Significantly, such sales were to prove both ephemeral and local to France and Switzerland: the STN disseminated very few copies in the rest of Europe.

Necker's *Compte rendu*, as Michael Kwass has pointed out, was a runaway best-seller. Although he was not the first *controlleur-général des finances* to issue a defence of his tenure of office, Necker's accounts appeared to lay bare French finances as never before. They ran to at least seventeen editions and sold an estimated 40,000–100,000 copies. The STN statistics suggest commentaries, refutations, and other pamphlets responding to Necker sold several times more.[18] These statistics help to contextualize the relative importance of books and journalistic products. For the year the *Compte rendu* appeared, thanks to the chance survival of post office records, we also have apparently full circulation statistics for newspapers inside France. They show that there were in total about 45,000 subscribers to newspapers circulated via the post office. Of these, 14,000 were for highly regarded twice-weekly imported 'foreign gazettes' such as Leiden's *Gazette de Leyde*, Zweibrücken's *Courier du Bas Rhin*, and London's *Courier de l'Europe*.[19] Assuming ten readers per copy, this represents a newspaper audience of 450,000. Among a population of over 25 million, this is a relatively limited readership, comprising perhaps one in thirty adults. The market for books must have been many times larger, though few individual titles matched the 5,000–7,000 print runs of the *Courier de l'Europe* or *Gazette de Leyde*.[20]

In fact, the average print run for a single eighteenth century edition has generally been estimated at no more than 1,000 copies.[21] On that basis we can speculate that perhaps 2,500,000–3,000,000 copies of French books were being churned out every year. Certainly, the most extensive bibliographic survey to date, which incorporates a range of print products not dissimilar to the STN's *marchandises générales*, suggests that 1,576 first editions were published in French in 1770, rising to 1,950 in 1786. This total does not include second and subsequent editions of the more popular works, which might have added perhaps half as many editions again. Thus, if there was one newspaper subscription for every 600 or so inhabitants of France in 1781, the annual rate of book production was around one book per ten inhabitants.[22]

Hence the social penetration of books was probably considerably greater than for newspapers, which were expensive and sold by subscription. Books were seemingly affordable for urban labourers, and between 1750 and 1789 book ownership expanded rapidly. Parisian will inventories from the 1750s record that 13 per cent of wage labourers and 20 per cent of domestic servants owned books. By 1780, those figures had risen steeply to 35 per cent of labourers and 40 per cent of domestic servants.[23] Cheap broadsides, occasional pamphlets, ephemera, chapbooks, and the *bibliothèque bleue* were more accessible still. By the late eighteenth century many peasant families in wealthy, highly literate, north-eastern France owned or had access to devotional material, and some owned other printed works besides. Yet book ownership remained a predominantly urban phenomenon, and provincial publishers, often operating on a knife-edge, tended to print a conservative mix of religious and traditional fare. Hence, in the rural south and west, where education and literacy rates were much lower, the main reading fare tended to be devotional chapbooks and folk-tales. Penetration of enlightenment material beyond the towns was negligible.[24] The correlation between literacy rates and areas of revolutionary and grass-roots dechristianizing activism is striking. Conversely, areas of counter-revolutionary activity coincide strongly with areas of low literacy.[25]

Generally, however, expanding book markets were underpinned by a surge in popular literacy. Of course, literacy involves a wide spectrum of skills, ranging from a basic ability to comprehend and decode letter shapes through to the ability to assimilate and produce complex texts. The standard measure of literacy favoured by most historians (more by default than desire), the ability to sign a marriage certificate or similar document, measures only one basic skill—using a pen to produce a few well-practised letters.[26] Rates of signature literacy rise significantly in the eighteenth century. Among men, across France, they had reached 50 per cent by 1789, up from 21 per cent a century earlier. By the Revolution, signature literacy was near universal among bridegrooms in Paris and the north-east. Their brides, too, were more likely than not able to write. Moreover, as reading and writing were taught as separate skills, and many lower-class women were probably taught reading alone, it seems probable that much female literacy is disguised, and the true discrepancy between the sexes less pronounced than in these figures. Yet in remote areas of the south and west of France, literacy levels could fall below 20 per cent of young men. Such literacy rates certainly inhibited the circulation of books and enlightened ideas.[27]

France's generally impressive literacy figures help to explain the print explosion of 1789. In the pre-revolutionary and revolutionary maelstrom, as the shackles of censorship were released and political crisis led to the politicization of ever-increasing swathes of the population, reading became a means of engagement with pressing current concerns. The volume of French pamphlet production is revealing here. For the first dozen years of Louis XVI's reign, pamphlets listed in the Bibliothèque nationale's extensive, if not exhaustive, *Catalogue de l'histoire de France* number just 312 titles. However, it lists 217 for 1787; 819 in 1788; and an astonishing 3,305 in 1789.[28] Parallel growth rates are found in Conlon's general bibliographic survey, which lists 11,338 works appearing in 1789 as opposed to 1,950 in 1786.[29] This exponential expansion is dwarfed by the explosion in newsprint from July 1789. Whereas in 1781 the French market supported just 45,000 newspaper subscriptions, most of them for weekly or twice-weekly publications, by 1790 the Parisian press alone was pumping out an estimated 300,000 papers a day.[30] From whence came the extra production capacity?

In his unpublished memoirs, the Lieutenant-Général of the Police of Paris, Jean-Pierre-Charles Lenoir, suggested that much of the revolutionary press capacity came from the underground presses of the Jansenist-parlementarian opposition. Many of these presses had been mothballed since the Maupeou crisis of 1771–74, waiting to strike again.[31] This explanation seems weak. Jansenist and parlementary oppositional pamphleteering was certainly a thorn in the government's side, but the actual numbers of clandestine titles were rather low. The most scandalous and successful, such as Pidansat de Mairobert's *Anecdotes sur Madame la Comtesse du Barry*, were essentially commercial affairs, produced in large numbers outside the kingdom. François Grasset's Lausanne edition alone probably ran to 5,000 or more copies.[32] Keeping such volumes of production secret inside France would have been challenging, even for those members of the social and political elite who dabbled in oppositional politics.

Yet the French elite were becoming more involved in political pamphleteering activities as the Revolution approached. The rot started at the top. Necker and his arch-rival Calonne both kept printing presses in their homes at various stages of their careers. Likewise, many high-ranking government officials and ministers of the late 1780s cut their political teeth in oppositional politics in the 1760s and early 1770s. The extent of their complicity was shown in 1786, after a relatively minor *parlementaire* lawyer named Lemaître was arrested with a completed printer's *forme* of a clandestine pamphlet at the gates of Paris. Police inquiries implicated much of the political elite and reached even the heart of government. Investigating Lemaître, who had been active in oppositional networks since the 1760s, revealed too much. When his testimony threatened to embarrass one of Marie-Antoinette's favourites, the inquiry was abandoned. Such evidence hints at a considerable underground press capacity developing in the 1770s and 1780s, abetted by rampant factionalism at court and weak royal control.[33]

Simultaneously, it appears that the Parisian print trade was increasing its stranglehold on the French publishing industry, abetted by a government intent on restricting provincial book production.[34] The mid-1780s saw the French government take effective measures against the extra-territorial publishers operating along their eastern border, who pirated popular works, flooding the French market with cheap imitations. Most decisive was a decree of 12 June 1783, ordering that all book imports must travel via Paris for inspection by the Parisian booksellers' guild. The ostensible reason for this measure was the need to prevent scandalous pamphlets against Marie-Antoinette reaching France. This was probably only a pretext. Redirection via Paris massively increased the cost of sending books to the provinces. It particularly harmed the Swiss booksellers, who were located further from Paris than their Dutch or Rhenish rivals. A recent digital survey shows that the decree severely damaged the Swiss trade: despite their protests the French did not relent. This harm proved permanent, judging from the massively reduced numbers of editions trickling out of Neuchâtel, Lausanne, Yverdun, and Geneva thereafter. The Revolution merely delivered the *coup de grâce* to their trade with France.[35] Meanwhile, the Parisian industry probably took up the slack, increasing its productive capacity in the half decade before the Revolution. As Elizabeth Eisenstein has shown, many print professionals and exiled writers began flocking back to Paris.

Her provisional survey associates this influx with the outbreak of the Revolution, but a full-scale prosopographical survey might well reveal that, in fact, writers and printing professionals returned in the years preceding 1789.[36] Certainly, this applies to some of the most successful among their number—Brissot, Mirabeau, Louis-Sébastien Mercier.

Their return was accompanied by a transformation in print culture. As noted, the genre experiencing most growth in the pre-Revolutionary period was the political pamphlet. However, by late 1789 newspapers were undoubtedly the chief vehicle of political publishing, and the most influential. The most successful broke with tradition in numerous ways. Most significantly, where the heavily censored pre-Revolutionary press fed its readers a diet of news information, revolutionary newspapers offered an essay-based opinion journalism.[37] Its most successful proponents sold thousands of copies daily, making them very wealthy within a few months. Many also were, or became, significant political actors in the process, among them Brissot, Marat, Roederer, and Camille Desmoulins, but Danton, Robespierre, and Napoleon Bonaparte were also skilled manipulators of the press.

This narrative of revolutionary displacement of books by pamphlets and pamphlets by newspapers raises two important questions. First, what books were being consumed most avidly before the Revolution? Second, what space was left for the more traditional book in revolutionary culture? The rest of this chapter explores these questions.

The first question was famously formulated by Daniel Mornet in his *Origines intellectuelles de la Révolution française* (1933). It has perplexed historians ever since, inspiring several sweeping bibliometric surveys. Mornet's own survey, based on private library catalogues, threw up some interesting surprises. Most intriguingly, it suggested that the Jacobin Bible, Rousseau's *Social Contract*, was little known before the Revolution. In a survey of 500 private library catalogues, Mornet found just a solitary copy.[38] Other works of enlightenment philosophy proved similarly hard to detect.

Subsequent bibliometric surveys, whether based on other library clusters, will inventories, surveys of book reviews in periodicals, or requests for '*publique*' or '*tacite*' publishing permissions, also struggled to detect subversive enlightenment works. In retrospect, the reasons are obvious. Most classic enlightenment works fell foul of the censorship apparatus at some point. Few had the official approbation and state protection of a *permission*, whether *tacite* or *publique*, so owners tended to hide them away. Nor were enlightenment classics likely to be reviewed in state-tolerated periodicals, listed in printed library or book sale catalogues (which were censored prior to publication), or recorded in legal inventories.[39] Looking at these measures of book ownership or publishing proves unhelpful as a way of seeking enlightenment.

Robert Darnton's work offers a more fruitful approach, by examining the statistics of the book trade to recover what people wanted to read. Darnton limited his investigation to the highly illegal sector of the trade (the very sector missing from previous surveys) and based it on a broad sampling of the correspondence of French booksellers ordering illegal books from the STN.[40] His methodology has been followed by several other scholars.[41] Darnton's results were somewhat ambivalent. His top three authors included both d'Holbach and Voltaire—who published so many works with Gabriel

Grasset, a major STN trading partner, that his works could hardly fail to register.[42] But few of Voltaire's individual works appear as major sellers. In contrast, d'Holbach may be over-represented in STN figures because they published the first edition of his *Système de la nature*. This edition provoked an angry reaction from local Calvinist clergy, and thereafter the STN avoided publishing or widely disseminating radical materialism.[43]

The STN were willing, however, to dabble in other forms of subversive literature. These included the works of Pidansat de Mairobert, Darnton's second best-selling author, whose scandalous biography of Louis XV's mistress, the *Anecdotes sur Madame la Comtesse du Barry* (1775) was among their most ordered texts. Together with the futuristic vision of a morally perfected France communicated by Louis Sébastien Mercier's *L'An 2440*, and the materialist anti-clerical pornography of d'Argens real-life inspired novel *Thérèse philosophe*, it is highly implicated, according to Darnton, in the progressive desacralization of the monarchy. As 1789 approached, these works and others in similar genres—including *L'Histoire de Dom Bougre, portier des Chartreux*; Théveneau de Morande's *Gazetier cuirassé ou anecdotes scandaleuses de la cour de France*; Mouffle d'Angerville's *Vie privée de Louis XV*; and the anonymous *Amours de Zeokinizul, roi des Kofirans*—progressively stripped throne and altar of their sacred veneer, leaving them exposed and vulnerable. Such texts, Darnton suggests, more than the celebrated works of the high enlightenment canon, were the main vectors for transmitting anti-monarchical and anti-clerical messages to the French public. Their corrosive power stemmed from their ability to put across a simplified Rousseauism to readers unable to comprehend Rousseau's original political texts. It is in this underground literature of scabrous libel that we should seek the origins of the Revolution.[44]

Darnton's arguments pose further questions, many of which he tackles head on. How widely read and disseminated were these illegal texts? Did they reach a sans-culotte or proto-Jacobin audience, particularly as prohibition inflated prices? If so, how were they actually read and understood? What else was being read by the same audience? On a theoretical level there were further quandaries. What was the link between reading and belief—was it as simple as Darnton seemed to suggest: were readers' minds really like 'soft wax', mused Roger Chartier?[45] If not, was the model of desacralization still credible?

It was with such questions in mind that I determined to embark on a comprehensive survey of the STN archive, using bespoke digital methodologies. This survey would be broader than Darnton's, and based on hard evidence from account books rather than the orders of booksellers, which showed only that a book had been ordered, not necessarily delivered. And because the survey was conducted through a database, the statistics produced would be infinitely more malleable than Darnton's, as well as more extensive (based on 410,000 copies of books disseminated across Europe as opposed to 28,212 French orders for illegal books). Accompanied by a detailed and carefully defined computer-moderated subject taxonomy, it would facilitate the study of demand across time and space.[46]

While it would be dangerous to dwell too far on the trade of a single publishing house, the evidence of the STN database contains some suggestive findings. First, it allows us to better understand the shape and extent of the illegal sector. As a publisher-wholesaler, the STN was a relative specialist in banned books, secure in the shelter of Neuchâtel's powerful Prussian overlords. As a result, fully 28 per cent of its trade with France comprised works on Darnton's highly illegal list of clandestine literature. Naturally, this overstates the extent of the illegal sector. Relatively few publishing houses traded so extensively in illegal works; those that did were based along French borders in the Netherlands, Bouillon, the Rhineland and Switzerland, but also London. These houses were massively outnumbered by publishing houses inside France, where it was dangerous to publish illicit material and few publishers were willing to do so. Keeping the printing of illicit works secret was difficult. Even beyond French borders, Bourbon spies, police agents and diplomats often detected and prevented the production of offending works.[47] On several occasions they sponsored attempts to kidnap and possibly assassinate dissident writers based abroad.[48]

Close analysis of the STN's trade, which mostly comprised cheap, popular editions, leads to several further conclusions. And because the STN accounted for perhaps 1 per cent of unit sales, legal and illegal, of French books across Europe between 1770 and 1789, these conclusions appear, with certain caveats, to have broader representative value.[49] First, and perhaps most importantly, they appear to rehabilitate the high enlightenment. For even in the highly illegal sector, it seems that enlightenment *'philosophie'* was always more popular than salacious tales of royal mistresses, libertine pornography, and bawdy anti-clerical works. The popularity of the *philosophes* is exemplified by Voltaire's place at the head of the STN's general best-selling author table for France. His sales accounted for around 10 per cent of their trade in works printed by other publishers (4,746 units).[50] Voltaire's French sales considerably outstripped sales of the Bible (3,068 units) and exceeded sales of any other writer by a factor of three. Trailing in distant second place was Swiss medical author Samuel Tissot, famed for his championing of smallpox inoculation and path-breaking, erroneous, but titillating tract on *Onanisme*. He sold a mere 1,534 units. The top 20 selling authors in France also include several leading *philosophes*, notably d'Holbach (789 units), Jean-Jacques Rousseau (590 units), the abolitionist propagandist Raynal (347 units) and Claude-Adrien Helvétius (339 units). Alongside them stood enlightened men of science, popularizers and agricultural writers: Tissot; the Swiss doctor, scientist, poet and polymath Albrecht Haller; and Maupin, a writer on viticulture. His STN sales exceeded those of both Raynal and Helvétius.[51] Nor should we exclude the works of the popular Rousseauist novelist and playwright Louis Sébastien Mercier, who occupies fifth place. If we included the STN's own editions in our table, he would occupy top spot. Mercier's utopian moral fantasy *L'An 2440*, rambling, reformist *Tableau de Paris*, and overtly political plays, including the historical drama *La Destruction de la ligue*, perhaps represent a more engaged brand of late enlightenment thought. As this list makes clear, there was considerable demand among late *ancien régime* readers for high-brow and sophisticated enlightenment works.

STN customers also ordered lower-brow, distracting works in large numbers. Sales figures suggest that they devoured the sentimental novels of Madame de Ricoboni, and the more *risqué* fare of the Marquis de Luchet. The novels and light, mildly erotic, poetry of the libertine author Claude-Joseph Dorat were also in high demand. So, too, were works and anthologies aimed at children, including the didactic output of Madame de Genlis (393 unit sales), the fairy stories of Madame Leprince de Beaumont (447 sales), and a popular anthology of *Lectures pour les enfants* [*Readings for Children*], which offered snippets of everything from La Fontaine to Voltaire (542 sales). More intriguingly, the STN's best-selling author list also includes the grammarian Johann Christoph Gottsched, author of the *Maître de la langue allemande*. While German grammars were probably less prominent in the trade of other publishers, language works, notably school textbooks, and foreign language grammars and dictionaries, accounted for 2.3 per cent of STN sales—over one in 45 works traded. This was the tip of an iceberg, for 'school books' and general reference books accounted respectively for 7.65 per cent and 5.25 per cent of their entire trade.[52] Alongside—and occasionally overlapping with—high and low enlightenment texts, these tried and tested genres provided the bread and butter for many ordinary publishers.

Of course, eighteenth century publishers and readers may not have thought in such categories. When it came to cataloguing their stock, publishers frequently resorted to the classificatory system of the Parisian booksellers, developed around the turn of the eighteenth century. It divided printed works into five distinct groups, each with numerous and flexible sub-categories. As a way of reading the world, this proves revealing. For if we strip out 'vanity press' commissioned works, it segments the STN's trade as follows. *Belles lettres* (creative literature including anthologies which included fiction and non-fiction) accounted for just under 35 per cent of units traded; *Histoire* [history], which included travel writing [*Voyages*], for almost 30 per cent, and the catch-all *Sciences et Arts*, comprising everything between epidemiology and materialist philosophy via artisanal trades, 21 per cent. *Théologie* [theology] accounted for 10.5 per cent and *Jurisprudence* for just 2.8 per cent. Thus two out of every three of the STN's general sales were works which might provide entertainment or distraction, as well, in some cases, as edification: creative literature, history or travel writing. Intriguingly, between 1769 and 1788, the French took marginally less *Histoire* (27.33 per cent), and read commensurately more *Sciences et Arts* (23.75 per cent), *Théologie* (11.3 per cent) and *Jurisprudence* (3.1 per cent) than the STN's other clients. The deviation in each case is around 10 per cent. What should we make of this? The statistics—which, nevertheless, tend to suggest that *Belles lettres* and *Histoire* were more popular than shown by most other surveys—are not decisive enough to support a general theory.[53] But perhaps French readers had more serious, high-brow interests than francophone readers elsewhere?

The statistics of the STN's illegal trade point to stronger conclusions concerning the distinctive traits of the France's clandestine book market. The French ordered irreligious, anti-clerical, libertine and erotic works in proportionately greater quantities than anyone else in Europe, and within these genres they favoured more 'hard-core' materials. Tellingly, the STN's top-selling authors list for France includes John Cleland, whose novel *Fanny Hill* was translated into French as *La Fille de joie* [*The Prostitute*] and Michel Milot, author of the *Ecole des filles* [*School for Whores*], as well as the anonymous biographer of Italian Renaissance pornographer Pietro Aretino. Following the decree of 12 June 1783, French sales of such works collapsed and demand from elsewhere increased proportionately. But this was almost certainly testimony to the effectiveness with which the French closed their borders, rather than a sign of changing tastes elsewhere. Nor is it certain that the French had a more pronounced taste for such works. Possibly francophone readers elsewhere, for whom French was often a second language, preferred to savour erotica or tackle challenging heterodox philosophical works in their native tongues. The same may be true of scientific or theological texts. That said, sales of erotic and religiously heterodox works to other areas with concentrations of native French speakers—the Protestant Swiss Romande or Roman Catholic Belgium—were considerably lower than French sales in the same genres. Revealingly, these are the very works that Darnton claims desacralized the French monarchy.

The evidence for such a claim remains at best ambiguous, not least on the grounds of timing. For example, the heyday for French sales of another class of desacralizing work, anti-Louis XV *libelles* such as the *Anecdotes sur Mme du Barry*, lay prior to 1780. In the final decade before the Revolution, and particularly after the decree of 12 June 1783, their market inside France dried up.[54] Furthermore, contrary to popular and historical myth, such works were not replaced by an outpouring of *libelles* against Marie-Antoinette until after 1789.[55] Likewise, multiple indicators suggest that the production and circulation of radical atheistic texts peaked during the years of the Maupeou crisis (1771–74), when government and *parlements* were too distracted by their own internecine feuds to pay much attention to the publications of the baron d'Holbach and his collaborators.[56] Whether such scandalous and sacrilegious fare led or reflected public opinion is also open to question. Perhaps it merely piqued readers' curiosity. What is clear is that in the final decade before the Revolution, such materials represented only a small and evidently declining segment of the French book market. In contrast, heavyweight and engaged works on politics, contemporary history, state finance and the colonial system, often written by leading *philosophes*, were all enjoying a considerable vogue.[57]

Thus, the relationship between reading, philosophy and the politicization of the French public in the final years before the Revolution now appears more complex than ever. Their political education appears to owe more, after all, to the theoretical and abstruse writings of the leading *philosophes* than to Grub Street authors, but they also had a marked predilection for libertine and desacralizing works. However, they were also, from at least the 1770s, being invited to engage more openly and frequently with public affairs through a range of print genres, and, in comparison with audiences elsewhere, they may well have had a preference for heavyweight intellectual works. This helped to prepare the way for the explosion of an often highly partisan political essay journalism during the Revolution, and the resultant rise to prominence of the newspaper press.

Nevertheless, it would be misleading to write off the literary production and book publishing of the Revolution. To do so is to accept too readily the counter-revolutionary view of revolution as 'cultural wasteland'.[58] What is clear is that the Revolution ushered in a period of ephemeral publication, marked by the triumph of the novel in literature as well as the temporary eclipse of books by newspapers and pamphlets. In large part this was due to new deregulated market structures, which in publishing, as in many other economic spheres, had effects diametrically opposed to what the revolutionaries hoped.[59] They had fondly imagined that freed of the *ancien régime* system of censorship, licences, and exclusive *privileges*, readers would flock to buy enlightenment French science and philosophy, as enlightenment publishing enterprises moved from the European periphery to the metropolis of Paris. Yet the new regime was stifling of literary and publishing creativity. Denied the legal protection previously accorded to authors, many writers turned to ephemeral journalism and pamphleteering as the most effective means to prevent their work being pirated. Book publishers likewise turned to churning out short works of pulp fiction, afraid that more serious or longer works or luxury editions would soon be undercut by cheap reprints in a cut-throat, zero-sum game. If we ignore music publishing, which consisted mostly of songs and sheet music, over half of copyright requests lodged with the *Depôt legal* at the Bibliothèque nationale between 1793 and 1799 related to works of creative literature, mostly novels (997/1,947 requests).[60]

Attempts to stem the tide in July 1793 by granting authors a lifelong interest in the works they published proved inadequate. This measure brought much of the literary culture of the enlightenment—the works of dead authors—into the public domain. There was, however, none of the expected flurry to publish such material, although by the end of the Revolutionary decade state-sponsoring of scientific and technical works was beginning to bear fruit. Generally, publishers were reluctant to publish out-of-copyright works, for fear that rival, cheap editions would flood their market: far easier to resort to publishing unseen *nouveautés* [novelties]. They did so in unprecedented numbers, particularly from 1797. By 1798 and 1799 the supply of novels to the market had grown exponentially: a trickle during the early Revolution had become a flood.[61] In that sense the Revolutionary publishing scene proved the antithesis of the enlightenment ideal. The heady delight of daring to know had been replaced with the guilty pleasures of escapism and novel reading. Only with the Napoleonic regulation of the book trade from 1810 would a more bookish elitist culture re-emerge as the economic and political pendulum swung back towards protection and exclusive privileges, and a return to a world of printed knowledge characterized by censorship, high prices, and restricted access.[62]

NOTES

1. Jacques Mallet du Pan, 'On the Degree of Influence which French philosophy as Had upon the Revolution', *British Mercury* 14 (15 March 1799), 335–63 at 335.
2. See Simon Burrows, *Blackmail, Scandal and Revolution: London's French Libellistes, 1758–1792* (Manchester, 2006); 'Introduction', in Hannah Barker and Simon Burrows (eds), *Press, Politics, and the Public Sphere in Europe and North America, 1760–1820*, (Cambridge, 2002).
3. See, for example, the criticisms of Robert Darnton's work in Haydn T. Mason (ed.), *The Darnton Debate: Books and Revolution in the Eighteenth Century* (Oxford, 1998), especially those by Daniel Gordon, Thomas Kaiser, and Renato Pasta.
4. Darrin M. McMahon, *Enemies of the Enlightenment: The French Counter-Enlightenment and the Making of Modernity* (Oxford, 2001).

5. Roger Chartier, *The Cultural Origins of the French Revolution* (Durham, NC, 1990), 89.

6. The construction of this 'mythical' view of the enlightenment is explored in Annelien de Dijn, 'The Politics of Enlightenment from Peter Gay to Jonathan Israel', *Historical Journal* 55, no. 3 (2012), 785–805. In its most recent incarnation de Dijn views it as the creation of Peter Gay, whose intellectual heirs include Robert Darnton, Roy Porter, and Jonathan Israel.

7. Jonathan Israel, *A Revolution of the Mind: Radical Enlightenment and the Intellectual Origins of Modern Democracy* (Princeton, 2010).

8. The key figure in Israel's *Radical Enlightenment: Philosophy and the Making of Modernity* (Oxford, 2001) is Spinoza, whose work is depicted as the 'intellectual backbone' (p. vi) of the radical enlightenment.

9. Immanuel Kant, 'Was ist Aufklärung?', *Berlinische Monatsschrift* IV (12 December 1784).

10. This approach exemplified by Thomas Munck, *The Enlightenment: A Comparative Social History, 1721–1794* (London, 2000).

11. See Rolf Engelsing, 'Die Perioden der Lesergeschichte in der Neuzeit. Das statische Ausmass und die soziokulturelle Bedeutung der Lektüre', *Archiv für Geschichte des Buchwesens* 10 (1969), cols. 944–1002.

12. Jürgen Habermas, *The Structural Transformation of the Public Sphere: An Inquiry into a Category of Bourgeois Society*, trans. Thomas Burger (Cambridge, MA, 1989).

13. John Hardman, *Louis XVI: The Silent King and the Estates* (New Haven and London, 1993), 35. The remark is from Louis XVI's *Réflexions*.

14. For critical overviews, see Craig Calhoun (ed.), *Habermas and the Public Sphere* (Cambridge, MA, 1989); editors' 'Introduction', in Barker and Burrows (eds), *Press, Politics and Public Sphere*, 1–22.

15. Book length studies of the STN archive include Michel Schlup (ed.), *L'Edition neuchâteloise au siècle des Lumières: la Société typographique de Neuchâtel (1769–1789)* (Neuchâtel, 2002); Robert Darnton, and Michel Schlup (eds), *Le Rayonnement d'une maison d'édition dans l'Europe des Lumières: la Société typographique de Neuchâtel 1769–1789* (Neuchâtel, 2005); Robert Darnton, *Forbidden Bestsellers of Pre-Revolutionary France* (New York and London, 1996); Jeffrey Freedman, *Books Without Borders in Enlightenment Europe: French Cosmopolitanism and German Literary Markets* (Philadelphia, PA, 2012); and Robert Darnton, *The Literary Underground of the Old Regime* (Cambridge, MA and London, 1982). Two further volumes arising from the French Book Trade in Enlightenment Europe (FBTEE) database project will appear with Continuum in 2015: Mark Curran, *Selling Enlightenment* and Simon Burrows, *Enlightenment Bestsellers*.

16. In some inventories, the STN separated their own editions from their '*marchandises générales*' and the *livres troquées* which they had swapped in bulk with allied houses across the Swiss Romand.

17. The FBTEE database, prepared by Simon Burrows and Mark Curran, is hosted at http://fbtee.uws.edu.au/main/.

18. Michael Kwass, *Privilege and the Politics of Taxation in Eighteenth-Century France: Liberté, Egalité, Fiscalité* (Cambridge, 2000), 214. On previous *compte-rendus*, see Joël Félix, 'The Problem with Necker's Compte rendu au roi (1781)', in J. Swann and J. Félix (eds), *The Crisis of the Absolute Monarchy. France from Old Regime to Revolution* (Oxford, 2013), 107–125.

19. Gilles Feyel, 'La Diffusion des gazettes étrangères en France et la revolution postale des années 1750', in Henri Duranton, Claude Labrosse and Pierre Rétat (eds), *Les Gazettes européennes de langue française (XVIIe–XVIIIE siècles* (Saint-Etienne, 1992), 81–99.

20. For sales statistics for international gazettes see Simon Burrows, 'The Cosmopolitan Press', in Barker and Burrows (eds), *Press, Politics and the Public Sphere*, 26–7.

21. The 1,000 print-run figure is widely cited. According to Philip Gaskell, *New Introduction to Bibliography* (Oxford, 1972), 161, technical and economic constraints usually limited print runs to 500–2,000 copies.

22. Pierre M. Conlon, *Le siècle des Lumières: bibliographie chronologique*, 32 vols (Geneva, 1983–2009), lists 1,963 new works published in 1781 (adjusted figures); cf. just 523 regular and illegal titles in Robert Estivals, *La Statistique bibliographique de la France sous la monarchie au XVIIIe siècle* (Paris and The Hague, 1965), 405.

23. Daniel Roche, *The People of Paris* (Berkeley and Los Angeles, 1987), 212.

24. Michel Vovelle, *The Fall of the French Monarchy, 1787–1792* (Cambridge, 1984), 63.

25. Contrast the map charting the intensity of deChristianizing activity in Michel Vovelle, *The Revolution against the Church: from Reason to the Supreme Being* (Columbus, OH, 1991), 193, with that for literacy rates in 1789 in Vovelle, *Fall of the Monarchy*, 61.

26. Robert A. Houston, *Literacy in Early Modern Europe. Culture and Education 1500–1800* (Harlow, 1988), 125–6.

27. Vovelle, *Fall of the Monarchy*, 60–3.

28. Antoine de Baecque, 'Pamphlets: Libel and Political Mythology', in Robert Darnton and Daniel Roche (eds), *Revolution in Print. The Press in France, 1775–1800* (Berkeley, 1999), 165–76, at 165–6.

29. Conlon, *Siècle de lumières* (adjusted figures).

30. Jeremy D. Popkin, *Revolutionary News; The Press in France, 1789–1799* (Durham, NC and London, 1990), 82, 84; France's first daily newspaper the *Journal de Paris* was founded in 1777.

31. Mediathèque d'Orléans, Lenoir MS 1423/3, 263–4, 'Sur les écrits clandestins', 264. On Lenoir's testimony see also Simon Burrows, 'Police and Political Pamphleteering in Pre-Revolutionary France: The Testimony of J.-P. Lenoir, Lieutenant-Général of Police of Paris', in David Adams and Adrian Armstrong (eds), *Print and Power in France and England, 1500–1800* (Aldershot, 2006), 99–112, at 110.

32. Between May 1776 and January 1777 the STN sourced 825 copies of the *Anecdotes* from Grasset, before switching to other suppliers. This suggests a huge print run, as Grasset had several major clients.

33. On the Lemaître affair see Jeremy D. Popkin, 'Pamphlet Journalism at the End of the Old Regime', *Eighteenth-Century Studies* 22 (1989), 351–67.

34. See Thierry Rigogne, *Between State and Market: Printing and Bookselling in Eighteenth-Century France*, SVEC, 5 (Oxford, 2007).

35. 'Reading, Writing and Publishing', in Darnton, *Literary Underground*, 167–208 at 192–6. An original aim of the FBTEE project was to study the impact of this decree. The topic has been discussed in more depth in many of the conference presentations and publications stemming from the project by Simon Burrows; Mark Curran, most notably 'Beyond the Forbidden Bestsellers of Pre-Revolutionary France', *Historical Journal* 56 (2013), 89–112; and Louise Seaward, notably 'Policing the Public Sphere: The French Government and the Extra-Territorial Book Trade (1770–1787)', unpublished doctoral thesis (Leeds, 2013) and 'Political Bargaining in the Book Trade: The *Société typographique de Neuchâtel* (STN) and the French Government, 1769–1789', *French History* (forthcoming).

36. Elizabeth A. Eisenstein, *Grub Street Abroad: Aspects of the French Cosmopolitan Press from the Age of Louis XIV to the Enlightenment* (Oxford, 1992), 152.

37. Elizabeth A. Eisenstein, 'The Tribune of the People: A New Species of Demagogue', in Harvey Chisick (ed.), *The Press in the French Revolution*, SVEC 287 (Oxford, 1991), 145–59.

38. The representativeness of Mornet's conclusion is challenged by James Swenson, *On Jean-Jacques Rousseau: Considered as First Author of the French Revolution* (Stanford, 2000), which shows that the *Social Contract* was widely available before 1789, if not necessarily read, both in individual editions and in sets of his complete works. However, he also suggests that many copies were acquired more through interest in the author of *La Nouvelle Héloïse* than for their own sake.

39. See Darnton, 'Reading, Writing and Publishing', 173–82.

40. Darnton, *Forbidden Bestsellers*.

41. See especially Darnton and Schlup (eds), *Le Rayonnement d'une maison d'édition*; Freedman, *Books without Borders*.

42. Andrew Brown, 'Voltaire and Gabriel Grasset', in François Bessire and Françoise Tilkin (eds), *Voltaire et le livre* (Ferney-Voltaire, 2009), 63–91.

43. Michel Schlup, 'La Société typographique de Neuchatel (1769–1789): points de repère', in Schlup (ed.), *L'Edition neuchâteloise*, 61–105 at 72–6.

44. See Robert Darnton, 'The High Enlightenment and the Low-life of Literature in Prerevolutionary France', *Past and Present* 51 (1971), 81–115. See also Darnton's work on political libel, *The Devil in the Holy Water or the Art of Slander from Louis XIV to Napoleon* (Philadelphia, 2010).

45. Chartier, *Cultural Origins*, 83.

46. The main output of this AHRC-funded study is the FBTEE database, whose academic content was authored by Simon Burrows and Mark Curran and edited by Simon Burrows, with digital design and technical support from Sarah Kattau, Henry Merivale and Vincent Hiribarren. This chapter owes a considerable debt to all these people, as well as project board members David Adams, Simon Dixon, Russell Goulbourne, and Jonathan Topham.

47. On the activities and policing of these publishing houses see: Raymond Birn, *Pierre Rousseau et les Philosophes de Bouillon*, SVEC 29 (Oxford, 1964); Burrows, *Blackmail, Scandal and Revolution*; Darnton, *The Devil in the Holy Water*; Seaward, 'Policing the Public Sphere'; and works on the STN in note 15 above.

48. Simon Burrows, 'Despotism without Bounds: The French Secret Police and the Suppression of Dissent in London', *History* 89, no. 4 (2004), 525–48. See also Burrows, *Blackmail, Scandal and Revolution*, especially chs 3–4; Darnton, *The Devil in the Holy Water*.

49. See Simon Burrows, 'French Banned Books in International Perspective', in David Andress, *Experiencing the French Revolution* (SVEC 2013:05 Oxford, 2013), 19–38, at 24–5, for how this figure is calculated.

50. The STN's own editions, which accounted for about 70 per cent of their sales, have been ignored here in order to reduce the distortions introduced by the STN's publishing preferences.

51. The figures here are drawn from a search query for primary authors in the STN database online interface version 2. It excludes STN editions from consideration. Results were adjusted by deleting 542 sales from each author anthologized in a work entitled *Lectures pour les enfants*. The results of the query then read: 1. Voltaire (4742.6 unit sales); 2. *Bible* (3068 sales); 3. Tissot (1534); 4. Pidansat de Mairobert (1175); 5. L.-S. Mercier (1143); 6. D'Holbach (789); 7. Dorat (605); 8. J.-R. Ostervald (593); 9. J.J. Rousseau (590.8); 10. Pietro

Aretino (545); 11. Mme Leprince de Beaumont (477); 12. J. Cleland (468); 13. J. Gottsched (444); 14. Albrecht Haller (425); 15. Marquis de Luchet (419); 16. Maupin (418); 17. Michel Milot (407); 18. Mme de Genlis (393); 19. Raynal (347); 20. C.-A. Helvétius (339).

52. The overlap between the two categories is only 0.69 per cent of the STN's trade, so together they comprise 12.21 per cent of units traded.

53. See Darnton, 'Reading, Writing and Publishing'.

54. See note 34.

55. Vivien Gruder, 'The Question of Marie-Antoinette: The Queen and Public Opinion before the Revolution', *French History* 16, no. 3 (2002), 269–98; Burrows, *Blackmail*, esp. ch. 5.

56. See Mark Curran, *Atheism, Religion and Enlightenment in Pre-revolutionary Europe* (Woodbridge, 2012).

57. See Burrows, 'French Banned Books in International Perspective', 35–7.

58. Simon Burrows, 'The Cultural Politics of Exile: French Emigré Literary Journalism in London', *Journal of European Studies* 29, no. 2 (June 1999), 157–74; Carla Hesse, *Publishing and Cultural Politics in Revolutionary Paris, 1789–1810* (Berkeley, 1991), 1.

59. Consider for example effects of the abolition of the bakers and butchers guilds as described in Michael Fitzsimmons, *From Artisan to Worker. Guilds, the French State, and the Organisation of Labor, 1776–1821* (Cambridge, 2010), 73–6, 92–3.

60. Figures derived from Hesse, *Publishing and Cultural Politics*, 202–3.

61. According to Hesse's figures (*Publishing and Cultural Politics*, 202), registrations for works of literature (mainly novels) rose from 84 and 87 in 1795 and 1796 respectively, to 132 in 1797, 269 in 1798, and 297 in 1799. A survey of Parisian first editions for the years 1794 to 1799 as listed in Angus Martin, Vivienne Mylne, and Richard Frautschi (eds), *Dictionnaire du genre Romanesque français, 1751–1800* (London and Paris, 1977) reveals the same trend: 10 (1794), 35 (1795), 45 (1796), 61 (1797), 81 (1798), 159 (1799). Broadly similar growth is seen in 'Reéditions'.

62. This paragraph summarizes some of the main conclusions of Hesse, *Publishing and Cultural Politics*, 240–8.

Selected Reading

Chartier, Roger, *The Cultural Origins of the French Revolution* (Durham, NC, 1990).

Darnton, Robert, *Forbidden Bestsellers of Pre-Revolutionary France* (New York and London, 1996).

Darnton, Robert, *The Literary Underground of the Old Regime* (Cambridge, MA and London, 1982).

Darnton, Robert and Schlup, Michel (eds), *Le Rayonnement d'une maison d'édition dans l'Europe des Lumières: la Société typographique de Neuchâtel 1769–1789* (Neuchâtel, 2005).

Eisenstein, Elizabeth A., *Grub Street Abroad: Aspects of the French Cosmopolitan Press from the Age of Louis XIV to the Enlightenment* (Oxford, 1992).

Estivals, Robert, *La Statistique bibliographique de la France sous la monarchie au XVIIIe siècle* (Paris and The Hague, 1965).

Hesse, Carla, *Publishing and Cultural Politics in Revolutionary Paris, 1789–1810* (Berkeley, 1991).

Israel, Jonathan, *A Revolution of the Mind: Radical Enlightenment and the Intellectual Origins of Modern Democracy* (Princeton, 2010).

McMahon, Darrin M., *Enemies of the Enlightenment: The French Counter-Enlightenment and the Making of Modernity* (Oxford, 2001).

Mason, Haydn T. (ed.), *The Darnton Debate: Books and Revolution in the Eighteenth Century* (Oxford, 1998).

Munck, Thomas, *The Enlightenment: A Comparative Social History, 1721–1794* (London, 2000).

Rigogne, Thierry, *Between State and Market: Printing and Bookselling in Eighteenth-Century France, SVEC 2007: 5* (Oxford, 2007).

CHAPTER 6

TUMULTUOUS CONTEXTS AND RADICAL IDEAS (1783–89). THE 'PRE-REVOLUTION' IN A TRANSNATIONAL PERSPECTIVE

ANNIE JOURDAN

> The Facility with which the same truths may be repeated enforced by placing them daily in different Lights, in Newspapers which are every where read, gives a great Chance of establishing them. And we now find that it is not only right to strike while the Iron is hot, but that it is very practicable to heat it by continual Striking.[1]

THE French Revolution, as is well known, did not erupt into a harmonious and peaceful universe. Less known, however, is the influence of this context. Most historians have preferred to give a nationalist account of the event, and to emphasize the struggle between the *parlements* and the king; between the nobility and the *Tiers-Etat*; the financial crisis, the Estates-General; the provincial uprisings, the scarcity of food, and so on.[2] The transnational dimension was considered irrelevant. In the 1950s, Robert Palmer and Jacques Godechot contended that similar phenomena were happening in other Western countries before and after 1789, but it is nowadays difficult to accept their argument that these movements were essentially a struggle between aristocracy and democracy. It is difficult too to accept their comparative methodology because it focuses on the parallels at the expense of the differences, and neglects interconnections and interactions.[3] Another great historian, Franco Venturi, has given us an interesting survey of the end of the old regime, but his case studies are extremely limited and do not reflect the intensity of contemporary intellectual interconnections.[4] Only recently, indeed, has the French Revolution been approached in its global dimension. But few studies have shown interest in the years before the fall of the Bastille and in what has been called—rightly or wrongly—the 'pre-revolution'.[5]

This world was far more connected than we may think in our global age. To be sure, international exchanges were older than the eighteenth century. There were already intensive relations between humanist scholars and a 'Republic of Letters', in the sixteenth-century age of Erasmus. There also were international connections between bankers, merchants, and European nobility.[6] These men and women did not belong to a single world or a single nation. All of them travelled, exchanged ideas and goods, and communicated intensely. Thanks to the Enlightenment and to the technical advances made in trade, transport and printing, connections increased all around the world. This is one point. The other one is less positive. It concerns the wars which had awakened patriotism across the Western world.[7] Indeed, what Turgot called the 'American quarrel' implicated an increasing number of European—and non-European—actors. In France, this quarrel followed a time of crisis: the Seven Years War and the crisis between the *parlements* and the Bourbon monarchy during 1770–4.[8] The American War of Independence had a great effect on the kingdom of Louis XVI, but also on the Spanish monarchy and on the United Provinces. All three sided with the American insurgents via various treaties; they participated directly or indirectly in the struggle against the British and welcomed American agents sent to Europe by their states to obtain loans and armed support.[9] John Adams was in The Hague, Paris and London; Franklin, and, after him, Jefferson were in Paris; John Jay in Madrid; Arthur Lee in Berlin. There was also an important American colony in France whose ideals were altogether revolutionary and commercial. Numbered among those were Joel Barlow, a poet from Connecticut, whose mission was to sell American land tracts in Europe, and James Swan, a trader who longed for greater connections between France and the United States. For these men, business was not incompatible with love of liberty.[10] Moreover, Turgot's letters reveal that the French elites were fascinated by the American war and wished to support the insurgents. The very fact that the 'liberal' nobility took up arms to help the American patriots speaks volumes about this involvement.[11]

DIFFUSION AND CIRCULATION OF IDEAS

Although they too were interested in American adventures, most cultivated Frenchmen drew upon other experiences, first, with travels, like the Grand Tour, but also business and study trips.[12] There were also books and reading, and sometimes writing; finally, social ties were formed between men and women who did not automatically move in Parisian circles. For these people correspondence was fundamental. Even though Franklin lived in Paris and was a regular visitor among fashionable circles and official networks, he also used letters to discuss ideas and events with Turgot, La Fayette, Dupont de Nemours, and Condorcet. He was so popular at that time that he received mail from all around the world. After his departure, he was replaced by Thomas Jefferson, William Short, and Gouverneur Morris. The three of them would lead equally intense social and political lives. In another striking example, it was during a visit to Geneva that Jacques-Pierre Brissot, the future leader of the Girondins, met in 1782 the banker Etienne Clavière who was to become one of his best friends, and Minister of Finances in 1792–3. In 1787, Jean-Marie Roland, also a later minister, contacted the same Brissot with whom he then cultivated a long friendship. All these men and women were fascinated by Enlightenment ideas: those of the Italian Beccaria, for instance, or those of Adam Smith, to name only two influential thinkers. Turgot's student Condorcet was also reading the *Méditations sur l'économie politique* from the Italian Pietro Verri and discussing the book with the author.[13] The Genevan banker Clavière was so fond of Adam Smith that he tried to find the latest edition of the *Wealth of Nations*. Elsewhere, Brissot commented on the marquis de Chastellux' narrative on North America. He lamented that Chastellux was caricaturing the new republic, its Quakers, its citizens and its negroes, and published a book to set the false record straight. The abbé Morellet did not agree, but did not dare to stand up for his friend, Chastellux.[14] The quarrel was not over. Two other thinkers of the French Enlightenment, Grimm and Diderot, published a critical review on the book and mentioned that some abstracts of it had already been issued in the *Journal de Lecture* from Gotha, in Germany. Ideas and publications thus were travelling too. The late Enlightenment was a worldwide phenomenon connecting all kinds of intellectuals with each other.

In the French provinces, the diffusion and circulation of ideas depended on academies, which were essential because they popularized a number of fashionable topics.[15] The Lyon academy, for instance, opened a competition about the discovery of America: was it or was it not an improvement for humanity? The theme had been chosen by the abbé Raynal who was so fascinated by the new American republic that he had published an essay on it in 1781. The text had been severely criticized by Thomas Paine. Meanwhile, the Toulouse academy had launched a new competition on the importance and influence of the American Revolution.[16] Jean-Baptiste Mailhe, lawyer at the *Parlement* de Toulouse and later *Conventionnel* had won the challenge. His text, printed in Toulouse, depicted the American Revolution as the 'triumph of politics and humanity'.[17] It celebrated American patriotism and did not see it as incompatible with the Bourbon monarchy. The topic fascinated the French as far away as in Amsterdam, where the merchant Joseph Mandrillon put pen to paper to express his admiration about the American constitutions. Chastellux tried his luck at the Lyon competition in 1787. Like Raynal in a way, he came to the conclusion that the discovery of America had been, above all, beneficial to international trade. Some years before, La Rochefoucauld d'Enville had translated the complete set of American constitutions which Franklin had given him.[18] The American diplomat wanted everyone in Europe to know these texts and he did all he could to have them officially published. The admiration for the heroic courage of the American colonists against the English revived the European patriotism which had emerged in the late 1740s and broadened its appeal during the Seven Years

War.[19] It also revived references to liberty and virtue. And above all, it rekindled ideas and ideals which were until then less well known in France: the great and less great philosophers took this opportunity to express themselves on republicanism and on the principles of liberty and equality.

After Raynal came Mably, who compared the United States with Switzerland before advising the former to give up commerce and wealth so that they would be spared the corruption common to modern republics.[20] Turgot had already added his critical voice on the topic, and in a letter to Richard Price from 1778, condemned the very fact that most of the constitutions had divided the legislative power and annihilated the nation's unity. He told Price to keep his letter secret as he did not want public opinion to hear of his love for freedom. After all, he had been the king's minister.[21] Even disgraced, he did not feel it right to express such a feeling too openly. All the same, the letter was published by Price after Turgot's death in 1784. His heir Condorcet pursued the debate and published a book on the American Revolution in 1786.[22] These examples are living proof of the increasing communication across the Atlantic world, but also of the great effect caused by the surprising event on the European continent.[23] This is not to say that these discussions and influences are to be seen as the origins of the French Revolution, but they show that there were intensive political discussions and debates long before the fall of the Bastille.

DIVERSIFIED EXPERIENCES

Travels are no less educative and emulative than discussions and debates. Although they too were not creating revolutionaries, they showed visitors other institutions, other principles and practices, which could be used as alternatives in a context of discussions and reforms. They produced experiences which would lead to expectations—hopes or regrets.[24] The Dutch study trip of Jean-Marie Roland from 1768 illustrates this very well. There he discovered a republican, working and frugal people who cultivated equality. He admired their religious tolerance and impartial justice. His Dutch perceptions and experiences stimulated him to criticize his own country and what he saw as an arbitrary legislation. Furthermore, his caustic comments on the Catholic Church and the French nobility would almost confirm Robert Darnton's interpretation on the thirst for revenge of the Grub Street writers.[25] Malesherbes, member of the Parisian *Cour des Aides* who travelled to Holland in 1777 to learn about its constitution and judicial institutions, agreed with Roland in a way. He too was fascinated by the great works he discovered in the little republic, by the lack of beggary and the public wealth, the freedom and tolerance. Like Roland, he lamented the French arbitrary laws and the very fact that nothing could be undertaken without permission. But both travellers did not condemn the French monarchy or wish to exchange it for a republic. Notably, they did not much appreciate the monotonous uniformity they discovered in Holland. They missed the majestic buildings and works of art they were used to and found it difficult to mix with the population whose arrogance and coarseness they highly disliked. But they compared what they were experiencing with their own national customs and they returned to France with the conviction that religious tolerance was precious and that freedom of enterprise was necessary for the general wealth. By doing so, they obviously shared the ideas of the Scottish Enlightenment on 'laissez-faire'—ideas which were also Turgot's.[26] Above all, they experienced personally what a republic was 'in action'.

Brissot's travels are even more exemplary, since he was young, ambitious, and looking for a better future. His description of Genevan republicanism speaks volumes about his aspirations, notably through his enthusiasm for the tumultuous political clubs where the citizens debated about the commonwealth. He lamented the death of the patriot movement in 1782.[27] Once in England, where he stayed several times, he tried to understand the parliamentary monarchy, and learned enough about it to adapt some of its features to the French context when he conspired in August 1787 on behalf of the marquis Ducrest.[28] Brissot's case is interesting because he is always intermingled idealism and opportunism. When he set out for America in August 1788, for instance, it was for business, but he returned with a book on the new republic and a political analysis which demonstrates that he understood very well how it worked and what it implied: a representative republic based on election and removability, where the citizens nurtured public and private virtues. His model: Samuel Adams, who would cultivate probity, simplicity, modesty, but also firmness and energy. These would be the genuine republican virtues. As with the American adventurers investing in France, business did not restrain Brissot's political enthusiasm and patriotism.[29]

A NEW FRAME OF REFERENCE

Books and travels provide a basis for reflection which can be enriched by real discussions and debates. These were numerous during the eighteenth century, as we will see. Acquisition of knowledge depends upon numerous factors, but is unquestionably stimulated by reading and reflection, social exchanges, and experiences. All this can lead to action, if the context lends itself to it. And indeed, the 1780s were a time of reforms for France. Louis XVI had to implement reforms because the royal treasury was empty and he needed money. From January 1787 on, the royal plans would become a matter of intense discussions. Or, in other words, from the moment the reform plans were made public, the increasing conflicts to which they gave rise, and the sense of crisis thus provoked, had a transformative effect on the French, propelling a shift in their frame of reference. Ideas and experiences from outside gained relevance in the new situation. The conflicts would lead to a process of increasing involvement and to action in the form of writings, debates, and projects. The avalanche of pamphlets published between 1787 and 1789 is living proof of this awareness. But they were more reformist than revolutionary.

They were intended to comment on the reforms or to propose new ones. Their 'patriotic' authors contended for the right to advise government.

However, their tune would slowly but surely change as the crisis dragged on, confirming the transformative effect of conflicts.[30] In 1786, for instance, when Condorcet published his book on the American Revolution, he did not have the same convictions as he would two years later. In 1788, he was far more convinced than before that the government had to teach the people to know their rights: its aims had to be 'the enjoyment of the natural rights of man'. Then, Condorcet wanted to believe that Louis XVI aspired to nothing else than to grant the French these rights. Furthermore, his definition of human rights became more elaborated than in 1786.[31] Condorcet's writings show very well what had changed since Turgot's death. Turgot wanted to create provincial Assemblies but wished to limit their power—so that they did not federate as the American states did and form a 'national' congress. Louis XVI's minister saw no reason at all to modify the Bourbon constitution.[32] Ten years later, Turgot's heir was adopting a far more revolutionary vocabulary to ask for further reforms. He was not afraid of anticipating the creation of a 'national assembly' as he called it, where all provincial Assemblies would be represented. After all, the government had published the first regulations on these Assemblies and 'seemed to have invited the citizens to discuss them and to publish the result of their observations'. From this moment one can date the first tumultuous eruptions of a public opinion until then 'excluded from each public function' in a country where 'political discussion on administrative matters has never been free'.[33] Condorcet anticipated that it would be different in the near future, and that the people would soon have the right to speak. Did not the king's censors grant permission to the American constitutions to be published? Such an initiative together with the French participation in the war of Independence and the planned reform policy suggested that Louis XVI was an open-minded monarch and that his reforms would be enlightened. It was a great misunderstanding, but it opened a horizon of expectation among the Parisian elites.

TUMULTUOUS CONTEXTS

During the 1780s, public opinion was to be heard elsewhere in Europe, but in a more violent way, since armies were involved. In Geneva, the 1782 revolution was the latest of many attempts to end civil inequalities amongst citizens and inhabitants. In the *Lettres écrites de la montagne*, published in 1764, Rousseau had already criticized the Genevan government on this topic.[34] There, the French monarchy had intervened to crush the rebellion. Conversely, Louis XVI and his ministers supported the Dutch patriots in the 1780s who were protesting against their prince, William of Orange, and his pro-British policy. Ironically, one root of patriotic opposition had been Dutch naval defeat in late 1780 against the British navy, caused, they claimed, by William's neglect of the fleet. Awakening patriotism translated into a demand for more representative government. Moreover, the patriots claimed an alliance with the Americans who had established true liberty. A number of years before the fall of the Bastille, thus, several nations experienced a more or less radical revolution. After Geneva, Switzerland and the United Provinces were to come the Austrian Netherlands and Poland. The origins of these uprisings must not be sought in the American Revolution: each one had its own 'national' causes. In Belgium, indeed, it was the drastic reform policy of Joseph II which sparked things off, and in Poland a pressing need to consolidate the kingdom against its voracious neighbours. If the American Revolution was not the trigger, it would soon become a reference: it provided the revolutionaries with their mottos and inspired their principles. From then on, they were all speaking of 'helping freedom to triumph or dying under its ashes'.[35] Each people had to enjoy their natural rights and to participate in the formation of laws. Even in France, it became an expectation.

Obviously, the emancipation of the French was not so much stimulated by the American Revolution, as by the American policy of the French government. Or in Mailhe's words: 'When France chose to adopt America's cause, she granted nations permission to break their bonds with their sovereigns'.[36] Furthermore, by publishing in French the American constitutions, the king had permitted France to discover that 'the people have the right to change their government', since a body politic would be 'a voluntary association of individuals', bound by 'a social contract'.[37] In 1784, when Mailhe published his text, he was thinking that the other peoples of the New World would soon imitate the Thirteen Colonies and revolt against the 'European yoke'. Some years later, it was not the New World that was set on fire, but the Old.

Forced to flee by the Prussians who restored the Prince of Orange during the winter of 1787 (while France looked on, paralysed by crisis), some 4,000 Dutch patriots took refuge in France, where they were to meet some of the Genevan refugees from 1782: Etienne Dumont, De Bourges, Du Roveray, and Clavière. These refugees were working with Mirabeau, the author of several radical pamphlets. But Mirabeau's workshop included also Dutch patriots, such as Paul-Henri Maron, the Protestant minister of the Dutch embassy and Antoine-Marie Cerisier, a French journalist who had supported John Adams' propaganda in the United Provinces.[38] They provided information to Mirabeau on the Dutch Republic and allowed him to issue well-informed texts. It explains why the *Analyse des papiers anglais* published by Mirabeau was able to give an extract of a bill of rights[39] based on the 1785 Leiden draft drawn up by Dutch patriots. At the same time, in April 1788, Mirabeau's workshop published another text, *Aux Bataves sur le stadhouderat*, with a complete bill of rights, more or less inspired by the Virginian constitution. Mirabeau reminded his readership that civil liberty was nothing without political freedom—a remark he could have taken from Richard Price. And he noted that the Dutch cause was the cause of all men. As a consequence of this publication, a lot of discussions and debates followed, as far away as Germany.[40] At the same time, Dutch patriots were intriguing with Mirabeau to prepare a 'revolution' in their country. In March 1788, a report was issued by Mirabeau called *Mémoire sur la nécessité de rétablir à main armée la liberté Belgique*. Various plans were devised to restore the patriots by force. They were communicated to minister Montmorin. The duke of Orleans was involved, but also the duke of Lauzun, the marquis de Bombelles, the chevalier Ternant, and perhaps, La

Fayette.[41] These conspiracies were called 'revolution' by those who planned them. But at that time they had no consequences. Louis XVI did not want to hear of them. The French financial situation was not up to launching a military campaign. But these plans are certainly proof of the extreme political unrest that dominated Paris.

There was thus a, more or less, wide Parisian circle including French and foreign refugees. The uncertain context encouraged them to draft audacious plans. They were stimulated by some radical 'patriots' who wished to liberate their brothers and come back home, leading a victorious army. These were the first to think of a revolution in the so-called 'Belgian Provinces'—meaning the United Provinces and the Austrian Netherlands. In the meantime, Thomas Jefferson and La Fayette were discussing and projecting a French bill of rights. Jefferson was convinced that the king would have to adopt one. The debates of 1787–8 had persuaded him that seeds had been sown from which fruits would emerge. So he predicted that the Estates-General would give France a constitution. And he anticipated the reforms to come: a regular convening of the Estates-General which would gain the exclusive right of taxation and of legislation; a bill of rights; and a civil list for the government. In May 1788 he told John Adams that Paris was 'a furnace of politics'. In December, he even wrote that 'all hands are employed in drawing plans of bills of right'. Meanwhile, La Fayette had his own ready. Jefferson sent it to Madison as a kind of emulation for the new American Constitution.[42]

La Fayette and Jefferson were not the only ones to expect great changes. During the 1770s and 1780s, the abbé Sieyès collected his thoughts and devised a political constitution for the French government. This constitution would have given great power to the municipalities and would have provided elected administrators. More than others, however, he was criticizing the king, who 'considered the nation as his own property', so he said. And he concluded that the comparison of the king to a father was ill-founded, since a real father 'creates, brings up, nurtures and establishes his children', whereas 'a king is created, brought up, nurtured etc, by his children'.[43] These notes are not precisely dated, but on those from 1788, Sieyès observed that France needed a constitution without social orders. These few examples demonstrate that second-rank actors were politicized some months, or even some years, before 14 July 1789. The next case is particularly striking.

EXPERIENCES AND HORIZON
OF EXPECTATION

Back in 1787, the young Brissot had been plotting with the marquis Ducrest, the brother of Madame de Genlis and chancellor of the duke of Orléans. In August 1787, he drafted a plan of reform to give Ducrest access to the ministry. He had to think of a strategy and looked back to his experiences in England, and advised the duke of Orleans and Ducrest to create 'an opposition party'.[44] To be able to do so, both plotters had to seduce the people. This would have been quite easy: Orleans' party would promise that they would not be taxed without their consent. But the party also had to publish books and pamphlets and win over public opinion, and get supporters. In England, so Brissot said, political parties collected money to pay for this kind of expense. In this context, he quoted the famous seventeenth-century machinations of the cardinal de Retz in the Fronde rebellion, and said that he had to be imitated but for a far better goal: the people's well-being. 'This would be the sole cause to justify a division, a party'. This party would support the people 'against the administration'. Furthermore, the party would demand the king to give a constitution to the nation: 'a French constitution' would be the opposition's motto. Brissot's inspiration thus was not simple. He looked back to his experience in England (oppositional politics and finances), to what he knew from America (written constitution, right to consent to taxation, patriotism) and to the Fronde (how to buy and win supporters).[45] This special case shows very well that political strategies are not only drawn from a single model, but intermingle ideas drawn from books, experiences and perceptions to attain certain expectations. The results of the plot were null and void. Some days later, in the next of many twists in the pre-Revolutionary crisis, the Paris *Parlement* was exiled. Ducrest and Brissot decided to set out for Holland.

Over a period of three years, the French and their friends developed their ideas and projects. These started to take form and to become clearer. About feudalism for instance, Sieyès wrote that it was condemned since it was unproductive and thus harmful to modern society. Others were now asking for an actual representation instead of a virtual one and for the right to consent to taxation, but also, and increasingly, for a written constitution, and for the natural rights of man, which had been so brilliantly illustrated by the Declaration of Independence. In 1783, La Fayette had already hung an empty frame in his hallway next to the American text, which was intended for the French one to come. Like Franklin and Condorcet, La Fayette was obviously convinced that 'while we try to propagate some ideas which in themselves are isolated and sterile, in the long run these can make it easier to elaborate combinations which will be more successful and fruitful'.[46] Condorcet thought that the time would come when all these ideas would be executed, but over one hundred years. History decided otherwise.

Conclusion

What can be deduced from the above is that the triggers of the crisis were multiple and various, national and international. First, the problems of the Bourbon monarchy were legion and this explains why Louis XVI wanted to implement reforms.[47] The very fact that he wished to reform provoked a general misunderstanding—except in the *parlements* which understood very well that they were going to lose power. To be sure, the king's successive decisions and concessions increased the problems instead of resolving them. Above all, they stimulated public expectations.[48] The powerful *parlements* did nothing to help, since they were alternatively in the vanguard and rearguard. But the king's ministers did not do better, whether they fought against the power of the *parlements*, or attacked one another. The dispute between Necker and Calonne, for instance, gave publicity to issues the state needed to keep secret. In 1781, Necker had already published a *Compte-rendu au roi* which opened to the public what had always been a 'mystery' of state: the royal finances. In 1787, the finance minister Calonne criticized Necker's accounts and the latter answered with an exculpation.[49] Discord reigned at the top of the state and stimulated contests. The Ducrest affair invented by Brissot is another one, especially notable since a prince of the blood—d'Orléans—was involved.[50] Others were stirring up the bones of contention from other directions: the philosophers' enemies or the adversaries of revolutionary America.[51]

Second, there was the very paradoxical situation that had involved monarchical France in a struggle on behalf of American independence. It was an ambiguous situation because the French king and his minister Vergennes had supported insurgents against their sovereign and, by so doing, had implicitly admitted that a people may liberate themselves from whatever yoke. Their revolt would be legitimate. The government had even allowed the French publication of the American constitutions and given each citizen the opportunity to read that the people had the right to change their government and to be granted their natural rights. The 'liberal' aristocracy had shown the way when its members joined the insurgents on the other side of the Atlantic. Public opinion had followed, as the provincial academies' competitions and the various publications demonstrate. These publications celebrated the American fight against British despotism. The philanthropic societies implied a similar involvement. The Gallo-American society created by Brissot, for instance, intended to strengthen the bonds of friendship between France and the United States. Other societies were granting prizes to acts of benevolence and virtue. The Société des Amis des Noirs founded once again by Brissot was far more political, since it campaigned for liberty and the emancipation of slaves, and, moreover, it brought together the patriotic avant-garde.[52] The Society of Thirty formed late in 1788 did even more: it tried to influence the composition of the Estates-General.[53]

Third, there were the foreign refugees: Swiss, Genevan, Belgian, and Dutch patriots who were trying to liberate their fatherland. They had allies among the Parisian elites, and good contacts with the Americans in Paris. Mirabeau is the best known among them, but there was also Brissot's circle which was implicated in various schemes: financial, social, and political. Other private societies were more discreet, such as the marquise de Champcenetz's where the Dutch patriots were welcome.[54] These patriots cultivated strong friendships and correspondence that made their influence by no means insignificant. This is why Morellet did not take up the pen to support his friend Chastellux against Brissot's attacks. He feared that the affair might become worse. Elsewhere, in his Paris home, Thomas Jefferson too gave a warm welcome to all kind of patriots, and dispensed his advice long before the fall of the Bastille. All together, these men and women stimulated the French to adopt a bill of rights and to devise a new constitution, or even to draft plans of revolution.

These three factors may have led to action, or at least, to plans for action. But the plans did not set out to destroy the French monarchy. Sieyès is the exception which proves the rule. The patriots took aim at the *parlements*, or at the ministers, or another country, considered despotic. They did not challenge the institution of royalty, but its injustices and arbitrary rules or taxes. Among the patriotic avant-garde, there were not many Republicans either. Most of them did not value this kind of government, because modern republics were federal and unable to take quick decisions and be efficient. The French did not appreciate checks and balances, or mixed governments either, because they divide sovereignty. They could not understand why it was useful, since a nation, or a people, was 'one'. Another criticism was that republics could be as tyrannical as monarchies if they enforced bad laws. The problem for these men was not which kind of government was better, but what kind of laws had to be implemented.[55] This conviction explains that there were only two wholehearted Republicans in Paris at the time: Brissot and Clavière. Clavière was born Republican, and Brissot became one because he had been confronted with this kind of government. For both men, Republicanism meant above all election and removability—that is, genuine representation. The others did not attack French society outright, only heredity and feudalism.

From the outset, nobility in itself was not criticized. The marquis de La Fayette, for instance, was admired as the 'American hero'. But attacks on privileges became more frequent in 1788 when it was evident that the nobility refused to give up its advantages or to share them with others. The same is true of the Church. Nevertheless, something had changed. This can be seen in the watchwords that reveal a consciousness that had now decided to put its experiences and ideas into practice, and that was anticipating change. The French patriots and their friends indeed asked for a constitution—remember that Turgot did not want to modify the French one, or only via provincial Assemblies without real power. They invoked the natural rights of man and claimed freedom of the press and religious tolerance—Louis XVI seemed to agree by granting both of them—but also the people's participation in the formation of the law and the liberty to consent new taxes. Here the American motto can be heard: 'no taxation without representation'. The provincial Assemblies implemented in 1788 looked like a step in this direction. This explains the public conviction that the nation was going to be represented, boosted throughout the period as the Estates-General was increasingly mentioned. On the one hand, the king gave the impression that he was prepared to liberalize the regime; on the other hand, the *parlements* were appealing to the people against his reforms. They even used American precedents—the violent reaction to the Stamp Act considered the starting moment of the American Revolution—to frighten the king.[56] In short, circumstances and ideas conspired to increase the expectations that had awakened from the moment the Assembly of Notables was convened in early 1787.

As engagement with the new situation intensified, novel practices arose. The French people went into politics. Discussions became legion on what had to be modified in their country. The king himself asked his subjects to propose solutions and to express their grievances. This was the signal for the start of political debates, increased by the turbulence of real elections at the start of 1789—the duke of Orleans and Mirabeau, notably, made a lot of noise to ensure their election—and the publicity around public

affairs—like the Necker and Calonne affair—but it was also the signal for intense disputes and internal rivalries. The reformist spirit—genuine but limited—of the
king did not explain everything either. The 1780s tumult had been prepared by the
Enlightenment, which was perhaps less radical than has been said, but that encouraged
human beings to think for themselves and to contest this or that policy.[57] The affairs
treated by Voltaire speak volumes on this involvement, as did Rousseau's plans to draft
constitutions for Corsica and Poland. Philosophers were not the only ones to think
of reforms. Enlightened despots did too. In Prussia and in Tuscany, torture and the
death penalty were abolished, while the failure of the reform policy of Joseph II could
have been a signal for Louis XVI to be more cautious. The men who came into politics
in the 1780s were the heirs of these forerunners, but they formed a new generation,
who believed that radical changes were possible. Their optimism was sustained by the
American Revolution, which had opened a great horizon of expectation. This is why
this precedent was so essential. The American Revolution proved that a radical change
was possible, and thus conceivable. Moreover, the policy of Louis XVI seemed to confirm this view. Finally, foreign patriots corroborated what Brissot was suggesting in
1787: that the Western world was swept by a violent current leading to liberty. English
dissenters, Scottish philosophers and thinkers, American revolutionaries, continental patriots, all these men encouraged public opinion to devise a new society and to
claim a political liberty that had been unknown to France until then. The American
Revolution became for all the reference by excellence—even among Oratorians, as the
writer Arnault recalled.[58] In 1788, moreover, the new republic had proved to the world
that it was strong enough to implement a new constitution and to subdue the last popular revolts. The United States became a key reference because they happened to be
viable and had enforced several principles the Europeans were then dreaming of.

Was this enough to provoke the French Revolution? Uncertainties, expectations and disappointments may lead to unrest, but to a revolution, that is less certain.
Undoubtedly, the context had created great expectations among the French elites.
From the spring of 1788, Jefferson was living proof of these, when he wrote that 'in gay
Paris ... men, women and children talk nothing else' than politics.[59] In August 1787, he
had even admitted that 'an explosion of some sort [was] not impossible'. Arthur Young's
and Lord Dorset's analysis confirm Jefferson's comments. From summer 1787 up to July
1789, however, what turned out to be most important was the inconsistent attitude of
the king towards the *parlements* and the nobility. Because of this attitude, the conflicts
became hopelessly bogged down, and the French radicalization amplified—it was no
longer limited to Paris. From July 1788 onwards, discontent and revolts became widespread in the towns which possessed a *parlement*. Their resistance indeed increased the
tensions between the three orders. This was perceptible in Rennes for instance, where
pageants were leading actions against the nobility and the Church. In Languedoc and
the Franche-Comté, there were urban uprisings. The Dauphiné, Normandy, and Béarn
were to be involved too. The crisis was still not untangled in 1788. Foreign observers
in France signalled that the popular discontent was becoming worse.[60] At that time, it
was about the electoral system. Conflicts ran in cycles, as one was resolved, another was

raised, reviving the former. This accumulation of conflicts inflamed the public sphere. In contrast to the general expectations around the first Assembly of Notables and to the following debates, it progressively became evident that the king did not wish to modify French society.

During the following months, repeated uncertainties and dashed expectations, followed by anxiety and fear, were the French daily lot. The situation was extremely dangerous. Furthermore, this was the first great crisis of the state in which the French had something other than a mythical past to compare themselves with.[61] Since 1776, there had been a well-known precedent: the American Revolution. This precedent was strengthened by the European revolts on behalf of the people, their liberty and equality, which had persuaded public opinion that changes were imminent. Thanks to all these events, the French had certainly altered their frame of reference. But they also had to deal with their insecure perceptions and betrayed expectations, and an increasing anxiety. The combination could become explosive, all the more so since a food shortage was adding its effects to the political deadlock. The winter of 1788–9 was especially tumultuous not only because of food riots, but also because of highly disputed elections and the catalogue of grievances in the *cahiers de doléances*. One only needs to read the diplomatic notes from Lord Dorset to understand that civil discord triumphed and the 'language of party [ran] high'. Perhaps Franklin's predictions were sound: 'it was not only right to strike while the iron is hot, but it is very practicable to heat it by continual striking'. The paradox of the story is that not only patriots and public opinion did it, but also the king, his ministers and his *parlements*. All of them had a different agenda, but at the outset, none had a revolutionary one.

NOTES

1. Benjamin Franklin, www.benjaminfranklinpapers.org vol. 37, Letter to Richard Price, 13 June 1782.
2. For a revision on this approach, L. Hunt, 'The French Revolution in Global Context', in D. Armitage and S. Subrahmanyam (eds.) *The Age of Revolutions in Global Context* (New York and Basingstoke, 2010), 20–36; P. Campbell (ed.), *The Origins of the French Revolution* (New York and Basingstoke, 2006).
3. M. Werner and B. Zimmermann, 'Beyond Comparison: Histoire croisée and the Challenge of Reflexivity', *History and Memory* 45, no. 1 (2006), 30–50. Parallelism puts facts side by side, whereas the connected approach takes interactions, transactions and connections into account. See E. Gould, 'Entangled Histories, Entangled Worlds: The English-Speaking Atlantic as a Spanish Periphery', *American Historical Review* 112, no. 3 (2007), 764–86.
4. R. R. Palmer, *The Age of the Democratic Revolution*, 2 vols (Princeton, 1959–64). J. Godechot, *La Grande Nation. L'expansion révolutionnaire de la France dans le monde* (Paris, 1983). See also his *Les Révolutions (1770–1799)* (Paris, 1967); F. Venturi, *The End of the Old Regime in Europe*, 2 vols (Princeton, 1991).
5. See a first attempt in my *La Révolution. Une exception française?* (Paris, 2004). Pierre Serna has put to the test Hunt's contention on behalf of a reversal of perspectives and goes so far as to argue that the challenge was coming from the periphery and not from the centre. Serna,

'Toute révolution est guerre d'indépendance' in S. Desan, L. Hunt and W. M. Nelson (eds), *The French Revolution in Global Perspective* (Ithaca, 2013) 165–82. Some interesting views in Philipp Ziesche, *Cosmopolitan Patriots. Americans in Paris in the Age of Revolution* (Chapel Hill, 2010).

6. H. Lüthy, *La Banque protestante en France*, 2 vols (Paris, 1959); P. Cheney, *Revolutionary Commerce: Globalization and the French Monarchy* (Cambridge, MA, 2010).

7. J. M. Smith, *Nobility Re-imagined. The Patriotic Nation in Eighteenth-Century France* (Ithaca and London, 2005); R. Chartier, *The Cultural Origins of the French Revolution* (Durham, 1991).

8. *Oeuvres de Turgot et documents le concernant*, 5 vols (Paris, 1913–23), 5, 185.

9. Spain hesitated to take sides, because she feared a revolutionary contagion in South America. In Holland, the Amsterdam merchants tried to make a trade treaty with the new republic. Ireland was also concerned. Thanks to America, she was granted some of the rights she claimed since long. Germany too was involved: 30,000 German soldiers were sent to America to support Britain. H. Dippel, *Germany and the American Revolution* (Wiesbaden, 1978), 118–12.

10. A. Jourdan, 'A Tale of Three Patriots in a Revolutionary World. Théophile Cazenove, Jacques-Pierre Brissot and Joel Barlow', *Early American Studies* 10, no. 2 (2012), 360–81.

11. On French soldiers back to France, G. Bodinier, *Les officiers de l'armée royale, combattants de la guerre d'Indépendance des Etats-Unis* (Vincennes, 1983).

12. J. M. Smith, 'Between Discourse and Experience: Agency and Ideas in the French Revolution', *History and Theory* 40, no. 4 (2001), 116–42. On the notion of crisis, P. Campbell, 'Rethinking the Origins of the French Revolution' in P. McPhee (ed.), *Companion to the French Revolution* (Oxford, 2012), 3–23.

13. *Oeuvres de Condorcet*, 12 vols (Paris, 1847–49), I, 282.

14. J.-P. Brissot, *Examen critique des voyages de M. le marquis de Chastellux (Londres, 1786)*. *Mémoires inédits de l'abbé Morellet*, 2 vols (Paris, 1822), I, 322; *Correspondance littéraire, philosophique et critique de Grimm et de Diderot*, 15 vols (Paris, 1829–31), XIII, 103.

15. D. Roche, *Les Républicains des lettres. Gens de culture et Lumières au XVIIIe siècle* (Paris, 1988).

16. Abbé Raynal, *Révolution de l'Amérique* (London, 1781); T. Paine, *A letter addressed to the Abbé Raynal on the Affairs of North-America in which the mistakes of the Abbé's Account on the Revolution of America are corrected and cleared up* (London, 1982).

17. J.-B. Mailhe, *Sur la grandeur et l'importance de la révolution qui vient de s'opérer dans l'Amérique septentrionale* (Toulouse, 1784), 1–10.

18. *Correspondance de Benjamin Franklin* (Paris, 1866), 310–18.

19. Smith, *Nobility Re-imagined* and D. A. Bell, *The Cult of the Nation in France. Inventing Nationalism 1680–1800* (Cambridge MA, 2001).

20. *Œuvres complètes de l'abbé de Mably* (Lyon, 1792), 8, 373–413. See also the English translation, *Observations on the Government and Laws of the United States of America* (Amsterdam, 1784). On virtue and corruption, M. Linton, *The Politics of Virtue in Enlightenment France* (New York and Basingstoke, 2001).

21. R. Price, *Observations on the Importance of the American Revolution and the Means of making it a Benefit for the World* (London, 1784).

22. Condorcet, *De l'influence de la Révolution d'Amérique sur l'Europe* (s.l. 1786).

23. See H. Dippel, *Germany and the American Revolution; J.W. Schulte Noordholt, The Dutch Republic and American Independence* (Chapel Hill, 1982).

24. See Smith, 'Between Discourse and Experience'; R. Koselleck, *L'expérience de l'histoire* (Paris, 1997), 203; and *Le Futur du passé. Contribution à la sémantique des temps historiques* (Paris, 1990), 324–6.

25. For the papers of Roland, BNF, N.a.f. 6242, 60–70. Roland had very hard words for the nobility and priests, such as 'la sangsue mallotière'; 'la vermine monacale'; 'la morgue de nos petits robins à cuisses croisées sur les rangs ». Malesherbes' papers, ANF 162 MI/24, vol. 3, 1777.

26. P. Cheney, *Revolutionary Commerce*.

27. Brissot, *Le Philadelphien à Genève ou lettres d'un Américain sur la dernière révolution de Genève, sa constitution nouvelle* (Dublin, 1783). It is worth noting that several authors invented American narrators to diffuse their message. Condorcet, *Lettres d'un bourgeois de Newhaven à un citoyen de Virginie* (s.l., 1787) ou *ibidem, Lettres d'un citoyen des Etats-Unis d'Amérique à un Français sur les affaires présentes* (s.l., 1788).

28. We will come back to this intrigue.

29. Brissot, *Nouveau Voyage dans les Etats-Unis d'Amérique* (Paris, 1791). It was translated in English by Joel Barlow.

30. On the transformative effect of crisis, Campbell (2012), and his book in progress, *Crisis and Revolution. State failure and the Origins of the French Revolution* (Oxford, forthcoming).

31. In 1786, he only mentioned surety of person and of property; the right to have general laws and to take part directly or indirectly in the formation of the laws. *De l'influence de la Révolution américaine*, 5–7. In 1788, he spoke of surety, liberty, property, and equality and distinguished natural rights from human rights in society. *Lettres d'un citoyen des Etats-Unis*, 98–105.

32. *Oeuvres de Turgot*, 4, 627–8. On Turgot and Necker, J. Félix, *Louis XVI and Marie-Antoinette. Un couple en politique* (Paris, 2006).

33. Condorcet, *Essai sur la Constitution et les fonctions des assemblées provinciales* (s.l., 1788), 120–8 and 271. See also Condorcet, *Sentiments d'un républicain* (s.l. 1788) where he is speaking anew of a National Assembly.

34. J. J. Rousseau, *Lettres écrites de la montagne, Oeuvres complètes*, vol. 3 (Paris, 1964), 815–97. His first draft from 1763 was for Geneva. Corsica's draft is from 1764, and the Polish one from 1771.

35. Mailhe, *Sur la grandeur*, 10.

36. Mailhe, *Sur la grandeur*, 39.

37. *Constitutions des treize Etats d'Amérique*, tr. La Rochefoucauld d'Enville (Paris, 1783). The quotations are taken from the Massachusetts' declaration.

38. A. Jourdan, *La Révolution batave entre la France et l'Amérique* (Rennes, 2008), 60–7; J. Bénétruy, *L'atelier de Mirabeau. Quatre proscrits dans la tourmente révolutionnaire* (Paris, 1962).

39. On the Leiden draft, J. Popkin, 'Dutch Patriots, French Journalists, and Declarations of Rights: The Leidse Ontwerp of 1785 and its Diffusion in France', *The Historical Journal*, no. 3 (1995), 553–65.

40. *Oeuvres de Mirabeau*, 3 vols (Paris, 1912–21), I, 437–53.

41. National Archives The Hague, Dumont-Pigalle, 13. Dumont-Pigalle was a Walloon refugee.

42. *Papers of Thomas Jefferson* 21 vols (Princeton, 1950-), 13, 125–6 and 642; 14, 420–4. *The Republic of Letters. Correspondence between Thomas Jefferson and James Madison*, 3 vols. (New York and London, 1995), 1, 567.

43. ANF 284 AP 3. Private papers Sieyès.

44. It was not the first time that someone in France was speaking of an opposition party. The Paris parlement had invoked this idea one month before Brissot. See Lord Dorset, *Despatches from Paris*, ed. O. Browning, 2 vols (London, 1909), 1, 221.
45. Brissot, *Mémoires suivis de correspondance*, 3 vols, ed. C. Perroud (Paris, 1912), III, 149–60.
46. W. H. Adams, *The Paris Years of Thomas Jefferson* (New York, 1997), 95–6; Condorcet, *Essai sur la constitution*, 102–4.
47. P. Campbell (ed.), *The Origins*. See also T. Kaiser and D. van Kley (eds), *From deficit to deluge. The Origins of the French Revolution* (Stanford, 2011).
48. See A. Young, *Travels during the years 1787, 1788 and 1789* (Dublin, 1793), I, 136–7 and 190. Young was convinced that 'the American Revolution had laid the foundation of another in France, if the government does not take care of itself'.
49. *Compte-rendu au roi par M. Necker* (Paris, 1781).
50. On other plots with the duke of Orleans, Adams, *The Paris Years of T. Jefferson*, 284. And D. Jarrett, *The Begetters of Revolution. England's involvement with France, 1759–1789* (Plymouth, 1973), 244–83.
51. D. McMahon, *Enemies of the Enlightenment. The French Counter-Enlightenment and the Making of Modernity* (Oxford, 2001).
52. On philanthropic societies and the Société des Amis des Noirs, C. Duprat, *Le Temps des Philanthropes*, 2 vols (Paris, 1993), I, 115–28.
53. On this society, see D. Jarrett, p. 246.
54. *Despatches from Paris*, II, 23.
55. Turgot, 3,488; 5,535; Condorcet, 1,300. And *De l'influence de la Révolution d'Amérique*, 7. Like Richard Price and Turgot, Condorcet writes here that a republic with despotic laws is worse than a monarchy.
56. *Despatches from Paris*, I, 222.
57. See D. Edelstein, *The Enlightenment. A Genealogy* (Chicago and London, 2010).
58. A. V. Arnault, *Souvenirs d'un Sexagénaire*, 4 vols. (Paris 1833), I, p. 23.
59. *Republic of Letters*, I, 526–7.
60. *Venise et la Révolution Française* (Paris, 1997), 216–50; *Despatches from Paris*, II, 143–53 and 160–75. Dorset awaited a St Barthelemy against the nobility.
61. K. Baker, *Inventing the French Revolution* (Cambridge, 1990).

SELECTED READING

Armitage, David and Sanjay Subrahmanyam (eds), *The Age of Revolutions in Global Context, c.1760–1840* (New York and Basingstoke, 2010).

Bell, David A., *The Cult of the Nation in France. Inventing Nationalism, 1680–1800* (Cambridge MA, 2001).

Campbell, Peter R. (ed.), *The Origins of the French Revolution* (New York and Basingstoke, 2006).

Campbell, Peter R., *Crisis and Revolution. State Failure and the Origins of the French Revolution* (Oxford, forthcoming).

Chartier, Roger, *The Cultural Origins of the French Revolution* (Durham, 1991).

Cheney, Paul, *Revolutionary Commerce: Globalization and the French Monarchy* (Cambridge, MA, 2010).

Desan, Suzanne, Lynn Hunt and William Max Nelson, *The French Revolution in Global Perspective* (Ithaca, 2013).

Jarrett, Derek, *The Begetters of Revolution. England's Involvement with France 1759–1789* (Plymouth, 1973).

Jourdan, Annie, *La Révolution batave entre la France et l'Amérique* (Paris, 2008)'.

Kaiser, Thomas and Dale van Kley (eds), *From deficit to deluge. The Origins of the French Revolution* (Stanford, 2011).

Linton, Marisa, *The Politics of Virtue in Enlightenment France* (New York and Basingstoke, 2001).

McPhee, Peter (ed.), *Companion to the French Revolution* (Oxford, 2012).

Palmer, Robert R., *The Age of the Democratic Revolution*, 2 vols (Princeton, 1959–64).

Smith, Jay M., *Nobility Re-imagined. The Patriotic Nation in Eighteenth-Century France* (Ithaca and London, 2005).

Venturi, Franco, *The End of the Old Regime in Europe*, 2 vols (Princeton, 1991).

Ziesche, Philipp, *Cosmopolitan Patriots. Americans in Paris in the Age of Revolution* (Chapel Hill, 2010).

CHAPTER 7

THE DIPLOMATIC ORIGINS OF THE FRENCH REVOLUTION

THOMAS E. KAISER

It is hardly a secret that the French Revolution had a profound, transformative impact on Europe and the world at large. Yet the influence of Europe and the world at large on the French Revolution remains something of a mystery, if for no other reason than that comparatively few historians have directly addressed the topic since the publication of Albert Sorel's magisterial, eight-volume *L'Europe et la Révolution francaise* over a century ago. This relative neglect can be attributed in large part to the decline in the status of diplomatic history, which over the twentieth century lost its earlier pre-eminence to the study of social history and subsequently to the study of political culture. Although not altogether unmindful of the international context, social historians and historians of political culture have primarily focused on local and national developments, and so, too, have most studies of the eighteenth century French monarchy and the French political system in general.[1]

The absence of attention to the international dimension of the French Revolution in general is all the more evident when it comes to explaining the origins of the Revolution in particular. Yet, thanks to the efforts of a handful of historians during the last few decades who have tried to draw connections between events abroad and 1789, this situation has begun to change. In 1979, Theda Skocpol reopened the question of the French Revolution's diplomatic/military origins, contending that this collapse occurred in large part because, given its internal contradictions, the monarchy could not bear the fiscal burden of projecting power abroad, especially when competing with Britain. In their own ways, T. C. W. Blanning and Bailey Stone have expanded on this argument by exploring the international terrain more thoroughly and factoring in ideological and domestic political forces that Skocpol largely ignored. All these historians agree that developments in the international sphere were not sufficiently toxic by themselves to bring down the old regime, which had faced and overcome considerably more serious foreign policy challenges in the sixteenth and seventeenth centuries. Likewise, the collapse of the old regime in 1789 clearly differed from regime collapse in 1870 or 1940, when crushing military defeat played the most prominent role in delegitimizing the state. Their work does persuasively demonstrate, however, that with the old regime on the brink of internal collapse by the late 1780s for other reasons, threats from abroad that the more robust old regime of earlier decades might have overcome, became far less manageable for a regime facing financial and ideological bankruptcy. Because of the seriously compromised condition of the French state/social system, shock waves generated by challenges to France's position in the world order rippled throughout the old regime's shaky institutional structure, leaving little of it intact. Once this is acknowledged, it becomes clear that explaining the origins of the Revolution requires not only the examination of developments outside French borders, but also the analysis of how and when they combined with domestic factors to send the old regime to its doom.[2]

THE DIPLOMATIC BACKGROUND

One advantage present-day historians enjoy when tackling such difficult matters is that substantial progress has lately been made in the study of eighteenth century European diplomatic and military history in general, thanks principally to the work of Anglo-American scholars. If these historians hardly agree on all matters, there are three critical points on which they do.[3]

First, they demonstrate that by the mid-eighteenth century, the European system of power was a multi-polar field in which five major and roughly equal contenders—France, England, Austria, Russia, and Prussia—competed amongst themselves alongside a host of second- and third-order powers like Spain, the Netherlands, Portugal, and Denmark. This system has often been said to have enjoyed self-correcting checks and balances that ensured stability. But as Paul Schroeder has argued, it also put less well centralized and integrated nations at risk when two or more major powers conspired to carve them up. For this reason one of the persistent dilemmas of late eighteenth century French foreign policy-makers—who frequently alleged that as a 'satisfied' power, France no longer had any European territorial ambitions—was how best to contain its more aggressive rivals, notably Prussia, Russia, and Austria, which actively and shamelessly pursued territorial aggrandizement at the expense of traditional French confederates, like Sweden, Poland, and Turkey.[4]

A second major point of agreement is that during the eighteenth century French power was in decline. This decline became especially evident following the Seven Years War (1756–63), during which France lost most of its overseas empire to its chief rival Britain. Despite a temporary reversal of fortunes during the early 1780s, French decline once again became manifest—indeed, it became an international scandal—when in 1787 France failed to defend its new ally the Netherlands from Prussian invasion and abandoned its 'old friend' Turkey to the ambitious designs of Russia and Austria. Different historians place different weight on the reasons for French decline, just as contemporaries did; but the usual list of primary factors includes state financial weakness, poor military leadership and organization, and a compromised system of alliances that drew resources away from where they were most needed—in the maritime war with England—and invested them on the continent to reinforce misplaced commitments, principally to Austria. Whatever else it entailed, France's failure to maintain its stature abroad was one of the most conspicuous indications of the corruption of the old regime and the imperative keenly felt by the Revolutionaries to 'regenerate' the nation and restore its lost honour.

A third point of general agreement is that even if France no longer wielded the same international clout by the 1780s that it had in previous decades, it was not inert in the face of new challenges coming from abroad, just as it was not unresponsive to the challenges it faced at home. Although under Louis XVI France's security posture continued to rest upon the twin defensive alliances with Austria and Spain contracted during the previous reign (in 1756 and 1761 respectively), the French government did execute some bold moves to reverse the strategic imbalance favouring Britain since the Seven Years War. These included support for the American rebels in 1778, which ended in Britain's humiliating loss of thirteen valuable Atlantic coast colonies, and its sequel, the sealing of the Dutch alliance in 1785, whereby Britain lost a strategically important continental ally under its influence for more than a century. Although Britain mitigated the effects of American independence by restoring profitable commercial ties with its wayward offspring, these losses not only dealt a blow to British power and prestige, but also enabled the French monarchy to represent its fight against British 'despotism' of the seas as part of the fashionable politics of 'freedom' and to acclaim Louis XVI as the world's great 'protector of liberty'.[5]

Another innovation, noted by recent historians, lay in the monarchy's rethinking of the logic of war. Like so many other regimes, the French state had developed primarily as a military machine that since the accession of Louis XIV had been activated and deployed in every decade except the 1720s. But by the middle of the eighteenth century, the reasons for going to war—at least on the continent—appeared less compelling than they had previously, especially since France no longer faced imminent threats on its borders and military costs were rising and adding ever more to the French debt. A witness to France's humiliation during the Seven Years War as the French ambassador to Turkey, Louis XVI's foreign minister the comte de Vergennes was keenly aware of the diminishing returns that war was bringing to France. 'We regard war as a very great evil', he declared, 'and we will avoid it as long as we are not forced into it out of duty to our engagements or the bad faith of our rivals.' In Vergennes's view, French interests would be better served by treaties and adherence to international law than by armed conflict, and thus stabilization of the European balance of power appeared more attractive than its disruption.[6]

For a monarchy that in earlier times had basked in the bloody defeats of its enemies, this strategic reorientation required recasting its image and diplomatic discourse, as

Vergennes well appreciated. Henceforth, according to a ministerial memorandum of 22 February 1778, the king would act upon and advertise his moderation, disinterestedness, and firmness, which would 'inspire respect for his personal character' at a time when 'the contrast [with that of other rulers] would render him all the more honorable' and result in a 'consideration' that would be 'the most powerful pivot of the prosperity and glory of his reign'. It would go too far to claim that Vergennes—who was no friend of the *philosophes* and unhesitatingly clamped down on all speech subversive of the king's absolute authority—was an Enlightenment fellow-traveller; but his policies at least faintly reflected the irenic norms of international public law as propounded by the jurists of his age, which has given Murphy leave to call Vergennes 'a man of political vision'.[7]

One critical aspect of Vergennes's new 'political vision', recent scholarship has shown, was his reconsideration of the role of colonies and commerce in the French imperium. Received mercantilist opinion maintained that economic development was a zero-sum game in which growth in one nation entailed contraction in others and that colonies were necessary to secure essential markets abroad. For this reason, France's loss of empire in the Seven Years War was widely interpreted as a major sign of French decline. Yet rather than attempting to recapture France's lost colonies—which Vergennes considered too risky, given that it would almost certainly have required war on a large scale—he sought to expand the economy and enhance French political influence through the reduction of tariffs and other trade barriers via commercial treaties with Britain, Russia, Spain, Portugal, and the United States. Traditional scholarship has emphasized the negative consequences of these treaties—especially the 1786 Eden Treaty with Britain, which flooded sectors of the French economy with cheaper British manufactures that drove up unemployment and drove down profits in France. But recent analyses have provided a more balanced assessment of its impact, demonstrating that if some sectors of the economy suffered as a result of this treaty, others benefited. Everything taken into account, concludes one recent analysis, the French experience with the Eden Treaty showed that 'there were justified reasons for cautious optimism about France's long-term ability to compete'. Indeed, although he has certainly not overlooked the failings of Vergennes's policies, Murphy has gone so far as to hail the foreign minister as a forward-thinking, far-sighted progenitor of the European Common Market.[8]

If the French government cannot be fairly accused of sclerotic thinking and immobility in its foreign and military policy, did that policy have little or nothing to do with the origins of the French Revolution? In the end, of course, the 'success' of a foreign policy cannot be measured simply in terms of the number and/or boldness of the new initiatives it undertakes and the innovative thinking that lies behind them. It must also be judged with regard to the aggregate effectiveness of its component parts in meeting the offensive and defensive needs of the power that pursues it and the costs thereby incurred. In the case of eighteenth century France, few, if any historians would deny that it was war that put the greatest burden on the state's fiscal system, and in that way diplomatic developments contributed to the coming of 1789. The real question in dispute is whether *in addition to* 'mere' fiscal stress, France's foreign/military policy contributed anything to the old regime's breakdown, and if so, what? The answer to be given here rests on two principal claims: first, that just as foreign and military factors imposed heavy burdens on the French budget in the run-up to the French Revolution, so did constraints on the French budget severely limit the options of makers of French foreign/military policy; second, that the contradictions already present in the foreign/military policy of Vergennes—although not altogether irreversible—came home to roost in 1787 and later years under his successor the comte de Montmorin, weakening France as a player in European politics and discrediting the old regime in the eyes of the nation. Therein lay its contribution to the French Revolution.[9]

Rethinking Vergennes's Legacy

Vergennes may have expected his commercial policy to reduce the likelihood and cost of war, but the pacific intentions and effects of his policies should not be exaggerated. Next to some of his ministerial rivals who argued for much more bellicose policies toward Britain, such as the naval minister the marquis de Castries, Vergennes might seem to have been a 'moderate' inasmuch as his ultimate goal was reconciliation. Yet distasteful as it was to Vergennes, reconciliation on any acceptable basis depended upon righting the imbalance of power between the two nations, and that meant waging war by direct and indirect means, as the British hardly failed to appreciate. This contradiction between methods and goals was compounded by another: Vergennes had hoped and expected that his commercial diplomacy would ultimately lead to reductions in French military expenditures, but if peace with Britain first required war, military outlays in the short and medium term would have to increase, as indeed they did. To counter British 'despotism' of the seas and protect French trade, France under Louis XVI began closing the long-lamented naval gap through a massive ship-building campaign. By 1780 the navy had grown to 86 frigates and 79 ships of the line—roughly half the size of the British fleet—thereby quadrupling annual naval expenditures between 1776 and 1783, and although some ships were retired thereafter, a roughly equal number of new ships were projected for later deployment. Whether this strategic build-up brought the additional military clout France sought and needed is debatable, but at a minimum, it—like the French intervention in the American war—indicated a firm French refusal to concede the mastery of the oceans to Britain.[10]

To understand the impact of this escalation of the arms race on the Anglo-French rivalry as a whole, we need to consider not only what it meant to France—a desperate attempt to gain parity with its arch-rival—but also what it meant to Britain. With a smaller navy due in part to heavier military commitments on the continent, France was at a structural disadvantage. Yet France enjoyed vast superiority in terms of aggregate domestic resources that should have allowed it to compete successfully, as the British appreciated. Even as France descended into Revolution, one anonymous pamphleteer warned that should Britain's rival restore order to its finances, 'the public credit of

France, from the superior natural resources of the country over those of England, will start up in an instant far superior to that of England'. Indeed, as we now know, France's population was about four times greater than that of Britain and its GDP more than three times larger in the late eighteenth century; and contrary to older views, which overestimated Britain's industrial development in this period, France's economic growth rate was roughly comparable to that of its competitor. Moreover, although Britain had clearly 'won' the Seven Years War, this victory and Britain's rough handling of neutral shipping during the conflict had raised widespread suspicions that it was pursuing a maritime 'universal monarchy'. This fear provided France with the materials to forge what one French diplomat called 'a sort of [international] conspiracy against that power' and contributed to Britain's isolation between 1763 and 1787.[11]

If Britain recovered fast enough commercially from the humiliating loss of the thirteen American colonies in 1783 and in the next ten years added no fewer than thirty-three ships of the line to the navy, it was not without a lot of hand-wringing about the nation's future. 'We shall never again figure as a leading power in Europe', bemoaned the Earl of Sandwich, 'but think ourselves happy if we can drag on for some years a contemptible existence as a commercial state.' In the wake of its defeat in America and the rebuilding of the French fleet, reported the comte d'Adhémar from London on 10 March 1786, 'the English nation no longer has that blind confidence in its navy that its mariners used to derive from the great advantages [it used] to have over us. The chance of an invasion by the French is [now] discussed as something [that is] not only possible, but even probable; this grand project that we consider chimerical is today discussed on both sides of the Channel as a plausible enterprise.'[12]

This exaggerated perception of imminent British vulnerability is important to grasp because it helps explain why Britain felt it could not respond positively to most of Vergennes's gestures toward reconciliation, and hence why his British policy ultimately failed. As many benefits as reconciliation offered both parties, it proved a non-starter as a whole because it came packaged with so many aggressive moves on France's part: French support for the successful American Revolution; the forging of a French-led coalition of opposing powers at a time of British isolation; a major expansion of the France's fleet, which in combination with that of its ally Spain, challenged British maritime supremacy; and in 1786 the construction of a large harbour at Cherbourg, which, according to some British reports, could berth 100 ships of the line and comported a tower of 60 feet from which all naval operations on the Channel could be monitored. With all these trumps in the French hand, how could Britain hope to negotiate from a position of any strength? It was only because the agreement promised to deliver great commercial benefits to Britain—so many that Eden worried the French could not sustain it—that Britain believed it could afford the Eden Treaty, and even in this case it was France, not Britain, that took the initiative in concluding it. As for the rest of Vergennes's peace offensive, the only reasonable British response, it seemed, was to refuse the hand extended to them from across the Channel, maintain the navy, build more defences at home, and frustrate French interests abroad wherever possible.[13]

DEBACLE IN THE NETHERLANDS

The irony of this situation is not hard to grasp. In an effort to compete with its hegemonic rival, France had managed to undermine British superiority and confidence, for which France would, in turn, pay the price under Montmorin in the Dutch crisis of 1787. In this arena, too, France had demonstrated a fatal indifference to British sensibilities in 1785 when it plucked The Netherlands from the British orbit and placed it within the constellation of French allies. This realignment not only altered the balance of power on the continent, but also opened the door to fresh French commercial penetration of the Dutch overseas empire and expansion into India. Understandably, then, when Dutch Patriots revolted against the stadtholder William V, the British saw a golden opportunity to reverse the tide flowing against them and escape from their not so splendid isolation. This they did not only by supporting William V, but also by immediately building ties with Prussia, whose new king Frederick William II had a personal dynastic stake in crushing the rebellion because his sister Wilhelmina was married to William V.

Despite desperate French efforts to arrange a compromise, events rapidly spun out of French control when the Patriots arrested Wilhelmina on 28 June and subjected her to such degrading captivity that the Prussian ministry demanded immediate reprisals. Hoping to avert war, Montmorin accepted an invitation from the Dutch Estates to mediate the conflict without understanding the real stakes involved. For despite disturbing signs of Anglo-Prussian collusion aimed at exploiting the crisis to their benefit, he naively believed England had an interest in settling it on some equitable basis acceptable to France, and he even went so far to placate the British as to invite them to act as co-mediator. Not all French officials were so deluded as Montmorin. On 14 August the French chargé d'affaires in London, the marquis de Barthélemy, warned that Britain was presently working 'to unite all the powers jealous of the French Crown to strip from us an ally [the Netherlands] ... in order to cover us with the dishonour of being unable to prevent such a misfortune without the risk of being dragged into a land and sea war simultaneously'. 'It is now that we must regret the result of the last war', he observed, 'as well as the last five years of peace.' The costs of humiliating Britain for so long had finally begun to sink in.[14]

Despite this and other admonitions, however, Montmorin steadfastly refused to recognize the depths of impending Anglo-Prussian perfidy, the result of which was catastrophe. On 13 September Prussian armies crossed into The Netherlands and soon thereafter Britain mobilized its fleet, placing France under extraordinary pressure to assist an embattled ally in its back yard. As became instantly notorious, France failed to deliver on its promises to defend The Netherlands, chiefly because the fiscal crisis that had so dominated French politics since the previous winter had not been resolved. The result was the crushing of the Dutch Patriot rebellion and the loss of a hard-won French ally. In addition, panicked by the threat of superior British naval forces, the French signed an agreement on 27 October to stabilize the size of their fleets on terms dictated by Britain. In this connection it is important to recall—but also to revise—Skocpol's general argument about France's inability to compete as a world power. Obviously, if the monarchy had resolved its financial problems by this time, France would have had more and better options in the Dutch crisis. Yet misguided assumptions and calculations on France's part—stemming in part from policies inherited from the Vergennes era—also caused France to blunder: French insensitivity to the impact of the Dutch alliance on British sensibilities; inflated expectations of the moderating effects of the Eden Treaty on British behaviour; underestimation of Frederick William's distress over the fate of his sister; and finally, a profound misreading, especially on Montmorin's part, of British and Prussian intentions.[15]

The Dutch debacle had many consequences. Most immediately, France lost a hard-won continental ally, and with it potentially lucrative commercial markets in and around the Dutch colonies. Second, Britain was now able to break out of its quarter-century isolation, for in the wake of Anglo-Prussian collaboration in defence of the stadtholder, the groundwork had been laid for a formidable Triple Alliance among Britain, Prussia, and The Netherlands directed against French interests abroad. Third, whatever additional standing as a military and diplomatic player France had acquired in 1783 evaporated. 'The humiliation that France has brought upon itself by its conduct in the Netherlands' and 'the [damaging] impression that the weakness just shown by the Court of France would infallibly have on Europe', the Swedish ambassador Staël-Holstein informed Louis XVI's principal minister Loménie de Brienne and Montmorin, would have a devastating impact on French credibility. For who could now have faith in French promises, the Swedish ambassador pointedly asked, given that shortly before abandoning The Netherlands, France had sworn to defend it? Would the Turks receive the same treatment as the Dutch? To the second question, the deeply embarrassed foreign minister could only lamely answer, 'that he hoped not'. Alas, as we shall see, they did.[16]

Loss of French credibility abroad translated into loss of self-confidence at home. 'In Europe', recalled one French diplomat, 'our rivals stopped fearing us, our friends [stopped] counting on us, and we [stopped] counting on ourselves.' Within the government, two ministers associated with the queen, Ségur and Castries—appalled by Montmorin's blindness with regard to British intentions and lack of backbone in thwarting them—resigned even before Prussian troops entered The Netherlands. Outside the government, public attention—which for most of 1787 had been riveted on the battle over the monarchy's financial reform programme—shifted decisively for a time to foreign affairs. 'The political conversation of every company I have seen', reported the British traveller Arthur Young, 'has turned much more on the affairs of Holland than on those of France'. Not surprisingly, the Dutch debacle triggered a sense of national shame. 'Suffused with a sense of honor and justice', noted one contemporary, 'the nation is complaining of [our] abandonment of the [Dutch] Patriots.' But no less did it fuel fears of vulnerability to malevolent foreign forces beyond French control. 'We are beginning to perceive', wrote one observer in the late summer of 1787, 'that a concert [of powers] fatal to our interests could be forming among the foreign powers, [and] even could have existed for a long time under the appearance of sham divisions, to execute great designs that our dilatory politics has made all the easier'. For the Dutch crisis was not—and neither did it appear to be—an isolated event in European affairs: rather, it fitted all too well within a much larger, unpredictable confluence of forces which threatened to drag France into an unwanted, potentially disastrous 'general war' that the monarchy and the nation were ill-prepared to wage.[17]

Imagining Invasion

In the face of these potentially 'fatal' threats, to which powers could France turn for assistance? By 1787, France's ageing alliances with Austria and Spain were showing signs of strain. The 1756 Austrian alliance had never recovered from the outcome of the Seven Years War, most French observers contending that France's failures in that war stemmed largely from the extravagant support France provided for Austria's vain campaigns to recapture Silesia. Efforts to re-enforce that alliance through the marriage of the future Louis XVI to the Austrian archduchess Marie-Antoinette had backfired, especially as a result of the queen's plunging reputation for extravagance in the wake of the Diamond Necklace Affair and rumours that she was sending 'all the gold in France' to support her brother, the Austrian emperor Joseph II, in his aggressive designs on France's 'old friend' Turkey.

Although less unpopular, the *pacte de famille* with Spain had not provided the solid block of Bourbon powers and grand new markets for French goods that it had promised, while Spain fiercely resented how it had been manipulated by France against its own interests in the past. To be sure, in part because of their closer dynastic ties, France and Spain were on reasonably cordial terms, and France did appreciate and acknowledge the vocal support Spain had provided in the Dutch debacle. But Spanish military weakness and Austrian fecklessness were such that Montmorin, in an agonizing reappraisal of France's security in early 1788, stunningly concluded that France 'has no friend, no ally on whom it can count, and if it faced a war on the continent, it would probably be left to its own devices'. Others arrived at even darker conclusions. 'The house of Bourbon', affirmed one anonymous observer, 'is about to be dragged into a general war, [and] without friends and without allies.' If the first duty of any state is to protect its inhabitants, the French state—nearly bankrupt and increasingly isolated—was verging on failure more than a year before the French Revolution erupted in 1789.[18]

Just as feelings of vulnerability had bred rumours of a French invasion of Britain in 1786, so did they breed French suspicions of some sort of British offensive manoeuvre during the spring of 1788. 'We are more convinced than ever', reported the French ambassador to Britain La Luzerne on 15 April, 'that England ... is seeking by all means possible to contravene us in the rest of Europe so as to catapult us, if possible, into a land war.' Two months later, as talk of war intensified in Britain, its offensive plans remained fuzzy, but through the haze of rumours La Luzerne thought he could now perceive its bare outlines: Britain would stir up trouble on the continent, create a *casus belli* that would obligate France to supply its allies, and then, while its resources were diverted elsewhere, attack France by means of a fleet now being rigged in British ports. In France, these dire warnings did not fall on deaf ears. No sooner did Lamoignon de Malesherbes, a member of the Royal Council, receive reports such as La Luzerne's, than he advised the king on the basis of these reports that 'England is preparing to attack France immediately'. 'Even if I did not have this information', Malesherbes interestingly remarked, 'it would seem impossible that this will not happen'—a conclusion he deduced principally from France's desperate financial situation, which was crippling the French defence system and, inasmuch as it was known to all France's adversaries, invited foreign attack on multiple fronts. Were those attacks to occur, Malesherbes despaired, 'the outcome would be irremediable', for 'if our colonies are invaded, our commerce destroyed, our reputation lost among far-flung nations, [and] our navy destroyed, France would be unable to recover for perhaps several centuries'.[19]

Under the weight of these warnings and further 'evidence' of imminent invasion, even Montmorin—who, in the wake of the Dutch debacle, had barely begun to awaken to the threat from across the Channel—became convinced that Britain was France's true nemesis and the prime instigator of France's troubles abroad. 'The conduct of the English ministry', he informed La Luzerne in July 1788, 'is so tortuous, and its malevolence towards us so manifest, that we cannot be too distrustful of its intentions, nor, consequently, monitor too closely its slightest initiatives.' Montmorin now conjured up a nightmare scenario that would haunt the ministry and condition its policies for years to come. 'Drunk on its success in the Netherlands', he alleged, Britain was covertly organizing an expanded coalition of powers whose 'secret goal' was 'to lay down the law to the house of Bourbon ... shackle the [house of] Austria; contain Russia in the East; dominate Germany; in a word, it will make England the predominant power in Europe ... The house of Bourbon will be deprived of the role it has played until now; its trade and possessions will be [henceforth] at the mercy of its natural enemy.'[20]

What is so striking about these and other jeremiads of the period is that while Britain had, in fact, conspired with Prussia to subvert French policies in The Netherlands on its way to constructing the Triple Alliance, it had no serious plans, or intentions, to attack France, at least as this juncture. Yet as in the case of British perceptions of its imminent vulnerability to French attack two years earlier, the 'chimerical' had come to seem 'plausible'—even to such 'well-informed' contemporaries as Malesherbes and Montmorin—and disturbing rumours of imminent war continued to ripple across France into 1789. Had Britain been the only foreign threat France faced in the run-up to 1789, it is conceivable that during the Dutch crisis and thereafter the government could have sounded the alarm, rallied the country, and clinched the case for its tax programme with the *parlements* on the grounds of national emergency. Indeed, before he resigned this is exactly the course Castries urged upon Louis XVI, if for no other reason than that it might reverse the political tide which had been running against the monarchy since the spring of 1787. 'Present the idea of *la gloire* to Frenchmen and you will effect the most useful ... diversion from the present turmoil. Give the appearance of necessity to taxation, the mood will calm and perhaps you will see government recapture a part of what it is ready to lose.'[21]

That the monarchy did not choose this course—and thereby lost a chance to escape entrapment in the widening revolutionary vortex—was no doubt due to a number of reasons, including the failure of royal nerve, the government's aversion to rescuing a nearby 'democracy' at a time of rising resistance to the royal will at home, and, of course, the empty treasury, which spoke loudly against any foreign adventure. But there was another factor that weighed heavily in the balance: namely, the deteriorating situation in the Levant, which even more than the Dutch debacle, threatened to enmesh France in a 'general war' it could not afford and made offensive action against Britain, whatever its potential political benefits, appear too risky.

Abandoning Turkey, the Quadruple Alliance, and the Austrian Plot

For decades, Russia had been cutting away at the western and northern reaches of the Turkish Empire, most recently in 1783 when it had seized the Crimea with the tacit support of its new ally Austria. During late summer of 1787—at the same moment as the Dutch debacle—Turkey declared war against Russia, which in March of 1788 was joined by Austria, whose reluctant entry into the war convinced nearly everyone—except the Turks—that the Turkish Empire was doomed. These events forced France to choose between assisting Turkey or abandoning it to its apparently inexorable fate and possibly sharing in the spoils. Painful as this decision was, it could not be indefinitely postponed. For as the French ambassador Choiseul-Gouffier repeatedly warned from Istanbul, the Turks were in desperate need of immediate French aid. This was news that Montmorin clearly did *not* want to hear because of the agonizing dilemma it presented: if the current state of French finances dictated desertion of the Turks, French honour and commercial interests dictated renewed support of France's 'old friend', especially at a time when France was covering itself with ignominy in The Netherlands.[22]

While the French government pondered this difficult decision, another arose to complicate it, namely, whether France should join a projected defensive Quadruple Alliance uniting France, Russia, Austria, and Spain to counter the emerging Triple Alliance of England, Prussia, and the Netherlands. Russia and Austria became increasingly attracted to this notion, mainly to protect themselves from Prussian attack while their armies were occupied in the Levant. Had this alliance been clinched, the threat of a Russian coalition with Britain—which most contemporary observers considered 'natural' and thus likely—would have been allayed, and France might have considerably strengthened its strategic position. But joining the Quadruple Alliance came at a price and created fresh risks. It would have meant almost certain French collusion in the dismemberment of the Turkish Empire, and hence the further staining of

French honour and loss of credibility. Although a 'general war' might possibly have been averted by restraining Prussia's territorial ambitions, it was also possible that by committing France to defending Russia and Austria against Prussian attack, the alliance would, on the contrary, have dragged France into an unsustainable 'general war' against the Triple Alliance. These considerations were debated backwards and forwards within the French government from the fall of 1787 into the Revolution, and they belie Skocpol's claim that France suffered from an 'unquenchable penchant for war'. On the contrary, what the government sought above all was to *escape* from war, and it was paradoxically its success in doing so—first in The Netherlands and then in the Levant—that led to its state of semi-paralysis in foreign affairs and helped doom the old regime.[23]

Ultimately, faced with the twin dilemmas of what policy to pursue in regard to Turkey and the Quadruple Alliance, the French government managed to combine the worst of all available options, a policy that would have profound impact not only abroad, but also at home. France's first decision in this arena was to abandon the Turks to their apparent dark fate by refusing to provide military aid on the convenient pretext that Turkey had rashly declared war on Russia against strenuous French advice. That act alone, Montmorin instructed Choiseul-Gouffier to inform the Turks on 2 October 1787, had fundamentally changed the situation both strategically and morally, for it had turned Turkey into 'the aggressor in the eyes of Europe' and tied the king's hands as regards any assistance in accordance with 'his principles of justice'. It might have seemed that having so contemptibly sold out Turkey, in the name of high moral principle, the French government would now at least reap the strategic benefits of joining the Quadruple Alliance. Yet in the end, despite the mounting Russian and Austrian pressure to conclude it and the majority support for it in the Royal Council, the French government, after endless dithering, allowed the project to wither on the vine during the spring of 1789. Once again, the imperative to avoid entrapment in a 'general war'—and thereby avoid the additional financial costs such a war would have entailed—overrode all other strategic considerations.[24]

Where did these decisions put the French government and what did they contribute to the coming of the French Revolution? First, France, having just abandoned one formal ally and one 'old friend', compounded its loss of prestige and credibility in diplomatic circles and outside them by scuttling negotiations over an alliance that it had dangled before Austria and Russia for a year and a half. To be sure, partly because of France's ignominious disengagement from two major regions of conflict, the imminence of war temporarily receded by 1789. But France appeared more vulnerable than ever to its prospective enemies, especially Britain, which, flanked by two new allies, could now contemplate continental interventions from which it had flinched only recently. As Barthélemy observed from London in October 1788, Britain, having usurped the supremacy that France had once enjoyed, 'will deploy [its supremacy] to injure us constantly during peacetime and to make war upon us whenever circumstances appear favourable'. No more frank an admission of the failure of Vergennes's policy of confrontation and reconciliation could be imagined.[25]

A second consequence of French diplomacy in the run-up to the Revolution was the further delegitimation of the French monarchy, not only because it was patently failing in its first duty to secure the nation, but also because its latest manoeuvres reinforced long-standing suspicions that the queen was subverting French policy on behalf of her native Austria. As noted above, the Austrian alliance had been unpopular in France almost from its inception, and its close association with Marie-Antoinette, whose own popularity was also on the decline, did neither any good. The widespread rumour that the queen—who became popularly known as 'Madame Deficit'—was depleting the royal treasury to subsidize Joseph II's wars abroad gave new meaning the fiscal crisis that lay behind France's weakness abroad: rather than being 'merely' a problem of faulty administration, that crisis could be, and was by some, attributed to the Marie-Antoinette's purposeful diversion of state funds to benefit Austria and her native family.[26]

Although unfounded in fact, this rumour did have plausibility, since having given birth to three surviving children (including two sons), the queen enjoyed growing political influence during the 1780s, placing three ministers beholden to her on the Royal Council. Despite a setback due, in part, to the Diamond Necklace Affair in 1785–6, Marie-Antoinette's political influence once again began to grow and reach its height in 1787, following the death of her enemy Vergennes in February and the dismissal of his ally Calonne two months later. Although the queen was unable to replace Vergennes with the comte de St Priest—the candidate favoured by Austria—the king did appoint her creature Loménie de Brienne as head of the council of finances in April and subsequently as principal minister. This leverage was sufficient to turn French foreign policy in an increasingly pro-Austrian direction, a seismic shift that French public opinion—a growing force in the run-up to the Revolution—could hardly ignore.

One strong reason for believing in the co-optation of French foreign policy by the Austrians devolved from the Dutch debacle. In the wake of its humiliation by Prussia, France had every reason to reverse the pro-Prussian tilt adopted by Vergennes and then by Montmorin during the first year of his ministry. In fact, that redirection was strongly urged upon Montmorin by some ministerial insiders who wished to punish Frederick William II for his betrayal of French trust. This meant that unless France decided upon an unthinkable isolation, it had little choice but to strengthen ties with Prussia's enemy, Austria, and Austria's ally Russia, and indeed, that is the exactly the outcome many observers predicted. 'All our pundits [spéculateurs]', noted an anonymous observer in December 1787, 'say that our resentment of [Prussia] ... is going to wind up putting us squarely in the camp of the two imperial courts.' Resentment of Prussia clearly played into the hands of the Austrian faction, which, backed by the queen, would see to it that France threw itself into the arms of Vienna and St Petersburg. 'The cabinet of Versailles', observed the baron de Staël-Holstein, 'is more than ever determined to ally closely with Russia', and 'the credit of the queen in nearly all matters ... makes it unlikely that we will witness France seeking an alliance with Prussia for a very long time.'[27]

The French abandonment of Turkey in the fall of 1787 provided a second reason to suspect creeping Austrian co-optation of French foreign policy via the strengthened hand of the queen. Far from remaining a state secret, this shift in policy instantly became a matter of public knowledge; indeed, no sooner did the French government inform the Turks of its refusal of aid, than word arrived in Paris that the Turkish government had convoked the French ambassador in Istanbul to denounce French 'perfidy' in pretending to help the Turks resist Russian aggression, all the while giving aid and comfort to its enemies. The news prompted immediate popular indignation in Paris, for although the Turkish regime had long epitomized 'despotism' in the French political imagination and had never been formally allied with France, its ancient strategic partnership in counterbalancing the Habsburgs in Germany had earned it a large reservoir of popular goodwill. Because of Austria's collusion with Russia in the Turkish War of 1787, it took little imagination to attribute French desertion of Turkey to the malign influence of Marie-Antoinette and the Austrian lobby on French policy, especially after Austria entered the Turkish War in March 1788, and to connect it with the queen's much rumoured export of French funds to Vienna. Indeed, a bogus letter from Joseph II to Marie-Antoinette that circulated publicly in 1789 falsely intimated that the Austrian emperor had ordered his sister and her ministerial creature the baron de Breteuil to raise 50 million *livres* in France through a variety of 'despotic' means to finance his war with Turkey. That estimate would soon explode. One account put the sum at 100 million *livres*; another raised it to several hundred millions; and in April 1789, the radical journalist Jean-Louis Carra insisted in a popular pamphlet that Joseph II had been receiving 500,000 *livres* from his sister *every week*. To the many believers in the claims of this literature, it seemed as if the mystery behind France's unanticipated bankruptcy and its shocking decline abroad had finally been dispelled—enough so for the Austrian ambassador to demand that the French government suppress it.[28]

A final reason for believing that France was falling irretrievably into the Austro-Russian orbit was the proliferation of signs that France was about to conclude the Quadruple Alliance. From the outset of these negotiations, all parties involved had tried to keep them secret for their own particular motives. Yet as in the case of France's abandonment of Turkey, word of these negotiations leaked out almost immediately, the Russian Vice-Chancellor complaining already in November 1787 that reports were circulating in Paris. The implications of this disclosure were not lost on the French government. The treaty, Montmorin predicted at that moment, 'will not enjoy public favour'—a prediction whose accuracy he confirmed one year later—and for reasons that were perfectly obvious. Not only was the proposed alliance publicly seen as a 'confirmation of the system that binds us to the court of Vienna' and 'a consolidation of the Treaty of 1 May 1756 [with Austria], which I must admit, has never been and never will be in accordance with the will of the nation'; but by committing France to assisting Austria and Russia if they were attacked by Prussia, it also raised the prospect of French involvement in a 'general war' at a time of extraordinary French weakness.[29]

Although he dismissed this 'terror' as 'chimerical', Montmorin admitted—perhaps because he half-believed it himself—that it had 'some apparent foundation'; and he acknowledged that in informing public opinion it would inflict further damage on the credit, and hence the military readiness, of the French state. For these combined reasons, the French government eventually gave up on the Quadruple Alliance, fearing not only its financial and strategic implications, but also the hostile reception it would receive in the forthcoming Estates-General. In so doing, the monarchy managed to incur all of the costs—in the form of the negative public opinion that news of its negotiation stirred up at home—and none of the potential benefits—in the form of greater security abroad—that the Quadruple Alliance had to offer.[30]

Conclusion

There can be no doubt that the immediate origin of the French Revolution lay in a governmental fiscal crisis that France had the economic means—but not the political will—to resolve. Ever more desperate to avoid bankruptcy, the monarchy jerked from one unsuccessful expedient to another, an unprecedented process that engaged an ever wider public in an ever more sweeping critique of the old regime. Because of the compelling domestic stakes involved, public attention was not always focused on events abroad, but these events did fitfully intrude on the national consciousness and contributed to the growing disenchantment with the old regime. To be sure, the monarchy, however clumsily, did keep France out of war at a time of government financial crisis; but as one contemporary severely noted, the price of Montmorin's peace had been 'the loss of allies that his predecessors had always regarded as essential to our interests and the preservation of [Europe's] equilibrium'. This loss translated not only into a further decline in France's prestige abroad, but also into a sense of imminent vulnerability to foreign invasion, more intense than most people could remember, as indicated by the panicked reaction to the mobilization of the British fleet in 1788. It did not take much knowledge of foreign affairs to grasp the essential truth that French security hung by the slenderest of threads.[31]

This outcome was all the more troubling because there were reasons to believe that at this moment of terrifying vulnerability, the French government was being subverted from within and that the most immediate problem of the old regime—state bankruptcy—was a product of that subversion. If it were true, as the marquis de Bombelles observed in January 1789, that 'never was a queen of France less beloved [than Marie-Antoinette]', this disaffection surely was rooted in the queen's apparently purposeful misspending of state funds and their alleged diversion in support of Joseph II's war against France's 'old friend' Turkey. Indeed, because of the real and evident spike in the queen's political clout in the run-up to the Revolution, it seemed that every false move of the government was the result of her malign intervention, which not only made her one of the most reviled rulers in history, but also brought discredit to the entire old regime. 'A blind hatred against the queen', Bombelles duly noted, 'has made all the orders of the state forget what they owe and what they should do for the good of the *patrie*'. Having, on the instigation of her native Austria, allegedly weakened France not only by stealing from its coffers, but also by discouraging patriotism, Marie-Antoinette had made regeneration of France's foreign policy and its internal constitution seem more urgent than ever. Once we understand that perception—a blend of fact and falsehood—it becomes much less mysterious why the French people in 1789 felt compelled to execute the most radical severing of ancient ties they would ever undertake and embrace a future that could not have been more uncertain.[32]

NOTES

1. For a recent reassessment, see Joseph Klaits and Michael Haltzel (eds), *The Global Ramifications of the French Revolution* (Cambridge, 2002); Albert Sorel, *L'Europe et la Révolution française*, 8 vols (Paris, 1885–1905). Robert Palmer's great *The Age of the Democratic Revolution*, 2 vols (Princeton, NJ, 1959, 1964) was one of the few general works of the last century that examined cross-national trends in detail and revealed a great deal about the 'Revolutionary International'. Yet Palmer's goal was not to explain how the international context—in particular, diplomatic developments—bore on the French Revolution, but rather to demonstrate that revolutions in different national contexts had a common 'democratic' origin.

2. As Annie Jourdan has remarked, the foreign roots of the French Revolution is 'a subject about which little, if anything has been written'. Annie Jourdan, 'The Alien Origins of the French Revolution: American, Scottish, Genevan and Dutch Influences', *Proceedings of the Western Society for French History* 35 (2007), 186; Theda Skocpol, *States and Social Revolutions: A Comparative Analysis of France, Russia, and China* (Cambridge and New York, 1979), chap. 2; T. C. W. Blanning, *The Origins of the French Revolutionary Wars* (London, 1986) and *The Culture of Power and the Power of Culture: Old Regime Europe, 1660–1789* (Oxford, 2002), chap. 7; Bailey Stone, *The Genesis of the French Revolution: A Global-Historical Interpretation* (Cambridge, 1994). See also, Jeremy J. Whiteman, *Reform, Revolution and French Global Policy, 1787–1791* (Aldershot, 2003).

3. Some of the most notable recent works illuminating the diplomatic context of the French Revolution include: H. M. Scott, *The Birth of a Great Power System, 1740–1815* (Harlow, 2006); Jeremy Black, *British Foreign Policy in an Age of Revolution, 1783–1793* (Cambridge, 1994); Orville Murphy, *Charles Gravier, comte de Vergennes: French Diplomacy in the Age of Revolution, 1719–1787* (Albany, NY, 1982) and *The Diplomatic Retreat of France and Public Opinion on the Eve of the French Revolution, 1783–1789* (Washington, DC, 1998); Paul Schroeder, *The Transformation of European Politics, 1763–1848* (Oxford, 1996); Derek Beales, *Joseph II*, 2 vols (Cambridge, 1987, 2009). See also the introduction in John Hardman and Munro Price (eds), *Louis XVI and the comte de Vergennes: Correspondence, 1774–1787* (Oxford, 1998).

4. Schroeder, *Transformation*, chap. 1.

5. Stone, *Genesis*, 119–23; as in abbé Racine, *Discours sur la paix, prononcé le 11 janvier 1784* (Toulouse, 1784), 75. Translation mine, as are all that follow. This is not to say that the Treaty of Paris of 1783 was an unmixed victory for French diplomacy in general, or that the spike in French international prestige was enduring. As Schroeder has aptly remarked, 'Britain lost the war and France lost the peace.' Schroeder, *Transformation*, 38. Moreover, the American Revolution gave a cohort of French nobles practice at resisting 'tyranny' that some of them could draw upon when resisting it at home in 1789. See Munro Price, 'The Court Nobility and the Origins of the French Revolution', in Hamish Scott and Brendan

Simms (eds), *Cultures of Power in Europe during the Long Eighteenth Century* (Cambridge, 2007), 269–88.

6. For a recent reaffirmation of the importance of war in French state-building and its costs, see Guy Rowlands, *The Financial Decline of a Great Power: War, Influence, and Money in Louis XIV's France* (Oxford, 2012); James C. Riley, *The Seven Years War and the Old Regime in France: The Economic and Financial Toll* (Princeton, 1986); cited in Murphy, *Vergennes*, 229.

7. This ideological reorientation had already begun under Louis XV. See Jeffrey Merrick, 'Politics on Pedestals: Royal Monuments in Eighteenth-Century France', *French History* 5 (1991), 234–64; Thomas E. Kaiser, 'Louis le Bien-Aimé and the Rhetoric of the Royal Body', in Sara E. Melzer and Kathryn Norberg (eds), *From the Royal to the Republican Body: Incorporating the Political in Seventeenth- and Eighteenth-Century France* (Berkeley, 1998), 131–61; Archives du Ministère des Affaires Étrangères (henceforth AAE) Correspondance Politique (henceforth CP) Autriche 334, f. 232; Murphy, *Vergennes*, 474.

8. Jeff Horn, *The Path not Taken: French Industrialization in the Age of Revolution, 1750–1830* (Cambridge, MA, 2006), 77; Murphy, *Vergennes*, 458.

9. For two recent analyses of the fiscal crisis, see Joël Félix, 'The Financial Origins of the French Revolution', in Peter R. Campbell (ed.), *The Origins of the French Revolution* (Houndmills, 2006), chap. 1; Gail Bossenga, 'Financial Origins of the French Revolution', in Thomas E. Kaiser and Dale K. Van Klay (eds), *From Deficit to Deluge: The Origins of the French Revolution* (Stanford, 2011), chap. 1.

10. On the Vergennes/Castries rivalry, see Munro Price, 'The Dutch Affair and the Fall of the Ancien Régime, 1784–1787', *The Historical Journal* 38 (1995), 875–905; William Doyle, *The Oxford History of the French Revolution* (Oxford, 1989), p. 32; Jonathan Dull, *The French Navy and the War of American Independence: A Study of Arms and Diplomacy, 1774–1787* (Princeton, 1975), 336–8.

11. Cited in Black, *British Foreign Policy*, 334; Jack A. Goldstone, *Revolution and Rebellion in the Early Modern World* (Berkeley, CA, 1991), 204–6; AAE CP Angleterre 567, f. 70. As Scott nicely frames the paradox, 'Britain's own rise to pre-eminence, along with the corresponding decline of France, had undermined her foreign policy.' H. M. Scott, *British Foreign Policy in the Age of the American Revolution* (Oxford, 1990), 342.

12. Dull, *French Navy*, 340–4; cited in Scott, *British Foreign Policy*, 339n1; AAE CP Angleterre 555, f. 248.

13. Black, *British Foreign Policy*, 103, 105–12.

14. For recent accounts of the Dutch debacle from a French perspective, see Murphy, *Diplomatic Retreat*, chap. 6, and Whiteman, *Reform*, chap. 2; Black, *British Foreign Policy*, 142; AAE CP Angleterre 561, f. 55.

15. It is remarkable that even after the Prussian invasion, Montmorin refused to recognize ill-will on Frederick William's part, and he even expressed admiration for the good order Prussian troops were observing in their occupation! Once Prussia withdrew its troops, he told the Prussian ambassador in October, France was prepared to 'wipe the slate clean [*passer l'éponge*]' over the whole affair. AAE CP Prusse 207, ff. 260, 228. Montmorin was more suspicious of British motives and intent, but as late as January, 1788 he dismissed warnings that Britain and Prussia were planning to ally, and he still nursed hopes that Britain and France could restore 'a frank, cordial, and solid understanding' between them. AAE CP Angleterre 564, ff. 66, 51; Black, *British Foreign Policy*, 154.

16. Eric Magnus, baron de Staël-Holstein, *Correspondance diplomatique du baron de Staël-Holstein*, ed. L. Leouzon Le Duc, (Paris, 1881), 74, 71–2.

17. Louis-Philippe, comte de Ségur, *Mémoires, souvenirs et anecdotes*, 3rd edn, 3 vols (Paris, 1827), 3: 225; Duc de Castries, *Le Maréchal de Castries* (Paris, 1956), 149–52; Arthur Young, *Travels during the Years 1787, 1788, & 1789*, 2nd edn, 2 vols (London, 1794), 1: 72; Adophe Mathurin de Lescure (ed.), *Correspondance secrète inédite sur Louis XVI, Marie-Antoinette, la cour et la ville de 1777 à 1792*, 2 vols (Paris, 1866), 2: 184, 176.

18. On these developments, see Thomas E. Kaiser, 'Who's Afraid of Marie-Antoinette? Diplomacy, Austrophobia, and the Queen', *French History* 14 (2000), 241–71; See Louis Blart, *Les Rapports de la France et de l'Espagne après le pacte de famille, jusqu'à la fin du ministère du duc de Choiseul* (Paris, 1915); Francis P. Renaut, *Le Pacte de Famille et l'amérique: La politique coloniale franco-espagnole de 1760 à 1792* (Paris, 1922); AAE CP Espagne 625, f. 337. According to the Venetian ambassador to France, it had been the Spanish king's declaration of support for France in the aftermath of the Dutch debacle that had accelerated British willingness to sign the naval agreement of 27 October. Allesandro Fontanas et al. (eds), *Venise et la Révolution française: Les 470 dépêches des Ambassadeurs de Venise au Doge, 1786–1795* (Paris, 1997), 138; AAE Mémoires et Documents (henceforth MD) Russie 16, f. 313; Lescure, *Correspondance secrète*, 2: 209.

19. AAE CP Angleterre 565, ff. 76–7, ff. 299–303; Guillaume-Chrétien Lamoignon de Malesherbes, 'Mémoire sur la situation présente des affaires en juillet 1788', in Valérie André (ed.), *Malesherbes à Louis XVI, ou les avertissements de Cassandre: Mémoires inédits, 1787–1788* (Paris, 2010), 125, 132.

20. AAE CP Angleterre 566, f. 20; see Thomas E. Kaiser, 'A Tale of Two Narratives: The French Revolution in International Context, 1787–1793', in Peter McPhee (ed.), *A Companion to the French Revolution* (Blackwell, 2012) 161–71; AAE CP Espagne 625, ff. 33–4.

21. Cited in John Hardman, *Louis XVI* (New Haven, CT, 1993), pp. 128–9. Interestingly, Catherine the Great—for her own self-interested reasons, of course—gave the French government much the same advice, as did Staël-Holstein. AAE CP Russie 122, f. 217; Staël-Holstein, *Correspondance diplomatique*, 69.

22. On the abandonment of Turkey, see Hugh Ragsdale, 'Montmorin and Catherine's Greek Project: Revolution in Foreign Policy', *Cahiers du monde russe et soviétique* 27 (1986), 27–44; see, for example, Choiseul-Gouffier's urgent dispatch of 10 August 1787, in which he laid out the French stakes in protecting Turkey—trade and honour—and the relatively minor French military commitment that was necessary to do so. AAE CP Turquie 176, ff. 97–9.

23. Skocpol, *States*, 64.

24. AAE CP Turquie 176, f. 230. Montmorin also made the argument that France had no formal alliance with Turkey, and thus France was not obligated to come to its aid. This was perfectly true, but it had not stopped France from aiding Turkey in the past when it suited French interests; François-Emmanuel Guignard, comte de Saint-Priest, *Mémoires du comte de Saint-Priest* (Paris, 2006), 191. Jacques Necker had already written against joining the Quadruple Alliance the previous fall, chiefly on the grounds of financial exigency. AAE MD Russie 16, ff. 392–402.

25. AAE CP Angleterre 567, ff. 43–4.

26. For a fuller exposition of the following, see Thomas E. Kaiser, 'From Fiscal Crisis to Revolution: The Court and French Foreign Policy, 1787–1789', in Kaiser and Van Kley, *From Deficit to Deluge*, chap. 4.

27. AAE CP Hollande 575, f. 124; Lescure, *Correspondance secrète*, 2:211; Staël-Holstein, *Correspondance diplomatique*, 95.

28. Louis Petit de Bachaumont, *Mémoires secrets pour servir à l'histoire de la république des letters en France depuis MDCCLXII jusqu'à nos jours* 36 vols (London, 177–89), 35: 469–70; on negative French public reaction to the plight of Turkey, see Siméon-Prosper Hardy, 'Mes loisirs, ou journal d'événements, tels qu'ils parviennent à ma connoissance', Bibliothèque Nationale Ms. Fr, 6686, f. 403. On the French image of Turkish 'despotism', see Thomas E. Kaiser, 'The Evil Empire? The Debate on Turkish Despotism in Eighteenth-Century French Political Culture', *Journal of Modern History* 72 (2000), 6–34; Jean-Louis Giraud Soulavie, *Mémoires historiques et politiques du règne de Louis XVI*, 6 vols (Paris, 1804), 6: 172–3; Nicolas Ruault, *Gazette d'un parisien sous la Révolution* (Paris, 1976), p. 80; Bachaumont, *Mémoires secrets* 35: 479–80; [Jean-Louis Carra], *L'Orateur des États-Généraux pour 1789* (n.p., 1789), 24; Alfred d'Arneth and Jules Flammermont (eds), *Correspondance secrète du comte de Mercy-Argenteau avec l'Empereur Joseph II and Le Prince de Kaunitz*, 2 vols (Paris, 1891), 2: 254.

29. AAE CP Russie 122, f. 230; AAE CP Russie 127, f. 368. AAE MD Russie16, f. 374.

30. AAE CP Russie 128, f. 238; Arneth and Flammermont, *Correspondance secrète*, 2: 229–30.

31. On this conceptualization of the crisis, see Kaiser and Van Kley, *From Deficit to Deluge*, intro. and concl.; Lescure, *Correspondance secrète*, 2:231.

32. Marc-Marie, marquis de Bombelles, *Journal*, eds Jean Grassion and Frans Durif, 7 vols (Geneva, 1977–2008), 2: 306, 2: 271.

SELECTED READING

Black, Jeremy, *British Foreign Policy in an Age of Revolution, 1783–1793* (Cambridge, 1994).

Blanning, T. C. W., *The Origins of the French Revolutionary Wars* (London, 1986).

Kaiser, Thomas E., 'Who's Afraid of Marie-Antoinette? Diplomacy, Austrophobia, and the Queen', *French History* 14 (2000), 241–71.

Kaiser, Thomas E., 'From Fiscal Crisis to Revolution: The Court and French Foreign Policy, 1787–1789', in Thomas E. Kaiser and Dale K. Van Kley (eds), *From Deficit to Deluge: The Origins of the French Revolution* (Stanford, 2011), chap. 4.

Murphy, Orville, *Charles Gravier, comte de Vergennes: French Diplomacy in the Age of Revolution, 1719–1787* (Albany, NY, 1982).

Murphy, Orville, *The Diplomatic Retreat of France and Public Opinion on the Eve of the French Revolution, 1783–1789* (Washington, DC, 1998).

Price, Munro, 'The Dutch Affair and the Fall of the *Ancien Régime*, 1784–1787', *The Historical Journal* 38 (1995), 875–905.

Skocpol, Theda, *States and Social Revolutions: A Comparative Analysis of France, Russia, and China* (Cambridge and New York, 1979), chap. 2.

Sorel, Albert, *L'Europe et la Révolution française*, 8 vols (Paris, 1885–1905).

Stone, Bailey, *The Genesis of the French Revolution: A Global-Historical Interpretation* (Cambridge, 1994).

Whiteman, Jeremy J., *Reform, Revolution and French Global Policy, 1787–1791* (Aldershot, 2003).

PART II

THE COMING
OF REVOLUTION

CHAPTER 8

·····

THE VIEW FROM ABOVE

·····

JOHN HARDMAN

THE main focus of this chapter is on the second administration (25 August 1788–12 July 1789) of Jacques Necker, finance minister and de facto prime minister.[1] His dismissal led to the Parisian insurrection which culminated in the fall of the Bastille on 14 July. Having been finance minister 1776–81, he was recalled to office on 25 August to cope with a political crisis which had led to a partial suspension of cash payments by the royal treasury and the promise to summon the Estates-General of the kingdom for the following year. There has been much speculation, among contemporaries and historians, about the policies of Necker's second administration. But the major questions remain.

What did the government hope to obtain from the Estates-General? Did the government have a programme? Was it favourable to the ambitions of the Third Estate? Did it consider that France already had a constitution or did one have to be created *de novo*? And if the latter, by whom? Why were troops summoned to the Ile-de-France at the end of June and beginning of July 1789? What was the king's personal position on all these questions?

Already I have fallen into the trap of talking about 'the government' as if it were a united entity. In theory the king was meant to take advice formally in council, abiding by majority decisions, concealing his personal position, with only a casting vote. In practice Louis XVI both manipulated and was manipulated in the council, inviting like-minded people to attend, retaking votes, using preparatory committees. And in this existential crisis of the regime there were deep ideological divisions within the ministry which often overrode any formal unifying structures which could be thrown at them. Moreover Louis XVI had always taken extra-ministerial advice as well.

This being the case, any attempt to offer a general account of these events risks distortion. Instead, we shall follow the developing crisis through the analyses of a handful of individuals on whom the king relied for information and advice; and his unsuccessful attempt to effect a synthesis from them. If he failed to synthesize conflicting advice into a coherent policy maybe that was because the deep divisions in his council reflected only too well those in the country. The individuals whose analyses we follow are: Necker himself, Saint-Priest, a ministerial ally, Barentin, the Keeper of the Seals (justice minister), and his main ideological opponent, Laurent de Villedeuil, minister for Paris.

The issues involved in 1789 cannot be understood without knowing what happened in what is sometimes called the 'pre-revolution' of 1787–8, starting with the opening of the Assembly of Notables on 22 February 1787. For, as Malesherbes, ex-minister and still adviser to the king, observed. 'The situation of France in 1787 bears no relationship even to France in 1786, because the Assembly of Notables produced events which have no parallel in our history.' The king had revealed to a stunned Assembly and nation the existence of a massive deficit and the Assembly had rejected his proposals for tackling it. He was now exposed as a broken-backed king, and the price of raising him up was the surrender of his sovereignty.

The finance minister, Calonne had persuaded the king to convoke this semi-representative Assembly to endorse a comprehensive reform programme which would increase revenue by ending the tax exemptions of the nobility and clergy. Provincial Assemblies elected without reference to the traditional organization of society into clergy, nobles, and Third Estate would assess a new land tax which would therefore be free from bias towards the first two orders. This tax would gradually replace the *taille* and *corvée* which fell largely on the peasantry. Internal customs barriers would be abolished and free trade in grain established.

The Notables had no legislative powers but Calonne hoped that their endorsement would overawe the thirteen *parlements* who registered royal legislation and had a track record of resisting reform. But Calonne had been naive in supposing that a body of privileged individuals would support an attack on privilege. However, neither they nor the *parlements* could admit that their opposition was entirely selfish.[2] Thus they concentrated on the fact that the new tax—an inflation-proof percentage one—would free the king from any financial control and turn him into a despot. They managed to change the terms of the debate from a discussion of privilege to one of despotism. Calonne responded by appealing to the people in a widely distributed pamphlet titled *Avertissement*, one meaning of which is 'warning'. It fell flat at the time but was not forgotten.

When, after Calonne's fall, Brienne tried to put a modified version of his measures before the *parlements*, they employed the same argument as the Notables; and they increased the stakes by asserting that they were not competent to register new taxation: only the elected Estates-General, 'regularly convoked', which had not met since 1614, could do that.

Why did the *parlements* demand a meeting of the Estates-General? Prima facie they would eclipse the *parlements* which in the words of one of them 'only exercised a secondary and fiduciary power in the absence of the estates-general.'[3] In one memorandum he gave to the king, Malesherbes offers 'perhaps the clue' to an 'enigma' which has continued to fascinate historians. Some form of National Assembly was inevitable and Malesherbes wanted it to be elected by the provincial Assemblies without distinction of order as Turgot, and possibly Calonne, had advocated.[4]

The last thing, however, that the *Parlement* of Paris wanted was a truly representative National Assembly which would have a greater legitimacy than its own, representing as *it* did, only the king. So when it first called for the Estates-General, it demanded that the estates should be 'regularly convoked'. It did not add, as it famously did after Necker ended its exile in September 1788, 'and that according to the forms of 1614' but that was what it meant.

The public, who as Malesherbes observed were not as learned in political history as were the judiciary and whose 'political schooling'[5] was not as advanced as Vivian Gruder asserts, did not at this stage take in the implications of the *Parlement*'s pronouncement. Or, as Malesherbes delicately put it, there were at least some *parlementaires* who 'have a better understanding of what they are asking than the public but will not explain as frankly what they want'.[6]

The *Parlement* was well aware of the limitations of previous Estates-General both as to real power and genuine representation. The Estates-General had no legislative power. They could raise grievances (*doléances*) which the king could embody or discard in edicts he laid before the *Parlement* for registration after the Estates had gone home when 'the *parlements* . . . re-entered upon all their rights, without any fear of contradiction from the nation's representatives'.[7] And since the king was not obliged to reconvene them in their absence the *parlements* would continue to exercise their role as the only *permanent* representatives of the nation. They saw themselves as *plus royaliste que le roi* because a truly representative Assembly would infringe his sovereignty.

An increasingly bitter dispute between Crown and *parlements* ensued, with the king exiling the *Parlement* of Paris to Troyes in August 1787, arresting members in November, and replacing it in May 1788 with a puppet plenary court to register legislation for the whole country. These measures were accompanied by massive troop deployments. There was considerable opposition in the country but how far it extended beyond the towns which housed a *parlement* and derived a livelihood from them is debated.[8] But the disturbances were sufficient to cause the run on the treasury which led to Necker's recall in late August 1788.

In its dying days, however, the Brienne government had taken two crucial measures. It promised the convocation of the Estates-General for 1789 and, in a decree of 5 July, invited the public to provide the government with information on how the estates had been organized in the past and what modifications the passing of time necessitated. Press censorship was lifted for the occasion. Now the terms of debate changed once more. They did not change back exactly to how Calonne would have presented them: 'despotism' was still an issue. But whereas for the previous eighteen months 'equality' had seemed of lesser importance to 'liberty', now the emphasis was reversed.

The moment of epiphany came on 25 September when the *Parlement*, recalled on Necker's advice, made explicit that 'regularly convoked' meant 'according to the forms pertaining in 1614'. In 1614 the three 'orders', clergy, nobles, and Third Estate or commons each had roughly one-third of the votes and votes were taken 'by order' rather than individually or 'by head'. The privileged orders would have a built-in 2:1 majority. But despite the hysterical language they increasingly adopted, the leaders of the Third Estate always knew they were going to overturn this. And so, deep down, did everyone else.

On his return to office, Necker saw the situation as follows. The king had promised to convoke the Estates-General and there was no going back on this promise: first and foremost because public opinion demanded it; second, because it would have dishonoured the king to renege on a promise; but—equally important—because the *Parlement* had stated that it was no longer competent to authorize taxation or loans. It was, as Necker graphically put it, 'as if Atlas had suddenly declined to shoulder the burden of the world.'[9] And since public opinion now demanded modifications to the 1614 format, they must be made.

Only one of the king's ministers is recorded as having advised him to cancel the convocation of the estates—the hard-line and cynical Laurent de Villedeuil, minister for the King's Household and Paris, proposed that, given the unrest in the country, the meeting of the Estates should be shelved and instead 'an assembly of the nation without distinction of orders' should be summoned.[10] The king would choose the 'deputies' from nobility, clergy and magistrates 'as well as from the third estate'. According to Barentin, this proposal 'made a profound impression on His Majesty'. Necker and Montmorin, the foreign secretary, however, insisted that the question of whether to call the estates could not be reopened.[11]

Public opinion demanded the estates and for Necker public opinion was paramount, at once the basis of his power and his master. That being so, he felt obliged to pursue an asymmetrical approach to policy-making. By reinforcing majority opinion, it might be possible to mask the fundamentally weak position of the king, to manage his decline, after the *révolte nobiliaire*: 'It was vital to the preservation of the majesty of the throne that the limits to the royal prerogative should remain unclear.'[12]

As applied to the situation which confronted him on his return to office, this meant supporting the Third Estate in its claim to have as many deputies to the Estates-General as the nobility and clergy combined ('doubling') and when this had been granted to stipulate that voting in the estates, at least on matters of general interest, should be individually 'by head' rather than by order.

The king also believed that he should follow public opinion, which, he proclaimed as a teenage prince, was 'never wrong'. Twenty years later, in the last year of his reign, he told his counter-revolutionary brothers that, 'you cannot govern a people against its inclinations'.[13] And he added that this was a principle of general application whether one was talking of the Ottoman Empire or the United States of America.

But were these principles of government as axiomatic as Necker and his king believed? Was it not as axiomatic that they would strengthen that tyranny of the majority which soon established itself in France? And was there not already in the reign of Louis XVI an example of the majority—and an almost unanimous one at that—being wrong: the decision taken in 1778 to enter the American War of Independence. Is it not the duty of government to guide rather than follow? Was not the cardinal mistake made by the government in 1789 not to present the Estates-General with a programme; either one adapting the traditions of monarchical government to changed circumstances or one extracted from the *cahiers de doléances*? Malesherbes certainly thought so.

In October 1788, after he had left office, Malesherbes had a long conversation with the king in which he voiced his concerns. He compared Louis' situation with that of Charles I of England, from whom Louis was directly descended. Both kings had come to the throne at the point 'when a dispute arose as to the relative prerogatives of the crown and of the nation'. If Charles I had backed down, he would have lost face with those among whom he had grown up. But on the other hand, he was the weaker party. So, in the period 1640–2, the two years which preceded the Civil War, 'a new concession was extracted from him every minute' until he felt compelled to leave London and raise his standard—in the same way that Louis would be forced to attempt in 1791.

Similarly, Malesherbes warned, 'they will successively strip you of several of your prerogatives. It is up to you, in your Council, to draw up a definitive list of what you will never surrender.' The king had to retain the royal prerogatives essential for a properly functioning monarchy, which Malesherbes defines as an English style, one with the king having complete control over the executive and foreign policy. Malesherbes also urged the king to veto any move by the 1789 estates to entrench organization by order for future meetings of the estates.[14]

THE *RÉSULTAT DU CONSEIL*

Despite his belief in the power of public opinion, Necker was sufficiently rattled by the *Parlement*'s pronouncement to postpone the meeting of the estates from January to May 1789 in order to consult a reconvened Assembly of Notables, primarily on the question of the relative number of seats each order should have in the forthcoming estates.[15] Necker made the same mistake as Calonne: an Assembly of the privileged voted to preserve privilege. Of its six bureaux, only one, and that by a single vote majority, voted to double the representation of the Third Estate. Moreover, the Assembly went beyond its remit to assert that voting by head was unconstitutional.

The king assembled his council to decide what to do. Barentin describes a ferocious battle over fundamental issues, Necker playing on royal resentment against the nobility's opposition to Brienne, who had been Marie-Antoinette's protégé. Barentin claims that Necker and Montmorin had tried to stitch up the decision in a committee with the king before it was submitted to the other ministers for rubber stamping. Louis, however, this time insisted on an elaborate consultation process, presiding over a series of *comités* each lasting 4–5 hours and consisting of Necker, Barentin (as the 'essential minister for the estates'), and a pair of other ministers, each time different: 80–100 hours of preparatory work.[16]

When the full council finally met, Barentin was supported strongly by Laurent de Villedeuil, minister for the Household and Paris, in rejecting doubling and weakly by the 'subtle courtier' the duc de Nivernais, minister without portfolio. The rest followed Necker. The deciding factor may have been the presence of Marie-Antoinette herself which was, according to Saint-Priest, 'without precedent in the history of the monarchy, except in the cases of a queen-regent'. She maintained a strict but minatory silence and 'it was easy to see that she did not disapprove double representation for the third estate'.[17] The queen's views at this stage may surprise many who regard her as a consistent reactionary.

The decision, embodied in the *Résultat du conseil* of 27 December 1788, stipulated 'that the number of deputies for the third estate will be equal to that of the other two orders combined'. Nothing, however, about how votes should be taken. Nevertheless, combined with the memory of the *Avertissement* and the king's struggle against the *révolte nobiliaire*, it was enough for cries of 'the king and the Third Estate' to sound throughout the kingdom. Furthermore, the king promised in the *Résultat* that he would never raise taxation without the consent of the estates.

One disturbing development however was that the king's younger brother, the comte d'Artois, and the Polignac set of courtiers, who had staunchly defended Calonne's egalitarian measures, were leading the opposition to the Third Estate. Artois had signed the Calonne-inspired *Mémoire des princes*, which had attacked the commoners' pretensions. The Polignac set were the king's personal and political friends. From his English exile, Calonne argued there was perfect consistency in his stance. He had not advocated the destruction of a single right, only abuses. He warned prophetically that, 'nothing would be worse than a revolution followed by a counter-revolution'.[18] The trajectory of these men would influence the king's.

There was, according to Barentin, a lively discussion in council over the venue for the estates. Necker favoured Paris because the provinces might be less inclined to honour the government's obligations to (mainly) Parisian creditors. But few if any ministers supported him—even his closest ally, Montmorin, thought that Versailles was preferable and the others thought Versailles was the nearest they could possibly go to the capital. Barentin himself, with support from some (unspecified) ministers favoured Soissons, with the king residing in nearby Compiègne. This proposal, defeated for the present, was to recur at intervals throughout the remaining three years of the monarchy. Louis, who had not made his preferences clear during the discussions, without telling anyone ordered 'Versailles' to be placed in the blank space left in the letters of convocation. Necker could not conceal his anger.[19]

THE ESTATES-GENERAL

The Estates-General were opened on 5 May 1789 by three speeches from the king, from Barentin and from Necker extending respectively to 3, 9 and 58 pages of print.[20] Louis' speech was an anodyne compilation of ministers' drafts. Necker's two-hour speech was mostly taken up with technical details about the financial crisis which he incongruously both claimed to have solved and thought should be the deputies' priority. To get an inkling of developing royal policy we can look at the elaboration of Necker's speech.

A starting point—because it is the only enunciation of a royal programme—is the section in the *Résultat du conseil*, after the regulations for the elections to the estates, in which the king indicates that not only will he not raise any new taxes without the consent of the Estates-General but that he will not prolong existing ones. Meetings of the estates will be 'periodic' and the time lag between sessions will be discussed with the estates. Subject to certain restrictions, *lettres de cachet* will be abolished and freedom of the press established. The king will also 'lend a favourable ear to ... [the estates'] suggestions on how to give these provisions permanence and stability'. But what does that mean?

In his draft speech to the Estates-General, Necker proposed to reinforce these promises with 'legislative authority'. Louis objected and he had obviously raised this matter before, because he writes that he '*still* wants to change the phrase'.[21] Maybe Louis is saying no more than that his word should be taken as his bond. But maybe he is also saying that he does not want these pledges to be given constitutional status. An indication that the king was already being held to his pledges is afforded by the protest on 18 May by the electoral Assembly of Paris at attempts by Villedeuil to prevent the publication of proceedings in the estates.[22]

Louis also picks up Necker on his general views about the legislative process. Necker believed that the Estates-General could make laws—elsewhere he wrote 'with the opening of the estates, legislative power begins'.[23] Not only that but: 'the king, whilst speaking of the new constitution, should pronounce only on the suitability indeed the necessity of maintaining [*sic*] a bicameral legislature. For the rest, he should content himself with the arrangements presented to him' by the estates.[24] This was anathema to the king, but he politely put Necker's error down to sloppy wording: 'At the beginning I have added "at the request" of the estates because ... they cannot make law on their own.'[25] The phrase 'on their own', however, does mark the king's recognition that the 1789 estates, unlike those of 1614, would have a role in the legislative process. But what role?

Barentin thought that the king was overly 'indulgent' in putting Necker's error down to a mere 'slip of the pen'. Rather, Necker had 'slipped in what he did not want to be noticed for the moment, but ammunition he held in reserve to use as occasion served'. Even the king's change to 'at the request of the estates' was too mild for Barentin. Louis should have told Necker roundly that laws were made by the king after the estates' 'doléances, supplications [or] representations'. Barentin also thought it was a mistake for the king to concede (whether by promise or legislation) 'periodic' estates because it 'stripped him of the right of convoking and dissolving them and above all of not assembling them at all'.[26]

This was the heart of the matter but it was temporarily obscured by wrangling in the estates on whether voting should be by order or by head. To pre-empt this decision, the Third Estate wanted the credentials of the deputies to be 'verified' in common. Saint-Priest and the duc de Nivernais, ministers without portfolio, advised that Barentin should 'verify the powers' himself and when the king ruled that it should be left to the estates, Nivernais sulkily ceased attending council.[27] For seven weeks the estates wrangled over these essentially technical issues, albeit ones with political implications. The king offered a futile arbitration service and many suspected that he wanted an excuse to dissolve the estates. In January the king had dissolved the estates of Provence after six days because of disputes between the orders, and on 15 June the future naval minister, Bertrand de Molleville suggested to Montmorin that the king should now do the same. Since (unlike in 1614) the *cahiers* were mostly printed, the king could make his own digest in his council. Molleville proposed that Montmorin bypass Necker by reading his memorandum making the above suggestion in council, but Montmorin said that Necker would stop him 'at the first sentence' and ask for it to be handed over, and the king would support him. Then give it to the king, suggested Molleville. No good: the king would give it to Necker. For such were the hallmarks of the premier that, de facto, Necker was. But not to worry, Necker had a plan of his own.[28]

Two days later, on 17 June, the Third Estate took matters into their own hands by unilaterally declaring themselves the National Assembly and inviting the nobility and clergy to join them. It was, as the king said 'only a phrase'—and one which had been contemplated by Malesherbes and Brienne. In the *cahiers* 'National Assembly' is interchangeable with Estates-General.[29] But Barentin immediately seized the implications. To his legalistic and precedent-bound mind—and, he rightly surmised, to the legalistic minds of the lawyers who dominated the Third Estate—as long as the Estates-General remained the Estates-General, they would never have dared to usurp the legislative power, because previous Estates-General had never exercised it.[30] This act, the assumption of the title National Assembly, was, for Barentin, the primary cause of the series of council meetings which culminated in the famous *séance* of 23 June, when the king, for the first and last time, attempted to intervene in the proceedings of the estates. Barentin wanted the king to annul the third's act, Necker to merely 'pass over' it.

A crisis meeting of the council seems to have been scheduled for noon 17 June at Marly,[31] where the king had retired to mourn the dauphin who had died on 4 June, but if this took place it went unrecorded, and the earliest details we have are of discussion on 19 June, when Necker argued that the main battle was lost and all the king could do was cover his retreat. He should deploy the panoply of a *lit de justice* (which Barentin made no bones about styling it) to command the first two orders to join the third in discussing matters of general interest including the crucial one of the organization of future estates. Hopefully, that would give the king enough credit to make his underlying political surrender conditional on a series of reservations: (1) that the feudal and honorific privileges of the nobility should not be discussed in common; (2) that the king would not accept a single chamber legislature; (3) that the public should not be allowed to attend sessions; and (4) that the king 'reserved to himself the full exercise of the executive power, especially the administration of the army'.[32]

With the support of Montmorin (foreign affairs), La Luzerne (navy), and Saint-Priest (minister without portfolio) Necker carried the day, and the *séance* was fixed for 21 June, 'and the portfolios were already closing'[33] when an official entered and called the king away. 'Only the queen', Montmorin concluded, 'would have permitted herself to interrupt a meeting of the council.' A key difference between the discussions leading to the *Résultat du conseil* and the *séance royale* was that Marie-Antoinette had changed sides, now forming a temporary but fatal alliance with Artois against Necker.[34] On his return the king postponed all decisions to a further council meeting on the evening of 20 June, when the king expected to wrap things up: placards announced the *séance* for 21 June and the National Assembly's hall was closed to prepare for the ceremony. Necker's defeat did not affect the proposed timetable, he himself wanted the hall closed for preparations which it was thought would take sixteen hours.[35]

Outraged, suspicious and feeling insulted (emotions which came easily to them) the National Assembly took refuge in the Tennis Court where it took its famous Oath not to separate until it had given France a new constitution. Suddenly, if inevitably, the dispute between the orders had morphed into an assumption of sovereignty and this was bound to colour the discussions in the council when it resumed its discussions.

Necker was absent from the reconvened council because his sister-in-law was dying but he sent the king a letter advising him to cancel the *séance*—either because he feared his enemies would distort it or, more likely, because the Oath meant it would fail. Instead, he suggested 'a simple letter of invitation [*sic*]' to discuss certain matters in common.

Saint-Priest complained to the king that the reconvened council was stuffed with supernumeraries who had no real right to give official advice, whereas Necker and his allies were the only '*ministres d'état*', that is, the only ones with a seat in the *Conseil d'état*.[36] He specifically mentions the king's brothers Artois and Provence. They had been locked in discussions with the king before the council and he just invited them to come along. But Louis had also summoned the minister without portfolio, the duc de Nivernais, who had provided a draft for the king's opening speech, to travel in from Saint-Omer 'if his health permitted' to join the discussions, and Lambert, a former finance minister was also consulted.[37] Did either attend?

Necker complained about the attendance of the four councillors of state who formed the commission running the estates.[38] The state councillors had been increasingly reactionary or authoritarian since 1787. As technical advisers, councillors could attend and, Barentin elsewhere implies, have a vote.[39] They voted this time. Voting with Necker were Montmorin, La Luzerne, and Saint-Priest; and against him: Artois, Provence, Barentin, Villedeuil, Puységur, and the councillors, at 9:4.[40]

The council meeting went on for hours and had to be reconvened for 21 June. At midnight an exhausted king scribbled a note to Bailly, president of the National Assembly, telling him that the *séance* was postponed until Tuesday 22 June at 10 a.m. He addressed the note to 'Monsieur Bailly, président de l'ordre du tiers-état'. Bailly thought that the use of 'président' instead of 'doyen' indicated a semi-recognition on the king's part of the National Assembly.[41] Another sign of the king's hesitation was that on 22 June he asked Saint-Priest for a written opinion which he knew would favour Necker's proposals. Two further meetings of the council were held at Versailles on the 21st (with Necker and the princes present) and the 22nd, and the *séance* was postponed once more until 23 June.[42]

At the *séance*, the king rejected Necker's model, and the one he adopted was a total inversion, or rather perversion, of it. The peremptory language of the *lit de justice* which Necker intended to be deployed against the nobility, who were used to it, was deployed against the majesty of the nation. The forming of the National Assembly and the Tennis

Court Oath were declared to be 'illegal and unconstitutional'. Deputies were reminded that 'none of your projects, none of your arrangements can have the force of law without my explicit approval'—an extension beyond legislation to internal discipline with which previous kings had not interfered.

Two of Necker's restrictions were retained (feudal privileges not to be discussed in common, no public access) with no mention of the need for more than one chamber, but the nobility and clergy were 'invited' not ordered to join the third for matters of general interest. Note, however, that Necker's own letter of the same day talked only of an 'invitation' and Barentin thought both terms 'should have the same effect'.[43] The king said that the requirement for a two-thirds majority would be acceptable not to say pleasing to him and, crucially, 'matters of general interest' did not include the organization of future estates.

These rulings were followed by a 'declaration of the king's *volontés*'. Here the king reiterated his pledges in the *Résultat du conseil* and by doing so with this slightly despotic word—*volonté*—connoting the king's good pleasure, doubly refuted Necker's contention that legislation was required. The king also added to the list of pledges: consent to loans as well as taxes, annual budgets, phasing out of the *taille*, *corvée*, and so on. He strongly hinted that nobility would in future be conferred by service not ennobling office. Provincial estates were to be made universal and voting was to be by head for everything. The Third Estate was to have half the seats, the nobility three-tenths and the clergy two-tenths. But, as a reaction to the large number of curés elected to the Estates-General, the episcopacy was to be guaranteed a fixed but unspecified number of seats. These provisions would have made the provincial estates more 'aristocratic' but the third would still have dominated provincial proceedings. It has never been satisfactorily explained why the king considered that what was appropriate at the provincial level was not at the national.

There was a lucid definition of the king's view of the future legislative process: 'The king desires that the laws which he promulgates whilst the estates are in session and in accordance with their desires and wishes should not be met with any delay or obstacle in their registration [by the *parlements*] and execution throughout the kingdom.' Finally, the king threatened that if he were abandoned in this 'fine enterprise' he would enact laws on his own derived from the *cahiers de doléances*.

So why did the king reject Necker's version of the *séance*? There was personal pressure from his wife and brother, but the ground had been prepared by Necker's ministerial opponents. Barentin argued that the 'noble revolt' was a myth. Rather, there had been a rising of the whole nation against the 'despotism' of Calonne and Brienne who had distorted the ancient constitution. Naturally, the king did not see it this way but Artois and Calonne had squared that particular circle, making a synthesis of the two positions possible, with the convocation of the estates erasing the stigma of despotism.

This synthesis, however, veered more towards the aristocratic constitutionalism of the noble revolt than Calonne's proposals; and involved almost as great a sacrifice of royal authority as Necker's scheme. But it was a sacrifice to the known, legitimate, and finite rather than the unknown and infinite, for many members of the National Assembly, and not just Siéyès with his dictatorship of constituent power embodied in a single chamber, had already 'become revolutionar[ies]'.[44] And at least the synthesis offered a clear, principled and consistent line for the king to follow, with guaranteed support from what even Necker still considered to be a great weight in the balance—the nobility.

Against this Necker offered fudge. And—what may have been determinant—he did not even guarantee success. For his supporter Saint-Priest confessed to the king his fears that the Third Estate 'in its present mood of exaltation' would reject the king's conditions and even 'complain about … [his] sovereign intervention'. The king would then have to appeal to the country—How?—but that resource was 'as slow as it is uncertain'.[45] Necker made little secret of his intention that his two-chamber solution would develop into a full-blown English-style government—he added that the king subsequently came round to this way of thinking but only when it was too late. However in August the two-chamber solution was decisively—humiliatingly for Necker—rejected by the National Assembly by 849 votes to 89. Finally, did the 'invitation' suggested in his letter to the king amount to much more than the failed conciliation service the king had been providing for the past weeks?

The perversion of his programme placed Necker in a quandary. Within the ministerial conventions obtaining since the 1787 Assembly of Notables he could make conditions under threat of resignation—the king had come to recognize ministers had this right, as in England, now that they too were expected to manage Assemblies. But his resignation before the *séance* would have caused a riot. On the other hand, to attend the *séance* would be to endorse policies of which he disapproved. So he sat in his carriage with the horses harnessed and dithered until his daughter, the feisty Madame de Stael, told him it would be dishonourable to attend.

The *séance royale* was a disaster. The king's orders were ignored. He had in Mirabeau's phrase 'been sold to the magnates'. A crowd surged towards the royal apartments, on this occasion being stopped by the Bodyguards. The king begged Necker not to resign but Necker made the same demand Calonne had made in 1787: to remodel the ministry with like-minded men, that is, to be a prime minister in the English sense.[46] The king refused and Necker, weakly or responsibly, agreed to stay. At any rate, by not attending the *séance*, Necker had signalled that the ministry was divided and this, he believed would win the king sympathy and permit a climb-down.[47]

The ministry being now openly divided, the king followed two parallel or rather contradictory policies, which established his reputation for duplicity. On 27 June Louis ordered the nobility and clergy to join the Third Estate—he had to repeat his order to the nobility. But he signed a series of orders for troop reinforcements. The first, for the Swiss Reinach regiment to leave Soissons and arrive in Paris on the 26th was dated 22 June: in other words, it was the necessary concomitant of the hard-line version of the *séance royale*. Saint-Priest deduced the link or had already got wind of the actuality. For also on 22 June he told the king that there was no money in the treasury to pay for military sanctions.

We have the orders given to the troops: their destination and, in some instances, what they were to do when they reached it. Some of these were published by P. Caron in 1906 and the material at Vincennes has been used by J. Godechot in *The Taking of the Bastille*.[48] Both authors, however, draw perverse conclusions from their own evidence and stick to the cliché that the king was planning a *coup d'état*. How, for example, can they ignore the implications of the following purely defensive order from Broglie, the king's generalissimo to Besenval, his field commander in Paris dated 1 July:

> The king consents that you assemble all the forces on which you can rely to safeguard the Royal Treasury and the Discount Bank and … at a time when we are unfortunately not in a position to look to everything, that you confine yourself to defending these two positions. I shall authorize the marquis d'Autichamp to remain in his command at Sevres and then, if it becomes necessary, to bring up the Salis regiment *as reinforcements to protect Versailles, falling back on the palace if necessary.*[49]

This military order—one of many we have—encapsulates the king's two concerns: law and order in Paris and the defence of Versailles. The link between the two would be demonstrated on 5 October. The king's principal agents in Paris, directly responsible to Laurent de Villedeuil, as minister for Paris, were the lieutenant-general of police, Thiroux de Crosne, and the *prévôt des marchands* (mayor) de Flesselles. But their jurisdiction was steadily being invaded by the central committee of the electors of Paris, which continued to meet after the deputies to the estates had been chosen, despite Villedeuil's belief that this was unconstitutional.[50]

On 25 June some radical assertions were made in the electors' committee: that the king had recognized that they retained 'an active power', that the 'pretended municipality' nominated by the king should only continue their functions 'provisionally' until elections for successors had been held, that the king was only 'the sovereign implementer of the general will' and that a 'bourgeois guard' instead of royal troops should maintain order in Paris.[51] On 13 July Flesselles told the central committee that 'the only authority he desired to exercise was that which had been conferred by the inhabitants of the Capital'.[52]

Meanwhile, Crosne ignored an order on 24 June from Villedeuil to stop the circulation of the National Assembly's resolutions of 17 and 20 June. He also could or would do nothing to prevent the circulation of a 'scandalous pamphlet', *Premier coup de Vêpres*, which had been drawn to the minister's attention by 'une personne auguste'—the conventional way ministers referred to the queen.[53] With his position untenable, Crosne handed in his resignation to the king, was thanked by the electors' committee, and instructed by them to continue his functions in so far as they related to food provisioning.[54]

The king's second concern was the defence of Versailles—not so much from a threat from Paris but from insurrection in the town itself.[55] The king was also worried about the safety of the smaller royal châteaux in the Ile-de-France. Godechot goes into some detail about where the troops were to be placed. Three cavalry regiments were to be stationed at La Muette; two regiments of dragoons at Rambouillet; and a further cavalry regiment at Marly. These orders were given between 22 and 28 June. But then 'on 29 and 30 June, fresh orders were sent, proving that the king's plans were taking shape'. The troops were to get 'as close as possible to Paris'. The regiment of Nassau-Infanterie was to speed up its progress and go to Choisy-le-roi instead of Charenton whilst the Royal-Allemand was also to go to Choisy. Finally, on 7 July Lauzun's hussars were summoned from Verdun to Marly. What did all these places have in common: La Muette, Rambouillet, Marly, and Choisy? Why does Godechot neglect to say that they were all royal châteaux? The troops were there to prevent their being sacked.[56]

By July, everyone knew that troops were being assembled; but the continued presence of Necker in the ministry guaranteed that they would not be used. There was a balance of inertia within the ministry. Villedeuil and probably Barentin did not know that Breteuil, who replaced Necker on 12 July, was going to be appointed.[57] Breteuil himself had said recently that he did not want to return to power unless Necker was dismissed through having lost public support.[58] Broglie was opposed to Necker's dismissal, 'or at the very least demanded prior notification'.[59] Both Broglie and Breteuil wanted to keep Necker in place until the troop concentrations were complete.

With ineffable dramatic irony National Assembly member and inventor, Dr Guillotin, told the Parisian electoral assembly on 11 July that 'all was quiet at Versailles, that M. Necker was thought to be more firmly established in the king's confidence than ever, and that there would not be a *séance royale* on Monday, the day after tomorrow, as had been rumoured'.[60]

The following day Necker was dismissed, together with his ministerial supporters, and this was the trigger for the rising symbolized by the storming of the Bastille. It was—and is—commonly believed that the administration which succeeded Necker's, headed by the baron de Breteuil, planned to dissolve the National Assembly, arrest its leaders by *lettres de cachet* and subdue Paris by force of arms. Bailly thought that the plan was hold another *séance royale* on 15 July (others thought the 13th) where the programme of 23 June would be re-presented. If the Assembly, even surrounded by troops, still refused to recognize it, it would be dissolved and the edicts registered by a *parlement* which had learned its lesson.[61]

Munro Price considers that Breteuil was prepared for an offensive against Paris but that Broglie, whose appointment on 27 June preceded his own and was independent of it, refused to countenance any offensive action. Breteuil, however, also sought to negotiate with the Assembly in general and in particular the duc d'Orléans, with whom he had family connections.[62] The programme of the *séance royale* remained important to Laurent de Villedeuil and Barentin also who tried to promulgate the provisions of the *séance* in the provinces even after the king had ordered the nobility and clergy to sit with the Third Estate. But they were scared.[63]

Royal authority in Paris, which had been crumbling for some weeks, finally collapsed on 14 July. On the night of 15/16 July there was a crisis meeting of the council. Flight to Metz was discussed, but Broglie advised the king, 'I can certainly get you to Metz, but what do we do when we get there?' Louis' brother Provence begged him to stay put; Artois (probably) to go to the Assembly to announce he was withdrawing the troops.[64] Barentin told the historiographer royal, 'I believe we must have recourse to another dynasty'.[65] The implications of this are manifold but Barentin must have thought that Louis was so compromised that the National Assembly would never give him adequate powers to govern the country, let alone uphold the constitution. He and Broglie fled, the one to Brussels, the other to Metz. Others—including Breteuil and Artois—shortly followed.

The king availed himself of a loophole in his note dismissing Necker—'I wrote that when things had calmed down I would give proof of my sentiments towards you'—to recall him on 16 July.[66] But things had not 'calmed down' and the fourteen months of his third ministry saw the king lose all the powers, legislative and executive, which Necker had previously hoped to salvage.

CONCLUSION

The general pattern of royal policy over the period considered is clear. The king moved from supporting the Third Estate to opposing it. Some third deputies even believed he intended to murder them. Whether this induced a clinical trauma in them, as Shapiro has argued, or just a shock, as I have, the result was the same: a total collapse of trust.[67] This meant that the National Assembly stripped the king not just of legislative but of most of his executive power also, including control over the army and foreign policy— the only thing for which he had been trained.

But the deeper question is to explain the king's volte-face. The facile answer is to say that he spent all his time with nobles. That is factually wrong—he spent most of his time with administrators—and conceptually so: after Louis XIV kings were not *primus inter pares*, or *pluribus impar*, they were *sui generis*. To understand the king's stance, we must consider that of the Third Estate.

One does not have to go as far as Gruder in asserting that France was already revolutionary in 1787 to dissent from Tackett's view that they only started 'becoming' revolutionaries from mid-June.[68] And whilst endorsing Tackett's (and Malesherbes') view that Assemblies develop an emulative *esprit de corps* making the group more radical than the individual, the devotion of the third deputies to the king was entirely sentimental and contingent on his implementing their will which they took to be the general. Whether they were influenced by the Enlightenment or de-sacralization is beside the point: at issue was a practical seizure of power.[69] The duc de Luxembourg, doyen of the nobility in the estates, said that the *Résultat du conseil* granted 'all that the estates-general on bended knees could have asked for'. That may have been true of his order, but not of the Third Estate which had no intention of bending its knee (collective or individual) to anyone.

Necker thought he could ride the Revolutionary tiger or at least placate it with tasty morsels of the royal authority, forgetting that *l'appétit vient en mangeant*. But a group of advisers, ministerial (Barentin, Villedeuil) and extra or ex-ministerial (Artois, Calonne) thought no compromise was possible and that the old constitution must be preserved intact. Here at least was a chance: a coherent ideological position with military backing. The historian of the royal army, S. F. Scott, considered that the army could and should have been used against the Parisian insurrection and the failure to do so irreparably demoralized it.[70] But the military option required a courage and ruthlessness which the king conspicuously lacked and an intelligence equally lacking in his brother, Artois. Nor did it help to have a septuagenarian generalissimo who did not don uniform. A minister had told Louis in 1787 that he 'would have to arm 100,000 men' to 'crush' the *parlements*, and one is entitled to ask whether the 100,000 envisaged in 1789 have been enough to crush the National Assembly and Paris; or the 100,000 *livres* of paper money apparently printed enough to pay them?[71]

So Louis vacillated between the two positions. It was hard, even for insiders, to know what was going on. Necker himself wrote, 'there were secrets within secrets and I think that the king himself was not a party to all of them' and added that perhaps the plan was to 'spring measures on the king they hadn't dared to mention'.[72]

In the end, however, the king decided. When Louis told the Assembly that 'the orders which have been given to the troops' were no cause for concern, Bailly expostulated, '"Which have been given", he does not say, "which I have given"; so it is not him … we see that the Council and the King are not the same thing'.[73] But Bailly was wrong: the council had not given the orders, and the king had. The council did not dismiss Necker: the appointment and dismissal of ministers was the king's prerogative, one of the few he retained to the end.

Barentin had to urge Louis ('at stake is your reputation and the fate of France') to convene an extraordinary session of the council where, inter alia, Villedeuil and Broglie could report on the state of Paris,[74] whilst regular meetings to run the country seem not to have been held as regularly as before the crisis.

In the end, we cannot better the analysis of the decision-making process made by an acute observer at the beginning of the reign: 'Louis XVI … takes … information from every hand and the decisions come from his person.'[75] Louis left no record of his thinking at this time, beyond a peevish assertion of the 'sacrifices' he claimed he was making voluntarily. So we cannot look inside his mind, only at the 'information' that was impinging on it.

Notes

1. For a more sympathetic treatment of Necker, see R. Harris, *Necker and the Revolution of 1789* (Lanham, 1986).
2. For a different view see V. Gruder, *The Notables and the Nation; the political schooling of the French 1787–1788* (Cambridge, MA and London, 2007).
3. Speech in the Assembly of Notables by Le Blanc de Castillon, Hardman, J., *Overture to Revolution, the 1787 Assembly of Notables and the Crisis of France's old regime* (Oxford and New York, 2010), 151–2.
4. Hardman, *Overture to Revolution*, 127
5. Cf. the sub-title of Gruder, *Notables and the Nation*.
6. V. André (ed.), *Malesherbes à Louis XVI ou les Avertissements de Cassandra, Mémoires inédits 1787–1788* (Paris, 2010), 174.

7. Malesherbes, *Mémoires*, 177.

8. See for example P. Jones, *Reform and Revolution in France: the Politics of Transition 1774–1791* (Cambridge, 1995), 156.

9. J. Necker, *De la Révolution française*, 4 vols (Paris 1797), I, 152.

10. Hardman, *Overture*, 123.

11. *Mémoire autographe de M. de Barentin ... sur les derniers conseils de Louis XVI* ed. M. Champion (Paris, 1844), 68.

12. Necker, *Révolution française*, I, 87.

13. Louis XVI to his brothers, 25 September 1791, Vienna State Archives, Familien Acten 88, dossier 3, fos. 108–25.

14. Extract from Véri's diary, published by duc de Castries in *Revue de Paris*, November 1953, 84–6.

15. Barentin, *Mémoire*, 48.

16. Barentin, *Mémoire*, 87 ff.

17. Saint-Priest, comte de, *Mémoires*, 2 vols, ed. baron de Barante (Paris, 1929), I, 216.

18. Calonne, C.-A. de, *Lettre au Roi*, London, 1789, 54.

19. Barentin, *Mémoire*, 166–8.

20. [*Discours d'ouverture des Etats-généraux*], Grenoble [1789]; the king's speech, 1–3; Barentin's 4–12 and Necker's 13–71 plus appendices.

21. Louis XVI to Necker, *c.*1 May 1789, in J. Hardman (ed.), *The French Revolution Sourcebook* (London and New York, 1999), 91.

22. Electeurs de Paris, 125.

23. Necker, *Révolution*, I, 86.

24. *Sur l'Administration de M.Necker par lui-meme*, in *Oeuvres*, Paris, 1821, VI, 91.

25. *Revolution Sourcebook*, 91.

26. Barentin, *Mémoire*, 146–7.

27. Saint-Priest, *Mémoires*, I, 220–1.

28. Bertrand de Molleville, *Mémoires*, 2 vols (Paris, 1816), I, 47–52.

29. Blackman, R., 'What's in a name? Possible Names for a Legislative Body and the Birth of National Sovereignty during the French Revolution, 15–16 June 1789', *French History* 21 (2007), 24–45, 37–8.

30. Barentin, *Mémoire*, 99.

31. Barentin, *Bulletins*, 34.

32. Necker, *Révolution*, 200.

33. Saint-Priest's recollection was that the queen intervened when the meeting was 'just beginning', *Mémoires*, I, 223.

34. Mercy to Joseph II, 4 July 1789 in *Correspondance secrète du comte de Mercy-Argenteau avec l'empereur Joseph II et le prince de Kaunitz*, 2 vols, ed. Arneth et Flammermont (Paris, 1889–91), II, 255.

35. Bailly, *Mémoires*, 183.

36. This was misleading since the council involved was that of dépêches to discuss home policy and no one challenged the relevance of Barentin's or Villedeuil's presence.

37. Barentin, *Lettres et bulletins à Louis XVI*, ed. A. Aulard (Paris, 1915), 34 (16 June).

38. Vidaud de la Tour, la Michodière, La Galaisière and d'Ormesson.

39. Barentin, *Mémoires*, 51.

40. Saint-Priest, Mémoires, I, 225–6; one wonders whether the liberal d'Ormesson, ex-finance minister would have been in the majority.

41. The hybrid phrase 'l'Assemblée des états-généraux' was used by the king, Bailly and Mirabeau among others for some weeks.

42. The final draft, by the *conseiller d'état* Vidaud de la Tour, was given by Barentin to the king on 22 June, Barentin, *Bulletins*, 41–2.

43. Barentin, *Bulletins*, 42.

44. Cf. Timothy Tackett, *Becoming A Revolutionary: The Deputies of the French National Assembly and the Emergence of a Revolutionary Political Culture (1789–1790)* (Princeton, 1996).

45. Saint-Priest to the king, undated but 22 June, *Revolution Sourcebook*, 98–100.

46. For example Saint-Priest was to replace Villedeuil, Saint-Priest, *Mémoires*, I, 229.

47. Necker, *Révolution*, I, 225.

48. P. Caron, 'La tentative de contre-revolution de juin-juillet 1789', *Revue d'histoire moderne et contemporaine*, vol. 8 (1906–7), 5–34 and 649–78; J. Godechot, *The Taking of the Bastille: July 14th, 1789*, trans. J. Stewart (London, 1970).

49. Caron, 'La tentative de contre-revolution', 25, my italics. Besenval did, however, order the governor of the Bastille to resist 'to the last man', *Électeurs de Paris*, 394. Intercepted note dated 14 July.

50. Bailly, *Mémoires*, I, 235.

51. *Procès-Verbal des séances et déliberations de l'Assemblée-générale des Électeurs de Paris*, Paris, 1790, 152–4.

52. *Électeurs de Paris*, 186.

53. J. Peuchet, *Mémoires tirées des archives de la police de Paris*, 6 vols (Paris, 1828), III, 182.

54. *Électeurs de Paris*, 393–4.

55. Bailly, *Mémoires*, I, 312.

56. J. Godechot, *Bastille*, 178–81.

57. Bailly *Mémoires*, I, 309–10.

58. Bailly *Mémoires*, I, 325.

59. Bailly, *Mémoires*, I, 326–7, on Broglie's stance, see M. Price, *The Fall of the French Monarchy: Louis XVI, Marie-Antoinette and the baron de Breteuil* (Basingstoke and Oxford, 2002), 89–91.

60. *Électeurs de Paris*, 171.

61. Bailly, *Mémoires*, I, 391–2.

62. Price, *Fall*, 91; M. Price, 'The "Ministry of the Hundred Hours": A Reappraisal', *French History* 4:3 (1990), 317–39.

63. On 1 July Barentin insisted it was still in force, *Bulletins*, 50.

64. Journal de Fersen, in R. M. Klinkowstom, *Le comte de Fersen et la cour de France* (Paris, 1877–78), 2 vols, II, 6; Bailly, I, 393–4.

65. J. N. Moreau, *Mes souvenirs* (Paris, 1898–1901), 2 vols, II, 439–41.

66. A.N. C 185 (123) 1.

67. B. Shapiro, *Traumatic Politics, the Deputies and the King in the Early French Revolution, PA, 2009, passim*. J. Hardman, *Louis XVI* (New Haven and London, 1993), especially 161.

68. Gruder, V. *The Notables and the Nation*.

69. Tackett, *Becoming*, 304–7.

70. S. F. Scott, *The Response of the Royal Army to the French Revolution . . . 1787–1793* (Oxford, 1973).

71. Castries, *Journal*, Archives de la Marine Ms 182/7964 1–2, II, 346–7. Bailly, *Mémoires*, I, 392,

72. Necker, *Révolution*, II, 2.

73. Bailly, *Mémoires*, I, 367–8.
74. Barentin, *Bulletins*, 52 and 56.
75. Abbé de Véri, *Journal 1774–1780*, 2 vols, ed. J. de Witte (Paris, 1928–30), I, 111.

Selected Reading

Caiani, A., *Louis XVI and the French Revolution 1789–1792* (Cambridge, 2012).

Hardman, J., *Louis XVI* (New Haven and London, 1993).

Hardman, J., *Overture to Revolution: the 1787 Assembly of Notables and the Crisis of France's Old Regime* (Oxford and New York, 2010).

Harris, R., *Necker and the Revolution of 1789* (Lanham, 1986).

Price, M., *The Fall of the French Monarchy: Louis XVI, Marie-Antoinette and the baron de Breteuil* (Basingstoke and Oxford, 2002).

Shapiro, B., *Traumatic Politics, the Deputies and the King in the Early French Revolution* (Pennsylvania, 2009).

CHAPTER 9

·····························

THE VIEW FROM BELOW

The 1789 cahiers de doléances

·····························

PIERRE-YVES BEAUREPAIRE

'To Reopen a Much-Desired Direct Communication between His Faithful Peoples and their King'[1]

'His Majesty [having] desired that, from the extremities of his kingdom and the most obscure dwellings, all should be brought together to transmit to him their wishes and demands', the electoral regulation of 24 January 1789 fixed the conditions of election of the deputies to the Estates-General and the drafting of the *cahiers de doléances*. By its sheer size, this consultation and opportunity for expression constituted a major event. From the base of an electoral pyramid, with primary Assemblies in each country parish, and in each urban parish or artisan and mercantile guild, 'all the inhabitants [male, though widows were admitted as heads of household, and female trades wrote their own *cahiers*] making up the Third Estate, born or naturalised French, aged at least twenty-five, of stable residence, and included on the tax-rolls' were convoked.[2] Members of the clergy and the nobility were convoked to a higher level, that of the *bailliages*. As François Furet notes, this collective expression took place in an old-regime framework. The *cahiers de doléances* are not intended to express 'a common political wish based on the interests or the will of individuals, but to express and transmit, from low to high, and to the highest, the necessarily homogeneous requests of the corporate bodies of the kingdom'.[3]

The drafting of the *cahiers* constituted a moment of collective expression from the different electoral units under consideration. If few parishes failed to seize the opportunity to be heard, nonetheless, participation was highly variable even within regions, from one parish to another. Thus in the future Nord *département*, against an average participation of 42 per cent noted by Philippe Marchand, wide variations appear in the minutes of the Assemblies: from 9.7 per cent to 100 per cent. In the Vexin (Île-de-France) studied by Jacques Dupâquier, participation averaged 22.5 per cent.[4] But in all these cases, as Ran Halévi observes, 'despite its extreme precision, the procedure Necker had put in place ignored the fundamental notions of modern electoral analysis: prior registration, electoral registers, calculation of voting proportions, in short all that could assist the creation of ordered and comparable statistics'.[5] Moreover, at the end of many lists of voters' signatures there was frequently a very vague mention of those who did not know how to sign, who may have been at such events in widely varying numbers. Thus Halévi concludes: 'as is evident, we shall never know the number of Frenchmen who took part in this consultation.'

Overall, the context in which this collective consultation took place, that of the society of the old regime, a society of orders, must be recalled. It was logical in these conditions that secretaries did not gather the names of the most humble. It was not a democratic consultation. Testimony of tensions within the Third-Estate Assemblies, from which a 'fourth estate' sometimes felt excluded, nonetheless exists, and can be seen in public demonstrations of distrust, drafting of separate *cahiers*, or the desire to have the difference of views recorded in the official minutes. At Varengeville, in the *bailliage* of Rouen, one can read that 'all the poor inhabitants have attended the Assembly and given their names; all in good accord have named their deputies; but seeing in the *cahier* too little of the misery of their estate, have refused to sign, crying out that ordinary bread cost 3 sols 6 deniers a pound'.[6] At Elliant, in the *sénéchaussée* of Concarneau, the under-representation of the rural versus the urban population was denounced: 'the representatives of the order of the Third at the Estates [of Brittany] are always found amongst the towns and never in the countryside, which leads to the oppression of the peasant and the cultivator, whose needs are never known because he is never consulted.'[7]

At every level, the *major et sanior pars*, the most elevated part of the population, was if not the only one to express itself, then the one which authenticated the act of collective speech represented by the written form of the *cahier*, in signing the minutes of the Assembly. This did not mean that this group had captured the exclusive expression of grievances. Examples are known of dissident *cahiers* written by inhabitants who refused to endorse a text that did not meet their expectations. As always in writing of the *cahiers*, we must take account of the vast spectrum of local situations and particular configurations which produced very different results. Paul Bois has rightly insisted on the prudence with which any given example must be treated, and movement towards generalization is thus perilous.[8] If, for example, Georges Lefebvre has shown for the villages of the Orléanais that day-labourers did not appear on the registers of the primary Assemblies, Régine Robin notes in Burgundy a contrary case where not only were they present, but insisted on being heard and having their grievances recorded.[9]

A Vast Historiographical Output

This consultation is the origin of the 45,000 texts which, for Alexis de Tocqueville, 'will remain as the final testament of the old French society, the supreme expression of its desires, the authentic manifestation of its last wishes', and which is thus 'a document unique in history'.[10] At the level of the *bailliage* and *sénéchaussée* Assemblies, it is thought some 650 *cahiers* were drafted, of which 531 remain today: 165 from the clergy, the same number from the nobility, and 201 from the Third Estate. They were very quickly the object of editorial attentions, for in 1789 there appeared in Paris a three-volume collection by 'a society of men of letters', the *Résumé Général ou Extrait des Cahiers de Pouvoirs, Instructions, Demandes et Doléances, remis par les divers Bailliages, Sénéchaussées et pays d'Etats du Royaume, à leurs Députés à l'Assemblée des États Généraux ouverts à Versailles le 4 mai 1789*. Since Tocqueville, the *cahiers* have not ceased to interest historians, to the point where Roger Chartier observed, some thirty years ago, that 'few documentary collections have been more interrogated than the *cahiers*'.[11]

There is thus a particularly rich field of historiographical debate around the *cahiers*. From quantitative to cultural approaches, via the borrowing of linguistic methods, it could be said that the study of the *cahiers* has followed every turn of twentieth-century historiographical evolution. Since Tocqueville, two questions have, nevertheless, broadly served to orient exploration of this vast documentary deposit: how far have the ideas and vocabulary of Enlightenment entered and shaped the grievances of the French and their expression? In what ways are these grievances a herald of the Revolution? Evidently, these questions have sometimes led into teleological readings of events. Thus while Jacques Godechot considers that 'the preparation of elections for the Estates-General and the drafting of the *cahiers de doléances* produced across all of France an extraordinary tremor', that tremor may be analysed as a forerunner of the earthquake of summer 1789.[12] Tocqueville went even further, seeing in the *cahiers* the systematic calling into question of the old order: 'I saw with a sort of terror that what was demanded was the simultaneous and systematic abolition of all the laws and all the customs currently exercised across the country'.[13] This was for him the fruit at the same time of the 'revolutionary education of the people' at work since the Frondeur generation of the seventeenth century, and the convergence between noble and bourgeois grievances: 'Fundamentally, all the men of the ranks above the people resembled each other, they had the same ideas, the same habits, the same tastes, the same pleasures, read the same books, spoke the same language. They no longer differed amongst themselves in anything except their rights.'[14] Tocqueville did not merely offer a reading and a strong interpretation of the *cahiers*, he also had the merit of placing the accent upon their major importance as a historical source, and to have confronted that documentary ocean himself.[15]

Even when questioned, the reference to Tocqueville remains constant in works on the *cahiers* down to the present day. The preface of the major study by Gilbert Shapiro and John Markoff, *Revolutionary Demands*, places their research (which took more than thirty years) under Tocqueville's auspices: 'this work began in the mid-1950s when Shapiro, preparing a course on social change at Oberlin College, first read Alexis de Tocqueville's *Old Regime and the French Revolution*'.[16] Such references are ever-present in works stretching from François Furet to Philippe Grateau, via George V. Taylor and Roger Chartier, and up to Charles Walton who used it to begin his 2006 article on press freedom as depicted in the *cahiers*. This point is worth noting because Tocqueville's questions and perspectives continue to weigh on research in this area, even when undertaken quantitatively. The preface of *Revolutionary Demands* thus continues: 'The importance and the fascination of the historical events, and the sophistication of Tocqueville's theoretical assumptions led him [Gilbert Shapiro] to deliver a paper on Tocqueville as sociologist at the plenary session on the occasion of the centennial of Tocqueville's death held by the Eastern Sociological Society. Tocqueville's heavy reliance on the *cahiers de doléances* posed a challenge: could such hypotheses as Tocqueville advanced be tested more rigorously using contemporary methods of content analysis?'[17]

More than fifty years after Tocqueville's work, and from the other end of the political spectrum, Jean Jaurès opted in his *Histoire socialiste de la Révolution française* for a lyrical approach in the mould of Jules Michelet: 'Yet I know of nothing more complete, more solid, more substantial than these *cahiers* of the Third Estate which are a supreme expression of French literature of the eighteenth century, and if I may say, the greatest national literature possessed by any people.'[18] This enthusiasm aroused by this moment of self-expression by France from below—not only the privileged—is another characteristic of the attractions that the *cahiers* exert over researchers: the sense that in *1789, the French Speak Out*—to echo the title of a famous work by Pierre Goubert and Michel Denis.

The classic debate between George V. Taylor and Roger Chartier is itself characteristic of selective readings of the *cahiers* for the study of what is today called 'the fabrication of opinion'. For Taylor, the Third Estate wished above all to obtain concrete advances, while showing itself respectful of the hierarchical structures of the old regime, and with little concern for Enlightenment: 'Our results indicate that Enlightenment political ideas were quantitatively insignificant in most sectors of French opinion before the Estates General met on May 5.'[19] Taylor centred his study on the *cahiers* of the primary Assemblies. Against this, Chartier focused on the *cahiers* of the higher *bailliage* and *sénéchaussée* level, and generally followed Tocqueville in underlining the significance of Enlightenment discourse and vocabulary at this echelon of elaboration of grievances. Addressing the question of press freedom, Charles Walton took the view that the *cahiers* had to be reread beyond this opposition: 'Do we still need to choose one or other of these interpretations? This debate is outmoded by an analysis of the demands for press freedom that reveal simultaneously influences of the Enlightenment (abolition of pre-publication censorship) and conservative principles of the old regime (maintenance of repressive laws against abuses).'[20]

In the work drawn from his doctorate, one of the most recent texts devoted to the *cahiers*, Philippe Grateau proposed 'a cultural rereading' of them, based on a corpus of

6,581 examples. Choosing to combine different levels of analysis, he first selected two test-issues at a national level: schooling and health. Then he drew on a major sample of 1,032 *cahiers* across seven provinces (Brittany, Champagne, Île-de-France, Languedoc, Normandy, Quercy, Roussillon) allowing him to take into account the diversity of France in 1789. Finally, he explored the local level, as 'only this local level reveals evidence of falsehoods, by omission or exaggeration'. Grateau insisted rightly on the necessity of treating each *cahier* in the context of its production.[21] From this perspective, they are all different and must be reread in the environment of their creation and immediate reception. In reviewing Grateau's book, Jean-Luc Chappey, nonetheless, reproached his 'acerbic judgments on the reforming thought of the social elites (always denigrated for not being hungry!) and the *philosophes* of the eighteenth century (vilified throughout the work under the label of "mental incendiaries"!).' While Chappey laments that Grateau 'gives way to an anti-intellectualism all the more regrettable for being entirely gratuitous', this should not obscure the breadth of the research or its importance for the exploration of France from below.[22] Thus we can see that if the political fever of the 1989 Bicentenary has subsided, ideological postures have yet to disappear from academic works, and must be taken account of by their readers.

Writing the *Cahiers*: Circulation of Model *Cahiers*, Selective Appropriation and Adaptation

The set of model grievances and demands known as the *Instruction donnée par SAS Monseigneur le duc d'Orléans, a ses représentans aux bailliages: suivie de délibérations à prendre dans les Assemblées* is well known. The role played by writers such as its author Choderlos de Laclos—with whom the abbé Sieyès is generally also associated—very quickly drew attention, and was fuel for conspiracy theories about the origin of the Revolution of 1789. More seriously, the *Instruction*, of which perhaps 100,000 were printed, posed, along with the other models that achieved lesser circulation, a recurrent question to historians: that of the general authenticity of the *cahiers*. Nobody now argues, with Hippolyte Taine of the nineteenth century, that the *cahiers* were generally fabricated on the basis of such models, and thus 'inauthentic'. However, the issue does arise in other forms. The editing, distribution, reception, and selective appropriation of such prefabricated demands raises the question of the 'fabrication of opinion' in the spring of 1789.

The circulation of model *cahiers* is confirmed by the historical record, which even permits the reconstitution from partial survivals of models that no longer exist in their complete form. We can also note that, in the case of the duc d'Orléans' territories, Beatrice Hyslop has been able to identify twenty-six official representatives of the duke in the local Assemblies of the nobility, among whom four were elected to the

Estates-General. Yet all this must be addressed carefully: circulation of information does not mean passive reception and unreserved adoption. Not only is it the case that the specific grievances in the *Instruction* were far from being systematically taken up in the *cahiers*, but sometimes they totally failed to make an impact—notably in the demand for divorce—and overall their partial adoption did not swing the profile of *cahiers* in these areas significantly away from the general national picture.[23]

Moreover, the emergence of model *cahiers* is not merely part of the national context and its stakes. The *cahiers* are first and foremost the expression of France from below, not merely in purely social terms, but also in terms of geographically anchored expectations, concerns and aspirations. Where local contexts were especially tense, political excitement transformed the drafting and adoption of the *cahiers* into a significant gamble, with victory over public opinion at stake. This local situation could thus stimulate the circulation of models. Philippe Grateau notes one printed patriot model, *Les Charges d'un bon citoyen de campagne*, widely distributed in the *sénéchaussée* of Rennes and which one parish, Plestan in the current *département* of Côtes d'Armor, was content simply to submit as representing its own grievances.[24] The success of this model was incontestable, as some 40 per cent of *cahiers* from the area show its direct or indirect inspiration. A good model had to present itself as a canvas offering multiple possibilities, for both substantial borrowings, and for adaptation to local, urban or rural situations.

In the *bailliage* of Château-du-Loir (Sarthe), Paul Bois found evidence for the circulation of three model *cahiers*. Two of these left no trace in the parish *cahiers*, while one—the most moderate—was used by ten of the thirty-nine *cahiers* in the sample. Of these ten, only one is a copy of the model, all the others rejected at least one article. In total, of the 116 articles across the ten *cahiers* inspired by this model, forty-eight are drawn from it. One can thus deduce that, even when borrowing from a model is evident, it did not stop villagers from performing an evaluation and selection, and writing for themselves what they thought should be added. Certainly, Paul Bois himself has recognized that in other *bailliages*, such as those of Angers and Orléans, influence—but the study of cultural appropriation has shown how delicately this term should be used—appears to be greater on local *cahiers*. One can, however, observe movements in the other direction, concerning the practical stakes of rural life, on which villagers were more knowledgeable than townsfolk (for example, shortage of shade trees lining the roads). Noted with precision in village *cahiers*, such things are sometimes taken up in those of the towns.[25]

More broadly, research into the phenomena of appropriation and cultural circulation has renewed the study of the *cahiers*. While there is no doubt of the circulation of models, and lawyers and village worthies clearly played an important role in the primary Assemblies of rural parishes, the peasantry was not passive. In the first place, collective resistance to attacks on villagers' communal property and rights in the decades before 1789 had a role in raising the consciousness of communities in defence of their interests, notably through legal action: they used notaries to record their complaints, or even attempted to play off royal justice against seigneurial courts.[26] Physical resistance, the intensity of which has been demonstrated in the major work of Jean Nicolas on *La rébellion française*, readied the countryside to express not only their grievances but also their demands.[27] In the Rennes region, where both seigneurial justice and peasant opposition to it were strongly active, incidents were common. Sometimes a seigneurial official might attempt to gather an electoral Assembly at the local château, seeking to draft a *cahier* favourable to the conservation of his master's rights. The peasants refused to take part and met elsewhere. Naturally, the official then rejected that Assembly, refusing to sign its records. A more general question can be asked about the chairing of Assemblies by seigneurial officials. Did it reinforce peasant hostility towards seigneurial rights and 'feudalism' or, on the contrary, did it pressurize discussion into moderating the expression of grievances? On the evidence of Georges Lefebvre's study of the *bailliage* of Orléans, such a presiding officer seems not to have dissuaded those present from protesting against the weight of seigneurial rights. It is also common to see Assemblies avoid designating their presiding officer as their delegate to the higher-level Assembly.[28]

GRIEVANCES EXPRESSED IN 1789, AND THE LANGUAGE USED TO CONVEY THEM

Working on the *bailliage* of Semur-en-Auxois, Régine Robin's pioneering study showed that the juridical language of the old regime was more present in the *cahiers* than the lexicon of Enlightenment, owing to the important role played by men of the law, the *robins*, in their drafting. Her conclusion was thus that 'the vocabulary of the *cahiers* remains the prisoner of the ideological and conceptual field of the Old Regime'.[29] Philippe Grateau notes, however, that the absence of the term 'equality' does not signify an absence of aspiration to that ideal, and the contrary may be true. The demand for equality in matters of taxation was omnipresent. An analysis is required not just of the immediate content of the *cahiers*, but also of their forms and modes of expression. Grievances concerning liberty show this very clearly, with notable contrasts between reputedly 'bourgeois' texts and those of the countryside. In Brittany, Grateau compared the demand for suppression (or at least substantial reorganization) of universally hated militia recruitment by Rennes patriots in *Des charges d'un bon citoyen de Campagne*, with the request composed in very poor French by the peasants of Penguily (on the north coast of Brittany) to be able to grind their grain freely—in other words, without being obliged to use their seigneur's mill. While the former based their grievance on the sacred and imprescriptible principle of liberty—'that our liberty should be as sacred as that of other citizens; that all forcible enrolments should be suppressed, to be replaced with paid enrolment'—the latter spelled out phonetically a very concrete claim: *demandon que les labureure iret aux moullin ou bon leure sanbleret*: 'we ask that the farmers will [be able to] go to the mill where it suits them'.[30]

Study of the *cahiers* leads to further questions about the meanings that contemporaries gave to the texts, and to the relationship between the deputies that they sent to the Estates-General and the *cahier* they carried. This is the famous question of the 'imperative mandate', often taken up by the electoral Assemblies, which bound the deputy exclusively to the expression of the grievances contained in the *cahier*. At the national level, deputies with imperative mandates in their *cahiers* included some 35 per cent of the clergy, 42 per cent of the Third Estate, and a huge 82 per cent of the nobility.[31] This issue is thus significant. Shapiro and Markoff note the example of a group of clergy enraged against their deputy for voting for the abolition of the tithe, when their *cahier* authorized him merely to discuss the level of its application.[32]

The Unbearable Pressure of Taxation

While Grateau has observed that 'purely quantitative methods erase the diversity of situations and conceal the uneven qualities of reality', the monumental statistical investigation of Shapiro and Markoff in *Revolutionary Demands* has the merit not only of bringing into action an unprecedented corpus of *cahiers* but of submitting it to a systematic analysis through the long-term project of coding the various grievances.[33] Nevertheless, their results are sometimes hard to disentangle from their complex presentation. Thus their chapter 14 answers the burning question of: 'What were the Grievances in 1789? The Most Common Demands in the *Cahiers de Doléances*' in some twenty pages.[34] Yet in an appendix, their table: 'The Subject Codes and Rank of Document-Level Frequency of Each Subject for Each Estate' extends over thirty-six pages, classed according to the codes themselves, and not their frequency or ranking—thus giving primacy to the technique over the analysis. It is difficult to extract results from such data. Underlying this is the fact that through their long researches Shapiro and Markoff collided with one of the characteristics of the *cahiers*: since the writers were not constrained to respond to a questionnaire (many of which circulated in the eighteenth century via the administrative hierarchies), but could note their grievances freely, each *cahier* has its own structure, forms of expression, headings and language to express its grievances. Under such conditions, the work of aggregating data is particularly delicate.

Shapiro and Markoff use what they call a funnelling technique to define four levels of issues. In the parish *cahiers*, grievances related to 'Government' (level 1) come first, representing 40.3 per cent of all recorded items. At level 2 this rather vague category is broken down; and the question of taxation emerges crushingly ahead, present in over two-thirds of the corpus, against 14 per cent for issues of 'regional & local government', which come in second. Within the level 2 category of 'Taxation' are further level 3 topics, with indirect taxation at 24 per cent coming ahead of direct taxation (12.7 per cent). This 2:1 ratio at parish level increases sharply when looking at the Third-Estate *bailliage* documents (4.5:1) and those of the nobility (4.2:1). Descending to the final level of specificity, first place goes to grievances about the *aides*, indirect taxes on alcoholic drink (16.4 per cent), followed closely by the infamous salt tax, the *gabelle* (15.9 per cent).

This statistical treatment of frequency and ranking of mentions, while not revolutionary, allows us to confirm or contest, and above all to refine, a range of previous analyses. For example, Shapiro and Markoff note the problems of an impressionistic reading for the work of Alfred Cobban, *The Social Interpretation of the French Revolution*: 'Clearly, Cobban's important book depends heavily on his reading of the *cahiers*. While, in our examination, we have often found his rejection of the "orthodox" social interpretation, i.e., the Marxist view, generally supported by our data, we have also found instances in which he throws out the baby with the bathwater. His own social interpretation, emphasizing conflicts between country and town, and between rich and poor, comes off much less well when measured against the results of our content analysis.'[35] The issue of grievances over seigneurial milling monopolies is characteristic. For Cobban, it was the form of monopoly most often contested. Shapiro and Markoff confirm that it is evoked in almost 17 per cent of parish *cahiers*, twice as often as any other monopoly. Yet by rank, it is only the thirty-fourth most frequently mentioned subject. At the higher *bailliage* level, it appears in more than 35 per cent of cases, yet its ranking falls to only eighty-seventh.[36]

The key point to retain here is the range of different 'burdens' recorded in Shapiro and Markoff's table of 'Subjects Most Widely Discussed in Cahiers Ranked by Frequency of Discussion'. At the level of the parish *cahiers*, the grievances of France from below, the question of 'Taxation in general' is indisputably ahead of any other subject discussed. While the same is true for the Third-Estate *bailliage* texts with their input from the urban bourgeoisie, in contrast, the frequency of future Estates-General meetings dominates for the nobility. Other matters of taxation—including the *gabelle*, the *aides*, stamp taxes on official paperwork, state-ordered *corvée* labour levies, the *taille* tax on land, the tax privileges of the clergy, and of the nobility—occupy nine of the next ten places in the ranking at parish level: one can thus speak of a genuine fiscal obsession expressed in the *cahiers*. In simple numbers, 72 per cent of all the parish texts studied by Shapiro and Markoff demand, in one form or another, the total or partial suppression of the tax privileges of the elite and the transformation of unequal taxation into more balanced contributions. As token of the fundamental nature of this question in the fabrication of opinion and the process of movement from subjects to citizens, the Assembly of the Third Estate of Nemours opined that he who pays no taxes is not a citizen.[37]

If the *cahiers* called for an in-depth refashioning of direct taxation, by contrast, the outright rejection of indirect taxation, and of those who collected it, was strongly marked. Criticisms of the distribution of the (direct) *taille* within communities were notably lower in frequency than those of the (indirect) *gabelle* and *aides*.[38] The *cahier* of Salmonville-la-Rivière in the *bailliage* of Rouen echoed the general hatred aroused by the General Farm (the private company that contracted to collect many indirect taxes) and its agents thus: 'There remain the Farmers-general and all the satellites in their pay. They are the leeches of the State, an all-devouring species of vermin, an infestation of plague. [...] We beg most humbly and earnestly His Majesty to deliver us from them forever, and to so extirpate the roots of this pernicious plant, that it shall never regrow.'[39]

While some *cahiers* denounced lyrically 'a single true tyrant, the TAX SYSTEM'[40] which worked night and day to strip the king and the nation of their wealth, most raised first and foremost local problems that the king needed to understand. Thus, at Gastines in Bas-Anjou, even though the Assembly took considerable inspiration from a model *cahier* circulated by Volney, this did not stop them emphasising 'that in the division of taxes in general, not enough attention is paid to the difference in the soil of the parishes, so that poor [and unproductive] lands are taxed as highly as the productive'. This *cahier* relates the daily pressures of life: 'when our feeble resources allow us sometimes to fatten a pig, it is very difficult for us to eat it in peace. Have we a small piece of bacon on our bread? At the moment we least expect them, three or four agents of the *gabelle* arrive, sworn enemies of the human race, who search, seize and plunder [...] either for their own profit or that of the office [of the General Farm], and often even haul us into prison'.[41] While taking account of the clear effort to invoke emotion, the atmosphere of suffering and hostility is nonetheless evident.

The sums demanded in taxes were considered not merely confiscatory, but unbearable. This was expressed in the *cahier* of Repel, in the *bailliage* of Mirecourt (Lorraine): 'We form a community of thirty-three hearths [households], of which five are *laboureurs* and three *demi-laboureurs* [terms for better-off peasants], all renting lands ... the rest is composed of day-labourers, amongst whom more than half live in absolute poverty and beggary; many widows and widowers, with numbers of orphans charged to the community. We find that we are overloaded with taxes, notably the *subvention* [the equivalent in Lorraine of the *taille*], the bridges and roads, the *vingtièmes* [taxes on property] and the *corvées* [...] We have many salt-pans in Lorraine, and we pay a great deal for salt, more than the foreigners who take it from these salt-pans'.[42]

Beyond local problems, fiscal pressure posed the issue of reform and redistribution of the burden. Consequently, this brought into question the organization of French society into orders that were unequal in the face of taxation. The three united orders of the *bailliage* of Langres in Burgundy were well aware of this: 'The time has arrived, Sire, to set down the basis of a just division of taxation amongst all citizens [...] Yes, Sire, all your subjects, of every estate and rank, pay homage now to this great truth, that a proportionate equality must be the law of contribution.' They concluded: 'Our wishes are sincere, Sire: we desire truly that all pecuniary exemptions should be forever abolished, and that the proportion of fortunes should henceforth be the only measure of imposition. We ask that this new order of things, which must be the salvation of the people and the regeneration of the public wealth, be made stable and inalterable.'[43]

The game about to play out at Versailles would thus be decisive, not only because the Estates-General had been called because of the financial distress of the monarchy, but above all because the fiscal issue carried within it the question of national regeneration. Moreover, in the immediate context, the issue was all the more sensitive because added to all these different taxes were the seigneurial rights frequently noted as 'exorbitant'.

SEIGNEURIAL RIGHTS

The *cahier* of the guild of glaziers of Saint-Maixent reflects the tone of many fierce attacks on seigneurial rights: 'we demand here, in the name of Humanity, the extinction of certain feudal rights that the ignorance of barbaric centuries has consecrated to the ferocious pride of the noble possessors of some old châteaux'.[44] At Ruca and Landébia, in the *sénéchaussée* of Rennes, the Assembly denounced 'an unjust slavery, shameful slavery in a free kingdom, in a kingdom of French or Franks'.[45] Tensions were all the higher because such rights weighed particularly heavily in years, like this one, of poor harvests and difficult *sou-dure*—the period before the new harvest when old stocks ran low, and might be exhausted. The attitude of some Second-Estate Assemblies, like that of the nobility of the *bailliage* of Montargis, did not calm the situation: rather the opposite. The refusal to change, or even to negotiate, was firmly stated: 'We declare [that we will] never consent to the extinction of the rights that have characterised until now the Noble Order and which we hold from our ancestors [...] We prescribe formally to our deputy to oppose anything which might bring harm to the useful and honorific properties [we hold] in our lands, and we agree that he may not lend himself to any modification or reimbursement of any kind, such things shall only be done by our wish and our free and individual consent'.[46] Nonetheless, we should note that the *cahiers* of the Third Estate regularly envisaged a financial indemnity in exchange for the suppression of various seigneurial rights. Revolutionary radicalization had not yet taken place, and we must be wary of hasty generalizations.

Alongside concerns over feudal payments, attempts to divide common lands and reduce communal use-rights were regularly denounced: enclosures and limitations on free grazing for livestock or access to woodland made the situation of the poorest only more fragile. The *cahier* of Frenelle-la-Grande, in the *bailliage* of Mirecourt, took a very determined position: 'Enclosures work the ruin of the cultivator. Who are they who can enclose? Those who possess vast lands, those who have fortunes: enclosures are expensive. Few inhabitants have enough lands to be able to enclose them. By enclosure, our forests are degraded, and the price of wood rises. The *parcours* [rights to the grazing of animals on the fields after harvest] diminishes, and shrinks the resources of the farmer, who can only with difficulty feed his draught animals, of which we need many [to work] the difficult soil of our region. Things must be put back to their primitive state'.[47] But it must be noted that this issue was far from a simple collision between village communities and seigneurial power. At the heart of the community, differences in circumstances were real, and there were many 'village cockerels', small groups of economically dominant individuals who wished to profit from the reduction of the commons. Such issues thus divided as much as they united. In the urban context, where the lower classes of the Third Estate were also suffering from the economic crisis, the *cahiers* singled out the unfortunate consequences of mechanization for traditional manufacturing processes. This was particularly true in textile regions, where 'mechanicals' were strongly targeted. In the arena of trade, the fatal effects of the 1786 Anglo-French Free-trade Treaty were equally denounced.[48]

PRIVILEGE AS A CRIME AGAINST 'THE NATION'

According to many *cahiers*, not only were the privileges of the nobility and upper clergy unjust, but they also sterilized the nation: 'The gifts, the pensions, the great [cleri-cal] livings reserved only to nobles, strip away from both nobles and commoners [the hope of] emulation. They strip it from the former because, being able by mere birth to aspire to everything, they have no need of merit; and from the latter, because being able to aspire to nothing, it is useless to them. To thus deprive a state of the genius that might enlighten, instruct and defend it, is a crime of *lèse-nation* [a new coinage, parallel to the serious crime of *lèse-majesté*, insulting the monarch].' Thus pronounced the *cahier* of Lauris, in the *sénéchaussée* of Aix-en-Provence.[49] Ploughing the same furrow as the abbé Sieyès' famous *What is the Third Estate?* and other pamphlets, the authors gave no concessions to the privileged: 'Thus the nobility enjoys everything, possesses everything, and wishes to free itself of everything; however if the nobility commands the armies, it is the Third Estate which makes up their ranks; if the nobility sheds a drop of blood, the Third loses it in streams. The nobility empties the royal treasury, the Third Estate fills it; in the end, the Third Estate pays everything and enjoys nothing.'

The upper clergy, and its pomp, was particularly targeted. At Villiers-le-Sec, the Assembly of the Third Estate did not hesitate: 'the Church grew without wealth; it is with wealth that it has degenerated; reducing it to its primitive form would be to recall it to its primitive sanctity. In those distant times, they preached to us by example; today they merely instruct us in morals, they are content to say to us, "Do as we say; do not look at what we do." To make those happy times live again and to reform that morality, which is an abuse and the source of all others, the wealth that corrupts them must be withdrawn from them, [for] it prevents them deserving and receiving the respect due to their character.'[50] The tithe, and the 'fat *décimateurs*'—those among the clergy who kept the greatest part of the tithe—were thus singled out. And, indeed, it was within the fortunes of the First Estate that the nation was to find the means to alleviate the burden of its debts. The debate here prefigures the central revolutionary issue of the transformation of Church property into *biens nationaux*.

Conclusion

As John Markoff wrote in the introduction to *The Abolition of Feudalism*, 'The *cahiers* are unmatched in their capacity to give us the range of views expressed by social groups around the country: they are not only invaluable as a source for the positions being staked out in France's forty thousand rural communities; they are an utterly unparalleled source for the study of peasants in revolution. There is simply no similar body of evidence bequeathed to us by any other revolutionary upheaval.'[51] At the parish level, the *cahiers* offer the documentary source for a vast immersion in the view of France from below in 1789. They make clear the tensions running through the society of orders, but also reveal a vast spectrum of particular situations across this mosaic of territories and social, economic and institutional configurations.

In these conditions, this peerless documentary deposit is far from being exhausted, and this is even more the case as the tools of the historian change. Lexical analysis attests clearly to this. In the pioneering works of the 1960s and 1970s, the corpuses deployed were limited to a few dozen *cahiers*, or sometimes even fewer, and the results obtained often merely served to confirm impressions obtained from straightforward reading of the sources. But today, it is possible to work on much more extensive selections with much finer forms of analysis. Moreover, renewed interest in 'ego-documents' may allow us to study how, in the private correspondence of the men and women of the time, and their other personal writings, the electoral Assemblies and the drafting of the *cahiers* were lived from the inside by subjects in the process of becoming citizens. These are two trails to explore. Finally, the publication of Jean Nicolas's investigation into *La Rébellion française* leads one to suggest, without contesting the exceptional character of the massive production of grievances from below in 1789, a new perspective on the long-term history of grievance, of self-expression in times of crisis and tension, and the possibility of varied chronological contextualizations. This offers the opportunity for new work to bring together not only the immediate political, economic, social, territorial, and seigneurial conjuncture of 1789, but also deeper, and thus less easily identifiable, tensions and fault-lines.

NOTES

1. *Cahier des doléances et observations que prennent la liberté de présenter au roi, notre sire, les gens du Tiers-Etat de la paroisse de Champaissant, du ressort du bailliage secondaire de Mamers, au pays & comté du Maine.*

2. 'Règlement fait par le roi pour l'exécution des lettres de convocation', *Collection complète des lois, décrets, ordonnances, réglemens du Conseil d'Etat ...*, réunis par Jean-Baptiste Duvergier, vol. 1 (Paris, 1834), p. 13.

3. François Furet, 'La monarchie et le règlement électoral de 1789', in Keith Michael Baker (ed.) *The French Revolution and the Creation of Modern Political Culture*, vol. 1, *The Political Culture of the Old Regime* (London and New York, 1987), 376.

4. Philippe Grateau, *Les Cahiers de doléances. Une relecture culturelle* (Rennes, 2001), Table 2: 'Quelques exemples de 'participation électorale' en 1789', 41.

5. Ran Halévi, 'La monarchie et les élections: position des problems', in Baker (ed.) French Revolution, 394.

6. Pierre Goubert and Michel Denis (eds), *1789: Les Français ont la parole. Cahiers des Etats Généraux* (Paris, 1964), 225–6.

7. Goubert and Denis (eds), *1789: Les Français ont la parole*, 226.

8. Paul Bois (ed.), *Cahier de doléances du tiers état de la sénéchaussée de Château-du-Loir pour les état généraux de 1789* (Paris, 1960), 79–80.

9. Georges Lefebvre, *Etudes orléanaises, I: Contributions à l'étude des structures sociales à la fin du XVIIIe siècle* (Paris, 1962), 74; Régine Robin, 'Quatrième état et cahiers de doléances dans le bailliage d'Auxois en 1789', *Bulletin de la Commission d'Histoire Economique et Sociale de la Révolution française* (1966), 31–3.

10. Alexis de Tocqueville, *L'Ancien Régime et la Révolution* ([1856] Paris, 1967), 45.

11. Roger Chartier, 'Cultures, Lumières, Doléances: les cahiers de 1789', *Revue d'Histoire Moderne et Contemporaine* 28, no. 1 (1981), 68.

12. Jacques Godechot, *La Révolution française: Chronologie commentée, 1787–1799, suivie de notices biographiques sur les personnages cités* (Paris, 1988), cited as the epigraph to Colette Merlin, *1789, Les cahiers de doléances du Jura*, (Montmorot, 1989), unpaginated.

13. Tocqueville, *L'Ancien Régime*, 89.
14. Ibid., 144.
15. Ibid., 88–9.
16. Gilbert Shapiro and John Markoff, *Revolutionary Demands: A Content Analysis of the Cahiers de doléances de 1789* (Stanford, CA, 1998), xxix.
17. Shapiro and Markoff, *Revolutionary Demands*, xxix.
18. Jean Jaurès, *Histoire socialiste de la Révolution française*, I (Paris, 1968), 281.
19. George V. Taylor, 'Revolution and Nonrevolutionary Content of the Cahiers de doléances: An Interim Report', *French Historical Studies* 7, no. 4 (1972), 481.
20. Charles Walton, 'La liberté de la presse selon les cahiers de doléances de 1789', *Revue d'histoire moderne et contemporaine*,53, no. 1 (2006), 65–6.
21. Philippe Grateau, *Les Cahiers de doléances. Une relecture culturelle* (Rennes, 2001), 22.
22. Jean-Luc Chappey, compte-rendu de Philippe Grateau, *Revue d'histoire moderne et contemporaine* 52, no. 2 (2005), 217.
23. Béatrice Hyslop, *L'apanage de Philippe-Egalité, duc d'Orléans (1785-1791)* (Paris, 1965).
24. Grateau, *Les Cahiers de doléances*, 48–55.
25. Paul Bois (ed.), *Cahier de doléances du tiers état de la sénéchaussée de Château-du-Loir pour les état généraux de 1789* (Paris, 1960), 5–68.
26. Pierre-Yves Beaurepaire and Charles Giry-Deloison, *La Terre et les Paysans, France— Grande-Bretagne XVIIe–XVIIIe siècle* (Neuilly-sur-Seine, 1999), 288–302.
27. Jean Nicolas, *La Rébellion française. Mouvements populaires et conscience sociale (1661–1789)* (Paris, 2002).
28. Shapiro and Markoff, *Revolutionary Demands*, 150–8.
29. Régine Robin, *La société française en 1789* (Paris, 1970), 317.
30. Grateau, *Les Cahiers de doléances*, 20.
31. Shapiro and Markoff, *Revolutionary Demands*, 145.
32. Ibid., 128.
33. Grateau, *Les Cahiers de doléances*, 22.
34. Shapiro and Markoff, *Revolutionary Demands*, 253–79.
35. Ibid., 265.
36. Ibid., 260.
37. Goubert and Denis (eds), *1789: Les Français ont la parole*, 152–5.
38. Shapiro and Markoff, *Revolutionary Demands*, 380–1.
39. Goubert and Denis (eds), *1789: Les Français ont la parole*, 139.
40. Ibid., 133. *Cahier* of Montousse, in the future *département* of the Hautes-Pyrénées.
41. Goubert and Denis (eds), *1789: Les Français ont la parole*, 33–4.
42. Ibid., 99–100.
43. Ibid., 141–2.
44. Ibid., 86.
45. Ibid., 85. The last phrase is playing on the etymological link with freedom—*franc*, franchise, etc.
46. Goubert and Denis (eds), *1789: Les Français ont la parole*, 83.
47. Ibid., 125.
48. Ibid., 130–1.
49. Ibid., 72–3.
50. Ibid., 158–9.
51. John Markoff, *The Abolition of Feudalism. Peasants, Lords and Legislators in the French Revolution* (University Park, PA, 1996), 6.

SELECTED READING

Baker, Keith Michael (ed.), *The French Revolution and the Creation of Modern Political Culture*, vol. 1, *The political culture of old Regime* (London and New York, 1987),

Bois, Paul (ed.), *Cahier de doléances du tiers état de la sénéchaussée de Château-du-Loir pour les état généraux de 1789* (Paris, 1960).

Chartier, Roger, 'Cultures, Lumières, Doléances: les cahiers de 1789', *Revue d'Histoire Moderne et Contemporaine* 28, no. 1 (janvier–mars 1981), 68–93.

Cobban, Alfred, *The Social Interpretation of the French Revolution* (Cambridge, 1965).

Goubert, Pierre, Denis Michel (eds), *1789 Les Français ont la parole. Cahiers des Etats Généraux* (Paris, 1964).

Grateau, Philippe, *Les Cahiers de doléances. Une relecture culturelle* (Rennes, 2001).

Hyslop, Beatrice, *A Guide to the General Cahiers of 1789 with the Texts of Unedited Cahiers* (New York, 1936).

Jaurès, Jean, *Histoire socialiste de la Révolution française* (Paris, 1901–4).

Markoff, John, *The Abolition of Feudalism. Peasants, Lords and Legislators in the French Revolution* (University Park, PA, 1996).

Markoff, John, Shapiro Gilbert (ed.), *Revolutionary Demands: A Content Analysis of the Cahiers de doléances de 1789* (Stanford, CA, 1998).

Michelet, Jules, *Histoire de la Révolution française, 1847–1853* (réédition Paris, 1963).

Nicolas, Jean, *La Rébellion française. Mouvements populaires et conscience sociale (1661–1789)* (Paris, 2002).

Robin, Régine, *La société française en 1789* (Paris, 1970).

Taine, Hippolyte, *Les origines de la France contemporaine*, 6 vols (Paris, 1876–94), vol. I *L'Ancien Régime*. English translation, *The Ancient Régime* (New York, 1896).

Taylor, George V., 'Revolution and Nonrevolutionary Content of the Cahiers de doléances: An Interim Report', *French Historical Studies* 7, no. 4 (1972), 479–502.

Tocqueville, Alexis de, *L'Ancien Régime et la Révolution* (Paris, 1856).

Walton, Charles, 'La liberté de la presse selon les cahiers de doléances de 1789', *Revue d'histoire moderne et contemporaine* 1, 53–1 (2006), 63–87.

CHAPTER 10

A SOCIAL REVOLUTION? RETHINKING POPULAR INSURRECTION IN 1789

PETER MCPHEE

PIERRE-LOUIS-NICOLAS DELAHAYE, born in 1745, was the schoolteacher and parish clerk of the village of Silly-en-Multien, twenty miles north-east of Paris. From 1771 Delahaye kept a diary of 'remarkable and curious events' in his village, including the suffering during the hard winter of 1788–89. In late June 1789 he recorded that 'we are in frightful distress, all we hear is talk of revolts and massacres everywhere. There is no more wheat to be found'. The ripening harvest of 1789 promised an end to hunger. Then, in the anxious, expectant atmosphere after news arrived of the taking of the Bastille on 14 July, the villagers acted on the rumour that harvesters working for vengeful nobles were cutting the crops prematurely:

> the alarm was sounded and the priest ran through the village to gather all the men and boys, all armed, a few with rifles, the others with forks, spits, axes, pitchforks, with whatever they could, then left with the priest at their head, wearing his cockade.[1]

From hindsight, this 'remarkable and curious event' on 27 July was one of thousands of acts that came to be known as the 'Great Fear' of July–August 1789. As news of the seizing of the Bastille reached the countryside, rural communities like Silly had armed themselves against imminent but imaginary revenge from angry seigneurs, then often confronted the seigneurial system itself.

Historians disagree on the extent to which the popular upheavals that reverberated through cities, towns and villages in 1789 were genuinely revolutionary in content and purpose rather than an expression of age-old fears and resentments. Following Georges Lefebvre's pioneering studies from the 1920s to the 1950s, most historians agreed that, while popular involvement in the Revolution had its own impulses and rhythms, it was at the heart of the Revolution from July 1789.[2] But, while some historians subsequently furthered the famous critiques by Alfred Cobban and George V. Taylor of Lefebvre and his Jacobin-Marxist successors by contesting whether this reflected a deep-seated and revolutionary crisis in French society, most others have since been more interested in identifying the new urban discourses that sapped the foundations of the monarchical régime.[3] Not surprisingly, in recent scholarly collections surveying the origins and outbreak of the Revolution, contributions on the peasantry and urban *menu peuple* sit awkwardly alongside those on political and cultural history.[4]

Nevertheless, the Revolution of 1789 is still most commonly understood following Lefebvre's 1939 model of aristocratic, then bourgeois, and finally popular revolt: that is, as initially the response of élites to the breakdown of the régime, in which the working people of town and country only became major actors from July 1789. Like Lefebvre, Jean-Clément Martin and William Doyle have thus argued that the sporadic, if widespread, unrest in Paris and the provinces before mid-1789 was essentially an expression of traditional material grievances, with political uncertainty providing the language and pretext.[5] In contrast, John Markoff, Anatoli Ado, Micah Alpaugh, and others have identified an earlier revolutionary challenge 'from below', while agreeing that the substance of grievances and the forms in which they were expressed were redolent of the past.[6] This chapter responds to this debate by probing the relationship of diverse popular upheavals in 1789 to the unfolding political crisis among ruling élites. To what extent should the Revolution of 1789 be understood as a crisis of legitimacy expressed widely across society as well as a collapse of arrangements of power among élites? Was it from the outset a social as well as a political revolution?

* * *

The history of eighteenth century France was studded with protest; indeed, Guy Lemarchand has calculated that in the years 1720–88 there were no fewer than 4,400 'troubles' in the countryside significant enough to be documented, some three-quarters of them after 1765.[7] These protests were of three main types: food riots, anti-tax rebellions and resistance to seigneurial obligations. All of them expressed an opportunistic and defensive community rejection of threats: against a merchant or large farmer taking a wagon of grain to market at times of shortage; a seigneur's agent making exactions that were novel or had fallen into disuse; or an official collecting taxes without sufficient personal protection.

These were protests within a system that people assumed would never end. Even the spectacular rioting in Paris, Rennes, Grenoble, and elsewhere, which in 1788 contested royal decrees to reform or exile the *parlements*, then celebrated when they were rescinded, had had as their objective the defence of traditional, aristocratic buffers against 'ministerial despotism'. But Louis' decision in August 1788 to call a meeting of the Estates-General for May 1789 dramatically expanded the parameters of the possible and revealed social divisions that challenged the legitimacy of a society of 'orders'. Torn between his loyalty to the established corporate order of rank and privilege and the exigencies of his kingdom's fiscal crisis, the king vacillated on the crucial political question of whether the three orders would meet separately, as in 1614, or in a common chamber.

His vacillation aggravated debate. In September 1788, the English agronomist Arthur Young was in the bustling Atlantic port of Nantes just six weeks after Louis XVI had announced the convocation of the Estates-General, and noted how *enflammée* was the town in 'the cause of liberty'. The merchants with whom Young conversed convinced him of the rights of 'the most decided talents', like them, to participate more fully in public life. Nor was this political awareness limited to élites. The Parisian cobbler Joseph Charon recalled in his memoirs that by 1788 political ferment had descended:

> from men of the world of the highest rank to the very lowest ranks through various channels … people acquired and dispensed enlightenment that one would have searched for in vain a dozen years earlier … and they have acquired notions about public constitutions in the past two or three years.[8]

Louis' decision, on 5 December, to double the size of Third Estate representation served only to further highlight the issue of political power, because he remained silent on how voting would occur. The popular expectation of reform which now erupted reveals how much deeper the crisis of absolutist France extended beyond confrontation between nobles and monarch. The ferment was aggravated by the harsh winter of 1788–89, which was one of sharp misery in cities as well as the countryside. Contemporaries spoke of 80,000 unemployed in Paris, and half, or more, of the looms lay idle in textile towns such as Amiens, Lyon, Carcassonne, Lille, Troyes, and Rouen, generating desperate hopes among the working poor for the Estates-General and claims to vote for it, mixed with equally fevered rumours of grain hoarding and conspiracy. On 21 March, posters in Marseille urged workers who paid no taxes to protest at being excluded from voting: 'if you have courage, show it now'. Two days later the homes of a tax collector and the Intendant were attacked, and crowds ransacked warehouses storing fish and flour, shouting 'Vive le Roi!' as if they were rioting in the king's name. There was a similar mix of subsistence and politics in violent protest during March–April in many other towns and cities, including Cambrai, Valenciennes, Vannes, Besançon, and Alençon.[9]

In the spring of 1789, people in small towns and villages also began behaving and voicing attitudes that challenged the structures of their world in unprecedented and illegal ways. As the bitter winter dragged into spring, the sharp edge of hunger and anxiety accentuated the expectation occasioned by Louis' calling of the Estates-General. The easing of controls on public debate and open friction about the form and function of the Estates-General opened up a moment in which boundaries of obedience could be tested. In many regions there were reports of opposition to the seigneurial system itself, in particular hunting and grazing restrictions. In Provence the châteaux of Solliès and Besse were ransacked and in many parishes communal herds were driven onto seigneurs' lands. East of Gap, three villages banded together in April against their seigneur d'Espraux, a councillor in the Parlement of Aix, and seized back the grain they had paid as harvest dues in 1788.[10] In Artois, peasants from a dozen villages gathered together to kill the Count d'Oisy's game and announced that they would pay no more dues. Since the previous December, peasants had refused to pay taxes or dues or had seized food supplies in parts of the neighbouring Cambrésis and Hainaut regions in the north-east, the Franche-Comté, and the Paris basin, perhaps in expectation of royal recognition of their plight. Indeed, just as in Marseille, at times they claimed that the king had promised an end to dues and tithes.[11] Had not the king himself declared that he wished to hear his people's grievances at the Estates-General? Peasants now had the perfect pretext and excuse for bolder actions than ever before.

The acts of rebellion during the winter were sporadic and local, but everywhere across the kingdom anxiety over food supplies coincided with unprecedented opportunities to participate in political life. The electoral provisions for the Estates-General announced on 24 January were broad, at least in the countryside: adult male taxpayers were eligible to attend special parish meetings which were to agree on the content of a *cahier de doléances* and to appoint delegates, usually two to four depending on the size of the parish, to represent it at district (*bailliage* or *sénéchaussée*) level. Millions of households which had hitherto experienced the structures of power and privilege as constraints to be obeyed, sidestepped or occasionally contested were now authorized, even required, to reflect on their efficacy and legitimacy and to identify and suggest remediation for their grievances.[12] The drawing up of the *cahiers* in the context of political anticipation and subsistence crisis was, for rural people, the first episode in a decade of revolution. Of course, they would know that only in retrospect.

The 40,000 peasant *cahiers* ranged in length from many pages of detailed criticisms and proposals to the three sentences written in a mixture of French and Catalan from the tiny village of Serrabone in the stony foothills of the Pyrenees. Their veracity as statements of popular attitudes is often questioned: not only did the number of those participating in their drafting vary widely, in many areas model *cahiers* were circulated through the countryside from towns, even if frequently added to or adapted at a local level.[13] And although in theory all male taxpayers over 25 years of age were eligible to participate in the process of drawing them up, their compilation was likely to be—whether or not by general consent—in the hands of the better-off minority of villagers. This was not always the case. The surviving Third Estate *cahiers* from the Corbières region of Languedoc concluded with the formula that 'the literate members have signed', but the records of the meetings show that many more men in fact were present than indicated by the numbers of those who could sign, in places as many as 85 per cent of male heads of household.[14] Occasionally, too, exclusion of poorer peasants resulted in overt friction: for example, at Beignon, near Ploërmel in Brittany, after a gathering of twenty-six of the well-to-do had formulated a placatory *cahier* on 5 April, eighty-six others met two days later in protest, writing their own *cahier* to attack the seigneur, in particular for felling 860 trees.[15]

Despite these limitations, the *cahiers* are a source of extraordinary richness. John Markoff and Gilbert Shapiro have analysed 1,112 of them, including 748 from village communities.[16] Although more than three-quarters of the village *cahiers* criticized seigneurialism in some way, Markoff and Shapiro showed that a more common target of peasant anger in 1789 was state taxation—hardly surprising given the purpose of the *cahiers*. The issues were closely linked, however, for what rankled most with commoners was the privileged fiscal treatment of the noble élite, whether seigneurs or as bishops and abbots within the Church. Hostility to seigneurial exactions tended to go together with criticism of the tithes, fees, and practices of the Church; that is, they were seen as interdependent within the seigneurial regime.[17] Typical in this regard was the *cahier* of the parish of Sagy in the Vexin region to the north of Paris, situated between the Seine and Oise rivers. Its chief targets were the burden of state taxes on commoners, and noble hunting and other privileges: they wanted 'to pay taxes in proportion to their capacity, with the clergy and nobility, and to enjoy in freedom the cultivation of their land without being troubled by any form of servitude'.[18] There were frequent criticisms of other 'rights', such as the monopoly (*banalité*) over the village oven, grape and olive press, and mill; the multiplicity of 'rights' and those who owned them; and the unpaid labour required from the community on the lords' lands. In stark contrast, 84 per cent of noble *cahiers* were simply silent on seigneurial dues.[19]

Equally striking in the *cahiers* is the tone of resolute optimism, common across the kingdom. Most rural people spoke a language other than French in daily life, such as Breton, Basque, Flemish, or Occitan, and many lived in provinces such as Lorraine or Roussillon which had only recently been incorporated into the kingdom. Despite their lively expression of regional difference, their *cahiers* expressed an assumption of French citizenship within a regenerated kingdom.[20] Words like 'patrie', 'nation' and 'citoyen' were studded throughout the *cahiers*, which were imbued with assumptions of a secular citizenship as the basis of a regenerated public realm. Such evidence suggests that 1789 was not the sudden rupture in peasant outlook and values so often assumed by historians, but rather a long time in the moulding and the result of complex social interactions.

The economically vulnerable were acutely aware of the potential costs of being outspoken about privilege and prerogative. It is therefore startling to find examples of parish Assemblies who were so bold as to criticize the tithe and the seigneurial system directly. In the southern corner of the kingdom, the few lines submitted from the tiny community of Périllos were unreservedly hostile to the system under which they claimed that the seigneur treated them 'like slaves'.[21] In the impoverished little village of Erceville, north of Orléans, the parish Assembly was presided over by the local judge employed by the seigneur, a prominent member of the *Parlement* of Paris whose personal holdings covered most of the parish. Not surprisingly, his tenants decided to stay away from the meeting, but those peasants, labourers and artisans who did attend to draw up the *cahier* were bold and blunt, requiring the judge to write articles stipulating that, 'without any distinction of title or rank, the said seigneur be taxed like them'; that 'the tithe and the *champart* (harvest due) be abolished, or at least converted into an annual payment in money'; and—clearly aware of the looming political issue of whether the three orders would deliberate separately or jointly at Versailles—that all taxes should require 'the consent of the whole Nation assembled in Estates-General'.[22]

In turn, men long used to the exercise of power in the countryside were unsettled by the boldness of some rural communities and the confident new language with which the charged political context of early 1789 had invested their grievances. From the village of Pont-sur-Seine in the Champagne region a seigneur's agent wrote to his master:

In vain I've done everything I can to exclude from the *cahier* the articles on the abolition of *banalités*, of the right to hunt, and other seigneurial dues … The intention
and the tenacity of the people are immovable on this question and it is impossible to
dissuade them, because they have been given the right to express their grievances.[23]

Hostility towards noble status was not uniform. Some urban Third Estate *cahiers*—for
example, from Agen, Alençon, Bayonne, Lyon, and Le Havre—supported the retention
of the three orders, although, like Dijon, noting that noble standing should be reflected
only in 'honorific privileges, more worthy of them than pecuniary privileges'.[24] There
was a shared commitment in all three orders to the need for change, and general agreement on a plethora of specific abuses to be reformed within the Church and state apparatus. However, the divisions over the key issues of political power, seigneurialism and
claims to corporate privilege were already irreconcilable by the time the deputies arrived
in Versailles. Most obviously of all, nobles and commoners could not agree on arrangements for voting at the Estates-General.

The rural inhabitants of rural and urban France could not have envisaged the consequences of such divisions. Louis XVI had asked his people for their advice and support
in a consultative process, not whether they would prefer the end of a complete social
and political system. Of themselves, the *cahiers* were not explicitly revolutionary: no one
in France in the early spring of 1789 knew that they were about to live through what
became in hindsight 'the Revolution of 1789'. Again and again, however, the *cahiers* of
the Third Estate had made demands for a regular meeting of a representative body such
as the Estates-General, equality of taxation and opportunity, and the end of seigneurialism. Consciously or not, these demands taken together presupposed the end of a particular social and political order.

After drawing up their *cahiers*, parish Assemblies elected two delegates for the first
one hundred households and one more for each extra hundred; these delegates in turn
chose deputies for each of the 234 district constituencies and consolidated parish *cahiers*
into one for their district. Participation at the parish level was generally high everywhere, but varied sharply, for example, in parishes around Béziers from 5 to 83 per cent,
near Vitré in Brittany from 6 to 96 per cent, and in Artois from 14 to 97 per cent. In what
was to become a common feature of the Revolutionary period, such variations had no
common cause: they could be a reflection either of levels of enthusiasm or of the extent
to which voters shared a common view about who should or would be elected, that is,
whether it was worth voting at all.[25]

The district Assemblies in local town centres were often confused and stormy occasions, for many urban bourgeois dismissed parish complaints about seigneurial rights
and other specific grievances as private matters between them and the seigneur, provoking indignation from their rustic fellows. Despite the experience of municipal office
of many delegates, at the *bailliage* level there was a lack of clarity about what was being
decided: at times peasant delegates seem to have assumed that they were deliberative
gatherings of the sovereign people. Desmé de Daubuisson, lieutenant-général of the
bailliage of Saumur on the Loire River, complained that:

What is really tiresome is that these assemblies that have been summoned have gen-erally believed themselves to be invested with some sovereign authority and that when they came to an end the peasants went home with the idea that henceforward they were free from tithes, hunting prohibitions and the payment of seigneurial dues.[26]

The voting procedures and eligibility requirements for Third Estate deputies reinforced deeply engrained assumptions about education, wealth and capacity, and ensured that virtually all of the 646 Third Estate deputies were lawyers, officials and property-owners, men of substance and repute in their town or region. While histories of 1789 commonly write as if the Third Estate revolution began only after the Estates-General opened in Versailles on 4 May in fact, these deputies had been through a protracted, often bit-terly divisive, electoral process also involving the mass of the population. In Artois, for example, Robespierre was narrowly elected one of eight deputies only after five months of angry debate and electioneering involving the 245 communities of the district of Artois. His opponents were furious with his brother Augustin's open campaigning in the countryside.[27]

Robespierre had a frantic dash to make the opening of the Estates-General. But when he arrived, he was exhilarated that, despite differences of language, the bourgeois depu-ties articulated a common outlook, insistent on their dignity and responsibility to 'the Nation'. They refused to meet in a separate Third Estate chamber, and on 17 June pro-claimed themselves the National Assembly. Paris, thirteen miles from Versailles and a crucible of revolutionary enthusiasm, was invested with 20,000 mercenaries and, in sym-bolic defiance, Louis dismissed Jacques Necker, his one non-noble minister, on 11 July.

The men of the Assembly were themselves saved from summary dismissal by a col-lective action by thousands of Parisian working people. Though barred by gender or poverty from participation in the formulation of *cahiers* or the election of deputies, from April, the mass of manual workers (*menu peuple*) had demonstrated their conviction that the bourgeois deputies' revolt was in the people's name. Pamphlets expressed the anger of wage-earners at their exclusion from the political process. Sustaining this anger was an escalation in the price of a 4 lb loaf of bread from 8 to 14 *sous*, an increase widely assumed to be the result of deliberate withholding of supplies by noble landowners. An offhand (and misreported) remark about wages by the wealthy manufacturer Réveillon at a Third Estate meeting on 23 April triggered a riot in the *faubourg* Saint-Antoine dur-ing which, echoing Sieyès' *What is the Third Estate?*, shouts of 'Long live the Third Estate! Liberty! We will not give way!' were heard. The riot was put down by troops at the cost of about 300 lives (estimates went as high as 900), the bloodiest event of 1789.[28] In general, however, the Parisian disturbances of 1789 were intimidatory rather than violent. Early in July, for example, crowds up to 10,000 strong freed fourteen *Gardes françaises* impris-oned for insubordination, just one of about forty mass protests in the city that year, of which only seven involved violence.[29]

The Paris bookseller Sébastien Hardy, whose diaries are an unparalleled source for the early months of the Revolution, noted that people were saying, 'that the princes were hoarding grains deliberately in order to more effectively trip up M. Necker, whom they are so keen to overthrow'.[30] Necker's dismissal on 11 July confirmed these suspicions, and forty of the fifty-four customs houses ringing Paris were destroyed over the following days. The abbey of Saint-Lazare was searched for arms; popular suspicions that the nobility were trying to starve the people into submission were confirmed when stocks of grain were also discovered there. Arms and ammunition were also seized from gunsmiths and the Invalides military hospital. The ultimate target was the Bastille fortress in the *faubourg* Saint-Antoine, both for its supplies of arms and gunpowder and because this powerful fortress dominated the popular neighbourhoods of eastern Paris. It was also an awesome symbol of the arbitrary authority of the monarchy.

On 14 July, up to 8,000 armed Parisians laid siege to the fortress; the governor, the marquis de Launay, refused to surrender and, as crowds forced their way into the courtyard, ordered his soldiers to fire upon the crowd, killing about one hundred. Only when two detachments of Gardes Françaises sided with the crowd and trained their cannon on the main gate, did he surrender. The *vainqueurs de la Bastille*, as they came to be known, anticipated the social composition of the *sans-culottes* of 1791–94. On one list compiled by a *vainqueur*, Stanislas Maillard, there were perhaps a score of bourgeois, including manufacturers and merchants, and 76 soldiers among the 662 survivors. The rest were typical of the *menu peuple*: tradesmen, artisans, and wage-earners from about 30 different trades, notably 49 joiners, 48 cabinetmakers, 41 locksmiths, and 28 cobblers.[31]

The seizure of the Bastille on 14 July had important consequences. In political terms, it saved the National Assembly and legitimized a sharp shift in power. Paris was now controlled by a new city government under an elected mayor, Bailly, inaugural President of the National Assembly, and a bourgeois civil militia commanded by the French hero of the American War of Independence, the marquis de Lafayette. Early on the morning of 17 July, Louis' youngest brother, the Count d'Artois, and Marie-Antoinette's favourite, Madame de Polignac, left France in disgust at the collapse of respect evident among commoners. A steady trickle of disgruntled courtiers would join Artois in his *émigré* court in Turin. On the same day, however, Louis formally accepted what had occurred by entering Paris to announce the withdrawal of troops and the recall of Necker.

The taking of the Bastille was only the most spectacular instance of popular conquest of local power all over France. From Paris to the smallest hamlet, the summer and autumn of 1789 saw an unprecedented collapse of centuries of royal state-making. In provincial centres nobles retired or were forcibly removed from office or accommodated an influx of new men, in what Lefebvre called the 'municipal revolution'.[32] In villages and small towns the vacuum of authority caused by the collapse of the Bourbon state was temporarily filled by municipal bodies chosen by popular mandate. This seizure of power was accompanied everywhere by refusal of the claims of the state, seigneurs and Church over the payment of taxes, dues and tithes; as royal troops openly fraternized with civilians in the exultation of the people's power, the judiciary was powerless to enforce the law.

The rural response to the news of the taking of the Bastille was spectacular. Parishes had placed their hopes in the meeting of the Estates-General; now news of the seizure of the fortress tempered such hopes with anxieties that the nobility would take revenge on the Third Estate. During the second half of July villages formed popular militias in anticipation of external menace. As in Silly-en-Multien, the bands of destitute people roaming country roads were the focus of suspicion as anxious peasants waited for crops to ripen: were they possibly in the employ of vengeful nobles conspiring to destroy peasants' crops as punishment for the boldness of the Third Estate? Panic fanned out almost simultaneously from sparks in six different parts of the country as accounts of suspicious behaviour of 'outsiders' became magnified into fearful accounts of armed brigands. These rumours travelled like bushfires from village to village, at the pace of a brisk walk, affecting every region except Brittany and the east. While many local incidents took the traditional form of compelling vulnerable members of the privileged orders or their agents to surrender food and drink, there were at times two new elements: the seizure and destruction of feudal registers, and the public humiliation of seigneurs or their stewards. This unprecedented panic and its outcomes came to be known as the 'Great Fear'.

After the drawing up of the *cahiers de doléances*, this was the second great act of revolution in which masses of rural people were involved. Unlike the meetings that had produced the *cahiers*, when parishes hid radical demands behind protestations of fealty to the king, this time those involved in this frontal assault on the seigneurial system were well aware of what they were doing. Most spectacularly, on 24 July the inhabitants of Pont-de-Veyle, just south of Mâcon, besieged the local château and seized the seigneurial registers and other papers, which they deposited at the town hall, symbolic of 'the people's' power. The scene was repeated next day, at nearby Vonnas. Up to 800 peasants from twelve villages attacked the abbey at Saint-Sulpice, forcing the monks to burn the registers, and plundering the abbey's cellar. The following day they erected a gibbet in the middle of the cloister, ostensibly to hang the monks, who were allowed finally to flee in terror into the surrounding forest before the insurgents set fire to the buildings.[33] In other places, specific targets of local hatred were attacked, such as a particularly disliked seigneur or his manager. In Alsace, Jews were singled out: in Durmenach, Hagenthal, and Hegenheim, Jewish houses were pillaged.[34]

Rural insurgents occasionally used a traditional tactic of self-protection by arguing that they believed they were acting against hoarders on the orders of the king.[35] More often, however, the collapse of authority encouraged peasants to abandon well-practised tactics of dissembling and duplicity against authority and instead to be explicit about what James Scott has called their usually 'hidden transcript'.[36] In particular, they adopted the language of the Third Estate revolt to their own ends. From Montmartin, to the north-east of Paris, the steward of the estate of the duke of Montmorency wrote to his master on 2 August that, 'approximately three hundred brigands from all the lands associated with the vassals of Mme the Marquise de Longaunay have stolen the titles of rents and allowances of the seigneurie, and demolished her dovecotes: they then gave a receipt for the theft signed *The Nation*', a dramatic and confident flourish.[37]

The Great Fear was driven by 'conservative' impulses to protect local communities against outsiders, but its outcomes were radical, particularly in the creation of popular militias, which in many places violently attacked the seigneurial system.[38] Rural communities drew on an extensive repertoire of well-tried forms of protest against well-known enemies in 1789, but their ambitions had shifted dramatically, drawing on the language of élite politics to clarify the prism of their own experiences and memories. The *cahiers* are replete with references to the past, ranging from evocations of an imaginary golden age to specific dates when arrangements with seigneurs had been codified. But such references jostled with new and startling claims about national representation, privilege and even seigneurialism itself. What was revolutionary about the rural insurrection of 1789 compared with the protests that had always been part of rural life was both the open confrontation and the 'implicit negotiation', in John Markoff's words, between distant political élites and rural communities which facilitated a dramatic rethinking about power. The new peasant politics was evident in the *cahiers*, and then in the waves of rebellion of July–August.[39]

Actions during the Great Fear amounted to a revolutionary confrontation, and the noble, clerical and bourgeois deputies of the National Assembly were well aware of its import. In an atmosphere of terror and exhilaration, a series of nobles mounted the rostrum on 4 August to respond to the crisis in the countryside. The legislators' original intention—to quieten peasant insurrection by abolishing seigneurial dues in return for monetary compensation—was overwhelmed by the panic-stricken surrender of a maze of other privileges. In the succeeding week, however, sobered legislators made a distinction between instances of 'personal servitude' (serfdom, dovecotes, seigneurial and royal hunting privileges, and unpaid labour), which were abolished outright, and 'property rights' (seigneurial dues payable on harvests) for which peasants would have to pay compensation before ceasing payment. The decrees also responded to the grievances expressed in the *cahiers* by abolishing seigneurial courts and taxation exemptions.[40]

Later in August the Assembly approved the Declaration of the Rights of Man and of the Citizen, together with the August Decrees marking the end of the absolutist, seigneurial and corporate structure of eighteenth century France. They were also a revolutionary proclamation of the principles of a new golden age, to be founded on an equality of rights, responsibilities and civic dignity. The Declaration asserted the essence of liberalism: that 'liberty consists of the power to do whatever is not injurious to others'; accordingly, it guaranteed rights of free speech and association, of religion and opinion, limited only by 'the law'. This was to be a land in which all were to be equal in legal status, and subject to the same public responsibilities: it was an invitation to become citizens of a nation instead of subjects of a king. The decrees were a brilliant expression of broad, 'enlightened' principles of civil society in the context of the raw demands of urban and rural revolt against the material inequities of economic and social power.

The August Decrees and the Declaration met with refusal from Louis. The Estates-General had been summoned to offer him advice on the state of his kingdom: did his acceptance of the existence of a 'National Assembly' require him to accept its decisions? Claims multiplied of open contempt for the Revolution on the part of aristocrats; for example, after a welcoming banquet at Versailles on 1 October for the officers of new troops, newspapers reported that the national tricolour cockade had been besmirched by drunken noble officers. As the food crisis worsened the victory of the summer of 1789 seemed again in question. For the second time, the *menu peuple* of Paris intervened to safeguard a revolution they assumed to be theirs. This time, however, it was particularly the women of the markets: in the words of the observant bookseller Hardy, 'these women said loudly that the men didn't know what it was all about and that they wanted to have a hand in things'.[41] On 5 October, up to 20,000 women marched to Versailles; among their spontaneous leaders were Stanislas Maillard, a *vainqueur* of 14 July, and a woman from Luxembourg, Anne-Josephe Terwagne, who would become known as Théroigne de Méricourt. They were belatedly followed by the National Guard. At Versailles the women invaded the Assembly. A deputation was then presented to the king, who promptly agreed to sanction the decrees. It soon became apparent, however, that the women would be satisfied only if the royal family returned to Paris; on 6 October it did so, the Assembly in its wake.

This was a decisive moment in the Revolution of 1789. The National Assembly owed its existence and success, once again, to the armed intervention of the people of Paris. The mayor, Bailly, recalled that, when the women returned to Paris on 6 October, they were singing 'vulgar ditties which apparently showed little respect for the queen'. Others claimed to have brought with them the royal family as 'the baker and his wife, and the baker's apprentice'.[42] The women were here making explicit the ancient assumption of royal responsibility to God for the provision of food. Convinced now that the Revolution was complete and secure, and determined that never again would the common people of Paris exercise such power, the Assembly ordered an inquiry into the 'crimes' of 5–6 October, and gave authorities to power to declare martial law. On 21 October a labourer from the Bastille district was hanged for inciting 'sedition'.[43] The key decrees sanctioned, and the court party in disarray, the Revolution's triumph seemed assured; to signify the magnitude of what they had achieved, people now began to refer to the '*ancien régime*'.

* * *

The municipal council of Fitou, near Narbonne, spent part of Christmas Day 1789 lauding the 'wise, unceasing labors of the National Assembly' against 'l'antique et barbare régime féodal'. The secretary went on to transcribe in full about one hundred pages of the Assembly's decrees, as the decrees themselves required.[44] The revolutionary year had involved masses of French people in ways of thinking and acting that were unprecedented, even unimaginable. The causes of the Revolution are best understood as originating deep in French society, as well as being the result of élite political dysfunction. Similarly, after the initial revolutionary stand of Third Estate deputies at Versailles on 20 June, the great acts of revolution which in July–October turned pre-Revolutionary France into the *ancien régime* were the work of popular revolt.

While the Declaration proclaimed the universality of rights and the civic equality of all citizens, it was ambiguous on whether those without significant property would have political as well as legal equality, and was silent on how the means to exercise one's talents could be secured by those without the necessary education or property. With the Assembly's prevarication on the full abolition of seigneurial dues, these ambiguities and silences were to underpin ongoing uncertainty and confrontation in town and country. Urban manual workers would contest political exclusion and economic insecurity, with radically different demands according to local circumstances. The same day the Estates-General opened in Versailles on 4 May, in the distant town of Limoux 700–800 people forced officials to seal the granaries, demanded an end to dues and indirect taxes, then ransacked the tax collector's offices and threw records into the River Aude.

Protest also continued unchecked in the countryside. The weight of the *ancien régime* had varied sharply across the kingdom: in all, the exactions of the royal state, the Church and seigneurs amounted to anywhere between 15 and 40 per cent.[45] Responses to the changes or lack of changes brought by the Revolution also varied. Disappointment that the National Assembly's putative abolition of feudalism would not reform *domaine con-géable* caused a surge of peasant protest in Upper Brittany in January 1790. Already in October 1789 the *recteur* of the parish of Coëtbugat in the diocese of Vannes had warned the National Assembly of 'the murmurings of discontent in our countryside'. 'Our peasants are coarse', he added, 'but sensitive as well'. Reforms to the Church in 1790 would turn the murmurings into a roar of rage.[46]

In contrast, during the four months after December 1789 peasants from 330 parishes in the triangle between Montauban, Rodez, and Périgueux invaded over one hundred châteaux to protest against the requisite payment of harvest dues, which were among the highest in France. These 'wild federations' seemed to appear spontaneously during the winter as bands of villagers armed themselves after church and went to neighbouring villages to join in the destruction of weathercocks and other symbols of the *ancien régime* before lighting a bonfire with pews from the church and erecting and dancing around a maypole ('mai'). Often the pole would be decorated with slogans that would have seemed contradictory to the Assembly, such as 'Long live the Nation, the Law, the King', and 'Woe to he who pays his rent!' A peasant from Alassac added: 'We don't need bourgeois or gentlemen any more.'[47] Here, as in all revolutions, popular ideologies fused ancient resentments with new assumptions about power and rights.

There was no one point at which 'peasants' or 'urban working people' became politicized or revolutionary, but their demands were inherently and incipiently revolutionary during the months, even years, before the massive revolt of July–August 1789.[48] Some historians have questioned the level of political awareness of the urban and rural masses, even as late as July 1789, but from late 1788 their grievances, as expressed in collective protest and the *cahiers*, could not have been accommodated within the *ancien régime*.[49] Even in 1780, an exasperated lawyer fulminated against a group of errand boys in Paris who refused to carry his messages: 'they form among themselves an insolent republic'. No doubt one could find examples at any time in Paris's history of the well-to-do regretting the erosion of deference, but for David Garrioch the use of 'republic' is revealing at a time of increased social distance and fractiousness in the changing capital: long before 1789, 'ordinary people felt themselves ready and able to be citizens'.[50]

Rural communities kept testing the boundaries of legitimate protest, utilizing the tried and true tactics of dissembling and manoeuvring. Just as some had 'believed' they were doing the king's will in refusing to pay dues in the winter of 1788–89, so in July others claimed a new authorization for disobedience. According to an official in Ploërmel, Brittany:

> all the peasants around here and in my area generally are refusing their quota of sheaves to the tithe-collector and say quite openly that there will be no collection

without bloodshed on the senseless grounds that as the request for the abolition of these tithes was included in the *cahiers* of this *sénéchaussée*, such an abolition has now come into effect.[51]

The insistence of rural communities that the seigneurial system be totally abolished was only recognized in 1792–93. This, and their search with urban working people for fuller political and social equality, drove the Revolution in directions that could not have been anticipated in 1789. The French Revolution of 1789 was both a social revolution and the pivotal turning-point in the social history of modern France. Most important, rather than the outcomes of the Revolution of 1789 being understood as the work of political élites in Paris and Versailles, they were also the result of an intense year of negotiation and confrontation between those élites and the working men and women of Paris and the provinces.

NOTES

1. Jacques Bernet (ed.), *Le Journal d'un maître d'école d'Île-de-France (1771–1792): Silly-en-Multien de l'Ancien Régime à la Révolution* (Villeneuve-d'Asq, 2000), 189, 195–6. The commune is today Silly-le-Long.
2. Georges Lefebvre, *The Coming of the French Revolution* [1939], trans. R. R. Palmer (Princeton, NJ, 1947).
3. Alfred Cobban, *The Social Interpretation of the French Revolution* (Cambridge, 1964); George V. Taylor, 'Revolutionary and Nonrevolutionary Content in the *Cahiers* of 1789: An Interim Report', *French Historical Studies* [hereafter *FHS*] 7 (1972), 479–502. For a discussion of the uneasy interaction of social and cultural history, see the contribution of William Scott to Peter R. Campbell (ed.), *The Origins of the French Revolution* (Basingstoke, 2006).
4. See, for example, the chapters by John Markoff in Campbell, *Origins of the French Revolution*; and Jack A. Goldstone in Thomas E. Kaiser and Dale K. Van Kley (eds), *From Deficit to Deluge: the Origins of the French Revolution* (Stanford, CA, 2011).
5. Jean-Clément Martin, *Nouvelle histoire de la Révolution française* (Paris, 2012), especially 88–9, 150–3, 169–73; William Doyle, *The Oxford History of the French Revolution*, 2nd edition (Oxford and New York, 2002), chs 4–5, esp. 114–15; François Furet, *The French Revolution 1770–1814*, translated by Antonia Nevill (Oxford, 1992), 66–70. In 1932, Lefebvre had paid far more attention to earlier unrest, noting that some of it was anti-seigneurial, but saw at its heart age-old traditions of subsistence protest: *The Great Fear of 1789: Rural Panic in Revolutionary France* [1932], trans. Joan White (New York, 1973), Part 1, ch. 4.
6. Gilbert Shapiro and John Markoff, *Revolutionary Demands: a Content Analysis of the Cahiers de Doléances of 1789* (Stanford, CA, 1998); John Markoff, *The Abolition of Feudalism: Peasants, Lords, and Legislators in the French Revolution* (University Park, PA, 1996); Anatoli Ado, *Paysans en Révolution. Terre, pouvoir et jacquerie 1789–1794* (Paris, 1996), ch. 2, esp. 95; Jean-Pierre Jessenne, 'Une Révolution sans ou contre les paysans?', in Michel Biard (ed.), *La Révolution française, une histoire toujours vivante* (Paris, 2009), 253–67; P. M. Jones, *The Peasantry in the French Revolution* (Cambridge, 1988); Micah Alpaugh, 'The Politics of Escalation in French Revolutionary Protest: Political Demonstrations,

Non-violence and Violence in the grandes journées of 1789', *French History* [hereafter *FH*] 23 (2009), 336–59. See also Jacques Godechot, *The Taking of the Bastille, July 14th, 1789*, trans. Jean Stewart (London, 1970), ch. 6.

7. Guy Lemarchand, 'Troubles populaires au XVIIIe siècle et conscience de classe: une préface à la Révolution française', *Annales historiques de la Révolution française* [hereafter *AHRF*] 279 (1990), 32–48; Jones, *Peasantry*, 53–8; Jean Nicolas, *La Rébellion française: mouvements populaires et conscience sociale 1661–1789* (Paris, 2008).

8. Arthur Young, *Travels in France during the years 1787–1788–1789* (New York, 1969), 96–7; Daniel Roche, *France in the Enlightenment*, trans. by Arthur Goldhammer (Cambridge, MA, 1998), 669–72; David Garrioch, *The Making of Revolutionary Paris* (Berkeley, Los Angeles and London, 2002), 285–9.

9. Godechot, *Bastille*, 124–33; Donald Sutherland, 'Urban Crowds, Riot, Utopia, and Massacres, 1789–92', in Peter McPhee (ed.), *A Companion to the French Revolution* (Oxford, 2013), 233.

10. Godechot, *Bastille*, 129; Markoff, *Abolition of Feudalism*, 226.

11. Jones, *Peasantry*, 60–81; P. M. Jones, *Reform and Revolution in France. The Politics of Transition, 1774–1791*, Cambridge, 1995, 166–74, 180–183; Godechot, *Bastille*, ch. 6; Lefevbre, *Great Fear*, ch. 4; David Andress, *1789: the Threshold of the Modern Age* (London, 2008), 205–7.

12. Several thousand parish *cahiers* were published in the first half of the twentieth century under the auspices of the Ministère de l'Instruction Publique as the *Collection de documents inédits sur l'histoire économique de la Révolution française*. This series is outlined in Shapiro and Markoff, *Revolutionary Demands*, 117–19.

13. On the limitations to the usefulness of the *cahiers*, see Jones, *Peasantry*, 58–67; Markoff, *Abolition of Feudalism*, 25–9.

14. Gilbert Larguier *et al.*, 'Les Assemblées primaires de la sénéchaussée de Carcassonne (8–16 mars 1789): typologie et composition sociale', *Bulletin de la Société des Études Scientifiques de l'Aude* 89 (1989), 101–20. See also Shapiro and Markoff, *Revolutionary Demands*, 136–40.

15. Marcelle Richard (ed.), *1789. Doléances et élections dans le futur Morbihan*, 2nd edition (Vannes, 1988), 15–27.

16. Markoff, *Abolition of Feudalism*; Shapiro and Markoff, *Revolutionary Demands*. For a different type of reading, see Philippe Grateau, *Les Cahiers de doléances: une relecture culturelle* (Rennes, 2001).

17. Jones, *Peasantry*, 94–8.

18. Denise, Maurice and Robert Bréant, *Menucourt. Un village du Vexin français pendant la Révolution 1789–1799* (Menucourt, 1989), 45–6.

19. Jones, *Peasantry*, 58–67.

20. Etienne Frénay (ed.), *Cahiers de doléances de la province de Roussillon (1789)* (Perpignan, 1979); Peter McPhee, *Revolution and Environment in Southern France: Peasants, Lords, and Murder in the Corbières, 1780–1830* (Oxford, 1999), 49.

21. McPhee, *Revolution and Environment*, 42.

22. Philip Dawson (ed.), *The French Revolution* (Englewood Cliffs, NJ, 1967), 16–18, 30–2.

23. Ado, *Paysans en Révolution*, 114.

24. Michael P. Fitzsimmons, *The Remaking of France: the National Assembly, the Constitution of 1791 and the Reorganization of the French Polity* (Cambridge and New York, 1994), 28–32.

25. On the elections of 1789, see Malcolm Crook, *Elections in the French Revolution: An Apprenticeship in Democracy, 1789–1799* (Cambridge, 1996), ch. 1; Jones, *Peasantry*, 28, 62–4.

26. Jones, *Peasantry*, 65–7; Lefevbre, *Great Fear*, 39. A strong regional study is Clay Ramsay, *The Ideology of the Great Fear: The Soissonnais in 1789* (Baltimore, MD, 1992).

27. Peter McPhee, *Robespierre: a Revolutionary Life* (London and New Haven, 2012), 50–61.

28. Godechot, *Bastille*, 133–51; Garrioch, *Making of Revolutionary Paris*, ch. 11.

29. Alpaugh, 'Politics of Escalation in French Revolutionary Protest', 339.

30. George Rudé, *The Crowd in the French Revolution* (Oxford, 1959), 46; Alpaugh, 'Politics of Escalation in French Revolutionary Protest', 344–8.

31. Rudé, *Crowd in the French Revolution*, ch. 4.

32. Lynn Hunt, *Revolution and Urban Politics in Provincial France: Troyes and Reims, 1786–1790* (Stanford, CA, 1978).

33. Eugène Dubois, *Histoire de la Révolution dans l'Ain*, vol. 1, *La Constituante* (1789–1791) (Bourg, 1931), 60–8.

34. Claude Muller, 'Religion et Révolution en Alsace', *AHRF* 337 (2004), 70; Timothy Tackett, 'Collective Panics in the Early French Revolution', *FH* 17 (2003), 149–58.

35. This tactic is outlined by George Rudé, *The Crowd in History* (New York, 1964).

36. James C. Scott, *Weapons of the Weak: Everyday Forms of Peasant Resistance* (New Haven, CT, 1985); *Domination and the Arts of Resistance: Hidden Transcripts* (New Haven, CT, 1990).

37. *AHRF*, 1955, 161–2; Philip Dwyer and Peter McPhee (eds), *The French Revolution and Napoleon. A Sourcebook* (London and New York, 2002), 22–3.

38. Ramsay, *Ideology of the Great Fear*, ch. 8.

39. Markoff, *Abolition of Feudalism*, p. 5. Note, too, the reflections of Melvin Edelstein, 'La Place de la Révolution française dans la politisation des paysans', *AHRF* 280 (1993), 135–44.

40. Michael P. Fitzsimmons, *The Night the Old Regime Ended: August 4, 1789 and the French Revolution* (University Park, PA, 2003); Jones, *Peasantry*, 81–5; Markoff, *Abolition of Feudalism*, ch. 8.

41. Rudé, *Crowd in the French Revolution*, 69 and ch. 5; Alpaugh, 'Politics of Escalation in French Revolutionary Protest', 354–9.

42. *Réimpression de l'Ancien Moniteur, seule histoire authentique et inaltérée de la Révolution française, depuis la réunion des Etats-Généraux jusqu'au Consulat*, 32 vols (Paris, 1847), vol. 2, 1789, 544; J. S. Bailly, *Mémoires d'un témoin de la Révolution* (Genève, 1975), vol. 3, 118–19.

43. Rudé, *Crowd in the French Revolution*, 79.

44. McPhee, *Revolution and Environment*, 54.

45. Jones, *Peasantry*, ch. 2; D. M. G. Sutherland, *The Chouans: The Social Origins of Popular Counter-Revolution in Upper Brittany, 1770–1796* (Oxford, 1982), 70.

46. Roger Dupuy, 'Les Émeutes anti-féodales de Haute-Bretagne (janvier 1790 et janvier 1791: meneurs improvises ou agitateurs politisés?', in Jean Nicolas (ed.), *Mouvements populaires et conscience sociale, XVI–XIXe siècles. Actes du colloque de Paris 24–26 mai 1984* (Paris, 1985), 453–4.

47. Jean Boutier, 'Jacqueries en pays croquant: les révoltes paysannes en Aquitaine (décembre 1789–mars 1790)', *AHRF* 34 (1979), 765; *Campagnes en émoi. Révoltes et Révolution en Bas-Limousin, 1789–1800* (Treignac, 1987); Jones, *Peasantry*, 105–117; Mona Ozouf, *Festivals and the French Revolution*, trans. by Alan Sheridan (Cambridge, MA, 1988), 37–8, 232–343.

48. In Peter Jones's words, 'it is essential to realise that the mobilisation of country dwellers did not wait upon events in Versailles or Paris': *Peasantry*, 61. Note the significant differences on peasant attitudes between the second and third editions of William Doyle, *Origins of the French Revolution* (Oxford, 1988, 1999), 198, cf. 183.

49. David Andress, *The French Revolution and the People* (London, 2004), 103; Rudé, *Crowd in the French Revolution*, 47, 209.
50. Garrioch, *Making of Revolutionary Paris*, 287, 294 and ch. 12.
51. Lefevbre, *Great Fear*, 40.

SELECTED READING

Alpaugh, Micah, *Non-Violence and the French Revolution: Political Demonstrations in Paris, 1787–1795* (Cambridge, 2014).

Alpaugh, Micah, 'The Politics of Escalation in French Revolutionary Protest: Political Demonstrations, Non-violence and Violence in the *grandes journées* of 1789', *French History* 23 (2009), 336–59.

Andress, David, *1789: the Threshold of the Modern Age* (London, 2008).

Campbell, Peter R. (ed.), *The Origins of the French Revolution* (Basingstoke, 2006).

Crook, Malcolm, *Elections in the French Revolution: An Apprenticeship in Democracy, 1789–1799* (Cambridge, 1996).

Fitzsimmons, Michael P., *The Night the Old Regime Ended: August 4, 1789 and the French Revolution* (University Park, PA, 2003).

Fitzsimmons, Michael P., *The Remaking of France: the National Assembly, the Constitution of 1791 and the Reorganization of the French Polity* (Cambridge and New York, 1994).

Godechot, Jacques, *The Taking of the Bastille, July 14th, 1789*, trans. Jean Stewart (London, 1970).

Lefebvre, Georges, *The Coming of the French Revolution* [1939], trans. R. R. Palmer (Princeton, NJ, 1947).

Lefebvre, Georges, *The Great Fear of 1789: Rural Panic in Revolutionary France* [1932], trans. Joan White (New York, 1973).

Jones, P. M., *The Peasantry in the French Revolution* (Cambridge, 1988).

McPhee, Peter (ed.), *A Companion to the French Revolution* (Oxford, 2013).

McPhee, Peter, *Living the French Revolution, 1789–1799* (Basingstoke, 2006).

Ramsay, Clay, *The Ideology of the Great Fear: The Soissonnais in 1789* (Baltimore, MD, 1992).

Rudé, George, *The Crowd in the French Revolution* (Oxford, 1959).

Shapiro, Gilbert, and John Markoff, *Revolutionary Demands: a Content Analysis of the Cahiers de Doléances of 1789* (Stanford, CA, 1998).

CHAPTER 11

··

A PERSONAL REVOLUTION

National Assembly Deputies and the
Politics of 1789

··

MICAH ALPAUGH

ON 20 June 1789, hundreds of legislators crowded into a royal tennis court on a side street of Versailles. Most had not known each other for more than six weeks. None had a full conception where their actions would lead them. Yet the men, predominantly drawn from the Estates-General's Third Estate, continued forward in their revolt against the royal prerogative and privileged orders' pre-eminence. Together swearing an oath to remain united as a National Assembly and gather wherever necessary to continue their work, the body became a revolutionary institution embodying national sovereignty. Through an emotional display of solidarity and power, a measure virtually unthinkable several weeks earlier became a reality. Through deputies' leadership, the revolts sweeping France coalesced into a revolution.

As the 'affective turn' has gathered strength in French Revolutionary studies, the emotions and psychology of the members of France's first National Assembly have garnered increasing attention. Who were the persons at the centre of the Revolution's early political dynamics? As Timothy Tackett asked, how did these men 'become Revolutionary?'[1] How did such individuals, predominantly drawn from practical, and in many ways ordinary, backgrounds, move beyond their initial objectives to shape the most radical revolution the world had seen? How did the deputies' radicalization react to and concurrently help fuel France's revolutionary fervour?

Attempting to understand National Assembly deputies' 'personal revolution' requires approaching the subject from a combination of personal, group, and collective viewpoints. In a 1,200-man legislature, drawn from varying circumstances and without stable factions or clearly defined leaders, the heterogeneity of experiences should not be underestimated. Each came from different backgrounds across a large and diverse country, and had their own reasons for serving. Many divides were likely overcome by necessity: the turmoil of mid-1789 did not privilege independent thinking. The Revolution predominantly advanced through hastily mobilized collective actions, to which each deputy had to respond, based upon his own ambitions, fears, alliances, and desired outcomes. Yet there was also much the deputies shared: refusing to accept political factions, most continued to work towards common solutions to the Revolution's most pressing problems.

Understanding the National Assembly's actions must also comprehend the vast pressures placed upon the legislators—including from royalty above, popular protesters below, and middling constituents back home. At the Revolution's centre, the National Assembly became its crossroads, interacting either through epistolary connections or face to face with virtually every group involved, from Parisian protesters to royal officials and reactionary nobles to small municipalities facing rural insurrections. The Assembly's revolutionary push would be repeatedly aided by outside groups—indeed, the revolutions of July and August 1789 are primarily attributable in the first case to Parisian insurgents, and the second to rural protests' continued force across France. Indeed, much of the legislature's power came from being able to respond more effectively to popular claims than the Crown did. Difficult as these stand-offs were—indeed, some Assembly members seemed pushed to near mental breakdown by the stresses of summer 1789—they played a fundamental role in forging the Assembly's politics.

This chapter will explore the dynamics at work in the formation of French Revolutionary legislative politics. It will examine the backgrounds, social context and political actions of men drawn into serving in France's first revolutionary legislature, attempting to interpret the deputies' radicalization over spring–summer 1789 and its legacies for the Revolution's course. France's national legislators became revolutionary through developments in both group cohesion and personal attitudes, with their politics developing in dialogue with the year's radicalizing events and processes.

ORIGINS AND ELECTIONS

The Estates-General's calling in contemporary perspective represented not a beginning, but rather a new phase of the economic and political crisis which increasingly battered France over the 1780s. Indeed, the Estates was the third Assembly convened by the Crown over the previous two years, following failed Assemblies of Notables in 1787 and 1788. Vivian Gruder has argued that the earlier Assemblies constituted not so much a 'pre-Revolution' as the French Revolution's 'first step', in which many of the era's fundamental issues were already in play, including the push for representative government and limitation of royal 'absolutism'.[2] Widespread fiscal and administrative reform became seen as essential for solving France's financial crisis. A total of 217 future Estates-General members—one-sixth of the future deputies—served in at least one of the bodies.[3] Many more, especially among the two-thirds of future Third Estate deputies with legal training, in some capacity participated in the growing opposition to the Crown, whether through parlementary judicial resistance, public protest, or the seditious pamphlet trade. Through such contestations, a vocabulary for resistance developed, popularizing emerging notions of citizenship, political reason and the French nation.[4] Commencing in a climate of turmoil, the Estates needed to accomplish significant reforms to restore faith in French government.

Though in certain respects the Estates-General's calling appeared a fresh start after bitter recent conflicts, the Crown's refusal to declare whether voting would be done by head or order—while adding to the uncertainty by doubling the Third Estate delegation's size—seemed designed to incite discord in the incoming Assembly. During the two Assemblies of Notables, noble representatives repeatedly appealed to the broader 'public' for support, and appeared to sway popular sentiment in their favour.[5] In early 1789, royal authorities used the voting procedure issue to divide the privileged from their former commoner allies. Through granting the Third Estate a chance to become directly involved in politics, albeit with a still undecided amount of power, the commoners soon became the other orders' adversaries.[6] Virtually all commoner *cahiers de doléances*—statements of grievances requested by the king—drawn up that spring called for all appointed positions to be opened to talent regardless of birth, a measure certain to incite noble resistance.[7] The Crown fostered an atmosphere of division, but lacked a plan for arbitrating between factions.

Nevertheless, Estates-General elections proceeded with great enthusiasm in winter 1789. Though varying by region and order, with the clergy's Assemblies appearing the most rancorous, great effort and significant debate commonly went into choosing deputies and drafting the *cahiers*. Many elections were highly contested, with nominees (especially for the Third Estate) often facing a multi-tiered election process. With little secret—or even individual—balloting employed, those standing for election faced potentially humiliating voice-votes from their peers.[8] Few could undertake their candidatures lightly, as participation in the Estates necessitated significant sacrifices: deputies would be away from their home and affairs for an unspecified period, and often had to pay at least part of their expenses. As local elites of at least some wealth, they also had much to lose in means and/or reputation should the Estates conclude unfavourably.

Who were the men elected, and how did they come to embody France's hopes in spring 1789? Though the over 1,200 representatives' diversity should not be underestimated, voting patterns across each Estate did hold recurring patterns. Some trends appeared reactionary. Ancient 'sword' nobles dominated elections for their seats, although even here provincial nobles commonly bested courtiers. Those chosen were wealthy even for their caste, and 80 per cent had served as military officers.[9] The commoners' deputation almost completely excluded peasants, artisans, and shopkeepers, while being dominated by urban professionals—though commoner deputies on average were still far less wealthy than those the nobility elected. Only amongst the clergy did an Estate's lower ranks gain the majority of seats, with many *curés* elected to sit alongside high ecclesiastical authorities. Though representing many gradations of middle-to-upper old regime society, virtually all men elected were at least moderately successful in their stations, and looked to push for changes favouring their own groups' interests.

To what extent these deputies were intellectually prepared for the task ahead can be debated. 'Men of letters' did not commonly gain election, with Third Estate voter preferences instead running to more 'practical' men predominantly drawn from the liberal professional classes. Future legislators' later interest in Rousseauian and democratic Enlightenment principles does not appear presaged by their reading preferences before 1789. Though 116 had published before 1789, most of their writings appeared far more in convention with *belles lettres* than demonstrative of any radical bent. Only about ten men of the 1,200 could be considered significant Enlightenment *philosophes*. Instead, voters often returned deputies with experience in old regime government and politics: a majority participated in municipal, provincial or ecclesiastical Assemblies, judicial *parlements*, or authored political pamphlets.[10] Though the deputies would soon receive a far deeper immersion into politics than any had heretofore received, they were no political virgins, having typically been exposed to earlier French political contestations.

Those deputies already possessing well-defined radical views appeared a small minority. Certain members had dabbled in international radical movements for political, and what would become human, rights, such as the comte de Mirabeau, marquis de Lafayette, and other future deputies who helped found the *Société des amis des noirs* in late 1788.[11] Yet as seen in the antislavery society's reversals in 1789, many more deputies often distrusted broad humanitarianism. Domestic radical pamphleteering also only rarely provided a successful political route forward. The era's most successful pamphlet, abbé Sieyès' January 1789 call for the full inclusion of non-nobles in political life in *What is the Third Estate?* made its author a minor celebrity in certain Paris salons and clubs, but did not lead to a groundswell of support for Sieyès' candidacy—he would be the last of twenty deputies elected for Paris' Third Estate, after being rejected by both the Orléans and Paris clergy. Indeed, the extent to which the famous pamphlet was an agent of change rather than a prognostication is questionable.[12] Characterizing radical deputies and their close allies as a bloc 'orchestrating' the Assembly's movements—as done in one major recent work—seems far too facile.[13] Such representatives' views appeared highly marginal until the shocks of the early Revolution.

Estates-General deputies may have anticipated some of the troubles ahead, given the climate of worsening political and wider social conflict. Rural revolts rose, with peasants across much of France—who had been largely excluded from Third Estate voting—looking to gain political voice and achieve land reforms.[14] Urban unrest also erupted, most notably in Paris, where voting restrictions were even more pronounced than in most provinces. April 1789's Réveillon Riots directly targeted a Parisian elector (Jean-Baptise Réveillon) believed to have spoken dismissively in a closed-door Third Estate meeting of the working poor's financial difficulties. Following poor policing of initial Parisian demonstrations, three days of open street-fighting broke out before authorities restored order. Though incoming deputies (many of whom were seeing Paris for the first time) commonly reacted with horror to the Réveillon uprising, few yet looked to offer protesters alternative methods to dialogue with authorities.[15] The limitations upon suffrage for the lower Third Estate left few means besides protest for gaining an active voice in national politics.

Yet despite the challenges ahead, most deputies appeared optimistic upon arriving at Versailles: for the first time in 175 years, the king directly looked to involve the three orders in the governing process, for the explicit goal of determining political reform. This optimism was largely untroubled, however, by specifics: although the Estates' voting procedures remained undecided, few if any deputies had developed detailed plans or strategies for the upcoming months. Expecting royal authorities to guide the legislative process, no one was prepared for the extent of uncertainty, upheaval, and resulting improvisations ahead.

THE ESTATES-GENERAL

The Estates-General's 5 May opening appeared a moment of great hopes for all involved. Each Estate believed it could gain royal and ministerial favour for their own positions: the nobles looked to gain increased power autonomous from the faltering Crown, the clergy for mild ecclesiastical reform but also an increased cultural role, and the Third Estate for a broad but largely undefined programme of state restructuring and greater political incorporation of its members. Most expected royal leadership to enunciate an agenda for the Estates, but royal Minister Jacques Necker's vague and uninspired opening speech—presenting the crisis facing France but no proposed solutions—offered no real direction. The conflict over whether to vote by head or order remained unsolved.

The deputies, most of whom had never before seen Versailles, concurrently confronted an unknown—and often treacherous—social scene. Almost all had to find lodgings for the Estates' uncertain duration and owing to the resulting housing shortage often took up rooms with local residents, or split accommodations with one or more fellow deputies. Many complained of expenses at the centre of old regime splendour, especially since legislators at most received only small stipends for serving. Their own stretched circumstances contrasted starkly with the continued grandeur of royal court life. Such discrepancy appeared especially galling given the financial crisis deputies came to Versailles to solve. Legislators also experienced the many slights to personal prestige the court system fostered: though granted access to the palace gardens (like any well-dressed commoner), most remained shut out of the inner chambers and consultative circles surrounding the king and royal family. Social relations between deputies and courtiers worsened.[16] Indeed, many legislators came to believe the court was plotting their downfall.

Despite growing pressures to commence serious discussions, the Estates remained deadlocked on voting procedures. Royal indecision led many to increasingly doubt the monarchy's basic ability to function. Most noble and clerical deputies were not prepared to renounce voting by order, nor would the Third Estate accept only a minority voice. Moderate deputies in all three orders, though distressed at the growing polarization, generally continued to support their own Estate.[17] Conciliatory conferences between the three orders on 23 May failed. Radical minorities from each privileged order, however, appeared ready to create a liberal majority with the Third Estate if voting by head.

In navigating the crisis, Third Estate deputies had to move carefully: alienating privileged supporters (or conservatives in their own ranks) would make their push for power untenable, and leave the two privileged Estates in control. Yet to force resolution the Third Estate engaged in almost total obstruction, refusing to participate in any activity that might set precedent for voting by order.

The May–June procedural stand-off helped foster growing group confidence among Third Estate radicals. A new form of caucusing developed with the Breton Club, at first a social organization for deputies from Brittany, which became an important venue for cultivating radical opinion. Already possessing a 'Patriote' reputation for their 1788 defence of the Rennes Parlement, the Bretons soon drew other radicals to their meetings, and within a week of the Estates' opening began calling for a National Assembly.[18] More broadly, deputies' cohesion grew as Versailles social life expanded: dining parties, salons, lectures, music, theatre, and other groups proliferated as weeks passed.[19] In formal meetings as well, since most Third Estate sessions occurred separate from the privileged orders, collective identity grew.

Third Estate radicals became increasingly autonomous from monarchy as they developed their own political identities during the early Estates-General. Though the Crown had brought them to Versailles—if as a counterweight to the intransigent privileged orders which had let the Assemblies of Notables fail—commoner deputies became more willing to resist royal directives. To justify their deviance, radicals broadly constructed a new identity for themselves as the French nation's true representatives. Whereas according to the medieval conception of the Estates the deputies were 're-presenting' their constituents' opinions for the king, in 1789 legislators came to position themselves as 'representatives' in the modern sense, claiming to embody sovereign power. To bolster such ideological justifications, deputies looked to play the part of a sovereign more convincingly before the public. The French theatre became a key inspiration, with some deputies taking acting lessons, and many adjusting their oratory (an especially difficult art in the cavernous Menus Plaisirs meeting hall) to popular stage conventions.[20] Theatrical and literary sentimentalist content also increasingly filled deputies' speeches as they strove to influence sceptical colleagues.[21] Developing actors' sense of gravitas—though little offsetting the sense of detachment or irony—legislators refined postures for their upcoming performances.

Deputies conceptualized themselves as representatives of the entire French nation, and with the help of growing press freedom looked to build a national audience. Mirabeau's Lettres aux constituants reported Estates-General proceedings, aired controversies, and proposed solutions. Full-time journalists soon followed with regular reports of debates.[22] Reporting legislative proceedings itself was a recent innovation: in Britain, such journalism had been illegal until 1774, on the argument that legislators' impartiality would be compromised. French National Assembly orations increasingly became delivered not just for their impact on fellow legislators, but for a vast virtual audience. Readers across France could follow the Estates as a serial, in which many felt a growing emotional investment. In turn, deputies' accountability, with debates soon known to crowds around the capital and constituents back at home, also grew.

As the Third Estate and its allies coalesced, groundwork congealed to enable the major changes soon to come. Commoner deputies' growing sense of common cause would embolden them to resist royal directives with a resolution inconceivable earlier on. Whereas the Crown could likely have implemented a wide range of directives in early May, by mid-June it faced legislators possessing an extensive sense of solidarity, and their own divergent plans about France's future.

THE FORMATION OF THE
NATIONAL ASSEMBLY

The leap forward to a nationally sovereign, unicameral Assembly came about quickly. Following a 10 June proposal by the abbé Sieyès, momentum built for the Third Estate to declare itself nationally sovereign. On 17 June, the commoner deputies (along with a smattering of clergy) elected to assume the title National Assembly—a term specifically chosen for its totalizing connotations in representation. Through representing the nation, deputies looked to embody it.[23] The tactic initially appeared successful: on 19 June, a settlement between liberal nobles and the Third Estate cleared the way for a majority vote on credentials, which would lead to voting by head. Conservative nobles and clergymen, however, convinced the Crown to intervene. Guards locked the Menus Plaisirs in 'preparation' for a royal speech that afternoon. To head off royal intervention, the Third Estate and their allies moved ahead with a show of power.

In a collective action owing much to the popular demonstrations regularly occurring in Versailles, Paris, and elsewhere, deputies marched from the Menus Plaisirs to an indoor tennis court several blocks away. A much larger crowd followed, chanting loudly to encourage the deputies. Nearly unanimously, the representatives present swore not to separate before granting France a constitution. Through creating a political spectacle by their emotional oath-taking, the legislators asserted their own sovereign power. For the first time, legislators directly opposed the king's will.

A further show of solidarity soon brought full attainment of their designs. After the new National Assemblymen over the next two days convinced most of the First Estate to join, the Crown moved against the new legislature, with Louis XVI convening all deputies on 23 June. Despite Necker's conspicuous absence, implying a division between king and minister, Louis proceeded with his assertion of power. The king explicitly reversed the National Assembly's creation in demanding the Estates vote by order on issues concerning privileges. If disobeyed, Louis implicitly threatened full dissolution. The nobility and much of the clergy applauded, and filed out after the king. Though the Crown may have successfully enacted such instructions on 5 May, now radicals mobilized for resistance. Mirabeau, Sieyès, Barnave, and other influential orators harangued the remaining deputies, asserting a royal declaration could not dissolve a National Assembly. In a display of solidarity, Mirabeau famously declared those present 'will not be driven from this chamber but by the force of bayonets'. Royal authorities opted against using force. The majority of the clergy returned to the Assembly with the commoners the next day, as did a noble contingent on 25 June. With the king's authority collapsing owing to legislators' non-compliance, Louis capitulated, ordering the remaining privileged deputies to join the others—though still not explicitly sanctioning a National Assembly as such.

The implications of the deputies' actions were staggering: the king had been directly and successfully disobeyed. Despite new shows of fealty towards Louis XVI following the crisis' resolution, the National Assembly accepted no limits upon its prerogative. Equally important, the Assembly's formation resulted from, and furthered, growing sentiments of both hope and fear sweeping the legislators and France more broadly. With the collapse of royal primacy, realms of possible revolutionary action continued to multiply. In a society previously based on precedent, tradition, and (commonly) inertia, now the high expectations of a new era drove action.

Though June's events produced moments of exhilaration, the stresses upon many deputies grew. The cumulative psychological strain of recent developments pushed certain members to breaking point. One deputy apparently suffered a psychotic breakdown the day after the Tennis Court Oath. As Barry Shapiro's work has highlighted, deputies—previously 'respectable and law-abiding pillars of French Society' across the early Revolution were fighting a 'set of powerful emotional constraints', particularly relating to their duties towards the king.[24] Fears of royal retribution, together with guilt over subverting a monarch all still swore fealty to, helped shape and distort deputy action across the period. Yet such reservations did not impede legislators from continuing their now-revolutionary movement.

The deputies helped create a new identity as 'Revolutionaries' which had not existed before. Previously, 'Revolution' was seen as a systemic event, functioning beyond the limits of human control. From June 1789 onwards, however, the process became embodied in 'Revolutionaries': activists committed to breaking with the past and establishing a new order. How did deputies come to see a sharp rupture as the way forward? Tackett delineates four key factors in radical deputies' 'psychological transformation' into Revolutionaries: their growing 'group consciousness', the effects of Assembly oratory, protesters' impact, and the nobility's intransigent attitudes.[25] Such a description evenly divides the causes between internal and external factors, working together to drive radical legislators forward. Pushed by both radical insurgents and conservative nobles, the deputies reacted by developing a radical synthesis beyond anything they might have proposed otherwise. Bombarded with extreme stimuli, representatives had to quickly process the changing political landscape and adjust to new situations. The new National Assembly's revolutionary actions arose not from a preconceived plan, but rather from circumstances and their mental impacts on deputies.

Deputies' personal revolution closely related to the extent of their identification with the radical branch of the former Third Estate. For the core of radical deputies, the struggles towards creating the National Assembly seemed a marvellous collective act, presaging the transformation of all France. Others viewed the events with trepidation—or amongst conservative deputies, even horror—intensifying obstruction or even counter-Revolutionary opposition. The newly minted National Assembly continued to direct the growing revolution forward, but only with the help of outside events.

The National Assembly
and the July revolution

After the National Assembly's revolution, the impetus for revolutionary action passed outwards. Whereas before July the Assembly acted as the Revolution's avant-garde, in the mid-month turmoil legislative politics were superseded by a series of popular revolts. Looking to establish a new governmental structure for France at virtually all levels, should aristocratic reaction be overcome, urban and rural insurgents soon undertook municipal revolutions. Facing a quickly radicalizing political dynamic, with broader swathes of the population becoming increasingly revolutionized, legislators sought to conciliate solutions between the growing number of groups contending for revolution or reaction.

Despite the momentousness of declaring a National Assembly, old suspicions and antagonisms amongst the deputies continued. In late June, conservatives openly held meetings discussing how to subvert the new Assembly's proceedings.[26] The revolutionary nature of the National Assembly's formation exposed the legislature's dubious legality—which conservatives attempted to turn to their advantage. Many Estates-General deputies were sent to Versailles with specific 'mandates', requiring deputies to vote only in accordance with the *cahiers*' now-outdated content. No legislators were mandated to participate in anything approximating a 'National Assembly'. Several conservatives used this legal crisis to justify withdrawal from further participation. Others asserted that the Assembly must wait for several weeks until new credentials could be verified. Most deputies, however, continued in office, recognizing their mandates only in part.[27] Presaging the summer's much-further-sweeping changes, Revolutionaries showed their willingness to break from constraints of the past.

Though the Tennis Court crisis occurred only three weeks earlier, National Assembly deputies did not appear prepared for the summer's next major crisis. The Crown's recall of Jacques Necker, which became known on 12 July brought not another moment of solidarity and commitment from the National Assembly legislators, but inaction. A motion by Mirabeau condemning the troop build-up around Paris and Versailles had been rejected on 9 July. Despite the Assembly's defiance of royal force the previous month, with the legislators now surrounded by a growing military presence, none of the recently minted Revolutionaries moved to strongly repudiate the ministerial change—even with the National Assembly's future at risk. Royal coercion appeared to be working.

Though the Revolution may have faltered if left solely in the deputies' hands, popular groups stepped forward to ensure its continuance. The Palais Royal—owned by liberal noble deputy the duc d'Orléans and freed from police oversight by his princely privilege—had emerged as Paris' radical political meeting ground. From its gardens, the first demonstrations opposing Necker's recall set out on the afternoon of 12 July, leading to the Bastille insurrection.[28] Direct and decisive revolutionary action could come not just from the legislators, but also popular groups seeking to represent the French *peuple*. Whereas previously the Assembly had seen the Revolution as inseparable from themselves, now they looked upon decisive events as spectators.

The legislature passively waited for the Parisian insurrection's outcome, with their future course likely to be guided by the event's success or failure. Reprisals against radical deputies seemed very possible should the Paris uprising have been crushed, and to heighten tensions the Crown—perhaps taking Mirabeau's famous earlier proclamation literally—posted new guards armed with bayonets outside the Menus Plaisirs.[29] Only after the Crown's capitulation—announced before the Assembly on the morning of 15 July to wild applause—would the legislature send a deputation to parley with Parisian protesters. Additionally, 100 deputies accompanied the king during his tense visit to Paris two days later. With the capital's newly reconstituted *Milice bourgeoise* lining the authorities' route, legislators could witness the Revolution's growing force.

Municipal revolutions throughout France followed in the Bastille insurrection's wake, to which the National Assembly had little choice but to acquiesce. Though local revolutionary correspondence committees had become widely established and politically influential in spring 1789, the steps taken following the Bastille's fall proved much more thorough. News of Parisian events—often spread in letters by the deputies themselves— sparked uprisings across France, with crowds wresting power from royal authorities in favour of elected councils. Local Third Estate elites typically led the new municipal organizations, and enlisted active voters into militias to attempt to keep order.[30] Through a combination of euphoria in the advancements occurring and fears of potential aristocratic reaction, insurgents established a revolutionary infrastructure across France. Much like national deputies, local officials 'became revolutionary' through assuming governing power in the people's name. Also akin to the national authorities after July, they owed their positions to the results of popular collective action.

Though the Assembly abstained from direct involvement in July's upheavals— and typically condemned popular violence more generally—in profiting from the Bastille uprising, the body became implicated in the use of violence for political ends. Previous major revolutionary changes, including the National Assembly's creation, had occurred peacefully. Indeed, the popular demonstrations beginning the Bastille uprising had also attempted to abstain from physical violence. But now, in profiting from the Parisian insurrection, the National Assembly in certain respects became complicit in its excesses. Though most deputies continued to express horror at such actions, they could not be fully separated from the revolutionary gains occurring alongside. Revolutionary elites' internalizing of these legacies, for historian François Furet, helped sow the seeds for an ideology of terror.[31] To comprehend the uprising, as David Andress has shown, Maximilien Robespierre himself increasingly adopted melodramatic distinctions between 'good' and 'evil' he would later adapt for his terroristic programmes.[32]

Following the Bastille insurrection, the Assembly appeared solidly established for the first time. As the threat of forced dispersion receded, autonomy from royal control increased, as the Assembly had no fear of Necker and another attempted ministerial change could have incited further rebellion in Paris and the provinces. Yet, conversely, the collapse of royal authority and institutions also created a 'power vacuum' which could also threaten the Assembly, with local and regional authority potentially devolving from the central state. The Revolution expanded in scope and power, but deputies would need to creatively assert their own authority to direct it.

THE REVOLUTION OF 4 AUGUST 1789

In the aftermath of the July insurrection, the National Assembly lost much of its revolutionary avant-garde status to wider popular upheavals in Paris and across the provinces. The legislature would be pushed to their radical abolition of privileges by the anti-seigneurial uprisings continuing across France. John Markoff has described peasants and legislators as working in an implicit dialogue, whose failure to reach effective compromises early on progressively radicalized both sides.[33] Deputies also engaged in direct dialogues with their constituents, working to bring peace to the countryside. Many legislators, across all three former estates, also had personal land interests to protect. Though the Assembly's mid-July debates largely focused upon using force to suppress rural insurgents, some deputies began discussing scaling back seigneurial laws instead.[34]

The extent of the changes inaugurated on 4 August proved shocking. If June 1789 had created a revolutionary identity for legislators, August 1789 revolutionized social life for much of France. At a sparsely attended evening session, proposals allowing peasants to purchase seigneurial property received wide approbation. Next, the duc du Châtelet offered to abandon such rights to his own land, provided he receive 'just compensation'. Numerous deputies then rushed to the rostrum to make their own renunciations in an emotional flurry. Soon, sacrifices moved from being individual to systemic. Tithes, feudal rights, virtually the entire edifice of privileges organizing old regime hierarchy were abolished—the result of efforts led by the privileged orders' representatives. Additionally, nobles' preferential access to governmental appointments—and thus their existence as a privileged social stratum—ended, with the legislature opening all appointed positions to talent. No previous revolutionary changes had been so far-reaching: indeed, never before in European history had the nobility officially been abolished anywhere.[35] Rather than reacting sluggishly or piecemeal to the rural upheavals, the Assembly with the 4 August measures acted to 'embrace' social revolution, as Michael Fitzsimmons has argued.[36] Thereby, an agenda to construct a thoroughly 'New Regime' developed—a gargantuan undertaking which would continue to consume the legislature.

Yet if 4 August provided the basis for feudalism's abolition, deputies spent a week working out its detailed terms, and produced a more ambiguous settlement. In a measure regarded by many in the countryside as a betrayal, the Assembly decreed on 11 August that property dues must continue to be paid until adequate compensation for the nobles could be determined. Much of the peasants' financial burdens remained. But the Assembly did abolish *corvée* labour and a wide variety of other noble privileges forever. Despite new-found resistance in some areas, however, the political conversation broadly shifted from revolutionary insurgency to elaborating the new revolutionary compact. The June–July 1789 wave of rural insurrections—featuring at its height over 145 simultaneous uprisings across France—would abate for the rest of 1789.[37]

The decrees of 4–11 August reflected the Assembly's anarchic and emotionally charged environment. In a legislative body without regular leaders, possessing few procedural regulations, and privileging the effects of oratory and sentiment, support for measures could coalesce quickly, without extensive pre-planning or appreciation for full implications. Deputies' respect for the power of emotion, and the precedents of immediate revolutionary change in June and July, also helped inspire the August groundswell. The legislators moved boldly—believing they possessed the mandate and group power to enact drastic changes.

Closely following the development of new 'revolutionary' standards, however, for a significant minority of deputies was a growing sense of what becoming 'counter-revolutionary' could mean. The emigration of the king's brother the Count of Artois after the Bastille insurrection contributed to fears of the Revolution being crushed from outside. More moderate conservatism also spread, as the *Monarchien* faction rose to a position of great influence. The aftermath of 4 August pushed many *patriote* clergymen into opposition: whereas the Assembly initially planned to reimburse Church tithes, revised plans abolished the revenues outright. This appeared especially egregious as accompanying new arrangements compensated the nobility better than expected for their suppressed privileges. Whereas many priests initially saw the Revolution heralding an era of needed religious reform, now, in the words of one clerical deputy, the Assembly appeared 'to have vowed the clergy's ruin'.[38] Though the Assembly inevitably faced difficulties moderating between different groups' interests, 4 August heightened antagonisms that the Revolution would never escape.

Fears of aristocratic reaction later that month helped push the deputies to adopt on 28 August—despite their practical bent—the most far-reaching statement of revolutionary principle yet, the Declaration of the Rights of Man and the Citizen. Whereas many deputies did not initially see the value in an abstract and inclusive statement of rights, the legislature came to find useful a statement of guarantees establishing freedoms of speech, press, religion, due process, and even 'resistance to oppression'.[39] Yet the Declaration still incorporated numerous compromises, agreed upon in the Assembly committee: though strongly asserting the 'negative freedoms' of resistance to tyranny, the extent to which the document would ensure the 'positive liberty' of democratic participation to much of the population remained vague.[40] Though debate over the Declaration's applicability to the poor, women, colonial slaves, and other disenfranchised groups would continue, radicals could pronounce what they now described as the Revolution's basic principles enshrined. Through their pronouncements of August, deputies decisively set much of the Revolution's programme. Yet also, particularly due to the Declaration's sweeping and universalist rhetoric, the document helped further what Lynn Hunt has described as 'unreasonable expectations' for a society still very unequal.[41]

Did the decrees of August, in eliminating millennia-old bases of French society, make the Revolution too large to be controlled? Though some implications of 4 August and the Declaration were not as sweeping as they first appeared, in other senses they showed the aggressiveness of a Revolution now refusing to accept traditional precedents and increasingly overcoming even entrenched interests. With no political or cultural restraints strong enough to directly impede the Revolution's progress, radical change in France had only begun.

Prelude to Terror?

Debates over the Constitution—whether such a document was even necessary, or if so in what form—consumed a great deal of legislators' attention over the summer of 1789. Did France already have an inherent 'constitution' ingrained in its ancient practices, as Britain claimed to? The radical changes of 4 August made this claim appear untenable. Revolutionary change now seemed to necessitate a consciously new constitutional order. But what would such a system entail? The deputies' solutions to these questions highlighted much about their hopes and fears for the new Revolutionary order.

Despite the power the Assembly assumed during the summer of 1789, their justifications for holding authority remained problematic. How the deputies embodied national representation appeared complicated, particularly given the often-competing representations of its unity in one person (the king) or the assembled people (as assumed by such groups as electoral Assemblies, clubs or popular protesters).[42] To maintain authority, the assembly had to prove itself as a useful middle ground of representation between alternative conceptions.

How the Assembly would share power with the king, who still held absolutist pretensions, represented a key difficulty. After rancorous debates, the legislature—without consulting the royal court—settled upon enacting a 'suspensive veto'. This gave the monarch power to temporarily strike down legislation, but still made him answerable to the nation's electoral districts, which could vote to override. Though itself a compromise between more extreme positions, this solution pleased neither royalists who wanted an absolute veto, nor popular radicals who opposed granting the king any such power. Indeed, Palais Royal factions organized a massive demonstration towards Versailles on 30 August to make their displeasure known. To enact the compromise veto, deputies had to assert their own sovereign authority—which they justified through asserting that the legislature possessed France's 'general will'.

Did the deputies, through their composite actions over the Revolution's early months, sow the 'seeds' of their own destruction, as Norman Hampson has argued?[43] Did the constitutional compromise lead them, as Keith Baker has suggested, into 'opting for Terror'?[44] By arguing for the predominant force of the 'general will' over prior authority and constraint, did deputies create a model future authorities could subvert into dictatorship and terror?[45] Such arguments' overly suggestive features fall flat, however, when one examines the vast alternative possibilities present during the Revolution's first year, and indeed the legislature's generally moderate governance over their last two years in office. Despite 1789's many dangerous precedents, legislators looked to only make one, singular French Revolution. The relationship between the monarchy and Assembly appeared to largely stabilize, only becoming recontested after the royal family's Flight to Varennes in 1791.[46]

THE MODERATE REACTION

Linear accounts of the Revolution's progression can best be complicated by examining the moderate reaction of late 1789 onwards. Despite the radical changes of June–August 1789, the majority of deputies thereafter looked to slow or even 'end the Revolution', focusing on solidifying the changes already made. Consolidation—rather than escalation—appears to have been legislators' predominant intent.

The year's last major political event, the October Days, again saw deputy inaction amidst an armed stand-off between Parisians and the king's forces. The action apparently took the legislature by surprise: no mention of growing disquiet in Paris was made in the Assembly preceding the protest's arrival. Female protesters' avant-garde quickly occupied the Menus Plaisirs, targeting prominent right-wing legislators for verbal abuse, but seemed primarily concerned with blocking the legislature from interfering with events at the royal château. The Assembly ultimately decreed its intention to follow the king wherever he should reside. A limited number of conservatives resigned from the Assembly in protest, several more threatened to do so, and many wrote of the events in lurid terms, but the altered location would be permanent.[47]

Deputies now found themselves in Paris, in most cases for their first extended stay. Much of the summer's fermentation had subsided or been suppressed: the Palais-Royal had lost its police-exempt privileges after 4 August, and the Assembly would pass a martial law decree following a popular lynching on 23 October, ending major street protests for the year. Other aspects of popular dissent, however, continued to multiply: revolutionary newspapers grew in number, with the most radical calling for direct popular sovereignty beyond National Assembly representation.[48] The Assembly's new hall, on the Tuileries Gardens' north side, lay near both the Palais-Royal and the king's residence. Radicals came to dominate the area, with many lodging nearby, while conservative deputies increasingly withdrew to quieter quarters. Whereas most deputies had lived in relatively close proximity at Versailles, the capital's size allowed deputies to associate more selectively.[49] Few, however, could have avoided the influences of all the competing interests in Paris, especially as the Revolution's broadening scope increasingly attracted more interested parties and profiteers.

A relative normality in Assembly politics developed by the time of the move to Paris, with only a minority of deputies endorsing further radical solutions. Harriet Applewhite demonstrated in her study of deputy political alignments how, based upon their voting and published opinions, only 35 per cent of deputies can be classified as consistently on the Revolution's political 'left'. Indeed, 47 per cent displayed regular 'conservative' leanings, with 'moderates' constituting the 18 per cent in between. Although left-wing deputies spoke in the Assembly more often, published more regularly, and held a dispro-portionate number of leadership positions (including sessions as Assembly president), they depended upon others' support to pass legislation.[50] The two privileged orders still constituted nearly half the delegates, and largely directed their efforts towards ensuring a moderate Revolutionary settlement. While the great occasions of emotional solidarity in June and August had swept along the moderate rump, under more normal circum-stances such support could be difficult to procure.

By fall 1789, many deputies' political positions hardened. When sitting in the Assembly, members of similar persuasions deliberately clustered together and away from their opponents, creating the modern political connotations of 'left' and 'right'. Enthusiasm for pursuing politics based upon the 'general will'—at least in the spirit of the unamist proclamations of June—receded before a multiplying variety of clubs and factions. While the *Monarchiens* appeared the most powerful group in early fall 1789, the centre-right *Impartials* multiplied after the move to Paris. The radical Jacobins formed in November, both in the capital and through a growing provincial network, justifying their close-knit association as necessary due to recent conservative gains.[51] Growing divides and mistrust amongst Assemblymen may have helped lead to the 'self-denying ordinance' of May 1791, which did not allow any deputy to stand for election to the upcoming Legislative Assembly.[52] Much early idealism gave way to partisan battling over the form the New Regime would take.

As much as 'becoming a Revolutionary' altered legislators' notions of themselves and the French political community, the deputies did not necessarily see Revolutionary change as an ongoing phenomenon. National Assembly members typically conceptual-ized themselves as trying to moderate an end to the Revolution and fix a permanent new order for France—indeed, no amendments to the forthcoming Constitution would be allowed. Only the upheavals of future years would upset the balances the Constituent Assembly attempted to establish.

CONCLUSION

The political dynamics and rapid changes of 1789 cannot be understood apart from those individuals at the heart of the process in the National Assembly. Alternately directing and responding to the year's vast upheavals, the deputies played a central role in shaping both what 'Revolutionary' came to mean and the course of the Revolution itself. Though not reducible to any individual or small group of leaders, the deputies' French Revolution was an intensely personal one: fraught with risk and transformative for their own selves as well as France. The experience of revolution led legislators to solutions they could not have anticipated in May 1789.

The emotions of legislators' lives over the Revolution's first months should not detract, however, from the rationales that drove their actions forward. Drawn from overwhelmingly practical backgrounds, the deputies looked to navigate towards solutions which would both stabilize French politics and favour their own interests. While such an outcome required radical dissent—and perhaps France's greatest revolution—in June 1789, thereafter the National Assembly realized the need to mediate between competing factions in order to create a new Revolutionary order. Though threats to their new compact continued, far from opting for terror, the deputies looked to inaugurate a new era of conciliation and opportunity.

Notes

1. Timothy Tackett, *Becoming a Revolutionary: The Deputies of the First French National Assembly and the Making of a Revolutionary Culture, 1789–1790* (Princeton, 1996).
2. Vivian R. Gruder, *The Notables and the Nation: The Political Schooling of the French, 1787–1788* (Cambridge, 2007).
3. Tackett, *Becoming*, 81.
4. David A. Bell, *Lawyers and Citizens: The Making of a Political Elite in Old Regime France* (Oxford, 1994).
5. Jay M. Smith, *Nobility Reimagined: The Patriotic Nation in Eighteenth-Century France* (Ithaca, 2005).
6. Gruder, *Notables*, esp. 3–6.
7. John Markoff and Gilbert Shapiro, *Revolutionary Demands: A Content Analysis of the Cahiers de Doléances of 1789* (Stanford, 1998), 292.
8. Tackett, 97–9; Malcolm Crook, *Elections in the French Revolution: An Apprenticeship in Democracy, 1789–1799* (Cambridge, 1996), esp. 8–29; William Doyle, *The Origins of the French Revolution* (Oxford, 1980), 150–5.
9. D. M. G. Sutherland, *The French Revolution and Empire: The Quest for a Civic Order* (Oxford, 2003), 35.
10. Tackett, *Becoming*, 48–94.
11. Marcel Dorigny and Bernard Gainot (eds), *La Société des amis des noirs: contribution à l'histoire de l'abolition de l'esclavage* (Paris, 1998).
12. William H. Sewell, Jr, *A Rhetoric of Bourgeois Revolution: The Abbé Sieyès and What is the Third Estate?* (Durham, 1995), esp. 8–16; Ken Margerison, *Pamphlets and Public Opinion: The Campaign for a Union of Orders during the French Revolution* (West Lafayette, 1998).
13. Jonathan Israel, *Democratic Enlightenment: Philosophy, Revolution and Human Rights, 1750–1790* (Oxford, 2011).
14. John Markoff, *The Abolition of Feudalism: Peasants, Lords and Legislators during the French Revolution* (University Park, Pennsylvania, 1996).

15. See my 'The Politics of Escalation in French Revolutionary Protest: Political Demonstrations, Nonviolence and Violence in the Grandes journées of 1789', *French History* 23, no. 3 (2009), 336–59; Tackett, 166.
16. Edna LeMay, *La vie quotidienne des députés aux États généraux* (Paris, 1987), 57–77.
17. Sutherland, *French Revolution*, 38.
18. Harriet B. Applewhite, *Political Alignment in the French National Assembly, 1789–1791* (Baton Rouge, 1993), 72.
19. Alyssa Goldstein Sepinwall, *The Abbé Grégoire and the French Revolution: The Making of Modern Universalism* (Berkeley, 2005), 86.
20. Paul Friedland, *Political Actors: Representative Bodies and Theatricality in the Age of the French Revolution* (Ithaca, 2002).
21. Angelica Gooden, 'The Dramatizing of Political Theatricality and the Revolutionary Assemblies', *Forum for Modern Language Studies* 20 (1984), 193–212; William M. Reddy, *The Navigation of Feeling: A Framework for the History of Emotions* (Cambridge, 2001).
22. Jeremy D. Popkin, *Revolutionary News: The Press in France, 1789–1799* (Durham, 1990), 29–30.
23. Michael P. Fitzsimmons, *The Remaking of France: The National Assembly and the Constitution of 1791* (Cambridge, 1994), 41; Robert H. Blackman, 'What's in a Name? Possible Names for a Legislative Body and the Birth of National Sovereignty during the French Revolution, 15–16 June 1789', *French History* 21, no. 1 (2007), 22–43.
24. Barry M. Shapiro, *Traumatic Politics: The Deputies and the King in the Early French Revolution* (University Park, Pennsylvania, 2009), 17, 36–7.
25. Tackett, *Becoming*, 138.
26. Fitzsimmons, *Remaking*, 45.
27. Keith Michael Baker, 'Representation Redefined', in *Inventing the French Revolution* (Cambridge, 1990), 224–51; Blackman, 'What Does a Deputy to the National Assembly Owe His Constituents? Coming to an Agreement on the Meaning of Electoral Mandates in July 1789', *French Historical Studies* 34, no. 2 (2011), 205–41.
28. Darrin McMahon, 'The Birthplace of the Revolution: Public Space and Political Community in the Palais-Royal of Louis-Philippe-Joseph d'Orléans, 1781–1789', *French History* 10, no. 1 (1996), 1–29; Alpaugh, 'Politics', 348–52.
29. Shapiro, *Traumatic*, 54.
30. See among others Alan Forrest, *Paris, the Provinces and the French Revolution* (London, 2004), 62–70.
31. François Furet, *Interpreting the French Revolution*, trans. Elborg Foster (Cambridge, 1981).
32. David Andress, 'Living the Revolutionary Melodrama: Robespierre's Sensibility and the Construction of Political Commitment in the French Revolution', *Representations* 114, no. 1 (Spring 2011), 108–9.
33. Markoff, *Abolition*.
34. Tackett, *Becoming*, 171.
35. Fitzsimmons, *The Night the Old Regime Ended: August 4, 1789, and the French Revolution* (University Park, 2003), 134.
36. Fitzsimmons, *The Night the Old Regime*, ix.
37. Markoff, *Abolition*, 300.
38. Tackett, *Becoming*, 180–2.
39. Tackett, *Becoming*, 182–4.

40. J. K. Wright, 'National Sovereignty and the General Will: The Political Program of the Declaration of Rights', in *The French Idea of Freedom: The Old Regime and the Declaration of Rights of 1789*, Dale Van Kley, ed. (Stanford, 1994), 233.

41. Lynn Hunt, *The French Revolution and Human Rights, A Brief Documentary History* (Boston, 1996), 14.

42. Jon Cowans, *To Speak for the People: Public Opinion and the Problem of Legitimacy in the French Revolution* (New York, 2001).

43. Norman Hampson, *Prelude to Terror: The Constituent Assembly and the Failure of Consensus, 1789–1791* (Oxford, 1988), 138.

44. Baker, 'Fixing the French Constitution', in *Inventing*, 305.

45. Baker, *Inventing the French Revolution*, and Furet, *Interpreting*.

46. Tackett, *When the King took Flight* (Cambridge, 2003).

47. Tackett, *Becoming*, 195–9.

48. Jack R. Censer, *Prelude to Power: The Parisian Radical Press, 1789–1791* (Baltimore, 1976); Popkin, *Revolutionary News*.

49. Tackett, *Becoming*, 242.

50. Applewhite, *Political Alignment*, esp. 64–93.

51. Tackett, *Becoming*, 206–7, 241–2.

52. Shapiro, 'Self-Sacrifice, Self-Interest or Self-Defense? The Constituent Assembly and the "Self-Denying Ordinance" of May 1791', *French Historical Studies* 25, no. 4 (2002), 625–56.

SELECTED READING

Applewhite, Harriet B., *Political Alignment in the French National Assembly, 1789–1791* (Baton Rouge, LA), 1993.

Baker, Keith Michael, *Inventing the French Revolution* (Cambridge, 1990).

Blackman, Robert H., 'What's in a Name? Possible Names for a Legislative Body and the Birth of National Sovereignty during the French Revolution, 15–16 June 1789', *French History* 21, no. 1 (2007), 22–43.

Cowans, Jon, *To Speak for the People: Public Opinion and the Problem of Legitimacy in the French Revolution* (New York, 2001).

Crook, Malcolm, *Elections in the French Revolution: An Apprenticeship in Democracy, 1789–1799* (Cambridge, 1996).

Fitzsimmons, Michael P., *The Remaking of France: The National Assembly and the Constitution of 1791* (Cambridge, 1994).

Fitzsimmons, Michael P., *The Night the Old Regime Ended: August 4, 1789, and the French Revolution* (University Park, 2003).

Friedland, Paul, *Political Actors: Representative Bodies and Theatricality in the Age of the French Revolution* (Ithaca, 2002).

Furet, François, *Interpreting the French Revolution*, trans. Elborg Foster (Cambridge, 1981).

Hampson, Norman, *Prelude to Terror: The Constituent Assembly and the Failure of Consensus, 1789–1791* (Oxford, 1988).

LeMay, Edna, *La vie quotidienne des deputes aux États généraux* (Paris, 1987).

Markoff, John, *The Abolition of Feudalism: Peasants, Lords and Legislators during the French Revolution* (State College, 1996).

Patrick, Allison, 'The Second Estate in the Constituent Assembly, 1789–1791', *Journal of Modern History* 62, no. 2 (1990), 223–52.

Sepinwall, Alyssa Goldstein, *The Abbé Grégoire and the French Revolution: The Making of Modern Universalism* (Berkeley, 2005).

Shapiro, Barry M., *Traumatic Politics: The Deputies and the King in the Early French Revolution* (University Park, 2009).

Tackett, Timothy, *Becoming a Revolutionary: The Deputies of the First French National Assembly and the Making of a Revolutionary Culture, 1789–1790* (Princeton, 1996).

PART III

REVOLUTION AND CONSTITUTION

CHAPTER 12

....

SOVEREIGNTY AND CONSTITUTIONAL POWER

....

MICHAEL P. FITZSIMMONS

> Two and one-half years of work have redressed the unhappiness of four-
> teen centuries; in fourteen centuries the gratitude that we express to you
> today for the completion of so sublime a work will not yet have weakened
> in the hearts of the French.
>
> Message of Jacobin Club of Loches to
the National Assembly, 21 September, 1791[1]

DURING the summer of 1789, Edward Rigby, an English physician visiting France, passed through Paris during the eventful month of July. He left Paris on 19 July and in a letter he wrote on 11 August described his visit to Versailles on 11 July, stating that watching the conversations among deputies on the grounds of Versailles reminded him of 'Athenian groves filled with philosophers'. Another English visitor, Helen Maria Williams, wrote of her visit to the National Assembly a year later:

> And this, repeated I with exultation to myself, this is the National Assembly of France! Those men now before my eyes are . . . the men whose magnanimity invested them with the power to destroy the old constitution, and whose wisdom is erecting the new, on a principle of perfection which has hitherto been thought chimerical, and has only served to adorn the page of the philosopher, but which they believe may be reduced to practice, and have therefore the courage to attempt.[2]

Historians have generally been less generous in their appraisals of both the Assembly and the constitution. The Constitution of 1791 was the product of the Tennis Court Oath, a momentous action but also one to which deputies arrived circuitously and undertook reluctantly, only after efforts to work with the clergy and nobility had failed. Furthermore, the original aspirations for the constitution were unexpectedly and profoundly trans-formed by the meeting of 4 August 1789. Finally, the short duration of the constitution—less than a year, the briefest period for any French constitution—affected perceptions of it.

Nevertheless, the Constitution of 1791 is arguably the most historic of all French constitutions. Not only did it formalize the appropriation of sovereignty by the people, but its achievement was so significant that every successive government in France has believed it necessary to affirm its legitimacy with a constitution. Moreover, the emphasis on its deficiencies has obscured the suddenness with which the issue of a constitution emerged and how fully the National Assembly realized the constitutional ideal. When, on 3 March 1766, in the 'Session of the Scourging', Louis XV quashed constitutional arguments inherent in the union of *parlements* and asserted that sovereignty was his alone and that he owed no explanation for his exercise of it, the polity did not react to this restatement of classic royal absolutism. In 1771, Chancellor René-Nicolas-Charles-Augustin de Maupeou exiled the *parlements* and met with only verbal opposition. During the following decade, however, inhabitants of provincial parlementary towns were vigorously and sometimes even violently defending their *parlement* against royal authority, and twenty-five years after the Session of the Scourging, Louis XV's successor had lost sovereign power and become a constitutional monarch.

*　*　*

Under the old regime, privilege was a primary instrument of government and the chief medium of political exchange between the Crown and the corporate entities that comprised much of French society.[3] Rights and privileges were essentially synonymous and emanated from the Crown—although he was referring especially to the fiscal sphere, the characterization of David Bien that privilege was 'the functional equivalent' of a constitution is particularly apposite.[4]

The centrality of privilege explains why the catalyst for the series of events that ultimately led to the appropriation of sovereignty was a memorandum sent by the Controller-General of Finances, Charles-Alexandre de Calonne, to Louis XVI during August 1786, advocating the convening of an Assembly of Notables. Highlighting the divisive effects of privilege upon the polity, Calonne sought to impress the monarch with the gravity of the developing fiscal crisis by asserting that an alteration of the traditional mode of governance was necessary because privilege upset the equilibrium of the kingdom, impeded its effective governance and rendered provinces unfamiliar to one another.[5] Louis agreed to its convocation, and at the opening session Calonne made clear that privilege was the critical issue to be addressed. He contended that it was no longer possible to utilize previous expedients and that only two courses of action were available, one of which, bankruptcy, was intolerable. The only workable solution, he claimed, was to eliminate social, political and fiscal abuses, and it was apparent that his allusion to 'abuses' referred to privileges enjoyed by many Notables. As he concluded his speech, Calonne implied that there was little to discuss and that the primary task of the Assembly was to give assent to his plan.[6]

Instead, the Notables questioned the existence of a deficit and after weeks of inaction Calonne commissioned a pamphlet, *Avertissement*, to pressure the Notables to end their obstruction and had it distributed free of charge in both Paris and provincial cities.[7] Its publication and remarkable dissemination, which William Doyle characterized as the most ambitious attempt to cultivate public opinion since Necker's *Compte rendu* of 1781, embittered relations between Calonne and the Notables and almost certainly played a role in Calonne's dismissal days later.[8]

Despite dismissing him, Louis still desired the enactment of Calonne's programme, which led Louis to appoint a member of the opposition within the Notables, Loménie de Brienne, as minister without portfolio to manage the reform agenda. Although Louis indicated a willingness to modify the project to meet objections raised by the Notables and allowed them to examine the royal accounts, Brienne had no more success than Calonne and dismissed the Assembly on 25 May.[9]

The motives of the Assembly of Notables have long been debated and the body has drawn renewed interest, but two aspects of the meeting struck contemporary observers. The sessions of the Assembly had been closed—*Avertissement* provided the first glimpse into its deliberations and heightened interest in its proceedings.[10] Although the pamphlet did not directly accuse the Notables of opposition or defence of vested interests, it nevertheless enabled the perception that privilege and the national interest were increasingly incompatible to gain traction[11]—indeed, one Notable stated that *Avertissement* sought to 'reduce everything to a combat between privilege and the people'.[12] The second aspect was the complete lack of success of the Assembly, which, after three months, had not resolved the issue for which it had been convened. Its failure seemed historic and, under the influence of *Avertissement*, a belief that the Notables had been unwilling to yield their fiscal privileges to restore the fiscal health of the state began to take root, which in turn led many to believe that privilege had triumphed over the well-being of the nation. Even more importantly, by portraying the fiscal privileges of the clergy and nobility as antithetical to the greater good, *Avertissement* legitimized criticism of privilege in a manner that would have been virtually unthinkable before the Assembly opened. Ultimately, the failure of the Assembly led to a reconsideration of the nature of the kingdom—was it an aggregation of privileged individuals and bodies or was it a grander entity defined by deeper bonds and shared ideals? The debate precipitated a movement away from acceptance of privilege as an instrument of governance to opposition to it as inimical to the common good.[13]

The Crown presented its programme to the *parlement*, but its resistance initiated a protracted conflict with the Crown that began with the exile of the *parlement* to Troyes after it defied an order to register the edicts. The Crown recalled the *parlement* in September, but a presumed agreement between Crown and *parlement* in November collapsed and two magistrates were arrested. The arrests provoked cries of despotism and the dispute culminated with the suspension of the *parlements* during May 1788, although only that of Paris complied. The Venetian ambassador, who had characterized the events of May as 'astonishing and almost unbelievable', captured the discontent that would soon crystallize in favour of a constitution when he wrote that the actions of the Crown 'overturned laws and customs sanctified by time and the nation'.[14]

The absence of the *parlement* of Paris changed the locus of events from Paris to the provinces, intensifying their politicization as parlementary cities mobilized in defence of their *parlement* and calls for the Estates-General to meet grew. The Crown capitulated during July, 1788, declaring that the Estates-General would convene but not specifying a date for the meeting. The decree announcing its convocation also solicited ideas on protocol for the Estates-General, implying that its form was an open question. With the announcement of a date for the meeting of the Estates-General and declaration of bankruptcy during August, what had begun eighteen months earlier as a ministerial manoeuvre to resolve a fiscal problem had evolved into a constitutional question that engaged much of the politically-aware populace.

The Venetian ambassador wrote that the events of August had compromised royal authority, and William Doyle argued that August 1788, represented the collapse of the old monarchy,[15] but the bankruptcy and retreat of the Crown also clarified the terms of the debate that ensued. Until August 1788, privilege and despotism had been coterminous issues, but the setting of a date for the meeting of the Estates-General removed despotism as an issue and made privilege the focus because bankruptcy ended doubts about the fiscal crisis. The contradistinction between the incontestable revenue needs of the state and the fiscal privileges of the clergy and nobility created an antithesis between them, making privilege and the nation mutually exclusive categories for much of the politically informed public. Because reform was imperative, and the critical issue to be resolved was the fiscal privileges of the clergy and nobility, the composition and procedure of the Estates-General assumed primordial importance—vote by order, the procedure followed in 1614 that effectively provided the clergy and nobility with veto power, was unacceptable.

After the *parlement* of Paris returned during late September, it quickly forfeited the favour it had accrued when it declared that the Estates-General should observe the forms of 1614. The decision did not merely reignite the constitutional debate—it intensified and enlarged it. Since the end of the Assembly of Notables, most of the politically-engaged populace had been generally content to allow the *parlement* to exercise its self-proclaimed constitutional role, supplemented by meetings of the Estates-General. During the period of concern about despotism, the promised convocation of the Estates-General had appeared to resolve the constitutional question, but the declaration of the *parlement* demonstrated how misplaced trust in it was and how inadequate the current constitutional model was. Furthermore, the calling of the Estates-General no longer sufficed; rather, its structure and procedures became the object of even more intense debate and assumed extraordinary importance. Moreover, the opinion of the *parlement* expanded the debate. From the dismissal of the Assembly of Notables until the proclamation of the *parlement*, the issue of privilege had been confined primarily to the fiscal privileges of the clergy and nobility, but after September 1788, it also encompassed the structure and protocols of the Estates-General.

After a reconvened Assembly of Notables likewise endorsed the procedures of 1614, anger became widespread—the Venetian ambassador opined that if Louis XVI followed its recommendation it could incite a general insurrection.[16] Indeed, the degree to which privilege had grown as an issue is apparent in a pamphlet that appeared after the second meeting of the Notables—its author observed that the monarch had convened the Notables twice to consult them on the interests of the throne and the nation. In 1787, he wrote, the Notables had defended their privileges against the throne and in 1788 they had defended their privileges against the nation.[17]

As the debate over the Estates-General continued, the Crown took no position, which allowed each side to believe that the Crown might support it. With the most important issue before its opening being the doubling of the representation of the Third Estate, during December 1788, Jacques Necker, who had succeeded Brienne, secured approval for doubling the number of Third Estate deputies, which was well received by the Third Estate—the Parisian bookseller Nicolas Ruault wrote that it was a victory for the French people, who would no longer be a valet for the clergy and nobility. The more perspicacious Venetian ambassador, however, presciently observed that although the measure calmed discontent among the Third Estate, it left much unresolved because voting procedure for the Estates-General was not stipulated.[18]

In his letter, Ruault also specified his hopes for the Estates-General, the first of which was to bring forward 'a wise constitution'.[19] Moreover, Ruault's letters from November 1788, to January 1789, illuminate the emergence of privilege as the overriding concern for the Third Estate and its fusion with the issue of a constitution, a development not generally experienced by much of the clergy and nobility. Consequently, the elections for the Estates-General were held with significantly different assumptions—many within the clergy and nobility saw the doubling of the Third as a discrete action that did not overturn vote by order, whereas the Third Estate concluded that it inferred vote by head. In addition, although the nobility and, to a lesser extent, the clergy were reconciled to the loss of their fiscal privileges, substantial elements within each also regarded the distinction of orders as a fundamental social and constitutional tenet. The Third Estate was willing to recognize social distinctions of order and to preserve honorific privileges of the clergy and nobility, but would not assent to orders as a political structure, especially for voting at the Estates-General.[20]

The sudden crystallization of the demand for a constitution has generally been overlooked. Its formation in a kingdom with little customary or formal constitutional tradition, and in which the Crown viewed discussion of a constitution as virtually disloyal— its sensitivity evident in the fact that as late as July 1789, the Venetian ambassador believed that the ubiquitous term 'regeneration' served essentially as a code word for constitution—was extraordinary.[21] Although it materialized quickly and unexpectedly, it was the goal of a constitution that galvanized the Third Estate and provided the strength and unity to overcome clerical and noble resistance. To be sure, the idea of the constitution was amorphous—'constitution' became the catchword for a political structure more equitable to the Third Estate. The opinions of the *parlement* of Paris and the Notables had revealed that traditional political elites could not be trusted to bring about a fairer political system. Although Necker had seemingly countered the *parlement* and the Notables, the Third Estate recognized the fragility of its apparent victory and did not want its fortunes dependent upon the vagaries of ministerial goodwill. The newly arrived American minister to France, Gouverneur Morris, was immediately struck by the desire for a constitution and wrote to his counterpart, the French minister to the United States, during late February 1789, 'your nation is now in a most important crisis, and the great question, shall we hereafter have a constitution or shall will continue to be law, employs every mind and agitates every heart in France'.[22]

On the eve of the Estates-General, as Kenneth Margerison has demonstrated, the prevailing hope among the Third Estate was a 'union of orders', envisaging distinction of orders, a doubled Third Estate and vote by head. The famous pamphlet by Sieyès, *What Is the Third Estate?*, signalled his dissent from this programme, but his stance was rejected,[23] with his marginalization apparent in the fact that he was the final member of the Third Estate delegation elected during the spring of 1789.[24] The goals of the Third Estate had evolved considerably during the two years between the end of the first Assembly of Notables and the opening of the Estates-General and had culminated with the demand for a constitution, the blueprint for which, prior to the beginning of the Estates-General, would have been drawn from the union of orders ideal.

The Estates-General opened on 4 May 1789, but deputies did not receive any guidance from the Crown with respect to procedure. It was a major blunder because the authority of the Crown was at its zenith at this juncture,[25] and the lack of leadership allowed events to develop a momentum of their own that quickly undermined hopes for a union of orders. In the vacuum created by lack of direction from the Crown, the nobility sought to impose vote by order and the Third Estate vote by head, plunging the Estates-General into a stalemate. An unanticipated initial benefit of the deadlock was that participation in the conciliatory conferences that sought to resolve it allowed members of the large Third Estate delegation to become acquainted with each other. During the following weeks hundreds of deputies who had previously been unknown to one another were able to build trust and forge bonds that subsequently made unilateral action possible—indeed, the declining support for the conferences as their futility became clear reflected the growing self-assurance of its members.

In a society based on prescriptive tradition, the nobility was in an advantageous position but, galvanized by the desire for a more equitable political system, the Third Estate was prepared to defy custom and past practice. The idea of a constitution bound them, but otherwise there was little consensus, particularly with the lack of recourse to tradition. Trapped in a historical void in which precedent was unavailing, deputies unexpectedly had to formulate a new course and on 17 June the National Assembly came into existence as a solution to the impasse. Although its denomination reflected the emerging unitary ideal of the nation rather than the separate identities and interests of social groups, deputies did not have the confidence to break from the framework of existing institutions and therefore held to the union of orders—the Assembly sat by order even as it voted by head.

In the Tennis Court Oath, taken three days after the formation of the Assembly, deputies proclaimed that they had been summoned to establish the constitution of the kingdom and took a solemn oath not to separate until the constitution was established upon firm foundations. Indeed, concerned that the Assembly might be dissolved by the Crown, they emphasized their resolve by declaring that they would assemble wherever circumstances dictated to complete the task. It was signed by virtually every deputy—far stronger support than the vote to declare itself the National Assembly, in which there had been scores of dissenters—and printed and made public.[26] The Tennis Court Oath underscores the importance that the issue of a constitution had come to assume, with deputies clearly viewing it as their foremost obligation and fundamental legacy. It also revealed that the confidence of deputies had moved beyond challenging the clergy and nobility to defiance of the Crown itself, as would become evident three days later, on 23 June, when Louis presented a programme and ordered vote by order. Louis' intervention, however, was too late—the anger and resolve engendered by weeks of stalemate rendered it both dilatory and inappropriate,[27] and there can be little doubt that the defiant response of the Assembly—that it held to its previous resolutions—referred especially to the Tennis Court Oath.

As the confidence of the commons had increased, that of the nobility had declined precipitously as they began to fear the consequences of the stalemate. The rupture of the solidarity of the nobility on 25 June appears to have been pivotal in the Crown's decision to use force to regain control of events. In a bid to gain time, Louis, never using the words National Assembly, asked recalcitrant members of the clergy and nobility to 'join the other two orders'. Most did, and after abolishing imperative mandates to overcome a stratagem by many of those deputies to subvert it, the Assembly returned to its goal of producing a constitution. The Assembly had subdivided into thirty subcommittees but, not wishing to consider thirty different constitutional projects, it elected a Committee on the Constitution to guide the effort. The mandated membership of the committee, which was elected on 14 July, conformed to the union of orders—two clerical deputies, two from the nobility and four from the commons—but the insurrection in Paris overshadowed their election. Although saved from dissolution, the Assembly did not possess identity or cohesion and had no consensus on principles for the constitution. Moreover, many deputies were eager to conclude their mission and return home, and their restiveness broke through on Friday 24 July, when the Assembly ordered the Committee on the Constitution to present its work, only ten days after its formation.[28]

The committee gave its report the following Monday, 27 July, and it offers insight into the outlook of the Assembly at the beginning stage of the constitution. Indeed, in an illustration of the degree to which events had either outraced the political consciousness of deputies, or that they viewed the National Assembly as a temporary mechanism to complete the constitution, the report utilized the term 'Estates-General' several times when referring to a future legislature. With the Assembly lacking common purpose, the ideas advanced were cautious and constrained. After submitting avowed principles, including that the French government was monarchical and that 'the nation' makes laws 'with royal sanction', the committee formulated eighteen questions to be resolved, with the most important posited first—did the king have legislative powers, limited by constitutional laws of the kingdom? Other issues to be decided were whether laws would be submitted for registration to sovereign courts, who could dissolve the 'Estates-General', and whether the 'Estates-General' would be permanent or periodic. Reflecting continuing adherence to orders, other matters to be determined included whether 'the first two orders' would be joined in one chamber or whether two chambers would be formed without distinction of orders and what the proportional representation of the clergy, nobility and commons should be. The committee also asked whether a new order—an 'ordre des campagnes' representing rural commoners—should be recognized.[29]

The 27 July report reveals the rudimentary state of the constitutional project and the indeterminacy of sovereign power. The committee stated that it would be guided by the *cahiers*, which meant that the constitution would be built upon custom and existing institutions. Deputies believed that it would be completed in a few weeks and, had this occurred, this period might have been recognized at best as a transition from absolute to constitutional monarchy, with little modification of the existing order—analogous perhaps to the Revolution of 1688 in England, but without even the change of dynasty. Just over a week later, however, as a result of the meeting of 4 August, the Assembly abandoned prescriptive tradition and initiated a new course that ultimately transformed a society tied to its past and defined by tradition into one altogether different.

The meeting of 4 August has been treated at length elsewhere;[30] the focus here will be on its constitutional aspects, the most significant of which was the appropriation of sovereignty by the National Assembly. Only days earlier the Assembly had signalled its willingness to negotiate major issues with the Crown, including the apportionment of sovereignty. After the night of 4 August this was no longer the case; having conceived a new ideal of the polity, the Assembly assumed sovereignty to systematize it. The vehicle for the appropriation of sovereignty was a little-known instrument, the pact of association, the obscurity of which is due largely to the Assembly itself—through it, deputies affirmed the relinquishment of all provincial privileges and pledged to resist any Crown effort to reimpose privilege. Because of the seditious implication of a vow to counteract the Crown, the pact of association remained an unwritten covenant among deputies, although article 10 of the August decrees, which cited the abolition of provinces as the precondition to a national constitution, was the closest public expression of it.[31] The appropriation of sovereignty was done with strong consideration for the dignity of the monarch, which was undoubtedly another factor in masking the pact of association. Although Louis was in no position to resist, the Assembly maintained a sense of honour for him by proclaiming him 'Restorer of French Liberty' in article 17 of the August decrees. Article 18 stated that the Assembly would go en masse to present the articles to him but, in accordance with the pact of association, there was no mention of securing his approval of them, although deputies expected his sanction.

The meeting of the night of 4 August produced a functional consensus—not a shared set of ideas or values, but assent to a framework that met the interests of different groups and allowed the Assembly to overcome aimlessness. For members of the clergy and nobility, the renunciations reconciled them with the Assembly and legitimized future disagreement in a manner previously not possible, whereas for those committed to the Assembly the relinquishments made possible a vastly larger programme than that presented on 27 July—the renunciations became the foundation from which reform could proceed. The consensus is characterized as functional because acrimonious debates soon arose over the degree to which the kingdom should be reshaped after the elimination of privilege, but the presence of dissension should not obscure the fact that the Assembly never contemplated going back to the model of privilege in any sphere.

During 1790, as work on the constitution continued, the deputy Edmond-Louis-Alexis Dubois-Crancé, who mistakenly believed that the Assembly was within months of completing the constitution and wished to provide his constituents with an overview, stated that all the work of the National Assembly after 4 August should be attributed to that meeting, writing that it had provided 'the fundamental principles of a constitution that will honour France forever among nations'. Similarly, a liberal noble deputy wrote a decade later that the constitution was made on the night of 4 August just as the Revolution had been made on 14 July.[32]

The appropriation of sovereignty by the Assembly did not proceed effortlessly—it encountered a significant challenge during the following month. Seeking to maintain a meaningful role for the monarch, the Committee on the Constitution wanted to grant him veto power, but dissent arose over the nature of the veto. There was a cohort within the committee that continued to adhere to a notion of reform pre-dating 4 August—still attached to a more restrained agenda consonant with the union of orders, it believed that the task of the Assembly was to improve government rather than reshape the kingdom.

During late August the Assembly began discussion on the role of the monarch in making law; although other issues were at stake, it was effectively a final settlement on the meeting of 4 August and the placement of sovereignty, centred on the veto power of the monarch. The resolution occurred on 11 September, when the Assembly, by a nearly three-to-one margin, voted to confer Louis with a suspensive veto, denying him the right to veto the constitution that the contending absolute veto would have provided him, leading a relieved Parisian to observe that the sceptre of despotism had again been removed from the hands of the monarch.[33] Keith Baker noted that with this decision the Assembly chose to craft a constitution 'created *de novo* by an act of sovereign will',[34] but it is more accurate to state that the Assembly reaffirmed its decision with respect to the constitution and was definitively resolving the location of sovereign will. The vote led to the resignation of the members of the Committee on the Constitution who had favoured the absolute veto; upon learning of their action, the remaining members also resigned, necessitating the election of a new committee on 15 September, and the members chosen that day led the drafting of the Constitution of 1791.

Article 10 of the August decrees had identified provincial privileges as the primary obstacle to a national constitution; consequently, the first task undertaken by the Assembly was the abolition of provinces through a new division of the kingdom. The 'new' Committee on the Constitution, as the heading of the report stated, made a presentation on 29 September proposing the formation of departments to replace provinces. After making some modifications, the Assembly enacted it during November, and completed work on municipal administration the following month. Article 10 also stipulated the new governing principle of the kingdom—laws common to all. Therefore, after completing its reform of administration, the Assembly turned to reorganizing the judiciary during March 1790. The Committee on the Constitution presented a report that denounced the role of privilege in the old regime judiciary, after which the Assembly voted to reshape the judicial system in its entirety, a task it completed six months later. The reconstruction of administration and the judiciary were the foundations on which the new polity envisioned on 4 August rested—although the Assembly worked another year to complete the constitution, these elements were its nucleus.

Without question, the Assembly made mistakes—even admirers of the constitution admitted deficiencies.[35] A critical error was the manner in which it reorganized the Church—although the Civil Constitution of the Clergy had an internal logic for the Assembly, deputies failed to perceive how poorly the election of priests and bishops, especially in areas with populations of Protestants or Jews, might be received. Moreover, when the Civil Constitution of the Clergy became an object of contestation with the papacy, national sovereignty required the Assembly to reaffirm its work. Ultimately and unintentionally, the Civil Constitution of the Clergy became a major solvent of the new polity created by the Assembly.[36]

During June 1791, as deputies approached completion of the constitution, Louis XVI staged his furtive escape from Paris, leaving behind a manifesto complaining about the diminution of royal power that began with the changes in administration and justice. The document revealed Louis' insincerity in his dealings with the Assembly and placed deputies in a difficult position when a backlash developed against him that culminated with the massacre at the Champ de Mars.[37] Unwilling to abandon its work, deputies linked Louis' retention on the throne to his acceptance of the constitution and, viewing republicanism as a harbinger of chaos and war, enacted several anti-democratic measures to curtail political activity or participation by popular elements. In an unprecedented situation of conditional captivity for the monarch and an atmosphere of fear and unrest, the Assembly reconfigured the body politic to a less embracing, more propertied standard than had been envisaged before Louis' flight. Louis accepted the constitution on 13 September and, its task completed, the Assembly disbanded on 30 September, but the constitution became a critical divide between those who believed that the Revolution was over and those who believed it had only begun.

Because the greatest excesses of the Revolution occurred in the wake of the collapse of the Constitution of 1791, some historians, most notably François Furet, sought to trace a line backward to the National Assembly to explain their origin.[38] They attributed the Terror to an intolerant outlook rooted in the inability of the Assembly to imagine anything other than undivided national sovereignty in a unicameral legislature, which, they contended, laid the foundation for suppression of opposition.

Such reductionism and *ex post facto* determinism is misguided, beginning with its basic premise that the Assembly was intolerant and illiberal.[39] Although Charles Walton, in his recent study of the culture of calumny, cited four instances of deputies condemned for speech in the National Assembly and the forced resignation of François-Henri, comte de Virieu, from its presidency as evidence that 'illiberal practices were seeping into high politics', he also conceded that the sanctions levied were mild and 'not that shocking', because old regime corporate bodies had often exercised similar discipline over members. Walton attributed the temporary arrests to an old regime culture of religion, oaths, and honour, with radicalization of the sense of honour playing a major role. Moreover, he acknowledged that the detained deputies were not 'vexed or traumatized by their treatment' and disavowed any connection between these 'punitive exclusions' and the beginning of the movement toward the Terror.[40]

A more substantive measure of the liberal outlook of the Assembly than calumny is its reaction to institutional opposition, and it is telling that during the autumn of 1789, when two provincial bodies—an Intermediate Commission and a *parlement*—overtly opposed it, the Assembly explicitly declined to respond with force against them. Moreover, in contrast to its revolutionary successors, only the National Assembly did not enact punitive legislation against *émigrés* or refractory priests and, again uniquely, shortly before it disbanded, it proclaimed a general, unconditional amnesty for all individuals arrested for political crimes.[41]

The presence of discord should not be overemphasized, as Williams understood:

> But one ceases to wonder that the meetings of the National Assembly are tumultuous, on reflecting how important are the objects of its deliberations. Not only the lives and fortunes of individuals, but the existence of the country is at stake: and of how little consequence is this impetuosity in debate, if the decrees which are passed are wise and beneficial, and the new constitution arises, like the beauty and order of nature, from the confusion of mingled elements![42]

The conduct of the National Assembly was so removed from that of the National Convention during 1793–94 that to impute any equivalency between them is misinformed and ahistorical. Scholars should recognize the considerable difference between reproach and proscription, between resentment toward *émigrés* or refractory priests and legislating harsh laws against them, between a blanket amnesty for political acts and making such acts a capital offence, between freely relinquishing power and disqualifying oneself for membership in the succeeding legislature and legislating a mandatory high percentage of incumbents to dominate the next legislature. In outlook and behaviour, the National Assembly profoundly differed from its revolutionary successors and any linkage of the Assembly to the Terror is without foundation.

Louis' flight from Paris was arguably the most decisive event of the French Revolution and to the degree that the origins of the Terror may be situated during the period of the Assembly, it may be found in this action because deputies faced the extraordinary situation of an unwilling, even hostile, monarch with a critical constitutional role on the throne. To return to the example of 1688 in England, the only near antecedent, James II had been permitted to flee to make possible a fresh political start. Not only did growing fear of war preclude allowing Louis to leave France, but there was no generally-accepted successor at hand. The mistrust that Louis' flight generated never dissipated—in a letter written during October 1791, Ruault asked how could one who had shamefully turned his back on them on 21 June be their friend on 14 September, and the following month rumours circulated in Paris that the monarch was planning another escape.[43] The lack of trust placed every action of his, especially use of the veto, under suspicion and ultimately led to his overthrow.

The lack of support for the monarch after June 1791, brings out another aspect of the National Assembly that has received insufficient attention—its success in implanting a constitutional tradition in France. Although the boldness of the August decrees had captured the attention of the populace, a constitution was longer, more abstract, and had little tradition in France—a written constitution had none.[44] From an early point the Assembly wanted to instruct the public on the constitution through civic catechisms and other publications.[45] The catechism format for these efforts was significant—as Adrian Velicu noted, it served to assimilate tenets without questioning them.[46] Their didactic nature, consisting of short, prosaic questions and answers, has often led scholars to ignore or dismiss them, but they provide insight into the manner in which, through elementary precepts, awareness and knowledge could take root. However pedestrian many publications on the constitution may appear, they offer a glimpse of one method through which much of the general populace learned of the constitution and how a novel convention gained acceptance so rapidly. Indeed, the deputy Jean-Paul Rabaut de Saint-Etienne, a member of the Committee on the Constitution, particularly endorsed civic catechisms, stating that it was especially necessary 'to give a sense of the constitution and to distil two hundred decrees to a few pages' and that anyone who knew the catechism well would know the constitution well.[47] Whereas catechisms were primarily directed toward villages, in a more sophisticated fashion, dictionaries—like catechisms, authoritative in nature but more exhaustive—pursued the same goal of explicating the constitution to the better-informed public.[48]

Although neither the readership nor effectiveness of these publications can be ascertained, the aftermath of Louis' escape from Paris suggests that efforts to secure support for the Constitution of 1791 should not be underestimated. In a country with a custom of monarchical loyalty stretching back more than 1300 years and little constitutional tradition, nowhere in France was there any meaningful demonstration of support for the king. The lack of any response in favour of Louis XVI was an implicit and important endorsement of the National Assembly and the constitution—when the monarch and the nascent constitution were set in direct opposition to each other, the French populace overwhelmingly countenanced the latter.

The contemporary and historical importance of the Constitution of 1791, both of which are large, have generally been slighted or overlooked. Its contemporary legacy was that it filled the three-year vacuum created by the collapse of royal authority during August 1788. Disquietude had been profound and had been exacerbated by Louis' flight from Paris, which demonstrated his belief that the constitution could be renegotiated, perhaps even overturned, and revealed the potential fragility of the constitutional project. It was for such reasons that the sense of relief and gratitude at the completion of the constitution was so palpable, expressed in countless messages to the National Assembly—the constitution would again set the state on a firm political foundation. Robespierre reportedly said in 1791 that 'the Revolution is over', which, if true, reflected his view, noted by a biographer, that 'critical of the Assembly as he was, he recognized the legal force of its decision on the king and the forthcoming constitution'.[49] The essential conditions for the success of the constitution were that it become firmly established, that all concerned abide by it peaceably and that there be no dangerous enemies within France or beyond its borders, but none were obtained. In the final analysis, the failure of the constitution was due less to inherent flaws than to circumstances altogether beyond the control of its authors, particularly because they disqualified themselves from continuing in office.

The historical significance of the Constitution of 1791 is even more noteworthy. Although short-lived, it implanted a constitutional tradition in France so firmly that every subsequent regime, even those indifferent to, or insulated from, public opinion, has believed it necessary to legitimize its authority with a constitution. The National Convention produced two constitutions, the first of which was the Constitution of 1793, completed during June 1793, and approved by a referendum. During October 1793, however, the Convention indefinitely suspended it and proclaimed a 'Revolutionary government' that was to last until the achievement of peace, but the Constitution of 1793 never came into force. Indeed, the juxtaposition of the absence of a constitution and the Terror strengthened the association between a constitution and lawful government. The second effort of the Convention, the Constitution of the Year III, established the Directory in 1795. After Napoleon Bonaparte overthrew the Directory in 1799, he sought to legitimate his seizure of power by promulgating a new constitution and covered each subsequent permutation of his political ascendancy with a constitution. The restored Bourbon regime, which loathed a constitution as tied to revolution, nevertheless reluctantly accommodated the constitutional practice with the issuance of what it called a 'voluntary grant' and 'gift', the Charter of 1814—a constitution in all but name.

It is illustrative of both the instability introduced by the Revolution and the centrality of a constitution to political legitimacy that, beginning with the Constitution of 1791, France has had fifteen constitutions since the Revolution—twelve of them between 1791 and 1870. Two of the last three constitutions have been the longest-lasting, suggesting that political stability and constitutional tradition have become firmly established. Other than a few allusions—ironically—to the stillborn Constitution of 1793, the constitutional legacy was scarcely mentioned during the bicentennial celebrations of the Revolution, but the success of that legacy after a 1,300-year monarchical heritage was a major stride toward modernity and lasting accomplishment of the National Assembly.

France was the first continental power to put a written constitution in place and French armies spread the practice to conquered areas. Despite the repugnance felt by much of the European populace for French imperialism, most embraced the constitutional ideal that the French had brought. Yet, as the bicentennial celebrations suggest, the constitutional heritage is an all but forgotten legacy of the National Assembly. Whereas scholars have often concentrated on perceived structural flaws of the Constitution of 1791 or argued about whether it fully lived up to the principles of the Revolution, it was the constitutional ideal itself that struck contemporaries and endured long thereafter. As the nineteenth century progressed, royal absolutism appeared increasingly antiquated—nearly six decades later, when popular revolution erupted in Berlin and Vienna, the chief demand was a constitution, and a similar phenomenon occurred in early twentieth-century St Petersburg.[50]

The overlooked heritage of the Constitution of 1791 is all the more surprising in view of the magnitude of the constitutional legacy. According to the Constitutions Repository of ConstitutionMaking.org, approximately 800 constitutions have been written since 1789. Just as a constitution became the touchstone for political legitimacy in France, so, too, a similar tradition developed elsewhere as well. Furthermore, the Constitution of 1791, more than any other up to that time, associated the right to have rights with a constitution—the United States constitution institutionalized slavery and under the British constitution religious toleration was only customary and uncodified, like the British constitution itself.

The constitutional heritage has proved to be one of the most enduring accomplishments of the National Assembly. The Bourbon and Orléanist regimes sharply curtailed popular sovereignty during the first half of the nineteenth century and the legacy of nationalism became subsumed to a broader European outlook during the second half of the twentieth. The constitutional ideal, however, has never been abridged—on the contrary, it has spread and strengthened. The power and modernism of the core value and defining achievement of the National Assembly deserves greater recognition than it has received.[51]

Notes

1. A.N. C 127, dossier 427, document 3.
2. Elizabeth Eastlake (ed.), *Dr. Rigby's Letters from France &c. in 1789* (London, 1880), 41; Helen Maria Williams, *Letters Written in France in the Summer of 1790 to a friend in England, containing various anecdotes relative to the French Revolution and memoires of M. and Madame du F.* (Dublin, 1791), 45–6.
3. Michael P. Fitzsimmons, *The Remaking of France: The National Assembly and the Constitution of 1791* (Cambridge, 1994), 4–5.
4. David Bien, 'The Secrétaires du Roi: Absolutism, Corps and Privilege under the Ancien Régime', in Ernst Hinrichs, Eberhard Schmitt and Rudolph Vierhaus (eds), *Vom Ancien Régime zur Französischen Revolution* (Göttingen, 1978), 159.
5. Albert Goodwin, 'Calonne, the Assembly of French Notables of 1787 and the Origins of the Révolte nobiliaire', *English Historical Review* 61, no. 2 (May 1946), 209–11.
6. Albert Goodwin, 'Calonne, the Assembly of French Notables of 1787 and the Origins of the Révolte nobiliaire', *English Historical Review* 61, no. 3 (September 1946), 336–8; John Hardman, *Overture to Revolution: The 1787 Assembly of Notables and the Crisis of France's Old Regime* (Oxford, 2010), 108, 111–12.
7. Goodwin, 'Calonne', 349, 357–9; Hardman, *Overture to Revolution*, 160–76, 199–230; Vivian R. Gruder, *The Notables and the Nation: The Political Schooling of the French, 1787–1788* (Cambridge, 2007), 41–2.
8. Goodwin, 'Calonne', 359–62; William Doyle, *Origins of the French Revolution*, 3rd edn (Oxford, 1999), 96.
9. Goodwin, 'Calonne', 365–74; Gruder, *The Notables and the Nation*, 40–1; Hardman, *Overture to Revolution*, 272–5.

10. Alessandro Fontana, Francesco Furlon and George Saro (eds), *Venise et la Révolution française: Les dépêches des ambassadeurs de Venise au Doge, 1786–1795* (Paris, 1997), 90; Gruder, *The Notables and the Nation*, 72.

11. Hardman, *Overture to Revolution*, 204–5; Gruder, *The Notables and the Nation*, 31.

12. Hardman, *Overture to Revolution*, 203.

13. Fitzsimmons, *The Remaking of France*, 11–12.

14. *Venise et la Révolution française*, 182, 190.

15. Ibid., 222; William Doyle, *Origins of the French Revolution*, 107, 110.

16. *Venise et la Révolution française*, 249.

17. *A la mémoire auguste de feu de Monseigneur le Dauphin, père du roi* (n.p., n.d.), p. xi.

18. Nicolas Ruault, *Gazette d'un Parisien sous la Révolution: Lettres à son Frère 1783–1796*, ed. Anne Vassal (Paris, 1976), 120; *Venise et la Révolution française*, 256, 261.

19. Ruault, *Gazette d'un Parisien*, 120.

20. Fitzsimmons, *The Remaking of France*, 143–4.

21. *Venise et la Révolution française*, 302.

22. Beatrix Cary Davenport (ed.), *A Diary of the French Revolution by Gouverneur Morris 1752–1816*, 2 vols (Boston, 1939), 1: xlii.

23. Kenneth Margerison, *Pamphlets & Public Opinion: The Campaign for a Union of Orders in the Early French Revolution* (West Lafayette, 1998), 98–103; William Doyle, *Aristocracy and its Enemies in the Age of Revolution* (Oxford, 2009), 178–81.

24. The Parisian delegation was the last to hold elections for the Estates-General and Sieyès was the last deputy elected for the Third Estate of Paris.

25. Etienne Dumont, *Souvenirs sur Mirabeau et les deux premières assemblées législatives*, ed. J. Bénétruy (Paris, 1951), 47.

26. For a more detailed examination of the idea of the constitution beginning with the Tennis Court Oath, Keith Michael Baker, *Inventing the French Revolution: Essays on French Political Culture in the Eighteenth Century* (Cambridge, 1990), 252–305.

27. Adrien-Joseph Colson, *Lettres d'un bourgeois de Paris à un ami de province 1788–1793*, ed. Chantal Plantier-Sasson (Saint-Cyr-sur-Loire, 1993), 38.

28. Fitzsimmons, *The Remaking of France*, 44–51.

29. *Archives parlementaires de 1787 à 1860*, 1st series, 82 vols (Paris, 1862–1913), 8: 284–5.

30. Michael P. Fitzsimmons, *The Night the Old Regime Ended: August 4, 1789, and the French Revolution* (University Park, 2003).

31. Ibid., 17–18.

32. *Lettre de M. Dubois de Crancé, député du Département des Ardennes à ses commettans, ou Compte rendu des travaux, des dangers et des obstacles de l'Assemblée Nationale, depuis l'ouverture des Etats-Généraux, au 27 avril 1789, jusqu'au premier août 1790* (Paris, 1790), 9; François Emmanuel, vicomte de Toulongeon, *Histoire de France, depuis la révolution de 1789*, 7 vols (Paris, 1801), 1: 99.

33. Colson, *Lettres d'un bourgeois*, 71.

34. Baker, *Inventing the French Revolution*, 301.

35. P. N. Gautier, *Dictionnaire de la Constitution et du gouvernement français* (Paris, 1791), 102.

36. Timothy Tackett, *Religion, Revolution, and Regional Culture in Eighteenth-Century France: The Ecclesiastical Oath of 1791* (Princeton, 1986).

37. David Andress, *Massacre at the Champ de Mars: Popular Dissent and Political Culture in the French Revolution* (Woodbridge, 2000).

38. François Furet, 'The French Revolution is Over', in *Interpreting the French Revolution* (Cambridge, 1981), 1–79.

39. See also Isser Woloch, 'On the Latent Illiberalism of the French Revolution', *The American Historical Review* 95, no. 5 (December 1990), 1458–9.

40. Charles Walton, *Policing Public Opinion in the French Revolution: The Culture of Calumny and the Problem of Free Speech* (Oxford, 2009), 136–58, with quotations from 136, 157.

41. Fitzsimmons, *The Night the Old Regime Ended*, 43–5.

42. Williams, *Letters Written in France*, 44–5.

43. Ruault, *Gazette d'un Parisien*, 260–1. On the rumours, Colson, *Lettres d'un bourgeois*, 207.

44. Nannerl O. Keohane, *Philosophy and the State in France: The Renaissance to the Enlightenment* (Princeton, 1980), 14–17; 25–53.

45. Adrien Velicu, *Civic Catechisms and Reason in the French Revolution* (Burlington, 2010), 5–6.

46. Ibid., 2.

47. François Rouvière, *Quatre lettres inédites de Rabaut de Saint-Etienne* (Nimes, 1885), 12.

48. Gautier, *Dictionnaire de la Constitution*.

49. Ruth Scurr, *Fatal Purity: Robespierre and the French Revolution* (New York, 2006), 170.

50. A similar point is made by David Andress, *1789: The Threshold of the Modern Age* (New York, 2008), 397.

51. As should its role in the even more modern concept of human rights. Lynn Hunt (ed.), *The French Revolution and Human Rights: A Brief Documentary History* (Boston, 1996).

SELECTED READING

Andress, David, *Massacre at the Champ de Mars: Popular Dissent and Political Culture in the French Revolution* (Woodbridge, 2000).

Andress, David, *1789: The Threshold of the Modern Age* (New York, 2008).

Baker, Keith Michael, *Inventing the French Revolution: Essays on French Political Culture in the Eighteenth Century* (Cambridge, 1990).

Bien, David, 'The Secrétaires du Roi: Absolutism, Corps and Privilege under the Ancien Régime', in Ernst Hinrichs, Eberhard Schmitt and Rudolph Vierhaus (eds), *Vom Ancien Régime zur Französischen Revolution* (Göttingen, 1978).

Doyle, William, *Origins of the French Revolution*, 3rd edn (Oxford, 1999).

Doyle, William, *Aristocracy and its Enemies in the Age of Revolution* (Oxford, 2009).

Fitzsimmons, Michael P., *The Remaking of France: The National Assembly and the Constitution of 1791* (Cambridge, 1994).

Fitzsimmons, Michael P., *The Night the Old Regime Ended: August 4, 1789, and the French Revolution* (University Park, 2003).

Furet, François, *Interpreting the French Revolution* (Cambridge, 1981).

Goodwin, Albert, 'Calonne, the Assembly of French Notables of 1787 and the Origins of the Révolte nobiliaire', *English Historical Review* 61, no. 2 (May 1946), 202–34.

Goodwin, Albert, 'Calonne, the Assembly of French Notables of 1787 and the Origins of the Révolte nobiliaire', *English Historical Review* 61, no. 3 (September 1946), 329–77.

Gruder, Vivian R., *The Notables and the Nation: The Political Schooling of the French, 1787–1788* (Cambridge, 2007).

Hardman, John, *Overture to Revolution: The 1787 Assembly of Notables and the Crisis of France's Old Regime* (Oxford, 2010).

Hunt, Lynn (ed.), *The French Revolution and Human Rights: A Brief Documentary History* (Boston, 1996).

Keohane, Nannerl O., *Philosophy and the State in France: The Renaissance to the Enlightenment* (Princeton, 1980).

Margerison, Kenneth, *Pamphlets & Public Opinion: The Campaign for a Union of Orders in the Early French Revolution* (West Lafayette, 1998).

Scurr, Ruth, *Fatal Purity: Robespierre and the French Revolution* (New York, 2006).

Tackett, Timothy, *Religion, Revolution, and Regional Culture in Eighteenth-Century France: The Ecclesiastical Oath of 1791* (Princeton, 1986).

Velicu, Adrien, *Civic Catechisms and Reason in the French Revolution* (Burlington, 2010).

Walton, Charles, *Policing Public Opinion in the French Revolution: The Culture of Calumny and the Problem of Free Speech* (Oxford, 2009).

CHAPTER 13

···

THE NEW REGIME

Political Institutions and Democratic
Practices under the Constitutional
Monarchy, 1789–91

···

MALCOLM CROOK

THE return to politics and ideology in the Revolution, or rather a renewed interest in exploring its political culture, was marked by a series of four conferences that
commenced in Chicago in 1987.[1] Of course, relevant research had already begun in a
post-revisionist environment where revolutionary historiography was shifting away
from economic and social issues towards political ideas and institutions. As the French
put it, this entailed research into 'le politique' rather than 'la politique', in other words,
the underlying principles and practices relating to governance rather than the day-to-
day business of politics.[2] Elections, press, clubs, and public opinion have all been the
focus of unprecedented attention as a result. The Revolution is still associated with the
birth of modernity, but now it is culture rather than capitalism that is regarded as its
essence. Yet if the early 1790s are no longer labelled 'bourgeois', in contrast to a subsequent 'popular' phase, their fundamental radicalism remains underestimated, eclipsed
by a preoccupation with political violence and the Terror. This chapter will argue that a
study of political institutions and practices under the constitutional monarchy reveals a
precocious and vibrant experiment in radical politics that was curbed later in the decade. Edmund Burke was right to warn that events in France far exceeded the British
experience of 1688: a massive transformation was already under way, which deserves
greater recognition.

There was certainly talk of 'regeneration' in France before 1789, but until the momentous events of that great summer occurred, no one suspected just how far-reaching
the process would be. Even after they had taken the revolutionary step of creating the
National Assembly in June, most deputies reckoned that their constitutional work
would soon be complete. In fact, they required more than two years to finish their task

of reconstruction which culminated in the (short-lived) Constitution of 1791. For, on the famous night of 4 August, the old regime was comprehensively dismantled and then, on 26 August, the Declaration of the Rights of Man and the Citizen set an agenda for the creation of a profoundly new order.[3] To build would prove far more difficult than to destroy, because the great principles of sovereignty of the people, equality before the law, and individual liberty would have to be implemented in a society where none of these ideals had previously been recognized. Thus began an intense, indeed exhilarating, period of innovation and experimentation that would turn France into a political laboratory for the next decade or so. Though the period of constitutional monarchy has often been regarded as a 'moderate' or 'liberal' phase of the Revolution (Jean-Clément Martin has recently asserted that 'the real revolution began in 1792'), vast changes were in motion.[4] It is equally misleading to dub these early years 'a prelude to Terror', since political practice was developing in a democratic, even pluralistic fashion.[5] A number of innovations, ranging from the administrative system to elections, political clubs, and the newspaper press, about which much remains to be learned, will be explored in this chapter.

THE NEW ADMINISTRATIVE FRAMEWORK

On 29 September 1789, speaking on behalf of the Constitutional Committee of the National Assembly, the Norman deputy Thouret presented a plan for a truly thoroughgoing administrative reorganization of the French kingdom. A contemporary pamphlet described the existing arrangements as 'a monstrous and contradictory pile of inequalities, that time, hazard, abuse, privilege, and the favour of despotism have composed out of chaos'.[6] The proposal instead was to divide the territory into 80 departments, 720 *grandes communes* and 6,480 cantons. Aside from Paris, the network's point of departure which was to be treated separately, each department would comprise 324 square leagues (some 5,000 square kilometres), split into 9 *grandes communes* and 81 cantons, all of equal size. In the event, this grand, geometric design was stillborn. The alternative that was adopted retained the principle of uniformity, and remained integral to the system of representation, but it took account of topographical realities. Nonetheless, the reorganization was a radical one, and in terms of the departments (83 were created in 1790) it has proved enduring, despite some intense debate over its nature and consequences.

Change on this scale represented a vast undertaking, but it was rapidly achieved, for there was no dispute over the urgent need for the National Assembly, which had seized the legislative initiative and sidelined (though not removed) the king, to create an administrative backbone for the new regime. The country had dissolved into chaos during the summer of 1789 and it was not just Paris that witnessed the emergence of ad hoc arrangements to fill the vacuum left by the collapse of the old monarchy. An urban and rural upheaval was already occurring in the provinces which rendered the existing patchwork of government still more variegated. The recent generation of revolutionary historians has demonstrated that a process of politicization had begun in several regions even before debate was engaged over the convocation of the long-dormant French parliament, the Estates-General. In Provence, for example, the question of restructuring the provincial estates, as part of the proposed royal reform of local government in 1787, had already divided elite opinion.[7] Then, in the spring of 1789, coinciding with rising food prices and growing misery, a spectacular mass revolt obliged seigneurs to renounce feudal dues, while town councillors could only watch as food stores were pillaged and their authority was shattered. Elections brought ordinary people on to the streets at Marseille and Toulon, as they thrust themselves into the political process and succeeded in inserting their own demands (notably regarding regressive local taxes) into the general *cahiers de doléances* of the Third Estate. Bourgeois militias were expanded, and would later be transformed into a National Guard, but urban oligarchies (as well as the nobility), had already been thrust on to the defensive.

Violence did not occur everywhere, but only in few cases were municipal elites left unscathed. In the face of threats to their own inhabitants, not to mention the fear of peasant unrest, political power was widely wrested from what had come to be regarded as deeply unrepresentative urban bodies. Revolutionary committees were mostly established after the arrival of news of the storming of the Bastille in Paris, but they spontaneously emerged from a similar situation of insecurity and assumed a variety of forms, challenging the existing authorities which were struggling to cope with an unprecedented crisis. Very often those who had represented the town during the successive stages of Third Estate elections to the Estates-General played a leading role, as at Bordeaux, where the ninety individuals involved in the final level of the electoral process constituted themselves as a committee and began taking initiatives to restore order and maintain the bread supply. Elsewhere, at Reims for example, fresh elections took place, though the individuals chosen mostly emanated from the old elite and shared power with existing municipal personnel.[8] Artisans and shopkeepers were voted into office, but only in rare cases, such as Strasbourg, was the old town council replaced rather than reinforced.[9] Yet, as Lynn Hunt suggests, many townspeople had taken advantage of the situation to participate in shaping urban government and create novel, autonomous political spaces, a process that would prove difficult to reverse.

Paris witnessed some audacious initiatives in the 'districts', specifically set up to facilitate elections to the Estates-General in the spring of 1789, but which enjoyed a more lengthy existence and left a deep imprint. Elsewhere in France an extensive franchise had encompassed most male householders (and sometimes widows too, though lower-class participation was mostly confined to the preliminary stages of the electoral process). By contrast, Third Estate electors in the capital were limited to those who met a fiscal requirement of 6 *livres* a year in the *capitation*. This restriction was contested by some poorer artisans, who felt that their concerns might be overlooked as a result, but elements among the wealthy electorate itself immediately challenged the very basis on which they were meeting. Those attending the district of Petit-Saint-Antoine, for example, protested against the narrow franchise and, like many of their counterparts, made a claim for sovereignty, refusing to accept the appointed officials and electing their own instead.[10] This practice of autonomy became more pronounced after 14 July, when non-voters became involved in setting up a militia. Though it was the middle-class electors of Paris who improvised a revolutionary administration they were obliged to contend with the districts, which continued their deliberations despite the completion of their electoral business. When the National Assembly decided on a new structure for the capital city a year later, the forty-eight electoral divisions, or 'sections', bore a striking resemblance to the former districts and were soon claiming sovereignty. Barrie Rose concluded that these agencies constituted 'a workshop of democracy', leaving a substantial legacy for the celebrated sans-culottes, but a detailed investigation of one district by David Andress suggests that they were more preoccupied with the restoration of order.[11]

Sharing a similar concern to end lawlessness, in the autumn of 1789 the National Assembly had agreed to modified proposals for a uniform, nested hierarchy of departments, districts and communes to replace the chaos of local initiatives recently superimposed on the disparate authorities of the old regime. Although the provinces lost their former role in government, most departments were visibly carved out within their boundaries, taking their names from the topographical features that defined them, mostly rivers, mountains, or coasts, such as Saône-et-Loire, Hautes-Alpes, or Manche. The result has often been hailed as a victory for decentralization, but this was more apparent than real. All departmental, district and municipal officials were to be elected, including the *procureurs-syndics*, attached to each administration to act as liaison officers between locality and centre. However, the uniformity which replaced the incoherent and overlapping bodies that previously existed did generate the potential for greater central control in future. As Marie-Vic Ozouf-Marignier argues, provincial privileges (or *libertés*, as they were called), which had long sustained and protected local traditions, had disappeared and the departments were not strong enough to stand up to the centre; power had been 'de-concentrated' rather than decentralized.[12]

Since many provincials were anticipating the opportunity to draft their own administrative statutes, this outcome was doubtless disappointing. Some satisfaction was derived from the National Assembly's indulgence where communes were concerned: their total swelled to some 44,000, many of them miniscule, though they were grouped into cantons for electoral and judicial purposes (when Justices of the Peace were instituted). A struggle for the spoils inevitably ensued around the new circumscriptions, with different towns vying for the coveted status of *chef-lieu*, whether within departments or between districts. It proved difficult, if not impossible, to arrive at dispassionate decisions as waves of petitions were launched and deputations converged on Paris. While size might suggest a solution, smaller rivals could argue in favour of their central location. Much was at stake, for the loss, or gain, of councils, law courts and diocesan headquarters (all to be aligned with the administrative system) carried employment as well as prestige, on which many diminutive towns had relied in the past. The tiny provinces of Aunis and Saintonge on the western seaboard, for example, which were (somewhat unwillingly) amalgamated into the department of the Charente-Inférieure, produced a four-way contest for the headship between La Rochelle, Rochefort, Saintes, and Saint-Jean-d'Angély, which was eventually decided in favour of La Rochelle. Such rivalry might sow the seeds of future conflict, like the hostility between Aix-en-Provence, the former provincial capital initially appointed as *chef-lieu* of the Bouches-du-Rhône, and the great seaport of Marseille. Tension persisted because more than half a million posts were up for election and incumbents would enjoy only short periods of office, usually of no more than two years' duration.

ELECTIONS AND CITIZENSHIP

A completely unprecedented, mass electoral process began at the grass roots, with the formation of the lowest tier of the administrative hierarchy, that of the commune. In January and February 1790, usually starting on a Sunday in the parish church and invariably commencing with a mass, country dwellers and townspeople assembled to create their new municipal councils. Turnout of voters, like turnover of personnel, was less marked in the south than in the north of France, though 80 or even 90 per cent of active citizens turned out in some tiny communes.[13] At Saint-Brieuc, a small town of some 3,000 inhabitants, which was *chef-lieu* of the Côtes-du-Nord department on the Channel coast, voters began by choosing their own officials (president, secretary, and scrutineers) before proceeding, according to the legislation of 14 December 1789, to separately elect a mayor, a *procureur*, eight councillors and eighteen *notables*, or deputy councillors. The level of attendance fluctuated as different polls were taken, and declined the longer the election went on, but 70 per cent of the active citizens took part in the highest recorded vote. A doctor became mayor, while members of the legal profession and businessmen dominated as councillors, though artisans and shopkeepers formed a minority of the deputy councillors.[14]

This example tells us a good deal about the revolutionary electoral system, a vital part of the political process which, after years of neglect, has recently attracted considerable interest from historians, who disagree over its significance.[15] It was indicative of the passion for uniformity that the elections taking place everywhere in France after 1790 should operate in a similar fashion whatever the post in contention and that each voter employed a ballot paper to express his preferences. To be sure, a degree of continuity with the past was in evidence, for elections had been conducted at local level prior to 1789 and they often involved large numbers of adult males (and sometimes females). One important element retained throughout the Revolution was the practice of voting in Assemblies. This was a far cry from the brief, individual gesture with which we are familiar today but, while apparently archaic, it was a means of ensuring the validity of proceedings, since the casting and counting of votes was conducted in public. Meeting together also facilitated the successive series of ballots that were required, with up to three rounds prescribed in search of absolute majorities for those elected. However, this protracted procedure did take a toll on attendance and favoured the influence of those who could afford to participate for longer periods, not least on working days. In any case, the sovereignty of the people expressed in these Assemblies was not, as it transpired, to be expressed in a wholly inclusive fashion.

Towards the end of 1789, when it was decided at the National Assembly who should be entitled to vote for those exercising authority over them, reservations became apparent. The basic franchise was limited to men aged over twenty-five, of French nationality, resident in their electoral domicile for at least a year, who paid taxes equivalent to the local value of three days unskilled labour (to a maximum of 3 *livres*). Emmanuel Sieyès, the great advocate of the Third Estate in 1789, celebrated for his pamphlet *What is the Third Estate?*, suggested excluding the poor (as well as women) from the vote, and he coined the phrase 'passive citizen' to describe those from whom the franchise was withheld.[16] The term has since enjoyed more currency among historians than it did at the time, though the radical journalist, Camille Desmoulins, immediately denounced it, on the grounds that many of those who had 'actively' stormed the Bastille were thus denied the vote. In the Assembly itself, Robespierre would characteristically expose the deputies' timidity in restricting the franchise, notwithstanding the equality of rights enshrined in the great Declaration of Rights. Yet his objections were echoed by few of his colleagues (the abbé Grégoire was a salient exception) and made little impression beyond the chamber. Indeed, votes for women were never discussed in the Assembly, though their cause was at least publicized, notably by Condorcet and Olympe de Gouges.[17]

Albert Soboul claimed that, as a result of this franchise legislation, 'the common people were eliminated from political life.'[18] In fact, by contemporary European standards, the proportion of the population encompassed by the basic suffrage in these early years of the Revolution represented a rather generous measure. At around two-thirds of adult males, or in excess of four million individuals, it indicated a democracy in the making, which the progress of prosperity was expected to advance. To be sure office-holding was limited to those who could meet a higher threshold by paying ten days' wages in tax. Moreover, the choice of all officials above the municipal and cantonal level was made via an indirect, two-tier process, with the election of district, department and national office-holders vested in electoral colleges, the members of which had to meet this more demanding fiscal criterion. Nonetheless, some three million individuals were suitably qualified to fill the 40,000 or so college places on offer, though unremunerated attendance at a distant location, for several days on end, lay beyond the capacity of many of them. What initially generated the greatest uproar was payment of the *marc d'argent*, equivalent to some 50 *livres* in tax, demanded of future legislative deputies. Some members of the National Assembly protested vigorously, arguing that talented but impecunious individuals like Rousseau would have been rendered ineligible. When the *marc d'argent* was discarded in 1791 (enabling any voter to become a deputy), it was in return for a stiffening of the requirements for electoral-college members, which also made reference to property-holding.

The number of registered, as opposed to potential, voters (taken from the tax rolls) was diminished by the additional requirements that tax receipts had to be presented, and enrolment in the National Guard certified, before active citizens could attend an electoral Assembly. How assiduously these demanding criteria were applied is uncertain, but in Paris, where turnout tended to be low—only 16 per cent of the putative total of voters took part in the return of Bailly as mayor in August 1790—a handful of surviving lists suggests that no more than half of those who were eligible to vote had actually fulfilled the necessary formalities. The time-consuming nature of the electoral process was also a disincentive to participation. The initial polls of 1790 had frequently attracted a healthy turnout in excess of 50 per cent but thereafter, as local authorities underwent renewal, only a minority of voters regularly used their new-found rights. Indeed, in 1791 primary elections in the cantons to replenish the departmental colleges attracted less than a quarter of the electorate on average, though rural involvement at this stage tended to be greater than in towns, where communal pressure to vote was weaker than in villages.[19] Unless personal, parochial or partisan passions were aroused there seemed little need for the whole community to turn out to register a consensus, while a smaller attendance meant that electoral business could be transacted more quickly; it was not simply a matter of apathy.

Generally speaking, participation diminished the longer elections went on, but not invariably so, because those in contention might mobilize reinforcements in order to secure victory at the second or third round. Even a modest turnout of 20 per cent meant that almost a million Frenchmen were taking part, and doing so repeatedly, at frequently held polls for municipal and judicial personnel, not to mention voting for National Guard officers and members of the electoral colleges. In 1790 and 1791 all French voters were summoned to attend their electoral Assemblies on at least six occasions, sometimes more. Elections also fulfilled a symbolic function: no longer could notables declare their preferences out loud and expect them to be readily adopted, for citizens now voted in strict alphabetical order, regardless of rank, and used a paper ballot. It was in these Assemblies that candidatures were advanced and campaigning was conducted in an intensive fashion, sometimes causing controversy. Elections should accordingly be regarded as veritable schools of citizenship, a process of political apprenticeship that, for all its flaws and fragility, challenges Patrice Gueniffey's conclusion that this great electoral experiment left a disappointing legacy.[20]

Moreover, such occasions for gathering to vote in Assemblies were easily transformed into opportunities for discussion. Deliberation had always been inseparable from election, a well-established feature of old-regime polling that was exemplified in the drafting of *cahiers* that accompanied the choice of deputies to the Estates-General of 1789. Historians have tended to overlook the fact that permission for the mass electorate to meet for the purpose of drawing up petitions, a major conduit for conveying grievances to the National Assembly, was granted in the municipal regulations of December 1789.[21] In bigger towns, an extraordinary Assembly would be convened following a request signed by just 150 active citizens and when municipal statutes were drawn up for Paris, in May 1790, this requirement was further relaxed: just fifty citizens could trigger an Assembly of their section.[22] Although this fell short of the 'permanence' demanded by some districts, the Postes section in the capital held, on average, one extraordinary meeting a fortnight after December 1790. Some of the larger provincial cities were soon following suit, such as Toulon in January 1791 and neighbouring Marseille later in the year. Participatory politics, or direct democracy, was deeply disturbing for those who were now seeking to contain popular initiatives and stress the representative nature of the new system. Thus the idea for a popular ratification of the forthcoming Constitution, mooted in the National Assembly in 1791, was firmly rejected on the grounds that deputies incarnated the sovereignty of the people.[23]

Nor did the 'second-degree' electoral colleges restrict themselves to the business of election, but freely engaged in debate. In 1790 there was continuing discussion about the structure of several departments, while in 1791 the Assembly of the Seine (Paris) examined a machine for counting votes. Attendance at departmental and district Assemblies was usually strong, though turnout invariably fell the longer that lengthy sessions went on—weeks, even months, at this level, as opposed to days in the case of cantons or communes. Hence the oft-quoted, but completely misleading example from the departmental Assembly of the Seine, which suggests that a mere 20 per cent of college members took part in the summer of 1791.[24] By this stage in the proceedings only minor posts remained to be filled and electors were heading for home, whereas earlier, when deputies for the Legislative Assembly were being chosen, intense competition involved over 90 per cent of the membership. As the president of the Assembly in the Haute-Saône advised his colleagues, in 1791, 'Having accepted the mission entrusted to you, you should endure the boredom, fatigue and expense that the task involves.'[25] These Assemblies were, after all, an elite gathering—if not an 'elective' aristocracy—composed of urban and rural notables (former office-holders, professional men, rentiers, and farmers), who often held office at municipal level and were thus expected to represent their communities at the secondary level of the electoral process.

The same individuals were duly elected to departmental and district Directories and councils, in some cases thence to the national Assemblies. However, it should be emphasized that former nobles and priests were usually conspicuous by their absence at the electoral colleges, which marks a significant change from the provincial Assemblies of the old regime, or indeed the Estates-General of 1789. Conversely, when these bodies were renewed in 1791 and 1792, artisans and shopkeepers began to make serious inroads as representatives from the larger towns. A similar evolution is apparent in the socio-professional profile of elected personnel at municipal level. To be sure, in 1790 half of the mayors initially chosen in departmental *chefs-lieux* across the country were nobles, but this situation would soon change. Melvin Edelstein has demonstrated that although the urban social elites dominated municipal councils in the bigger cities that year, the role of mercantile elements among them was a novelty, while artisans were starting to obtain a strong foothold as deputy councillors.[26] When these bodies were renewed later in 1790, and again in 1791, the popular classes continued to make progress, notably in Provence, securing posts as councillors and leaving the old elites increasingly powerless. Such turnover was less marked in most rural areas: in Artois, for example, wealthier farmers, former agents of the seigneur, generally dominated the new municipalities elected under the constitutional monarchy, though their monopoly of office was being challenged.[27]

POLITICAL CLUBS AND SOCIABILITY

A further source of democratization in the early years of the Revolution was furnished by the right of association, which found expression in the formation of political clubs and their consequent activities. 'On the 11 April of the first year of Liberty, 1790, a very great number of citizens met in the hall of the tennis court on the rue Thubaneau. Their purpose was to establish a Society for the defence of the Constitution, the maintenance and the propagation of Liberty.'[28] No fanfares accompanied the creation of the Jacobin Club of Marseille, but its influence rapidly spread into the region and far beyond Provence. As the plaque outside the door of its premises, now occupied by a bathhouse, reminds visitors, what became the French national anthem, *La Marseillaise*, was sung here in 1792. It was adopted as a battle hymn by volunteers from the city as they marched to defend Paris, where they took part in the overthrow of the monarchy on 10 August 1792. However, in his scholarly survey that put provincial clubs firmly on the map, Michael Kennedy emphasizes the respectable origins of the founding fathers at Marseille. Men serving on the municipality and holding other public offices were prominent among those who created the club, while the mayor became its first president. As one nineteenth-century historian put it, these 'patriots were motivated by the need to meet together and to defend the principles enumerated by the National Assembly'.[29]

This new form of sociability quickly spread across the country. Calling themselves patriotic societies, or clubs (a term borrowed from Britain), such bodies had been established in some twenty large towns by the end of 1789. The following year another 300 were created and the total had risen to over 1,000 by the end of 1791, with most departmental and district *chefs-lieux* now housing at least one club. The old regime had accepted the existence of artisan and penitent fraternities, protected learned academies, and tacitly tolerated Masonic lodges and reading societies, but all of these organizations would wilt and mostly disappear during the early 1790s. Instead, the revolutionaries endorsed the collective elaboration and expression of public opinion in a novel type of gathering that borrowed some practices from its predecessors, but whose rationale was primarily political. These clubs thus offered another space in which citizenship could develop and they played a significant role in the creation of a new political culture, though the nature of that contribution has always been a subject of historiographical debate.

The majority of clubs were linked to Paris where, in the autumn of 1789, a group of like-minded deputies in the National Assembly had started meeting at the nearby, former Jacobin (or Dominican) convent to discuss parliamentary business. These Jacobins soon extended membership to the ordinary public, attracting over 1,000 adherents by the end of 1789, and they also began to accept affiliation from provincial clubs. In the early 1790s the club 'phenomenon' was essentially an urban one but, since foundations at this stage were spontaneous and by no means dependent on any national directive, distinctive regional variations were apparent. Jacobin clubs were especially well implanted in the Midi, from Bordeaux to Toulon, in smaller as well as larger communities, doubtless a reflection of southern sociability and urbanized villages. Some northern areas, notably the coast of Normandy, would also participate heavily in the movement, while the western interior of France, in company with Alsace and Lorraine on the eastern frontier, responded rather less enthusiastically.[30]

In the network that was created, clubs corresponded with other societies in their regions, as well as with the *société-mère* in Paris. These strong links have led historians like François Furet, who has questioned the liberal credentials of revolutionary ideology, to regard clubs as tight-knit organizations, determined to enforce will of the people as they perceived it, brooking no dissent, and preferring purges to pluralism.[31] However, as Jean Boutier and Philippe Boutry demonstrate in their comprehensive, cartographical study, Jacobin clubs constituted 'neither a machine, nor a party, but instead an original and open form of political activity'.[32] A good example of their autonomy, at least in the earlier years of the Revolution, are their hesitations at moments of crisis, not least when the Parisian Jacobin club itself was deeply divided in the wake of the king's flight to Varennes, in July 1791. Disaffected moderates who wished to uphold the constitutional monarchy decamped to the former Feuillants convent in Paris and established an opposing organization. Faced with schism, the society at Honfleur, in Normandy, did not automatically maintain its allegiance to the remaining Jacobins, but carefully weighed up the opposing arguments before coming down in their favour.[33]

Even before the 'explosion' of fresh foundations in 1793–94, these societies had become a mass phenomenon, involving tens of thousands, especially when their public sessions—which non-members, including females, could attend—are taken into consideration. Adherents were inducted into the rituals of political debate and decision-making, as well as undertaking internal responsibilities that provided a gateway into public office holding. Jacobin club membership was open to all active citizens, but subscription fees (12 *livres* a year for admission to the Jacobin Club of Paris; 3 *livres* at Marseille), were beyond the means of most ordinary individuals. Nonetheless, during the early years of the Revolution, when clubs were dominated by the middle classes, better-off artisans, shopkeepers and well-to-do farmers began to join. Clubs were, therefore, already penetrating beyond the reach of Freemasonry and tapping into new layers of French society. Outside Paris aristocrats were generally unwelcome, but clergy who accepted the Civil Constitution of the Clergy and became 'constitutional' priests were able to play a significant role. Other clubs were created outside the Jacobin network, such as the Cordeliers of Paris, once again named after the former monastic premises on which they met, founded in June 1790. Their official appellation, La Société des Amis des Droits de l'Homme et du Citoyen, indicated a more radical mission and less elite membership, which was reflected in a modest one *livre* 4 *sols* entry fee. The Cordeliers sponsored 'Popular Societies', loosely based on the sections of Paris, to allow admission to passive citizens, and also encouraged women to join 'fraternal societies' of the two sexes.

Similar initiatives were being taken in some of the larger provincial cities, which thus made a significant contribution to this developing democratic culture. At Lyon, for example, popular societies sent representatives to a coordinating *club central* that met once a week.[34] At Bordeaux, where several political clubs were established between 1789 and 1791, there seems to have been coexistence, if not cooperation between them. By contrast, at Aix-en-Provence, where artisans and farmers were dismayed by the exclusive nature of the Jacobin-affiliated Friends of the Constitution, a *Société des Antipolitiques* was founded in November 1790 and conflict soon followed. Conversely, when moderates in some places grew fearful of radicals dominating the Jacobins, they quit (or might be expelled) and opposing societies emerged. The Feuillant schism of

1791 was echoed in the provinces, notably at Toulon, where an earlier attempt to found a second, more conservative club, finally bore fruit during that summer. The new club, significantly entitled 'The Friends and *Defenders* of the Constitution', was justified by the allegedly 'violent behaviour of a handful of sedition-mongers, who had outraged the sensibilities of the membership with a hypocritical display of patriotism that … forced many decent citizens to withdraw [from the existing club]'.[35]

'Friends of the Constitution' they may have styled themselves, but in spite of their declared aim of supporting the Assembly, by promoting public awareness of its endeavours, these clubs soon began to challenge the national and local authorities.[36] Relaying information from the press was an important function, since few individuals could afford subscriptions and those unable to read could listen; club meetings were often timed to coincide with the arrival of the latest editions. However, newspapers took a critical approach that was inevitably imparted to their audiences. It became the duty of club members to hold their representatives to account and the Cordeliers expressly chose the eye of vigilance as their emblem. Denunciation of administrators and politicians became commonplace in 1791, especially in the case of departmental authorities, which had been elected among the notables and tended to be conservative: the Jacobins of Toulon accordingly denounced the administrators of the Var for not 'providing the slightest proof of loyalty since the outset of the Revolution'.[37] The campaign against refractory clergy in 1791 was similarly vituperative. Government ministers were certainly not spared, nor the queen, though until his flight to Varennes the king was usually exempt from reproach.

The composition of addresses and petitions, which were frequently circulated around the club network, were also a means of trying to influence policy at all levels—locally with the call for 'transparency', via the admission of the general public to council meetings, and nationally in terms of debate over the franchise, for example. Clubs were soon involving themselves in electioneering. For the most part they simply emphasized the importance of choosing 'good patriots', but lists of 'candidates' were issued, while members of the electoral colleges were invited to discuss their business with club officials; canvassing of this sort might be perfectly acceptable today, but during the Revolution it was usually regarded as 'factionalism'.[38] The fate of the monarchy in the wake of Varennes prompted tremendous activity; after all, in the declaration he left behind, Louis XVI had condemned the clubs as agents of anarchy. A widespread campaign for a republic ensued and, though most clubs did subsequently accept retention of the monarchy, their faith in the Crown was significantly diminished.[39]

THE PRESS AND THE PUBLIC SPHERE

The newspaper press contributed mightily to the vibrant participatory political culture that emerged after 1789. During the early years of the Revolution the most popular title at the Jacobin clubs, some of which published their own newssheets, was Jean-Louis

Carra's *Annales patriotiques*. It provided daily helpings of home and foreign news without indulging in the extremism which characterized some of the more radical and historically better-known, but much less widely circulated titles, such as Marat's *Ami du Peuple*. Second in importance among the Jacobins, but more original in terms of content, was the *Feuille villageoise*, which first appeared in September 1790 and continued for the next five years.[40] Its main editor was Joseph Cerutti, a former Jesuit who had pursued a literary career since the late 1760s and began to engage in politics at the end of the old regime (and indeed became a member of the Legislative Assembly in 1791). The *Feuille* appeared every Thursday, in 24 quarto pages which initially sold at 7 *livres*, 4 *sols* a year (as opposed to 32 *livres* for the more upmarket *Mercure national*). It was 'addressed to all the villages of France, in order to educate them' and drew on an appropriate agricultural metaphor: 'Happy the land which leaves no field nor individual uncultivated.' Like the *Annales patriotiques* its tone was pro-revolutionary, but moderate: it supported a restricted franchise, the constitutional Church and free trade. A common practice was to read it aloud at public sessions of clubs, in town squares, or at village markets.

The origins of this type of mass print medium in the Revolution should be sought in the preceding decades, but while there had been a steady development of the newspaper press, it was nothing compared to the veritable explosion that occurred from the late 1780s onwards.[41] Although the hamstrung monarchy invited comments on the state of the kingdom in 1788, and censorship was becoming difficult to impose, when the Estates-General actually opened the following year it reiterated that reporting required official permission. The deputy Mirabeau and publicist Brissot simply flouted this royal instruction; liberty was seized rather than granted. The Declaration of the Rights of Man, which stated that 'The free communication of thoughts and opinions is one of the most precious rights of man; thus any citizen may speak, write and print freely', consecrated as much as created this new-found liberty, which quickly became something of a free for all. A score of new titles appeared in Paris alone in May and June 1789, with over 200 more starting later in the year in the kingdom as a whole, albeit many of them of short duration. The following year, 1790, represented the apogee for a pluralistic press, with 400 fresh titles of all political persuasions appearing, before the flow of print began to subside and attempts were made to rein in its diversity.

Besides exploring the material history of newspaper production and its circulation during this period, historians like Hugh Gough and Jeremy Popkin have recently revealed the riches of the revolutionary provincial press, which are currently being gathered into a comprehensive inventory.[42] Existing local newspapers changed title and content, like the south-western *Affiches de Périgueux*, which became the *Journal patriotique*, while others turned from weekly to more frequent publication. However, the capital dominated in terms of production, as the number of print shops leapt from just 36 in 1789 to over 200 in 1791, but newspaper technology remained traditional, like the format, though some titles appeared as wall posters. By contrast, the term 'fourth estate' seems to have been coined at this point to characterize the emergence of the journalistic profession, an especially apt appellation in view of the porous boundaries between press and politics in revolutionary France. Carra, for instance was elected to the National Convention by eight departments in 1792 as a result of the reputation he had built through journalism, while Brissot and Condorcet, overlooked by electors in 1789, both became deputies in 1791.

The readership for the revolutionary press was predominantly urban but, as the example of the *Feuille villageoise* demonstrates, newspapers did penetrate into the countryside, as editors responded to a vastly increased demand for news in a rapidly changing political environment. The audience for the revolutionary press can thus be numbered in the hundreds of thousands and, like both elections and clubs, newspapers offered a profound schooling in citizenship. The pedagogic objective was neatly summed up by Brissot, in his prospectus for the *Patriote français*: 'We have to look for an alternative to pamphlets for the continuous education of Frenchmen, in a form that will be both cheap and interesting.'[43] Newspapers appeared with a rapidity unmatched by other media, supplying content that was overwhelmingly political. Rather than merely recording events, many titles, which ranged across the political spectrum from the radical *Révolutions de Paris* to the royalist *Ami du Roi*, deployed deeply critical comment and engaged in invective. Initially deferential towards the National Assembly, the press was increasingly prone to challenge the constituted authorities. Desmoulins wrote: 'it is the journalist … who inspects the senate, the consuls and the dictator himself'.[44] Extremists—both the royalist Royou and the radical Marat—refused to accept self-censorship, leading Popkin to conclude that: 'The press … subverted the new institutions it appeared to support.'[45]

There will always be argument over the extent to which newspapers create rather than reflect public opinion, but there is agreement that they were vital to shaping perceptions of the Revolution and making sense of its development. The press was an integral part of the process of open debate which the Revolution initially encouraged. Advocates of press freedom (wrongly) assumed that, as in the case of clubs and elections, a unified public opinion would emerge from the experiment. Consensus was assumed to constitute the norm in a free society and thus opponents were all too easily regarded as dangerous dissenters, an attitude only strengthened by the lack of self-restraint on the part of both radicals and royalists.[46] Nonetheless, a press divided along partisan lines did give voice to the views of those not represented on elected bodies. The pluralism of the early 1790s, even though it was relatively short-lived, pointed in the direction of a polity where conflict and competition might become more acceptable. This would prove difficult without a stable political framework and, by the summer of 1792, those newspapers which continued to support a constitutional monarchy were mostly eliminated, not so much by legislation—though steps were taken in this direction—as by popular pressure.

Ending the Revolution in 1791?

The radicalization that occurred after 1789 was by no means a linear process, although this is seldom recognized. As completion of the Constitution approached, widely envisaged as marking the end of the Revolution, there was an upsurge of reaction. In the spring and summer of 1791, conservative deputies in the National Assembly sought to restrict some of the developments that have been discussed here and they redoubled their efforts in the wake of the disarray caused by the king's flight to Varennes on 21 June. The subsequent demonstration on the Champ de Mars in Paris, which called for a replacement of the monarchy and was mirrored in the provinces by petitions in favour of dethroning the king, produced a backlash which Albert Mathiez long ago dubbed the 'Tricolour Terror'.[47] It was certainly evident in revisions to the franchise, where the criteria for election to membership of the departmental electoral colleges were concerned. These changes, which demanded ownership or access to land and property, varying in rental value from 100–200 *livres* a year, depending on the size of the community, were endorsed in return for abolishing the *marc d'argent* hitherto required of deputies. These amended criteria did not apply to the 'legislative' elections of June 1791, which were already in train, but they were symptomatic of an attempt to close down access to the broad political space that had emerged after 1789. Since these provisions were later revived, virtually unchanged, in the Constitution of 1795, it is possible to assess their impact on the second-degree electorate, which would have been reduced to less than a third of the three million Frenchmen previously eligible.[48]

The clampdown was more immediate when it came to the political challenge posed by newspapers, clubs, and petitions. The National Assembly's constitutional committee, reinforced by new members in order to complete its work, was determined to curb their criticism in order to 'end the Revolution'. Long envisaged, but endlessly postponed, legislation to 'combat crimes committed in the press' was introduced by Thouret on 22 August, which enabled prosecution for incitement to disobey the law, defamation of public bodies, and opposition to their endeavours.[49] A month or so later, on the very eve of the Assembly's dissolution, Le Chapelier launched a comprehensive attack on the role of political clubs and the idea of popular sovereignty:

> When the revolution is complete, when the constitution is fixed … Nothing must hinder the actions of the constituted bodies. Deliberation and the power to act must be located where the constitution has placed them and nowhere else … There is no power except that instituted by the will of the people and expressed through their representatives. There are no authorities except those delegated by the people and there can be no actions except those of its representatives who have been entrusted with public duties. It is to preserve this principle, in all its purity, that the constitution has abolished all corporations, from one end of the state to another, and henceforth recognises only society as a whole and individuals within it. A necessary consequence of this principle is the prohibition of any petition or placard issued in the name of a group.[50]

A law forbade clubs to interfere in the process of government, to issue collective petitions, or to appear as a group at public events (although an accompanying proposal to ban their sponsorship of public debates and curtail their networking was not endorsed).[51]

What this raft of conservative measures actually achieved remains a subject of debate, but in his classic study of the Revolution Alphonse Aulard argued that radicals and Republicans were deflated and only experienced a revival during the winter of 1791–92.[52] It is true that the instigators of this legislation immediately lost their parliamentary authority, when the new constitution came into force and the National Assembly was dissolved on the last day of September 1791. Back in May, the Assembly had agreed to a proposal from Robespierre for a 'self-denying ordinance', which meant that none of them were eligible for election to the single-chamber Legislative Assembly that would succeed them.[53] The experience and influence acquired by deputies over the past two years was thus denied to the new body, and Michael Fitzsimmons sees this as a key factor in unravelling the consensus around the constitution.[54] These same individuals had recently discussed a convention that might revise their efforts in the near future, but even they cannot have anticipated the demise of their efforts within less than a year. Clearly the events of 1792 were unpredictable when the deputies separated, duly declaring that the Revolution was over. The outbreak of war, like the king's divisive use of his veto, was a major, unforeseen factor in prompting fresh political upheaval, but the seeds of radicalism had been sown and intensely cultivated. The shift in historiographical focus, as Terror has once more become 'the order of the day' among historians, should not obscure the profound, democratic change already developing in what is erroneously described as 'the moderate phase' of the Revolution.

Notes

1. Keith Michael Baker et al. (eds), *The French Revolution and the Creation of Modern Political Culture*, 4 vols (Oxford, 1987–94).

2. Colin Jones, 'Twenty years After', *French Historical Studies* 32 (2009), 679–87, one of a series of historiographical reflections in this special issue of the journal devoted to '89: then and now'.

3. Michael P. Fitzsimmons, *The Night the Old Regime Ended: August 4, 1789, and the French Revolution* (University Park, PA, 2003).

4. Jean-Clément Martin, *Nouvelle histoire de la Révolution française* (Paris, 2012). Noah Shusterman, *The French Revolution. Faith, Desire, and Politics* (London, 2014), 23–54, devotes a chapter to 'The Liberal Revolution of 1789'.

5. The phrase is taken from Norman Hampson, *Prelude to Terror. The Constituent Assembly and the Failure of Consensus, 1789–1791* (Oxford, 1988).

6. Cited in Ted W. Margadant, *Urban Rivalries in the French Revolution* (Princeton, 1992), 84.

7. Monique Cubells, *Les horizons de la liberté* (Aix-en-Provence, 1987), 92–109.

8. Lynn A. Hunt, *Revolution and Urban Politics in Provincial France. Troyes and Reims, 1786–1790* (Stanford, 1978), 77–82.

9. Lynn A. Hunt, 'Committees and Communes: Local Politics and National Revolution in 1789', *Comparative Studies in History and Society* 18 (1976), 345–6.

10. R. B. Rose, *The Making of the Sans-Culottes. Democratic Ideas and Institutions in Paris, 1789–1792* (Manchester, 1983), 28–31.

11. Rose, *The Making of the Sans-Culottes*, 58–86 and David Andress, 'Neighborhood Policing in Paris from Old Regime to Revolution: the Exercise of Authority by the District de Saint-Roch, 1789–1791', *French Historical Studies* 29 (2006), 231–60.

12. Marie-Vic Ozouf-Marignier, *La formation des départements. La représentation du terri-toire français à la fin du 18e siècle* (Paris, 1989).

13. Isser Woloch, *The New Regime. Transformations of the French Civic Order, 1789–1820s* (New York, 1994), 60–3, and Michel Cassan et al. (eds), *Limousin en Révolution* (Treignac, 1989).

14. Melvin Edelstein, 'La reception de la Révolution en Bretagne: étude électorale', in Roger Dupuy (ed.), *Pouvoir local et révolution, 1750–1850: la frontière intérieure* (Rennes, 1994), 194–6.

15. Malcolm Crook, *Elections in the French Revolution. An Apprenticeship in Democracy, 1789–1799* (Cambridge, 1996); Patrice Gueniffey, *Le Nombre et la raison. La Révolution française et les élections* (Paris, 1993); and Melvin Edelstein, *The French Revolution and the Birth of Democracy* (Farnham, 2014).

16. William H. Sewell, 'Le citoyen/la citoyenne: Activity, Passivity, and the Revolutionary Concept of Citizenship', in Colin Lucas (ed.), *The French Revolution and the Creation of Modern Political Culture*, vol. 2 (Oxford, 1988), 105–23.

17. Lynn Hunt, *The French Revolution and Human Rights. A Brief Documentary History* (Boston, 1996), 26–9.

18. Albert Soboul, *The French Revolution 1787–1799*, trans. (London, 1974), 180–1.

19. Malcolm Crook, '"Aux urnes citoyens!" Urban and Rural Electoral Behaviour during the French Revolution', in Alan Forrest and Peter Jones (eds), *Reshaping France. Town, Country and Region during the French Revolution* (Manchester, 1991), 152–67.

20. Gueniffey's verdict informs his study, *Le Nombre et la raison*, but it is also evident in his contribution on 'Elections', in François Furet and Mona Ozouf (eds), *A Critical Dictionary of the French Revolution* (Cambridge, MA, 1989), 33–44.

21. A[rchives] P[arlementaires], t. X, 358, 3 December 1789.

22. Titre IV, article I of the municipal regulation for Paris, 21 May 1790, cited in Ernest Mellié, *Les sections de Paris pendant la Révolution française, 21 mai–19 vendémiaire an IV. Organisation, fonctionnement* (Paris, 1898), 17.

23. AP, t. VIII, 581–4, 5 September 1789, and M. Fridiev, *Les origines du référendum dans la Constitution de 1793* (Paris, 1932), 229.

24. J. M. Thompson, *The French Revolution*, rev. edn (Oxford, 1985), 227.

25. Jean Girardot, *Le department de la Haute-Saône pendant la Révolution*, 3 vols (Vesoul, 1972–74), II, 102.

26. Melvin Edelstein, '"Laying the Foundations for the Regeneration of the Empire": The First Municipal Elections in the Biggest Cities of France during the Revolution', *French History* 17 (2003), 260.

27. Jean-Pierre Jessenne, *Pouvoir au village et Révolution. Artois 1760–1848* (Lille, 1987).

28. 'Règlemens des amis de la Constitution de Marseille', cited in Michael L. Kennedy, *The Jacobin Club of Marseilles, 1790–1794* (Ithaca, NY, 1973), 13.

29. Cited in Kennedy, *The Jacobin Club of Marseilles*, 13–14.

30. Jean Boutier and Philippe Boutry, *Atlas de la Révolution française, vol. 6, Les sociétés poli-tiques* (Paris, 1992).

31. Patrice Gueniffey and Ran Halevi, 'Clubs and Popular Societies', in Furet and Ozouf (eds), *A Critical Dictionary*, 458–9.

32. Boutier and Boutry, *Les sociétés politiques*, 55.
33. Michel Biard, 'The "Jacobin Machine", a Historical Fantasy Revisited in the Light of a Local Study: The Popular Society of Honfleur (1791–95)', *French History* 26 (2012), 85–6.
34. W. D. Edmonds, *Jacobinism and the Revolt of Lyon 1789–1793* (Oxford, 1990), 71–97.
35. Malcolm Crook, *Toulon in War and Revolution. From the Ancien Régime to the Restoration, 1750–1820* (Manchester, 1991), 103–4.
36. Michael Kennedy, *The Jacobin Clubs in the French Revolution. The First Years* (Princeton, NJ, 1982), 26–8.
37. Crook, *Toulon in War and Revolution*, 115.
38. Kennedy, *The Jacobin Clubs … The First Years*, 210–23, and Crook, *Elections in the French Revolution*, 69–70 and 179–80.
39. Kennedy, *The Jacobin Clubs … The First Years*, 260–80, and Timothy Tackett, *When the King took Flight* (Cambridge, MA, 2003), 184–98.
40. Melvin A. Edelstein, *La Feuille villageoise: communication et modernisation dans les régions rurales pendant la Révolution* (Paris, 1977).
41. See Simon Burrows, 'Books, Philosophy, Enlightenment', in this volume.
42. Hugh Gough, *The Newspaper Press in the French Revolution* (London, 1988); Jeremy D. Popkin, *Revolutionary News. The Press in France, 1789–1799* (Durham, NC, 1990); Gilles Feyel (ed.), *Dictionnaire de la presse française pendant la Révolution, 1789–1799. La presse départementale*, 4 vols to date (Ferny-Voltaire, 2005–14).
43. 'Le Patriote Français', prospectus, cited in Gough, *The Newspaper Press*, 36.
44. 'Révolutions de France et de Brabant', 2, cited in Gough, *The Newspaper Press*.
45. Popkin, *Revolutionary News*, p. 181.
46. Charles Walton, *Policing Public Opinion in the French Revolution. The Culture of Calumny and the Problem of Free Speech* (Oxford, 2009).
47. Albert Mathiez, *Les grandes journées de la Constituante* (Paris, 1913), 197 and David Andress, *Massacre at the Champ de Mars. Popular Dissent and Political Culture in the French Revolution* (Woodbridge, 2000).
48. Crook, *Elections in the French Revolution*, 47–9.
49. AP XXIX, 631–9, 22–3 August 1791, and Walton, *Policing Public Opinion*, 123–4.
50. AP XXXI, 616–17, 29 September 1791.
51. Michael L. Kennedy, *The Jacobin Clubs in the French Revolution. The Middle Years* (Princeton, 1988), 8–9.
52. Alphonse Aulard, *Histoire politique de la Révolution française. Origines et développement de la démocratie et de la République (1789–1804)*, 5th edn (Paris, 1910), 171–7.
53. Barry Shapiro, 'Self-Sacrifice, Self-Interest or Self-Defense? The Constituent Assembly and the "Self-Denying Ordinance" of May 1791', *French Historical Studies* 25 (2002), 625–56.
54. Fitzsimmons, *The Remaking of France*, 255–6.

Selected Reading

Aulard, Alphonse, *Histoire politique de la Révolution française. Origines et développement de la démocratie et de la République (1789–1804)*, 5th edn (Paris, 1910).
Boutier, Jean and Boutry, Philippe, Atlas de la Révolution française, vol. 6, Les sociétés politiques (Paris, 1992).
Crook, Malcolm, *Elections in the French Revolution. An Apprenticeship in Democracy, 1789–1799* (Cambridge, 1996).

Edelstein, Melvin, *The French Revolution and the Birth of Democracy* (Farnham, 2014).

Furet, François and Ozouf, Mona (eds), *A Critical Dictionary of the French Revolution* (Cambridge, MA, 1989).

Fitzsimmons, Michael, *The Remaking of France: The National Assembly and the Constitution of 1791* (Cambridge, 1994).

Gough, Hugh, *The Newspaper Press in the French Revolution* (London, 1988).

Gueniffey, Patrice, *Le Nombre et la raison. La Révolution française et les élections* (Paris, 1993).

Hunt, Lynn, *Politics, Culture and Class in the French Revolution*, 2nd edn (Berkeley, 2004).

Kennedy, Michael L., *The Jacobin Clubs in the French Revolution. The First Years* (Princeton, NJ, 1982).

Kennedy, Michael L., *The Jacobin Clubs in the French Revolution. The Middle Years* (Princeton, NJ, 1988).

Lucas, Colin (ed.), *The French Revolution and the Creation of Modern Political Culture*, vol. 2 (Oxford, 1988).

Margadant, Ted W., *Urban Rivalries in the French Revolution* (Princeton, 1992).

Ozouf-Marignier, Marie-Vic, *La formation des départements. La représentation du territoire français à la fin du 18e siècle* (Paris, 1989).

Tackett, Timothy, *When the King took Flight* (Cambridge, MA, 2003).

Walton, Charles, *Policing Public Opinion in the French Revolution. The Culture of Calumny and the Problem of Free Speech* (Oxford, 2009).

Woloch, Isser, *The New Regime. Transformations of the French Civic Order, 1789–1820s* (New York, 1994).

CHAPTER 14

REVOLUTION AND CHANGING IDENTITIES IN FRANCE, 1787–99

JEREMY D. POPKIN

ONE of the most striking slogans generated by the dramatic events of July 1789 was the motto of the *Révolutions de Paris*, a pamphlet account of the storming of the Bastille that developed into a weekly newspaper: '*Les grands ne nous paraissent pas grands que parce que nous sommes à genoux. Levons-nous!*' ('Those above us only look big to us because we are on our knees. Let's rise up!') In two short sentences, this slogan captured the essence of the experience that the French people had suddenly found themselves caught up in. By taking action—by getting off their knees and adopting a new posture—the participants in the Revolution changed their sense of who they were. They had been royal subjects and social subordinates, looking up to authority figures who seemed to tower over them; they would now confront their former superiors on a basis of equality. At the same time, by changing their own sense of who they were, the participants in the Revolution would impose a new identity on their former overlords: *les grands* would no longer be *les grands* if they no longer overawed their supposed inferiors.

'Identity' is a widely used concept in contemporary social and historical analysis, and it is particularly fruitful for thinking about the transformations wrought by the French Revolution.[1] The concepts of identity and identity transformation are particularly effective ways of conceptualizing the relationship between the political and institutional aspects of the revolutionary experience, on the one hand, and the embodiment of that experience in the lives of individuals, on the other. The revolutionaries of 1789 frequently described what they were doing in language that strongly suggests that they themselves conceived the Revolution as an effort to change the way people defined themselves. When they resolved to combat 'ignorance, neglect, and scorn of the rights of man' by issuing their *Declaration* on 26 August 1789, the deputies of the National Assembly intended the document to 'continually remind [the citizens of France] of their rights and their duties ... ' In other words, the Declaration would call on its audience to understand themselves as autonomous individuals, possessors of 'natural, inalienable, and sacred' rights, and as members of a consensual community toward which they also had obligations. Its authors were replacing the identity of royal subject with that of national citizen, and, as philosopher Étienne Balibar has put it, this was a momentous transformation, of profound philosophical as well as political significance: 'The citizen (defined by his rights and duties) is that "nonsubject" who comes after the subject, and whose constitution and recognition put an end (in principle) to the subjection of the subject.'[2]

The *Révolutions de Paris*'s epigraph is a striking example of how central processes of identity transformation were to the drama of the French Revolution. At the same time, its two sentences encapsulate many of the complexities concealed in these processes. Was identity, for example, a collective or an individual attribute? The newspaper's epigraph used plurals—'*nous*' and '*les grands*'—suggesting that it referred to groups rather than individuals. But the action it called for in its final words—'*levons-nous!*'—was, in the literal sense, a physical act that had to be performed by discrete individuals. Nevertheless, this 'rising up' would only take on significance if many individuals performed it at the same time. Individual and collective identity were thus tightly interwoven: collective identities could only be transformed through changes in the behaviour of individuals, but individual action only became effective as part of a collective transformation. Similarly, the *Révolutions de Paris*'s epigraph was ambiguous about whether identities were chosen or imposed, effects of will or of circumstance. By exercising their will and getting up off their knees, the anonymous 'we' the epigraph addressed could, the slogan implied, transform their own identity, but in doing so, they would also demonstrate that identities are relational: their action would change the identity of '*les grands*', whether or not the latter consented to the process.

The success of the revolutionary effort to transform France from an absolute to a constitutional monarchy in 1789 or from a monarchy to a republic in 1792 depended on the willingness and ability of the country's population to adopt new forms of behaviour appropriate to their new political status. These forms of behaviour, ranging from voting and National Guard service to the wearing of the national cockade, both expressed and generated new senses of identity in those who practised them.[3] By acting in new ways that expressed their rejection of their pre-Revolutionary identities as subjects, commoners, and as members of many of the corporate groups to which they had belonged before 1789, people simultaneously asserted new identities: as citizens, as members of a nation composed of legally equal individuals, as 'patriots'.

In some cases, these transformations were voluntary or negotiated, as when representatives of the French provinces renounced most of their special privileges on the night of 4 August 1789, or when the Constituent Assembly granted French Jews the right to become citizens if they took an oath to support the new constitution and agreed to abandon their previous identity as a collective group with its own laws. In other cases, identities were imposed or abolished by force. Former nobles lost their special legal status when titles were abolished in June 1790, and many of them found themselves classified as '*aristocrates*', a new label indicating that, in the eyes of those with the power to impose identities, they were now seen as enemies.[4] If they reacted by leaving the country, they found themselves with a new identity as émigrés; at the same time, they exposed their relatives and friends to guilt by association as *parents d'émigrés* (relatives of émigrés), another case of involuntary identification.

As the earlier discussion of the *Révolutions de Paris*'s slogan has already indicated, the term 'identity' is a suggestive but extremely complicated one. As I will use the term here, identity has both internal and external dimensions: it refers both to the ways in which individuals and groups define and present themselves to others, through their speech and actions, and to the ways in which they are categorized and treated by others. Both these dimensions of identity pose many difficulties. Are internally defined identities, for example, to be understood as honest and sincere expressions of some inner self? The revolutionaries had inherited from Rousseau the conviction that the good person should be entirely transparent, with a public identity directly reflective of his or her inner being.[5] In his *Confessions*, whose posthumous publication narrowly preceded the Revolution, Rousseau had sought to provide a model of the transparent self, claiming that full revelation would vindicate his conviction of the consistency between his inner and outer personas.[6]

But the revolutionaries were correspondingly obsessed with the problem of the individual whose public persona belied his or her inner thoughts: the false patriot, the masked traitor, or the hypocrite. Diderot, in his *Paradoxe sur le comédien* (*The Paradox of Acting*) had explored the conundrum posed by the fact that the most convincing actor might be the person most detached from the sentiments he or she was expressing. Nor was Diderot's argument limited to the theatre. 'In courtrooms, in assemblies, in all places where people strive to master the minds of others', he wrote, 'they feign anger, fear, pity, in order to inspire these sentiments in others.'[7] As William Reddy has shown, the early years of the Revolution were marked both by an insistence that participants' actions be framed as sincere and honest expressions of their innermost sentiments and by pervasive 'doubts about the sincerity of these emotions'.[8] The revolutionaries feared that apparent identity was all too often, in sociologist Erving Goffman's terms, a 'presentation of self' that failed to correspond to the truth.[9]

The question of true versus false identity was complicated by the special character of the revolutionary situation. The process of revolution implied a sweeping transformation of identities. The desire to see 1789 as a complete break with the past meant that identities could not be validated by reference to the practices of the old regime, which now stood stigmatized as a time when all identities had been misunderstood or degraded. Those who had been subjects until 1789 now proclaimed themselves self-determining citizens, and some of those who had been holders of privileges now often insisted that, in their hearts, they had never considered themselves nobles or priests. It is true that many revolutionaries understood this transformation not as the creation of a new identity but as the recognition of a 'natural' identity that had been masked by the corruption of the old regime. But the possibility of such a corruption underlined the difficulty of distinguishing true from false identities, and the numerous forms that 'unnatural' identities could take.

While the fear that individuals could misrepresent their true identities haunted the revolutionaries, they also frequently behaved as though people necessarily possessed identities defined by their personal histories or by the way others regarded them. In his famous discussion of anti-semitism, Jean-Paul Sartre argued that a Jew is a person defined as a Jew by others.[10] This process of involuntary imposition of identities was as important an aspect of the Revolution as the process of voluntary proclamation of identity. In the most extreme case, Louis XVI, whose identity in his own eyes was 'king of France', found himself identified by the members of the National Convention as a 'traitor' and executed. But he was not alone in discovering that he could not control the definition of his identity. Former nobles and refractory priests found themselves being stigmatized as 'aristocrats' and 'counter-revolutionaries'. The law passed during the Terror classifying all former nobles as political suspects implied that their identity was fixed by their ancestry, regardless of their political opinions or their behaviour since 1789. During the Terror, a large part of the population, including resident foreigners and relatives of émigrés, also found themselves suffering the consequences of being identified as 'suspects'. When the National Convention voted, in November 1793, to forbid women from participating in political Assemblies, it asserted the right to define them as something less than full citizens because of their supposed natural qualities. The Revolution thus demonstrated, not only that there was an aspect of identity that depended on others rather than the self, but also that the ability to define identities was an essential aspect of political power.

The drastic consequences for many individuals and groups that followed from some of the identities imposed on them during the Revolution underline the unique aspects of the problem of identity in a situation like that created in 1789, and the contribution that revolutionary history can make to the theoretical understanding of identity formation. Theories of identity formation have usually emphasized the influence of the private and intimate experiences of childhood, on the one hand, and of longstanding public cultural traditions and institutions, on the other. By challenging individuals to redefine themselves, the Revolution tested the critical issue of whether identities can be remade by acts of will. By seeking to transform the institutional frameworks that had shaped personal and collective identities, the revolutionaries exposed to view the normally concealed connections between power and identity. Any comprehensive theory of individual and collective identity formation needs to take into account the implications of such historical upheavals.

In 'normal' circumstances, individuals fit themselves into a relatively stable system of social roles and identities because they have acquired what French sociologist Pierre Bourdieu defined as the *habitus* corresponding to their situation. In his definition of this key concept in his thought, Bourdieu emphasized the weight of tradition: 'The *habitus*, a product of history, produces individual and collective practices—more history—in accordance with the schemes generated by history. It ensures the active presence of past experiences, which, deposited in each organism in the form of schemes of perception, thought and action, tend to guarantee the "correctness" of practices and their constancy over time, more reliably than all formal rules and explicit norms.'[11] Patterns of behaviour that constitute what Bourdieu defines as *habitus* involve interaction between individuals who occupy different social positions, and these interactions define and reinforce their participants' respective identities, with implications that affect others as well as those involved in any particular interaction.

Old regime France was certainly a society with powerful mechanisms for transmitting established patterns of *habitus*. The unwritten rules about what constituted proper behaviour for a royal subject, a noble, a peasant, or a woman had existed for many centuries. To be sure, these rules changed over time, but slowly and almost imperceptibly. The French Revolution raised the question of whether this grip of the past could be broken, and whether the collective exercise of human will could alter patterns of identity. As historian Mona Ozouf has written, the essence of the Revolution was an effort at 'regeneration, a program without limits, at once physical, political, moral, and social, which aimed for nothing less than the creation of a "new people"'.[12] The revolutionaries themselves were conscious of the difficulties such a transformation of the practices that constituted identities posed. As Committee of Public Safety member Billaud-Varennes wrote, 'to overturn the throne, it was enough to kill the tyrant. To break the bonds that attach a degenerated nation to antique customs, it seems that it is necessary, so to speak, for one to strike against himself, by sacrificing the interests of the moment.'[13]

In old regime France, most individuals found their status and social identity largely determined by the circumstances of their birth: they were nobles or commoners, Catholics or members of one of the kingdom's small religious minorities, inhabitants of a particular region, town or province. If they were male, they were likely to follow their father's occupation. To be sure, old regime identities were never completely fixed: some individuals and families succeeded in changing their social status, as peasant sons became artisans or wealthy merchants plotted to acquire noble status, if not for themselves, at least for their descendants. Taking on the identity of a member of the clergy required a deliberate individual act: in theory, at least, no one was born into its ranks. It is true that many aspects of that system were coming under criticism before 1789, as the lively debate generated by the abbé Coyer's *La noblesse commerçante*, with its proposal to grant noble status to successful merchants, demonstrated.[14] Ambitious manufacturers, such as the Montgolfier family, papermakers in southern France, experimented with schemes to remodel their workers, breaking them of their traditional habits in an effort to make them more productive; they 'were transforming new men into a new kind of worker', as one study puts it.[15] The abbé Henri Grégoire's celebrated *Essai sur la regeneration physique, morale et politique des juifs*, published in 1788, proposed a systematic programme for the remaking of the kingdom's Jewish population, by changing their occupations and their patterns of behaviour.[16] Nevertheless, the notion that the entire system of social identities might be uprooted and transformed, virtually from one day to the next, not in some distant future but in the immediate present, remained inconceivable until mid-1789.

The Revolution represented a drastic break with this situation. As Jan Goldstein has written, 'the specter of a society without corporations effectively problematized the self for contemporaries: it posed the question of whether, in the absence of a corporate matrix, a person's own inherent resources were adequate to ensure that person's stability or whether, buffeted by an overactive imagination, the person would be thrown ominously off-kilter.'[17] Both individuals and groups now had to make deliberate choices about defining their identities and consciously adopt new forms of behaviour. The revolutionaries suggested that the entire system of old regime identities had been artificial. In its place, the revolutionaries of 1789 proposed, on the one hand, a set of identities rooted in 'nature', and thus supposedly more fundamental than the familiar categories of the past, and, on the other hand, a collection of identities generated by the Revolution itself and thus radically revealed as historically constructed. In the first category were such identities as that of the citizen endowed with natural rights, extended to adult males of all races with the abolition of slavery in 1794, and the gender identities proclaimed by the legislators in 1793. In the second were identities such as that of the 'Jacobin', a category only comprehensible with reference to the creation of the club of that name in November 1789, and 'counter-Revolutionary', a label that would have been meaningless before 1789.

Identities were changed in a complex process that mixed spontaneity with organization and calculation, and a variety of institutions, from the revolutionary legislatures to the press, took part in it. Law-making was one key mechanism by which political elites consciously tried to guide these transformations. Let us look, for example, at the most famous enactment of the first revolutionary legislature, the Declaration of the Rights of Man and Citizen. The Declaration is usually read as a statement of abstract principles intended to guide the drafting of a new constitution, but it can also be read as an effort to define the identity of the new citizen whose adherence to those principles would be necessary if the new system was to succeed. As Marcel Gauchet has written, 'A society that imagines itself as the product of individuals is implicitly in reality a society with the mission to manufacture individuals.'[18]

The Declaration begins with the assertion of a new identity—not that of the citizens, but that of its authors, who had originally been deputies to an Estates-General convoked to advise the king but who had now redefined themselves as 'the representatives of the French people, organized as a national assembly'. Only by establishing their own credentials in this way could the deputies claim the authority to issue such a document. The reference to 'the French people' carried important implications. It asserted that there was such a collectivity and implied that what unified its members was more important than anything that might divide them—assertions that remained to be translated into reality in 1789. Only if the population accepted this definition of its identity would the transformation proposed in the rest of the document actually take place. By referring to the 'natural, inalienable, and sacred rights of man', the document added a second element to the identity being constructed for its readers. They were not just members of a collectivity, but individuals with rights, even though 'ignorance, neglect, and scorn' for those rights might have meant that the new citizens had not previously been aware of possessing them. The Declaration would 'continually remind them of their rights', but also of 'their duties', indicating another dimension of the identity of citizen. Citizens, the preamble indicated, could not be passive: the purpose of issuing a declaration of their rights was to allow them to compare government acts 'with the purpose of any political institution', but, on the other hand, when they put forward demands, knowledge of the declaration would ensure that they would be 'based ... on simple and incontestable principles' that would 'always contribute to the maintenance of the constitution and the happiness of all'.

Even in its preamble, the Declaration of Rights thus outlined a complex identity for that new creature, the citizen of a constitutional French state. The citizen had both rights and duties; he—and possibly she, since the document's language with regard to gender was ambiguous, and certainly provided women with new ways of thinking about themselves, as Olympe de Gouges' 'Declaration of the Rights of Woman and Citizen' of 1791 demonstrates[19]—was to maintain an active and critical stance toward government, but at the same time the citizen needed to exercise a certain degree of self-restraint and not put forward demands that reflected selfish interests. The rest of the document elaborated on this new model of identity. Article 1's announcement that 'men are born and remain free and equal in rights' was rich in identity implications. It went against centuries of tradition that had taught the opposite, namely that rights were essentially unequal. Whether he had been a noble or a humble peasant, the new citizen would have to revise his understanding of himself, and also his understanding of his fellows, an adjustment likely to be as difficult for those who had been subordinates in the old order of things as for those who had been in privileged positions.

Article 2 elaborated on the notion of natural and imprescriptible rights, enumerating them as 'liberty, property, security, and resistance to oppression'. What liberty implied was set out in articles 4 and 5: being 'able to do anything that does not harm another person', subject only to limits to prevent 'actions harmful to society'. Articles 7, 8, and 9 added to this provisions against arbitrary arrest and punishment, and articles 10 and 11 broadened the concept of liberty to include religious freedom and freedom of speech, while article 17 reinforced the protection of the citizen's property. The citizen's identity thus implied a generous sphere of action and a degree of personal autonomy very much at odds with the practice of pre-Revolutionary society, in which not only the government but the Church, families, village communities, guilds, and many other groups had claimed rights to control their members. Given the large investment that most the of the population had in one or more of these groups up to 1789, learning to accept the model of the autonomous individual as the norm meant that everyone in France had to develop new ways of thinking about him- or herself.

Article 6 reinforced the notion, already incorporated in the preamble, of citizenship as an active identity. The citizen had a right to participate, directly or indirectly, in law-making; article 14 added that citizenship meant a right to consent to taxes and to know how public money was being spent. Article 6 also gave every citizen a right to compete for public honours, positions, and employment on the basis of his 'virtues and talents', which were purely individual attributes. The identities derived from membership in corporate groups that had largely determined access to such positions under the old regime were now ruled illegitimate. To be sure, the ideal citizen implied by the Declaration had responsibilities as well as rights. He was to peacefully submit to any lawful arrest warrant, to avoid letting his religious convictions disturb the public peace, and to pay his taxes; he would presumably recognize those social distinctions 'established ... for the common benefit' that were justified in Article 1.

The 'implied citizen' constructed in the Declaration of Rights was thus a new creation, transformed in many ways from the pre-Revolutionary royal subject. So, too, was the 'implied reader' of the Revolutionary press. One of the most striking examples of the use of the press to both express and redefine identities was the proliferation of popular pamphlets attributed to the fictitious 'Père Duchesne'. The Père Duchesne is usually assumed to be a persona invented by the radical journalist Jacques-René Hébert, who came to be known by his character's name, thereby establishing a powerful identity for himself, but the fictional character actually had a life of its own and Hébert was just one of a number of journalists and pamphleteers who wrote under this disguise.[20] In all his incarnations, however, the Père Duchesne had certain consistent characteristics. He was a man of the people, an artisanal '*marchand des fourneaux*' ('furnace peddlar'). In contrast to the upper classes, he enjoyed simple pleasures within everyone's reach—drinking, talking with his friends, making love with his wife. He was plain-spoken, and, in contrast to members of polite society, he laced his speech liberally with swearwords. From his earliest appearance on the revolutionary scene, the Père Duchesne was the very model of the modern egalitarian citizen. In the very first revolutionary Père Duchesne pamphlet, the eponymous character planned a visit to the Estates General and told readers, 'If the King is there, I'll explain myself with even more assurance. I'll open my heart to him ...' Throughout the Revolution, the Père Duchesne never hesitated to say what he thought to those in power, whether they were kings or Convention deputies. The malleability of the notion of sans-culotte identity was demonstrated, however, by the fact that rival versions of the *Père Duchesne* espoused widely varying political points of view. Although the most celebrated of these pamphlet newspapers, that of Hébert, was identified with radical populism, there were also successful *Père Duchesne* publications that supported many other factions, and the several pamphlet series attributed to *Mère Duchesne* were sometimes overtly counter-revolutionary.[21]

One of the special characteristics of the *Père Duchesne* pamphlets was the inclusion on the front page of each number of a woodcut illustration showing the title character. In 1792 and 1793, this image became the Revolution's most familiar visual depiction of a popular militant or sans-culotte. The woodcut showed a muscular man in working-class clothing, brandishing a hatchet and with a pistol stuck in his belt. To one side of him was a table with a wine bottle, a musket, and a furnace pipe, symbols of the Père Duchesne's popular sociability, his militant support for the Revolution, and his artisanal skills. On the other side appeared a kneeling priest and the enigmatic motto, 'Memento Mori' ('Remember that you must die'), which could be read both as a general reference to the sans-culottes' victory over the vestiges of the old regime and as a specific endorsement of the radical de-Christianization campaign that Hébert in particular strongly supported. The picture of the Père Duchesne, circulated three times a week throughout the Revolution's radical phase, was a powerful visual icon of sans-culotte identity: it regularly reminded readers that the ideal citizen was a man of the people who engaged himself directly and personally on behalf of the movement and did not hesitate to use force to defend its ideals. The political content of the *Père Duchesne* pamphlets reinforced the same message. Most issues were in fact short stories in which the title character intervened in some controversy of the moment and demonstrated how a true revolutionary should act. The earthiness, the rough humour, and the storyline in which the man of the people triumphed over or showed himself wiser and more patriotic than his social superiors were all constants of the genre. Radical politicians and more conventional journalists argued in abstract terms for the sovereignty of the people; the *Père Duchesne* pamphlets recounted concrete triumphs of the people in action.

The *Père Duchesne* pamphlets are a fascinating example of the ways in which revolutionary activists propagated new forms of identity, not least because they provide an opportunity to see what cultural resources the Revolution could draw on in proposing new ways for citizens to think of themselves. The character of the Père Duchesne emerged from the traditions of popular boulevard theatre in the old regime. The short stories in most of the pamphlets were written versions of the humorous skits or *parades* performed on these fairground stages.[22] But the roots of the Père Duchesne persona went even further back, to the long tradition of cagy peasants and artisans who showed up their betters in the folktales and popular literature that had circulated in France since the Middle Ages. The Père Duchesne's association with furnaces and fire and his uncanny ability to appear anywhere in the world and to assume any disguise also amply justified his frequently repeated claim to be a *'bon diable'* (a 'good devil') and linked him to supernatural traditions in popular literature and religion, as well as to literary predecessors such as Alain-René Lesage's *Diable Boîteux*. The colourful language used in the *Père Duchesne* pamphlets differed in significant ways from the familiar tradition of *poissarde* pamphlets in which lower-class figures were allowed to express subversive truths about the old regime in deformed or outdated speech. The *Père Duchesnes* were earthy and expressive but usually also grammatically correct; they spoke a language that was meant to be taken as popular but at the same time to demonstrate the common people's ability, not only to master the language but to use it creatively. When the more middle-class Jacobins of 1794 suppressed Hébert's *Père Duchesne*, they explicitly condemned the paper's language for promoting the notion of a separate popular identity, insisting that 'today, when equality has brought all men together, language should be the same for all'.[23] Before he was silenced, however, the fictitious Père Duchesne had done much to model a persona for the politically active man of the common people.

Whereas the sans-culotte identity embodied by the fictitious Père Duchesne was put forward as a positive model that good citizens should emulate, the label 'counter-revolutionary' was a pejorative one, even if some of those to whom it was applied chose to accept the epithet as a mark of pride. Unlike the roles of 'patriot' or 'citizen' proudly taken on by supporters of the revolutionary movement, 'counter-revolutionary' was usually a negative identity imposed on individuals and groups by their opponents. In its initial, euphoric phase, the Revolution ostensibly welcomed everyone: its early leaders included many prominent nobles and clergy, and at the end of its marathon session on 4 August, the National Assembly declared Louis XVI 'the restorer of French liberty'. Nor was the peasant population whose uprisings during the Great Fear had pushed the

Assembly to pass the 4 August decrees seen as a reservoir of resistance to the movement. To be sure, revolutionary ideology had warned against the possibility of opposition from the outset of the movement. In his definition of the issues at the end of 1788, *What is the Third Estate?*, the abbé Sieyès engaged in a radical form of identity politics, labelling the Third Estate alone as the 'nation' and stigmatizing the 'privileged order' as an alien body. By employing hyperbolic rhetoric against the nobles as a privileged group, Sieyès hoped to intimidate them into abandoning their special status and get them to accept a new identity as citizens. As individuals, they would be accepted as members of the nation, although as a corporate body they were to be regarded as enemies.[24]

On 14 July 1789, the revolutionary crowd vividly demonstrated how dangerous it would be to be identified as an opponent of the Revolution. The lynchings of the commander of the Bastille, de Launay, the head of the royally appointed municipal government, and the *prévôt des marchands* Flesselles, followed a week later by the killing of two more prominent royal officials, Berthier and Foulon, sent a clear message. The epithet '*aristocrate*' entered revolutionary discourse as a general term of opprobrium for those accused of opposing the movement's egalitarianism. For obvious reasons, those who feared the Revolution's potential radicalism avoided giving themselves a distinctive label or acknowledging the designations used by their opponents. Nevertheless, there was organized and self-conscious opposition to the Revolution within the National Assembly—not surprisingly, since half of its members were from the pre-Revolutionary privileged orders—and during the first year of the Revolution, these *noirs* ('Blacks', so called because of the black clerical robes worn by the numerous clergy members of the group) often held their own in parliamentary debates.[25] Outside the Assembly, counter-revolutionary journalists developed several strategies for attempting to assert a counter-revolutionary identity in positive ways. They put themselves forward as *amis de l'ordre* ('friends of order'), as *amis de la religion et du roi* ('friends of religion and the king'), they used satire and ridicule against the *patriotes*, and their supporters adopted distinctive forms of symbolic behaviour such as the singing of the song *Ô Richard, ô mon roi*, whose words expressed loyalty to the monarch.[26]

For their part, supporters of the Revolution waged an increasingly aggressive campaign to define the characteristics of counter-revolutionaries and put them on the defensive. Caricatures played a major role in this campaign. Easily understandable imagery contrasted the healthy and muscular bodies of Third Estate patriots with the effeminate bodies of aristocrats and the fatness of clergy who had feasted too much on the tithes they extracted from the population.[27] The National Assembly's abolition of noble titles in June 1790 and the enactment of the Civil Constitution of the Clergy translated imagery into action: to cling to any shreds of noble identity now became a violation of the law, and clergy who wished to retain their status had to go through the public ritual of taking an oath to the new constitution, thus acknowledging a new basis for their status.

The enactment of the Civil Constitution of the Clergy affected not only the identity of the clergy, but also that of their parishioners. As Timothy Tackett has demonstrated, congregations exercised considerable influence on their pastors, pressuring them to accept the Revolution in some areas and strengthening their will to resist in others. In this way, the struggle over the clerical oath became a powerful engine for broadening the applicability of notions of counter-revolutionary identity from the relatively limited elites singled out by the law to whole sectors of the population that resisted the new religious system. The radicalization of the Revolution after 1792 brought in its wake new forms of counter-revolutionary identity. The outbreak of the Vendée rebellion in March 1793 produced a new model of the counter-revolutionary: the peasant insurrectionist, fighting for Church and king, identified by the emotionally charged symbol of a red heart surmounted by a cross. While the Vendée rebels asserted an identity of their own, their Republican enemies imposed additional characteristics on the identity of the counter-revolutionary, such as the accusation that the Revolution's opponents were agents of foreign powers. Indeed, as Sophie Wahnich has demonstrated, the epithet 'foreigner' came to be applied to anyone who failed to espouse the revolutionary creed, regardless of their actual place of origin.[28] At the same time, as Jean-Clément Martin has shown, the label of 'counter-revolutionary' was applied more and more broadly. The Montagnards who controlled the Convention and the Committee of Public Safety in 1793–94 used the term to identify all revolutionary factions that opposed them—the Girondins, the Hébertistes, the Dantonists. In one sense, the term lost all meaning, but in another it remained a uniquely powerful example of imposed identity: those to whom it stuck were singled out for the guillotine.[29]

Struggle over the identification of those who opposed, or were accused of opposing, the Revolution continued throughout the Directory period, although usually in less violent fashion than during the Terror. Supporters of the Directory tried to monopolize the identity of Republicans, and to stigmatize the counter-revolutionary opposition as royalists or to tie them to the violent bands active in the Midi during the thermidorian period, such as the *Compagnie de Jésus*, by calling them *égorgeurs* ('throat-cutters'). For their part, the journalists and politicians who were the most visible representatives of this political tendency struggled to impose terms that were both meaningful and politically non-committal. They campaigned as the representatives of *les honnêtes hommes* ('respectable men') or as *modérés* ('moderates'). Because one of their favourite themes was the evil of partisan organization, symbolized by the Jacobins, the politicians of the right tried to avoid emphasizing the fact that they had their own club, the Club de Clichy; their opponents, however, lost no opportunity to label them *Clichyens* and to try to identify them with the evils of factionalism. The parliamentary elections of April 1797, the freest vote in France since the early revolutionary elections of 1790–91, showed that the right had strong support among the wealthy elite who now made up the electorate, but its inability to develop a positive identity in the struggle with a Republican group that continued to control both the levers of power and an effective machinery for asserting its own identity as the sole legitimate representation of national interests was a critical weakness.[30]

While identities such as that of the 'sans-culotte' or the counter-revolutionary grew out of the Revolution's political conflicts, the question of whether women could have a political identity appeared to most male revolutionaries to have been settled by nature itself. 'What character is suitable for women?' the Montagnard deputy Amar asked in a speech opposing political rights for women in October 1793. 'Morals and even nature have assigned her functions to her'. The Paris Commune spokesman Pierre Chaumette was even more explicit in his claim that women's natural identity was a reason for excluding them from politics. 'Since when is it permitted to give up one's sex?' he demanded. 'Is it to men that nature confided domestic cares? Has she given us breasts to breast-feed our children?'[31] Even advocates of women's rights, such as Olympe de Gouges, could not entirely break free of the belief that women's physiological attributes were relevant to the question: in her Declaration of the Rights of Women, she called women 'the sex that is as superior in beauty as it is in courage during the sufferings of maternity'.[32] In the domain of family law, where they recognized that women had a legitimate place, revolutionary legislators did concede women equality with men: marriage was defined as an egalitarian contract and all children, regardless of sex, were guaranteed an equal share of their parents' estates. In public life, however, the identity transformations of the revolutionary era did little for women.

One of the areas where the revolutionary era did create radical transformations of identity was in France's overseas colonies, and in particular the most valuable of them, Saint-Domingue, whose Black population went, in the course of thirteen tumultuous years, from the status of slaves to that of free French citizens and then became citizens of an independent nation of their own.[33] The pre-revolutionary identity system in the sugar islands of the Caribbean and the Indian Ocean was very different from that of old regime France. For whites, the Antilles, especially Saint-Domingue, the fastest-growing of the colonies, offered an opportunity to escape from the constraints of metropolitan society into a world where noble privileges were not recognized and where an energetic young man could hope to make a fortune with a speed that was almost unimaginable in Europe. This possibility existed because of the opportunity to exploit the labour of blacks from Africa who had been violently deprived of their original identities and forced to accept their condition as plantation slaves. The wealthy white colonists dominated a population that also included the so-called *petits blancs*, whites who did not own plantations, as well as a significant number of free people of mixed race, often more prosperous than the poor whites. The elaborate vocabulary developed to distinguish individuals according to their proportion of black blood was testimony to the importance of identity issues in maintaining the colonies' social order. The colonists' treatment of the slave population was intended to deliberately deprive them of any sense of identity other than that of slave.

It would be entirely misleading, of course, to conceive of the slaves as people without a sense of identity. Those brought from Africa had been brutally wrenched out of societies that had their own, highly structured identity systems. Slave traders and slave owners knew that their victims were quite capable of expressing themselves—violent uprisings on slave ships were a common and much-feared danger of the trade—and the slaves were therefore subjected to a dehumanizing process that was meant to disorient them and leave them incapable of exercising any kind of autonomy. Recent scholarship on the colonies has shown that at least some Africans successfully resisted this process and created new identities in the New World. The slaves synthesized elements of African and French culture to create a new language, Creole, and an original set of religious practices, vodou. Within the framework of the plantation system, some blacks, such as the future Toussaint Louverture, managed to acquire enough money to change their status by purchasing their freedom and sometimes that of other family members. Others escaped from the plantations and formed *marron* communities that modelled a form of independence. Black sailors, urban artisans and domestic servants were sometimes literate and served as intermediaries, circulating news from the wider world among the slave population.

News of the revolution in France in 1789 gave all groups in the colonial population opportunities to adapt the new identities being proclaimed there for their own purposes. The white *colons* appropriated language about liberty and self-government to insist that they should be freed from administrative restrictions and allowed to make laws for themselves. Free people of colour used the language of equality to insist that they should be granted the rights of citizens; the legislators in France were thus challenged to decide whether race was in fact an essential aspect of the identity of citizens, a decision with implications that they were reluctant to confront until events in the colonies gave them no choice.[34] The unsuccessful rebellion of free men of colour led by Vincent Ogé in Saint-Domingue in October 1790 showed that these questions of who could claim the identity of citizen in the colonies were not merely theoretical debates.[35] The beginning of the great slave insurrection in Saint-Domingue in August 1791 raised the stakes in this debate even further. While the white planters were driven to jettison their French identities to the point of appealing for British and Spanish intervention against the insurrectionists, the slaves eventually compelled the French revolutionaries to broaden the new identity of French citizen to include them. On 20 June 1793, when whites opposed to racial equality threatened to overthrow the revolutionary civil commissioners sent to the island by the revolutionary government, witnesses in Saint-Domingue's main city of Cap Français heard the commissioners' supporters running through the streets, calling out to the slaves, 'You are all free! The commissioners say you are all free, all whites are now equal to us, the whole country belongs to us'.[36] As Laurent Dubois has put it, 'by taking up the defense of the nation, the insurgent slaves, who were not citizens, intervened as Republican citizens, which compelled the representatives of national authority to give official confirmation to a citizenship that the slaves had already claimed for themselves'.[37]

To say that the insurgent slaves of Saint-Domingue and Guadeloupe used their claim to the identity of citizens in their own interests is not to say that they understood this identity in the same way as the French did. Indeed, the great challenge confronting any effort to understand how the black participants in these transformations interpreted their own actions is the paucity of direct testimony from them. The former slaves were largely illiterate, and historians have had to make what deductions they can from source material largely supplied by hostile whites. Even those French observers who worked to implement the new status granted to the former slaves by the emancipation decree of the 1794 rebellion recognized the large gap between themselves and the blacks. Victor

Hugues, the French Republican commissioner who liberated Guadeloupe from the English with the help of armed blacks in 1794, provided a good example of this contrast in the proclamation he issued on 20 June 1794. The former slaves interpreted the promise of freedom they had received above all as a promise of liberation from the conditions of plantation labour. Hugues, trying to restore the island's economy, had to counter their strong tendency to devote themselves to a subsistence agriculture that produced no surplus for export. His proclamation was an attempt to impose a European-derived identity of the citizen as economic producer on a population that had other ideas. 'He who does not work, deserves only contempt and is not entitled to the benefits of our regeneration', Hugues warned, 'since one is entitled to presume that those who don't work exist by committing thefts'.[38] Hugues, the revolutionary official, attempted to impose a European definition of what freedom meant rather than trying to understand what meaning the former slaves were trying to give to their own identity. The blacks' view of what emancipation meant was quite different, as the peasant saying, '*Moin pas esclave, moin pas travaye*' (I'm not a slave, I don't have to work)' indicates.[39] Hugues's policies were similar to those of the new black leadership class emerging in Saint-Domingue itself, where first the white emancipators Léger-Félicité Sonthonax and Étienne Polverel and then Toussaint Louverture faced similar pressures to restore the functioning of the plantations and also resorted to forced labour.

The experiment constituted by the abrupt transformation of identities in the colonies during the Revolution led to radically different outcomes in different places. After a bloody struggle provoked by Napoleon's attempt to reverse emancipation, Saint-Domingue became the independent nation of Haiti, whose first constitution proclaimed that all citizens would henceforth share the same identity, that of 'black'. In Guadeloupe, slavery and the pre-revolutionary system of racial identities were restored, and in Martinique, occupied by the British from 1793 to 1802, and in the French slave colonies in the Indian Ocean, the system had never been dismantled. Slavery was not finally abolished in the French colonies until 1848, and issues of identity in these 'old colonies', now constituted as 'overseas departments', continue to differ considerably from those in metropolitan France, even though their inhabitants are officially French citizens. Whether one focuses on the Revolutionary era or the 'long durée' that has followed, these overseas territories offer fascinating opportunities to analyse the complexities of identity issues.

Viewing the Revolution through the lens of identity is thus an effective way of bringing out what was at stake in many of the period's conflicts, and of bringing together issues, such as the revolts in the colonies and the development of the counter-revolution, that are not normally connected. At the same time, it is a way of bringing together the individual destinies of those who experienced the Revolution with the collective experiences that normally dominate historical narratives. An example of this is provided by the life of Madame Roland. Author of an autobiography heavily influenced by the example of Rousseau, she was herself keenly aware of the way in which participation in the Revolution had changed her own identity. Already in the pre-Revolutionary period, she had tried declaiming an incendiary pamphlet aloud and noting how the exercise transformed her.

'Wanting to amuse myself by reading it aloud, with the expression that seemed to fit with the words, I found myself much resembling a troublemaker; there is stuff to fill the chest of a stentor and bring down the ceiling', she told a friend.[40] Unlike the small but vocal group of proto-feminist militants who demanded political rights for women, including, sometimes, the right to bear arms, Madame Roland tried to avoid being seen as violating the rules about gender roles that barred women from active involvement in the public sphere, but her involvement with the Girondins led to her arrest during the Terror. In prison, she made careful plans to be sure that she would be remembered as she wished to be: as a model of feminine virtue and as a martyr to the cause of liberty.[41] The writing of her memoirs was the most important aspect of these plans, but she even made arrangements with a friend to ensure that her famous last utterance, 'Liberty, what crimes are committed in your name!' would be recorded and transmitted to posterity.[42]

From these examples, we can see that the French Revolution was a vast laboratory for experiments concerning issues of identity and the possibilities of identity transformation. Understanding these experiments is vital to any attempt at bringing together the levels of individual and collective experience during this period. Not all the efforts to change identities during the Revolution succeeded. Many a proud citizen of the 1790s learned to accept a new status as a subject of the Napoleonic Empire and then lived on to see a Bourbon monarch restored to the throne. Women, who had obtained equal status within the family if not within the state according to the legislation adopted in 1792, were redefined as legal minors by the Civil Code of 1804. Nobles never regained the legal identity they had held before 1789, but they did regain much of the informal prestige they had enjoyed, the pre-Revolutionary provinces continued to compete for loyalty with the new *départements*, and identity-shaping institutions such as artisans' *compagnonnages*, driven underground by the Revolution's campaign against collective *corps*, reappeared in the nineteenth century.[43] Nevertheless, the Revolution did bring about some lasting changes in identity. Equality before the law and a powerful identification with the French nation remained deeply anchored in people's minds. Whether or not they consciously supported the ideals of 1789, subsequent generations knew, too, that as citizens of the country where the great Revolution of that year had taken place, they possessed an identity that set them apart from others.

Notes

1. For an important critique of the use of the term, see Rogers Brubaker and Frederick Cooper, 'Beyond "Identity"', *Theory and Society* 29 (Feb. 2000), 1–47. Although Brubaker and Cooper profess to find the term vague and complain that it is often used in inconsistent ways, their proposal to substitute the notion of 'self-identification' for 'identity' suggests that they find some version of the concept too useful to discard altogether.

2. Etienne Balibar, 'Citizen Subject', trans. James B. Swenson, in Eduardo Cadava, Peter Connor and Jean-Luc Nancy, eds., *Who Comes after the Subject?* (New York and London, 1991), 33–57, cit. 38–9.

3. On the significance of National Guard service in creating citizen identity, see Dale L. Clifford, 'Can the Uniform Make the Citizen? Paris, 1789–1791', *Eighteenth-Century Studies* 34 (2001), 363–82.

4. Patrice Higonnet, 'Aristocrate, Aristocratie', in Sandy Petrey, ed., *The French Revolution 1789–1989: Two Hundred Years of Rethinking* (Lubbock, TX, 1989), 47–66.

5. This is a major theme in Carol Blum, *Rousseau and the Republic of Virtue: The Language of Politics in the French Revolution* (Ithaca, NY, 1986).

6. The classic analysis of Rousseau's enterprise of self-revelation is Jean Starobinski, *Jean-Jacques Rousseau: la transparence et l'obstacle* (Paris, 1971; orig. 1957).

7. Denis Diderot, 'Paradoxe sur le comédien', in Diderot, *Le neveu de Rameau*, ed. F. A. Burguet (Paris, 1966), 221. Written between 1769 and 1778, this text was not published until 1830.

8. William Reddy, 'Sentimentalism and its Erasure: The Role of Emotions in the Era of the French Revolution', *Journal of Modern History* 72 (2000), 136.

9. Erving Goffman, *The Presentation of Self in Everyday Life* (Garden City, NY, 1959). For a use of Goffman's notion of identity as strategic self-presentation in the revolutionary context, see Gregory S. Brown, 'The Self-Fashionings of Olympe de Gouges, 1784–1789', *Eighteenth-Century Studies* 34 (2001), 383–401.

10. Jean-Paul Sartre, *Anti-Semite and Jew*, trans. George J. Becker (New York, 1965).

11. Pierre Bourdieu, *The Logic of Practice*, trans. Richard Nice (Stanford, 1990), 54.

12. Mona Ozouf, 'Regeneration', in François Furet and Mona Ozouf, eds., *A Critical Dictionary of the French Revolution*, trans. Arthur Goldhammer (Cambridge, Mass., 1989), 781.

13. Cited in Sophie Wahnich, *L'Impossible citoyen. L'étranger dans le discours de la Révolution française* (Paris, 1997), 356.

14. For two discussions of this debate, see John Shovlin, 'Toward a Reinterpretation of Revolutionary Antinobilism: The Political Economy of Honor in the Old Regime', *Journal of Modern History* 72 (2000), 35–66, and Jay M. Smith, 'Social Categories, the Language of Patriotism, and the Origins of the French Revolution: The Debate over Noblesse commerçante', *Journal of Modern History* 72 (2000), 339–74.

15. Leonard N. Rosenband, *Papermaking in Eighteenth-Century France: Management, Labor and Revolution at the Montgolfier Mill, 1761–1803* (Baltimore, 2000), 61.

16. Rita Hermon-Belot, 'The Abbé Grégoire's Program for the Jews: Social Reform and Spiritual Project', in Jeremy D. Popkin and Richard Popkin, eds., *The Abbé Grégoire and His World* (Dordrecht, 2000), 13–26.

17. Jan Goldstein, *The Post-Revolutionary Self: Politics and Psyche in France, 1750–1850* (Cambridge, Mass., 2005), 9.

18. Marcel Gauchet, *La Révolution des droits de l'homme* (Paris, 1989), xxii–iii. For the debates out of which the Declaration emerged, see, in addition to Gauchet, Keith Baker, 'The Idea of a Declaration of Rights', in Dale Van Kley, ed., *The French Idea of Freedom: The Old Regime and the Declaration of Rights of 1789* (Stanford, 1994), 154–96, and Antoine de Baecque, ed., *L'An I des Droits de l'Homme* (Paris, 1988). For revolutionary concepts of the citizen and their origins, see Pierre Rétat, 'The Evolution of the Citizen from the Ancien Régime to the Revolution', and Michael P. Fitzsimmons, 'The National Assembly and the Invention of Citizenship', both in Renée Waldinger et al., eds., *The French Revolution and the Meaning of Citizenship* (Westport, CT., 1993), and Pierre Rétat, 'Citoyen-Sujet, Civisme', trans. Gerd van den Heuvel, in Rolf Reichardt and Eberhard Schmitt, eds., *Handbuch politisch-sozialer Grundbegriffe in Frankreich 1680–1820*, Heft 9 (Munich, 1988), 75–105.

19. See the discussions in William Sewell, Jr, 'Le Citoyen, La Citoyenne: Activity, Passivity and the French Revolutionary Concept of Citizenship', in Colin Lucas, ed., *The French Revolution and the Creation of Modern Political Culture, vol. 2, Political Culture of the French Revolution* (Oxford, 1988), 105–25, Joan Scott, 'A Woman Who Has Only Paradoxes to Offer', in Sara E. Melzer and Leslie W. Rabine, eds., *Rebel Daughters: Women and the French Revolution* (New York, 1992), 102–20, and John R. Cole, *Between the Queen and the Cabby: Olympe de Gouges's Rights of Women* (Montreal and Kingston, 2011).

20. Jeremy D. Popkin, *Revolutionary News: The Press in France, 1789–1799* (Durham, NC, 1990), 151–68.

21. Ouzi Elyada, 'La Mère Duchesne: masques populaires et guerre pamphlétaire, 1789–1791', *Annales historiques de la Révolution française* no. 271 (1988), 1–16.

22. Jacques Guilhaumou, 'Les mille langues du Père Duchêne', *Dix-huitième siècle* 18 (1986), 143–56. See also Antoine de Baecque, *Les Eclats du rire. La culture des rieurs au XVIIIe siècle* (Paris, 2000), 13–14, 94–102.

23. *Journal de la Montagne*, 18 pluviôse II (6 Feb. 1794), cited in Popkin, *Revolutionary News*, 166.

24. On the implications of the assault on noble status and identity, see William Doyle, *Aristocracy and its Enemies in the Age of Revolution* (Oxford, 2009).

25. Tackett, *Becoming a Revolutionary*, 207, 248–56.

26. On the counter-revolutionary press, see William J. Murray, *The Right-Wing Press in the French Revolution, 1789–1792* (London, 1986), and Jeremy D. Popkin, *The Right-Wing Press in France, 1792–1800* (Chapel Hill, NC, 1980). On counter-revolutionary songs, see Laura Mason, *Singing the French Revolution* (Ithaca, NY, 1996), 46–7, 52, 57.

27. See especially the discussion in Antoine de Baecque, *La caricature révolutionnaire* (Paris, 1988) and the contrasting analysis of counter-revolutionary caricature in Claude Langlois, *La caricature contre-révolutionnaire* (Paris, 1988).

28. Wahnich, *L'Impossible Citoyen*, 204–5, 233.

29. Jean-Clément Martin, *Contre-Révolution, Révolution et Nation en France, 1789–1799* (Paris, 1999), 197, 230.

30. Popkin, *Right-Wing Press*.

31. Citations in Darline Gay Levy, Harriet Branson Applewhite and Mary Durham Johnson, eds., *Women in Revolutionary Paris, 1789–1795* (Urbana, IL, 1979), 215, 219.

32. Cited in Levy et al., *Women*, 89.

33. This account draws heavily on the recent scholarly literature on the Revolution in the Caribbean. For a bibliography of this literature, see Jeremy D. Popkin, *A Concise History of the Haitian Revolution* (Malden, Mass., 2012), 171–7. Two important works published after the completion of that bibliography are Philippe R. Girard, *The Slaves Who Defeated Napoleon: Toussaint Louverture and the Haitian War of Independence* (Tuscaloosa, AL, 2011), and Malick Ghachem, *The Old Regime and the Haitian Revolution* (New York, 2011).

34. Robin Blackburn, *The Overthrow of Colonial Slavery, 1776–1848* (London, 1988), 177–82; Yves Bénot, *La Révolution Française et la fin des colonies* (Paris, 1987), ch. 3; John Garrigus, 'Opportunist or Patriot? Julien Raimond (1744–1801) and the Haitian Revolution', *Slavery and Abolition* 28 (2007), 1–21.

35. John Garrigus, 'Vincent Ogé jeune (1757–1791): Social Class and Free Colored Mobilization on the Eve of the Haitian Revolution', *The Americas* 68 (2011) 33–62.

36. *Extrait d'une lettre, sur les malheurs de Saint-Domingue en général, et principalement sur l'incendie de la ville du Cap Français* (Paris, An II (1793)), 13.

REVOLUTION AND CHANGING IDENTITIES IN FRANCE, 1787–99 **253**

37. Laurent Dubois, *Les Esclaves de la République: l'histoire oubliée de la première émancipation, 1789–1794*, trans. Jean-François Chaix (Paris, 1998), 71.
38. Hugues, proclamation of 2 mess. IV (20 June 1794), cited in Dubois, *Esclaves*, 179.
39. Blackburn, *Overthrow of Colonial Slavery*, 241.
40. Madame Roland, letter of 2 June 1788, in *Lettres de Mme Roland* (Paris, 1867), 566–7.
41. On Madame Roland's self-fashioning during the Revolution, see Lesley H. Walker, 'Sweet and Consoling Virtue: The Memoirs of Madame Roland', *Eighteenth-Century Studies* 34 (2001), 403–19; Dorinda Outram, 'Words and Flesh: Mme Roland, the Female Body and the Search for Power', in Outram, *The Body and the French Revolution* (New Haven, 1989), 124–52; Siân Reynolds, *Marriage and Revolution: Monsieur and Madame Roland* (Oxford, 2012).
42. Walker, 'Sweet and Consoling Virtue', 413.
43. Cynthia Truant, *The Rites of Labor: Brotherhoods of Compagnonnage in old and new regime France* (Ithaca, NY, 1994).

SELECTED READING

Balibar, Etienne, 'Citizen Subject', trans. James B. Swenson, in Eduardo Cadava, Peter Connor and Jean-Luc Nancy, eds., *Who Comes after the Subject?* (New York and London, 1991), 33–57.

Brubaker, Rogers and Cooper, Frederick, 'Beyond 'Identity'', *Theory and Society 29* (Feb. 2000), 1–47.

Clifford, Dale L., 'Can the Uniform Make the Citizen? Paris, 1789–1791', *Eighteenth-Century Studies 34* (2001), 363–82.

Doyle, William, *Aristocracy and its Enemies in the Age of Revolution* (Oxford, 2009).

Goldstein, Jan, *The Post-Revolutionary Self: Politics and Psyche in France, 1750–1850* (Cambridge, Mass., 2005).

Outram, Dorinda, *The Body and the French Revolution* (New Haven, CT, 1989).

Ozouf, Mona, 'Regeneration', in François Furet and Mona Ozouf, eds., *A Critical Dictionary of the French Revolution*, trans. Arthur Goldhammer (Cambridge, Mass., 1989), 781–9.

Popkin, Jeremy D., *Revolutionary News: The Press in France, 1789–1799* (Durham, NC, 1990).

Reddy, William, 'Sentimentalism and its Erasure: The Role of Emotions in the Era of the French Revolution', *Journal of Modern History 72* (2000), 109–52.

Scott, Joan, 'A Woman Who Has Only Paradoxes to Offer', in Sara E. Melzer and Leslie W. Rabine, eds., *Rebel Daughters: Women and the French Revolution* (New York, 1992), 102–20.

Sewell, William, Jr 'Le Citoyen, La Citoyenne: Activity, Passivity and the French Revolutionary Concept of Citizenship', in Colin Lucas, ed., *The French Revolution and the Creation of Modern Political Culture, vol. 2, Political Culture of the French Revolution* (Oxford, 1988), 105–25.

Waldinger, Renée et al., eds., *The French Revolution and the Meaning of Citizenship* (Westport, CT, 1993).

CHAPTER 15

···

RELIGION AND
REVOLUTION

···

EDWARD J. WOELL

INTRODUCTION

IN late May 1790 the leading citizens of Salles-sur-l'Hers, a village set between the Pyrenean foothills and Toulouse, wrote to the National Assembly out of despair. They explained that a few years earlier the bishop of Rieux, upon a request by their own curé, or parish priest, had suspended the sacred rites established by the community a 'long time ago' for securing favourable growing conditions and thus abundant crops. They also noted that a subsequent appeal to the bishop and the curé to resume these rites only produced an additional clerical rebuff. This prompted village leaders to convoke a parish meeting where they resolved to make their case to the deputies in Paris. In the letter to the Assembly they included not only an explanation why these rites were crucial, but also a suggestion as to how the two clerics might be persuaded to withdraw their opposition:

> The pests from the sky have not ceased to fall on our crops ever since the suppression of these holy rites that the people now vehemently want to bring back, which prompts us to appeal again to the august National Assembly so that it would provide an ordinance recognizing the legitimacy of our declaration made here, and making clear to the lord bishop that until a reestablishment of the said rites, we will be permitted to refuse the tithe (or whatever will replace it) to the said bishop and curé. The inhabitants of Salles never cease to raise our voices to heaven for the preservation of members of the august Assembly since they are in charge.[1]

The appeal ultimately reached the Assembly's Ecclesiastical Committee, but since its members were drawing up legislation that would soon eliminate both the village's

religious funding obligations and this particular bishopric, there was no need to respond
to the request.

That such a plea was ignored does not mean, however, that we too should consign it
to oblivion—especially not when it shows how these southern villagers were a world
away from the representatives in Paris. Whereas the deputies envisaged revolutionary
religious reform as a means to address the nation's fiscal crisis, subsume the Catholic
Church under the state, and rationalize the Church's structures in order to prevent putative corruption, the villagers of Salles-sur-l'Hers viewed it as an opportunity to stave off
pestilence and ensure that their tax liability would be put to better use. As it turned out,
of course, neither the villagers nor the Assembly's deputies gained what they had sought
from this reform. Both had to settle for a deeply divided nation instead.

This chapter focuses on unremarkable citizens like those of Salles-sur-l'Hers who
derived an identity—albeit to varying degrees—from Catholic institutions, practices,
and beliefs. It specifically explores how Catholic citizens, meaning here the many French
who sought to maintain those Catholic beliefs and practices (in spite of these often varying from one believer to another), interacted with the state's effort to reform their church
during the first three years of the Revolution. Particular emphasis here is given to how
such engagement unfolded in, and around, those middling and small towns where two
administrative structures of the new regime (municipal and district) yielded enough
documentation to make the dynamics of this development perceptible to us today. The
justification for taking up such a subject is rather simple: popular engagement with religious reform was critical to the Revolution because it was critical to much of the nation
itself.

This revolutionary relevance becomes even more evident once it is understood what
many Catholic citizens sought in this reform, as well as how they perceived its changes
once state officials began its implementation. To this end, the following makes the case
that as the citizens of Salles-sur-l'Hers well illustrate, religious reform was popularly
evaluated by how much it would maintain or extend religion's capacity to promote a
local community's well-being, which was understood as a multi-faceted yet collective
phenomenon. It asserts, moreover, that since religion was pervasively viewed as a vital
contributor to a local community's welfare, many Catholic citizens believed (quite correctly) that in matters of religious reform, the collective life so central to their meaning
was at stake.

While recognition of the crucial give-and-take over religious reform has not been lost
on the current generation of historians, this chapter nonetheless suggests that scholarly understanding about such exchange remains insufficient for two reasons.[2] First,
much contemporary attention given to the popular politics of religious reform focuses
on the Civil Constitution of the Clergy and most particularly on the Ecclesiastical
Oath of 1791 that yielded the 'oath crisis'. But as shown here, popular exchange with
religious reform predated the Civil Constitution by arising immediately after the abolition of privileges in August 1789 and then growing more extensive and momentous
with the nationalization of Church land and the legal suppression of many religious
orders. The Civil Constitution and the 1791 oath requirement only corresponded to this

engagement reaching a critical mass—not, as many scholars seem to suggest, suddenly forming anew. Moreover, as conflict over the oath was unfolding, this interaction was also being informed by lesser-known aspects of reform that included the sale of *biens nationaux* and the circumscription of parishes. And second, few contemporary scholars have attempted to make a direct connection between the popular politics of religious reform and the broader dynamics in the Revolution, most notably its successes and failures in creating democratic governance and its predilection for centralization and state-sponsored repression. While elements like ideology, war, and unforeseen contingency were undoubtedly instrumental in dictating such trends, the volatile mixture of state religious reform and what ordinary citizens wanted from it created a nexus essential for moulding the Revolution's comprehensive character. To fully consider this nexus we must turn to when it first emerged, which was not long after the Revolution did.

THE ABOLITION OF PRIVILEGES AND NATIONALIZATION OF CHURCH PROPERTY

As much as the Catholic clergy was essential for launching the Revolution, particularly through its actions at the Estates-General in June 1789, there was little to indicate before the evening of 4 August that the Catholic Church would be subject to dramatic reform. But over the course of that the night, as some clerical deputies in the National Assembly renounced fees associated with the Catholic rites and property, the entire fiscal apparatus of the Catholic Church was put in doubt. The abolition also repudiated corporatism and with it the unique autonomy that the Church had enjoyed in the old regime. Given all that the abolition had done, the immediate results of that chaotic night yielded what Michael Fitzsimmons has termed an 'existing sense of unease' among many clerical members of the Assembly. Subsequent developments like guarantee of religious freedom in the Declaration of the Rights of Man and the Citizen only exacerbated such apprehension. As the National Assembly moved gingerly toward nationalizing all Church land near the end of 1789, hostility toward the corporative status that many Catholic leaders still claimed for their institution was on the rise among many deputies.[3]

But often left in the shadows of this increasing contention is the effect that the erasure of clerical privileges and the nationalization of Church property had on local politics. Ending the tithe and eliminating benefices and other fees were initially welcomed by rural and urban citizens alike, yet the more politically conscious saw trouble on the horizon. The loss of such funding meant, among other things, that many priests and members of religious orders would be unable to provide local poor relief needed more than ever in the winter of 1789–90. This concern was evident, for example, among twelve Estates-General electors from the *bailliage* of Evreux and Rouen, who wrote to the National Assembly some time in the autumn of 1789. The electors deftly pointed out that elimination of the tithe had serious ramifications for the entirety of many rural communities, thus underscoring how economically far-reaching the Assembly's decision was:

> Consider, my lords, the certainty that both the big and small farmer would take up all the remains on the land from the harvest, and by consequence the poor day labourer from a small town or village, who would have foraged the tithed land to keep alive one or two milk cows during five or six months of winter, would be forcibly deprived of any assistance, thus reducing the poor to the greatest misery; he would no longer have any cows that he could obtain for keeping his family alive, and thus the pivotal role played by these most useful animals in the life of this man will be more so reduced; there would be infinitely less wealth of two kinds [land and animal] and infinitely more misery for the poor, in addition to more impediments for cultivating the land since a considerable number of beef cows would necessarily decrease.[4]

More familiar with small-town and rural life than many deputies, these electors concluded that the abolition would produce within their jurisdiction not only greater stress on the poor, but also a downturn in the local economy through a reduction in the number of milk cows, beef cows, and the products that these animals provided—all because the land set aside for the tithe would no longer be accessible to the poor.

The next critical step taken by the National Assembly regarding religious reform was a rather vague decree on 2 November to place all Church property 'at the disposal of the state'. Although only later was it clarified as the nationalization of such holdings, popular attention to the issue emerged immediately after the decree, if indeed letters received by the Assembly's Ecclesiastical Committee are any indication. The primary concern among many Catholic citizens was what this seizure would do to religious orders and the services that they provided. For many communities that were home to religious orders—small and middling towns in particular—there seemed to be growing anxiety about what the National Assembly had done. The sentiment can be found, for example, in a petition signed by many inhabitants of Pont-à-Mousson (Meurthe) and submitted to the National Assembly shortly after the nationalization decree was passed:

> Frightened by the unfortunate effect that this suppression cannot help but have, certainly in this town, [the petitioners] believed that they had a duty ... to support the preservation [of their religious communities]. Eleven religious houses still remain here; would their suppression be a benefit for the state, in light of all these considerations, and when the wishes of the citizens are to maintain their existence in this town? Since the National Assembly has not decided on their ultimate fate, it can still be argued that the general interest would be served as much as our own interest, by way of our request. The property of religious orders sold for the profit of the state would provide momentary relief, but as for the future, it will deprive us of a resource that would be indispensable.[5]

Two observations may be made about this petition. The most obvious is that the nationalization of Church property did not always meet with consonant approval among ordinary citizens, in part because such property either directly or indirectly benefited many of them. The petitioners of Pont-à-Mousson foresaw—quite correctly, as it turned out—that turning over the property of religious orders to the state would result in a net loss for them. A less apparent but equally important inference, however, is that the language shows these citizens as proficient in using revolutionary political culture for their own end as early as 1789, particularly in articulating that their request was in the nation's 'general interest'. If, indeed, many Catholics sought to 'reclaim the sacred' later in the Revolution through their democratic bona fides—as Suzanne Desan has argued—then the first claims of such a sort appeared at this time.[6]

Curbing Religious Orders

Admittedly, the number of petitions expressing worry over the nationalization that reached Paris in November and December of 1789 is relatively few, perhaps because many citizens were still waiting to see what the comprehensive religious settlement would be. Yet the same cannot be said about the correspondence after the decree of 13 February 1790, which among other things legally dissolved religious orders not tied to education or charity, forbade the reception of new novices to these orders, revoked any future profession of religious vows and legal recognition of those already made, and ordered a relocation of many nuns, monks, and friars who refused to disperse. It ensured that, together with legislation subsequently passed, community life for these individuals became all but impossible.[7] The decree was significant, in part, because it represented a radical departure from the ecclesiastical perspective of most French citizens—even more so than the nationalization of Church property. The parish-level and general *cahiers de doléances*, composed only a year earlier, vividly attest to this. As John McManners observed, as few as 1 in 50 parish-level *cahiers* proposed ending all vows made by the regular clergy. Timothy Tackett similarly found that only 4 per cent of the general *cahiers* of the Third Estate called for the abolition of religious orders.[8]

Accordingly, in the weeks and months that followed the February decree—at the same time when troubles were arising between Catholics and Protestants in Nîmes and other communities in the south—the National Assembly received many letters and petitions from diverse regions expressing numerous concerns about the legislation. Some writers, such as those in the municipal council of La Réole (Gironde), argued that contemplative religious institutions in their communities should be exempt from the decree because, despite these orders' primary purpose, they served local communities by providing education and other services. Many letters and petitions, some from members of religious orders destined to be dispersed, expressed sadness and bewilderment at the decree—especially as these orders had fully conformed by reporting all of their property to state authorities. Still others were collective declarations from religious houses in which members promised to stay together, or from municipal councils supporting their resolve. Many writers, moreover, took issue with the amount of the pension that dispersed monks, nuns, and friars would receive, objected to state confiscation of property specifically donated by laypeople for poor or sick relief, or requested some kind of temporary assistance for religious institutions that had gone months without any kind of revenue. A few of the letters even anticipated what the effect of the Civil Constitution of the Clergy would be. In the Isère, for example, numerous letters and petitions calling for the preservation of Vienne's archbishopric were sent to the National Assembly not only from the small town itself but also from the municipal councils of two neighbouring communities: Beaurepaire and Saint-Jean-de-Bournay. Likewise, a petition from the small town of Saint-Gaudens (Haute-Garonne) called for the preservation of the bishopric, collegiate church, and seminary of nearby Comminges.[9]

By no means does such correspondence suggest that Catholic citizens were prepared to revolt against religious reform before passage of the Civil Constitution of the Clergy. Nevertheless, it serves to check a tendency in recent historiography to dismiss popular reaction to reform predating the Civil Constitution as inconsequential.[10] Once the popular rapport with the nationalization of Church property, the abolition of many religious orders, and in some corners, the granting of full civil rights to Protestants is properly understood, Timothy Tackett's emphasis on the Civil Constitution and the 1791 oath being a 'seminal event in its own right' and one that played a role in 'recasting the gestalt of provincial France' can be seen as selling the importance of religious developments that immediately preceded it somewhat short.[11] The emphasis appears convincing, in part, because Tackett's own narrative on the background to the Ecclesiastical Oath requirement leaves little space for not only the decisive reforms adopted between the abolition of privileges and the Civil Constitution, but also how the Catholic laity promptly responded to them.[12]

THE CIVIL CONSTITUTION OF THE CLERGY, THE 1791 OATH, AND THE SCHISM

Even with much religious reform a fait accompli before mid-1790, the decree on the Civil Constitution of the Clergy clearly marked a critical turning point—in no small part because its effects would be dramatically wide-ranging. Passing the National Assembly on 12 July 1790, the legislation sought to reform the Catholic Church in France in three key ways. First, it established a new and uniform system of clerical salaries: the state would pay most curés 1200 *livres* (an improvement for many), pay all bishops 12,000 *livres* (a dramatic decline for most), and guarantee pensions for those too old or ill to continue their ministry. Second, it simplified and rationalized the Church's structure in France by eliminating many elite or honorific ecclesiastical offices, reducing the number of dioceses to be coterminous with the newly created departments, and closing rural and urban parishes that did not meet certain population requirements or were otherwise deemed redundant. And third, it stipulated that all bishops and curés would be elected by lay electoral Assemblies, thereby abrogating the Concordat of 1516—an agreement by which the French Church maintained its independence vis-à-vis Rome.[13]

There can be little doubt the most important historiographical contribution to contemporary consideration of the Civil Constitution of the Clergy has been Timothy Tackett's magisterial analysis of the 1791 Ecclesiastical Oath, which the National Assembly required of all clerics in the wake of substantial opposition to the Civil Constitution by the French episcopacy. One of his most important findings regarding the oath, which signified clerical acceptance of the new legislation under penalty of losing one's clerical office, was that the rate of taking or refusing it varied greatly from one region to the next. In the Parisian basin, Berry-Bourbonnais, southern Poitou, Guyenne-Gascony, and the Alps, for example, a sizeable majority of priests took the oath. In Brittany, Normandy, northern Poitou, the Midi, Alsace, Franche-Comté, and Flanders, on the other hand, a disproportionate number of clerics refused it. Tackett found that the most reliable indicator of a priest's reaction was clerical density, that is, how many priests on average served in the region's parishes and other ecclesiastical institutions; the more priests were regionally present, the less likely they were to take the oath. Overall, though, slightly more than half of all clerics took the oath. Tackett saw such clerical reaction as crucial not only in itself but also because of how it influenced the laity. Even so, he also considered the roles that regional religious cultures, other revolutionary reforms, gender, and the presence of Protestants played in popular reception of the oath.[14]

Tackett's explanation for why oath reaction took its varied shape, however, is less revealing of what the immediate popular impact of the controversy was. From the perspective of citizens in towns and villages, one can argue that the struggle over the oath affected their communities in three salient ways. First, conflict over the oath tended to delegitimize the new regime in the eyes of many citizens because it prompted district and departmental officials not only to remove many long-standing and well-respected pastors, but also denounce or oust elected officials assumed to be siding with refractory priests. Given these extraordinary actions, one can understand why many would come to view revolutionary democracy as highly flawed. Second, the 1791 oath divided communities so keenly that not only did democratic political engagement become problematic, but also the collective and unitary identity on which many inhabitants depended was shattered. Third, this divisiveness itself led local authorities and partisans to call on more departmental and national intervention into local affairs, whereupon the centralization process was augmented. Thus a spiral of diminishing local autonomy and external enforcement of unpopular laws, increasingly illegitimate in local eyes, was created.

The loss of the new regime's legitimacy among citizens is apparent in many incidents involving either refractory priests or the constitutional priests who replaced them over the course of 1791 or 1792. For example, on 21 May 1791 the mayor of Saint-Marcellin (Isère) reported that on the night before the installation of the constitutional curé, the many women who continued to support the refractory pastor gathered at the parish church and provocatively opened all of its doors.[15] Municipal officials ordered the women to disperse and closed up the church, only to find later that its doors had been opened again. The following day, as preparations were made for his installation, the constitutional curé found that all the candles for the high and low altars had been removed, thus prompting the cleric to buy new candles from a local merchant. As people gathered for the installation they found the church doors locked and were prevented from approaching the church by women crying that there was going to be a revolt. About ten days later town authorities were scandalized when an abbé Dufort—apparently another of the town's refractory priests—refused to take off his hat when the rogation procession led by the new pastor went by his residence's window.

Later in the summer, when numerous townspeople and priests were accused of disrupting public order, local court testimony revealed that the constitutional curé had been called a 'bugger' and a 'fat pig'. It also claimed that during the rogation procession the new pastor was subject to 'indecent cries', in addition to being declared a 'schismatic' and a 'thief'. Adding insult to injury, during one of his masses the new curé was subjected to a show of indecent hand gestures. These events led to the prosecution of the refractory pastor and his most ardent supporters, during which an anonymous letter sent to authorities stated, 'We learned with much regret the incarceration of the [refractory] curé of Saint-Marcellin; you undoubtedly ignore the attachment that we have for our zealous and true pastor; it is based on a certainty, which is the anonymous proclamation that we will not recognize any other.'[16]

These incidents, which were not uncommon throughout much of France, are insightful for understanding how the local politics of the 1791 oath was practised among Catholic citizens. On the most superficial level, the events at Saint-Marcellin suggest how integral religion was to Catholics who supported the refractory clergy, specifically as demonstrated by how much vitriol was apparent in their political activism; arguably the protest would have been less turbulent if religious practice had been seen as merely an ancillary matter. On another level, though, these events show how citizens expressed their contention that state religious reform lacked legitimacy. The loss of legitimacy took the form of besmirching the reputation of the new pastor not only by verbally accusing of him of being sexually depraved, immorally corpulent, religiously fraudulent, and brazenly criminal, but also by physically disrupting the public ritual—so central to his office—that he led. On a still deeper level, one might recognize that the crux of the issue was not necessarily the reform per se, but rather a collective conception of the community that the oath requirement helped obliterate. This was evident in how both the object and means of attack launched by opponents of the new pastor were communal in character. It was essential for these Catholics not only to carry out their protest in unison but also to claim that they were speaking with one voice.

To be sure, not all citizens—even including the women within the small town of Saint-Marcellin—opposed the constitutional clergy, much less protested in this scandalous way.[17] Nevertheless, a seeming absence of legitimacy stemming from the oath conflict generated a new crisis for many citizens, in part because local elected officials were also subject to punishment. In many communities district and departmental officials denounced or removed municipal officers from their positions because of their alleged affinity for refractory priests. On 18 August 1791, for example, the district directory of

Grenade (Haute-Garonne) denounced their own town's mayor, four other municipal officers, and the communal prosecutor. Their purported offence was calling for prayers to be said for the health of crops without receiving permission from the constitutional bishop of Toulouse, which was an indication to district officials that town administrators were not only continuing to support refractory priests but also viewing the new bishop as illegitimate.[18] A month earlier in the same department, the Constitutional curé of Muret complained to departmental officials not so much about refractory priests, but rather about the town's municipal council protecting them.[19] Later in the year, on the opposite side of France, a municipal officer in the town of Montfort (Ille-et-Vilaine) named Pierre Allais was denounced by his colleagues for having his own child baptized by a refractory cleric—the infant's maternal uncle, no less—at a private residence. When Allais defended himself by invoking the right to free religious opinion as found in the Declaration of the Rights of Man and the Citizen, his enemies on the municipal council explained why his actions had been so reprehensible:

> He lent so much of himself that he compromised public security, accrediting by his actions the ideas of schism, fanaticism, and secession which, in leaving our temples empty, in simultaneously separating citizens, in leaving brother estranged from brother, will end by substituting the precious empire of law with the despotism and horrors of anarchy. Already these disastrous divisions have produced troubles in our town, and the diverse [administrative and judicial] tribunals are required to move ruthlessly against their authors.[20]

But municipal administrators were far from being the only officials punished because of oath conflict. In September 1792, the municipal officials of Neufchatel (Seine-Inférieure) turned the tables by denouncing one of their superiors—a district prosecutor—for 'protecting the enemies of our revolution, as well as promoting their machinations and their audacity'. They described him as 'a zealous apostle of refractory priests' and 'a declared enemy of constitutional priests and citizens shown to be the true friends of liberty and equality'.[21] According to Tackett, moreover, in 1791 a special commission of the National Assembly concluded that the departmental directors of the Bas-Rhin had been dragging their feet in implementing the Civil Constitution's reforms, whereupon it took the unprecedented step of suspending the entire Directory and naming hand-picked replacements.[22] Such examples show how the summoning of what today would be termed 'national security' circumvented the democratic process much earlier in the Revolution than widely believed, thereupon setting a dangerous precedent. Yet they also yield more evidence for why conflict over the oath prompted many citizens to question the legitimacy of the Revolution itself.

Negative perceptions of democratic governance were also fomented by another aspect of fallout from the oath conflict. Many communities became so divided over the oath that the civic unity required for democratic practice bore no resemblance to the local reality. Indeed, small towns especially became so finely splintered over the oath that marriages and families were often divided. The prosecuting attorney of the

District of Saint-Malo (Ille-et-Vilaine) said as much when he reported in December 1791 that 'visceral divisions' over the oath were thriving in his district 'among the most tightly united families, troubling the best marriages, raising a wall of separation said to be impenetrable between father, mother, children, and the espoused'.[23] Microhistorical research on the district town of Machecoul (Loire-Inférieure), where religious conflict likely contributed to a counter-revolutionary massacre, also suggests that the divide often cut across social partitions involving gender, work affiliations, and broader socio-economic standing.[24]

Even more important, social divisions over the oath did not always coincide with an urban–rural dichotomy. In the middling town of Dieppe (Seine-Inférieure), for example, a municipal official revealed that when a female merchant's servant tore up an official poster denouncing refractory priests, the workers of a competing merchant gathered up the pieces and threw them underneath her door, after which they declared her house as belonging to an 'aristocrat'.[25] Less than a year later—and several months after many refractory priests were expelled from France—the municipal council of nearby Cany (Seine-Inférieure) explained that because it was so critical 'for the public tranquillity that the divisions created by the diversity of religious views in this town end', a high mass would be celebrated by a constitutional curé, to which all the town's citizens would be invited in that hope that the rite would 'reunite sentiments' among them. Despite such attempts at reconciliation, the intricate divisions created by the 1791 oath suggest that religious reform quickly became a self-defeating gambit in revolutionary politics. Because of what the oath did to communities, religious reform inherently became antithetical not only to a collaborative democracy that officials were promoting, but even more to the collectivity that remained central to the self-conception of many citizens.[26]

The absence of civic unity made it all the more important that revolutionary officials intervene not only to maintain peace between citizens, but also to uphold a faltering democratic culture. This augmented the trend of political centralization, whereby the national government extended its authority over citizens and thereby became more controlling of their daily lives.[27] The centralizing process—at least as activated by oath conflict—tended to follow a common pattern. Complaints about refractory priests and their supporters were first made by either municipal or district officials, or by local political clubs. This then prompted departmental officials to take steps to curb the influence of refractory priests, including placing residency requirements upon them.[28] A 1791 letter from the Jacobin club in Beaune (Côte d'Or) to its departmental Directory demonstrates how the centralizing process typically began:

> the refractory priests are entrenched daily in the convents of this city, but mainly that of the Carmelites; there, not only those of tender consciences [the nuns], but also the indecent number of enemies of the revolution, fill the church; unfortunately it seems that the number of those misled increases daily, along with the evil that causes such scandalous scenes; thus we please ask you, gentlemen, to find a remedy as promptly as you can ...[29]

The letter suggests that the repressive measures pursued against refractory priests and their supporters—to say nothing of the broader development of centralization—should not be understood as strictly a 'top-down' phenomenon. On the contrary, local complaints about oath conflict were often a catalyst for the process.

The local impetus for greater centralization was strongly evident in departments that, well before the Revolution, showed signs of anti-clericalism or religious indifference. One such jurisdiction was the Puy-de-Dôme where, in June 1791, district officials in Ambert acknowledged reception of a petition from the town requesting that fifty troops be stationed there. The justification for such a request was the considerable civil unrest caused by the 'enemies of law and order', meaning refractory priests and their supporters. Not long thereafter, on 4 August 1791, the 'good citizens' of Ambert petitioned departmental officials for the closure of all unessential chapels (where refractory priests administered sacraments) in the Puy-de-Dôme.[30] Elsewhere in the department about a month later, a complaint from Billom stated that refractory priests and former canons in the town were entertaining 'error and trouble'. Once more, the plea urged departmental authorities to pursue 'the means suitable to the circumstance'. On 20 July 1792 district officials in Riom expressed concern about 'clandestine and superstitious masses that lively fanatics employ daily to mislead the people and trouble public tranquillity', and added that it was 'the duty of the [departmental] administration to utilize the full severity of the law against these shameful and treasonous manoeuvres'.[31]

Yet even in departments marked by a vibrant religious culture before and during the Revolution, centralization was also advanced—perhaps even more so than in less religiously responsive areas. This was because the support for refractory priests in many of these departments was so pervasive that it often extended to municipal officials, which would then compel district and departmental administrators (and often gendarmes and line troops), to intervene in many communities and carry out laws against refractory priests. A case in point is the Ille-et-Vilaine, where in early 1792 departmental officials believed that one of their decrees against refractory priests was not being enforced in Saint-Malo, despite the insistence of municipal authorities that it was.[32] Several months later, the district of Redon's prosecuting attorney reported that the municipal council in the district seat had declared a departmental decree against refractory priests illegal and refused to enforce it. The attorney added that the stationing of soldiers in Redon, as ordered by the department Directory, only further alienated the municipal council and townspeople.[33] The presence of troops in the district of Redon, where none of the fifty-seven priests ministering there took the oath,[34] puts into focus another side of the centralizing process: the use of brute force. Given the religious unrest in departments like the Ille-et-Vilaine and the Loire-Inférieure, one can see in troop deployments made there in 1791 and 1792 early manifestations of what Howard G. Brown aptly described as the 'Security State'.[35]

Moreover, since 'patriots' in such departments were frequently outnumbered, their allegiance and deference to the National Assembly and administrative authorities in the central government most likely grew. In the Seine-Inférieure—another department where rural supporters of the Civil Constitution often found themselves in the minority—the district Directory of Neufchâtel wrote to departmental authorities in August 1791 to complain about refractory priests. Aside from the formulaic claims that refractory priests were 'employing all means to disturb public order' and 'misleading gullible people by making them believe that constitutional curés are worth nothing', district officials added that 'the National Assembly promptly anticipated the game played by these churchmen, namely in realizing how these especially outrageous manoeuvres would constitute such cruel attacks on the faith that these priests, being more hypocritical than religious, would still maintain the confidence of simpletons'.[36] While such partisans may have welcomed the intervention of those whom they viewed as visionary administrators, it is difficult to imagine that others at the local level were as enthusiastic about such a prospect.

REFORMS BEYOND THE OATH

As politically transformative as the oath conflict was for citizens, often overlooked by even the most accomplished scholars is that other religiously related reforms were being carried out at the same time. As a result, the tendency of some specialists has been to conflate the oath conflict with the fallout of other religious reforms.[37] This inclination is understandable if only because revolutionary officials were prone to do the very same thing—and not without good reason. For example, the reduction of religious orders in early 1790, though mostly separate from the oath, had a vital impact on the schism during 1791 and 1792. Since many chapels of religious orders were closed following the 1790 decree, by 1791 such venues offered a sacred space in which those clerics who refused the oath could administer the sacraments to their adherents. While state authorities first saw rites exhibited at these sites as manifestations of religious pluralism (most evident by the so-called 'Law of Toleration' passed on 7 May 1791), increasingly they became anathema to the new regime, particularly in areas where the refractory clergy was formidable.[38] But among the followers of the refractory clergy who frequented these sites to receive sacraments, merely being present at these abandoned chapels might have suggested a narrative that the Revolution was out to destroy their communities, if not the Catholicism that had bound them together. Within such a story, the nationalization of Church property and the dismantling of many religious orders were probably viewed as part of a logical progression toward the denouement in the destruction: the Civil Constitution and the 1791 oath requirement.[39]

Nevertheless, these abandoned chapels raise another issue that had only a tangential connection with oath conflict: the confiscation and selling of *biens nationaux* that had belonged to the Catholic Church. Even before disputes stemming from the oath were unfolding, officials in many jurisdictions were already well prepared to sell off former Church property. Most districts began the auctioning around January 1791, just as the oath requirement went into effect. About five months later the National Assembly voted to authorize the sale of specific Church structures, including redundant churches, chapels, and parsonages. By the beginning of 1792 much of the Church's former property had already been purchased.[40] According to McManners, the effects of selling these parts of the *biens nationaux* were 'incalculable'. He concluded that the whole selling process 'added a faint, sacrilegious perversity to ordinary existence that reinforced the great groundswell of anti-clericalism that was sweeping into the revolutionary events'.[41] At the same time, though, the sale of properties like chapels may have fed a perception among many Catholic citizens that their life together stood in the balance, especially given how religious ritual and sociability helped foster a collective identity.

Clearly, not all ordinary Catholics had qualms about the sale of former Church property, especially if it had come at the expense of wealthy religious orders. Yet the same cannot be said about proposals to shut down parishes and liquidate their property—another overlooked part of religious reform that unfolded as the oath did. Indeed, the closing of parishes was probably the most feared of all religious reforms from the perspective of most Catholic citizens.[42] To understand why this was so, the Civil Constitution of the Clergy's stipulations about parish circumscription must be understood. The decree mostly targeted small towns by declaring that 'in all the towns and *bourgs* that do not comprise more than six thousand souls, there will be only one parish; the other parishes will be suppressed and annexed to the principal church'. But for towns that had more than six thousand people or for parishes in the countryside, the stipulations for circumscription were decidedly vague. Each parish in larger towns, according to the decree, was to 'comprise a greater number of parishioners, and will be conserved according to the needs of the people and the localities that will require it'. There were no clear stipulations for circumscribing parishes in the countryside aside from an ambiguous description of the circumscription process itself:

> The administrative assemblies [department and district], together with the diocesan bishop, shall decide by the next legislature, the parishes, annexations, or branch chapels in cities or the countryside that are to be strengthened or extended, established, or suppressed, and they shall indicate their boundaries, after investigating the needs of the people, the dignity of religious practice, and the different localities.[43]

The National Assembly therefore left much of the decision about circumscription, particularly for large towns and the countryside, to departmental and district authorities.

The projected impact of circumscription on large towns is relatively well known. As McManners pointed out over forty years ago, Bourges (Cher) was to have its parish totals reduced from 15 to 4, Angers (Maine-et-Loire) from 17 to 8, and Paris from 52 to 33.[44] For Rouen (Seine-Inférieure), the initial recommendation was that its 32 parishes should be reduced to 11.[45] Less known, however, is that small towns hovering around six thousand or fewer inhabitants were especially hit hard by parish circumscription, in part because stipulations for these locales were more specific. At least fifteen small or middling towns faced the prospect of one or more of their parishes being eliminated through proposals submitted to the Legislative Assembly in 1791 and 1792.[46]

The proposed elimination of parishes in these towns could be intensely divisive for their citizens. In the Seine-Inférieure's *bourg* of Gournay, for example, circumscription pitted the two parishes of Saint-Hildevert and Notre-Dame against each other. For over a year their parishioners wrote bitter diatribes invariably attacking those from the opposing parish, which were then sent to departmental and national authorities in an attempt to sway the outcome. Ultimately, administrators and the constitutional bishop chose Saint-Hildevert for conservation, after which the Legislative Assembly formally decreed the closure of Notre-Dame. But rather than uniting the two parishes, the new law only drove a greater wedge between them. Parishioners from Saint-Hildevert stepped up their complaints against those of Notre-Dame, who in turn sided with refractory priests and their supporters in wake of the decision. By the spring of 1792 departmental authorities pacified the entire town, but only by threatening it with military force and financial penalty.[47]

Many smaller *bourgs* and villages were affected by plans for parish circumscription as well. In the Ille-et-Vilaine, district officials of La Guerche recommended the conservation of 27 parishes, but the elimination of 4. For the district of Bain, the recommendation was to conserve 22 parishes and shut down 7. The district of Dol reported that of the 53 parishes in its jurisdiction 36 were to be maintained and 17 eliminated.[48] In the Puy-de-Dôme, the district of Riom was to have 52 of its parishes conserved while 34 would be either closed or dropped to the lower status of a *succursale* or an oratory—neither of which would have a resident pastor.[49] Understandably, such plans were often met with popular consternation and occasionally protest. When the parish of Pocé-les-Bois (Ille-et-Vilaine), a village just outside of the district seat of Vitré, was recommended for closure its parishioners forwarded a plea to the National Assembly asking deputies that they 'be allowed to place into your bosom their sorrows, their worries, and their demands'. The petitioners explained that 'that by suppressing our parish, you are depriving us of benefits that the National Assembly wants to provide to all the French'. They furthermore pointed out how difficult it would be to travel to neighbouring parishes, particularly during inclement weather and with small children in tow, and that such a prolonged trip would not permit them to attend both the high mass in the morning and vespers at night on Sundays and feast days. They also noted that the long trek would leave little time to have their children instructed in the faith. Many departmental archives and numerous cartons at the national archives are full of petitions from villages like Pocé: a telling sign of how troubling parish circumscription was to inhabitants in the countryside.[50]

How widespread circumscription was, as well as how politically significant it became to those affected, is subject to some uncertainty. According to Tackett, 'perhaps several hundred parishes' were abolished—an extremely low number for the nation as a whole.[51] He surmised, moreover, that 'though there were proposals for the suppression and reduction of parishes, such plans seldom materialized outside the larger town', in part because 'enormous local opposition disallowed the suppression'.[52] Even if most plans for parish circumscription based on the Civil Constitution never went forward, however, two points about this reform may still be made. First, the mere threat of closing their parish was probably enough for many parishioners to turn against religious reform, especially given how important parishes were to community life. Second, there may have not been a need for official circumscription in many regions since there was a de facto process of closure underway from 1791 to 1794. The reasons for this included a shortage of constitutional priests, efforts by authorities to close specific parishes where refractory priests were presiding, and later the movement of de-Christianization in Year II, in which large numbers of constitutional priests resigned their posts either voluntarily or under duress.[53]

In the case of parish closures due to the presence of refractory clerics, some evidence indicates that plans for parish circumscription in 1791 and 1792 were a weapon wielded by local officials to reduce these priests' power and influence. As such, parish circumscription was another instance when oath conflict and religious reform became conflated. The Jacobins from the town of Fougères (Ille-et-Vilaine), for example, discussed parish closures in the context of complaining about refractory priests. They urged its departmental Directory 'to accelerate, as soon as possible, the circumscription of parishes, after receiving the advice of priests known for their patriotism and their virtues'. Claiming that this recommendation was based on their 'zeal for the public wellbeing', the Jacobins explained that they were 'ardently expressing a consensus found among all good patriots'.[54] Conversely, the plan to close a parish may have also dictated clerical and popular responses to the 1791 oath. Tackett cites one instance in the Aisne of a curé objecting to the oath ostensibly because his parish was to be abolished.[55] In the case of the previously discussed parish closure in Gournay, documents suggest that members of the suppressed parish were sympathetic to the refractory clergy, which perhaps by no coincidence included their own curé.

CONCLUSION

In facing the recommended closure of their parish, as noted above, the people of Pocé-les-Bois complained to deputies in Paris that they were being deprived of benefits that the National Assembly sought to provide for the entire nation. Little did these parishioners know, however, that many revolutionary authorities often failed to acknowledge the recompense that citizens derived from their religious beliefs, practices, and institutions, or assumed that the deleterious effects of religion far outweighed such gain. The plea from Pocé therefore returns to us to what was illustrated by another set of villagers—those of Salles-sur-l'Hers—in the introduction. In both cases an appreciable disconnect between these citizens and the greater share of revolutionary politicians and administrators was obvious. Whether this dissonance was attributable to ideological intransigence, expedient manoeuvres to attain power, or a stunning absence of political imagination on the part of revolutionary elites cannot be settled here.[56] Regardless of the reason, though, the disparity merits special emphasis because it explains not only why many Catholic citizens soured on revolutionary religious reform but also, as a result, why democratic culture failed to penetrate their communities—and yet state repression simultaneously did.

By focusing mostly on such citizens, this chapter has shown that Catholics often evaluated revolutionary religious reform on the basis of how it would ostensibly affect their communities' well-being. On such a basis, some welcomed this reform because it lifted the burden of the tithe and other payments from their communities and enabled some citizens, through the sale of former Church property, to prosper in a manner impossible during the old regime. But many others affiliated this religious reform with the destruction of services and institutions upon which many of them relied, the division of communities in ways that undermined political legitimacy, the cessation of collective civility, and the augmentation of outside intervention by those who did not necessarily have the best interest of local citizens at heart.

Even so, a series of questions remain. What precisely about religious reform caused so many citizens to reject it? Was it because reform destabilized collective life, which was heavily dependent on ritual and the social exchange surrounding it? Was it because the changes resulted in the loss of cultural services, including education, or certain economic benefits such as poor relief? Or was it because the process invited a heavy-handed, external intervention as well as an accompanying loss of local autonomy? The problem with such questions is that they tend to assume that Catholic citizens compartmentalized their world much as we do today. In all likelihood, many Catholics saw their own socio-cultural, economic, and political motivations as indistinguishable from one another, or so mutually reinforcing that they made for an organic whole. The 'well-being' of most citizens, at least from their perspective, encompassed a wide range of phenomena—not unlike the multiple ways in which religion was seen to secure this ideal on behalf of an entire community.

Notes

1. Les archives nationales (hereafter referred to as 'AN'), D XIX 59.
2. See, for example, Susan Desan, *Reclaiming the Sacred: Lay Religion and Popular Politics in Revolutionary France* (Ithaca, 1990); Nigel Aston, *Religion and Revolution in France 1780–1804* (Washington, DC, 2000); Michel Vovelle, *The Revolution against the Church: From Reason to the Supreme Being* (Columbus, 1991).
3. Michael Fitzsimmons, *The Night the Old Regime Ended*, (University Park, 2003), 47–92; Timothy Tackett, *Becoming a Revolutionary: The Deputies of the French National Assembly and the Emergence of a Revolutionary Culture (1789–1790)* (Princeton, 1996), 176–207.
4. AN, D XIX 50.
5. Ibid.
6. Desan, 13–18.
7. Aston, *Religion and Revolution in France*, 134–7.
8. John McManners, *The French Revolution and the Church*. (New York, 1969), 31; Timothy Tackett, *Religion, Revolution, and Regional Culture in Eighteenth-Century France: The Ecclesiastical Oath of 1791* (Princeton, 2006).
9. AN, D XIX 49, 51.

10. See, for example, Aston, *Religion and Revolution in France*, 166–7; Gwynne Lewis, *The French Revolution: Rethinking the Debate* (London, 1993), 61; William Doyle, *The Oxford History of the Revolution* (Oxford, 1989), 144.

11. Tackett, *Religion, Revolution, and Regional Culture*, 298–300.

12. Ibid., 11–12, 183.

13. Aston, *Religion and Revolution in France*, 140–62; Tackett, *Religion, Revolution, and Regional Culture*, 11–16.

14. Tackett, *Religion, Revolution, and Regional Culture*, 159–300.

15. For more on the role of women in resisting the Civil Constitution and the Constitutional Clergy, see Timothy Tackett, 'Women and Men in Counterrevolution: The Sommières Riot of 1791', *Journal of Modern History* 59 (1987), 680–704.

16. Les archives départementales de l'Isère, L 1765.

17. Tackett, *Religion, Revolution, and Regional Culture*, 173.

18. Les archives départementales de la Haute-Garonne (hereafter referred to as 'ADHG'), 1 L 1057.

19. ADHG, 1 L 1073.

20. Les archives départementales de l'Ille-et-Vilaine (hereafter referred to as 'ADIV'), L 439.

21. Les archives départementales de la Seine-Maritime (hereafter referred to as 'ADSM'), L 339.

22. Tackett, *Religion, Revolution, and Regional Culture*, 279–80.

23. ADIV, L 441.

24. Edward J. Woell, *Small-Town Martyrs and Murderers: Religious Revolution and Counterrevolution in Western France, 1774–1914* (Milwaukee, 2006), 95–144.

25. ADSM, L 335.

26. ADSM, L 333.

27. For a lucid and more prolonged discussion of the relationship between oath conflict and centralization, see Tackett, *Religion, Revolution, and Regional Culture*, 196–202.

28. Tackett, *Religion, Revolution, and Regional Culture*, 275–83.

29. Les archives départementales de la Côte-d'Or, L 1180.

30. Les archives départementales du Puy-de-Dôme (hereafter referred to as 'ADPD'), L 2433.

31. ADPD, L 2438.

32. ADIV, L 441.

33. ADIV, L 1402.

34. Tackett, *Religion, Revolution, and Regional Culture*, 188, 355.

35. Howard G. Brown, *Ending the French Revolution: Violence, Justice, and Repression from the Terror to Napoleon* (Charlottesville, VA, 2006).

36. AN, D XIX 22.

37. Note, for example, how both Tackett and Aston see parish circumscription as a part—albeit a secondary one—of the oath crisis. See Tackett, *Religion, Revolution, and Regional Culture*, 199, 15n; Aston, *Religion and Revolution in France*, 172–9.

38. Tackett, *Religion, Revolution, and Regional Culture*, 275–6.

39. Aston, *Religion and Revolution in France*, 220–30.

40. Bernard Bodinier and Éric Teyssier, *'L'Événement le plus important de la Révolution': La vente des biens nationaux (1789–1867) en France et dans les territoires annexés* (Paris, 2000), 25–32, 123–32, 333–62.

41. McManners, *The French Revolution and the Church*, 30.

42. To be sure, the reconstitution of parishes was only one facet of drawing up new revolutionary jurisdictions that led to much contention. See Ted W. Margadant, *Urban Rivalries during the French Revolution* (Princeton, 1992).

43. *Decret sur la constitution civile du clergé du 12 Juillet 1790* (Paris: Baudouin, 1790), 10 (title one, articles XVI, XVII, and XVIII).
44. McManners, *The French Revolution and the Church*, 39–40.
45. AN, D IVbis 104.
46. AN, D IVbis 106. Note especially 'Rapports faits à l'assemblée nationale par les membres du comité de division, sur la circonscription des paroisses,' c.August 1792.
47. ADSM, L 1191, 1193, 1196, 1777, 337; AN, D IVbis 104; F[19] 472.
48. ADIV, L 1015.
49. AN, D IVbis, 106.
50. AN, D IVbis, 96.
51. Tackett, *Religion, Revolution, and Regional Culture*, 15.
52. Ibid., 199. It is unclear here whether an exact number of parish circumscriptions can ever be determined since it would require exhaustive research of every department and district. Tackett's approximation of 'several hundred parishes' may overlook the suppression of many parishes in the countryside, which was often executed by local authorities and normally much less controversial and contested by elites.
53. Aston, *Religion and Revolution in France*, 211–19.
54. ADIV, L 438.
55. Tackett, *Religion, Revolution, and Regional Culture*, 61.
56. See Dale Van Kley, 'The *Ancien Régime*, Catholic Europe, and the Revolution's Religious Schism', and Edward J. Woell, 'The Origins and Outcomes of Religious Schism, 1790 99', in Peter McPhee (ed.), *A Companion to the French Revolution* (Chichester, 2013), 123–60.

SELECTED READING

Aston, Nigel, *Religion and Revolution in France 1780–1804* (Washington, DC, 2000).

Bodinier, Bernard, and Teyssier, Éric, *L'Événement le plus important de la Révolution': La vente des biens nationaux (1789–1867) en France et dans le territoires annexés* (Paris, 2000).

Desan, Suzanne, *Reclaiming the Sacred: Lay Religion and Popular Politics in Revolutionary France* (Ithaca, 1996).

Fitzsimmons, Michael P., *The Night the Old Regime Ended: August 4, 1789, and the French Revolution* (University Park, 2003).

McManners, John, *The French Revolution and the Church* (New York, 1969).

Plongeron, Bernard, *Histoire du christianisme des origines à nos jours, vol. 10, Les défis de la modernité, 1750–1840* (Paris, 1997).

Tackett, Timothy, *Priest and Parish in Eighteenth-Century France: A Social and Political Study of the Curés in a Diocese of Dauphiné, 1750–1791* (Princeton, 1977).

Tackett, Timothy, *Religion, Revolution, and Regional Culture in Eighteenth-Century France: The Ecclesiastical Oath of 1791* (Princeton, 1986).

Van Kley, Dale, 'Christianity as Casualty and Chrysalis of Modernity: The Problem of Dechristianization in the French Revolution', *American Historical Review* 108 (2003), 1081–104.

Vovelle, Michel, *The Revolution against the Church: From Reason to the Supreme Being*, translated by Alan José (Columbus, 1993).

Woell, Edward J., *Small-Town Martyrs and Murderers: Religious Revolution and Counterrevolution in Western France, 1774–1914* (Milwaukee, 2006).

CHAPTER 16

URBAN VIOLENCE IN 1789

D. M. G. SUTHERLAND

The applause of the entire multitude convinces those who know how to peer into the heart of the people that vengeance is only momentary and that generosity is a natural human instinct.

(Mirabeau, *Courier de Provence*, l, du 5 au 6 octobre [1789], 24)

HISTORIANS are masters of narrative.[1] Knowing the end of the story, they can impose order on disordered events. They can also see connections that were not apparent to contemporaries. One of the teleologies that is most common in studies of the French Revolution is the growing consciousness of the urban crowd. That is, as events unfolded, ordinary people deepened their political consciousness. Georges Lefebvre and George Rudé, among many others, posited a before and after in crowd consciousness. Before the Revolution, bread prices and anxieties over shortages produced the classic grain riot. Men and women intervened in the marketplace to set prices at a level they considered fair, or else they prevented carts and barges from leaving a market town in order to assure supply. But there was more to this than a mechanical response to the failures of the free market. No one believed shortages or high prices were the result of natural calamities. Instead, profiteers, hoarders, and speculators took advantages of shortages to drive prices much higher than they might otherwise have been. Human agency produced high prices and shortages. The classic grain riot was designed to counteract the greed of these speculators.

The transition to the revolutionary crowd occurred with the social crisis of 1789. The narrative then is a smooth recounting of the effects of bad weather, the mobilization of the population, the transfer of popular hopes for relief to the Estates-General, the fear of aristocratic plots, and the final collapse of the old regime on 14 July 1789. According to George Rudé and those whom he inspired, a classic subsistence crisis in 1788–89 was transformed by the externalities of the Estates-General and the fall of the Bastille. The revolutionary crowd emerged from this twin economic and political crisis.

Common experience does not move so smoothly, of course. The collapse of old regime institutions was very uneven; in many places the subsistence crisis did not transform the food riot into insurrection; although shortages and fear of shortages were vital, people also reacted to insults and fears; the insurrections in Paris and in some provincial cities were much more violent and ugly than classical historiography suggests; and in the reactions of ordinary people and of some leaders, we can glimpse doctrines of popular justice. The radicalism of the Revolution may have roots in the Enlightenment for some; for most working people, it emerged from other experiences.

One of the greatest natural disasters of the century was the hailstorm of 13 July 1788.[2] The rest of the summer of 1788 was exceptionally hot and dry, so that the harvest was mediocre even in regions the storm had spared. The winter of 1788–89, by contrast was the coldest in generations. The cold began on 25 November 1788 and below freezing temperatures lasted for fifty days—a record that stands to this day. Freezing rain made transportation by road dangerous while the weight of ice made many trees fall over.[3]

The ministry implemented an increasing array of controls to cope with the crisis: import subsidies, forbidding exports, restricting sales to official markets, indemnities for selling grain at a loss, tax forgiveness, and so on. By the spring of 1789, the Intendant of Paris, Berthier de Sauvigny, was ordering a census of grain stocks in barns and mills and forcing farmers to sell on designated markets.[4] Municipal authorities in the provinces were the last links in the chain of relief. They had many instruments at their disposal. The most important was the ability to control bread and grain prices.

The poor harvest of 1788 and the devastating winter that followed, therefore, produced a major social crisis and a major mobilization of private and public institutions. The crisis did not, however, shake the regime, nor did it provoke a rise in revolutionary consciousness. An examination of over a dozen riots in Normandy, Maine, Brittany, Beaujolais, Forez, Lyonnais, and Champagne shows almost no connection to the contemporaneous political crisis.

The Réveillon riots in Paris on 27–8 April showed that the government could still handle huge riots. But the riots also open a window to a popular political consciousness that was rare in the provinces, one that was very special, as it was fixated on revenge and punishment.[5]

Apparently two of the largest employers in the Faubourg Saint-Antoine, Jean-Baptiste Réveillon, a wallpaper manufacturer, and Dominique Henriot, a saltpetre maker, both said workers could get by on 15 *sols* a day. This enflamed the crowd. Why did the rioters take these ill-considered remarks so seriously? After all, Réveillon was a model employer who carried his workers over the terrible winter even though there was no work for them. So far as one can tell, none of those indicted worked either for Réveillon or for Henriot. Misery was part of the answer. The uprisings occurred in the context of the city having set the price of the 4 lb loaf at 14 *sous*, a price that was about 40 per cent higher than the legal price earlier in the decade. Yet the rising did not resemble the classic bread riot. Although demands for a reduction in the price of bread emerged, there was no popular price fixing, nor pillage of bakers' shops and merchants' granaries.

The key to explaining the insult was that the offending remarks occurred during the electoral Assemblies that were part of the process of forming the Estates-General. In at least two of the electoral Assemblies in the Faubourg Saint-Antoine, the notables claimed a higher status by sitting apart from ordinary working people. In the Enfants Trouvés District, Henriot was supposed to have called working people 'rabble [canaille]'. In Réveillon's District, Sainte-Marguerite, a struggle broke out that involved class feelings and substantive issues over what to put in the *cahier de doléances*. The notables could not conceal their sense of their own superiority, enlightenment, and education. Yet, however much the notables sneered at working people's proposals as 'devoid of sense', workers knew they had a right to speak. In the end it appears the notables suppressed the working people's motions. They left profoundly humiliated.[6]

The rumour that two of these notables had proposed a wage reduction confirmed these frustrations and humiliations. Personalizing the issue and developing slogans were shorthand ways of expressing diverse resentments in a compressed manner, much like the cheers for Necker the following July or the denunciations of the 'orgies' at Versailles the following October.

The riots began with an attack that destroyed Henriot's apartment around 7 p.m. on 27 April.[7] The next day, the crowds enlarged their grievances. Réveillon and Henriot remained targets but there were additional demands for a reduction in the price of bread.[8] Crowds were much larger too. They made their way to Réveillon's house on the rue de Montreuil. After a long struggle against the guards, they broke in and vandalized the furniture, tossing it through the windows where it was burned or stolen. Royal troops who tried to break up the mêlée were met with hails of stones and roof tiles that killed several soldiers. The French Guards, under a particularly dangerous shower of projectiles, gave warning, then fired back. The result was terrible, said a contemporary commentator, 'Poor wretches rolled off the roofs, the walls were splattered with blood, and the cobblestones were covered with quivering limbs; cries of pain were mixed with howls of rage.'[9] Inevitably, looters made for the basement where some drank themselves into a stupor while others mistakenly drank acids and dyes intended for the wallpaper manufacture process and died in horrible convulsions.[10] Perhaps 200 rioters were killed, and about 300 wounded.[11] It was the largest Parisian insurrection since the Fronde nearly 150 years before and, if the figures are accurate, the bloodiest act of repression in the entire Revolution in Paris.

The Réveillon riots are often seen as a curtain raiser for the Parisian *journées* to come.[12] Fair enough, but there is too little attention directed at the political culture the crowds already possessed. Too much consideration is paid to shouts of 'Vive le Tiers État', as if this represents a growing political awareness. But this was the electoral season in Paris. Not all expressions of support for the Third Estate emanated from the rioters.[13]

Rioters were certainly caught up in the electoral excitement. Yet the new slogans did not replace older ideas. Rather, the rioters grafted the slogans on to older forms of expression. One of these was the mock execution. For example, on 26 April, before the riots broke out, some workers out for a Sunday drink in the Faubourg Saint-Antoine cooked up a project to make effigies of Réveillon and Henriot. The next day, they took the effigies to the Place de Grève, then to the steps of Notre Dame to have them perform a simulated supplication for forgiveness. This was a simplified adaptation of a royal execution, a ceremonial reserved for capital crimes.[14]

The bookseller Hardy and the journalist Montjoye each encountered separate crowds on either bank of the Seine. Each carried effigies; one depicted a hanged man, the other dragged a mannequin through the streets. Each displayed or read out mock decrees condemning Réveillon to death. Montjoye spoke acerbically of a crowd of 'badly dressed bandits, with hideous faces, armed with clubs ...' The representation of the crowd as beyond civilized society was thus born early.[15]

The parading, hanging, and destruction of mannequins, the threats, and the sentences were all judicial forms improvised from the past or borrowed or adapted from contemporary, official justice. Later on in the Revolution, mock executions were frequently warnings, suggesting that the condemnations of Réveillon could have been followed by a gruesome popular execution. Hanging, burning or destroying a mannequin was a more dramatic expression of intent to kill than a screaming threat.[16] Contemporaries understood its meaning and so closed their shops and shuttered their windows. The crowd did not kill Réveillon because he had himself incarcerated in the Bastille.

Of the eve of the collapse of the old regime, a few basic conclusions can be drawn. The first is that the government was as yet unshaken. Its police and judicial institutions were still working. The government was less successful in managing the food crisis. At the extreme end, many of the most vulnerable died. Yet, for the most part, the controls and interventions worked to keep the cities fed. This was especially true of Paris which for centuries had always received special attention. Aside from the Réveillon riots, there were no major riots over subsistence in Paris until October.

The food crisis then did not draw rioters into a broader critique of the regime. If the Réveillon riots were representative, the Revolution was not already in people's heads, to paraphrase Tocqueville. Ordinary folk retained very old notions of the polity that had manifested themselves in earlier times of troubles. In 1789, as in these earlier times, people sensed that a crisis was an opportunity to assert claims and express hopes. In the past, this developed into a simple utopianism, as it did in 1789.[17] In Aix-en-Provence, for example: 'the vast majority of this honest class of citizens [the peasants in the town] awaits with confidence and respect the end of all its misfortunes. They are convinced this will be found only in the National Assembly, when our fellow citizens will have had the satisfaction of telling the truth to the King and his ministers'. Direct access to the king was a very old aspiration, despite the interesting addition of the National Assembly. At Pertuis, one observer summarized popular principles as: 'that the king wishes that everything be equal, that he wishes there be no more seigneurs nor bishops; no more ranks, no tithes or seigneurial rights. So these misled men believe in anticipating their rights and follow the will of the king'.[18] People also understood that the *cahiers* the electoral Assemblies would draft for the Estates-General was the device for communicating with the king and the National Assembly.

These electoral meetings were frequently very turbulent. At Brignolles, near Toulon, the struggle over what to insert in the *cahier* went horribly wrong. After he refused to sign the *cahier*, M. de Montferrat, the seigneur, had to take refuge in a tavern, where a crowd dismembered him with an axe.[19] Although this was the only murder, other electoral Assemblies in Provence witnessed bloodcurdling threats and riots. At Aubagne near Marseille, for example, *vignerons* invaded the electoral assembly that was meeting to draft the town *cahier* without their input. The leader of the *vignerons* threatened to eviscerate a town councillor and announced that from now on, he would obey no one but the king.

At Toulon, consumption taxes, arrears in pay owed to the ever volatile dock workers in the arsenal, and high bread prices created a combustible mix. On 24 March, an angry crowd, armed with clubs and axes, invaded the Hôtel de Ville where the electoral assembly was meeting. They wanted to ensure the town's *cahier* demanded abolition of consumption taxes on flour, wine, and oil. They would also have killed two notables except for the intervention of friends who helped them escape over the rooftops. The crowd then pillaged the bishop's residence and tossed his carriage into the harbour.[20] In late March, there were similar attacks on collectors in Marseille, Brignolles, and Pertuis. On 25 March at Aix-en-Provence, sacks of flour and grain were stolen, while crowds also attacked the houses of the mayor, the tax assessor, the royal Intendant, and the town's tax farmer.[21]

As Georges Lefebvre remarked long ago, the calling of the Estates-General stimulated hope among ordinary people that their lives would be transformed. Lefebvre was never precise about what the Great Hope meant but these hopes were not limited to piecemeal reforms, like alleviation of the tax burden or adjustments in tithes and dues. Sometimes, they advanced total transformations, an egalitarian utopia over which a just king presided, but with ecclesiastical and aristocratic intermediaries eliminated. The electoral Assemblies were thus critically important. These meetings also exposed fissures within the Third Estate that would last for much of the rest of the Revolution. This was a struggle that the anti-aristocratic rhetoric of the period clouded over because beneath were chiliastic expectations for permanent improvement. This would come at the expense of the entire elite. This passion explains why men and women were so committed to a vast change—and also why events in Paris and Versailles were so important.

The *cahiers de doléances* assumed that the king and the Estates-General would work together for reform. The king's speech of 23 June 1789 raised the frightening possibility that this partnership had been broken. To the deputies of the Third Estate, it appeared that the king had been duped by the diehards at court, or had even chosen to side with them. Protests began immediately. The French Guards refused to fire on a crowd of protesters that had invaded the courtyard at Versailles. The Guards themselves had particular reasons to hate their well-connected colonel, the duc du Châtelet, and no reason to support diehard courtiers. A crowd released the ringleaders of the mutiny from the Abbaye prison in Paris and feted them at the Palais Royal, the boisterous headquarters of some of the most exuberant orators and pamphleteers.

Perhaps as a response to this defiance of the king, the government began to move troops to the perimeter of the capital. Many feared this was a prelude to dissolving the Estates-General altogether and with it all hope of fiscal and political reforms. The sign that the coup was underway would be the sacking of Necker.

News of Necker's dismissal arrived on Paris before noon on 12 July. The first reaction was not to seize arms but to demonstrate. Crowds closed theatres as a sign of mourning, or stole busts of Necker and the popular duc d'Orléans and paraded them through the streets. The demonstrations became violent when a crowd marching to Versailles entered the Place Louis XV.[22] The Royal Allemand regiment under the prince de Lambesc was waiting for them. In the inevitable mêlée, the cavalry charged the crowd. Almost immediately, rumours spread of a massacre.

The exaggerated reports of Lambesc's charge transformed the situation. The agitators at the Palais Royal and the electors at the Hôtel de Ville both frantically tried to oversee the search for arms. Each wanted to arm the population, although the Hôtel de Ville wanted the newly armed citizens to form into a National Guard. The National Guard was inaugurated on 13 July, although plenty of other citizens roamed the streets with all manner of weapons.

The city was also much more chaotic than either pole, Palais Royal, or Hôtel de Ville, could manage. Observers spoke of their fears of rising criminality and pillage. A riot inside the Châtelet prison led to a breakout. All day on 13 July, waves of looters, including some French Guards, stormed the Saint Lazare monastery, stealing food and relics, drinking themselves senseless, and destroying holy objects. Starting on the morning of 12 July, the customs posts that ringed the city began to be destroyed. Continuing for nearly a week, small bands of men and women armed only with hammers, bars, and sledgehammers burned the registers, roughed up the clerks and set fire to the posts. At one post, the rioters asked the clerks if they were for the Third Estate, and then proceeded to sack the offices. But the Third Estate had interesting allies: smugglers who participated in the destruction and then rolled their barrels of wine to eager customers inside the capital.[23]

The revolutionaries needed arms to restore order and to defend the capital against a royal attack. Thus a raid on the Invalides produced large numbers of muskets and cutlasses—but no powder. But the Bastille held huge amounts of weapons and powder that had been moved there a few days earlier. It also had a strategic importance. The government ordered its governor, the Marquis de Launay, to hold out at all costs. The Parisians besieged the Bastille for military reasons, neither to release the prisoners inside, nor to lower the price of bread. How a successful defence of Paris might save the Estates-General never arose, although in fact it did, albeit in circumstances no one anticipated.

The story of the surrender of the Bastille is confusing—so many summonses, so many delegations, so many truces, and so many betrayals. The story makes sense, however, if we realize that each side violated the conventions of siege warfare. The Swiss defenders fired on the crowds from the battlements while negotiations were taking place, possibly because they were not informed. In addition, de Launay surrendered, expecting he and his men would enjoy a safe conduct. But he was beheaded along the rue Saint-Antoine, several of his commanders were hanged from lamp posts and except for the intervention of the French Guards and some timely escapes, the crowd would have executed the entire garrison for its betrayals.

As late as 9 p.m., well after the news of the Bastille had reached Versailles, it was said that the king and his entourage were preparing a counter-attack. But there was also a danger that the newly armed Parisian National Guard and hordes of citizens would attack Versailles. Rumours of an invasion arrived in Versailles at about the same time as the news of de Launay's execution, that is, around 10 p.m. One version of the rumour had the Parisians marching to Versailles 'to extend [their] vengeance and to deliver the National Assembly'. Another claimed that up to 100,000 Parisians had already overwhelmed the defences at the Pont de Sèvres and were advancing on Versailles. Hussars were ordered to line the route from the palace to the bridge. Still another claimed the Parisians were attacking the Pont de Sèvres and that one could hear the sound of cannon.[24]

Nor was the rumour entirely fanciful. Some radicals in Paris were preparing for an attack. On the morning of 15 July, a delegation arrived at the Hôtel de Ville with exciting news. It announced the formation of a group called the 'Volunteers of the Palais Royal', some 12–15000 young men dedicated to the defence of the 'common liberty'.[25] One of their stated goals was 'to capture [faire prendre] the aristocrats'.[26] Desmoulins, one of their leaders, was also urging a rush on Versailles. That would finish the conflict, he said, remove 'the entire [royal?] family, and take out the entire aristocracy in a single blow'.[27] A diplomat from Parma reported that the extremely violent protests and bloodshed in Paris, the rapid arming of the population, 'their rage capable of anything, the fear they might come to Versailles, as they had sworn, to blow off the heads that their anger had designated, all that combined made the court and the new ministers blanch with fright'.[28] Montjoye gave a pungent summation: 'In a word, if Paris feared Versailles, Paris worried Versailles even more.'[29] In the end the Crown capitulated, agreed to withdraw the troops, and to recall Necker. The king also journeyed to Paris on 17 July in an attempt to stave off a worse outcome.

Not all institutions floundered; some were attacked, and in places the aftermath was dreadfully violent and gruesome. In Paris, for example, on 14 July, the crowd hanged the de facto mayor, de Flesselles, and dragged his body through the streets. Just over a week later, the crowd beheaded the Intendant of Paris, Berthier de Sauvigny and his father-in-law, Foulon, a former financial official with a reputation for corruption. They suspected Berthier of wanting to use his official position to strengthen the court party by starving the capital; and they despised Foulon for contemptuous remarks he apparently made during the Flour War of 1775 that the people should eat hay. Both had been expected to form part of a new reactionary ministry. On 22 July, after ripping out Berthier's heart, they paraded Foulon's head on the end of a pole, the mouth stuffed with hay. Later, the crowds carried the trophies to the Palais Royal. Restif de la Bretonne who saw part of the carnage, wrote: 'I went to the Palais Royal. All the shops were closed. Like Medusa's, the [two] heads seemed to have turned all beholders to stone. The groups in the garden were no longer concerned, as they had been, with motions. They spoke only of killing, hanging, and decapitating. My hair stood on end.'[30]

It is tempting to concur with the journalist Babeuf that the crowd was merely imitating what they had seen from the royal way of death; that the barbarity of the elite had made the people barbarous. In a general way, this may be true but popular justice did not imitate official. Each responded to different rhythms. On the eve of the Revolution the vast majority of executions were by public hanging. The Crown's humiliation *post mortem* was limited to leaving a hanged person on display for 24 hours and then, before it was demolished in 1760, suspending the corpse in the gibbet at Montfaucon. By contrast, for the crowd, the *post-mortem* humiliation was the essence, with decapitation, dragging the corpse, triumphal parades of severed heads, dismembering, and souvenir taking. Finally, throughout the Revolution, popular executions were secular; unlike royal executions, religious ceremonies and priests were entirely absent.

A popular execution was not a mob rising up against civilized society. Huge crowds of onlookers that included 'civilized society' cheered the triumphal parades—prints frequently show well-dressed spectators. The texts invariably mention women among them, as if their approbation added a special legitimacy. The noble deputy from Saint-Domingue, Gouy d'Arcy, observed that even in the century of enlightenment, many people, not just the populace, cheered the executions, the dismembering, the hand washing in blood, the singing, dancing, and cries of joy as the cadavers were dragged throughout Paris. Barbarism, he feared, would become a habit.[31]

As it did, because some leading politicians and journalists either sympathized with the killings or excused them. These killings broke the soft consensus among the pre-revolutionary elite against barbarous justice. Mirabeau blamed the problem on centuries of despotism which corrupted the people's character, 'If the anger of the people is terrible, it is the cold blood of despotism that is atrocious. Its systematic cruelties do more damage in a day than popular insurrections destroy in a year.'[32] Speaking in the National Assembly on 21 July, a deputy from Artois, 'M. de Robert-Pierre', also found mitigation in the killings of 14 July: 'What happened in this riot in Paris? Public liberty, a little blood spilled, a few heads knocked off no doubt, but guilty heads … So, messieurs, the nation owes its liberty to this riot.' In another version, he said 'Is there nothing more legitimate than to rise up against a horrible conspiracy formed against the nation?'[33] Babeuf deplored the cruelty, not the right of the people to exact justice. Then there is the most chilling justification of all, the one everyone quotes, from the deputy Barnave: 'Was the blood just spilled so pure then?' Despite the furor provoked by the remark, Barnave never backed down. His intention, he said later, was to put the murders of Berthier and Foulon in perspective, 'that all revolutions carry with them unfortunate events, and that perhaps we ought to congratulate ourselves that this revolution only has to reproach itself with a small number of victims and little blood [spilled]'.[34]

Politicians and sympathetic journalists thus asserted three defences for extra-legal killings: blame the tyranny of the old regime; argue self-defence, pre-emption, or sovereign right; and minimize the significance of the events. These are, of course, defences that are often still used, but used without much self-awareness. Claiming the crowd acted against real or imagined threats, like the aristocratic plot, or failing to notice the victims were helpless at the time of their murders deflects attention from the ceremonial of popular executions. Two things follow. First, endorsing the executions as somehow justified also produced a reluctance to prosecute such killings. Not so many years later, the consequence was destruction of the civic order. Second, avoiding the gruesome *post-mortem* details evades the question for which there is no easy answer: the origins of such ceremonials.

Elsewhere, the crisis in Versailles and Paris resonated powerfully but it is too simple to imagine provincials awaiting news from the capital before acting. In every provincial city, national politics filtered through earlier experiences. All the cities continued to deal with the agonizing subsistence problem. Even where the municipalities were reconfigured or even overthrown in the summer crisis, the subsistence issue did not change. The new or revamped authorities faced the same problem and the same demands for action from the population. Moreover, the same tensions that existed in Paris between ordinary people and local elites manifested themselves everywhere in the large provincial cities. The revolutionary ideology of a unified citizenry rising up against local despotism often masked a struggle against municipalities, military commanders, and 'aristocrats'.

Popular clamour did display new features. Among them are youth groups. Young men continued to participate in local politics and, frequently, their militias contributed to the formation of the National Guard. In Marseille, for example, news of Necker's downfall produced a severe but brief panic. Rumours that the most popular deputy of the region, Mirabeau, had been murdered or that a horrible massacre had occurred in Paris swept the region.[35] But local politics soon reverted to issues that had animated the population earlier: control of the municipality and the armed forces, among other things. The young men armed themselves in support of the patriot cause, fought their enemies in street brawls, and even marched to outlying towns to support their comrades.

There is no hard and fast rule that can encapsulate how the large provincial cities responded to the crisis in Versailles and Paris. Some cities like Marseille, Toulon, and Lyon began their local revolution before the crisis of July in the capital. For others, like Nantes and Strasbourg, the news of Necker's sacking or his recall precipitated a local struggle for power. The agonizing subsistence crisis strained authority everywhere but the form of popular struggles differed. In Marseille, Lyon, and Strasbourg, the economic crisis produced spectacular revolts against municipal taxes and fees. At Nantes, municipal authorities protected grain and flour stores successfully, while at Strasbourg, celebrations over the recall of Necker on 20 July triggered a demonstration for a reform of the municipal franchise. Without reform, the people would destroy the town hall and murder the magistrates 'because it is now the people who make the law and who watch over who dispenses justice to them'.[36] The next day, the crowds destroyed much of the Hôtel de Ville, tossed furniture, royal portraits, and mountains of paper into the streets, eight centuries of archives in all. It was said that some rioters drowned in the cellar from the massive amounts of wine gushing from the kegs they had smashed. At Caen, the 'citizens' phalanx', composed largely of young men, went to the market hall and lowered the price of wheat, barley, and salt; seized the records of the alcohol tax administration; freed prisoners; and released all the supplies of grain in storage.[37]

Rumours played a large role in the local revolutions at Lyon and Nantes. A rumour arrived in Lyon at the end of June—an echo of the king's order of 27 June that all three orders of the Estates-General meet as a single body—that the king had suspended excise taxes for three days but that the municipal officers and the tax farmers were suppressing the decree. Thousands of peasants with their cattle and wine barrels stormed the customs posts. The forces of order shot four people including a woman, hanged another rioter and ordered still another to be branded and banished.[38] At the end of July rumours flew that brigands would attack the city. This was a reflection of the Great Fear in nearby Dauphiné, but the rumours exposed divisions between elites and ordinary people. Thus, when the rumours arrived, crowds sized the Arsenal and the Powder Depot; threatened to kill the governor of the Fort Pierre-Scize; and nearly hanged a group of employees of the tax farms whom they took to be brigands sneaking arms and poison into the city. Two weeks later on 12 August, the volunteers had to disperse a crowd that was demanding the head of the provisional mayor, Imbert-Colomès.[39]

The crisis in the capital also revealed ruptures at Nantes. When the news of Necker's sacking arrived on 16 July, the crowd seized a powder magazine. On 20 July, rumours arrived that three heavily armed regiments were marching on the city from the south. This was an early version of the Great Fear and, as it did elsewhere, it provoked a mobilization of the population. The municipality persuaded the commander of the Château de Nantes to surrender the fortress to the bourgeois militia but the crowd broke into the château at the same time and distributed the muskets to whoever wanted them. The crowd threatened to kill the commander and his aide-major. Out on the streets, men and women shouted, 'Better die today than tomorrow. Let us imitate the Parisians. Let us prefer death to servitude.' Thousands of armed men went down to meet the invaders at the Loire bridges; hundreds of peasants armed with pitchforks joined them; women boiled water to dump on the assailants; delegations from small towns in the periphery, like Machecoul and Clisson, offered help.[40] Eventually, authorities controlled the situation but not before restructuring the municipal government.

Amid this bewildering series of events, the one common thread was the collapse of the regime. Unlike the riots of the spring, royal authority in the form of intendants, courts, and *maréchaussée* are largely, but not entirely, absent from the narrative. Many intendants fled their charges after the mob murdered their colleague, Berthier de Sauvigny.[41] The crisis of authority at the centre sapped institutional vigour at the periphery. What remained were the municipalities, provisional committees, youth militias and embryonic national guards. Sometimes this could go terribly wrong, as it was to do at Caen. Weakness opened a chasm for popular justice.

On 12 August 1789, a ferocious crowd slaughtered one of the officers in charge of the ducal palace in Caen, Major Henri, vicomte de Belsunce. His murder illustrated, as murders did in Paris and elsewhere, that the popular movement claimed the right to punish. He was a haughty young man but, more than that, he was unpopular at a time of extreme tension over the food supply. He had escorted grain convoys out of the city through the poor quarter of Vaucelles, holding the reins of his horse in his teeth, a pistol in each hand, making insulting gestures as he passed. He also disrupted patriotic fetes that celebrated the recall of Necker. On 11 August a rumour spread that Belsunce was preparing a surprise attack to retake the ducal château that had fallen to the patriots a few weeks before.[42] A gun battle near the barracks resulted in a fatality. As the news mushroomed, the city exploded. Women especially were heard calling their communities to arms.[43]

Finally, after much negotiation between the Hôtel de Ville and the regiment de Bourbon, Belsunce himself agreed to appear before the Provisional Committee under guarantee of a safe conduct.

From this point until the grisly end, events resembled the murders in Paris in July. As in Paris, while he marched from the barracks to the Hôtel de Ville, the crowd pummelled him with cudgels while shouting ugly threats. The Provisional Committee in effect put Belsunce on trial once he and his escort reached the Hôtel de Ville. But crying, 'It's the nation', the crowd seized Belsunce and shot him on the Place St Pierre. Even when he was dead, the shooting continued, 150 balls, apparently. He was then decapitated, his head paraded about on the end of a pole, accompanied by music played by the soldiers of his regiment. One witness recalled seeing, 'this young and beautiful head, with powdered hair, who in spite of death, retained an air of nobility and fidelity'.[44]

The Belsunce murder can be understood in the way Lefebvre analysed crowd action.[45] The social construction of a hate figure, the threat, the panic, the fear of destruction, the exercise of 'punitive will' were common to both murders. But one can go further in the case of Belsunce because the crowd behaved as if they were following judicial procedures. Thus, when he got to the Hôtel de Ville, the Committee read out a set of charges. They took his responses as so many admissions to 'the crimes that were imputed to him'.[46]

Nor was the murder the end because after the 'trial' came the *post-mortem* carnival. The various parades were celebrations and humiliations at the same time. One witness saw a young man, a plasterer with pale skin and light blond hair, tossing the heart from one hand to the other 'as if it were a ball, with a ferocious joy'.[47] The soldiers also paraded the corpse around and, as the authorities euphemistically put it, 'demonstrated their indignation towards him and then joined the multitude parading around the town'.[48]

Killings and the pitiless maimings like those in Caen were rare: aside from those in Paris and its environs, we should include the marquis de Montferrat in Provence in the spring, a massacre at Bellon near Laval in the summer, another in the Touraine, and still another particularly cruel murder of the mayor of Troyes in September. But the small number mattered less than the common forms of these executions. The October Days in Paris and Versailles illustrate once again that theatrical punishment was central to the popular repertoire.

At a basic level, the October Days were a bread riot in which many thousands of Parisian women marched to Versailles to demand bread from the king. After two days of boisterous activity, they succeeded in forcing the royal family to accompany them back to Paris. Yet, the emphasis on women and bread is only part of the story. The harvest of 1789 was probably mediocre, not abundant as contemporaries believed. It would be hard to explain the continuing high prices throughout the country otherwise. Unlike in July, however, Paris faced real shortages. As always, people blamed authority, in this case Lafayette and Bailly.

Both women and men expressed some very violent and revealing opinions. Moreover, the struggle in October was a continuation of the struggle in July with its suspicions of public officials, faithless deputies, the king, and some very open threats to murder the queen. Authorities like Lafayette could not control the crowd, at least in part because some battalions of the Paris and Versailles National Guard, plus some soldiers of the Flanders regiment sympathized and fraternized.

The crisis began on 4 October with the arrival in Paris of news that the King's Bodyguard had thrown a banquet on 1 October to welcome the Flanders Regiment. Among other outrages, toasts had failed to celebrate the nation, the celebrants had worn the Bourbon and Hapsburg cockades instead of the tricolor, and it was said the tricolor had been trampled underfoot.[49] Finally, the royal family had blessed these outrages by their presence.

Back in Paris, officials and many in the public were outraged at the news of the banquet. A woman at the Café Foy was the first to denounce the 'anti-national' cockades.[50] The queen was the source of all troubles, the women said, that they would go to Versailles and the men would follow.[51] One of the leaders of the women's march, the *femme* Chéret, stated that the women wished 'that the king and the queen come to Paris and live at the Louvre, where they would be ... infinitely better off than at Versailles'.[52]

Women were aware they had a special role. When they broke into the Hôtel de Ville on the morning of 5 October to get weapons, many said over and over 'that the men do not have enough guts [assez de forces] to avenge themselves, and that they would show themselves off better than the men'.[53] Eventually, several thousand women had set off for Versailles with only two small cannon, accompanied by the now formally named battalion of 'Conquerors of the Bastille' under Stanislas Maillard as the rear guard. The women were delirious with joy, noted one observer; 'a wild, mad Enterprize', said Gouverneur Morris. Bailly said there were 4,000 women and 4–500 men, not enough, one would have thought, to overwhelm regular troops.[54]

The marchers said they were going to Versailles to get bread and that dragging the king back to the capital would make bread abundant. Everyone, including the women, intended to force the withdrawal of the Flanders regiment, punish the Bodyguards and bring the king back to Paris—possibly to prevent a royal flight. More broadly, the women thought of themselves as patriots, not as a separate movement. At around 5 p.m., the National Guard in Paris compelled Lafayette to lead them to Versailles. Aside from regular citizen soldiers, the spaces between the ranks were filled with 'many badly dressed individuals, bizarrely armed, who resembled vagabonds which the army wished to get rid of'.[55]

The October Days were violent from the start. Most startling was the violence of the language directed at the queen, a language derived in part, perhaps, from a discourse that had reviled the queen for her promiscuity, her greed, and her favouring the interests of her Austrian family. Once again, 'mob' and 'civilized society' were not distinct categories. Thus, while the crowd was trying to rush the queen's apartments on 6 October, one woman boasted, 'Yes, the bitch will jump; we'll throw her head out the window.' A large redheaded woman then took out a rope and shouted, 'The bitch, here is what is going to decapitate her.'[56]

The first cohort of Parisians arrived in the late afternoon. It had been raining for an hour and a half and the marchers were exhausted, soaked and muddy.[57] Almost immediately, resistance from the royal troops evaporated. Many in the Flanders regiment fraternized with the women. Eventually, Lafayette persuaded the king to permit the Parisians to assume sentinel duty at the château. The Bodyguards withdrew.

Meanwhile, the Parisians made for the National Assembly where their spokesperson, Maillard, informed the deputies that Paris had had no bread for three days; they had come to avenge the insult to the nation. Behind his back, some women were denouncing the queen, saying that the lamp post was too good for her, that they would wring her neck, that she was the cause of all the misfortunes that afflicted them, that she was behind the orgy of the King's Bodyguard.[58] After Maillard's address, Mounier, the President of the Assembly, escorted a small delegation of women to see the king in person. Calm as always, Louis ordered stores in the Paris hinterland at Senlis and elsewhere be released.

In the meantime, hundreds of women and men swarmed on to the Assembly floor. They were cold and tired but some cried out or sang; others embraced the deputies; still others fell asleep, drained after their gruelling march. Deputies and the Parisians began debating and passing motions. A woman took over the President's chair. Lafayette and 20–30,000 of his men arrived in Versailles around midnight. Early risers on the morning of 6 October wandered into the exterior, largely unguarded courtyards. But a defender then shot a young Parisian. No doubt feeling they had been lured into a trap, the crowd boiled over with rage. They carried the victim's corpse to a staircase in the Cour de Marbre that led to the queen's apartments. The crowd intended to kill any Bodyguard they found. They got as far as the queen's apartments. They planned to seize the queen herself. She fled her bedroom, half dressed.[59]

Meanwhile, a fat little man with his sleeves rolled up, 'from the Faubourg Saint-Antoine with a long beard', decapitated two Bodyguards with his axe at the foot of the staircase in the Cour des Ministres. The 'people' dragged the corpses to their barracks.[60] Women and men then paraded the heads on poles around the streets of Versailles. One participant was a young child, covered with blood, who was carrying one of the poles. Some said the Bodyguards should be chained together, marched to Paris and executed on the Place de Grève.[61]

Soon after, the royal family, Lafayette and some Bodyguards appeared on a balcony overlooking the Cour de Marbre. The crowd began to shout: 'To Paris! To Paris!' Amid rapturous cheering, the king announced that he and the royal family would be going to Paris. Louis XVI beseeched the crowd to grant the Bodyguards amnesty. The consensus of the crowd was that pardon should be granted but at least one individual, a baker, shouted no, 'They are so cuddly now [but] if we don't take the opportunity to get rid of all these people, we will never have another.'[62]

The long line of marchers took hours to return to Paris. From midday onwards, and despite the still heavy rains, huge crowds lined the way from Passy to the Hôtel de Ville. The very first to arrive was a group carrying the heads of the two Bodyguards on the end of pikes. Female escorts looked at the heads with a 'ferocious joy and danced while they gaped'.[63] At least two hours after this, artillery trains passed by. Then came fifty or sixty carts of flour taken from various storehouses in Versailles—looted, said the municipality of Versailles. The royal carriages intermingled with National Guard cavalry, women, deputies (thirty-six had decided to accompany the king), grenadiers, soldiers of the Flanders Regiment, and some Swiss. The Bodyguards were not entirely forgiven. They marched on foot, bareheaded, disarmed.[64] 'The fishwives, drunk with fury, joy and wine, holding branches decorated with ribbons, seated astride the cannons, riding horses, and wearing the hats of the Bodyguards ...'[65] The women shouted to the cheering spectators, 'We are bringing the baker, the baker's wife and the baker's boy.'

Contemporary writers and artists knew the parade was strange. That is why they represented it as a bizarre carnival, a burlesque of the social hierarchy overturned. Thus Rivarol: 'The horror of a gloomy, cold and rain soaked day; this infamous militia, paddling in the mud, these harpies, these monsters with a human face, and these two heads hoisted in the air; in the middle of his imprisoned guards, a Monarch dragged slowly with his family, all that formed a spectacle so frightening, a lamentable mixture of shame and despair.'[66]

This parade is what makes urban crowds in the French Revolution strange to us too, but not for the same reason. Rudé and others have a script for ordinary people that has them rising to a higher consciousness of bourgeois democracy. Without leadership, and on their own, they tilt towards a rough social democracy of economic controls, no more. To the extent that their political education deepens under Jacobin guidance, the crowd becomes more mature, more modern. This is a teleological view, one that knows working people will be transformed into sans-culottes. It is hard to see this future in the parade, if by the future we mean the sans-culotte future of direct democracy standing alone. If, on the other hand, we abandon a teleological view and postulate a future in which advanced ideas were layered on top of older views of a justice through public mortification, then crowd actions in 1789 and after make more sense. New ideas grafted onto the old would explain the explosions of 1792 in which hundreds of individuals outside Paris were lynched, followed by the same forms of *post-mortem* display. Consider that a certain *vigneron* of Aubagne, who marched with the *Marseillais* on their inspiring mission to overthrow the monarchy in 1792 was the same man who threatened to eviscerate the municipal official during the electoral meeting in 1789. It is doubtful that Dominique Pichou changed all that much in the interval.[67]

NOTES

1. Colin Lucas, 'Talking about Urban Violence in 1789', in Alan Forrest and Peter Jones (eds), *Reshaping France: Town, Country and Region during the French Revolution* (Manchester, 1990), 122–36 examines the concepts contemporaries used in examining this phenomenon. My study is about the political culture of urban riots.
2. Camille Flammarion, *The Atmosphere* (London, 1873), 392.
3. AD Rhône 5 GG 5 Chartenay 1788 BMS.
4. Gustave Bord, *Histoire du blé en France. Le Pacte de famine; histoire—légende* (Paris, 1887), 50.
5. Good narratives in David Andress, *The French Revolution and the People* (London, 2007), 98–101. Haim Burstin, *Une Révolution à l'œuvre: le faubourg Saint-Marcel (1789–1794)*

(Seyssel, 2005), 51–5. The most recent treatment is Micah Alpaugh, 'The Politics of Escalation in French Revolutionary Protest: Political Demonstrations, Non-Violence and Violence in the Grandes Journées of 1789', *French History* xxiii, no. 3 (2009), 336–59.

6. *L'ami du roi, des françois, de l'ordre et surtout de la vérité ...*', ch. xiv, avril 1789, 94 col 1. Different version of this extract in Ch.-L. Chassin, *Les élections et les cahiers de Paris en 1789: documents recueillis, mis en ordre et annotés*, 4 vols (Paris, 1888–89), iii, 53–4.

7. Chassin, *Les élections et les cahiers de Paris en 1789*, iii, 57. Dispatch of 4 May 1789 in M. Kovalevsky (ed.), *I dispacci degli ambasciatori veneti alla corte di Francia durante la rivoluzione* (Torino, 1895), i, 19–20. Letter of 28 April 1789 in 'Documents inédits. Lettres de Thiroux de Crosne, lieutenant-général de police à Louis XVI (20–30 avril 1789)', *La Révolution française* xxviii (1895), 180. *Exposé justificatif pour le sieur Henriot, salpêtrier du Roi* repr. in Chassin, *Les élections et les cahiers de Paris en 1789*, iii, 121–2.

8. 'Lettres de Thiroux de Crosne', 15th letter, 28 Ap., p. 179.

9. Galart de Montjoie, *Histoire de la révolution de France: depuis la présentation au parlement de l'impôt territorial et de celui du timbre, jusqu'à la conversion des états-généraux en assemblée nationale* (Paris, 1797), ii, 86. 'Documents inédits. Lettres de Thiroux de Crosne', 17th letter, 28 April, 6 pm, p. 180.

10. Jean Collot, 'L'Affaire Réveillon, 27 et 28 avril 1789', *Revue des questions historiques* 121 (1935), 240.

11. This was Montjoye's estimate repeated by Collot, 240–1. Hardy estimated 5–600 (Chassin, *Les élections et les cahiers de Paris en 1789*, iii, 62). Other counts vary a lot.

12. Raymonde Monnier, *Le faubourg Saint-Antoine, 1789–1815* (Paris, 1981), 116–7.

13. Examples of slogans not connected with the rioters in Collot, 'L'Affaire Réveillon', 241; Chassin, *Les élections et les cahiers de Paris en 1789*, iii, 63.

14. L. de Launay, *Une famille de la bourgeoisie parisienne pendant la Révolution: Toussaint Mareux, membre de la Commune de 1792 et directeur de Théâtre Saint Antoine et François Sallior, membre du Bureau central sous le Directoire, d'après leur correspondance inédite* (Paris, 1921), 154–5; Richard Mowery Andrews, 'The Death Penalty in Old Regime France', in Richard Mowrey Andrews, *Punishment: Meanings, Purposes, and Practices: an Interdisciplinary Exploration* (New York, 1993), 78–9.

15. Chassin, *Les élections et les cahiers de Paris en 1789*, iii, 50–1. *Histoire de la conjuration de Louis-Philippe-Joseph d'Orléans, premier prince du sang, duc d'Orléans, de Chartres, de Nemours, de Montpensier et d'Etampes, comte de Beaujolais, de Vermandois et de Soissons, surnommé Égalité* (1796), 265–6.

16. On effigies and mannequins see the fascinating discussion in Paul Friedland, *Seeing Justice Done: The Age of Spectacular Capital Punishment in France* (Oxford, 2012), 106–12.

17. Yves-Marie Bercé, *Revolt and Revolution in Early Modern Europe: An Essay on the History of Political Violence* (Manchester, 1987), 114–19.

18. AN H 1474, pce 12, to 'Monsieur' [28 Mar. 1789].

19. AN H 1474, pce 10, undated, unsigned note.

20. William S. Cormack, *Revolution and Political Conflict in the French Navy 1789–1794* (Cambridge, 2002), 50–1; Malcolm Crook, *Toulon in War and Revolution: From the Ancien Régime to the Restoration, 1750–1820* (Manchester and New York, 1991), 80–1.

21. Monique Cubells, *Les Horizons de la liberté: naissance de la Révolution en Provence: 1787–1789* (Aix-en-Provence, 1987), 94–6. For Aix-en-Provence, see *Copie du procès-verbal de l'émeute arrivée à Aix le 25 mars 1789, adressée en original à messeigneurs Necker, de Villedeuil et de Beauvau (27 mars)* [1789] ADBR, 100E 41.

22. Deposition #xiv, Sieur François de la Genêtière, bourgeois, in *Procès du prince de Lambesc; Résumé général de ce procès, ou, Résultat des réflexions qu'il fait naître d'après le rapprochement de chaque déposition* (Paris: [s.n.], 1790), 123–4.

23. M. Markovic, 'La révolution aux barrières: L'incendie des barrières de l'octroi à Paris en juillet 1789', *Annales historiques de la Révolution française* 372 (2013), 27–48. AN, Z¹ᵃ 886, 'Plainte concernant l'incendie des barrières', 24 February 1790.

24. *Courrier de Versailles à Paris*, 154. Letter to municipality of Toul, 18 July 1789, in A. Denis (ed.), 'La Révolution à Toul en 1789', *Annales de l'Est* v (1891), 553. The Venetian ambassador: dépêche no. 190, 20 July 1789, in *Venise et la Révolution française: les 470 dépêches des ambassadeurs de Venise au Doge, 1786–1795* / éd. établie par Alessandro Fontana, Francesco Furlan et Georges Saro (Paris, 1997), 307. Jefferson to Jay, 19 July in *The Papers of Thomas Jefferson*, 35 vols (Princeton, 1959), xv, 289.

25. Bailly and Duveyrier (eds), *Procès-verbal des séances et des délibérations ... des Electeurs de Paris*, i, 413–6. See also Jean-Sylvain Bailly, *Mémoires de Bailly* (Paris, 1821), ii, 12.

26. Bailly and Duveyrier (eds), *Procès-verbal des séances et des délibérations ... des Electeurs de Paris*, ii, 73.

27. *Œuvres de Camille Desmoulins, recueillies et publiées d'après les textes originaux, augmentées de fragments inédits, de notes et d'un index, et précédées d'une étude biographique et littéraire*, par M. Jules Claretie, 2 vols (Paris, 1874), i, 97.

28. Jean-Loup Virieu-Beauvoir, *La révolution française, racontée par un diplomate étranger: correspondance du bailli de Virieu, ministre plénipotentiaire de Parme (1788–1793)* (Paris, 1903), 119.

29. *Ami du roi*, 'suite de juillet 1789, et du second mois de l'interrègne', li, 13.

30. Restif de La Bretonne, *Les nuits révolutionnaires: 1789–1793* (Paris, 1989), 40. See also Andress, *French Revolution and the People*, 118–19.

31. *Archives parlementaires*, session of 23 July, viii, 265.

32. Speech of 16 July 1789 in Gabriel-Honoré Riquetti Mirabeau, *Lettres de comte de Mirabeau à ses commettans, pendant la tenue de la première législature* (Paris, 1791), i, 511.

33. *Courrier de Versailles*, 25 July 1789, xviii, 305–6; *Point du jour*, no xxviii, p. 245, 20 July; Peter McPhee, *Robespierre: A Revolutionary Life* (New Haven, CT, 2012), 68.

34. Antoine Barnave, 'Introduction à la Révolution française', in *Œuvres de Barnave mises en ordres et précédées d'une notice historique sur Barnave par M. Bérenger de la Drôme ...* (Paris, 1843), 109.

35. Blanc-Gilli, *Discours prononcé dans le Conseil des Trois-Ordres Réunis, au Conseil Municipal ordinaire de la Ville de Marseille, le 18 juillet 1789 et publié à la demande qui en a été faite* (1789). BM Marseille Xd 2959.

36. Rodolphe Reuss, 'Le sac de l'Hôtel de Ville de Strasbourg, juillet 1789', *Revue historique* cxx (1915), 52.

37. *Révolutions de Caen, capitale de la Basse-Normandie, ou récit exact de ce qui s'est passé dans cette capitale, et particulièrement de la prise de la forteresse, (18–21) juillet 1789* (Paris, 1789). Lb³⁹ 2023; AM Caen, FF 10(1).

38. AN, D XXIXᵇⁱˢ 18, Letters of Imbert Colomès and other aldermen to the ministry, especially those of 4 July 1789 (pce 104); 5 July, 10 heures du soir (pce 105); 5 July 9:30 du soir (pce 107) as well as the letters further down in the box in the small folder entitled 'Émeute de Lyon'.

39. *La révolution du Lyonnais (29–30 juillet 1789)* (sl, sd.), BM Lyon 110910. Antoine Pericaud, *Tablettes chronologiques pour servir à l'histoire de la ville de Lyon, 1751–1789* (Lyon, 1832), 47.

40. Léon Delattre, *Souvenirs de la Révolution. La prise du Château et les événements de Juillet 1789 à Nantes* (Nantes, 1908). BM Nantes, Cote: 94668/C508. *Journal de Correspondance de Nantes* xiv, p. 134, 20 July; xvi, p. 155; xviii, p. 182, 29 July; xix, p. 194, 31 July. AM Nantes, BB 112 ff. 87v–89, rd., session of 20 July 1789; ff. 94v–95v, session of 27 July; ff. 96–96v, session of 28 July.

41. Alain Cohen, 'Les intendants au cœur de la crise de l'Ancien Régime: 1783–1791. Les généralités d'Alençon, Caen, Rouen, Rennes, Orléans, Bourges, Moulins, Poitiers, Limoges, Tours, Riom et Dijon', *Annales historiques de la Révolution française* 362, (2010), 108.

42. *Extrait du procès-verbal du comité général et national de la ville de Caen, relatif à la mort de M. de Belzunce* (Caen, 1789), 19–20, 24–5. Lb^{39} 2278.

43. *Extrait du procès-verbal du comité général et national de la ville de Caen*, 32–3.

44. Cited in Félix Mourlot, *La Fin de l'Ancien régime et les débuts de la Révolution dans la généralité de Caen, 1787–1790*, (Paris, 1913), 346, n. 3.

45. Georges Lefebvre, 'Le meurtre du comte de Dampierre' in his *Etudes sur la Révolution française* (Paris, 1954), 288–97.

46. *Extrait du procès-verbal du comité général et national de la ville de Caen*, 8.

47. Cited in 'Discours de M. Bernard Haussoullier', *Bulletin de la Société des antiquaires de Normandie* (1860), 101.

48. *Extrait du procès-verbal du comité général et national de la ville de Caen*, 34.

49. Antoine-Joseph Gorsas, *Extrait du Courrier de Versailles à Paris, et de Paris à Versailles* (Paris, 1790), 3.

50. Camille Desmoulins and Louis Marie Prudhomme, *Révolutions de France et de Brabant* (Paris, 1789), 47.

51. Albert Mathiez, 'Étude critique sur les journées des 5 & 6 octobre 1789', *Revue historique* lxviii (1898), 293.

52. Chéret, *Evénement de Paris et de Versailles, par une dame qui a eu l'honneur d'être de la députation à l'assemblée générale* ([Paris], 1789), 2–3. Lb^{39} 7941. Mathiez, 'Étude critique sur les journées des 5 & 6 octobre 1789', lxix (1899), 44.

53. Deposition #lxxxi of Stanislas-Marie Maillard, capitaine des volontaires de la Bastille, 27 Feb. in *Procédure criminelle, instruite au Châtelet de Paris sur la dénonciation des faits arrivés à Versailles dans la journée du 6 octobre 1789* (Paris, 1790), i, 118.

54. Gouverneur Morris, *A Diary of the French Revolution* (Boston, 1939), i, 243. Bailly, *Mémoires de Bailly*, iii, 86. Morris thought the Parisians would be defeated.

55. Bailly, *Mémoires*, iii, 89.

56. Deposition #ccxxxvi, Anne-Marguerite Andelle, 11 May 1790 in *Procédure criminelle, instruite au Châtelet de Paris*, ii, 97.

57. Gorsas, *Extrait du Courrier de Versailles à Paris*, 12.

58. Deposition #ccxxxvi, Anne-Marguerite Andelle, 11 May 1790 in *Procédure criminelle, instruite au Châtelet de Paris*, ii, 97.

59. François-Marie-Périchou Kerverseau, *Histoire de la Révolution de 1789 et de l'établissement d'une constitution en France* (Paris, 1790), iii, 368–75.

60. Deposition #lxxxii, Jeanne Martin, garde malades, 5 Mar in *Procédure criminelle, instruite au Châtelet de Paris*, i, 133–6.

61. Gorsas, *Extrait du Courrier de Versailles*, 16.

62. Deposition #cxi, Pierre-Victor Malouet, 22 Mar. in *Procédure criminelle, instruite au Châtelet de Paris*, i, 170.

63. Jean-Joseph Mounier, *Exposé de la conduite de M. Mounier, dans l'Assemblée nationale et des motifs de son retour en Dauphiné* (Paris, 1789), 83.

64. Louis-Henri-Charles de Gauville, *Journal du baron de Gauville, député de l'ordre de la noblesse aux États généraux, depuis le 4 mars 1789 jusqu'au 1er juillet 1790* (Paris, 1864), 29.

65. Antoine de Rivarol, *Tableau historique et politique des travaux de l'Assemblée constituante, depuis l'ouverture des États-Généraux jusqu'après la journée du 6 octobre 1789* (Paris 1797), 363.

66. Rivarol, *Tableau historique et politique des travaux de l'Assemblée constituante*, 362.

67. See my *Murder in Aubagne: Lynching, Law, and Justice during the French Revolution* (Cambridge, 2009), 42, 97.

Selected Reading

Andress, David, *The French Revolution and the People* (London, 2004).

Doyle, William, *Origins of the French Revolution* (Oxford, 1980).

Fitzsimmons, Michael, *The Night the Old Regime Ended: August 4, 1789, and the French Revolution* (University Park, PA, 2003).

Godechot, Jacques, *The Taking of the Bastille, July 14th, 1789* (New York, 1970).

Godineau, Dominique, *The Women of Paris and their French Revolution* (Berkeley, 1998).

Hunt, Lynn A., *Revolution and Urban Politics in Provincial France: Troyes and Reims, 1786–1790* (Stanford, 1978).

Kaplan, Steven L., *The Famine Plot Persuasion in Eighteenth-Century France* (Philadelphia, 1982).

Lefebvre, Georges, *The Coming of the French Revolution, 1789* (Princeton, 1947).

Lefebvre, Georges. *The Great Fear of 1789; Rural Panic in Revolutionary France* (New York, 1973).

Rudé, George, *The Crowd in the French Revolution* (Oxford, 1959).

CHAPTER 17

·····················

RACE, SLAVERY, AND COLONIES IN THE FRENCH REVOLUTION

·····················

MANUEL COVO

For a very long time the colonies remained extremely marginal in the narrative of the French Revolution. Except for Jean Jaurès, almost all its great historians, from Alphonse Aulard to Albert Soboul, disregarded the colonial question. Even Jacques Godechot and Robert Palmer managed to skirt around it in formulating their Atlantic Revolution.[1] One of the reasons for this neglect had to do with the post-Seven Years War realities of the French colonial Empire, amputated of its continental space by the peace of 1763. At the time, it seemed that there were only a few remaining confetti of Empire: in the West Indies, in Guiana, in the Mascarene islands, in Senegal (Gorée), and on the coast of India. Between the loss of Canada and the conquest of Algeria in the 1830s, France seemed to have no empire of any significance. Therefore, what happened in the colonies appeared as peripheral consequences, generated by metropolitan turmoil.

Over the last twenty years or so the reversal has been total: the colonies slipped progressively from the periphery to the very centre of the revolutionary story. Few fields in the historiography of the French Revolution ever experienced such a swing. Looking beyond the so-called disappearance of the French Empire, we have started to acknowledge the economic importance of the wealthiest colony in the late eighteenth century, namely Saint-Domingue, and its political impact in what would become the Haitian Revolution. The question could no longer be eclipsed. Building on the once-isolated foundation of C. L. R. James's *Black Jacobins*, first published in 1938, authors such as Robin Blackburn and Yves Benot, and more recently Laurent Dubois, have drastically altered the revolutionary hierarchy of significance.[2] The colonial world was thenceforth seen as the frontier of citizenship and human rights, whose universality was put to the test. It has even been argued that the colonies were the matrix of the French Revolution: they defined it, for any Revolution was a 'war of independence'.[3]

Such a change in perspective allows for a full re-reading of the revolutionary narrative. But this major project has scarcely yet begun. It has been proven that the colonies did matter in the revolutionary course, but to what extent, in what field, and in what direction? The research in progress on the Haitian Revolution demonstrates the ambiguities of the abolitionist dynamic, which placed life-long government into the hands of general-in-chief Toussaint Louverture: should Haiti consequently appear as the paragon of republicanism?[4] In reality one must admit from the start the extraordinary complexity of the colonial revolution, which cannot be reduced to the sole matter of abolition. At times parallel stakes greatly complicated the motivations of the political actors. In fact the revolutions interrogated the whole colonial system: slavery, but also the slave trade, the rights of the free people of colour, the political autonomy of the colonies, and commercial legislation (the colonial *Exclusif*). More generally, the French Revolution questioned the compatibility of legal pluralism and political modernity. In other words, to redefine sovereignty, the colonial problem had to be addressed.

The other element of complexity lies in the diversity of situations during the revolutionary decade. In many respects, Saint-Domingue played the main part in a drama that entwined the fate of all the other colonies. However, the peculiarities proper to each and every colonial society as well as the proceedings of the maritime war led to a great variety of revolutionary situations. The Law of 16 Pluviôse II (4 February 1794) which abolished slavery after five years of struggle and hesitation in fact concerned only Guadeloupe and Guiana: Saint-Domingue had conquered its freedom by force, Martinique had been taken over by British armies, while the colonists of Île-de-France (Mauritius) simply refused to abide by the law. Likewise the restoration of slavery eventually decreed by Bonaparte on 20 May 1802 concerned some colonies only—Saint-Domingue being then on its way to independence. One must recall, however, that a number of actors circulated between various spaces and inter-connected the revolutionary issues: administrators, traders, lobbyists for white colonists, or for free people of colour. While one must bear in mind this global outlook, obviously my project here is not to engage in a detailed account of the revolutions in the colonies: I deal exclusively with the impact of the colonial question on the general course of the French Revolution, and more precisely on its early stages, when the interactions between metropole and colonies were still fluid, and notably before the Haitian Revolution took on the contours of a major upheaval in its own right.

The Colonies: Wealth and Enlightenment in Pre-Revolutionary France

The place that the colonies held in the French public sphere in the wake of the Seven Years War and until the beginning of the Revolution must not be underestimated. This interest was directly linked to a new geopolitical situation and the major economic boom of the Antilles. The French Crown preferred to give up Canada in 1763 rather than Guadeloupe and Martinique, whose sugar production was deemed essential to the prosperity of the metropole. The 1760s also marked the beginning of the peak of Saint-Domingue's productive wealth. Its sugar production ranked first worldwide, and that of coffee represented half of global trade. Outside the war years, the slave trade also flourished—so that in 1791, there were in Saint-Domingue over half a million slaves alongside a free population of only some 70,000, by far exceeding the numbers in its main West Indies rival, Jamaica. The French Antilles exported 125,000 tons of sugar in 1787, against only 107,000 tons for the British West Indies: metropolitan France imported ten times more coffee than Great Britain in the same period.[5] Moreover, the boom in the colonies greatly enriched the main ports of the kingdom: Nantes (the main slave-trade port) and Bordeaux (the main Caribbean trade port), but also Marseille and Le Havre, which experienced an unprecedented growth, plus a string of medium-sized ports from Bayonne to Dunkirk. This fed the opulence of great merchants, who would claim (unsuccessfully) in 1789 to have formed a new order distinct from the old 'Third Estate'.[6]

As regards the overall effect of this colonial trade on the national economy, historians diverge: Guillaume Daudin maintains that the colonies did fuel the economic engine, but Olivier Pétré-Grenouilleau states that their effects were limited to certain regions and that the colonies either hindered industrial investment or led to neglect of European trade.[7] Interestingly, this very debate was already current in the period addressed here. The relevance of colonial trade was the target of numerous controversial publications. Their main topic was the system of monopoly, called the *Exclusif*, violently contested after the loss of Canada and Louisiana.[8] Admittedly, smuggling had always got around this legislation and the relations between the West Indies and New England had also always been substantial, but this monopoly now seemed absurd, considering that the metropole was incapable of supplying its Caribbean islands properly. The major Physiocrats spoke out against the system of the colonial *Exclusif* in the Caribbean: François Quesnay, the marquis de Mirabeau, Pierre-Samuel Dupont de Nemours, and André Morellet all rejected such systems, which also embraced the privileges of the French East India Company in Asia.[9]

During the American Revolution, the publication and translation of Adam Smith's *Wealth of Nations* strengthened the liberal argumentation used by the colonists to support their cause. But in their turn the chambers of commerce of the kingdom brandished the writings of François Duverger Véron de Forbonnais, the author of the article 'Colony' in the *Encyclopédie*, Montesquieu's *Esprit des Lois*, and the success of the parallel British practice of Navigation Acts to justify the upholding of this regime. A torrent of publications flooded the public sphere in the 1760s, then again after American independence, when Franco-American alliance wavered over adamant American demands for access to the French markets in the Caribbean. A compromise was eventually adopted by the Secretary of State for the Navy and the Colonies, on 30 August 1784, the *Exclusif mitigé,* which allowed trade in some goods and prohibited others. This was only a provisional conclusion to a colonial debate whose stakes continued to increase.

The whole colonial system and its political implications for the metropole were gradually being subjected to the tribunal of public opinion.

The debate was not limited to the sole question of commercial legislation but also dealt with the sciences. This period was the golden age of the French colonial Enlightenment—which was attested in particular by the *Cercle des Philadelphes* created in Saint-Domingue's largest city Cap-Français in 1784, which became a major site of research in the Atlantic world.[10] On a political level, the issue of self-government, already brought up in 1768 by an uprising of Saint-Domingue's whites against ministerial despotism, was raised again by the revolt of the Thirteen Colonies.[11] Many pamphleteers seized on the American Revolution to claim new rights for the colonies. The most important among them, Michel René Hilliard d'Auberteuil, suggested numerous measures of great scope dealing with many fields, from public transportation to the reform of slavery and the rights of the free people of colour.[12] Even though it had been commissioned by the Secretary of State of the Navy, Hilliard d'Auberteuil's *Considérations sur la Colonie de Saint-Domingue* was censored in 1777, which nonetheless earned it publicity through notoriety. His audience was however somewhat eclipsed by the triumph of Raynal's *Histoire des deux Indes*, the equivalent of a colonial encyclopedia: it was the fifth best-seller of this whole period.[13]

From 1770 to 1780, this massive work, narrating the colonial expansion of Europe worldwide, appeared in three different editions (and was to be republished forty-four times before 1789), using some ten different authors. Each edition conveyed a more radical and committed aim. In Diderot's contributions in particular emerged the figure of a black Spartacus arising to avenge all the Africans reduced into slavery in the Americas. This image, already evoked by Sébastien Mercier in his novel *L'An 2440* (1770), was used to suggest the urgency of speeding up reforms which could prevent such an imminent general insurrection. In the American revolutionary context, the criticism of the colonial system was mixed with a denunciation of monarchical absolutism and a reflection on modern republicanism whose genesis in the United States caught the attention of the great names of the time—Turgot, Dupont de Nemours, Condorcet. In other words, the colonial field was clearly at the heart of public debate in pre-revolutionary France.

FREEDOM, SLAVERY, AND THE RACE ISSUE IN THE 1780S

One topic became predominant in these years: the rights of the free people of colour. They were emancipated slaves or descendants of emancipated slaves who had been enduring ever more severe discriminations in the colonies. Yet their number was also growing: almost 30,000 in 1789, they were about to catch up with the free whites in terms of demography, and above all to challenge the economic supremacy of the latter. Many of them were indeed planters whose fortune was often much greater than that of many poorer *petits blancs*: owners of coffee or indigo (rather than sugar) plantations, many were even slave owners.[14] According to the 1685 Black Code the only statutorily admitted distinction was between free and non-free. However, discriminatory measures had been adopted by the courts in the Antilles and multiplied after the Seven Years War: sumptuary laws reserved some clothing for whites alone, and banned others from carrying swords; other local decrees excluded them from some professions. This legislation, although unevenly enforced, produced a growing legal precariousness, but was justified in theory by 'colour prejudice' (*préjugé de couleur*).[15] Prejudice was conceived as a tool of colonial governance: degrading those derogatorily called 'mulattoes' was meant to force the slaves to interiorize the natural inferiority of coloured men. Julien Raimond, a man of mixed-race ancestry born in Aquitaine, and a planter in the southern part of Saint-Domingue, became the main spokesperson of the rights of the free coloured and found benevolent ears among the successive secretaries of state for the navy, despite fears that white inhabitants would resist any reform.

The claims of the free people of colour question the reality of the 'racialization' of French society in this period. This topic is still very controversial among historians. First, there is an important distinction between the situation in the colonies and that of the metropole. The legal incapacities mentioned did not concern the free coloured in Europe. The monarchy worked to enforce the rule that French soil was free, so that colonies and metropole were clearly distinguished—at least in theory, because planters obtained derogations to bring their 'domestic slaves' to France with them. However, as Pierre Boulle maintains, the law of 1777 on the *Police des Noirs* aimed at limiting considerably the entry of Blacks into metropolitan France: this was legally based more on colour than on status.[16] For all that, concluding that policy was definitively racialized may seem excessive in so far as challenging 'monogenism' was much more an exception than the rule. The philosophers from Montesquieu to Diderot did not cease repeating the unity of the human species, and even the most respected scientists such as George-Louis Leclerc de Buffon thought about degeneration only in terms of climate, not of race.[17] The authors condoning slavery such as Malouet did not do so in a polygenistic perspective but resorted to climatic theories and even in some cases to natural law theory.[18] It is not even clear whether Louis Médéric Moreau de Saint-Méry, a member of the *Cercle des Philadelphes*, who proposed a sophisticated hierarchy of interbreeding, believed in the plurality of races.[19] The prejudice of colour, very much a political question, could also be a component of the aristocratic reaction that marked the 1780s in France.

Moreover, the slavery issue proved to be an essential catalyst in the process of defining political elites' identities in revolutionary France. As such the creation of the Society of the Friends of the Blacks was essential. Founded by Jacques-Pierre Brissot and Etienne Clavière in February 1788, it followed the short-lived *société gallo-américaine*. The journalist Brissot had developed a passion for the cause of the United States, where he travelled, following many literary men of his time.[20] Fascinated by the Quakers, he was aware of the Pennsylvania abolitionist movement and wanted to emulate the London Committee for the Abolition of the Slave Trade that had just been created by Thomas Clarkson and Granville Sharpe. The Friends of the Blacks belonged to a general elitist and philanthropic movement but offered more specifically to link a theoretical reflection with an international activism.

As an heir of physiocracy and the Scottish Enlightenment the society did not embrace purely abstract ethical objectives. Its goal was to modernize the economy of the kingdom, and even some great planters such as Charles de Lameth were present at the first sessions of the Society. Slavery was denounced because it was inhuman but also because it was a kind of labour that was deemed less profitable than the wage system. The goals of this society first aimed at being realistic. The abolition of slavery should be introduced gradually so as to prepare both masters and slaves for a peaceable post-slavery society: the former had to make an economic conversion, the latter had to learn how best to use their freedom. The urgent task, however, was to abolish the slave trade internationally, in coordination with the London committee and the US manumission societies. The Friends of the Blacks did not matter only for their abolitionist programme but more generally for their role in the political apprenticeship and networking of men who would lead the patriotic movement of the first revolutionary Assemblies: Honoré-Gabriel Riqueti de Mirabeau, Gilbert du Motier de Lafayette, Nicolas de Condorcet, Jérôme Pétion de Villeneuve among others. They wove links which later proved crucial even if they did not prevent further far-reaching break-ups.[21]

The Estates-General Under the Pressure of Colonial Lobbies

All these colonial agendas were completely entangled: they took a new political consistency when the Estates-General convened. The white colonists took the initiative and tried to pull the rug from under the feet of the Friends of the Blacks. The main planters first wanted to have the right to be represented, which the monarchy had refused previously. A minority of white colonial inhabitants had gathered secretly to organize elections and appoint spokesmen who sought to take part in the sittings. A colonial committee, composed of absentee planters and upper-class aristocrats, most of whom were based in Paris, was formed to that intent in 1788. The very rich and equally indebted marquis de Gouy d'Arsy, who had never set foot in Saint-Domingue, became the spearhead of this lobby. In the *cahiers de doléances* that they were bringing with them, colonial delegates contested ministerial despotism, the suppression of the main judicial court in Cap-Français, the intervention of officers into the regulation of slavery—which to their eyes should remain in the sole hands of the planters—the over-lenient attitude towards the free people of colour, and the upholding of the *Exclusif*.[22] Likewise, the chambers of commerce dispatched extraordinary delegates in order to lend a hand to the ordinary deputies of the ports, which the great merchants deemed under-represented considering the economic impact of the Atlantic trade on France as a whole. The chambers feared both the deputies of the colonists who threatened France's colonial trade in protesting against the *Exclusif*, and also the Friends of the Blacks who were adamant in calling for a halt to the slave trade.[23] Representatives of the free people of colour, led by Julien Raymond, were also trying to make themselves heard. They all published pamphlets and articles, adding a colonial cacophony to the metropolitan one. The claims supported by these various actors went far beyond their private interests: the future of the whole French nation was at stake, considering that real French sovereignty resided in its commercial power. Relentlessly repeating that six million French people relied on the colonies to survive, they made the colonial cause a national one.

The insistence of the colonists in participating in the Estates-General led to a series of chain reactions that proved decisive for the French Revolution. Some of them succeeded in June 1789 in taking the Tennis Court Oath. They argued that their patriotism pleaded in favour of their official admission. This debate started in late June, and ran on: the colonists were confronted with the combined resistance of the deputies of the ports and the Friends of the Blacks. This debate clearly brought to mind the one in Philadelphia in 1787, where the future US Constitution pivoted around the respective weights of the Southern and the Northern states. The colonial committee maintained that Saint-Domingue should be entitled to twenty-one deputies, on account of its demography and its economic power. Mirabeau reminded them that they represented only the white colonists: 'If the colonists want the Negroes and free people of colour to be men, they must let the former free; let them all vote, let them all be elected. Otherwise we shall pray them observe that in apportioning the number of deputies to the population of France, we have not taken into consideration the quantity either of our horses or mules; that thus the pretence of the colonies to have twenty representatives is absolutely ridiculous.'[24] The debate engaged a great number of deputies but finally the Assembly admitted six representatives, who were joined in the autumn by two deputies from Martinique and two others from Guadeloupe. This first great national debate had from the start asked the question of the nature of the link between metropole and colony. For various reasons the deputies hesitated to admit the political rights of the colonies: should these territories be regarded as overseas provinces or as properties of the kingdom? It was also envisaged that more rights should be granted to local colonial Assemblies, already existing in Martinique and Guadeloupe. Could the nation be one while an institution such as slavery existed in the colonies?

THE CONSTITUENT ASSEMBLY AND LEGAL PLURALISM

In the summer of 1789, when the parliamentary debate opened on the drafting of a Declaration of the Rights of Man and the Citizen, the contradictions within the colonial system appeared more and more obvious. On 4 August, Gouy d'Arsy had barely succeeded in keeping the emancipation of the slaves out of that night's 'abolition of privilege'. Great metropolitan merchants such as Stanislas Foäche, and major absentee planters, such as the marquis de Gallifet, deemed that organization was needed to channel the seismic effect of the Declaration. At the Hôtel Massiac, amid the *Société des Colons*, established on 20 August 1789, the colonial leadership worked to coordinate a response from all the parties anxious to defend the colonial system. In particular, the main leaders tried to get colonists and traders to bury the hatchet of their mutual antagonism so as to defend the essentials of their economic life. Meanwhile, as far as possible, revolutionary politics had to be persuaded to 'forget' the colonies and make sure that the Declaration was valid solely in the metropole. Thus the 'Club Massiac' endeavoured to coordinate with the Ministry of the Navy to prevent correspondence and subversive news from reaching the colonies.[25]

These aims were all the more difficult to enforce as neither the deputies from the colonies nor the representatives of the Chambers of Commerce were keen on disowning the mandate they had been entrusted with. In fact one and all came to break the strategy of silence in stigmatizing one another as *aristocrates*. This divide was layered on another between white slave-owners and free coloured slave-owners. Vincent Ogé, a free 'mulatto' of Saint-Domingue who appealed to the Club Massiac in September 1789 had hoped for a reconciliation, but the icy welcome he received made him understand that the free people of colour had nothing to expect from them. In fact this breach was at the heart of all the fluctuations of the Constituent Assembly regarding the colonies.

But it is crucial to emphasize at the outset that the colonial question was never 'forgotten' in the debates of the Constituent Assembly, or in successive revolutionary Assemblies. The subject was actually decisive in shaping the newly emergent political identities of 'parties'. This process of definition was not clear initially and resists any simple equation between revolutionary abolitionists and counter-revolutionary pro-slavery advocates. This ambiguity emerged when it was proposed to establish a Committee of Colonies in the National Assembly, at the request of members of the colonies themselves. The Club Massiac was firmly opposed because the Assembly was simply not to legislate for the colonies. Conversely, the Friends of the Blacks feared that such a committee would be a planters' and merchants' tool, as the colonists had already managed to thwart Gregoire's efforts to admit the free people of colour to the Assembly. It was the news of unrest in Martinique that forced the Assembly to clarify its position on the subject, especially as the white colonists of Saint-Domingue had also risen up and expelled the royal *intendant* in October 1789.

This was a constant during the decade: the Assembly almost never took the initiative but it reacted to events in the colonies, even though information from the Atlantic was always late and uncertain. The risks presented by the revolutionary context justified the creation of a Colonial Committee on 2 March 1790. Ironically, Brissot in the *Patriote français* was delighted at Antoine Barnave's designation among the members: in the journalist's view, the man who thought that the Declaration of Rights was to become the 'national catechism' might oppose the planters and traders of the Committee.[26] Mirabeau had just delivered a resounding speech against the slave trade at the Jacobin Club.[27] But on 8 March, when Barnave presented his report on colonial legislation, all the Friends of the Blacks' hopes were nullified. It was indeed announced that the constitution of the metropole would not apply in the colonies and that the slave trade would be maintained with 'no innovation'. The national interest of trade required the preservation of a system that was at the core of French power, and thus of its regeneration. The Committee managed to pass the law without discussion, despite Gregoire's attempts to speak out. The 'patriot' Barnave appeared now as the instrument of the Chambers of Commerce and broke the unity of the revolutionaries, leading Brissot outside the Assembly to launch multiple pamphlet attacks against this 'Janus'.

The Colonial Committee and Club Massiac would have liked to bury the issue for good, but the successive revolts in the colonies and the unresolved question of free people of colour never ceased to return to the foreground. The autonomist insurgency of the Saint-Marc colonial Assembly in Saint-Domingue in spring 1790 and near civil war between ports and countryside in Martinique—both extremely complex revolts—sought resolution from the National Assembly. Uncertainty about the status of active citizenship for the free people of colour constituted the main point of cleavage, as the 28 March 1790 instructions on the topic were intentionally vague. The colonies had won the right to prepare specific constitutions that were different from that of the metropole. For this purpose, colonial Assemblies were expected to convene, but a majority of white colonists rejected free people of colour's participation even when they met the fiscal conditions of active citizenship. Worse, on 12 October 1790, by concerted manoeuvre between the Colonial Committee and Club Massiac, the Assembly adopted the principle that only the colonial Assemblies had the right of initiative on all legislation concerning the status of persons in their territory. This was to reassure colonists and prevent them from calling for a British intervention. By placing colonists' properties under the protection of the nation, the Assembly made the gradual abolition envisaged by the Friends of the Blacks very unlikely.

Because of this blockage, Vincent Ogé and Jean-Baptiste Chavannes at the head of a small and poorly organized force took up arms on behalf of the free people of colour in Saint Domingue in October 1790. Easily defeated, they fled to the Spanish part of the island, but were soon extradited by local authorities. Ogé and Chavannes suffered gruesome punishment in February 1791: they were broken on the wheel at the demand of uncompromising white colonists. The brutality of the repression caused a huge stir in France and provoked two great debates at the National Assembly in May and September 1791. The issue was one of the decisive factors in the split of the Jacobins during that summer. On 15 May 1791 a compromise text had granted the rights of active citizenship to free people of colour whose father and mother were free—a clause which appeared as the first victory for the Friends of the Blacks, although it was very limited in scope and did not address the issue of slavery at all. Two days earlier, Moreau de Saint-Méry had driven through a constitutional law in which the National Assembly renounced all claim to legislate on 'non-free persons' without the colonies' initiative. Nevertheless, the most uncompromising white planters, believing that the National Assembly had gone too far in favour of free people of colour, themselves took up arms in the summer—creating a climate of civil war in the Antilles. On 28 September 1791, the Constituent Assembly, still unaware of the beginning of a general uprising in Saint-Domingue, abrogated the law of 15 May 1791.

These debates embraced a discourse denouncing miscegenation and degeneration of French blood, which was said to be threatened with impurity. Grégoire had the courage to praise the racial crosses that, in his view, created the superiority of Americans over Europeans.[28] By excluding Barnave and the Lameth brothers from the Jacobin Club after this debate, the Society of Friends of the Constitution helped to clarify positions: one could not pretend to be a 'patriot' while calling for legal discrimination based on colour differences.[29] In individual trajectories too, the colonial issue proved to be central; several political heavyweights of the Revolution defined themselves in the process: Brissot of course, but also Grégoire and Pétion, and on the opposite side, Malouet and Barnave. While he was not part of the Friends of the Blacks, Robespierre nevertheless became the bane of white planters. Echoing a phrase from Dupont de Nemours and refusing to allow the word 'slave' to appear in the constitution, he exclaimed on 13 May 1791: 'Perish the colonies!' Therefore Robespierre embodied revolutionary extremism in the eyes of the colonists, even though his abolitionism did not exclude some moderation in the detail of his proposals.[30]

ABOLITIONISTS CONFRONTING GENERAL INSURRECTION

The Legislative Assembly that met from October 1791 had to face the general insurrection of slaves in the northern plain of Saint-Domingue. Started during the night of 22–3 August 1791, news of it only reached metropolitan France in late October. Friends of the Blacks, now numerous in the Assembly, then found themselves in a particularly difficult position because they were accused of being responsible for the insurrection. The colonists also questioned their patriotism, denouncing the *philanthropes'* collaboration with the London abolitionist society and calling them *négrophiles*. At first Brissot replied by denying the reality of the revolt, then he accused royalist counter-revolutionaries of manipulating slaves and imputed the upsurge of violence to discriminatory legislation against free people of colour. The Friends of the Blacks had to accept that the insurgency negated their gradual abolition projects. The restoration of calm therefore became their priority: to suppress insurrections, definitively ensure the rights of free people of colour and repeal recent measures taken by the Constituent Assembly. In particular, they took up the cause for the ratification of the *concordats* that had been concluded between some white planter royalists and free people of colour in the west of Saint-Domingue, although these initiatives had been in conflict with laws passed by the Constituent Assembly.[31]

The parliamentary battle against the newly emerged Feuillant party, headed by Vincent-Marie Viénot Vaublanc, both a creole and a great planter in Saint-Domingue, was as crucial in defining the political line of the Jacobins as the policy of repression against *émigrés* and refractory priests. In particular, a group that would form the embryo of the Gironde and that coalesced behind Brissot stood out. Those members who came from the Bordeaux region—Elie Guadet, Armand Gensonné, Pierre Vergniaud—became the first defenders of free people of colour. Most had been on the fringes of the Bordeaux trade with the colonies, but in favour of reform and willing to pacify relations between whites and free-coloured planters in order to enhance the grip of the owners. Hence the ambiguities of the period: for some, recognition of the rights of free people of colour was a prerequisite to future abolition, for others, it was primarily to restore order. The challenge was therefore more political than ideological: in Clavière's view, the goal was to separate the planters from merchants by proving that the Jacobins' policy was the best solution economically—despite the fierce resistance of the Club Massiac.[32]

In spring 1792, the Jacobins slowly gained ground and managed to give the free people of colour full citizenship in the law of 4 April 1792. This finally removed any legal discrimination based on colour. It also rescinded the right of colonial Assemblies to define the status of inhabitants. To implement this decision, it was decreed that a civilian commission would be appointed with emergency powers—powers that suspended the law and common institutions. On this point, the innovative nature of such a move has probably not been sufficiently emphasized in the historiography: the colonies were a laboratory.[33] In November 1790 Barnave had arranged to send a civilian commission to restore order in Martinique; a first civilian commission had also been sent to Saint-Domingue in late 1791, but with limited powers which made it helpless on the ground. In 1792, the National Assembly delegated extraordinary powers to the commission, foreshadowing those of future *Représentants en mission*. This already manifested the desire to ensure the superiority of the civil power and the influence of the legislative body, which then had no confidence in the officers of the Ministry of the Navy. The main difference with the policy of the future Republic lay in the fact that the commissioners were not themselves members of the Assembly.

REPUBLICAN, FRENCH, OR HAITIAN REVOLUTIONS?

The spatio-temporal distance between the colonies and the metropole also contributed to the specificity of the truly revolutionary nature of the commission. With an army of 6,000 men, Etienne Polverel, Léger-Félicité Sonthonax, and Jacques-Louis Ailhaud left France while it was subject to a constitutional monarchy; when they landed in Saint-Domingue, France had become a republic. Sonthonax and Polverel, although quickly abandoned by Ailhaud, were Jacobins already well-known for their anti-slavery ideas, and gained growing powers in the course of their mission. The commission was to apply the law of 4 April 1792, crush insurrections and form a new mixed-race colonial assembly which was to be designated by an electoral body of active citizens including free people of colour. The British entry into the war in February 1793 changed the situation completely, so that Sonthonax and Polverel had to supervise the entire war effort to ensure the territorial integrity of the Republic.

Domestically, they were faced with a multitude of local conflicts and insurgencies that demonstrated a wide variety of situations. They had to recognize their partial impotence and deal with the fact of self-liberated slave power. At the same time they aroused the extreme hostility of white colonists fearing the formal abolition of slavery. When the arrival of a new governor led to a great battle between sailors and free people of colour, new complexities of conflict were unleashed. This spurred the intervention of slave armies, caused the destruction of Cap-Français, drove the departure of thousands of white colonists, and precipitated the abolition of slavery by Sonthonax on 29 August 1793. This was followed by partial invasion of the colony by the British and the Spanish. This change was partly unpredictable: it showed that, concerning the colonies, the main stage of the Revolution had definitely moved from the metropole to the West Indies and to Saint-Domingue in particular.[34]

Indeed, the National Convention in Paris, subject to all kinds of rumours, only imperfectly understood the events taking place in the Antilles. The fall of the monarchy truly sounded the death knell of the Club Massiac, most of whose members had emigrated in September 1792 to serve the cause of counter-revolution. In London, in particular, the former representative of Guadeloupe at the National Assembly, Louis De Curt, and Malouet negotiated with the authorities a British 'sequestration' of the French colonies in February 1793—which was the prelude to the invasion. But instead of the Massiac group, new planter lobbyists who posed as Republican patriots, Pierre-François Page and Augustin-Jean Brulley, exerted a very considerable influence on the Convention. They had the ear of some members of the Committee of the Navy and of the Committee of Public Safety—especially through André Jeanbon Saint-André. They played the anti-Girondin card to fight the Friends of the Blacks and took advantage of the confrontation with the Montagnards in spring 1793. Julien Raimond, now converted to the abolitionist cause, saw his prestige decline because of his links with the Girondins.

The latter's elimination on 31 May–2 June further strengthened Page and Brulley's position, so that Louis Antoine Saint-Just even asked them to help him prepare a report on the colonies—which was never released. Given the French military situation in 1793, it seems that a number of Montagnards were willing to tolerate slavery—at least temporarily—to prevent full-scale invasion of the colonies. In fact, it is almost impossible to define exactly what could be Montagnard policy for the colonies. Article 18 of the 1793 Declaration of Rights stipulated that no man 'could sell or be sold', that he was not 'alienable property'. On 4 June 1793, the mayor of Paris, Anaxagoras Chaumette, brought a sans-culottes petition to the Convention calling for the abolition of slavery; a black woman, Jeanne Odo, supposedly aged 114 years, also paraded in favour of the 'equality of the epidermis'. Still concrete measures did not come. Misunderstandings reached their climax when Robespierre adopted the lobbyists' discourse, accusing the French ambassador to the United States, Charles-Edmond Genêt, of participating in the 'general subversion of the colonies' by arming slaves.[35] The great division of Montagnards on the subject and the game played by the different committees, in which key members were linked to Page and Brulley, contributed to the wait-and-see policy.

Once again, the end to the deadlock came from the colonies: it was the arrival of the Saint-Domingue tricolor deputation that accelerated the revolutionary process in France. The white Pierre-Louis Dufay, the mulatto Jean-Baptiste Mills, and the blac Jean-Baptiste Belley surmounted many attempts by the colonists to thwart their mission in the Caribbean, in the United States, and in France—including arrest by the Committee of General Security after their arrival in January 1794. Their release and admission to the Convention was followed by the great meeting of 4 February (16 Pluviôse II) when Dufay, Georges Jacques Danton, and Jacques-François Delacroix gave important speeches. The decree abolishing slavery was passed by the Convention, both for ethical and for practical and military reasons. Many abolitionists, like Grégoire, regretted that the gradual path had not been adopted, but they also thought that the situation as it was should be acknowledged. This was made possible by the stabilization of the Republican position with black general Toussaint Louverture's volte-face in favour of France in May 1794 and with the re-conquest of Guadeloupe by Commissioner Victor Hugues.

Page, Brulley, and many colonists residing in Paris were imprisoned, but the same happened to Sonthonax and Polverel on their return. A special commission was appointed by the Convention to clarify what really happened in the colonies. Rumours and radical uncertainty had indeed played a key role throughout the revolutionary crisis: it would be wrong to attribute to ideology that which derived from imperfect or untrustworthy information. This especially had reinforced the influence of the 'experts'. In fact, the Convention could not prevent the representative from Île-de-France (Mauritius), Benoît Gouly, from doing his best to sabotage the decree of abolition.[36]

Did the abolition decree mark the victory of universal human rights in the French Empire? In Saint Domingue as in Guadeloupe, the extreme realities of the Caribbean war imposed exceptions. Nonetheless, while new citizens were deprived of regular elections and subject to extra-constitutional government institutions, they were no longer chattels, they received wages and could not be legally tortured by whips. This was not the case in Île-de-France, where the delegates of the Republic who were to enforce the decree of abolition, René Gaston Laurent Baco La Chapelle and Pierre Etienne Burnel, were expelled by force by the colonists. Indeed, white planters in the Mascarene islands had agreed to ally with free people of colour in order to preserve slavery and the economy. However, one should not underestimate the Republicans' commitment to extend citizens' rights to overseas territories.

The Constitution of the Year III declared the colonies integral parts of the Republic, which opened the way to press for institutional assimilation. Again the colonial issue was one of the major sites of clashes in the legislative councils. The so-called moderate and royalist *clichyiens* Viénot-Vaublanc and Matthieu Dumas, who were first and foremost colonists, did their best to counter Republican reforms.[37] Their programme provisionally failed thanks to the coup of 18 Fructidor V (4 September 1797). In this respect, the 4 Brumaire year VI departmentalization law (25 October 1797) and the colonial constitution of 12 Nivôse year VI (1 January 1798) were thought to root the principle of equal citizenship and Republican isonomy. Two incoming members of the colonies played a major role in the issue: former Governor of Saint-Domingue and staunch neo-Jacobin, Etienne Laveaux, and Sonthonax himself returning from the colony. To view the Directory as uniformly reactionary is a mistake.

As such, the real backlash duly occurred after the coup of 18 Brumaire VIII (9 November 1799), after which the constitution of the year VIII reinstated 'special laws for the colonies', making the restoration of slavery by Bonaparte possible. During this period, revolution continued, but in Saint-Domingue in what became itself the Haitian Revolution, clashing with a French colonial counter-revolution in 1802.

CONCLUSION: THE COLONIAL ISSUE, THE NEW HISTORIOGRAPHICAL FRONTIER OF CITIZENSHIP

The narrative here is primarily concerned with political elites, but we may wonder to what extent the colonial question engaged with a popular revolution in metropolitan France. It is often assumed that the British abolitionist movement achieved a much wider social mobilization than French revolutionary abolitionism. This opposition does not only deserve qualifications, but also calls for more research. Evidence for some sensitivity to colonial issues has not yet been seriously investigated except for the *cahiers de doléances* and congratulatory addresses of clubs about the 16 Pluviôse II decree. Only thirty-two *cahiers* confronted the problem of slavery, even though Condorcet had tried to publicize abolitionist proposals to the various *bailliage* Assemblies. However, some *cahiers*, including the one written by the Third Estate of Amiens, fiercely denounced the slave trade. Others, particularly in the major seaports, intentionally avoided the subject, suggesting fear of public attention.[38] Thanks to Jean-Claude Halpern's research, it is also known that 356 addresses, including 285 from popular societies, congratulated the Montagne for abolishing slavery between 19 Pluviôse and 5 Thermidor II. This figure is not necessarily particularly significant, however, as there was a continuous flow of conformist congratulatory petitions from the provinces in this period.[39]

In addition, we would like to know more about the treatment of the colonial revolution by the press. The Parisian press has already been examined to some extent. Some papers devoted many pages to the issue: Brissot's *Patriote français* or *Les Révolutions de Paris* in which Sonthonax published numerous articles, but even mainstream journals such as the *Journal de Paris* or the *Moniteur*. Similarly, there were specialized journals on the topic during the Revolution: Claude Milscent's *Créole Patriote* in 1792–93 or Bottut's *Républicain des colonies*, which was subsidized in 1796 by the Minister of

Marine, Laurent Truguet. In the pro-slavery camp, there was the daily *Journal historique et politique de la Marine* between 1795 and 1797. How was this press received by readers and did it reach an audience that went beyond the already committed? More attention is also needed to the provincial press, especially in the major ports where the treatment of colonial issues was most likely different. A more quantitative and more general approach would thus test whether a racialization of discourse spread beyond the propaganda of the Club Massiac.

Finally, it would be good to intertwine economic, financial, and political stakes through a colonial angle in general narratives of the Revolution. In a way this would hardly be new, as Albert Mathiez almost a century ago opened his work on the *vie chère* by evoking the sugar revolts that rocked Paris and Dunkirk in January–February 1792.[40] These patterns of consumption, through politicization, suggest other kinds of links to the colonies and call for an ambitious investigation. Reinvestment of colonial wealth in the real estate market or reassessment of the colonial debt will shed new light on the way colonies impacted on revolutionary France.[41] Beyond the legal understanding of the colonial sphere or the common metaphorical use of words like 'race' and 'slavery', we need to investigate what colonies meant for ordinary French people or for institutions in different regions and at different times.

The *affaire des colonies* was completely entangled with French Revolutionary dynamics. In this respect historians should not take for granted the colonial specificity that some political actors of the time intentionally constructed so as to justify legal pluralism and constitutional dualism. The colonies sometimes had been the laboratory of broader revolutionary issues, especially regarding political economy, law, institutions, and sovereignty. As we have seen with the Club Massiac, colonial actors could also be pioneers of counter-revolution. A better awareness of this interlacing implies that the debate around the very meaning of freedom, equality, and property cannot be understood without taking the colonies into consideration. But the colonial issue also illuminates how the circulation of information mattered: this greatly contributed to the ambiguities of the political actors and was in many ways more essential than so-called ideological orientations. To some extent, the metropole–colony relationship can be seen as a caricature of Paris–province links. This calls for a rethinking of the geography and chronology of revolutions beneath and beyond the imperial line, as the colonial issue always surpassed national boundaries.

This was part and parcel of Atlantic revolutions and of the waves of reforms that crossed all empires in the second half of the eighteenth century. The redefinition of the metropole–colony relationship—which happened not only in a French context, but in a much more global framework—created many tensions that had to do with the strengthening of central states and a correlated emergence of new conceptions of citizenship. One major reason why the colonies played a central role in revolutionary politics is that the objective of international competition had definitely moved from territorial conquest to capturing markets in a globalized world. In this respect, colonies were crucial as they defined the scope of political community and the role of economics in newer assertions of modern sovereignty.

NOTES

1. A good overview on the historiography can be found in Alyssa Goldstein-Sepinwall, 'The Specter of Saint-Domingue: American and French Reactions to the Haitian Revolution', in David Patrick Geggus and Norman Fiering (eds), *The World of the Haitian Revolution* (Bloomington, 2009), 317–38.

2. Robin Blackburn, *The Overthrow of Colonial Slavery, 1776–1848* (London, 1988); Yves Benot, *La Révolution française et la fin des colonies* (Paris, 1988); Laurent Dubois, *Avengers of the New World: the Story of the Haitian Revolution* (Cambridge, 2004).

3. Pierre Serna, 'Every Revolution is a War of Independence', in Suzanne Desan, Lynn Hunt, and William Max Nelson (eds), *The French Revolution in Global Perspective* (Ithaca, 2013), 165–82.

4. For a critique of such an interpretation, see David Patrick Geggus, 'The Caribbean in the Age of Revolution', in David Armitage and Sanjay Subrahmanyam (eds), *The Age of Revolutions in Global Context, c.1760–1840* (Basingstoke, 2010), 83–100.

5. François Crouzet, *La guerre économique franco-anglaise au XVIIIe Siècle* (Paris, 2008), 106–14.

6. Paul Cheney, *Revolutionary Commerce: Globalization and the French Monarchy* (Cambridge, 2010), esp. 168–94.

7. Olivier Pétré-Grenouilleau, *L'argent de la traite: milieu négrier, capitalisme et développement: un modèle* (Paris, 2009); Guillaume Daudin, *Commerce et prospérité: la France au XVIIIe siècle* (Paris, 2011).

8. The classic study on the topic remains Jean Tarrade, *Le commerce colonial de la France à la fin de l'Ancien Régime: l'évolution du régime de l'exclusif de 1763 à 1789* (Paris, 1972).

9. Pernille Røge, 'A Natural Order of Empire: The Physiocratic Vision of Colonial France after the Seven Years' War', in Sophus A. Reinert and Pernille Røge (eds), *The Political Economy of Empire in the Early Modern World* (Basingstoke, 2013), 32–52.

10. For a broader overview on French colonial sciences, see James Edward McClellan and François Regourd, *The Colonial Machine: French Science and Overseas Expansion in the Old Regime* (Turnhout, 2011).

11. Charles Frostin, *Les révoltes blanches à Saint-Domingue aux XVIIe et XVIIIe siècles: Haïti avant 1789*, (Rennes, 2008), 181–209.

12. Gene E. Ogle, 'The Eternal Power of Reason and The Superiority of Whites: Hilliard d'Auberteuil's Colonial Enlightenment', *French Colonial History* 3 (2003), 35–50.

13. Robert Darnton, *The Forbidden Best-Sellers of Pre-Revolutionary France* (New York, 1995), 65–6.

14. There have been several socio-economic studies of this group: Stewart R. King, *Blue Coat or Powdered Wig: Free People of Color in Pre-Revolutionary Saint Domingue* (Athens, 2001); John D. Garrigus, *Before Haiti: Race and Citizenship in French Saint-Domingue* (New York, 2006).

15. There was an important difference between actual social practices that were more lenient and stricter legal texts. This can be contrasted through Florence Gauthier, *L'aristocratie de l'épiderme: le combat de la Société des citoyens de couleur, 1789–1791* (Paris, 2007); Dominique Rogers, 'On the Road to Citizenship: The Complex Route to Integration of the Free People of Color in the Two Capitals of Saint-Domingue', in Geggus and Fiering (eds), *World of the Haitian Revolution*, 65–78.

16. Pierre Henri Boulle, *Race et esclavage dans la France de l'Ancien régime* (Paris, 2007). For another interpretation, see Sue Peabody, *'There Are No Slaves in France': The Political Culture of Race and Slavery in the Ancien Régime* (New York, 1996).

17. Andrew S. Curran, *The Anatomy of Blackness: Science & Slavery in an Age of Enlightenment* (Baltimore, 2011).

18. Jean-Yves Grenier, 'Faut-il rétablir l'esclavage en France?', *Revue d'histoire moderne et contemporaine*, 57 (2010), 7–49.

19. On the complexity of his thinking, see: Dominique Taffin (ed.), *Moreau de Saint-Méry ou Les ambiguïtés d'un créole des Lumières: actes du colloque, 10–11 septembre 2004* (Fort-de-France, 2006).

20. On Brissot and Clavière's *américanophilie*, see Étienne Clavière and Jacques-Pierre Brissot de Warville, *De la France et des États-Unis: ou de l'Importance de la révolution de l'Amérique pour le bonheur de la France, des rapports de ce royaume et des États-Unis, des avantages réciproques qu'ils peuvent retirer de leurs liaisons de commerce* (London, 1787).

21. For a comprehensive analysis of the history of the society, see Marcel Dorigny and Bernard Gainot, *La Société des amis des Noirs, 1788–1799* (Paris, 1998).

22. Prosper Boissonnade, *Saint-Domingue à la veille de la révolution et la question de la représentation coloniale aux États généraux (janvier 1788–7 juillet 1789)* (Paris, 1906).

23. Joseph Letaconnoux, *Le Comité des députés extraordinaires des manufactures et du commerce de France et l'œuvre économique de l'Assemblée constituante, 1789–1791* (Paris, 1913). See also Lauren R. Clay, 'The Bourgeoisie, Capitalism, and the Origins of the French Revolution', in the present volume.

24. Blanche Maurel, *Saint-Domingue et la Révolution française, les représentants des colons en France de 1789 À 1795* (Paris, 1943); Malick W. Ghachem, 'The "Trap" of Representation: Sovereignty, Slavery, and the Road to the Haitian Revolution', *Historical Reflections/Réflexions historiques* 29, no. 1 (2003), 123–44.

25. Gabriel Debien, *Les colons de Saint-Domingue et la Révolution; essai sur le club Massiac (août 1789–août 1792)* (Paris, 1953).

26. *Patriote français*, no. 205, 2 March 1790, 1.

27. Honoré-Gabriel de Riquetti Mirabeau, *Les bières flottantes des négriers* (Saint-Etienne, 1999).

28. This important dimension is examined in Alyssa Goldstein Sepinwall, *The Abbé Grégoire and the French Revolution: The Making of Modern Universalism* (Berkeley, 2005).

29. Léon Deschamps, *Les colonies pendant la Révolution: la Constituante et la réforme coloniale* (Paris, 1898), 236.

30. Bernard Gainot, 'Robespierre et la question coloniale', in Philippe Bourdin and Michel Biard (eds), *Robespierre: Portraits croisés* (Paris, 2012), 74–89.

31. Marcel Dorigny, 'La Société des Amis des Noirs, les Girondins et la question coloniale', in *Esclavage, colonisations, libérations nationales* (Paris, 1990), 69–78.

32. This had been clearly articulated in Etienne Clavière, *Adresse de la Société des amis des noirs, à l'Assemblée nationale, à toutes les villes de commerce, à toutes les manufactures, aux colonies, à toutes les sociétés des amis de la constitution* (Paris, 1791).

33. For instance, this is not mentioned in Michel Biard, *Missionnaires de la République: les représentants du peuple en mission, 1793–1795* (Paris, 2002).

34. For a detailed account of the events, see Jeremy D. Popkin, *You Are All Free: The Haitian Revolution and the Abolition of Slavery* (Cambridge, 2010).

35. See Robespierre's 27 Brumaire II report in: *Moniteur universel* 18, no. 60 (1793), 457–63.

36. Claude Wanquet, *La France et la première abolition de l'esclavage (1794–1802): le cas des colonies orientales Île de France (Maurice) et La Réunion* (Paris, 1998).

37. Bernard Gainot, 'La Constitutionnalisation de la liberté générale sous le Directoire', in Marcel Dorigny (ed.), *Les abolitions de l'esclavage. De L.F. Sonthonax à V. Schoelcher, 1793, 1794, 1848* (Paris, 1995), 213–29.

38. Jeremy D. Popkin, 'Saint-Domingue, Slavery, and the Origins of the French Revolution', in Thomas E. Kaiser and Dale Van Kley (eds), *From Deficit to Deluge: the Origins of the French Revolution* (Stanford, 2011), 220–48.

39. Jean-Claude Halpern, 'Sans-culottes et ci-devant esclaves', in *Esclavage, colonisations, libérations nationales* (Paris, 1990), 136–43.

40. Albert Mathiez, *La vie chère et le mouvement social sous la Terreur* (Paris, 1927), 29–49. See also Colin Jones and Rebecca Spang, 'Sans-Culottes, sans Café, sans Tabac: Shifting Realms of Necessity and Luxury in Eighteenth-Century France', in Maxine Berg and Helen Clifford (eds), *Consumers and Luxury: Consumer Culture in Europe 1650–1850* (Manchester, 1999), 37–62.

41. Allan Potofsky, 'Paris-on-the-Atlantic from the Old Regime to the Revolution', French History 25, no. 1 (2011), 89–107; Lynn Hunt, 'The Global Financial Origins of 1789', in Desan et al. (eds), *French Revolution in Global Perspective*, 32–43.

Selected Reading

Armitage, David and Subrahmanyam, Sanjay (ed.), *The Age of Revolutions in Global Context, c.1760–1840* (Basingstoke, 2010).

Benot, Yves, *La Révolution française et la fin des colonies* (Paris, 1988).

Cheney, Paul, *Revolutionary Commerce: Globalization and the French Monarchy* (Cambridge, 2010).

Desan, Suzanne, Hunt, Lynn, and Nelson, William Max (eds), *The French Revolution in Global Perspective* (Ithaca, 2013).

Dorigny, Marcel (ed.), *Les abolitions de l'esclavage: de L. F. Sonthonax à V. Schoelcher 1793, 1794, 1848* (Saint-Denis, 1995).

Dorigny, Marcel and Gainot, Marcel, *La Société des amis des noirs, 1788–1799: contribution à l'histoire de l'abolition de l'esclavage* (Paris, 1998).

Dubois, Laurent, 'An Atlantic Revolution', *French Historical Studies* 32, no. 4 (2009), 655–61.

Dubois, Laurent, *A Colony of Citizens: Revolution and Slave Emancipation in the French Caribbean, 1787–1804* (Chapel Hill, 2004).

Gaspar, David Barry and Geggus, David Patrick (eds), *A Turbulent Time: the French Revolution and the Greater Caribbean* (Bloomington, 1997).

Geggus, David Patrick and Fiering, Norman (eds), *The World of the Haitian Revolution* (Bloomington, 2009).

Niort, Jean-François, Régent, Frédéric, and Serna, Pierre (eds), *Les colonies, la Révolution française, la loi* (Rennes, 2014).

Popkin, Jeremy D., *You Are All Free: the Haitian Revolution and the Abolition of Slavery* (Cambridge, 2010).

Régent, Frédéric, *Esclavage, métissage, liberté: la Révolution française en Guadeloupe, 1789–1802*, (Paris, 2004).

Spieler, Miranda Frances, 'The Legal Structure of Colonial Rule during the French Revolution', *The William and Mary Quarterly* 66, no. 2 (2009), 365–408.

Wanquet, Claude, *La France et la première abolition de l'esclavage (1794–1802): le cas des colonies orientales Ile de France (Maurice) et La Réunion* (Paris, 1998).

PART IV

·····································

COUNTER-REVOLUTION AND COLLAPSE

·····································

CHAPTER 18

LOUIS XVI AND MARIE ANTOINETTE

AMBROGIO A. CAIANI

THE reign of the last *ancien régime* monarchs of France, and the influence of his Habsburg queen-consort on politics, continues to be the source of much historical inquiry and debate. Their importance has never been in doubt. Indeed, his first biographer, the abbé Soulavie, stated unequivocally that the 'fleeting and uncertain character of Louis XVI, is the primary cause of the collapse of the ancient monarchy and also of the fall of the constitutional monarchy'.[1] After two centuries of painstaking archival investigations one could be forgiven for thinking that all possible avenues of research have been exhausted, however this is very far from being the case.

Indeed, since the early 1990s, there has been renewed academic interest in ministerial politics, diplomacy and the public imaginary.[2] Such scholarship has stressed, rightly, the problems of governance in *ancien régime* France and, inspired by Tocqueville, has examined how contradictory attempts at reform did much to undermine the public's confidence in the Bourbon monarchy.[3] For many, the Crown, and its tarnished image, became part of the problem, rather than the traditional source for pragmatic solutions and compromises. Great stress has been placed on how Louis XVI's freedom of action was constrained by the interlocking and conflicting goals of ministerial elites and clans of noble courtiers, whose interests were often detrimental to the need for fiscal rigour.[4] Considerable time has been devoted to examining how the difficulties France faced on the international stage of global competition further exacerbated an already delicate situation.[5] These approaches have tended to interpret the monarchy's fate as sealed once power migrated from the ministries and cabinets of Versailles to the National Assembly in Paris. In effect a monarchy, committed to reform through *ancien régime* instruments, was unlikely to engage in a constructive dialogue with a Revolution defined by a regenerative mission which sought to redraw beyond recognition France's political, social, and cultural landscape.

Such an interpretative framework has, however, tended to neglect events inside the Tuileries during the revolutionary maelstrom. Instead, it has favoured research into the legacy of the pre-1789 reign, and into the real, and imagined, diplomatic efforts by this monarch, and especially his Austrian consort, to erect some form of counter-revolutionary conspiracy. Admittedly, there is much to justify this approach, after all, the king sometimes considered himself a virtual prisoner of the capital. On several occasions, he self-consciously referred to any political concessions he made as 'things which circumstances force me to undertake'.[6] While it is not the intention here to deny the importance of the legacy of the *ancien régime*, foreign conspiracy, and the radicalizing impact of the outbreak of war in 1792, it does seem that a revaluation of France's first constitutional monarchy is overdue. To merely describe Louis XVI's reaction to revolutionary events as an invariant paroxysm of hostility is unenlightening. The king's relationship with the National Assembly and the Revolution's emergent political culture was dynamic and inherently unstable.[7] The efforts and opportunities to find an accommodation, or at the very least a working relationship, between Crown and nation varied throughout the period.

In historiographical terms, the constitutional monarchy has not fared well. It has generally received unsympathetic treatment, dismissed as an ineffectual compromise almost predestined to failure.[8] At the beginning of the twentieth century, Jean Jaurès, in his multi-volume history of the period, famously rewrote the lawyer Raymond de Sèze's defence speech at the king's trial. According to Jaurès the king's actions were irrelevant, as he was a victim to the vagaries of social and economic forces which were outside his control.[9] From this historical materialist perspective, the king had neither the intelligence nor ability to resist the invisible tides of history. Georges Lefebvre, the leading voice of the classical school of French Revolutionary history, placed the blame for this failed experiment squarely on Louis XVI's recalcitrance when it came to accepting the Revolution's regenerative mission.[10] Indeed, for Lefebvre the revolutionaries had generously made every effort to integrate the Crown within the recreated French state.

The revisionist challenge to this orthodoxy has somewhat struggled to gauge the evolutionary potential of the French monarchy in the early 1790s. Over forty years ago François Furet and Denis Richet, in their narrative of the revolutionary maelstrom, presented 1790 and 1791 as a great missed opportunity to create a liberal parliamentary regime of a quasi-Anglo-Saxon stamp in the hexagon. These two scholars were among the first to analyse the flight to Varennes in a sympathetic fashion. For them this was not just the noxious fruit of a counter-revolutionary conspiracy, but rather an attempt to put the reform programme of 1789 back on course. Ultimately, Louis XVI merely wanted to renegotiate, from a position of strength, a constitutional settlement which would reinvigorate his executive powers.[11] In their view the Varennes blunder had the deeply unfortunate effect of catalysing the *dérapage* (skidding off course) of the Revolution. This botched escape plan pulled the carpet from underneath the feet of the 'liberal' Feuillant majority of the Constituent Assembly and, in their stead, the surviving extremists of the Jacobin club grabbed hold of the Revolution's helm.[12]

This rather neat account of the monarchical causes of the failure of the 'liberal revolution' was soon challenged by new interpretative frameworks (one of which was strongly championed by Furet himself) emphasizing the radical and discursive continuities which persisted from the beginning of the revolutionary rupture of 1789 right through to the Jacobin Republic and Terror. An influential group of mainly English and American historians became convinced that the deputies of the Constituent Assembly, through their reading (or some would say misreading) of some of the key eighteenth century works of political thought, had opened a Pandora's box from which a deeply intolerant, quasi-totalitarian and proto-Republican ideology emerged.[13] This vision of politics had little or no wish to reach genuinely a working compromise with the *ancien régime* past, let alone with the monarchy which stood at its summit. Norman Hampson, in an eloquent essay, described the entire period as a prelude to the Terror.[14]

Not all have accepted this negative assessment of the Constituent Assembly. Some continue to stress more contingent explanations. Timothy Tackett and Michael Fitzsimmons praise the constitutional settlement, and place the blame for its unworkability squarely at the king's feet for his refusal to accept its spirit and dictates.[15] As Fitzsimmons states, with little equivocation: 'ultimately the edifice constructed by the National Assembly failed less from internal contradictions than from the refusal of the monarch to abide by it unconditionally and in good faith'.[16] If one were to suppose, but not concede, that Fitzsimmons is correct, his conclusion does assume that Louis XVI should, and could, have jettisoned his dynastic heritage and the legacy of Bourbon rule at a whim. Alas in 1790 it was not a mere question of the Constituent Assembly's will meeting with the monarchical wont; nor was it simply the case that the separation of powers, espoused by the deputies in 1789, deprived the king of all legislative initiative, and merely bestowed on him executive powers, which were severely limited through the strict supervision of the Assembly and its vast network of parliamentary sub-committees. The problem with such an argument, excepting its oversimplification, is that even an 'unworkable' compromise must first be agreed upon. The Constitution, which was in force in France from June 1789 to September 1791, existed only in the unfettered imaginations of the 1200 deputies of the Constituent Assembly. As Hampson put it: 'in the France of the summer of 1789 there was no past that anyone was prepared to invoke as proof of legitimacy. Behind them, the deputies had the exhilarating triumphs of July. Ahead lay a future whose possibilities seemed endless.'[17]

Yet another interpretation of the immediate origins of the French Revolution has painted the summoning of the Estates-General in the colours of a Royal Revolution that misfired.[18] After all, as the story goes, it was Louis XVI who summoned the Estates-General to Versailles to deal with the *ancien régime*'s debt-crisis. According to this view, he was an enlightened ruler, who wanted to regenerate the state's fiscal structure. Despite these good intentions, he became the instigator of drastic changes which, ultimately, subverted the political foundations of the kingdom of France. There is something to recommend this point of view, after all Louis XVI was not averse to change and reform. Indeed, his pre-Revolutionary reign was littered with many examples of institutional and humanitarian reforms (whose outcomes were decidedly mixed).[19] The hypothesis that the king appealed directly to the Nation, by allying himself with the Third Estate, in order to circumvent the obstacles and intermediate bodies which had previously blocked the path to fiscal reform, is compelling. Such a line of argument also helps to explain why, in 1790, he was still prepared to engage in a 'possibilist' fashion with the reform programme of the Constituent Assembly. The concern remains that this argument is, at times, rather more intuitive than grounded in a firm evidential basis.

While Louis certainly desired to be the prime mover behind any reform initiative, it seems clear that, from 1787 to 1789, both control, and indeed understanding, of events rapidly slipped away from him.[20] It has been argued that he suffered some form of nervous breakdown, and lived the years of the Revolution through a sort of mental haze, which made him seem disconnected from reality. The evidence for a sustained psychological illness is difficult to prove with any degree of confidence, as throughout all his life the king demonstrated a phlegmatic, calm and detached composure, impervious to external stimuli. It was part of the eighteenth century art of being a monarch to be impenetrable, and to dissimulate one's true thoughts. Louis XVI's lethargy was as much a political tactic as it was a fatalistic resignation.[21] Whether this was an efficient way of playing the game is another matter. As events spiralled out of control, the king bided his time, only intervening if he felt that he could influence their direction. Such temporizing was ineffective when confronted with the new format of revolutionary politics, whose chief characteristic was its unstoppable forward momentum.

The birth of the National Assembly and its arrogation of the realm's legislative authority were unexpected and disturbing. The better part of the subsequent year saw the king trying to digest not only this unwelcome setback, but also seeking to find a means of adapting to the evolving new political climate. It should be realized that, despite early legislative decisions, no aspect of the final settlement had been determined irrevocably. Thus in 1790, everything in theory was still 'up for grabs'. Louis XVI had some understanding of these stakes and that is why, on 4 February, he appeared in the *Salle du Manège* and proclaimed: 'I shall favour, I shall second through every possible means within my power, the success of this reorganization upon which depends the future of France.'[22] Contemporaries interpreted this move as an exercise in manipulation. They suspected that its immediate aim was to put an end to public unrest, allow the Crown to resume control of government affairs and, in time, undermine the drafting of a constitution.[23]

Such a reading maybe overly cynical, and attributes to the king a devious desire, at every turn, to re-establish 'absolutism'. This seems unconvincing in the light of recent studies. As Munro Price has argued, Louis XVI had effectively conceded a constitutional settlement in his declaration for the *séance royale* of 23 June 1789.[24] The principle of regular meetings of the Estates-General, and that new taxation would require their consent, had been granted. In his subsequent writings the king always made reference to his declaration of June 1789. Clearly, he was not seeking to destroy the Constitution, but rather to improve it from his monarchical perspective. The programme set forth in his speech on 4 February 1790 described a moderate constitutional charter that was respectful of the traditional structure of French society. This blueprint recognized some concept of national sovereignty, but watered it down in favour of a mixture of property and merit-based qualifications for political participation. The monarch's political vision aligned him not with diehard counter-revolutionaries but placed him on the same wavelength as the liberal and moderate fringe of the Assembly. This was not a *politique du pire*, but a practical effort on the part of the monarchy to salvage what it could from the previous year's turmoil. The year 1790 is among the most neglected by scholars of the Revolution. There is much evidence that, in this crucial year, a nascent constitutional monarchy was diluted and disempowered by an increasingly confrontational political context. Radical deputies, popular societies and other pressure groups intended that a break with the past was not merely a question of reform, but rather of destroying every administrative institution that was contaminated by *ancien régime* corruption. In the end, the failure of the constitutional monarchy was not a stillbirth but rather a form of infanticide.

In this fraught context it is tempting to turn to Marie-Antoinette and interpret her role as the counter-revolutionary *éminence grise* during her husband's political woes. Again, there is a risk here of excessive over-simplification. Centrally, and this is often forgotten, this Habsburg princess was a consort rather than a queen-regnant. She had been in a difficult position since the moment of her arrival in France. Why did this individual, who was supposed to be the physical embodiment of the pacific and positive fruits of France's 'diplomatic revolution' of 1756, receive such a sustained barrage of contemptuous criticism? The answer seems to lie in Chantal Thomas' compelling observation that: 'Marie Antoinette's crimes lie not in an act but in a quality of being.'[25] As the daughter of the hated Habsburg nemesis the queen was hardly a free agent. It was far easier for her to confirm the public's worst expectations than to dispel atavistic hatreds.[26] Indeed, there were other elements in this operatic drama which significantly muddied the waters.

The queen's ambiguous role during the Revolution has been the subject of far from sympathetic treatment over the past two centuries.[27] It has provided a convenient alliance of patriotism and misogyny that has allowed much pseudo-scholarship to attack a degenerate woman and foreigner who betrayed France's war plans to her imperial brothers. As Thomas Kaiser notes compellingly she was a hostage to the fortunes of the Bourbon-Habsburg alliance.[28] This diplomatic pact's association with military defeat and international humiliation meant that the public's frustration was vented on its living embodiment in Versailles. Unhappily for her, the young queen possessed neither the necessary ruthlessness nor a natural flair for realpolitik. Marie-Antoinette seems for all of her life to have had an admirable, though ultimately self-defeating, obsession with friendship and family loyalty, which made it difficult for her to pursue an effective political line.

Even in the very midst of the revolution she never abandoned her former court allies, and remained a committed lobbyist for Habsburg interests in France.[29] With the benefit of much hindsight it can be seen that, in the early 1790s, this was a suicidal form of conduct. It would be unfair to depict Marie-Antoinette as either dim-witted or naive, but it should be realized that she constructed her court partisanship on the basis of emotive and dynastic affinities, rather than purely political ends. It was logical, and from her point of view legitimate, to seek outside assistance from her Habsburg clan, aiming to permit her aristocratic allies to regain French soil.[30] Marie-Antoinette was not a stateswoman, but a traumatized witness of revolution, who wished to turn back the clock in order to resume the relatively tranquil existence she had enjoyed at Versailles. The queen's notable political role in both court politics and international relations cannot be denied, but to view her as either an *éminence grise* or unofficial foreign minister seems to be taking a stride too far. She was an influential player and intermediary, but never constituted the power behind the throne which, for a long time, a misogynistic historiography has implied. A powerful atavistic distrust of foreign princesses meddling in politics ensured that her role could only ever be indirect. Ultimately, it was the fiscal reform which precipitated the revolutionary turmoil, and in this domestic matter the queen did not determine the course of events. The death of her eldest son, the dauphin Louis Joseph, on 4 June 1789, and the violence of the early Revolution, deeply traumatized her. It would take time before she would again have the stomach to re-enter the game of politics. During the subsequent constitutional monarchy, her role remained circumscribed to the sphere of covert diplomatic negotiation. It was only in mid-1790 that she recovered from the shock of the October days, and began actively intriguing to influence the outcome of the constitutional settlement which would govern France.[31] Whether or not this was done with the knowledge of her husband remains an area of intense debate.[32]

Indeed, as the year 1790 commenced, there was no certainty in which constitutional direction the Revolution would head. It was the year when, as Timothy Tackett has argued, the deputies became revolutionaries but failed to transform Louis XVI into a constitutional monarch.[33] When Louis awoke on the morning of 1 January 1790 in the Tuileries palace, he could have been forgiven for still harbouring some optimism. After all, his executive powers had remained unaltered since the previous year. The royal routine continued unperturbed, and its usual array of rituals and ceremonies were deployed to uphold the spectacle of monarchical representation. On this day, he received in audience the grandees of the court, the magistrates of the *parlements* and delegations from the other judicial institutions littered around Paris.[34] Each presented their compliments for the new year. The only real element of novelty was embodied by a delegation sent by the National Assembly, which symbolically reminded all those present that there was a rival source of sovereignty in the realm.[35] Despite this development, the king's authority in most spheres remained strong. It is true that, by September 1789, Louis had lost his law-making ability. During this crucial month the National Assembly limited the monarch's involvement in legislative process by granting him a suspensive veto rather an absolute one.[36] They also rejected proposals for the creation of an upper house composed of royal appointees.[37] While this is undoubtedly the case, it is also true that the king retained the power to issue administrative regulations and guidelines on how to implement the substantial stream of legislation emanating from the Assembly.

In the early months of 1790 Louis never used these residual legislative powers to hijack any of the assembly's reforms. It seems likely that the king, initially, approved of many of the Revolution's early transformations. In his speech of 4 February 1790 he expressed his admiration for the deputies' desire to create a uniform administrative and legal system, which would increase the state's efficiency. Studies in the monarch's education and personality show that he had a natural aptitude for the sciences and practical arts.[38] Law reform projects for the departmentalization of France's administrative jurisdictions, a uniform system of weights and measures and a rational scheme for tax collection all elicited not only the king's approval but admiration.[39] During 1790 the court of the Tuileries was rather more welcoming than in subsequent years. The king received in formal audience many of the celebrities of the time. These included not only the Corsican patriot (and former rebel) Pasquale Paoli, but also a number of scientists and a centenarian Burgundian former serf called Jean Jacob who came to Paris to inspect his newly acquired liberty.[40]

Meanwhile, there is also evidence that the king intended to use at least some of his remaining royal prerogatives in a progressive fashion. Louis' right of appointment and patronage over governmental posts and pensions had not yet been called into question. The monarch not only theoretically selected the highest ranking ministerial civil servants and army officers, but thanks to the terms of the Concordat of Bologna of 1516 he still chose which clerical candidates should be appointed to vacant Sees.[41] The key adviser in the sphere of ecclesiastical appointments was the minister of the *feuille des bénéfices*. The incumbent at this time was Jean-Georges Lefranc de Pompignan, the liberal archbishop of Vienne, under whose guidance the king was to make the last royal episcopal appointment of the *ancien régime*. He chose the distinguished divinity professor Asseline of the Sorbonne to fill the vacancy which had emerged for the bishopric of Boulogne.[42]

It is an appointment which could easily be ignored were it not a sign that the king was trying to show his willingness to adapt to changing circumstances. After all, this nomination was the first time in the second half of the eighteenth century that a non-noble had been chosen to occupy an episcopal throne. It was a direct message to the Assembly that the king could be trusted to choose clerics who were progressive and sympathetic to its reform programme. There is also some evidence that, during this time, Lefranc tried to persuade the progressive abbé Grégoire to accept the See of La Rochelle.[43] The First Estate's position had been under threat from the outbreak of the Revolution. Their properties had been placed at the nation's disposal and the tithe had been abolished. Louis XVI defended his right to nominate bishops not in terms of traditional aristocratic patronage, but by demonstrating his openness to candidates who were favourable to the new religious order of things.

The most important sphere where royal power remained undiluted was foreign policy and its concomitant military dimension. This, since time immemorial, had been considered the prime site of regal competence, the *métier du roi* par excellence. When it came to foreigners, the revolutionaries experienced ambivalent feelings. On the one hand, they believed that their revolution enshrined a universal system of government, which was applicable to all mankind.[44] On the other hand, conspiracy theories and panics led to mass xenophobia. The Paris populace feared infiltration on the part of foreign agents bent on counter-revolution, and in late 1789, to prevent such a contingency, they invaded the ambassadorial residences of the capital in search of compromising documents. The papal nuncio Archbishop Dugnani in November 1789, as doyen of the *corps diplomatique*, protested against such outrages, which constituted a clear violation of the Law of Nations.[45] This formal complaint was also seconded, on 12 December, by the Foreign Minister, the comte de Montmorin, and the Assembly in response decreed that ambassadors and other emissaries remained under the protection of the Executive Power, that is the monarchy.[46]

Therefore, despite the fall of the Bastille and the court's forcible removal from Versailles to Paris in October 1789, the king still possessed a strong measure of residual authority. What most threatened the monarch's position was that the Constituent Assembly was not merely a law-making organ, but had determined, on 27 July 1789, to redraw *ex novo* the fundamental political organization of the realm.[47] The Constitution remained unwritten and, if the king wanted to retain the lion's share of his exclusive competencies, he would need to prove to the representatives of the nation that he could be trusted with any public function. The initial indicators were promising, especially considering that the deputies endowed the monarch with a very generous financial settlement. The creation of a British-style civil list provided the king with 25 million *livres*. This sum was augment by separate emoluments for the queen and some of the princes of the blood. The deputies' generosity extended also to the private debts of the monarch and his court, which were subsumed into the national debt.[48]

After initially refusing to leave the seclusion of the Tuileries, the king started appearing in public more often. One suspects that this was meant to serve as an outward sign of his acceptance of the new order of things. In February 1790 he rode, escorted by courtiers and national guardsmen, in the bois de Boulogne, and attended *Te Deums* in Notre Dame to celebrate his endorsement of the Assembly's achievements.[49] The queen also participated in such events. Most notably, she donated and distributed to the Versailles National Guard their new flags and standards.[50] The royal couple also used the civil list to bestow some charitable donations on the destitute and visited the foundlings' hospital in Paris.[51] Louis XVI's reviews of the National Guard, which took place in May and July on both the Champ de Mars and Plaine de Sablons, were supposed to highlight the Crown's positive working relationship with the citizen militia and its Fayettiste general staff.[52] These occasions were marred, to some extent, by the royal refusal to wear this military unit's uniform. Several National Guard officers and journalists drew attention to this supposedly unpatriotic behaviour.[53] Indeed, Lafayette's cousin, the prince de Poix, made the unwise choice of suggesting directly this course of action to the king and received an angry and withering written response.[54] Louis was incensed that a former *garde du corps* should interfere in matters relating to his dress. For two centuries the monarch's clothing had been a matter for the *premier gentilhomme de la garde robe*, and Bourbon kings had very seldom worn military uniform.[55] So this suggestion, from a junior member of the Noailles, smacked of impertinence. From the king's traditionalist perspective it made no sense to wear the recently created National Guard uniform when he had rarely donned those of long-established and distinguished regiments.[56]

Despite this stand over his personal appearance, there is also significant archival evidence that the king was tinkering with ways of reorganizing his court along less exclusivist and traditionalist lines. Private reports, and other writings, suggested to the king that he should abolish redundant honorific positions and amalgamate duplicate departments in an effort to cut costs.[57] All in all the start of 1790 was promising and showed a will on both sides to find some form of common ground. The quibbles that initially appeared were ones of style rather than substance. What eventually put an end to this brief honeymoon was the legacy of the recent past, and developments in the international arena.

One of the key remits bestowed on the Estates-General had been the examination of the Crown's rudimentary budgets and other governmental accounts. After spending several months perusing the figures of the previous administration, the Assembly published, on 11 April 1790, a detailed list, the *livre rouge*, containing the names of those who had received pensions since 1774.[58] The total sum spent, during the fifteen years of Louis' pre-revolutionary reign, on this, at times dubious, form of royal patronage amounted to a staggering 225 million *livres*. The presence of the Polignacs, Vaudreuils and other members of the queen's party drew much negative press speculation.[59] When it came to the expenditure of the royal chapel few were impressed by Cardinal Montmorency's argument: 'let not thy left hand know, what thy right doeth', for keeping the royal alms secret.[60] The fallout from the *livre rouge* was enormous, and deeply damaged the Crown's reputation. It became difficult to sustain the monarchy's credibility as a fiscally responsible institution, and darker doubts started to arise. Indeed, the radical journalist Louis Prudhomme asked: 'how can it be that a king, who is generally respected as an honest man, has signed ordinances whose very purpose was to swindle the public purse[?]'.[61]

Three international crises further stoked political discontent. The less serious of these involved, first, the annexation, after a pro-revolutionary insurrection, of the papal territories of the Comtat-Venaissin in Provence, and latterly the suppression of the sovereign rights of several German princes in Alsace.[62] While neither was catastrophically destabilizing, they did give the other European monarchies a rather frightening glimpse into the National Assembly's disregard for international law. Avignon had been part of the Pope's temporal domains since the fourteenth century, and the Alsatian princes' sovereign right to collect feudal dues from their vassals was guaranteed by the terms of the Treaty of Westphalia of 1648.[63] The Assembly asserted that it possessed a higher jurisdiction, grounded in natural law, and argued that it was not bound to honour the diplomatic treaties negotiated by corrupt *ancien régime* ministers.[64] For the king, whose international standing was inextricably linked with his ability to honour the agreements which he and his predecessors had entered in good faith, this was a worrying development. The Assembly's unilateral decisions were a dangerous intrusion into an area which the king considered to be his exclusive competence.[65]

The flashpoint, which deeply compromised royal control of foreign policy, occurred when Britain and Spain almost declared war on each other in May 1790 over the 'Nootka Sound Incident'.[66] This revolved around the Spanish Crown's claim that it had the exclusive right to colonize and settle the western coast of North America. Between May and

July 1789, a flotilla of Spanish vessels seized a number of British and US merchantmen off what is now Vancouver Island, British Columbia. As the ensuing diplomatic crisis over events in the Pacific Ocean worsened, Charles IV of Spain appealed to the clauses of mutual support enshrined in the third Bourbon family compact of 1761.[67] Louis XVI, aware of his international obligations, began arming a squadron of warships in case this crisis escalated into war. He appealed to the National Assembly to guarantee the funds necessary for France to meet its diplomatic commitments. Instead of consenting automatically to the executive's request the Assembly launched one of its most animated debates on who, ultimately, had the right to declare war and negotiate peace. The baron de Menou seemed somewhat inebriated by the possibilities opened up by this question. On 15 May he declared:

> I say that it is essential to immediately decide on the issue of who holds the right to make peace and [declare] war; only subsequently shall we decide which of the two nations in question is in the wrong. If it is Spain we should use all our influence to force her to stand down; if it is England and she refuses herself to justice we must not just arm fourteen ships of the line but all of our forces on land and sea. It will be at this juncture that we will show to Europe that this is not a ministerial war but a national one.[68]

Certainly, the prospect of arrogating the monarchy's power to determine foreign policy made the deputies indulge in some of their most hyperbolic fantasies. On 18 May, the Alsatian Reubell was among the most extreme in his denial of reciprocal obligations among states:

> Treaties of alliances are nothing but a means of raising taxes and ruining the national treasury; to give the king the right [to make treaties] is to allow him constitutionally to sell men like flocks of sheep. The executive power may determine the quantity and deployment of military forces. A great nation needs no other allies but providence, its own resources and justice.[69]

The debate was decidedly chaotic; there were excursions into different hemispheres of the world, and some musings on whether or not Henri IV's foreign policy had been ethical. Ultimately, the vindication of natural law over precedent meant that, in terms of foreign relations, everything was now up for grabs.[70] Treaties that emanated from the cabinets of princes had little or no validity. Only nations, with representative Assemblies, could legitimately enter into negotiations. The individual was made vicious by his particular interests, while the collective body of all citizens was infallible. No one better epitomized this vision than Maximilien de Robespierre: 'it is from France that the liberty and happiness of the world must commence'.[71] In the end, it was agreed that the monarch could propose war, but the ultimate decision had to be ratified by the National Assembly.[72] Suddenly, Louis found himself stripped of the key aspect of early modern kingship: the ability to direct foreign policy. It is clear from his correspondence with Charles IV that the king not only resented this interference, but equally was much embarrassed at having to abandon his cousin in a time of need, especially when his Bourbon cousins had done much to support him during the American War of Independence.[73]

The second half of 1790 brought little in terms of reassurance when several high-profile army and naval mutinies erupted.[74] The troops in several provincial garrisons, displeased with the lack of progress made in army reform, refused to obey their officers and, in some cases, seized regimental funds.[75] In the end order was restored, but at high price. In Nancy the military commander the Marquis de Bouillé fought a pitched battle, for three hours, with the rebels.[76] The ringleaders of these revolts were either hanged, broken on the wheel or sent to the galleys. Many patriots and radicals of the popular societies in Paris believed that the soldiers' grievances were justified, and saw the severe repression that followed as evidence that the Crown was reverting to despotic habits. The military committee of the Assembly proposed that the king lose his monopoly over military appointments and that seniority of service be codified in a proper promotions system.[77] By the end of the year, Louis XVI's role as commander in chief of the army seemed to be increasingly symbolic. The emigration of the lion's share of noble officer corps in the subsequent months meant that the issue of who ultimately controlled the army was opaque to say the least.[78]

In his speech of 4 February 1790 the king had signified to the Assembly his willingness to accept that the old medieval notion of a society of orders was superseded. After all, the tax exemptions of the clergy and nobility had been one of the great obstacles that he himself had faced when trying to solve the budget deficit. Yet, despite this acceptance that the social compact needed to be altered he did warn that: 'at the same time, all that reminds a nation of the ancientness and continuity of the [public] services provided by an honoured race, is a distinction which nothing can destroy, [...] all classes of society should aspire to serve their fatherland efficiently and those who have already experienced the joy of doing so in the past, have an interest in respecting [the] transmission of titles, or other such reminders, which are the most beautiful of all the legacies which they can bestow on their children'.[79]

Consequently the Assembly's decision, on 19 June, to abolish titles of nobility seems to have been diametrically opposed to the Crown's appeal for a society in which honorific distinction and civic equality could coexist. The abolition of hereditary titles remains one of the more mysterious events of the French Revolution. A recent study by William Doyle, inspired by Mirabeau's correspondence, suggests that this was the work of a group of liberal nobles working in the *Société de 1789*.[80] It is unclear what the monarchy's role was in the whole affair. The king never made any public comment on this political decision (only finance minister Necker dissented in writing).[81] However, one could speculate that the Crown had prior knowledge of this political decision as, on 4 June 1790, the king abolished court presentations and removed all genealogical criteria for admission to honorific and courtly offices. By doing so he was obviously trying to demonstrate his adherence to the Declaration of the Rights of Man, which stated that admission to public positions could only be determined through meritocratic principles and notions of public utility.[82] While it is true that the erasure of the kingdom's nobility did not lead to irreconcilable difficulties between monarch and assembly, on the other hand, it was a symbol that the loose constitutional blueprint laid out in 4 February speech was being jettisoned to satisfy a more radical reform agenda. Bare months later, the king, honoured with the title 'Restorer of French Liberty', was largely ignored by the nation's legislature, who were refashioning the kingdom's fundamental governance with little, or no, reference to past practices, and who resented any form of regal interference.

The straw which broke the camel's back was the Civil Constitution of the Clergy of July 1790.[83] It seems that the king—and even many clerics—were initially sympathetic to the stated aim of rationalizing the ecclesiastical jurisdictions present in the realm by reducing the number of bishoprics and giving all priests a state salary. However, the principle that appointment to ecclesiastical benefices, such as parishes or dioceses, would be subject to an electoral process was troubling. Even more so was the requirement that all clergymen with an active ministry swear an oath to uphold the supremacy of the French Constitution. This law created a conflict of loyalty and diminished the authority of the king, the bishops and the Pope.[84] The Assembly acted in a unilateral fashion when it came to negotiations with the Holy See. It effectively presented Pius VI with a fait accompli, rather than any gesture of consultation. Other enlightened monarchs, especially the Emperor Joseph II, had shown that concessions could be obtained from the Church through patient diplomacy.[85] The Roman curia moved at a snail's pace, and it took more than six months before the Pope's fulminations duly arrived in March 1791, when the Civil Constitution was formally denounced in the bull *Quod Aliquantum*.[86]

The prospect of a Church schism must have been deeply unsettling for a monarch who, at his coronation, had insisted on maintaining the time-honoured oath to extirpate heresy from his domains.[87] Throughout the early months of 1791 a steady stream of letters from some of the most senior prelates of the hexagon, such as the Bishops and Metropolitans of Clermont, Aix and Paris, reached the Tuileries.[88] 'How unfortunate it would be if ever this schism could be legitimated through your Majesty's conduct', wrote the Bishop of Clermont early in 1791.[89] The effects of the legislation led to a growing polarization in French society, violence in Paris, and a monumental crisis in church–state relations, when all but seven bishops refused to take the constitutional oath.[90] In April, as a symbol of the worsening situation, the king and his family were surrounded by a crowd who stopped their coach leaving the Tuileries for their country residence in Saint-Cloud (during this incident one of the first gentlemen of the bedchamber the duc de Villequier was physically attacked).[91] Growing sectional violence, and journalistic attacks, put pressure on Louis XVI to allow his most important courtiers to resign. By April 1791 the first gentlemen of the bedchamber, the grand almoner, the master of the horse and several other senior officials had all quit the court over fears for their personal safety. Increasingly eminent voices like Prudhomme, Desmoulins and Marat referred to the king as the 'first functionary of the Nation', a profound insult for a monarch raised on the belief that his power was divinely sanctioned.[92] After a year in which the possibilities of creating a favourable constitutional settlement had floundered, the now isolated king of the French stopped believing that he could honourably function as a constitutional monarch. His thoughts started turning to flight and counter-revolution.

Fleeing from either Versailles, or Paris, was a contingency which the king had considered from the earliest days of the Revolution. However one dilemma remained, and it was best expressed by the maréchal de Broglie who, during the July crisis of 1789, asked 'we can go to Metz, but what do we do when we get there?'[93] The prospect of flight as the king knew well, from his careful study of Hume's history of England, was replete with the danger of instigating civil war.[94] Once in flight from his capital he would eventually need to appeal to armed forces in order to subdue rebellion and restore his authority. This is why I would suggest that, for over a year, Louis wanted to avoid this dangerous and uncertain prospect in order to attempt to find some *modus vivendi* in which the Crown and the nation's representatives could collaborate in the government of the realm. Yet, it became increasingly apparent that political manoeuvring would not be sufficient to exit the political impasse which had been reached at the beginning of 1791. Some drastic course of action was necessary. Some months previously, around July 1790, the Queen's diplomatic channels had been used to secure the expensive advice of the comte de Mirabeau. This wily deputy advised a flight to one of the kingdom's internal provinces (to avoid suspicion of a foreign plot), from where the court could negotiate, from a position of strength, an agreement anchored on a reinvigorated monarchical executive.[95]

This rudimentary plan, however, seems to have offered insufficient guarantees. Mirabeau's death in April 1791 meant that the king had to rely on other advisers, most notably the baron de Breteuil, a former minister of the royal household, and the marquis de Bombelles, a veteran diplomat both of whom were close to the queen. Their prolonged absence from the kingdom inevitably meant that their knowledge of France's internal situation was increasingly second hand and perhaps out of touch with reality. The ultimate aims and objectives of the royal plans for flight are difficult to gauge with precision. Most of the papers dealing with preparations were considered too compromising and consequently were destroyed. Whatever Louis XVI may have hoped to achieve, the central flaw in the arrangements for Varennes, and other foreign plots, was that the need for secrecy meant that insufficient local support was raised in the provinces. In the end, a rather ill-concocted scheme was devised to flee to Montmédy, a border fortress town, under the command of the reliable marquis de Bouillé (whose role in the flight earned him an unflattering mention in the 'Marseillaise').[96] It seems that this strategy was adopted on the queen's insistence, and there is no evidence that the king dissented in any significant way. It was believed that the proximity of Montmédy to the Austrian Netherlands, and the perceived threat of Habsburg military intervention, would allow the king to dictate a new constitutional settlement.[97]

There is no need to describe in detail the blunders which resulted in the royal family's arrest at Varennes. It is worth recalling, however, that the choice of Monsieur, the king's brother, to follow a more direct route, and his refusal to waste time, ensured that he successfully escaped from France.[98] The reasons and aims of this historical event will always remain a subject of intense controversy.[99] Its effects are less difficult to discern.[100] The radical sections and opinion makers of Paris recalibrated their political focus. They abandoned any residual allegiance they may have held towards the constitutional monarchy and turned their attention to the establishment of a republic. The attempts to recast the flight to Varennes as a kidnapping, and later events on the Champ de Mars in July 1791 (where Republican petitioners were fired upon by the National Guard), did much to undermine popular support for the moderate Feuillant and Fayettist party within the Assembly.[101]

Perhaps, the most unexpected outcome of the failed escape was that it gave rise to secret negotiations, from July to September, between the court and a number of moderate deputies.[102] These tangled discussions resulted in a constitution purged of the worst excesses proposed by the Jacobin press. For instance, the king was not referred to as either the 'Nation's agent' or 'chief civil servant' as Desmoulins, Marat and others had proposed. In essence, the document that emerged established a strange political stalemate. The king was not bereft of power, he was in charge of the realm's administration and the implementation of all legislation. In some ways it could be argued that, through his 'suspensive veto', he had the ability to participate in the law-making process. However, this positive assessment should not blind one to the significant limitations placed on his powers. Most acts of the executive authority were placed under the direct surveillance of parliamentary sub-committees, who could effectively block royal initiatives.[103] The chapter of the Constitution which dealt with the monarch's authority was a peculiar piece of legal thinking. A large share of its attention was devoted to describing the remedies to be applied in the eventuality that the king fled the nation or raised an army against the Assembly. Also of note was the decision to enshrine in law the king's right to raise a personal guard of 1800 men, outside of the regular army, for protection against unspecified threats.[104] It is true that on a superficial level the constitution of 1791 presented the appearance of a liberal constitutional monarchy. However, its contents remained the expression of the legislative's deep distrust of executive authority and for this reason the Crown's wings had been clipped significantly.[105] Its purpose was to avoid the dangers of another royal flight and to stem the tide of nascent republicanism.

After the king ratified this document, the deputies of the Constituent wrapped up a few loose ends and returned home. They had passed, in May 1791, a self-denying ordinance which made them ineligible to stand in the elections for a new legislature.[106] These polls had been deeply influenced by events at Varennes and the Massacre at the Champ de Mars. The 749 deputies of the new Legislative Assembly, unlike their predecessors, did not feel they had a clear mandate and were uncertain how to proceed.[107] This placed them at the mercy of their more energetic colleagues, like the members of the Brissotin party, whose political ends were inimical to the survival of the monarchy. It is unnecessary to cover here ground which has been analysed in depth by others.[108]

Louis XVI, after Varennes, had few real political options open to him and seemed to be outmanoeuvred at every turn. In 1790 the king had tried to come to terms with events. However, in the subsequent two years, he hoped that the increasingly turbulent course of the Revolution would lead to its implosion. As he stated in a secret memorandum: 'in adopting its [the Constitution's] principles and executing them in good faith, [I will make the people] see the true cause of its misfortunes; public opinion will change; and since without this change new convulsions will be inevitable, I will have more chance of achieving a better state of things by my acceptance than by my refusal'.[109] This approach, ultimately, did little to endear him to the radical population of the capital, and when he became a prisoner of the insurrectional commune on 10 August 1792 his fate was hardly in any real doubt. Indeed, the king's most loyal courtiers and military supporters were purged and executed, with little in the way of legal due process, by the second Revolutionary Tribunal of August 1792. Attempts by some experts to view his trial of December 1792 as a form of justice akin to twentieth-century innovations in the realm of prosecutions for crimes against humanity seem wishful thinking. In the end, despite some flimsy legal window dressing, it was Saint Just and Robespierre's argument, that the monarch be tried as a *hostis humani generis* (enemy of the human race), that carried the day.[110] The failure to negotiate a constitutional compromise, which could blend tradition and innovation, flung the king away from a conciliatory stance into a state of dejection and passive counter-revolution. For the constitutional monarchy the crucial turning point had been the year 1790.

NOTES

1. Jean-Louis Soulavie, *Mémoires Historiques et Politiques du Règne de Louis XVI, depuis son mariage jusqu'à sa mort. Ouvrages composé sur des pièces authentiques fournies à l'auteur avant la révolution, par plusieurs ministres et hommes d'état et sur les pièces justificatives recueillies après le 10 août dans les cabinets de Louis XVI à Versailles et au château des Tuileries*, 6 vols (Paris, 1801), VI, 379.

2. John Hardman, *French politics, 1774–1789 from the accession of Louis XVI to the fall of the Bastille* (London, 1995); Munro Price, *Preserving the Monarchy, the Comte de Vergennes, 1774–1787* (Cambridge, 1995); Jean-François Labourdette, *Vergennes*: ministre principal de Louis XVI (Paris, 1990); Robert Harris, *Necker and the Revolution of 1789* (Lanham, MD, 1989); Mona Ozouf, Varennes, la mort de la royauteé, 21 juin 1791 (Paris, 2005).

3. P. M. Jones, *Reform and Revolution in France, The Politics of Transition 1774–1791* (Cambridge, 1995).

4. Julian Swann, 'The French Nobility, 1715–1789', in *The European Nobilities in the Seventeenth and Eighteenth Centuries*, ed. Hamish Scott, 2 vols (London, 1995), 168.

5. Bailey Stone, *The Genesis of the French Revolution, A Global-Historical Interpretation* (Cambridge, 1994).

6. '[D]es choses que les circonstances me forcent de faire', in A[rchives] N[ationales], C 184, no. 316; and John Hardman, *Louis XVI, the Silent King* (London, 2000), 115.

7. For a recent pyscho-historical interpretation of the dysfunctional relationship between king and deputies see, Barry Shapiro, *Traumatic Politics, The Deputies and the King in the Early French Revolution* (Pennsylvania, 2009), esp. part I.

8. François Furet and Ran Halévi, La monarchie républicaine, la constitution de 1791 (Paris, 1996).

9. Jean Jaurès, *Histoire Socialiste 1789–1900*, 2 vols (Paris, 1901), II, 876–83.

10. Georges Lefebvre, *The French Revolution* (London, 2001), 147–8.

11. Denis Richet and François Furet, *La Révolution Française* (Paris, 1988 [orig. pub. 1965]), 125–57.

12. Ibid, pp. 143–5.

13. François Furet, *Interpreting the French Revolution* (Cambridge, 1982), part I, *passim*; and Keith Michael Baker, *Inventing the French Revolution* (Cambridge, 1990), chaps 9–11.

14. Norman Hampson, *Prelude to Terror* (Oxford, 1988), *passim*.

15. Timothy Tackett, *When the King took Flight* (Cambridge, MA, 2004); and Michael Fitzsimmons, *The Remaking of France, The National Assembly and the Constitution of 1791* (Cambridge, 1994), 111–39.

16. Ibid, p. 256.

17. Hampson, *Prelude to Terror*, 189.

18. Pierre Lafue, *Louis XVI, l'échec de la Révolution Royale* (Paris, 1964).

19. Hardman, *French politics, 1774–1789*, esp. part II the politicians and the public; Jones, *Reform and Revolution in France*, chap. 4.

20. For the most recent studies see John Hardman, *Overture to Revolution, the 1787 Assembly of Notables and the crisis of France's old Regime* (Oxford, 2010); Vivian Gruder, *The Notables and the Nation, the Political Schooling of the French, 1787–1788* (Cambridge, MA, 2007).

21. John Hardman, *Louis XVI* (London, 1993), 20–5.

22. A[rchives] P[arlamentaires], vol. XI, 429.

23. Adolphe Fourrier de Bacourt, *Correspondance entre le comte de Mirabeau et le comte de La Marck, pendant les années 1789, 1790 et 1791*, 3 vols (Paris, 1851), I, 464; Joël Felix, *Louis XVI et Marie-Antoinette, un couple en politique* (Pairs, 2006), 514–16.

24. Munro Price, *The Fall of the French Monarchy, Louis XVI, Marie Antoinette and the Baron de Breteuil* (London, 2003), 63–71.

25. Chantal Thomas, *The Wicked Queen, the Origins of the Myths of Marie-Antoinette* (New York, 1999), 11.

26. 'Marie-Antoinette's marriage to the Dauphin was a matter of political controversy well before it took place, pouring fresh fuel on the fires of an already raging battle between *anti-dévot Choiseuliste* and *dévot anti-Choiseuliste* factions, in Thomas E. Kaiser, 'Who's Afraid of Marie-Antoinette? Diplomacy, Austrophobia and the Queen', *French History* 14 (2000), 248.

27. For a summary, see Thomas, *The Wicked Queen*, esp. ch.4; Louis Prudhomme, *Les Crimes des Reines de France depuis le commencement de la Monarchie jusqu'à Marie-Antoinette* (Paris, 1791), 434–60.

28. Kaiser, 'Who's Afraid of Marie-Antoinette', 252–8.

29. Antonia Fraser, *Marie Antoinette, The Journey* (London, 2001), 288–91.

30. Price, *The Fall of the French Monarchy*, 116 and 166–8.

31. Munro Price, 'Mirabeau and the Court: Some new Evidence', *French Historical Studies* 29 (2006), 37–75.

32. For an original and extremely controversial exposition of the thesis that in the early 1790s the queen pursued a separate foreign policy from her husband see, Paul and Pierette Girault de Coursac, *Le Sécret de la Reine* (Paris, 1998).

33. Timothy Tackett, *Becoming a Revolutionary, The Deputies of the French National Assembly and the Emergence of a Revolutionary Culture (1789–1790)*, chap. 9.

34. *Gazette de France*, no. 1.

35. *Révolutions de France et de Brabant*, no. 8, 340–2.

36. Furet and Halévi, *La monarchie républicaine*, 369–417.

37. Doyle, *The Oxford History of the French Revolution*, 118–20.

38. Pierrette Girault de Coursac, *L'éducation d'un Roi, Louis XVI*, 2nd edn (Paris, 1995).

39. Doyle, *The Oxford History of the French Revolution*, chap. 5.

40. Ambrogio Caiani, *Louis XVI and the French Revolution* (Cambridge, 2012), chaps 3 and 5.

41. John McManners, *Church and Society in Eighteenth-Century France*, 2 vols (Oxford, 1998), I, 208.

42. Nigel Aston, *The End of an Élite, The French Bishops and the Coming of the Revolution 1786–1790* (Oxford, 1992), 221.

43. Ibid, p. 220.

44. Michael Rapport, *Nationality and Citizenship in Revolutionary France: The Treatment of Foreigners 1789–1799* (Oxford, 2000).

45. AP X, 516.

46. Ibid.

47. Baker, *Inventing the French Revolution*, ch. 11.

48. Philip Mansel, *The Court of France 1789–1830* (Cambridge, 1988), 24–6.

49. AN LL 335 No. 45 ASTo, Francia, Lettere Ministri, Mazzo 236, dépêche no. 22, Paris le 12 février 1790.

50. Roger Dupuy, *La Garde Nationale 1789–1872* (Paris, 2010), 107.

51. Sigismond Lacroix (ed.), *Actes de la Commune de Paris pendant la Révolution*, première série, 8 vols (Paris, 1894–1899), 243; and Anon, *Supplément aux règlements adoptés par la Société de la Charité Maternelle* (Paris, 1790).

52. AN C 221, no. 160, *Journal de Louis XVI*; and Caiani, *Louis XVI and the French Revolution*, 121–3.

53. Dupuy, *Garde Nationale*, 51–2 and 64–5.

54. AN C 184, no. 316.

55. Philip Mansel, *Dressed to Rule* (London, 2005), 18–36.

56. Philip Mansel, 'Monarchy, Uniform and the Rise of the Frac', *Past and Present* 96 (1982), 129–31.

57. AN, C 184, Part I, No. 142, Tableau des Six Sections composant la Maison Civile du Roi.

58. Jules Michelet, *Histoire de la Révolution française*, 2 vols (Paris, 1952), I, 364.

59. *Révolutions de France et de Brabant*, no. 21, 335–43.

60. AP XIII, 296.

61. *Révolutions de Paris*, 6 au 12 avril 1790, no. 36, p. 67. This issue was dedicated entirely to the *livre rouge*.

62. Bailey Stone, *Reinterpreting the French Revolution, A Global Historical Perspective* (Cambridge, 2002), 118–21; and for a full correspondence, on the issue of the Alsatian Princes, between the Ministry of Foreign Affairs and The Assembly's Diplomatic Committee, see AN D XXIII 1 and 2 *Contentieux Politiques*.

63. For the complicated negotiations surrounding the surrender of this province to France see, Peter H. Wilson, *Europe's Tragedy, A New History of the Thirty Years War* (London, 2010), 710–11 and 755–8.

64. David A. Bell, *The First Total War, Napoleon's Europe and the Birth of Modern Warfare* (London, 2007), 89–109; and for a succinct summary and very compelling argument see, Henry A. Kissinger, *A World Restored, Metternich, Castlereagh and the Problems of Peace 1812–1822* (Boston, 1973), 3–6.

65. Indeed one of the longer passages of his later Varennes declaration bemoans his power-lessness when it comes to the management of diplomatic relations with other European princes. See, AP XVII, 380.

66. John Lynch, *Bourbon Spain 1700–1808* (Oxford, 1989), 377–9.

67. Ibid, 317–24.

68. AP XV, 518.

69. Ibid, XV, 564

70. Dan Edelstein, *The Terror of Natural Right, Republicanism, The Cult of Nature, and The French Revolution* (Chicago, 2009), esp. prologue and pp. 38–40.

71. AP XV, 516.

72. T. C. W. Blanning, *The Origins of the French Revolutionary Wars* (London, 1986), 79.

73. Albert Mousset, *Un Témoin Ignoré de la Révolution, Le Comte de Fernan-Nuñez Ambassadeur d'Espagne à Paris 1787–1791* (Paris, 1924), 228 and *passim*.

74. Samuel F. Scott, *The Response of the Royal Army to the French Revolution, The Role and Development of the Line Army* (Oxford, 1978); and William S. Cormack, *Revolution and Political Conflict in the French Navy 1789–1794* (Cambridge, 1995).

75. Scott, *The Response of the Royal Army to the French Revolution*, 81–97.

76. Ibid, 95–6.

77. AP XVII, 264–9, 338–9, 427–36, 446–8, and 489; AP XVIII, 141–3.

78. Again the loss of his military powers was another humiliation of which Louis XVI complained bitterly in his Varennes' declaration. AP XXVII, 379–80.

79. AP IX, 430.

80. William Doyle, 'The French Revolution and the abolition of the Nobility', in Hamish Scott and Brendan Simms (eds), *Cultures of Powers in Europe during the long Eighteenth Century* (Cambridge, 2007), 299.

81. Léonard Burnard, 'Necker et le débat sur l'abolition de la Noblesse', in Philippe Bourbin (ed.), *Les Noblesses françaises dans l'Europe de la Révolution* (Rennes, 2010), 41–51.

82. 'Men are born, and remain, free and equal in their rights. Social distinctions can only be founded on public utility.' Article One of The Declaration of the Rights of Man and the Citizen; & for a more detailed analysis of this event and the end of the *honneurs de la cour* see, Caiani, *Louis XVI and the French Revolution*, chap. 5.

83. John McManners, *The French Revolution and the Church* (London, 1969), chap. 5; Timothy Tackett, *Religion, Revolution, and Regional Culture in Eighteenth-Century France: The Ecclesiastical Oath of 1791* (Princeton, NJ, 1986), *passim*; and Dale Van Kley, *The religious origins of the French Revolution* (London, 1996), esp. chap. 6.

84. Ibid, chap. 6.

85. Derek Beales, *Joseph II*, 2 vols (Cambridge, 1987–2009), II, chap. 6.

86. Doyle, *The Oxford History of the French Revolution*, 146.

87. Baker, *Inventing the French Revolution*, 109–12.

88. AN, C 183, nos 11–33.

89. Ibid, no. 11.

90. McManners, *The French Revolution and the Church*, 48.

91. Mansel, *Court of France 1789–1830*, 27.

92. *Orateur du Peuple*, no. 42, 323–6; *Révolutions de France et de Brabant*, no. 17, 145–6; *Révolutions de Paris*, 1791, no. 93, 60; and *Le Patriote Français*, no. 978, 422.

93. Price, *The Fall of the French Monarchy*, 93.

94. Girault de Coursac, *L'éducation d'un Roi*, 194–6.

95. Price, 'Mirabeau and the court: some new evidence', 37–75.

96. 'Mais ces despotes sanguinaires, Mais ces complices de Bouillé'.

97. Cf. Price, *The Fall of the French Monarchy*, 117–18.

98. Philip Mansel, *Louis XVIII* (London, 1999), 53–7.

99. For the most controversial view see, Paul and Pierrette Girault de Coursac, *Sur la Route de Varenne*, 2nd edn (Paris, 2000).

100. Tackett, *When the King too Flight, passim*.

101. David Andress, *Massacre at the Champ de Mars* (Woodbridge, 2000).

102. Price, *The Fall of the French Monarchy*, 207–11.

103. For a sophisticated and interesting discussion on ministerial responsibility during the Constituent Assembly see, Guillaume Glénard, *L'Exécutif et la Constitution de 1791* (Paris, 2010), 430–46.

104. For an in-depth discussion and analysis of Louis XVI's Constitutional Guard, see Caiani, *Louis XVI and the French Revolution*, chap. 4.

105. Furet and Halévi, La monarchie républicaine, 239–58.

106. AP XXVI, 118–27.

107. Edna Hindie Lemay, *Dictionnaire des Législateurs 1791–1792*, 2 vols (Oxford, 2007), esp. Introduction.

108. Félix, *Louis XVI et Marie-Antoinette*, 582.

109. Price, *Fall of the French Monarchy*, 222–3.

110. Edelstein, *Terror of Natural Right*, chap. 3 especially pp. 146–58.

Selected Reading

Blanning, T. C. W., *The Origins of the French Revolutionary Wars* (London, 1986).

Caiani, Ambrogio, *Louis XVI and the French Revolution* (Cambridge, 2012).

Doyle, William, *Aristocracy and its Enemies in the Age of Revolution* (Oxford, 2009).

Felix, Joël, *Louis XVI et Marie-Antoinette, un couple en politique* (Paris, 2006).

Fitzsimmons, Michael, *The Remaking of France, The National Assembly and the Constitution of 1791* (Cambridge, 1994).

Girault de Coursac, Paul and Pierette, *Le Sécret de la Reine* (Paris, 1998).

Hampson, Norman, *Prelude to Terror* (Oxford, 1988).

Hardman, John, *Louis XVI* (London, 1993).

Hardman, John, *Louis XVI, the Silent King* (London, 2000).

Jones, P. M., *Reform and Revolution in France, The Politics of Transition 1774–1791* (Cambridge, 1995).

Kaiser, Thomas E., 'Who's Afraid of Marie-Antoinette? Diplomacy, Austrophobia and the Queen', *French History* 14 (2000), 241–71..

Mansel, Philip, *The Court of France 1789–1830* (Cambridge, 1988).

Price, Munro, *The Fall of the French Monarchy, Louis XVI, Marie Antoinette and the baron de Breteuil* (London, 2003).

Tackett, Timothy, *Becoming a Revolutionary, The Deputies of the French National Assembly and the Emergence of a Revolutionary Culture (1789–1790)* (Princeton, 1996).

Tackett, Timothy, *When the King took Flight* (Cambridge, MA, 2004).

Thomas, Chantal, *The Wicked Queen, the Origins of the Myths of Marie-Antoinette* (New York, 1999).

CHAPTER 19

EMIGRATION IN POLITICS AND IMAGINATIONS

KIRSTY CARPENTER

Du drame bien long et bien noir,
Que nous jouons, sans le vouloir,
Sous les yeux de l'Europe entière

(Very long and very black tragedy,
That we act out, unwillingly,
Under the gaze of all of Europe)[1]

Escaping from the Revolution was a dangerous business, but escaping from the entrapment of emigration politics took much longer. Nearly 130,000 French men and women were registered on the official lists as émigrés in France during the French Revolution.[2] This was not a large proportion of the twenty-eight million who made up the French population at the beginning of the Revolution, but compared to the number of nobles (around 140,000) its significance is plain.[3] Figures can vary but 73 per cent of the non-ecclesiastic émigrés enrolled on the relief lists in London in 1797 perceived themselves to have aristocratic connections and used the particle '*de*' before their name.[4] They were a politically active minority that long term made a very significant difference—simply by not being defeated and being able to return. They fought to assume their right to be French and to live safely in a hostile France where the Republicans used their majority vote to condemn the émigrés to death. This group braved the perils of exile, experienced poverty and misery to stand up for their right to belong in a Nation determined to blame them for all the evils of absolute monarchy. Some did not return from emigration, dying from exhaustion, in childbirth, of old age and stress, or in war serving with the armies of the allies against Republican troops. If caught, like the émigrés at Quiberon, they were put to death just because their names appeared on the national émigré lists.[5]

In the European cities of London, Vienna, Berlin, St Petersburg, Madrid and Lisbon, émigrés waited imagining a better France.[6] This imagination and hope for a different political future was the life-blood of the emigration.[7] It was expressed in all forms of literature from the polemics of Lally Tolendal and the writings of the exiled deputies of the Constituent like Montlosier, to the novels of Madame de Staël, Madame de Souza and Senac de Meihan.[8] It can also be found in the work of another later generation affected by those who had known the experience of emigration, and written their memoirs. Rance emphasizes that, 'Émigré authors were not so much seeking to give a sense to the explosion of violence as to understand how the destruction of a political regime, a system of State, had been possible'.[9] Others like Lucie de la Tour du Pin simply recounted how patterns of life were changed in emigration. The trickle-down effect of this recounting can be found later in the nineteenth century in, for example, George Sand: 'He found her awake. She was accustomed to get up early as a result of the habits of active labour she had acquired in emigration, and she had not been able to lose on recovering her opulence.'[10]

There is no question that the vast majority of the émigrés wanted to live in a France governed by a Bourbon king.[11] The sympathetic reception of the memoirs of Cléry, Louis XVI's confessor, when they appeared in Britain in 1793 provides proof of the horror that both the British and the French felt at the king's execution.[12] Émigrés provided the written proof that the Revolution could not eradicate all trace of the aristocracy and its supporters, or their habits and ways, simply by killing the king.[13]

Yet, despite what would come to unite them, in particular the ten years' average stay outside France that most endured, émigrés came to that status through different routes, and for many it was not a completely free choice.[14] From officers pressured to take the *chemin de l'honneur* and leave loved ones behind them, to those who found that personal views or social position put them at odds with powerful local officials, émigrés found themselves surrounded by hostile attitudes.[15] They often had only one option that could be relied upon to leave them alive, or to keep their family intact. For many individuals who were not themselves heads of households, emigration had little of choice about it at all. Dependence upon the decisions of others—fathers, husbands, or other male relatives—was responsible for leaving many women and children individually subject to revolutionary proscription.[16] Priests too, who were not officially classed as émigrés until the Law of Suspects came into effect, often had choices forced upon them because they had nowhere to hide inside France without putting others at risk.[17] The lists of those condemned as émigrés have become famous over time for their errors.[18] There was a large cross section of people who found themselves on these lists or trapped in emigration through no direct political decision of their own—underscoring the point that emigration was fundamentally violent.[19] The *Courrier de Londres* clarified in November of 1792:

There are in England several thousand brave people who have not quitted France because their courage was not equal to the events, but because they were personally persecuted, and they could have become the last victims of the calumnies that time alone could unveil and against which their heroism served no purpose.[20]

So what explains the slippage between the imaginings and expectations of the émigrés, and the reality of politics in France? By whom and how were the distances and divisions created: physical, political and intellectual? And central to this, is the question of whether it is correct to see the émigrés as only a negative influence in regard to the French state in revolution—by whom was this decided, and just how much was determined by the émigrés being legally given the death sentence?

Émigrés have been largely rediscovered since the bicentenary of the French Revolution in 1989.[21] Many individuals in emigration have been shown to be colourful, interesting, and rashly courageous. They were a subset of counter-revolutionaries, but their predicament was legally defined by their geographic movements, and the date they left French soil, rather than by their taking arms against the state.[22] The Republican government made it a crime for a virtuous Frenchman not to reside on French national soil, and this posed many new administrative and political dilemmas. The codification of the émigré laws by the Convention between 28 March and 5 April 1793 marked a turning point. These émigré laws, some 200 in all, affected not only émigrés but friends and relatives of émigrés as well as public functionaries who were responsible for implementing the law and servicing the debt.[23]

There are three important issues regarding émigré legislation. First, the definition of an émigré was fixed in 1793 after the war had begun, and throughout the period 1793–1802, the definition remained essentially unchanged. Second, the procedural issues associated with émigré legislation were never properly or legally resolved and, as a consequence, the lack of any significant revision of the émigré legislation was an indicator of the vulnerability of the Revolutionary government's position. Third, the cumulative rigidity of these laws prevented a political rapprochement taking place between émigrés and moderate ex-nobles within France in the critical period 1795–97. This critical lost opportunity arguably prevented the institution of a constitutional monarchy years before the eventual Restoration.[24]

Penal legislation targeting the opponents of Revolution was an inevitable product of the deposition of the king, and the property of émigrés had already been the subject of penal taxation then confiscation after the outbreak of war. On 23 October 1791 émigrés were first banished in perpetuity from French soil, and those caught on French soil were condemned to death. A short amnesty of fifteen days was accorded to allow those who wished to re-enter the country to do so, but the decree was vetoed by the king and did not take effect. Nevertheless the unbending severity of the universal condemnation sent shock waves through the émigré community.[25] Émigrés who had hoped to return to their homes after only a short absence were made brutally aware by the first two articles of the legislation that their exodus was permanent. From 1793 onwards émigrés could be condemned to death on the strength of a simple identification test and put to death by local officials in complete accordance with the law and without right of representation or appeal.

The 28 March 1793 legislation was unsurprising coming as it did in the wake of the king's execution, and amid massive alarm at provincial revolts. The émigrés had been tarred liberally with accusations of treachery and desertion since before the outbreak of war, and these had been further reinforced by the image of émigré soldiers serving with the princes' army alongside the Revolution's enemies. Prevailing attitudes permitted no moderation or challenges to commonly accepted legal definitions.[26] Confusion, panic, and paranoia surrounded the legislation which stripped the émigrés of their political rights, of their possessions and of their families and friends.

The legislation covered all aspects of emigration from identity of an émigré and the exemptions, to providing a formula for a *certificat de résidence* which was the effective proof that an individual was not an émigré because he or she had resided in France during the required period. It also included procedures for assessment and disposal of émigré property and a multitude of very detailed procedural issues including debts and creditors. These were subject to several modifications during 1793 as they went into practice, but the important articles remained unchanged.[27]

Exceptions were made for children less than fourteen years old as long as they had not taken arms and as long as they returned within three months. In future, younger children would have to return by their tenth birthday in order to avoid being subject to the law. Persons banished and deportees were exempted as were those whose absence pre-dated 1 July 1789, as long as they were not living on enemy territory. The wives and children of government officials and diplomats were exempted but domestic servants had be of a number 'habitually employed by that functionary' and had to have been in the service of that employer prior to his foreign appointment. Increasing the entourage of an official was a recognized way to slip émigrés in and out of the country. Frenchmen whose purpose for being abroad was the study of science, arts or crafts and the acquisition of new knowledge were exempted provided they were '*notoirement connus*' (publically recognized) before their departure.

The crime of emigration could also be applied by association to those who had aided the émigrés or furthered their hostile projects; those who had sent their children abroad; those who had supplied arms, horses, munitions or financial assistance to émigrés; those who had solicited émigrés by promises or financial rewards; those who had knowingly hidden émigrés or helped them to return to France; those who were responsible for false certificates of residence. The vague nature of the crime of aiding émigrés or furthering hostile projects threw the net very wide and left much to interpretation and misinterpretation.[28]

The law itself initiated its own contradictions because it was more specific about who was and was not an émigré than what an émigré's defining characteristics really were. An émigré was a criminal more because of what he or she had chosen not to do—return to France in the designated, brief, amnesty period—than for what any émigré had consciously or deliberately done in person to harm the French nation. From the very beginning, the gaps and insufficiencies in the justice of the legislation, and the deputies' unwillingness or powerlessness to do anything about it became apparent.[29] Parallels can easily be drawn between the urgency with which the Revolutionary government passed the initial émigré laws, and the similar degree of haste which accompanied the Aliens Act in Britain requiring all French citizens as foreigners to carry passports whilst in the British Isles.[30] As in that case, the practicality of the legal process was lost in the precipitous rush to put the legislation into immediate operation.[31] All this gave rise to many problems faced by the deputies of the Convention in their impatience both to enforce the law and to see justice done. Some members were more aware than others of the treacherous nature of such a legal definition, which left so much to the discretion of those designated to administer justice.

As early as 1793, while asserting the need to bring to justice those Frenchmen prepared to take arms against the Republic, concerns were raised for those to whom the legislation might be applied unjustly and without provision for appeal (requiring, as it did, the execution of the sentence within twenty-four hours of the judgment). Jean-Baptiste Michel Saladin, a Montagnard and a lawyer, was one such individual who flagged the potential abuses.[32] He argued fiercely for the premise of the presumption of innocence which he felt was taken away by a law which prematurely condemned the accused:

> Because, if it is true that to condemn an individual to a punishment no matter which, there needs to be a moral certitude that he has violated the law, that he has committed the crime against which the law has established this punishment. If such is the maxim of even the least civilised of peoples, without this moral certitude, the condemnation is an injustice, and its execution an act of violence. It is necessary to conclude that the first and the most rigorous of duties of the legislator is to find the term where the law must stop and to do so in a way that this point is precisely the one that leaves the innocent the greatest conviction possible that he will not be condemned, and the guilty the least hope possible, to see his crime go unpunished. [33]

The absence of this 'moral certitude' was precisely what was holding up the sale of *biens nationaux*, and the problem would only become greater as more and more Frenchmen became less and less sure that the properties being sold had been legally obtained and would not be imminently subject to reversion to their former owners. Saladin, while loudly condemning those émigrés who had deliberately betrayed their country in language which the Jacobins appreciated only too well, pleaded for the need to pay attention to the application of these laws and to ensure that the innocent may not be accused without recourse to a fair trial.[34]

This issue was first exposed after the defeat at Verdun (1 September 1792), when émigrés caught with the invading armies were subject to prosecution by military tribunals created specially for the purpose. These tribunals were the first to question the legislation and Saladin, with his own legal training to draw on, made an impassioned plea for the competence of the *commissions militaires* to be restricted to only those émigrés caught red-handed or '*en flagrant délit*'. He argued that up until 9 October 1792 the death sentence was part of the penal code, and could only be rendered by tribunals established by the law of 20 September 1791 and composed of juries.[35] The clause of the legislation providing that the sentence be carried out within twenty-four hours of the judgment of the *commissions militaires* rendered it even more important to establish with exactitude the crime of the accused. Saladin argued for a distinction to be made between those taken in arms and more anonymous émigrés who may have fought against the Republic but whose case needed a proper inquiry to prove their guilt or innocence and the nature of the legislation allowed no time. He therefore argued that the difference in the two circumstances was too pronounced for both offences to share the same legal procedure.[36]

In the second case he argued that the proof of the crime must be established. When he wrote 'the law alone is powerful, the law only must reign', he said only what many more would say before the end of the century, whether pro or anti the émigré cause. Marie Joseph Chénier, a man with no émigré sympathies, asserted for example that 'liberty consists of depending solely on the law'.[37]

Saladin's plea to have émigrés whose crimes were not conclusive transferred for trial in the ordinary courts did not gain a majority, but it echoed across the Revolutionary years. The bureaucratic haste, the euphoria of victory and the impending trial of the king, whose death Saladin voted for, all compounded to set reason and law to one side. In 1792, the Convention was already acting on the premise that Robespierre enumerated in the wake of 14 Frimaire (that the government owes national protection to good citizens; to enemies of the people it owes only death)[38] and he dismissed those who counselled caution as 'stupid or perverse sophists who seek to confound opposites'.[39]

Saladin was one of the first to read the writing on the wall both in regard to the application of the émigré laws and the extension of the military machine to assume jurisdiction over the punishment of émigrés. That both these aspects of law were the subject of reports to the Convention in 1793 at the very beginning of the history of the emigration is of extreme importance. These reports show that the deputies were made fully aware of the difficulties and potential for injustice in taking an extreme approach to guilty verdicts where the émigrés were concerned. The same issues of guilt and innocence would receive fuller treatment under the Directory, but then too the political circumstances dictated a negative response. 'The revolutionary tribunal made equality triumph by showing itself as severe for the porters, and for servants as for the aristocrats and financiers'.[40]

Throughout the latter years of the Revolution the émigré laws could not be repealed, in part due to the immediate political threat the émigrés posed, but essentially because any re-examination of the validity of the laws questioned the foundations of the Revolution itself. If the émigrés were unjustly accused then the injustice was not a matter of Girondin versus Montagnard or confined to the Terror, but it undermined the more universal claims of Revolution going back as far as the Declaration of the Rights of Man of 1789.[41]

After the fall of Robespierre the laws against émigrés were still in force, émigrés were still registered on the police lists, but there were few deaths. During the Thermidor period only the most extreme cases were deported, and this was deplored by those who wanted the enemies of the Republic brought to justice more quickly. Marie Joseph Chénier wrote scornfully:

It has finally happened that the constituted authorities, disconcerted by rumours that one would like to mix up with public opinion, have so feared that they might be punished for executing your laws, and even your recent laws, that the paralysed tribunals have not felt the vigour necessary to render justice . . . [42]

A revision of November 1794 scaled down the punishment of émigrés to banishment in perpetuity and the forfeit of their possessions to the state, but still referred to émigrés as 'atrocious men who breathed only the ruin of their country'.[43] Infraction of that banishment was punishable by death. This perhaps had more to do with revulsion for bloodshed in the aftermath of the Terror than any revision of policy on émigrés.[44] Eschasseriaux wrote that 'there have been so many questions raised and complaints lodged on the subject of these laws that all prove the necessity of the essential measure that has been adopted'.[45]

Most importantly all possibility for trial of émigrés by jury was ruled out, and they remained at the mercy of the criminal tribunals.[46] Fears of election victories for deputies with constitutional royalist sympathies led to the passing of the Decree of Two-Thirds that ensured Republican dominance in the Assemblies. The 13 Vendémiaire revolt and the repressive law of 3 Brumaire an IV (25 October 1795) prohibited three groups from holding elective public office. These were any member of the primary or electoral Assemblies, anyone who had been listed as an émigré without obtaining full radiation (removal from the émigré list), or any relative of a listed émigré. Women related to émigrés were required by the same law to return to their domicile of 1792 and remain under the surveillance of the municipal authorities. These measures ensured a continued rigidity on issues regarding émigrés and their relatives, *biens nationaux* and refractory priests during First Directory. There were many inconsistencies in the sale of *biens nationaux* and many sales and potential sales were being contested and held up due to doubts about their validity.[47] The laws against the priests that had effectively been suspended were re-imposed. Catholic issues were of central importance for a variety of political and private reasons because almost without exception emigration and Catholicism went politically hand in hand.[48] Catholicism of the sort Chateaubriand celebrated in the *Génie du Christianisme* advocated a return to a religion of mystic purity, innocence and imagination—a view that drew widespread support.[49]

The contradictions around émigré issues were apparent to at least some members of the Council of Five Hundred. The irony could hardly cease to strike the observer that Malouet, the Lameth brothers, and Girondins who escaped the purge of 1793 were, as far as legislation was concerned, no different to émigrés like Calonne, Breteuil and the royal princes. The law allowed for no such nuance or for any lenience for good service to the Revolution at an earlier date. Yet while all émigrés were declared to be enemies of the state, as time went on, more and more people were prepared to argue that this was not so. *Les fugitifs français* was a term adopted in an attempt to disentangle the former from the émigrés or *les royalistes-aristocrates*.[50] The term 'French fugitives' was designed to provide a category of émigré where the crime was less severe and previous good service to the Revolution taken into account.

Roederer, a lawyer and a former member of the Constituent Assembly, proposed three categories of extenuating circumstances for emigration on the condition that these men, the French fugitives, had not taken arms against France.[51] He pleaded for 'those who have quitted France between 10 August and 20 October 1792; those who quitted in the interval 20 October to 31 May (1793); those finally who quitted between 31 May and 10 Thermidor.'[52] He argued that there could not be any fugitives post-dating Thermidor, because the suppression of the Jacobins and the committees had put an end to the rivalry. 'A state cannot condemn to perpetual banishment citizens who quitted their country only because the social guarantee was insufficient to protect them from violence.'[53] Arguments like this gave rise to a certain re-examination of the crime of emigration and to questions about what exactly the émigrés were guilty of: 'To what exactly reduces the action from which tyranny has made a crime for the refugees—to have withdrawn their head from that tyranny?'[54]

Roederer did not convince the majority, but he made it clear that the émigré he was pleading for was a modern political refugee:

> All was calm in France when the émigré left; all was in turmoil when the fugitive escaped. The émigré could serve his country, the Refugee was prevented from doing so. The émigré experienced a delay in coming back. The Refugee did not have one leaving. The émigré only left his country to seek war against it, the Refugee only quitted it when it had made war on him. The émigré has not ceased to turn his arms on France, the Refugee unarmed in France did not take up arms outside it. The émigré wanted to shed blood in our homes, the Refugee only sought an asylum—the one has brought us death, the other tried to defend himself against it.[55]

This sort of analysis emphasizing the difference between former patriots and soldiers of the armée de Condé made little difference to the actual legislative condition of the émigrés, but in the long term it did matter. It showed in many cases that what was missing was conclusive proof against the émigré not caught gun in hand, and in that circumstance the date of emigration was the only indicator of intent—and that was arguably a rather flimsy one.

> What is there to find in common between these men armed against their country, between the soldiers of Artois or the Legion of Condé and these refugees so much more respectable for the fact that most of them came from the privileged classes, that they have made for the happiness of their fellows and for their philosophy the sacrifice of their pretentions and their pride? God, what difference between the French and the Americans, the men who made the revolution in America constantly esteemed and venerated their compatriots, and we have sent Brissot to the scaffold, and the principal actors of the Revolution of 1789 languish in exile and in misery, and no voice is raised for them. Oh height of ingratitude, Oh shame of the century.[56]

Yet by the coup of 18 Fructidor so many very high hopes for change to the émigré situation had vanished to a point where the Marquis de la Maisonfort, who had taken to publishing on French politics from exile could write, 'The 18th Fructidor destroyed our hopes, the royalists reassembled in Paris, for want of being able to agree, like the workers at Babel, dispersed.'[57] In 1796 there had been a window in the political situation that almost transformed itself into a complete repeal of the émigré laws. Constitutional royalists were in a strong position due to their moderation by contrast with the Jacobins, and their link to the period of revolution that was not associated with the Terror. This royalism also appealed to provincials for whom the more radical aspects of revolution and, in particular, the de-Christianization and continuing attacks on religion made little sense.

Many émigrés had clandestinely returned to France between mid-1796 and mid-1797 in anticipation of a royalist victory, and the imminent relaxation of the émigrés laws.[58] There was even a question of letting returned émigrés vote, and in fact those who had managed to obtain provisional radiation in the provinces were allowed to do so which showed how much ground had been gained. On 27 April 1797 Boissy d'Anglas gave a speech in the Council of Five Hundred where he referred to the 'barbarous justice' by which the émigrés could be condemned to death on the strength of a simple identification if caught on French soil and pleaded for trial in the ordinary courts. On 4 May the above-mentioned law of 3 Brumaire was amended to allow relatives of émigrés to hold office, and on 27 June 1797 it was withdrawn altogether. It was this same time that polemics like Lally Tolendal's *Défence des Émigrés* appeared in print in exile insisting:

> People of France, and it is time to correct an error in which you have been studiously kept in order that the name of Emigrant might remain in your minds, attached to each sacrifice, to each grief, to each vexation, to each punishment, the law might bring down upon you.[59]

Election results favouring constitutional royalists, and the repressive Directorial Terror that followed the coup was initiated by a two-week amnesty allowing émigrés to return to their places of exile. The fact that this was declared before the émigré laws were re-imposed suggests not only how many émigrés had attempted to return, but also a disinclination to make widespread émigré arrests. Deportations to French Guiana replaced public executions in Paris. The law of 3 Brumaire was reinstated, and that saw the émigré position return to what it had been in 1792–93. Priests had to take an oath of hatred to royalty in order to ensure that they were not conspiring against the government but many refused. By a further law of 9 Frimaire an VI (29 November 1797) ex-nobles were excluded from public office and regarded as foreigners, if they could not prove that they had served the Revolution. Because no test for proving service to the Revolution was included in the legislation, this law was implemented very sparingly because it threatened former nobles in very high places like Barras and Bonaparte.

The events of Year VI offered little hope of change to the émigré situation. The war, the economy and the renaissance of Catholicism in France all contributed to keep government policy rigid. Elections were always contentious, those of Year VI produced the Floréal Coup which purged the Assembly of legally-elected radical Jacobin deputies in order to prevent a shift to the far left, those of Year VII preceding the Brumaire coup by a few months were characterized by an even more unsatisfactory result. The Second Directory had to go on maintaining its rigidity on the émigré question. The deterioration of the economy and the desperate need of conscripts for the army resulted in the Law of Hostages (24 Messidor an VII, 12 July 1799) which outlawed any resistance to new measures. By that law local authorities were empowered to arrest relatives of émigrés, imprison them at their own expense and impound their property to pay for damages.

The next return opportunity for the émigrés did not come until the Peace of Amiens was signed on 25 March 1802. From the arrival of Bonaparte as First Consul the signs of a pending reconciliation between the moderate royalists and the Jacobins emerged. In November 1799 the Law of Hostages was repealed, and the government also lifted the legal penalties on the relatives of émigrés and commuted the oath of hatred to royalty to one of loyalty to the Constitution. Relatives of émigrés and nobles were restored to full voting citizenship, and on 3 March 1800 a further decree closed the émigré list and a commission was appointed to speed up the radiation process. Although émigrés began to return, it was still dangerous.[60] After Bonaparte's dazzling victory at Marengo, Pope Pius VII, despite the views of the émigré Bishops in Britain, was persuaded of the desirability of reconciliation—the Concordat signed on 15 July 1801, achieved it.[61] This was the point at which the vast majority of émigrés, including the clergy, returned to France: free, after a decade, to do so without risking exposure to penalties. Those who remained in exile after 1802 were those who refused to give up plotting to restore the absolute monarchy.

The émigrés may have disagreed with the political notions of the popular regime, but legislation made their position untenable, and once outlawed, their recourse to justice was remote. Literary channels were among the only avenues for protest and output was prolific.[62] Historians like Philip Mansel have shown that many supporters of Louis XVIII were less ultra than historically portrayed, and that the assumptions which abound about emigration must be treated with great caution.[63]

It is inescapable that the injustice of the émigré laws was brought to the attention of the Revolutionary government and ignored in 1792, and this makes a significant difference to traditional approaches to emigration which assumed a degree of treachery implicit in every individual case of emigration. It should now be recognized that this was not necessarily so, and that many émigrés were at peril of their lives if they stayed in France, leaving only as a last resort. Women, children, servants and priests were among those who made no deliberate decisions but followed those they loved and trusted. Lally fulminated:

> Women. Great God! Women guilty of cowardice or treason ... The whole body of society is bound to protect the mothers of families, the wives, the sisters, the female friends who support or cement or embellish the social bond. The coward is he who abandons them; the traitor he who gives them up.[64]

Emigration harboured diversity and talent. Nowhere is this plainer than in the numerous geographic routes that émigrés took to leave France and the panoply of countries and regional locations within them where the French took refuge to work and write until they were free to return. A significant proportion never saw their homes again, and the only trace they left was their writings, giving proof of a patriotic French counter-identity without which the Revolution would not have been such a truly European event. Madame de Staël wrote of her hero Le comte d'Erfeuil:

> This man had borne the loss of a very large fortune with perfect serenity. He lived by his musical talent and supported an old uncle whom he cared for until his death. He constantly refused the offer of money that others pressed upon him. He showed the most brilliant valour, French valour, during the war, and the most unshakable good humour in the midst of adversity. [65]

Anatole France in *Les dieux ont soif* portrayed the émigré from the point of view of Evariste, Jacobin, judge, and someone who prided himself on the sincerity of his commitment to revolutionary ideals.[66] He was one of the first authors to point to the fact that it was the abuse of the legal system which was significant both in the cases of the émigrés and of Dreyfus—and importantly what was being protected by such abuse was the political establishment. The complex jigsaw of individual émigrés within the wider context of French Revolution politics continues to emerge from the archives and the literature.[67] Emigration had no universally happy ending and was fraught with internal factionalisms and financial crises. Those who survived were scared both psychologically by the loss of family and friends, and financially by the loss of their properties and fortune. But these often well-connected refugees who had shown determined commitment to a way of life and to a preferred form of government were able to return to France in the nineteenth century and play key roles in the growth of the modern French Republic. The time the émigrés had spent outside France imagining a better society contributed to diplomatic careers and politics when the individuals were no longer banished, and women authors like Madame de Staël, and Madame de Souza gained secure literary reputations.

> Never at any moment in our [French] history have minds shown themselves more compulsive, more prompt to submit to the impression of the moment and to transform it. . . . into a rigid law that endured.[68]

Notes

1. French newspaper *L'Ambigu, Les loisirs d'un émigré*, ouvrage posthume, dédié aux honnêtes gens. Poem dedicated to honest men. IHRF, FOL-L2C-1027 no. III, p. 71.
2. Donald Greer, *The Incidence of the Emigration During the French Revolution* (Cambridge, Mass., 1951), 20 puts the figure at 129,099.
3. The population figure is from William Doyle, *Oxford History of the French Revolution*, 2nd edn (Oxford, 2002), 2, and the number for nobles from William Doyle, *Aristocracy and its Enemies in the Age of Revolution* (Oxford, 2009), 16.

4. PRO T(93) 57. (78% of this list came from the former first or second estate.)

5. These were compiled by local authorities in the provinces in mid- to late 1792, and centralized in Paris in 1793. In February 1795, it was decided that only the Paris authorities could approve removal from the émigré lists known and referred to as radiation. On the Quiberon expedition, see Maurice Hutt, *Chouannerie and Counter-Revolution, Puisaye, the princes and the British government in the 1790s* (Cambridge, 1983).

6. On London see Carpenter, *Refugees of the French Revolution*. On Vienna see Philip Mansel, *The Prince of Europe. The life of Charles Joseph de Ligne 1735–1814* (London, 2003). On Russia see Angelica Goodden, *The Sweetness of Life, A biography of Elisabeth Louise Vigée Le Brun* (London, 1997), chs 8 and 9. On Prussia see Thomas Höpel, 'French Émigrés in Prussia', in Carpenter and Mansel, eds., *The French Émigrés and the struggle against Revolution*, op cit., 101–8. On Portugal see David Higgs, 'Portugal and the Émigrés', in Carpenter and Mansel, eds., *The French Émigrés and the struggle against Revolution*, op cit., 83–100.

7. See Fernand Baldensperger, *Le Mouvement des idées dans l'Émigration française 1789–1815* (Paris, 1924).

8. On Madame de Staël see Angelica Goodden, *Madame de Staël, the Dangerous Exile* (Oxford, 2008). On the comte de Montlosier see Pierre Serna, 'Du noble radical à l'aristocrate tempéré: le comte de Montlosier', in Philip Bourdon, ed., *Les noblesses françaises dans L'Europe de la Révolution* (Rennes, 2010).

9. Karine Rance, 'La violence révolutionnaire au crible des émigrés. Entre discours performatif, exemplarité du passé et prospective', in Philippe Bourdin, ed., *La Révolution 1789–1791 Écriture d'une Histoire immédiate* (Clermont-Ferrand, 2008), 210.

10. George Sand writing of Raymon de Ramière's mother; George Sand, *Indiana*, reprint edns (Paris, 1984), 223.

11. See Philip Mansel, 'From Coblentz to Hartwell, the Émigré Government and the European Powers 1791–1814', in Carpenter and Mansel, eds., *The French Émigrés in Europe and the struggle against Revolution 1789–1814* (London, 1999) 1–27.

12. Jean-Baptiste Clery, *Journal de ce qui s'est passé à la Tour du Temple pendant la captivité de Louis XVI* (London, 1798). (It was reprinted several times after the original appeared in 1793.) For the British reaction see David Bindman, *The Shadow of the Guillotine, Britain and the French Revolution* (London, 1989), 16-25.

13. William Doyle, *Aristocracy and its Enemies in the Age of Revolution* (Oxford, 2009), 275.

14. This is made clear particularly in novels such as Madame de Souza's *Eugénie et Mathide*, vol I, chs XXII–XXV MRHA Critical Texts, vol. 26, 2014, 89–94. Senac de Meihan, *l'Émigré* (Bruswick, 1797), and see also Malcolm Cook, 'Utopian Fiction of the French Revolution' *Nottingham French Studies*, 2006, No 45.

15. Charles Tilly, *The Vendée* (London, 1964), 195.

16. See Lynn Hunt, *The Family Romance of the French Revolution* (London, 1992). Chapter two makes it clear how affected women and children were by the authority of male family members. Works that treat issues affecting émigrées include: Carla Hesse, *The Other Enlightenment, How French Women Became Modern* (Princeton, 2001) and Jolanta T. Pekacz, *Conservative Tradition in Pre-Revolutionary France: Parisian Salon Women* (New York, 1999).

17. On the clergy in emigration see particularly the work of Dominic Aidan Bellenger, *The French Exiled Clergy in the British Isles after 1789* (Bath, 1986).

18. John Dunne, 'Quantifier l'émigration des nobles pendant la Révolution française: problèmes et perspectives', in J-C Martin, ed., *La Contre-révolution en Europe, XVIII-XIX siècles, réalités politiques et sociales, résonances culturelles et idéologiques* (Rennes, 2001), 133–41.

19. See Karine Rance, 'La violence révolutionnaire au crible des émigrés. Entre discours per-formatif, exemplarité du passé et prospective', op cit., 200.

20. *Courrier de Londres*, 9 November 1792. Section: Bulletin de Londres.

21. Accounts of emigration in English include Carpenter, Carpenter and Mansel, eds., *The French Émigrés and the struggle against Revolution*, op cit.; Simon Burrows, *French exile journalism and European politics, 1792-1814* (Woodbridge, 2000) and William Doyle, *Aristocracy and its Enemies in the Age of Revolution* (Oxford, 2009).

22. See e.g. Didier Michel, *Du Héros de Rennes en 1788 à la Contre-Révolution Blondel de Nouainville, L'itinéraire d'un noble normand (1753-1793)* (Cherbourg-Octeville, 2012), 126-7.

23. Charles Delacroix, *Opinion Sur les valeurs qu'il convient d'admettre en paiement des biens fonds des émigrés et autres biens nationaux, imprimée par arrêté du Comité d'Alienation des Domaines*, (Paris, 1793), 2.

24. See Philip Mansel, *Louis XVIII* (London, 1998) and Munro Price, *The Perilous Crown: France between Revolutions, 1814-1848* (London, 2007).

25. Mme de la Châtre confided to Fanny Burney that she would be able 'to gather together a small débris of her fortune, but never enough to settle in England—that, in short, her parti étant pris—that she must go to America', *Diary and Letters of Mme d'Arblay* edited by her niece (London, 1842), vol V, 366.

26. Kristian Jensen, *Revolution and the Antiquarian Book, Reshaping the Past, 1780-1815* (Cambridge, 2011), 34 notes the drop off in sales of law books. The book trade favoured books that did not challenge contemporary politics.

27. An émigré was: any French citizen who had quitted the territory of the Republic after 1 July 1789 and had not justified his return by 9 May 1792; or who was found absent from their domicile and unable to produce a certificate of residence without interruption since 9 May 1792; or who, although present during this time, had been absent at any given point; or who left the Republic without fulfilling the necessary formalities; or a government agent who did not return to France within three months of receiving his recall; or a French citizen who during enemy invasion left non-occupied territory to reside on enemy territory; or a girl or woman who married a foreigner or left France or sold her possessions. See John Hall Stewart, *A Documentary Survey of the French Revolution* (New York, 1951), 414. And in Greer, *Incidence of Emigration* op cit., 30.

28. Anne Simonin in her work, *Le Déshonneur dans la République. Une histoire de l'indignité 1791-1958* (Paris, 2008), looks at this issue of collaboration as a criminal act and explores this separation of military and other emigration crimes. While Greg Burgess's *Refuge in the Land of Liberty, France and its Refugees, from the Revolution to the End of Asylum, 1787-1939* (Basingstoke, 2008), 10 looks at Republican refugees and the fine line between national objectives and the Revolution's universal promises.

29. Marcel Ragon, *La législation sur les Émigrés 1789-1825*, thèse de droit, ed., Arthur Rousseau (Paris, 1904), 3.

30. The Aliens Act passed through the British Parliament on 4 January 1793 and required all foreign citizens on British soil to carry passports.

31. See Kirsty Carpenter, *Refugees of the French Revolution, the Emigrés in London 1792-1802* (London, 1999), 36-9.

32. See Marcel Dorigny, 'Saladin, Jean-Baptiste Michel', in Albert Soboul, ed., *Dictionnaire historique de la Révolution française* (Paris, 1989), 953.

33. *Rapport et Projet de loi sur le mode de juger les exceptions particulières, non-prévues par la loi contre les Emigrés à la Convention nationale au nom des quatres comités réunis de Législation, des Finances, Diplomatique et de la Guerre. Développement*, p.5, Maclure collection.

34. Ibid.

35. By the terms of the law of 28 March 1793 émigrés had to be brought before a criminal tribunal in their *département* of domicile. By a subsequent law of 17 September 1793 they could be tried before the criminal tribunal of the *département* in which they were arrested. In the Revision of 1794, it is pointed out that when an émigré was caught with no proof of his identity or his crime on his person and constantly denied that he was an émigré that the authorities had only the list of émigrés to consult, and that only people who knew the accused could verify that he was the person inscribed on the list and that these people could only logically be found in the accused's *département* of origin. *Rapport fait au nom de la Commission chargée de la révision des Lois contre les Emigrés* Eschasseriaux, 24–5.

36. Saladin, *Rapport et Projet de Décret sur la compétence des commissions militaires pour le jugement des Emigrés pris les armes à la main*, au nom du comité de législation, Convention Nationale, 5–6; *Les uns sont accusés, jugés mêmes par le fait et par la réunion de toutes les circonstances qui parlent plus haut que les preuves légales ou juridiques.* […] *Les autres au contraire n'ont contre eux aucun de ces caractères du même crime, que peut-être ils ont commis, mais dont la preuve à leur égard est plus difficile.*

37. Convention nationale, 15 Brumaire an II.

38. Robespierre, 'Sur les principes du Gouvernement révolutionnaire', 5 nivôse an II, Convention Nationale, from *Robespierre; Ecrits*, présentés par Claude Mazauric, (Paris, 1989), 286.

39. 'Sur les principes du Gouvernement révolutionnaire', 288.

40. A. France, *Les Dieux ont soif*, 140. Although this statement is written in a work of fiction, it is statistically correct: see Donald Greer, *The Incidence of the Terror in the French Revolution. A statistical interpretation* (Cambridge, Mass., 1935).

41. This was made explicit in the declaration of rights for the Constitution of 1791 which promised freedom to go, to stay and to leave. This was not the only article of the 1789 Declaration which was infringed. Articles 9 [man is presumed innocent until proved guilty …] and 17 [the right of property is inviolable and sacred …] were blatantly ignored in regard to émigrés.

42. M-J Chénier, *Rapport et Décrets sur le prompt jugement des Emigrés trouvés sur le territoire de la République; l'expulsion des individus rentrés après déportation; et les peines portées contre ceux qui provoquaient l'avilissement de la Représentation nationale ou le retour à la royauté etc*, 12 Floréal an III, au nom des comités de Salut Public, de sureté générale et de législation réunis.

43. *Rapport au nom de la Commission chargée de la révision des Lois contre les Émigrés*, *L'imprimerie de la Convention nationale*, Paris, 3, Maclure collection vol. 386.

44. Ibid., 3.

45. Ibid., 2.

46. Ibid. Section première of the Décret, Article XIV concerning the judgement and condemnation of émigrés stated that, *Les émigrés ne pourront, dans aucun cas, être jugés par jury* (at 96).

47. See Marc Bouloiseau, *l'Etude de l'émigration et la vente des biens des émigrés 1791–1830* (Paris, 1963), and André Gain, *La Restauration et les biens des émigrés* (Plancy, 1929), 2 vols.

48. The liberty of *cultes* had been declared but there was much mistrust of the counter-revolutionary designs of the Catholic Church whose interests would be best served by a restored monarchy. Chénier's speech of 12 Foréal an III underlined this: '*On dit souvent qu'il ne fallait point parler de religion dans la Convention nationale, et rien n'est plus vrai; les religions sont un domaine de la conscience: mais lorsqu'une opinion religieuse devient un prétexte pour violer la loi, ce n'est pas l'opinion religieuse que le législateur doit punir, c'est la loi voilée qu'il doit venger.*' Op cit., 6.

49. See Emmanuelle Rebardy, 'La Révolution contraire. Chateaubriand et le *Génie du Christianisme*, 1802. Genèse d'une pensée réactionnaire', *Annales historiques de la Révolution française*, 309 (1997), 492–501.

50. Roderer defined les royalistes-aristocrates in *Des Fugitifs Français et Des Emigrés* as '*les hommes pour qui ce qu'il avait de bon et de grand dans la révolution de 89, a été un malheur insupportable, et qui ont trouvé dans les maux qui l'ont suivie, plutôt une consolation ou une vengeance, qu'un nouveau motif de la détester.*'

51. Pierre-Louis Roederer [1754–1835] Lemay, ed., *Dictionnaire des Constituants, 1789–1791*, vol. II L-Y (Paris, 1991), 820–4.

52. Roederer, *Des Fugitifs Français et Des Émigrés*, 5 Floréal an III, p. 5, Maclure collection. '*Ceux qui ont quitté la France depuis le 10 du mois d'août, jusqu'au 20 octobre 1792; ceux qui l'ont quitté dans l'intervalle du 20 octobre au 31 mai; ceux enfin qui l'ont quitté du 31 mai au 10 thermidor.*'

53. Roederer, *Des Fugitifs Français et Des Emigrés*, 5 Floréal an III, op cit., 6.

54. Ibid., 7.

55. Ibid., 19.

56. J. Marchena, '*Quelques réflexions sur les Fugitifs Français depuis le 2 Septembre an III*' (Paris chez Gorsas Imprimeur-Libraire rue Neuve des Petits-Champs No. 74), 13.

57. Marquis de la Maisonfort, *Mémoires d'un agent royaliste, sous la Révolution, l'Empire et la Restauration, 1763–1827* (Paris, 1998), 129.

58. Some were able to get themselves taken off the émigré lists using devious tactics. Madame de Souza e.g. used Talleyrand plus her own outright lies and the authorities—too frustrated to follow up further—granted her radiation. Baron de Maricourt, *Madame de Souza et sa famille, Les Marigny, les Flahaut, Auguste de Morny, 1761–1836* (Paris, 1907), 210–14.

59. 'Defence of the French Emigrants' addressed to the People of France translated by John Gifford Esq. (London, 1797), 195.

60. See: Emmanuel de Waresquiel, 'Joseph Fouché et la question de l'amnistie des émigrés (1799-1802)' in *Annales historiques de la Révolution française*, n° 372, Armand Colin, Paris, 2013/2, pp. 105-120

61. An account of the reception of this news in London can be found in: *Mémoires de la comtesse de Boigne née Osmond, tome I Du règne de Louis XVI à 1820* (Paris, reprint 1986), 135–6.

62. See Simon Burrows, *French Exile Journalism and European Politics, 1792–1814*, op cit, 143-73.

63. Biography of *Louis XVIII* (1981), *Paris Between Empires 1814-1852* (2001) and the biography *The Prince of Europe. The life of Charles Joseph de Ligne 1735–1814* (2003). Mansel has worked to put the royalist faction around the exiled French King Louis XVIII in a more broadly contextualized perspective.

64. 'Defence of the French Emigrants' op cit., 39.

65. Madame de Staël, *Corinne ou Italie* (Paris, reprint 1985), 34. '*Cet homme avait supporté la perte entière d'une très grande fortune avec une sérénité parfaite; il avait vécu et fait vivre, par son talent pour la musique, un vieil oncle qu'il avait soigné jusqu'à sa mort; il s'était constamment refusé à recevoir les services d'argent qu'on s'était empressé à lui offrir; il avait montré la plus brillante valeur, la valeur française, pendant la guerre, et la gaieté la plus inaltérable au milieu des revers.*' On Madame de Staël as an émigré: Aprile, *Le siècle des exilés*, 49–56.

66. Evariste finds himself in sympathy with the plight of the émigré he is bound by a revolutionary's honour and law to condemn, and his inner struggle leaves him no peace beyond a vague sense that he is doing his duty and that future generations will benefit from his blood-stained hands.

67. For recent biographical work on émigrés in English, see Simon Burrows, *A King's Ransom, The life of Charles Thaveneau de Morande* (London, 2010); Caroline Moorehead, *Dancing to the Precipice, the Life of Lucie de la Tour du Pin Eye-witness to an Era* (London, 2009); Goodden, *Madame de Staël the Dangerous Exile*, and Angelica Gooddens, *The Sweetness of Life, a biography of the painter Elisabeth Louise Vigée Lebrun* (London, 1997).

68. Ragon, *La législation sur les Émigrés*, 2.

Selected Reading

Aprile, Sylvie, *Le siècle des exilés, Bannis et proscrits de 1789 à la Commune* (Paris, 2010).

Baldensperger, Fernand, *Le mouvement des idées dans l'émigration française 1789–1814* (Paris, 1924).

Bellenger, Dominic A., *The French Exiled Clergy* (Bath, 1986).

Bourdin, Pierre, ed., *La Révolution 1789–1791 Écriture d'une Histoire immédiate* (Clermont-Ferrand, 2008).

Burrows, Simon, *French Exile Journalism and European politics, 1792–1814* (Woodbridge, 2000).

Carpenter, Kirsty, *Refugees of the French Revolution, Émigrés in London 1789–1802* (London, 1999).

Carpenter, Kirsty, and Philip Mansel, eds., *The French Émigrés in Europe and the struggle against Revolution 1789–1814* (London, 1999).

Diesbach, Ghislain de, *Histoire de l'émigration* (Paris, 1975).

Doyle, William, *Aristocracy and its Enemies in the Age of Revolution* (Oxford, 2009).

Greer, Donald, *The Incidence of Emigration during the French Revolution* (Cambridge, 1983).

Goodden, Angelica, *Madame de Staël, the Dangerous Exile* (Oxford, 2008).

Martin, Jean-Clément, ed., *La Contre-révolution en Europe, XVIII-XIX siècles, réalités politiques et sociales, résonances culturelles et idéologiques* (Rennes, 2001).

Mansel, Philip, *Paris Between Empires, 1814–1852* (London, 2001).

——, *Louis XVIII*, revised edn (London, 2005).

Simonin, Anne, *Le Déshonneur dans la République. Une histoire de l'indignité 1791–1958* (Paris, 2008).

CHAPTER 20

CHALLENGES IN THE COUNTRYSIDE, 1790–2

NOELLE PLACK

AFTER the initial euphoria and upheaval of 1789, the following years were spent working out the goals, principles, and direction of the Revolution in the countryside. The extraordinary shift in power relations which had taken place during that 'unparalleled year' emboldened the peasantry to make ever more radical demands through sporadic uprisings and violent attacks, passive resistance, and petitioning lawmakers. Yet as a group the peasantry were diverse with differing linguistic and cultural practices as well as inhabiting distinct topographical regions with contrasting economic structures.

This chapter describes how the critical period of 1790–1 was one of transition with legislators in Paris working to devise policies that tried to bridge the considerable hopes and expectations of 1789 with practical, and often harsh, reality. Along the way some peasants became disenchanted with the transformations taking place and either pushed for greater change or sought to arrest such change. Rural unrest continued during the years 1790–2 and the relationship between legislators and country dwellers evolved and often exhibited signs of tension, negotiation, and compromise. The dialectical and transformative nature of their interactions can be seen in a number of arenas from the ending of seigneurial dues and rents to agrarian and tax reforms. This is before considering the gulf created by the revolutionaries' religious policy.

In terms of the Revolution in the countryside, this chapter will trace and access the impact of the new laws on feudalism, taxation, land holding as well as the religious schisms of 1791–2. Yet the categories are porous, for there was much overlap and interaction between these issues. Boundaries are needed, however, in an attempt to capture the diverse, complex, and sometimes, contradictory experiences of the people living in the villages and small market towns of the French countryside.

FEUDALISM

The peasantry's struggle to eradicate the feudal regime was one the defining and most original features of the French Revolution. Indeed, Georges Lefebvre argued three-quarters of a century ago that the peasant revolution of 1789 was independent of, but interactive with, the 'bourgeois' revolution.[1] In truth, the rural revolution was only just beginning in 1790 as many in the countryside felt that the decree of 4–11 August 1789, which 'abolished' feudalism, was actually 'a monstrous fraud'.[2] Rebellion and unrest continued throughout the period 1790-2 with widespread insurrection in the winter of 1789–90, the summers of 1790 and 1791, and the spring of 1792.

Historians generally agree that the abolition of feudalism was a dialectical process with waves of rural revolt followed by legislation dismantling certain aspects of the regime. The work of John Markoff in this area has furthered our understanding of the relationship between peasant and legislator; he argues that it was 'a dialogic process that led, not to a compromise, but to a mutual radicalization'.[3] Thus, the petitions sent to the Feudal Committee and the attacks on seigneurial chateaux, in which peasants destroyed manorial rolls, coats of arms, weathercocks, and much else, radicalized and pushed legislators into proposing more extreme measures. In turn, these legislative acts sent a signal to the rural world that their actions were producing results and presented opportunities for further insurrection. Markoff is very clear that it was the revolutionary *process* that forged these actions and their convergence brought down the seigneurial regime.

The wave of rebellion that engulfed parts of Brittany and the southwest in January–February 1790 forced the National Assembly to clarify the terms of the original August decree on feudalism in the spring of 1790. There were two main pieces of legislation. First, the law of 15–28 March 1790 spelled out which feudal rights would be abolished outright (*corvées*, *triage*, and *banalités*) and which ones would only be relinquished through indemnity because they derived from a concession of land once freely consented to. This muddled distinction between 'personal obligations' and 'real rights' pleased seigneurs and outraged peasants, as did the fact that the burden of proof for the remaining rights (*cens*, *champart*, and *tasque*) lay not with former lords but with village communities themselves.

Second, the law of 3–9 May 1790 set the rates for buying out these remaining 'real rights'—twenty times the amount of annual cash dues and twenty-five times the annual amount of dues payable in kind. Without doubt the peasantry *en bloc* rejected the idea of indemnification of seigneurial dues; there is very little evidence that redemption payments were made. Residents in Thuellins (Isère) explained in a petition to the Feudal Committee that 'not only is redemption impossible for poor proprietors, but it would be so disadvantageous [in general] that even the most easy in circumstances would not take advantage of it'.[4] Indeed, J. J. Clère has estimated that redemption payments for a single village could have totalled 50,000 to 60,000 *livres*—a sum equivalent to the amount of direct taxes paid by a village over twenty years or more.[5] Not only did peasants decline to buy out the remaining rights, they also refused to pay them by foot-dragging, quibbling, resistance, or outright revolt throughout the rest of 1790, all of 1791 and half of 1792. They demanded to see title deeds or pretended to 'misunderstand' the law; the newly elected municipalities and National Guard often aided and abetted the peasantry, essentially creating a 'popular front' against local seigneurs.

During the spring and summer of 1792 insurrection spread across the countryside on a scale not seen since the summer of 1789. There were anxieties and tensions around the food supply and the escalation of war, but these revolts were mostly, in J. P. Jessenne's assessment, an accumulation of impatience, irritation and frustration with the direction of the Revolution thus far.[6] For many rural dwellers their hopes and desires, especially in terms of the abolition of the feudal regime, had not been met. In the Centre and the Midi there was a wave of violent attacks, known as the *guerre aux châteaux;* while these revolts were predominantly anti-feudal in character, they also contained religious and patriotic elements. Some 600–1000 armed men in the district of Castelsarrasin (Tarn-et-Garonne) ransacked chateaux, burned feudal title deeds, stopped grain convoys, and chased away refractory priests in February 1792.[7] A tragic drowning of 69 army volunteers in the Rhône River near Avignon in March, which was blamed on 'aristocrats', sparked off a violent surge of chateaux burning in neighbouring departments. In the Gard alone more than one hundred chateaux were attacked and destroyed, prompting the district officials in Sommières to print a circular declaring that 'the hated vestiges of feudalism have disappeared from this country; the people (are) satisfied to never again see such humiliation'.[8]

These uprisings continued into the summer and in this charged atmosphere, the working people of Paris and army volunteers (*fédérés*) stormed the Tuileries palace on 10 August 1792 essentially ending the reign of Louis XVI. The crisis of the spring and summer 1792 served as a major turning point in the Revolution as it forced legislators to pass laws that satisfied the common people of France both urban and rural. In terms of seigneurialism, the law of 25 August 1792 proclaimed that all feudal dues were abolished without indemnity, except in cases where the *ci-devant* seigneur could produce an original title. This law effectively ended anti-feudal protests in the countryside. It was now almost impossible for former lords to collect what dues, in principle, remained as they rarely had possession of actual title deeds; they had either been destroyed by peasant attacks since 1789 or had never existed in the first place. The Jacobin law of 17 July 1793 abolished all feudal rights and dues (even if the former lord could produce a title) and is often seen as the crowning act that finally made good on the promise of the August decrees of 1789.

Most historians concur that the abolition of feudalism was one of the most profound consequences of the Revolution in the countryside. Judging from the breadth and scale of anti-seigneurial attacks all peasants (and many bourgeois proprietors) deeply resented the feudal regime. First and foremost the abolition of seigneurial rights principally benefited peasant landowners who no longer owed the lord dues on their harvest. Tenants and sharecroppers gained less from the abolition of feudal rents, dues and tithes, especially in Brittany where the *domaine congéable* (quasi-feudal tenures) remained.[9] This is perhaps one of the central reasons why counter-revolution took hold in the west. There were, however, clear socio-economic benefits as all peasants, regardless of their status as proprietors, tenants, or landless labourers, profited from the ending of tolls, compulsory labour, hunting rights, and monopolies over bread ovens, mills, and olive and wine presses.

Peasants across France also gained from the liquidation of seigneurial justice in which cases were tried by judges appointed and paid by the lord and its replacement with elected justices of the peace who were fairer, quicker, and less expensive.[10] There were also more non-tangible gains, as the shift in mental universe that the abolition of feudalism brought about was profound. John Markoff reminds us that the ending of 'the innumerable affronts to dignity' embodied in the lord–peasant relationship was a very significant non-economic benefit of the abolition of feudalism. He is also adamant that popular violent insurrection was a necessary component of the revolutionary process and contributed to human advance; for without their determined and aggressive fight, peasants in France would have most likely been burdened by feudal dues until at least the middle of the nineteenth century.[11] The abolition of feudalism may not have fostered the ascent of capitalism in the countryside but it did fundamentally alter rural social relationships and marked the end of the 'feudal *rentier* mentality' that had endured for centuries.

Taxation

Taxes were at the heart of the French Revolution. There is little doubt that issues of taxation were at the forefront of the majority of people's minds during the early months of 1789. It was *the* issue for most rural parishes as they drew up their *cahiers de doléances* for the Estates-General, appearing in eight out of ten of the subjects most widely discussed; this popular concern for taxation is simply unmatched by the grievances put forward by elites, be they clerics, nobles, or bourgeoisie.[12] In many ways the popular struggle against the tax system was similar to the battle against seigneurs; rebellion and protests often combined to bring down two of the most hated features of the *ancien régime*. There were widespread tax revolts in the spring and summer of 1789 but the challenge for deputies was to engineer a new system without losing revenue in the intervening time. Ultimately, this meant that the old taxes would remain in place for the rest of 1789 and all of 1790 until the new fiscal system could begin in 1791. This situation seriously tested the good will of the majority of the country-dwellers who believed, or chose to believe, that the Revolution had brought an end to state taxation in all of its forms.[13]

Tax revolt, in the form of petition, riot, resistance, and non-compliance was far more prevalent in the French Revolution than many historians realize. Barrie Rose has suggested that urban and rural refusal to pay taxes was as important to bringing down the *ancien régime* as subsistence riots and attacks on seigneurial chateaux.[14] These events, however, often go under-researched, perhaps because tax rebellions do not fit into the classic interpretative frameworks of French Revolutionary historiography—they cannot solely be described as anti-feudal, anti-capitalist, or anti-state. Nevertheless, throughout the first few years of the Revolution there were large-scale tax revolts in many parts of France, the challenge for historians is to find some meaningful way of cataloguing and analysing them.

Which taxes proved the most problematic? Indirect taxes on consumer goods were the target of much popular fury because many felt that the money went, not to the state, but into the coffers of the corrupt institution responsible for their collection, the General Tax Farm. The salt tax (*gabelle*) and taxes on alcoholic beverages (*aides*) were two of the most detested and contested levies. The decree of 23–7 September 1789 re-established the customs barriers around cities and towns, many of which had been attacked in previous months, to continue the perception of indirect taxes. Opposition to these extractions grew, however, once the principle of equal taxation without distinctions had been declared in October 1789. From Languedoc to Picardy, from Provence to the Vendée to the Nord, many communities reported difficulties in collecting indirect taxes and attacks on customs barriers from the autumn 1789 and throughout 1790.

These actions had profound implications; the General Tax Farm collected over 18.7 million *livres* in indirect taxes during the first third of 1790 but that figure had fallen to 8.6 million for the final trimester of the year.[15] In regions of both the *grande* and *petit gabelle*, there was continued resistance to pay the salt tax. A deputy from Anjou declared in February 1790 that peasants in his province 'were ready to sacrifice their lives ... if the *gabelle* was even provisionally re-instated'.[16] Contraband salt had always been available, but by early 1790 it would be a fair assessment to say that more untaxed salt was being sold and consumed than the legal variety. Dupont de Nemours, a prominent member of the Assembly's finance committee, admitted as much when he stated that 'entire provinces had been freed from the salt tax by insurrection'.[17] The National Assembly abolished the hated *gabelle* with the decree of 21–2 March 1790 along with taxes on leather, iron, oils, and soap. Yet with this law, came others throughout 1790 insisting on the continued collection of the remaining *aides* and *octrois* (municipal excise duties). For once the *gabelle* had been rescinded, the focus of revolt moved to the equally reviled tax on alcoholic beverages.

Wine was the most prominent type of alcohol as well as being one of the most heavily taxed commodities in eighteenth century France. By the time both the *aides* and the *octrois* were added to an ordinary barrel, its price was effectively tripled. Resistance and rebellion against taxes on wine were extensive in 1790 and these actions were among the few that united people from both town and countryside. Disturbances were reported in Touraine and Berry with crowds ready 'to exterminate' the tax-agents and those who supported their collection of the *aides*.[18] This was not unique but what was different in the context of 1790–1 was that people began to employ the ideals of liberty, equality and justice in their struggle against taxes on wine.[19] Indeed, for many, these taxes were immoral because of their regressive nature and should not exist in a nation inhabited by free citizens. This determined resistance had a dramatic effect. The *aides* had produced

52 million *livres* in 1788, but by the end of 1790 the corresponding figure was 13.75 million.[20] Even though the National Assembly had ideally wanted to retain indirect taxes in some form and particularly until the new tax system was up and running, certain deputies realized that their continued imposition would be impossible. After much debate, the *aides* and *octrois* were abolished 17–19 February 1791 with the latter decree coming into effect on 1 May 1791. On this day there were prolonged and exuberant celebrations in Paris and throughout France, which commemorated the end of duties on many consumer goods including wine, meat, and tobacco. Throughout most of the 1790s these products were sold without excises until Napoleon re-established indirect taxes on alcohol, tobacco, and salt in 1804 and 1806.

Revolts against direct taxes were never as violent, spectacular, or widespread as those against indirect extractions. In large measure this was due to the method of collection as the *taille*, the *capitation*, and the *vingtième* were paid directly to the state and not farmed out to third parties, but also because many believed them to be more legitimate. The French Revolution marked a major turning point, for by transferring sovereignty from the king to the nation, taxation lost its arbitrary power. The principle of equality transformed the relationship between state and society as taxes were now paid voluntarily by citizens to finance the general interests of the nation. However, this moment also created a tension, characteristic of modern democracy, between the ideal of consenting to tax and the maintenance of the coercive power of the state to supply its needs.[21] In the hope of securing some much needed income, the National Assembly passed a special one-off tax called 'the patriotic contribution' on 6 October 1789 with disappointing results. On 1 January 1790 all households, regardless of occupation or judicial status, were listed on the register for tax assessment, but this did not alter the fact that tax receipts for that year were dismal. The National Assembly projected 180 million *livres* for 1790, but only 33 million had been collected by September.[22] The following year the much-lauded revolutionary tax system was rolled out, based on three new taxes or 'contributions' as they had been renamed. Making up 75 per cent or 240 million *livres* of projected revenue was the *contribution foncière*, a tax on all landed property. The *contribution mobilière* was a tax on income and movable wealth, estimated to produce 60 million *livres* or 20 per cent of the state's revenue. The *patentes* were trade and commerce licences meant, in some measure, to replace the indirect taxes and were to make up the remaining 5 per cent of revenue. The fundamental problem with the first two new taxes, while founded upon the principles of equality and transparency, was that the assessments were based on pre-1789 tax capacity. Not until the Napoleonic land survey, the *cadastre*, begun in 1807 but not fully complete until the 1830s, would the Revolution's fiscal overhaul be wholly accomplished.

In theory the new fiscal system was an improvement on its predecessor but in practice there were still many inconsistencies, irregularities, and inequalities. For instance, peasants complained bitterly that the urban bourgeoisie through their control of departmental and district authorities had off-loaded the weight of the *contribution mobilière* on to countryside. This was ironic as this tax, designed to assess non-landed sources of income and wealth, ended up hitting peasant households in many departments from the

Côtes-du-Nord, Pyrénées-Orientales and Gers, to the Bouches-du-Rhône.[23] There has been great debate amongst contemporaries and historians surrounding the new tax system—did people pay more? In some regions, Brittany and the north, there is no doubt that tax burdens were increased. Georges Lefebvre found that households in the department of the Nord paid 11 *livres* each in 1792, but only paid 7 *livres* 10 *sols* under the *ancien régime*.[24] Yet in other departments (Puy-de-Dôme and Ardèche) per capita taxation remained unchanged while in the Lozère, Aveyron, Lot and Haute-Loire the tax burden was actually lighter under the new regime. To truly assess the Revolution's tax reforms one must look beyond the 1790s and into the Empire and Restoration when tax yields produced what legislators had hoped for in 1791.[25]

On the ground, however, what mattered was how people perceived the changes to the fiscal system. Some historians have argued that disenchantment with the new tax regime gave rise to counter-revolutionary sentiment and action. This certainly many have been the case in the west where per capita taxation appears to have doubled in Brittany and in some of the villages of the Vendée. However, in this debate on whether taxes increased markedly, we should not forget the ending of tithes and dues; landowning peasants were certainly better off, outside the west, as they retained on average about one-quarter more of their produce.[26] Despite the regional variations, the global tax burden most likely remained the same, yet who was paying had changed. As one prominent historian has claimed, 'lightening the overall load was probably never a realistic option, but the deputies of the National Assembly did put in place the foundations of what was to become a fairer tax system in the years ahead'.[27]

AGRARIAN REFORM

Attempts to transform the agricultural structures, practices, and outputs of the kingdom were nothing new, as the *ancien régime* monarchy had enacted various reforms since the 1760s. But with the watershed moment of 1789, the stage was set to completely rework the agrarian economy of France. The possibilities seemed endless. Legislators in the National Assembly were imbued with the idea that the territory of France needed to be as free as the men who inhabited it. Taking their cue from the Physiocrats and the *agronomes*, the principle of reform would be to emancipate the landed property of the nation from its centuries-old restrictions. The National Assembly wasted no time, setting up an Agricultural Committee in September 1789 and tasking it with the project to codify and 'modernize' all rural practices in France. This would prove to be an unreachable goal. The complex web of communal rights and customary practices, such as gleaning, stock grazing, and woodcutting, applied to both private property and common land and ensured the survival of many poor peasants as well as the proper functioning of the rural economy. Yet the members of the National Assembly were adamant that individual freedom in all agricultural domains was the only way to favour progress and that 'each proprietor must be the master of his domain'.[28]

The issues targeted for reform, including the restriction of collective pasturing (*vaine pâture*), the division of common land, clearing of wasteland, and draining of marshes as well as the establishment of a rural police force, were laid out in the summer of 1790 with the final draft of the entire project submitted to the National Assembly on 5 June 1791. The Rural Code, as it became known, was voted into law on 28 September 1791. While the new decree was a definitive legal statement fixing the rights and obligations of all members of the rural community, the overall effect of the legislation was contradictory and served, according to Peter Jones, as 'the juridical basis for the "historic compromise" between the bourgeoisie and the peasantry'.[29]

The heart of the problem lay in the fact that large landowners wanted their property rights vindicated. They believed that with the abolition of feudal dues, the long-standing collective and communal rights of the countryside must also be rescinded. In contrast, the peasantry, or at least the majority of smallholders and the landless, wanted private property that was free from servitudes or feudal dues whilst still retaining their collective grazing and gleaning rights on the lands of their neighbours. Perhaps the original remit was too great. Merlin de Douai, member of the Agricultural Committee, conceded as much when he declared that 'it is impossible to create universal rural laws'.[30] However, the Rural Code has turned out to be one of the most enduring pieces of Revolutionary legislation—the basic provision for collective grazing, including the right of the landless to pasture beasts, is still in existence today. Its main tenets have survived because they struck the right balance between protecting landowners' rights and safeguarding collective agricultural practices, which ensured the survival of large sections of rural society.[31]

One of the issues purposefully left out of the final Rural Code but central to the agrarian reform agenda was the partition of village common land (*biens communaux*). During the early years of the Revolution both legislators and many rural inhabitants were determined to share out the commons between individual proprietors. Yet they were not united over what proportion of the commons should be divided or who the beneficiaries should be. Indeed, in some areas like the west or Centre, the poor insisted on preserving communal land and collective access to it, while in the north-east and Midi, many smallholders were keen to divide these spaces.

The period 1790–2 witnessed a playing out of key issues in the debate over the commons and two inter-related phenomena can be detected. First, in line with the abolition of feudal dues and indirect taxes, there was an interactive dialogue between state and citizen. While officials and elites believed in a censitary distribution procedure whereby shares of common land would be awarded in proportion to landownership, David Hunt has analysed the petitions from villagers sent to the feudal and agricultural committees and has argued that these petitioners pushed legislators beyond their original positions and towards more democratic and egalitarian reform.[32] The most prevalent demands were to partition common land and to abolish the feudal right of *triage*, whereby a lord could usurp up to one-third of a community's common land.[33] This right was abolished outright under the law of 15 March 1790, but many rural dwellers also wanted the reintegration of lands that had been lost. The second manifestation of this period was the spontaneous division of common land in many regions, particularly in the north-east

(Aube, Marne, Oise, Seine-et-Oise, Seine-et-Marne, Somme) and the South (Ardèche, Aude, Bouches-du-Rhône, Hérault, Gard).[34]

Laws on common land reform were amongst the cascade of legislation pertaining to the countryside, which reached the statute books after the second revolution of 10 August 1792. The first measure was the law of 14 August 1792 that ordered the mandatory partition of all non-wooded common land. Although met with much excitement, the decree was inoperable as the *mode de partage* had yet to be determined. A more radical law, passed 28 August 1792, allowed communities to reintegrate any common land that had been unjustly taken from them by their former seigneurs. Historians have contended that this law resulted in thousands of actions to retrieve long-lost assets; in the Haute-Marne, for instance, communities invoked this decree against their seigneurs and successfully recovered land.[35] A feasible law for the partition of common land was finally decreed in the summer of 1793. Although this legislation has been at the heart of intense debates about the peasantry and their relationship to the French Revolution and agrarian capitalism,[36] there is consensus that in certain regions, particularly the north-east and south, the law of 10 June 1793 was implemented with some success.[37] Yet even in these areas, there was intra-communal tension, as many smallholding peasants desired a plot, while their better-off neighbours, who tended to monopolize the commons for pasture, were not as supportive of egalitarian division. On the whole, however, the privatization of common land during the Revolution did not occur on a very large scale, as many communities still saw value in continued collective ownership of these spaces for the grazing of livestock.

One of the reasons why many peasants were hopeful and anxious to receive a plot of land during these years was that the sales of nationalized church lands (*biens nationaux*) began in November 1790. The National Assembly had placed the landed property of the church at the 'disposal of the nation' in November 1789. By late spring of the following year it was decided to sell off these lands in large blocks at auctions held in the principal town of each district (decree of 14–17 May 1790). This stipulation tended to favour the bourgeoisie of cities and towns who had enough capital to purchase large tracts of land; it offered modest possibilities to wealthier peasants, but not much hope to the poor or landless unless they combined their funds and bid as a group. Nevertheless, modern research has determined that the peasantry acquired roughly 30 per cent of the church lands sold at auction.[38] This varied tremendously, however, according to region and the value and quality of lands on offer. In the department of the Nord, Georges Lefebvre found that 52 per cent of the purchasers of church lands were peasants and 48 per cent were of bourgeois origin; Lefebvre used this evidence to argue that a whole new class of smallholders were created by the sales of *biens nationaux*.[39] Yet the Nord seems to be an exception rather than the rule in terms of dramatically transforming peasant land ownership, for almost everywhere else it was the well-to-do of country towns or the wealthiest peasants who dominated the purchases of church lands in 1791.

However, the popular uprising of 10 August 1792 ushered in another phase in the revolutionary land settlement. It was decided just four days later to confiscate the lands of *émigré* nobles and sell them as *biens nationaux* of second origin. A workable law was finally passed on 3 June 1793; the lands were still to be sold at auction but they were to be divided up 'as far as possible ... into lots or portions' with the specific purpose of helping the poor receive a plot. Bodinier and Teyssier are certain that the peasantry benefited from this Jacobin policy subdivision and estimate that they secured around 40 per cent of all *émigré* lands sold.[40] In total, then, the peasantry procured through the sale of nationalized lands around 1.5 million hectares, around 3 per cent of the soil surface area. Yet these results were not evenly distributed throughout the country. In the vast cereal plains north of Paris, there were hardly any beneficiaries of peasant origin. While in the departments of the Ardèche, Averyron and the Hérault, the peasantry acquired between 50 per cent and 70 per cent of all *biens nationaux* sold.[41]

Religion

During these years the National Assembly's religious policy was an arena that created unrivalled tension, anxiety, and disappointment. The Catholic Church not only lost all of its land, but also much power, prestige, and above all its independence. The new governance structure for the Church was ratified on 12 July 1790 and become known as the Civil Constitution of the Clergy. Described by Timothy Tackett as 'a remarkably radical' document,[42] it failed to win much support amongst the men and women of rural France as it prescribed a whole package of wide-ranging reforms to popular religious habits. While some parish *cahiers* suggested moderate changes to the Gallican church, such as the abolition of surplus fees and adjustments to the tithe, the Civil Constitution set forth an unprecedented level of religious change that went well beyond anything recommended in the *cahiers de doléances* of 1789.[43] Not only were bishops and priests made salaried employees of the state, which improved the living standards of some of the poorest parish *curés*, they would henceforth be elected by the laity, rather than appointed by their superiors, and the number of bishoprics would be reduced from 136 to 83, one for each department.

More disturbing for rural dwellers was the initiative to reorganize and rationalize the number of parishes and close small churches in outlying hamlets. This caused much fear, anger and resentment in many communities which lost the right to worship as independent entities, for the physical environment of the church, with its yard and cemetery, was central not only to spiritual, but also temporal life. In the department of the Cher, the inhabitants of Saint-Doulchard pleaded with officials not to close their local church, 'to take it away would be an act of atrocious barbarism'.[44] The reduction in the number of parishes was significant in some areas: in the district of La Roche-sur-Yon (Vendée), 19 out of 52 parish churches were closed, while the country towns of Bayeux (Calvados) and Laon (Aisne) lost 15 and 10 churches respectively, leaving each with only two.[45] Even though *ancien régime* parishes were extraordinarily diverse in terms of size, the new dioceses were more or less equal and coterminous with the administrative districts. In the final analysis, over fifty bishoprics, all archbishoprics and several hundred parishes were abolished under the Civil Constitution of the Clergy.[46]

If there was a point where the Revolution 'went wrong' it was when the National Assembly imposed the oath to the Civil Constitution of the Clergy on 27 November 1790. Historians have viewed the oath as a critical turning point in the Revolution and have interpreted it, amongst other things, as the beginnings of a 'cultural revolution', the basis for the popular counter-revolution, and another episode in broader church–state relations.[47] While on paper asking clerics to take an oath of fidelity to the nation, the law, the king, and the new Revolutionary constitution may have seemed relatively benign, in reality it became a referendum on whether one's first loyalties were to Catholicism or to the Revolution. Given the fact that almost all of the bishops and a little less than half of the parish clergy refused to take the oath, there is broad consensus that it led to an acute political and religious divide throughout France and led to the first great rupture in the Revolution since 1789.

For almost two hundred years historians have tried to uncover how many parish priests actually swore the oath during the thousands of ceremonies that took place in January and early February 1791. While about 52 per cent of the parish clergy took the oath overall, what is notable is the remarkable regional variation which Timothy Tackett's work has illuminated. The majority of priests swore the oath in the Paris basin, the Berry-Bourbon centre, southern Poitou, the Guyenne-Gasçon south-west, and the Alps, while for the most part the clergy refused the oath in Brittany, western Normandy, northern Poitou, the Midi, Alsace, Franche-Comte, and Flanders. Clerical density was a crucial factor in priests taking the oath, according to Tackett, as non-jurors were most likely from robust clerical communities, while jurors probably resided in parishes having a lone pastor or relatively few *vicaires*.[48]

Throughout the rest of 1791 and most of 1792 there was an ambiguous situation as the National Assembly, in its policy of toleration, allowed the non-juring clergy to continue practising as a parallel, unofficial cult.[49] This state of uncertainly remained until the provisional government of August 1792 issued a decree that led to the deportation of all non-jurors. There is no doubt that the issue of the oath led to much pressure, unease and violent protest in certain areas and that it did fuel hostility towards the Revolution. Yet it should not be exaggerated, since, as one noted historian of the counter-revolution has remarked, 'in many areas of the country, where the clergy took the oath, life carried on much as before'.[50]

One region that was profoundly affected by the oath, however, was the west of France. Indeed, by 1792 areas of Brittany, Anjou, Maine, lower Poitou, and lower Normandy were sites of open popular rebellion against the Revolutionary regime. A year later these conflicts had escalated to civil war; known as the *Vendée* and *Chouannerie*, historians have tried to uncover why rural opposition to the Revolution in the west began so early, spread so widely, and attained such a degree of violence, intensity, and organization. Some have insisted on the socio-economic origins of the rebellion, such as the degree of 'modernization' or system of land tenure and rural distribution of wealth, while others have stressed the uniqueness of regional church structures and religious culture.[51]

Tackett has underlined the distinctive features of the Church in the west—the distribution of Church wealth, the rural density of the clergy, and the patterns of rural recruitment; he has also uncovered a 'missing ingredient' that helps to explain the explosive nature of religious reform in this region. It was a strikingly anti-clerical urban elite culture, which clashed with rural dwellers that led to such hostility and conflict. These urban elites filled district and departmental positions and used the Civil Constitution, not as a plan for regenerating the Church, but as the means of 'relegating priests to their proper place'.[52] By early 1792 these officials were drawing up unilateral and technically illegal orders to round up and imprison all refractory priests in the region, long before it became national policy to do so.

The religious crisis of 1791–2, however, should not just be reduced to the oath and the replacement of trusted clerics with 'intruders', however traumatic these operations must have been, but should also include the broader ecclesiastical reorganization, including the sale of *biens nationaux*. Edward J. Woell has recently argued that the Revolution faltered during these years, because the oath and religious reforms divided France so profoundly; there was little chance of it truly becoming a 'deliberative democracy' in which the citizenry is able to participate openly and make collective decisions.[53] The teasing out of the Revolution's religious policy in the west underscores the complexity of the social, cultural, economic, and political forces at play.

A similar confluence was on display in the outbreaks of violence that occurred in the Midi in 1790–1. Protestant–Catholic relations in Languedoc had been troubled since the Revocation of the Edict of Nantes in 1685 and the War of the Camisards (1702–5); the Revolution of 1789 only aggravated these long-standing conflicts and provided a context for further aggression. On 24 December 1789 the National Assembly granted Protestants complete civil and religious equality, voting rights and entry to the National Guard based on property qualifications. By the spring of 1790, after the National Assembly's refusal of Dom Gerle's motion to proclaim Catholicism the state religion, tensions between emancipated Protestants and fearful Catholics came to a head across the Midi.

The department of the Gard was the site of the bloodiest conflicts. It was here that the first serious threat against the Revolution took hold as the ultra-Catholic François Froment secretly planned to launch a grand offensive to restore the king's authority in early 1790.[54] Violence soon followed as Protestants, who had been excluded from municipal office in February, were elected to the new departmental administration in June, sparking off riots in Nîmes in which a sectarian call to arms ended with the superior Protestant forces massacring two to three hundred Catholics over several days. This incident, known as the *bagarre de Nîmes*, fuelled suspicion that Protestants were manipulating the Revolution and gave birth to the first 'Camp de Jalès' in August 1790 at which some 20,000 Catholic peasants from 180 parishes protested against the killings of the previous month. In February 1791, a second 'Camp de Jalès' took place in the hills south of the Ardèche at which 10,000 Catholics gathered to demonstrate against another violent episode at Uzès.[55] Violence in the Midi had sectarian tensions at its heart. Protestants went on to dominate many municipal, district and departmental administrations in Languedoc for the next two decades; it was not until the 'White Terror' of 1815 that Catholics were able to regain control and extract their revenge.

* * *

The years 1790–2 in the countryside were a time of challenges and opportunities, better understood in terms of further revolution and unrest than counter-revolution and collapse. This is clearly seen in three out of the four areas under analysis in this chapter. However, the sheer range of issues necessarily had a different dynamic and outcome according to place and social structure. There continued to be attacks against seigneurial chateaux, tax revolts and conflicts over land; these confrontations put pressure on legislators to extend the scope of their reform projects. These encounters are evidence of the negotiation and compromise between the state and its citizens and were at the heart of the revolutionary process. In the realm of religion, there was breakdown, and fissures did occur between the policies of the National Assembly and the rural population in several regions, but this overwhelmingly manifested itself in an anti-revolutionary stance rather than full-blown counter-revolution (which it would become in subsequent years).

We should not forget that peasants, often treated by outsiders as an anonymous mass, were as multi-faceted and complex as any other members of revolutionary French society—they could exhibit pro-Catholic and pro-royalist tendencies on the one hand yet at the same time participate in anti-feudal, anti-tax, and agrarian reform campaigns. The characterization of counter-revolutionary and patriot is too simplistic for these early years of the revolutionary dynamic. As one respected historian has recently noted, it is difficult to categorize rural France in 1792–3 as massively pro- or counter-revolutionary as its structural diversity created at least five different responses to the cataclysm, ranging from centres of communal Jacobinism to the extraordinary and singular reaction in the *Vendée*.[56] Indeed, the idea of counter-revolution is far too stringent for these years as it 'telescopes a number of possible stances and denies the transformative character of politics that the French Revolution was in the throes of creating'.[57] This chapter has thus highlighted the diverse and complex (re) actions of rural populations to key issues and has demonstrated that the peasantry, in concert with urban legislators, helped to shape the aims, meaning, and course of the Revolution in the countryside.

NOTES

1. G. Lefcbvre, *The Coming of the French Revolution* trans. by R. R. Palmer (Princeton, NJ, 1947).
2. P. M. Jones, *The Peasantry in the French Revolution* (Cambridge, 1988), 81.
3. J. Markoff, *The Abolition of Feudalism: Peasants, Lords and Legislators in the French Revolution* (University Park, PA, 1996).
4. P. Sagnac and P. Caron, *Les Comités des droits féodaux et de legislation et l'abolition du régime seigneurial, 1789–1793* (Paris, 1907), 252.

5. J. J. Clère, 'L'abolition des droits féodaux en France', *Cahiers d'histoire. Revue d'histoire critique* 94–4 (2005), 135–57.

6. J. P. Jessenne, *Les Campagnes françaises: entre mythe et histoire (XVIIIe–XXIe siècle)* (Paris, 2006), 143.

7. A. Ado, *Paysans en Révolution: terre, pouvoir et jacquerie, 1789–1794* (Paris, 1996), 263.

8. F. Rouvière, *Histoire de la Révolution française dans le département du Gard.* (Nîmes, 1888, reprint: Laffitte, 1974), vol. II, 198.

9. T. J. A. Le Goff, *Vannes and Its Region: a study of town and country in eighteenth century France* (Oxford, 1981); D. M. G. Sutherland, *The Chouans: The Social Origins of Popular Counter-revolution in Upper Brittany, 1770–1796* (Oxford, 1982). See as well, D. M. G. Sutherland, 'Peasants, Lords, and Leviathan: Winners and Losers from the Abolition of French Feudalism, 1780–1820', *The Journal of Economic History* 62, no. 1 (2002), 1–24.

10. A. Crubaugh, *Balancing the Scales of Justice: Local Courts and Rural Society in Southwest France, 1750–1800* (University Park, PA, 2001). Note however, J. Hayhoe, *Enlightened Feudalism: Seigneurial Justice and Village Society in Eighteenth-century Northern Burgundy* (Rochester, NY, 2008).

11. Markoff, *The Abolition of Feudalism*, 588–94 and J. Markoff, 'Violence, Emancipation and Democracy: The Countryside and the French Revolution', *American Historical Review* 100 (1995), 360–86.

12. Markoff, *The Abolition of Feudalism*, 37.

13. Jones, *Peasantry*, 181–4.

14. B. R. Rose, 'Tax Revolt and Popular Organization in Picardy 1789–1791', *Past & Present* 43 (1969), 92–108.

15. M. Marion, 'Le Recouvrement des Impôts en 1790', *Revue Historique* 121 (1916), 36–7.

16. Cited in Ado, *Paysans en Révolution*, 199.

17. *Archives Parlementaires*, XXV, 53.

18. Archives Nationales, D XXIX bis 34, 355.

19. N. Plack, 'Liberty, Equality and Taxation: Wine in the French Revolution', *Social History of Alcohol and Drugs* 26, no. 1 (2012), 5–22.

20. F. Braesch, *Finances et monnaie révolutionnaires. Les exercises budgétaires de 1790 et 1791 d'après les comptes du Trésor* (Nancy, 1934), 44.

21. N. Delalande, *Les batailles de l'impôt: consentement et résistance de 1789 à nos jours* (Paris, 2011), 23–36.

22. Marion, 'Le Recouvrement', 25.

23. Jones, *Peasantry*, 189–90.

24. G. Lefebvre, *Les paysans du Nord pendant la Révolution française* (Bari, 1959), 604–5.

25. T. J. A. LeGoff and D. M. G. Sutherland, 'The Revolution and the Rural Economy' in Alan Forrest and Peter Jones (eds), *Reshaping France: Town, Country and Region during the French Revolution* (Manchester, 1991), 69–71; Sutherland, 'Peasants, Lords and Leviathan', 7–11.

26. P. McPhee, *Living the French Revolution, 1789–1799* (Basingstoke, 2006), 211.

27. P. M. Jones, *Reform and Revolution in France: the politics of transition, 1774–1791* (Cambridge, 1995), 206.

28. *Restauration de l'agriculture en France, et moyens de prévenir toute disette*, par un cultivateur, député à l'Assemblé Nationale (Paris, 1790).

29. Jones, *Peasantry*, 129.

30. *Archives Parlementaires*, XXIX, 256.

31. N. Plack, 'Collective Agricultural Practices and the French state: Aspects of the Rural Code from the 18th to the 20th Century' in Nadine Vivier (ed.) *The State and Rural Societies: Policy and Education in Europe, 1750–2000* (Turnhout, 2008), 95–110.

32. D. Hunt, 'Peasant Movements and Communal Property during the French Revolution', *Theory and Society* 17 (1988), 255–83.

33. N. Vivier, *Propriété collective et identité communale: les biens communaux en France, 1750–1914* (Paris, 1998), 104–15.

34. Ado, *Paysans en Révolution*, 275–80.

35. J. Clère, *Les paysans de la Haute-Marne et le Révolution francaise* (Paris, 1988), 217–34.

36. See P. McPhee, 'The French Revolution, Peasants and Capitalism', *American Historical Review* 94 (1989), 1265–80; P. M. Jones, 'Georges Lefebvre and the Peasant Revolution: Fifty Years On', *French Historical Studies* 16 (1990), 545–63.

37. For regional studies see G. R. Ikni, *Crise agraire et révolution paysanne, le mouvement populaire dans les campagnes de l'Oise de la décennie physiocratique à l'an II* (Lille, 1993); P. McPhee, *Revolution and Environment in Southern France: Peasants, Lords and Murder in the Corbières 1780–1830* (Oxford, 1999); N. Plack, *Common Land, Wine and the French Revolution: Rural Society and Economy in Southern France, c.1789–1820* (Burlington, VT, 2009).

38. B. Bodinier and E. Teyssier, *L'événement le plus important de la Révolution: la vente des biens nationaux* (Paris, 2000), 220.

39. Lefebvre, *Les paysans du Nord*, 514–25.

40. Bodinier and Teyssier, *L'événement le plus important*, 222–3. See as well, P. M. Jones, 'The "Agrarian Law": Schemes for Land Redistribution during the French Revolution', *Past & Present* 133, no. 1 (1991), 96–133.

41. B. Bodinier, 'La Révolution française et la question agraire: le bilan national en 2010', *Histoire et Sociétés Rurales* 33 (2010), 7–47.

42. (Princeton, NJ, 1986), 12.

43. N. Aston, *Religion and Revolution in France 1780–1804* (Washington, DC, 2000), 165–6; Tackett, *Religion, Revolution, and Regional Culture*, 11–14.

44. M. Bruneau, *Les débuts de la Révolution dans les départements du Cher et de l'Indre, 1789–1791* (Paris, 1901), 392.

45. P. McPhee, *The French Revolution, 1789–1799* (Oxford, 2002), 111; McPhee, *Living the French Revolution*, 84.

46. Tackett, *Religion, Revolution, and Regional Culture*, 15.

47. J. McManners, *The French Revolution and the Church* (London, 1969), 38; M. P. Fitzsimmons, *The Night the Old Regime Ended: August 4, 1789, and the French Revolution* (University Park, PA, 2003), 91–92; Sutherland, *France 1789–1815: Revolution and Counterrevolution* (London, 1985), 97–99; Tackett, *Religion, Revolution, and Regional Culture*, 287–300.

48. Tackett, *Religion, Revolution, and Regional Culture*, 34–56.

49. See Aston, *Religion and Revolution in France 1780–1804*, 170–2.

50. Sutherland, *France 1789–1815: Revolution and Counterrevolution*, 117.

51. P. Bois, *Paysans de l'Ouest* (Paris, 1971); C. Tilly, *The Vendée* (Cambridge, MA, 1964); T. J. A. Le Goff and D. M. G. Sutherland, 'The Social Origins of Counter-Revolution in Western France', *Past & Present* 99 (1983), 65–87; T. Tackett, 'The West in France in 1789: The Religious Factor in the Origins of the Counterrevolution', *The Journal of Modern History* 54 no. 4 (1982), 715–45.

52. Tackett, *Religion, Revolution, and Regional Culture*, 275.

53. E. J. Woell, 'The Origins and Outcomes of Religious Schism, 1790 99', in Peter McPhee (ed.), *A Companion to the French Revolution* (Oxford, 2013), 151.

54. G. Lewis, *The Second Vendée, the Continuity of Counter-Revolution in the Gard, 1789–1815* (Oxford, 1978); James N. Hood, 'Protestant-Catholic Relations and the Roots of the First Popular Counterrevolutionary Movement in France', *Journal of Modern History* 43 (1971), 245–75; and 'Patterns of Popular Protest in the French Revolution: The Conceptual Contribution of the Gard', *Journal of Modern History* 48 (1976), 259–93.

55. F. de Jouvenel, 'Les campes de Jalès (1790–1792), épisodes contre-revolutionnaires?' *AHRF* 337 (2004), 1–20.

56. J. P. Jessenne, 'Une Révolution sans ou contre les paysans?' in Michael Biard (ed.) *La Rvolution française: une histoire toujours vivante* (Paris, 2009), 260–1.

57. P. M. Jones, 'Choosing Revolution and Counter-Revolution', in Peter McPhee (ed.) *A Companion to the French Revolution* (Oxford, 2013), 288.

SELECTED READING

Ado, A., *Paysans en Révolution: terre, pouvoir et jacquerie, 1789–1794* (Paris, 1996).

Jessenne, J. P., 'The Land: Redefinition of the Rural Community', in Keith Michael Baker (ed.), *The French Revolution and the Creation of Modern Political Culture, vol. 4 The Terror* (Oxford, 1994), 223–47.

Jones, P. M., *The Peasantry in the French Revolution* (Cambridge, 1988).

Jones, P. M., 'Georges Lefebvre and the Peasant Revolution: Fifty Years on', *French Historical Studies* 16 (1990), 545–63.

Lefebvre, G., 'The Place of the Revolution in the Agrarian History of France', in Robert Forster and Orest Ranum (eds), *Rural Society in France: Selections from the Annales: Économies, Sociétés, Civilisations*, translated by Elborg Forster and Patricia M. Ranum (Baltimore, MD, 1977), 31–49.

Markoff, J., 'Violence, Emancipation and Democracy: The Countryside and the French Revolution', *American Historical Review* 100 (1995), 360–86.

Markoff, J., *The Abolition of Feudalism: Peasants, Lords and Legislators in the French Revolution* (University Park, PA, 1996).

McPhee, P., *Living the French Revolution, 1789–1799* (Basingstoke, 2006).

Tackett, T., *Religion, Revolution, and Regional Culture in Eighteenth-Century France: The Ecclesiastical Oath of 1791* (Princeton, NJ, 1986).

CHAPTER 21

··

CLUBS, PARTIES, FACTIONS

··

CHARLES WALTON

WHAT role did political clubs play in the French Revolution? Were they engines of democratization and social justice or seedbeds of factionalism and terror? Views on the clubs have divided historians ever since the early nineteenth century. In her *Considerations on the Principal Events of the French Revolution*, Mme de Stael demonized the most influential of clubs, the Jacobins: 'The dreadful sect of Jacobins pretended to found liberty on despotism, and from that system arose all the crimes of the Revolution.'[1] A few decades later, Jules Michelet cast the clubs in a more favourable light. He attributed their emergence across France in 1789 and 1790 to political crisis: '[They] grew out of the situation itself, from the most imperious necessity, that of public safety.' He also stressed the 'genius' of the Paris Cordeliers Club for its 'popular reason' and concern for the working classes.[2]

Conflicting views on French Revolutionary clubs persisted over the next two centuries. At the turn of the twentieth, Augustin Cochin attributed the Revolution's 'terrorist legislation' to the clubs, which he saw as growing out of the late old regime's 'sociétés de pensée' (salons, circles, clubs, literary associations). He echoed Alexis de Tocqueville's criticism of Revolutionaries' excessive philosophical zeal, or what de Tocqueville referred to as their 'abstract literary politics', but he developed this criticism along sociological lines: commitments to egalitarianism and political unanimity, largely inspired by the writings of Jean-Jacques Rousseau, led the clubs to impose a pre-manufactured 'general will' and to denounce or expel anyone who disagreed with it. This dynamic, already present in the clubs of the early Revolution, gradually seeped into revolutionary politics more generally, with calamitous consequences. Between August 1793 and August 1794, 'Rousseau's idea, direct democracy, achieves its realisation; it is the year of the Terror.'[3]

In the 1970s, François Furet drew heavily from de Tocqueville and Cochin in analysing Jacobinism. He saw early revolutionary commitments to democratic equality and collective sovereignty as generative of paranoia, denunciations and purges. Although Jacobin clubs initially supported constitutional monarchy and tended to limit membership to elites (membership fees were high), their high-minded principles of equality and moral regeneration unwittingly drove them towards the Terror. Cochin and Furet's critiques of the Jacobin clubs chimed with conservative and liberal views of the Revolution: Cochin was a devout Catholic, sympathized with the counter-revolution and greatly admired Hippolyte Taine, an influential conservative historian of the late nineteenth century. For his part, Furet was inspired by liberalism, especially in the vein of Madame de Staël and Benjamin Constant, whom Furet sought to resurrect in French Revolutionary historiography.

Republican and Marxist views on the Revolutionary clubs were more sympathetic. After publishing several volumes of the minutes of the Paris Jacobin Club's meetings, François-Alphonse Aulard, writing in the 1890s, concluded that the club was not ideologically inflexible, as often claimed. The club was willing to 'bend to circumstances' and 'reflected the vicissitudes of public sentiment'. True, Jacobins may have been naive in seeking to spread Republican principles across Europe, he conceded, but their zealous pedantry should not deprive them of the credit due to them for being, in politics, 'the first primary school instructors of France'.[4] More recently, Raymonde Monnier, seeking to nuance Albert Soboul's 'class' interpretation of popular politics, contends that the clubs played a crucial role in developing 'democratic public space'. Factionalism, she argues, had less to do with class or egalitarian ideology than with tensions between Paris and the surrounding countryside over grain and general fears about subsistence.[5]

Ideology and circumstances, then, are the two principal lines of interpretation for factionalism in French Revolutionary politics. This chapter will introduce an alternative thesis: namely, the weak state. The conditions generated by it radicalized the discourse and actions of the clubs. But before re-examining the sources of factionalism in the clubs, it is worth reviewing, first, the clubs' origins and the kinds that existed (they were not all Jacobin); second, what the clubs actually did and not just what they professed (actions cannot be reduced to ideas); and finally, the political context in which the political clubs evolved ('weak state' conditions, which radicalized civil society).

THE ORIGINS AND RISE
OF REVOLUTIONARY CLUBS

One of the earliest Revolutionary clubs, or circles, of 1789 was the Club de Valois. Co-founded by the abbé Sieyès on 11 February 1789, the club met in the Palais-Royal under the sponsorship of the duc d'Orléans, cousin (and purported rival) of Louis XVI. It counted more than six hundred members. Many were of noble origins, robe and sword, which is ironic given that Sieyès published *What is the Third Estate?* at the time of the club's founding. Members came from the haute bourgeoisie as well, and included financiers and wholesale merchants (*négociants*). The Club de Valois was short-lived, quite contentious, and its internal clashes escalated not infrequently into duels.[6]

Members would go on to span the political spectrum in later years, joining the Jacobins (left, centre-left), the Feuillants (constitutional monarchs who split off from the Jacobin Club) or the Club monarchique (right, centre-right).

Most historical accounts of the Revolutionary clubs begin with the Breton Club, which formed during the Meeting of the Estates-General in early May 1789. Spearheaded by a group of Third Estate deputies from Brittany, the club met regularly at a café in Versailles over the summer to strategize. It folded when the National Constituent Assembly followed the king to Paris in October, but the following month several of its former members founded the *Société de la Révolution*, named after a London club that publicly sympathized with the reforms of the French Revolution. In January 1790, the club changed its name to the *Société des amis de la Constitution* and rented space in a Jacobin convent on the rue Saint Honoré, near the National Assembly hall—hence their more familiar name, the Jacobin Club. Initially liberal and selective, the club would become more democratic and republican after July 1791, when a factional split and defection of members committed to constitutional monarchy, a split sparked by dramatic events (the royal family's attempt to flee France in late June and the fusillade of patriots in July), forced the Jacobins to seek the support of commoner and poor sectors of the population.

Political clubs proliferated throughout France in 1789 and 1790. Many grew out of, or followed the traditions of, late old regime voluntary associations: freemasonry clubs, Mesmerist harmony societies, philanthropic societies, and reading salons. Provincial clubs often sought affiliation with the Jacobin Club in Paris, which offered benefits. Affiliation provided access to influential national deputies and to news about legislation and events taking place in the capital. It also conferred legitimacy, which was important in a legal climate in which voluntary associations were at the mercy of municipal authorities, which had been given vast legal powers to maintain public order in 1789. Although the Declaration of the Rights of Man and of the Citizen did not grant the right of association, a decree passed on 14 December 1789 extended this right in a limited way to active citizens, that is, males over 25 years of age who paid the equivalent of three days' wages of an unskilled worker in taxes and who were deemed neither bankrupt nor insolvent. The decree required club meetings to be approved by municipal authorities and to be limited to the drafting of addresses and petitions, deputations for which could not exceed ten citizens.[7]

Several municipalities tried to restrict or suppress the Jacobin clubs, especially in areas with intense opposition to the Revolution's religious policies, which the Jacobin clubs supported (expropriation of Church property and the ecclesiastical oath to the constitution that all clerics were required to swear). Seeking to strengthen local support for these reforms, the National Assembly passed a more liberal decree on 13 November 1790, extending 'the freedom to assemble peaceably and to form free societies' to all citizens, active and passive (the question of gender was not addressed). Over the next three months, the number of cities with clubs affiliated with the Paris Jacobins doubled, from 213 to 427.[8] Several cities had more than one patriotic club. Some of the newer clubs grew out of factional splits in the established ones; others out of class dynamics: many could not afford the high membership fees of the elite clubs. In Nîmes, for example, the bourgeois patriot club charged 24 livres. The rival popular club, on the other hand, charged only 6 livres, payable in three instalments.[9] Although tensions existed between competing local clubs in some towns and cities, in many cases, pro-Revolutionary clubs managed to coexist peacefully. Sometimes they established alliances or fused.

Provincial patriot clubs expanded dramatically in the early years of the Revolution. Although not all provincial clubs were affiliated with the Paris Jacobins, the increase in the number of cities with affiliations to the mother club provides a general sense of growth rates: from 20 cities with affiliations in January 1790 to 921 by July 1791.[10] Representatives-on-mission, sent by the National Convention into the provinces in 1793, frequently founded patriotic clubs in (mostly rural) areas where enthusiasm for the Revolution was weak and contributions to the war effort minimal or nil. In this radical phase (1793–94), some clubs became de facto branches of administration. They collaborated closely with local *comités révolutionnaires* and *comités de surveillance* and became the arms through which the representatives-on-mission imposed emergency measures.[11] In places where local officials were lax or inactive, the clubs might take control, with the blessing of the representative-on-mission. By the start of the Year II (September 1793), in towns that had a club, local officials were likely to be club members. In Bayeux, for example, the local club declared, after a purge of the local administration: 'Henceforth, the municipality and the club will be one-in-the-same.'[12]

After 9 September 1793, the National Convention sought to curtail sans-culotte militancy in the Paris sections by passing a decree limiting meetings to twice per week (they had been meeting *en permanence*). To sweeten this bitter pill, the Convention called for paying the poor 2 livres to attend each of these bi-weekly meetings, as a means of extending social assistance. Circumventing these restrictions, sectional militants founded popular societies in the fall of 1793. In the late spring and summer of 1794 (even before 9 Thermidor and the fall of the *robespierristes*), the sectional clubs began closing, for a variety of reasons: exhaustion with factionalism, but above all, pressure and manipulation on the part of the Jacobin Club and the government (especially the Committees of General Security and of Public Safety, themselves at odds with each other). Clubs were abolished by the decree of 6 Fructidor Year III (23 August 1795), but they resurfaced clandestinely during the Directory. One finds neo-Jacobins meeting in Paris in the lead-up to the Fructidor coup of the Year V and across France in the months prior to the Brumaire coup of 1799, which brought Napoleon to power.[13] Counter-revolutionary clubs re-emerged as well, most notably, the Club de Clichy in Paris.[14] Napoleon's prefectures, which were established in February 1800 and given vast policing powers, stifled all significant club activity until 1814.

Anti- and counter-revolutionary clubs, often overlooked by historians, also emerged in the early years of the Revolution.[15] Little is known about these fleeting associations, but according to Paul R. Hanson, they existed in at least thirty-five towns and cities across France, including large ones such as Paris, Bordeaux, Aix-en-Provence, La Rochelle, Strasbourg, and Toulouse.[16] Like their radical counterparts, the royalist clubs were prone to paranoia, denunciations, and violence. Though staunchly in favour of patriarchal authority, they shared with their Jacobin rivals the belief that particular interests should be subordinated to the general interest. In the preamble to its prospectus, the monarchical club in Limoges expressed its aversion to all 'private associations'. The short-lived Club des Impartiaux in 1790, and subsequently, the Club monarchique, both founded in Paris by centre-right deputies of the Constituent Assembly, mounted a relentless libel campaign against the Jacobins. Like their adversaries, the Club monarchique sought and secured provincial affiliations.

Local royalist clubs often clashed with the patriotic societies, sometimes violently. In December 1790, members of the royalist *Club des amis de la paix* in Aix-en-Provence insulted and shot members of Aix's two patriotic clubs, killing one and wounding several others in front of a royalist café (the club's meeting place) on the Cours Mirabeau. The popular clubs forced authorities to hand over two detained suspects deemed responsible for the violence. After tracking down a third (the instigator), the popular clubs hanged all three men near the site of the shootings. This was an extreme case. Still, tensions between pro and anti-Revolutionary clubs ran high in several towns, exacerbated by a polarized press in which royalist and patriot journalists relentlessly demonized each other.[17]

SOCIAL COMPOSITION AND ACTIONS

The social composition of Revolutionary clubs varied greatly. Some Jacobin clubs were dominated by liberal nobles and haute bourgeoisie; others, by professionals, retail merchants, and artisans. The question of women's inclusion in the Jacobin clubs was much debated in the early years of the Revolution. When and if women were admitted, they tended to be confined to a certain area of the meeting hall and forbidden to address the club or talk to the male members. Their presence, often justified on the grounds that women needed education, sometimes caused tensions. Women forged their own clubs and circles, occasionally securing 'auxiliary' status with the local Jacobin club. Such circles proliferated in early 1791 but were generally non-political and devoted to reading newspapers and preparing revolutionary festivals. One club, the *Société des citoyennes républicaines révolutionnaires*, founded in Paris in May 1793, was notably different, professing a militant patriotism that led to street clashes with more moderate women. The Convention banned it in September, at a time when deputies were seeking to curb popular militancy more generally. A month later, on 30 October, it banned all women's clubs.[18]

Political clubs took up many activities. They lobbied, often for local economic interests, and electioneered. They communicated with other clubs to coordinate positions on important political matters, most notably the constitution. At a time when Church-run schools were closing (the result of expropriations), Jacobins took it as their duty to offer public instruction. Given the collapse of tax collection, the clubs often spurred citizens to make voluntary gifts and contributions to the nation. They opened 'souscriptions' for various charitable causes as well. They became so effective at charity drives that in 1793 and 1794, some local administrations conferred the management of public charity on them.

Although the creation of paper money (the *assignats*) helped the government meet expenses in the Revolution's early years, by 1793, lack of tax revenues and depreciation of the *assignats* led to a raft of decrees urgently calling for the collection of current taxes, arrears, and forced loans. Local clubs often took the lead in collecting these sums. They also took a public stance with regard to subsistence crises: initially supportive of market freedom in the grain trade, most clubs changed their minds by 1793 and 1794 and became militant about the surveillance of commodity supplies and price ceilings. The abrupt return to liberal economic policies during the Thermidorian Convention and Directory was accompanied by the abolition of the clubs (August 1795). Meanwhile, many of the club leaders of the Year II who had played an active role in the economic 'terror' were persecuted in the Year III, by crowds but also by officials.[19]

CLUB RADICALIZATION: IDEOLOGY OR 'WEAK-STATE' CONDITIONS?

How did the pro-Revolutionary clubs of the French Revolution, which proclaimed the promotion of freedom, equality, and fraternity, end up in deadly faction-fighting by the Year II? We have already noted how François Furet and his followers drew inspiration from Cochin and de Tocqueville, who saw in the clubs the seeds of authoritarianism and terror. Versions of this interpretation follow intellectual and sociological lines. According to Keith M. Baker and Mona Ozouf, Jacobin commitments to absolute collective sovereignty and moral regeneration undermined whatever liberal potential the Revolution may have had.[20] They argue that Revolutionaries inherited from the old regime (and Rousseau) illiberal, absolutist conceptions of sovereignty and an aversion to pluralist notions of public opinion, which they took to be divisive and anarchic. Contemporaries believed that moral tutelage was needed to rein diverse opinions into a rational consensus oriented towards the general interest. Jacobins, Baker argues, were allergic to the English model of party politics, which they saw to be chaotic and destabilizing. Indeed, the term 'parti' in late eighteenth century France was synonymous with 'faction'. Jacobins worried about the effects of all political opposition and all mediating bodies, which corrupted the 'general will'. Society was to be comprised of virtuous individual citizens and the state operating for the general good. Particular interests were viewed with suspicion.

Whereas Baker and Ozouf focused on concepts and discourse, Furet emphasized the sociological implications of commitments to Enlightenment ideals. But in borrowing from Cochin, his sociology was ultimately idea-driven. Other potential factors driving radicalization, such as circumstances and counter-revolution, were not only subordinated in Furet's model; they were presented as the necessary consequence of ideology. For Cochin and Furet, ideology created its own circumstances and intensified obsessions with 'counter-revolution'. Cochin asks, 'Is it true, as M. Aulard believes, that circumstances explain all revolutionary laws and actions? What we assert is that the very idea of revolutionary acts and laws [...] would not have arisen without the principle of direct sovereignty and the [kind of] regime that results from it: the social regime.'[21] (The 'social regime', for Cochin, was without hierarchical authority and guided by abstract principles that equal citizens were expected to share.) Like Cochin, Furet drew a straight line from democratic sociability and principles to the pathological politics of the Year II: 'The truth is that the Terror was an integral part of revolutionary ideology, which [...] gave its own meaning to "circumstances" that were largely of its own making.'[22] For Furet, ideology produced 'counter-revolution' as well. Scarcely a threat in real terms (or so he believed), 'counter-revolution' was blown out of all proportion by paranoid Jacobins, for whom any deviation from the 'general will' and 'virtue' constituted an existential threat.

The persuasiveness of these arguments lies in the way they are hermetically sealed within a tight, idea-based logic of cause and effect. Ideology is seen as motivating actions, structuring them, and justifying them. The way power explains itself and the way it actually works are one and the same. The argument is thus circular and self-reinforcing: if one begins with the premise that circumstances are the epiphenomena of ideology (or what ideologically committed clubs inevitably produce), then one can dispense with judiciously weighing a broad range of factors. Put another way, if 'abstract literary politics' are all one considers, then the Revolution's tragic course will perforce appear to be the result of 'abstract literary politics'. The task of analysis is limited from the outset to tracking down the ideas most responsible for the tragedy: collective sovereignty, representation, moral regeneration, perpetual peace, natural law.

The ideological determinism implicit in the Furetian model has been challenged in recent decades. Often, though, historians simply reject the thesis and go on to tell an alternative story in which 'circumstances' or 'counter-revolution' are stressed. Political theorist Jean Cohen, however, offers a critique of the Furetian thesis that engages closely with its terms. She concedes that discourses of popular sovereignty and representation are ultimately 'fictions' and 'carry the risk that dictatorial or oligarchic elites will deploy them to legitimate their authoritarian and self-interested forms of rule', but she insists that they are 'necessary fictions'. Their 'philosophical and sociological indeterminacy', she argues, 'are precisely what permit critique, questioning, reflexivity and creativity on the institutional and theoretical levels, in the unending quest to make institutions more just, more egalitarian, more open, more responsive, more accountable, more responsible—that is, democracy itself'.[23] Democratic principles can be used in different ways, positive and negative, and therefore cannot be assumed to have only one (negative) set of implications.

Cohen moves us beyond ideological determinism but leaves us with an unresolved question: On what does a positive or negative deployment of democratic principles depend? Why do those principles serve as salutary checks on state power in one context but lead to exorbitant state power in another? The historian is likely to turn to circumstances for answers to this question, and indeed, the thesis of 'circumstances' has made a comeback over the past decade or so. But the defenders of this thesis often sidestep rather than confront Cochin and Furet's critique of it. Cochin and Furet insist that circumstances are sociologically produced. They do not emerge *sui generis*, the accidental concatenation of myriad causes. If we accept their sociological inclinations but reject their tendency to reduce sociology to ideology, we are left looking for an alternative sociological basis to explain how circumstances are produced and how they inflect, positively or negatively, the course democratic ideas ultimately take. What alternative sociological category of analysis might be useful?

I propose focusing on what Jean-Clément Martin refers to as the 'défaut d'état'—the absence or weakness of the state.[24] Weak-state conditions, I argue, radicalized the discourses and actions of the revolutionary clubs, which pressured officials to implement policies and decrees that those officials were either unable or unwilling to carry out. Rather than seeking the flaws (ideology) within institutions of civil society (the clubs) to explain the rise of terror and authoritarianism, we might begin with the deficiencies of the state to explain the radicalization of civil society (and hence, the clubs). These deficiencies were many, but among the most important were the inability and/or unwillingness to regulate violence, redistribution (tax collection and public spending), subsistence, and honour.

VIOLENCE

Inability to control violence is arguably the most important of the state's deficiencies during the early years of the French Revolution, when the old regime's forces of public order fragmented, collapsed or merged with new forces. Louis XVI could not count on the army to put down revolt in Paris on 14 July 1789, in part because so many of his soldiers defected, joining new National Guard forces, which came into being that day. New authorities' control over the army, navy, bourgeois militias, National Guard, and, in 1793, the popular revolutionary armies (ambulatory bands of sans-culottes who enforced the economic terror in the countryside) was also tenuous. This chronic weakness put society (and, hence, the clubs) in the predicament of having to take sides, supporting or condemning various forces and their sometimes violent actions, such as the revolts and mutinies of the army and navy in Nancy and Brest in 1790. Coercion and punitive justice are not matters easily reconciled with pluralism in opinions. To consolidate 'legitimate' violence in the state, society must reach a sufficient degree of consensus on whether such violence merits support or condemnation. One of the most contentious issues dividing the Jacobins in autumn 1792 and winter 1793 was how to respond to the September massacres, when sans-culottes spontaneously stormed the prisons of Paris, executing hundreds of priests, nobles, and ordinary criminals, just as foreign counter-revolutionary troops were advancing on Paris. Were the massacres 'just'? The question polarized the Jacobin Club and led to the expulsion of several moderate 'Girondin' ministers and deputies (Jacques Pierre Brissot, Jean-Marie Roland, Étienne Clavière), who condemned the massacres as a 'Robespierrist' plot to seize power.

Other deficiencies of the state helped radicalize society as well: officials' inability or unwillingness to collect taxes, secure subsistence, and avenge assaults on honour. These deficiencies often prompted the clubs to intervene, at first through petitioning and denunciations, but eventually, by taking over local administrative powers.

TAXES AND REDISTRIBUTION

Modern states, much like authorities in non-modern societies, are redistributive. They procure resources (through taxes, tribute, loans, confiscation, plunder) and redistribute them again (through patronage, subsidies, contracts, charity, pensions, public works, subsistence, and rents on public debt). While historians agree that the Revolution's most immediate cause was the old regime's financial crisis, this fact is often treated as a circumstantial 'spark' while other factors (class tensions, public opinion) are taken to be the combustible material for more explosive dynamics. This view limits our ability to see how political legitimacy was bound up with the state's ability to meet redistributive demands, especially for subsistence and rents (interest payments) on public debt.

The importance of redistribution in claiming and maintaining power was evident at the very start of the Revolution. When Third Estate deputies broke away from the other two orders (the clergy and nobles) on 17 June 1789 and declared themselves to be the National Assembly, they immediately asserted their authority over redistribution, declaring the abolition of the old tax regime then authorizing its temporary maintenance until they completed the creation of a new system. They also put the old regime's debts (those of the monarchy but also of venal tax receivers and tax farms, which had conflated public and private debts) under the Assembly's safeguard and promised to maintain interest payments, or rents, which were a kind of redistribution, on capital investments in the debt. Finally, they announced that they would investigate the sources of the subsistence crisis and devise solutions. In short, the National Assembly staked its legitimacy on the promise to meet the most pressing redistributive demands in the crisis of 1789. The clubs played an active, if contentious and controversial, role in supporting, and at times opposing, the various policies adopted to deal with these demands over the next four years.

Already insufficient to meet redistributive obligations in 1787, tax collection virtually ground to a halt in the chaos of 1789.[25] The National Assembly's creation of a new tax regime in late 1790 and early 1791 did little to improve the situation. Faced with the spectre of default in 1789, the National Assembly opted to nationalize, then privatize through auctions, church property. The terms of this land redistribution, worked out contentiously in the National Assembly over the winter, spring, and early summer of 1790, met with significant opposition in many parts of France, especially from clerics but also the wider population. The clubs played a crucial role in bringing about the relative success of the redistribution—success, that is, in terms of bringing land to auctions, not, as it turned out, in terms of eliminating national debt. Michael L. Kennedy observes: 'For the Jacobins of the Constituent, religion was the number-one issue.'[26] Clubbists, he continues, were instrumental not only in protecting Protestants from bigotry but also in supporting the confiscation of Church property to pay off the national debt. They often put pressure on reluctant or resistant administrators to auction these lands. Unsurprisingly, perhaps, they also figured prominently among the buyers of these *biens nationaux*.

The collapse of tax revenues in 1789 had multiple causes: fear and uncertainty about the future, of course, but also the imminent abolition of venal tax receiverships and tax farms. Tax officials had little motivation to enforce a moribund system. Meanwhile, patriotic and popular clubs took the lead in voluntarily giving to the state. Such giving pre-dated the emergence of clubs, and had already made a mark on national politics. In one of its final decrees before leaving Versailles for Paris with the royal family in early October 1789, the National Assembly, desperate to reassure creditors, invited taxpayers to make a one-time voluntary 'patriotic contribution' of 25 per cent of one's annual income to the nation. The decree emphasized the voluntary nature of these contributions and forbade officials from forcing citizens to pay.[27] With few contributions given over the course of the following year, however, the National Assembly resorted to making the *contribution patriotique* mandatory in August 1790. The initial voluntary status of the contribution prompted the nascent clubs in many parts to transform what might have been a legal matter (paying taxes) into a litmus test of loyalty and virtue to the new regime. They spurred local citizens to pay the *contribution patriotique* over the next few years. By 1793, receipt of a *certificat de civisme*, without which one might become a suspect, required proof of having paid all taxes including the *contribution patriotique* of 1789.

Indeed, at a time when local administrations proved to be incapable or unwilling to collect sufficient revenues to meet redistributive demands for social assistance, the clubs often took the initiative in organizing charity. They raised money to subsidize the purchase of grain and distributed bread. In November 1792, the local club in the town of Tarascon (Bouches-du-Rhône) proposed side-stepping the municipality to organize public road works. Two months later, the club wrote a terse letter to local officials requesting the town to give up its church bell, obviously to be melted down for metal to help with the war effort.[28]

The rise in the influence and power of the clubs on the local level may well have stemmed from their ability to deal with crucial redistributive demands, especially for subsistence and war munitions, demands that local administrations often could (or would) not meet. There is, indeed, some evidence of unwillingness on the part of officials to enforce taxes on their fellow citizens. Officials in Tours, for example, wrote to other municipalities in late 1790, after the *contribution patriotique* had been made mandatory, explaining how 'odious' it was to enforce this tax. They discouraged other towns from collecting it, assuring them that it was not being collected in Paris and other cities in France.[29]

Tax collection remained weak throughout the early years of the Revolution. To meet expenses, national authorities printed more *assignats* (which led to their depreciation). Exacerbating matters, local authorities often refused to burn the *assignats* used to purchase *biens nationaux* (as they were supposed to do, having fulfilled their function of swapping public debt for land) and applied them to meeting expenses, such as wages for local public works.[30] In early 1793, the National Convention passed a raft of decrees insisting on the payment of current taxes, arrears, and forced loans. The clubs proved in many cases to be more zealous about enforcing these decrees than local administrations, which were often purged and replaced with club members. In Pau in February 1793, a local club announced that it would appoint its own commissioners to knock on the doors of all citizens 'and to note the names of all those who give [for the war effort] and how much they give, as well as [the names] of those who refuse to give', which must have struck many citizens as menacing.[31] Although historians tend to focus on the executions of the Terror, many of those arrested were simply fleeced and sometimes (though not always) released. The arrest registers of the *comité révolutionnaire* in Nantes 1793, full of radicalized clubbists, contain indications of 'dons patriotiques' and release dates in the margins.[32] In short, the state's failure to manage fiscal redistribution—tax collection and public spending—created an opening for more determined forces in society, notably the clubs, to take the initiative, bullying citizens into paying and pressuring, and even purging, local administrations to ensure payments were made.

Visible or Invisible Hands? The Problem of Subsistence

Subsistence was the other important redistributive demand that national deputies committed themselves to meeting on the day they seized power (17 June 1789). What role did the clubs play in dealing with the bread question? At first, they supported the liberal economic policies of the National Assembly.[33] Although deputies initially seemed to lean towards interventionist measures between late June and mid-August, by the end of August, when they were completing the final articles of the Declaration of the Rights of Man and of the Citizen, they opted for 'hands-off' policies instead, in tune with the most 'advanced' economic thinking of the era. On 29 August 1789, they passed a decree criminalizing market interventions, be they by crowds or local authorities. Violations were to be treated as *lèse-nation*, a kind of treason or sedition, for which special jurisdictions were to be established. While many local administrations wrote to the Assembly to complain about the decree and request its abrogation, Jacobin clubs over the next year largely supported it, believing that the self-regulating market was the most efficient and equitable means of distributing grain throughout France. To the degree that market forces were not yet perfect, clubs were willing to organize charity. In Paris, it appears that the Club monarchique took the lead in distributing bread to the masses well before the

Jacobins. In 1790 and 1791, the Jacobins repeatedly denounced the *monarchiens* in the National Assembly for not playing fair, for seeking to bribe the population to support counter-revolution.[34] If that was the aim of the monarchists, their efforts largely failed. The journalist Jean-Baptiste Gorsas captured the cynicism of the situation in recounting a verbal exchange in the faubourg Saint-Marceau. When a national guardsmen reproached a friend for accepting such handouts, the friend replied, 'Oh well, I may have eaten monarchist bread, but when it comes out it is patriot crap!'[35]

Throughout the Revolution, the question of aid for subsistence often took the form of a debate over loans or subsidies. Contemporaries were well aware of the difference between the two. Whereas subsidies drew state resources away from the payment of rents on public debt, loans offered the possibility of turning a subsistence crisis into a source of more rents (interest on the loan). Both solutions might resolve the crisis in the short term, but loans ran the risk of indebting bakers, who would eventually have to raise the price of bread. One of the earliest political causes taken up by radicals in the Cordeliers District of Paris, which would eventually become a club when the city was carved up into sections, concerned this very issue. It appears that in early July 1789, Jacques Necker, minister of finances, promised subsidies to Jacques Rutledge, a negotiator hired by the bakers of Paris. When the Commune of Paris offered the bakers loans in October 1789, Rutledge encouraged them to opt for Necker's subsidies instead. The Commune was outraged by this and charged Rutledge with *lèse-nation*.[36] Necker denied having made such promises to Rutledge (though traces of a meeting to this end can be found in the National Assembly minutes for early July).[37] Journalists associated with the Cordelier District, Camille Desmoulins and Jean-Paul Marat, publicized the affair widely, condemning the Commune and Necker while vigorously supporting the imprisoned (though soon-released) Rutledge, presenting him as a martyr. Rutledge would go on to become a radical figure in the Cordeliers Club over the next three years.

The transition among Jacobin clubs from supporting the self-regulation of grain markets to supporting government regulation and price ceilings in 1793 provoked much debate and controversy. Many clubs were indecisive about which course of action to support. The club in Pau, for example, repeatedly flip-flopped on the issue in 1793, taking bold stances each time. On 17 May, members petitioned the department to enforce the 4 May decree placing a maximum price on bread. When the department failed to respond, the club sent a deputation in early June. It is not clear what happened in the meeting with departmental officials, but by July the club was touting the virtues of the free market. Members even discussed sending a deputation to the National Convention to request the abrogation of the maximum. By October, however, they had changed their minds yet again (the National Convention had passed a more robust law regarding the 'maximum' in late September) and were pressuring the municipality to enforce price ceilings on commodities that had not yet been regulated. They repeated the demand in February 1794.[38]

The subsistence question divided the Paris Jacobin Club, which was increasingly influenced by the social agendas of the Cordeliers Club and popular subsistence demands. Although most Jacobins subscribed to liberal economic principles, when Jean-Marie

Roland, a Jacobin, began enforcing free grain markets as minister of the interior in 1792, his adversaries in the club (Robespierre, Marat) exploited the unpopularity of his liberal policies.[39] Tensions in Paris over how – or indeed if – the government should regulate food commodities soon exacerbated those in the provinces. While Roland sent repeated instructions to the local administrations and clubs to take the lead in educating the masses about the benefits of the free market, the Jacobin Club denounced Roland's policies in its regular correspondence with its affiliates.

In the summer of 1793, after the passage of the first maximum law of 4 May 1793, the new Jacobin minister of the interior, Dominique-Joseph Garat, discreetly circulated translated copies of Adam Smith's *The Wealth of Nations* among his itinerant agents, instructing them to draw on its wisdom in drafting observation reports.[40] In the midst of the sans-culotte ascendancy of 1793, it was wise not to tout free-market principles publicly. Still, those principles were shaping government views and objectives. Once the Jacobin Club and government committees managed to curtail the influence of the radical movement in the spring and summer of 1794, however, economic liberal policies started making a comeback (the lifting of the maximum, then of all regulation concerning subsistence in 1795), which angered and disillusioned many Jacobin supporters in the sectional clubs.

How do controversies over subsistence support the 'défaut d'état' thesis? The absence of state, I have argued, stemmed not only from the inability but also from the unwillingness of officials to meet certain redistributive demands. Although the bread crisis is usually treated as an 'economic' issue by historians, for contemporaries it was profoundly political. The liberal economic commitments of early revolutionaries weakened the bonds between society and the state and radicalized redistributive demands by trying to de-politicize them. Economic liberals sought to redirect demands for bread to the self-regulating market, a space beyond politics and administration. The clubs, however, were the only mediating bodies left on the political scene after the (Jacobin-inspired) abolition of the guilds, corporations, chambers of commerce, and government regulatory bureaux in 1791. Deprived of alternative institutions for their expression (and even collective petitions were banned in 1791), economic demands worked their way into the clubs, which increasingly militated for the re-regulation of the economy, and especially subsistence.

Arguably, then, if the Jacobin clubs can be faulted for being naive and utopian about anything, it was their early faith in the myth of the self-regulating market. In his *The Great Transformation*, Karl Polanyi argues that attempts to create a society based on self-regulating markets has been historically destabilizing.[41] Although he does not seek to explain the French Revolution, his model is useful for understanding the passions and tensions to which debates over political economy gave rise at that time. Analysing the efforts to realize the self-regulating markets in other periods of modern history, he concludes that the greater the efforts to remove economic demands from the sphere of politics (and economic liberals during the Revolution tried to do so by criminalizing interventions in grain markets and abolishing socio-economic mediating bodies), the more likely it is that those demands will storm back into politics with a vengeance. The form those frustrated demands take depends on the circumstances, but he believes that it is likely to be illiberal. The clubs of the French Revolution clearly served as the conduits in this process, which Polanyi refers to as a 'double movement': liberalization produces political frustration, which produces radical demands for re-regulation. Clearly, the 'défaut d'état' in regulating subsistence between 1789 and 1793—the effort to replace moral economy with political economy—contributed to dividing and radicalizing the clubs.

FREE SPEECH AND THE CULTURE
OF CALUMNY AND HONOUR

The Revolution's 'weak-state' conditions extended not only over problems of violence, taxes and markets but also extended over the problem of free expression. Revolutionaries struggled to reconcile this freedom, proclaimed in the Declaration of the Rights of Man and of the Citizen of August 1789, with the protection of honour. In demanding the freedom of the press throughout France on the eve of the Meeting of the Estates-General, most French *cahiers de doléances* (formal demands for reforms drafted by the three orders throughout France) also called for the punishment of abusive expression, such as insults, libel, and calumny.[42] The advent of free speech hardly altered people's obsession with honour, which was central to social life. Honour had important social, political, and economic implications. Access to patronage, credit, marriage opportunities, offices, and jobs all depended on honour. The inability to maintain it or avenge slanderous and calumnious assaults on it could have dire repercussions.[43]

Maintaining honour was always a challenge in the old regime, but the breakdown of policing institutions in 1789, competing views on how to deal with calumny, and the advent of civil equality (which disrupted hierarchical patterns of esteem and deference) greatly complicated matters. As political participation in the new regime expanded, honour became all the more important. For calumniated representatives and officials, the honour of their constituents was often seen to be at stake, and the failure of authorities to avenge calumnious attacks was taken to be a sign of weakness. Thomas Paine, theorist of 'the rights of man' and deputy to the French National Convention, believed that calumny was one of the greatest threats to the new regime. In a letter to Georges-Jacques Danton in May 1793, just weeks before the purge of the Girondins (whom sans-culotte militants denounced as calumniators of Paris), Paine explained: 'The departments did not send their deputies to Paris to be insulted, and every insult shown to them is an insult to the departments that elected and sent them.'[44]

A central paradox of the Revolution, then, was its simultaneous commitment to freedom of expression and obsession with punishing calumniators. Weak-state conditions deprived individuals and groups who believed themselves to be slandered of the means to seek redress. Between 1789 and 1791, censorship was abolished, the old courts broke down, and new courts were not yet functional. Although the National Assembly recognized the high speech crime of *lèse-nation* (the nationalized version of *lèse-majesté*) as early as July 1789 and had created a police committee to investigate such crimes, they failed to define the actual nature of such speech crimes clearly, and this generated a climate of political frustration. Jacques Brissot, a leading journalist and (in the early stages of the Revolution) radical leader, summed up the matter concisely in an issue of his *Patriote français* in 1790: 'To punish calumny without violating the freedom of the press is the most difficult problem to resolve in politics.'[45]

To be sure, the culture of calumny poisoned revolutionary politics on all levels, but the clubs were central in spreading it and in spreading obsessions with it. With their networks and armies of writers and journalists, they calumniated relentlessly yet were indefatigable in denouncing calumny. They orchestrated elaborate libel campaigns (although, so, too, did the monarchy, the Church and various factions and committees of the National Assembly), even as they sent a constant stream of denunciations of *lèse-nation* speech crimes to the Constituent Assembly's police committee, the *comité des recherches*, insisting on punishment. Clubbists hardly needed to understand the fine points of Rousseau's 'general will' to denounce 'enemies of the Revolution'. The old regime had bequeathed a rich legacy of calumniating. It did not, however, bequeath the legal and institutional mechanisms for dealing with such offences. Civil equality rendered the laws and institutions that had regulated honour in a hierarchical world irrelevant. Yet, honour remained important and attacks on it, which had always been a means of pursuing social and political competition, were still considered egregious offences.

Calumny, unchecked by a weak state, poisoned relations between and within clubs. No sooner had the *Société de la Révolution* (the future Jacobin Club) formed in November 1789 than it became the target of calumnious attacks. Royalists spread the rumour that Jacobins were holding nocturnal meetings to plan a regicide.[46] Apparently, these rumours worried Jacobins enough that they chose to publicize their meetings. (They did not, however, open their meetings to the public until October 1791.) By mid-1790, the Jacobins and *monarchiens* repeatedly denounced each other's 'calumny' in the National Assembly. Legislation regulating slander was proposed on several occasions that year but was voted down by narrow margins or repealed shortly after its passage.

As calumny spiralled, the Revolution radicalized. Politics became a kind of pressure cooker in which outrage and accumulated grudges fuelled factionalism, at first between Jacobins and royalists, subsequently among Jacobins themselves. In a pamphlet entitled *Discourse on the influence of calumny on the Revolution* of October 1792, Robespierre denounced Roland's propaganda bureau for spreading calumnies against the club, from which he (Roland) would soon be expelled. 'What will you say', the Incorruptible asked his readers, 'when I demonstrate that there now exists a coalition of virtuous patriots [ironic reference to Roland], of austere Republicans who are perfecting the criminal policies of Lafayette [who had defected to Austria] and his allies?'[47] He predicted that prisons would soon be filled with true patriots, like himself, under the government of the tyrannical Girondin ministers. For their part, Brissot, Roland and their allies had been slandering the *robespierristes* since the spring, when Robespierre opposed their (successful) efforts to persuade the National Assembly to declare war against Austria. During that time, Brissot insinuated in a published speech to the National Assembly that Robespierre was in the pay of the monarchy. Moreover, one of the titles that Roland's propaganda bureau spread to the provincial clubs in the autumn was entitled, 'To Maximilien Robespierre and to his royalists'.

To be sure, the clubs were not the only political forces in the early Revolution to be obsessed with calumny. So, too, was the monarchy. Majesty demanded esteem and deference, but the proliferation of calumny after the collapse of censorship and the freeing of the presses deprived the king of the respect he believed was due to him. It may well have contributed to his attempt to flee France. On the eve of his attempted flight, he imprudently left a note in the Tuileries Palace, deploring 'the thousands of calumniating newspapers and pamphlets' of rebels who 'labour to present the monarchy under the most false and odious colours'. Upon his return, he enumerated reasons for trying to flee, among them, 'the insults that have gone unpunished'.[48] Yet, the monarchy was hardly an innocent bystander. The seizure of the king's private papers after his fall in August 1792 revealed evidence of his use of the civil list to pay for libels against revolutionaries.

During the Terror, the Convention finally enacted legislation against calumny. By that time, obsessions with it and accumulated grudges had reached a point that made moderate solutions unlikely. The Law of Suspects (17 September 1793) targeted those who 'by their conduct, relations, words, or writings show themselves to be the partisans of tyranny and federalism and the enemies of freedom'. The Law of 22 Prairial Year II (10 June 1794), passed just as the Terror was ratcheting up for its final lethal phase, went still further. It imposed death on anyone found guilty of 'disparaging the National Convention and the republican government', 'calumniating patriotism', 'spreading false news', 'misleading public opinion', 'corrupting the public conscience' and 'impairing the energy and purity of revolutionary and republican principles'.[49] The ex-noble and revolutionary writer Louis-François Ferrières Sauveboeuf defended these measures: 'No law would dare circumscribe the freedom of the press; it is an arm that belongs to all citizens; but is it not necessary to punish those who use this arm to assassinate others, in so far as an honest man puts his reputation before his life?'[50]

CONCLUSION

Clearly, circumstances mattered in factionalizing the clubs of the French Revolution. The flight of the king in 1791 and chronic popular violence polarized the Jacobin Club in Paris, and the factionalism produced there spread to the provincial clubs, exacerbating tensions nationwide. Controversial issues and events were all the more divisive for the clubs in that they were debated in a context in which virtually no legal limits on speech existed—limits that an honour-based society widely expected and repeatedly demanded ever since the *cahiers de doléances* had been drafted in the spring of 1789. Legislators were unable or unwilling to implement these desired limits, until, that is, the situation had radicalized to the boiling point in 1793.

The absence, or weakness, of the state complicated efforts to meet other demands coming from society as well. The failure to collect taxes while guaranteeing rent payments on investments in public debt created conditions that led to dramatic measures: the expropriation and sale of church property proliferation of paper money. The clubs pressed local officials to sell church property, but when sales proved to be insufficient and tax collection and patriotic giving became imperative, clubs again took the lead, albeit chaotically and sometimes brutally.

Yet, even as the clubs gained influence and power, they remained divided over crucial issues: should they support constitutional monarchy or a republic? Should they support a war or peace? Should they educate society about the benefits of the free market or should they militate for the re-regulation of the economy? These were complicated and contentious issues. In a context of rampant, unchecked calumny and heightened obsessions with honour, they became explosive.

Notes

1. Staël, Anne-Louise-Germaine Necker, Baroness de, *Considerations on the Principal Events of the French Revolution*, Duke de Broglie and Baron de Staël (eds), 2 vols (New York, 1818), vol. 1, 176–7.

2. Jules Michelet, *Histoire de la Révolution française*, 9 vols (Paris, n.d.), vol. 2, 240, 281–2.

3. Augustin Cochin, *La Révolution et la Libre-pensée: la socialisation de la pensée-1750–1789; la socialisation de la personne—1789-1792; la socialisation des biens—1793-1794* (Paris, 1979), 201.

4. François-Alphonse Aulard, 'Le Club des Jacobins sous la monarchie', *La Révolution française* 22: 2 (July–December, 1892), 122.

5. Albert Soboul, *The Parisian Sans-culottes and the French Revolution, 1793-94* (Oxford, 1964); Raymonde Monnier, *L'Espace public démocratique: Essai sur l'Opinion à Paris de la Révolution au Directoire* (Paris, 1994).

6. Augustin Challamel, *Les clubs contre-révolutionnaires: Cercles, Comités, Sociétés, Salons, Réunions, Restaurants et Librairies* (Paris, 1895), 32.

7. Jérôme Mavidal et al. (eds), *Archives parlementaires de 1787 à 1860: Recueil complet des débats législatifs et politiques des Chambres françaises* (Paris, 1867) [hereafter AP], vol. 10, 567.

8. Michael L. Kennedy, *The Jacobin Clubs in the French Revolution: The First Years*, (Princeton, 1982), Appendix B, 362.

9. Claude Mazauric, 'Jacobins/Jacobinisme', in Albert Soboul (ed.), *Dictionnaire historique de la Révolution française* (Paris, 1989), 586.

10. Kennedy, *Jacobin Clubs: The First Years*, Appendix B, 362.

11. Michel Biard, *Missionnaires de la République* (Paris, 2002), esp. chap. 5.

12. Michael L. Kennedy, *The Jacobin Clubs in the French Revolution, 1793-1795* (New York, 2000), 53–77, for quote, see 66.

13. Isser Woloch, *Jacobin Legacy: The Democratic Movement under the Directory* (Princeton, 1970); Bernard Gainot, *1799, un nouveau Jacobinisme?* (Paris, 2001).

14. Challamel, *Les clubs contre-révolutionnaires*, 483–506.

15. In addition to Challamel, *Les clubs contre-révolutionnaires*, see Robert Griffiths, *Le Centre perdu: Malouet et les "monarchiens" dans la Revolution francaise* (Grenoble: 1988).

16. Paul Hanson, 'Monarchist Clubs and the Pamphlet Debate over Political Legitimacy in the Early Years of the French Revolution', *French Historical Studies* 21:2 (Spring 1998), 301.

17. Hanson, 'Monarchist Clubs', 299–324.

18. Dominique Godineau, *The Women of Paris and Their French Revolution* (Berkeley, 1998); Jean-Clément Martin, *La Révolte brisée: Femmes dans la Révolution française et l'Empire* (Paris, 2008); Olwen Hufton, *Women and the Limits of Citizenship in the French Revolution* (Toronto, 1992).

19. Stephen Clay, 'Vengeance, Justice and the Reactions in the Revolutionary Midi', *French History* 23:1 (2009), 22–46; Howard G. Brown, *Ending the French Revolution: Violence, Justice, and Repression from the Terror to Napoleon* (Charlottesville, 2006).

20. Keith M. Baker, *Inventing the French Revolution: Essays on French Political Culture in the Eighteenth Century* (Cambridge, 1990), esp. chap. 8; Mona Ozouf, 'Public Opinion' at the End of the Old Regime', *Journal of Modern History* 60, Supplement 9 (1998), S1–S21; and Ozouf, 'Public Spirit', in Furet and Ozouf (eds), *Critical Dictionary of the French Revolution* (Cambridge, MA, 1989), 771–80.

21. Cochin, *Les sociétés de pensée et la démocratie moderne* (Paris, 1921), 82–3.

22. François Furet, *Interpreting the French Revolution*, trans. Elborg Forster (Cambridge, 1981 [1978]), 62.

23. Jean Cohen, 'The Self-Institution of Society and Representative Government: Can the Circle be Squared?', *Thesis Eleven* 80 (February 2005), 24.

24. Jean-Clément Martin, *Violence et Révolution: essai sur la naissance d'un mythe national* (Paris, 2006).

25. For tax collection during the French Revolution, see Eugene Nelson White, 'The French Revolution and the Politics of Government Finance, 1770–1815', *Journal of Economic History* 55:2 (1995), 227–55.

26. Kennedy, *Jacobin Clubs: The First Years*, 304.

27. Charles Walton, 'Between Trust and Terror: Patriotic Giving in the French Revolution', in David Andress (ed.), *Experiencing the French Revolution* (Oxford, 2013), 47–67.

28. Archives départementales, Bouches-du-Rhône, L 1571, Letter of 9 November 1792 by the Société des amis de la liberté et de l'égalité.

29. Archives municipales de Bordeaux, G 20 'Contributions patriotiques', Letter from municipal officers in Tours to those in Bordeaux, no date (but clearly from late 1790).

30. For example, see the explanation of district administrators in Tarascon, who feared insurrection if wages for public works were not paid by using *assignats* that were supposed to be burned: Archives départementales des Bouches-du-Rhône, L 1513, 'Délibérations et arrêtées Directoire du district de Tarascon', 2 January 1793.

31. Jean Annat, *Les sociétés populaires* [Pau, Nay, Saint-Jean-de-Luz, Lescar, Orthez] (Pau, 1940), 207.

32. Archives départementales de Loire-Atlantique, L 1322, 'Comité révolutionnaire de Nantes'.

33. Kennedy, *Jacobin Clubs: The First Years*, 124; his *The Jacobin Clubs of the French Revolution: The Middle Years* (Princeton, 1998), 65–79; and his *The Jacobin Clubs of the French Revolution: 1793–1795*, 111–29.

34. Challamel, *Les clubs contre-révolutionnaires*, 164. See also *Réponse de M. Malouet à la dénonciation du club de la constitution monarchique, par. M. Barnave* in Archives nationales de France, AD XVIIIc, no. 12.

35. Hanson, 'Monarchist Clubs', 313.

36. For details on this affair, see A. Tuetey, *Répertoire général des sources manuscrites de l'histoire de Paris pendant la Révolution française* (Paris, 1890), entries 1177–204.

37. AP, vol. 8, 207, 'Extrait du registre', 6 July 1789.

38. Annat, *Les sociétés populaires*, 197–8.

39. For the political tensions over Roland's economic policies, see Charles Walton, 'Les graines de la discorde: Print, Public Spirit and Free-market Politics in the French Revolution', in Charles Walton (ed.), *Into Print: Limits and Legacies of the Enlightenment. Essays in Honor of Robert Darnton* (University Park, PA, 2011), 158–74.

40. Archives nationales de France, F^{1a} 551, dossier 'Franqueville', in Walton, '*Les graines de la discorde*', 170.

41. Karl Polanyi, *The Great Transformation: The Political and Economic Origins of Our Time* (Beacon Hill, 1957 [1944]).

42. This section is drawn from Charles Walton, *Policing Public Opinion in the French Revolution: The Culture of Calumny and the Problem of Free Speech* (New York, 2009).

43. There are many studies of honour in the old regime. See especially, David Garrioch, *Neighborhood and Community in Paris, 1740–1790* (Cambridge, 1986). For its importance for access to credit, see Clare Haru Crowston, *Credit, Fashion, Sex: Economies of Regard in Old Regime France* (Durham, NC, 2013).

44. For sans-culotte denunciations of the Girondins as calumniators, see Archives nationales, F^7 4432, cited in [Louis] Mortimer-Ternaux, *Histoire de la terreur*, 3rd edn (Paris, 1869), 7: 310, n. 1.

45. Jacques Pierre Brissot, *Le Patriote français* (Paris), 10 August 1790.

46. F.-A. Aulard, 'Le Club des Jacobins sous la monarchie', *La Révolution française* 22:2 (1892), 111.

47. *Discours de Maximilien Robespierre sur l'influence de la calomnie sur la Révolution* (Paris, 28 October 1792), 17.

48. John Hall Stewart, *A Documentary Survey of the French Revolution* (New York, 1951) and Timothy Tackett, *When the King Took Flight* (Cambridge MA, 2003), 41–5.

49. *Moniteur*, 20: 264, 24 Prairial, Year II (12 June 1794), 697.

50. Ferrières Sauveboeuf, *Réflexions politiques sur le gouvernement révolutionnaire, la liberté de la presse et les élections par le peuple dans les circonstances actuelles* (Paris [1793–94]), 4.

Selected Reading

Aulard, François-Alphonse (ed.), *La Société des Jacobins: Recueil de documents pour l'histoire du club des Jacobins de Paris*, 6 vols (Paris: 1889–97).

Bourdin, I., *Les Sociétés populaires à Paris pendant la Révolution* (Mayenne, 1937).

de Cardenal, L., *La province pendant la Révolution. Histoire des clubs Jacobins (1789–1795)* (Paris, 1929).

Cochin, A., *Les sociétés de pensée et la démocratie moderne* (Paris, 1978 [1921]).

Cochin, A., *L'esprit du jacobinism. Une interprétation sociologique de la Révolution française* (Paris, 1979).

Furet, François, 'Jacobinism', in François Furet and Mona Ozouf (eds), *Critical Dictionary of the French Revolution*, trans. Arthur Goldhammer (Cambridge, MA, 1989).

Gueniffey, Patrice, 'Clubs and Popular Societies', in Furet and Ozouf (eds), *Critical Dictionary of the French Revolution*.

Higonnet, Patrice, *Goodness Beyond Virtue: Jacobins during the French Revolution* (Cambridge, MA, 1998).

Kates, Gary, *The Cercle Social, the Girondins, and the French Revolution* (Princeton, 1985).

Kennedy, Michael L., *The Jacobin Clubs in the French Revolution: The First Years* (Princeton, 1982).

Kennedy, Michael L., *The Jacobin Clubs in the French Revolution: The Middle Years* (Princeton, 1988).

Kennedy, Michael L., *The Jacobin Clubs in the French Revolution, 1793–1795* (New York, 2000).

Monnier, Raymonde, *Espace public démocratique: essai sur l'opinion publique à Paris de la Révolution au Directoire* (Paris, 1994).

Soboul, Albert, *The Parisian Sans-culottes and the French Revolution, 1793–94* (Oxford, 1964).

Walton, Charles, *Policing Public Opinion in the French Revolution: The Culture of Calumny and the Problem of Free Speech* (New York, 2009).

Woloch, Isser, *Jacobin Legacy: The Democratic Movement under the Directory* (Princeton, 1970).

CHAPTER 22

MILITARY TRAUMA

ALAN FORREST

THE early years of the French Revolution were a period of crisis for France's armed forces both off and on the battlefield. The Revolution proclaimed a new ideal of civil society, in which military service was transformed into a duty of citizenship, creating what Thomas Hippler has described as a necessary tension between citizenship and discipline.[1] It also set out to abolish existing forms of privilege and the institutions in which that privilege was enshrined. The regiments, the officers, and the soldiers who made up France's line army found themselves serving new political masters and defending new ideological values. For many the change was abrupt and unwelcome, and for some sufficiently traumatic to make continued service in the army unthinkable. By its proclaimed ideals and its political initiatives the Revolution made it impossible to keep the old regime army as it had been, and to that degree it is true that the Revolution brought on a crisis in France's military affairs. It was something that revolutionary politicians would claim repeatedly during the 1790s. Yet in the eyes of many contemporaries, including very senior army officers, the crisis was already there under the Bourbons, and it contributed to the army's relative lack of success in the field. And if the crisis was already being talked of during the reigns of Louis XV and Louis XVI, so were many of the ideas for reform already being circulated and discussed.

THE ARMY OF THE OLD REGIME

The army of the old regime was inextricably tied to the political institutions of the Bourbon monarchy. Those officers who were in post in 1789 had all taken a personal oath of loyalty to the monarch, and they did not necessarily feel bound to the nation or to the French people, a concept that had no basis in law and seemed alien to many of them. For the officers of the Maison du Roi, the royal household regiments which guarded the royal palaces and the king's person and took part in the major ceremonies of state, that loyalty may have felt even more personal. But the line regiments, too, answered to the king as commander-in-chief, and they constituted the principal fighting strength of the army. In 1789 the army numbered some 113,000 infantry, 32,000 cavalry, and 10,000 artillery, who were organized in 102 regiments. Of these 79 had been recruited in France itself. The others consisted of foreign mercenaries, those soldiers of fortune—Swiss and Germans and Scots and Irish—to whose services the monarchy habitually turned in times of war. The French regiments were generally named after their province of origin or heroes of past campaigns. Similarly, the foreign regiments were usually called after their country of origin or their past commanders: La Marck and Royal Hesse-Darmstadt for the Germans, Diesbach and Châteauvieux for the Swiss; Walsh and Dillon for the Irish. It is scarcely to be wondered at if they had little sense of fighting for the French nation; their loyalties were to the monarch as their paymaster, and to the army colonels who recruited them for the king's service.[2]

Common soldiers enjoyed few rights and privileges under the old regime and were subject to a severe code of military discipline against which they had no recourse. Many of them were drawn from the poorer sections of French society—from the workshops of the cities and agricultural labour in the countryside—and they had every reason to sympathize with the demands of the Third Estate. There was something heady and infectious about the Revolution's rhetoric, and the troops were not immune to its intoxicating effects. In Paris they looked on as crowds stormed the Bastille or demonstrated at the Tuileries, demanding bread or political rights in the name of the French people. Many found it hard not to make common cause with the crowd. Besides, with the Assembly declaring that all men were now citizens, entitled to arm themselves in defence of their rights, and creating a new National Guard for local policing and ceremonial functions, their future role was almost necessarily brought into question. The new political situation could not but affect the army's perception of its role, and it was clear, even in 1789, that for many soldiers the Revolution and the notion of military duty would make uneasy bedfellows.

This proved to be a problem from the first indication that troops might be asked to move against the civil population to protect food convoys or suppress rioting or insurrection. This was not, of course, a new situation. Throughout the years of the Bourbon monarchy regiments of the Royal Army had regularly been called upon to intervene in what were essentially political disturbances, where they were expected to suppress opposition movements and to demonstrate a total allegiance to the Crown. But the context in which they were asked to intervene had dramatically changed. The increasingly political atmosphere throughout France in the last months of the old order, the holding of political hustings in advance of elections to the Estates-General and the consultation of popular opinion in the *cahiers de doléances* had aroused new levels of political awareness, among the troops as well as in the population at large. When in June 1788, for instance, an angry crowd in Grenoble had rioted in support of the *parlement* of Dauphiné after their magistrates had been served with *lettres de cachet* by the king, the troops and their officers had to make a vital political decision. Did they obey the king's orders to suppress the riot, if necessary shedding the blood of the rioters, or did they side with the people? For some the moral quandary this posed proved unbearable, and some disillusioned officers resigned their commissions in protest. The marquis de Langeron, the garrison commander in Besançon, did not try to hide his dismay at the tasks he was being asked to perform. The army, he declared, was there to be deployed against the enemies of the French state, not against its own citizens; its honour was at stake; and it was essential that its loyalty should not be abused.[3]

Yet the advent of the Revolution brought more policing, not less. The spring of 1789 saw the deployment of several regiments of infantry and cavalry to Paris to prevent trouble should the king dissolve the Estates-General. By the summer both French and foreign units were being used to disperse political protests in the capital, defending state buildings and private property against the demands of the crowd. Some, at least, of the soldiers came to see their first loyalty as being to the nation, to the French people, rather than to the sovereign, and began to be infected with revolutionary ideas.

NOBLE OFFICERS AND PROFESSIONALIZATION

For the more conservative officers the French Revolution brought dilemmas of a very different kind, since its most fundamental message, the one that united the different factions in the National Assembly, was an abhorrence of privilege and a commitment to abolish the legal distinctions between the different estates. Since the overwhelming majority of officers were still nobles, the principal exceptions being in the artillery, many felt a deep resentment that it was their status and honour that were under attack, the more so in that the privileged position of the military nobility had been the subject of much debate and repeated reforms during the second half of the eighteenth century. From the time of the Seven Years War it was obvious that the profession of arms no longer commanded as much respect in society, and that army careers were less eagerly sought after. This had led to the entry to the officer class of many newer nobles, often men who had been recently *anoblis* and whom the older families somewhat gratuitously insulted and underestimated. Of the older hereditary nobility only around a quarter were still serving or had served in the royal army by 1775, a fact that seemed to many to undermine the quality and sense of vocation of the entire officer class.[4]

It was to reverse this situation that the Ségur Ordinance of 1781 laid down that officer rank in the king's army in future required four quarterings of nobility—four grandparents who were nobles—which might appear a deeply exclusive and reactionary measure. Yet there was little public clamour against it, and few murmurs of disgruntlement in the *cahiers*. Ségur, after all, was one of the more notable military reformers of the decades before 1789. And the old military nobility, often the sons of provincial noble families with little wealth but a long pedigree of service in the royal armies, were defending their position not against men from trade or the professions but against a threat from within the noble estate, from *arrivistes* with money and court nobles with political connections.[5] They were defending their access to military commissions, moreover, not in opposition to the notion of meritocracy in the French army, but in support of it, for they firmly believed that, bolstered by family tradition, they had a unique understanding of the qualities that made a good officer. Restricting access to officer rank did not, in their eyes, conflict with the idea of merit. Rather it was a measure that would ensure that only the best candidates, those most committed to a military career and with most understanding of military strategy and man management, would be appointed to positions of command. In their eyes the Ségur Ordinance was a step towards greater professionalization, and a growing emphasis on talent and discipline, in the army.[6]

Expertise, skill and proficiency already mattered for the officer corps. They were not simply the pampered sons of the aristocracy, promoted too young and given charge of units of war-seasoned veterans, as enlightened satirists were wont to claim. Drill, training and—increasingly—formal military education now counted for more than in previous reigns in the appointment and promotion of officers. In France, much more than in England, those who were groomed for careers as high-ranking officers started as officer-cadets in military schools or academies, the most prominent and prestigious of which, the *Ecole Royale Militaire*, was established in Paris in 1750. In the course of the eighteenth century military education had developed in a somewhat piecemeal manner, often the result of private initiatives, but the result was that by the time of the Seven Years War there were a number of local academies and riding schools which prepared young gentlemen for service in the military, often dispensing a mix of basic academic knowledge and social etiquette as well as some military science, swordsmanship, dance and equestrianism. The academic curriculum often emphasized subjects that had some military application, like technical drawing and mathematics. It would be an exaggeration to think of this as a necessary preparation for entry to the officer corps; many young officers continued to enter the service directly without passing through the school, usually on the basis of family connections. But it was a step in the direction of professionalization. And it was conceived as a way of widening the range of officer recruitment, and especially of giving some protection to the poor provincial nobility who had traditionally provided the Crown with military service by providing an education for their sons at the king's expense.[7]

The move to professionalize army officers and to eradicate incompetence reached its peak during the ministry of Saint-Germain in 1775, when major reforms signalled a new determination in government to end the damaging influence which the court nobles held over military appointments. Saint-Germain believed staunchly in the need for a root-and-branch reform of the culture of the military: he imposed a rigorous new training regime, disbanded units of the Maison militaire, and tried to rid the army of redundant, lazy and often profligate officers. In particular, he legislated to improve officer education by creating a network of a dozen provincial cadet schools across France that would prepare young men for the realities of modern warfare and hone the skills that would be necessary for leadership in the infantry, cavalry and artillery. These schools trained many of the young officers who went on to serve under the Revolution. The young Bonaparte attended one of them, at Brienne, before moving to Paris and the Ecole

Militaire; he was taught three languages (French, German, and Latin) as well as subjects deemed to provide him with the social skills to prepare him for the officer's mess (music, dancing, and fencing).[8] Other pupils came from overseas. Arthur Wellesley, the future duke of Wellington, spent a year at a private military school in Angers in 1786, where the curriculum included horsemanship, fencing, and the theory of fortifications, but which 'more than anything else sought to inculcate the virtues of honour and nobility'.[9]

THE REFORM DEBATE

This increased emphasis on talent and discipline led reformers—the great majority of them noble—to attack privilege and favouritism in the army.[10] The years before the Revolution saw a huge rise in the number of pamphlets and manuscript memoirs published by serving and recently retired army officers on the subject of military reform, the majority of them proposing reforms to improve discipline and morale in the army. The trend began long before the Revolution, and it illustrates the strength of opinion in the army in favour of change and reform. It shows, too, that army officers were not benighted reactionaries clinging to privilege at any cost; many of them had spent long years advocating reforms that might make the Bourbon army more open to talent, better supplied, and more professional. Military reformers had emphasized the need for change since the mid-century, largely as a consequence of the indifferent performance of the French armies in the War of the Austrian Succession and the subsequent disasters of the Seven Years War. They had the example of other eighteenth century armies before them, not least the Prussian army of Frederick the Great which had humiliated them at Rossbach in 1757, and they were willing to learn from them. Nothing encouraged reappraisal in military circles like a comprehensive defeat in the field, and the twenty-five years before the Revolution were notable for the vigour of debates within the army and the wide range of reforms that were proposed. The army itself, moreover, clearly encouraged such writings, urging its officers to write down their ideas and recommendations for improvement, and to submit them to their commanding officers or to the Ministry for consideration. Those judged to be the best ideas were discussed and given consideration; men could even cite their works among their military achievements on which a case for future promotion might be based. Of the memoirs submitted in the second half of the eighteenth century on questions of military organization, discipline, and training some 630 have survived; and it is clear than many of them were written and distributed with the aim of opening up a debate inside the military.[11]

One of the features of these writings, especially in the later years of the monarchy, was the attention they gave to motivation and to the question of honour. There was less insistence on mindless drill and exercise, and a greater sense that ordinary soldiers, like their officers, would respond better to the conditions of the battlefield if they were allowed to show initiative, to be actors in the engagement rather than simply automatons who were expected to respond mechanically to the orders of others. French soldiers, it was now suggested, had a character of their own, a certain flair and enthusiasm, which could not usefully be curbed or overlooked; they were not capable of approaching battle like the Prussians, for instance, as they were individualists, responded badly to the stick and, crucially, understood, just like their officers, the concept of honour. Some of the pamphlets were blisteringly critical of established practices which, they implied, had contributed to French military shortcomings during the previous half-century. Where discipline was harsh, it could also be arbitrary: this was an army where, since 1716, the official penalty for desertion was death, and officers were unwilling to decimate their armies in order to abide by the letter of military law. It was an army, too, where large numbers of soldiers were impressed and where public esteem in soldiering was stubbornly low. Improving morale, many felt, must involve different methods of recruitment, an army that was more representative of society at large. Joseph Servan, in 1780, was already suggesting a citizen-army in which men would serve as a matter of civic duty for a short campaign before returning to civilian life on the farm. He was already talking, ten years before the Revolution, of soldiering as a rite of passage for young men of all backgrounds and all classes of society. Only in this way, he believed, would France be able to call upon the talents of its people when the country was attacked.[12]

Many of these ideas do not seem so far removed from the rhetoric of the Revolution, and can appear to herald a new, more democratic age. And there were certainly similarities with the reforms which would be proposed after 1789, by the National Assembly and its successors. The idea of an officer class chosen on merit, for instance, would be revived after 1789, when some of the reformers of the old regime became policy-makers under the new. But the transition would not be a smooth one. The noble concept of merit did not easily conflate into the egalitarian vision of the men of 1789, for whom the concept of careers open to talent had a far wider resonance and any idea of restricting promotion to the nobility was anathema. There was a strong element of mutual misunderstanding here, a tension between two very different measures of merit which only became apparent in the heated debates on army reform that punctuated the early months of the Revolution. Indeed, many noble officers were at first inclined to embrace the new meritocratic discourse and seek to benefit from it, awaiting the Assembly's reforms with a degree of measured optimism. Only belatedly did they discover to their dismay that the revolutionaries were not advocating their sort of merit and were talking a quite different language of rights and civic equality, of offices open to all. But here, as always, different sections of the nobility spoke with different voices. There was little unity within the Second Estate, and its attempt to maintain its privileged position in the military was doomed to fail.

The National Assembly and the Army

Those members of the military nobility who took their seats in the National Assembly as representatives of the Second Estate took a lead, indeed, in pressing for army reforms, and they would play a significant role in the debates of the Assembly's *comité militaire*, set up in October 1789 with the aim of drafting a new military constitution for France. Membership of the committee was dominated by officers, active or retired: Rafe Blaufarb notes that all but two of its twenty members were noble officers and that one of its most outspoken members, the Baron de Wimpfen, had himself been a reformer under the old regime as well as a close collaborator of both Saint-Germain and Ségur.[13] Many saw the Revolution as an opportunity to press their case for reform, taking up some of the proposals which they had made under the monarchy. But there was little that was revolutionary in what they proposed, little to take account of the extent of change in the polity. When, for instance, Bouthillier reported to the Assembly on 19 November on proposals to reform recruitment to the army, his recommendations were modest, even rather conservative. He drew attention to some of the abuses of the old system, it is true, including the disadvantages of impressment and of an army composed of the poor and marginal; he made the case for a more balanced regional representation; he noted the high percentage of urban artisans who joined the service, but warned against the risk to agriculture if large numbers of farm workers found themselves forced to serve. So he preferred to retain the traditional system of recruitment, enlisting men in return for a signing-on bounty, as being the most practical, certainly in peacetime; and that it should also be used for as long as it could be sustained. Anything more radical he rejected as being too disruptive. In particular, he urged that any form of compulsion that might be 'susceptible to appear to attack in some way the liberty of citizens' should never be employed unless it could be demonstrated to be necessary for the defence of the nation.[14]

But not all members of the committee agreed, and opinion evolved rapidly. On 15 December Dubois-Crancé, himself a former *mousquetaire du Roi*, shocked conservative opinion in the Assembly by presenting a much more radical programme of military reform, one which, he claimed, was made necessary by the circumstances that now beset the nation. A revolutionary army, he believed, could not just continue as it had done in the past. There was a new spirit of patriotism in the minds of ordinary soldiers which made it imperative to tap their energy and free them from the burdens they faced, for they were now free men well able to think for themselves. And yet the army was top-heavy with a surfeit of officers, far more than the establishment required, many of whom spent little time on active service; while the men under them were inadequately fed, poorly paid, and driven to insurrection. He urged that the number of high-ranking officers should be drastically reduced and that the resources that were being wasted on rewarding noble sinecures be redistributed. He proposed that the existing military schools, which overwhelmingly served to protect the nobility, should all close and that appropriate education to prepare the young to assume military responsibilities be offered in schools across France. He denounced current recruitment practices, advocating instead a system of conscription, arguing that every Frenchmen owed his person to his *patrie* in times of war and that all must be prepared to serve, including men of property 'from the second head of the empire to the last active citizen'. And already, in 1789, he proposed that officers should not be appointed by their superiors—a system which he adjudged open to abuse and to favouritism—but elected by the men of their own rank.[15]

In other words, he believed that France was a revolutionary society, and that a revolutionary society required a revolutionary army, an army in its own image. The debate had moved on from the reform proposals of the 1780s in ways that would prove traumatic for many in the military.

For the present, of course, none of this passed into law. The army still contained many of the same regiments, the same officers and the same troops as in the previous year; the same military laws and the same penalties, too. When in 1790 the Assembly voted to punish soldiers who had taken part in a series of mutinies it showed no greater clemency than in times past: it ordered the ringleaders to be hanged or broken on the wheel. And when the military constitution was adopted in 1790 it took care to reserve the supreme command of the army to the king—one of his few executive prerogatives—while matters of day-to-day management were largely left to the military itself. The powers of the legislative were largely restricted to general policy matters, like the size of the military budget, the numbers of men to be recruited, forms of enrolment, levels of pay, rules governing promotion, or the use of foreign mercenaries.[16] These were all matters in which successive Assemblies would take increasing interest as the Revolution progressed.

The National Assembly had also to answer another question, and one that might be just as traumatic for seasoned officers; just what did they want an army for? The deputies accepted, of course, that they must be able to defend their territory in the event of a hostile attack from neighbouring states, and some were even realistic enough to recognize that the Revolution had probably made such an attack more likely. Some might seek to attack for ideological purposes—Austria was always prone to sabre-rattling gestures and to promise to restore Louis XVI to the plenitude of his powers—but there were more mundane reasons to fear a hostile attack. A country which was perceived to be in the midst of internal turmoil could seem easy game for other powers eager for conquest, with its army in disarray, its finances unsecured, and its administrative and judicial systems in apparent chaos. And there was no fresh start for France in the area of international relations: the revolutionaries inherited the treaty obligations and international commitments that had been entered into by Louis XVI's ministers, from which, whatever their declared intentions, the revolutionary authorities would find it difficult to escape. Since the time of Louis XIV France had been a major player in a diplomatic game where, through a succession of wars, the great powers had traded alliances and sought to gain advantage in both the European and the colonial spheres. Under Louis XVI France had been fully signed up to this policy, involving French forces in the American War of Independence to gain revenge on Britain for the humiliation of the 1763 Peace of Paris. Louis' foreign minister, Vergennes, could even claim to have gained valuable kudos in a campaign that was aimed at limiting Britain's global expansion while containing the power of Austria, Prussia and Russia on the European continent.[17] The policy had proved expensive, crippling the finances of the monarchy. Yet any sign of military weakness, any reluctance to assent to military expenditure, or the merest hint that the Revolution had no longer any interest in pursuing the country's traditional foreign policy would alert the other nations of Europe to their opportunity and risked unleashing further hostilities.

The Assembly debated at length about the nature of warfare in the new era that was opening up before them and about the uses to which their armies could legitimately be put. It was recognized that they would have to have recourse to military action if their territory were attacked—that fell clearly within the scope of the just war—but was it legitimate to conceive of an offensive campaign? And could the king, as head of the executive, be entrusted with the responsibility of declaring war and peace? For many deputies this was the real issue at stake, whether they could trust the king to exercise that right in a responsible manner, or whether he would be tempted to lead the country into rash wars or dynastic conflicts, as kings had so often done in the past.[18] They were also concerned that royal authority should not be enhanced by involvement in a foreign war, and the principal procedural decision that was taken on 22 May 1790 was to restrict the king's power in military matters and to entrust the making of war and peace to the nation, the sovereign people in the person of its deputies. But the decree, famously and symbolically, laid down the circumstances in which France, as a revolutionary state, could justifiably go to war. For a declaration of war, with the human cost which that involved, was not to be made lightly. It had to have a moral cause. France should not make war against other peoples but only against tyrants; and if the executive should ever declare war in circumstances which the Assembly held to be unjust, it would be held to account. In the words of the decree, 'if the Legislative Body judges that the hostilities declared constitute a culpable act of aggression on the part of the ministers or other agents of the executive, the author of that aggression will be pursued in the criminal courts for the crime of *lèse-nation*'. The decree went on to insist that henceforth 'the French nation renounces all wars made for the purpose of conquest, and that it will never deploy its forces against the liberty of any people'.[19] Political control was being asserted over the deployment of the military, which, for the officers of the old line army, meant a new definition of their role. Meanwhile, the other nations of Europe watched, observed, and drew their own conclusions. They had no reason to renounce their own foreign policy objectives because of the drama that was being played out in Paris.

CRISIS IN THE ARMIES

It was not only legislative changes that threatened the stability of the army in the early months of the Revolution; much more serious was the threat of collapse in its own regiments as both officers and men reacted to the political changes around them. Many army officers, seeing their privileged status revoked and hearing of attacks on chateaux and landed estates across large swathes of the countryside, were faced with a conflict of loyalties at a time when their families were being stripped of their possessions or were fleeing to the frontiers. And the most devotedly royalist among them took strong exception to the new constitution and to the deputies' attempts to bridle at what they saw as the legitimate powers of the monarch. As the Revolution became more radical more and more officers became disillusioned with the new political culture, and many were tempted to join the flow of émigrés abroad. A few left as early as the summer of 1789, joining the first wave of émigrés in Turin and Koblenz and vowing to support the cause of a Bourbon restoration. Others were driven to follow, whether by the abolition of privilege and the social reforms of the early Revolution, or by the attack on the position of the Church, or by the reluctance of the king to embrace the ideals of the new era. Individual motives clearly varied. Some turned against their own army in the face of a greater assertiveness and belligerence on the part of their soldiers, a refusal to obey orders, or acts of open insubordination by their men which increasingly went unpunished. Others belonged to families that were politically counter-revolutionary or where fathers and older brothers had been persecuted by local revolutionaries. But most of all they modelled their behaviour on the reactions of the king whom they continued to see as the fount of all that was honourable; with the consequence that, for as long as Louis seemed prepared to adjust to the demands of being a constitutional monarch, the great majority of his officers remained in his service. But Louis' flight to Varennes in the summer of 1791 changed all that. It marked a major turning point, the moment when it became clear that the king's allegiance to the Revolution was an empty sham and that his position was untenable. It had great cultural resonance, too. For if the king himself was prepared to abandon France to its fate and—many believed—plunge the country into civil war, honour surely demanded that his officers, members of his nobility who had sworn their loyalty to him, should follow his example. What had been a worrying trickle of officers back to their estates or over the French frontier turned into a haemorrhage.

The result was a traumatic reduction in officer strength that left gaping holes in the command structure of the army and seriously undermined military morale. Sam Scott has shown how individual regiments were left bereft of leadership in the months following the king's flight and officer posts in both infantry and cavalry regiments remained unfilled. The figures he gives illustrate the extent of the crisis. Between 15 September and 1 December some 2,160 officers emigrated, while some regiments—especially those where indiscipline was rife—suffered mass resignations. And the political events of 1792, culminating in the deposition of the king and the declaration of the Republic, only magnified the extent of the crisis. In all, in the fifteen months from September 1791 to December 1792 Scott concludes that 'one-third of the units in the line army lost one-third or more of their authorized officer strength as a result of resignations, illegal absences, and emigrations'.[20]

The trauma posed by the Revolution was not restricted to army officers, though they certainly faced the hardest choices. The soldiers, too, had to reconcile their new status as free men and citizens with what they encountered on joining the army and what many continued to resent throughout their period of service: the lack of freedom, low pay and harsh discipline that characterized army life in the old regime. None of these was swept away in the early months of the Revolution, and the seeming inability of the army to respond to the values of the Revolution added to the malaise in the ranks and pushed a number of regiments to open mutiny. Most common among the causes cited for acts of mutiny or insubordination were issues of treatment and supply—the fact that soldiers had not been paid, that their rations were withheld, or that they had been cheated by their officers. Wrongful imprisonment or insulting rebukes were often sufficient to incite soldiers to throw down their swords or refuse to obey orders. Few revolts were directly tied to revolutionary ideas, though it is clear that there was widespread sympathy for the ideals of the Revolution, which in turn encouraged a high degree of complicity with civilians, particularly where the troops had been ordered to quell popular outcries and political disturbances. Soldiers fraternized with local National Guard units which had expressed their support for radical change. Radical politicians and newly established political clubs were by 1790 taking the soldiers' side against their officers, and men were being urged to denounce officers who expressed counter-revolutionary views or who abused their position of command. By 1791 some clubs went further, demanding the dismissal of the general staff and the replacement of all nobles who still held military rank. Jacobin clubs in garrison towns in the north and along the Belgian frontier complained that their agendas were becoming dominated by army matters; while from May 1791 military personnel were allowed by a vote of the Assembly to attend club meetings when they were off-duty.[21] The political atmosphere in the regiments was becoming seriously overcharged, and desertion rates among the troops rose alarmingly at a time when the number of new recruits all but dried up. The army faced a serious manpower shortage.

Disgruntlement among the soldiers reached its peak in the summer of 1790 and the spring of 1791 in a series of violent mutinies and increasing belligerence towards those in authority.[22] In some cases insubordination was reflected in desertion rates in excess of 10 per cent; and in a few instances soldiers openly flouted their officers' orders and showed their support for the new regime. A sense of crisis spread through the army and the political leadership, and though the National Assembly may initially have been sympathetic to the demands of the men, it could not ignore the serious military weakness which threatened the security of the country. There were reports of mutinies from garrisons across France, from Hesdin in the north to Perpignan on the Spanish frontier. But the most serious occurred in the eastern city of Nancy in August 1790, where two French regiments and the Swiss mercenary regiment of Châteauvieux mutinied against their officers. Politics clearly played its part as the regiments involved had been infiltrated by members of the National Guard in the weeks following the festival of the Federation, held to celebrate the anniversary of the fall of the Bastille. And the soldiers' demands were political, too. In the *Infanterie du Roi* they had established a soldiers' committee which established close links with the local Jacobins; the men insisted that they were being denied their rightful pay and rations, demanded to see the regimental accounts and confined all their officers to barracks. When the demands spread to the Swiss, their officers had the soldiers' representatives publicly whipped, an action that turned them into martyrs and further stoked the mutiny. Discipline had clearly collapsed, and the Assembly, fearful of the effect on morale in the army at large and the damage that was being done to the nation's security, determined on this occasion to take a firm—many would say a brutal—stand against the mutineers, leaving a tremor of unease and fear running through the entire army. In the name of the government the marquis de Bouillé refused to negotiate with the rebels, taking the city with a force of over four thousand men and insisting on an unconditional surrender.

It was an ugly end to what had been an ugly moment—French soldiers fighting with one another and firing on one another in support of conflicting loyalties—and it was a graphic demonstration of the damage which revolutionary enthusiasm could do to military discipline. Bouillé was in no mood for compromise, and as part of the terms of surrender he insisted that each of the three regiments hand over their four most mutinous soldiers. Worse was to follow as the high command tried to reimpose its control. The Swiss of Châteauvieux, mercenaries who owed their livelihood to the king, suffered most; they had also been involved in some of the bloodiest fighting. In all, over forty soldiers were sentenced to thirty years in the galleys—a plight that would turn them into *sans-culotte* heroes later in the Revolution—while twenty-two of the ringleaders were condemned to be hanged and one—the man who was supposedly at the heart of the rebellion—was broken on the wheel. Discipline was no doubt restored, but at a terrible price; while the mutinies and the repression that followed drove a wedge between the army leadership and popular opinion, especially in the more radical cities. Nancy came to epitomize for many what was wrong with the line army as a means of defending a society in the midst of a political revolution, and it went far to convince the politicians that the army needed root-and-branch reform, an approach that went far beyond what had been discussed in the dog days after defeat at Rossbach.

An Army for the Revolution

They started with the problem of recruitment, which had been languishing since the start of the Revolution. Men were no longer volunteering for service when the morale of the army was low and there were more prestigious billets in the ranks of the National Guard. And the government, inheriting a bankrupt treasury and with tax revenues plummeting, lacked the resources to buy the services of mercenaries. So in 1791 they called upon the young men of France to volunteer their services to protect both the nation and the Revolution. In the first of these years, with war not yet declared, the numbers required were found without difficulty: there seemed something vaguely glorious and patriotic about volunteering, and members of the National Guard often rushed to present themselves for service. But when they tried to do the same in 1792, appealing once again to single men aged between 16 and 45, the response was less enthusiastic. Departments failed to reach their target numbers in a climate where the early optimism had worn off as politics became more sectarian and the realities of war sank in. By 1793, with France at war on every front and desperately in need of recruits to stave off invasion, voluntary inscriptions were clearly not going to provide the men that the army required. The *levée des 300,000* in the spring turned to compulsion by enforcing departmental quotas; and by the autumn the Jacobins abandoned all pretence of voluntarism when they proclaimed the *levée en masse*: henceforward, the law declared, all French citizens had a duty to help the *patrie en danger*: young men by going to fight, women and children by producing supplies to support the men in the field. There would be no provision for replacements. Those who were designated were to serve in person as France aimed to create a citizen army a million strong. And, somewhat ominously, no limit of time was placed on their service; many of the young men sent to fight in 1793 would still be in the units that Napoleon led across Europe during the Empire.[23]

The creation of an army of citizens was presented as a political measure to build an army in the image of a revolutionary society, an army whose soldiers would have levels of prestige, and of pay, that far exceeded those of the men of the line. Replacing the yawning gaps in the ranks of the officers produced a problem of a different kind, since the Revolution implicitly distrusted noble officers and the military schools of the old regime had been the exclusive preserve of nobles. After the declaration of the republic and the trial of the king this proved a difficult challenge. How could the revolutionaries conjure up a new type of officer, more in tune with the men they led and with the ideals they were defending? How could they identify potential talent? Their response was to open officer positions to capable NCOs, men who had gained battle experience through service as sergeants and corporals and who had earned the trust of those they led. To this end, they instituted a system of election, whereby men at each rank would choose one of their number to lead them, the assumption being that they would choose only the best, those who enjoyed their trust and on whom they felt they could depend in tight situations. Empirical evidence would suggest that they often made inspired choices. Finding generals, on the other hand, remained in the hands of the politicians. The revolutionaries had suffered from having royalist officers who did not share their ideals and who had resigned or deserted to the enemy. In future, generals had to be committed Republicans, men on whom the government could depend, and chosen, on both military and political criteria, by the National Convention. Some, especially at the height of the Jacobin Republic, would prove to be poor choices, the result of political favouritism rather than any military tuition.

Other decisions followed which added to the sense of crisis in the military. The army by 1793 was a jumble of different forces and structures, traditional line regiments and units of volunteers, paid differential rates and clinging to different military values, and often showing little mutual esteem. The old regime soldiers were accused of lacking commitment, and the volunteers of being raw and poorly trained. Fights broke out between them when their units crossed in garrison towns, with regular reports of volunteers and line troops treating one another with contempt when under the influence of drink. In extreme instances men were killed by their supposed comrades. The different regiments were difficult to administer: when the Convention sought to introduce reforms it found that there were often no registers, no lists of enrolments, no account books, and no reliable lists of losses through death and desertion. For these reasons the new minister of war, Dubois-Crancé, undertook a major restructuring of the army in February 1793, breaking up the traditional regiments and battalions to create smaller, more mobile units called *demi-brigades*, and in the process abolishing any lingering distinction between the volunteers and the men of the line. The *amalgame* set out to create a single, unified army, all wearing the same uniform and receiving the same pay; it abolished the last traces of regional autonomy and created a force with a single focus of loyalty: the French nation. The result was an army of 196 *demi-brigades* of infantry, each provided with a company of artillery, as well as units of cavalry, light artillery and engineers.[24] With this reform the Revolutionary army of the Year II was born.

It had not been an easy transition. The new era may have brought hope for some, and launched a new generation of young men on the road to military glory, but the change was traumatic. The Revolution ended many officers' careers and damaged their family prospects. Under the Jacobins there would be an almost pathological suspicion of the officer class which conspired to undermine traditional discipline, encouraged soldiers to denounce their superiors and subjected the military to intense political surveillance. By 1793, generals were answerable to political commissars sent to root out desertion, prosecute corrupt suppliers, and investigate accusations of cowardice and treason made against officers. Deputies on mission added a strong dose of political accountability, though their mandates were not always clear, some reporting to the Convention, others to the Committee of Public Safety or to ministers.[25] Army commanders felt that they were no longer free to make military judgements. Even a surfeit of caution in the pursuit of victory could lead a commander to face capital charges as the Jacobins took Terror, and the guillotine, into the armies; and in the Year II four generals in the Army of the North alone were condemned and executed. Their humiliation was intended to be public, as their regiments would be lined up to witness their executions. Traumatic it certainly was, a way of terrorizing the army into obedience; but its supporters would argue that it was also effective, since it was during the Jacobin Republic that the war was turned around and when the early defeats were turned into victories. There is more than a grain of truth in this, since the war had started badly for the inexperienced French armies, with a string of defeats against the Austrians and Prussians. And though revolutionary propaganda tried to make moral capital out of the victory over the Prussians at Valmy in September 1792 which gave the French their first taste of success, in reality it was a minor engagement rather fortuitously won.[26] It was only during 1794, during the most radical months of the Jacobin Republic, that the years of military trauma gave way to the elation of victory.

But with success the army also became less revolutionary. Officers were chosen for their professional capacity, not for their politics, and in the process the army became more and more divorced from civil society. The idealism of the nation-in-arms gave way by the end of the decade to annual conscriptions of a kind that had been debated and rejected back in 1789.[27] The perception and motivation of the army changed, too. Soldiers who had been encouraged to see themselves as citizens became inured to army life and to the military as a profession: they began to see their future in the army; they valued the approval of their comrades more than of the public back home; and like the Napoleonic armies that followed them they dreamt of rewards and promotion.[28] Their lives, like those of French society more generally, were increasingly dominated by the fact of war and the sacrifices it necessitated. In Italy and in Egypt Napoleon's campaigns would briefly make war and the conduct of that war the principal focus of public interest, but the concern for conquests in exotic countries served only to underline the greater schism between the interests of the people and those of the state. Soldiers were increasingly kept apart from the civil population, camp followers—especially women—were discouraged, and the government sought to exclude sans-culottes and radicals from the ranks of the officer corps. A revolution that had begun by insisting that the use of war should be severely limited now unleashed a conflict that would engulf Europe for a generation and leave Britain as the undisputed imperial power of the nineteenth century. It is too easy to blame these changes on Napoleon and the militarization of French society over which he presided. They were already present under the Directory and even in the Thermidorian Republic. French soldiers might still be volunteers in name, but the ideal of the citizen-soldier, of an army that reflected the values of the population at large and fought for the interests of all—the ideal that had inspired old regime reformers and fired Jacobin militants in 1793—had long since passed into history.

NOTES

1. Thomas Hippler, *Citizens, Soldiers and National Armies: Military Service in France and Germany, 1778–1830* (London, 2008), 1–9.
2. Alan Forrest, *The Soldiers of the French Revolution* (Durham, 1990), 27–8; Samuel F. Scott, *The Response of the Royal Army to the French Revolution: the Role and Development of the Line Army, 1787–93* (Oxford, 1978), 217–24.
3. Scott, *Response*, 48.
4. André Corvisier, *Armies and Societies in Europe, 1494–1789* (Bloomington, 1979), 102.
5. David Bien, 'The Army in the French Enlightenment: Reform, Reaction and Revolution', *Past and Present* 85 (1979), 68–98.
6. Rafe Blaufarb, *The French Army, 1750–1820: Careers, Talent, Merit* (Manchester, 2002), 34–5.
7. Ibid., 20–4.
8. James Marshall-Cornwall, *Napoleon as Military Commander* (London, 1967), 15.
9. Gordon Corrigan, *Wellington: A Military Life* (London, 2001), 6.
10. Jay M. Smith, *The Culture of Merit: Nobility, Royal Service and the Making of Absolute Monarchy in France, 1600–1789* (Ann Arbor, 1996), 228–62.
11. Arnaud Guinier, 'L'honneur du soldat: la discipline militaire en débat dans la France des Lumières' (doctoral thesis, Université de Poitiers, 2012), 49.
12. Joseph Servan, *Le soldat citoyen* (Neufchâtel, 1780), 451–8.
13. Blaufarb, *The French Army*, 58.
14. *Archives Parlementaires*, vol. 10, 118–22.
15. *Archives Parlementaires*, vol. 10, 595–614.
16. *Archives Parlementaires*, vol. 11, 521–1.
17. Jeremy J. Whiteman, *Reform, Revolution and French Global Policy, 1787–1791* (Aldershot, 2003), 18–19.
18. *Archives Parlementaires*, vol. 15, 651–61.
19. *Archives Parlementaires*, vol. 15, 662.
20. Scott, *Response*, 109–10.
21. Pierre Dufay, *Les sociétés populaires et l'armée, 1791–1794* (Paris, 1913), 24–5.

22. Jean-Paul Bertaud, *La Révolution armée: les soldats-citoyens et la Révolution Française* (Paris, 1979), 47–8; Scott, *Response*, 93–95.
23. Alan Forrest, *Conscripts and Deserters: The Army and French Society during the Revolution and Empire* (New York, 1989), 20–42.
24. Forrest, *Soldiers*, 50–2.
25. Paddy Griffith, *The Art of War in Revolutionary France, 1789–1802* (London, 1998), 98.
26. For Goethe Valmy represented the beginning of the modern era. See Jean Planchais, *Adieu Valmy: La fin de la nation en armes* (Paris, 2003), 7.
27. Annie Crépin, *La conscription en débat, ou le triple apprentissage de la Nation, de la citoyenneté, de la république, 1798–1889* (Arras, 1998), 19–33.
28. Michael J. Hughes, *Forging Napoleon's Grande Armée: Motivation, Military Culture and Masculinity in the French Army, 1800–1808* (New York, 2012), 39–42.

SUGGESTED READING

Bertaud, Jean-Paul, *La Révolution armée: les soldats-citoyens et la Révolution Française* (Paris, 1979).

Blanning, T. C. W., *The French Revolutionary Wars, 1787–1802* (London, 1986).

Blaufarb, Rafe, *The French Army, 1750–1820: Careers, Talent, Merit* (Manchester, 2002).

Chickering, Roger, and Stig Förster (eds), *War in an Age of Revolution, 1775–1815* (Cambridge, 2010).

Crépin, Annie, *La conscription en débat, ou le triple apprentissage de la Nation, de la citoyenneté, de la république, 1798–1889* (Arras, 1998).

Cubells, Monique, (ed.), *La Révolution Française: la guerre et la frontière* (Paris, 2000).

Forrest, Alan, *Conscripts and Deserters: The Army and French Society during the Revolution and Empire* (New York, 1989).

Forrest, Alan, *The Soldiers of the French Revolution* (Durham, 1990).

Griffith, Paddy, *The Art of War in Revolutionary France, 1789–1802* (London, 1998).

Hippler, Thomas, *Citizens, Soldiers and National Armies: Military Service in France and Germany, 1778–1830* (London, 2008).

Hughes, Michael J., *Forging Napoleon's Grande Armée: Motivation, Military Culture and Masculinity in the French Army, 1800–1808* (New York, 2012).

Lynn, John A., *The Bayonets of the Republic: Motivation and Tactics in the Army of Revolutionary France* (Urbana and Chicago, 1984).

Scott, Samuel F., *The Response of the Royal Army to the French Revolution: the Role and Development of the Line Army, 1787–93* (Oxford, 1978).

Smith, Jay M., *The Culture of Merit: Nobility, Royal Service and the Making of Absolute Monarchy in France, 1600–1789* (Ann Arbor, 1996).

Whiteman, Jeremy J., *Reform, Revolution and French Global Policy, 1787–1791* (Aldershot, 2003).

PART V

THE NEW REPUBLIC

CHAPTER 23

POLITICS AND INSURRECTION

The Sans-culottes, The 'Popular Movement', and the People of Paris

DAVID ANDRESS

THERE can be no more iconic figure of the French Revolution than the sans-culotte. Immediately visually identifiable from both sympathetic and hostile depictions, this archetype of rough, plebeian masculinity dominates discussion of popular revolutionary engagement in the period of radical Republicanism from 1792 to 1794, and is often invoked as an epitome of mobilization by 'the people'. So potent was the idea of the sans-culotte in that period itself that it frequently displaced any other label to describe a popular patriot, leading to a blurring of the lines between socio-economic identities and political commitments that has continued to mark the term's use ever since.

The classic historiography of popular, especially Parisian, political mobilization, having escaped from beneath earlier generations' contempt for such activity, replaced revulsion with idealization, and sought to foreshadow through the sans-culotte later forms of class militancy (and, arguably, partisan vanguardism). With the world-historical collapse of the kind of Marxism that had made such conjugations self-evident, it appeared at the end of the twentieth century as if historiography might revert fully to a demonization of mob-violence as the only significant contribution of the Parisian *menu people* to revolutionary processes. However, as this chapter will document, even before that collapse new and intriguing questions were being posed about the real social identities and cultural contexts of mobilizations in 1789 and after. Such work has continued to yield insights into this new century, and to suggest that both the positive and negative stereotypes of the sans-culotte are little more than crude approximations—indeed obfuscations—of a very complex reality. The image of a 'popular movement' both firmly rooted in the lower classes, and eager to deploy the mass violence of insurrection, is increasingly being revealed as a mirage, one that has concealed a far more widespread landscape of

popular engagements, and given undue precedence to the confected imagery of plebeian purity deployed in the service of factional goals.

The immortal touchstones of historiography in this field are Albert Soboul's *Les Sans-
culottes Parisiens* and George Rudé's *The Crowd in the French Revolution*.[1] Appearing
at the end of the 1950s, neither of these texts has really been superseded as a broad, yet
empirically dense, examination of its subject-matter. If one wishes to know all that a
measurement of recorded social identities amongst riotous crowds, or a blow-by-blow
account of the radicalization of Republican neighbourhood politics, can tell us, they
remain indispensable. Such texts, like so many in the Marxist tradition, seem to promote
the agency of the common people in a way which cannot be gainsaid. Yet closer examination shows that both Rudé and Soboul embodied in their work a schema of popular
mobilization that relied on top-down agitation, seeing wage-labour as essentially a passive class, only able to be awakened to its historical destiny by the ideas of middle-class
radicals, or the practical leadership of its literal masters from the artisan community.
For Soboul in particular, journeymen and wage-workers lived under effectively patriarchal domination in pre-Revolutionary Paris, and did not noticeably break free from it in
a 'popular movement' his researches clearly identified as bearing its own internal social
and organizational hierarchies.[2]

The extent to which such perspectives were seen as unproblematic is reflected in the
work of Jeffry Kaplow, who in 1972 proposed that this pre-Revolutionary labouring population was literally helpless, subjected by a ruthless police apparatus, and imprisoned
in a 'culture of poverty' that only an external revolutionary stimulus could dissolve.[3]
Ironically it was in the 'reactionary' decade of the 1980s that such visions of old-regime
plebeian passivity began to be challenged, first with Daniel Roche's treatment of *The
People of Paris* as a bustling, thriving population of cultural and practical *bricoleurs*,
and soon after with Arlette Farge's multiple descents into the archival depths of the era,
showing us a world of dissent and critique at constant odds with authority, and only too
conscious that, in the face of life's fragility, only activity provided any safety.[4] Farge, along
with Jacques Revel, also showed how such activity could, in extreme circumstances,
become deadly riot even in the face of the impressive policing apparatus of the capital.[5]
The events of 1750 which led to the death of a police agent in what was effectively a public
execution give the lie to an image of a city resting mute under the thumb of authority.

Yet it is important from the outset to acknowledge the complexity of the new picture
of social relations that has emerged over the last thirty years. As David Garrioch demonstrated, the penetration of neighbourhoods by police and magistrates might simply
constrain popular outbursts at times, but far more often it served to channel popular
anger and dispute into avenues of legal and administrative assertion.[6] Just as in Michael
Sonenscher's demonstration of the vital role of legal contestation in eighteenth century
labour markets, so Garrioch's work acknowledged that, at multiple levels, members of
the common people could use the authority-structures placed 'over' them to make their
own demands.[7] Parisians lived at the intersection of multiple levels of control and assertion, where audience behaviour at an official execution, the spreading of seditious songs
and poems, the retailing of elite gossip obtained through complex circuits of servants

and intermediaries, the pursuit of individual economic advantage in filigreed webs of credit and interchange, the close guarding of traditional and purely local rights and privileges, the ingrained sense of a broader urban identity against destabilizing external threats, and the occasional outburst of truly collective violence, all had a role to play in defining a plebeian public sphere.[8]

Given all of these contexts—which are of course in terms of lived experience one great context—the rapidity with which Parisians embraced an assertively defensive role in the crisis of 1789 becomes less than surprising. As traditional accounts make clear, significant elements of the working population were prepared to mobilize both on specific occasions—as for example in the multi-faceted protests commonly called the Réveillon Riots—and also in longer-term efforts such as the steady undermining of the morale of the military garrison that caused the effective defection of the French Guards even before the July crisis.[9] Evidently, a focus on a language of 'Third Estate' and of 'nation' occupies a key place in the articulation of such efforts, but their scale effectively precludes the possibility that new elite political language was the midwife of new practices. Rather, the language was circumstantial; the responses, structural.

If we examine the new structures of public life that emerged within Paris by the end of this critical year, we can also begin to develop a sense of the persistent complexities that make talk of a clear plebeian radical vanguard problematic. There is no question, for example, that one of the core missions of the revolutionary National Guard was to suppress social disorder, or that it was organized with an increasing emphasis on propertied citizenship and action in defence of established community norms.[10] But it was not just that, and indeed the evidence of everyday exchanges around the work and politics of the Guard is that social identities and political critiques ebbed and flowed in significance depending on the collisions of the moment.[11] While some clear affinities would emerge between the more prosperous parts of the city and a more generally conservative political response, even a writer as extreme as Marat persistently identified a range of National Guard battalions as more 'patriot' than others, without always having any particular regard to their social composition.[12] In general, there appears to have been a strong presupposition in favour of the defence of a revolutionary mainstream against disruptive speech or actions from either radical or reactionary positions. Although the new revolutionary authorities were more likely to label as *motions incendiaires* the public pronouncements of those visibly socially marginal, they showed no favour towards public disruption from any source.[13]

These complexities of socio-political inclusion and exclusion are also visible in larger-scale events. As Micah Alpaugh has recently reminded us, the October Days of 1789 were only the most spectacular and consequential of a long series of more-or-less mass protests and demonstrations in the second half of the year.[14] While Alpaugh's particular focus is on the capacity of Parisians to organize protest that did not become violent, the extent to which different events also engaged at different levels with tradition, innovation, solidarity and distinction is noteworthy. Some of the protests that appear to have caused the most unease, and also to have had the least real effect, were those of economically subordinate groups against the travails of their condition—most notably, when domestic servants seem to have organized a quite 'modern' form of demonstration against their political exclusion, to meet with a stone wall of official hostility and general indifference. Major demonstrations that invoked time-honoured forms, such as the parades to Sainte-Geneviève that marked the early autumn, seem to have drawn larger numbers, and to have given far more pause for thought to observers. The form of the protests that became the October Days is striking in this regard, melding, by accident or design, the traditional female role in market protest with a significant National Guard mobilization. The agenda of the protest, too, was syncretic, calling for essentially old-regime methods of market regulation along with agitation for the royal sanction of decrees, including the Declaration of Rights, that represented profound innovation. Their outcome in the royal move to Paris likewise shares elements that range from an almost literally folkloric belief in the king-as-provider to a profound revolutionary suspicion of his motives and his associates at Versailles.[15]

From landmark events in July and October 1789, and the background agitation that went on between them, we know that Parisians were able to mobilize for street protest in large numbers, and it is only reasonable to conclude that such events included a cross-section of the common people, and in some cases were led by the concerns of groups within that general population.[16] However, while such purposive actions, and a broader culture of outdoor debate, speculation and engagement, continued through 1790 and 1791, the efforts of some to translate it into a sharper-edged popular political organization were far less visibly successful. Unquestionably, the initiative first of the Cordeliers Club to open its sessions to public participation, and subsequently the foundation of a wave of groups that explicitly sought out a plebeian membership, and became defined as *sociétés populaires*, was a move towards acknowledgement of a genuinely popular voice.[17] Yet even the most positive accounts of these groups concur in numbering their adherents at a few thousand at most, of whom the consistently committed activists can probably be numbered in the hundreds. Moreover, even in this particularly focused space of popular activism, many of those who emerged as leaders continued to come from the same class of professionals who were increasingly dominating the stages of local and national politics. How such groups trod a delicate line between bottom-up initiative and a more disciplined sense of leading 'the people' is shown by the outrage of one such group, the *Société fraternelle*, at a proposal from two of its members to topple royal statues after the Flight to Varennes. Not only did they report the matter to the municipal police, and receive a letter from those authorities confirming their formal disavowal of such vandalism, but they caused that letter to be published in the press, and in August expelled the 'two women of colour' apparently responsible for the suggestion. The juxtaposition of the particularly radical inclusion of such individuals with the fact of their subsequent exclusion is particularly piquant.[18]

By the summer of 1791, as my own research demonstrated some time ago, we can speak with confidence of a multi-layered, and multi-purpose, adoption of revolutionary rhetorics, assumptions and justifications by members of the broad population. While men remained the substantial majority in such participation, women's voices were clearly heard at every level from street-corner to *sociétés populaires*, and they had already carved out a visible niche as spectators of the National Assembly, both within its galleries and in the immediate surroundings of the Tuileries.[19] Yet we should always recognize the individuality of popular response. On the evening after the Champ de Mars Massacre of 17 July 1791, a witness living on the rue Tirechappe in central Paris reported that 'Madame Garpant', his apartment-house neighbour, had vigorously denounced the authorities, and crudely insulted him when he took their side. Yet on the same street, a group of journeymen artisans were almost literally slapped down by neighbourhood women—including artisans' wives and a domestic servant—when they started an argument about the misdeeds of the National Guard militia in the affair. Across the city, amongst the most outspoken public critics of the Guard was Constance Evrard, a 23-year-old domestic cook, and friend of her neighbour and future radical activist Pauline Léon. But other such critics included men who held sergeant's rank in the Guard itself.[20]

As the course of the Revolution advances beyond the summer of 1791, a new problem for the historical perception of popular engagement comes to light. Almost all of what we know in detail about such engagements up to this point comes from the records of the police—both in pre-revolutionary and revolutionary circumstances, the abiding desire for good order led to the meticulous recording of incidents and confrontations that allows us to document individuals' precise words, social identities and collisions. In 1791, for example, as well as telling us about those who denounced the events of 17 July, records of the wider municipal 'police' let us see the emergence of a nascent independent workers' movement, contesting for economic power after the guild system was abolished in March. They also document the speed and vigour with which such assertions of collective action were criminalized and shut down, as they show the similar unhesitating force with which unrest amongst the unemployed, placed in 'public workshops' that were mostly just ditch-digging, was met.[21] Of course, in such circumstances many of the sources vent the prejudices of self-interested observers, but their confrontational nature generally allows for a plausible reconstruction of the issues being aired on both sides.

As the 'popular movement' develops in political salience from the start of 1792, the hard edges of social conflict that produced the records enabling such clarity begin to blur dramatically. When in this epoch the term 'sans-culottes' comes into regular use, it is as an already-muddy reference to general solidarity between the political class and an ill-defined popular bloc.[22] As the political strife of the period develops from anxieties about royal enmity to decisions about dethronement, and then on into the seemingly endless cycle of factional confrontations that made up the life of the National Convention, political identities come to usurp social ones, and a determination of what is or is not 'popular' becomes a vexed question.

Seen in this context, some of the leading historical claims about popular engagement become contentious. Colin Lucas in 1988 offered what is in many respects an important and subtle reading of the historiography of the 'revolutionary crowd' to that date, and especially how it could be situated within pre-revolutionary contexts, and the development of more organized political forms. However, in so doing he nevertheless persisted in articulating the notion that 'the crowd' was a concrete and in some sense coherent phenomenon, and very clearly put forward a schema for 'crowd politics' in the Revolution that placed events from July and October 1789 to August 1792 and May–June 1793 on an escalating scale of popular penetration of the political system by the revolutionary crowd: from an essentially external impetus for institutional decisions, to a fundamental attack on the composition of the national representation. But such a classification only holds up until we begin to question the nature of this supposed 'crowd'.[23]

Rudé's classic account of Parisian events in 1792 illustrates the difficulties involved. After discussing for several pages the notable economic disturbances of January–February, when crowds conspicuously led by women looted shops, seized wagons of foodstuffs, and generally carried out what the eighteenth century understood as *taxation populaire*, Rudé slips into a discussion of 'the next great popular demonstration' in June.[24] Hedging his bets—'Ostensibly it was a purely political affair ... yet it may well be that [economic motives had a role]. Yet this is supposition'—Rudé recounts events of an entirely different character as part of the same narrative.[25] In the winter, local National Guard units had, if not always enthusiastically, nonetheless been active in restraining the disorder. By the summer, the National Guards of the more radical Sections were in the vanguard of organization for a great demonstration of revolutionary commitment, a march under arms to plant a liberty-tree in commemoration of the Tennis-Court Oath of three years before. Rudé labels as 'insurgents' the combined contingents of the Faubourgs Saint-Marcel and Saint-Antoine, marching under their officers to present a petition to the Legislative Assembly, albeit against the wishes of the conservative administration of the Paris *département*.[26]

It is clear from the variety of surviving second-hand sources that these National Guards were at the core of a much larger mixed crowd of men, women and children, leading elements of which did force their way into the Tuileries palace that afternoon of 20 June, and subjected Louis XVI personally to an ordeal of verbal abuse and attempted intimidation that lasted at least several hours. This was a significant expression of an apparently authentically 'popular' view of the king as responsible for the ongoing political crisis and alarmingly negative military situation of a country two months into a war that had promised liberation, and threatened to deliver invasion. Yet, as all sources agree, the crowds eventually dispersed having secured not even so much as nominal concessions from the authorities.[27]

In the greater conflict that erupted on 10 August, Rudé shows that, in relation to the killed and injured on the radical side, the case can be made overwhelmingly for their social identity as 'shopkeepers, small traders and manufacturers, master craftsmen, artisans, or journeymen', with a minority being waged workers, and only a smattering from any other occupational group.[28] But as is so often the case in the work of this generation of historians, Rudé's identification of the rank and file of this movement does not address the critical questions of leadership, motivation and mobilization (or when it does, it simply slides over any complicating issues). From Rudé's own account, it is clear that on several occasions in the preceding fortnight, groups had attempted to raise the alarm for an insurrection—even on one occasion dragging the famous sansculotte brewer and National Guard leader Santerre from his bed to lead them.[29] But until the organized radical vanguard of the city's Section committees and political societies agreed to move, nothing decisive happened.

The insurrection that did take place on 10 August was, first, a *coup* by the Sections against the compromised municipal leadership of the Girondin-sympathizing mayor Pétion, followed by an advance of several columns of armed National Guards on the Tuileries—though the latter's ranks were also swelled by 'non-active' citizens admitted in the previous week, and a more general accompanying crowd. The fact that the city was being raised by its leadership with overwhelming military force was decisive in the bloodless resolution of the day's key political question—for the king had, of course, surrendered himself and his family into the custody of the Legislative Assembly long before the first shots were fired in the iconic, but tragically unnecessary, confrontation between the insurgent forces and the Swiss Guard.[30]

Here we can see why a schema of 'crowd' action as a single phenomenon—whether in Rudé's own work or a generation later in that of Lucas—needs to be revised. While it is to an extent reasonable and legitimate to attribute a well-developed political consciousness (in its own context) to the crowds involved in these events, the translation of that consciousness to actions that are both clearly politically targeted, and effective in their outcomes, is a much more complex issue. Crowds that had already acted in 1789 within thick cultures of expectations about power and its responsibilities were by 1792 equally, if not more, enmeshed in a revolutionary political culture that had created leadership groups and structured political expectations at multiple levels. In the early stages of events such as the 20 June march, as in the abortive risings before 10 August, such leaders could be propelled forward to a certain extent by broader popular pressure. It is clear from autobiographical recollections, for example, that many in the general population of the Faubourg Saint-Marcel were intent on marching on the Tuileries on the 20th, despite their official leaders' reluctance.[31] Yet the limits of that purely 'crowd' pressure are shown by the essentially stymied response of the people who successfully invaded the palace. We might commend, at one level, their restraint in offering no real physical violence to the king—one bullet, or one knife, after all, would have been enough to end the monarchy there and then, but at the cost perhaps of a Vendée-type eruption or more determined foreign assault.[32] Yet at another level, we might suspect that the members of the crowd did not really know what to do when confronted with the reality of the monarch in person—the urge to protest did not follow through into impetus for decisive action, despite all that has been long noted about the popularity of uncompromising radical prescriptions in the gamut of popular journalism from Hébert to Marat. Throughout these events, in sharp distinction to the model proposed by Lucas, radical insurrection succeeded not when it was the product of a 'crowd', but rather when the 'crowd' was led, or indeed relegated to spectatorship, by organized political groups emergent from well-understood structures of local administration and radical mobilization.

It is worth here recalling some of the basic social facts about the make-up of Parisian sectional leadership drawn out by Soboul's analysis. On the regular 'civil' committees of the sections in 1793—bodies already purged of more moderate members after the fall of the monarchy—there yet remained almost 30 per cent of members who lived without working, either from unearned incomes or the employment of others. On the even more ardent surveillance committees created in the spring of 1793, known generally in Paris as *comités révolutionnaires*, independent master-artisans and shopkeepers predominated, with no more than 10 per cent made up of workers, apprentices or journeymen. Indeed, at 12 per cent, clerks, artists, teachers and lawyers outnumbered waged workers. Even amongst those identifiable as lesser militants who did not hold a committee post, only some 20 per cent were wage-earners, as against 15 per cent clerks and professionals and a similar number of shopkeepers, with artisans making up the balance. By even the most generous assumption, the collective body of identifiable active sans-culottes numbered somewhere under 2 per cent of the general population.[33] On the basis of these figures, and his own investigations into how far many militants and committee-men down-played their social status to escape post-Thermidorian persecution, Richard Andrews produced a meticulous analysis arguing that the essential social identity of the sans-culottes in practice was as the employers and controllers of subordinated wage-labour, and they thus represented a ruthlessly dominant local social elite, rather than a movement from below.[34] While this can only be one interpretation, we must almost certainly acknowledge, that, whatever else these people were, they were essentially a self-selected *political* elite.[35]

The dominance of this political (if not social) elite is further visible when we address what is often regarded as the high-water-mark of crowd intervention, the purging of the Girondin leadership from the National Convention in the sustained insurrection-ary crisis of 31 May–2 June 1793. By this stage, self-identified sans-culotte militants were engaged in an increasingly successful war for control of those Parisian Sections more inclined to favour moderation, using the rhetoric of 'fraternization' to cover a series of local *coups* in which committee leaderships were ousted through the intimidatory presence of large numbers of militants from neighbouring, or indeed distant, Sections. Crowd actions were still occurring—the end of the winter had been marked by a fur-ther wave of significant food-riots—but even the people's champion Robespierre was inclined to blame these on aristocratic agitation precisely because they did not have an overtly political agenda, and Marat's advocacy of lynching for speculators merely placed him ever-more firmly in a minority of one on the national stage.[36] There were those who tried to organize what Rudé rather tellingly calls 'premature insurrection' in March and April, but as he also notes, 'resolute opposition' from the Commune, the Jacobins and the leadership of the Faubourg St-Antoine left such agitation abortive.[37]

Morris Slavin has examined in scrupulous detail what surviving records can tell us of what happened next, as the struggle on the national stage reached a climax with Girondin attempts to have Marat and radical leaders of the Paris Commune condemned by the new Revolutionary Tribunal.[38] Many individuals had been engaged in a wide campaign of escalating radical activity, from street skirmishes with 'moderate' youths to direct political pressure, and a movement from the sans-culotte Sections emerged to sidestep the existing Commune, with its awkward legal obligations, and plot insurrec-tion. At the heart of this movement was a *Comité central révolutionnaire* that represented the very pinnacle of agitational militancy—but its membership included four lawyers, five men of letters and a series of others linked to either rentier income or entrepreneurial activity, including one former noble, and not one wage-earner or working artisan. At the level of socio-economic background, then, this grouping was not noticeably distinct from that of the leadership of the Cordeliers Club, the Jacobins, or even the Convention. Men like Claude-Emmanuel Dobsen, iron-merchant's son, lawyer and judge, or Jean-Baptiste Loys, lawyer, merchant and former *procureur-syndic* of Marseille, were different from Robespierre, Saint-Just, Desmoulins and other major figures only in the scope of their political prominence.[39]

The 'insurrection' that this committee led was for most of its first day a matter of delegations presenting documents—the 'insurrectionary' committee showed its credentials in the name of the 'sovereign people' to the general council of the Commune, dissolving it and immediately reconstituting it as a 'revolutionary' body relieved of tiresome legal obligations. Information passed back and forth from city to neighbourhood and national bodies, in what was self-evidently a well-planned political takeover.[40] As 'patriot' Sections answered a call to arms, one thing conspicuously absent was any crowd action—indeed in some respects it was closer to a purge from above, as 'suspect' individuals in some localities were placed under arrest. It was from the Commune that orders came, first naming the Convention deputies to be ousted, and then commanding the levy of a 24,000-man supplementary armed force, paid for by an immediate tax on the wealthy (later shifted by a compliant Convention to a grant from national funds). Although the rhetoric of the insurrection emphasized that, as Slavin puts it, 'the sections in revolt' were the source of its legitimacy, it is far from clear how this was anything but an empty gesture towards a notion of popular identity.[41]

Tellingly, one of the issues that marked 1 June, a day of general stalemate between a Convention reluctant to be purged and a Commune conspicuously reluctant to purge by force, was that of the 'poor sans-culottes' called to arms.[42] Two Section committees from the Faubourg Saint-Antoine warned in ambiguous terms that the men would need to be paid, or stood down—and that in the latter case, unspecified more dangerous forces might take their place. Although the Commune could not meet this request with funds, it did agree on the urgency of keeping such forces under control. The *Comité central révolutionnaire* began to use those forces more decisively on the night of 1–2 June, but again it is noteworthy that this meant, on the one hand, sending armed guards to all the prisons to protect against any uncontrolled violence, and on the other, instructing delegates of the Commune to cross the city, proclaiming its anti-Girondin resolutions and further summoning citizens to (disciplined) arms.[43]

What happened on the next, decisive, day was witnessed by tens of thousands of ordinary Parisians as spectators, thronging the streets on a summer Sunday—and indeed by the hundreds taking up their by-now customary raucous role in the galleries of the Convention itself—but it remained essentially a military operation. Reports numbered at up to 100,000 the armed men surrounding the Convention, but also indicated that the vast majority were passive, and perhaps even uncertain of why they had been assembled by the 'insurrectionary' municipal leadership. At their core were a few thousand under the direct command of the sans-culotte general Hanriot, following the explicit orders of the *Comité central révolutionnaire* to place 'a respectable armed force' around the legislature, 'in such a way that the leaders of the faction [i.e. the Girondins] can be arrested in light of open day in case the Convention should refuse to carry out the demands of the citizens of Paris.'[44] Everything about proceedings was done in a way that ensured political initiative remained with those who held control of disciplined armed force. That armed force would finally, after much tergiversation by the *conventionnels*, offer the latter a stark choice between compliance and physical coercion. The fact that the leadership of the insurrection held back any possible outbreak of uncontrolled violence finally gave the Montagnards in the Convention the political space to assert that the vote to expel the Girondins came from a 'free' body—a body that Hanriot had informed he would 'blast' if it failed to comply, and at whose members his troops had only minutes before levelled serried muskets.[45]

Traditional accounts of these processes, including Slavin's, want to honour the sans-culotte protagonists both for their organized political commitment, discipline, and management of a delicate and potentially dangerous situation, and for their identity as representatives of an authentic popular movement. Yet this is contradictory, for one of the central things that emerges from Slavin's work—and even from Soboul's, read against the grain—is that these sans-culotte militants were nervous of real popular initiative, and indeed on some occasions actively fearful of it, precisely because they could not control it. They did everything they could to get in front of potential spontaneous collective action, to co-opt it into acceptable channels, and to present themselves through a rhetoric of identity with 'the people' that amounted in practice to a claim of entitlement to suppress any alternative suggestions of what the people might want.

We need not attribute malice to explain this. It fits into a clear longer-term pattern of anxiety about what might lurk amongst the people—the presence of tens of thousands of 'brigands', indistinguishable in practice from the poorer classes of the populace, had been an article of faith since the first revolutionary upheavals, as had their susceptibility to aristocratic subversion.[46] We may rightly criticize the assumption amongst male militants that most women were irrational and untrustworthy, but we do also need to acknowledge that this was a clear component of their cultural heritage, which further led to the view that market crowds and food-based disturbances were easily co-opted to nefarious ends. It makes absolute sense for a politically active, locally based leadership class to have emerged, and it makes very good political sense for them to have identified themselves as 'the people' at a time when that term was already a totem for radicalism.[47] But a measured historical account must nonetheless separate out that movement, with its leaders, organizations and followers, from any sense of a simple, collective, 'popular' social identity.[48]

Some parallel points were made by Colin Lucas, in the context of addressing revolutionary rhetorics of violence, in an important, if under-utilized, 1994 article. As he explores the development of a 'theory of revolutionary violence' in political circles, he notes that 'strict control over popular insurrection' emerged as a *leitmotif*, alongside the 'naive vulnerability' of ordinary people to counter-revolutionary agitation, and the troubling persistence of perceived 'bad violence' not directed towards sufficiently pure revolutionary political goals (including, for example, the food riots of 1792). Thus the Revolutionary Tribunal was brought into existence famously to prevent the 'people' from being 'terrible' as they had been perceived to be in the September Massacres, and the 'Terror' itself was summoned into legislative being after a troublingly 'popular' demonstration had been channelled by the Commune and the Jacobin Club into more acceptably political form on 5 September 1793, amid debate which insisted on the need to transfer 'revolutionary violence away from the real people and onto the revolutionary state presented as the reification of the People'.[49]

Lucas's overarching point is that an anxious distrust of popular initiative ran through the rhetoric of the Jacobin political elite, along with a sentiment that such initiative had to be governed, rather than acknowledged as legitimate in any but the most paternalist terms. These were 'revolutionary democrats fearing *demos* as an active mass, attempting to find ways to accommodate its creative power, seeking to secure a conserving principle of violence in controlled conditions'.[50] Underpinning this is an evident gulf of experience and understanding, in which the realities of popular life disappear beneath the preoccupations of an educated political class for whom 'the people' is a point of rhetorical reference, and a potential threat, rather than an agglomeration of individual lives.

One of the intriguing features of historiography on the subject of popular insurrection is how bluntly critiques such as Lucas's can be set aside by the drive of some to see an admirable reality in the language of co-opted popular identity. Thus while Christian Muller in 2000 echoed Lucas in noting some of the questionable shifts of political rhetoric around such insurrections, 'from "people led astray" to the "child-like people"', Diane Ladjouzi in the same year published an article on the September 1793 events presenting them unproblematically as a 'movement of union between the people, the Commune of Paris and the Convention'.[51] One of the most publicly notable interventions in the question of popular and revolutionary violence in recent years was Sophie Wahnich's short 2003 book, *La liberté ou la mort*.[52] Although provocatively phrased, at the heart of this text was essentially the same contention as Lucas's above— that the 'official' Terror came into existence to defend state order against a dangerously uncontrolled potential 'popular' terror, in the wake of the horrifying spectacle of the September Massacres. Wahnich's originality was to assert, in place of Lucas's measured examination, that this was an unalloyed good, taking forward the benefits of 'the Revolution' that might otherwise indeed have been endangered. In her more lengthy recent work on the events surrounding the fall of the monarchy in 1792, Wahnich takes this process a stage further, and commits to the view that 'the people' is essentially whatever the most radical political activists say it is.[53] We thus find ourselves having gone not only full-circle back to the classic Marxist analyses of popular/radical identity, but perhaps even a stage further, to a point where the careful attention of a Rudé or a Slavin to what archival sources tell us about individuals' actual social identities is no longer viewed as necessary.

Historians have, in general, had great difficulty making coherent positive observations about the cloud of concepts, events and groups that ranges from 'crowds' to 'sansculottes', from the legitimacy of insurrection to the problem of violence. The tangle of discourses and practices involved makes it hard to find a solid intellectual foothold unless one comes equipped with a clear schema in advance; yet the clearer such a schema is, the more it seems to lead to special pleading or easily highlighted self-contradiction.[54] Critique is easier, but not without its pitfalls. William Sewell pithily addressed the 'sans-culotte rhetoric of subsistence', arguing that it was in large part an artefact of spokespeople claiming popular hunger as a justification for political claims, rather than a grounded reality.[55] But in riposte, Colin Jones and Rebecca Spang pointed out that in some respects this simply replicated the unsympathetic views of those who scorned food-rioters as aristocratic dupes, unable to decide for themselves what the material bases of their consumption should be.[56]

Over forty years ago, Richard Cobb memorably declared that the sans-culotte 'is not a social or economic being; he is a political accident'.[57] There is plenty of evidence to support that view from the period itself. Girondin authors such as Antoine Gorsas, who had lauded the sans-culottes in 1792, were by 1793 articulating the charge that the label had been seized by well-heeled plotters: 'today's sans-culotte is a sans-culotte who has fine breeches, but who still wants to get hold of the breeches of those who do have breeches, so as not to give a thread or a penny, or even any breeches, to those poor devils who have no breeches, the sans-culottes'.[58] Late in 1793, local administrators across France wrestled to define the 'true sans-culottes' as a category distinct from the indifferent mass of the population.[59] Early the next year, Gorsas's charge was echoed by Robespierre himself.[60] Shortly afterwards the leaders of the Cordeliers Club saw their efforts to attack the Convention from the left in the name of the sans-culottes damned as a conspiracy of aristocrats wearing a pantomime version of popular costume—and the Père Duchesne himself went to the guillotine mocked by a cheering crowd.[61] The fate of the 'Hébertist' leadership echoed in more bloody form the ostracism they had helped to mete out nine months earlier to the so-called *Enragés*, who had at least a plausible claim to be making the effort to speak for the Parisian populace in favour of price controls and revolutionary rigour, yet who had also been too far from the sites of radical power to be more than a nuisance to be swatted aside.[62]

For each new study, such as that of Lisa DiCaprio, that shows us the *menu peuple* (and in this case women workers) actively engaged with patriotic activity and resistance to the impositions of the political class, there is another which shows how that class captured popular identity to its own ends.[63] Haim Burstin's essays on 'the invention of the sans-culotte' illustrate the energetic 'protagonism' of the many individuals willing to thrust themselves forward into politics—but also how many of them, like the Polish gentleman Claude Lazowski, had 'sans-culottised' themselves to fit the rhetorical necessities of the moment.[64] In earlier work, Burstin also demonstrated how little sympathy supposedly 'sans-culotte' local authorities had for working people when their concerns threatened to interfere with the war effort.[65]

In the end, the historical picture of popular protest and politicization through these years remains unclear. We have evidence about life before and immediately after 1789 amply sufficient to reject the simplified narratives of earlier historiography, but the icon of the sans-culotte, battered and frayed at the edges as he may be, still obscures our view of how ordinary people reacted to the critical years of radical revolutionary politics. The one indisputably authentic voice of an artisanal activist that we have is that of the glazier Jacques-Louis Ménétra, whose rambling memoirs reveal a career of local service and insurrectionary activity in 1792–95 sufficient to elevate him to the front rank of the sans-culottes. But what they also show is that he cowered in fear throughout the period—as much from what he saw as the wicked and self-interested denunciations of his own neighbours as from any larger threat—and that in crafting his memoirs, he did not feel the need, even once, to write the word 'sans-culotte'.[66] To understand how not just Ménétra, but tens of thousands of others, experienced this turbulent time, is the challenge of the next generation of historians.

NOTES

1. Albert Soboul, *Les sans-culottes parisians en l'an II: mouvement populaire et gouvernement révolutionnaire* (original publication 1958; Paris, 1968). George Rudé, *The Crowd in the French Revolution* (Oxford, 1959).

2. See, in English translation, Albert Soboul, *The Parisian sans-culottes and the French Revolution, 1793-4*, trans. G. Lewis, (Oxford, 1964), esp. 33–6, 40–1, 50–1; Rudé, *Crowd*, 18–19 makes similar points about social structure, and (at 199) explicitly assimilates crowd motivations to 'bourgeois' leading ideas and slogans.

3. Jeffry Kaplow, *The Names of Kings: The Parisian Laboring Poor in the Eighteenth Century* (New York, 1972).

4. Daniel Roche, *The People of Paris: An Essay in Popular Culture in the Eighteenth Century* (Leamington Spa, 1987). Arlette Farge, *Fragile Lives: Violence, Power and Solidarity in Eighteenth-Century Paris* (Cambridge, 1993), *Subversive Words: Public Opinion in Eighteenth-Century France* (Cambridge, 1994).

5. Arlette Farge and Jacques Revel, *The Rules of Rebellion: Child Abductions in Paris in 1750* (Cambridge, 1991).

6. David Garrioch, *Neighbourhood and Community in Paris, 1740–1790* (Cambridge, 1986).

7. Michael Sonenscher, 'Journeymen, the courts and the French trades, 1781–1791', *Past and Present* 114 (1987), 77–109, and more generally, *Work and Wages: Natural Law, Politics and the Eighteenth-Century French Trades* (Cambridge, 1989). See also Garrioch's more general survey of the era, *The Making of Revolutionary Paris* (Berkeley, 2002).

8. On the transmission of information within the city, see Robert Darnton, 'An Early Information Society; news and the media in eighteenth-century Paris', *American Historical Review* 105 (2000), 1–35, and at greater length, *Poetry and the Police: Communication Networks in Eighteenth-Century Paris* (Cambridge, Mass., 2012). For a dense micro-study of 'crowd' behaviour in the late 1780s, see Thomas M. Luckett, 'Hunting for Spies and Whores: a Parisian riot on the eve of the French Revolution', *Past and Present* 156 (1997), 116–43.

9. Jacques Godechot, *The Taking of the Bastille, July 14th 1789* (London, 1970).

10. Dale L. Clifford, 'The National Guard and the Parisian Community', *French Historical Studies* 16 (1990), 849–78; and 'Command over equals: the officer corps of the Parisian National Guard, 1789–90', *Proceedings of the Annual Meeting of the Western Society for French History* 18 (1991), 152–65.

11. David Andress, 'Neighbourhood Policing in Paris from Old Regime to Revolution: The Exercise of Authority by the District de St-Roch, 1789–1791', *French Historical Studies* 29 (2006), 231–60.

12. David Andress, *Massacre at the Champ de Mars: Popular Dissent and Political Culture in the French Revolution* (Woodbridge, 2000), 52–4.

13. David Andress, 'The Micro-physics of Öffentlichkeit? Habermas, Foucault and the Administration of Democratic Space in the Palais-Royal, 1789–1790', *Cultural and Social History* 3 (2006), 1–22.

14. Micah Alpaugh, 'The Politics of Escalation in French Revolutionary Protest: Political Demonstrations, Non-violence and Violence in the Grandes Journées of 1789', *French History* 23 (2009), 336–59. See more generally his PhD dissertation, 'Nonviolence, Violence and Revolution: Political Demonstrations and Collaborative Protest in Paris, 1787–1795', Univ of California, Irvine, 2010.

15. See David Garrioch, 'The Everyday Lives of Parisian Women and the October Days of 1789', *Social History* 24 (1999), 231–49; and Barry M. Shapiro, *Revolutionary Justice in Paris, 1789–1790* (Cambridge, 1993), which is extensively concerned with how the political class negotiated the contentious aftermath of the protests.

16. This is the basic message of the early chapters of Rudé, *Crowd*.

17. See, classically, Isabelle Bourdin, *Les Sociétés populaires à Paris pendant la Révolution* (Paris, 1937), and R. B. Rose, *The making of the sans-culottes: democratic ideas and institutions in Paris, 1789–1792* (Manchester, 1983).

18. An episode discussed in Andress, *Massacre*, 121–2.

19. Dominique Godineau, *The Women of Paris and Their French Revolution* (Berkeley, 1998), esp. 197–215.

20. Andress, *Massacre*, 8–11, 184–7.

21. David Andress, 'Economic Dislocation and Social Discontent in the French Revolution: Survival in Paris in the Era of the Flight to Varennes', *French History* 10 (1996), 30–55.

22. Michael Sonenscher, *Sans-culottes; An Eighteenth-century Emblem in the French Revolution* (Princeton, 2008). Note that Sonenscher's analysis here is in sharp and explicit contrast to some of his earlier work, e.g. 'The sans-culottes of the Year II: rethinking the language of labour in Revolutionary France', *Social History* 9 (1984), 301–28, and 'Artisans, Sans-culottes and the French Revolution', in Alan Forrest and Peter Jones, eds., *Reshaping France: Town, Country and Region in the French Revolution* (Manchester, 1991), 105–21.

23. Colin Lucas, 'The crowd and politics', in Colin Lucas, ed., *The French Revolution and the creation of modern political culture, II: The political culture of the French Revolution* (Oxford, 1988), 259–85. See 276–7 where the chronological progression is mapped most concisely.

24. For a longer-term perspective on *taxation populaire*, see Cynthia Bouton, *The Flour War: Gender, Class and Community in Late Ancien Régime French Society* (University Park, 1993), and Judith Miller, *Mastering the Market: The State and the Grain Trade in Northern France, 1700–1860* (Cambridge, 1998).

25. Rudé, *Crowd*, 98.

26. Rudé, *Crowd*, 100.

27. See the detailed exploration by Micah Alpaugh, 'The Making of the Parisian Political Demonstration: A Case Study of 20 June 1792', *Proceedings of the Western Society for French History* 34 (2006), 115–33. Available online at <http://hdl.handle.net/2027/spo.0642292.0034.007>.

28. Rudé, *Crowd*, 106.

29. Rudé, *Crowd*, 103.

30. The events are discussed in detail, albeit from the other side of the barricades, in Munro Price, *The Road from Versailles; Louis XVI, Marie Antoinette and the fall of the French Monarchy* (New York, 2002), 294–303. See also Leigh Whaley, 'Political factions and the Second Revolution: The Insurrection of 10 August 1792', *French History* 7 (1993), 205–24.

31. Haim Burstin, *Une révolution à l'oeuvre, Le faubourg Saint-Marcel 1789–1794* (Paris, 2005), 363–72.

32. As Alpaugh observes, 'Making', 129.

33. See Soboul, *Sans-culottes parisiens*, 442–51, and the summary in David Andress, *The French Revolution and the People* (London, 2004), 210–11.

34. Richard M. Andrews, 'Social Structures, Political Elites and Ideology in Revolutionary Paris, 1792–4: A Critical Evaluation of Albert Soboul's Les Sans-Culottes Parisiens ...', *Journal of Social History* 19 (1985–86), 71–112. This is the only extant summary of a project which began with a doctoral thesis, 'Political élites and social conflicts in the Sections of Revolutionary Paris, 1792—An III', (unpubl. DPhil. diss. Oxford 1971), but was unfortunately never brought to full publication.

35. For a particularly telling micro-study of the kinds of individuals at the core of radical leadership in the archetypical sans-culotte zone of the Faubourg Saint-Antoine, see Sophie Faguay, 'Bourgeois du faubourg Saint-Antoine, 1791–1792', in Michel Vovelle, ed., *Paris et la Révolution: actes du colloque de Paris I, 14–16 avril 1989* (Paris, 1989), 89–95.

36. See Andress, *French Revolution*, 192.

37. Rudé, *Crowd*, 119.

38. Morris Slavin, *The Making of an Insurrection Parisian Sections and the Gironde* (Cambridge, Mass., 1986).

39. See Slavin, *Making*, 76–8, for these individuals, and the following pages for the remainder of the committee.

40. Slavin, *Making*, 94, and generally 90–6 for these events.

41. Slavin, *Making*, 100.

42. Slavin, *Making*, 106.

43. Slavin, *Making*, 111.

44. Slavin, *Making*, 112. Ironically, Hanriot himself appears to be a man of genuinely plebeian origins, the son of a servant who became a tax-clerk, but his progress from 1789 to officer-rank in the National Guard, and his sources of income in these years, remain obscure. See Raymonde Monnier, 'Hanriot, François', in Albert Soboul, ed., *Dictionnaire historique de la Révolution française* (Paris, 2005), 531–2.

45. Slavin, *Making*, 114–16.

46. Andress, *Massacre*, 47–52.

47. Jon Cowans, *To Speak for the People; Public Opinion and the Problem of Legitimacy in the French Revolution* (New York, 2001) documents the wider political quest for 'popular' legitimation.

48. Critical reflection is also required, e.g. on the notion that in 'acculturating' the common people to revolutionary rhetoric, elite 'spokespeople' were in fact articulating the necessary demands and interests of those people—see Jacques Guilhaumou, *L'avènement des porte-parole de la République (1789–1792): Essai de synthèse sur les langages de la Révolution française* (Lille, 1998).

49. Colin Lucas, 'Revolutionary Violence, the People and the Terror', in Keith Michael Baker, ed., *The French revolution and the Creation of Modern Political Culture, vol. 4, The Terror*

(Oxford, 1994), 57–79; citations at 70, 71, 73. Paolo Viola makes some parallel points about popular perception of the legitimacy of punitive violence in 'Violence révolutionnaire ou violence du peuple en révolution?', in Michel Vovelle and Antoine de Baecque, eds, *Recherches sur la Révolution* (Paris, 1991), 95–102.

50. Lucas, 'Revolutionary Violence', 76.

51. Christian A. Muller 'Du "peuple égaré" au "peuple enfant": le discours politique révolution-naire à l'épreuve de la révolte populaire en 1793', *Revue d'histoire moderne et contemporaine* 47 (2000), 93–112. Diane Ladjouzi, 'Les journées de 4 et 5 septembre 1793 à Paris: un mou-vement d'union entre le peuple, la Commune de Paris et la Convention pour un exécutif révolutionnaire', *Annales historiques de la Révolution française* 321 (2000), 27–44.

52. Sophie Wahnich, *La Liberté ou la Mort. Essai sur la Terreur et le Terrorisme* (Paris, 2003). Republished in English translation as *In Defence of the Terror; Liberty or Death in the French Revolution*, and with a foreword by Slavoj Zizek (London, 2012).

53. Sophie Wahnich, *La longue patience du peuple; 1792. Naissance de la république* (Paris, 2008). Eric Hazan has recently made similar claims about the French Revolution as a whole: *Une histoire de la Révolution française* (Paris, 2012)—see e.g. ch. 7 on June–Sept 1792, esp. 149ff on 'sans-culottes', and later 167ff, 209, 244.

54. A parallel example to Wahnich is Raymonde Monnier, *L'espace public démocratique: essai sur l'opinion à Paris de la Révolution au Directoire* (Paris, 1994), which is extensively taken up with discussion of elite views about popular opinion, to the exclusion of much evidence for actual opinions amongst the people.

55. William H. Sewell, Jr, 'The Sans-culotte Rhetoric of Subsistence', in Baker, ed., *The Terror*, 249–69.

56. Colin Jones and Rebecca Spang, 'Sans-Culottes, Sans Café, Sans Tabac: Shifting Realms of Necessity and Luxury in Eighteenth-century France', in Maxine Berg and Helen Clifford, eds., *Consumers and Luxury; Consumer Culture in Europe, 1650–1850* (Manchester, 1999), 37–62; see esp. 38–9.

57. Richard Cobb, *The Police and the People; French Popular Protest, 1789–1820* (Oxford, 1970), 120. His views of the futility of attempting to make essentially individual responses into a social analysis can be found throughout his work: see, e.g. Richard Cobb, 'The Revolutionary Mentality in France', in *A Second Identity* (Oxford, 1969), 122–41. For dis-cussion of 'Cobbist' analysis in a national context, see Stephen Miller, 'Politics and Class, 1790–1794: Radicalism, Terror, and Repression in Southern France', *Proceedings of the Western Society for French History* 32 (2004), 140–58.

58. Sonenscher, *Sans-culottes*, 361.

59. Philippe Goujard, 'L'homme de masse sans les masses ou le déchristianisateur malheureux', *Annales historiques de la Révolution française* 58 (1986), 160–80, 163.

60. In his speech 'On the Principles of Political Morality' of February 1794; see the full text in Keith Michael Baker, ed., *Readings in Western Civilization, 7, The Old Regime and the French Revolution* (Chicago, 1987), 369–84.

61. Morris Slavin, *The Hébertistes to the Guillotine: Anatomy of a 'Conspiracy' in Revolutionary France* (Baton Rouge, 1994).

62. R. B. Rose, *The Enragés: Socialists of the French Revolution?* (Sydney, 1965).

63. Lisa DiCaprio, 'Women Workers, State-Sponsored Work, and the Right to Subsistence during the French Revolution', *Journal of Modern History* 71 (1999), 519–51; and at greater length, *The Origins of the Welfare State: Women, Work, and the French Revolution* (Urbana, 2006).

64. Haim Burstin, *L'invention du sans-culotte; regards sur le Paris révolutionnaire* (Paris, 2005); see e.g. 92–7.
65. Haim Burstin, 'Problems of Work during the Terror', in Baker, ed., *The Terror*, 271–93.
66. Jacques-Louis Ménétra, *Journal of My Life*, introduction and commentary by Daniel Roche, translated by Arthur Goldhammer (New York, 1986). The revolutionary period from 1789 to the Directory is covered at 217–35.

Selected Reading

Alpaugh, Micah, 'The Politics of Escalation in French Revolutionary Protest: Political Demonstrations, Non-violence and Violence in the Grandes Journées of 1789', *French History* 23 (2009), 336–59.

Andress, David, *The French Revolution and the People* (London, 2004).

Burstin, Haim, *L'invention du sans-culotte; regards sur le Paris révolutionnaire* (Paris, 2005).

Cobb, Richard, *The Police and the People; French Popular Protest, 1789–1820* (Oxford, 1970).

Farge, Arlette, *Fragile Lives: Violence, Power and Solidarity in Eighteenth-Century Paris* (Cambridge, 1993).

Darnton, Robert, 'An Early Information Society; news and the media in eighteenth-century Paris', *American Historical Review* 105 (2000), 1–35.

Garrioch, David, 'The Everyday Lives of Parisian Women and the October Days of 1789', *Social History* 24 (1999), 231–49.

Godineau, Dominique, *The Women of Paris and Their French Revolution* (Berkeley, 1998).

Lucas, Colin, 'Revolutionary Violence, the People and the Terror', in Keith Michael Baker, ed., *The French Revolution and the Creation of Modern Political Culture*, vol. 4, *The Terror* (Oxford, 1994), 57–79.

Rose, R. B., *The Enragés: Socialists of the French Revolution?* (Sydney, 1965).

Rose, R. B., *The Making of the Sans-culottes: Democratic Ideas and Institutions in Paris, 1789–92* (Manchester, 1983).

Rudé, George, *The Crowd in the French Revolution* (Oxford, 1959).

Slavin, Morris, *The Hébertistes to the Guillotine: Anatomy of a 'Conspiracy' in Revolutionary France* (Baton Rouge, 1994).

Soboul, Albert, *The Parisian Sans-culottes and the French Revolution, 1793–4*, trans. G. Lewis, (Oxford, 1964).

Sonenscher, Michael, *Sans-culottes; An Eighteenth-century Emblem in the French Revolution* (Princeton, 2008).

CHAPTER 24

WAR AND DIPLOMACY
(1792–95)

MARC BELISSA

'WAR and Diplomacy': historians have paid much more attention to the former than the latter, as if the historical moment that began with the declaration of war on 20 April 1792 and ended with the treaties of Basel in 1795 had been totally controlled by the inexpiable nature of the tensions between revolutionary France and European monarchies. Jacques Godechot in 1956 asserted that 'during the revolutionary period the diplomatic game was characterised by its superficiality and its transient nature'.[1] At the start of the twentieth century, Albert Sorel characterized the era of the Revolutionary government as 'diplomacy of the void', and this view has prevailed for much of the past century.

Military history, however, has for several decades been recovering from earlier neglect. The traditional military history of the nineteenth and early twentieth centuries did produce many important works, but between 1920 and the 1970s the discredit of 'battle-history' in France marginalized the history of revolutionary warfare. From the mid-1970s onwards, academics in France, England and the USA have come back to the field with renewed interest in the political and social history of armies and in the history of conscription, of war efforts, of the role of the armies in the building of nations, of strategic and tactical innovation, and of the impact of war on science and culture.

Jean-Paul Bertaud, Sam Scott, Alan Forrest, John Lynn, Annie Crépin, Patrice Bret, and Bernard Gainot are among many who have renewed this area of research. These historians highlighted the politicization processes that the armies inherited as well as new ones created between 1792 and 1795. They have analysed the political, social, and cultural consequences of the economic mobilization for war, and scrutinized various forms of national integration and acculturation put forward by members of the Convention sent on mission.

However, none of these works question the links between war, diplomacy and international relations in a geopolitical perspective. Here, Timothy Blanning's conclusions of 1986 are still fundamentally accurate: our historiography of revolutionary wars dates mostly from the end of the nineteenth and the beginning of the twentieth century.[2] The recent renewed interest in the history of foreign relations of the last two decades has not changed anything, because most specialists are careful to not venture beyond the fatal date of 1792 or even 1789. And those who are willing to take the risk to analyse revolutionary conflicts are usually mostly concerned with the long-term 'rise of the great powers', losing the specificity of 1792–95 on the larger canvas of international modernity.

IDEOLOGICAL WAR OR POWER WAR?

There is no doubt that the launch of the 1792 war represents a rupture in the history of the French Revolution and more generally of Europe. But what was the nature of that war? Was it fundamentally an 'ideological' war, a war between two antagonistic political, social and cultural systems or was it only a consequence of international conflicts that predated the Revolution? This is how historians have usually articulated this question.

The declaration of war on the 'King of Bohemia and Hungary' on 20 April 1792 is one of the key dates of the French Revolution. It opens a military cycle that will carry on until 1802 (and even 1815). In the late nineteenth and early twentieth centuries, arguments about the origin and the nature of the 1792 war were ferocious, because essential issues for the construction of both French and German national identities were at stake. For Leopold von Ranke (1795–1886) and his disciples, the revolutionary wars were first and foremost a conflict between the monarchic and the Republican ideals.[3] Accordingly, many German historians believed that as early as 1789, the opposition of the *ancien régime* and the Revolution carried the germs of a European war which needed no more than a spark to flare up. Consequently, they saw the Revolution as a fracture that opened up the era of 'ideological' wars.

Heinrich von Sybel (1817–95), a pupil of Ranke, shifted emphasis onto 'Reasons of State' rather than ideology.[4] For Sybel, the outbreak of the war was mostly the fruit of a Girondin political decision, because Prussia and Austria at the time were more concerned with events in Poland and the Orient than in France. Against von Sybel, who had supported German rights to Alsace-Lorraine, Albert Sorel wrote his master work *L'Europe et la Révolution française* (1885–1904).[5] The French school saw the war as the result of the European powers' scheme to dismantle France (and Poland) under the guise of a battle against the Revolution.[6]

The histories of the 1789–92 years used to explain that, having proclaimed the rights of nations against those of kings, the Revolution was attacking the basic ideological foundations of the *ancien régime*, particularly in situations like those of the 'princes possessionnés' in Alsace, or in papal Avignon. The attempts by the Assembly to gain control of foreign affairs and French manoeuvrings in Belgium were also the objects of many narratives. From that perspective the years 1792–95 appear as the time when the old order collapsed, a point of view which emphasizes the 'ideological' understanding of the war.

In some slightly different versions of these ideological interpretations, the 'national' character of the war was presented as a sign of its 'modernity'. Indeed, the 1792–95 war has often been presented as the historical moment when the ideas of the Nation and of nationalism were constructed. For some of the French nineteenth-century historians, both 'liberals' and 'nationals', it was even the only justification of revolutionary violence. Thus, Thiers or Mignet, but also Michelet, sang the praises of the French military victories which were presented as expressions of the bright side of the Revolution in contrast to its dark side (the Terror, Jacobin dictatorship). The myth of the 'armies as the secret refuge of the national honour', while in Paris infighting factions were destroying each other, was very powerful. Here the Third Republic found a glorious connection between its army and that of the First Republic, while being able to keep the 'excesses' of 1793 at bay.

From a very different perspective, Jean Jaurès and then Albert Soboul also insisted on the 'national' nature of the war. According to Soboul, because of the war 'the revolutionary bourgeoisie needed the people, and had therefore to make some concessions. Thus did the social scope of the Nation broaden. [The Nation] as such was born in the war which was both national and revolutionary'.[7] If this statement contains some elements of truth, nonetheless it disregards the issue of the relationship between France and its neighbouring peoples. Undeniably, the revolutionary wars were not only national wars but also, at least intermittently, wars of conquest. Emphasizing the tensions between a liberatory ideology and the pragmatic necessities of a military occupation, the recent military studies have nuanced this perspective on the Nation.[8]

Already weakened by von Sybel, the 'ideological' interpretation was further undermined by various early twentieth-century studies of the motivations and expectations of the main political characters of the era.[9] In 1986, Timothy Blanning opened up the whole question once again and concluded that the power configuration of European politics was more important than ideology. For Blanning, if the 1792–93 war 'was indeed the first of the modern wars', it cannot be explained as the consequence of an ineluctable conflict between revolutionary France and the European monarchies. The answer of the European powers to the declaration of war in April 1792, was not only an answer to the Revolution as a political process, it was also an answer to France as a power that had been involved in a system of alliances that went back to 1756. In spite of their hostility to the Revolution, neither the King of Prussia not the Emperor went to war in order to bring back the *ancien régime* in France but in order to protect their own geopolitical priorities. As far as the French war-mongers were concerned, they too had as many internal as external reasons to favour war. Similarly, the declaration of war with England in 1793 mostly had its roots in the conquest of Belgium by France and had little to do with Edmund Burke's calls to war against 'anarchy', even if the radicalism of 1792 had been a worry for the British elites. Obviously, the European powers were concerned by the proclamation of the principle of popular sovereignty and of the rights of nations by the revolutionary Assemblies, but according to Blanning, first and foremost they saw the war in terms of self-interest and power.

Over the last thirty years, British and American historians have often studied the revolutionary war era from the perspective of the rise and fall of various European powers.

For Derek McKay and Hamish M. Scott, the French Revolution marks the end of the division of Europe into two distinct spheres, west and east, and the arrival, despite some elements of continuity with the *ancien régime*, of a new and long-lasting ideological dimension in foreign relations.[10]

Paul Schroeder too sets the revolutionary wars back in the context of the collapse of the European order in the last three decades of the eighteenth century.[11] For him, they were only one moment in the international reshuffling that occurred between 1763 and 1848. According to Schroeder, Europe in 1789 was characterized by a crisis of its international security mechanisms. Thus, if the French Revolution was a contingent event, the European wars which started in 1787 (with the beginning of the Russo-Turkish conflict) were not. Europe in the early 1790s was not set for a European revolution but for a general, 'systemic' and 'structural' war. The revolutionary wars were not the consequence of the French Revolution but of the conjunction between a specific political dynamic in France and the structural context of the collapse of the international system. It is because European powers (including France) were powerless to resolve this systemic crisis that these wars developed. For Schroeder, in spite of the Revolution, France, at least at first, was simply defending its traditional interests. Likewise, no European power really intervened with the intention of putting a stop to the Revolution. But once the conflict had started, nobody was able to end it and to put in place a new system of collective security, partly because nobody was able to figure out how the monarchist powers and Republican France could co-exist.[12]

Recently, Jean-Yves Guiomar (2004) and David Bell (2007) have questioned afresh the nature of revolutionary war using the controversial concept of 'total war'.[13] Guiomar and Bell aim to make this concept the foundation of a new understanding of the historical impact of the wars. They juxtapose 'total war' with 'limited' or 'regulated' war which begin for 'clear and traditional motives'; the kind of war which supposedly characterized the *ancien régime*. For Guimar the 1792 war became 'total' first and foremost because 'its original goals were vague and vast enough (extend the influence of the Revolution, deliver oppressed people)' and 'eventually it could thus not be stopped by those who had started it'.

David Bell partly follows Guiomar's definition while insisting on the fact that 'total war' was the result of a cultural shift which made 'the cataclysmic intensification of the fighting over the next twenty three years' possible. According to Bell, this shift is the origin of our current idea of war. Bell points to changes in 'war cultures' at the end of the eighteenth century as the starting point of this transition. According to him the emergence of a 'military' sphere distinct from the 'civilian' gave birth to our modern 'militarism'.[14] The radicalization of the Revolution further distanced this moment from the 'regulated war' culture that limited earlier conflicts.

Guiomar's and Bell's analyses have been contested.[15] Bell has been criticized for idealizing the *ancien régime* war culture and underestimating the brutality and the scale of its wars, for underrating the continuity between the conflicts of the 1763–89 period and those of the revolutionary years, and for neglecting the economic aspects of the whole issue. The validity of Guiomar's idea, that the war of 1792 lacked real goals and that it aimed at the liberation of the oppressed people of Europe, has also been questioned. Although these works have opened up a new debate, the concept of 'total war' has not been accepted by most historians of this period.

Other studies of the causes of the 1792 war take a much narrower chronological perspective. Patricia Chastain Howe has studied the links between Dumouriez policies regarding Belgium and those of Lebrun and the Girondins.[16] Silvia Neely has analysed the different strategic positions within the 'bellicist party' in 1792, particularly the La Fayette-Brissot opposition.[17] Michael Hochedlinger investigated Austrian foreign policies towards revolutionary France.[18] These studies tend to share Blanning's perspective on the precedence of geopolitical and diplomatic motives over ideological ones to explain the 1792 war.

Very recently, Virginie Martin has looked at how the war broke out from a very different angle: instead of only seeing the months of October–November 1792 as those of a 'push for war' decided by resolutely bellicose political parties, she has tried to show that the war was also the result of the failures and contradictions of the diplomacy pushed forward by Dumouriez and the Brissotins trying to impose France's 'national dignity' issues on Europe.[19] Indeed the 'war cry' of public opinion, fearing invasion and the military intervention of the 'despots' and keen to take its revenge on the foreigners who had insulted France, had made the question of 'national honour' a central issue of this war. The war did not only begin to solve an internal political crisis, but also to impose France's power in Europe and as a retaliation to the foreign powers's (misled by the 'emigrés') 'insults to the very name of Frenchman'. The French never really tried to export their ideals but simply to gain some form of respect and recognition in Europe.

In my own works, I have studied the nature of the war from a perspective that aimed to go beyond what I saw as the unproductive opposition between 'ideological' and 'power' war.[20] I have found it more suitable to try to understand how these ideological and strategic aspects were connected and combined. I have thus attempted to come back to the juridical and political debates that arose during the war and to compare them to those of the Enlightenment period. Emma MacLeod follows a similar path in her analyses of British attitudes towards the wars against revolutionary France.[21] She underlines the importance of the ideological representations of the international scene in the ways in which Burke, Pitt or the radicals saw the issues of war and peace.

How did those who lived through it understand this war? How did the collective and reciprocal images of the belligerents impact on the definitions of its goals and means?

From the first revolutionary movements onwards, the 'patriots' dreaded invasion.[22] In 1789, rumours of military preparations in England alarmed the National Assembly. The following year, many suspected the Anglo-Spanish conflict over the Nootka Bay in North America to be a confected pretext for the king to regain some political leadership. The conventions of Reichenbach and then of Pillnitz managed to convince the revolutionaries that the 'coalition of despots' did exist. The idea of a foreign military intervention was not a pure delusion: revolutionaries in Belgium were indeed crushed in November–December 1790 by the Emperor's army, with the blessing of Prussia, of the United Provinces and of England. This is why the presence of 'emigrés' on the Rhine could look like the prelude to a general invasion. If we know now that this war was in fact wished and pushed for by the king, La Fayette and the Girondins, most of the French population was convinced that in April 1792 France was merely pre-empting an imminent attack.

If the European powers felt no urge to intervene against the French Revolution, there is nonetheless no doubt about their increasing hostility towards it. Acts of censorship, the tightening of the control of foreign movements, the condemnation of the Declaration of the Rights of Man all show how very important the ideological opposition to the Revolution was amongst the chief European powers. This hostility, which was to a certain extent openly acknowledged, was at the root of a mood of insecurity and of rejection amongst large elements of the patriot movement. They worried about army movements (whether real or imaginary) near the borders, and about the difficulties French people encountered when they travelled abroad. Based on these worries, the feeling that a foreign military intervention was *possible* increased.

However, the war that started in 1792 was the result of many factors, none of which was ineluctable in 1789. Undeniably, the Assembly had proclaimed the rights of the nations and many patriots ardently hoped that the European people would reclaim their rights, but nobody imagined or wished that this could happen through military intervention.[23] How then did this connection between war and 'revolutionary expansion' occur? It was both internal *and* diplomatic factors that produced it. Without going into all the details of the situation, there are no doubts that the bellicist camp (the Court, La Fayette, the minister Narbonne, the Brissotins) did look at the war as a way to solve both the diplomatic and the internal crisis of the kingdom. Of course, the goals were very different from one group to the other. The Court, La Fayette and Narbonne wished for a 'simulated' war against the Rhineland states, a short and victorious war that would increase their 'popularity', allow them to regain the control of the armies and mostly bring about a European congress that would lead to a political Restoration. On the other hand, the Brissotins were trying to give to a 'patriot minister' control of the executive power and to break off with the Austrian system of alliances. It is worth pointing out here that the idea that the Republican Girondins were pushing for war in order to abolish the monarchy cannot resist any careful study of the chronology and sources. The myth of the 'Republican plot' is a product of the Girondins' own language after 10 August.[24]

It is most probably in public opinion that bellicism was most ideologically marked: the conviction that France had a duty to fight the despots that had crushed revolutions in Belgium had popularized a preventive war. Nevertheless, the idea that war should aim to free European peoples from their kings was only defended by a handful of enthusiasts. Even if some Brissotins used that theme in their speeches, liberation was never regarded as a primary goal, but only as the consequence of a defensive struggle between France and the kings. In spite of the strategic plot of the April war-mongers, most of the French population was convinced that the foreign powers were only waiting for an excuse to intervene against the Revolution. Thus the war was first and foremost justified by the necessity to defend the Revolution and by the aggressive diplomacy demanded by the

Brissotins. Human rights, the freedom to choose one's form of government, the legacy of the Revolution but also the respect of national rights, were thus invoked.

On the coalition's side, it was the defence of the European order which was said to be at the heart of the war. But which European order: the Princes' order that Austria and Prussia had proclaimed or the one defending the nations' properties to which Britain referred, from 1792 onwards? The British counter-revolutionaries insisted on the idea of the defence of European society against French 'ambitions'. It was the opening of the Scheldt River and the conquest of Belgium by the Convention's army, not the execution of Louis XVI, that brought about the rupture. France stood accused of not recognizing public law as understood by the society of monarchs. The argument is thus very different from a straightforward defence of the traditional order; it was their ideals of freedom and order that the British counter-revolutionaries intended to fight for.[25]

From the beginning of the war, ideological and strategic motivations were thus closely connected on both sides.[26] With the victories of late 1792, the Republican army was on the offensive in Belgium, in Savoy, Nice and in the Rhineland. Thus, the nature of the war changed and it gradually took the aspect of a war of conquest in spite of the Republican generals' proclamation of their respect for the people's sovereignty.

However, the 'liberated' people of Europe soon rejected French occupation which expressed itself, especially in Belgium, through military rule, by the obligation to use the *assignat*, and by widespread official confiscations of property, not to mention church pillaging. If Savoy seems to have accepted its *réunion* to France easily enough, things were much more complicated in Belgium and in the county of Nice where French troops faced the insurrection of the Barbets. With the defeats of March 1793, Republican troops retreated and the agenda went back to defensive war. The 'Nation in arms' rose against the 'despots' soon dubbed 'enemies of the human race'. The 'tyrants' who by endangering French liberties and also by 'enchaining their people', opposed the fight for human rights were, according to Robespierre, 'slaves who combat the real sovereign of the earth': humankind. The real enemies of the 'patriot' were not the foreign soldiers—those were either victims of deception or slaves—but the 'despot's satellites', all the conscious servants of their kings.[27]

The revolutionary wars were thus undoubtedly seen by their main actors as a conflict between two 'political cultures'. From that perspective, it can be said that two worlds fought each other, but we must also go beyond that conclusion, as the war was also very much seen as an internal conflict. For Robespierre, the war was that of all the people of Europe against all the enemies of Liberty. The concepts of the *Enemy of the human race* and of the *Enemy of society* used by both sides clearly suggest that it was also seen as an issue for the whole of humankind. The revolutionaries were convinced that they led a universal fight for human rights and were not just defending the French nation. These visions of war had consequences for its conduct, which brings us back to its 'total' or 'limited' nature.

For the French, foreign people were not the enemy (at least as long as they did not collaborate with their despots) but their potential allies. Convinced that 'regenerated' France could not fight like a king's army, the members of the Assembly did debate how

French soldiers and officers should behave in foreign lands. In 1792, Belgium's population was encouraged by the French and returning revolutionary exiles to support the armies that had come to free them. As he entered Brussels, General Dumouriez proclaimed he would respect the freedom and sovereignty of the Belgian people. In Mainz, in Brussels and in Chambery, local patriots were encouraged to create their own popular societies and provisory administrations. The generals forced loans and taxes on the wealthy only. However, the situation swiftly degenerated, especially in Belgium after November 1792. Real people were not always as enthusiastic as expected at the idea of becoming French or Frenchified. The decree of 15 December 1792 that organized French rule, as well as antireligious acts like the confiscation of the churches' silverware, gave rise to violent reactions, including nocturnal assassinations and even ambushes during the retreat of March 1793.

Some level of continuity with the laws of war, as they were understood and practised under the *ancien régime*, survived: exchanges of prisoners remained a common practice, similar understandings of 'combatant' and 'civilian' were in use, and contributions whether financial or in kind were imposed on local populations just as they were before 1789. This continuity can be explained by the technical necessities of eighteenth century war and by the fact that the officers had been trained during the wars of kings. Nevertheless, the politicization of war kept increasing: the Convention offered French citizenship to all foreign deserters that chose the side of Liberty, the patriot refugees were organized in legions, the abolition of privateering and the proclamation of new laws of war were actively discussed, and most of all the decree of 7 Prairial An II declaring that no English or Hanoverian prisoners would be taken was the sign of a cultural rupture with the wars of the *ancien régime*. The question of the significance and real effects of this decree is still open but its very existence is evidence of a changing conception of warfare.

In practice the 1792–95 war was really a 'limited' war: there were no plans to eliminate the local populations, and generals tended to avoid the risks of headlong pursuit of defeated enemies to annihilate them. On more than one occasion during the Year II, the Committee of Public Safety expressed its frustration at the generals' lack of ferocity; some of them even paid for this with their lives. Thus, revolutionary defensive war was nonetheless total in its political expression: total mobilization (the *levée en masse*), refusal of any kind of comprise until all national territory was liberated, and a rhetoric of the extermination of the enemy.[28]

For all the belligerents, the revolutionary wars inherited some of their characteristics from former conflicts. In each case, they were about establishing or re-establishing a European order that would work in their interest or at least that would not work against it. But it is their new characteristics that make these wars a crucial element of European history. If in some aspects, any war is ideological, (even during the *ancien régime* there were attempts to justify ideologically the resort to force), the age of the revolutionary wars was an unprecedented era of mass mobilization around politically defined goals. If the French Revolution undoubtedly constituted a moment of (at least temporary) rupture in the diplomacy of the age, it is nonetheless clear that the war that began in 1792 can only be understood in an international context that was marked by its continuity with the conflicts of the years 1763–92. For the French, even more than for their adversaries, the revolutionary wars were a complex phenomenon and cannot be described as a mere inter-state conflict. Their three different aspects (ideological war, geopolitical war and national war) were in fact inseparable and it is probably naïve to attempt to 'evaluate' the respective and precise importance of each of those components in their origin or development. A point of view that would attempt to analyse the connections, tensions and sheer contradictions between ideology and strategy seems to me to be in a better position to renew this historical field.

Did a 'Revolutionary Diplomacy' Exist?

The diplomatic history of the 1792–95 period is even bleaker than its war history. The re-evaluation of the international dimension of the French Revolution has brought along an important historiographical renewal since the bicentenary, whereas the study of diplomacy and diplomats has remained very marginal amongst contemporary research. To give only one example of this 'disappearing', neither of the two important dictionaries of the French Revolution—*the Dictionnaire de la Révolution française* directed by Albert Soboul and the *Dictionnaire critique de la Révolution française*, directed by François Furet—includes a single article about diplomacy or foreign affairs.

According to Virginie Martin, the historiographical vacuum that surrounds revolutionary diplomacy 'proceeds from an analysis focused on two dogmas: the dogma of *diplomatic tradition* on the one hand, the dogma of *revolutionary propaganda* on the other hand.'[29] To take their position to the extreme, it could be said that that for the French historians of foreign relations, revolutionary diplomacy was nothing but a form of propaganda that disappeared with the Revolution. The history of diplomacy would thus have been the history of a continuous development without any ruptures, a history inscribed in the long term that would have hardly been altered by the French Revolution. This historiography tends to deny all revolutionary innovations and to concentrate exclusively on the analyses of legacies, continuities and 'traditions'. It is striking that many historical syntheses on foreign relations move from the 1780s to the Congress of Vienna in a few pages.[30] On one side, the Revolution is diluted in the changes of the end of the eighteenth century, on the other side it disappears in the reiteration of the significance of the supposed 'return to normalcy' of 1814. It is not uncommon to read in these syntheses that the Revolution did not constitute any kind of rupture.[31]

With a few exceptions, recent French historiography of modern diplomacy seems to be mostly concerned with the study of the procedures and norms of the 'essence' of diplomacy as refined from the sixteenth to the eighteenth century in parallel with the construction of the monarchy. As a monarchic institution 'par excellence' the diplomacy of the revolutionary period can thus only be a proper diplomacy as far as it assimilated these diplomatic 'traditions'. France's 'return' to the forefront of the European scene after 1795 is thus never analysed as the result of the emergence of a new kind of diplomacy but as the restoration of the *ancien régime's* system; this system having been allowed to survive in the ministerial offices amongst the clerks trained under Vergennes and influenced by *ancien régime* traditions. The idea that such a thing as a 'Republican diplomacy' or even worse a 'diplomacy of the Terror' could have existed, is wholly absent from those historical syntheses.

This perspective is not a new one. It was already characteristic of the diplomatic history studies of the late-nineteenth and early-twentieth centuries. In these too, the hate figure of the 'revolutionary diplomat' is identified with that of the 'Jacobin emissary' unable to differentiate diplomacy and propaganda. Thus, Bassville or Genet have become iconic figures of a 'subverted diplomacy, subverted because it had become subversive' (Virginie Martin) and their extreme practices are constantly referred to as emblems of a diplomacy that did not deserve its name. Such an image of revolutionary diplomacy is not impartial. It has its roots in the point of view of the first generation of historians of diplomacy, who as diplomats saw themselves as the defenders of a 'tradition' that was endangered by the Third Republic.

This point of view dominates the important work of Albert Sorel *L'Europe et la Révolution française (1885-1904)* which remains to this day a major reference. Sorel's interpretation can be summarized in three points. First, there was continuity between the Revolution's foreign policy and that of the monarchy. Secondly, the Revolution was characterized by the contradiction between its 'abstract and philosophical' principles (i.e. the idea of a right of nations that had its origin in the 'natural law of nations' school to which the revolutionaries claimed allegiance) and solid 'realities' based on permanent 'interests'. Finally, Sorel defended the idea that by being unable to separate the eternal interests of France from the temporary interests of the Revolution, revolutionary diplomats did turn their back on the 'French tradition'.

The influence of this point of view has been all the strongest for being largely subconscious and accepted as orthodoxy. Yet, it was highly controversial when first voiced. At the time, two schools opposed each other strongly. On the one side was the Sorbonne's Republican history of the French Revolution lead by Alphonse Aulard, on the other side was the conservative and nationalist *École libre des sciences politiques* with Albert Sorel as well as the 'Société d'histoire diplomatique' founded in 1886.

These two schools defended radically opposite views of revolutionary diplomacy: on Aulard's side the thesis of originality,[32] on Sorel's side the ideas of 'tradition' and 'continuity'. But from 1890 onwards, notes Virginie Martin, Aulard totally changed his discourse and started praising Sorel. This turn can be explained by the desire of the Republican historiography of the Revolution to reclaim the concept of a 'diplomatic tradition'. The truce between Aulard and Sorel allowed for the gradual integration within the Republican story of the Revolution of an interpretation of its diplomacy that was not originally Republican. From then on, the studies of revolutionary diplomacy remained in a kind of lethargy that was increasingly reinforced by the *Annales* criticisms of the old diplomatic history. A few studies that opposed Sorel's determinism stand out as exceptions to this trend, like *Le Directoire et la Paix* by Raymond Guyot in 1911, which remains the great reference text on this topic.

From the 1920s to the 1950s, the study of revolutionary diplomacy did not constitute a specific historiographical field any longer, but it was included in more general studies of the Revolution, often along with a personalization of political processes. It was a time when what was studied were 'Mirabeau's' and then 'Danton's' and then 'Talleyrand's' diplomacies.[33] The history of revolutionary diplomacy became more and more 'national', in the sense that it was more and more concerned with the divergences between various French diplomatic actors. Thus, diplomatic issues became minor issues within the internal conflicts of the Revolution.

During these same years the so-called 'Marxist' or 'Jacobin' historiography had no interest in diplomatic history. For that school, the positive nature of revolutionary expansion, the myth of the soldiers of l'An II bringing freedom to the world, clearly outweighed diplomatic issues. The inexpiable ideological opposition between the Republic and the monarchical powers disqualified diplomacy as a pathetic game of compromise between two irreconcilable systems. Only Jacobin emissaries could be positive heroes, precisely because they had devoted themselves to 'propaganda' and not diplomacy. Here we have a vision symmetrical to Sorel's, but one that eventually led to the same conclusion: revolutionary and Republican diplomacy should only be regarded as a minor issue. One of the few historians who tried to break away from those standardized stories is Jacques Godechot in *La Grande Nation* in 1956. But according to him, even if the initial project of the revolutionaries was not to convert people and occupy their lands, 'revolutionary expansion' nonetheless made all diplomatic enterprise vain, as the diplomats themselves became agents of this expansion, as much as the generals.

In the great *Histoire des relations internationales* published under Pierre Renouvin's direction in the 1950s, André Fugier was in charge of the volume on the French Revolution.[34] His choice to distance himself from traditional diplomatic history and to incorporate analysis of the 'deep forces' of demography and economy into his history of international relations did not facilitate study of short spans such as 1792 to 1795.

The fading of any real interest in revolutionary diplomacy allowed Sorel's interpretation to flourish and continue to dominate the field even if, of course, some works centred on diplomatic structures and on the long-term chronology were published during the 1970s and 1980s.[35] It can for instance be found among members of the so-called '*école critique*', particularly François Furet who reproduced Sorel's ideas in many of his articles.[36] It also influenced the *Annales historiques de la Révolution française*, although in a different way: all issues relative to diplomacy and international relations disappeared from the content of their review. Since the early 1990s, the historiography of revolutionary diplomacy has thus largely been restricted to details that have not questioned the great lines of Sorel's interpretation.[37]

In my own works, I have focused my attention not so much on diplomacy as such but on the conceptual framework that allowed the people of the time to understand (and for some of them to attempt to re-invent) relations between people. I have endeavoured to show how what we now call 'international relations', had previously been the topic of numerous discussions and arguments amongst men of the Enlightenment. Most of all,

I have endeavoured to describe how some of the protagonists had tried to invent a new European order and a new kind of diplomacy on the foundation of those discussions.

The old idea that the revolutionaries of 1789 were ignorant of diplomacy and had no concept of foreign policy has been invalidated by the careful study of the arguments on the 'political system' of the kingdom that took place in both the Constituent and Legislative Assemblies. The revolutionaries had in fact a thorough knowledge of treaties and public law, and a solid understanding of the Enlightenment's philosophers and their critical views of the European order.

Already, in the *cahiers* of 1789, many declarations of hostility to wars of conquest, and claims that the nation should have its say on foreign policy, can be found. Those ideas, along with the topic of permanent armies, were discussed during the debate on the Declaration of Rights in July–August 1789. But it is at the end of 1789 that the left wing of the Assembly started to raise a serious case against the diplomacy of the *ancien régime*. In January 1790, the Assembly rejected the claims of the Republic of Genoa on Corsica, Mirabeau invoking popular sovereignty to do so. It was during the May 1790 debate on declarations of war that the left rose up to demand a break with the practices of the *ancien régime*. Petion, Robespierre and Volney wanted the laws of peace and war to be put in the hands of the Nation, they asked for a declaration of the rights of nations to complete the Declaration of the Rights of Man, and demanded the end of secret diplomacy.

Alongside the debate on wars of conquest and on the rights of nations, there was also a second debate on alliances and on the place of France within Europe. The importance of the anti-Austrian lobbies within the Foreign Ministry and among the French population as a whole, has been clearly established for many years. Thomas Kaiser studied the depth of the opposition to the 1756 Treaty that was considered as one of the causes of the French decline in Europe—even amongst 'patriots'.[38] For many of those 'political patriots', new alliances should follow the revolutionary regeneration. Some desired a connection with the British in order to divide the world between the two 'free nations' of Europe. Others considered that the natural enmity of England was ineradicable and that France should strengthen the Franco-Spanish alliance to destroy English tyranny over the sea.

What should the attitude of a 'regenerated' France be regarding the treaties that had been signed by the king?[39] The issue was crucial because Spain had appealed to the existing Bourbon 'Family Compact' to ask for France's help against England, because the German '*princes possessionés*' in Alsace required compensation for the abolition of feudal laws on their land, and finally because the inhabitants of Avignon and of the *comtat Venaissin*, which belonged to the papacy, demanded their *réunion* with France in the name of the right of people to free themselves of an oppressive domination. The attitude of the revolutionaries towards those external consequences of the Revolution was not monolithic. For the left, the treaties went against the rights of nations and against the principle of national sovereignty and were *de facto* obsolete. Robespierre for instance asked for the dismissal of the Family Compact, the rejection of the German princes' requests and the reunion with Avignon without any consideration of the opinions of the other European countries. But there were also many others on the left who preferred a compromise to the destruction of European public law.

The debate on the organization of the various ministries brought about a proliferation of projects for the reorganization of diplomacy. Indeed during the early stages of the Revolution, it had remained a sphere reserved to the top ranks of the aristocracy. Until 1792, there was little change, but growing confusion: after the summer of 1791 and even more so after the summer of 1792, the majority of Louis XVI's ambassadors resigned, some of them even changed sides and started working for the *émigrés*. They were replaced, as well as it could be, by subaltern agents (legation's secretaries, chancellors and consuls) who sometimes took the title of '*chargés d'affaires*' and became reliable servants of the new regime that had ensured their promotion. Alongside them appeared a new class of diplomats chosen for their political credentials. The arrival of Dumouriez at the ministry in March 1792 created a proper rupture—but certainly not a revolution—as he reorganized various offices, simplified the hierarchy and purged the management. From then on, commitment to the Republic and its values became the first requirement of a strong candidate.

In spite of these changes and until 10 August 1792, diplomacy remained undoubtedly the least 'revolutionized' element of the monarchical government. As has been clearly shown by Virginie Martin, the failure of the regeneration of diplomacy had much more to do with the resistance of the diplomats who refused to represent the Nation, than it did with the pusillanimity of the Assemblies that refused to give themselves the constitutional means to gain the control of the diplomacy.

With the fall of the monarchy, and the proclamation of the Republic, it was necessary to imagine and define, in a war context, the foundations and the structures of a new Republican diplomacy. The diplomacy of the Girondins and that of the first Committee of Public Safety aimed at a reversal of alliances in favour of Prussia and even more so of England. Many emissaries were sent to London, without any success. Danton's secret diplomacy pushed (with no more success) for a rapprochement with Berlin.

The formation of the coalition simplified the situation, as by the beginning of 1793, only Switzerland, the Scandinavian states, Turkey and the USA had remained neutral. The decrees of 13 April and of 24 September 1793 and then Robespierre's report of 17 November 1793 signalled a change of political lines. They can be read as attempts to redefine Republican diplomacy while reconstructing a new system of alliances between France, 'neutral' people and friendly nations that would defend each other's national rights. All ambassadors were removed: in hostile countries they were replaced by secret agents, and in neutral states by '*chargés d'affaires*'. Finally the Convention rejected (officially at least) anything that had to do with secret diplomacy. The Committee of Public Safety refused to negotiate with any emissary of any power that had not recognized the Republic, but this obviously did not prevent informal contacts.

Did a Republican diplomacy exist in those years when France was very isolated in Europe? On the eve of Thermidor, there remained officially only four diplomats in post. In reality, between 1792 and 1794, untitled agents (spies or emissaries) had become very common, as had the double posting by a parallel authority (Provisional Executive Council and then Committee of Public Safety) of a second man, with the goal of supporting or keeping in check the initial agent named by the Foreign Ministry. Far from having disappeared under the Convention, French diplomats had multiplied and the diplomatic structure had become increasingly complex. This proliferation was the consequence of both the wavering of a juvenile foreign policy and of the plurality of the recruiting authorities. Paradoxically, a new diplomacy was born in the revolutionary context, and the word 'diplomacy' had even acquired a new meaning. Included for the first time in the 1798 edition of the *Dictionnaire de l'Academie*, it was defined as 'the science of relationships and interests between political powers'. This clearly signals the switch of emphasis that took place during that period, from a diplomacy that was serving the private interests of kings and princes to one that was led by the idea of national interests. The importance of 'commercial diplomacy' in the debates of the years 1793-95 also points in that direction.[40]

The institutional and prosopographic perspective of Virginie Martin supports the idea of the creation of a new and unique Republican diplomacy between 1792 and 1795. Her thesis is a study of French Diplomacy between 1789 and 1796 on three levels: institutional analysis of the relationship between the legislative and the executive powers, description of the implications of this relationship in diplomatic practices, and a case-study of the diplomats and agents of the Revolution in Italy.

Martin's thesis is an essential milestone in the historiography of revolutionary diplomacy. First of all, because it questions radically and definitively Sorel's myths about Republican 'propaganda' and 'diplomatic chaos', including that of the 'Jacobin diplomatic emissary'. It shows that the diplomacy of the revolutionary era—whether between 1789 and 1792 or 1792 and 1795—was not based on a propagandist vision of the spread of revolutionary principles and that the legislative power, whatever its form, had never wanted (or been able) to take control of diplomacy, with the exception of the period of the Committee of Public Safety that was indeed entrusted with that authority. It also shows that the public debates on the Nation's control over diplomacy and on the nature of the foreign relations of a 'regenerated' France, never led to any kind of real control of the legislature by the executive (still with the exception of the An II). And finally it shows that these debates did not produce any declaration on the right of people or on the ways France should behave with other nations. Furthermore, it is this lack of control and of clearly defined principles on which French foreign relations could have been based that allowed the executive to seize power, and most of all created a dysfunctional situation in foreign relations.

For Martin, the diplomacy of the Republic was not a 'diplomacy of the void' but only began to take shape when the Committee of Public Safety decided to define its Republican characteristics. [41] Thus it is only during the Terror that a new diplomacy appeared. This affirmation may seem paradoxical, but it is nonetheless fundamental. There was thus a Republican diplomacy whose goals were to have the Republic recognized, to impose the Nation as a legal entity with an official status, to defend French citizens and its own honour and not to use propaganda to spread the Revolution thorough Europe. However, the Republic did of course defend its own principles, which it understood as potentially universal.

Through her Italian case study, Martin also provides us with an invaluable description of a very specific group: the diplomatic actors.[42] She understands the 1792-95 period as a time of transition from the *ancien régime's* view of diplomats as artful 'negotiators' to the new diplomats who specialized in a matter that was now understood as the science of inter-state relations. Because traditional historiography was only interested in 'official' agents, it did not give itself the proper means to understand how Republican diplomacy was constituted: through unofficial agents whose role was crucial in the preservation of (more or less informal) diplomatic relations, as is clearly shown in the Italian example.

French diplomacy, obliged by powerful foreign hostility to act through unofficial channels, can however be comprehended through Republican symbols and modes of self-representation. A cultural history of revolutionary diplomacy allows the reconsideration of how Republican France did in fact create relations with neutral, indifferent or indeed hostile powers. Martin underlines the importance of the battle for Republican emblems that the agents wore or placed on buildings. The promotion of a Republican language was an essential task of the French diplomats. They had to show to foreign governments and foreign nations that the Republic existed and that it claimed its due place amongst the nations.[43] This thesis shows that the question of revolutionary diplomacy needs to be re-evaluated and analysed afresh, mostly through the concepts of the cultural history of political life.

New Research Paths

Which paths could future researchers in war, peace and diplomatic issues of the years 1792–95 follow?

First, the artificial opposition between theoretical principles and practical decisions, between ideas of war and peace and strategies, between ideological and power wars needs to be overcome. Analysing revolutionary wars in such binary terms does not allow us to understand their historical specificity, which is precisely this unique connection between their new political dimension and the diplomatic power-structure that they inherited from the 1763–89 wars. To pretend that the 1792–95 war was purely ideological is to underestimate its geopolitical features, to deny any role to its actors, and to imagine an ineluctable antagonism between revolutionary France and monarchist Europe. On the other hand, to deny any meaning to the political ideals at stake is to misunderstand the kind of rupture the French Revolution introduced in the European order, a rupture nobody at the time had any doubts about.

If French and English attitudes towards the war are quite well known, it is not the same when we consider the German or Italian regions or the neutral states like the Scandinavian kingdoms. Studies on the representation of war in the press or in public opinion would be very useful indeed. Examination of the armies' representational practices could also be valuable. What did the combatants think about their 'enemy'? Did their representations follow national formats or not? It would also be interesting to contextualize the concept of neutrality in both long- and short-term studies.[44]

As far as the history of revolutionary diplomacy is concerned, everything (or almost everything) needs to be done again. Diplomatic archives have to be studied and re-read in the light of a 'Republican diplomacy'. Virginie Martin's work could also be completed, and maybe nuanced, by other area studies on Swiss cantons or Scandinavia. The prosopographic method applied to the whole body of French agents abroad would undoubtedly give us a very different picture of Republican diplomats that the one that still dominates many historical syntheses on the topic.

Whereas on other periods, cultural perspectives on diplomatic issues have gained much authority, this is not yet the case for the historiography of the Revolution. There is still much to be discovered: representations of international society and the way they influence their understanding of relations and conflicts between states and people, cultural transfers, the construction of national identities, the spread of political models and of elements of diplomatic cultures around Europe, images of the sovereign, ceremonials and changes in laws on war and peace.

Notes

1. Jacques Godechot *La Grande Nation* (Paris, 1956), 16.
2. Timothy C.W. Blanning, *The Origin of the French Revolutionary Wars* (London, 1986).
3. Leopold von Ranke, *Ursprung und Beginn der Revolutionskriege 1791–1792* (Leipzig, 1879).
4. Heinrich von Sybel, *Geschichte der Revolutionszeit von 1789 bis 1795* (Dusseldorf, 1877).
5. Albert Sorel, *L'Europe et la Révolution Française*. 8 vols. (Paris, 1885–1904).
6. Pierre Muret, 'L'affaire des princes possessionnés d'Alsace...' *Revue d'Histoire moderne*, 1899–1900, 433–56, 566–92.
7. Albert Soboul, *Nation, patrie, nationalisme*, Acte du colloque de Moscou 1970, (Paris, 1974), 6.
8. One of the most recent examples of this approach is Gilles Candela, *L'armée d'Italie. Des missionnaires armés à la naissance de la guerre napoléonienne* (Rennes, 2011).
9. For instance, see Georges Michon, *Robespierre et la guerre révolutionnaire* (Paris, 1938) or *Le rôle de la presse en 1791–1792 dans la déclaration de Pilnitz et la guerre* (Paris, 1941).
10. Derek McKay and Hamish M. Scott, *The Rise of the Great Powers 1648–1815* (London and New York, 1983). See also Paul Kennedy, *The Rise and Fall of Great Powers* (New York, 1987).
11. Paul Schroeder, *The Transformation of European Politics, 1763–1848* (Oxford, 1994).
12. Schroeder, *Transformation*, 100. Jeremy Black argues for a different balance of change and continuity: *The Rise of the European Powers, 1696–1793* (London, 1990), *European International Relations 1648–1815* (Houndmills, 2002), 249.
13. Jean-Yves Guiomar, *L'invention de la guerre totale* (Paris, 2004). David Bell, *The First Total War* (Boston and New York, 2007).
14. Bell, *The First Total War*, 18.
15. See the discussion in the H-France forum, on the IHRF site and the 'Regards croisés' rubric in *Les annales historiques de la revolution française*, n. 366 (2011–14), 153–70.
16. Patricia Chastain Howe, *Foreign Policy and the French revolution. Charles François Dumouriez, Pierre Lebrun and the Belgian Plan, 1789–1793* (New York, 2008).
17. Silvia Neely, 'The uses of power: La Fayette and Brissot in 1792', *Proceeding of the Western Society for French History*, vol. 34 (2006), 99–114.

18. Michael Hochedlinger, 'Who is Afraid of the French Revolution, Austrian Foreign Policy and the European Crisis 1787–1797', *German History*, vol. 21, n. 3 (2003), 293–318.

19. Virgine Martin, *La diplomatie en Révolution. Structures, agents pratiques et renseignements diplomatiques. L'exemple des diplomates français en Italie (1789–1796)*, Thèse de Doctorat, Paris I (2011), 3 vols., vol. 1, chs. IV–VI.

20. Marc Belissa, *Fraternité Universelle et intérêt national, 1793–1795. Les cosmopolitiques du droit des gens* (Paris, 1998).

21. Emma V. McLeod, *A War of Ideas: British Attitudes to the Wars against Revolutionary France, 1792–1804* (Aldershot, 1998).

22. The next few pages are an abridged version of the argument of parts II and III of my book *Fraternité universelle*.

23. Ibid., 243ff.

24. Ibid., 302.

25. Marc Belissa, 'Les stratégies de la contre-révolution. L'exemple du débat parlementaire anglais (1792–1794)' in Jean-Clément Martin (ed.), *La Contre Révolution Europe XVIIIe-XIXe siècles*, Jean-Clément (ed.) (Rennes, 2001), 163–73.

26. The following pages are an abridged version of the argument developed in Marc Belissa and Patrice Leclercq, 'The Revolutionary Period: 1789–1802', in A. V. Hartmann and B. Heuser, (eds), *War, Peace and World Orders* (London, 2001).

27. Sophie Wahnich, 'Anglais', in *Dictionnaire des usages socio-politiques, 1770–1815*, vol. IV (Paris, 1989), 35–63.

28. Marc Belissa and Sophie Wahnich, 'Trahir le droit, les crimes des anglais', *Annales historiques de la Révolution française*, n. 2 (1995), 233–48.

29. Martin, *La diplomatie en Révolution*, vol. 1, 73–162.

30. For instance, see Mathew S. Anderson, *The Rise of Modern Diplomacy 1450–1919* (London and New York, 1993). Jean Berenger (ed.), *L'ordre européen du XVIe au XIXe siècle* (Paris, 1998).

31. See for instance Thierry Lentz, *Histoire de la diplomatie française* (Paris, 2007).

32. See in particular the works of Aulard's pupil, Boris Mirkine-Guetzevitch (1892–1955).

33. See for instance Pierre Rain, *La diplomatie française de Mirabeau a Bonaparte* (Paris, 1950).

34. André Fugier, *La révolution française et l'Empire napoléonien, Histoire des relations internationales*, vol. IV, Pierre Renouvin (ed.) (Paris, 1954).

35. Jean Baillou (ed.), *Les affaires étrangères et le corps diplomatique français*, tome 1 de l'Ancien Régime au second Empire (1984). Yves Lemoine, *La diplomatie française pendant la Révolution* (Paris, 1989).

36. In François Furet, Mona Ozouf (eds), *Dictionnaire critique de la Révolution française* (Paris, 1988) or in the article, 'Les Girondins et la guerre', in François Furet and Mona Ozouf (ed.), *La Gironde et les Girondins* (Paris, 1991).

37. Linda and Marsha Frey, 'The Reign of the Charlatans is Over. The French Revolution Attack on Diplomatic Practise', *Journal of Modern History* 65 (December 1993), 712–15. Gary Savage, 'Political Culture, Revolution and Foreign Policy in France, 1787–92' unpublished doctoral dissertation (Cambridge, 1996) and 'Favier's heirs, The French Revolution and le secret du Roi' *Historical Journal* 41 (1998), 225–58.

38. Thomas Kaiser, 'La fin du renversement des alliances: La France, L'Autriche et la déclaration de guerre', *Annales Historiques de la Révolution Française*, n. 351 (January/March 2008), 77–98.

39. Marc Belissa, *Fraternité universelle et intérêt national*, 98 et al.

40. Marc Belissa, 'Handel, Diplomact und die nationale Macht wahrend der Franzosichen Revolution (1789–1799)', in Asbach Olaf (ed.) *Der Moderne Staat und 'le doux commerce'*, (forthcoming).

41. Virginie Martin, op cit., ch. VIII, 'La diplomatie, coeur ou periphérie de la centralité législative (printemps 1793–novembre 1795)?'.

42. Martin, op cit., ch. X, 'Qu'est-ce qu'un diplomate républicain?'.

43. Martin, op cit., ch. XI, 'Représenter et dire la République: le métier de diplomate à l'épreuve de la République 1792–1795)'.

44. A new collection from Palgrave—*War, Culture and Society, 1750–1850*—has published several volumes about the culture of the revolutionary and Napoleonic wars. On this latter period, see some of the contributions in Alan Forrest, Karen Hagemann and Jane Rendell (eds), *Soldiers, Citizens and Civilians, Experiences and Perceptions of the Revolutionary and Napoleonic Wars, 1790–1820* (Basingstoke, 2008); Karen Hagemann, Gisela Mettele and Jane Rendall (eds), *Gender, War and Politics; Transatlantic Perspectives, 1775–1830* (Basingstoke, 2010); and Alan Forrest, Étienne François and Karen Hagemann (eds), *War Memories, The Revolutionary and Napoleonic Wars in Modern European Culture* (Basingstoke, 2012).

Selected Reading

Belissa, Marc, *Fraternité Universelle et intérêt national, 1793–1795. Les cosmopolitiques du droit des gens* (Paris, 1998).

Belissa, Marc, *Repenser l'ordre européen 1795–1802. De la société des rois aux droits des nations* (Paris, 2006).

Bell, David, *The First Total War* (Boston, 2007).

Black, Jeremy, *British Foreign Policy in an Age of Revolution 1783–1793* (Cambridge, 1994).

Blanning, Timothy C.W., *The Origins of the French Revolutionary Wars* (London, 1986).

Bois, Jean-Pierre, *De la paix des rois à l'ordre des empereurs, 1714–1815*, (Paris, 2003).

Edelstein, Dan, 'War and Terror: The Law of Nations from Grotius to the French Revolution' *French Historical Studies*, Vol. 31, No. 2 (Spring 2008).

Frey, Linda and Marsha, 'The Reign of the Charlatans is over. The French Revolution Attack on Diplomatic Practise', *Journal of Modern History* 65 (December 1993).

Godechot, Jacques, *La Grande Nation* (Paris, 1956).

Guiomar, Jean-Yves, *L'invention de la guerre totale* (Paris, 2004).

McLeod, Emma V., *A War of Ideas: British Attitudes to the Wars against Revolutionary France, 1792–1804* (Aldershot, 1998).

Martin, Virginie, *La diplomatie en Révolution. Structures, agents pratiques et renseignements diplomatiques. L'exemple des diplomates français en Italie (1789–1796)*, Thèse de Doctorat, Paris I, 2011. 3 vol. (en cours de parution).

Mathiez, Albert, *Danton et la paix* (Paris, 1919).

Sorel, Albert, *L'Europe et la Révolution Française*. 8 vols. (Paris, 1885–1904).

CHAPTER 25

FROM FACTION TO REVOLT

PAUL R. HANSON

WHEN the National Convention first met on 20 September 1792 its deputies thought themselves to be on the threshold of a new era. Two days later, heartened by news of the military victory at Valmy, they would declare the First French Republic, 'one and indivisible', to which they pledged their dedication and loyalty. That spirit of unity was to be short-lived. Within weeks the National Convention became polarized, divided between the factions known as Girondins and Montagnards, with a large mass of uncommitted deputies between them, the much-maligned Swamp, or Plain. The autumn and early winter months were consumed by the trial of Louis XVI, which added to the divisions, but following the king's execution stalemate set in, and little progress was made on the deputies' principal task, the drafting of a new constitution. In late May Paris erupted in insurrection, forcing the proscription from the National Convention of the leading Girondin deputies. In response, four provincial cities declared themselves in revolt, refusing to recognize the authority of the violated legislature and pledging to lead a march of provincial volunteers on Paris to restore the integrity of the National Convention. With the Vendée already in rebellion France teetered on the brink of civil war.

In the space of barely eight months the Republic had collapsed, or very nearly so. How had this happened? In the following sections we will explore that question through three different lenses: first, from the perspective of Paris, where the political disputes were most intense and the conflict was concentrated; second, from the perspective of the provinces, where French citizens were also absorbed and embroiled in the task of inventing democracy, engaged in their own disputes and rivalries, but with one eye constantly cast toward the capital; and third, from the perspective of international developments, in particular the war in Europe and the brewing insurrection in Haiti, both of which threatened the stability of the Republic and influenced revolutionary politics.

It is often said that all politics is local, and there is truth in that statement for this period. But French revolutionaries were peculiarly aware that they were acting on a world stage, that decisions taken in Paris would have a ripple effect throughout the country, across Europe, and indeed in other parts of the world. France had been at war with Austria since April 1792, joined by the rest of Europe in the months following the execution of Louis XVI. Recruitment for the army intensified in the spring of 1793, so few citizens anywhere in France would have been unaware of the ways in which war was impinging on their lives and the future of their country. Most of the deputies in the National Convention had had experience in local politics before coming to Paris, in municipal, district or departmental administrations. They were products of local political culture, remained concerned about issues and political controversies back home, and were often in regular correspondence with friends and colleagues in their home towns. Certainly, there were many ordinary Frenchmen in the provinces, potentially involved in local politics and concerned about the dissension in Paris, who would have been unable to locate Haiti on a map and had little sense of the colony's importance to the French economy. But in Paris working people did grow alarmed about the rising price of sugar in the winter months of 1792–93, and in that way the slave revolt in Haiti directly affected the mood of the capital and the growing opposition between Girondins and Montagnards. As we examine the deteriorating political climate of 1792–93 in the context of national, local and international events we must remember that these were not discrete spheres, but rather interacted with each other in complicated ways.

Paris

How was France to be governed without a king? And what was to be the fate of the king who had just been deposed from the throne? These were huge questions confronting the deputies elected to the National Convention, and they came at an inopportune time. France was at war, and Prussian and Austrian troops were on French soil advancing toward Paris. Moreover, at this moment of crisis the Legislative Assembly had chosen to expand suffrage, eliminating the distinction between active and passive citizens and lowering the voting age to 21, introducing a system of virtual universal manhood suffrage. For some, such as Robespierre, this expansion of the electorate represented an acknowledgement of the contribution of ordinary people to the Revolution, particularly in the uprising of 10 August 1792. For others, this decision may have been motivated by a desire to generate popular support for the war effort. But for many, the entry of the working poor into the electorate was an unsettling development. Would they vote responsibly, or be vulnerable to the manipulations of radicals and anarchists?

Both David Jordan and Raymonde Monnier have argued that this period saw the democratization of Parisian politics.[1] There was intense activity in the sectional Assemblies of Paris throughout the summer, beginning with the agitation that led up to the failed insurrection of 20 June. That uprising, during which a crowd invaded the grounds of the Tuileries palace, elicited letters of protest from many departmental administrations expressing their support for the king and queen and their outrage at the disrespectful treatment to which they had been exposed. Mindful of those letters from the provinces, many deputies in the Legislative Assembly were reluctant to embrace the increasing clamour for insurrection that came from the sections in late July and early August. Pierre Vergniaud, presiding over the Legislative Assembly, rebuked the Mauconseil section's 4 August declaration that it no longer recognized the authority of the king, denouncing it as unconstitutional. When the monarchy fell just six days later, the Legislative Assembly was put in the awkward position of having to take credit for an insurrection it had not endorsed.

This created a very awkward political space, or moment, in the capital. The Legislative Assembly had lost its legitimacy, not only because it had allowed events to overtake it, but also because its sessions in late July and early August were very poorly attended, with a majority of deputies staying away.[2] Where, then, did sovereignty lie in the aftermath of 10 August? With the Paris Commune, which had taken the lead in coordinating the insurrection of 10 August? With the sectional Assemblies, most of which had adopted the petition calling for the ouster of Louis XVI that Vergniaud had declared unconstitutional? With the Jacobin Club, which the king himself had denounced a year earlier, at the time of the flight to Varennes, for acting as a shadow parliament? Or with the as yet unelected National Convention, scheduled to convene on 21 September?

In the midst of this uncertainty, panic swept across Paris. For five days in early September militant sans-culottes invaded the prisons, seized those suspected of conspiring with the enemy, conducted summary trials in streets and courtyards, and in the end executed between 1,100 and 1,400 people, nearly half of the prison population. No constituted authority, neither the Legislative Assembly nor the Paris Commune, intervened to stop the massacres. In the days following, most political leaders lamented the violence but described the killings as justified. Jean-Marie Roland, then minister of the interior, described the massacres as a regrettable but necessary measure 'over which perhaps a veil must be drawn'.[3] By the end of September, however, the prison massacres had become a source of political controversy and acrimony, pitting Girondins against Montagnards.

Girondin leaders faced a dilemma at this moment. Although very few revolutionaries had opposed the declaration of war in April 1792 (Robespierre and Marat notable among them), the Girondins had unquestionably led the calls for war, and the war had gone badly. Jacques-Pierre Brissot, erstwhile Jacobin club leader and prominent Girondin, had represented Paris in the Legislative Assembly, but after his ardent advocacy of war and lukewarm support of the 10 August uprising he felt compelled to stand for election to the National Convention from the Eure-et-Loir. Indeed, all of the leading Girondin deputies represented provincial departments. The Parisian delegation, by contrast, was dominated by Montagnards—twenty of the twenty-four Parisian deputies sat with the Mountain. Robespierre had described 10 August as a triumph of the people, and associated himself explicitly with that people. The Girondins needed desperately to establish their own base of support and to erode the popular support that the Montagnards enjoyed in the nation's capital. The September massacres seemingly presented an opportunity to do both.

Vergniaud was the first to give a speech denouncing the Paris Commune for its role in the massacres. Then, at the end of October, Jean-Marie Roland, minister of the interior, issued a report on the state of the country and Paris, highly critical of the Paris Commune and calling for the creation of a departmental guard to protect the National Convention against the threat of anarchy in the capital. The next day Jean-Baptiste Louvet, himself a native Parisian, rose in the National Convention and delivered a speech denouncing Robespierre as the instigator of the prison massacres, for having plotted with Georges Danton and Jean-Paul Marat to install themselves as dictators. The speech was rhetorically brilliant, and drew enthusiastic applause from other deputies, but proved to be a tactical failure. Four days later Robespierre parried the attack with a speech of his own, a speech that drew nearly 800 Parisians into the galleries to cheer him on. The quandary that the Girondins faced was clear: how could they attack the perpetrators of the massacres without seeming to condemn the people of Paris who had saved the Revolution? And how could they call for a departmental guard to protect the National Convention without similarly impugning those same people?[4]

These same lines of opposition quickly emerged in the trial of Louis XVI as well. There was little disagreement over the charges—the guilty verdict was unanimous. But leading Girondins proposed that the king's sentence be referred to primary Assemblies, the *appel au peuple*, so that the people of France might either ratify the judgement of the Convention or decide Louis' fate themselves. Robespierre countered that such a referendum would be cumbersome and subject to manipulation, exposing the nation to the risk of civil war, and that in any case the people had already spoken on 10 August—their actions had condemned the king to death. Moreover, the people had elected the deputies of the National Convention, and it was now their responsibility to act. In his response, Vergniaud contrasted the law-abiding departments to the intrigue and tumult of the capital, and evoked once again the spectre of the September massacres. Whether the Girondins' call for an *appel au peuple* is best seen as an attempt to save the life of the king, or as an effort to shift the locus of sovereignty from Paris to the departments, it failed. The proposal was defeated decisively, some deputies voting against it chastened perhaps by reports of a violent riot in Rouen touched off by royalist agitation. The vote sentencing the king to death was much closer, and his execution resolved none of the animosities and rivalries that had emerged in the preceding months. Two great challenges now confronted the deputies: the need to draft a new constitution, and the expanding war against the monarchs of Europe.[5]

Marie Jean Antoine Condorcet chaired the committee charged with drafting a new constitution. It submitted a proposal on 15 February 1793, but no consensus formed in its support. Joining Condorcet on the committee were Pierre Vergniaud, Armand Gensonné, Jacques Pierre Brissot, and Jérome Pétion, all associated with the Girondin faction. The proposed constitution would have increased the power of government ministers, at that time predominantly Girondin, and increased the power of departmental administrations. Montagnards attacked the document for its failure to guarantee political equality and for its federalist tendencies.[6] A stalemate developed that persisted throughout the spring, generating frustration within the National Convention and impatience in the provinces.

The antipathy between the sans-culottes of Paris and the Girondin deputies came to a head in late February and early March. Steadily rising prices, particularly for sugar (a result of the troubles in Saint-Domingue) incited a wave of riots and attacks by women on grocers, beginning on 25 February. Even Robespierre spoke critically of these riots, characterizing them as unworthy of the patriotic sans-culottes of Paris. For the Girondins, whose ardent defence of free trade drew the ire of the protesters, the riots seemed the work of the same lawless and anarchistic elements responsible for the September massacres.

The violence took on a more explicitly political aspect on 9 and 10 March, one day after the first reports of recent military defeats in Belgium. With Danton urging the sections to mobilize for the war effort, the focus of Parisians turned once again, as it had in September, to enemies within the country. The Girondin deputies, widely perceived as the war party within the Convention, were now blamed not only for the setbacks on the battlefield but also for trying to conceal the bad news from the public. During the night of 9 March an armed band of some 200–300, mostly soldiers, sacked the printing presses of Gorsas, Brissot, and Condorcet. The first calls were now heard in Paris for the arrest of leading Girondin deputies, who in turn alleged that freedom of the press was under siege and that their very lives had been in danger. Vergniaud and others warned that the blades of assassins hung over their heads.[7]

Calm returned to the capital as winter gave way to spring, but the military situation in Belgium and Holland continued to deteriorate. The war affected the political mood in Paris in several ways. Beginning in March, the Convention sent approximately forty pairs of representatives on mission to provincial departments to assist with military recruitment. These deputies were drawn principally from the ranks of the Montagnards, which depleted their numbers in the meeting halls of the Convention and allowed the Girondins to maintain their control of parliamentary debate and committee work. Conversely, these missions to the provinces gave the Montagnards an opportunity to carry their message beyond Paris and improve their relations with the citizens of distant departments. That was decidedly not the effect of recruitment missions to the West, however, where local resistance soon coalesced into open rebellion. The Vendée rebellion became the first major counter-revolutionary uprising against the young republic, adding an internal threat to that posed by the foreign war.[8]

Bad news from the front reached Paris in March as well. On 18 March, General Charles Dumouriez's army was defeated at Neerwinden and three days later suffered a second setback at Louvain. Amid rumours that Dumouriez was in negotiation with the Austrians, the Convention sent four deputies to the front to investigate and possibly arrest the general. Instead, Dumouriez arrested them, turned them over to the Austrians, and attempted to lead his troops on Paris to restore the monarchy. When his officers refused to follow his lead he abandoned his post and fled to the Austrian lines in early April. The treason of Dumouriez posed a political liability to both Montagnards and Girondins. Georges Danton had visited the Belgian army on mission the previous month, and allegations soon swirled that he had compromised himself during that visit. Moreover, when Dumouriez deserted to the Austrians he took with him the son of Philippe Egalité, duc d'Orléans. The Girondins now accused the Montagnards of an alliance with Orléans, and in April the National Convention ordered the entire Orléans family to be arrested and sent to Marseille to be imprisoned. The treason of Dumouriez posed a greater risk to the Girondin leadership, however, since they had controlled the ministry of war when Dumouriez was appointed. Several of the Girondins, most notably Armand Gensonné, had developed close relationships with Dumouriez and turned to him for his foreign policy expertise. As the spring wore on, radicals in Paris explicitly made these connections and began to call for the arrest of leading Girondin deputies.

Finding themselves once again under attack by Parisian militants, the Girondins turned against one of their champions, Jean-Paul Marat. Marat's name had been linked with Robespierre and Danton in the autumn, as alleged instigators of the September massacres. Both had spoken critically of Marat in the intervening months, however, and the Montagnards generally tried to distance themselves from the 'friend of the people'. On 5 April, however, Marat assumed the presidency of the Jacobin Club, and on that same day signed a circular that denounced the generals (especially Dumouriez) and moderates within the Convention and exhorted the departments to march to the defence of Paris. This could be seen as a riposte to previous proposals by the Girondins that a departmental guard be brought to the capital to defend them against Parisian anarchists. One week after Marat's pronouncement, Marguerite-Elie Guadet (a deputy from Bordeaux) rose in the Convention to call for Marat's impeachment and trial before the Revolutionary Tribunal. With many Montagnard deputies absent on mission, the Convention voted the indictment the following day, charging Marat with incitement to pillage, murder, and attacks upon the National Convention. It proved to be a serious misstep. Making a case against Marat was one thing—his newspaper had been filled in the preceding months with calumniation and calls for heads and more heads, earning for Marat a reputation in the provinces as the chief 'drinker of blood'. But convening a Parisian jury that would convict him was quite another, and after barely forty-five minutes deliberation the jury returned a unanimous verdict of acquittal, demonstrating at once the overwhelming popularity of Marat in Paris and the vulnerability of the Girondin deputies.[9]

THE PROVINCES

It was not only in Paris that the first months of the Republic were marked by violence and political contention. Fear and suspicion of enemies at home as the war went badly on the frontier led to violence in provincial cities as well. In Limoges an angry crowd killed a priest on the streets at a moment of renewed crisis in July 1792, and in Caen Georges Bayeux, the *procureur-général* of the department, was murdered in broad daylight even as the prisons were being attacked in the capital in early September. Claude Lomont, one of the Calvados deputies to the National Convention, wrote home to a friend at the time, 'the people of Paris and Versailles have bestowed an air of justice to the vengeance that they exercised upon the prisoners ... but in Caen nothing at all like that, people say'.[10]

The introduction of universal manhood suffrage heightened political tensions in some provincial cities. Both the Legislative Assembly and the Paris Jacobin Club issued circulars in August aimed at influencing the election of deputies to the National Convention. In some departments local authorities chose not to print those circulars. National elections remained indirect, however—voters chose electors, who convened in an electoral assembly to cast ballots for the deputies who would be sent to Paris. Municipal elections, by contrast, were direct, and it was at this level that universal suffrage proved to be most contentious in the late autumn and early winter of 1792–93. Let us consider the examples of Lyon and Marseille, where disputed municipal elections had a clear impact on the path that led to revolt in the summer of 1793.

Lyon was the second largest city in France, with a population of 150,000. Roughly a third of Lyon's population relied for their livelihood either directly or indirectly on the silk industry, which had been in decline for most of the eighteenth century. The 1786 trade treaty with England dealt the silk industry a further blow, as did the disruption of the Revolution. More than 20,000 Lyonnais silk weavers were unemployed in the early 1790s. There was social tension in the city, then, between an old aristocratic elite that had long dominated municipal affairs, supported by the roughly four hundred *marchands fabricants* who controlled silk production, and the substantial artisanal population that found itself in a deteriorating economic situation. Lyon aristocrats, not surprisingly, were royalist in their political sympathies, and the city became something of a haven for would-be *émigrés* heading toward the eastern frontier. The merchant elite showed little interest in assuming political leadership in the city after 1789, leaving space in the local political arena for others drawn from the professional classes to vie for political power.[11]

The political atmosphere in Lyon was unsettled, then, in the early years of the Revolution, but the simmering social tensions rarely flared into open violence. That changed in the last months of 1792. On 9 September, perhaps incited by reports of the massacres in Paris, an angry crowd invaded the prison in the Pierre-Scize neighbourhood of town and killed eight officers of the former Royal-Pologne regiment and three refractory priests.[12] No arrests were made, but the violence did not end there. Market disturbances broke out on 14 September, and for a week chaos and disorder reigned in the city. More than a hundred stores and bakeries were pillaged in the midst of the riots. This week of violence heightened the social polarization in Lyon just on the eve of municipal elections.

Even prior to the violence, in late August, there were allegations of voter fraud in Lyon in regard to the selection of electors for deputies to the National Convention. One of the sections in town petitioned the municipal council demanding that the list of electors recently chosen in their section be overturned, alleging that a slate of candidates had been imposed on those assembled to vote. The election stood, but the same allegations of electioneering would surface in the subsequent mayoral and municipal council elections. Among those elected to the Convention was Louis Vitet, a moderate figure who had helped to maintain calm in the city during the past two years. His departure necessitated a mayoral election in November, in which one of the two candidates was Joseph

Chalier, a Jacobin firebrand who had served on the municipal council in 1790–91 but had been in Paris through much of 1792 consorting with radical groups in the capital.

Lyon is fascinating in this period not only because of the city's size and importance and the complexity of its own political landscape, but also because of the myriad personal links between Lyonnais and Parisian politics. The most notable among these involved Joseph Chalier and Jean-Marie Roland. Like Chalier, Roland had been active in Lyon municipal politics early in the Revolution. Indeed, the two had worked together in some measure to initiate a sectional club movement and energize political engagement in the city. Whereas Chalier had moved in a radical direction, however, Roland had befriended Jacques Brissot when he shifted base to Paris in 1791–92. Roland became minister of the interior for a second time after the fall of the monarchy, clearly aligning himself with the Girondin faction in the National Convention. Moderates in Lyon viewed Roland as a crucial ally in the capital, and a number of them corresponded regularly with him, while Jacobins in Lyon viewed Chalier as a leader with strategic connections to radicals in Paris.[13]

The prospect that Joseph Chalier might be elected mayor of Lyon was enough to galvanize the merchant elite into action. Opposing Chalier in the mayoral election was Antoine Nivière-Chol, a moderate. Voter turnout was extraordinarily high, and Nivière-Chol won a decisive victory, although again there were signs of irregularities. Having secured that victory the Lyon elite grew complacent, perhaps, and voter turnout was much lower in the subsequent municipal council elections, with the result that nearly every position was won by candidates supported by the radical Club Central. Chalier himself was elected as president of the district tribunal.

Unlike most other provincial cities, Lyon did not see the early emergence of a Jacobin club affiliated with the mother society in Paris. Rather, encouraged by both Roland and Chalier, a network of neighbourhood clubs had developed in the thirty-two sections of Lyon. They operated independently, but sent two to three delegates apiece to monthly meetings held at the Club Central—meetings that were open to the public. This fostered a certain level of civic activism in 1790–91, but in late 1792 Chalier and his supporters moved to transform the Club Central into a more centralized organ asserting control over the sectional clubs. This produced an organized slate of candidates in the municipal elections. Lyon Jacobins then overplayed their hand. At an alleged secret meeting at the Club Central on 6 February 1793 Chalier and his supporters laid plans for the creation of a revolutionary tribunal and prepared a list of suspects. When the municipal council ordered household searches shortly thereafter, and the arrest of 300 suspects, panic began to spread in the city. The mayor, Nivière-Chol, over-reacted and called out the National Guard, which in turn elicited a wave of public criticism, leading the mayor to resign. A special election was quickly arranged, amid heated emotions, in which Nivière-Chol easily prevailed. Jubilant in victory, a mob of his supporters sacked the Club Central, only to see their candidate decline his election.

A third mayoral election, on 27 February, returned to office another moderate, J. E. Gilibert, but François Laussel (a supporter of Chalier who had been elected *procureur* of the city council in November) had taken the precaution of arresting Gilibert on charges of inciting insurrection, and after several days in jail he resigned. In this fashion, Lyon Jacobins were finally able to place one of their own in the mayor's office, Antoine-Marie Bertrand. For them the past few months represented democracy in action, the people triumphant. For their opponents, the moderate merchant elite and aristocratic royalists, this series of elections amounted to an electoral travesty, a judgement that on the face of it seems merited.[14]

For the next several months radicals and moderates did battle in Lyon. In one crucial sense their positions were the opposite of those occupied by Girondins and Montagnards in Paris. The most important allies of Lyon Jacobins were militants in Paris, three days' journey distant, whereas Lyon moderates could rely on the support of the conservative departmental administration. Throughout the spring Lyon moderates organized to mobilize support in the sectional Assemblies, as a counter to the solidly Jacobin Club Central. While the 'soak the rich' rhetoric of Chalier and his allies undoubtedly appealed, some artisans complained that such incendiary language had thrown them out of work by forcing the wealthy to flee town out of fear for their lives. Both sides made entreaties to the numerous teams of representatives on mission who passed through Lyon en route to the eastern front. Some among the elite feared that those deputies, predominantly Montagnard in their sympathies, would bring the Army of the Alps to the aid of Lyon Jacobins.

Rumours that the Army of the Alps had indeed left Grenoble for Lyon on 27 May triggered an insurrection in Lyon two days later. Moderates mobilized their supporters in sectional Assemblies along with several National Guard battalions to seize control of the arsenal and mount an assault on the Jacobin municipality. After two hours of pitched battle and some two dozen fatalities the municipal council was ousted from office, Joseph Chalier was placed under arrest, and moderates resumed control of Lyon politics. Within days, upon news of the 2 June insurrection in Paris that ended with the proscription of twenty-nine Girondin deputies, Lyon would declare itself in rebellion against the National Convention.

Marseille, too, was a contentious political arena in 1793, but its revolutionary history was quite different from Lyon's and its socioeconomic situation also contrasted with that of its sister city further north on the Rhône. Marseille was a city of approximately 100,000 people at the end of the old regime, about half of whom were recent immigrants, about a third from the Provençal hinterland, with the remainder from across southern France and a few from northern Italy. Like Lyon, it was an overwhelmingly commercial city, but unlike Lyon its economy remained relatively vibrant until France went to war with England in early 1793. Whereas Lyon gained an early reputation as a counter-revolutionary haven, Marseille rivalled Paris as the most revolutionary of France's cities between 1789 and 1792, and in August the *fédérés* from Marseille played a leading role in the assault on the Tuileries palace that led to the fall of the monarchy. Unlike Lyon, where the merchant elite remained largely aloof from revolutionary politics, the first municipal council in Marseille was dominated by merchants, who were also active in the Marseille Jacobin Club, which held its first meeting in April 1790 and soon affiliated with the mother society in Paris.[15]

Marseille Jacobins tended to focus their revolutionary energies outward, sending a number of contingents to neighbouring towns and villages in 1791–92 to encourage vigilance against royalists and counter-revolutionaries and the creation of Jacobin clubs. But there were social and political tensions within the city as well, and the local elections of 1792–93 brought these to a pitch as they had in Lyon. The voting began in early January, later than in most provincial cities, and Jean-Raymond Mouraille was re-elected mayor by a wide margin. Mouraille, in his early 70s, was older than most active revolutionaries, and had held the position of mayor since 1791. He was close friends with Charles Barbaroux, a prominent Marseille deputy to the National Convention, and had been a popular mayor. He played a role in the arming of the *fédérés*, presided over the Jacobin club for a time, and exercised a moderating role in defense of the merchant community.

Elections for the municipal council were quite controversial, however, and Mouraille would have a difficult time navigating the fallout from that. Votes were cast in the first week of January, and on 11 January 150 citizens signed a petition to the departmental administration demanding that the balloting be annulled on the grounds that several sections had collaborated to draw up a list of twenty candidates (there were twenty officers on the council), that list then being nominated back in the section Assemblies. The Marseille Jacobin Club almost certainly initiated this organized electoral campaign, which many Marseillais clearly found objectionable.[16]

The election results enhanced the influence of Marseille Jacobins, and in February the club created a central committee, which worked with municipal officers to denounce and disarm suspects in March and April. As in Lyon, however, the deteriorating economic situation made it increasingly difficult for the Jacobin municipality to maintain its base of popular support. Grain was in increasingly short supply, and the radical measures urged on the municipal council by the club cast fear in the hearts of wealthy merchants and alienated some of the workers and artisans who depended on them for employment. The embattled municipal council turned to Montagnard representatives on mission for support, while moderates, denouncing that outside meddling in local affairs, built their base of support in sectional Assemblies.

The months of April and May witnessed an ongoing struggle that essentially focused on the question of whether the sections or the club were the more legitimate expression of popular sovereignty in Marseille. The club demanded that only 'good citizens' be allowed to attend sectional meetings, while the sections demanded that the club refrain from meeting when sectional Assemblies were in session. Sectional Assemblies challenged the legitimacy of the Marseille Revolutionary Tribunal, protesting to the National Convention, but the Jacobin Club found allies in the representatives on mission, Moise Bayle and Joseph Boisset, who ultimately declared the sectional Assemblies to be counter-revolutionary.[17]

As in Lyon, there were personal connections between leading politicians in Marseille and the political factions in Paris. As already noted, Jean-Raymond Mouraille had a friendship with Charles Barbaroux, a leading Girondin in the National Convention who had previously served on the Marseille municipal council and was among the founders of the Marseille Jacobin Club. Moise Bayle, on mission to the southwest in the spring of 1793 had also served on the Marseille municipal council, but was associated with the Montagnards. Barbaroux had made efforts to keep the battalion of Marseille *fédérés* who had marched to Paris the previous summer in the capital to protect the Convention from 'anarchists,' but to no avail. By April 1793 they were back in Marseille, where they would prove to be useful allies to the moderates of the sections.

Among the first actions taken by the representatives on mission in Marseille was the levying of a new brigade of 6,000 men, to respond to reports of counter-revolutionary violence in the neighbouring department of the Gard. Although justified on the face of it—the southeast had been plagued by counter-revolutionary violence throughout the early years of the Revolution—moderates suspected that this force would become a political weapon for the Jacobin municipality, which just the month before had ordered the disarming of suspects and the creation of a revolutionary tribunal. As events played themselves out in April and May we see the complicated intersection of local, regional and national politics. Mouraille, realizing that the creation of a new brigade would exacerbate tensions in the region, made efforts to delay its departure. This alienated Marseille Jacobins, who called on the representatives on mission to dismiss the mayor from office. Bayle and Boisset eventually did so, but in an effort to be even-handed they also ordered the arrest of the Savon brothers, accused by moderates of 'terrorist' violence against suspects.

Two other developments in the area added to the political tension. On 8 April, the National Convention ordered that Philippe Egalité and the Orléans family be sent to Marseille. Bayle and Boisset assured the Marseillais that this order showed the confidence of the Convention in their city, but the approach of the second royal family of France proved a source of consternation rather than pride. Moderates, mindful of Girondin propaganda, feared that Orléans would launch a coup from Marseille and lead the brigade of 6,000 back to Paris to assume the throne at the head of a radical government dominated by bloodthirsty Montagnards. Marseille Jacobins, equally fearful, associated Orléans with the treason of Dumouriez and the manoeuvrings of the Girondins. No one in the city welcomed the arrival of this royal prisoner.

Aix-en-Provence, just a half day's journey to the north, formerly the seat of the *parlement* of Provence and initially designated as the departmental *chef-lieu* of the Bouches-du-Rhône, had long been a political rival to Marseille. There had been violence between royalists and patriots, radicals and moderates, in Aix throughout the early years of the Revolution, and the Marseille Jacobin Club had sent expeditions to the town on several occasions. Early in 1793 Aix Jacobins allegedly murdered several prisoners and in April, meeting *en permanence*, the sections of Aix ordered the arrest of a number of leading Jacobins in town accused of those murders. Bayle and Boisset responded by ordering section Assemblies closed, which in turn alarmed moderates in Marseille, who feared that this would soon be the fate of their section Assemblies and that the brigade still under formation would be turned against them. With emotions in Marseille stoked by both of these developments, Bayle and Boisset fled Marseille at the end of April to seek refuge in a nearby town.

From the safety of Montélimar the two deputies issued an order on 2 May declaring the sections of Marseille counter-revolutionary and suppressing the Central

Committee of the sections as well as the Popular Tribunal, which had been constituted by the sections in fall 1792. Bayle and Boisset observed in their order that 'calling themselves Sovereign, the sections act as if national Sovereignty belonged to them'. As if to confirm that sentiment, the sections ignored the order and created a new General Committee, composed of three delegates from each section. The Popular Tribunal remained in session long enough to try the former mayor, Mouraille, who was acquitted, and the Savon brothers, who were found guilty and sentenced to death. Based on the evidence from that trial, the General Committee issued an order for the arrest of a number of leading Jacobins on 18–19 May. Two weeks later, upon receiving news of the sectional revolt in Lyon and the proscription of the Girondin deputies in Paris, the General Committee dismissed both the municipal council of Marseille and the departmental administration of the Bouches-du-Rhône. Marseille, like Lyon, was now poised to join the federalist revolt against Paris. In both cities a movement initiated by section Assemblies had unseated a municipal council supported by local Jacobins. Unlike the uprising in Lyon, the revolution of the sections in Marseille had been virtually bloodless.

The early part of this chapter discussed the democratization of politics that occurred in Paris during the summer months of 1792. That same process played out in provincial towns and cities in the following months, and as in the capital it proved to be contentious. The events in Lyon and Marseille were more dramatic than in most towns, but they should not be seen as in any way exceptional. The expansion of the electorate introduced a new level of contestation into revolutionary politics in 1792–93. In the local elections of late 1792 it was the Jacobin Club network that was best positioned to engage in what we would today regard as political campaigning, which brought new men into political office, particularly at the municipal level. It should not surprise us that the *honnêtes gens* of these provincial cities viewed this electioneering as manipulative, and as we have seen, the elites of Lyon and Marseille drew upon traditional clientage networks to mobilize their supporters in sectional Assemblies, ultimately succeeding in wresting political power from the Jacobins and their supporters. Their timing could not have been worse, coming as it did right on the eve of the political defeat of the Girondins in Paris.

What was at stake here was essentially sovereignty, how it was to be exercised and by whom. But there was a second issue at stake, which had to do with representation. Did citizens cede their sovereignty, as Vergniaud would have it, to their elected representatives once they were voted into office? Or was sovereignty inherent in the people, as Robespierre argued, and if so, how were they legitimately to exercise it in times of national crisis, or local crisis for that matter? That these issues came to the fore in 1792–93 should not be surprising. The abdication, trial and death of Louis XVI left a void at the centre of the political arena in France, and that opening created space for precisely the sort of political conflict we have been describing. Even as the Revolutionaries struggled over these issues of sovereignty and representation, however, the nation faced serious international challenges that fed the sense of crisis in the country and rendered more intractable the political divisions that threatened to throw France into civil war.

INTERNATIONAL CONTEXT

In the year of its birth, the international position of the French Republic was precarious indeed and this certainly affected the political climate. Two issues were of particular importance. First, the disruption of sugar production on Saint-Domingue following the slave rebellion on the island drove prices up in Paris by late 1792 and produced market protests in February. Those protests were awkward for both political factions, but on balance the popular discontent served the interests of the Montagnards, who at this stage welcomed the support of the people of Paris. Concern over the cost of food led eventually to the adoption of the *maximum*, a policy favoured by the Montagnards and opposed by the Girondins.[18] We are coming to appreciate more fully the effect of the Saint-Domingue slave uprising on the Revolution in metropolitan France (Bordeaux would never fully recover from the loss of France's most valuable colony), but more work needs to be done to explore in greater detail the impact of the disruption in trade on the French economy in 1792–93. The declaration of war on Great Britain in February 1793 also disrupted Mediterranean trade and adversely affected the grain supply in France. The adequate provisioning of the armies and urban markets was a crucial political issue throughout the spring and summer months of 1793, and authorities that failed in that task quickly drew the wrath of the people.

The war in Europe, of course, was the second international event that influenced the internal political struggle. Military recruitment was among the factors that incited resistance in the Vendée in western France, where the first open rebellion against the National Convention occurred. Parisian sans-culottes were among the most eager volunteers joining the Republican battalions sent to put down the Vendée rebellion, but it is interesting to note that authorities in Bordeaux and Caen, two centres of the federalist revolt, were willing to send volunteers to join the Republican forces in the Vendée even as they attempted to raise departmental forces to march against Paris in June 1793.[19] Parisians also enthusiastically enlisted to go to war against Austria and Prussia, which helped to counter the Girondin propaganda depicting them as lawless anarchists. Parisian activists never tired of extolling the sacrifices they had made for the Republic— from the 10 August assault on the Tuileries, to the battle against the Vendéan rebels, to the defence of *la patrie*.

Letters and proclamations flowed back and forth between Paris and provincial cities throughout the winter and spring of 1793.[20] Deputies in the National Convention wrote frequently to their constituents back home, often exhorting them to let their voices be heard. Departmental administrations and municipal councils responded by sending appeals to Paris, decrying the political stalemate that paralysed the Convention. We have grown accustomed today to email appeals from one organization or another asking us to add our names to petitions to Congress or Parliament supporting calls for reform or opposing controversial new laws. French revolutionaries collaborated in these ways, too, in the 1790s, gathering signatures on petitions in public meetings and circulating printed copies of stirring addresses to the National Convention. Those addresses most often lamented the factionalism in Paris and the undue influence of the unruly populace of the capital. But provincial Frenchmen were also exasperated by the inability of their representatives to rise above political squabbling at a time of national crisis in order to deliver a new constitution and unite in opposition to France's enemies.

Given those concerns, the treason of Charles Dumouriez in April 1793 was a serious blow to the political fortunes of the Girondin leaders. Try as they might to link Dumouriez to Danton and implicate both in a complicated web of conspiracy involving Philippe Egalité, the connections between the general and the Girondins were much stronger. Dumouriez' denunciation of the Jacobins, followed by his desertion to Austrian lines, made more credible the allegations that the Girondins had all along favoured the preservation of the monarchy. Now finding themselves on the defensive, Girondin leaders directed their accusations against Jean-Paul Marat, which as we have seen proved to be a political blunder.

CONCLUSION

Sorting out the factors that brought France to the brink of civil war in the summer of 1793 is a complicated task. Politics, ideology, personalities, social divisions—all of these came into play. On 2 June 1793, as 80,000 Parisians surrounded the National Convention, calling for the proscription of the leading Girondin deputies, news arrived in Paris of the insurrection in Lyon three days earlier. The first reports were that 800 patriots had died in Lyon. Those reports proved to be vastly exaggerated, but for the moment they probably added to the conviction of Montagnards and their supporters that something needed to be done to break the stalemate in the National Convention. Accordingly, the deputies voted to proscribe twenty-nine Girondin deputies later that afternoon and place them under house arrest. Remarkably, the insurrection of 31 May–2 June did not end in violence.[21]

In the week or two following 2 June more than a dozen of the proscribed deputies fled Paris for Caen, which became their base for the following month. Caen emerged as one of the centres of the federalist revolt, and delegates who gathered there from other Norman and Breton departments formed a Central Committee of Resistance to Oppression, which drafted a manifesto, sent commissioners throughout the country seeking support, and made preparations for an armed march on Paris to restore the integrity of the National Convention. The fugitive deputies encouraged these measures, and in doing so opened themselves up to charges that they were fomenting civil war.

Had the Girondins prevailed in the political struggle in Paris, the moderates who seized control of municipal politics in Lyon and Marseille would have had powerful allies. Instead they found themselves isolated and vulnerable, their local victory threatened by the shifting political landscape in Paris. So those cities, too, became provincial centres of the federalist resistance to the Montagnard Convention, along with Bordeaux in the southwest, home to many of the proscribed Girondin deputies. The federalist revolt was in part a reaction to the national political crisis, a culmination to the months of protests by departmental administrations over the factionalism in the National Convention and the unruly street politics of the Paris crowd. But it was also an integral part of the debate over sovereignty that had been waged over the past three years at both the national and local levels.

The Girondins and their supporters in the provinces favoured government by a propertied and educated elite, the *honnêtes gens* so frequently mentioned in the pamphlets of the early Revolution. For them equality meant legal equality, a system of laws that would apply to all, preserve social order, and protect property. The Montagnards based their political vision not on the rule of law (though they were not unmindful of its importance), but rather on the will of the people.[22] At least in 1792–93, they succeeded in mobilizing the people, and that mobilization, whether on the streets of Paris or at the ballot box in municipal elections across France, proved threatening to the propertied elite. In most provincial cities the elite managed to preserve their political ascendancy in the elections of 1792, and rural property owners maintained firm control over departmental administrations, most of which protested the proscription of the Girondin deputies in word if not in action. In Lyon and Marseille, where moderates lost control of the municipal councils in the face of an organized Jacobin-led campaign, they managed to rally their supporters in sectional Assemblies, which they now claimed to be the locus of popular sovereignty, and reclaim political power, only to see their victory jeopardized by the Montagnard triumph in Paris.

The federalist revolt, the product of political and social divisions in both Paris and the provinces, failed for two principal reasons. First, in none of the rebel cities (Caen, Bordeaux, Lyon and Marseille) were the leaders able to generate popular support for a march on Paris. In Lyon and Marseille the people rallied in some measure to the defence of their cities, when Republican troops laid siege. But they showed no enthusiasm for the broader political agenda of the moderate elites. At no time did the federalist rebels seriously challenge the authority of the central government. Second, the Montagnard leaders in Paris, now firmly in control of the National Convention, delivered the constitution for which everyone had been clamouring for the past six months, the most democratic constitution of the Revolutionary decade. Their failure to enact that constitution, owing to the war-time emergency, stands as a betrayal of their commitment to popular sovereignty and a major factor in their own eventual demise.

Notes

1. David P. Jordan, *The Revolutionary Career of Maximilien Robespierre* (Chicago, 1985), 106; Raymonde Monnier, *L'Espace Public Démocratique: Essai sur l'opinion à Paris de la Révolution au Directoire* (Paris, 1994), 135–9.
2. Jordan, *Revolutionary Career*, 110. The assertion of sporadic attendance is challenged by C. J. Mitchell, *The French Legislative Assembly of 1791* (Leiden, 1988).

3. Marcel Dorigny, 'Violence et Révolution: Les Girondins et les massacres de septembre', in Albert Soboul (ed.), *Girondins et Montagnards* (Paris, 1980), 103–20.

4. See Michael Sydenham, *The Girondins* (London, 1961), 123–30, for a detailed account of the acrimony in the Convention from September through October 1792.

5. On the king's trial see Michael Walzer, *Regicide and Revolution: Speeches at the Trial of Louis XVI* (New York, 1992); and David P. Jordan, *The King's Trial: Louis XVI vs. the French Revolution* (Berkeley, 1979).

6. There has been much historiographical debate over just how 'federalist' the federalist revolt truly was. For an extensive discussion of that debate see Paul R. Hanson, *The Jacobin Republic under Fire: The Federalist Revolt in the French Revolution* (University Park, PA, 2003), chapter four.

7. A. M. Boursier, 'L'Emeute Parisienne du 10 mars 1793', *Annales Historiques de la Révolution française* 44, no. 2 (1972), 204–30.

8. The most comprehensive recent work on the representatives on mission is Michel Biard, *Missionnaires de la République: Les représentants du peuple en mission (1793–1795)* (Paris, 2002). See also Jean-Pierre Gross, *Fair Shares for All: Jacobin Egalitarianism in Practice* (Cambridge, 1997).

9. The classic work on Marat remains Louis R. Gottschalk, *Jean Paul Marat: A Study in Radicalism* (New York, 1927), but see also Clifford D. Conner, *Jean-Paul Marat: Tribune of the French Revolution* (London, 2012).

10. Paul R. Hanson, *Provincial Politics in the French Revolution: Caen and Limoges, 1789–1794* (Baton Rouge, 1989), chapters two and three.

11. For a fuller discussion of Lyon politics during the Revolution see W. D. Edmonds, *Jacobinism and the Revolt of Lyon, 1789–1793* (Oxford, 1990); and Hanson, *The Jacobin Republic under Fire*, 139–54.

12. Edmonds, *Jacobinism and the Revolt of Lyon*, 124.

13. For the life of Roland see C. A. Le Guin, *Roland de la Platière: A Public Servant in the Eighteenth Century* (Philadelphia, 1966). The best biography of Chalier remains the short essay by Maurice Wahl, 'Joseph Chalier: Etude sur la Révolution française à Lyon', *Revue Historique* 34 (1887), 1–30.

14. On the events of February–March 1793 see Edmonds, *Jacobinism and the Revolt of Lyon*, 148–53. The considerable contemporary documentation includes J. L. Tallien, *Rapport et projet de décret sur les troubles arrivés à Lyon, présentés à la Convention Nationale, au nom du Comité du Sûreté générale*, B. M. Lyon, Fonds coste, 350560; A. C. Lyon, I²3, pièce 8 (*Rapport et pétition sur les troubles à Lyon, présentés et lues à la barre de la Convention Nationale*); B. M. Lyon, Fonds Coste, 545 (letter from Achard and Gaillard to Javogues, Pressavin, Dupuy, Pointe and Dubouchet); and B. M. Lyon, Fonds Coste, 561 and 565 (letters from private citizens).

15. For a fuller discussion of Marseille politics during the Revolution see William Scott, *Terror and Repression in Revolutionary Marseilles* (London, 1973); Jacques Guilhaumou, *Marseille républicaine (1791–1793)* (Paris, 1992); and Hanson, *The Jacobin Republic under Fire*, 154–60.

16. There is rich documentation regarding these elections in the departmental and municipal archives in Marseille. In particular see A. D Bouches-du-Rhône, L1964; and A. C. Marseille, K38.

17. Also see Jacques Guilhaumou, *Marseille républicaine (1791–1793)* (Paris, 1992) in regard to the events of that spring.

18. The *maximum* on grain, much debated in the winter/spring of 1793, was adopted in early May. The *maximum général*, which imposed price controls on other staple goods, was not enacted until late September, following widespread protests in Paris about the cost of living earlier that month.

19. See Alan Forrest, *Society and Politics in Revolutionary Bordeaux* (Oxford, 1975), 143–4; and Hanson, *Provincial Politics*, 158 for discussion of volunteer battalions sent from Bordeaux and Caen to the Vendée.

20. Dozens of these letters are reprinted in Henri Wallon, *La Révolution du 31 mai et le fédéralisme en 1793*, 2 vols (Paris, 1886).

21. The best account of the 31 May–2 June insurrection remains Morris Slavin, *The Making of an Insurrection: Parisian Sections and the Gironde* (Cambridge, MA, 1986).

22. See Keith M. Baker, 'French Political Thought at the Accession of Louis XVI', in Keith M. Baker (ed.), *Inventing the French Revolution* (Cambridge, 1990), 109–27, for a discussion of the 'political', 'judicial', and 'administrative' discourses that he argues dominated French political thought at the end of the old regime.

SELECTED READING

Biard, Michel, *Missionnaires de la République: Les représentants du peuple en mission (1793–1795)* (Paris, 2002).

Biard, Michel (ed.), *La Révolution française, une histoire toujours vivante* (Paris, 2009).

Cousin, Bernard (ed.), *Les Fédéralismes: Réalités et Représentations, 1789–1874* (Aix-en-Provence, 1995).

De Francesco, Antonio, 'Popular Sovereignty and Executive Power in the Federalist Revolt of 1793', *French History* 5, no. 1 (March 1991), 74–101.

Edmonds, W. D., *Jacobinism and the Revolt of Lyon, 1789–1793* (Oxford, 1990).

Forrest, Alan, *Society and Politics in Revolutionary Bordeaux* (London, 1975).

Forrest, Alan, *The Revolution in Provincial France: Acquitaine, 1789–1799* (Oxford, 1996).

Guilhaumou, Jacques, *Marseille républicaine (1791–1793)* (Paris, 1992).

Hanson, Paul R., *Provincial Politics in the French Revolution: Caen and Limoges, 1789–1794* (Baton Rouge, 1989).

Hanson, Paul R., *The Jacobin Republic Under Fire: The Federalist Revolt in the French Revolution* (University Park, PA, 2003).

Jordan, David, *The Revolutionary Career of Maximilien Robespierre* (Chicago, 1985).

Monnier, Raymonde, *L'Espace Public Démocratique: Essai sur l'opinion à Paris de la Révolution au Directoire* (Paris, 1994).

Scott, William, *Terror and Repression in Revolutionary Marseilles* (London, 1973).

Slavin, Morris, *The Making of an Insurrection: Parisian Sections and the Gironde* (Cambridge, MA, 1986).

Vovelle, Michel, *Les Sans-culottes marseillais, le movement sectionnaire du jacobinisme au fédéralisme, 1791–1793* (Aix-en-Provence, 2009).

CHAPTER 26

....

WHAT WAS THE TERROR?

....

DAN EDELSTEIN

EVERYONE knows what the Terror looked like. Parisian sans-culottes forced national representatives to do their bidding; cartloads of suspects were packed off to the guillotine by the revolutionary tribunal; Republican armies fought tooth and nail against royalist and federalist forces; and strange, neo-pagan cults were celebrated in erstwhile churches. Everyone knows all this, because the Terror is probably the most represented moment in the history of the French Revolution: countless works of history, fiction, film, and art have left a searing imprint in our imaginations of this 'heady' time (to borrow the most commonly employed, if rather inappropriate, adjective).

On closer inspection, however, the defining features of the Terror lose their apparent coherence. The different actors of this period—most notably, the Parisian sections, the Paris Commune, the National Convention, the governmental committees, the political clubs, the revolutionary tribunal, and the revolutionary army—were not all marching to the same tune. Indeed, they were often in open disagreement with one another. This was largely because they had different goals: certain groups wanted stronger economic measures to combat *la vie chère*; others pushed for political change (which was itself a matter of dispute); yet others wanted to push forward with cultural, and especially religious, reform.

Complicating matters further is the problem of chronology. At a distance, it is fairly easy to date the Terror, and most textbooks use this label as a convenient way to identify events that took place between September 1793 and July 1794. But these bookends do not hold up to much scholarly scrutiny. Most of what Colin Jones termed the 'dark machinery of state political Terror' was created in the spring of 1793, that is, six months *before* the Convention debated the motion that Terror be made 'the order of the day'.[1] And many historians have pointed out that the practices we associate with the Terror— imprisonment for political views, executions for counter-revolutionary activity, and extra-constitutional repression by the government, to name but a few—continued well *past* the fall of Robespierre and his associates on the 9 thermidor Year II (27 July 1794).

These are only two of the most prominent issues muddying the clear picture we may have of the Terror. Also problematic is the term itself: what exactly did it mean?

Who was meant to be terrorized? Equally perplexing are the political agendas of this period: what was the Terror for? How does it relate, if at all, to other initiatives of this time? Finally, there is the biggest quandary of all: why did the Terror—or the loosely connected set of actions that we lump together under this name—even occur? What were its causes? Could it have been avoided? These are the questions that I address in this chapter, through an analysis of the events and sources of the time, as well as the copious secondary literature that has amassed over the past two centuries.

WHEN WAS THE TERROR?

One of the thorniest issues that scholars of the Terror must confront concerns its timing.[2] The traditional start date of 5 September 1793, is problematic on many levels. As noted above, most of the key institutions of the Terror had been introduced that previous spring: the creation of a revolutionary tribunal was approved by the National Convention on 10 March; military commissions to execute *hors-la-loi* were established on 19 March; the first law of suspects was passed on 21 March; and the Convention voted to create a Committee of Public Safety on 10 April.

It is true that these institutions and laws did not prove very effective for the first six months of their existence. As François Furet pointed out, this was the period when the French Republic was militarily at its weakest.[3] Only with the retaking of Lyon (9 October), the victory over the Austrians at Wattignies (16 October), and over the Vendéens at Cholet (17 October) did the Republican forces begin to reverse a trend that had left them on the defensive. In this regard, the traditional start date for the Terror does reflect the moment when the French Republic became more aggressive, particularly with respect to its own citizens.

But if violence is the measure we adopt to determine when the Terror begins, what are we to make of earlier violent episodes? The fall of 1793 was hardly the first time when blood was shed during the course of the French Revolution. The infamous prison massacres of September 1792 could be seen as foreshadowing the political violence of *quatrevingt-treize*;[4] this parallel would in fact be drawn explicitly by Danton, who exclaimed, in the run-up to the creation of the revolutionary tribunal, 'let us be terrifying in place of the people' (*soyons terribles pour dispenser le peuple de l'être*).[5]

There had been equally 'terrifying' events before, as well. Republican politicians had not forgotten the Champ-de-Mars massacre of 17 July 1791, when National Guards, commanded by the marquis de Lafayette, acting with the mayor of Paris, Jean-Sylvain Bailly, proclaimed martial law and then opened fire on demonstrators, killing around fifty of them.[6] Other massacres punctuate the history of the Revolution all the way back to its beginnings. In addition to lynching of the marquis de Launay, the governor of the Bastille, on 14 July 1789, a Parisian crowd hanged the controller-general of finances, Joseph-François Foullon de Doué, along with his son-in-law, a week later.

Compiling such lists of violent outbursts has led many historians, starting with Edmund Burke, to conclude that the history of the Terror is none other than the history of the Revolution, and that the two cannot be separated.[7] Here our chronological problem morphs into a definitional one. Is all violence the same? Indeed, one of the main problems with conflating the Terror with the Revolution is that it treats popular violence and state-sponsored killings as a single phenomenon. To be sure, there are some grey zones: we may never know how complicit Danton or Roland were in the September massacres.[8] But the decision to 'be terrifying *in place of* the people', nonetheless, constitutes an important and non-negligible distinction between much of the violence that occurred before *quatrevingt-treize* and that which occurred during and after. The Republican officials and soldiers who brought 'terror' to the Vendée countryside did so believing that they carried 'the law in their hands'.[9] There is a fundamental difference in the kind of authority underpinning popular versus state-sponsored acts of violence. Of course, not all state violence was literally 'authorized': after Thermidor, some of the more zealous administrators, such as Jean-Baptiste Carrier, were accused of overstepping their authority.[10] The variability of the implementation of the Terror has led Jean-Clément Martin to argue that the extreme violence of 1793–94 was in fact due to the weakness of the state, and not to its strength.[11] Even in this interpretation, however, there remains a significant difference between acts of popular violence, which tended to be sporadic and unpredictable, and state violence, which was generally more methodical and spread out over time.

One manner of determining when the Terror 'began', then, would be to identify when the state first institutionalized measures of political repression. This approach comes with its own set of challenges: as explained in the section 'Why was there a Terror?', there is no clear red line that demarcates 'terrorist' legislation or institutions from non-terrorist ones. Moreover, as historians of the Thermidorean Convention and the Directory have observed, the practices and laws we associate with the Terror did not end with the death of Robespierre. Howard Brown in particular has argued that it was the Directory's unwillingness to contain its actions within a constitutional framework that contributed heavily to destabilizing the regime.[12] In some respects, the problem of determining when the Terror ended is more intractable than identifying when it began.

But this is also a problem of a different sort. Post-Thermidor, the French revolutionaries inherited a complex set of laws, institutions, and precedents; sorting through, disentangling, and retiring parts of this repressive apparatus was, unsurprisingly, a protracted and delicate affair. Understanding how and why this apparatus came about in the first place is the real 'mystery' that continues to puzzle historians.[13]

Why 'the Terror'?

Another set of difficulties confronting scholars of the Terror concerns the word itself. First, it is a confusing label. The term originates in the demands and speeches of a host of French revolutionaries, who employed it regularly during the period that has gone down in history as 'the Terror'. But 'the Terror' has also become a category of historical analysis, employed by scholars. And these two categories, one historical, the other meta-historical, do not neatly overlap. Lexical studies of revolutionary discourse have shown that the primary spokesmen of the Terror—that is, the members of the Committee of Public Safety who most commonly addressed the Convention during this time, namely Robespierre, Saint-Just, and Billaud-Varenne—essentially stopped using the term altogether after February 1794.[14] During the six-week period that historians often identify as the 'Great Terror' (between the passage of the law of 22 Prairial [10 June 1794] and 9 Thermidor), the word was hardly used at all.

A second problem has to do with the official status of the term. Until recently, the standard narrative held that the National Convention had declared terror 'the order of the day' on 5 September 1793. But as Martin recently argued, this does not, in fact, appear to be the case. A delegation made up of representatives of the Paris Commune, the Parisian sections, and the primary Assemblies (gathered in Paris to ratify the new constitution) *requested* that the Convention issue this directive; but the *conventionnels*, following Danton's lead, only responded indirectly.[15] To be sure, this distinction may well have been lost on most people; there is considerable evidence that many revolutionary officials *believed* that the Convention had officially decreed this measure. Perhaps the strongest indication of this belief was the fact that Saint-Just introduced a bill on 13 March 1794 that made '*justice* [...] the order of the day'.[16] The members of the Committee of Public Safety thus clearly saw the need to move beyond terror, though their concept of 'justice' did not appear altogether very different.

Finally, what did the word 'terror' actually mean? A number of scholars have examined the pre-revolutionary history of this term, in the hope of identifying clear patterns of signification.[17] What we can tell simply by looking at its usage in 1793 is that it was used in many different ways. While some historians have suggested that it was the revolutionaries themselves who were 'terrified', and thus reacted in kind,[18] most uses of the term were in fact transitive: for the sans-culottes and other actors who employed it most, 'terror' was what the enemies of the Revolution were supposed to feel. But their agreement largely ended there: for some, terror was synonymous with death; for others (including, most of the time, Robespierre), terror was 'salutary', and, like the Aristotelian concept of catharsis, could bring about an inner conversion toward republicanism.[19] What these disagreements underscore, in any case, is the danger of relying excessively on the semantics (or even emotions) of 'the Terror' in an effort to understand it.

What was the Terror for?

'Out of the eleven thousand two hundred and ten decrees that the Convention issued, one third had a political purpose, and two thirds had a humane purpose.' Thus Victor Hugo assessed the Terror in his novel *Quatrevingt-treize*.[20] One can quibble with his fractions, but his basic point was fair: not every law that was passed, or institution that was created, during the time known as the Terror was part of a repressive apparatus. This was, after all, a time when the Convention introduced the metric system, invented a calendar, created neo-classical festivals, and reorganized public instruction, among other initiatives. It was also a time when the state implemented economic controls, most notably the 'law of general maximum' (29 September 1793), which fixed the prices on staple food items such as flour, butter, salt, and meat, as well as on other substances like soap, paper, and fabrics.[21] If some of these measures, such as the redistribution of confiscated land, had a political dimension, many did not.[22] So how do we reconcile (in Hugo's terms) the political and the humane efforts of this time?

It would help if we knew exactly what it was that the leaders of the Committee of Public Safety were up to. Did they have a plan? Or were the different pieces of legislation presented to the Convention simply a hotchpotch of initiatives, reflecting the various pressures they were facing? Choosing between these alternatives is no simple task: the multiple *rapports* that the spokesmen of the Committee presented to the Convention between October 1793 and July 1794 are filled with Republican exhortations, but are rather vague on details. The best one can do is to examine the institutions that were implemented during this time and try to piece together what the Committee's political goals might have been (and if they were coherent).

The first institution that demands attention is the administrative structure known as 'revolutionary government'.[23] This structure was first established on 10 October 1793, by a decree that Saint-Just presented to the Convention. It came about in a strangely indirect manner: the primary purpose of Saint-Just's measure was to suspend the constitution, ratified two months prior, though this action was not even addressed in the body of the law. Instead, the bill simply declared the French government to be 'revolutionary until peacetime'.[24]

Despite the wartime rhetoric that Saint-Just employed to justify this move, the decision to make do without a constitution was more complicated than it appeared. Even *before* the Convention had ratified the new constitution, on 10 August, in a baroque ceremony scripted by Jacques-Louis David, there were already voices clamouring for its suspension. At a meeting of the Jacobin Club, on 4 August, François Chabot laid out the obvious political reality: if the constitution were implemented, new elections would be have to be held, and the Mountain could very well lose the majority it had enjoyed in the National Convention since the 31 May—2 June purge of the Girondins.[25] Accordingly, when a deputy moved, on 11 August, that the Convention be dissolved, and new elections held, Robespierre rose to counter this proposal, warning that it could only lead to the election of a counter-revolutionary Assembly.[26]

The revolutionary government therefore largely owed its existence to the desire among Jacobin politicians to hold on to power. No doubt some genuinely feared that new elections might endanger the Republic. But military concerns did not seem to have played a major part in the decision to suspend the constitution: in his report presenting the 10 October decree, Saint-Just never even mentioned any war-related circumstances (the only 'enemies' he identified were those in government). Once in place, however, the revolutionary government was a useful political tool: in his 18 November 'Report on a mode of provisional and revolutionary government', Billaud-Varenne introduced a decree that placed all public officials (including ministers) under the supervision of the Committee of Public Safety.[27]

In the first few months of its existence, the revolutionary government was repeatedly described as 'provisional' (as the title of Billaud-Varenne's report indicates). In a speech given on what would have been Christmas Day 1793, but was now 5 nivôse, Robespierre even defined it in contrast to 'constitutional government', this time justifying its necessity as a wartime exigency.[28] In this regard, we might view revolutionary government as a kind of 'emergency' rule.[29] But as time went by, the spokesmen of the Committee of Public Safety spoke less and less about the provisional nature of this government. Neither Billaud-Varenne nor Saint-Just breathed a word about *when* the Republic would revert to constitutional rule (let alone mentioned the constitution), in their respective speeches on revolutionary government in April 1794; Saint-Just even went so far as to uncouple revolutionary government from the war.[30]

This silence could be interpreted as a sign that the Committee, or at least some of its members, had comfortably settled into dictatorship.[31] While it might be argued that the Committee, between October 1793 and July 1794, enjoyed near dictatorial powers, the term 'dictatorship' implies, at least in its modern sense (as opposed to, say, Roman usage), the indefinite exercise of power. But just because the Committee no longer promised the swift reinstatement of the constitution does not mean that it simply wished to perpetuate the status quo of revolutionary government. Indeed, such an interpretation fails to account for the remarkable number of 'state-building' measures that the Committee pursued during its brief rule. Chief among these were the classical-Republican institutions that Saint-Just and Robespierre, in particular, insisted were essential for the guarantee of political liberty.[32] Saint-Just imagined a countless number: in his ideal republic, there would be institutions for the regulation of childhood, friendship, marriage, clothing, luxury, morality, the military, and more.[33] Robespierre focused on one in particular: the cult of the Supreme Being. He presented it as the cornerstone of justice, since it would instil in man 'a rapid instinct which, without the slow assistance of reason, would lead him to do good and avoid evil'.[34]

A cynic might object that these strange and seemingly naive institutions were merely a diversion masking the Committee's true intention of staying in power as long as possible. If this was indeed the goal, then its members acted in odd ways. Robespierre largely disappeared from sight for five weeks, between 18 June and 26 July 1794: he stopped attending the Committee's nightly meetings, did not speak at the Convention, and said little at the Jacobins' club.[35] During this time, a major rift also opened up on the Committee between Collot d'Herbois, Billaud-Varenne, and (to a lesser extent) Lazare Carnot, on the one hand, and Robespierre, Saint-Just, and Georges Couthon, on the other. After a politically disastrous speech by Robespierre on 26 July at the National Convention, during which he implied that more purges were on the way, his opponents on the Committee (assisted by members of the rival Committee for General Security) sprang into action, overthrowing him and his chief supporters the next day—9 Thermidor.

The fall, and subsequent execution, of Robespierre and his faction prevents us from ever knowing how (or if) they imagined the transition to democratic government to occur. Most of the evidence, however, suggests that they conceived of 'Terror' as the necessary labour pains to give birth to a regenerated republic. What this republic would ultimately have looked like is difficult to say: it may not have had a constitution, since many Jacobins expressed the belief that the laws of nature provided a sufficient—and unsurpassable—foundation for government. In keeping with Saint-Just and Robespierre's classical-Republican interests, they seem to have imagined a form of government that relied primarily on institutions to maintain social and political order. This reliance on institutions, however, casts the law of 22 prairial and the cult of the Supreme Being in new, frightening light: rather than a temporary measure destined to speed up transition away from revolutionary government, it appears more likely to have been precisely the kind of institution on which Saint-Just and Robespierre hoped to rest the new republic.[36] In the end, what is most frightening about their utopian vision is that the reign of Justice—which Robespierre promised from atop an artificial hilltop at the Festival of the Supreme Being—may have been far more terrorizing than the reign of Terror.

WHY WAS THERE A TERROR?

Of all the questions surrounding the Terror, perhaps the most vexing concerns its cause. How did it come to pass? Did the French revolutionaries of 1793 betray the principles of 1789? Or was the Terror in some way foreordained? It has proved difficult, over the past two centuries, to answer these questions without a political bias: conservative historians have tended to lump Terror and Revolution together, while their socialist colleagues generally sought to downplay its importance (or even defend it). Leaving aside, to the extent possible, the politics of revolutionary historiography, one can group most accounts of the Terror's origins into one of the three categories: some historians suggest that it was simply a response to genuinely threatening circumstances; others argue that Terror is an inevitable part of revolution; while a third group seeks a middle way between the first two, rejecting the notion that the terror was foreordained, but examining how, in light of certain revolutionary events, it became increasingly likely.

For many twentieth-century historians, the Terror was not a question to which they gave much thought. These historians mostly took the revolutionaries' justifications for their measures at face value. With *la patrie en danger*, what else was the National Convention to do? 'Circumstances' demanded expedient, emergency action. This interpretation had the notable benefit of decoupling the Revolution as a whole from the period of the Terror, and thus, of countering a favourite strategy of conservative writers (see below).

Resting as it did on the claims of the revolutionaries themselves, it is no surprise that this argument originated in neo-Jacobin circles. It already features, for instance, in Buchez and Roux's early *Histoire parlementaire de la Révolution française*, published in the 1830s. But it was only with the dominance of Marxist historiography in the twentieth century that this thesis gained widespread acceptance. Albert Soboul offers a paradigmatic version in his assessment of the Terror as 'in essence an instrument of national and revolutionary defence against rebels and traitors'. The acceleration of the Terror with the law of 22 prairial, he suggests, 'can be explained by the special circumstances prevalent at the moment', namely the attempts made on the lives of Collot d'Herbois and Robespierre. But he does not suggest that the revolutionaries over-reacted. All in all, that Terror was nothing to be ashamed of: 'it was an important factor if victory were to be won'.[37] Even those who, like the young François Furet, did not go so far as to defend the Terror, nonetheless, accepted that it was a momentary lapse (*dérapage*) from purer revolutionary principles, largely brought about by the threat that the foreign and civil wars presented.[38]

These threats, to be sure, were anything but imaginary. At various points in 1793, the military situation on the northwestern front, then in the east and in the south, was very dire indeed. There can be little doubt that the dangers facing the nascent Republic were an important catalyst: the Terror was not simply a nefarious plan hatched fully armed out of the minds of bloodthirsty, power-hungry revolutionaries.

Acknowledging this, however, does not validate the *thèse des circonstances*. If counter-revolutionary hostility was a trigger for the terrorist laws and institutions, it did not determine the specific forms that these laws and institutions would take. The intensity of the revolutionaries' response, in particular, cannot simply be explained in terms of a reaction to external and internal threats. Evidence of this can be found, for instance, in the continuity between the Terror laws of spring 1793 and the much earlier, punitive legislation against the *émigrés*.[39] Similarly, the legal category of an 'outlaw' was not born during the debates over the Vendée uprising, but was crafted during the king's trial, without any reference to war activity.[40] When the time came to respond to counter-revolutionary violence, the revolutionaries already had a lethal arsenal of laws and inimical concepts at their disposal. The 'circumstantial' interpretation of the Terror thus skates over the question of why the revolutionaries had proved willing to devise such punitive measures even before the Republic came under fire.

The circumstantial interpretation was in many respects a response to an older, much more conservative one, which tied Terror to the Revolution from its very inception. In this reading, Terror is the necessary handmaiden of Revolution, an evil conjoined twin who cannot be cast aside. Although this interpretation has its roots in counter-revolutionary writing, it has taken a number of different forms: where early conservative authors viewed the people as inherently vicious, more recent scholars have argued that political ideology or a political 'dynamic' inherent to the revolutionary movement doomed it from the start.

'It is said the people are revolting.' 'You said it. They stink on ice.' This old Mel Brooks joke, from his *History of the World, Part I*, only slightly caricatures one of the first theories of the Terror. As we saw already with Burke, this theory looks to the outbursts of popular violence that punctuated the Revolution from July 1789 onward to claim that a political movement driven by *le peuple* could only result in massive bloodshed. This was a view that remained dominant among many writers throughout the nineteenth century. One finds it, for instance, in Thomas Carlyle's 1837 study, in which 'the People' appear as a blood-thirsty tiger.[41] It was from this work that Charles Dickens borrowed his portrayal of the savage sans-culottes in *A Tale of Two Cities*. This same distrust of the lower classes marks Hippolyte Taine's history almost half a century later (and in the shadow of the socialistic Paris Commune of 1871): he believed the French Revolution to have been hopelessly dominated by those 'who, were it not for the Revolution, would still grovel in their native filth', and who had become 'intoxicat[ed] as they dr[a]nk deep draughts from the bottomless cup of absolute power'.[42]

In addition to the profoundly elitist bias that this attitude betrays, it does not hold up well to the historical record. The chief architects of the Terror were not born in filth, as Taine would have it: they were, on the contrary, well educated, well fed, even well bred. Saint-Just and Joseph Fouché attended Oratorian *collèges*; Robespierre went to Louis-le-Grand, the same Jesuit *lycée* as Voltaire and many members of the high aristocracy. Barère, Billaud-Varenne, Danton, and Robespierre were all lawyers; Marat was a doctor, Lazare Carnot an engineer, Fouché a professor, and Collot d'Herbois a theatre director. And they were not exceptional, in this regard: as Donald M. G. Sutherland has noted, 'the *sans-culottes* [...] were a heterogeneous social group, who were often the elite of their neighbourhoods and trades'.[43]

When conservative historians addressed this issue (if they did at all), they generally argued that revolutionary politicians simply did the bidding of an unruly mob. 'Let the Convention, if it pleases, pompously install itself as sovereign, and grind out decrees', Taine wrote. 'It makes no difference; regular or irregular, the government still marches on in the hands of those who hold the sword.'[44] But this argument, too, is hard to sustain. The *conventionnels* proved extremely adept at redirecting popular (mostly economic) demands toward their own (mostly political) aims. When the Parisian sections and representatives of the primary Assemblies (which had just ratified the Constitution) stormed into the Convention to demand that 'terror be made the order of the day', they did not have Robespierre's republic of virtue in mind: they wanted harsh measures taken against grain hoarders and greedy merchants.[45] Furthermore, after September 1793, the sans-culottes ceased to play a major role in revolutionary politics: there would be no more popular insurrections, or *journées*, until 12–13 germinal III (1–2 April 1795).

A more widespread interpretation of the Terror's origins holds that the political and philosophical *ideas* championed in 1789 were the cause of the violence committed in 1793–94. This argument, too, has its roots in counter-revolutionary historiography: all the while castigating the Jacobins as uneducated brutes, Taine accused them of obsessing over Rousseau's *Social Contract*.[46] This is the text to which many historians still point when searching for the intellectual sources of the Terror: Rousseau is the primary bugbear, for instance, in Jacob Talmon's 1952 *Origins of Totalitarian Democracy*. But it was François Furet who developed the Rousseauist thesis most fully, by linking the arguments of the *Social Contract* not only to the Jacobins, but also to the initial politics of the Revolution.[47] For Furet, it was Rousseau's 'democratic ideology', resting as it did on the concept of undivided sovereignty (the general will), that inexorably led the French Revolution down the path to Terror. In Keith Baker's reformulation of this argument, the National Assembly, in 1789, chose 'the language of political will, rather than of social reason [...] of absolute sovereignty, rather than of government limited by the rights of man—which is to say that, in the long run, it was opting for the Terror'.[48]

In the wake of the bicentennial, this 'revisionist' interpretation of the Terror was widely accepted, particularly by Anglo-American scholars, though it has since come under fire from numerous quarters. Some have questioned the premise that the French revolutionaries, in 1789, were 'Rousseauist' in any meaningful sense of the term: in his 1996 *Becoming a Revolutionary*, Timothy Tackett claimed that few deputies of the National Assembly were at all familiar with the *Social Contract*.[49] Furet's interpretation of Rousseau has also been questioned, with Samuel Moyn showing how Furet drew mostly on Claude Lefort's theory of totalitarianism, rather than Rousseau's own work, in his analysis.[50] Finally, it is far from clear that the Jacobins were even that inspired by Rousseau's political theory: it was, in fact, the Girondin deputies who drew on Rousseauist principles in the debates over the constitution of 1793, whereas the Jacobins turned instead to natural right theory, and were openly dismissive of *la volonté générale*.[51]

The history of revolutions after 1789 (and particularly after 1917) led some scholars to hypothesize that, since political terror was not a unique feature of the French Revolution, perhaps it was an inevitable part of every revolution. This argument was first developed in sociological studies, most notably Crane Brinton's *The Anatomy of Revolution* (1938). As a historian of the French Revolution, Brinton claimed to offer a 'scientific' explanation for why all revolutions went through different phases, including terror. Echoes of this social-scientific approach could still be heard in the 1990s: in his study of *Revolution and Rebellion in the Early Modern World*, for instance, Jack Goldstone argued that 'the growing pursuit of internal and external enemies—the Reign of Terror and the war—were the natural outcome of the terms in which the revolutionary power struggles were framed [...] the Reign of Terror was an inherent part of the process of revolution'.[52]

The thesis that the French Revolution launched a process that inexorably led to the Terror has also found favour among some contemporary historians. Donald Sutherland and Arno Mayer have described the Terror as the unavoidable conclusion of a dialect of revolution and counter-revolution.[53] Invoking a 'revolutionary dynamic', Patrice Gueniffey generalized this claim to all revolutions: Terror, he wrote, 'undoubtedly lies as a potentiality at the heart of every voluntaristic enterprise, as a recourse to violence to overcome the resistance of people and objects'.[54]

Owing to their sweeping nature, statements of this sort are difficult to assess at the general level, though they betray a worrisome faith in teleology. The particularities of Gueniffey's argument, however, reveal more obvious problems. In his view, terrorist violence is strictly opposed to legality: 'it is the deployment of violence unfettered by any legal framework [...] The terror is the universal and indefinite reign of the arbitrary'.[55] But this definition is contradicted by the fact that the deputies of the National Convention did in fact put into place a remarkably robust legal framework to prosecute their enemies (and were strongly opposed to any state of *anomie*). As we saw, this was precisely a distinguishing feature of state-sponsored terror, in contrast to the sporadic episodes of popular violence: most victims of the Terror were executed according to laws. The most notorious of these was the 19 March 1793, *hors-la-loi* decree, which declared that anyone caught 'arms in hand' resisting French Republican forces could simply be dragged before a three-person military commission, identified, and shot within 24 hours. According to the historian Donald Greer, this law was responsible for the majority of executions during the Terror.[56]

Passed in reaction to the deadly riots in western France against mandatory conscription, this law does support the broader historiographical claim that counter-revolutionary violence played some role in the establishment of the Terror. But as shown, with regard to the 'circumstantial' argument, the foreign and civil wars alone cannot explain why the Republican reaction—the Terror—took the forms it did.

A third group of scholars seek to find a middle way between the all-or-nothing theories described above. With the 'circumstantial' historians, they agree that it is hyperbolic to argue that the Revolution careened toward the Terror from the moment it began. But with the proponents of the 'inevitability' thesis, they also recognize that, by a certain point in revolutionary history, the gears of the Terror do seem to have been set into motion. When (and what) exactly that moment was is hotly debated; but there is an agreement among these scholars that the Terror cannot be neatly excised from the history of the Revolution. From a certain point onward, the revolutionaries appear to have become caught in an ever-expanding logic of legal repression. This was the logic that led Robespierre, in December 1792, to insist that the execution of Louis XVI was only a 'cruel exception' to his abolitionist principles, but that later made him a staunch defender of the Terror; or the logic that led the *conventionnels* to restrict the 'outlaw' decree of March 1793 to the leaders of insurrection, only to describe the peasant fighters as 'a rebel race in need of eradication' five months later.[57] Essentially, this was the logic that culminated in article 6 of the law of 22 prairial, which presented a laundry list of political crimes that were all punishable by death.

This logic did not come down from on high: the Terror, as David Andress has argued, 'was the outcome of a process, not its preordained goal'.[58] At every step, specific individuals were responsible for the decision to expand legal categories further. Others might well have chosen to act differently. But one can still speak of 'a logic', since the growth in potential targets of the Terror did not occur in an arbitrary fashion. New groups were identified based on their family resemblance to old ones: the leaders of the Vendée rebellion were 'like' the king, in that they, too, were betraying the Republic. What greatly facilitated the expansion of the Terror's legal dragnet was the existence of fairly amorphous criminal categories, such as the counter-revolutionary, the enemy of humanity, and later, the 'enemy of the people'. As legal scholars have argued, the tendency for such categories to gradually expand is one of the dark hallmarks of exceptional justice.[59]

But at what point, then, did the Revolution embark on the 'process' that pointed toward, if it did not inexorably lead to, the Terror? The problem, for historians, is that there is a multiplicity of options. Some have identified the king's flight to Varennes (on 20–1 June 1791), and the subsequent Champ-de-Mars massacre, as the crucial turning point in the path toward Terror.[60] The French declaration of war against Austria in

April 1792 also considerably raised the stakes of political dissent, and led to a tightening of laws against *émigrés* and emigration.[61] Then in August, as a Prussian-led force was invading, the monarchy fell, ushering in a republic and a whole new political discourse, classical republicanism, whose contributions to the violent rhetoric of the Terror have been catalogued by Keith Baker.[62] The sacking of the Tuileries also resulted in a great deal of popular resentment toward the king's guards: Sophie Wahnich has argued that the September massacres were largely an act of revenge for the deaths of 10 August.[63] Finally, the king's trial itself, in November–December 1792, provided the *conventionnels* with their first major legislative challenge, a challenge that involved devising legal arguments for executing a sovereign. These arguments would provide the legal framework for political repression during the Terror.[64]

In addition to their multiplicity, these events are also defined by their variety. As we saw, some introduced new political discourses; others established new emotional dynamics. What is more, not all transformations of revolutionary culture were tied to discrete events. William Reddy has shown how the emotional tensions brought about by a culture of 'sentimentalism' aggravated the relations between leading Jacobin figures; in a related vein, Marisa Linton recently argued that a shared belief in the importance of personal virtue underpinned the mutual denunciations of counter-revolutionary activity.[65] Both scholars focus on aspects of revolutionary culture that had been present well before 1789, but which became increasingly prominent over the course of the revolution.

Considered together, the list of events and cultural currents that may have contributed to the Terror is both long and perplexing. How is one to determine which elements were more influential than others? As they all occurred in sequence, it is nearly impossible to isolate the impact of a single factor. Perhaps we need to adopt a subtler model of historical causality; after all, there is no reason why a complex phenomenon such as the Terror should have only one cause. But even if we accept that the Terror was brought about by a multiplicity of factors, we are still left with the question of why so many discourses, practices, and emotional tensions were encouraging violence. What made political repression such a palatable, even desirable option? This question might seem to encourage a reassessment of the 'inevitability' thesis: if so many arrows were pointing toward the Terror, how could it *not* have occurred? But likelihood is not necessity; just because the Terror may have been causally over-determined does not imply that it was bound to occur. In conclusion, therefore, I will explore a slightly different angle: how might the Terror have been avoided?

Was the Terror Avoidable?

The political violence that came to characterize the French Revolution during year II has often been contrasted with the relative absence of similar repression in the American case. Hannah Arendt famously compared both revolutions and found the American more admirable, as it 'remained committed to the foundation of freedom and the establishment of lasting institutions', whereas the French, believing that 'all is permitted', 'unleash[ed] a stream of boundless violence'.[66] Her comparison is a bit forced: the American Revolution in fact witnessed a number of casualties per capita that was comparable to the French,[67] and in France state violence was the result not of lawlessness but, on the contrary, of particularly repressive legislation. That said, it is true that the Americans steered clear of enacting punitive laws. On occasion, they came close, as in the case of the Alien and Sedition Acts of 1798. But the Federalists and Republican-Democrats never got to the point of sending each other to the gallows.

If we are to make this comparison truly meaningful, however, we must broaden its geographical and chronological scope.[68] Indeed, when placed alongside the English Civil War, the Glorious Revolution, the Haitian Revolution, and then the series of (European) nineteenth-century and (global) twentieth-century revolutions, the political violence of the French Revolution no longer appears quite so unusual. Of course, many of the revolutions that came after 1789 took the French as their model, Terror and all. But more generally, when viewed within this portrait gallery of revolutions, it is the American case that appears exceptional.

The purpose of this comparative survey is not to heap laurels on the American Revolution, but rather to ask how it managed to avoid the otherwise common (though not inevitable) turn to political violence. Here it may be worth considering less the political, than the judicial context, of the American Revolution. Indeed, one of the peculiarities of the American case was the strong legacy of English common law in the former colonies. Two of the state declarations (written after independence was declared) insisted on the continuity of this legal tradition in the new country: article 3 of the Maryland Declaration, for instance, affirms that the inhabitants of this state 'are entitled to the common law of England, and the trial by Jury, according that law, and to the benefit of such of the English statutes, as existed at the time of their first emigration'.[69] As can be seen here, one of the key features of common law that the Americans wished to preserve was its robust set of judicial forms. Indeed, all of the American Declarations include the right of a trial by jury, the right not to be subject to warrantless searches, the right against self-incrimination, and the right against excessive bail. These 'rights' were the hard-won trophies of English political struggles, which had since been enshrined in common law practice.

The French had no similar legal tradition to fall back on.[70] Article 7 of the 'Declaration of the Rights of Man and of the Citizen' stipulates that: 'No person shall be accused, arrested, or imprisoned except in the cases and according to the forms prescribed by law', but does not describe what those forms should be.[71] What is more, the French included far more qualifiers in their declarations: the rights to liberty, property, religious worship, and even expression all came with potential restrictions.[72] In the case of freedom of expression, article 11 notes that: 'Every citizen may [...] speak, write, and print with freedom, but shall be responsible for such abuses of this freedom as shall be defined by law.' By contrast, the Americans were much more full-throated in the defence of this right: 'the freedom of the press is one of the great bulwarks of liberty, and can never be restrained but by despotick governments', proclaims the Declaration of Virginia (article XIV).

If the American Revolution managed to steer clear of state-sponsored political violence, then, it may have had less to do with fundamental differences in its political culture, and more to do with the specificity of its judicial culture. The Americans faced many of the same pressures, threats, and worries as the French (and as other revolutionaries before and after them); but their fierce attachment to a legal system that afforded untouchable rights to defendants served as a firewall against inflamed political passions.

Whichever factors we identify as the more important causes of the French Revolution, we ought accordingly to remember that, in practice, the Terror boiled down to the amending of judicial forms to facilitate the prosecution of suspected counter-revolutionaries. In this regard, it could be argued that the causal sequence that led politicians to enact the Terror legislation matters less than the fact that the justice system was insufficiently robust to resist this kind of tampering. There were many roads to Terror; the fact that the Terror occurred was ultimately due to the failure of the only safeguard which could have prevented it. The Terror was not a French abnormality: it is rather that the French legal culture was particularly ill-designed to resist its coming.

Notes

1. Jones, *The Great Nation: France from Louis XV to Napoleon* (London, 2002), 471. See also Michel Biard, 'Les rouages de la Terreur', in *Les politiques de la Terreur, 1793–1794*, ed. M. Biard (Rennes, 2008), 24.

2. See esp. Bronislaw Baczko, *Ending the Terror: The French Revolution After Robespierre* (Cambridge, 1994); and Baczko, 'The Terror Before the Terror?' in *The Terror*, ed. Keith Baker, vol. 4 of *The French Revolution and the Creation of Modern Political Culture* (Oxford, 1987–94), 19–38.

3. See Furet, 'Terror', in *A Critical Dictionary of the French Revolution*, ed. François Furet and Mona Ozouf, trans. Arthur Goldhammer (Cambridge, MA, 1989) [henceforth abbreviated *CDFR*], 143.

4. For a controversial account of this connection, see Sophie Wahnich, *La Liberté ou la mort: essai sur la Terreur et le terrorisme* (Paris, 2003).

5. 10 March 1793; in *Archives parlementaires de 1787 à 1860*, 102 vols, ed. M. J. Mavidal et al. (Paris, 1862–), 60:62–3 [hereafter abbreviated *AP*].

6. See David Andress, *Massacre at the Champ de Mars: Popular Dissent and Political Culture in the French Revolution* (Woodbridge, 2000); see also Timothy Tackett, *When the King Took Flight* (Cambridge, MA, 2009).

7. For Burke, the paradigmatic event of the French Revolution was the 1789 October days, when the *poissardes* (market women), along with a crowd of men, invaded the Versailles palace: see *Reflections on the Revolution in France* (1790). See more on this thesis in the section 'Why was there Terror?'

8. Pierre Caron, *Massacres de Septembre* (Paris, 1935).

9. Robespierre, speech of 8 May 1793, at the Jacobin society; in *Œuvres de Maximilien Robespierre*, ed. Société des études robespierristes, 10 vols (Ivry, 2000), 9:491 [henceforth abbr. *Rob.*].

10. See Baczko, *Ending the Terror*.

11. Martin, *Violence et révolution: Essai sur la naissance d'un mythe national* (Paris, 2006).

12. Brown, *Ending the French Revolution: Violence, Justice, and Repression from the Terror to Napoleon* (Charlottesville, 2006).

13. Timothy Tackett, 'Interpreting the Terror', *French Historical Studies* 24 (2001), 569–78.

14. See Dan Edelstein, *The Terror of Natural Right: Republicanism, the Cult of Nature, and the French Revolution* (Chicago, 2009), ch. 5.

15. Martin, *Violence et révolution*, 186–93.

16. 'Rapport sur les factions de l'étranger', 23 ventôse an II (13 March 1794), in Louis-Antoine de Saint-Just, *Œuvres complètes*, ed. Michèle Duval (Paris, 1984) [henceforth abbr. *SJ*], 736; emphasis added.

17. See notably George Armstrong Kelly, 'Conceptual Sources of the Terror', *Eighteenth-Century Studies* 14, no. 1 (1980), 18–36; and Ronald Schechter, 'Conceptions of Terror in Eighteenth-Century Europe', in Michael Laffan and Max Weiss (eds), *Facing Fear: The History of an Emotion in Global Perspective* (Princeton, 2012), 31–54.

18. See for instance R. R. Palmer: 'The Terror was Born of Fear, from the Terror in which Men Already Lived', in *Twelve Who Ruled: The Year of the Terror in the French Revolution* ([1941] Princeton, 1989), 56.

19. On terror as catharsis, see Kelly, 'Conceptual Sources of the Terror'.

20. *Quatrevingt-treize* (Paris, 1992), 193–4.

21. See Jean-Pierre Gross, *Fair Shares for All: Jacobin Egalitarianism in Practice* (Cambridge, 2003).

22. See Saint-Just's 'Rapport sur les personnes incarcérées', *SJ*, 705. More generally, see P. M. Jones, "The 'Agrarian Law': Schemes for Land Redistribution during the French Revolution," *Past and Present* 133 (1991), 96–133.

23. On revolutionary government, see Furet's article on this topic in *CDFR*; Carla Hesse, 'The Law of the Terror', *MLN* 114, no. 4 (1999), 702–18; and my *Terror of Natural Right*, chs 4–5.

24. See Saint-Just's 'Rapport sur la nécessité de déclarer le gouvernement révolutionnaire jusqu'à la paix', *SJ*, 520–30; AP, 76:315.

25. See Alphonse Aulard (ed.), *La société des Jacobins: recueil de documents pour l'histoire du club des Jacobins de Paris*, 6 vols (Paris, 1889–97), 5:328.

26. See *Rob.*, 10:65.

27. See his 'Rapport sur un mode de gouvernement provisoire et révolutionnaire', 28 brumaire an II (18 November 1793); *AP*, 79:451–57; more particularly, see section II, art. 2. On Billaud-Varenne, see notably John M. Burney, 'The Fear of the Executive and the Threat of Conspiracy: Billaud-Varenne's Terrorist Rhetoric in the French Revolution, 1788–1794', *French History* 5, no. 2 (1991), 143–63; and Françoise Brunel's 'Introduction' to her edition of Billaud-Varenne's 1795 *Principes régénérateurs du système social* (Paris, 1992).

28. 'Rapport sur les principes du gouvernement révolutionnaire', 5 nivôse an II (25 December 1793), *Rob.*, 10:277.

29. See Hesse, 'Law of the Terror', 708.

30. For Saint-Just, see his 'Rapport sur la police générale ... ' 26 germinal an II (15 April 1794), in *SJ*, 809; for Billaud-Varenne, see his 'Rapport sur la théorie du gouvernement démocratique', 1 floréal an II (20 April 1794), in *Histoire parlementaire de la Révolution française*, 40 vols, ed. P. J. B. Buchez and P. C. Roux (Paris, 1834–38), 32: 349.

31. This is the view, notably, of Robert R. Palmer, in his (generally excellent) introduction to the Terror, *Twelve Who Ruled*, 70.

32. I discuss the role of institutions in Jacobin political thought (and some of the relevant secondary sources) in *Terror of Natural Right*, ch. 4.

33. See his 'Fragments des *Institutions républicaines*', in *SJ*.

34. See 'Sur les rapports des idées religieuses et morales avec les principes républicaines, et sur les fêtes nationales', *Rob.*, 10:452–53.

35. See Peter McPhee, *Robespierre: A Revolutionary Life* (New Haven, CT, 2012), 207.

36. Neo-Jacobin historians (see below) have argued that the law of 22 prairial was merely a reaction to the assassination attempts on Collot d'Herbois and Robespierre, but as Patrice Gueniffey has shown, the plan to expedite the proceedings of the revolutionary tribunal predates these attempts: see Gueniffey, *Politique de la Terreur*, ch. 10.

37. Soboul, *The French Revolution, 1787–1799*, trans. Alan Forrest and Colin Jones (New York, 1974), citations at 388, 386, 389.

38. See François Furet and Denis Richet, *La Révolution française* (Paris, 1973).

39. See Anne Simonin, *Le Déshonneur dans la république: une histoire de l'indignité, 1791–1958* (Paris, 2008).

40. Edelstein, *Terror of Natural Right*, ch. 3.

41. 'Ye People, in a state of Insurrection! Blood is shed, blood must be answered for [...] for it is as with the Tiger in that; he has only to begin', *The French Revolution*, 3 vols (New York, 1871), 2:247; see also 141.

42. See Hippolyte Taine, *The French Revolution*, trans. John Durand (Indianapolis, 2002), 3 vols, 2:653–4. The original French title of Taine's work was *Les Origines de la France contemporaine*, 5 vols.

43. Sutherland, *France, 1789–1815: Revolution and Counterrevolution* (Oxford, 1986), 194.

44. Taine, *French Revolution*, 2:687.

45. For a discussion of the primary and secondary sources relating to this *journée*, see my *Terror of Natural Right*, ch. 3.

46. Taine, *French Revolution*, bk 6, ch. 1 (3:901 ff).

47. See Furet, *Interpreting the French Revolution*, trans. Elborg Forster (Cambridge and Paris, 1981).

48. Baker, *Inventing the French Revolution: Essays on French Political Culture in the Eighteenth Century* (Cambridge, 1990), 305.

49. Tackett, *Becoming a Revolutionary: The Deputies of the French National Assembly and the Emergence of a Revolutionary Culture (1789–1790)* (Princeton, 1996).

50. Moyn, 'On the Intellectual Origins of François Furet's Masterpiece', *The Tocqueville Review/La Revue Tocqueville* 29, no. 2 (2008), 1–20.

51. See Edelstein, *Terror of Natural Right*, ch. 4.

52. Goldstone, *Revolution and Rebellion in the Early Modern World* (Berkeley, 1991), 432–3.

53. Sutherland, *France, 1789–1815: Revolution and Counterrevolution*; and Arno Mayer, *The Furies: Violence and Terror in the French and Russian Revolutions* (Princeton, 2000).

54. Gueniffey, *Politique de la Terreur*, 54; see also 14.

55. Ibid., 32.

56. Greer, *The Incidence of the Terror During the French Revolution: A Statistical Interpretation* (Cambridge, MA, 1935), 14.

57. For Robespierre, see 3 December 1792 speech at the Convention (*Rob.*, 9:129–30). For the 19 March decree, see *AP*, 60:331, and for the August 1793 decree, see *AP*, 70:91.

58. Andress, *The Terror: The Merciless War for Freedom in Revolutionary France* (New York, 2006), 5.

59. See e.g. Michael Ignatieff, *The Lesser Evil: Political Ethics in an Age of Terror* (Princeton, 2004), or Bruce Ackerman, *Before the Next Attack: Preserving Civil Liberties in an Age of Terrorism* (New Haven, CT, 2007).

60. See esp. Tackett, *When the King Took Flight*. Andress also begins his account of the Terror with this episode.

61. See Ozouf, 'Emigrés', *CDFR*. More generally, see David A. Bell, *The First Total War: Napoleon's Europe and the Birth of Warfare as We Know It* (Boston, 2007).

62. Baker, 'Transformations of Classical Republicanism in Eighteenth-Century France', *Journal of Modern History* 73, no. 1 (2001), 32–53.

63. Wahnich, *Liberté ou la mort*.

64. See Edelstein, *Terror of Natural Right*, ch. 3.

65. See Reddy, *The Navigation of Feeling: A Framework for the History of Emotions* (Cambridge, 2001); and Linton, *Choosing Terror: Virtue, Friendship, and Authenticity in the French Revolution* (Oxford, 2013).

66. Arendt, *On Revolution* ([1963] London, 2006), 92.

67. See Andress, *The Terror*, 2.

68. See notably Suzanne Desan, Lynn Hunt, and William Max Nelson (eds), *The French Revolution in Global Perspective* (Ithaca, 2013).

69. For the full text of this declaration (and the others cited here), see http://avalon.law.yale.edu/17th_century/ma02.asp. The Delaware declaration contains a similar passage in article 25.

70. On French legal culture, see notably Pierre Lascoumes, Pierrette Poncela, and Pierre Lenoël, *Au nom de l'ordre: Une histoire politique du code pénal* (Paris, 1989), and Jean-Marie Carbasse, *Histoire du droit pénal et de la justice criminelle* (Paris, 2000).

71. On the French Declaration, see in general Stéphane Rials, *La Déclaration des droits de l'homme et du citoyen* (Paris, 1988). The classic work comparing French and American state declarations is Georg Jellinek, *The Declaration of the Rights of Man and of Citizens* (1895). A more recent comparison can be found in Marcel Gauchet, *La Révolution des droits de l'homme* (Paris, 1989).

72. For a more detailed comparison of the French and American declarations, see David Andress, *1789: The Threshold of the Modern Age* (New York, 2008).

SELECTED READING

Andress, David, *The Terror: The Merciless War for Freedom in Revolutionary France* (New York, 2006).

Baczko, Bronislaw, *Ending the Terror: The French Revolution After Robespierre* (Cambridge, 1994).

Baker, Keith, 'Transformations of Classical Republicanism in Eighteenth-Century France', *Journal of Modern History* 73, no. 1 (2001), 32–53.

Bell, David A., *The First Total War: Napoleon's Europe and the Birth of Warfare as We Know It* (Boston, 2007).

Edelstein, Dan, *The Terror of Natural Right: Republicanism, the Cult of Nature, and the French Revolution* (Chicago, 2009).

Furet, François, *Interpreting the French Revolution*, trans. Elborg Forster (Cambridge and Paris, 1981).

Greer, Donald, *The Incidence of the Terror During the French Revolution: A Statistical Interpretation* (Cambridge, MA, 1935).

Gueniffey, Patrice, *La Politique de la Terreur: essai sur la violence révolutionnaire (1789–1794)* (Paris, 2000).

Hesse, Carla, 'The Law of the Terror', *MLN* 114, no. 4 (1999), 702–18.

Martin, Jean-Clément, *Violence et révolution: Essai sur la naissance d'un mythe national* (Paris, 2006).

Palmer, R. R, *Twelve Who Ruled: The Year of the Terror in the French Revolution* (1941; Princeton, 1989)

Simonin, Anne, *Le Déshonneur dans la république: une histoire de l'indignité, 1791–1958* (Paris, 2008).

Sutherland, D. M. G., *France, 1789–1815: Revolution and Counterrevolution* (Oxford, 1986).

Wahnich, Sophie, *La Liberté ou la mort: essai sur la Terreur et le terrorisme* (Paris, 2003).

CHAPTER 27

TERROR AND POLITICS

MARISA LINTON

EVEN after over two hundred years the Terror in the French Revolution remains a controversial subject, one that points to political and philosophical dilemmas which remain unresolved to this day. Within France itself the Terror left divisions in society and politics that can still be traced. This chapter traces some of the earlier debates on the Terror, primarily between Marxists and revisionists. It then examines how a new generation of historians is seeking to revise our understanding of the complex politics of the Terror.

WHAT WAS THE TERROR?

The definition of the Terror is problematic. Some aspects of the Terror have assumed an almost mythic status: even people who know very little about the French Revolution identify it with the drama of the guillotine, though all too often they assume that the guillotine was in daily use throughout the Revolution. People who know a little more may identify the Terror with the Year II of the Republic (from 22 September 1793 to 21 September 1794) or, more specifically, the period of the so-called Jacobin Republic, that is, the time from June 1793 to July 1794 when members of the Parisian Jacobin Club played a leading role in government. Though the so-called 'Jacobin Terror' is the best known, indeed, the most notorious, it was far from the only form of revolutionary terror. The early stages of terror were characterized by popular and street violence, much of it carried out by radical Paris militants, known as the sans-culottes. The most notorious incident of popular violence was that of the September Massacres, which began on 2 September 1792, shortly after the overthrow of the monarchy, and against an atmosphere of rising panic at the prospect of Paris being at the mercy of the invading armies. Over the course of several days some 1200 people were taken out of the Paris prisons by bands of men who appointed themselves their judges—and executioners. It was partly in response to such episodes of street violence that the revolutionary leaders adopted coercive forms of government. As the Jacobin leader, Danton put it: 'Let us be terrible in order to stop the people from being so.'[1]

Though the Jacobin Republic is often seen as synonymous with the Terror, one of the most significant pieces of 'terrorist' legislation was put in place during the spring of 1793, before the Jacobins came to power. On 19 March 1793 a decree was passed by the Convention whereby insurgents captured with 'arms in their hands' were to be put to death within twenty-four hours, with no right of appeal. This law was passed to respond to the beginnings of the revolt in the Vendée. This revolt escalated into a full-scale civil war. The exact numbers of those who perished in the Vendée cannot be precisely calculated, but it has been estimated that up to 250,000 insurgents and 200,000 Republicans met their deaths in a war in which both sides suffered appalling atrocities. By contrast, the numbers guillotined by order of the Revolutionary Tribunal were relatively small. The total number of death sentences in Paris was 2639. Beyond Paris a further 14,000 people were sentenced to death following some form of trial; though to that figure we must add, together with those who died in the Vendée, those who were killed elsewhere without legal process, and the many people who died in the prisons of poor sanitation, overcrowding, and infection.[2]

How Debates About the Terror Have Changed

For much of the twentieth century, debates about the Terror were dominated by historians whose attitudes were strongly informed by their own political views. For patriotic socialists and Marxists, leading scholars of the Revolution, including Jean Jaurès, Albert Mathiez, Georges Lefebvre and Albert Soboul, the Terror was the necessary means by which France avoided defeat in the most critical period of the war, from spring 1793 to July 1794: as such it was the price that had to be paid for the Revolution, and France, to survive. According to this perspective the Terror was the logical consequence of 'the force of circumstances'.[3] This phrase was taken from the words of Saint-Just, who declared: 'In effect, the force of circumstances leads us perhaps to consequences which we had never before considered.'[4] Thus, external pressures obliged the Jacobins to choose terror.

In the 1970s there was a reaction against this traditional historiography led by François Furet whose political opposition to the traditional French Left coloured his polemic against the 'apologists' for the Terror. He would have no truck with the idea that the Terror was a pragmatic response to the need to reverse the military disasters of 1793. According to Furet the Terror was already inherent in the ideology of 1789; it emanated out of Rousseau's notion of the 'general will', above all, in the idea that in the name of 'liberty' and 'equality' one section of society could exercise domination over the rest.[5] For Furet there was no sense in which there could be any justification for the Terror, rather the Terror was the outward sign that the Revolution and its ideology had failed.[6] Furet's writing was received with enthusiasm in the 1970s and 1980s when intellectuals were struggling to reject the monolithic old politics of the Left. Furet's work had a profound impact on the ways in which subsequent historians have addressed the ideology of the Revolution and its relationship to the concept of terror. His work inspired the opening up of the study of political culture, and political language.[7] It had a more negative impact on the study of social and economic aspects of the Revolution, particularly the role of the sans-culottes.

The early twenty-first century has seen the beginnings of a reaction against Furet's focus on ideological and linguistic aspects of the Revolution. There has been a renewed interest in the social history of the Revolution, though without the rigid class categories employed by earlier Marxist historians.[8] In another rejection of the Furetist approach, a major school of thought has emphasized the seriousness of the counter-revolution, and its impact on the way in which revolutionary ideology shifted and radicalized in response to this challenge.[9] There has been a revival of the 'force of circumstances' thesis, though now the subject is approached more dispassionately, without the vituperative disagreements that characterized much of the twentieth-century historiography of the Revolution.[10] Some historians have been prepared to reassert the claim that overall the Revolution left a positive legacy, though few would go so far as to lay claim to the Terror as one of those positive effects.[11]

Whilst controversy about the causes and nature of the Terror shows no sign of abating, in recent years it has moved in different directions. Interest in the relationship between Enlightenment ideology and revolutionary terror continues, and has been explored in a number of studies, building on the influential work of Keith Baker.[12] Attention has shifted from Rousseau's concept of the 'general will' to the concept of nature: Mary Ashburn Miller has studied the connections between the language of violent nature and revolution, whilst Dan Edelstein has analysed the links between terror and natural law.[13]

Other historians, uneasy at approaches that explain the Terror principally in terms of ideology, have sought answers elsewhere, in the interface of relationships between politics, ideology, tactics, emotions and the role of individuals. Studies by Jean-Clément Martin, Tim Tackett, Annie Jourdan and Guillaume Mazeau amongst others have been re-examining the 'mythologizing' of the Terror and rejecting monocausal explanations. In their different ways they stress both the multiplicity of forms of terror, and the diversity of people's experiences of the Revolution.[14] Martin has argued that the Terror itself came about partly as a consequence of the political weakness of the State and the Jacobins' shaky hold on power. The Terror was not only about the recourse to actual violence, it was also calculatedly, about the *threat* of violence. Jourdan has stressed the ways in which the language of Terror was used as a rhetorical device to intimidate enemies. Both Martin and Jourdan have argued that too much of what is commonly perceived as terror was more a rhetoric than a reality, and that the revolutionary leaders envisaged the political violence which they established through legislation as being about enforcing justice, albeit a harsh justice.[15] Much of the evidence regarding the legalized recourse to terror bears out this view. In most cases brought before the Revolutionary Tribunal, people had some chance to mount a legal defence, and overall, only just over half the people it tried were sentenced to death. Even after the Law of 22 Prairial was passed, one in four defendants escaped death.[16] There has also been a particularly rich anglophone tradition of historiography that has delved into local and departmental archives to bring to light the diversity of provincial experiences of the Terror, including studies by Peter McPhee, Colin Lucas, Donald Sutherland, Richard Cobb, and Bill Edmunds.[17] Taken together, the work of these historians draws a picture of a terror that is far more ad hoc and responsive to contingent events and the context of war and betrayal, than the traditional image of an ideologically coherent 'reign of Terror' masterminded by Robespierre and his fellow Jacobins.

The very name 'the Terror' implies that terror was a unified system of government. The reality was somewhat different. As the Jacobin Levasseur later recalled, 'No one had dreamt of establishing a system of terror. It established itself by force of circumstances; no one's will organized it but everyone's will contributed to its creation.'[18] Jean-Clément Martin has demonstrated that, contrary to a claim that has routinely been made, the Jacobins never made 'terror the order of the day'.[19] This refers to the events on 5 September 1793 when crowds of sans-culottes invaded the Convention. During the following days, acting under pressure from the Paris militants, a series of measures were passed, including the Law of Suspects (which gave sweeping powers to arrest a wide range of 'suspects'), and the Law of the General Maximum (to regulate prices). Despite this, the Convention, including its Jacobin members, resisted the efforts of the sans-culottes to make it formally decree that it was adopting 'Terror'. Therefore, rather than refer to 'the Terror' it may well be more accurate (though linguistically ponderous) to speak of a 'recourse to terror'.

INDIVIDUALS AND EMOTIONS IN REVOLUTIONARY POLITICS

Current thinking amongst historians of the Terror has been turning away from overarching schematic explanations, based on such overall categories as class or ideology. There is a new concern to explore the role of individual agency, the interplay between emotions and politics, and the experience of revolution. When we examine revolutionary politics at the level of individuals, it becomes evident that ideology alone does not explain the choices that individual Jacobins made. They were subject to a range of conflicting influences, including personal ties, friendship, enmity, trust, distrust, loyalty, betrayal, and the need to maintain a revolutionary 'identity'.

It is no easy task to uncover the multitude of factors that shaped the mindset of individuals in the past. Historians are confronted by two principal problems. The first is the shortage of source material, particularly of sources that reveal the private lives and thoughts of their writers. The second problem is how to avoid taking an anachronistic approach to how people of the past thought. Should we assume that they thought like us? Why should they have done so? An approach taken by a previous generation of historians was the study of mentalities, developed by the Annales school historians, Marc Bloch and Lucien Febvre. Michel Vovelle's work on revolutionary mentalities applied this kind of approach to the study of revolutionary politics.[20] One of the difficulties with the study of mentalities is that its focus is more on a kind of 'collective mindset' (artificial though that concept necessarily is) than on the study of many individual mentalities: thus it tells us more about group attitudes than the thinking of specific individuals. The English historian Richard Cobb also did original work on the revolutionary mentality, though from his own idiosyncratic perspective, unaligned to any particular school of historical thought. His focus was on sans-culottes and Jacobins in the provinces, where one man might come to dominate a local community through his political networks and affiliations. In wrestling with the problem of the shortage of documents dealing with private life, Cobb concluded that: 'We must resign ourselves to the fact that the private individual almost completely eludes us, a fact that spares us the difficult task of trying to separate the public image of the revolutionary man from the one he presented to intimate friends and associates.'[21] Despite Cobb's cautionary judgement, it is only through attempting to reconstruct the complex relationship between the private individual and his public image, that we can get closer to an understanding of what drove people to embrace radical politics and, ultimately, terror. We need, therefore, to turn to new methods and approaches in an effort to reconstruct the mental world of the French revolutionaries in all its dimensions—political, ideological, personal, and emotional.

My own research has shown that friendship played a key role in both Jacobin ideology and politics.[22] The revolutionaries were suspicious of political friendships, which were seen as redolent of old regime politics, a means for politicians to engage in mutual social advancement. To conduct politics through friendship meant to take part in political activities 'behind closed doors' and for personal advantage, or the advantage of one's friends and family. In ideological terms, political friendship had a very ambiguous position: on the one hand, the Jacobins idealized friendship as holding out the potential of a pure and selfless relationship between equals; on the other hand, private friendships were seen as incompatible with political virtue which entailed selfless devotion to all. To put loyalty to one's friends before the good of the *patrie* was potentially to betray that homeland. The conflict between virtue and friendship was illustrated in a story from antiquity: Lucius Junius Brutus, founder of the Roman Republic, was a man of such virtue that when his own sons conspired to overthrow the Republic he had them both executed. Many revolutionaries saw themselves as latter-day emulators of Brutus, and used his conduct as a model on which to fashion their own identity as 'men of virtue'.[23] Political friendships became increasingly dangerous as revolutionary leaders were vulnerable to accusations that their friendships with one another masked a secret conspiracy against the republic. Friendship networks could be seen a cloak for counter-revolutionary conspiracy. During the trials of political factions in the Year II, great play was made of the supposed link between networks of friends, illicit factions, and political conspiracy. It is for this reason that when on 14 December 1793, Camille Desmoulins was called upon to justify his political choices at a purifying scrutiny of the Jacobin Club he sought to vindicate himself by stating that he had always put virtue before friendship. He declared: 'I was always the first to denounce my own friends; from the moment that I realized that they were conducting themselves badly, I resisted the most dazzling offers, and I stifled the voice of friendship that their great talents had inspired in me.'[24]

The narrative of conspiracy was central to how revolutionaries conceived of the dynamic of revolutionary politics. Whilst revolutionary leaders saw themselves as politically transparent 'men of virtue', they depicted their opponents and political rivals in sharp contrast as conspirators—the 'enemy within'—who were secretly plotting to subvert the achievements of the Revolution.[25] These conspirators were said to be in league with France's external enemies, counter-revolutionaries and agents of the foreign powers. Recently historians have been unravelling the complex links between the rhetoric of conspiracy and the radicalization of revolutionary politics.[26] The part played by the concept of conspiracy in the Revolution went beyond a purely rhetorical function, for there were also real conspiracies, that is, groups of people organized clandestinely to undermine the political transformation brought about in 1789. At the same time, the narrative of conspiracy was not simply a cynical strategy for destroying enemies, it was also indicative of the powerful emotions that drove revolutionary politics. Obsessive fear of conspiracy was a key factor in the origins of the Terror.[27]

The importance of emotion in revolutionary politics has attracted increasing attention.[28] Work by Lynn Hunt and Barry Shapiro draws upon modern understandings of psychology to throw light upon the ways in which people conceptualized revolutionary politics.[29] There has been particular attention to the experience of revolutionary politics, both the experience of participants and those who were on the receiving end of the consequences of Revolution.[30] Other studies have focused on developing theories of the emotions, an example of which is William Reddy's theory of 'sentimentalism', arguing that the concept of transparent 'natural' feeling was used by the Jacobins to interpret people's felt emotions in ways that paved the way for the Terror.[31] Arguably, there were other emotions, even more intrinsic to the Terror—including anger, suspicion, mistrust, enmity, anxiety, stress, bewilderment and confusion, as well as more positive emotions, such as loyalty, love and friendship.

Probably the single most significant emotion in the Terror was fear. The work of Timothy Tackett, Sophie Wahnich and Jean-Clément Martin has illuminated some of the ways in which fear played a determining part in revolutionary politics.[32] My own research indicates that, contrary to what one might expect, among the principal groups that were subject to fear during the Year II were the Jacobin leaders themselves. They feared royalists and the counter-revolution. They feared that they would lose the war. They feared the sans-culottes. They feared assassination by one of their many enemies— a risk they were obliged to run daily.[33] Most of all, perhaps, they feared one another, the 'enemy within'.[34]

CHOOSING TERROR

For terror to become possible individuals must choose it. One way to get closer to an understanding of the Terror is to ask who chose to deploy terror, and in what circumstances they did so. How far was it the choice of a few key individuals, the leaders amongst the Jacobins? Since the fall of Robespierre there has been no shortage of commentators to argue that responsibility for the Terror should be laid at the door of Robespierre, Saint-Just and a few other Jacobin extremists. This is in part because Robespierre and Saint-Just, along with Barère and Billaud-Varenne (all four members of the Committee of Public Safety), delivered some of the key speeches advocating the recourse to terror: they were thus some of the principal spokesmen for the Terror. Yet Robespierre's personal role in the Terror continues to be a matter of intense debate. Did Robespierre lead events, or was he, to a large extent, led by them?[35] Until very recently attention had focused primarily on the Committee of Public Safety and the Committee of General Security as groups that organized the mechanics of the Terror. Yet it was the Committee of Legislation that proposed the principal terrorist legislation, including the decree of 19 March and the Law of Suspects. The Committee of Legislation was led by men who were classed as political 'moderates' and enjoyed long careers after the fall of the Jacobin Republic, including Merlin de Douai and Cambacérès, neither of whom was sympathetic to Jacobinism.[36] A study by Annie Jourdan has helped bring to light the activities of this hitherto largely overlooked Committee.[37] The terrorist legislation that the Committee of Legislation proposed was voted for by the deputies of the Convention as a whole, only a minority of whom were Jacobins. The Jacobins chose to use terror, but this choice was equally made by non-Jacobin deputies. The idea of an exclusively Robespierrist terror was a myth, invented by the Thermidoreans, the men who overthrew Robespierre out of fear for their own lives, most of whom were themselves very much implicated in the recourse to Terror.[38] The pragmatic choice to use terror extended far beyond the Jacobin leaders to the deputies of the Convention who voted for it, and the many activists beyond the national representation who implemented it. In the Year II terror was a collective choice.

Why then did people, most of whom had hitherto led unexceptional lives and shown no tendency towards violence, eventually decide to choose terror? In part it seems that terror came about through a series of small choices made in the context of an unprecedented set of circumstances, including war and betrayal by a series of political and military leaders. These circumstances resulted in a rising tide of fear and suspicion, which in turn made revolutionary leaders readier to take measures which, in normal circumstances, they would have rejected. Ironically, the consequences of choosing terror unleashed the events that culminated in the self-destruction of the Jacobins in the 'politicians' terror'.

THE POLITICIANS' TERROR

The 'politicians' terror' was at the heart of the revolutionary Terror.[39] It was an internalized form of terror: its principal victims were the leaders of the Revolution themselves. The politicians' terror reached its climax during the Year II with the mutual extermination of a succession of factions: the Girondins, the Hébertists, the Dantonists and the Robespierrists. Most of the people caught up in this terror, either as perpetrators or as victims (in many cases both) either were, or had previously been, members of the Parisian Jacobin Club. The numbers involved were comparatively small; but this grim series of events had a pivotal impact on the course of the Revolution. In Paris itself, the central locus of the Revolution, much of the terror was directed at public officials, including politicians. Ironically, they had more cause to fear the recourse to terror than most of the Parisian population.

We have seen that in many of the cases heard before the Revolutionary Tribunal some effort was made to hand out justice, based on evidence. But justice had little to do with the terror that politicians dealt to one another. The trials of political factions during the Year II were among the most ruthlessly manipulated of the whole Revolution. Few of the victims of the politicians' terror had 'arms in their hands' when they were arrested. In the majority of cases their 'crime' against the Revolution was much more ambiguous: it turned on their true identities. Conviction hinged on unreliable evidence regarding the authenticity of the accused politicians' inner motivation. They were accused of having engaged in a secret conspiracy against the Revolution. Their identity and the authenticity of their claims to be 'men of virtue' were subjected to intense scrutiny.

The politicians' terror took place in an atmosphere of toxic intimacy. It was carried out for the most part amongst a relatively small group of people who already knew one another; many of them were former friends.[40] It was in these factional trials that the Jacobin leaders themselves played a direct role, intervening in the legal process. In taking part they were actively choosing to deploy terror. They were the accusers; they were witnesses to the conduct of the accused; they wrote the narrative of virtue and conspiracy. Ironically, the accused shared the same view of revolutionary politics as their accusers, one based on the idea of the conspiratorial guilt or virtuous innocence of revolutionary leaders.

Denunciation was supposed to be motivated by virtue, never by personal enmity. It was the accuser's own virtue, his concern for the public good, that legitimated the denunciation. Yet the personal dimension of politics was of considerable importance—a significance that has been underestimated by historians. Within the personal dimension we can also situate individual and collective emotions. Emotions were extremely intense in the claustrophobic environment of the inner circles of Parisian politics; they had a considerable impact on individual choices, one which needs to be better understood. The Jacobin leaders during the Year II were subject to a cocktail of toxic emotions: fear, suspicion, anxiety, stress, envy, and friendships that had soured into enmity, all played a significant part in the reality of how politics was conducted, including the process of denunciation. Some of the politicians' terror was conducted in a cynical way—as a way of removing political enemies. Yet there was more to it than that. The circumstances of the politicians' terror also pointed to an inner anxiety about other people's motives; the difficulty of reading what was really in someone else's heart.

The politicians' terror derived much of its intellectual impetus from the ideological belief that revolutionary politicians should be men of virtue. This meant that as public officials they should be devoted to the public good, not to their own self-interest. They must not be motivated by personal ambition, egoism, the desire for glory, or the wish to acquire wealth and influence out of their office. They were supposed to be the reverse of the archetype of the old regime courtier—who was portrayed as a consummate dissembler, corrupt, self-serving, conspiratorial and cynical. Revolutionary politicians were answerable to public opinion, which had the right to scrutinize not only the politicians' words and actions, but also their inner motives and private lives to ensure that these matched up with their public identity as 'men of virtue'. The rhetoric of political virtue developed during the eighteenth century partly as a way of critiquing old regime politics.[41] With the onset of the Revolution this rhetoric developed into an ideological imperative underpinning ideas about the ways in which the new revolutionary politics should be practised. It was not just the Jacobins who believed that politicians should be motivated by political virtue. Contrary to popular belief, Robespierre was far from being the only revolutionary leader to adopt the identity of a man of virtue. Indeed, he owed his political authority in large part to his ability to persuade his audience that, unlike many of his peers, his claim to be motivated by virtue was authentic, not just a cloak for his ambition.[42] Virtue was part of a political culture common to many people of varying political persuasions. Yet the Jacobins bought heavily into this belief and were to pay a high price for it.[43]

Earlier manifestations of the politicians' terror can be seen in the language used on occasion by the early leaders of the Jacobins, Barnave, Alexandre de Lameth, and Duport (the triumvirs), who supported the constitutional monarchy, and manoeuvred tactically to become powerful figures in the new regime. In order to dominate the Jacobin Club and appeal to radical public opinion, they adopted the identity of men of virtue. There were instances when they used this rhetoric to denounce their political opponents and personal rivals, as in February 1791 when they denounced their former friends, Lafayette and Mirabeau as 'secret enemies', 'traitors' who had imposed on the people by 'a mask of patriotism'.[44] The language that they used to denounce rival politicians was not so far removed from that which would be used during the politicians' terror. The difference is that under the Constituent Assembly it was a politician's personal reputation and career that were put at risk by revelations that he was feigning political virtue. During the Terror it would be his life. The triumvirs themselves came under attack by more radical Jacobins, using similar language. Shortly after the king's flight to Varennes Marat evidently had in mind the triumvirs when he declaimed against the enemies within, describing them as: 'Enemies even more redoubtable in that they are more afraid to show themselves and cover themselves beneath the mask of friendship. In this class must be placed nearly all our mandataries, all the representatives of the people, all the public functionaries ... '[45]

The push to war over the winter and spring of 1791 to 1792 resulted in a stepping up of the ominous consequences of being unmasked as one of the 'enemy within'. Brissot and the group (later known as the Girondins) that formed around him to promote the war took the lead in driving the rhetoric of virtue and conspiracy on to a new level of intensity and perceived threat.[46] On 14 January there was a dramatic session in the Assembly when the Girondin Gensonné declared, to a wildly enthusiastic audience, that those who sought a reconciliation with Austria by means of a concert were 'traitors to the *patrie*' and therefore guilty of the crime of *lèse-nation* (treason against the nation).[47] On 10 March Brissot rose in the Assembly to denounce Delessart, Minister for Foreign Affairs, for weakness in his dealings with the Austrians. Brissot accused the minister outright, 'I declare that we are surrounded by treasons, that the traitors are not far from us, and that it is important to know them ... I regard M. Delessart as a traitor.'[48] Brissot subsequently prepared an official indictment of Delessart, which was adopted by the Assembly on 14 March.[49] Delessart was sent to Orléans, to be judged by the Haute Cour Nationale. Delessart and other ministers were replaced by the so-called 'patriot ministry', which included men who were friends of Brissot. Delessart was subsequently murdered during the September Massacres.

The politicians' terror reached its deadly climax during the year of the Jacobin Republic. Successive revolutionary factions fell victim to a terror that, in many cases, they had themselves helped to orchestrate. In the atmosphere of fear and suspicion that prevailed they were accused of conspiracy against the Revolution that they had helped to build. Amongst the first victims of the politicians' terror were the Girondins. This group had originally been part of the Jacobin Club, but a succession of political choices led to a decisive split between Girondins and Jacobins. The Girondin leaders were executed on 31 October 1793, including Brissot, the man who had himself made much use of the rhetoric of unmasking and denouncing traitors. They were followed to the guillotine by other factions within the Jacobins: the Cordeliers (also known as the Hébertists after their leader, the journalist, Hébert) on 24 March 1794; followed on 5 April by Danton and his group; and lastly, Robespierre, his friends and associates on 28, 29 and 30 July 1794. Many of the men who perished in these successive factional bloodbaths had previously denounced one another, whether out of conviction, the need to maintain their own identities as 'men of virtue', or out of fear, or in some cases perhaps a mixture of all these motives. None of the deputies who were brought before the Revolutionary Tribunal during the Year II, and virtually none of the other prominent political figures who appeared before it in that time, escaped the death sentence. The Jacobin leaders feared many enemies, but during the politicians' terror the most ruthless and desperate enemy they faced was themselves.

ENDING TERROR

If the question why the Terror began is subject to ongoing debate, the question of when and how it finally ended is no less contentious. It has often been claimed that Terror ended with the overthrow of Robespierre. In large part this argument was generated by the Thermidoreans, the men who overthrew Robespierre.[50] They included men such as Fouché, Collot d'Herbois, Tallien, Fréron and Barras who, as deputies on mission, had taken a very active role in using terror, and were afraid that Robespierre intended to denounce them for it. When in the days that followed it became evident that public opinion had tired of the Terror, the Thermidoreans were eager to exculpate themselves from any responsibility for terror, and load all the blame on to Robespierre. Yet the reality was that all members of the Convention who voted for the measures were implicated. Nor did terror end with the fall of Robespierre. It was impossible to continue to live in that state of semi-intoxication mingled with fear that had characterized that traumatic year. The Jacobin deputies who had engineered the overthrow of Robespierre were themselves soon outflanked and a number of them were, in their turn, denounced as terrorists.

In the months after Thermidor the institutional and legal structures of the Terror were wound down, though this happened more slowly than has commonly been assumed. The power of the Committees was dismantled and, in November 1794, the Jacobin Club was closed down. The Terror as an instrument of government was ending. In its place began the so-called 'White Terror' whereby murder gangs (particularly in the region around Lyon and the Rhône valley) began to attack former Jacobins in a war of retributive violence and vengeance, beginning in December 1794 and escalating into 1795. The traumatic impact of the Terror continued to reverberate for many years and is the subject of analysis by Ronen Steinberg.[51] Violence, legitimacy and repression continued to haunt successive regimes in the years after the formal ending of the Terror.[52] In Paris itself violence continued above all against the political class as activists struggled with the problem of political legitimacy and finding a voice in an increasingly reactionary and discredited regime.[53] The deputies themselves were also subject to the trauma of the Terror and the effects of the politicians' terror. Mette Harder has demonstrated that the purging of deputies was more extensive than has previously been acknowledged and that it continued well after the overthrow of Robespierre. In the Year III, though there were fewer death sentences, the number of deputies arrested was greater than it had been in the Year II. Her work adds considerably to our understanding of the scale and significance of the Convention's sacrifice of its own members.[54]

Each generation brings its own preoccupations to its efforts to understand the past. The question of what motivates an individual to choose terror is as pressing in the modern world as it was in the eighteenth century. Contemporary political analysts agree that a myriad of reasons may contribute to making an individual choose terror—including personal ties, family and friends, as well as the search for a collective identity and the need for the individual to maintain a sense of belonging. Likewise for the period of the French Revolution: though ideology was clearly central to revolutionary politics, it is equally evident that the recourse to terror cannot be fully explained in terms of ideas. It is also clear that no one explanatory framework can account for the French revolutionary Terror. In place of the monolithic explanations of the past we are seeing the development of multiple lines of investigation: ideological, political, personal, and emotional. It is possible to see now that the reasons for the Terror were far less coherent, less schematic, less purely ideological, more chaotic, and much more emotional than was once assumed. One thing we can say with certainty is that the causes of the Terror were complex, as complex as the people who created it, as complex as we are ourselves.

NOTES

1. See Marisa Linton, 'Robespierre and the Terror', *History Today* 56, no. 8 (2006).
2. For official figures on the victims of the Terror (people who perished as a result of a formal trial) the classic text is Donald Greer, *The Incidence of the Terror During the French Revolution: A Statistical Interpretation* (Cambridge, MA, 1935). Modern historians agree, however, that Greer seriously underestimated the probable number of deaths in the Vendée, many of which took place without a legal process.
3. This approach to Jacobinism is summarized in Marc Bouloiseau, *The Jacobin Republic, 1792–1794*, trans. Jonathan Mandelbaum (Cambridge, 1983).
4. 'Rapport ... sur les personnes incarcérées, présenté à la Convention Nationale dans la séance du 8 ventôse an II', in Louis-Antoine Saint-Just, *Oeuvres complètes* ed. Michèle Duval (Paris, 1989), 705.
5. Furet places the origins of the Terror at the start of the summer of 1789: François Furet, 'Terreur', in François Furet and Mona Ozouf (eds), *Dictionnaire critique de la Révolution française* (Paris, 1988), 156.
6. François Furet, *Interpreting the French Revolution*, trans. Elborg Forster ([1978] this edition, Cambridge, 1981). For the argument that the Jacobin terror cannot be correlated to the war see Mona Ozouf, 'War and Terror in French Revolutionary Discourse (1792–1794)', *Journal of Modern History* 56 (December 1984), 579–97.
7. The works that owe a debt to Furet are too many to list here. Numerous studies of political revolutionary culture since the 1970s exist, at least in part, because of his influence in making this kind of study acceptable, even where the writers do not agree with his political conclusions. For a study that takes a particularly 'Furetist' approach to the ideology of Terror, see Patrice Gueniffey, *La Politique de la Terreur: essai sur la violence révolutionnaire, 1789–1794* (Paris, 2000); and 'La Terreur: circonstances exceptionnelles, idéologie et dynamique révolutionnaire', *Historical Reflections/Réflexions Historiques* 29, no. 3 (2003), 433–50. Studies of the political culture of the Terror include: Lynn Hunt, *Politics, Culture and Class in the French Revolution* (Berkeley, 1984); Keith M. Baker (ed.), *The French Revolution and the Creation of Modern Political Culture*, vol. 4, *The Terror* (Oxford, 1994).
8. See the historiographical review essays by Suzanne Desan, 'What's After Political Culture? Recent French Revolutionary Historiography', *French Historical Studies* 23 (2000), 163–96;

and Jack R. Censer, 'Social Twists and Linguistic Turns: Revolutionary Historiography a Decade After the Bicentennial', *French Historical Studies* 22 (1999), 139–67.

9. D. M. G. Sutherland, *France, 1789–1815: Revolution and Counterrevolution* (London: Fontana, 1985); his more recent and revised work, *The French Revolution and Empire: the Quest for a Civic Order* (Oxford, 2003); and D. M. G. Sutherland and T. J. A. Le Goff, 'The Social Origins of Counter-Revolution in Western France', *Past and Present* 99, no. 1 (1983), 65–87.

10. The debates on the Terror are summarized in Hugh Gough, *The Terror in the French Revolution* (2nd edn, Houndmills, 2010). The very readable account by David Andress, *The Terror: Civil War in the French Revolution* (London, 2005) reasserts the importance of war and counter-revolution in explaining the genesis of the Terror. For the historiography of revolutionary violence, see Paul R. Hanson, *Contesting the French Revolution* (Oxford, 2009), 159–85.

11. Lynn Hunt, 'The World We Have Gained: The Future of the French Revolution', *American Historical Review* 108, no. 1 (2003), 1–19. See also the review essay by Jeremy D. Popkin, 'Not Over After All: The French Revolution's Third Century', *Journal of Modern History* 74 (2002), 801–21; and Rebecca Spang, 'Paradigms and Paranoia: How Modern is the French Revolution?', *American Historical Review* 108, no. 1 (2003), 119–47. Spang includes a call for more studies on revolutionary psychology.

12. Keith Michael Baker, *Inventing the French Revolution* (Cambridge, 1990), 305; and, more recently, Baker, 'Enlightenment Idioms, Old Regime Discourses and Revolutionary Improvisation', in Thomas E. Kaiser and Dale K. Van Kley (eds), *From Deficit to Deluge: The Origins of the French Revolution* (Stanford, 2011).

13. Mary Ashburn Miller, *A Natural History of Revolution: Violence and Nature in the French Revolutionary Imagination, 1789–1794* (Ithaca, 2011); and Dan Edelstein, *The Terror of Natural Right: Republicanism, the Cult of Nature, and the French Revolution* (Chicago, 2009).

14. Jean-Clément Martin, *Violence et révolution: essais sur la naissance d'un mythe national* (Paris, 2006); Annie Jourdan, 'Les discours de la terreur à l'époque révolutionnaire', *French Historical Studies* 36, no. 1 (December 2012), 52–81; Timothy Tackett, 'La Révolution et la violence', in Jean-Clément Martin (ed.), *La Révolution à l'oeuvre: perspectives actuelles dans l'histoire de la Révolution française* (Rennes, 2005); Guillaume Mazeau, 'La "Terreur". Laboratoire de la modernité', in Jean-Luc Chappey et al. (eds), *Pour quoi faire la Révolution* (Marseilles, 2012); and the collected essays in Michel Biard (ed.), *Les Politiques de la Terreur, 1793–1794* (Rennes, 2008).

15. Martin, *Violence et révolution*; Jourdan, 'Les discours de la terreur'.

16. For a detailed analysis of the statistics on the variety of verdicts given by the Revolutionary Tribunal, see James Logan Godfrey, *Revolutionary Justice: A Study in the Organisation and Procedures of the Paris Tribunal, 1793–95* (Chapel Hill, 1951), 136–50. See also Anne Simonin, 'Les acquittés de la Grande Terreur: Réflexions sur l'amitié dans la République', in Biard, *Les Politiques de la Terreur*.

17. Works that address terror in the provinces include: Richard Cobb, *Paris and its Provinces, 1792–1802* (Oxford, 1975), and some of his collected essays in Cobb, *The French and Their Revolution* (London, 1988); Colin Lucas, *The Structure of the Terror: the Example of Javogues and the Loire* (Oxford, 1973); William Edmonds, *Jacobinism and the Revolt of Lyon, 1789–1793* (Oxford, 1990); and D. M. G. Sutherland, *Murder in Aubagne: Lynching, Law and Justice During the French Revolution, 1789–1801* (Cambridge, 2009).

On the experience of the Revolution at a local level, see Peter McPhee, *Living the French Revolution, 1789-99* (Houndmills, 2006).

18. Cited by Norman Hampson, *A Concise History of the French Revolution* (London, 1975), 139.

19. Martin, *Violence et révolution*, 86-93; on discourses of terror as a rhetorical strategy see Jourdan, 'Les discours de la terreur'.

20. On the Jacobin mentality, see Michel Vovelle, *La Mentalité Révolutionnaire* (Paris, 1985), chap. 9; also Mona Ozouf, *La Fête révolutionnaire, 1789-1799* (Paris, 1976); and Albert Soboul, 'Sentiment religieux et cultes populaires pendant la Révolution: Saintes patriotes et martyrs de la Liberté', *Annales historiques de la Révolution française* 3 (1957), 193-213.

21. Richard Cobb, 'Some Aspects of the Revolutionary Mentality, April 1793-Thermidor, Year II', in Jeffry Kaplow (ed.), *New Perspectives on the French Revolution: Readings in Historical Sociology* (New York, 1965), 306.

22. On the politics of Jacobin friendship, see Marisa Linton, *Choosing Terror: Virtue, Friendship and Authenticity in the French Revolution* (Oxford, forthcoming 2013); and Marisa Linton, 'Fatal Friendships: The Politics of Jacobin Friendship', *French Historical Studies* 31, no. 1 (Winter 2008), 51-76.

23. On the ways in which Saint-Just deployed the classical model of the 'man of virtue' as a way of establishing his political identity, see Marisa Linton, 'The Man of Virtue: The Role of Antiquity in the Political Trajectory of L. A. Saint-Just', *French History* 24, no. 3 (2010), 393-419.

24. François Aulard (ed.), *La Société des Jacobins: recueil de documents pour l'histoire de club des Jacobins de Paris*, 6 vols (Paris, 1889-1897), 5, 559. See also Linton, *Choosing Terror*, chap. 8, 'The Enemy Within'.

25. On the polarization of 'conspiracy' and revolutionary 'transparency', see Hunt, *Politics, Culture and Class*, 38-45.

26. On the links between fear of conspiracy and the Terror, see Peter R. Campbell, Thomas E. Kaiser, and Marisa Linton (eds), *Conspiracy in the French Revolution* (Manchester, 2007), especially Kaiser, 'Catilina's Revenge: Conspiracy, Revolution, and Historical Consciousness from the Old Regime to the Consulate', and Linton, '"Do You Believe That We're Conspirators?" Conspiracies Real and Imagined in Jacobin Politics, 1793-94'. See also Timothy Tackett, 'Conspiracy Obsession in a Time of Revolution: French Elites and the Origins of the Terror, 1789-1792' *American Historical Review* 105 (2000), 691-713.

27. Timothy Tackett, 'Interpreting the Terror', *French Historical Studies* 24, no. 1 (2002), 569-78, esp. 575.

28. New work on emotions in the French Revolution is discussed in Sophia Rosenfeld, 'Thinking about feeling, 1789-1799', *French Historical Studies* 32, no. 4 (Fall, 2009), 697-706.

29. See Lynn Hunt, *The Family Romance of the French Revolution* (London, 1992); and Barry M. Shapiro, *Traumatic Politics: The Deputies and the King in the Early French Revolution* (University Park, 2009).

30. See in particular the contributions in David Andress (ed.), *Experiencing the French Revolution* (Oxford, 2013).

31. See William Reddy, *The Navigation of Feeling: A Framework for the History of the Emotions* (Cambridge, 2001), esp. 146-7.

32. See Sophie Wahnich, *In Defence of the Terror: Liberty or Death in the French Revolution*, trans. David Fernbach ([2003] this edition, London, 2012); Tackett, 'Interpreting the Terror', Martin, *Violence et revolution*.

33. On the Jacobin leaders' fear of assassination and how this affected their political choices, see Linton, 'The Stuff of Nightmares: Plots, Assassinations, and Duplicity in the Mental World of Jacobin Leaders, 1793–1794' in Andress, *Experiencing the French Revolution*.

34. On fears experienced by the Jacobin leaders, see Linton, *Choosing Terror*, 227–8.

35. On Robespierre, see Peter McPhee, *Robespierre—a Revolutionary Life* (New Haven, 2012); the collected articles in 'Robespierre', ed. Michel Biard, special issue of the *Annales historiques de la Révolution française*, no. 371 (janvier–mars 2013); and Michel Biard and Philippe Bourdin (eds), *Robespierre: Portraits croisés* (Paris, 2012).

36. Hervé Leuwers, *Un juriste en politique. Merlin de Douai (1754–1838)* (Arras, 1996).

37. Annie Jourdan, 'La Convention ou l'empire des lois: le Comité de législation et la commission de classification des lois', *La Révolution française*, 3 (2012), http://lrf.revues.org/730

38. On this point, see Jourdan, 'Les discours de la terreur'; and Mazeau, 'La 'Terreur', laboratoire de la modernité', 83.

39. On the politicians' terror, see Linton, *Choosing Terror*.

40. For the connections between friendship and the politicians' terror, see Marisa Linton, 'Friends, Enemies and the Role of the Individual' in Peter McPhee (ed.), *Companion to the History of the French Revolution* (Oxford, 2013).

41. Marisa Linton, *The Politics of Virtue in Enlightenment France* (Houndmills, 2001).

42. On Robespierre's identity as a 'man of virtue', see Marisa Linton, 'Robespierre et l'authenticité révolutionnaire', *Annales historiques de la Révolution française*, no. 371 (janvier–mars 2013): 153–73. On Saint-Just, see Linton, 'The Man of Virtue'.

43. See Hunt, *Politics, Culture, and Class in the French Revolution*, 43–4. See also the recent analysis by Annie Jourdan, *La Révolution, une exception française?* (Paris, 2004), Part Two.

44. Aulard, *La Société des Jacobins*, 2: 97–8, 103, 107. See also Linton, *Choosing Terror*, 93–4.

45. Jean-Paul Marat, *L'Ami du peuple*, no. 505, 27 June 1791.

46. On the Girondins as heirs to the longstanding fear of the 'Austrian Committee' and the implications of this fear for international relations, see the many works by Tom Kaiser, especially Thomas E. Kaiser, 'From the Austrian Committee to the Foreign Plot: Marie-Antoinette, Austrophobia and the Terror', *French Historical Studies* 26, no. 4 (Fall 2003), 579–617; and Kaiser, 'Who's Afraid of Marie-Antoinette? Diplomacy, Austrophobia, and the Queen', *French History* 14 (2000), 241–71.

47. The term *lèse-nation* was not invented by the revolutionaries. It circulated in *parlementaire* discourse before the Revolution, forming part of a linguistic transfer of authority from royal sovereignty to the sovereignty of the nation. As Dale Van Kley has shown, it had its origins in Jansenist constitutionalism: see Dale Van Kley, *The Religious Origins of the French Revolution: From Calvinism to the Civil Constitution, 1560–1791* (New Haven, 1996), 325–6.

48. 10 March 1792, *Archives Parlementaires de 1787 à 1860*, ed. M. J. Madival et al., 127 vols (Paris, 1862–1972), 39: 528.

49. Étienne Dumont, *Souvenirs sur Mirabeau et sur les deux premières Assemblées Législatives, par Étienne Dumont*, ed. Jean Bénétruy ([1832] this edition, Paris, 1952), 305, note 3.

50. On Thermidor and its aftermath, see Bronislaw Baczko, *Ending the Terror: The French Revolution After Robespierre* (Cambridge, 1994); Laura Mason, 'The Thermidorean

Reaction', in McPhee, *A Companion to the French Revolution; and Françoise Brunel, Thermidor: La chute de Robespierre* (Paris, 1989).

51. Ronen Steinberg, 'Trauma Before Trauma: Imagining the Effects of the Terror in the Revolutionary Era', in Andress, *Experiencing the French Revolution.*

52. Howard G. Brown, *Ending the French Revolution: Violence, Justice, and Repression from the Terror to Napoleon* (Charlottesville, 2006); and Stephen Clay, 'The White Terror: Factions, Reactions and the Politics of Vengeance', in McPhee, *A Companion to the French Revolution.*

53. Laura Mason, 'Never was a Plot so Holy: Gracchus Babeuf and the End of the French Revolution', in Campbell, *Conspiracy in the French Revolution.*

54. Mette Harder, 'Crisis of Representation: The National Convention and the Search for Political Legitimacy, 1792–1795' (PhD, University of York, July 2010).

Selected Reading

Andress, David, *The Terror: Civil War in the French Revolution* (London, 2005).

Andress, David, (ed.), *Experiencing the French Revolution* (Oxford: Studies on Voltaire and the Eighteenth Century, 2013).

Campbell, Peter R., Thomas E. Kaiser, and Marisa Linton (eds), *Conspiracy in the French Revolution* (Manchester, 2007).

Gough, Hugh, *The Terror in the French Revolution* (2nd edn, Houndmills, 2010).

Hanson, Paul R., *Contesting the French Revolution* (Oxford, 2009).

Linton, Marisa, 'Fatal Friendships: The Politics of Jacobin Friendship', *French Historical Studies* 31, no. 1 (Winter 2008), 51–76.

Linton, Marisa, 'The Man of Virtue: The Role of Antiquity in the Political Trajectory of L. A. Saint-Just', *French History* 24, no. 3 (2010), 393–419.

Linton, Marisa, *Choosing Terror: Virtue, Friendship and Authenticity in the French Revolution* (Oxford, 2013).

McPhee, Peter, (ed.), *Companion to the History of the French Revolution* (Oxford, 2013).

Tackett, Timothy, 'Interpreting the Terror', *French Historical Studies* 24, no. 1 (2002), 569–78.

Wahnich, Sophie, *In Defence of the Terror: Liberty or Death in the French Revolution*, trans. David Fernbach ([2003] this edition, London, 2012)

CHAPTER 28

RECKONING WITH TERROR

*Retribution, Redress, and Remembrance in
Post-Revolutionary France*

RONEN STEINBERG

IN 1795, two citizens from Arras published a pamphlet detailing alleged atrocities committed against the detainees in one of the prisons in the city during the Reign of Terror.[1] The allegations included corruption, appalling conditions of detention, improper sanitation, food shortages, and, particularly, various aggressions against female prisoners. In one anecdote the authors recounted how public officials in the prison subjected a woman who had just been arrested to an intrusive search and did not refrain from touching her private parts, telling her that, 'you are well capable of hiding papers even there!' The pamphlet ended by calling on the National Convention to remove from office all those who had been involved in such brutalities during the Terror. This was described as a 'salutary purge' that was necessary for the town of Arras as well as for many other communes.[2]

It is impossible to know whether these allegations were true but in a way this is beside the point. This pamphlet was part of a genre of denunciatory literature that flooded the literary marketplace in the years after the fall of Robespierre. These texts offered readers detailed stories of excess and violence, usually accompanied by calls to bring the perpetrators to justice. Anecdotes about various forms of sexual aggression, which were a leitmotif in this literature, were meant to show how revolutionary authorities abused the power vested in them and violated the principles of virtue that they themselves preached. Stories and revelations about the brutalities of Jacobin repression were highly popular after 9 Thermidor, perhaps because they struck a chord with the widespread sentiment that the Reign of Terror was an outrage, a massive atrocity that called for some kind of reckoning.

This chapter is about this reckoning. It argues that the French Revolution created the conditions for an unprecedented, modern debate on how events of mass violence affect individuals and society. In the months and years after the fall of Robespierre, revolutionary leaders, relatives of victims, and ordinary citizens grappled with a series of dilemmas around retribution, redress and commemoration. Was the responsibility for the Terror individual or collective? How far back could the leadership go in trying to repair the harm caused to citizens by state actions, without undoing much of what the revolutionary movement had achieved in the process? How was one to commemorate a difficult past, an event that evoked disagreement and horror rather than glory? These dilemmas would have been unthinkable under the old regime. They derived from the democratizing thrust of the French Revolution: this is what made them particularly modern.

In recent years, several studies have highlighted the end of the Terror as a problem rather than a fact in revolutionary historiography. Bronislaw Baczko's path-breaking work on the Thermidorian Reaction focused on the emergence of a 'counter-imagination', that is, a language that sought to counter the political tendencies of the Terror but could not avoid reproducing some of its most salient features. According to Baczko, 'ending the Terror was not an *act* but a *process*, tense and with uncertain issue. The Terror was not brought to an end by the fall of Robespierre; it was a road to be discovered and travelled'.[3] Howard Brown has taken this inquiry forward by examining how the Thermidorian Reaction and the Directory struggled to end the Revolution by quelling various forms of civil violence. Brown's research shows that in so doing, the authorities resorted increasingly to measures that bore much resemblance to the mechanisms of Jacobin repression, a hybrid situation that he terms 'liberal authoritarianism'.[4]

This chapter builds on these studies, but poses a different question: what does it mean to speak of the end when it comes to events of mass violence like the Terror? Surely, for many who experienced the Terror at first hand—the victims, their families, those who played an active role in the apparatus of repression, even revolutionary leaders— the events of 9 Thermidor were in many ways just a beginning. What followed was a lengthy and complex process of coming to terms with the legacies of the Terror, both at the individual and the collective level. This process involved not only questions of politics and language, but also questions of property rights, practices of commemoration, and even psychological and public health.[5] Those who participated in it were not only state authorities or political elites but also victims and ordinary citizens who took advantage of the liberalizing atmosphere of the late 1790s in order to stake their claims.[6] Nor was this process limited to the Thermidorian Reaction or the Directory. Rather, the process of coming to terms with the Terror extended well into the 1830s, that is, into the last years of the generation that had lived through the events in question.[7]

The sections that follow highlight various aspects of this process. They focus particularly on retribution, redress and remembrance. This is by no means an exhaustive list and other facets of the same process could have been discussed. Nevertheless, the aspects of coming to terms with the Terror examined in the following pages—all those 're-words', as Charles Maier referred to them—have in common the desire to turn time backward, to return things to where they were before the damage had been done.[8] This is, of course, an impossible desire but it is one that marked deeply the process of reckoning with the Terror.

RETRIBUTION

In the immediate aftermath of the Terror, calls to hold accountable those responsible for the violence came pouring in from around the country. A group of citizens from Avignon wrote to congratulate the National Convention on removing Robespierre and his acolytes from power:

> Citizens representatives! On 9 Thermidor you have saved the fatherland yet again. At the moment in which Robespierre—may his memory be execrated—planned to ascend to the throne, you have made him mount the scaffold instead ... Now you must learn about the actions of the agents of his cruelty, and deliver them to justice.[9]

Such texts were essentially denunciations of the conduct of public officials. In this sense, they were continuous with the revolutionary practice of denunciation, which reached its peak during the Terror.[10] But in the context of the Thermidorian Reaction they took on a different meaning. As the representations of 9 Thermidor crystallized into a narrative of a revolution within the Revolution, an internal insurrection that put an end to the Terror, the denunciations sent by political clubs and popular societies from various parts of the country played a role in legitimating the new regime as a return to the path that France embarked upon in 1789 and a repudiation of the Jacobin aberration of 1793. As the prominent leader Jean-Lambert Tallien put it in a seminal speech delivered a month after the execution of Robespierre, it was time to replace Terror with justice as the order of the day.[11] In the months after 9 Thermidor, then, we see the emergence of a diffuse yet very real sense that the time of repression was over and that of reckoning about to begin.

Yet justice in the aftermath of the Terror proved to be as elusive as it was urgent. Initially, the Convention advanced rapidly with the dismantling of the institutional apparatus of the Terror. It repealed repressive laws—most notably, the law of 22 Prairial, which had led to the dramatic increase in the rate of executions during the summer of 1794—reorganized the revolutionary tribunal in a way that curtailed much of its powers, and began the mass release of political prisoners. It also recalled to Paris about 60 per cent of the *représentants en mission*—the men who had been responsible for implementing the decrees of the Committee of Public Safety in the provinces—and replaced them with more moderate men.[12] But after that initial bout of activity, the Convention stalled, unsure how to proceed.

The following months were characterized by an incoherent set of policies that swung repeatedly between retribution and amnesty.[13] At the end of year II, the conventionnel Robert Lindet delivered a report in the name of the executive branch of the revolutionary government, where he urged his colleagues to draw a veil over the past months of civil strife and look forward to the future. 'The Revolution has left victims in its wake ... are you now going to authorize inquiries into each case? The welfare of the fatherland does not allow you to look back on the ruins that you have left behind'.[14] Yet a month later the Convention launched the first major trial of a public official for his role in the Terror, Jean-Baptist Carrier, the former *représentant en mission* in Nantes, who was accused of committing atrocities in his struggle against counter-revolution in the west.

Carrier's trial was a watershed moment. It was crucial in establishing the perception of the Reign of Terror as a massive atrocity. The anecdotes of excess that flowed from the courtroom—most notably, *les noyades des Nantes*, referring to the drowning of suspects in the Loire River—constituted micro-narratives that, to use Baczko's phrase, made 'horror the order of the day'.[15] Carrier's trial was also an extraordinary moment in modern legal history. It is one of the earliest known cases of a person being accused of *crimes contre le genre humain*—crimes against the human species—a juridical category that would assume a central place in the aftermath of the Holocaust.[16] The case of Carrier signalled a retributive turn in the policies of the National Convention. It was followed by other high-profile trials and executions, most notably the trial of Antoine Fouquier-Tinville, the chief prosecutor of the revolutionary tribunal in Paris, and the trial of Joseph Le Bon, the former *représentant en mission* in the north of France.[17]

These were of course show trials. They were meant to erect a wall between the Thermidorian Reaction and the previous regime. They did not follow due process—to the extent that one can talk of due process in the tumultuous series of judicial reforms that characterized the revolutionary decade—and the fate of the defendants was effectively sealed in advance. Nevertheless, the decision to take up the criminal prosecution of its own members for their role during the Terror was significant in itself because in so doing, the National Convention came up against a new and uniquely modern dilemma, that of establishing individual accountability in the aftermath of mass crime. Criminal prosecution presupposes individual responsibility, yet the mechanisms of mass violence seem to dilute the possibility of attributing such precise levels of accountability. Who, after all, was to be held responsible for the Terror? If the *représentant en mission* represented the Convention, and the Convention embodied the will of the people, could an individual official be held accountable for the Terror without, *ipso facto*, implicating the entire social order in the crime? As one conventionnel put it in the debates leading up to the trial of Carrier, 'it is actually the Convention that is being accused. It is the French people that are being put on trial for having tolerated the tyranny of the infamous Robespierre'.[18] The point is that this dilemma derived from the democratizing thrust of the French Revolution. It would have been unthinkable under the monarchy. It could only emerge as a specific difficulty in the aftermath of the Terror because the Revolution democratized responsibility by investing the people with sovereignty.[19] In this sense, the aftermath of the Terror saw the emergence of specific legal and moral difficulties around accountability, difficulties that were unprecedented but that would go on to become a mainstay of modern international and humanitarian jurisprudence.

Retribution in the aftermath of the Terror was not limited to legal measures. In the winter and spring of 1795, a wave of largely spontaneous acts of revenge, which came to be known as the White Terror, spread through the south of France. Jacobins and former *terroristes* were hunted down in the streets, massacred in prisons, or murdered at home.

In Tarascon they were rounded up and thrown off the roof of the medieval castle in the town. Stephen Clay has shown that these acts were for the most part a very local settling of scores: many assailants knew their victims personally.[20]

But the White Terror also enjoyed the support of the Convention, at least tacitly. A series of laws that were passed in this period seemed to authorize a witch-hunt of sorts against anyone suspected of having collaborated with, or benefited from, Robespierrist rule. Such was the law requiring all those who had been purged from their positions after 9 Thermidor to return to their original places of residence and be placed under administrative surveillance, as well as the law that stipulated the disarming of former Jacobins. This legal persecution of Jacobins was related to the recall of the expelled Girondins to the Convention (8 December 1794), as well as to the popular uprisings of Germinal and Prairial, year III, which raised the spectre of sans-culotte militancy again. In this sense, reckoning with the Terror went hand in hand with repressing popular radicalism.

The White Terror forced the Republican authorities to make difficult choices between, on the one hand, a commitment to the rule of law, and on the other hand, the recourse to extraordinary repressive measures.[21] Popular violence in the provinces, whether in the form of brigandage or political action—often, it was impossible to tell the difference—was getting out of hand. It is difficult to know the number of victims of the White Terror, but estimates range from a few hundreds to tens of thousands.[22] Clearly, retribution for the Terror was threatening the stability of the Republic. Bringing the disorder to an end—indeed, ending the Revolution—meant breaking the cycles of recrimination and reprisals.

Partly to that end, and partly to avoid close investigations into the past conduct of its own members, many of whom were personally implicated in the Terror, the National Convention adopted a sweeping amnesty decree on 26 October 1795, its last session as France's legislative Assembly. The decree pertained to 'acts purely related to the Revolution', and was meant to 'erase the memory of errors and mistakes that had been committed during the Revolution'.[23] Interpretations of the decree vary widely. For Brown it amounted to a whitewash, while for Sophie Wahnich it constituted an argument in favour of collective responsibility, the people taking charge of the violent foundation of their own Republic.[24] Be that as it may, the amnesty was presented at the time as a measure of national reconciliation, although it clearly favoured Republicans and revolutionaries. It did not extend to refractory priests, émigrés, and the rebels in the Vendée, who were to remain outlaws. But it did, in effect, put an end to the formal process of accounting for the Terror by making it impossible to bring those who had played a part in the repression to justice. More than anything else, the amnesty of 1795 was an attempt to institute amnesia.

Redress

For the most part, the vast historiography of the Terror has been devoid of victims. We know a great deal about the origins of the Terror, the ideas and circumstances that made it possible and, perhaps, necessary. We know a great deal about the various bodies and public officials that implemented the decrees coming out of Paris in 1793–94, and we also know quite a bit about the geographical unevenness of the Terror, the fact that its realities differed widely between various locales in France. But we know very little about its victims. This is a strange state of affairs to say the least, for at some basic level the very term 'terrorism'—an invention of the French Revolution—denotes a tripartite relationship between the terrorists, their victims, and their target.[25]

This relative absence of the victims of the Terror from accounts of the event can be explained in several ways. First, the historiography of the Terror—and there is a distinct historiography of the Terror within the historiography of the French Revolution—tends to focus on the origins and evolution of revolutionary repression.[26] The victims of the Terror seem to offer little to this particular discussion. Second, it must be acknowledged that for a long time narratives of victims of the Terror tended to be the provenance of a counter-revolutionary historiography.[27] These were for the most part subjective, highly emotional tales of suffering that added little to our understanding of the revolutionary decade but much to its *legende noire*. Also, it is the case that in studies of terrorism and political violence more generally, there is a tendency to focus on the perpetrators, their motivations and ideas, rather than on victims.[28] One thing is clear: the relative neglect of the victims of the Terror is not due to a lack of sources. Rather, it seems to be a matter of optics, the questions and the particular ways of seeing that have characterized revolutionary historiography.

If then we shift our gaze to the aftermath of the Terror and to the process of coming to terms with it, the issue of its victims looms large. The political and economic liberalization that characterized the Thermidorian Reaction and the Directory, and, even more so, the relaxation of censorship, created an atmosphere where the voices of the victims could be heard. Citizens who had been incarcerated as suspects under the laws of the Terror and were now released from prison were often anxious to publicize their tales of woe and misfortune, as were the families of victims. Thus, the *Mémoires d'un détenu*, published in 1795 by Honoré Riouffe, became an overnight success in France and beyond its borders.[29] These narratives found an audience eager for some sort of catharsis in the aftermath of what was widely perceived to be a massive atrocity. The stories of victims also accorded well with the political objectives of the Reaction, which was anxious to legitimate its own rule by portraying the previous regime as criminal.

But victims of the Terror did not only tell stories; they also demanded some form of reparation. As early as December 1794, a delegation of widows and orphans appeared before the Convention in Paris, imploring the government to 'listen today to the painful cries of thousands of wives and children whose husbands and fathers had been dragged inhumanely to the scaffold … [France] awaits a cure for the deep wounds inflicted by the barbarity of tyrants'.[30] The language surrounding the victims of the Terror was often couched in therapeutic terms, as a collective healing of sorts. Thus, in March 1795 the prominent Thermidorian leader, Antoine Boissy d'Anglas, delivered a speech where he urged his colleagues in the Convention to annul the judgements passed by

Revolutionary tribunals and to restore the property, which had been confiscated from the victims, to their surviving relatives. By removing Robespierre from power, Boissy told his audience,

> We have taken on before the entire universe the sacred commitment to be just, to dry the tears, to soften the pains, to cure the wounds of the unfortunate victims of tyranny ... we cannot bring back to life those whom crime had struck down, but at least let us console their souls [*mânes*] which, at this very moment, surround us, follow us, beseech us, and roam this place.[31]

According to Boissy, providing some sort of relief to the victims of the Terror was the moral and political duty of the revolutionary government. It was also, as his rhetoric suggests, a form of exorcism.[32]

In proposing these restorative measures to the National Convention, Boissy was acting on demands that were originally presented by people outside of government. In the weeks and months after 9 Thermidor, hundreds of widows of victims sent petitions to the authorities, demanding the restoration of their late husbands' property and the clearing of their names (*restitution des biens* and *réhabilitation de la mémoire*). The demand for the restitution of property was often directly related to matters of inheritance. Thus, the widow Lamotte from the department of the Meuse wrote about the difficulties of raising her three sons without the possessions that had been confiscated from her late husband and demanded that the Convention not deprive the 'three poor boys' of their father's inheritance.[33] The widow of the musician Louis Edelmann from Strasbourg asked not for the restoration of property—this was a poor family that had very few possessions to begin with—but rather for an annual pension based on her status as a victim of the Terror.[34] The demand for the rehabilitation of memory was a more complex matter that referred to various legal measures but that can be summed up as posthumous exoneration.

The debate around *les biens des condamnés*, as it came to be known, went on for several months within and beyond the walls of the Convention. Those who argued in favour of exonerating the victims and restoring their property made two main points. First, if the Terror constituted a mass crime, and the verdicts of the revolutionary tribunals were essentially unjust—and this was a widely held opinion after 9 Thermidor, across the political spectrum—then the revision of judgements must follow. Second, by holding on to possessions that had been confiscated from victims, the Republic was basically punishing children for the sins of their fathers. Restoring the property of victims to their families accorded well with the commitment of the Thermidorians to liberal values such as individual property. In this sense, the restitution of *les biens des condamnés* was presented as a restorative measure, aimed at the renewal of social ties after the Terror.[35]

Those who argued against posthumous exoneration and the restoration of property saw these measures as unfeasible and economically and politically dangerous. It was impractical to revise the judgements of revolutionary tribunals because often they did not follow due process and they relied on oral rather than written testimonies, so that there was insufficient documentation to re-examine past cases.[36] The only possible exoneration was a collective one, en masse, but this meant a criminalization of the entire edifice of revolutionary justice, something very few revolutionary leaders were willing to accept. The restoration of property was also presented as economically dangerous. Sales of nationalized property—*biens nationaux*—had long been basic to the economy of the Republic. Some leaders worried that the restoration of *les biens des condamnés* would destabilize this market, and damage the government in the eyes of all those holding *biens nationaux* thus potentially threatened with confiscation. As the conventionnel Laurent Lecointre put it, 'if you look back even once on the matter of these possessions, you will give the government an incalculable shock'.[37] More generally, looking back was politically unwise. Those who argued against restitution agreed that the government owed some kind of redress to the victims of the Terror, perhaps in the form of indemnity, but saw retrogressive measures as reactionary. The problem was that in an effort to undo the Terror, measures like restitution threatened to undo the Republic.

The decree on restitution as it was finally adopted in June 1795 reflected these dilemmas in that it relied on contorted distinctions between deserving and undeserving victims. The demand for posthumous exoneration was rejected outright. The decree stipulated that the possessions of all those who had been sentenced to death since 10 March 1793—the establishment of the revolutionary tribunal in Paris—should be restored to their surviving relatives, with the following list of exceptions: the property of Louis Capet and the royal family, the property of the Dubarry family, the possessions of the conventionnels who had been executed in relation to the events of 9 Thermidor, émigrés, counterfeiters, distributors of fake *assignats*, 'squanderers of the public fortune', and, more generally, conspirators.[38] Given that this list of exceptions included most of the alleged crimes that brought people before revolutionary tribunals in the first place, one wonders who was left to benefit from this restorative measure.

Yet benefit from it some did. The widow of the chemist Lavoisier, for example, was able to regain possession of his library and extensive scientific collections.[39] Over the coming decades, the restitution of *les biens des condamnés* spilled over into debates about the confiscated property of the émigrés and the rebels in the Vendée—debates that continued well into the nineteenth century, thus extending the chronology of the process of coming to terms with the Terror well beyond the immediate aftermath of 9 Thermidor.[40] Still, the actual restoration of property to the families of victims of the Terror remains to be studied in full.

The redress of injustice is inseparable from questions of memory. As legal scholar Robert Gordon argues, measures aimed at remedying past wrongs come embedded in a narrative that brings together a society's past and future. This narrative usually describes the period of injustice as an aberration from a history that should have taken place instead. Gordon points out that, 'when injustice is portrayed as a deviation from a counterfactual history ... the regime's response to injustice is a way of defining the new society's identity by reweaving the severed threads of memory ... getting history back on track'.[41] This chapter now turns to consider the remembrance of victims of the Terror.

REMEMBRANCE

Much like everything else, the French Revolution politicized the memory of the dead. Numerous studies have shown how monuments, tombs and even cadavers were harnessed to the cultivation of a Republican pedagogy.[42] Joseph Clarke has studied the remembrance of the dead across the revolutionary decade. Clarke's study shows the tensions between the personal desires of ordinary citizens, when they engaged in commemoration, and the political goals of revolutionary leadership, which sought to mobilize these deaths for its own purposes. Clarke maintains that for most of the bereaved families, this was seen as demeaning the remembrance of the dead, and the commemorative practices that they engaged in showed a remarkable resilience of Catholic traditions, in spite of the general opposition to the Church within revolutionary circles.[43]

Emmanuel Fureix has examined the cult of the dead under the Restoration and the July Monarchy. This is a key period for the study of attitudes to the revolutionary past in France because the return of the Bourbons opened up a space for the remembrance of the Revolution, and particularly the victims of the Terror, in a way that was not possible under the Napoleonic regime. Fureix's study of the burial or commemoration of such diverse figures as Louis XVI, ordinary victims of the Terror, the former conventionnels Cambacérès and Lanjuinais, and even the celebrated actor of the Comédie-Française, François-Joseph Talma, who was a close friend of Danton and Desmoulins, shows how during the Restoration, funerary rites allowed for the exploration of conflicts and reconciliatory efforts in a post-Revolutionary society that 'had become opaque to itself'.[44]

Fureix's work, as well as other studies of attitudes to the revolutionary past under the Restoration, highlights the notion of expiation.[45] Expiation is the reparation of a crime or a sin through an act of sacrifice, that is, the ritualistic shedding of blood. It was indeed central to the commemorative discourse of the period, especially as it pertained to the Terror. Thus we read in one of the earliest issues of the royalist-Catholic newspaper, L'ami de la Religion et du Roi, from 1814, that 'everywhere people make haste to repay the debt accrued toward those sacrificed to the furies of parties ... everyone joins this concert of regrets, homage, expiation and prayer with zeal'.[46] But expiation was inherently contradictory. On the one hand it expressed a desire for reconciliation and pacification and on the other hand it threatened to ignite civil discord, thus resurrecting the violence that it sought to leave behind. According to Fureix, mourning the victims of the Terror during the Restoration meant finding a way to 'remember without representing, expiate without accusing, recalling without reawakening'.[47]

The period between the end of the Terror and the 1830s saw the construction of numerous expiatory monuments for victims of the Terror. To name just a few, they included the chapel of Picpus in Paris, built in 1814; the Brotteaux monument in Lyon, built in 1819; and the chapel of Gabet in the town of Orange, built in 1832, to say nothing of the vast commemorative landscape in the Vendée.[48] Some monuments were public while others were private initiatives. Some boasted ornate structures while others consisted of little more than an improvised sign, usually a cross. Some attracted the attention and, at times, the approbation of authorities, while others were hardly noticed at all. But virtually all were constructed on the burial sites of victims of the Terror, and most involved repeated exhumations and reburials.

The remembrance of the victims of the Terror began spontaneously, as a grass-roots movement. In Lyon, for example, residents of the city inaugurated a commemorative cenotaph on the grounds of Brotteaux, where most victims of the revolutionary repression of the city were buried in mass graves in 1793. In the town of Orange, relatives of victims and other residents took to regular gatherings on the site of the mass graves in the fall of 1794. Eventually, these gatherings reached such proportions that local authorities sent an armed force to disperse the crowd.[49] In Picpus, several noble ladies—most notably, the wife of General Lafayette, whose mother was guillotined in 1794—led an association of families that purchased the plot of land, which contained two large mass graves of victims of the Terror, and began using it as a private cemetery in the early 1800s. In this sense, the origins of the commemoration of victims of the Terror were popular, but socially heterogeneous.

The attitude of the French state toward the commemoration of the Terror changed in rather predictable ways. The Thermidorian Reaction and the Directory tolerated such practices, but appropriated them as legitimating devices. Thus, a representative of the National Convention attended the inauguration of the cenotaph in Lyon. This was a city that, famously, rebelled against the authority of the Convention and, indeed, against the Republic. Now, the representative in Paris assured those present at the inauguration that the victims buried there died, 'for having defended the Republic and human rights...the Lyonnais have never fought under any flag except the *drapeau tricolore*'.[50] In contrast, the Napoleonic regime tended to suppress symbols and practices that recalled revolutionary violence. The Restoration proved more hospitable to the remembrance of victims of the Terror but it too preferred to avoid explicit recollections of revolutionary violence or the regicide of Louis XVI. As with most *lieux de mémoire*, the monuments commemorating the victims of the Terror proved highly malleable to the changing political landscape in France.[51]

But memories of the Terror cannot be reduced to politics and state formation.[52] They were also, perhaps first and foremost, a deeply personal matter for many contemporaries of the revolutionary era. This was especially true for the children, spouses and parents of victims, who needed a place to mourn their loved ones, and maybe even find some sense of closure. During the Terror, victims were thrown pell-mell into mass graves, with no sign marking their final resting place and without the benefit of last rites. In the post-revolutionary era, it became paramount for their families to locate their burial sites and to uphold proper funerary rites, even many years after the events in question.

Proper funerary rites were seen as essential for the restoration of social ties and moral values in the aftermath of the Terror. Thus, a public official, commenting in 1799 on the poor state of French burial grounds, pointed out that 'the French people must feel at present the need for sweet and sentimental ideas, for social ties of every kind, so as not to fall again into the absolute destitution which had nearly led them to barbarism'.[53] But for the bereaved families, this was a matter of mourning their loss, and perhaps also the past that the Revolution did away with. The journal of Amable de Baudus, a nobleman who had emigrated early in the Revolution and whose father had been executed in 1794, attests to this. Having returned to France during the Napoleonic period, we read in his diary entries:

> Wednesday, 13 May 1819, at Picpus with my brother; Monday, July 15 1819, the anniversary of my father's death. Travel to Picpus. I attended mass and then prayed in the grave of the victims of 1794; Wednesday, 5 July 1820, I heard mass said in honour of my father at Picpus; 14 July 1821 [in a letter to his son] three days ago, my dear friend, I made the pilgrimage to Picpus, as I do every year in this month.[54]

For De Baudus, and for many like him, the commemoration of victims of the Terror meant an effort to find continuity in a world deeply marked by rupture. As the examples above illustrate, individual mourning, social regeneration, moral renewal, and political conflicts were inextricably intertwined in the remembrance of victims of the Terror.

CONCLUSION

In the aftermath of the Terror, contemporaries of the revolutionary era grappled with dilemmas of retribution, redress, and remembrance. In seeking to bring those responsible for brutalities to justice, they had to face the question of how to locate individual accountability after mass crime. In trying to remedy the damage caused to citizens by state actions, they had to strike a balance between moral dictates and the political realities of the moment. Remembering the victims of the Terror through monuments and public rituals meant clashing with a social and political environment that, more often than not, preferred to forget revolutionary violence. None of these dilemmas were resolved neatly, nor could they have been. But their very existence, the debate and compromises that they engendered, were in themselves a novel, indeed, modern feature that emerged from the democratizing impulses of the Revolution. As Edgar Quinet noted in his magisterial *La Révolution* (1865), we find no similar debates about how to deal with the effects of political brutality before the French Revolution.[55]

The question of how the Terror, as an event of mass violence, continued to reverberate in post-Revolutionary society long after the fact resonates with ongoing concerns today. Since the Second World War, and in the shadow of the genocides and ethnic cleansing campaigns of the late twentieth century, the question of how societies face the consequences of such large-scale destruction—indeed, the awareness that the responses of human societies to such man-made catastrophes change over time and place—has assumed increasing centrality in academic and cultural life.[56]

The historiography of the French Revolution has not escaped these present-day concerns, but it has also not accepted them fully. As Jean-Clément Martin and Lynn Hunt, respectively, have noted, the emblematic atrocities of the twentieth century have been reorienting our view of the Revolution.[57] This does not mean, of course, that the Reign of Terror was somehow similar to the Holocaust or to the genocides in Rwanda and Bosnia. Of course it was not. Rather, it means that these large-scale atrocities cast such a long shadow over our historiographic horizon that they cannot help but generate new questions about the revolutionary past. Yet although the influence of these present-day concerns on the historiography of the Revolution is evident, especially since the bicentennial, much of the existing scholarship seems to shy away from using the extensive literature on the collective and individual effects of mass violence in order to open up new fields of inquiry.

This is what this chapter has tried to do. With that in mind, it would be useful to mention two additional themes that emerge from ongoing discussions in the social sciences and the humanities and that might be brought to bear on the Revolution, particularly in the aftermath of the Terror. The first is the notion of trauma. The definition of the term is a matter of considerable controversy, but generally speaking, traumatic events can be defined as involving a close encounter with death and the threat of bodily harm. These experiences are so threatening to our sense of self that they cannot be integrated into normal processes of cognition and memory. Instead, they become split off in the mind, giving rise to a wide array of symptoms that seem to take on a life of their own. For the traumatized person, noted the psychiatrist Judith Herman, 'it is as if time stops at the moment of trauma'.[58] Researchers also note that the effects of traumatic events are often collective, impacting families, communities, and even society as a whole.

Using the concept of trauma in order to examine the aftermath of the Terror is promising but also problematic. It is promising because it offers new ways of understanding the experience of revolutionary violence and how it continued to shape social, cultural and political processes in post-Revolutionary France. But it is also problematic because applying this modern diagnostic tool to the experiences of men and women in the late eighteenth century implies a kind of universal, timeless valence that few historians are willing to accept. Nevertheless, several recent studies have made use of the literature on trauma in order to generate new perspectives on the revolutionary era.[59] Literary scholars, in particular, have made use of the notion of trauma in order to examine how the experiences of the Revolution in general, and of revolutionary violence more specifically, found echoes in the fiction of the time.[60]

The second theme that pertains to the aftermath of the Terror and that calls for further research is reconciliation. The late 1790s and even the early 1800s did see recurring waves of violence and reprisals, but ultimately most communities in France found ways of enduring in a social environment where often *terroristes* and victims continued to live side by side many years after the events in question. How did communities endure after the divisive experience of revolutionary violence? What political, social, and cultural mechanisms were used to help communities come to terms with the violence that often tore them apart? Mona Ozouf has shown that festivals were used after 9 Thermidor to cultivate an image of a 'happy nation', a reconciled society in the face of a divisive reality.[61] The founders of the new civic religion, theophilanthropy, which enjoyed a brief heyday under the Directory, noted that one of their goals was to 'heal the wounds of the Revolution ... bringing the hearts closer to each other by preaching mutual forgiveness and the forgetting of all wrongs'.[62] The subject of reconciliation in the aftermath of the Terror remains to be studied, particularly on the local level.

NOTES

1. I would like to thank the Institute for Historical Studies at the University of Texas at Austin for its generous support. I am also grateful to Sandy Chang for providing critical comments at a crucial moment of writing this chapter.
2. Montgey et Poirier. *Atrocités commises envers les citoyennes, ci-devant détenues dans la Maison d'Arrêt, dite la Providence, à Arras, par Joseph Lebon et ses Adhérens, pour servir de suite aux angoisses de la mort ou idées des Horreurs des prisons d'Arras, par les Citoyens Montgey et Poirier de Dunkerque* (Paris [1795]), 26, 52–3.
3. Bronislaw Baczko, *Ending the Terror: the French Revolution after Robespierre* (Cambridge, 1994), 34.
4. Howard G. Brown, *Ending the Revolution: Violence, Justice, and Repression from the Terror to Napoleon* (Charlottesville, 2006), 235.
5. On the latter point, see Ronen Steinberg, 'Trauma before Trauma: Imagining the Effects of the Terror in the Revolutionary Era', in David Andress (ed.), *Experiencing the French Revolution* (Oxford, 2013), 177–99.
6. On the role of petitions by ordinary citizens in social reconstruction after 9 Thermidor, see Suzanne Desan, 'Reconstituting the Social after the Terror: Family, Property, and the Law in Popular Politics', *Past and Present* 164 (1999), 81–121.
7. See Sergio Luzzatto's illuminating study of the memoirs written in the 1820s by the former conventionnels who had been exiled by Louis XVIII in 1816. Sergio Luzzatto, *Mémoire de la Terreur. Vieux montagnards et jeunes républicains au XIXe siècle* (Lyon, 1991). See in particular chapter 6, which deals with the trials and tribulations of the children of former conventionnels.
8. See Charles S. Maier, 'Overcoming the Past? Narrative and Negotiation, Remembering, and Reparation: Issues at the Interface of History and the Law', in John Torpey (ed.), *Politics and the Past: on Repairing Historical Injustices* (New York, 2003), 295–304.
9. *Pétition à la Convention nationale des citoyens de la Commune d'Avignon, victimes de la faction de Robespierre, sur les atrocités commises dans cette commune et dans le département de Vaucluse, par les agens et les complices de cette faction* (Avignon, 1794), 1. The reference to Robespierre's plan to ascend the throne is an allusion to a popular rumor that Robespierre was planning to restore the monarchy. See Baczko, *Ending the Terror*, chapter 1.
10. See Colin Lucas, 'The Theory and Practice of Denunciation in the French Revolution', *Journal of Modern History* 68, no. 4 (1996), 768–85.
11. *Moniteur*, 13 Fructidor, an 2 (30 august 1794), vol. 21, no. 343, 615.
12. See Michel Biard, *Missionnaires de la République. Les représentants du peuple en mission, 1793–1795* (Paris, 2002).

13. See Howard G. Brown, 'Robespierre's Tail: the Possibilities of Justice after the Terror', *Canadian Journal of History* 45 (2010), 303–35.

14. Robert Lindet, *Rapport fait à la Convention nationale dans la séance du 4ème des Sans-Culottides de l'an 2ème, au nom des Comités de salut public, de sûreté générale et de législation, réunis, sur la situation interieure de la république, par Robert Lindet, Représentant du peuple, et membre du comité de salut public* (Montauban), 22.

15. See Baczko, *Ending the Terror*, chapter 3. See also Corinne Gomez-Le Chevanton, 'Le procès Carrier. Enjeux politiques, pédagogie collective et construction mémorielle', *Annales historiques de la Rèvolution francaise*, no. 343 (January–March 2006), 73–92.

16. On the significance of this phrase in the case of Carrier, see Sergio Luzzatto, *L'automne de la Revolution: luttes et cultures politiques dans la France thermidorienne* (Paris, 2001).

17. Baczko interprets these trials as emblematic of the Thermidorian thirst for revenge. See Bronislaw Baczko, *Politiques de la Révolution française* (Paris, 2008), chapter 5.

18. *Réimpression de l'ancien Moniteur, 14 Fructidor, an 2* (31 août, vieux style), vol. 21, no. 344, 622.

19. See Ronen Steinberg, 'Transitional Justice in the Age of the French Revolution', *The International Journal of Transitional Justice* 7, no. 2 (2013), 267–85.

20. Stephen Clay, 'Vengeance, Justice and Reactions in the Revolutionary Midi', *French History* 23, no. 1 (2009), 22–46.

21. See Brown, *Ending the Revolution*.

22. Clay, 'Vengeance, Justice and Reactions in the Revolutionary Midi', 26.

23. Quoted in Brown, 'Robespierre's Tail', 523.

24. See Sophie Wahnich, 'La question de la responsabilité collective en l'an III', in Michel Vovelle (ed.), *Le tournant de l'an III: Réaction et Terreur blanche dans la France révolutionnaire* (Paris, 1997), 85–97.

25. See Patrice Gueniffey, *La politique de la Terreur. Essai sur la violence révolutionnaire, 1789–1794* (Paris, 2000), 27–8.

26. I take the claim for a distinct historiography of the Terror from Haim Burstin, 'Entre théorie et pratique de la Terreur: en essai de balisage', in Michel Biard (ed.), *Les politiques de la Terreur, 1793–4* (Rennes, 2008), 39–52.

27. See Gueniffey, *Politique de la Terreur*, 13.

28. The victims of terrorism have been completely absent from general histories of the phenomenon. See Bruce Hoffman, *Inside Terrorism* (New York, 2006); Gérard Chaliand and Arnaud Blin, *The History of Terrorism, from Antiquity to Al Qaeda* (Berkeley, 2007).

29. See Julia Douthwaite, *The Frankenstein of 1790 and other Lost Chapters from Revolutionary France* (Chicago, 2012), chapter 4.

30. *Réimpression de l'ancien Moniteur, 23 Frimaire, an 3* (13 decembre, vieux style), vol. 22, no. 83, 721.

31. *Réimpression de l'ancien Moniteur, 3 Germinal, an 3* (23 mars, vieux style), vol. 23, no. 183, 21–2.

32. In this context it is telling to note that in their chapter on the Thermidorian Reaction, François Furet and Denis Richet also turned to ghosts and haunting as literary tropes. 'The deputies of the Convention were constantly haunted by two specters: the banishment of the Girondins on 31 May 1793, and the Terror'. François Furet and Denis Richet, *The French Revolution* (New York, 1970), 224.

33. Petition de Marie Joseph Beguinet, 'Veuve Lamotte, aux citoyens membres du comité de legislation près l'assemblée nationale', November 12 1794, *Archives Nationales* (hereafter cited as *AN*), D III 161/3996.

34. Petition de Marianne Edelmann, 'Veuve de Louis Edelmann, à la Convention nationale', 24 November 1794, AN, D III 213/5511.

35. See Luzzatto, *L'automne de la Revolution*, 167–76.

36. See Laura Mason, 'The "Bosom of Proof": Criminal Justice and the Renewal of Oral Culture during the French Revolution', *Journal of Modern History* 76, no. 1 (2004), 29–61.

37. *Réimpression de l'ancien Moniteur, 25 Frimaire, an 3* (15 decembre, vieux style), vol. 22, no. 85, p.738.

38. *Réimpression de l'ancien Moniteur, 24 Prairial, an 3* (12 juin, vieux style), vol. 24, no. 264, p. 658.

39. See Louis Tuetey (ed.), *Procès-Verbaux de la Commission temporaire des arts*, 2 vols (Paris, 1912), 2: 321.

40. On the significance of the *biens nationaux* in the nineteenth century, see the quantitative study by Bernard Bodinier and Éric Teyssier, *L'événement le plus important de la Révolution. La vente des biens nationaux (1789–1867)* (Paris, 2000).

41. Robert W. Gordon, 'Undoing Historical Injustice', in Austin Sarat and Thomas R. Kearns (eds), *Justice and Injustice in Law and Legal Theory* (Ann Arbor, 1996), 36.

42. See Jean-Claude Bonnet, *Naissance du Panthéon. Essai sur le culte des grands homes* (Paris, 1998); Annie Jourdan, *Les monuments de la Révolution, 1770–1804. Une histoire de représentation* (Paris, 1997); and Antoine de Baecque, *Glory and Terror: Seven Deaths under the French Revolution* (New York, 2001).

43. See Joseph Clarke, *Commemorating the Dead in Revolutionary France: Revolution and Remembrance, 1789–1799* (Cambridge, 2007).

44. Emmanuel Fureix, *La France des larmes. Deuils politiques à l'age romantique, 1814–1840* (Seyssel, 2009), 21.

45. See Sheryl Kroen, *Politics and Theater: the Crisis of Legitimacy in Restoration France, 1815–1830* (Berkeley, 2000).

46. *L'ami de la Religion et du Roi. Journal ecclésiastique, politique, et littéraire*, 183 vols (Paris, 1814–62), 1: 282.

47. Fureix, *La France des larmes*, 221.

48. See Ronen Steinberg, 'Spaces of Mourning: the Cemetery of Picpus and the Memory of Terror in Post-Revolutionary France', *Proceedings of the Western Society for French History* 36 (2008), 133–47; and Michel Lagrée and Jeanne Roche, *Tombes de Mémoire. La dévotion populaire aux victimes de la Révolution dans l'Ouest* (Rennes, 1993).

49. See L'abbé S. Bonel, *Les 332 victimes de la Commission populaire d'Orange en 1794, d'après les documents officiels, avec reproduction du monument expiatoire de la chapelle de Laplane et de quinze portraits*, 2 vols (Carpentras, 1888).

50. *Le Journal de Lyon, 19 Prairial, an III* (7 June 1795), no. 33.

51. See Pierre Nora (ed.), *Rethinking France: Les lieux de memoire. Vol. 1: the State* (Chicago, 2001); see also Patrick H. Hutton, 'The Role of Memory in the Historiography of the French Revolution', *History and Theory* 30, no. 1 (1991), 56–69.

52. This comment is pertinent because so much of the literature on memory seems to be about nation building or state formation, so that the personal, emotional dimensions of commemoration are often elided or forgotten entirely. For a critique of this tendency in the literature, see Clarke, *Commemorating the Dead in Revolutionary France*.

53. Quoted in Madeleine Lassère, *Villes et cimetières en France, de l'ancien regime à nos jours. Le territoire des morts* (Paris, 1997), 91.

54. Quoted in Steinberg, 'Spaces of Mourning', 146.

55. See Edgar Quinet, *La Révolution*, 2 vols (Paris, 1987 [1865]), vol. 2, livre vingtième.

56. See Martha Minow, *Between Vengeance and Forgiveness: Facing History after Genocide and Mass Violence* (Boston, 1995); John Torpey, *Making Whole What Has Been Smashed: on Reparations Politics* (Cambridge, MA, 2006).

57 See Jean-Clément Martin, *Violence et Révolution. Essai sur la naissance d'un mythe national* (Paris, 2006); and Lynn Hunt, 'The Experience of Revolution', *French Historical Studies* 32, no. 4 (2009), 671–78.

58. Judith Herman, *Trauma and Recovery: the Aftermath of Violence – from Domestic Abuse to Political Terror* (New York, 1992), 37.

59. See Barry Shapiro, *Traumatic Politics: the Deputies and the King in the Early French Revolution* (College Park, 2009); Patrice Higonnet, 'Terror, Trauma and the "Young Marx" Explanation of Jacobin Politics', *Past and Present* 191 (2006), 121–64.

60. See Douthwaite, *The Frankenstein of 1790*; Debora Jenson, *Trauma and its Representations: the Social Life of Mimesis in Post-Revolutionary France* (Baltimore, 2001); and Katherine Astbury, *Narrative Reponses to the Trauma of the French Revolution* (London, 2012).

61. See Mona Ozouf, *Festivals and the French Revolution* (Cambridge, MA, 1988), 110; see also James Livesey, *Making Democracy in the French Revolution* (Cambridge, MA, 2001).

62. Chemin-Dupontés, *Que-ce que la théophilanthropie?* (Paris, 1868 [1797]), 13.

Selected Reading

Baczko, Bronislaw, *Ending the Terror: the French Revolution after Robespierre* (Cambridge, 1994).

Baczko, Bronislaw, *Politiques de la Révolution française* (Paris, 2008).

Brown, Howard G., *Ending the French Revolution: Violence, Justice and Repression from the Terror to Napoleon* (Charlottesville, 2006).

Brown, Howard G., 'Robespierre's Tail: the Possibilities of Justice after the Terror', *Canadian Journal of History* 45 (2010), 503–35.

Clarke, Joseph, *Commemorating the Dead in Revolutionary France: Revolution and Remembrance*, 1789–1799 (Cambridge, 2007).

Clay, Stephen, 'Vengeance, Justice and Reactions in the Revolutionary Midi', *French History* 23, no. 1 (2009), 22–46.

Desan, Suzanne, 'Reconstituting the Social after the Terror: Family, Property, and the Law in Popular Politics', *Past and Present* 164 (1999), 81–121.

Douthwaite, Julia, *The Frankenstein of 1790 and other Lost Chapters from Revolutionary France* (Chicago, 2012).

Fureix, Emmanuel, *La France des larmes. Deuils politiques à l'âge romantique, 1814–1840* (Seyssel, 2009).

Kroen, Sheryl, *Politics and Theater: the Crisis of Legitimacy in Restoration France, 1815–1830* (Berkeley, 2000).

Luzzatto, Sergio, *Mémoire de la Terreur. Vieux montagnards et jeunes républicains au XIXe siècle* (Lyon, 1991).

Steinberg, Ronen, 'Transitional Justice in the Age of the French Revolution', *The International Journal of Transitional Justice* 7, no. 2 (2013): 267–85.

CHAPTER 29

·····································

JACOBINISM FROM OUTSIDE

·····································

MIKE RAPPORT

IN 1796, as a war-weary British government sought peace talks with the French Republic, Edmund Burke railed against treating with the 'regicides'. The European conflict, he argued, was in fact a civil war, 'between the partizans of the antient, civil, moral, and political order of Europe' and a Jacobinism he labelled as 'a sect of ambitious and fanatical atheists which means to change them all' and which was 'aiming at universal empire'.[1] Burke was not alone: John Robison, a Scottish natural philosopher, and the former Jesuit, Augustin de Barruel, both published works in 1797 arguing that the Revolution was an international conspiracy of Freemasons and freethinkers. For Barruel, Jacobinism was nothing less than Freemasonry finally revealing its ultimate, dark purpose. Cranky though such claims now appear, in the late 1790s for Europeans bending before the roar of revolution and war, they offered an all-embracing explanation for the crisis.[2] Yet Barruel, Burke, and Robison used the term 'Jacobin' very loosely, reinforcing a conservative tendency to define any dissent as dangerous. Almost always inaccurate, such a use of the label probably seemed more plausible because 'Jacobinism' rapidly changed in France itself, as the Revolution rattled forward on its breakneck course.

Yet local radical movements were rooted in national or even regional contexts. Those who conformed closely to the shifting shapes of the French model were few: the Italian *Giacobini* probably came closest to sharing the political egalitarianism and social reformism of the French Jacobins in their heyday of 1793–94. The radical response to the French Revolution varied from one context to another, including differences in political and cultural inheritance, diversities in social interests, the obstacles and scale of resistance to radical demands and the extent and nature of political violence. Complex though these varieties were, they permit a nuanced understanding of the international impact of the French Revolution.

For many years, the international varieties of 'Jacobinism' were debated within national contexts. In some interpretations, it was a foreign import, dangerous and traitorous at worst, or irrelevant to the nation's past at best. For liberals, the 'Jacobins' may have been on the right side of the struggle for progress, but their legacy was negligible because they were (variously) misguided, prone to social levelling, too closely linked to France or out of touch with the real needs and customs of the people. In Italy, this tendency dates to the very aftermath of the upheaval itself. In 1801 the disenchanted Jacobin Vincenzo Cuoco published his *Historical Essay on the Neapolitan Revolution of 1799*. In explaining its failure, Cuoco coined the term 'passive revolution', a phrase later adopted by the Marxist Antonio Gramsci, to mean one imposed 'from above' by an elite on an apathetic or hostile population:

> Our revolution being a passive revolution, the only means of bringing it to a successful conclusion was by winning popular opinion. But the views of the patriots and those of the people were not the same; they had different ideas, different customs, and even different languages.[3]

This was a central problem faced by radicalism across Europe: it was primarily the preserve of a literate, usually urbanized, minority. Even where it had the makings of a nationwide network, it usually attracted only a small section of the middle-class professionals, artisans and craft workers and so it struggled to impose itself on society at large. The essence of Cuoco's charge was taken up by the twentieth-century liberal-nationalist historian, Benedetto Croce. Croce declared that 'modern Italy, the new Italy, our Italy' was born in 1799 because of the patriotic awakening during the Neapolitan revolution. Otherwise, the Neapolitan Jacobins had little real understanding of their own country, so the democracy and egalitarianism that they represented could never be relevant to modern Italy.[4] The *destra storica*, conservative Italian historiography, saw Jacobinism as so utterly foreign to the Italian nation-state that it was both irrelevant and insidious.[5]

Such judgements stuck because 'Jacobinism' frequently depended upon French military intervention for any chance of success, throwing the poisonous problem of collaboration and resistance into the controversial stew. Nineteenth-century German assessments painted the Rhineland Jacobins as 'black-hearted traitors'[6] because they worked with the French, and in the early twentieth century Herman Theodoor Colenbrander accepted the good intentions of the Dutch Patriots, but argued that, once crushed by Prussian intervention in 1787, they had to learn from the real masters of revolution, the French. When they returned to power in 1795, they were merely 'marionetten', puppets on French strings. The trauma of the two world wars intensified such views. One post-war Dutch periodical condemned the Patriots as the 'NSBers', or Dutch Fascists, of the eighteenth century.[7]

Yet there were more positive views of 'Jacobinism'. Left-wing historiography saw it as the forerunner of twentieth-century communism or social democracy. The British post-war labour history tradition placed the British radicalism of the 1790s within the longer-term movement for democracy and social justice.[8] E. P. Thompson's subtle analysis of working-class radicalism argued that the political agitation of the 1790s 'altered the sub-political attitudes of the people, affected class alignments, and initiated traditions which stretch forward into the present [twentieth] century'.[9] For more orthodox Marxists, Jacobinism represented the bourgeois phase of human history: the East German historian Heinrich Scheel, for example, argued that the Mainz republic of 1793 was 'the first bourgeois-democratic republic on German soil' and so was the fore-runner of the 'first German workers' and peasants' state', the DDR.[10]

These interpretations were applied within national contexts, an approach challenged by the 'Atlantic' perspective proposed by Robert R. Palmer and Jacques Godechot, who suggested that the revolutionary upheavals across the eighteenth-century Atlantic world were part of a single movement, broadly similar in causes and aims, in an age of 'democratic' revolution. Marxist historians like Marcel Reinhard and George Rudé responded that it was wrong to lump the French Revolution together with the more moderate American Revolution or the British radical movement.[11] The 'Atlantic' thesis took this battering from the left and then suffered death by a thousand cuts by revision-ist research on the local experience of revolution, war, occupation and resistance. Such work emphasized pre-existing social developments and conflicts, political geography, earlier patterns of reform, customs, and identities.[12]

Much of this scholarship, focusing on resistance to French domination, tends to downplay the importance of 'Jacobinism' outside France. Yet it has effectively built up a complex mosaic representing a stunning diversity of local contexts in which the French Revolution was received, 'Jacobinism' expressed and responses shaped. Moreover, new life has been breathed into the Atlantic perspective. Research on cross-cultural encoun-ters, the movement of people, goods and ideas, slavery, resistance to it and empire have all contributed to a revival of interest in the Atlantic as a historical space for human interaction.[13] Some historians are bursting the bounds of this maritime framework in the 'global turn', which seeks to examine the French Revolution in imperial and world-wide context.[14]

The challenge, it now seems, is how to reconcile the local with such transnational approaches. The latter have explanatory power for the varieties of 'Jacobinism', because they help to explain why they arose in so many different places. In the European world, radicals inhabited a shared cultural space that shaped their ideologies, rhetoric, sym-bols and practices, giving them broadly similar features, overlaid by differences in local detail, that included the classical culture of the elites, the 'classical republicanism' of the Renaissance, historical memories of earlier conflicts such as the Dutch War of Independence and the British civil wars, and the critical culture of the Enlightenment.

Such cultural currents did not amount to a coherent ideology in themselves and indeed they fed both radical and conservative thinking, but for the former they had built ideological pillars such as popular sovereignty, the concept of civic virtue, an emphasis on political rights and representation and the nation as the source of sovereignty and identity. Reform movements across the West broadly sought to break open existing gov-ernments to wider (not necessarily democratic) political participation, but at their most radical they sought nothing less than 'regeneration', meaning the moral and cultural reshaping of an entire people. All such movements emphasized the importance of politi-cal organizations that would press for change and they employed systems of civic educa-tion, festivals, ceremonies and symbols to transmit their message to as wide an audience as possible. Thus, forms of sociability, association and education were central to radicalism, as they had been to the Enlightenment and 'public opinion' more generally. So the forms and expressions of 'Jacobinism' in the 1790s sprang from the forms of sociability and communication that characterized eighteenth-century cultural life. The global or Atlantic context therefore explains the cultural and social environment in which the varieties of 'Jacobinism' developed, but it cannot explain the variety itself.

One way of doing so is to explore the forms of political conflict that pre-existed the French Revolution. A radical movement aiming at a reform of Parliament had been at work in Britain throughout the 1780s and this, in turn, had roots in earlier agitation. In Ireland an energetic political campaign had secured legislative independence for the Parliament in Dublin in 1782, but left open the question of extending the franchise to all Protestants and to Catholics. The Dutch 'Patriot' Revolution of the 1780s saw the expulsion of the ruling Stadhouder until he was restored by Prussian troops in 1787. To the south, in 1789 there was a Belgian war of independence from Habsburg rule and a democratic uprising in the neighbouring Pays de Liège, both of which were crushed by 1790. In Switzerland, there were power struggles between the patricians, burghers and 'natives' of Geneva (1768–82), in which the patricians came out on top, while in Fribourg the patricians defeated a similar challenge to their authority in 1781. In Italy, the 'Jacobinism' of the 1790s was connected to long-standing conflicts and vendettas—over seigneurial rights, landholding, and patronage—whose roots probed deep into the eighteenth century.[15] Across the Atlantic, the American Revolution left a divisive legacy that was crystallizing into the bitter partisanship between conservative Federalists and radical Democratic-Republicans. These conflicts provided the foundation from which the local varieties of 'Jacobinism' emerged under the influence of the French Revolution.

Besides revolutionary pressure for change, enlightened government officials in Europe had sought to strengthen the state through reform 'from above'. In doing so, they invariably challenged vested interests, such as the nobility, the clergy, corporations, guilds, municipalities and provinces, as well as striking at old habits, customs and usages that ordinary people held dear. In Poland, King Stanisław August Poniatowski had since 1764 sought to bolster the Polish-Lithuanian Commonwealth, which was effectively being sucked into the orbit of Catherine the Great's Russia, by a series of reforms that culminated in the Constitution of 3 May 1791. A minority of disenchanted nobles solicited Russian intervention, which came in May 1792.

Moreover, although there was a democratic ('Vonckist') wing to the Belgian revolution of 1789, its leadership lost out to the conservative Statists, for the uprising was principally a conservative backlash against Joseph II's reforms—and such changes were also resisted in Hungary and the Tyrol. Grand duke Leopold of Tuscany saw privileged groups delay, block, or dilute the impact of reform, which also provoked popular hostility because of their assault on religious tradition. 'Jacobins' might therefore be reformers disillusioned with the failure or limits of change, the more so when their initiatives were blunted still further in 1789, as rulers reeled in horror at the news from France. In Piedmont, a brief period of open public debate permitted by Victor Amadeus III was abruptly replaced by censorship and repression.[16] In

Germany, enlightened reforms in states such as Mainz and Bavaria shuddered to a halt. In Austria and Hungary the 'Jacobins' are perhaps more accurately described as 'Josephists'—officials schooled in the radical reformism of Joseph II and radicalized when the tide was turned back from 1790.[17]

The French Revolution acted as a seismic shock on these pre-existing conflicts and frictions, prompting a wide range of responses. Reformers already proud of their enlightened credentials gave a verbal pat on Gallic backs. German intellectuals hailed the Revolution as a good thing for the degenerate French, while arguing that the traditions of enlightened reform in Germany made revolution unnecessary there.[18] British radicals saluted '1789' as the equivalent of their own 'Glorious Revolution' of 1688. When Lafayette presented President George Washington with the key to the Bastille, Thomas Paine approved: 'that the principles of America opened the Bastille is not to be doubted'.[19] For some, the Revolution was a warning of what might happen if flagging reform programmes were not reinvigorated. Pietro Verri in Milan and Francesco Gianni in Florence urged their rulers to enact constitutional concessions in order to pre-empt any spread of the revolutionary contagion. In April 1792, the Society of the Friends of the People in London cited the French Revolution as a fatal example should moderate parliamentary reform fail.[20]

Yet for others, the French experience demonstrated precisely the dangers of making over-hasty changes, since it could unleash uncontrollable, revolutionary forces. Edmund Burke's *Reflections on the Revolution in France* (1790) criticized the French for their inexperience, their destruction of the old order and their determination to found new institutions on abstract principles rather than on custom and tradition. In Italy, the moderate Lombard reformer Gian Carli recoiled in horror as he denounced the 'excesses of Jacobinism' in France, as did the Neapolitan intellectual, Giuseppe Maria Galanti.[21]

The international response was therefore shaped by the lessons that could be drawn from the Revolution and applied in local contexts. Yet there were direct relationships between the French Revolution and the varieties of 'Jacobinism' abroad. Some foreign radicals had their eye on the prize of French diplomatic, or even military, support and tailored their rhetoric accordingly. Dutch Patriot leader Johan Valckenaer, who moved to Paris in April 1791, broke with his own national traditions and proposed a Dutch constitution modelled on the French version, including a centralized constitutional monarchy. These proposals were alien to Dutch Patriot ideology, prompting Pierre Dumont-Pigalle, another Patriot leader, to remark that the Dutch should only borrow from French and American examples in so far as it was 'compatible with the physical and political characters of the seven [Dutch] provinces and with the character and customs of their respective peoples'.[22] After the Russian occupation of Poland in May 1792, Tadeusz Kościuszko, seeking support for an insurrection, promised the French National Convention in 1793 that a free Poland would abolish serfdom and grant equal rights to all Poles, measures which the 3 May constitution had not delivered.

Pragmatic as some of these schemes may have been, France was a source of genuine inspiration for those seeking to reinvigorate their flagging campaigns for reform.

Political associations and clubs, pamphlets, processions and celebrations were nothing new, but the French Revolution injected them with new forms and symbols: trees and statues of liberty (topped with red Phrygian bonnets) were raised, tricolour cockades sported and flags held aloft, civic oaths taken, and songs such as the *Marseillaise* and *Ça Ira* bellowed. The special appeal of the French Revolution was that it rested on the universalist language of the natural rights of man, rhetoric that allowed foreign radicals symbolically to connect their cause with that of the French and to outflank conservative arguments that drew, like Burke's, on appeals to tradition. While Anacharsis Cloots, a radical from Cleves in Germany, took the logical, if utopian, step of envisaging a universal republic, few others went that far. Radicals were galvanized by the French Revolution because it seemed to construct everything anew and to show that national regeneration was possible. But each nation would 'regenerate' according to its own original character. Rather than adopting French models lock, stock, and barrel, they cherry-picked what they thought most useful to their own cause. Encouraged by the publication of Thomas Paine's incisive response to Burke, *Rights of Man, Part One* (1791), British radicals combined appeals to natural rights with customary British symbols and texts, such as Magna Carta, the Bill of Rights of 1689 and the 'Anglo-Saxon' constitution. Most British radicals, in fact, insisted that a reform of the House of Commons would be enough, perhaps accompanied by programmes of education and social reform. Only a minority sought to abolish the monarchy and the aristocracy: the majority insisted that they were loyal to the 'balanced' constitution of King, Lords and Commons.

Dutch Patriots argued that regeneration required more far-reaching political change, including new laws, the embedding of democratic values in Dutch political culture and their inculcation through a renewed national system of education and a reinterpretation of the past. In other words, it was necessary to 'nationalize' the entire people.[23] Progressive Italian intellectuals looked back to ancient Rome, to classical republicanism and to *campanilismo*—the civic virtue of the Renaissance city states— for inspiration. Yet this was merely the first phase of *Giacobinismo* in the early 1790s. The experience of exile in revolutionary France and the shock of the French invasion of 1796 encouraged some *Giacobini* to break more decisively with the past: during the French conquest of 1796–99 (the *trienio*), the radicals saw their chance to liberate and regenerate Italy: in other words, to go far beyond the reformism of earlier years. Figures such as Giovanni Ranza, Filippo Buonarroti and Carlo Botta embraced republicanism, national independence and unity, although they disagreed over whether an Italian republic would be a federal or a unitary state. In Ireland, Nancy Curtin has argued, radical currents had already been at work before the French Revolution influenced the emergence of nationalism and republicanism in the 1790s.[24] Still, Protestant Irish radicals adopted natural rights theory and national sovereignty, refracted from France through the prism of Paine's *Rights of Man*, when they aimed to bridge religious divisions by establishing the Society of United Irishmen in October 1791. Its goal was the enfranchisement of all Irishmen, regardless of creed, which by the mid-1790s developed into a non-sectarian Irish republicanism exemplified by Theobald Wolfe Tone, a leader of the insurrection of 1798.[25]

If they did not abandon their appeals to the national past and custom altogether, radicals none the less demanded political rights *both* as human beings *and* as citizens in their own country: they sought to naturalize French revolutionary forms, symbols and rhetoric within their local contexts.[26] They saw no contradiction in symbolically harnessing their cause to the French Revolution while calling themselves 'patriots': natural rights theory rested on a distinction between 'man', the human being in a state of nature, and the 'citizen', the human being within the nation-state.[27] For eighteenth-century radicals, the latter took priority over the former, but while 'patriotism' certainly meant love of country, it also meant a willingness to put the nation above personal and sectional interests. It thus demanded virtuous self-abnegation and an end to social privilege and political exclusion.

The French Revolution influenced the structures, symbols and rhetoric of radical movements, but again local factors weighed heavily. The London Corresponding Society, founded in January 1792, was partially modelled on the French Jacobins: its members addressed each other as 'citizen', branches were formed across the British capital, and it aimed to create a nationwide network with other reform societies across the country. A significant difference, however, was its low membership dues: its founder, the master-shoemaker Thomas Hardy, declared its members were to be 'unlimited' in order to create a peaceful, law-abiding but irresistible groundswell of pressure for 'a fair, equal and impartial Representation of the People in Parliament'.[28] In Scotland, some eighty Societies of the Friends of the People sent delegates to a Scottish Convention in Edinburgh to press for parliamentary reform in December 1792. Whenever it adjourned, the delegates rose and, in explicit imitation of the French Jacobins, swore to 'live free or die'.[29] Yet the term 'Convention' shows how ambiguous political vocabulary could be: while it of course evoked the republican Assembly in Paris, it tapped directly into the Scottish past, most recently 1784–85, when two burgh conventions had met to campaign for electoral reform.[30]

The Polish insurrection of 1794 adopted the slogan 'Liberty, Integrity, Independence', echoing the French 'Liberty, Equality, Fraternity'.[31] The Poles also invoked the *levée en masse* (raising an army of 72,000 men) and established a self-proclaimed Jacobin club in Warsaw. The radical wing of the uprising adopted other French—and explicitly Jacobin tropes: one song called for the planting of the 'tree of liberty, sign of eternal equality', while the *Marseillaise of the Poles* evoked the executioner for those traitorous nobles (the 'confederates of Targowica') who had called in the Russians—and four of them were condemned to death by a special 'criminal tribunal'.[32]

In the United States, Democratic-Republicans sang songs such as *Ça Ira* and the *Marseillaise*, drank toasts to the French Revolution and planted trees of liberty. One of the largest such demonstrations, replete with French symbols, arose in Boston in January 1793, when the Democratic-Republicans celebrated the first French victory at Valmy.[33] Republicans also fêted Edmond Genêt, the French ambassador, and in 1796, Pierre Adet, the Directory's representative in the United States, evoked an enthusiastic response to his 'Cockade Proclamation', which called on American supporters of the French Revolution to wear *tricolor* cockades. Such celebrations energized the Republican base, choreographed their protests against their Federalist opponents and expressed their support for France. 'Jacobin' symbols were therefore adapted for local political purposes—a point illustrated in truly global terms by Tipu, ruler of the Indian kingdom of Mysore, who, preparing for a mortal struggle with the British East India Company, allowed a small body of French volunteers to form a political club at Seringapatam in May 1797. The French saluted Tipu (rather awkwardly) as 'Citizen Prince', planted a tree of liberty topped with a Phrygian bonnet and swore 'hatred to all Kings, except Tipoo Sultan, the Victorious'.[34] Tipu was no republican, but he pragmatically accepted such tributes in the (vain) hope that more French support would materialize.

The war in Europe gave international 'Jacobinism' its greatest opportunity and its greatest nightmare. Whenever and wherever the French army conquered during its great, if fluctuating, surges between 1792 and 1802, there were local patriots willing to work with the French military and civilian commissioners, hoping to enact their visions for change. Yet it became terrifyingly clear that French strategic and logistical needs would always take precedence over the 'liberation' of the territories that they occupied. The 'Edict of Fraternity' of 19 November 1792 may have offered 'liberty and help' to 'all peoples who wish to recover their liberty', but the teeth were bared in the law of 15 December 1792, which decreed how the 'liberated' peoples would defray the costs of French military occupation. The territories within France's 'natural frontiers' (the Alps, the Pyrenees, and the Rhine)—Nice, Savoy, Belgium, and the Rhineland—were annexed, while the conquests beyond were converted into 'sister republics'. The first was the Batavian (Dutch) Republic in May 1795, followed in Italy between 1796 and 1799 by the Cispadane, Cisalpine, Ligurian, Roman, and Neapolitan Republics, as well as the Helvetic (Swiss) Republic in 1798. They were expected to raise armies and taxes to support the French war effort, as well as paying directly for French armies of occupation. The 'Jacobins' in all these areas were therefore confronted with a dilemma. They might collaborate by serving as officials, judges, gendarmes, and army officers, incurring the wrath of their own people, or they might stand aloof, or even resist French demands, which would deny them the chance of at last realizing their goals, or of mediating between the French occupiers and their own people.[35]

Recent research has in fact suggested that in these circumstances European radicals proved to be more than French 'marionettes'. In Piedmont, the patriots of Alba and Bra protested against some of the worst abuses by the French military.[36] In the Rhineland, patriots such as Joseph Görres and A. G. F. Rebmann suffered fines, imprisonment and the closure of their newspapers by protesting against the excesses of the occupation: in January 1798, Johann Haan rose in the patriotic society in Koblenz and bitterly denounced the 'French leeches'.[37] In September 1795, the officials in the arrondissement of Spa in Belgium vehemently protested against French requisitions, while the Central Administration in Brussels prosecuted attacks against religious ceremonies, ordered surveillance committees to respect the right to privacy and quietly shelved denunciations rather than act on them.[38] While it is true that the French crushed opposition in the Batavian, Cisalpine, and Helvetic Republics, there was still some scope for local aspirations.

Analysis of the Batavian Constitution of 1798 has shown that there was some inspiration from the Dutch Patriots themselves: it was no mere French imposition. It recognized the social rights of Dutch citizens, including the right to work and to social welfare, and it declared that the supreme authority in the land was the legislature, not the executive (this stemming from a long history of conflict with the Stadhouder). The administrative system of departments was adopted, but in a concession to Dutch federalist scruples, they were guaranteed the freedom to run their own affairs.[39] The Helvetic Republic has also been shown to have at least some roots in Swiss traditions. It was the creation of Swiss radicals, among them Frédéric-César de La Harpe and Heinrich Zschokke, who ruptured with the past in creating a unitary state and abolishing seigneurialism, but in so doing they adopted a mixed language of the old and the new, seeing themselves as 'regenerating' existing Swiss virtues and liberties rather than creating new ones.[40] The law code envisaged for the Roman Republic in 1798 sought to protect the Catholic sensibilities of the population by not legalizing divorce and ensuring that the clergy held on to the registration of births, marriages and deaths. Indeed, the very fact that all but one of the 'sister republics' (the sole exception being the short-lived Neapolitan republic) experienced French-sponsored coups d'état shows that the leaders of the satellite states were not behaving as French puppets.[41]

In fact, when the French did prop up more pliable regimes, they were sometimes challenged by local Jacobins, especially in Italy, where the *Giacobini* had espoused a social egalitarianism (inspired in part by the emergency measures in France during the Year 2) that was enough to make the property-respecting leaders of Directorial France blench. Worse, some Italian Jacobins forged contacts with their French counterparts: Buonarroti was among those arrested with Gracchus Babeuf and the 'Conspiracy of the Equals'.[42] *Giacobini* imitation of French Jacobinism was explicitly a means of opposing French exploitation of Italy, of realizing their own visions of Italian independence and of challenging the limits of the reforms touted by the moderates in the sister republics. When Piedmontese Jacobins sought to oppose the annexation of their country by the French in 1799, they were supported by a peasant uprising in the Langhe region—and the insurgents bore as their symbols busts of the French Jacobin heroes Le Peletier and Marat.[43]

To conservatives, such behaviour simply demonstrated how dangerous Jacobinism was. The backlash almost everywhere took the shape of both official repression and popular reaction. The official response included prophylactic legislation against French influences, which included laws against foreigners and French citizens in particular: Austria (in 1792), Britain, Russia and Spain (in 1793) and the United States (in 1798) all passed such measures. Censorship was made stricter almost everywhere: in Britain, there were no fewer than 200 prosecutions for 'seditious libel' in the 1790s, meaning writings that incited disorder.[44] Newspapers in Austria were prohibited from commenting on politics from the spring of 1792 and in the United States there were fifteen prosecutions of radical journalists under the Alien and Sedition Acts of 1798.

Civil liberties were also curtailed: the British Parliament suspended habeas corpus twice, in 1794 and 1798, and governments prosecuted alleged 'Jacobins', with 'treason trials' taking place in Scotland (1793), England (1794), Austria and Hungary (1795). Driven underground, a small minority of British radicals formed the 'United Britons', 'United Englishmen' and 'United Scotsmen' to link up with the United Irish revolutionary movement and to lay the foundations for a French invasion. Ironically, then, the more hysterical claims that the British radical movement was subversive became a self-fulfilling prophecy. Governments also used the threat of 'Jacobinism' as a pretext to further their own strategic interests. In 1792, Catherine the Great claimed that she was 'fighting Jacobinism in Poland' as she crushed the emergent constitutional state. In India, Tipu's French flirtation gave the British the excuse they needed to unleash the fourth Anglo-Mysore war in 1799, destroying the power of the southern Indian kingdom. They also forced the surrender of the French military contingent in Hyderabad, citing its 'most virulent principles of Jacobinism'.[45]

Even more overwhelming was the popular backlash against the radicals. There were insurrections against the French and their collaborators in Belgium and Luxemburg and widespread resistance in the Rhineland in 1798. The spark was the introduction of conscription, but the uprisings were also underpinned by outraged religious sensibilities. They targeted both the French and those locals who collaborated with them: those who bought church lands, who assumed public office, or Jews who enjoyed civil rights under the new order. In Britain, loyalist organizations, sponsored by the government and the local elites rallied (or cajoled) the wider population into the defence of the established order. Yet, while the Association for the Preservation of Liberty and Property against Republicans and Levellers, created in November 1792, and the Volunteer militias, recruited from 1794, served such a purpose, probably just as weighty in the defeat of British radicalism were the unknown quantities of day-to-day intimidation and ostracism of individual radicals at a local level. Similar processes rapidly emerged in the United States, where it was easy for Federalists to accuse Democratic-Republicans of subversive, treasonous intent, particularly in 1798, when the United States and France came close to war.[46]

Popular conservatism, like the Jacobinism it opposed, was rooted as much in local as it was in national and international concerns. It was not necessarily 'counter-revolutionary' in the sense that it aimed to restore the old regime, but it was frequently 'anti-revolutionary', meaning that it protested against particular measures such as conscription, taxation, the assault on the church and on long-cherished customs. The rank-and-file insurgents who followed Cardinal Fabrizio Ruffo in his 1799 Sanfedist uprising against the Neapolitan Republic were driven by deep social grievances. The Jacobins were mostly property-owning bourgeois and nobles and, while the republicans were slow in abolishing feudalism, Ruffo attracted recruits because he promised to do so immediately. In the Tuscan cities of Arezzo and Siena, anti-Jacobin resistance combined with social protest in 1799: the mobs assaulted both 'Jacobins' and anyone thought to be starving the people, including Jews, who in Siena were slaughtered.[47]

Ultimately, 'Jacobinism' outside France suffered precisely because it existed in a state of near-permanent tension between three points: a broad sympathy for the French Revolution, a patriotic commitment to 'regeneration' or reform, and localized concerns and conflicts. Seen in this light, 'Jacobinism', in fact, was not only a response to the French Revolution, but also a symptom of the geographically more widespread and longer-term transition from the *ancien régime* to modern politics. So when the international varieties of radicalism were set within their local contexts, the application of the label 'Jacobin' was rarely accurate and was often polemical, a trope used by radicals' and reformers' conservative opponents to couple them with the political violence of the French Revolution and so to discredit not only the radical programme, but in the process the longer-term process of reform from which it had, in part, sprung. Indeed, the term 'Jacobin' all too easily concealed a diverse and often conflicting range of reformist tendencies that drew on ideas, traditions and a cultural milieu of which the influence of the French Revolution was only one, albeit sometimes the predominant, part.

The Neapolitan case illustrates this point well. In this southern part of Italy the term 'Jacobinism' could be applied indiscriminately to those who supported the six-month republic between January and June 1799, created an impression of discipline and unity of purpose among the 'patriots' that may have suited Bourbon purposes after Ruffo's successful Sanfedist insurrection against the republic, which was followed by a reaction in which ninety-nine leading republicans were executed and hundreds exiled. Yet the label 'Jacobinism' papered over deep divisions both among the Neapolitan republicans of 1799 and between the aims of these southern Italian radicals and the French. The first are exemplified by contrasting political ideas of two 'martyrs' of 1799, Mario Pagano and Vincenzo Russo. While Pagano had emerged from the traditions of enlightened reform in the eighteenth century and sought to give them political shape, Russo sought nothing less than social and moral renewal and a democratic republic. Where Pagano's republicanism drew heavily on the notions of balanced government associated with Montesquieu and proposed a constitution similar to that of 1795 in France, which had created the Directory, Russo, more heavily influenced by Rousseau and the abbé Mably, was ultimately a proponent of direct democracy, in which the people's representatives could be recalled by their electors. Such was Russo's ideal vision, but he agreed with Pagano, Cuoco and other Neapolitan patriots that the vast majority of their compatriots were not educated enough to enjoy political rights, so for the time being Russo accepted the view that Naples had to be governed by a political elite whose task was to educate the people, inculcate republican values and guide them towards democracy.

While Russo's ideas of regeneration driven by a political elite in order to forge an egalitarian democracy overlapped strongly with French Jacobinism of 1793–94, Pagano's version of republicanism owed almost everything to the reformist traditions of Enlightenment Italy. In his constitutional project, the republic would be run by an elite which had both substantial wealth and a formal, university education. Access to formal political participation might be gradually opened through education and, like Russo, this would be injected with a potent dose of civic instruction in republican 'virtue', but there was none of Russo's egalitarian zeal for direct democracy here. Rather, Pagano's project adopted the Directory's system of indirect suffrage and electoral colleges, albeit with a franchise even more restricted than that in France between 1795 and 1799.[48] The differences between Pagano and Russo reflected the sort of confluence of influences that were at work within the local varieties of 'Jacobinism' right across Europe.

That the more moderate Neapolitan patriots rejected 'Jacobinism' as a model altogether is shown by Pagano's draft constitution, which would have banned political clubs and collective petitions—an incongruous position for one labelled as a 'Jacobin' by his conservative opponents. In fact, Pagano had copied verbatim the clauses of the French constitution of 1795 (Articles 360–2) that absolutely forbade the establishment of political societies. If in France this, of course, reflected Thermidorian determination to extract what had recently been the vital organ of Jacobinism from France's body politic—and Pagano took this as a salutary example.

In practice, however, as in France, political societies did emerge in Naples in 1799: the first was encouraged by the new government in February as a *Sala di istruzione*, or 'chamber of public instruction'—charged with 'spreading and propagating the principles of the Republican Revolution and of public morality'. Yet it was strictly enjoined not to stray from this central purpose, and it was banned from presenting petitions to the government or—in another rejection of the former French Jacobin model—corresponding with other organizations.[49] In fact, some eighteen political societies did emerge in Naples during the brief republican period, but they were frequently warned—by the French military authorities as well as the Neapolitan leadership alike—to avoid the creation of 'parties', 'factions', and the denunciation of individuals. In one such admonition, in fact, General Championnet had urged the Neapolitan patriots to 'learn from our [French] experience' and to not allow the clubs to 'give rise to factions that within a short space will destroy any republic' and which 'frequently deformed' the Revolution in France.[50]

Where most (not all) Neapolitan 'Jacobins' did indeed join in a common sense of purpose was in their determination to secure the independence of their new republic from its French 'liberators', an aim which—quite apart from the domestic need to legitimize the republic among its own people—gave such urgency to their debates over the constitution. In his *Historical Essay on the Revolution of Naples*, Vincenzo Cuoco famously denounced the patriots' pragmatic though dangerous dependence on the success of French arms, but in a lesser-known text, his *Fragments of Letters to Vincenzio Russo*, he also criticized Pagano's 1799 project for a Neapolitan constitution because it depended too heavily on the French Constitution of 1795 as a model. This was not just grumbling with the benefit of hindsight: at the time of writing, Cuoco was in exile in Milan in 1801 and, with the French reconquest of northern Italy after Bonaparte's victory at Marengo, the question of a constitution which suited Italian rather than French purposes was once again urgent. Cuoco was in fact warning his fellow Italians not to repeat the mistakes of his Neapolitan compatriots by drawing too heavily on the French example—which would now mean the Napoleonic constitution of 1800.[51]

The Neapolitan experience shows that, when set in the wider context of the processes of reform, state-building, and political transformation that began in decades before 1789, the varieties of 'Jacobinism' appear as one response to debates about freedom and political identity that were being hotly contested around the world. In Europe, the defeat of 'Jacobinism' ensured that beyond France 'patriotism' and 'nation' would be defined less in terms of rights and citizenship and more in those of church, king, province, hierarchy, custom and tradition. Meanwhile, 'Jacobinism' and democratic politics in general were tarnished by their associations with the Terror, but this is ironic given that outside France most so-called 'Jacobins' were dedicated to reform and the rule of law, particularly in Germany and Britain.

The revolutionary or conspiratorial strains of 'Jacobinism' arose in countries where earlier political violence still festered, as in the Netherlands, where the repressive response of the state drove a significant number of radicals underground, as in Italy and Ireland, or where 'Jacobinism' arose from long-standing and bitter social conflicts, as again in Italy and Ireland. Yet, in a world where hierarchies, loyalties and social deference had been strongly challenged by war, revolution and radicalism, 'Jacobinism' did leave a legacy—a stock of ideas and historical memories that suggested alternative paths to the nation-state in the nineteenth century and provided an arsenal of symbols and rhetoric for later democratic movements. Musings such as these can only be tentative: historians have begun to explore the varieties of the democratic political culture of the 1790s within a transnational framework, but there is much work still to be done. There has been no recent attempt at a comprehensive, comparative analysis of the 'sister republics', although a start has been made.[52] The counter-revolutionary outbreaks in Europe in the late 1790s, or indeed of the broader conservative backlash in a European and Atlantic context, have also yet to be studied in international perspective. Such studies would enable a more comprehensive history of the rise and fall of international 'Jacobinism' to be written.

NOTES

1. E. Burke, *Two Letters Addressed to a Member of the present Parliament, on the proposals for peace with the Regicide Directory of France* (London, 1796), 144.
2. W. Doyle, *The Oxford History of the French Revolution* (Oxford, 1989), 218–19.
3. Quoted in D. Beales (ed.), *The Risorgimento and the Unification of Italy* (London, 1971), 113–14.
4. J. A. Davis, 'The Neapolitan Revolution, 1799–1999: Between History and Myth', *Journal of Modern Italian Studies 4* (1999), 350–1 [350–79]; D. Mack Smith, 'Benedetto Croce: History and Politics', *Journal of Contemporary History 8* (1973), 42 [41–61].
5. M. Broers, *Napoleonic Imperialism and the Savoyard Monarchy 1773–1821: State Building in Piedmont* (Lewiston, 1997), 3.
6. T. C. W. Blanning, *Reform and Revolution in Mainz 1743–1803* (Cambridge, 1974), 295.
7. Quoted in S. Schama, *Patriots and Liberators: Revolution in the Netherlands 1780–1813* (London, 1992), 16, 19.
8. J. Saville (ed.), *Democracy and the Labour Movement: Essays in Honour of Dona Torr* (London, 1954); G. D. H. Cole and A. W. Filson (eds), *British Working Class Movements: Select Documents, 1789–1875* (London, 1951).
9. E. P. Thompson, *The Making of the English Working Class* (Harmondsworth, 1968), 111.

10. Quoted in T. C. W. Blanning, 'The German Jacobins and the French Revolution', *Historical Journal 23* (1980), 985.

11. R. R. Palmer, *The Age of the Democratic Revolution: A Political History of Europe and America, 1760–1800*, 2 vols (Princeton, 1959–64); J. Godechot, *France and the Atlantic Revolution of the Eighteenth Century, 1770–1799* (New York, 1965). The debate can be followed in P. H. Amann (ed.), *The Eighteenth-Century Revolution: French or Western?* (Lexington, 1963).

12. See, for example, Broers and Schama, already cited, and T. C. W. Blanning, *The French Revolution in Germany: Occupation and Resistance in the Rhineland, 1792–1802* (Oxford, 1983); M. Broers, *The Napoleonic Empire in Italy, 1796–1814: Cultural Imperialism in a European Context?* (Basingstoke, 2005); M. Rowe, *From Reich to State: the Rhineland in the Revolutionary Age, 1780–1830* (Cambridge, 2003).

13. See, for example, such comparative studies as A. Jourdan, *La Révolution, une exception française?* (Paris, 2004); W. Klooster, *Revolutions in the Atlantic World: A Comparative History* (New York and London, 2009); for the movement of people and ideas, see, for instance, M. Durey, *Transatlantic Radicals and the Early American Republic* (Lawrence, 1997); M. Jasanoff, *Liberty's Exiles: The Loss of America and the Remaking of the British Empire* (London, 2011): this last extends its scope further than the Atlantic littoral.

14. L. Hunt, 'The French Revolution in Global Context', in D. Armitage and S. Subrahmanyam, *The Age of Revolutions in Global Context, c.1760–1840* (Basingstoke, 2010), 36; C. A. Bayly, *The Birth of the Modern World, 1780–1914: Global Connections and Comparisons* (Oxford, 2004), 86–120 (chapter 3 on 'Converging Revolutions'); J. Darwin, *After Tamerlane: The Rise and Fall of Global Empires, 1400–2000* (London, 2008), 157–218 (chapter 4 on 'The Eurasian Revolution').

15. Broers, *Napoleonic Empire in Italy*, 18; M. Broers, 'Revolution as Vendetta: Patriotism in Piedmont, 1794–1821', *Historical Journal 33* (1990), 573–97; J. A. Davis, '1799: Santafede and the Crisis of the Ancien Regime in Southern Italy', in J. A. Davis and P. Ginsborg (eds), *Society and Politics in the Age of the Risorgimento: Essays in Honour of Denis Mack Smith* (Cambridge, 1991), 1–25.

16. M. Broers, 'The end of a golden age or the implosion of a false absolutism? The Kingdom of Piedmont-Sardinia from absolutism to revolution, 1685 1814', in J. Swann and J. Félix (eds), *The Crisis of the Absolute Monarchy: France from Old Regime to Revolution: Proceedings of the British Academy 184* (Oxford, 2013), 58–9.

17. E. Wangermann, *From Joseph II to the Jacobin Trials: Government Policy and Public Opinion in the Habsburg Dominions in the Period of the French Revolution* (London, 1959), 13.

18. T. C. W. Blanning, *Reform and Revolution in Mainz, 1743–1803* (Cambridge, 1974), 329.

19. Quoted in G. S. Wood, *The Empire of Liberty: A History of the Early Republic, 1789–1815* (Oxford, 2009), 174.

20. H. T. Dickinson, *Liberty and Property: Political Ideology in Eighteenth-Century Britain* (London, 1979), 237.

21. J. Robertson, 'Enlightenment and Revolution: Naples 1799', *Transactions of the Royal Historical Society*, 6th series, 10 (2000), 40.

22. Quoted in A. Jourdan, *La Révolution batave entre la France et l'Amérique (1795–1806)* (Rennes, 2008), 67.

23. Jourdan, *Révolution batave*, 436.

24. N. Curtin, *The United Irishmen: Popular Politics in Ulster and Dublin, 1791–1798* (Oxford, 1994), 5.

25. M. Elliott, *Wolfe Tone: Prophet of Irish Independence* (New Haven and London, 1989).

26. Jourdan, *La Revolution, une exception française?*, 271–2.

27. D. A. Bell, *The Cult of the Nation in France: Inventing Nationalism, 1680–1800* (Cambridge, MA, 2001), 154–6.

28. A. Goodwin, *The Friends of Liberty: The English Democratic Movement in the Age of the French Revolution* (London, 1979), 191–3.

29. H. W. Meikle, *Scotland and the French Revolution* (Glasgow, 1912), 110.

30. J. Cannon, *Parliamentary Reform 1640–1832* (Cambridge, 1973), 112.

31. N. Davies, *God's Playground: A History of Poland*, 2 vols (Oxford, 1981–82), i, 539.

32. B. Leśnodorski, *Les Jacobins Polonais* (Paris, 1965), 265–6, 269.

33. S. Newman, *Parades and the Politics of the Street: Festive Culture in the Early American Republic* (Philadelphia, 1997), 122–5.

34. M. Hasan, *History of Tipu Sultan* 2nd edn (Delhi, 1971), 289; S. P. Sen, *The French in India, 1763–1816* (New Delhi, 1971), 550.

35. On this point, see especially the discussions in Jourdan, *La Révolution: une exception française?* Part One, Chapter 4 (on the European impact of the French Revolution) and Godechot, *La Grande Nation: L'expansion révolutionnaire de la France dans le monde* (Paris, 1983), especially 357–75 on the troubled relationship between France and its 'sister republics'.

36. Broers, *Napoleonic Imperialism*, 256–9.

37. Blanning, *French Revolution in Germany*, 267.

38. M. Rapport, 'Belgium under French Occupation: Between Collaboration and Resistance, July 1794 to October 1795', *French History* 16 (2002), 65, 70–1.

39. Jourdan, *La Révolution: une exception française?*, 260–3.

40. M. Lerner, *A Laboratory of Liberty: The Transformation of Political Culture in Republican Switzerland, 1750–1848* (Leiden and Boston, 2012), 130–3.

41. Godechot, *La Grande Nation*, 357–75.

42. S. J. Woolf, *A History of Italy 1700–1860: The Social Constraints of Political Change* (London, 1979), 161–2, 167–81.

43. Doyle, *Oxford History*, 367.

44. C. Emsley, 'An aspect of Pitt's "Terror": Prosecutions for Sedition during the 1790s', *Social History* 6 (1981), 174.

45. Quoted in Hasan, *History of Tipu Sultan*, 291.

46. J. C. Miller, *The Federalist Era 1789–1801* (New York, 1963), 228.

47. R. Mori, 'Il popolo toscano durante la rivoluzione e l'occupazione francese', *Archivio Storico Italiano* 105 (1947), 147.

48. A. de Francesco, 'How not to finish a Revolution', in G. Imbruglia (ed.), *Naples in the Eighteenth Century: The Birth and Death of a Nation State* (Cambridge, 2000), 172–4.

49. M. Battaglini, *Il 'Pubblico Convocìo': Stato e Cittadini nella Repubblica Napoletana del 1799* (Naples, 2003), 224.

50. Quoted in A. M. Rao, 'Popular Societies in the Neapolitan Republic of 1799', *Journal of Modern Italian Studies* 4 (1999) 362 [358–69].

51. Francesco, 'How not to finish a Revolution', 169–71. It has been argued that Cuoco's 'Fragments' were conceived in the spring of 1799, while the Neapolitan Republic was still in existence: this supported later historiography that could claim that Cuoco was essentially a political moderate, even a conservative, whose criticisms of Italian 'Jacobinism' dated to even when its Neapolitan variety was apparently triumphant. Yet in his article, Antonino

de Francesco compellingly places the 'Fragments' in the context in which Cuoco's more famous work—his 'Historical Essay'—was written, namely in exile in Milan, under the shadow of Bonaparte in 1800–1.

52. Annie Jourdan's *La Révolution: une exception française?* includes a trenchant chapter on the subject (212–76) and a collection edited by Pierre Serna has made a good start towards a reassessment: P. Serna (ed.), *Républiques Soeurs: Le Directoire et la Révolution atlantique* (Rennes, 2009).

SELECTED READING

Blanning, T. C. W., *The French Revolution in Germany: Occupation and Resistance in the Rhineland, 1792–1802* (Oxford, 1983).

Broers, M., *Napoleonic Imperialism and the Savoyard Monarchy 1773–1821: State Building in Piedmont* (Lewiston, 1997).

Broers, M., *The Napoleonic Empire in Italy, 1796–1814: Cultural Imperialism in a European Context?* (Basingstoke, 2005).

Curtin, N., *The United Irishmen: Popular Politics in Ulster and Dublin, 1791–1798* (Oxford, 1994).

Durey, M., *Transatlantic Radicals and the Early American Republic* (Lawrence, 1997).

Elliott, M., *Wolfe Tone: Prophet of Irish Independence* (New Haven and London, 1989).

Francesco, A. de, 'How not to finish a Revolution', in G. Imbruglia (ed.), *Naples in the Eighteenth Century: The Birth and Death of a Nation State* (Cambridge, 2000), 167–82.

Godechot, J., *La Grande Nation: L'expansion révolutionnaire de la France dans le monde* (Paris, 1983).

Goodwin, A., *The Friends of Liberty: The English Democratic Movement in the Age of the French Revolution* (London, 1979).

Jourdan, A., *La Révolution, une exception française?* (Paris, 2004).

Jourdan, A., *La Révolution batave entre la France et l'Amérique (1795–1806)* (Rennes, 2008).

Klooster, W., *Revolutions in the Atlantic World: A Comparative History* (New York and London, 2009).

Lerner, M., *A Laboratory of Liberty: The Transformation of Political Culture in Republican Switzerland, 1750–1848* (Leiden and Boston, 2012).

Newman, S., *Parades and the Politics of the Street: Festive Culture in the Early American Republic* (Philadelphia, 1997).

Rao, A. M., 'Popular Societies in the Neapolitan Republic of 1799', *Journal of Modern Italian Studies* 4 (1999) 358–69.

Rowe, M., *From Reich to State: the Rhineland in the Revolutionary Age, 1780–1830* (Cambridge, 2003).

Schama, S., *Patriots and Liberators: Revolution in the Netherlands 1780–1813* (London, 1992).

Serna, P. (ed.), *Républiques Soeurs: Le Directoire et la Révolution atlantique* (Rennes, 2009).

PART VI

AFTER THERMIDOR

CHAPTER 30

....

THERMIDOR AND THE MYTH OF RUPTURE

....

LAURA MASON

THE Thermidorian period was long the outcast at the revolutionary table, severed from all that preceded and much of what followed. Although these fifteen months were, chronologically, merely the second half of the National Convention's stormy three-year tenure (September 1792–October 1795), historians traditionally described them as a discrete moment inaugurated by Maximilien Robespierre's defeat (9 Thermidor II/27 July 1794). In so doing, they excised the period from the broader revolutionary dynamic.[1]

Thermidor's narrow interpretive boundaries are rooted in an enduring determination to explain the relationship between liberalism and radicalism which, even today, focuses attention on the Revolution's early years. Although conservatives followed Edmund Burke in linking the 1789 challenge of traditional order to the chaos and violence of 1793–4, and Marxists celebrated the emergence of democracy from bourgeois revolution as the promise of future upheaval, historians across the spectrum agreed that the process of radicalization was one of the Revolution's most important features.[2] Because that process reached its zenith during Robespierre's tenure on the Committee of Public Safety, it seemed that his end marked the Revolution's end. Accordingly, nineteenth-century historians like Thomas Carlyle and Jules Michelet abruptly terminated their accounts of the Revolution at 9 Thermidor. If twentieth-century historians were more inclined to look beyond that fatal moment, few believed that the Thermidorians did anything more than turn back the clock to the liberalism of 1789, either by reversing Jacobin social revolution or restoring the autonomy of civil society.[3]

It was Polish philosopher Bronislaw Baczko who reoriented the historiography in the late twentieth century. He argued that Robespierre's defeat neither ended nor reversed the Revolution but initiated a process of consolidation and closure that was significant in its own right.[4] As Baczko saw it, Thermidorian legislators did not just liberate themselves from the stultifying orthodoxies of the year II but openly challenged them, struggling to identify those guilty of the Terror's crimes without endorsing revenge and to repudiate the Terror's politics without renouncing the republic. Finding dying radicalism and rising reaction equally threatening, the Thermidorians crafted a middle way forward with the conservative but Republican constitution of 1795 that brought the Directory into being.

Baczko's assertion that Thermidor sustained the republic by transforming it gave the period new value and illuminated the Revolution's continuing dynamism. His work laid the foundation for a scholarship that knits together Thermidor and Directory to explain how the republic continued to refashion itself until swept away by Empire in 1804.[6] Despite Baczko's success in highlighting Thermidor's links to the years that followed, however, he continued to sever the period from what preceded, echoing the Thermidorian claim that Robespierre's defeat marked a decisive rupture. And yet, if 9 Thermidor changed the balance of forces in the National Convention, it did not make a clean sweep of all revolutionary aspirations and political practices. Rather, the Thermidorians preserved as much as they jettisoned: they repealed radical legislation but enhanced the Assembly's growing power, and they repudiated Jacobin 'tyranny' with practices that the Jacobins themselves had perfected. In short, Thermidor did not signal rupture but triggered a realignment of forces whose shifting priorities masked fundamental continuities in revolutionary political culture. This chapter examines the complex amalgam of change and continuity that characterized the Thermidorian period to explain how revolutionaries innovated while remaining rooted in a political culture that had been under construction since 1789.

RUPTURE

Maximilien Robespierre's defeat on 9 Thermidor II (27 July 1794) lifted the Revolution from the state of paralysis into which the Committee of Public Safety had plunged it.[7] For the Committee, after having galvanized France to defeat domestic counter-revolution and secure its borders in 1793, had turned on old allies in 1794 as it defined revolutionary orthodoxy ever more narrowly. In March, it targeted rivals on the left—the journalist Jacques-René Hébert and his allies, who were demanding more aggressive measures against food hoarders and moderates—then, in April, it went after men to its right, eliciting the execution of Georges-Jacques Danton and fellow 'Indulgents' who promoted political normalization. Beyond the Convention, popular militants were cowed into silence and formerly outspoken revolutionary newspapers toed the party line. In the memorable words of Louis-Antoine de Saint-Just, the Revolution was frozen. In reply, an uneasy coalition formed amongst extremist, moderate, and opportunist deputies concerned about the nation's future and their own. When Robespierre hinted at a new purge, they shouted him down from the floor of the National Convention and arrested him. The Incorruptible went to the guillotine with more than a hundred allies in the worst official blood-letting that the nation would witness for a century.

The extended retreat from political and economic radicalism that followed—a moment traditionally named the Thermidorian Reaction—unfolded in four distinct stages over the next fifteen months. The first stage, which lasted well into the autumn, saw gradual mobilization for change as deputies and private citizens took in the implications of Robespierre's defeat. Showing unity that would soon vanish, the National Convention acted quickly in a few key areas: in a few short weeks it repealed the notorious Prairial Laws, which had suppressed legal protections for those accused of political crimes and inflated the definition of counter-revolution; it trimmed the powers of the Committees of Public Safety and General Security; it limited the reach of the Revolutionary Tribunal; and it released thousands of political prisoners. The liberalization signalled by these measures revitalized public life. The press recovered its old vigour as pamphlets and newspapers sprang up, condemning Robespierre's political heirs as they faced off against Jacobins who continued to warn against the dangers of 'moderation'. In city streets, fashionable people jettisoned Republican austerity to crowd restaurants and elegant salons, while young men known as gilded youth noisily challenged Republican pieties. The steady evolution of public opinion was catalysed in mid-autumn by the revelation of atrocities committed in Nantes the previous year under the command of Jean-Baptiste Carrier, a Jacobin representative-on-mission. Newspapers publicized horrific accounts of rape, torture, and slaughter, charging that Jacobin ideology was as guilty as the man himself. When gilded youth attacked the club's Paris meeting hall in early November, the Convention seized on the public disorder as an excuse to close it indefinitely.

The rightward shift in public opinion generated the second wave of reaction, returning initiative to the Convention by strengthening the position of those legislators most eager to advance reform. Their first act was to lead the Assembly in restoring seventy-three colleagues they had purged as Girondin sympathizers in June 1793. When they turned next to the controlled economy of the year II, the liberal opinions of the returned men hastened a change of climate within which even old Montagnards had come to believe that the Convention must free trade to foster growth. So they eliminated public workshops and the general maximum, which had guaranteed work and affordable food through wartime crisis. But such abrupt deregulation triggered a runaway inflation that was intensified by a ferociously cold winter, which froze the Seine and suspended grain transport. In the capital, working people starved to death in the shadow of wealthy excess. This ghastly disparity in suffering fed popular longing for vanished social welfare policies and the Republican egalitarianism of year II, so the spring thaw brought renewed insurgency. In April 1795 (12 Germinal year III) and again in May (1 Prairial year III), hungry crowds descended on the Convention to demand food and implementation of the democratic constitution of 1793, suspended since its adoption.[8]

The popular insurgency of Germinal and Prairial proved a poor imitation of previous revolutionary crowd actions, which had managed to wring important concessions from successive Assemblies. Lacking spokesmen to make concrete demands and a sufficient number of sympathetic deputies to channel their energy into effective legislation, the crowds of 1795 hardened the reaction, which entered its third and most violent phase.

The Convention answered the first uprising with force and retribution: it called on the National Guard to clear its halls and decreed deportation without trial for the surviving members of the Robespierrist Committee of Public Safety. In the wake of the second insurrection, the Convention determined to be done for good with popular revolution. After purging forty deputies, who would be remembered as the 'last Montagnards', it turned its wrath outward, sending armed forces to subdue the popular faubourg Antoine and establishing a military commission that judged and summarily executed presumed insurgents. The deputies were assisted in their efforts to subdue the capital by moderates in the Paris sections, who disarmed and denounced thousands of radical militants, and angry newspaper editors, who replaced the revolutionary celebrations of popular militancy that had dotted their pages since 1789 with jeremiads against unruly crowds. In the Midi, the White Terror exploded as reactionaries and royalists targeted Jacobin administrators, their families and allies in prison massacres and episodes of private violence that left bodies broken in public squares, washed up on river banks, and festering at crossroads. A chill fell over popular militancy.[9]

The Convention's final months marked the fourth stage of the reaction, characterized by efforts to restore order and found a new political equilibrium. In the late summer, legislators abandoned the democratic constitution for a more conservative code that preserved the Republic but rejected universal male suffrage, the right to insurrection, and ironclad guarantees of free speech and association. And yet, the deputies still faced serious challenges from the right. Having accepted assistance from reactionary activists known as gilded youth during the popular insurgency of Germinal and Prairial, they found the young men to be ever more unruly allies. Mounting tensions exploded after the Convention decreed that two-thirds of its members must be elected or co-opted to the new government, a move that mingled the deputies' desire to prevent reaction at the polls with their more cynical wish to retain power. When a frustrated right rebelled against the decree in late September (Vendémiaire year IV), the youth joined in. The Convention turned the army on them and, in a final gesture meant to restore the embattled left, issued an amnesty for acts committed in association with the Revolution. Then it dissolved itself in favour of the Directory.

POLITICAL CONTINUITY

The preceding account of Thermidor as a moment of rupture is one on whose contours historians across the spectrum agree, whether emphasizing the opening of prisons and the repeal of restrictive legislation, as revisionists have, or highlighting the defeat of the maximum and the last gasps of popular radicalism, like the Marxists.[10] And yet, while such accounts explain how Thermidor reignited the Revolution by restoring particular liberties, altering political alignments, and revitalizing free speech, they ought not blind us to continuities that endured beyond Robespierre's defeat. For the rump of the

Assembly that had presided over the crisis of the year II remained, continuing to consolidate the Convention's grip on political life.

Legislators' determination to preserve their ascendancy was visible in the piecemeal way by which they dismantled the repressive apparatus of the Terror, restoring their own authority while leaving intact institutions that enhanced their surveillance of the nation. They reorganized the Committees of Public Safety and General Security, limiting continuity of membership to prevent domination by a few personalities and dividing responsibilities for Public Safety among a dozen committees. At the same time, however, they enhanced the powers of the Committee of General Security by uncoupling it from Public Safety and putting more armed forces at its disposal. Then, in the interest of efficiency, they steadily restored the Committee of Public Safety's precedence over the committees with which it had temporarily shared power. Similarly, deputies reorganized the personnel of the Revolutionary Tribunal and trimmed its powers but preserved that body, to send political criminals before it until May 1795. And they restored their own parliamentary immunity by repealing the draconian Prairial Laws. If the last act reached beyond the Convention by reinstating legal protections for those accused of counter-revolution, legislators only attended directly to public demands for liberalization by freeing political prisoners. But here too they preserved their authority by founding such liberation on specific concessions rather than by abolishing the law on suspects or issuing an amnesty, so sustaining their privilege of unilaterally defining legitimate political activity.[11]

If the Convention famously ended the dictatorship of the Committee of Public Safety, it continued to hold itself above the law by refusing to enact the constitution of 1793, adopted and almost immediately suspended the preceding year. Insisting that they could not rule constitutionally so long as the nation was at war, deputies freed themselves and thousands of local authorities from the requirement to seek re-election and preserved their own terrible latitude to continue tampering with the safeguards of civil society that a constitution would have guaranteed. Their disregard for rule of law was particularly visible in recurrent use of exceptional justice—supplementing the revolutionary tribunal with military councils that did not respect due process—and repeated resort to punitive legislation. Amongst the latter was the 'law of grand police', which secured the Convention on the eve of the Germinal insurrection by targeting not just active insurgents but those believed to have encouraged them and even onlookers who refused to disperse, making all liable to exile. After Prairial, the Convention took aim at women in particular with the excuse that male insurgents had cross-dressed to justify excesses: it consigned all members of the 'weaker sex' to their homes until further notice and forbade them, when in public, to gather in groups of more than five.[12]

Holding firmly to its own power, the Convention built upon Montagnard policies to continue demobilizing extra-legislative competitors as it had done since the very beginning of the Terror. The Convention had steadily eroded independent political activity before Thermidor by restricting sectional Assembly meetings and closing women's clubs, imprisoning populist Enragés, and executing the Hébertists. Deputies continued in this project even as they struck down Robespierre, sweeping away the Paris Commune, which had lent critical institutional support to sans-culottes. They rid themselves of an equally powerful rival by closing the Paris Jacobin Club, whose popular alliances had produced legislative purges, radical decrees, and the Montagnard victory of June 1793. Although hundreds of smaller Jacobin clubs remained scattered throughout the provinces, they were doomed because the Convention prohibited them from associating with one another or engaging in local politics, destroying their *raison d'être*. Membership dwindled and the provincial clubs closed one after the other until only a few remained when the Convention formally disbanded them in the summer of 1795.[13]

Finally, the Convention repudiated concessions to popular militancy. In December 1794, legislators repealed the maximum on prices that guaranteed food to a hungry, restive urban people, proving that this had always been the temporary measure they claimed rather than a programmatic retreat from laissez-faire ideals.[14] The official repudiation of popular activism proved fiercer still for even as rifts deepened among legislators over freeing the press and the desirability of further purging their ranks, these same men closed ranks against popular efforts to revitalize democracy. In early autumn 1795, when a small band of democrats known as the Electoral Club demanded that the Paris Commune be restored and the suspended constitution of 1793 activated, the Convention stonewalled. It refused to hear the Club's spokesmen, seized their meeting hall, and finally arrested their leaders. The movement melted away. The Assembly showed equal firmness when confronting the noisy, leaderless activism that erupted in Germinal and Prairial. Rather than making concessions that famine and the law seemed to require—ensuring affordable bread and enacting the existing constitution—the Convention forcibly dispersed activists and bowed to a minority within its ranks by adopting the hastily drafted and firmly conservative constitution of year III (1795).[15]

By the time the Directory was elected in October 1795, legislators believed they had not only ended the Terror but the Revolution. They had completed the Montagnard project of reining in Parisian militancy by transforming political terror into a sustained assault on working people, compounding the confiscation of vital institutions with legislative neglect and sheer starvation. For if legislators were surprised by the inflation that repeal of the maximum produced, their refusal to provide assistance in its wake inflamed the people and drove them to desperate measures. The crowd's fury elicited the death-blow of Prairial: far-reaching legal repression seconded by the scorn of an angry press. The people of Paris would not rouse themselves again for two generations. The Convention, having freed itself of rivalry with the Jacobins and the Paris crowd, cemented its victory with the constitution of the year III (1795), which not only guarded against renewed popular militancy but circumscribed all political activity by excluding most of the nation from active citizenship and imposing new barriers on extra-electoral activism.

Although the Thermidorians completed the Montagnard project of strengthening the Republican state by eliminating extra-legislative rivals, their mastery of the provinces was less certain. On the one hand, the Convention extended its reach throughout France by delegating more representatives-on-mission than at any moment since 1793 while narrowly defining the powers of those men to limit their independence. But, the Assembly did not retrieve its monopoly on violence as successfully as Jean-Clément Martin has suggested, instead ceding critical advantages to counter-revolutionaries in the west and reactionaries in the south, who would continue to create provincial chaos for years.[16] Generous peace treaties with Brittany and the Vendée would prove no more successful at reintegrating those regions into the nation than had military repression: rather, by amnestying former combatants and allowing them to remain armed, ostensibly to police themselves, the Convention practically guaranteed renewed revolt and widespread lawlessness that would simmer for years. The situation in the south was bleaker still. Prepared to accept unofficial reaction, legislators replaced Jacobin administrators with men who connived at the private settling of scores. The consequences were disastrous: political reaction fused with long-standing factionalism and traditional notions of justice to produce White Terror in the Midi. Although the most explicitly political violence would recede under the Directory, the upheaval left marauding bands to prey on travellers and isolated farmhouses for years.[17]

THERMIDOR AND DENUNCIATION

The mutual impact of change and continuity on French political life after 9 Thermidor raises the question of why that event was so long understood to signal fundamental rupture. Paradoxically, the answer lies in continuity here too. As the Thermidorians continued the Montagnard consolidation of legislative power initiated in 1793, they sustained the revolutionary culture of denunciation that radicals had been elaborating since 1789. Turning denunciation back on their old political allies, Thermidorians reified then-current notions of political terror to create the myth of a discrete category of national experience known as 'the Terror', which they claimed to have ended by defeating Robespierre.

Of the men who mobilized Thermidorian denunciation, two would prove to be the most famous of revolutionary turncoats: Stanislas Fréron and Jean-Lambert Tallien. Journalists, Jacobin deputies, and disgraced representatives-on-mission recalled to Paris for excess and corruption, they warded off prosecution by conspiring against Robespierre and then reinventing themselves as gladiators of liberty who waged war on his heirs. With speeches delivered in tandem a few weeks after the Incorruptible's defeat, they galvanized Thermidorian denunciation: Fréron suggested its form by praising the capacity of the press to disclose corruption, and Tallien proposed content with a speech whose definition of a 'system of terror' would be amplified in books, newspapers, pamphlets and plays.

Stanislas Fréron honed his accusatory skills in the Revolution's early years through his newspaper, *L'orateur du peuple*. Like fellow radicals and masters of the craft, Jean-Paul Marat, who he much admired, and Camille Desmoulins, with whom he occasionally collaborated, Fréron believed denunciation to be one of liberty's most potent weapons: it was an instrument to expose counter-revolutionaries and police the powerful which journalists wielded with particular efficaciousness. Many radicals shared this conviction, and some Jacobins went so far as to campaign for unlimited free press in 1791 on these grounds, arguing that publication without fear of censorship or punishment for libel was essential to patriotic denunciation. Such exhaustive deregulation was necessary to check state encroachment, they argued, because it placed journalists on an equal footing with men powerful enough to infringe popular rights. As Jérôme Pétion so succinctly put it: 'the public interest demands that one be able to inculpate without fear'.[18]

Although the press libertarians lost out in 1791, Fréron revitalized their arguments when he urged the post-Thermidorian Convention to renew the free press he accused Robespierre of having crushed. 'The axe was suspended over all who would make use of this liberty … [because], if the press had remained free … those outrages committed daily against justice, humanity and the law … would have been publicized … throughout the republic.' The Convention must learn from such experience, Fréron insisted, preventing future abuse by not only reaffirming a free press but abolishing all legal restraint to guarantee journalists' power to 'alarm … unmask, and … halt the plots of ambitious men'. Although Fréron explicitly took aim at the politically powerful, his easy transition from press freedom to police at the end of his speech suggested a more extensive role for watchful journalists. 'Well-organized surveillance' was necessary, he argued, to dispense with overcrowded prisons and cruel punishments that still haunted the nation. If Fréron was suggesting that journalists should assist in such surveillance, as he and others would do in the coming months, there was radical precedent in Jacobin F.-X. Lanthenas' 1791 proposal that the law ought not to protect even ordinary citizens from libel. However, by making his case in the wake of the Republican crisis, Fréron did not recall Lanthenas so much as Robespierre, voicing the same contempt for privacy as the man he claimed to challenge by praising a press that would scrutinize governed as well as governors.[19]

As Fréron put an activist press at Thermidorians' service, J.-L. Tallien sketched the contours of denunciation by turning Jacobins' political ideas against them. Bronislaw Baczko has rightly characterized Tallien's speech—delivered at roughly the same time as Fréron's and ghost-written by P.-L. Roederer, a Girondin sympathizer who was still in hiding—as a critical contribution to the Thermidorian 'reflection on the Terror as a *system of power*'. The speech was not, however, so readily abstracted from its historical context as Baczko suggests.[20] From its refusal to name the deputies it targeted to its grandiose claims about the Republic's future, this was a knowing inversion of Maximilien Robespierre's seminal speech, 'On the Principles of Political Morality', delivered to the same audience six months earlier. Declaring the Republic still very much in danger, Tallien and Roederer inverted Robespierre's description of terror as a revolutionary pro- phylactic to claim that it was, on the contrary, a mortal threat.[21]

The notion of 'terror' had evolved quickly after 1789. Although disparaged since Montesquieu as an instrument of despotism, 'terror' was appropriated by revolution- ary radicals and popular militants to denote the defence of such worthy aims as liberty, equality, and democracy. Hence, insurgents demanded that the Convention make terror the order of the day in the autumn of 1793, and Robespierre enlarged upon this sense of the word in 'On the Principles of Political Morality'.[22] With that speech, in David Jordan's words 'a tour de force of dialectics', Robespierre fused what Montesquieu held to be opposing principles: virtue and terror. Virtue, he argued, was the soul of the Republic, without which all was lost. But 'if the mainspring of popular government in peacetime is virtue, the mainspring of popular government in revolution is virtue and terror both: virtue, without which terror is disastrous; terror, without which virtue is powerless. Terror is nothing but prompt, severe, inflexible justice; it is therefore an emanation of virtue ... '[23]

Tallien and Roederer repudiated the dialectic: rejecting Robespierre's fusion of virtue and terror, they denied that terror could safeguard democracy or the Republic. Because it was not possible to target the guilty alone, as Robespierre promised, terror touched all citizens, poisoning bonds between friends and shattering relations within families. The world was turned upside down. 'It was only possible to guarantee ... liberty with the yoke ... humanity with the spilling of blood, fraternity by inciting one part of the nation against the other ... When terror is exercised in the name of liberty, it does not merely create indifference to liberty; it makes liberty hateful and it makes that hatred a sick- ness both incurable and hereditary, as fathers impart cowardice and servitude to their children in the name of *prudence*.' In short, terror did not protect virtue but corrupted it. Robespierre had not battled counter-revolution but served it.[24]

As Fréron and Tallien defined form and content, their extra-legislative ally J.-C.-H. Méhée de la Touche initiated practice with a bitter satire that taunted the survivors of the pre-Thermidorian committees of Public Safety and General Security as 'Robespierre's tail', who served tyranny while the man was alive and continued to do so in the wake of his death. Méhée's lampoon opened the floodgates. Parodies of that title—*Defend your tail, Cut off my tail, Give me back my tail*—and other satires poured forth, joined by more sober pamphlets that detailed the horrors of prison life in the year II and debated the 'crimes' of particular deputies. Like Roederer and Tallien, many pamphlets turned Robespierre's defence of terror back on itself, appropriating the latter's allusions to a 'catalogue of horrors committed by tyrants against the defenders of liberty' but naming those tyrants 'Robespierrists', 'Jacobins', and 'terrorists'. Playwrites joined in, giving audi- ences the opportunity to applaud *Cange ou le Commissionaire de Lazare*, a melodrama about unjust imprisonment, or hiss the corrupt figures on view in *L'intérieur des comités révolutionnaires*.[25]

Fréron and Tallien set the pace for newspapers as well. Resurrected from the Revolution's early years, Fréron's *L'orateur du peuple* and Tallien's *L'ami des citoyens* described Robespierre as drunk on ambition, abetted by confederates who were poisoned with greed, depravity, and violence.[26] Guilty survivors of 9 Thermidor threatened still, these papers warned, for 'how is it possible ... to return to the crowd after having made so many enemies?'[27] Conservative sheets like the *Journal de Paris* and *Le Messager du soir* joined in the chorus of condemnation, as did the monarchist *Journal de Perlet* and *Quotidienne*, describing mounting violence against former Jacobins with language that encouraged more of it. In the provinces, Jean-Baptiste Broulhiet of Toulouse advertised his opinion with the very title of *L'Antiterroriste*, while the former federalist Ferréol de Beaugeard condemned Robespierre from Marseille, castigating a regime 'that lasted just eleven months but did more harm in that short time than plague, famine and war have done in eleven centuries'. Ferréol asked why justice was not levied more quickly against 'terrorists' and 'cannibals'.[28]

Sweeping aside the experience of war and the complex interplay of forces between Convention and people, capital and provinces that shaped politics during the year II, Thermidorian publicists indulged in hyperbole that dehumanized Robespierre and the Jacobins like the accusations turned against the Crown and aristocracy in preceding years.[29] In so doing, such publicists reified an experience of political chaos and fear into a unique moment in the nation's history that would henceforth be known as the Terror, for which they claimed Robespierre and the Jacobins solely responsible. Many of the men who first levied such charges were themselves popular militants, former Jacobins or Girondins, radicals using the familiar practice of denunciation to challenge the next in a long line of revolutionary opponents. They succeeded because denunciation had, since 1789, been understood as a civic duty: defined first as a safeguard of the nation and rights of man, it gained broader resonance after 1792 to become a guarantor of virtue and means to illuminate webs of deceit.[30] Given revolutionaries' confidence in denunciation, it is not surprising that they turned it against 'terrorists' after 9 Thermidor. Nor was even the charge itself wholly new: Saint-Just had accused the Girondins of practising a 'system of terror' in the summer of 1793; Bazire and Chabot said the same of counter-revolutionaries a few months later.[31] Some of the post-Thermidorian denouncers were turncoats like Fréron and Tallien, obscuring their own crimes by publicizing and demonizing those of others, but others were more sincere in the conviction that they revealed necessary truths, like the radical journalist Gracchus Babeuf who so noisily condemned Robespierre in the wake of Thermidor.

What altered the impact and legacy of denunciation after Thermidor was its singularly widespread appeal, for radicals' charges were appropriated by men to their right. As a renascent conservative and monarchist press swamped old Jacobin newspapers, editors of the former widened the scope of accusation, advancing from charges against deputies and representatives-on-mission to target sans-culottes and issue broadsides against the Revolution.[32] Lines of opposition became confused as Republican denunciation mingled with monarchist. For the first time since 1789, there was agreement across the political spectrum about the nation's demons. Some Jacobins refused such rhetoric from the outset: P.-A. Antonelle, for example, accepted responsibility for his duties as a jurist on the Revolutionary tribunal, describing them as terrible acts for a terrible time. Others retreated as they came to recognize the degree to which the denunciations they had mobilized against old allies were being taken up as a right-wing cudgel. Gracchus Babeuf was among the first to recant, late in 1794, with the regretful cry that, 'when I ... thundered passionately to bring down the monstrous scaffolding of Robespierre's system, I did not imagine that I was helping lay the foundation for a structure that ... would be no less disastrous for the people'.[33] Méhée de la Touche broke with Tallien not long afterward, and even Fréron and Tallien would turn coat again. Fréron retreated from his alliance with the reactionary gilded youth when they challenged the Convention after Prairial and he would later condemn as monarchist factional violence in the Midi that was excited, in part, by the very sort of denunciation he helped bring into being. Tallien repudiated the right at almost the very last moment, condemning royalist rebels after their failed assault at Quiberon and abruptly turning on other reactionary deputies.[34]

But reactionary denunciation was not so easily quelled. Its lasting impact on the revolutionary imaginary became visible when Boissy d'Anglas offered the constitution of year III (1795) to the Convention. Promising that this new code repudiated terror and reaction alike to begin anew, Boissy could not shake the fearful images promoted throughout the preceding year. He opined hopefully that 'crime is to be found only in dungeons', but warned in the very next breath, 'and yet I would not say ... that all factions are defeated ... that all corrupt men have disappeared ... that all bloodthirsty men have ceased plotting'.[35] Such enduring fear of a secretive, vicious Jacobinism would encourage the Directory to identify the iconoclastic early communist, Gracchus Babeuf, with it, and give Napoleon justification for his coup against the Revolution in 1799. Even today, Robespierre and 'his' Terror linger in popular memory as unique symbols of the Revolution's worst failings.[36]

This is not to deny that the year II witnessed terrible violence and abuses of power. But that historical experience was the complex outcome of circumstance, political negotiation, and ideology, forged not by the tyranny of a few but the decisions of many. And, as this chapter suggests, it did not come to an abrupt end with Thermidor. By so grossly vulgarizing a moment they named 'the Terror' and reducing it to the work of a few bad men with familiar vices, Thermidorian critics sustained the violence and enmity that were making it impossible to end the Revolution. For once having reached fever pitch, reactionary denunciation did not speed identification of the guilty nor aid reparation but inhibited both, encouraging the prosecution of scapegoats rather than the dispensing of justice. As reactionary denunciation poisoned the present, it repudiated the past. By casting the Terror as the work of tyrants, reactionaries encouraged all who shared in the enthusiasms, fears, and mistakes of that period to name themselves bad, bullied, or blinded. It became almost impossible to talk about the terrible choices and compromises of the year II in such a way as to come to terms with or learn from them. How exactly were Republicans to lay claim to the awful past that reactionary denunciation had caricatured into being? One could only condemn the moment wholesale. This was a problem with which revolutionaries would wrestle until Napoleon cut short their efforts in 1799, and one to which historians have returned persistently ever since.

Breaking irreparably with the past, reactionary denunciation simultaneously denied any constructive vision of the future. In contrast to pre-Thermidorian denunciation which, however manichean, was always paired with positive visions of a world the Revolution was bringing into being, Thermidorian denunciation became exclusively negative. It condemned without creating, failing to offer a coherent vision of how politics and society might advance once France was purged of its terrorists. A nihilist rhetoric, it denied all possibility of reconciliation. This, too, was a problem that revolutionaries would continue to wrestle with under the Directory.

CONCLUSION

The defeat of Maximilien Robespierre and the Mountain initiated a sweeping realignment of political forces within the National Convention. In the wake of that event, the nation experienced liberation and new defeat as the Convention repealed the most repressive measures of the year II but also retreated from its promises of political and social democracy. One of the most tragic dimensions of those fifteen months was that Thermidorian deputies permitted their political contest to become social war as they abandoned guarantees of public well-being and colluded in mounting violence, both rhetorical and real, against working people and popular militants. But however significant the advent of 9 Thermidor, it did not cleave the Revolution or even the National Convention in two. The rump of the Assembly remained, as did the practice of revolutionary government: legislators ruling without a constitution continued to amplify the Convention's power, and denunciation remained an integral part of political repertoires within and beyond that body. Even the Convention's constriction of popular political life, which Marxists long held to be among Thermidor's most distinctive features, was rooted in the Montagnard determination to rein in independent militancy, which dated from the fall of 1793.

The aspirations and practices that survived Thermidor give the lie to reactionary claims that the Terror was a unique moment. Although the year II was in many ways a singular revolutionary moment, its practices and political culture remained intimately linked to what preceded and what followed. Hence, rather than chopping the early Republic into isolated fragments—prelude, Terror, Thermidor—we might more usefully use the institutional life of the National Convention to structure the years 1792–5 by considering how the deputies, agitated by the ebb and flow of competing factions, struggled simultaneously to face crisis and consolidate their hold on the nation. As that interpretive frame lends new coherence to the Republic's founding years, however, the practice of denunciation suggests the limits of an institutional perspective by recalling that revolutionary political culture evolved independently of specific events or government bodies. In other words, the content of Thermidorian denunciation tells us less about the experience of the Terror than the practice itself tells us about the continuities and ruptures of revolutionary power struggles.

In sum, restoring the Thermidorian period to its rightful place at the revolutionary table allows us better to understand not just those fifteen months but the Revolution as a whole. For although Republican political life changed significantly in the wake of Robespierre's death, the idée fixe that this was a decisive moment of rupture has hidden as much as it has revealed, obscuring continuities that bound the Revolution's second half to its first. In particular, rejecting the myth of a unique and isolated Thermidor conjures away the myth of a unique and isolated Terror, the Thermidorians' most enduring contribution to revolutionary politics and revolutionary historiography alike.

NOTES

My thanks to Mette Harder, Michael Kwass, Ronen Steinberg, and David Andress for their thoughtful comments on an earlier draft of this essay.

1. Richard Cobb's scholarship is an instructive exception to this rule, as is more recent scholarship on reaction in the Midi. Richard Cobb, *The Police and the People: French Popular Protest, 1789–1820* (Oxford, 1974); Stephen Clay, 'Les Réactions du Midi: Conflits, continuités et violence', *Annales historiques de la Révolution francaise* 345 (2006), 55–91; Donald Sutherland, *Murder in Aubagne: Lynching, Law, and Justice during the French Revolution* (Cambridge and New York, 2009).

2. Hugh Gough, *The Terror in the French Revolution*, 2nd edn (New York, 2010); E. J. Hobsbawm, *Echoes of the Marseillaise: Two Centuries Look Back on the French Revolution* (New Brunswick, NJ, 1990); Conor Cruise O'Brien, 'Introduction' to Edmund Burke, *Reflections on the Revolution in France* (London and New York, 1986); Jeremy Jennings, 'History, Revolution, and Terror', in *Revolution and the Republic: A History of Political Thought in France since the Eighteenth Century* (Oxford, 2011).

3. Albert Mathiez, *La réaction thermidorienne*, présentation de Yannick Bosc et Florence Gauthier (Paris, 2010 [1929]); François Furet and Denis Richet, *The French Revolution*, translated by Stephen Hardman (New York, 1970).

4. Bronislaw Baczko, *Ending the Terror: The French Revolution after Robespierre*, translated by Michel Petheram (Cambridge and New York, 1994).

6. Roger Dupuy and Marcel Morabito (eds), *1795: Pour une République sans Révolution* (Rennes, 1996); Pierre Serna, *Antonelle, Aristocrate révolutionnaire, 1747–1817* (Paris, 1997); Michael Vovelle (ed.), *Le tournant de l'an III: Réaction et Terreur blanche dans la France révolutionnaire* (Paris, 1997); Bernard Gainot *1799, un nouveau Jacobinisme? la démocratie représentative, une alternative à brumaire* (Paris, 2001); James Livesey, *Making democracy in the French Revolution* (Cambridge, MA, 2001); Pierre Serna, *La république des girouettes (1789–1815 ... et au-délà). Une anamolie politique: la France de l'extrême centre* (Paris, 2005); Andrew Jainchill, *Reimagining Politics after the Terror: The Republican Origins of French Liberalism* (Ithaca, 2008).

7. For a fuller account of the political events of the Thermidorian period, see Laura Mason, 'The Thermidorian Reaction', in Peter McPhee (ed.), *A Companion to the French Revolution* (Chichester, 2013).

8. Marcel Dorigny, 'La Gironde sous Thermidor', *1795: Pour une République sans Révolution*; François Hincker, 'Comment sortir de la terreur économique?' *Le tournant de l'an III* Kåre Tønnesson, *La défaite des sans-culottes* (Oslo, 1959).

9. Tønnesson, *La défaite des sans-culottes*; Richard, *Police and the People*; François Brunel, 'Pourquoi ces six parmi les derniers Montagnards?' *Annales historiques de la Révolution française* 304 (1996), 401–13; Haim Burstin, 'Echos faubouriense des journées de Prairial', *Annales historiques de la Révolution française* 304 (1996), 373–85; Raymonde Monnier, 'L'Étendu d'un désastre: Prairial et la révolution populaire', *Annales historiques de la Révolution française* 304 (1996), 387–400; Stephen Clay, 'Le massacre du fort Saint-Jean, une épisode de la Terreur blanche à Marseille', *Le tournant de l'an III*.

10. Furet and Richet, *The French Revolution*; Baczko, *Ending the Terror*; Mathiez, *La Réaction thermidorienne*; Tønnesson, *La défaite des sans-culottes*.

11. Henri Wallon, *Histoire du tribunal révolutionnaire de Paris* (Paris, 1881), vols 5–6; Alphonse Aulard, *Histoire politique de la Révolution française* (Paris, 1901), 504–10; Mathiez, *La réaction thermidorienne*; Georges Lefebvre, *The French Revolution*, vol. II: *From 1793 to 1799*, trans. by Elizabeth Moss Evanson, John Hall Stewart and James Friguglietti (New York, 1964 [1957]); François Gendron, *The Gilded Youth of Thermidor*, translated by James Cookson (Montreal and Kingston, 1993); Baczko, *Ending the Terror*.

12. J. B. Duvergier (ed.), *Collection Complète des lois, décrets, ordonnances, réglements …* (Paris, 1835) Deuxième édition t. 8, 49–50; Tønnesson, *La défaite des sans-culottes*, 170–1; 'National Convention: Session of 4 Prairial', Laura Mason and Tracey Rizzo (eds), *The French Revolution: A Document Collection* (Boston and New York, 1999), 273–5; Howard G. Brown, *Ending the French Revolution: Violence, Justice and Repression from the Terror to Napoleon* (Charlottesville and London, 2006) 142–4; Annie Jourdan, 'Le discours de la terreur à l'époque révolutionnaire (1776 1798): Etude comparative sur une notion ambiguë', *French Historical Studies* 36, no. 1 (Winter 2013), 51–81, p. 69.

13. Tønnesson, *La défaite des sans-culottes*; Michael Kennedy, *The Jacobin Clubs in the French Revolution, 1793–1795* (New York and Oxford, 2000); David Andress, *The Terror: The Merciless War for Freedom in Revolutionary France* (New York, 2005).

14. Andress, *The Terror*, 213–14; Hincker, 'Comment sortir de la terreur économique?'

15. Tønnesson, *La défaite des sans-culottes*; Monnier, 'L'Étendu d'un désastre'.

16. Jean-Clément Martin, *Violence et révolution: Essai sur la naissance d'un mythe national* (Paris, 2006), 269–70.

17. Cobb, *The Police and the People*; M. J. Sydenham, *The First French Republic, 1792–1804* (Berkeley and Los Angeles, 1974); Gwynne Lewis, 'Political Brigandage and Popular Disaffection in the South-east of France 1795 1804', in Gwynne Lewis and Colin Lucas (eds), *Beyond the Terror: Essays in French Regional and Social History, 1794 1815* (Cambridge, 1983); Colin Lucas, 'Themes in Southern Violence after 9 Thermidor', *Beyond the Terror*; Stephen Clay, 'Réaction dans le Midi (1/95–1800)', *Dictionnaire des usages socio-politiques (1770 1815). Fasc. 6: Notions pratiques* (Paris, 1999); Michel Biard, *Missionnaires de la République* (Paris, 2002), 226–9; Howard G. Brown, *Ending the French Revolution. Violence, Justice and Repression from the Terror to Napoleon* (Charlottesville and London, 2006); Mathiez, *La réaction thermidorienne*;

Jean-Clément Martin, 'The Vendée, Chouannerie, and the State, 1791 1799', *A Companion to the French Revolution*.

18. Charles Walton, *Policing Public Opinion in the French Revolution: The Culture of Calumny and the Problem of Free Speech* (Oxford and New York, 2009), 110. See also: Jack Censer, *Prelude to Power: The Parisian Radical Press, 1789-1791* (Baltimore, 1976), chaps 2–3; Claude Labrosse and Pierre Rétat, *Naissance du journal révolutionnaire, 1789* (Lyon, 1988), 193–211; Jacques Guilhaumou, 'Fragments of a Discourse of Denunciation', in Keith Michael Baker (ed.), *The French Revolution and the Creation of Modern Political Culture, vol. 4: The Terror* (Oxford and New York, 1994); Colin Lucas, 'The Theory and Practice of Denunciation in the French Revolution', in Sheila Fitzpatrick and Robert Gellately (eds), *Accusatory Practices: Denunciation in Modern European History 1789–1989* (Chicago and London, 1997), 22–39.

19. Stanislas Fréron, *Opinion sur la liberté de la presse* (Paris, 1794), 11–12, 14, 15–16; Walton, *Policing Public Opinion*, 110.

20. P. L. Roederer, 'Discours prononcé par Tallien sur la terreur', in A. M. Roederer (ed.), *Oeuvres du comte P. L. Roederer* (Paris, 1858), t. 7, 3–10; Baczko, *Ending the Terror*, 52.

21. Maximilian Robespierre', On the Principles of Political Morality', in Slavoz Žižek (ed.), *Robespierre: Virtue and Terror* (London and New York, 2010); Roederer, 'Discours prononcé par Tallien'.

22. Annie Geffroy, '"Terreur" et sa famille morphologique, de 1793 à 1796', in Louis Guilbert and R. Adda (eds), *Néologie et lexicologie: hommage à Louis Guilbert* (Paris, 1979), 124–35; Gerd Van den Heuvel, 'Terreur, Terroriste, Terrorisme', in Danielle Bonnaud-Lamotte (ed.), *Actes du 2eme colloque de lexicologie politique: Saint Cloud, 15–20 septembre 1980* (Paris, 1982), vol. 3, 893–912; Annie Jourdan, 'Le discours de la terreur à l'époque révolutionnaire'.

23. David Jordan, *The Revolutionary Career of Maximilien Robespierre* (Chicago, 1989), 183; Robespierre, 'On the Principles of Political Morality', 115.

24. Roderer, 'Discours prononcé par Tallien', 8–9.

25. Jean-Claude-Hippolyte Méhée, de la Touche, *La queue de Robespierre, ou, Les dangers de la liberté de la presse* (Paris, 1794); Gendron, *The Gilded Youth of Thermidor* 16–19. For a partial list of pamphlet titles, see Mortimer Tourneux, *Bibliographie de l'histoire de Paris pendant la révolution française* (Paris, 1890–1913), vol. 1, 396–422; *Cange ou le Commissionnaire de Lazare: fait historique en un acte et en prose* (Paris, year III); Ducancel, *L'intérieur des comités révolutoinnaires, ou les Aristides Modernes, comédie en trois actes et en prose* (Paris, year III).

26. *L'orateur du peuple* (1, 3 vendémiaire III); *L'ami des citoyens* (1 vendémiaire, 5 brumaire III).

27. Roederer, 'Discours prononcé par Tallien', 7.

28. Stephen Clay, 'The White Terror', *A Companion to the French Revolution*; Stephen Clay, 'La guerre des plumes: la presse provinciale et la politique de faction sous le Premier Directoire à Marseille, 1796–1797', *Annales historiques de la Révolution française* 308 (1997), 221–47, 225; Hugh Gough, *The Newspaper Press in the French Revolution* (London, 1988), 121–3.

29. Sergio Luzzatto, *L'Automne de la Révolution: Luttes et cultures politiques dans la France thermidorienne* (Paris, 2001), 78–85.

30. Lucas, 'The Theory and Practice of Denunciation in the French Revolution'; Guilhaumou, 'Fragments of a Discourse of Denunciation'.

31. For particular denunciations by old radicals, see Gracchus Babeuf, *Du systeme de la dépopulation, ou la vie et les crimes de Carrier* (Paris, [1794]); Vilate, *Causes secretes de la Révolution de 9 au 10 Thermidor* (London, [1794]); [Honoré Riouffe], *Memoires d'un détenu, pour servir à l'histoire de la tyrannie de Robespierre* (Paris, 1795). On denunciation after Thermidor and the creation of the notion of a 'Terror', see Jourdan, 'Le discours de la terreur à l'époque révolutionnaire; Peter McPhee, *Robespierre: A Revolutionary Life* (New Haven, 2012), 222–30; Van den Heuvel, 'Terreur, Terroriste, Terrorisme'; Françoise Brunel, 'Bridging the Gulf of the Terror', *The French Revolution and the Creation of Modern Political Culture, vol. 4: The Terror*; Martin, *Violence et Révolution*, 196–7.

32. Gendron, *The Gilded Youth of Thermidor*, 19, 81–82; Luzzato, *L'Automne de la Révolution*, 83.

33. Serna, *Antonelle: aristocrate révolutionnaire, 1747 1817*, 245–54; Gracchus Babeuf, *Tribun du peuple* 28 (28 frimaire III), 237.

34. Stanislas Fréron, *Memoire historique sur la Réaction royale, et sur les Massacres du Midi* (Paris, 1824); Mette Harder, 'Reacting to Revolution: The Political Career(s) of Jean-Lambert Tallien', in David Andress (ed.), *Experiencing the French Revolution* (Oxford, 2013), 104.

35. Boissy d'Anglas, 'Discours préliminaire au project de Constitution pour la République française', *Choix de Rapports, Opinion et Discours prononcés à la Tribune Nationale depuis 1789 jusqu'à ce jour, t. XV: Année 1794–1795* (Paris, 1821), 109–71, 110.

36. McPhee, *Robespierre*; Jourdan, 'Le discours de la terreur'; *Le Directoire exécutif aux citoyens de Paris* (Paris, an IV); Isser Woloch, *Napoleon and his Collaborators: the Making of a Dictatorship* (New York and London, 2001), 17–25.

Selected Reading

Baczko, Bronislaw, *Ending the Terror. The French Revolution after Robespierre*, translated by Michel Petheram (Cambridge, 1994).

Brown, Howard, 'Robespierre's Tail: The Possibilities of Justice after the Terror', *Canadian Journal of History* 55 (2010), 503–35.

Clay, Stephen, 'Vengeance, Justice and the Reactions in the Revolutionary Midi', *French History* 23, no. 1 (2009), 22–46.

Cobb, Richard, *The Police and the People. French Popular Protest, 1789–1820* (London, 1970).

Dupuy, Roger, and Marcel Morabito (eds), *1795: Pour une République sans Révolution* (Rennes, 1996).

Gendron, François, *The Gilded Youth of Thermidor*, translated by James Cookson (Montreal and Kingston, 1993).

Harder, Mette, 'Reacting to Revolution: The Political Career(s) of Jean-Lambert Tallien', in David Andress (ed.), *Experiencing the French Revolution* (Oxford, forthcoming).

Jainchill, Andrew, *Reimagining Politics after the Terror: the Republican Origis of Liberalism* (Ithaca NY and London, 2008).

Jourdan, Annie, 'Le discours de la terreur à l'époque révolutionnaire (1776–1798): Etude comparative sur une notion ambiguë', *French Historical Studies* 36, no. 1 (Winter 2013), 51–81.

Lewis, Gwynne, and Colin Lucas (eds), *Beyond the Terror: Essays in French Regional and Social History, 1794–1815* (Cambridge, 1983).

Luzzatto, Sergio, *L'Automne de la Révolution: Luttes et cultures politiques dans la France thermidorienne*, translated by Simone Carpentari Messina (Paris, 2001).

Mason, Laura, 'The Thermidorian Reaction', in Peter McPhee (ed.), *A Companion to the French Revolution* (Chichester, 2013).

Vovelle, Michel, (ed.), *Le tournant de l'an III: Réaction et Terreur blanche dans la France révolutionnaire* (Paris, 1997).

CHAPTER 31

THE POLITICS OF PUBLIC ORDER, 1795–1802

HOWARD G. BROWN

FRANCE in 1795 was a country in tatters. After the harshest winter in living memory came alarming grain shortages and a collapsing currency. Crime and suicide soared along with prices. Intensive warfare that had already lasted three years continued to impose huge burdens on state and society alike. Civil war had flared up again, reinvigorated by new rebel leaders, support from England, and demands to restore Catholic worship. Traditional elites, whether churchmen and seigneurial lords in the countryside or magistrates, guild masters and merchants in the cities, sought to recover their status and reassert their power, challenging the Republic and its beneficiaries at all levels. At the same time, Republicans tore themselves apart in internecine strife over the excesses and atrocities of 1793–94. Royalist sentiment grew by leaps and bounds while government authority atrophied by the month. Such appalling conditions provoked the greatest crime wave France has experienced in modern times.[1]

To survive, the Republican regime needed to impose a new political order while also restoring law and order. The two tasks were tightly entwined. Efforts to achieve both began with the Constitution of 1795, which articulated a liberal democracy based on the rule of law. The political and social challenges of the time, however, meant that efforts to establish individual liberty hindered efforts to provide collective security. Murderous conspiracies against the regime, revealed by trials of extremists on both the radical left (Babeuf) and the extreme right (Brottier), heightened the tension between liberty and security. Annual elections at all levels of government, including the judiciary, agitated existing animosities while preventing the state executive from exercising much control over civilian law enforcement. As a result, political instability and endemic lawlessness led first to multiple violations of the constitution, especially in the wake of elections, then to an abandonment of democratic Republicanism in favour of liberal authoritarianism. The result was the creation of a new 'security state', one that combined coercive policing, administrative surveillance, exceptional justice, and militarized repression.

The emergence of the new system helped to restore order, and thereby to legitimize the Consulate, but it also paved the road to personal dictatorship in 1802.

The Constitution of 1795, which created the Directorial regime, was intended to consolidate revolutionary changes to the social order while also entrenching key principles of the early revolution such as personal liberty, legal equality, and representative democracy through a secular Republic. The regime's legitimacy was supposed to derive from annual elections and a strict adherence to the rule of law. Although planned as a post-revolutionary Republic, the Directory lacked both the moral authority and the constitutional power to meet its multifarious challenges without resorting to exceptional measures. Not only was the country wracked by economic chaos, foreign war, and widespread crime, but political extremists continued to tear the polity to shreds. Unrepentant Jacobins and diehard royalists struggled for control of villages, towns and whole regions across the country. Their mutual fear and suspicion infected the government as well. This miasma of political antipathy destroyed the basic trust in individuals and institutions needed to rally Frenchmen behind the new order.

Although often described as moderate and even reactionary, the Directory did not lie at the centre of the political spectrum in France in the late 1790s.[2] Despite having political opponents on the left and the right, the Directory was not viewed by contemporaries as centrist, but as radical, and for good reasons: it was led by regicides, pushed a vehement anti-clericalism, barred émigrés and their relatives from the polity, and exported revolutionary ideas by cannon and bayonet. The political centre in French politics during the mid-1790s belonged to constitutional royalists. They believed that hereditary monarchy and parliamentary democracy would balance one another, that Catholic worship would stabilize communities and win approval from the largely rural populace, and that a restricted franchise would give traditional elites an electoral advantage. To the right of this position lay the royal absolutists attached to the comte de Provence, the Pretender (as Louis XVIII) to the throne in exile. The Directory made no effort to separate these strands of royalism because a restoration of whatever sort threatened anyone who had supported the Republic during its darkest days from 1792 to 1794. And yet, fears of a restoration were not enough to compel Republicans to develop a modus vivendi among themselves.

The internecine struggle among Republicans that undermined the Directory owed much to the National Convention's inability to resolve the legacies of the Terror. The Thermidorians had justified their overthrow of Robespierre in July 1794 by claiming that they were replacing a reign of terror with a reign of justice. Such rhetoric posed a problem: how would the Convention answer growing demands for justice made by the victims of political persecution in 1793–94? Many deputies had supported and even implemented the 'system of terror', whereas scores of others, notably the Girondins, had been its victims. A swelling tide of court-room revelations, public denunciations, and propagandistic exaggerations turned the 'reign of terror' into a national trauma experienced well after the actual events. The Convention famously responded with lengthy show trials, first of Carrier, a representative on mission to the Vendée, then of Fouquier-Tinville, chief prosecutor of the Revolutionary Tribunal. Less famously, it also sought to rectify some of the injustices of the previous year by repealing laws, reversing verdicts, exonerating individuals, and restoring property to victims' families.[3]

The Thermidorians' attempts to undo tragedies from the Terror never became a coordinated policy of restitution and rehabilitation. Moreover, rather than quenching the thirst for revenge, the Convention added to the sense of grievance. In particular, its aggressive response to the uprising of 1–2 Prairial III (20–1 May 1795) in Paris, which combined popular outrage over bread prices with Jacobin political demands, fuelled the mounting backlash against Republican militants. A series of spectacular prison massacres, notably at Lyon and Marseille, along with hundreds of assaults and lynchings, turned the Jacobins of the Midi into a briefly endangered species during the summer of 1795.[4] The Convention desperately searched for alternatives. The most promising was a proposed national commission charged with identifying genuine 'terrorists', as opposed to 'persecuted patriots'. This plan was first adopted unanimously, then overturned a week later after an ugly brawl in the Convention. Rather than broadening the scope of political punishment, as opponents of the commission had demanded, however, the Convention ended its days by passing an amnesty for all 'acts related to the revolution', thereby nullifying all arrests and prosecutions of accused 'terrorists'. This sudden reversal came in response to the threat of royalism made manifest by the national elections of October 1795 and the Parisian uprising of 13–14 Vendémiaire IV (5–6 October 1795) that followed. Thus ended the best opportunity to operate a limited form of retributive justice for the excesses of the Terror.[5]

Historians have emphasized the damage done to the democratic legitimacy of the Directorial regime by the law that required two-thirds of the seats in the new legislature to be filled by members of the Convention.[6] The amnesty of the Year IV did similar damage to the credibility of the new regime as a constitutional Republic dedicated to the rule of law. Adopting an explicit form of what would today be called transitional justice would have earned the Republic greater moral authority. However, efforts throughout 1796 to revise the amnesty in order to make it possible to prosecute leading 'terrorists' on the basis of the Penal Code led only to a fudged compromise: those spared prosecution by the amnesty were excluded from political office while immunity was extended to royalist rebels now that the Vendée civil war had officially ended.[7]

The Thermidorians' failure to deal effectively with the legacy of the Terror destroyed the prospect of building a Republican consensus over public order. The Directory's inaugural address to the nation promised a combination of 'inflexible justice and the strictest observance of the laws'; it also promised 'an active war on royalism' and the repression 'of all factions with a firm hand'.[8] Restoring law and order would be combined with imposing a Republican order. But just what would that Republican order be? As the minister of police noted in a proclamation in April 1796, 'During times of parties and revolutions, it is difficult for words such as order, security, and public tranquillity to have as clear a meaning as during times of calm and political reason. Each faction thinks that public order is disturbed, that the security of the State is compromised, if their party does not triumph.'[9] In short, it would take considerable coercive force to entrench the Republic envisioned by Thermidorians. They may have hoped to end the revolutionary

cycle of violence through the Constitution of 1795, but they also prolonged revolutionary politics by imposing draconian restraints on public displays of religion, reviving
deadly laws against refractory priests, and excluding relatives of émigrés from public
office. The Convention adopted these measures on the eve of handing power to the
Directory because it deemed them an essential means to combat counter-revolution
and consolidate the Republic. This renewal of anti-clericalism and political exclusion
was deeply unpopular. As a result, efforts to impose the Republican order greatly jeopardized attempts to restore law and order.

The elections of October 1795 confirmed widespread hostility to the Republic, tainted
as it was by the crimes of Year II and the calamities of Year III. Most of the administrators, prosecutors, and judges elected to fill the posts of the Directorial regime had good
legal credentials, but not good Republican ones, and so proved reluctant to bring 'political' offences to trial. Victims of the Terror continued to seek revenge through public
assaults and midnight ambushes, which newly elected officials too often deemed 'acts of
justice in all but name', and so declined to prosecute.[10] The years 1796 and 1797 brought
only a modest number of prosecutions for religious offences, at least compared to the
potential caseload. On the other hand, where Jacobins held office, either through election or appointment, they aggressively implemented the most revolutionary laws on the
books, often with unconstitutional zeal. Thus, the Directory found itself in an almost
impossible position, largely unable to correct either the negligence or the excesses of
local magistrates and administrative officials.

The nature of the judicial system also posed problems for a regime seeking to restore
order on staunchly Republican terms. On the eve of the Directory, the justice system
was given an elaborate set of new rules governing arrest, investigation, prosecution, and
incarceration that helped to define the modern notion of due process. These added further obstacles to a concerted crackdown on crime already challenged by having to rely
on the elected magistrates and English-style juries first introduced in 1791. Jurors based
their verdicts on an 'inner belief' in the culpability of the accused, which meant that
they weighed personalities and performances as much as evidence. Being able to acquit
on the basis of 'criminal intent' provided the basis for extensive 'jury nullification', especially in cases of resisting authority. Even armed attacks on gendarmes in order to rescue
captured priests or draft-dodgers frequently led to jury nullification. Thus, when it came
to prosecuting resistance to authority or overt political opposition, the regime found
trial juries unhelpful. Serious forms of ordinary crime, such as robbery, theft, and homi-
cide, were much less likely to inspire sympathy in juries. These cases yielded respectably
modest acquittal rates: on average, only one-third of defendants went free, which was
a far lower rate of acquittal than for other forms of crime. In general, therefore, juries
proved reasonably reliable on traditional issues of law and order—even though rather
tolerant of battery and brawling—whereas they proved highly unreliable when it came
to imposing the Republican order.[11]

The problems of restoring law and order while also establishing the Republican
order were clearly manifest in the struggle against brigandage, which was rife around
the country. Brigandage came in many forms ranging from petty banditry enacted

by small groups of deracinated poor to organized bands of hardened criminals with many murders to their credit. Much of this violence was opportunistic, conducted with arms in hand and loot in mind; however, broadly anti-social banditry overlapped with politicized forms of assault and plunder. In its extreme form, political brigandage appeared as militia-style operations led by royalist militants, such as *chouannerie* in western France. On the grandest scale were raids into small towns to seize weapons, uproot liberty trees, and loot, kidnap, or kill Republicans. More common were assaults on isolated farmhouses, especially those belonging to wealthy purchasers of national property. Mail coaches and pay wagons presented equal opportunity targets for criminals and counter-revolutionaries alike. The presence of tens of thousands of deserters and draft-dodgers throughout the country, especially in areas least sympathetic to the Republic, provided all forms of brigandage with a reservoir of young men already on the run from the law.[12]

Brigandage of any sort posed a serious challenge for the forces of order. The mounted constabulary was shabby and unreliable. Too many gendarmes lacked professional training, proper pistols, quality horses, and basic scruples. In the more dangerous parts of France, they found themselves outmanned and outgunned. The porous nature of provincial jails also undermined public confidence that criminals would remain in custody long enough to be sentenced. As a result, a hardened group of local bandits could easily intimidate witnesses as well as jurors. Outlaws around Lodève carried jury lists, shot witnesses, and kidnapped judges with impunity.[13] Adding a dose of popular counter-revolution, or even traditional anti-statism, often made localized banditry threatening enough that whole districts united in a conspiracy of silence during police investigations.

Newspapers helped to magnify fears about an already dangerous epidemic of crime. Almost every issue of every paper, whether national or provincial, contained short snippets of reportage describing yet more armed assaults, highway robberies or brutal murders. The politicized nature of many of these made them particularly prone to falsification. After a royalist stabbed a government official to death at Le Mans, the local paper reported that Republicans in distant Provence had gathered up 300 finely worked knives from the site of a brawl with royalist 'cut-throats'.[14] Who could verify such a claim? The interaction between official concerns and journalistic coverage, both prone to exaggeration, led to mounting demands for better security regardless of the consequences for civil liberties. As one editor wrote, 'You want a republic? In good time. As for me, I want the rogues removed, the bandits defeated, the thieves hanged, and the assassins punished; after that, we'll talk of a republic.'[15] Whether newspapers created public opinion or simply reflected it, the government had no doubt that its credibility depended on doing more to repress brigandage.

Improvement had to be made in two areas: policing and punishment. In the first case, the regime undertook major reforms in the gendarmerie. In 1797, dramatic cuts in manpower, along with a complete reorganization of the corps, led to a thorough review of its personnel. Thousands of ageing, incompetent, or partisan constables and officers lost their jobs. Reassignments and promotions helped to fill the senior ranks with long-serving and talented professionals. Further reviews, prompted by worries about loyalty to the Republic, combined with new recruiting standards to ensure that each time the force grew larger (1798, 1800, 1801), it also became more capable. In April 1798, the force received a definitive set of duties and responsibilities that better integrated it into the civilian apparatus of justice and repression. This organizational code of conduct also increased pay, guaranteed pensions, and provided for routine replacement of horses, uniforms, weapons, and equipment. The reforms of 1797–98 made the gendarmerie into a modern police force established on a truly national footing. But increased professionalism did not make the gendarmerie's task an easy one. The level of violence faced by the rural constabulary ensured that it was no haven for the feckless or cowardly. Confronting brigands and rebels, escorting prisoners, rounding up draft-dodgers, and dispersing riotous crowds remained constant challenges well into the Consulate. By June 1801, the gendarmerie stood at 15,700 men, twice its size in 1797 and four times the size of the rural constabulary in 1789. And yet, the force was still experiencing an average of two incidents a day in which gendarmes were killed or wounded. That such prolonged and deadly violence did not destroy the corps is evidence that it had become a genuinely professional force, one which was both respected and feared. Much had changed. Community policing had turned into policing communities.[16]

The Republic also sought to combat brigandage by intensifying punishment. A law adopted in May 1797 prescribed the death penalty for armed robberies as well as those in which victims suffered physical harm. Making these into capital crimes was intended to address the horrifying spread of *chauffeurs de pied* who tortured property owners into revealing where jewels or cash might be hidden by thrusting their feet into the family fireplace. As the number of executions mounted, the government reported that highway robberies had begun to supplant incidents of *chauffage* as the latest and greatest trend in banditry. The response proposed by the Directory provoked a major parliamentary debate about sacrificing individual liberty to the needs of collective security. The government's supporters claimed that existing laws were powerless to end the epidemic of brigandage that 'threatened the social order with dissolution'. Opponents protested: 'Let us respect our constitution: punish without eroding liberty … [Do not put] the blade and scales of Themis [goddess of justice] in the hands of a soldier.'[17] But the resulting law of 18 January 1798 did largely that. Highway robbery and housebreaking were to be punished by the death penalty, thereby restoring capital punishment for property crimes, something rejected as barbaric earlier in the Revolution. Moreover, if such crimes had been planned or committed by more than two persons, they became subject to military courts. The greatest advantage of using military justice was the ability to prosecute the sort of criminals whose local influence or personal ruthlessness had silenced witnesses and paralysed juries. However, sophisticated new guidelines provided checks on such a harsh approach.

The great crime wave of the mid-1790s had persuaded legislators that preserving the republic required draconian treatment of violent criminals and counter-revolutionary guerrillas alike. Regular military courts found themselves pronouncing judgement on smugglers in the Pyrenees, highway robbers in the Cévennes, burglars in Paris, and even vagabond women in Normandy. This was a wider array of malefactors than the law was intended to encompass. The blame lay with civilian prosecutors who hoped to control the rising tide of property crime through exceptionally severe penalties. But results varied. The military courts at Marseilles condemned to death and executed 56 of the 75 civilians who appeared before them over a two-year period (1798–1800); whereas at Tours, it was 63 of 150, and at Rennes, it was 69 of 225. In less tumultuous areas, such as at Besançon, far fewer civilians were tried, and even fewer condemned to death. Thus, in the symbolic language of the day, military courts were slicing off heads from the hydra of anarchy with one hand, while still gripping the scales of justice in the other. Viewed from a constitutional angle, however, personal liberty had been severely eroded by the demands for public security. As a result, the temporary law was not renewed in early 1800.[18]

The recourse to military courts to prosecute civilians was symptomatic of a new attitude toward both law and order and the Republican order introduced by the coup d'état of 18 Fructidor V (4 September 1797). This massive violation of the constitution is usually viewed through the lens of high politics; however, it also provided the basis for redressing crippling issues of order. Constitutional royalists had sought to win the elections of spring 1797 by replacing open violence against the regime with covert political organizing. The returns favoured opponents of the Republic at both the national and local levels. As a result, governmental authority rapidly waned in the provinces. Royalists had good reason to believe that the elections of 1798 would radically alter the complexion of the Republican regime, if not end it altogether. Some royalists had no patience for democratic processes, however, especially after a ministerial shake-up in July 1797 suggested that the Directory would not simply wait to be voted out of existence. The Pretender, in exile in Britain, soon sent his leading spymaster to Paris. Once there, the Prince de La Trémoille called together a bevy of insurgent commanders from the West. The presence of numerous royalist warlords added to the pall of fear and conspiracy that hung over the capital by late August. Three members of the Directory responded on 4 September with a bloodless coup, ordering the arrest and deportation of two colleagues, fifty-three deputies from the legislative Councils, and a handful of other assorted members of a supposed royalist conspiracy tied to foreign powers. Such a conspiracy did exist, but it was not based in the Councils; therefore, the Directory's public justification for shredding the constitution rang hollow.[19]

Other measures adopted at the time of the coup reveal a broader concern: the need to overcome the widespread hostility to the Republic that had undercut law enforcement. The general collapse of authority in the provinces during the summer of 1797 was not a conspiracy, but it was inspired by a combined effort by lawmakers and local officials elected in 1795 and 1797 to block the Directory's version of a Republican order. The coup's leaders saw popular Catholicism and resurgent royalism as serious threats to the regime's survival and so abandoned their earlier commitment to constitutionalism and the rule of law in favour of increasingly authoritarian means to restore order. The Fructidor coup annulled the recent elections in 49 departments, thereby eliminating another 124 deputies, as well as hundreds of judges and departmental administrators.

A tendentious explanation for the sources of instability—the return of counter-revolutionary émigrés and refractory priests—also led to draconian measures against them. The law of 19 Fructidor V (5 September 1797) ordered the death penalty for all unauthorized émigrés caught back in France. As a result, military commissions operating in over fifty towns and cities tried just over a thousand cases of emigration during the next two years. Almost 30 per cent of defendants were condemned to death. Half of these individuals were from the social elite (nobles, clerics, merchants, investors, lawyers, etc.). Some, such as the comte de Rochecotte and the marquis de Surville, were counter-revolutionary leaders engaged in armed insurgency. Most of the others had actively sought to subvert the republic, although victims also included several women and old men.[20]

In addition to creating military commissions, the law of 19 Fructidor also authorized the Directory, which in turn authorized departmental administrators to deport refractory priests as well as those deemed local agitators. This required no trial or hearing. As a result, simple administrative orders resulted in the deportation of nearly 1400 priests. Of these, 187 died within two years,[21] three times the number shot by firing squads. Many more would have died had the Directory not simply interned priests who were elderly or infirm. In order to enforce these new measures against émigrés and clerics, a law restored the need for individual passports when travelling around France. Local authorities, with the general approval of the government, used this as the basis for employing the gendarmerie and national guardsmen in numerous house searches and sweeps of the countryside. Furthermore, the reinvigorated Directory muted public opposition to its form of republicanism by closing forty-two newspapers, imposing a stamp tax on political journalism, and banning private delivery systems favoured by right-wing publishers.

The battery of measures associated with the Fructidor coup d'état marked a decisive turn toward authoritarianism. The Thermidorian politicians who staffed the Directorial regime hesitated to abandon constitutionalism altogether; however, because they viewed any serious challenges to their leadership as threats to the regime itself, they found it impossible to accept pluralistic politics—hence their recidivism in massively altering the results of national elections in the spring of 1798. Alarmed by the election of Jacobins and even unrepentant 'terrorists' in some parts of the country, the government orchestrated a cynical triage of election results known as the 'coup' of 22 Floréal VI (11 May 1798). After such blatant disregard for election results, it is not surprising that 1799 brought the lowest voter participation in the decade.[22] Political legitimacy was coming to depend more on the effectiveness of the state apparatus than on the democratic credentials of those who operated it. Moreover, the turn toward authoritarianism reflected a belief that preserving the Republic and restoring law and order required exceptional measures. In the process, the regime gave civilian and military authorities powers that were easily abused. What had been adopted as defensive necessities quickly became opportunities to persecute former social elites as part of continuing to transform society. Many could hear the distinct echo of events in 1793–94 and so dubbed the new measures the 'Directorial Terror'. Whereas the revolutionary government of Year II had depended on a national network of Jacobin clubs, the Directory soon repudiated 'constitutional circles' as bases of support and turned instead to the regular army to help impose its will. As a result, army officers not only became judges but acquired added authority to take over policing in areas of endemic unrest.

One of the main ways to enhance the role of army officers in domestic repression was to proclaim a town under 'state of siege', rather than imposing martial law, which relied on calling out local national guardsmen. By the mid-1790s, the National Guard had become a patchy and unreliable source of armed force, inclined to become embroiled in local factionalism. Therefore, the Directory turned to a form of military policing intended for frontier towns in times of war. The 'state of siege' was first used for domestic purposes during the Federalist Revolt of 1793, then became an important part of pacifying the Vendée in 1796. The Directory completed the transformation of the 'state of siege' from a wartime measure to an instrument of domestic repression in 1797. Declaring specific localities under 'state of siege' gave the local army commander the power to order arrests, control prisons, and employ his troops without waiting for civilian authorities to request them. Excessive use of this measure in the Midi sparked opposition in the legislative Councils; however, the Fructidor coup gave the Directory complete freedom to impose the 'state of siege' wherever it was deemed necessary. The Directory granted this power to individual generals who commanded interior military districts where collective violence proved especially intractable. By 1798, this once exceptional measure had become an almost routine response to outbreaks of collective violence, resistance to authority, or attacks on the forces of order. It was also exploited for more dubious purposes, such as helping to police elections. Renewed resistance to the Republic in 1799 prompted the Directory to extend blanket authorization to generals whose interior military commands covered a full 40 per cent of the country. By the time of the coup d'état that ended the Directory on 18 Brumaire (9 November), over 220 municipalities had experienced the shift of policing from local authorities to the regular army. Most of these were towns and bourgs in the south or west, but they included major cities in France (Lyon, Marseille, Toulon) as well as in annexed territories (Nice, Geneva, Antwerp, Ghent). The state of siege was used against peasant revolts as well. It was imposed on two dozen rural cantons around Toulouse in the autumn of 1799, then on five entire departments in western France in 1800. Only in 1801 did the Consulate begin to roll back use of the state of siege. Nonetheless, it remained a basic part of the French toolkit of repression throughout the Napoleonic Empire.[23]

The later Directory's frequent use of the state of siege reflected a broader tendency to rely on the army to provide basic functions of domestic policing. These extended beyond defending towns or patrolling main arteries to include escorting stagecoaches, checking passports, and conducting exhausting sweeps of sizeable regions where every large wood, walled farm, and country tavern needed to be carefully searched. The persistence of *chouannerie* in regions such as Normandy, Maine, and Anjou inspired a combination of civilian and military responses that paid little heed to the constitution. The government rarely objected as long as officials acted discreetly. The high mortality rate for *chouans* in custody, the use of soldiers disguised as *chouans*, and the taking of relatives as hostages all became features of Republican counter-insurgency. This protracted 'dirty war' extended from the official pacification of 1796 to the sudden renewal of open insurrection in the autumn of 1799. By then, *chouannerie* had become more militarized, thanks largely to the leadership of aristocratic émigrés whose royalist brevets came from the Pretender himself.

Such resistance gained even more room to operate when the Directory transferred most of the regular forces stationed in the interior to its failing armies on the frontiers. The domestic crisis provoked by victories of the Second Coalition in the summer of 1799 led directly to the infamous 'law of hostages' in July. This Jacobin-style solution allowed local authorities in areas officially recognized as 'troubled' to intern local nobles and relatives of émigrés as a means to paralyse opposition. This created a pool of candidates for immediate deportation in response to armed attacks. Such a measure was easily abused and so lawmakers sought to limit its use. Nonetheless, one *chouan* leader described the law of hostages as the best recruiting tool his party had that summer.[24]

The law of hostages, combined with the massive conscription announced at much the same time, fuelled a widespread willingness to take up arms against the regime. The Count of Bourmont's capture and occupation of Le Mans for three days in October 1799 marked the apogee of this militarized *chouannerie*. Despite mobilizing contingents of the National Guard throughout the west, it took reinforcements from the regular army finally to reimpose the Republic on the region. After months of intense fighting, First Consul Bonaparte ordered army commanders to make the insurgent areas 'feel all the weight and horrors of war' in order to terrorize 'the inhabitants to unite against the brigands'.[25] The offer of amnesty to individual rebels who turned over their guns evolved into a brutal campaign of rural disarmament in the spring of 1800. Despite proclaiming an official end to the civil war in April, the full panoply of exceptional measures remained in use. It took intense civilian and military policing, including the arbitrary arrest and imprisonment of amnestied leaders, to secure the region. Thereafter, an elaborate registry of brigands and *chouans* in western France provided the Ministry of Police with a biographical dictionary of the proverbial usual suspects when cracking down on outbreaks of violence.[26]

Greater reliance on armed repression needed to be complemented by a more reliable judiciary. The post-Fructidorian Directory used its enhanced executive power to strengthen the regular system of criminal justice, but again at the expense of constitutional rectitude. The Directory put particular emphasis on purging the magistracy of politically suspect judges. Scores of judges were eliminated by the Fructidor nullification of election results in forty-nine departments. Government appointees filled their places. Four months later, a law terminated all court presidents and public prosecutors elected at the start of the Directory, thereby opening their posts for election that spring. The 'coup' of 22 Floréal VI (11 May 1798) then eliminated almost one third of all the magistrates elected that year.[27] Once again, government appointees took their places. These heavy-handed interventions in the judiciary may have eroded its democratic basis, but they also served to reverse the anti-Republican leanings of the nation's least effective courts, especially in areas of unrest such as the southeast and the annexed departments of Belgium.

The Directory's role in selecting judges gave criminal justice a more Republican character. This tendency was also fostered by revising jury lists after the Fructidor coup, an activity strongly encouraged by the minister of justice. His encouragement gave local officials the opportunity to cull active citizens known for their antipathy to the Republic and to replace them with men of a more sympathetic complexion. More refining of jury lists followed the Floréal coup. This general winnowing over time filled jury pools with men more likely to see issues of law and order through Directorial eyes. Though juries never became pliable instruments of the regime, the government commissioner in the Doubs claimed that 'the regeneration of juries has terrified villains'.[28] If the increased likelihood of conviction is any indication, then his optimism was at least partially borne out.

The regular criminal courts became more effective in the last two years of the Directory than they had been in the first two years. The number of prosecutions increased while the acquittal rate dropped, especially in departments previously gripped by political reaction. The combination meant that the number of persons convicted of felonies increased—possibly as much as 20 per cent—from the first to the second half of the Directory. The increased attention paid to the types of crime that most threatened the social order (robbery and interpersonal violence) ensured that the number of persons sentenced to lengthy terms of hard labour grew by almost 50 per cent and the number of death sentences more than doubled. Furthermore, the government's influence in choosing magistrates ensured a large increase in the prosecution of crimes related to politics or resisting public authority—crimes such as harbouring a priest, striking an official, or rioting. The presence of more overtly Republican jurors also helped to ensure a drop in acquittal rates in such cases. These trends seem to have been determined largely by the more aggressive republicanism of the judicial establishment across the south of France where the regime struggled to overcome revolutionary factionalism that had exacerbated traditions of vendetta and anti-statism. In short, where the Republic had been most challenged, the years between the Fructidor coup and the Brumaire coup (1797–99) made the system of criminal justice both more Republican and more repressive.[29]

Though often viewed as the start of a return to order, the coup d'état of 18 Brumaire VIII actually disrupted efforts to restore law and order. Enthusiasm for the prosecution of crime cooled notably amidst the political and administrative uncertainties that accompanied the formation of a new regime. Officials of all types worried about their future. The anti-Jacobin tone of the coup raised special concern among the most ardent defenders of the Republic, the very men who had infused the judiciary with added intensity over the previous two years. Then came sudden institutional changes. As new structures and procedures were announced, existing ones ground to a halt. The resulting inaction opened great holes in the net of law enforcement. Overhauling the judiciary, in particular, required replacing all elected judges, prosecutors, and court presidents—more than 3,000 positions in all—with government appointees. Courts were not fully staffed again until June 1800. Thus, the early Consulate brought a marked reduction in both prosecutions and punishments handled by regular courts. Purposeful depoliticization of criminal justice also reduced caseloads as the prosecution of crimes associated with imposing the Republican order became increasingly rare. Major political trials initiated after the Fructidor coup, especially those inspired by reactionary violence, were also allowed to lapse or overturned on appeal.[30]

The scourge of brigandage, whether politicized or not, also continued unabated into the early Consulate. In fact, an infusion of royalist leaders turned an already chaotic mix of endemic lawlessness and local hatreds into a crescendo of banditry. With criminal courts in transition and regular military courts no longer involved, the First Consul sought new means to redress the situation. Bonaparte adopted an explicit policy of ruthless intimidation that would tip the balance of fear in the regime's favour. In the spring of 1800, he ordered the formation of three military commissions in regions where politicized brigandage had been stubbornly intractable: the upper Rhône Valley, the foothills above Nice, and western Brittany. Although tightly limited in geographic scope, these commissions displayed scant respect for due process. The flying columns of troops that attended each commission showed a special disregard for legality. They arbitrarily arrested scores of people, including whole families, pillaged farmhouses, brutalized recalcitrant officials and threatened to kill anyone who aided the bandits. Dozens of supposed brigands were shot while 'trying to escape' or simply as an object lesson to locals. The brigands showed no less determination. When the local commander refused to release a brigand leader from the jail at Valréas (north of Avignon), members of his band shot the commander and three fellow officers to death, then celebrated by dragging their naked and mutilated corpses through the streets. The ruthlessness of these regionalized conflicts is well illustrated by the struggle against the *barbets* north of Nice. The local armed forces there shot 136 men, including 65 of the 70 people tried by the military commission created in June 1800.[31]

First Consul Bonaparte's willingness to use whatever means were necessary became especially obvious in the wake of the failed attempt to blow him up in the rue Nicaise on 24 December 1800. This provoked what might be called the 'Consular Terror'. The national outcry over the attempt to assassinate Bonaparte encouraged him to exploit the public mood and take draconian action. He promptly ordered a crackdown on former Jacobin radicals and sans-culottes, more than a hundred of whom were arrested and deported without trial to Guyana. The Senate issued the deportation order, cynically claiming that it was a measure to conserve the constitution, thereby implicating the entire regime in this political proscription. Over half of these men died in exile, several times the number of deportees who died as a result of the Fructidor coup. Many provincial Jacobins were also rounded up, though most were later released without trial. All of this happened despite the government's knowledge that the actual bomb—dubbed the *machine infernale*—had been the work of royalist conspirators.[32]

The Consular Terror was extended to the provinces by four military commissions and flying columns created in Bas-Languedoc and Provence. These 'extraordinary military commissions' were empowered to judge bandits, their accomplices, and even those who received stolen goods. Public trials were held in numerous upland towns such as Rodez and Digne as well as in coastal cities from Montpellier to Toulon. Verdicts—over 400 of them—were announced on hundreds of broadsheets plastered throughout the region. Only a fifth of these verdicts brought freedom, whereas half led to firing squads. Many of these were held in market squares, on bridges, and along roads near where the original hold-ups, housebreakings, and murders had been committed, thereby reclaiming these sites as *lieux de mémoire* for the Republic, rather than its opponents. It also brought home to local residents and officials alike the deadly consequences of continuing to oppose either the Republic or law and order. In western France, some 1200 *chouans* were arrested, 250 condemned to death and another 150 killed 'while resisting arrest' during the winter of 1800–1.[33] Adding 'extraordinary military commissions' helped to sustain this regional terror throughout the spring of 1801.

Reports from the generals, whether in the south or the west, indicate that this special form of 'booted justice' finally broke the back of political brigandage in the regions where it had been worst. This is not to say that it was completely stamped out—it was not—but that the Republican state had gained the upper hand. The Consulate had used military commissions and flying columns to terrify the populace into abandoning their support for anti-Republican brigands. In some places, active citizens actually joined forces with the regime against the bandits as a means to restore the honour and good standing of their sullied communities. Just how much the regime succeeded by depriving its opponents of the power to intimidate and how much it succeeded by rising above factionalism remains unclear. The regime's reputation for depoliticization—for putting *le politique* (the political) in place of *la politique* (politics)—has been well established. However, determining levels of popular support for it, especially in the countryside, requires more sustained and more sophisticated research, especially considering the Consulate's closing of most newspapers in January 1800.[34] Regardless of the press censorship, it is clear that continuing to use such dreadful means of repression risked discrediting the regime. The Consular government decided, therefore, to create better regulated forms of exceptionalism: henceforth, the judicial response to brigandage would have more form and be less exceptional.

In the winter of 1800–1, the Consulate had sought to make several major reforms to the system of criminal justice. At first, liberal lawmakers objected to the government's attempt to strengthen the apparatus of repression as authoritarian and manifestly subversive of individual liberty. Then came the Consular Terror. The new circumstances made it far harder to put liberty above security. In fact, given the recent proscription of 130 individuals without trial, the activities of flying columns and extraordinary military commissions in the provinces, and a threat from the First Consul that he would govern by decree if his reforms were not passed, lawmakers no doubt viewed the creation of 'special tribunals' as something of a bulwark against both reckless terror and personal dictatorship. The law of 8 February 1801 proved a major defeat for constitutional liberals, notably Chénier, Daunou, and Benjamin Constant, who insisted on trial by jury as the 'palladium of liberty'. However, creating special tribunals was also an important means to limit the trend toward arbitrariness and military dictatorship, both in Paris and the provinces.[35]

Special tribunals quickly took a prominent place in the emerging security state. By 1803, more than one third of all departments had a special tribunal to supplement the regular criminal court. Special tribunals delivered exceptional justice within a straitjacket of regulations. They combined military and civilian judges, rather than jurors, and their competence was reviewed before trial, but verdicts could not be appealed. Prosecutors had favourable rules of evidence, whereas defendants had legal counsel and a public audience. Condemned rebels, bandits, and robbers were guillotined by the public executioner in the departmental *chef lieu*, not shot to death by a squad of soldiers in a remote village. Thus, despite being yet another form of exceptional justice invented by the First Republic to avoid insouciant magistrates and lax juries, special tribunals marked an improvement over revolutionary tribunals, military commissions and even regular military courts. As such, they embodied the essence—and contradictions—of the security state.

Special tribunals also packed a repressive punch. Their writ covered an assortment of rural crimes associated with brigandage, including sedition and recruiting conscripts. Their relatively harsh verdicts sharply increased the total judicial repression meted out by criminal courts. Although results varied considerably, on average, special tribunals issued two-thirds of the harshest penalties handed down in those departments where they operated. France reached the high-water mark of repression in the years 1801 to 1804. During that time, non-military courts annually sentenced over 800 individuals to death and another 3,000 others to hard labour. The continued use of military justice also added hundreds of executions a year, although the figures dropped precipitously after 1802. Special tribunals were intended to last only as long as France remained at war; however, because Bonaparte never really felt secure at home or abroad, he ensured that they became a permanent feature of the Napoleonic state.[36]

The coup d'état of 18 Brumaire VIII should not serve as historical shorthand for the transition from democracy to dictatorship. The process took much longer, stretching from the Fructidor coup (September 1797) to the Life Consulate (August 1802). Treating the Brumaire coup as a brutal rupture obscures basic continuities between the Directory and early Consulate. Most of the deputies appointed to the new tricameral legislature had already served in the Councils of the Directory. Confronting the interplay between political instability and widespread violence led these men— Thermidorians-cum-Brumairians—to conclude that representative democracy was not the best means to preserve individual liberty. Rather, they believed that combining a strong executive with equality before the law would give individuals sufficient freedom to pursue their own ends without fear for their safety. They chose, therefore, to replace democratic republicanism with liberal authoritarianism.[37] This had begun as a variety of exceptional measures—which ranged from nullifying election results to the law of hostages—that undermined the constitution in the name of preserving it. However, such measures threatened to become the basis of a new Republican dictatorship, especially during the Jacobin resurgence over the summer of 1799. The Consulate was intended to prevent that, as well as to end the need for exceptional measures.[38] And yet, the repeated recourse to various repressive expedients in 1800–1 paved the road to a personal dictatorship.

In addition to replacing elected judges and local administrators with appointed ones, expanding the gendarmerie, and relying on the army to repress resistance and banditry in areas of endemic unrest, the Consulate dealt directly with sources of instability and lawlessness provoked by the Directory's version of a Republican order. First Consul Bonaparte began by scrapping the odious law of hostages. He then relaxed the republic's anti-clericalism by allowing churches to reopen, releasing priests awaiting deportation, and simplifying the civic oath. Historians often underscore this new political vision, but fail to mention that it would have been impossible without years of strengthening administrative surveillance and preventive policing. In fact, the life of priests remained rather precarious, especially given how vehemently most Republicans opposed the Concordat. Its negotiation in 1801 and promulgation at Easter 1802 was a major departure from the Republican order envisioned in 1795. The same must be said of the treatment of émigrés. Even though the Constitution of Year VIII barred the return of émigrés, the Consulate moved cautiously to end their exclusion. The official list of émigrés numbered over 100,000 when it was closed in March 1800. Six months later, a partial amnesty sharply cut the number of émigrés whose return needed to be approved on an individual basis. The amnesty came swaddled in police controls, including the requirement that every émigré register with local authorities who then passed the information to the Ministry of Police. The minister, Joseph Fouché, had no qualms about arbitrarily arresting scores of émigrés suspected of counter-revolutionary activity and locking them in state prisons without trial. The political success of a measure that both offended Republican sensibilities and contravened the principles of due process led to a near total amnesty for émigrés passed by the Senate on 26 April 1802. Again, however, Fouché instructed subordinates to repress 'with inflexible severity' any disobedience from émigrés, including attempts to recover their property illegally.[39] Thus, the Consulate's progress toward restoring law and order depended on combining an altered vision of the Republican order with the steady emergence of a 'security state'.

The myth of Napoleon Bonaparte as the saviour of France came from ending the French Revolution by restoring order. Of course, achieving peace through victory played a major part in this achievement. The prolonged war, with its heavy demands for men and money, had been a wellspring of resistance and crime. It had also denuded the interior of troops in 1799, whereas the return of units in 1801 enabled the consular crackdown that year. All the same, it had taken years to build up the state's capacity to manage repression. In addition to appointed judges, Special Tribunals, and an enhanced gendarmerie, it now included 'prefects of police' and 'security magistrates' to coordinate policing and prosecution, as well as a handful of state prisons and a growing practice of internal exile to control suspects who could not be convicted at trial. This new apparatus, better described as a 'security state' than a 'police state', depended on greater administrative surveillance and weaker legislative authority. The purge of liberal opponents from the Tribunate in March 1802, together with a national plebiscite two months later, allowed Bonaparte to consolidate the Consulate as a personal dictatorship. Among other powers, the Constitution of Year X (August 1802) allowed the First Consul to grant pardons, avoid the use of juries, and even suspend the constitution in regions where he saw fit. The return to law and order apparently won Bonaparte much popular support, but it came at the expense of both civil liberties and a truly Republican order.[40] Political theorists from Carl Schmitt to Giorgio Agamben have reflected on the 'state of emergency' as a kernel of dictatorship in a liberal democracy.[41] The French First Republic offers a disturbing case in point, but just how willingly people sacrificed democracy and liberty for stability and security remains a subject for deeper research.

NOTES

1. Gordon Wright, *Between the Guillotine and Liberty: Two Centuries of the Crime Problem in France* (Oxford, 1983), 34.
2. The neologism 'extreme centre' at the heart of Pierre Serna, *La République des girouettes (1789–1815 et au-delà)* (Paris, 2005) refers more to a discourse of enhanced executive power in response to political instability than it does to a position on the political spectrum at the time.
3. Jean-Louis Halperin, 'Les décrets d'annulation des jugements sous la Convention', in Michel Vovelle (ed.), *La Révolution et l'ordre juridique privé: rationalité ou scandale*, (Orléans, 1988), 457–68; Ronen Steinberg, 'Restitution of Property, Rehabilitation of Memory: Undoing the Terror in France, 1794–1799' presented at the Annual Meeting of the Society for French Historical Studies, April 2006.
4. Bronislaw Baczko, 'Une passion thermidorienne: la revanche', in his *Politiques de la Révolution française* (Paris, 2008), 165–338; Michelle Vovelle (ed.), *Le Tournant de l'an III: Réaction et Terreur blanche dans la France révolutionnaire* (Paris, 1997), esp. 483–611.
5. Howard G. Brown, 'Robespierre's Tail: The Possibilities of Justice after the Terror', *Journal of Canadian History* (2010), 503–35.
6. For example, François Furet, *La Révolution française, 1770–1880: de Turgot à Jules Ferry* (Paris, 1988), 174.
7. Brown, 'Robespierre's Tail', 532–5.
8. A. Debidour, *Recueil des actes du Directoire exécutif*, 4 vols (Paris, 1910–17), I, 19–20.
9. *Le Moniteur universel* (henceforth *Moniteur*), 18 germinal an IV.
10. Colin Lucas, 'The First Directory and the Rule of Law', *French Historical Studies* 10 (1977), 231–60.
11. For assessments of criminal justice in this period, see Isser Woloch, *The New Regime: Transformations of the French Civic Order, 1789–1820s* (New York, 1992), 350ff.; Robert Allen, *Les Tribunaux criminels sous la Révolution et l'Empire, 1792–1811* (Rennes, 2005); Laura Mason, 'The "Bosom of Proof": Criminal Justice and the Renewal of Oral Culture during the French Revolution', *Journal of Modern History* 76 (2004), 29–61, and Howard G. Brown, *Ending the French Revolution: Violence, Justice, and Repression from the Terror to Napoleon* (Charlottesville, 2006).
12. For different perspectives, see Marcel Marion, *Le brigandage pendant la Révolution* (Paris, 1934); Richard Cobb, *Reactions to the French Revolution* (Oxford, 1972); Alan Forrest, *Conscripts and Deserters: The Army and French Society during the Revolution and Empire* (Oxford, 1989).
13. Archives nationales F[7] 7734, d. 26.
14. *Chronique de la Sarthe*, 24 brumaire VI.

15. Joseph Lavalée, *Semaines critiques, ou gestes de l'an cinq*, 2 vols (Paris, 1797), 19–20.
16. Brown, *Ending the French Revolution*, 189–200.
17. *Moniteur*, an VI, 344–7, 507.
18. Brown, *Ending the French Revolution*, 213–33.
19. For both details and a debate on the Fructidor coup, see Georges Lefebvre, *La France sous le Directoire, 1795–1799*, 2nd edn, edited by Jean-René Suratteau (1984), 418–33, 729–36.
20. Brown, *Ending the French Revolution*, 152–68.
21. Victor Pierre, *La Terreur sous le Directoire* (Paris, 1887), 423–61.
22. Malcolm Crook, *Elections in the French Revolution* (Cambridge, 1996).
23. Brown, *Ending the French Revolution*, 200–21.
24. Eric-Marie Guyot, *Vendéens et chouans contre Bonaparte (1799–1814)* (Paris, 1990), 11–12.
25. Charles-Louis Chassin, *Les Pacifications de l'Ouest, 1794–1801*, 3 vols (Paris, 1896–99), III, 523–4, 545–7.
26. Archives Nationales F⁷ 2261–70.
27. Jean-René Suratteau, *Les Élections de l'an VI et le 'coup d'état du 22 floréal an VI' (11 mai 1798)* (Paris, 1971), 210–25.
28. AD du Doubs, L 243.
29. D. M. G. Sutherland, *Murder in Aubagne: Lynching, Law, and Justice during the French Revolution* (Cambridge, 2009); Brown, *Ending the French Revolution*, 171–9.
30. Jean Bourdon, *La réforme judiciare de l'an VIII*, 2 vols (Paris, 1941), II, 231, 282; Brown, *Ending the French Revolution*, 303–8.
31. Archives de la Guerre B¹³ 120, 134.
32. Isser Woloch, *Napoleon and His Collaborators: The Making of a Dictatorship* (New York, 2001), 72–4.
33. Brown, *Ending the French Revolution*, 317–24; Ernest Daudet, *La Police et les chouans sous le Consulat et l'Empire, 1800–1815* (Paris, 1895), 23.
34. Steven Englund, *Napoleon: A Political Life* (New York, 2005).
35. Irene Collins, *Napoleon and his Parliaments, 1800–1815* (New York, 1979), 27–67; Andrew Jainchill, *Reimagining Politics after the Terror: The Republican Origins of French Liberalism* (Ithaca, 2008), 248–62; Adolphe Thiers, *Histoire du Consulat et de l'Empire*, 20 vols (Paris, 1845–62), II, 341–42.
36. Howard G. Brown, 'Special Tribunals and the Napoleonic Security State', in Philip G. Dwyer and Alan Forrest (eds), *Napoleon and his Empire: Europe, 1804–1814* (Basingstoke, 2007), 79–95.
37. Jainchill, *Reimagining Politics*, 197–204, adds an important political dimension to my original articulation of 'liberal authoritarianism'.
38. Bernard Gainot, *1799, un nouveau Jacobinisme? La démocratie représentative, une alternative à brumaire* (Paris, 2001), describes the 'regeneration' of 1799 without noting the consternation it caused; compare, Michael J. Sydenham, *The First French Republic, 1792–1804* (London, 1974).
39. Louis Madelin, *Fouché, 1759–1820*, 2 vols, 2nd edn (Paris, 1903), I, 329–47.
40. For contrasting views on Napoleon's handling of civil liberties, see Woloch, *Napoleon and his Collaborators*, and Michael D. Sibalis, 'Arbitrary Detention, Human Rights, and the Napoleonic Senate', in Howard G. Brown and Judith A. Miller (eds), *Taking Liberties: Problems of a New Order from the French Revolution to Napoleon* (Manchester, 2002), 166–84.
41. Carl Schmitt, *Dictatorship* (London, 2013); Giorgio Agamben, *State of Exception* (Chicago, 2005).

Selected Reading

Brown, Howard G., *Ending the French Revolution: Violence, Justice, and Repression from the Terror to Napoleon* (Charlottesville, 2006).

Cobb, Richard C., *Reactions to the French Revolution* (Oxford, 1972).

Doyle, William, *The Oxford History of the French Revolution* (Oxford, 1989).

Chassin, Charles-Louis, *Les Pacifications de l'Ouest, 1794–1801*, 3 vols (Paris, 1896–99).

Lentz, Thierry, *Le Grand Consulat, 1799–1804* (Paris, 1999).

Lewis, Gwynne and Colin Lucas (eds), *Beyond the Terror: Essays in French Regional and Social History, 1794–1815* (Cambridge, 1983).

Jainchill, Andrew, *Reimagining Politics After the Terror: The Republican Origins of French Liberalism* (Ithaca, 2008).

Lefebvre, Georges, *La France sous le Directoire, 1795–1799*, 2nd edn, edited by Jean-René Suratteau (Paris, 1984).

Lyons, Martin, *Napoleon Bonaparte and the Legacy of the French Revolution* (New York, 1994).

Sutherland, D. M. G., *The French Revolution and Empire: The Quest for a Civic Order* (Oxford, 2003).

Sydenham, Michael J., *The First French Republic, 1792–1904* (Berkeley, 1973).

Vovelle, Michel (ed.), *Le Tournant de l'an III: Réaction et terreur blanche dans la France révolutionnaire* (Paris, 1997).

Woloch, Isser, *Napoleon and His Collaborators: The Making of a Dictatorship* (New York, 2001).

CHAPTER 32

THE NEW ELITES. QUESTIONS
ABOUT POLITICAL,
SOCIAL, AND CULTURAL
RECONSTRUCTION AFTER
THE TERROR

JEAN-LUC CHAPPEY

THE historiography of the French elites at the end of the eighteenth century has recently experienced an important revival. Individual[1] or collective[2] works have re-thought traditional interpretative categories (bourgeoisie, aristocracy ...) and opened up new research paths.[3] Unquestionably, even if the French Revolution abolished the hierarchies and privileges of a society of orders, it did not abolish social, economic or cultural inequalities, in spite of the demands of some of its more radical voices. Traditionally, the elite owned landed property as well as financial, economic or symbolic goods which set it apart from other social groups. Members of the elite could also be recognized by their roles in political, administrative or academic institutions, membership in social and solidarity networks and even—in a given urban area—by their localization in specific neighbourhoods or by their mastery of particular social codes: all signs which lie at the root of a culture of separateness. It is, nonetheless, extremely difficult to find any real unity or cohesion among them. But it is possible to turn to the elite's discourse about itself and study the way its members constructed and formalized their image of themselves.[4] Beginning this chapter with the political opening created by the fall of Robespierre on 9 Thermidor Year II/27 July 1794 serves as a reminder of how 'the invention of the Terror' allowed for a redefinition of the Republican elite, flanked by a stigmatized, violent populace and an old sullied elite.

During the political and intellectual conflicts of the eighteenth century, the elites adhering to the ideals of the Enlightenment had developed a specific discourse and a particular imagery about the 'people', an entity in need of both control and education.[5] In order to leave the Terror behind and to justify the repression against Robespierre and his followers, the members of the Convention robustly restated the distinction between a civilizing elite and a people in need of civilization. This process, often reduced to the questionable concept of a Thermidorian 'reaction', really started in November 1794 when a new coalition within the Convention succeeded in marginalizing the few remaining Montagnards who had spearheaded the elimination of Robespierre. It is in this specific context that the notion of the 'invention' of the Terror should be understood.

Far from being a simple social and political reaction of the (or even of a) 'bourgeoisie', the Thermidorian elite's intention was to save the republic by keeping the people within 'just boundaries'. Their claim that the people could be changed and should not be seen as 'the Other' who, by nature, differed totally from the elite, was as important as their denunciation of popular violence. The political project of the Directory was explicitly built on the idea that the people could be transformed and integrated into the elite. Legitimizing the domination of the Republican elite, Reason was the new means of government. Because of their ignorance, the people had previously been reduced to the level of wild animals: this interpretation of the past allowed for a condemnation of the principles of the 1793 Constitution, guilty of having 'degraded' their minds.

At this point, the ignorance of the people did not describe their lack of knowledge as much as it described a failure of their minds. Thus it also clearly established a connection between madness and the 1793 Constitution. This interpretative model justified the temporary ascendancy of an elite that defined itself in terms of emotional control, of a sort of stoicism on which their political legitimacy was founded.[6] What they condemned was as much the shocking mores of the uncivilized people as the so-called scandalous behaviour of some individuals or groups, such as the 'Incroyables' or the 'Merveilleuses'. The Republican elite saw 'good mores' and virtuous domestic ideals as the true foundations of the political and social order, and built its identity against that of another elite which was considered corrupt and degraded, and whose regeneration was seen as much more problematic than the regeneration of the people. Measures of political repression against this corrupt elite, whose members were seen as embodiments of a total otherness, show how, through stigmatization, the new Republican elite managed not only to dissociate itself from the people but also from groups that could have pretended to belong to a social or cultural elite, but whose 'bad mores' had re-shaped them into political enemies.

Thus under the Directory, the Republican programme was created within the framework of an ideological paradigm where the elite's identity developed in contrast with that of the people, women, children and the colonial world, as well as the European populations living in territories conquered by the French army from 1795 onwards. Thus, it was very important to assert the civilizing mission of the new elite whose political, social and cultural supremacy could only be justified by its ability to free those various groups from their isolation and dependency and to lift them up to the highest ranks of civilization. From that perspective, their supremacy needed to be seen as temporary, and the permeability of the elite towards the social groups in need of civilization was understood as a necessary stage of the civilizing process. This connection of a political programme and an ideological paradigm is the most original feature of the 'republican way' as it was developed by the Directory, and its principles were expressed in the 1795 Constitution.

In this context, intellectual capital, based on the 'good' use of reason, became the basis of citizenship. Title II, Article 16 of the 1795 Constitution, states that 'young people should not be enrolled on civic registers unless they can prove that they can read, write and carry on an occupation.'[7] Besides the various other criteria that reduced access to political rights (payment of a fixed sum, age, gender ...), the Thermidorian politicians added a cultural and intellectual criterion. It excluded the huge mass of the illiterate from political citizenship, or—to be more precise—from primary Assemblies and from the administration of ballots, but also from various forms of political deliberations. The 1795 Constitution turned the literacy requirement into a general prerequisite to the exercise of any kind of civic rights, which from then on became dependent on a minimal intellectual capital. Representatives of various cultural and academic domains were called to work together to avoid the return of 'Barbary': scientists, writers, artists were expected to work towards the advancement of civilization and to provide policymakers with means (analyses, observation ...) to keep reason within 'just boundaries', as enthusiasm and passion were now considered as dangers that threatened political and social order.

Leaving the Terror behind and preventing its return were seen as the opening of a new era of reason's supremacy. According to Condillac (whose legacy was very much appreciated by Republican authorities at that time),[8] to think properly is more than anything else to speak properly. An inappropriate use of language was undoubtedly seen as the cause of uncontrolled emotions and of violence. From 1795 onward, the mission of the scholar was thus to prevent political 'convulsions', as is clearly shown by the exposure given to the research led by the psychiatrist and head of the Bicêtre Hospital, Philippe Pinel. The regime of the 'best' was first and foremost a regime of scholars. This was not so much a reinstatement of the old royal academies, as a new creation that aimed to legitimize the new Republican project.

The *Institut National des sciences, lettres et arts* founded in October 1795 and structured around the *Classe des sciences morales et politiques* was to be the embodiment of this scholarly mission: to republicanize the nation's mores.[9] The regeneration project clearly became the object of a science of mores. The epistemological foundations of this project to reshape human nature can be found in the public authorities' adhesion to Condillac's sensualist philosophy and their promotion of vitalist theories that affirm the interdependency between body and soul. 'Ideology', the 'general science of Man', was the name given to the vast body of knowledge that was to bring together all scientists, writers and artists to work towards the development of knowledge, but even more towards the transformation of humankind and society.

For the Republican elite, regeneration or civilization implied a programme of depoliticization of the popular classes. The idea was to promote pacified manners and mores by encouraging the expression in the public sphere of values and moral principles that had their origin in the domestic sphere: the good wife, the good father, were to be examples (presented through literature or theatre) at the foundation of a public ethic rooted in bourgeois private morality. It would be important, of course, to question the impact of this process of separation of bourgeois culture on newly emerging and potentially cynical political practices or on a more bureaucratic culture of government. However, this insistence on 'good mores' as well as the revival of practices of elite sociability did entail a real dissociation between the people and the elite, and amongst the elite it pushed towards the construction of social and cultural distinctions that could justify this dissociation.[10]

The pedagogical project that was at the root of this 'republicanization' of minds was supposed to reduce and, in due course, to eradicate the distinction between the reasoning and sensible elites on the one hand and the ignorant and impulsive people on the other hand. Laws and institutions were regarded as the instruments of a true political process of renovation which would eventually render possible the perfection of the people, who for the moment were seen as ignorant and incompetent.[11] This was how the attention of the political and administrative authorities towards those plagued by 'communicational impairment' and to Pinel's 'moral treatments' should be understood: very much like the doctors who 'treat' madness, the political elite's mission was to 'treat' the people by enforcing new communication rules.

In accordance with these principles, the diplomacy of the Directory was founded on a 'philosophical history of humanity' that addressed the popular classes and populations beyond France in strongly similar ways. In spite of the often very constrictive nature of French authority,[12] the French army and administration developed their relationship with local populations, in the belief that they were imparted with a civilizing mission towards them, with local elites often playing the role of a political and cultural intermediary.[13] After they were freed from their bondage, the infantilized populations of Europe and beyond would experience the benefits of civilization—but under the French Republic's tutelage. This mission was seen within the framework of a historical process linking all nations—each at their different level of development—together. This historical process, based on a model that had the development of rational faculties as its core, can be described as a succession of stages through which a nation grows gradually from 'savagery' to 'civilization'. What makes this growth possible is the development of relationships between a society, a people or a nation and a more evolved and civilized one. 'Commerce' (understood here as all the interaction of a nation with others) is thus understood as the motor of civilization—a very strange logic indeed, whose obvious ambiguities plainly validate the resistance it encountered amongst those other nations.

Studies of the Batavian or Italian republics, or of the contacts established with the Egyptian elites, have established the original and creative character of the political experiments that were undertaken there.[14] When contrasted with the demands of Italian or Batavian patriots who wanted quick changes, the representatives of the Directory were mostly concerned with soothing all radical ardour and putting in place a gradual programme of transformation of mores. This necessarily slow process justified their apparently paradoxical ideal of 'republicanism without a revolution' and it is this programme that ultimately failed. The diplomatic forces found themselves struggling against too many different groups; radical Italian patriots fighting for Italian unity, an ambitious French military elite attempting here and there to 'revolutionize' social relations more brutally, and even the Directorial authorities' own contradictions, as they had never really considered the 'sister republics' from any other angle but that of France's economic and strategic advantages.[15]

From 1795 onwards, the new political and intellectual elites' regeneration programme was the object of much criticism, contesting their self-defined leading role. The Catholic and royalist opposition questioned the scholars' ability to transform society, and accused them of leading an immoral venture that they saw as the source of many social ills (suicide, divorce …).[16] Those adversaries of the republic, whose voice was to be later amplified by Chateaubriand, lifting up poetry and beauty against the scholarly enterprise, presented themselves as the defenders of a traditional popular culture rooted in common sense and prejudice. Popular wisdom was thus opposed to the reason of the Parisian scholars. The successive royalist electoral victories between 1795 and 1797 clearly show that, in spite of the hard work of the employees of the interior ministry and their representatives in the departments and municipalities, the propagation of good Republican principles can hardly be considered as a full success.

More generally, the country people (more than the urban populations) without being totally opposed to the elite's educational venture, were becoming more and more indifferent to the ceremonies, festivals or even to the new religious cults (theophilanthropy, decadarism …) invented by those elites. The successive 'coups d'état' of 1797 and 1798 seemed to be justified each time by a need to correct the faults of a people still not mature enough to be able to exert full sovereignty. On 18 Fructidor Year V/4 September 1797, the supporters of the 1795 Constitution had to carry out a coup d'état in order to eliminate the 'royalist' members of parliament and to 'save' the republic. The new regeneration programme was thus pushed forward: in order to reduce the influence of traditional religion and its rhythms (Sunday rest, calendar of fairs, and markets) on the people, the Republican calendar was enforced. School teachers were mobilized too with the mission to spread educational songs, novels and artistic works supported by the authorities.

Stuck between the resistance practices expressed locally by the Catholic 'renaissance' and the exaltation of the new military heroes (some of whom, like Championnet, had no qualms about reenacting the enthusiasm of the Terror amongst his soldiers), the pedagogical programme supported by the political, administrative and intellectual authorities was faced with many challenges that weakened its impact and vindicated its increasingly numerous critics. During 1799, the political opposition led by the neo-Jacobin movement attacked all aspects of those republicanizing policies of the elites which they saw as cut off from the French people, and even more so from the infantilized European people. Questioning both regeneration policies based on an acculturation programme and the idea that a military crusade could advance the cause of European civilization, they gathered around an unusual and innovative programme: within French borders they supported the ideal of a shared culture bringing together the people and the elite in the same 'cultural arenas' and around similar cultural practices (songs, music, theatre …); outside of those borders their goal was to promote a new understanding of the links between the French republic and its 'sister republics', links that would produce a vast polycentric political configuration (anticipating some sort of federalist model) and encourage cultural contacts and interaction.[17]

There was a common logic in all their suggestions: the idea was to regenerate the republic by tearing down the separation between the supposedly 'civilizing' elite and the French and European people in need of civilization. This project, while it might have dealt with some of the Republic's problems in 1799, met with strong opposition from a political alliance led by the conservative Republicans. This grouping refused to give up the ideas of elite social, and French national, superiority. Gradually, they chose to abandon the republic in order to save their own political and social supremacy, in the name of resisting a 'barbarian' return.[18] It is therefore the 'civilized' elites and not the people that turned out to have been the gravediggers of the republic.

Traditional historiography has tended to oppose the French Republican model (characterized by its radical tendencies and its failure to implement a pluralistic political space able to reflect a variety of political opinions) to the American one. However, it appears that the weakening of the republic during the Directory had much more to do with an 'anomaly' that Pierre Serna has revealed: an emerging political centre whose representatives had no qualms about the use of legal violence as long as it kept them in control of the executive power.[19] Behind the appearance of a political 'see-saw' created by consecutive *coups d'état*, the conservative elites pushed towards a reinforcement of executive power in the name of the preservation of political and social order.[20] This proclaimed goal became the cornerstone of a vast centrist coalition whose members refused, and denounced as sterile, any form of political debate. The ideological promotion of governmental action and civic obedience, the disqualification of the political life of the years 1789–94, had become a new doctrine that was supposed to sanction the invention of new political practices. From then on, talents and virtue and not individual opinions were to determine individuals' positions, a slippage from public to private on which a whole framework of depoliticization rested.

This move of a fraction of the Republican elites towards the idea of a necessary revision of the constitution was undoubtedly based on the evolution of their quasi-anthropological perspective on the people, with whom they felt they had less and less in common. The idea of human perfectibility which was at the base of Directorial Republican ideals seems to have gradually faded away. A kind of scepticism concerning the people's ability to change had led to an uneasiness amongst the elite. Mostly anxious about protecting their own interests, they had become chiefly concerned with the defence of their identity and authority and had started to erect lines of partition between classes. Among those members of what progressively became the 'extreme centre' were also a number of Ideologues such as Cabanis who hoped to complete the work they had themselves started with the pen through the sword of a victorious general.[21] Most of them were to lose their illusions very quickly. In less than two years, following the assaults represented by the Concordat (which gave religion back its role in the political process), the return of slavery, and the suppression of the '*écoles centrales*', they had to give up their dreams and to come to terms with the idea than even a post-revolutionary society cannot be transformed but should simply be organized and stabilized.

Between 1795 and 1802, civilization was still regarded as a dynamic process. If the elites' domination may have been particularly restrictive, nonetheless, it was still believed to be a temporary and transitory phenomenon. From 1802–3 onwards, the goal was not to 'transform' people or societies, but to control and to bind them. Political, social, sexual and racial fixity became the new norm. As early as 1802, the reinstatement of slavery was coupled with a public campaign which aimed to prove the natural inferiority of the black race; it was all the more damaging that it was led by eminent scientists. Between men and women, animals and human beings, black and white people there was no possible continuity or real communication any more, and the ideal of a shared culture faded away, replaced by a clear-cut partition between the elite and the popular cultures. From unity to uniformity, from a civilizing ideal to a domesticating project, the 'imperial dream' turned into a conquering and domineering venture that existed only to benefit French interests. By then, the populations of the states that had come under French rule were subjected to the same kind of constraints and authority as the French popular classes. This naturalization of the authority of the elites over the people is one of the cornerstones of the 'invention of the nineteenth century', which happened against the heritage of the Revolution and against Republican ideals.

The new elite of the Consulate was created by an amalgamation of the revolutionary elite and the old aristocracy of the *ancien régime*. Claude-Isabelle Brelot has established how much resourcefulness was shown by the old aristocracy to adjust to this new situation: they went as far as reinventing the very idea of nobility.[22] The members of the old aristocracy had undoubtedly lost the titles and their seigneurial rights, but those who had managed to stay in France had kept their lands. From the first months of the Consulate, measures were taken in favour of those émigrés who wanted to come back to France and were willing to recognize the legitimacy of the new regime. Bonaparte, while insisting that sold *biens nationaux* would not be given back to their former owners, was able to rally many of the members of the traditional nobility to his cause. The creation of a new notability during the imperial regime seems to have been the outcome both of the revolutionary upheaval and of the survival of the *ancien-régime* elite. Imperial businessmen, merchants, financiers or landowners only represented a small minority. The notables' lists, drawn up by prefects, were purged of the 'parvenus'. Even if some work is still required to provide us with the bases of a definite synthesis on that topic, the notices put together in the series *Grands Notables du Premier Empire* indicate that there was an ideological agreement about who the notables were: few entirely new names but a combination of loyal civil servants of the new regime, landowners, and members of the old nobility. In the Vienne, the imperial notables were much more similar to those of the Restoration than to those of the Revolution.

The ideal of a fusion between different elites is an important element of the Consulate's mythology. The traditional nobility still owned a lot of land and this was not to be over-looked by regimes that, from the Consulate to the Restoration, promoted the social and political figure of the property owner. Even if an active minority had chosen through emigration to support the princes' and royalists networks' armies,[23] in many provin-cial cities the old aristocracy was still powerful and respected: in the Gironde and the Somme for example. In Bordeaux, indeed, reconciliation with Napoleon was not the most common path to the forefront of the political scene, and when it did happen it was often as a simple façade. The nobility here swiftly showed its preference for traditional-ism and fidelity to the Bourbon dynasty: behind the scenes they united to prepare the Restoration.[24] In the Somme, immediately after Robespierre's fall, the members of the nobility who had not left the country had instantly regained their positions as the main personalities of the village life of Picardy. If most of them remained reticent or even hostile to the new regime, this did not prevent them from holding important positions within the new group of notables.[25]

Nevertheless, this old nobility, very much weakened by the Revolution, now had to share its supremacy with new groups of notables that had emerged. At the top, all of Napoleon's ministers of the interior came from the bourgeoisie whether they were new landowners like Chaptal or Laplace, merchants like Cretet or lawyers like Montalivet, with the single exception of Champagny who was from the old aristocracy.[26] If aristo-cratic titles had made their comeback as early as the Directory, it was really only under the Empire that they clearly became social organizing tools again: the political power had, by then, clearly understood what an important part the 'reinstated nobility' could play in the reconstruction of the social and political order. In order to construct its own legitimacy, the Napoleonic state took on the role of the only true authority in matters of creation of a new homogeneous and loyal elite, one that would serve its cause.

Giving out pensions, support and paid employment in the army, the Church, or the University, the state took, once again, control of the structures of social promotion: those serving the state demonstrated their 'public virtues' and could thus join an elite whose unity was founded on the concept of 'service'. An administrative career soon became the ideal course for social and political promotion. Isser Woloch has plainly demonstrated that most of Napoleon's collaborators were men of the Revolution: he established the role of public service in the construction of the imperial elite congregating around meri-tocratic values that emphasized the permanence of the administrative organization.[27] Between potentialities of promotion and fear of social degradation, imperial elites were judged on their loyalty to a regime that was also organizing the judicial and police appa-ratus to protect their properties, their wealth and their integrity.

At the core of the structure was the *Cour des comptes*, or high court of finances, an institution created by the law of 16 September 1807 that would become the perfect tool to produce the imperial elites. Carrying through the restoration of state finances, and returning political power back to the government, it would become along with the other 'grands corps' (the *conseil d'État* created on 4 Nivose Year VIII/25 December 1799 and the *Cour de Cassation* in Year XII), a vital cog in the merger of the elites that had been so very much wanted by the regime.[28] The social and professional origin of the magistrates is marked both by diversity (especially in terms of age, as the oldest member was born in 1730 and the youngest in 1786,) and by competence: 60 per cent had had experience dealing with finances either during the *ancien régime* (former *Commis de le Ferme générale*, former *contrôleur des aides*...) or during the Revolution. In the composition of the personnel, some solidarity networks are easy to recognize, like the colonial network around François Barbé Marbois (1745–1837). A former diplomat, he had worked in the colonies, and as a former deputy at the *Conseil des Anciens* who had been condemned to the 'dry guillotine' and deported to Guyana just after the 18 Fructidor Year V, he had then taken advantage of the 18 Brumaire *coup* and of the protection of his friend Lebrun to come back to France. He had been in charge of the sale of Louisiana, and his success there had earned him the role of president of the *Cour des comptes* where he surrounded himself with close friends that had worked in the colonies or naval administration (Pierre Adet, Vincent-Marie Vienot comte de Vaublanc, Jean-Baptiste Guillemin de Vaivre or Louis Cordelle).

Among those who had no acquaintance with financial circles were many former members of the Consulate's legislative 'Tribunate' who ended up at the *Cour des comptes* following the suppression of that chamber. The make-up of this institution further exemplifies the imperial programme of reconciliation and unification of the various members of an elite expected to understand itself through the idea of service. The *Cour des comptes* would become an important source for members of the *Légion d'honneur* (in 1808 two-thirds of the high-ranking judges of the *Cour* had the *Légion d'honneur*) and of the imperial nobility (in 1814, nine knights, four barons, and one count had a seat at the *Cour*). In 1813, the magistrates of the *Cour des comptes* were granted the title of imperial counsellors with life tenure, which rendered a purge of the structure officially impossible in the event of yet another brutal overthrow of the regime. Accordingly, this purge was to be very restricted during the Restoration as only two magistrates were to be asked to leave their positions (among them the former regicide Letourneur). The same stability characterized other groups, such as the regents of the *Banque de France*.[29] In the legal world, Bonaparte successfully brought together a very heterogeneous professional milieu around the project of the *Code Napoléon*.

High positions created during the Empire thus not only allowed a restricted and select elite to accumulate economic resources and goods but also guaranteed that they could pass them on to the next generation. The Empire cleared the way for a 'society of heirs' that was to be able to reproduce itself from one generation to the next through the new educational system. The creation of the University in 1808, as a unified national structure, had the effect of creating a system for the scholarly reproduction of political and social elites. The first decades of the nineteenth century were characterized by the growth of a new technocratic elite educated at the *École Polytechnique*, which gradually (through the changes made to its admission procedures and exams) became the royal road to advancement for the children of the political and social elite.[30] In this way were put in place the bases of a government 'by honours'.[31] From his arrival in power, Bonaparte consistently increased the number of official symbols of recognition of public service. The most famous is the *Légion d'honneur* created to recognize civic virtue and military courage, and established officially by decree on 11 July 1804. As the crucible of a new nobility, this order was expected to merge soldiers and civilians, aristocrats and commoners, in order to create a fusion of the elites around common values: notably meritocracy and competition.[32] From 1802 to 1814, 48,000 *légionnaires* were nominated.

The recomposition of the old nobilities was, however, perturbed in 1808 by the creation of the imperial nobility, called to become the political, social, and cultural foundation of the new dynasty.[33] By creating imperial titles, which were the only ones to be recognized, Napoleon Bonaparte was attempting to legitimize his regime and to surround it by a loyal nobility whose members could act as representatives when abroad, and as role models when within French territory, in order to create healthy emulation within post-revolutionary society. This nobility also had to embody the fusion between old and new aristocracy. As 'granite masses' created to consolidate the whole of French society, the Empire's nobility was thus envisioned as a group of devoted and loyal vassals: the 1808 law required them to swear 'allegiance to the Emperor and his dynasty' while conferring specific duties on them.

If he supported meritocratic, individual social promotions, Napoleon Bonaparte also intended to naturalize and stabilize a hereditary elite through the institution of the *majorat* by the *senatus consulte* of 14 August 1806. This broke the pattern of equal inheritance installed by the Revolution, allowing for an oldest son to become a privileged heir. By the decrees of 1 March 1808, imperial titles were created and the judicial regime of the *majorat* was established, as the new elite had to have the financial resources that would allow them to honour their social status. Those who received hereditary titles were thus made to create a *majorat*, or package of landed property to be passed on undivided. As he limited the number of *majoritaires* to one child per family, it seems that the Emperor was not so much interested in widening the group of his political allies to the whole mass of the descendants of those he had made nobles than in instituting a proper aristocracy. The constitution of the imperial nobility did indubitably contribute to many people's submission: to get an aristocratic title, royalists such as Meiffren Laugier de Chartrouse, an important landowner and the mayor of Arles, were quick to commit to the new regime and to constitute a *majorat*. But all in all the imperial nobility was mostly composed of people who, from 1789, had been on the side of the Revolution.

In provincial and rural life, the extent to which large landowners controlled the municipalities of the Toulouse area under the Empire provide a good example of the emergence of a new elite that had successfully overcome the tempests of revolutionary politics.[34] In other places, the rural bourgeoisie that had been in place even before 1789, showed similar qualities and got involved in various local functions.[35] Study of the Mauges notability has clearly revealed how the reorganization of state structures under the Directory and the Restoration generated the conditions of birth of a new notability, even more so because the state needed local contacts to rebuild the country. Gradually, a political notability emerged that was mostly made up of the forestry and agricultural elites. The central power also found local contacts among the old landowning nobility, a group that, until then, had remained on the margins of local, cantonal or departmental political life.

As during the eighteenth century, the high-society circles that rebuilt themselves during the Directory played a major part at the point of contact between social and cultural dynamics. The increasing number of publications about good manners and social rules and etiquette clearly conveys the level of expectation among the newly pro-moted elites. In Consular and imperial society, culture had become an essential value of an elite that was determined to create new frontiers in order to separate themselves clearly from the people and to justify their supremacy. The unity of the elite was partly built around what they themselves perceived as an uncertainty about everybody's place in society. David Garrioch has shown how, in parallel, a new territorial division of the Parisian bourgeois elite was put in place between the Revolution and the Empire through new networks of family support and sociability, extending beyond older neighbourhood and parish connections, to embrace the structure of the *arrondisse-ment* or the municipality.[36]

From then on, the elites' identity was built around the claim of a common culture, around shared tastes and practices, around similar lifestyles that needed to be natu-ralized to escape the aforementioned uncertainty and to create, and impose as natu-ral and obvious, new ways to read and understand how society worked.[37] Those elites could then be inspired by (or even straightforwardly copy) the model of naturalist and anatomical classification which ran against competing transformist or hybridist theories, building lines of separation between species, races, and sexes. The change of the departmental statistical models, from 1806 onwards, was yet another important turning point whose consequences are very important: the national administration itself enforced the existence of frontiers between various social groups. Gradually, these ideas became less and less debatable because they were validated by mathemati-cal and natural sciences.[38] Whereas individualism was increasingly denounced as a source of social and political disorder, a new theory of the individual was promoted by philosophers like Victor Cousin for whom only men of the elite could show a supe-rior kind of will that could lead them to the possession of a real 'self'.[39] Thus appeared a concept of the 'self' that could justify the masculine, bourgeois order. Moving past Maine de Biran's cognitive project, the dynamic unity of the self appeared, in Cousin's works, as that of an active self, totally severed from the passive and uncertain self of the sensualists.[40]

On the very sensitive and symbolic topic of family relationships, the authors of the *Code Civil* clearly followed the paternalistic theories of the Directory: the paternal power was not meant to be shared and it was to be implemented within the couple too, where the wife was reduced to being her husband's daughter: the husband had to protect his wife in the same way as he had to protect his children.[41] Women were told rhetorically that they were men's equals, but that it was by obeying them that they would successfully guide and manage their husbands. The first condition of a successful marriage was thus the wife's acceptance of her subordinate position. The core of the family had changed, however: it was no longer the titular head of the lineage but the young man, the young father who had power over the rest of the family (older relations, his descendants and his wife) in the name of their weakness and reliance on him. The *Code Civil* gave him the status of paterfamilias. He was the strong man at the heart of the family. The time of the bourgeois Code had come: at the source of the family's authority, the family lineage was being replaced by the couple.

Finally, following the re-establishment of slavery in the colonies in 1802, a formally racist rhetoric developed amongst the colonial and metropolitan elites, which was exacerbated after the trauma represented by the loss of Saint-Domingue in 1804. This returning idea of the fixity of races is an important symbol of the gradual rejection of the revolutionary paradigm, and the evolutionism and historicism on which the Republican programme and the civilizing project of the Directory were based. From then on there was no imagined linkage between the common people, women, blacks, and imperial elites; there only was the powerful project to create a unbreakable barrier between social, sexual, and racial groups.

Not only did the elite try to isolate itself within select and separated neighbourhoods or social locations, but belonging to it also implied some shared common experiences like serving in the National Guard or participating in philanthropic activities. The National Guard, abolished in 1802, was briefly reinstated in 1809 and then again in 1814, but its ranks were closed to labourers and artisans. The uniform and the rank of an officer were huge symbolic assets, and there were always plenty of notables or merchants willing to enter it. An officer also had symbolic as well as real power over civilians.[42] Meanwhile, the famous Parisian *Societé philanthropique* (1804), and in provincial cities the ever expanding network of philanthropic societies and associations, played an important part in the social life of the notables and especially of their wives who gathered particularly around the *Société de charité maternelle* (established in 1801) and its numerous affiliated societies.[43] The *bureaux de bienfaisance* created in 1800 and each made up of six men nominated by the mayors of each *arrondissement* also gave opportunities to their important citizens to get involved in charitable works, whether it was because they were concerned about their fellow human beings, because they wished to assert and establish their status as notables, or just because they were attracted by the social power that came with that role. In the salons or by writing letters, women like Annette de Gérando, for instance, also played an essential part in the promotion of that socialite culture around which the solidarity of the elites was built.

Napoleon Bonaparte's wish to stabilize his authority was, however, confronted by the social elites' own interests: they were ready to support any regime that would suit them, even if it meant legitimizing a restoration. Despite all the benefits they received, the imperial elites did not remain passive or indifferent. As early as 1807, the members of the *Conseil Général de Haute Garonne* vigorously attacked the structure and weight of indirect taxes and actions of local administrative agents. Such discontents, even if they occasionally reflected an authentic royalist political positioning, also expressed deeper motivations. Local elites involved in business and mercantile activity grew increasingly disenchanted with the regime's military ventures. In Paris, the fifteen merchants of the *Chambre de Commerce* no longer hesitated to express their fundamental opposition to the imperial wars that they saw as harmful to trade.[44] After the defeat in Russia, the Empire lost any remaining sympathy from the world of trade, which moved towards abstentionism, indifference and eventually open opposition and support of the return of the Bourbons.[45]

The imperial aristocracy was never the solid and unanimous entity hoped for by Napoleon. When the 1814 campaign was being prepared, many in the Senate, especially amongst the senators who had held parliamentary seats during the revolutionary period, were already expressing their reservations. Opposition to its wars left the regime fragile. As far as the high ranks of the administration were concerned, serving the country came to take precedence over the regime. And, in the end, it was first and foremost the senators and the marshals, the core of the imperial nobility that precipitated the fall of the Empire. The vast majority of the new nobility had preferred to obey the legal power in order to preserve its own interests, while the genuine Bonapartist activists and loyalists turned out to be no more than a small minority of that nobility. Divided by their origins and their history, the new elites revealed themselves as a very heterogeneous group whose common appurtenance to the imperial nobility was not enough to give them a sense of unity.

The years following the Revolution and the Empire would see the gradual development, within the wide group that could be called the nobility, of a new elite made of wealthy legitimists. With the support of the 'granite masses' the Empire had been able to realize a partial unification of the traditional aristocracy, the new nobility and the bourgeoisie involved either in business or in the civil service. The Empire was thus able to set up the transition from a society managed by aristocrats to one that was managed by notables. Membership of the elite came to be constructed around a cultural community that excluded a series of social groups regarded as inferiors. Women, children and 'savages' had become 'natural' categories. Philanthropy had become a way to unify those elites through a common project: to aid the people who, nonetheless, had to retain their subordinate status.

The Revolution indisputably meant that redefining the elites was necessary. After the people had clearly made their voice heard and their power felt, this at least could not be avoided. When confronted by the various revolts and revolutionary movements of the nineteenth century, the elites kept transforming and changing to keep their power. Nonetheless, not only was this power confronted by external attacks but it was also weakened by internal conflicts that endlessly divided the members of this elite. Besides the concept of 'bourgeoisie' or 'notability', used by the elite to define itself in class terms, there was very little they had in common and it was a largely heterogeneous group. At the beginning of the nineteenth century, the fear of the people was the lowest common denominator of the French and European elite. But the main consequence of all the hard work they put into the preservation of their power was to render increasingly real, throughout that century and beyond, the very Revolution that they intended to reduce to a memory.

NOTES

1. David Garrioch, *The Formation of the Parisian Bourgeoisie (1690–1830)* (Cambridge and London, 1996); Michel Zylberberg, *Capitalisme et catholicisme dans la France modern. La dynastie Le Couteulx* (Paris, 2001); Sylvain Turc, *Les élites grenobloises des Lumières à la monarchie de Juillet* (Grenoble, 2009). Many recent PhD theses deserve to be mentioned here: Laure Pinau-Defois, *Les grands négociants nantais du dernier tiers du XVIIIe siècle. Capital hérité et esprit d'entreprise (fin XVIIe–début XIXe siècles)*, (Université de Nantes, 2008); Richard Flamein, *Mobilités sociales et matrice des identités bourgeoises d'Ancien Régime par l'univers matériel. La « résistible ascension » des Le Couteulx* (Université de Rouen, 2011).

2. Jean-Pierre Jessenne et Hervé Leuwers (eds), 'Changements sociaux et dynamiques politiques', *Annales historiques de la Révolution française* 359 (Jan./Mar. 2010).

3. William Sewell, *Logics of History: Social Theory and Social Transformation* (Chicago, 2005); Jean-Pierre Jessenne (ed.), *Vers un ordre bourgeois? Révolution française et changement social* (Rennes, 2007); Philippe Bourdin (ed.), *Les noblesses françaises dans l'Europe de la Révolution* (Rennes, 2010).

4. Sarah Maza, *The Myth of the French Bourgeoisie. An Essay on the Social Imaginary, 1750–1850* (Cambridge, MA, 2003), 5–11.

5. Déborah Cohen, *La nature du peuple. Les formes de l'imaginaire social (XVIIIe–XXIe siècles)* (Seyssel, 2010).

6. Bronislaw Baczko, *Comment sortir de la Terreur? Thermidor et la Révolution* (Paris, 1989).

7. The last phrase in the original is 'exercer une profession mécanique', which was glossed to include agriculture.

8. A new edition of his works was presented to the Convention by Dominique Garat in 1798. Cf. *Discours prononcé par le c. Garat offrant les œuvres de Condillac à la séance du 3 fructidor an VI/20 août 1798* (Paris, 1798).

9. Jean-Luc Chappey, 'Raison et citoyenneté: les fondements culturels d'une distinction sociale et politique sous le Directoire', *Citoyen et citoyenneté sous la Révolution française, Actes du Colloque de Vizille du 24–25 septembre 2005* (Paris, 2006), 279–88; Jean-Luc Chappey, 'De la science de l'homme aux sciences humaines: enjeux politiques d'une configuration de savoir (1770–1808)', *Revue d'histoire des sciences humaines* 15 (2006), 43–68.

10. Antoine Lilti, *Le monde des salons. Sociabilité et mondanité à Paris au XVIIIe siècle* (Paris, 2005); Dominique Margairaz, *François de Neufchâteau. Biographie intellectuelle* (Paris, 2005).

11. François Azouvi (ed.), *L'institution de la raison. La révolution culturelle des idéologues* (Paris, 1992); Dominique Dammame, 'Entre science et politique. La première science sociale', *Politix* 8, no. 29 (1995), 5–30; Laurent Clauzade, *L'Idéologie ou la révolution de l'analyse* (Paris, 1998); James Livesey, *Making Democracy in French Revolution* (Harvard University Press, 2001).

12. Bénédicte Savoy, *Patrimoine annexé. Les biens culturels saisis par la France en Allemagne autour de 1800* (Paris, 2003); Pierre-Yves Lacour, 'Les amours de Mars et Flore aux

cabinets. Les confiscations naturalistes en Europe Septentrionale 1794–1795', *Annales historiques de la Révolution française* 358 (Oct./Déc. 2009), 71–92.

13. Hervé Leuwers, 'République et relations entre les peuples. Quelques éléments de l'idéal républicain autour de brumaire an VIII', *Annales historiques de la Révolution française* 318 (1999), 677–93.

14. Annie Jourdan, *La révolution batave: entre la France et l'Amérique, 1795–1806* (Rennes, 2008); Antonino de Francesco, *1799. Una storia d'Italia* (Milano, 2004); Emanuele Pagano, *Pro e contro la Repubblica. Cittadini schedati dal governo cisalpino in un'inchiesta politica del 1798* (Milan, 2000).

15. Virginie Martin, 'Du modèle à la pratique ou des pratiques aux modèles: la diplomatie républicaine du Directoire', in Pierre Serna (ed.), *Républiques sœurs. Le Directoire et la Révolution atlantique* (Rennes, 2009), 87–100.

16. Jean-Luc Chappey, *Des anthropologues sous Bonaparte. La Société des Observateurs de l'homme (1799–1804)* (Paris, 2002).

17. Bernard Gainot, 'Construction et déconstruction du discours sur la Grande Nation', Jacques Bernet, Jean-Pierre Jessenne and Hervé Leuwers (eds), *Du Directoire au Consulat*, (Lille, 2000), t. II, 27–42.

18. Bernard Gainot, *1799, un nouveau jacobinisme? La démocratie représentative, une alternative à Brumaire* (Paris, 2001).

19. Pierre Serna, 'Existe-t-il un 'extrême centre'? . . . Le point aveugle de la République directoriale. L'exemple de la Décade', in Jacques Guihaumou and Raymonde Monnier (eds), *Des notions concepts en révolution* (Paris, 2003), 149–67.

20. James Livesey, *Making Democracy in the French Revolution* (Cambridge, MA, 2001); Andrew Janchill, *Reimaging Politics after the Terror: The Republican Origins of French Liberalism* (Ithaca, 2008).

21. Pierre Serna, *La république des girouettes. 1789–1815 et au-delà. Une anomalie politique: la France de l'extrême centre* (Seyssel, 2005).

22. Claude-Isabelle Brelot, *La noblesse réinventée. Nobles de Franche-Comté de 1814 à 1870* (Paris, 1992).

23. Jean-Paul Bertaud, *Les royalistes et Napoléon* (Paris, 2009).

24. Michel Figeac, *Destins de la noblesse bordelaise (1770–1830)* (Bordeaux, 1996).

25. Marie Wiscart, *La noblesse de la Somme au XIXe siècle* (Amiens, 1994).

26. Igor Moulier, 'Bourgeoisie et bureaucratie au début du XIXe siècle', in Jean-Pierre Jessenne (ed.), *Vers un ordre bourgeois? Révolution française et changement social* (Rennes, 2007), 237–53; Igor Moullier, *Le ministère de l'Intérieur sous le Consulat et le Premier Empire (1799–1814). Gouverner la France après le 18 brumaire* (PhD thesis, Université de Lille, 2004).

27. Isser Woloch, *Napoleon and his collaborators. The Making of a Dictatorship* (New York and London, 2001).

28. Matthieu de Oliveira, 'La Cour des comptes ou le 'troisième grand corps' de l'Empire', in Jacques Bernet and Emmanuel Cherrier (eds), *1807: apogée de l'Empire?* (Valenciennes, 2009), 227–42.

29. Romuald Szramkiewicz, *Les Régents et censeurs de la Banque de France nommés sous le Consulat et l'Empire* (Genève, 1974).

30. Bruno Belhoste, *La formation d'une technocratie. L'École polytechnique et ses élèves, de la Révolution au Second Empire* (Paris, 2003).

31. Olivier Ihl, 'Gouverner par les honneurs. Distinctions honorifiques et économie politique dans l'Europe du début du XIXe siècle', *Genèses* 55 (June 2004), 4–26.

32. Natalie Petiteau, 'Pourquoi Napoléon créé-t-il la Légion d'Honneur?', in Jean Tulard, François Monnier, Olivier Echappé (eds), *La Légion d'honneur. Deux siècles d'histoire* (Paris, 2004), 35–48.

33. Natalie Petiteau, *Élites et mobilités: la noblesse d'Empire au XIXe siècle (1808–1914)* (Paris, 1997).

34. Georges Fournier, *Démocratie et vie municipale en Languedoc du milieu du XVIIIe siècle au début du XIXe siècle* (Toulouse, 1994).

35. Jean-Pierre Jessenne, 'Usages, équivoques et pertinence de "bourgeoisie rurale"', in Jessenne (ed.), *Vers un ordre bourgeois?*, 119–45.

36. David Garrioch, *The Formation of the Parisian Bourgeoisie, 1690–1830* (Cambridge, 1997).

37. Denise Davidson, *France after Revolution: Urban Life, Gender and the New Social Order* (Cambridge, MA, 2007).

38. Marie-Nöelle Bourguet, *Déchiffrer la France: la statistique départementale à l'époque napoléonienne* (Paris, 1989), 302; Isabelle Laboulais, *Lectures et pratiques de l'espace, l'itinéraire de Coquebert de Montbret (1755–1831), savant et grand commis d'État* (Paris, 1999).

39. Jan Goldstein, *The Post-Revolutionary Self. Politics and Psyche in France, 1750–1850* (Cambridge, MA, 2005).

40. François Azouvi, *Maine de Biran. La science de l'homme* (Paris, 1995).

41. Anne Verjus, *Le bon mari. Une histoire politique des hommes et des femmes à l'époque révolutionnaire* (Paris, 2010); Jean-Clément Martin, *La révolte brisée. Femmes dans la Révolution française et l'Empire* (Paris, 2008); Jennifer Heuer, *The Family and the Nation in Revolutionary France* (Ithaca, 2005).

42. Roger Dupuy, *La garde nationale 1789–1872* (Paris, 2010).

43. Catherine Duprat, *Usage et pratiques de la philanthropie. Pauvreté, action sociale et lien social, à Paris, au cours du premier XIXe siècle* (Paris, 1997).

44. Claire Lemercier, *Un si discret pouvoir. Aux origines de la Chambre de commerce de Paris, 1803–1853* (Paris, 2003).

45. Silvia Marzagalli, *Les boulevards de la fraude. Le négoce maritime et le blocus continental, 1806–1813* (Lille, 1996).

Selected Reading

Broers, Michael, *The Napoleonic Empire in Italy, 1796–1814. Cultural Imperialism in a European Context?* (Basingstoke, 2005).

Brown, Howard G. and Judith A. Miller, *Taking Liberties, Problems of a New Order from the French Revolution to Napoleon* (Manchester, 2002).

Chappey, Jean-Luc, *Ordres et désordres biographies. Dictionnaires, listes de noms, réputation des Lumières à wikipedia* (Seyssel, 2013).

Desan, Susan, *The Family on Trial in Revolutionary France* (Berkeley, 2004).

Doyle William, *Aristocracy and its Enemies in the Age of Revolution* (Oxford and New York, 2009).

Heller, Henry, *The Bourgeois Revolution in France 1789–1815* (New York, 2006)

Hunt, Lynn, *Politics, Culture and Class in the French Revolution* (Berkeley, [1984]2004).

Leuwers, Hervé, *L'invention du barreau français, 1660–1830. La Construction nationale d'un groupe professionnel* (Paris, 2006).

Lignereux, Aurélien, *L'Empire des Français, 1799–1815. Histoire de la France contemporaine, vol. 1* (Paris, 2012).

Lucas, Colin, (ed.), *Rewriting the French Revolution* (Oxford, 1991).

Merriman, John, *Police Stories. Building the French State, 1815–1851* (Oxford, 2006).

Sewell, William, Jr, *Logics of History: Social Theory and Social Transformation* (Chicago, 2005).

Wrigley, Richard, *The Politics of Appearances: Representations of Dress in Revolutionary France* (Oxford, 2002).

Woloch, Iseer, *The New Régime, Transformations of the French Civic Order 1789–1820* (New York, 1994).

CHAPTER 33

···

NAPOLEON, THE REVOLUTION, AND THE EMPIRE

···

PHILIP DWYER

IN 1866, Pierre Larousse wrote the following opening line for the entry on 'Bonaparte' in his *Grand Dictionnaire universel du XIXe siecle*: '... general of the French Republic, born in Ajaccio (Corsica), on 15 August 1769, died at the Chateau of St Cloud near Paris on 18 Brumaire in the Year VIII of the French Republic, one and indivisible (9 November 1799):[1] The assertion that Napoleon died on the day he took power is a political gibe; he is thus portrayed as having betrayed the Revolution. Many of Napoleon's contemporaries reacted in the same way. Both the left and the right resisted Brumaire, the coup that ousted the Directory. Those on the right interpreted it as a radicalization of the Revolution, while those on the left saw it as a complete break, the government transformed into an arbitrary dictatorship based on the rule of one man. Napoleon understood that to determine how contemporaries, and posterity, were going to look at him he had to create his own political narrative. He did this by portraying himself and the Brumaire regime as a conciliatory government, and himself as the 'saviour' of the Revolution, above the factions that had rent the country apart. He alone, went the message, was capable of healing the political rifts and of recruiting talented men in the service of the nation, regardless of their political past.[2]

In some respects, the message was the man. Napoleon cared little about who served him, and the state, as long as they were reasonably competent but above all loyal. We thus find in his government (some) regicides such as Jean-Jacques-Régis de Cambacérès, Second Consul and later Arch-Chancellor of the Empire, alongside the Paris Prefect of Police, the former noble, Étienne-Denis Pasquier, a moderate who had been imprisoned during the Terror. That is the first distinction to be made between Napoleon and the Revolution: ideology had no role to play in the good offices of the state. Napoleon may have been born of the Revolution, but he was a political and social conservative. He may have overthrown *ancien régime* princes and created a slew of new states organized on 'modern' rational lines, but he did so not for ideological, but for military-political reasons. He needed efficient state-structures that could mobilize vast numbers of men and raise vast sums of money so that he could pursue his wars (which had no overarching goal other than the defeat of Britain). Napoleon's Revolution came from the top down and was purely pragmatic.

For generations, historians have pondered whether, to put it in its traditional framing, Napoleon was the heir to the Revolution, or whether he betrayed it.[3] What precisely that means is not clear, but historians customarily rattle off from one of two lists. On the one hand is what can be described as the gains of the Revolution, which Napoleon not only maintained but also consolidated. The list is impressive and includes the abolition of the feudal system and with it the privileges of the aristocracy; the nationalization of Church lands; the subordination of religion to the state; the establishment of a new legal system to replace that which had been abolished; the establishment of an educational system as well as state institutions whose structures persist to this day; a unified monetary system; the insistence that all careers be open to (men of) talent. On the other is a list enumerating how reactionary Napoleon was, and which generally comprises attacks on civil and political liberties as his regime became more authoritarian: press censorship; the lack of real elections and representative government; and the expansionist foreign policy that led Napoleon to conquer cities as far afield as Madrid and Moscow.

Posed that way, the question obliges historians to answer in simplistic, Manichean terms. It is to assume that one man dominated the era to such an extent that he was able to impose his own particular personal traits on to its laws, its structures and the manner in which both government and society developed. It is to forget that Napoleon received the support of large swathes of the political elite, especially at the beginning of his reign. The problem is more complex, the Empire a great deal more contradictory and ambiguous, and Napoleon's responses to the political landscape more subtle than some historians have cared to consider. Napoleon's regime was a curious mixture of the modern and the traditional. At the beginning of his reign, there was a willingness to see the Revolution consolidated as well as a desire among the most influential in the political elite to return to the roots of the Revolution, constitutional monarchy.[4] The choice of Empire represented a third way between radical republicanism and royalism. In the face of the long line of political failures that was the Revolution, the Empire was a new polity, one—an inherent contradiction—initially based on the revolutionary principle of the 'sovereignty of the people'.

That idea underpinned the coronation ceremony in Notre Dame on 2 December 1804. During the ceremony, Napoleon swore an oath to 'maintain the integrity of the territory of the Republic: to respect and to cause to be respected the laws of the Concordat and of freedom of worship, of political and civil liberty, and the sale of nationalized lands; to raise no taxes except by virtue of the law; to maintain the institution of the Legion of Honour; to govern only in view of the interest, the well-being and the glory of the French people'.[5] This was not simply a sop to Republicans; it was a social pact, a contract between the French people and their sovereign. Power was conferred on Napoleon not by God, but through a secular contract with the French people underlined by the plebiscite of June 1804 in which they were asked to ratify the Empire. Eventually, Republican

principles such as 'citizen' and the 'sovereignty of the people' disappeared entirely during the Empire to be replaced by traditional monarchical notions such as 'subject' and
divine right, which slowly seeped back into the political rhetoric after 1808. During that
process, the Nation, as envisaged by the revolutionaries, disappeared and was replaced
by a concept similar to that prevalent in the *ancien régime* during which the monarchy
and the state were embodied in the king. So too Napoleon came to embody the state, and
like the *ancien régime* he too came to represent the father of the people.

We can thus see within the Empire the juxtaposition of two political worlds, the revolutionary and, increasingly as the empire expanded, the traditional. The irony is that
Napoleon was never accepted by those traditional European monarchies, even after
the alliance with the House of Habsburg in 1810. Generally, historians argue that it was
because Napoleon was considered a 'Jacobin on horseback', tainted with the revolutionary virus. It is true that—another contradiction inherent in the empire—while Napoleon
sought to reintegrate France within the traditional European monarchical states system,
he nevertheless exported the political, social and economic principles of 1789.[6] There is
every reason to believe that if peace had been the normal course of affairs rather than
war, then the monarchs of Europe would have quickly learnt to accept Napoleon as one
of theirs, in much the same way the Hohenzollerns were accepted as a dynasty before
Napoleon, or that his nephew, Napoleon III, was accepted after him. The reason why
European monarchs rejected Napoleon had nothing to do with dynastic politics, and
everything to do with the way in which he behaved on the international scene. Napoleon
was not trusted because his power was such that no monarch felt safe, especially after he
overthrew the King of Spain, Charles IV, in 1808.

* * *

Despite the increasing reliance on the traditional, there are a number of elements within
Napoleon's reign that point to a degree of continuity with the Revolution. The first is the
extent to which revolutionary and Republican personnel rallied to Napoleon, who in the
process transformed them from a political into an administrative elite.[7] The vast majority of men in the administration before the coup of Brumaire remained on after, while
two-thirds of the original prefects, appointed shortly after Napoleon came to power, had
been deputies in one of the revolutionary Assemblies. The second element is that the
reforms introduced by Napoleon in the first years of his reign were almost all conceived
by his revolutionary predecessors. It is worth underlining that even Napoleon's attempts
to moderate the Revolution were not all that new. Other regimes had tried before him
and failed. It was the approach adopted after the fall of Robespierre, but the Directorial
government was too hostile to both left and right to find a balance. The Brumairians,
a small group of political plotters, had to appeal to wider sections of French society in
order to construct a new regime. Napoleon was able to do this because he was prepared
to work with anybody, no matter what their past, as long as they were willing to support
him—a radical departure from previous revolutionary governments.[8] In reality, there
were very few regicides and few declared royalists among Napoleon's collaborators, but
one should not dismiss his willingness to work with all-comers as political opportunism.

Behind the rhetoric was a real desire to carry out social and political reforms that would heal the rifts brought about by the Revolution, and to attract to him men of talent, even if their political opinions had a short time before made them enemies of the state.[9]

Napoleon managed to heal the political rifts through a classic combination of carrot and stick: non-juring priests who had been imprisoned during the Directory were set free, an olive branch was offered in the Vendée, and émigrés were allowed to return, while brigands and rebels were ruthlessly pursued in the provinces. Napoleon acted to restore law and order in ways that were reminiscent of the methods used during the Terror. Seven flying columns were formed—four in the Midi, three in Brittany—made up of gendarmes, National Guard and regular troops, attached to which were military commissions, whose task it was to arrest, try and execute any brigands caught.[10] In Brittany, in the first six months of their existence, between September 1800 and February 1801, the military commissions tried more than 1,200 people, a third of whom were condemned to death, mostly for criminal offences such as armed robbery.[11] The trials and executions were widely publicized and often occurred on powerful local sites of memory, places where counter-revolutionaries had committed atrocities. The regime was making a point. Violence against the state and its citizens would no longer be tolerated.

The politics of reconciliation coupled with extraordinarily brutal measures was a winning combination that brought the regime acceptance and, more importantly, followers. People wanted law and order and were prepared to sacrifice the revolutionary principle of liberty, or at least to turn a blind eye when it was flouted. Historians often point out that the first attack against liberty occurred two months after Brumaire, on 17 January 1800, when a decree was published that suppressed sixty of the seventy-three Paris newspapers.[12] The motive used to justify this measure was that they were 'instruments in the hands of the enemies of the Republic'. This was hardly an exaggeration.[13] Forty of the suppressed newspapers passed for royalist, but then all of the Republican press was also eliminated, with the exception of one newspaper, the *Moniteur universel*, which then became the official organ of the state. In late 1807, Napoleon used the unflattering comparison made by Chateaubriand with Nero as a pretext to close down the *Mercure de France*.[14] That year, the number of political newspapers in Paris was reduced to four: the *Moniteur*, the *Journal de l'Empire*, the *Gazette de France*, and the *Journal de Paris*, with a run of around 34,000 copies. Increasingly, the government was interested in controlling the content of articles before they appeared in the press.[15] In the provinces, the number was reduced to one newspaper per department, a measure that led to the creation of a good number of newspapers in departments that did not have them.[16]

The suppression of newspapers in France was little short of spectacular, another kind of coup, except that instead of getting rid of the journalists, the regime got rid of the newspapers they wrote for.[17] It is easy to interpret this attack on the press as an attack on freedom of speech, but it elicited little or no public protest, which leads one to suggest that the public was either indifferent or else approved of the measure. In part, this was a return to the system employed by *ancien régime* governments to control the press and public opinion, but the desire to restrict press freedom was also a reaction to the excesses experienced during the Revolution when anything and everything was permitted. This freedom, political moderates believed, was in part responsible for the radicalization of the Revolution and enabled factions to flourish. Journalists had usurped the role of the elected authorities, had sustained the factionalism that had riven French society, and had become inimical to 'public order'.[18] That is why the press suffered a number of restrictions after the fall of Robespierre when forty-odd newspapers were banned.[19] Total freedom of the press was reintroduced after the fall of Robespierre, but within a short time the Directory found itself assailed by an orgy of invective from neo-Jacobin, as well as royalist newspapers. Napoleon's decision to shut down so many newspapers was about controlling the flow of information, but it was also about national reconciliation.

Just about everything the new consular and later imperial regimes did, from the closing of newspapers, to the revival of the salons in 1800,[20] the creation of the Legion of Honour in 1802, the foundation of the Civil Code, the foundation of the Empire itself, or the establishment of a new nobility in 1808, was either born of the Revolution or an attempt to create a new social and political fusion between the old and the new France. Historians have traditionally argued that Napoleon thereby continued the work of the *ancien régime*, consummating a fusion of elites.[21] More recently, however, historians have postulated that Napoleon did not simply draw on *ancien régime* precedents or, indeed, revolutionary ones.[22] As we shall see, a much broader range of influences shaped Napoleonic initiatives.

THE CIVIL CODE

The idea of a uniform body of law was present from the earliest phases of the Revolution in 1789, and indeed the deputies had embarked on a new code of laws that would govern the kingdom in 1791. On three occasions—in June 1793, in September 1794, and again in June 1796—a code had been presented to the Assembly of the day, but was never voted on.[23] This was one of those occasions when Napoleon's dynamism easily distinguishes itself from the Directory. On coming to power, he set up a commission of four people—François-Denis Tronchet, Jean-Étienne-Marie Portalis, Félix Julien Jean Bigot de Préameneu, and Jacques de Maleville—to work on a text. It was finished in January 1801, and was then handed over to the Council of State for discussion and modification. Ever since, historians have debated the real impact of Napoleon on the Civil Code.[24] We know that he took part in a little over half of the sessions of the Council of State dedicated to discussing the Code over a three-year period, but the Code, like any body of law, was the result of a collective effort, and it reflected the needs of an emerging elite.[25] On the whole, by Napoleon's own admission, he listened and generally let the members of the committee get on with the job.[26] According to some witnesses, he does not appear to have had much of an impact on the proceedings. The duc de Broglie recalled that he would often ask questions and listen patiently, but when things went on too long, he would interrupt, then talk for a long time without much coherence.[27] It is true that he may have pushed the debates in directions they might not have otherwise taken, but it is certainly an exaggeration to think that the Code would not have seen the light of day without him.[28] The minutes of the sessions at which he assisted, published during the Empire, appear to have given him a larger role than he actually had.[29] Where Napoleon did facilitate the completion of the Code is in allowing specialists to advise him, and by getting jurists on side.[30]

The Civil Code allowed Napoleon to give the state a new structure, one that was recognized as the foundation on which French society was built long after the Empire had disappeared. Napoleon conceived of the Code as an instrument of social cohesion. The enforcement of the Code went hand in hand with building a modern (Republican) edifice and to this extent was a continuation of the work of the revolutionaries.[31] Out of it came a number of fundamental 'truths', at least as interpreted by nineteenth-century elites: the principle of equality before the law (at least if one were male); the abolition of feudalism; the family as the foundation of society; the suppression of primogeniture; the state as the unique source of all law.[32]

Those who worked on the Civil Code (re-named the Code Napoléon in 1807) wanted to assert the originality of their work in contrast with what preceded it, and especially the Revolution.[33] Only in a few instances, however, did the Civil Code differ substantially from the projects of the Revolution. One of those was in its attitudes towards the place of women and children in society. The Code introduced a much more paternalistic set of laws restricting women's rights and their civil status, especially in terms of marriage, divorce, and property, and certainly in comparison to legislation of the early 1790s.[34] Moreover— something that is little known—the Code re-introduced a form of *lettre de cachet*, whereby fathers could have their children confined for up to six months without having to justify their reasons. In a similar vein, husbands who caught their wives *in flagrante delicto* would be excused if they killed either the lover or the wife.[35] The central role of the father and husband was reinforced—indeed, it was more pronounced under Napoleon than during the *ancien régime*—and the notion of a patriarchal order was consolidated in law. For women, at least, this was a step away from the revolutionary ideal of equality.

THE CONCORDAT

The negotiation of an accord with the Catholic Church in the Concordat, signed in July 1801, has to be seen as working hand in hand with the Civil Code. Both were about the social and political pacification of the country. A number of historians have maintained that the Concordat helped preserve the gains of the Revolution, not only by legalizing the nationalization of Church lands, but also by firmly establishing the principle of religious tolerance.[36] More than that though, the Concordat gave the state a degree of control over the Church by allowing it to appoint bishops (although admittedly this is a power the kings of France had practised).[37]

Napoleon's attitude towards religion has always been depicted as strictly utilitarian, but one should not forget that he was born and raised a Catholic and that if he was not what one might call a true believer neither was he an atheist.[38] 'Without religion', he wrote, 'there is no happiness and no possible future.'[39] Napoleon realized that the only way of resolving the religious question in France, without recourse to constant repression, was to defuse the schism that had been precipitated by the Constitutional Oath of the Clergy during the Revolution.[40] However, much like the revolutionaries who had precipitated the conflict in the first place, he was determined that the state should remain in control of the Church.

After lengthy negotiations, the Concordat was signed during the night of 15–16 July 1801. As a preamble, the French government recognized the Roman Catholic religion as that of the 'great majority of the French people'. The implication was that there were other faiths, and that the state would now remain neutral in questions of religion.[41] The Concordat was ratified in Rome on 15 August and in Paris on 8 September 1801. During that time, Napoleon, at the suggestion of the apostate bishop and foreign minister, Charles-Maurice de Talleyrand, and without consulting Pope Pius VII, inserted the infamous addendum referred to as the 'Organic Articles'.[42] They were published at the same time that the Concordat was made public in 1802 in order to give the impression that the Pope had agreed to them. Introduced at the last minute in an attempt to appease anti-clericals within the Assemblies, the Organic Articles imposed a much more 'caesaro-papist formula' on Church–state relations: they denied the Pope authority to intervene in many areas of the French church; they strengthened the First Consul's power to do so; they formalized the loss of Church property during the Revolution; and they brought all papal communications with the French clergy under the strict control of the government.[43]

At the end of the negotiations, Napoleon is supposed to have said to Pierre Cabanis, 'Do you know what is this Concordat I have just signed? It is a vaccine against religion: in fifty years, there will be no religion in France.'[44] It was a rather glib prognostication. Rather than see it as the end all to religious problems in France—the Concordat is, after all highlighted as one of *the* achievements of Napoleon's early reign—it was really the start of a new set of problems that would quickly deteriorate into a bitter and protracted struggle between the Church and the French state, the likes of which had not been seen since the Middle Ages.[45] Nevertheless, the period of reconciliation between the Church and the state—something that had not been achieved since 1790—allowed Napoleon to take a considerable step down the path toward monarchy.

THE EMPIRE, SOVEREIGNTY, AND DIVINE RIGHT

The foundation of the Empire was not so much about the ambitions of one individual as about founding a stable political system, creating a new political synthesis.[46] It was the expression of a particular group within the elite with shared values and goals, and was presented as a kind of political and juridical synthesis, a hybrid regime, which recalled the past and which was driven by the will to placate the country and to bring the Revolution to an end.[47] Moreover, the extent to which Napoleon was recognized as the 'father of the people' by ordinary citizens demonstrates the extent to which *ancien régime* attitudes towards the 'supreme authority' were deeply embedded in the French *mentalité*. In short, personal ambition cannot explain the transition from republic to empire. Other factors are much more important: the push for a monarchical system within Napoleon's entourage and the government itself; the two assassination plots against Napoleon's life in 1800 and 1804 and the perceived threat to the stability of the political system; and the desire to re-enter the European family of states. In order to do so, the French elite had to renounce that 'vain abstraction', the Republic, and embrace a new form of government.[48] Napoleon had in effect taken a 'third way' between revolution and restoration, a bizarre combination of what was supposed to resemble a monarchy and the vestiges of a republic. The fact that it was not a true constitutional monarchy in which vigorous political debate was possible, and the fact that the notion of heredity was never firmly entrenched in the minds of the elites, means that the French Empire, like Alexander's and Charlemagne's, collapsed when Napoleon disappeared from the scene.

There was one fundamental revolutionary principle upon which the Empire was founded—the sovereignty of the people, in part exercised by the plebiscites that had been conducted in 1800, 1802, 1804 and again in 1815.[49] Historians have had a tendency to dismiss the plebiscites as cynical exercises in populism, and it is true that the plebiscite of 1802 is notorious for having had its results manipulated by Napoleon's brother, Lucien, then minister of the Interior.[50] But dismissing Napoleon's use of the plebiscite as a purely political exercise would be overly simplistic and is to ignore their relative success in comparison to what preceded them. The number of people who voted for the Convention in 1792, for example, was fewer than 800,000, or around 30 per cent of the electorate.[51] In comparison, the turnout for two of the Napoleonic plebiscites—1802 and 1804—even with corrections for fraud taken into account, are respectively around 47 and 42 per cent, a resounding success even by the standards of the day.[52] The figures for 1800 and 1815, at the beginning and at the end of Napoleon's reign, are much lower— around 22 per cent—but one should not, for all that, dismiss the process. On the whole, electoral participation during the Empire is better than during the First Republic, in part because the whole system had been codified and made uniform.

Nevertheless, Napoleon's attitude towards the notion of the sovereignty of the people, on which the Empire was founded, was ambivalent, which is possibly why he always felt insecure and why he (half-heartedly) began to toy with the idea of divine right. The invitations to the coronation in 1804, for example, pointed out that 'divine providence' had called Napoleon to the throne, a sentiment that can also be found in the media of the day, although in somewhat subtler terms. In other words, the idea of divine right was curiously mixed with the notion that Napoleon had been called upon by the French people to adopt the title, Emperor. The traditional notion of divine right and the revolutionary notion of the sovereignty of the people were thus in precarious balance, and it is perhaps why Napoleon received the appellation of 'Citizen Emperor' at the beginning of his reign.[53]

By 1810, however, its conservative character had become more and more entrenched, and increasing focus was placed on the dynastic legitimacy of the regime. Two developments highlight the extent to which Napoleon's regime was prepared to use *ancien régime* custom to consolidate the legitimacy of his reign. The first was the attempt to instil a degree of sacrality into the new regime, something that had not been seen since before the Revolution. An imperial catechism was introduced in 1806, based on the old Catholic catechism, that made a direct link between God and Napoleon. Take this short extract from the Imperial Catechism:

> Q.—Are there not particular reasons that should attach us more strongly to Napoleon I, our Emperor?
>
> A.—Yes, for he is the one God created in difficult circumstances in order to re-establish public worship and the holy religion of our fathers, and in order to become its protector.[54]

The imperial Catechism was an attempt by Napoleon to define a subject's duties by placing himself within the tradition of European monarchs anointed by God. As such, it represents a radical shift away from the secular nature of the French polity towards a more traditional notion of rule by divine right. Those who now failed in their duty towards Napoleon would find themselves facing 'eternal damnation'.

The second development that reinforced the notion of divine right was Napoleon's marriage to the Austrian emperor's daughter, Marie-Louise, in 1810.[55] Napoleon's marriage alliance with one of the leading European royal Houses was a turning point in the nature of the Empire, in which the questions of dynastic succession and continuity were reformulated. An institution that had been specifically French now became increasingly 'Germanic'. Greater reliance was laid on Roman and Carolingian traditions, while the court took on an increasingly pan-European flavour.[56] Between 1809 and 1815, 26 per cent of the senior household officials were non-French, while slightly over a third of those presented at court were also not French.[57] Etiquette became much more stringent from this time on; 634 articles regulating court etiquette were modified and introduced in 1811 drawing on *ancien régime* texts that went as far back as 1710.[58] There was an increasing reliance on the former aristocracy for service internally and abroad. The number of former nobles in diplomatic missions doubled from 30 to 60 per cent between 1800 and 1812–13. Similarly, the number of prefects who were of noble birth almost doubled to 41 per cent in that same period.[59] There was even some talk of moving the court back to Versailles.[60] The Trianon was restored and refurbished for Napoleon's mother and sisters after 1805, and soft furnishings were ordered in 1811–12 for the chateau itself, which underwent repair work throughout the Empire. Events were to intercede before that could happen, but it is clear that the movement towards monarchy and away from the Republic had come full circle.

The Nature of the Napoleonic Regime

In reality, the neo-monarchists of the Consulate got more than they bargained for. The Empire and Napoleon's style of rule went well beyond the limits of constitutional monarchy. Individual rights and the rule of law were largely upheld even if they were at times egregiously flouted, and representative government was ridden over roughshod whenever it dared oppose Napoleon. His mixture of consultation and authoritarianism was both efficient and probably in tune with what many at the time considered to be good governance. This changed over time. The longer Napoleon was in power, the less consultative he became.

Ultimately, what kind of regime was the Empire, and what kind of ruler was Napoleon? Historians often point to 1807 as a decisive year on the road towards a hardening in Napoleon's attitudes, and an increase in his 'despotic' behaviour.[61] The representatives in the Tribunate were discreetly purged in 1802, and then abolished in 1807.[62] The judiciary was also purged that year; more than 160 magistrates lost their jobs, some for incompetence, others because of their political opposition to the Empire, despite the fact that they had been appointed for life.[63]

For all that, legal boundaries to Napoleon's power were not entirely removed. If the legislative system was not what the revolutionaries had envisaged, it nevertheless existed and Napoleon still had to contend with the senate and the legislative corps where men spoke out against bills if they did not agree with them. Napoleon, however, eventually stopped listening and found it objectionable that a small opposition continued to exist. In many respects, 1807 marks the parting of the ways for some in Napoleon's entourage who did not agree with the tone and tenor of the Empire. Talleyrand, for example, disillusioned with the direction that foreign policy was taking, offered his resignation in August 1807, and quite possibly expected it to be refused. It was not. He was replaced by Jean-Baptiste de Nompère de Champagny, a relative nonentity, devoted to Napoleon, and minister of the interior for a while, but who had no experience in foreign affairs. He was exactly the kind of foreign minister Napoleon desired, someone who would do his bidding without nagging about alternative approaches or the consequences of his actions. Increasingly, the legislative bodies were marginalized so that by 1811 the deputies only sat for five weeks, and after that not at all for another eighteen months.

Was the regime for all that a dictatorship? Almost as soon as Bonaparte was in power, his enemies castigated him as a tyrant, a despot and a usurper.[64] Historians are no more unified on this point than they are about the meaning of the Revolution. William Doyle claims that Napoleon created an imperial monarchy that was more absolutist than anything the Bourbons had dreamt of.[65] The pre-eminent French Napoleonic scholar, Jean Tulard, drew a parallel between the Napoleonic Empire and the Caesarism of ancient Rome, a notion that seems to have gained some ground in recent studies.[66] Frédéric Bluche believes Napoleon was the heir of both the Revolution and the absolutist monarchies of the seventeenth and eighteenth centuries and proposed the term 'democratised absolutism' (*absolutisme démocratisé*) to describe Napoleon's regime.[67] In a similar vein, Louis Bergeron believes the Napoleonic state was a dictatorship, an offshoot of 'enlightened despotism', while David Bell believes Napoleon to be the last of Europe's enlightened despots (although this view simply ignores the momentous events that preceded him).[68] Jacques Godechot referred to the regime as a 'monocratie démocratique', that is, the government of one based upon the plebiscites carried out by universal suffrage.[69] Francois Furet described Napoleon as the 'Louis XIV of the democratic state'.[70] Lynn Hunt has referred to the Empire as an 'authoritarian police state'.[71] Howard Brown describes the Consular regime as 'liberal authoritarian'.[72]

One can see from the variety of these attempts to categorize Napoleon and his rule the difficulties historians face when trying to encapsulate the relationship between Napoleon as leader and the state he helped create.[73] To refer to 'Napoleonic despotism', as so many historians unthinkingly do, is nevertheless inaccurate. Napoleon was not a precursor of the twentieth-century totalitarian dictators.[74] He did not systematically pursue and eliminate his opponents. At most, several hundred people were imprisoned for political offences, but the numbers pale in comparison to the Terror, and only a few were arbitrarily executed for political reasons. Despite the repressive state machinery, Napoleon's regime was far more democratic than any other in continental Europe, in so far as he made use of mechanisms like the plebiscite and a limited electoral process.[75] Napoleon was certainly far less despotic than his eastern European counterparts, a term almost never used by historians to describe the political leaders of Austria, Russia or Prussia. And yet, Alexander I, Frederick William III and Francis II were answerable to no earthly power. Even compared with the democratic experiment that was the Revolution, Napoleon does not come off that badly.

The one thing that becomes clear when looking beyond Napoleon to the structure of empire is that, for the most part, the imperial regime represented *both* a new form of liberal order and a means of exploitation, that it both broke with the past and relied on *ancien régime* institutions and people to help implant that new order, and that it was fundamentally a modern state, governed by practicality rather than ideology. Evident in the reforms that have been briefly mentioned above is the tension between the type of centralist government the Empire represented, and the exportation of a French political culture that, in principle, was much more participatory, and much more inclusive than anything that existed on mainland Europe. Like all things Napoleonic, the contradictions abound.

Conclusion

At the risk of historiographical fence sitting, in an attempt to create new political structures Napoleon was both looking back as well as looking forward. He paid lip-service to the French Revolution by maintaining certain principles—equality before the law, freedom of religion, the protection of property. Yet, at the same time, and increasingly as his regime progressed, Napoleon adopted *ancien régime*-style trappings—a more rigid court etiquette, and an increasing reliance on the old nobility, as well as reversing some of the more radical reforms introduced during the Revolution. He also increasingly turned away from the idea of the sovereignty of the people and towards the idea of divine right. Many of these developments had the approval of the French political elite.

Napoleon did not turn his back on the Revolution, but he did bring into question its radical agenda: central schools were abolished; slavery was reinstated; blacks and mulattos were refused entry into France; racial intermarriages were forbidden; the Institute was reorganized and the section on moral and political sciences was abolished; and women were put back in their place. On the other hand, the reforming influence of the Revolution continued. The institutional structures were maintained—departments, districts, communes, cantons—the courts system was kept (even if the judges were purged in 1807–8), other legal codes were introduced in the course of the Empire codifying behaviour at every level of society (Civil Procedure in 1806, Commerce in 1807, Penal Code in 1810, Criminal Code in 1811).

Perhaps the best answer to that question lay not at the beginning of his reign, but at the end, in the stark choice facing the French in the spring of 1815, after Napoleon had returned to France from exile in Elba. Support for the Bourbon monarchy, in the army at least, was so lacking that it crumbled in the face of minimal opposition. In those few months, the French were presented with a choice between Napoleon on the one hand and the restored monarchy on the other, that is, between the Revolution and counter-revolution.[76] At that point in time, for Republicans, Jacobins, Bonapartists and most veterans, Napoleon was a better alternative than what the restored Louis represented—the *ancien régime*.

NOTES

1. Pierre Larousse, 'Napoléon', in *Grand dictionnaire universel du XIXe siècle*, 17 vols (Paris, 1866–76), ii. 920. A second entry on 'Napoleon', xi. 804, appeared in 1874, after the fall of Napoleon III, in which Larousse explained that at Brumaire, Bonaparte was dead as captain of the Republic and son of the Revolution, and from that moment had become 'a political and military dictator, and imitator of Caesar'.

2. Cf. Pierre Serna, 'Ralliement vertueux ou transformisme honteux des élites au temps du Consulat et du Premier Empire: le cas de Thibaudeau', in Antonino De Francesco (ed.), *Da Brumaio ai cento giorni: cultura di governo e dissenso politico nell'Europa di Bonaparte* (Milan, 2007), 178–9; Philip Dwyer, 'Napoleon as Hero and Saviour: Image, Rhetoric and Behaviour in the Construction of a Legend', *French History* 18 (2004), 379–403.

3. See, for example, the classic text by David Lloyd Dowd, *Napoleon: Was he the Heir of the Revolution?* (New York, 1957); Robert Alexander, 'Napoleon Bonaparte and the French Revolution', in Pamela M. Pilbeam (ed.), *Themes in Modern European History, 1780–1830* (London, 1995), 40–64; and his more general discussion of the subject in *Napoleon* (London: Arnold, 2001), 36–62.

4. Catherine Clerc, *La caricature contre Napoléon* (Paris, 1985), 12–13; Philip Dwyer, 'Napoleon and the Foundation of the Empire', *The Historical Journal* 53, no. 2 (2010), 339–58.

5. Frédéric Bluche, *Le Bonapartisme. Aux Origines de la Droite Autoritaire (1800–1850)* (Paris, 1981), 31.

6. Aurélien Lignereux, *Histoire de la France contemporaine, t. I. L'Empire des Français (1799–1815)* (Paris, 2012), 201.

7. Lignereux, *L'Empire des Français*, 28–9.

8. Napoléon Bonaparte, *Correspondance de Napoléon I publiée par ordre de l'empereur Napoléon III*, 32 vols (Paris, 1858–70), vi. n. 4468 (27 December 1799).

9. Such as François Barbé-Marbois, deported on 18 Fructidor, called to the Council of State; General Jourdan, who had spoken out against 18 Brumaire, named minister extraordinary in Piedmont; François Antoine de Boissy d'Anglas, a constitutional monarchist condemned to exile by the Directory, named to the Tribunate in March 1801 and who served Napoleon loyally till Waterloo (John R. Ballard, *Continuity during the Storm. Boissy d'Anglas and the Era of the French Revolution* (Westport, CT, 2000), 133–7); and Etienne Bernier, a refractory priest who became Agent General of the royal and Catholic armies in the Vendée, helped negotiate the Concordat and was made Bishop of Orleans.

10. Howard G. Brown, *Ending the French Revolution: Violence, Justice, and Repression from the Terror to Napoleon* (Charlottesville, 2006), 317–20; Howard G. Brown, 'Special Tribunals and the Napoleonic Security State', in Philip Dwyer and Alan Forrest (eds), *Napoleon and his Empire: Europe, 1804–1814* (London, 2007), 79–95.

11. Brown, *Ending the French Revolution*, p. 323; Howard G. Brown, 'Echoes of the Terror', *Historical Reflections/Réflexions historiques* 29 (2003), 553–5.

12. P. M. 'Un document sur l'histoire de la presse: la prepration de l'arrêté du 27 nivôse an VIII', *La Révolution française*, 44 (January–June 1903), 78–82; André Cabanis, *La Presse sous le Consulat et l'Empire* (Paris, 1975), 12–14.

13. P.-J.-B. Buchez et P.-C. Roux, *Histoire parlementaire de la Révolution française, ou Journal des assemblées nationales depuis 1789 jusqu'en 1815*, 40 vols (Paris, 1834–38), xxxviii. 331–2.

14. Eugène Hatin, *Histoire politique et littéraire de la presse en France*, 8 vols (Paris, 1859–61), vii. 546–6.

15. See, Natalie Petiteau, *Les Français et l'Empire (1799–1815)* (Paris, 2008), 76–7.

16. Cabanis, *La Presse*, 11–41, 69–71; 'Introduction', in Hannah Barker and Simon Burrows (eds), *Press, Politics and the Public Sphere in Europe and North America, 1760–1820* (Cambridge, 2002), 16; Henri Welschinger, *La censure sous le Premier Empire, avec documents inédits* (Paris, 1882), 119.

17. Michael Marrinan, 'Literal/Literary/"Lexie": History, Text, and Authority in Napoleonic Painting', *Word & Image* 7, no. 3 (1991), 178–79; Fernand Mitton, *La Presse française* (Paris, 1945), ii. 210–11; Simon Burrows, 'The Cosmopolitan Press, 1759–1815', in Barker and Burrows (eds), *Press, Politics and the Public Sphere*, 38; Simon Burrows, 'The War of Words: French and British Propaganda in the Napoleonic Era', in David Cannadine (ed.), *Trafalgar in History: A Battle and Its Afterlife* (Basingstoke, 2006), 48.

18. P. M. 'Un document sur l'histoire de la presse', 78, 79, 80.

19. Hugh Gough, *The Newspaper Press in the French Revolution* (London, 1988), 141–59; Jeremy D. Popkin, *Revolutionary News: The Press in France, 1789–1799* (Durham, 1990), 169–79.

20. Steven Kale, *French Salons: High Society and Political Sociability from the Old Regime to the Revolution of 1848* (Baltimore, 2004), 77–104.

21. Guy Chaussinand-Nogaret, Louis Bergeron and Robert Forster, 'Les notables du "Grand Empire" en 1810', *Annales: économies sociétés civilisations* 26 (1971), 1052–75.

22. Rafe Blaufarb, 'The Ancien Régime Origins of Napoleonic Social Reconstruction', *French History* 14, no. 4 (2000), 408–23.

23. A core body of work was carried out under Cambacérès as early as 1796. See Jean-Louis Halperin, 'Le codificateur au travail, Cambacérès et ses sources', in Laurence Chatel de Brancion (ed.), *Cambacérès, fondateur de la justice moderne* (Saint-Rémy-en-l'Eau, 2001), 154–65, although he questions the extent of Cambacérès's involvement.

24. René Savatier, *L'Art de faire les lois: Bonaparte et le Code civil* (Paris, 1927); and Pierre Villeneuve de Janti, *Bonaparte et le Code civil* (Paris, 1934); Eckhard Maria Theewen, *Napoléons Anteil am Code civil* (Berlin, 1991).

25. The reported number of sessions over which Bonaparte presided vary between 52 and 55 (Jean-Pierre Royer, 'Napoléon et l'élaboration du Code civil', in Françoise Bastien-Rabner and Jean-Yves Coppolani (eds), *Napoléon et le Code civil* (Ajaccio, 2009), 75, n. 4).

26. Henri Gatien Bertrand, *Cahiers de Sainte-Hélène*, edited by Paul Fleuriot de Langle, 3 vols (Paris, 1959), ii. 250.

27. Victor de Broglie (ed.), *Souvenirs, 1785–1870*, 4 vols (Paris, 1886), i. 65–7.

28. The preponderant role in the preparation of the Code given to Napoleon in older works published during the reign of his nephew, Napoleon III, is an exaggeration. Amédée Madelin, *Le premier Consul législateur, étude sur la part que prit Napoléon aux travaux préparatoires du code* (Paris, 1865); and Honoré Pérouse, *Napoléon Ier et les lois civiles du consulat et de l'empire* (Paris, 1866).

29. Jean-Guillaume Locré, *Esprit du Code Napoléon, tiré de la discussion, ou Conférence ... du projet de Code civil, des observations des tribunaux, des procès-verbaux du Conseil d'État, des observations du Tribunat, des exposés de motifs*, 5 vols (Paris, 1805–7); and Pierre-Antoine Fenet, *Recueil complet des travaux préparatoires du Code civil*, 15 vols (Paris, 1836).

30. Halpérin, *L'impossible code civil*, 266–9.

31. David A. Wisner, *The Cult of the Legislator in France, 1750–1830: A Study in the Political Theology of the French Enlightenment* (Oxford, 1997), 129–32.

32. Lignereux, *L'Empire des Français*, 123–7.

33. Jean-Louis Halperin, 'L'histoire de la fabrication du Code. Le Code: Napoléon?', *Pouvoirs* 107 (2003), 14.

34. Françoise Bastien-Rabner, 'La femme dans le Code civil', in Bastien-Rabner and Coppolani (eds), *Napoléon et le Code civil*, 83–97; James F. Traer, *Marriage and the Family in Eighteenth-Century France* (Ithaca, 1980), 166–91; Patricia Mainardi, *Husbands, Wives, and Lovers: Marriage and its Discontents in Nineteenth-Century France* (New Haven, CT, 2003), 12.

35. Mainardi, *Husbands, Wives, and Lovers*, 15, 17.

36. Martyn Lyons, *Napoleon Bonaparte and the Legacy of the French Revolution* (Basingstoke, 1994), 77–93; Nigel Aston, *Religion and Revolution in France, 1780–1804* (Basingstoke, 2000), 316–35.

37. David Jan Sorkin, *The Religious Enlightenment: Protestants, Jews, and Catholics from London to Vienna* (Princeton, 2008), 308.

38. Contrary to what some assert (Antoine Casanova, *Napoléon et la pensée de son temps: une histoire intellectuelle singulière* (Paris, 2000), 28). On Napoleon, the Church and religion see, Jacques-Olivier Boudon, *Napoléon et les cultes: les religions en Europe à l'aube du XIXe siècle, 1800–1815* (Paris, 2002), 39–46.

39. François G. de Coston, *Biographie des premières années de Napoléon Bonaparte*, 2 vols (Paris, 1840), i. 30. As John McManners, *The French Revolution and the Church* (London,

1969), 140, pointed out, religion was peripheral to Bonaparte's decision to reconcile with the Church. See also, Geoffrey Ellis, 'Religion According to Napoleon: The Limits of Pragmatism', in Nigel Aston (ed.), *Religious Change in Europe, 1650–1914: Essays for John McManners* (Oxford, 1997), 244; Marie-Christine de Bouët du Portal, 'A propos de la Saint-Napoléon: la solennité du 15 août sous le Premier et le Second Empire', *Revue de l'Institut Napoléon*, 158–9 (1992), 145.

40. Arno Mayer, *The Furies. Violence and Terror in the French and Russian Revolutions* (Princeton, NJ, 2000), 572.

41. Jacques-Olivier Boudon, 'Les fondements religieux du pouvoir impérial', in Natalie Petiteau (ed.), *Voies nouvelles pour l'histoire du Premier Empire: territoires, pouvoirs, identités* (Paris, 2003), 205.

42. They were compiled by the newly appointed Director of Religious Affairs, Jean-Etienne-Marie Portalis. See Jean-Luc A. Chartier, *Portalis, le père du Code civil* (Paris, 2004), 251–7. Roberts, 'Napoleon, the Concordat of 1801', 45–6, explains that the term 'Organic Articles' is inaccurate and describes them as 'administrative regulations'.

43. Geoffrey Ellis, 'Religion According to Napoleon: The Limits of Pragmatism', in Nigel Aston (ed.), *Religious Change in Europe, 1650–1914: Essays for John McManners* (Oxford, 1997), 244.

44. Germaine de Staël, *Considérations sur les principaux événements de la Révolution française*, 2 vols (Paris, 1818), ii. 275–6; André Cabanis, *Le Sacre de Napoléon* (Paris, 1970), 90.

45. Bernard Plongeron, 'De Napoléon à Metternich: Une modernité en état de blocus', in Jean-Marie Mayeur, Charles et Luce Pietri et al. (eds), *Histoire du christianisme: des origines à nos jours*, 14 vols (Paris, 1997), x. 635–50, highlights the problems that immediately occurred.

46. A similar view is expressed by Pierre Serna, '"Gouvernement du Lion … ou règne de l'astre brillant?" Le 18 brumaire au regard des historiens contemporains du premier Consulat (1800–1802)', in Jean-Pierre Jessenne (ed.), *Du Directoire au Consulat. 3. Brumaire dans l'histoire du lien politique et de l'Etat-nation* (Villeneuve d'Ascq, 2001), 366.

47. Jean-Marc Olivesi, 'De l'impossible porphyrogénèse à un rituel de légitimation: le Sacre', in *Napoléon le Sacre* (Ajaccio, 2004), 10; Jean-Luc Chappey, 'La notion d'empire et la question de légitimité politique', *Siècles. Cahiers du Centre d'histoire 'Espaces et culture*, 17 (2003), 117. The phrase 'hybrid regime' is from Jacques Bainville, *Napoléon* (Paris, 1931, reed, 1995), 172.

48. On this point, Marc Belissa, *Repenser l'ordre européen (1795–1802): de la société des rois aux droits des nations* (Paris, 2006), 178.

49. For a general discussion of the principle see, Michael Rowe, 'Napoleon and the post-revolutionary Management of Sovereignty', *Modern & Contemporary France* 8, no. 4 (2000), 510–13.

50. First brought to light by Claude Langlois, 'Le plébiscite de l'an VIII ou le coup d'État du 18 pluviôse an VIII', *Annales Historiques de la Révolution Française* 44 (1972), 43–65, 231–46, 390–415.

51. Josiane Bourguet-Rouveyre, 'La survivance d'un système électorale sous le Consulat et l'Empire', *Annales historique de la Révolution française* 346 (2006), 19, 20; Malcolm Crook, *Elections in the French Revolution: An Apprenticeship in Democracy: 1789–1799* (Cambridge, 1996), 102–15.

52. Malcolm Crook, 'Confiance d'en bas, manipulation d'en haut: la pratique plébiscitaire sous Napoléon (1799–1815)', in Philippe Bourdin, Jean-Claude Caron and Mathias Bernard (eds), *L'incident électoral de la Révolution française à la Ve République* (Clermont-Ferrand, 2002), 77–87.

53. Dusaulchoy de Bergemont, *Histoire du couronnement*, 288. The notion of divine right would gain authority as the empire progressed.

54. André Latreille, *Le Catéchisme Impérial de 1806. Etudes et documents pour servir a l'histoire des rapports de Napoléon et du clergé concordataire* (Paris, 1935), 80–1; André Latreille, *L'Église catholique et la Révolution française*, ii. 135–39. Translation in Philip Dwyer and Peter McPhee (eds), *The French Revolution and Napoleon: A Sourcebook* (London, 2002), 159–60.

55. Bluche, *Le Bonapartisme*, 35.

56. Michael Rowe, *From Reich to State: The Rhineland in the Revolutionary Age, 1780–1830* (Cambridge, 2003), 155.

57. Philip Mansel, *The Court of France, 1789–1830* (Cambridge, 1988), 56–7.

58. Nicole Gotteri, *Napoléon. Stratégie politique et moyens de gouvernement: essai* (Paris, 2007), 62–3.

59. Stuart Woolf, *Napoleon's Integration of Europe* (London, 1991),

60. Mansel, *Court of France*, 72; Anne Martin-Fugier, *La vie élégante ou La formation du Tout-Paris, 1815–1848* (Paris, 1990), 82; Pierre Branda, *Napoléon et ses hommes: la Maison de l'"Empereur, 1804–1815* (Paris, 2011), 101–2.

61. Thierry Lentz, *Nouvelle histoire du premier Empire. I. Napoléon et la conquête de l'Europe, 1804–1810* (Paris, 2002), 348 and 349.

62. François Piétri, *Napoléon et le Parlement ou la dictature enchaînée* (Paris, 1955), 207–21; Irene Collins, *Napoleon and his Parliaments: 1800–1815* (London, 1979), 114–15.

63. Gabriel Vauthier, 'L'épuration de la magistrature en 1808', *Revue des études napoléoniennes* (January 1919), 218–23; Jean Bourdon, 'Les sénatus-consulte de 1807. L'épuration de la magistrature en 1807–1808 et ses conséquences', *Revue d'histoire moderne et contemporaine*, 17 (July–September 1970), 829–36.

64. Simon Burrows, *French Exile Journalism and European Politics, 1792–1814* (Suffolk, 2000), 181–83; Stuart Semmel, *Napoleon and the British* (New Haven, 2004), 44–6.

65. William Doyle, 'The Political Culture of the Napoleonic Empire', in Forrest and Wilson (eds), *The Bee and the Eagle*, 91.

66. Jean Tulard, *Napoléon, ou, Le mythe du sauveur* (Paris, 1977), 324; Walter Bruyère-Ostells, 'Les officiers républicains sous l'Empire: entre tradition républicaine, ralliement et tournant libérale', *Annales historiques de la Révolution française* 346 (2006), 40–1.

67. Bluche, *Le Bonapartisme*, 88.

68. Louis Bergeron, 'Napoléon ou l'état post-révolutionnaire', in Colin Lucas (ed.), *The Political Culture of the French Revolution* (Oxford, 1988), 437–41; Louis Bergeron, *France under Napoleon* (Princeton, 1981), 4; David A. Bell, *The First Total War: Napoleon's Europe and the Birth of Warfare as We Know It* (Boston, 2007), 242; Lyons, *Napoleon Bonaparte and the Legacy of the French Revolution*, 296.

69. Jacques Godechot, 'Révolution, contre-révolution et monocratie en France (1789–1799)', *Recueils de la Société Jean Bodin* 21, no. 2 (1969), 782.

70. François Furet, *Dictionnaire critique de la Révolution française* (Paris, 1988), 224.

71. Lynn Hunt, 'The World We Have Gained: The Future of the French Revolution', *American Historical Review* (2003), 19. The terms 'police state', and the more nuanced term 'security state', are used to describe the type of public surveillance that characterized the regime (Howard G. Brown, 'From Organic Society to Security State', *Journal of Modern History* 69 (1997), 597–622; Michael Sibalis, 'Arbitrary Detention, Human Rights and the Napoleonic Senate', in Howard G. Brown and Judith A. Miller (eds), *Taking Liberties: Problems of a New Order from the French*

Revolution to Napoleon (Manchester, 2002), 166–84; and Judith A. Miller, 'The Napoleonic Police State', in Philip Dwyer (ed.), *Napoleon and Europe* (London, 2001), 79–94.

72. Howard G. Brown, 'Domestic State Violence: repression from the Croquants to the Commune', *The Historical Journal* 42 (1999), 597–622, and Howard G. Brown, *Ending the French Revolution*, 16, 236, 358. It is a term that has been adopted by Andrew Jainchill, *Reimagining Politics after the Terror: The Republican Origins of French Liberalism* (Ithaca, 2008), esp. 197–242.

73. This problem is discussed in Howard G. Brown, 'Napoleon Bonaparte, Political Prodigy', *History Compass* 5 (2007), 1382–98.

74. The comparison is often made, as in, for example, John Lukacs, *The Hitler of History* (New York, 1998), 240–51. See, R. S. Alexander, *Napoleon* (London, 2001), 90–116; Steven Englund, 'Napoleon and Hitler', *The Journal of the Historical Society* 6 (2006), 151–69; and Michael Rowe, 'Napoleon's France: A Forerunner of Europe's Twentieth-Century Dictators', in Claus-Christian Szejnmann (ed.), *Rethinking History, Dictatorship and War: New Approaches and Interpretations* (London, 2009), 87–106.

75. Malcolm Crook, 'The Uses of Democracy. Elections and Plebiscites in Napoleonic France', in Máire F. Cross and David Williams (eds), *The French Experience from Republic to Monarchy, 1792–1824: New Dawns in Politics, Knowledge and Culture* (Houndmills, 2000), 58–71.

76. For this see, David P. Jordan, *Napoleon and the Revolution* (Houndmills, 2012), 10.

SELECTED READING

Alexander, R. S., *Napoleon* (London, 2001).

Aston, Nigel, *Religion and Revolution in France, 1780–1804* (Basingstoke, 2000).

Brown, Howard G., *Ending the French Revolution: Violence, Justice, and Repression from the Terror to Napoleon* (Charlottesville, 2006).

Collins, Irene, *Napoleon and his Parliaments: 1800–1815* (London, 1979).

Dwyer, Philip and Forrest, Alan (eds), *Napoleon and His Empire: Europe 1804–1814* (London, 2007).

Dwyer, Philip, 'Napoleon and the Foundation of the Empire', *The Historical Journal* 53, no. 2 (2010), 339–58.

Dwyer, Philip, *Citizen Emperor: Napoleon in Power* (London and New Haven, 2013).

Ellis, Geoffrey, *Napoleon* (Harlow, 1997).

Ellis, Geoffrey, 'Religion According to Napoleon: The Limits of Pragmatism', in Nigel Aston (ed.), *Religious Change in Europe, 1650–1914: Essays for John McManners* (Oxford, 1997), 235–55.

Englund, Steven, *Napoleon. A Political Biography* (New York, 2004).

Forrest, Alan, *Napoleon* (London, 2011).

Jordan, David P., *Napoleon and the Revolution* (Basingstoke:, 2012).

Lyons, Martyn, *Napoleon Bonaparte and the Legacy of the French Revolution* (Basingstoke, 1994).

Tulard, Jean, *Napoléon ou le Mythe du sauveur* (Paris, 1977).

Woolf, Stuart, *Napoleon's Integration of Europe* (London, 1991).

Woloch, Isser, *Napoleon and his Collaborators: The Making of a Dictatorship* (New York, 2001).

CHAPTER 34

LASTING POLITICAL STRUCTURES

ISSER WOLOCH

More than two centuries have elapsed since the French Revolution stamped its indelible if ambiguous marks on the French nation, leaving many potential entry points for considering its lasting legacies. At least two approaches are possible. We can identify certain foundational features of the Revolution and then consider their trajectories going forward, or we can use 'the roundabout approach' proposed by Marc Bloch. In his great book on early French rural history Bloch sometimes worked backward from outcomes that could best be documented much later in the eighteenth century. Is it wrong, he asked, to decide 'what were the essential features of the finished model before plunging into the mysteries of its inception ... to read history backward if one hopes to break the secret cypher of the past?'[1] In this vein I begin with a look at France in the 1940s—with the occupation, the Liberation, and the post-war moment—and circle back from there to several of the Revolution's evolving but durable political and administrative innovations. Later, turning to military conscription, one of the Revolution's weightiest legacies, I will start in 1789 and work forwards.

I

It is impossible to prove, and may well be wrong, but the odds seem high that the French Revolution never looked so good as it did after 1942, when the oppressive weight of the occupation and Vichy had fully registered. Would not many, perhaps most, French citizens have relished the scene in *Casablanca* (had they been able to see it) where central-European anti-Nazi Victor Laszlo persuades the band at Rick's nightclub to play the Marseillaise, at which the throng of customers (except for the scowling German officers at one table) lustily sing the banned stanzas and shed more than one tear? By that time even General De Gaulle had acknowledged the appeal of the French Revolution. After a year of insisting that Free France was apolitical, purely patriotic and military, he finally incorporated the triad of *liberté, égalité, fraternité* onto the organization's letterhead—which did not imply that the Resistance in either London or on the ground had any wish to resurrect the Third Republic as such.[2]

In certain obvious ways the Third Republic had consolidated the Revolution's legacy of representative democracy, had embodied it in symbols such as the Marseillaise itself[3] and Marianne, and had promoted it in the French Revolution workshop of Sorbonne historian Alphonse Aulard. But in light of the widespread alienation from the Third Republic just before and after its collapse in 1940, it was easy enough to ignore that connection and go back to basics once the Nazis and Vichy were on their way to being ousted. In 1942 the Revolution had little inspiration to offer the Resistance in its organizational or military preparations, but its values provided one implicit thread in Resistance propaganda and post-war planning. After the Liberation, the Revolution's institutional legacies could also come into play. In that spirit a proclamation by the National Council of the Resistance (CNR) broadcast from London on 11 July 1944 invoked the Bastille, Valmy, and the Marseillaise to rouse the French people, and even the Americans broadcast a proclamation for 14 July anticipating the time when '*liberté, égalité, fraternité*' would reappear over France's town halls.[4]

The Resistance and the post-war moment shifted France's political spectrum leftward, starting with the Common Programme forged by the CNR. This umbrella group for various internal Resistance movements and traditional 'political families', coaxed into being by De Gaulle's personal emissary Jean Moulin in 1943, acknowledged the general's leadership while it worked to build the 'secret army' that would strike from within when the allied invasion finally came. The CNR's sixteen members, ranging from communists to conservative Republicans, hammered out various disagreements and in March 1944 unanimously approved a two-part Common Programme. Part one dealt with those military preparations and the immediate disarray that would follow the liberation of French territory. The second part sketched a vision for the post-war future, where the Resistance hoped to inspire a 'peaceful revolution' and moral renewal. Part two of the Common Programme amounted to a manifesto for democratic socialism, more in keeping with an update of the Declaration of the Rights of Man of 1793 than the Declaration of 1789. It included clauses advocating national economic planning and regulation, nationalizations in certain sectors, comprehensive social insurance, advances in worker rights, and other initiatives to promote the security and dignity of all citizens.[5]

In effect, part two of the CNR Common Programme embodied the interpretation of the French Revolution synthesized decades earlier by Socialist Party leader and sometime historian Jean Jaurès: that socialist values could best be nurtured in the democratic and Republican traditions of the French Revolution, while conversely the Revolution's democratic values could only be consummated through the gradual achievement of socialism.[6] In that spirit Albert Camus wrote in the Resistance newspaper *Combat* just after the Liberation that 'we are all socialists', although he had no commitment whatsoever to the old Socialist Party: 'Our plan is to make justice reign through the economy and to guarantee freedom through politics.'[7]

The CNR's unanimous adoption of the Common Programme reflected the imperative for unity within a disparate Resistance that initially had no organizational, political or ideological cohesion other than the anti-Nazi resolve of its partisans, but which by 1943–4 had achieved a measure of each. Communists and conservative patriots went along with the progressive vision of the Common Programme because winning the war was their overriding imperative, unity was the indispensable means, and post-war renewal an obvious goal. That moment in 1944 was perhaps the equivalent of 1790 in the French Revolution, when its festivals of federation projected hopes for unity and renewal as an existing reality. Louis Saillant, a clandestine operative for the General Confederation of Labour CGT and as of September 1944 the new head of the CNR, frequently referred to a seeming paradox of the Resistance: In its darkest moment, a prostrate France found a source of strength in an unprecedented unity of spirit at the core of the Resistance, which brought together 'adherents of the Christian concept and devotees of socialism'. Such people, Saillant declared, 'never had met except to clash and then part back to back. [But] in the shadows of underground France they found each other'. A year earlier the liberal Catholic theologian Jacques Maritain, who had taken refuge in the United States, introduced in one of his Voice of America broadcasts a similar view of the Resistance as an extraordinary rapprochement of France's historically warring democratic and Christian traditions.[8] For all their sentimental hyperbole such images of unprecedented cooperation in the Resistance were reasonably accurate for 1943–4, and lasted briefly into the post-war moment as well.

Freed of the Nazis and Vichy's usurpation by the Allied invasion (seconded by the armed actions of the Resistance), France awaited the return of Republican legality and democracy, which De Gaulle had repeatedly pledged in the face of scepticism by Roosevelt and others. But first came a long interim of provisional government (the GPRF), led by the general, his unity cabinet, his seventeen 'regional commissioners of the republic', and the prefects under their supervision. In due course, the GPRF orchestrated that return to democracy without reviving the much-vilified Third Republic per se. How this unfolded can tell us a lot about certain lasting political structures of the Revolution, especially in the succession of elections that began in April 1945—the key to the whole process.

As in the early years of the French Revolution, citizens (including women for the first time) went to the polls repeatedly in 1945–6 for a variety of elections and referenda.[9] By consensus, national elections could not be held until the defeat of the Reich allowed the repatriation of over two million POWs, deportees, and forced labourers, which delayed that decisive event until October 1945. But local elections began before the repatriation process was completed. First came municipal elections in April–May to replace unelected local officials from the Vichy or Liberation periods in *mairies* and town halls. From the largest cities to the smallest villages, voters chose municipal councils in over 35,800 *communes*. According to *Le Monde* even these relatively parochial elections 'confirmed the defeat of Vichyism and the trend toward the Left ... though the latter trend was far less marked in rural communes than in cities', since (one may presume) many rural and small-town voters opted for familiar local figures even if their behaviour during the occupation had been equivocal.[10]

The next round of elections came at the end of September: two-round cantonal elections to choose members of the general (administrative) councils for each of the ninety departments. With a total of 3,006 seats up for decision, the victors came from across the political spectrum. The Left more than doubled its seats compared to the pre-war, while the pre-war Right lost roughly half of its former seats, but the results were not really conclusive. The voters in the traditional Manche department—as a reliable local study enigmatically concluded—'chose change in continuity'.[11]

In our context, however, it is not the results of these elections that matter as much as their form and function. In one sense, the municipal and cantonal elections of 1945 picked up from where Vichy had scrapped Republican political institutions in 1940, and used their familiar forms to revive them. But the civic logic and much of the template itself dated back to the Revolution's reorganization of the national territory and to its remarkable commitment to elections at all levels.

II

After the night of 4 August the National Assembly of 1789 could disregard the traditional identities and boundaries of France's historic provinces in favour of a more rationalized (critics would say rigidly Cartesian) re-division of the national territory into ninety-odd departments, each similar in size though not in population, and each with an elected departmental administration. The Assembly then divided each department into districts, to which it ascribed various administrative functions to be carried out by an elected district administration.[12] Each district was in turn subdivided by the Assembly into cantons, in which it vested only two functions. Each rural canton (like urban wards) would be the circumscription for a primary Assembly in which the voters chose electors who would then meet in a departmental electoral Assembly to elect (indirectly) departmental administrators, judges, and legislators. The voters in each canton would also directly elect their justice of the peace. Finally, the Assembly bestowed legal and political identity on what it called *communes*—over 40,000 units of collective life ranging from the smallest agglomerated villages to the largest cities, each of which was to elect a similar administration consisting of a municipal council and a mayor.[13]

In the revolutionary decade, the Napoleonic era, and the regimes that followed, this four-tiered politico/administrative structure went through numerous alterations, shuffles, excisions, and reiterations. The Jacobin Convention, for example, essentially dissolved the elected departmental administrations, which in its eyes had become tainted with the political heresy of 'federalism' (i.e. support for the rival Girondins). For its part the Thermidorian Convention retaliated by curbing the district administrations because they were closely identified with implementing the Terror, and the Constitution of 1795 abolished the districts altogether. The Consulate, however, revived the districts, renamed them *arrondissements*, and inserted a sub-prefect into each as adjuncts of its new prefectorial system of administration—although the Empire did not utilize these circumscriptions as much as some had hoped: for example, by aggregating at the *arrondissement* level the maintenance of local roads or rural policing, which strained the civic and financial capacity of numerous communes.

The functions of the cantons also waxed and waned, although as market hubs most cantonal *chefs lieux* remained crucial to rural life regardless of the administrative map. Cantons gained heightened status when the Directory despaired of leaving the burdens of local government in rural communes to an elected mayor and municipal council, regarding them as too isolated, unqualified, or vulnerable to get the job done. So instead, the village mayors within each rural canton (still elected but renamed *agents municipaux*) were aggregated into a collective *administration municipal* that met in the cantonal seat. These creations in turn vanished with the Directory itself in 1800, as the Consulate returned local administration to the communes and their mayors, now appointed rather than elected but not much different in social profile, and now ostensibly under closer supervision by the state's sub-prefects and prefects. Yet in short order the cantons returned to significance as the site for the state's highest priority (apart from tax collection), the local conscription lottery. Later, in the wake of the Revolution of 1830, the mayors of rural communes would again be elected—a small first step, at least symbolically, on a long and tortuous road back to democracy.

Attitudes thus kept shifting in the capital toward the communes (far too many?), the cantons (a remedy for rural fragmentation?), and the districts (functionally sensible but hopelessly compromised in 1793–4?), and also towards the Revolution's initial, axiomatic reliance on elections. Through almost all the reconfigurations of local political and administrative institutions, however, the communes at one end and the departments at the other survived as essential units of French public life after 1800. To be sure, both the Napoleonic regime and the Bourbons hoped to cull the least viable rural communes with their minuscule populations and inadequate local revenues. But even the most aggressive periodic attempts by prefects to effect mergers (the *réunion des communes*) failed to make much headway against the inertial resistance of small communes in maintaining their distinct identities.[14] So, when we return to the vantage point of 1945 we still find more than 35,000 communes, of which over 80 per cent had fewer than 1500 inhabitants and many far fewer. As for the departments, their number expanded with annexations beyond France's borders of 1789 and contracted with subsequent military defeats; the total number of departments in 1945 (after the reincorporation of Alsace-Lorraine) ended up almost where it began in 1790, a meta-historical illustration perhaps of the regression to the mean.

This compressed account of the Revolution's politico/administrative structures reflects the evolving sense of what worked, or did not work, in the eyes of successive regimes. But it also suggests inherent tensions in the original revolutionary project itself. For the vision of 1789 contained two aims that could either prove complementary (as hoped) or conflicting. On one side, in reaction against royal absolutism, the revolutionaries established a system of local self-government via elections at all the aforementioned levels. On the other side, in keeping with their doctrine of national sovereignty and their repudiation of particularism, they insisted on uniformity across the national territory and on the goal of national integration. Citizens no matter where they lived would have the same rights, obligations, and institutions. In other words, the revolutionary project simultaneously entailed decentralization and recentralization.[15]

The decentralization of 1789—local participation and a degree of local self-government—had roots of a sort in the reformist agendas of Louis XVI's ministers Turgot and Calonne. Each had advocated the establishment of 'provincial Assemblies', representing large landowners or taxpayers, to advise royal officials in implementing such tasks as the allocation of tax quotas or public works in their provinces.[16] As the Revolution cohered in 1789, that notion, of course, disappeared along with the formal existence of the provinces themselves. Local civic and electoral participation devolved according to the divisions on the new administrative map. But the National Assembly simultaneously offset this devolution of authority by insisting unequivocally on the supremacy of national law. No local jurisdiction had any legislative authority, only the powers to implement laws that originated, and would be interpreted if necessary, in Paris, so that a citizen living anywhere in France would at least in theory live under the same rules. Challenges to this supremacy were not long in coming, among them pretensions to revolutionary autonomy by the Paris Commune of 1792, by the Paris sections in 1793–4, and by certain departmental administrations during the violent factional conflicts of 1793—all of which the revolutionary government and its Committee of Public Safety came down on aggressively.

Every regime from 1789 onward insisted on the supremacy of the national state regardless of the spaces it left or did not leave for local self-government. Accordingly, the National Assembly created the posts of elected 'procurator-syndics' on various local levels to serve as formal agents of liaison with the government in Paris. The National Convention did the same with its co-opted or appointed 'national agents', as did the Directory with its appointed departmental and cantonal commissioners, who coexisted uneasily with the elected departmental administrations or *administrations municipals*. The consummation of this recentralization of course came with the unambiguous supremacy of the Napoleonic regime's prefects and sub-prefects, who were subject to control only by the Interior Minister and the Council of State. This schema proved so functionally attractive that it survived virtually every subsequent change of regime, including the Third Republic (for all its electoral localism), Vichy (which relied on its prefects unchecked by any electoral participation at all), the GPRF (of necessity), and the Fourth Republic (for all its renewed commitment to electoral democracy).

Still—notwithstanding the supremacy of national law and national authority—local participation, if not exactly self-government, generally persisted in some form as well. The elected departmental administrative councils, brought into being in 1790 and temporarily suppressed by the revolutionary government of 1793–4, were resurrected in a new form under the Directory, and as a mark of their significance each was constitutionally mandated to publish a detailed annual accounting of its 'moral' and financial stewardship. Even Napoleon maintained a vestige of these departmental councils in a mutilated and truncated form. To aid the prefect, who came from outside the department, the Consulate appointed a *conseil général du départment* of prominent individuals with local knowledge. The council helped apportion the department's direct tax quota to the *arrondissements* (where comparable councils then assigned quotas to the communes) and heard appeals from those allocations; vetted the prefect's budget and his recommendation for the local tax surcharge (*centimes additionels*); and offered its views on local administrative problems—views systematically sought and collated in 1800–2. To discharge their business, however, the councils convened only once a year in a session lasting no more than two weeks. Still, at least in the early Napoleonic years when such things still mattered, these departmental councils imparted a faint patina of good government to the prefectorial system, and softened its authoritarian character at the margins, particularly in sensitive matters of the purse.[17]

Re-established in full heft by the Third Republic, the elected general councils of the departments became voices of local interests par excellence, alongside the single-constituency system of elections to the Chamber of Deputies—the latter memorably evoked by Pierre-Jakez Hélias's memoir of his Breton village in the person of Monsieur Le Bail, the 'Red' mayor of Plozevet, the area's deputy, and a backer of Pierre's Republican primary school or 'devil's school', as it was considered among the local 'Whites'.[18] With the disproportionate weight enjoyed by rural cantons, the departmental general councils of the Third Republic also became the seed beds of its reliably moderate or conservative Senate, the indirectly elected upper house of the Parliament. In all this, Vichy was the veritable outlier: it extinguished the Parliament, the general councils, and all elections along with the free press, independent trade unions and much else, far more brutally and thoroughly than Napoleon. Interestingly, in the corridors of Free France the idea had been floated to reconvene the pre-1940 general councils of the departments immediately after the Liberation as a dramatic first step toward re-establishing Republican legality. Conversely, at a Parisian congress of the departmental liberation committees in December 1944, delegates proposed that these committees, emanating directly from the Resistance, should now replace the Third Republic's departmental councils which Vichy had cashiered. Unsurprisingly, neither of these notions suited De Gaulle and they went nowhere, but a year after the Liberation new councils were duly elected under the aegis of his GPRF.[19]

III

On the level of the national state, always the centre of legislative and administrative power in France, neither De Gaulle nor other elements of the Resistance desired a simple revival of Third Republic institutions. A return to democracy and republicanism?—without question. A reversion to the previous methods of national elections and parliamentary governance?—to be avoided. But what should take their place? How could a new system be legitimately established? What would a new Republican constitution look like? The experience of the French Revolution pointed to some possible alternatives and to some snares.

A wide consensus prevailed in 1945 that citizens should elect a Constituent Assembly, which would simultaneously act as a legislature and draft a new constitution. But should this Assembly be fully 'sovereign' in the manner of the National Assembly in 1789 or the National Convention of 1792? The Communist Party (PCF) and its allies believed that it should. But De Gaulle argued that a preliminary ordinance crafted by the GPRF should restrain the Assembly's powers over the provisional head of state whom it would name; limit the time for completing its work to seven months; and provide for a popular referendum to accept or reject its constitutional draft.

At its source in the French Revolution, two models were available on the question of a popular referendum. The National Assembly had not seen fit to submit its exhaustively debated Constitution of 1791 to any form of popular approval. The National Convention of 1792, elected after the collapse of the monarchy, was fully 'sovereign' as well. But while it voted not to submit its verdict on executing the king to popular approval, it did decide to it submit its 'Jacobin' Constitution of 1793 to the nation's primary Assemblies, which it convoked specifically for the purpose of discussing, and then approving or rejecting the new constitution. In due course the primary Assemblies overwhelmingly approved the charter, even as many suggested changes, but the Convention then put the charter aside as it voted in October 1793 to institute 'a government revolutionary until the peace'. Later, instead of implementing the Constitution of 1793, the post-Thermidor Convention drafted another constitution in a different spirit in 1795, and submitted it to the primary Assemblies, but only for an up or down vote without discussion. Again, the primary Assemblies approved the charter, albeit by a less impressive vote than in 1793, and the Directory era began.[20] Subsequently, at each step of his rise to supremacy—the Consulate, the Life Consulship, and the Empire—Napoleon used a plebiscite to ratify his accretions of power.

De Gaulle always insisted that he had nothing in common with Napoleon, but he did share a penchant for plebiscites or referenda to draw legitimacy directly from the people. Since the two Napoleons had both notoriously abused this procedure, many Republicans had become wary about using referenda. Accordingly, the 'constitution' of the Third Republic was in reality a series of organic laws from 1875 that were never submitted for popular approval. In 1945 remnants of the Radical Socialist party—the traditional centrist, secularist Republican party much discredited by the events of 1938–40—remained a lonely public voice for going back to Third Republic forms of parliamentary life, and for avoiding the use of referenda. The resurrection of the Third Republic proposed by Édouard Herriot, the Radicals' repatriated warhorse, was insupportable not only to De Gaulle but to almost all elements of the Resistance, and to a wide spectrum of general opinion in France. But the dissent of the Radical-Socialists prompted De Gaulle to resolve the issue by a two-question referendum to be held in October simultaneously with the elections for a new National Assembly.[21]

The first question: should the Assembly elected that day be a Constituent Assembly (thus interring the Third Republic once and for all)? If the vote was YES (as seemed predictable), the second question asked: should the Assembly be delimited by an attached *project de loi* incorporating De Gaulle's desired limits mentioned above.[22] In tandem with De Gaulle, the new social-Catholic party (the MRP) and the Socialist Party (PS) advocated a yes/yes vote; they wanted a new start but accepted De Gaulle's blueprint for the circumscribing the powers of the Constituent Assembly. The PCF and its allies in the CGT advocated a yes/no vote; they too wanted a new start but campaigned vigorously for a fully 'sovereign' Assembly. Shards of the old conservative parties, comfortable enough with the Third Republic, advocated no/yes, while the hard-core Radicals stuck by their traditional preferences and alone advocated no/no votes. When the ballots were tallied, the proposal for a Constituent Assembly carried overwhelmingly with a yes vote of 96.4 per cent, while the conditions posed in the second question carried by a yes vote of 66.3 per cent.

On the parallel question facing the GPRF of how to conduct national elections and how they would be contested, the French Revolution's precedents had by now virtually no relevance at all. During the entire revolutionary decade voting had taken place in the primary Assemblies (in rural cantons or in urban wards), which chose 'electors' who convened in the departmental electoral Assembly to elect that department's legislative deputies. That mode of elections had long since disappeared. More importantly, all the regimes of the 1790s had opposed the formation of political parties. Political clashes could be intense within the electoral Assemblies, belying their ostensibly lofty role in seeking the most qualified and virtuous individuals as their representatives. But the conflicts were not allowed to unfold transparently through open candidacies and electioneering let alone rival party programmes or slates. The stubborn and arguably dysfunctional official hostility to incipient political parties consistently depicted them as mere self-seeking factions if not outright cabals working against the mythic ideal of national unity. Concretely, the notion of loyal oppositions could not take root. Perhaps party formation under the Directory would only have exacerbated partisan rivalries and vendettas, with their sometimes murderous outcomes. We will never know; political conflict, inescapably intense across the 1790s, was never normalized.

This bias against political parties was a dead relic of the past by 1875. On the contrary, Third Republic political culture was marked by an excess of party formation reflecting the multiplicity of social interests and political positions as well as the personal ambitions of its politicians. In the late nineteenth century, for example, the advance of socialism was impeded by the fragmentation of socialists into two and even three parties, until they finally forged a unified party under prodding from the Second Socialist International. In the inter-war years mainstream conservatism was even more fragmented into various parliamentary groups and at least two large parties, not to mention the rise of parties on the hard Right and hard Left.

In 1945 a consensus formed around replacing the two-round, single constituency system for electing the Third Republic's Chamber of Deputies with a one-round system based on proportional representation. The new system called for slates of departmental candidates rather than national lists, thereby favouring large and well-organized parties. The election of October 1945 then produced a remarkable political consolidation with the success of three dynamic parties—a PCF at the height of its popularity; a revived Socialist Party; and a progressive party in a new key created by social-Catholics prominent in the Resistance (the MRP). Each party won roughly 25 per cent of the vote and an even greater proportion of seats in the Assembly. In the end, De Gaulle, who stood aloof from all parties including the sympathetic MRP, and who shared something of Napoleon's contempt for most politicians, could not abide being challenged. His disdain did not focus on democracy, or the electorate, or even the Parliament per se, but was displaced on to the contending political parties, including the MRP whose leaders perforce let him down every so often. As his clear-eyed MRP loyalist Pierre-Henri Teitgen put it: 'Did not De Gaulle ... come to confound in the same phobia and the same contempt all the political parties (guilty or innocent) represented in that Assembly, and as a consequence did he not condemn the representative system itself?'[23] Unlike General Bonaparte who helped orchestrate a seizure of power, however, General De Gaulle simply walked away from the provisional presidency of the republic, to which the Assembly had named him, after two months of half-hearted wrangling.

The initial attempt of the Constituent Assembly to draft a constitution in 1946 almost destroyed the coalition, as it faced some of the quandaries that first arose with the French Revolution. For one, should the Fourth Republic have a unicameral legislature on the model of 1791, the National Convention of 1792, and the Second Republic of 1848 (the communist position in 1945), or a bicameral legislature like the Directory regime and the Third Republic, albeit in a different mode (De Gaulle's position)? As for the executive power: should the Fourth Republic have a strong, independent president—to De Gaulle the sine qua non for an effective government that alone could assure France's place on the world stage? Or should the sovereign legislature control the executive as it had under the National Convention (when even the title of minister was abolished in the 'executive commissions' that implemented the Convention's laws) or under the Third Republic (where prime ministers were subject to removal by sudden no-confidence votes, and the President of the Republic was a laegely ceremonial figurehead)?

The constitutional draft, muscled through by the PCF and the Socialists against the opposition of the MRP, opted for unicameralism and a weak president, but the voters rejected it. A second Constituent Assembly (with a similar profile) was then elected to try again. Anxious to be done with the provisional state of affairs, the three parties this time compromised sufficiently for all three to back this second constitutional draft. Since their compromise fell short of De Gaulle's priorities, it aroused the general's unbridled enmity, and the constitution won approval by only a thin margin in a referendum marked by the disenchantment of massive absenteeism.[24] But with the CNR Common Programme as their shared rallying point, the three parties continued on in the tripartite mode that De Gaulle had inaugurated. Despite their differences—over issues that dated back to the Revolution such as aid to Catholic schools and wage/price controls, alongside new ones such as the modalities for nationalizations—the tripartist governments effectively carried France past the gravest problems of the post-war moment and across the threshold to recovery.

IV

In 1789 the National Assembly's bold doctrine of popular sovereignty, by which its members alone could speak for the people, empowered it to adopt any form of military recruitment it deemed necessary. Initially, the Assembly opted for a small, professional army of long-term volunteers—in keeping with its view in 1790 that a regenerated France represented a force for peace in the world and would never launch wars of aggression. But after the outbreak of war in 1792 successive regimes would have to ponder the boundaries of state action in this domain repeatedly. From then on, army recruitment could not be relegated into a separate sphere marked 'military'. Alongside the Revolution's policies on the Catholic Church, recruitment became a fundamental political issue.

Meeting military needs involved numerous questions, including near the top whether French families would accept an obligation for military service should volunteering not suffice for the war effort. At the nadir of the Republic's military fortunes but at the height of *sans-culotte* militancy, the National Convention decreed the *levée en masse* in August 1793—a one-time 'requisition' or draft of able-bodied bachelors between 18 and 25 years of age. The *levée* was revolutionary in the full sense of the term, but was framed in a defensive and patriotic context.[25] In the end it raised about 300,000 new troops, but it also provoked massive draft evasion by about 200,000 other citizens whose families balked at losing their sons to the alien demands of military service.

For the next four years France's military posture depended on the intake of this one-time draft. Young men who turned 18 after 1793 were not conscripted, even though casualties, desertion, conditional discharges, and hardship furloughs drove down the size of the army from its high of 750,000 in 1794 to about 350,000 by 1798. It is conceivable that the *levée en masse*—given the resistance it engendered and the hardships it caused for those who served—might have faded away like other Jacobin expedients such as the Maximum, but only if a durable peace had been achieved between the republic and its European foes. The War of the Second Coalition ended that possibility, as the new Sister Republics and *la patrie* itself faced the prospect of military defeat. In response, the Loi Jourdan-Delbrel of 1798 introduced systematic military conscription as a permanent obligation of citizenship. As Jourdan put it: 'The soldiers of the fatherland consist of all Frenchmen capable of bearing arms. It only remains for us to determine how to call to the colours those whose presence will be necessary ... Many will be subject to service, but few are likely actually to serve.'[26]

Medically fit 20- to 25-year-olds, regardless of marital status, were subject to call-up by 'classes' (birth years), as needed. Jourdan introduced the new term *conscrit* to describe the young men subject to military recruitment in a given year (rather than referring to those actually designated for service). The government would issue quotas for each department based on population, and a lottery would be used locally to determine which conscripts were actually called up. In dire situations the entire 'class' of a given year could be mobilized, and in 1799 three such 'classes' had to be called up since draft evasion was again so rife.

After Brumaire Bonaparte inherited the need for more troops, the basic system for providing them, and the resistance against such conscription. Over the years the Napoleonic Empire finally made good the Revolution's demand on French citizens for military service—an ongoing obligation that impacted severely on the lives of French families. But the manner and spirit in which Napoleon used this vast accretion of state power soon left behind the particular revolutionary context of 1793–8—a quasi-Rousseauist or Jacobin notion of citizenship ostensibly democratic and patriotic.

Like the *levée en masse*, the troop levies of the Directory, Consulate, and Empire provoked massive draft evasion. The Napoleonic regime had to wage a protracted war of attrition on the home front to overcome this, and for years it seemed to be a losing battle. But in the end, after a decade of wearying struggle against chronic, regional patterns of *insoumission*, the government prevailed. In the process Napoleon placed his stamp on conscription, and transformed it into one of his 'granite masses'. By 1810 the Napoleonic state had broken the back of draft evasion, even in regions where it had been endemic, and where (as Alan Forrest has shown) communal support had habitually sheltered *réfractaires*.[27]

In this battle the Napoleonic state finally prevailed through a three-pronged strategy. First, the Consulate broke with the revolutionary model when it placated wealthy bourgeois and prosperous peasants (who needed their sons on the land) by introducing the option of replacement, which the mass levy and the Loi Jourdan had both excluded. The Consulate had a bad conscience about this, and hedged it with restrictions that precluded overt trafficking in replacements. Yet despite the steep and escalating prices commanded by a limited pool of replacements, this oft-used option neutralized some influential potential opponents of conscription.

Second, the Napoleonic regime's stability allowed for persistence. Over the years, it refined its bureaucratic technique for organizing and implementing conscription; readjusted it at the margins (for example, by moving the local draft lottery or *tirage* from rural communes to the cantonal seats); and routinized its occurrence in the public life of the French people. Napoleon could hold his prefects personally responsible for this matter, and eventually carrot-and-stick incentives in the prefectures yielded improving results.

Parallel to its bureaucratic routines, the Napoleonic state honed its coercive techniques. This was not as simple as it sounds. The first line of coercion would normally be heavy fines for the parents of draft evaders, or billeting troops known as *garnissaires* on them to induce them to turn over their sons. But most of the parents were of limited means to begin with, had no capacity to pay steep fines, and little to offer any *garnissaires*. Community responsibility, however, would make for a more effective sanction. Fines and *garnissaires* could be piled on the leading households of a village or urban neighbourhood, even if the targeted citizens vehemently protested such extra-legal measures. The ultimate sanction for regions persistently rife with draft evaders would be the unloosing of a mobile column. Regular troops or national guards would maraud through the area like an occupation force, lawfully wreaking havoc on its otherwise peaceable citizens in pursuit of draft evaders and deserters.[28]

The combination of unrelenting bureaucratic routine and bursts of coercive intrusion eventually succeeded. Communal complicity in sheltering and employing *insoumis* or in tolerating the petty crime they resorted to for survival, finally broke down. The historian might regret seeing this collapse of popular grit in resisting the demands of an increasingly remote regime. But the Napoleonic state *did* break the back of draft evasion. Although desertion from military units continued, this did not impact on local draft quotas or procedures. The Napoleonic conscription machine could legitimately trumpet its victory starting in 1810. In due course, this made it possible for the Emperor to replenish his army after the Russian disaster, and in turn to reject meaningful diplomatic negotiation in its wake.

By the time Napoleon abdicated, of course, it looked very different. Under the frantic and ludicrous calls for more and more troops in late 1813 the entire machine imploded. In the process the whole notion of mass conscription seemed utterly discredited, and the Bourbons' promise to abolish this punishing institution doubtless aided their tepid bid for popular support in 1814. Royalist caricatures attacked Napoleonic conscription with inventive, often scatological zest: Napoleon being fed young men and defecating kingdoms; Napoleon as the minotaur or the ogre 'who eats two hundred thousand men a year'; conscription as 'the Massacre of the Innocents'.[29] But the abolition of conscription by the Bourbons proved as ephemeral as any of Napoleon's imperial conquests. In 1818 they revived military conscription, albeit on a far more limited scale, and with extremely permissive provisions for hiring replacements for the families of *conscrits* who drew bad numbers in the local *tirage*. Thereafter, conscription in various forms remained a feature of the French landscape through every changing regime, and should therefore be reckoned as one of the most durable innovations of the French Revolution, as consolidated by Napoleon.

In post-Napoleonic France, the modalities of conscription changed several times. Before 1872, the provision of replacements for the well-off by insurance companies or self-help associations remained one hallmark, while the relatively few conscripts who drew bad numbers in their local lottery faced military service of between five and seven years. Theoretically universal, French conscription operated on a blatant two-tier system. Then a law of 1872 abolished replacement and stipulated that a good number in the *tirage* entitled a conscript to a term of one year's service, while a bad number still brought a five-year term. But the same law introduced numerous exemptions (including clergy, teachers, and heads of families), along with a proviso that conscripts who could pay for their own equipment at a cost of 1,500F could automatically serve as 'volunteers' for one year. This contorted practice, along with most exemptions, finally disappeared in 1889 in favour of an essentially universal obligation for three years' service. Conscripts still gathered for the local *tirage* but only to determine who ended up with an undesirable assignment to the navy or the colonial forces.[30]

Two pressures had driven these later changes in French conscription: the advance of republicanism, and the size of the rival German military. To accommodate these pressures, the army law of 1905 finally suppressed most exemptions and the *tirage au sort* itself. All medically fit conscripts would now serve for two years in a true *armée nationale*, subject to reserve status afterwards (an innovation pioneered by Prussia after 1806 with its *Landwehr* system).

But as far as we have come, let us remember that from 1818 onward (despite the brief interval of Bourbon anti-conscription propaganda), the French state had little trouble imposing its demands for military service, whatever their scope or extent. Before 1889 families may have bitterly resented it when their sons drew a bad number and could not afford to hire a replacement or qualify for an exemption. They might grumble or even wail. But they rarely resorted to draft evasion, which Napoleon had rendered deviant rather than normative, manageable rather than subversive.

Indeed nineteenth-century conscription took on a normative aspect for winners and losers alike, as the local *tirage au sort* became a masculine rite of passage, marking a transition from adolescence to a kind of adulthood. Conscription became associated with virility: passing the medical review as 'fit for service' also meant 'fit for the girls'—for sex and marriage. Eventually a group photograph of one's local cohort of conscripts might end up on the mantel alongside a marriage portrait. This mundane or folkloric side of conscription has been recovered by Michel Bozon's volume in the collection *Arts et Traditions Populaire*. 'In all periods and in all regions', writes Bozon, 'the conscripts were partial to streams of ribbons [ordinarily a feminine accoutrement] which symbolized virility for them'. Hats with white ribbons became marks of honour on the day of the lottery, and before 1905 conscripts often sported on those hats the lottery number they drew, either on a pre-printed card or a decorative handmade card. Conscripts typically set out for the *tirage* with grudging acceptance and made the best of it, whatever the outcome, with local rituals and symbols including oversized cocardes, songs, the aforementioned regalia, *tournées* of the neighbourhood or village, and the obligatory carousing.[31]

In sum, the French Revolution had initiated the obligation of conscription, the First Empire eventually overcame the stubborn resistance to it in certain regions, and state officials during the long nineteenth century had an easy job of military recruitment as they drew on the procedures and guidelines inherited from the Empire. Successive generations of young men now complied, if reluctantly, with the obligation. Successive governments and general staffs could count on it. The way was opened for the mobilization of the mass armies and reserve forces of Europe that would finally be hurled against each other in 1914. And despite the carnage of that Great War, and the revulsion and waves of pacifism that it engendered, military conscription endured. As rearmament began in earnest, first in Italy and Germany, later in Britain and France, militarization continued apace. Well over a million French soldiers could ponder this as they forcibly sat out most of the Second World War in German POW camps, their toll in dead and wounded, though not in humiliation and discomfort, mitigated by Pétain's capitulation in 1940.

A small number of those prisoners escaped soon after the surrender, or even later, and then embraced a different model of military service: a return to volunteering. Some found their way into the Free French army in England, others into the 'secret army' of the Resistance, the supreme example of a patriotic volunteer force among whom the image of Valmy likely resonated. With D-Day and the Liberation they immediately became the 'Forces Françaises de l'Intérieur', and within months thousands of these men, in whole units or as individuals, were incorporated into the Free French Army to continue the war. Like the Bourbon's pivot against conscription, however, this voluntarist model did not last. The core of long-term officers and soldiers who launched the battle to regain French Indo-China in 1945 were eventually supplemented by a new generation of conscripts. Later, in the brutal war to keep Algeria French, the fighting (and use of torture) fell to an ill-assorted combination of hardened paratroopers and ordinary conscripts (about two-thirds of the total).

Within a few years, however, a gradual and barely visible transformation began: the demilitarization of European societies and polities. Britain had begun this trend in 1960 by ending conscription and reverting to its traditional volunteer army. As European union advanced and as the Cold War settled into an equilibrium between the two blocs, mass conscription wound down in Western Europe. This process began in France by way of stagnating or declining military budgets; large increases in deferments from the military draft; higher physical standards for induction; reduced terms of service and reserve status for those inducted; and the creation of relatively non-disruptive, non-military alternatives for national service.[32] From the perspective of this chapter, then, one of the most fundamental, momentarily inspiriting, but problematic creations of the French Revolution dissipated at last.

NOTES

1. M. Bloch, *French Rural History: an Essay on its Basic Characteristics* (Berkeley, 1966 transl.), xxviii.
2. See J.-L. Crémieux-Brilhac, *La France Libre, De l'appel du 18 Juin à la Libération* (Paris, 1996), 195–8.
3. F. Robert, 'La Marseillaise,' in M. Vovelle (ed.), *L'État de la France pendant la Révolution (1789–1799)* (Paris, 1988), 257–58.
4. J.-L. Crémieux-Brilhac (ed.), *Ici Londres: Les Voix de la liberté, 1940–1944* (5 vols, Paris, 1975–77), V: 99.
5. See the indispensable C. Andrieu, *Le Programme Commun de la Résistance: des idées dans la guerre* (Paris, 1984) for contexts and successive drafts. Also J. Debû-Bridel, *De Gaulle et le Conseil National de la Résistance* (Paris, 1978), chaps 6–7.
6. C.-E. Labrousse, 'Preface: Le Socialisme et la Révolution française,' in J. Jaurès, *Histoire Socialiste de la Révolution Française Vol. I* (Paris, 1963/77).
7. *Combat*, 8 September and 1 October 1944.
8. Saillant speech of 14 October 1944 in *Free France* (New York, 1942–45); Maritain cited in J.-D. Durand, *L'Europe de la Démocratie chrétienne* (Paris, 1995), 222–3.
9. For an overview see V.-A. Montassier, *Les Années d'après-guerre 1944–1949* (Paris, 1980), 111–26.
10. *Le Monde*, 4 June 1945, cited in *Free France*, VIII: 1 July 1945, p. 34.

11. M. Boivin, 'Les Élections de 1945 dans la Manche: Continuité ou changement?', in C. Franck (ed.), *La France de 1945: Résistances, Retours, Renaissances* (Caen, 1996), 249–60.

12. See A. Patrick, 'French Revolutionary Local Government, 1789–1792', in C. Lucas (ed.), *The Political Culture of the French Revolution* (Oxford, 1988), 399–420.

13. See the graphic depictions of this project in D. Nordman and M.-V. Ozouf-Marignier (eds) *Atlas de la Révolution française: vols.4–5: Le Territoire* (Paris, 1992).

14. I. Woloch, *The New Regime: Transformations of the French Civic Order, 1789–1820s* (New York, 1994), 133–43.

15. See *A Critical Dictionary of the French Revolution*, ed. F. Furet and Mona Ozouf (Cambridge MA, 1989 transl.): 'Département' by M. Ozouf and 'Centralization' by Y. Fauchois.

16. See P. M. Jones, *Reform and Revolution in France: The Politics of Transition, 1774–1791* (Cambridge, 1995).

17. Woloch, *The New Regime*, 54–7.

18. P.-J. Hélias, *The Horse of Pride: Life in a Breton Village*, (New Haven, CT, 1978 transl.), 131–5; also E. Weber, *Peasants into Frenchmen: The Modernization of Rural France 1870–1914* (Stanford, CA, 1976), chap. 15: 'Peasants and Politics'.

19. A. Kaspi, *La Libération de la France: Juin 1944-Janvier 1946* (Paris, 1995), 187, on the liberation committees' demarche.

20. See M. Crook, *Elections in the French Revolution: An apprenticeship in democracy, 1789–1799* (Cambridge, 1996), chap. 5.

21. *Free France* VIII: October 1945, 203.

22. Facsimile of the ballot in *Free France*, November 1945, 20.

23. P.-H. Teitgen, *'Faites entrer le témoin suivant' 1940–1958: De la Résistance à la Ve République* (Ouest-France, 1988), 302–3.

24. G. Wright, *The Reshaping of French Democracy* (Boston, 1948), chaps 5–7.

25. See J.-P. Bertaud, *The Army of the French Revolution: From Citizen-Soldiers to Instrument of Power* (Princeton, 1988 transl.), chaps V–VI.

26. Conseil des Cinq Cents: *Rapport par Jourdan sur le recrutement de l'armée de terre* (2 Thermidor an VI).

27. A. Forrest, *Conscripts and Deserters: The Army and French Society during the Revolution and Empire* (Oxford, 1989), chaps 4–6.

28. I. Woloch, 'Napoleonic Conscription: State Power and Civil Society', *Past and Present* (111), May 1986, 101–29; Woloch, *The New Regime*, chap. 13.

29. See C. Clerc, *La Caricature contre Napoléon* (Paris, 1985).

30. See Weber, *Peasants into Frenchmen*, chap. 17.

31. M. Bozon, *Les Conscrits* (Paris, 1981), 21, 32–5, 62, 102–8, 117–19.

32. J. J. Sheehan, *Where Have All the Soldiers Gone? The Transformation of Modern Europe* (Boston, 2008), 167–70, 177–80.

Selected Reading

Aberdam, Serge, et al., *Voter, élire pendant la Révolution française, 1789–1799: Guide pour la recherche* (Paris, 2006).

Bergeron, Louis, *France Under Napoleon* (Princeton, NJ, 1981 transl.).

Crook, Malcolm, *Elections in the French Revolution* (Cambridge, 1996).

Fitzsimmons, Michael, *The Remaking of France: the National Assembly and the Constitution of 1791* (Cambridge, 1994).

Forrest, Alan, *Conscripts and Deserters: The Army and French Society during the Revolution and Empire* (Oxford, 1989).

Forrest, Alan, *Paris, the Provinces and the French Revolution* (London, 2004).

Godechot, Jacques, *Les Institutions de la France sous la Révolution et l'Empire* (Paris, 1968).

Gross, Jean-Pierre, *Fair Shares for All: Jacobin Egalitarianism in Practice* (Cambridge, 1997).

Jones, Peter, *Reform and Revolution in France: the Politics of Transition, 1774–1791* (Cambridge, 1995).

Nora, Pierre, (ed.), *Rethinking France: Les Lieux de Mémoire Volume I: The State* (Chicago, 2002 transl.).

Ozouf-Marignier, Marie-Vic, *La Formation des Départements: la représentation du territoire français à la fin du XVIIIe siècle* (Paris, 1989).

Rioux, Jean-Pierre, *The Fourth Republic, 1944–1958* (Cambridge, 1987 transl.).

Waldinger, René et. al. (eds), *The French Revolution and the Meaning of Citizenship* (Westport, CT, 1993).

Weber, Eugen, *Peasants into Frenchmen: the Modernization of Rural France 1870–1914* (Stanford, CA, 1976).

Woloch, Isser, *The New Regime: Transformations of the French Civic Order, 1789–1820s* (New York, 1994).

CHAPTER 35

LASTING ECONOMIC STRUCTURES

Successes, Failures, and Revolutionary Political Economy

JEFF HORN

ECONOMIC structures during the French Revolution have been largely ignored since the 1980s. Yet the economy's successes and failures profoundly influenced the fate of the Revolution itself. Revolutionary political economy created and dismantled developmental models that shaped the world throughout the nineteenth century and beyond. While the impact of the economy on society and politics has received a measure of recent attention, the economy's inner workings have not. More problematically, those works focusing on economic structures pay scant attention to the Revolution while the lived economic experience of the French people has been overlooked.[1] Without a firm foundation in the events, ideas and policies of the Revolution, investigations of lasting economic structures reflect historiographical or theoretical concerns more than the historical record. Only a more deeply grounded economic history of the decade from 1789 to 1799 can frame the successes and failures of political economy in the French Revolution. This chapter focuses on the economy's mechanics, their evolution under a succession of political regimes, and their long-term impact.

HISTORIANS AND THE STUDY OF REVOLUTIONARY POLITICAL ECONOMY

A new understanding of the long-term competitiveness of the nineteenth-century French economy began with the work of Patrick O'Brien and Caglar Keyder in the

1970s. Although complemented by other debates regarding the course and timing of the Industrial Revolution, O'Brien and Keyder's work stimulated relatively few studies of political economy focused squarely on the Revolutionary decade. Important works on the old regime like that of Philippe Minard end in 1791, while examinations of the nineteenth century begin in 1815. Since the *bicentenaire*, the economic history of the Revolutionary era has been discussed solely in broad explorations of longer periods. Influenced by the cultural turn, English-language commentators on economic matters like John Shovlin and Michael Sonenscher, for example, rely on the sources and modes of analysis of intellectual history. Although notable exceptions like Leonard Rosenband's work on the Montgolfier paper mill exist, meagre attention has been paid to the lived experience of production. This very lack of attention represents an opportunity for deeper analysis.[2]

Three trends stand out in the historiography exploring the economic importance of the French Revolution within the hexagon. Since the 1990s, historians have investigated consumption, both as cultural practice and in generating demand-based economic pressures. Daniel Roche's examination of 'everyday things' spawned numerous studies of consumption patterns. Research into commodities and foodways such as Paul Butel on tea, Steven Kaplan on bread, Judith Miller on the grain trade, and Sydney Watts on meatpacking have illuminated the webs of production and consumption, both domestic and international, that drove old regime market relations and defined their evolution after 1815. Yet these studies pay little attention to the economic impact of war and scarcity. Popular pressure on the state to provision the cities, the difficulty of supplying the armies, and the indelible link between labour and the state should not be ignored. The questions raised by Albert Mathiez should never go out of style.[3]

Mathiez' work on the political economy of 'the threat from below' evokes the labour concerns once so central to the study of the French Revolution. Although never abandoned completely, labour history is a shadow of its former self. François Jarrige on machine-breaking, Michael Fitzsimmons on the *corporations*, Samuel Guicheteau on Nantes' workers, Lisa DiCaprio on female labour in the state-sponsored workshops of the Year II and Daryl Hafter on guildswomen continue a proud tradition. It is both a strength and a weakness of these works that they all focus on the longer term: the era from 1789 to 1794 or 1799 as 'the Revolution' and the unique significance of labour during that era has been shunted aside by other questions, other concerns.[4]

A renewed interest in the impact of science and technology is the third historiographical trend in the economic history of the revolutionary period. Ken Alder and Jessica Riskin played some part in this development, but Patrice Bret and Charles Gillispie have been the driving forces in this revival. The Revolution's mobilization of France's scientific talent had great successes, but left behind outstanding figures like Antoine Lavoisier and the marquis de Condorcet. The current emphasis on expertise in the historiography of science and technology furnishes new ways of understanding the importance of the shift in educational emphasis toward practical application. Opportunities abound to explore the economic ramifications of the altered relationship of experts to the French state that bore such fecund harvests in the nineteenth century. Much work remains to be done to understand the shifting relationships among science, technology and economy during the Revolutionary decade.[5]

For a historiography as broad and as deep as that of the era of the French Revolution, it is surprising that since the *bicentenaire*, only Guy Lemarchand has written an explicitly *economic* history.[6] Lemarchand's excellent study is, however, focused on the role of the economy in undermining the old regime and France's inability to maintain the industrialization begun under Napoleon. The Revolution itself is not the emphasis. This observation is not meant as criticism, but rather as a plea for further attention. It is also noteworthy that, despite the considerable attention scholars have devoted to the colonies, the economic effect of the rebellion in Saint-Domingue on France has been neither fully delineated nor distinguished from those produced by the blockade. In sum, important work remains to be done.

REFORM, RATIONALISM, AND THE 'THREAT FROM BELOW' FROM 1789 TO 1791

Beginning in 1789, revolutionary violence precipitated the demolition of the structures and cultural attitudes underpinning the old regime's economy. Between July and October, in the provinces of Normandy, Champagne, Picardy, and Forez, crowd action destroyed approximately 1,000 technologically advanced, labour-saving machines worth hundreds of thousands of *livres*. French machine-breaking erased years of government and private investment. More importantly, however, popular rage against labour-saving machinery amidst a major subsistence crisis signalled the rapid ascent of a new, more politically insistent, yet equally market sensitive moral economy. Traumatized by widespread unemployment following the passage of the Anglo-French Commercial Treaty of 1786, labourers forcefully insisted on preserving jobs at the expense of international industrial competitiveness. For at least a decade, entrepreneurs and state officials at every level were constrained by that moral economy. This shift had profound consequences: it limited innovation and heightened the state's economic role while amplifying the size and scope of the underground economy. Unlike their British counterparts, French entrepreneurs after 1789 could not rely on the state's ability or even willingness to control the working classes on their behalf, altering the course of continental economic development.[7]

Machine-breaking occurred in or near urban areas. In the countryside, the Great Fear pushed the National Assembly to abolish the privileges that typified the old regime on the night of 4–5 August. Popular violence incited the deputies to write the *Declaration of the Rights of Man and the Citizen* and to lay the foundations for an administrative system based on the principles of liberty and equality. 1789's 'threat from below', exemplified by crowd action, both drove economic reform and limited the application of liberal principles.[8]

Commentators generally describe the chief policy goals of 'liberalism' during the French Revolution as dismantling 'feudal society' with its myriad impediments on enterprise while substituting individual property-ownership for collective rights. As practised by Louis XVI and the National Assembly, Enlightened rationalism entailed uniform application of law and equality of opportunity. The goal was to create a unified French economy out of a welter of fragmented markets and privileged enclaves. Faith in individual initiative, not to mention a chronic shortage of funds, led the central state to abandon nearly all direct efforts to foster economic development.[9]

Constrained by the enormous state debt and the complex *bricolage* of old regime economic regulation, the revolutionaries chose a different approach to fostering development. Legislative action in 1791 focused on creating a new legal and administrative structure that transformed the economy over the long term. A new patent system inaugurated in January sought to encourage innovation and publicize new technologies. In March, the Allarde Law abolished the guilds, formal apprenticeships and nearly all restrictions on entering a trade. Passed in June, the Le Chapelier Law forbade all worker coalitions. Quality inspection of goods ended that September: anyone could make and/ or sell almost anything they liked.[10] Sweeping away the debris of the old regime and its moral economy, policy-makers situated the principle of equality of opportunity at the heart of the emerging liberal economic structure.

From 1789, a rationalized taxation system was a major ambition of the revolutionaries. To pay off the debt, the National Assembly established a modest customs duty at the frontiers and a direct land tax to be collected by salaried employees overseen by elected representatives of the populace. Although this system proved more efficient in collecting revenue, the new regime had too many needs and obligations to make progress paying off the debt.

The intransigence of the debt along with Enlightenment anti-clericalism motivated the confiscation of the lands of the Roman Catholic Church. In November 1789, the National Assembly sequestered Church lands. Four months later, the deputies nationalized these properties and ordered them to be sold at public auction. A substantial proportion of the arable land held by the monarchy and *émigré* nobility was also seized and put on the block beginning in 1793. The appropriation and sale of nearly all common land and the abolition of primogeniture also expanded opportunities to purchase land. Taken together, these measures accelerated long-term shifts in the pattern of property-holding while improving rural living standards. (The refusal of many peasants to pay either the tithe or seigneurial dues after the night of 4 August also robustly boosted disposable incomes.) Most 'national lands' were acquired by well-to-do members of the urban middle classes or prosperous tenant-farmers, but a regionally variable amount of land ended up in the hands of small peasant proprietors. It was no accident that nineteenth-century French agriculture was even more dominated by small-holding producers than it had been before 1789. Land redistribution along with the strengthening of small-scale agriculture were two of the most significant socio-economic consequences of the French Revolution. Although the sale of national lands has been studied extensively, the economic impact of those sales deserves further research, locally, regionally, and nationally.[11]

The revolutionaries were financial innovators, but the role of 'rationality' in their actions has been fiercely debated.[12] In December 1789, the French central state issued 400 million *livres* worth of treasury bonds to bridge the gap between old and new taxes while servicing the debt of about 4 billion *livres*. These '*assignats*' paid 3 per cent interest. The bonds were backed by clerical lands worth an estimated 2.5 billion *livres*. From April 1790, the *assignats* no longer earned interest. They became legal tender that November. After April 1793, gold and silver were not permitted to circulate. The National Assembly issued more and more *assignats* in ever smaller denominations, creating a paper currency.

In 1790–1, the national lands' value greatly exceeded the nominal amount of paper money in circulation. But waning confidence in the central state fuelled inflation, depreciating the *assignat*'s value by 25 per cent by December 1791 and 40 per cent by March 1792 (see Table 35.1). The ease of issuing new paper money and the state's inability to cut spending without generating social unrest accelerated the cycle of inflation and depreciation.[13] What began as a short-term, fiscally responsible financial instrument spiralled out of control.

An astonishing 45.6 billion *livres* of paper money were printed by the end of May 1795, enfeebling the financial system and the economy. The *assignat* was eliminated in February 1796 and replaced with *mandats territoriaux* backed by the sale of 600 million *livres* worth of forested national lands. Too little, too late; France declared bankruptcy in 1797, defaulting on some two-thirds of state debt valued at approximately 2.6 billion *livres*. The rest was paid off in nearly worthless paper currency or in national lands.[14] Eliminating the debt burden accumulated by the old regime and the Revolution facilitated the return of financial stability and cleared the way for future growth.

English-language accounts of late eighteenth-century liberal economic reform are largely divorced from this financial and political milieu.[15] They overemphasize the influence of Adam Smith and downplay the complexity of the physiocrats' legacy.[16] Such overemphasis appears not only in examinations of the intellectual framework and actions of key policy-makers, but also in the rare studies of the successes and failures of innovating entrepreneurs. Unfortunately, *economic* analyses of the *economic* changes inaugurated in 1789–91 embrace intellectual or theoretical perspectives that minimize the lived experiences of producers or consumers. The Revolutionary period abounds

Table 35.1 Nominal value of *Assignats* in metallic currency (in percentages)[17]

1791	1792		1793			1794			1795		
Dec.	Mar.	Dec.	Sept.	Nov.	Dec.	July	Sept.	Dec.	Apr.	July	Oct.
75	60	50	22	33	48	31	34	20	8	3	.01

with untapped opportunities for scholars to develop concrete examples to apply theory to practice and practice to theory.

An institutional approach to understanding economic change associated with Douglass C. North underpins a number of important recent studies of the revolutionary era. Through the lens of the cultural turn, historians have explored how institutions, like the *corporations*, shaped the French economy in general and crucial labour practices such as apprenticeship, before, during, and after 1789. In combination with the results of the steady output of local studies from French scholars, these works reveal the constricted possibilities of applying Smithian liberalism. Laissez-faire capitalism as envisioned by liberal economic theory was never an option for Revolutionary France, constrained as it was by the need to respond to crushing public debt, the threat from below and, after 1792, war. Despite the dismantling of both the 'absolute' monarchy and feudalism, France's economy remained dependent on state action, both institutionally and materially. Although not every succeeding regime effectively took up the reins, the French economy could not escape the state's yoke put in place during the age of Louis XIV.

REVOLUTIONARY POLITICAL ECONOMY DURING THE TERROR

In 1793–4, the revolutionaries waged a war for survival. This relentless conflict undermined the political class's commitment to liberal economic reform and necessitated the creation of a rudimentary command economy. Beset by domestic rebellion, the Jacobin Republic was invaded on all frontiers while Great Britain and its allies established an increasingly effective maritime blockade and attacked France's colonies and coasts. Industries and agricultural producers reliant on trade lost direct access to crucial raw materials and long-standing markets. With commercial links between France and its Empire severed and with the slaves of Saint-Domingue in revolt, ports from Marseille to Bordeaux to Nantes, withered on the vine. The Revolutionary wars destroyed the colonial system that generated so much of France's eighteenth-century prosperity; and Britain's economy benefited from France's losses.

The Revolutionary state faced almost impossible challenges. Cut off from foreign sources of food, invasion and civil war prevented normal trade in grain. Not only did the armies need to be supplied, but to forestall further outbreaks of popular violence, militants in France's cities, especially Paris, had to receive their daily bread at affordable prices. Market forces could not accomplish these Herculean tasks. The French central state opted for thorough-going economic intervention: food was rationed with the military and the cities receiving priority.[18]

On 4 May 1793, the National Convention fixed prices by establishing the 'Maximum' amount that could be charged for grain and bread.[19] Grain could be sold only in officially sanctioned marketplaces at prices determined by local officials. Prices were set at an average of recent market rates and were to be lowered month by month until the harvest, when the system would lapse. Grain hoarders faced the death penalty.

These halting measures were followed up on 11 September with universal price ceilings on grain and flour. Departments could fix transport costs, requisition food, and establish public granaries. Administrative parochialism, however, led to a kind of economic warfare between institutions of local government that had to be mediated by representatives-on-mission from Paris. That administrative boundaries drawn by the central state in 1789–90 had little correlation to market supply zones only aggravated the situation.

On 29 September 1793, the Maximum price system was extended to all essential goods ranging from raw materials and manufactured items to most foodstuffs. This 'General Maximum' set prices at the local levels of 1790 plus one-third, but undervalued transport costs drastically, encouraging producers to bring their goods to the nearest rather than the neediest market. Transaction profits were set at 10 per cent for retailers and 5 per cent for wholesalers. In the spring of 1794, the Committee of Public Safety began—with increasing success—to standardize prices first regionally and then nationally.

To unravel the inflationary spiral, the General Maximum regulated wages as well as prices. After consulting with employers, workers and representatives of the central state, municipalities could set wage rates no higher than 50 per cent above the level of 1790. Wage limits were less strictly enforced than price controls because in many areas and in several skilled trades, labour costs had risen far above mandated levels. In addition, across vast swathes of the country, food was unavailable at the Maximum price and required recourse to the black market or payment of a supplemental fee that had to be authorized by representatives of the Committee of Public Safety. Despite the government's 1794 crackdown on the popular movement, wages remained more resistant to standardization or limitation than prices. Historians have focused on the political ramifications of the Maximums; they deserve equal attention as state economic practice.

The Committee of Public Safety proclaimed the first universal draft (*levée en masse*) on all males between the ages of 18 and 64 on 23 August 1793. Farmers and day-labourers in grain-producing regions, arms-workers along with carters who transported raw materials, food and munitions were exempted from the military. But these workers still had to perform national service for 12–14 hours per day (not including breaks) with only one day off in ten. They also had to move where the government wanted them. Many transport workers and those with vital metalworking skills relocated according to the advance and retreat of the armies.

Foreign trade was subjected to state planning. War and blockade did not stifle all exterior commerce. Blockade runners provided limited access to foreign goods. Neutral ships were encouraged to visit French ports where they were permitted to sell goods at prices above the General Maximum and could purchase luxury goods, especially lace, silk, fine wine, and tobacco, at steep discounts. The art collections and household goods of *émigré* nobles and clergy as well as the former royal family were sold abroad to buy arms, horses and raw materials. Through intermediaries in Hamburg, Genoa and Switzerland, the Trade Commission established by the Committee of Public Safety acquired a significant and increasing amount of vital war materiel.

Smugglers supplied scarce merchandise, and smuggling had long been a major occupation of otherwise law-abiding citizens along the frontiers and in the ports. In wartime, smugglers became entrepreneurial heroes by bringing in otherwise unavailable goods. In the ports of Bordeaux, Dunkerque, and Le Havre and frontier cities like Strasbourg, smuggling was an accepted business practice that drew quasi-public investment. Wine and luxury goods were exchanged for British cotton textiles, Italian olive oil, German steel, and Polish grain. The extent of this vast illegal trade is impossible to measure, but it should be recognized that smuggling facilitated the circulation of goods while casting deep shadows of doubt on official trade figures.[20]

For state planners, politics often trumped economic considerations, again reminding us of the limits of liberal policies. In Paris, the government created a massive arms industry from scratch. Skilled labour was conscripted from across the nation and sent to the capital. By fiat, scarce raw materials, steam engines, and tools were diverted to the capital. Even if economic efficiency was firmly subordinated to political needs, the state's investment paid considerable dividends. In thirteen months of operation, at a cost of 1.8 million *livres*, Paris' thirty-nine public workshops, and 5,400 workers fabricated or repaired nearly 155,000 muskets and pistols along with 1,500 bronze cannon, surpassing the combined production of the seven other major arms-producing centres.[21] At the same time, the government established a host of factories and workshops in Paris that made bayonets, swords, boots, uniforms, hats, gunpowder, ammunition, barrels, harnesses, and saddles, as well as fittings and munitions for the navy. Many workers were paid according to the Maximum. Most skilled workers were conscripted and then, under the supervision of experienced foremen, given the necessary raw materials and told exactly what techniques to use and how to perform their tasks. State officials set high production quotas and workers were punished or lost wages for each failure to meet quota. With food scarce, the state fed most workers and then reduced wages accordingly. At the height of the war crisis, tens of thousands of workers were so employed.[22]

Arms-workers, carters, farmers, and soldiers were not the only ones called to provide national service to the economy. The Committee of Public Safety mobilized France's scientific elite to improve industrial production. Chemist Jean-Antoine Chaptal bettered the process to turn saltpetre into gunpowder and taught his method to hundreds of foremen and supervisors. To enhance French arms and industrial efficiency, chemist Claude Berthollet and mathematicians Gaspard Monge and Alexandre Vandermonde wrote a widely distributed pamphlet describing best practice in steel manufacture. A telegraph warned of threats to the northern frontier, aerial balloons directed artillery fire and other technological innovations were tried or proposed during this frenetic time. In 1794, amidst the distractions of war and terror, the Committee of Public Safety founded the National Institute of Arts and Sciences and the Polytechnic Institute that indelibly linked scientific education and government service. The application of improved scientific capabilities bolstered morale and provided tangible economic benefits in both the short and the long term.

ENDING THE TERROR AND THE SEARCH
FOR A NEW ECONOMIC DIRECTION

Government-mandated wage and price controls could be enforced only by violence or the threat of violence. Making people accept payment for goods and services solely in depreciated *assignats* required similar pressure. The Maximums limited inflation, boosted the production of war materiel, and prevented famine (if not widespread hunger). The Jacobin Republic's mobilization of France's wealth of scientific and technological talent yielded material benefits in the manufacture of war matériel. Many enterprises established at the state's behest achieved impressive productivity gains. A modern study of the long-term economic effects of the industrial achievements detailed by Camille Richard would shed new light not only on the impact of the Terror but also on the potential of this form of state mobilization.[23] Placing these concerns in the context of the early stages of the Industrial Revolution would also reshape the debates on the effectiveness of liberal economics, French 'retardation', and 'why was Britain first?'

The Committee of Public Safety modelled how a state could encourage industrial development in the crucible of war and revolution. Deploying Terror as an essential tool of government policy, the Jacobin Republic kept the economy afloat long enough for the army swollen by the *levée en masse* to defeat the various Federalist cities, repel invaders, and finally to go on the offensive.[24] A significant (though hotly debated) percentage of the French people believed that protecting the republic merited such extraordinary measures and was worth the cost.

The Terror was less traumatic to end politically than economically. After 9 Thermidor, the National Convention resumed control over the economy and slowly restored a more liberal approach to policy despite the shock to the moral economy of the popular classes. A new Maximum published two weeks later abandoned strict oversight of wages. Despite a large pay increase, Parisians, led by the mass of arms-workers, demanded additional hikes. Rather than succumb to this pressure and fearing to unleash state repression once more, the government simply disbanded the workshops built with such great effort over the previous eighteen months.

Market forces pushed the *assignat* into free-fall in the autumn of 1794. By December, official prices had become a joke, ignored equally by buyers, sellers, and authorities. The abolition of the Maximum on 24 December only recognized the government's inability to control the economy. That same night a severe freeze presaged the worst winter of the century, intensifying demand for basic commodities, especially coal and firewood. With the transport system overextended by the advance of the Republic's armies, essential goods became increasingly scarce, accelerating the *assignat*'s final collapse.

Abandoning a command economy enforced by Terror was harrowing. For a huge number of entrepreneurs reliant on government patronage, payment in ever more worthless paper money rather than in raw materials and/or food made continued operation almost impossible. Chemical plants, forges, and mines suffered labour short-ages as essential skilled workers were discharged from national service. The advance of French arms also enabled refugees to return home. With transportation focused on mil-itary needs, the economic environment squashed many promising initiatives. The trau-mas associated with the reactionary White Terror precluded effective state intervention. A stunningly high percentage of the enterprises established with high hopes during the era of the Maximum collapsed between 9 Thermidor and the assumption of power by the Directory in November 1795, severely damaging French economic competitiveness.

Why did the government fail to address the economy's problems? As debates in the various legislative Assemblies and in the press demonstrate conclusively, the leaders of the National Convention and Directory certainly recognized what was going on. Many had reasonable, practical ideas about how to revive the French economy. The state's lack of an effective response is linked inextricably to one of the chief controversies about the legacy of the French Revolution. Although it saved the Revolution, the state's resort to Terror left government planning and centralized control of the economy thoroughly dis-credited amongst economic elites.[25] After 1794, few French accepted Terror either as state policy or as moral economy. This view encompassed the economic goals of the Year II such as ensuring the right to work, state provision of basic commodities at fixed prices, and redistributing wealth or land. Despite the success of the Jacobin Republic's economic management, this emerging consensus about the Terror on the part of France's economic and political elites anathematized this model of economic development. At the same time, militants who hoped to enact the Revolution's egalitarian agenda recognized that seizing control of the state had to be their first step to transform society.

This vision of exercising the state's power to refashion society was articulated by Gracchus Babeuf, who led a pathetic, abortive conspiracy to overthrow the govern-ment on behalf of the working classes in 1796. Although Babeuf's conspiracy never threatened elite control, thinkers like Karl Marx recognized the importance of his analysis. Throughout the nineteenth century, many egalitarians believed that only a powerful state with direct control of the economy could overcome the inherent exploitation of capitalism. In Russia, Vladimir Lenin claimed that he was following Babeuf's strategy when he orchestrated the October Revolution in 1917. On the other side of the coin, even a leader as powerful and popular as Napoleon Bonaparte could not overcome the distrust of European elites toward types of economic management that appeared to give too many opportunities to the working classes, thereby reviving fears of the Reign of Terror. Until the age of Napoleon III, concern over the growing numbers, influence and concentration of the working classes restrained state over-sight of economic matters. In the face of British predominance and in the absence of stimulus from the Empire, restrictions on the scope of state action limited French economic growth.

The reduced reach and prioritization of politics by the Revolutionary state were reflected in neglect of the transportation network. Highway maintenance lapsed except to support the war effort. Without labour levies to sustain them, many local roads fell further into disrepair. The blockade choked coastal shipping, removing alternatives to overland and riverine transportation. By appropriating horses and oxen for the army and necessitating that conquered territories be linked to the transport web, the war exacerbated transport problems. The expense, difficulty and lengthy delays involved in overland haulage represented a major drag on commerce, industry and agriculture. Transportation inadequacies enabled Britain and other competitors to capture markets that had long been French preserves. The economic performance of Revolutionary and Napoleonic Europe conclusively demonstrated the competitive disadvantages of overland and riverine continental transportation until the creation of linked national railroad networks after 1850.

OPPORTUNITIES ABROAD

Geographical constraints and transportation shortcomings combined to fragment markets in the territories controlled by Revolutionary France. This fragmentation ensured that even relatively inefficient manufacturers and merchants with poor reputations enjoyed considerable opportunities for profit-taking. Satisfying pent-up consumer demand and/or providing previously unavailable goods to new buyers in the expanding Republic attracted entrepreneurs from across the length and breadth of Europe. The collapse of maritime trade due to naval blockade and the slave revolt in Saint-Domingue encouraged the development of overland trading relationships as did the wartime prohibition of English goods from the French sphere of influence. Many speculators and government contractors invested their windfall profits in national lands and then established manufacturing or mining enterprises. High inflation kept real wages low, especially for women and children. Metallurgy and coal mining flourished thanks to wartime needs. Protected from direct British competition, entrepreneurs in cotton textiles invested in new technologies or mechanized their mills in the hope of supplying the continental market. Yet the vast majority of these efforts soon failed. Generally speaking, these new enterprises took advantage of temporary, artificial conditions; they were not truly internationally competitive. The war crisis of 1799 and soaring economic uncertainty wiped out nearly all of these businesses, forcing the Consulate to devote major resources to rebuilding the economy.

Despite the vagaries of the business climate, the Revolution offered many compensatory benefits. Belgium was conquered in 1795 and remained part of France for the next two decades. The German-speaking left bank of the Rhine River was seized in 1795 and stayed under French control until 1813 except for a brief interlude in 1799–1800. Also in 1795, the Batavian Republic under French tutelage emerged from the Netherlands. On the Italian peninsula, sister republics garrisoned by French troops were established in 1797–9, and, north of Naples, proved stable until they were absorbed directly into Napoleonic France. The Swiss Confederation became the Helvetic Republic in 1798. For at least fifteen years, French expansion provided an impressive array of economic resources and opportunities.

Territorial expansion enabled the Revolutionary government to survive. Conquered lands were looted of metallic currency and bullion reserves while enduring heavy taxation. In 1798–9 alone, the taxes from occupied territories amounted to 158 million *livres*. Cities that resisted French rule were fined extraordinary sums. Rome, for example, had to pay 70 million *livres*. Through conquest, France acquired enormous supplies of vital raw materials such as Belgian coal, Rhenish iron, and Piedmontese silk. France also benefited from the scientific and technological expertise, not to mention the business acumen of its new citizens. Particularly under Napoleon, entrepreneurs from Belgium, the German lands and later the Netherlands and northern Italy rushed to take advantage of the opportunities offered by the vastly expanded French domestic market and Napoleon's ongoing military needs stretching from Portugal to Poltava. Direct access to French customers and the right to become military suppliers improved these entrepreneurs' ability to make large-scale profits. Despite war's dislocations and continuing political unrest, these core areas boomed under French control, providing not only a path to survival, but also an almost unprecedented opportunity to flourish.[26]

SUCCESSES AND FAILURES

Land redistribution was the most profound long-term socio-economic result of the decade from 1789 to 1799.[27] In rural areas, living standards either held steady or dipped slightly, thanks to a relative wage increase. For many, the sale of most of the Church's property and a substantial proportion of the arable lands held by the monarchy and the nobility was the Revolution's chief tangible benefit. Redistributing property satisfied the desires for change of those who worked the land. The Revolutionary and Napoleonic regimes relied on the support of purchasers of national lands who feared the loss of their acquisitions. Short-term political advantages, however, paled beside the long-term consequences of this transfer of economic power. Without that transfer, nineteenth-century France would not have been dominated so deeply or so long by smallholders. In conjunction with high tariff barriers and the exploitation of conquered territories, the break-up of large estates encouraged specialty cultivation of crops, such as grapes or mulberries, to earn higher returns while slowing down more broadly based improvements in agricultural output and productivity. The dispersal of property-holding that began in the 1790s shaped France's economy and society throughout the nineteenth century.

Urban living standards generally declined during the Revolutionary decade. Cities and regions dependent on industry or maritime trade sank into depression; in southern France, some areas never recovered. Deprived of foreign markets and colonial sales, French manufacturers concentrated on satisfying the domestic market. The emigration, diminished circumstances or death of the royal family, nobility and clergy eliminated the market for most luxury goods and services. Groups and individuals whose incomes came from property-owning or financial investments were ruined by inflation, bankruptcies and nationalizations. War and tariffs lessened the need for quality manufacture. High demand for most manufactured items ensured sales. Domestic scarcity and the popularity of foreign goods afforded increased opportunities for smugglers to nurture the underground economy. These changes slowed French economic development.

In 1799, French industrial output was only about two-thirds that of 1789, itself a troubled year (using the same pre-war boundaries). Given the manufacturing economy's dependence (at least until 1792) on exports either to the colonies or to other European states, this degree of recovery could be considered something of an economic success story. That said, oscillations in the success of Revolutionary arms ensured that French industrial development would be shallow, fragmented, and internationally uncompetitive. Northern and eastern France held up better than the south and the west auguring the nineteenth-century developmental pattern.

During the French Revolution, investors and entrepreneurs lost faith in the state's policies, ability to protect its citizens, and durability. The Republic spent its money on survival, both political and military, almost completely neglecting strategic investment in the economy. The possibility of Revolutionary violence choked off innovation in production especially labour-saving mechanization. By sapping the confidence of entrepreneurs, the threat from below slowed down French industrial development considerably. Thus, shifts in moral economy represented a far more significant drag to French economic performance and technological creativity than any diversion of effort into military endeavours or politics. In consequence, Britain widened its industrial lead with profound consequences in the nineteenth century.

Legacies

At the same time that the Revolution retarded short-term economic growth, the revolutionaries paved the way for nineteenth-century economic growth. Expanded landownership, an updated administrative and tax structure, and the elimination of feudalism accompanied the eradication of the state's crushing debt. Vital educational institutions were founded, strengthening the link between science and the state. Increasingly reliable statistics track economic performance after the end of allied occupation in 1818. For the century between the Hundred Days and the outbreak of the First World War, per capita economic growth averaged a 1.4 per cent annual increase. Agriculture did well with annual growth of 1.2 per cent between 1820 and 1870 while industrial advance is calculated at between 2.5 and 3.4 per cent.[28] Revolutionary reforms made this considerable economic success possible. But were the Revolution's reforms sufficient for France to keep pace with Britain? My findings suggest that, by themselves, the economic and administrative reforms of 1789–99 did not generate France's impressive economic performance during the nineteenth century.

Although French growth over the long term even compared to Britain must impress, the Revolution damaged the economy, particularly the industrial and commercial sectors. The loss of overseas colonies and trading partners along with the blockade bankrupted the ports and deprived France of needed capital, raw materials and markets. Overland commerce could not compensate fully. Without the windfall commercial profits, resources and markets provided by the colonies, and in competition with the Republic's enormous financial demands, French industrial development was starved of capital and state support. The currency's collapse, runaway inflation, and the state's debt default sapped private investors' ability to step into the breach and their faith in the security of investments. Threatened by a moral economy that legitimated popular violence, the decisions made by many entrepreneurs to focus on smuggling, cater to the demands of the state or accept the limited profits to be made from property-owning all appear eminently rational. Although it was by no means inevitable, Revolutionary politics delayed the onset of the Industrial Revolution in France. Unlike its British rival, France did not experience a transformation from Smithian growth based fundamentally on commercial profits to Schumpeterian capitalist expansion founded on innovation and entrepreneurialism. In economic terms, this belated transition represented the French Revolution's most important economic impact, both domestically and internationally.

The postponed onset of industrial society also meant that liberal economic principles remained more of an objective than a reality. In particular, the ongoing role of the state in directing the economy and the revival of various forms of economic privilege after 1804 and continuing well into the nineteenth century restricted the impact of individualism at every level of society from the manufacturer who faced militant brotherhoods of journeymen to the day-labourer who no longer owed homage to the local lord, but whose opportunities remained almost equally limited. The French Revolution did not inaugurate a liberal society; rather it gave rise to a modern society in which individual interests remained mediated and constricted by collectivities and a semi-autonomous state apparatus.

The Revolution redistributed an impressive, but impossible to measure amount of wealth. This reallocation among cities, regions, groups and individuals can be said to have contributed to the rise to power of the 'bourgeoisie', so long as those bourgeois are understood as landowning notables of diverse social origins whose interest in the means of production did not extend far beyond the protection of landed property. These bourgeois were mostly unconcerned with maximizing profits and little involved in economically groundbreaking activities. These notables coalesced under Napoleon and waxed in influence until the July Monarchy. Bearing only superficial resemblance to a Marxian economic conception of this pivotal group, this bourgeoisie politically dominated France until the Third Republic.[29] Compared to the last decades of the Bourbon monarchy, the Revolution lessened the collective policy-making influence of entrepreneurs actively engaged in innovative agriculture, commerce, manufacturing or finance.

From 9 Thermidor, a significant proportion of the bourgeoisie worked for the increasingly bureaucratized state, a trend that accelerated under the Consulate. On both sides of this revolving door, the bourgeoisie espoused social order and certain types of liberal reform as the best means of containing the threat from below. Shifts in the economic mindset and interests of many bourgeois surely slowed the pace of economic growth in France by maintaining the influence of landed property and embracing conservative approaches to economic development. In relative terms, investment in innovation lagged along with state encouragement of industry. The 'bourgeoisie' that emerged during the Revolutionary decade could not, and did not wish to, compete with the English at their own game, as Bourbon policy-makers under Louis XVI had sought to do, both in commerce and in industry. Nor were these bourgeois willing to revive a command economy as in the Year II. Rather, after 1794, the French landowning elite had to develop a different approach to industrial competition. The foundations of that alternative pathway to industrial society were laid during the Revolutionary decade, but the edifice was erected by Napoleon and decorated by the Restoration and July Monarchy.

The economy speeded the downfall of the Bourbon monarchy and left a variety of legacies to the nineteenth century. We need to situate any consideration of those legacies in the Revolution itself. Beyond the deployment of groundbreaking economic models, the impact of the threat from below and French moral economy more generally shaped the course of the Revolution, nineteenth-century economic development, and events around the world. The Revolution was more than an end of the old regime or a tumultuous interlude on the way to industrial society. Reviving the study of economic practice before, during, and after the Revolution as well as under its various regimes ensures that both continuities and changes occurring in a society in revolution all receive adequate attention. Judging the Revolution's successes or failures through the prism of the periods before or after does not do justice to the impact of the immense transformation that took place between 1789 and 1799.

Notes

1. It is revealing that a historian as deeply learned as Peter McPhee paid so little attention to economic matters in a work entitled *Living the French Revolution* (Basingstoke, Hampshire, 2009).
2. Patrick O'Brien and Caglar Keyder, *Economic Growth in Britain and France 1780–1914: Two Paths to the Twentieth Century* (London, 1978); Philippe Minard, *La fortune du colbertisme: État et industrie dans la France des Lumières* (Paris, 1998); John Shovlin, *The Political Economy of Virtue: Luxury, Patriotism, and the Origins of the French Revolution* (Ithaca, NY, 2006); Michael Sonenscher, *Before the Deluge: Public Debt, Inequality, and the Intellectual Origins of the French Revolution* (Princeton, 2007); and Leonard N. Rosenband, *Papermaking in Eighteenth-Century France: Management, Labor, and Revolution at the Montgolfier Mill, 1761–1805* (Baltimore, 2000).
3. Daniel Roche, *A History of Everyday Things: The Birth of Consumption in France, 1600–1800*, trans. Brian Pearce (Cambridge, 2000 [1997]); Paul Butel, *Histoire du thé* (Paris,

1989); Sydney Watts, *Meat, Modernity, and the Rise of the Slaughterhouse* (Lebanon, NH, 2008); Steven L. Kaplan, *Provisioning Paris: Merchants and Millers in the Grain and Flour Trade During the Eighteenth Century* (Ithaca, NY, 1984); Judith A. Miller, *Mastering the Market: The State and the Grain Trade in Northern France, 1700–1860* (Cambridge, 1999); and Albert Mathiez, *La vie chère et le mouvement social sous la Terreur*, 2 vols (Paris, 1927).

4. Lisa DiCaprio, *The Origins of the Welfare State: Women, Work, and the French Revolution* (Urbana, IL, 2007); François Jarrige, *Au temps des 'tueuses de bras': Les bris de machines à l'aube de l'ère industrielle* (Rennes, 2009); Samuel Guicheteau, *La Révolution des ouvriers nantais: Mutation économique, identité sociale et dynamique révolutionnaire (1740–1815)* (Rennes, 2008); Michael Fitzsimmons, *From Artisan to Worker: Guilds, the French State, and the Organization of Labor, 1776–1821* (Cambridge, 2010); and Daryl Hafter, *Women at Work in Preindustrial France* (University Park, PA, 2007).

5. Ken Alder, *Engineering the Revolution: Arms and Enlightenment in France, 1763–1815* (Princeton, 1997); Jessica Riskin, *Science in the Age of Sensibility: The Sentimental Empiricists of the French Enlightenment* (Chicago, 2002); Patrice Bret, *L'État, l'armée, la science: L'invention de la recherche publique en France (1763–1830)* (Rennes, 2002); and Charles C. Gillispie, *Science and Polity in France: The Revolutionary and Napoleonic Years* (Princeton, 2004).

6. Guy Lemarchand, *L'Économie en France de 1770 à 1830: De la crise de l'Ancien Régime à la Révolution industrielle* (Paris, 2008).

7. This interpretation was set out in Jeff Horn, *The Path Not Taken: French Industrialization in the Age of Revolution, 1750–1830* (Cambridge, MA, 2006), 102–18 and elucidated further in '"A Beautiful Madness": Privilege, the Machine Question and Industrial Development in Normandy in 1789', *Past & Present* 217 (November 2012), 149–85. See also Jarrige, *Au temps des 'tueuses de bras'*.

8. Georges Lefebvre, *Les paysans du nord pendant la révolution française* (Lille, 1924) and Abel Poitrineau, *Ils travaillaient la France: Métiers et mentalities du XVIe au XIXe siècle* (Paris, 1992). See also Michael P. Fitzsimmons, *The Night the Old Regime Ended: August 4, 1789 and the French Revolution* (University Park, PA, 1998).

9. Philip T. Hoffman, *Growth in a Traditional Society: The French Countryside 1450–1815* (Princeton, 1997); Paul Cheney, *Revolutionary Commerce: Globalization and the French Monarchy* (Cambridge, MA, 2010); and Hilton L. Root, *The Fountain of Privilege: Political Foundations of Markets in Old Regime France and England* (Berkeley, 1994).

10. On quality control, see Fitzsimmons, *From Artisan to Worker*.

11. Hoffman, *Growth in a Traditional Society*; John Markoff, *The Abolition of Feudalism: Peasants, Lords and Legislators in the French Revolution* (University Park, PA, 1996); P. M. Jones, *The Peasantry in the French Revolution* (Cambridge, 1988); and Bernard Bodinier and Éric Teyssier, *L'événement le plus important de la Révolution: la vente des biens nationaux en France et dans les territoires annexes 1789–1867* (Paris, 2000).

12. Philip T. Hoffman, Gilles Postel-Vinay, and Jean-Laurent Rosenthal, *Priceless Markets: The Political Economy of Credit in Paris, 1660–1870* (Chicago, 2000).

13. Florin Aftalion, *The French Revolution: An Economic Interpretation*, trans. Martin Thom (Cambridge 1990 [1987]), 184–5.

14. Marcel Marion, *Histoire financière de la France depuis 1715*, 6 vols (Paris, 1927–31), 4: 55–69.

15. This and the following paragraph rely on Sonenscher, *Before the Deluge*; Steven L. Kaplan and Philippe Minard, eds., *La France, malade du corporatisme?: XVIIIe–XXe siècles* (Paris,

2004); Minard, *La fortune du colbertisme*; Steven L. Kaplan, *La fin des corporations* (Paris, 2001); and Michael Sibalis, 'Corporatism after the Corporations: The Debate on Restoring the Guilds Under Napoleon I and the Restoration', *French Historical Studies* 15 (1987), 718–30.

16. See, for example, Alessandro Stanziani: *Rules of Exchange: French Capitalism in Comparative Perspective, Eighteenth to Early Twentieth Centuries* (Cambridge, 2012). There is an important distinction between Smithian gains based on commercial development and Schumpeterian gains founded on technology and entrepreneurialism. Here I elide that distinction. William N. Parker, *Europe, America, and the Wider World: Essays on the Economic History of Western Capitalism*, vol. 1, *Europe and the World Economy* (Cambridge, 1984).

17. Compiled from Aftalion, *The French Revolution*, 171; William Doyle, *The Oxford History of the French Revolution* (Oxford, 1989), 265, 285; Albert Soboul, *The French Revolution 1787–1799: From the Storming of the Bastille to Napoleon*, trans. Alan Forrest and Colin Jones (New York, 1974 [1962]), 435–6; and Donald M. G. Sutherland, *France 1789–1815: Revolution and Counterrevolution* (New York, 1986), 93–4.

18. Jean-Pierre Gross, *Fair Shares for All: Jacobin Egalitarianism in Practice* (Cambridge, 1997).

19. This discussion of economic regulation in the Year II is based on the wealth of sources distilled in Horn, *The Path Not Taken*, 127–67.

20. See Gérard Béaur, Hubert Bonin and Claire Lemercier (eds), *Fraude, contrefaçon et contrebande de l'Antiquité à nos jours* (Geneva, 2006); Renaud Morieux, *Une mer pour deux royaumes: La Manche, frontier franco-anglaise (XVIIe–XVIIIe siècles)* (Rennes, 2008); Pierrick Pourchasse, *Le Commerce du Nord: Les échanges commerciaux entre la France et l'Europe septentrionale au XVIIIe siècle* (Rennes, 2006); and Christian Pfister-Langanay, *Ports, navires et négociants à Dunkerque (1662–1792)* (Dunkerque, 1985).

21. Louis-Bernard Guyton, *Rapport fait au nom du Comité de salut public par L.-B. Guyton, à la séance du 14 pluviôse an III, sur l'état de situation des arsenaux et de l'armement des armées de terre et de mer de la République* (Paris, 1795).

22. Camille Richard, *Le Comité de Salut public et les fabrications de guerre sous la Terreur* (Paris, 1922), 7–14.

23. Richard, *Le Comité de Salut public*.

25. The full range of evidence underlying this interpretation is in Horn, *The Path Not Taken*, 127–67.

26. Isser Woloch, *Jacobin Legacy: The Democratic Movement under the Directory* (Princeton, 1970); and James Livesey, *Making Democracy in the French Revolution* (Cambridge, MA, 2001).

26. Aftalion, *The French Revolution*, 177; and Denis Woronoff, *The Thermidorean Regime and the Directory 1794–1799*, trans. Julian Jackson (Cambridge, 1984 [1972]), 71–2, 97.

27. This section relies on Horn, *The Path Not Taken*, 169–210. See also Colin Heywood, *The Development of the French Economy, 1750–1914* (Cambridge, 1992). On deindustrialization, see Christopher H. Johnson, *The Life & Death of Industrial Languedoc, 1700–1920: The Politics of Deindustrialization* (Oxford, 1995).

28. Jean-Charles Asselain, *Histoire économique de la France du XVIIIe siècle à nos jours*, vol. 1, *De l'Ancien Régime à la Première Guerre mondiale* (Paris, 1984), 130; Patrick Verley, *La Révolution industrielle* (Paris, 1997), 317; Maurice Lévy-Leboyer, 'Capital Investment and Economic Growth in France, 1820–1930', in Peter Mathias and M. M. Postan (eds), *The Cambridge Economic History of Europe VII: 1, The Industrial Economies: Capital, Labour,*

and Enterprise: Britain, France, Germany, and Scandinavia (Cambridge, 1978), 267; and
Jean-Pierre Daviet, *La société industrielle en France 1814–1914: Productions, échanges, représentations* (Paris, 1997), 17.

29. This political domination depended neither on cultural visibility, nor self-identification, as a class. Somewhat problematically, Sarah Maza focuses on the conceptual absence of this group rather than its *de facto* presence in *The Myth of the French Bourgeoisie: An Essay on the Social Imaginary, 1750–1850* (Cambridge, MA, 2005).

SELECTED READING

DiCaprio, Lisa, *The Origins of the Welfare State: Women, Work, and the French Revolution* (Urbana, IL, 2007).

Gross, Jean-Pierre, *Fair Shares for All: Jacobin Egalitarianism in Practice* (Cambridge, 1997).

Heywood, Colin, *The Development of the French Economy, 1750–1914* (Cambridge, 1992).

Hoffman, Philip T., *Growth in a Traditional Society: The French Countryside, 1450–1815* (Princeton, 1996).

Hoffman, Philip T., Gilles Postel-Vinay, and Jean-Laurent Rosenthal, *Priceless Markets: The Political Economy of Credit in Paris, 1660–1870* (Chicago, 2000).

Horn, Jeff, *The Path Not Taken: French Industrialization in the Age of Revolution, 1750–1830* (Cambridge, MA, 2006).

Markoff, John, *The Abolition of Feudalism: Peasants, Lords and Legislators in the French Revolution* (University Park, PA, 1996).

Miller, Judith A., *Mastering the Market: The State and the Grain Trade in Northern France, 1700–1860* (Cambridge, 1999).

Shovlin, John, *The Political Economy of Virtue: Luxury, Patriotism, and the Origins of the French Revolution* (Ithaca, NY, 2006).

CHAPTER 36

DID EVERYTHING CHANGE? RETHINKING REVOLUTIONARY LEGACIES

JENNIFER NGAIRE HEUER[1]

IN 1791, the French lawyer and politician Pierre-Louis de Lacretelle proclaimed, 'A great revolution, for the last three years, has shaken everything, absorbed everything, disturbed everything.'[2] In 1802, after Napoleon's ascent to power, the abbé Pradt called attention to the global ramifications of change, observing that the Revolution had transformed not only Europe but also its colonies.[3] In the wake of both revolution and Napoleon's rule, conservatives offered more negative, but similarly comprehensive judgements of the cataclysmic changes that had reshaped their world. In 1814, for example, the journalist Jean-Gabriel Pelletier lamented that 'a horrible revolution has changed everything, perverted everything'.[4]

In many respects, contemporaries were right. The Revolution seemed to have changed everything. Revolutionaries had transformed politics, social relations, law, religion, gender, family life, education, work, leisure, property, state power, war, basic human rights, even names—whether of cities, streets, or individuals. And that list is only a beginning. The events starting in 1789 did not simply modify governments or legal systems; they profoundly reshaped how men and women experienced and understood their world.

But then again, the Revolution had not changed every aspect of life, nor were its changes necessarily permanent. As one conservative priest berated his contemporaries in 1820, it was wrong to simply accept that 'the revolution changed everything; things today are no longer as they were before'. He questioned what things had actually changed irrevocably, given that a Bourbon Catholic monarchy had come back and was overturning revolutionary laws, and told his readers that 'You are the ones who have changed, not *everything*'.[5]

The abbé Beauchamp, the priest in question, had specific goals: he sought to remake his audience back into faithful Christians, according to his definition of the term. But his treatise raises broader questions for us: How much do we see the legacies of the Revolution as a question of individual understanding of, or reaction to, events, rather than fundamental structural changes? Or were the two essentially intertwined? What had the Revolution actually transformed forever? Many of the most dramatic innovations of the period were reversed, at least in the short term. To name only a few examples, the Revolution that had executed a king led to the rise of an emperor, followed by a new king—even if new republics were later declared. Legislators proudly proclaimed the end of colonial slavery in 1794; Napoleon restored it in 1802. Revolutionaries celebrated the transformation of the family into a more egalitarian unit; their successors abolished divorce in 1816 and reinforced paternal authority. More positively, men and women who embraced violence during the Terror subsequently repudiated it, or at least certain forms of it. What changes should we thus see as permanent, and when should we look to judge their consequences?

While it is unquestionable that the Revolution had profound consequences for French and world history, assessing its legacies is an extraordinarily complicated task. This is in part precisely because of its very breadth. It is easier to judge the influence of changes in a specific domain than a project to transform all of politics, culture, economics, and society. It is also because many of its legacies are fundamentally contradictory. The Revolution introduced both dramatically new ideas of human rights and new justifications for violence and state-sponsored Terror. As anyone who has followed the often deeply polemical debates over the political lessons of the Revolution knows, it provided precedents for both freedom and oppression, democracy and totalitarianism. Indeed, the 'Revolution' is an amorphous and slippery beast; revolutions in the plural, rather than the singular, may be a more accurate term.

In the following pages, we look first at key methodological issues. Considering the legacies of the Revolution raises fundamental questions about how we understand historical change and the long-term relevance of the past. We then look at some of the broad conceptual changes that might be associated with the Revolution. Finally, we consider more specific legacies, including changes in gender relations and family; tensions between universalism and rights for different groups; the emergence of the modern nation-state; and ideas about the legitimacy and purpose of violence. Each of these themes deserves substantial discussion; this essay seeks, however, more to touch on a range of potential transformations than to address each fully. As David Bell is addressing conceptual legacies of the Revolution on a global scale, this essay also focuses most on resonances within France, although developments within the hexagon and those beyond its borders cannot be neatly separated.

Many historians are more accustomed to thinking about methodological issues when assessing the origins rather than the legacies of Revolution. In trying to understand what led to 1789, men and women have waged passionate battles not only about specific points of debates, but also about the basic motors of history: should we emphasize social and economic relations, whether class struggle or changes in global economics? Or should we look at political crises and the nature of the state? Cultural and intellectual shifts? Short-term triggers or longer-term structural transformations?

Should we see historical change as largely contingent or as the product of largely ine-luctable forces?[6]

We have not necessarily considered the methodological issues of revolutionary lega-cies in the same way. This is in part because of the specific historiographical models that have shaped our understanding of the beginnings of Revolution. Marxist explanations dominated much of the twentieth century. As Paul Hanson has noted, such explana-tions provided both a powerful framework for understanding the origins of revolution in terms of class struggle and the development of capitalism, and for imagining its con-sequences.[7] Those who sought either to dismantle Marxist interpretations or to establish counter models often also connected their accounts to equally broad claims about the meanings of history.

It is also because it can be more difficult to trace what an event produced than what led up to it. Many have expressed justifiable suspicion of claims that the Revolution was responsible for comprehensively ushering in 'modernity'. One cannot reduce the last two centuries of history to the unfolding of change set in place during a few eventful years. Indeed, one of the first questions in assessing revolutionary legacies is when to start, and especially, when to end the narrative. When, to paraphrase François Furet, was the Revolution over?[8] The story can look very different depending on what end-point or points of comparisons one chooses. To continue with our examples above, what might appear as the reversal of revolutionary goals in 1804 or 1814 can appear as the realization of those same goals if one looks at subsequent republics; though slavery was reinstated in the French Empire in 1802, it was abolished in 1848.

The story may also be very different depending not only when one is looking, but also who is looking. Individuals' social and geographical positions have likely had dramatic effects on how they perceived the meanings of the Revolution and its relevance. This is true on a global scale; it is also true within France and the French Empire. Consider the standpoints of a Catholic priest in Paris during the Restoration, a silk worker in Lyon on the barricades in the 1830s, a young woman schoolteacher in rural Brittany in the 1890s, a sugar plantation owner in Guadeloupe, and a Vietnamese anti-colonial nationalist in French Indochina in the 1920s. All would likely have voiced different judgements on the successes or failures of the Revolution and its lessons for the future.

Certainly, the legacies of the Revolution cannot be reduced to the positions of later actors, nor did all members of any group share a uniform perspective. At any given moment, there were also widely competing views about the significance of the Revolution—as well as ignorance of, or indifference to, it. But for those who lived with, or believed themselves to be living with, the consequences of the French Revolution, position and place mattered. For historians, the stakes may be less obvious or immedi-ate—especially, perhaps, for Anglophone historians who have often been less enmeshed in the political repercussions of the field than their French counterparts—but they can nonetheless be significant.[9]

There are other basic methodological questions at stake in how one views the past in general, and the legacies of Revolution in particular. Does one look for conscious appro-priation and rejection of its legacies, or at more structural changes? In other words, should attention focus on historical actors who drew on the rhetoric and examples of the Revolution or deliberately sought to counter its influences? Or on transformations that were not necessarily evident either to those who lived through them or even to subsequent generations? These layers could be deeply intertwined, as theoretical reflections on structure and agency suggest.[10] Yet what one emphasizes can give different perspectives. For example, many of those who have looked at structural changes in gender relations passed negative judgements about its impact for women's rights. The exclusion of women from political rights became more systematic after the Revolution. All men could theoretically be, or become, political citizens; until women finally received the right to vote in 1944, they could not. Historians interested in later appropriations of revolutionary ideals and examples have advanced more optimistic claims, arguing that the precedents of women's political activities and the rhetoric of rights developed during the 1790s echoed through the centuries, inspiring subsequent movements or providing resources for later activists.[11]

The most obvious examples of those inspired by the Revolution are other revolutionaries, particularly the men and women who sought dramatic social and political change in new revolutions in 1830, 1848, 1871, or even 1968. Those challenging political and social order in less seismic moments also drew on the Revolution as a template.[12] It helped define political landscapes—from the very terms of 'left' and 'right' to formal parties and ideologies. Politicians in the nineteenth, twentieth, and early twenty-first centuries regularly referred to the Revolution, whether to claim or reject aspects of its legacies.[13] It shaped a specific and powerful legacy of 'Republicanism'—the idea that a large, established, modern nation could function without a king or other individual leader—as well as rejections of that legacy, or counter models to it. It also provided models and rhetoric for later activists, lawmakers, and educators—although such references could run the gamut from imperialist claims that colonial expansion was compatible with Republican ideals to the writing of the Universal Declaration of Human Rights in 1948.[14]

Assessing the purposeful appropriation of the Revolution raises implicit challenges for historians. How did later actors understand the events of the 1790s? How were the memories, experiences, and lessons of the period passed on? Given the political stakes of the Revolution, it is not surprising that there were bitter struggles over what to accept as its legacies. These struggles began with the Revolution itself, and with claims in its immediate aftermath. Several historians have explored the genre of memoirs, and the ways in which revolutionaries sought to counter their personal experience against emerging master-narratives.[15] By the later nineteenth century, more academic and professional accounts offered competing narratives, alternatively rejecting the Revolution wholesale, embracing its radical legacies, or seeking a more 'liberal' interpretation.[16] Without rehashing all the historiographic debates and controversies of the past two centuries, it is clear that influential individuals, from Tocqueville to Marx, often shaped how people understood both the story of the Revolution and its potential relevance for their lives. Specific figures and events often served as flash points; Guillaume Mazeau, for example, has recently shown how differently the 'martyr of liberty' Jean Paul Marat and his assassin Charlotte Corday were regarded at various moments.[17]

This process of selective appropriation could entail deliberate forgetting: the Restoration government promoted a policy of 'union and forgetting', an attempt at reconciliation and implicitly, of obliterating the power of the Revolution by downplaying its history.[18] In his famous 1882 essay 'What is a nation?' Ernst Renan proclaimed, 'Forgetting, I would even go so far as to say historical error, is a crucial factor in the creation of a nation.'[19] While he only touches in passing on the events of 1789, his account suggests the implicit choices involved in constructing versions of the Revolution deemed useful for patriotic or political purposes.

There were also unintentional gaps in individuals' knowledge or understanding of events. This was especially an issue for later generations, who did not have a direct memory of the Revolution, and for individuals or groups who lacked resources that might have given them a fuller account. As Karen Offen has pointed out, women in the nineteenth and twentieth centuries drew on stories of women's revolutionary activism, especially the October Days March, but they often did not have access to libraries, universities, or archival collections to research their predecessors' activities or experiences.[20] Knowledge of the French Revolution could also be particularly limited or fragmented in the colonies, especially among conquered peoples allegedly integrated into greater France. Such limits did not necessarily preclude powerful references. Ho Chi Minh's 1945 Declaration of the Independence of Vietnam, for example, drew on the 1791 Constitution as well as American Declaration of Independence.[21] Such references were, however, intrinsically selective, designed to serve specific political purposes. Indeed, they are not so much direct legacies of the Revolution, as retrospective appropriations or re-imaginings of it.

Structural changes are even more complex to assess than deliberate allusions to the past, largely because they are often less visible, if potentially more profound. Identifying such changes depends in part on whether you see the Revolution as a 'bloc', to use the term publicized by the politician Georges Clemenceau in the 1890s and subsequently adopted by certain historians, or look instead either at different moments of the Revolution or different strands within it.[22] This interpretative choice is connected to arguments about causality. Many influential interpretations of the Revolution have had an element of determinism, although more subtle thinkers avoided reductionist versions. In Marxist accounts, class struggle both led to the Revolution and produced a new social order. Some 'revisionist' interpretations stressing political or ideological motors of change also contended that the course of the Revolution was pre-determined, or at least followed set paths. This argument is especially associated with explanations for violence: in short, the claim that the Terror of 1793–94 was inherent in the actions and events of 1789.[23]

More recent historians have increasingly emphasized contingency, calling attention to specific decisions or events that changed the course of history. Different historians have proposed different turning points—including the abolition of legal privilege on 4 August 1789, Louis XVI's failed attempt to leave France and subsequent capture in Varennes in June 1791, and the massacre of the Champ de Mars in July 1791—but collectively, they suggest that the choices made in such moments shaped the meaning and development of the Revolution in ways that could not have been foreseen from the onset.[24] Some have also called attention to unintended consequences of changes less closely tied to specific events. William Sewell, for example, argues that the creation of the term *citoyenne* was intended to be a replacement for Madame, as *citoyen* replaced Monsieur, but the implicit associations with citizenship empowered women in new ways.[25]

Just as more subtle proponents of more deterministic views still acknowledge a degree of unpredictability, these theorists are careful to avoid reducing the Revolution simply to personalities or chance. Focusing on contingency and unintended consequences, however, rather than a coherent 'bloc' or inexorable development of events, makes it trickier to address the repercussions and consequences of the Revolution. If the course of the Revolution depended on particular decisions or actions, should subsequent history be seen as similarly contingent? How much can we really look for causal structural changes set into motion by the events that began in 1789?

Assessing such changes also raises the question of where to look. The best known and most debated such changes concern class. The Marxist interpretation is, in a very simplified form, that the Revolution was a struggle between the aristocracy and the bourgeoisie; the bourgeoisie triumphed, only to face an emerging proletariat. This interpretation has been the subject of immense debate, particularly from the late 1960s through the 1980s. Some challenged whether the 'bourgeoisie' existed, or existed in clearly defined opposition to a coherent aristocracy; others questioned the distinctive economic path that France supposedly followed. Other social issues have also inspired considerable debate: For example, what was the long-term impact of the abolition of privilege? The end of venal office and seigneurialism? The sale of property seized by the state, the *biens nationaux*?[26]

Some of these issues are considered elsewhere in this volume. But it is worth noting that many of these legacies are both material and conceptual. They entailed fundamental shifts in the framework of social and legal relations, including an acceptance that men were formally equal before the law, and that the state had a legitimate role in securing equality and potentially, in securing economic opportunity. As Rafe Blaufarb demonstrates, the Revolution changed both ideas and laws about property.[27] It also helped reshape the social and cultural identities of groups, in both work and leisure.[28] The extent to which these shifts can be seen in terms of class or ascribed directly to the Revolution, rather than to subsequent developments, has been hotly debated. So too has the question of whether the Revolution actively created class relations, or by removing the system of legal privilege, simply created a space for later constructions of class.[29] Yet the very fact that by the mid-nineteenth century, contemporaries increasingly thought about social relations in terms of classes, regardless of the precise definition or social reality of those classes, suggests a profound transformation.

Other, more clearly conceptual, changes can be seen as equally structural, fundamental transformations in ways of thinking and even feeling about the world. Lynn Hunt has made a particularly compelling case for the cultural shifts inaugurated by the Revolution. She suggests that both its negative legacies—including violence and prototypes of totalitarian rule—and its more positive legacies—particularly human rights and democracy—are linked by how the Revolution transformed time.[30] She uses the term in part to refer to how people understood the dynamics of change.. To some extent, her formulation develops earlier discussions of regeneration, the tension between believing that the Revolution had fully broken with the past and created a new order, and the fact that individuals, groups, and even the Nation as a whole, were not immediately or fully 'transformed'.[31] Hunt also adds other dimensions to new understandings of time, corresponding to the immediate intensity of Revolutionary experience. In the longer term, a new sense of the pace of events fed a belief in voluntarism—the idea that people could shape their future—as well as a sense of epochal change that transcended individuals.

Other historians have called attention to related shifts in experience and identity. Indeed, our priest's claim that 'you are the ones who have changed' may have far more resonance than he would have likely imagined or intended. Several scholars have argued recently that the Revolution transformed both our experiences of emotion and understandings of the self. William Reddy contends that the Revolutionary period marked a transformation from 'sentimentalism' to its virtual erasure by 1814. In this use, the term refers less to its modern connotations of maudlin excess than to a particular eighteenth-century belief that certain stimuli could, and should, provoke intense emotional responses, and that public display of such emotions, both by men and women, was appropriate and even necessary. He suggests that the experience of the Terror played a key role a shift away from sentimentalism, although he does not fully explain the causality of the shift.[32] Others have similarly argued that the Revolution transformed how people expressed emotions, as well as how they used emotional narratives to make sense of—and potentially create or oppose—political change.[33]

Perhaps more fundamentally, Jan Goldstein has suggested that the Revolution helped create a new idea of the self, or at least played a pivotal role in a longer-term set of developments. Contemporaries critiqued the sensationalist psychology of the eighteenth century, imagined to have produced a fragmented sense of self and to thus have led, via emotional instability, to socio-political havoc. After 1789, intellectuals, particularly Benjamin Constant and those associated with him, sought to replace sensationalism with a new version of the self, an indivisible, stable, and immaterial *moi*. Goldstein identifies this new model of the self as particularly associated with male bourgeois identity, mobilized to create or maintain a sense of order in politics and society.[34]

Indeed, if we look more closely at particular conceptual legacies of the Revolution, some of the more controversial issues are around gender and family. One set of questions revolves around the extent to which the Revolution transformed women's rights. A related question is the origin of 'domesticity'. The term is perhaps most used in the Anglo-American world; it has a complex set of connotations, connected to the idea of a 'separate sphere' of the home and to limited public power and presence for women, especially those of the middle classes.[35] Historians have partly attributed the rise of domesticity to the socio-economic changes associated with industrialization. Few would dispute that the French Revolution also played a role in its development, but the precise nature and timing of that role is far less certain.

Some historians have ascribed the origins and salience of domesticity to Rousseau's lasting influence, or to an exclusion inherent in democracy—or at least the particular versions of democracy and political order embraced by revolutionaries.[36] Others have turned to the experience of the Revolution itself—ranging from the political struggles around specific events, like the closing of women's political clubs, to a desire for domestic stability during a period of dramatic change.[37] Still others have focused on achievements, arguing that the Revolution generated new discourses and practices for attacking gender inequality, and changing women's relationships to the state.[38] In this interpretation, nineteenth-century domesticity was not a product of the Revolution but rather of reaction against it, and especially against the gender instability of the period and women's relative political and legal power. Here we return to one of our key methodological questions of assessing 'Revolutionary' legacies: should we consider as part of the legacies of the Revolution reactions against it, especially reactions that took place years or decades later?

Some of the most substantial, if perhaps less immediately spectacular, changes in gender relations during the Revolution concerned both the legal and imaginative base of the family. These did not just transform women's rights or position in society; they fundamentally affected men's roles and identities. Among other changes, revolutionaries legalized divorce and adoption, reduced paternal authority, instituted a uniform age of majority and egalitarian inheritance, changed the legal nature of power within marriage, and granted rights to children born out of wedlock. Subsequent regimes reversed many of these legal changes. For example, although marriage would remain formally secular, Napoleon would make divorce far less egalitarian. The Catholic Restoration monarchy abolished it completely in 1816; divorce would not be re-established in France until 1884, and then under much more restrictive and sexist terms than those of 1792.

The enduring conceptual legacies of Revolutionary family reforms are harder to assess than the consequences of specific laws.[39] Social and cultural transformations in France cannot be neatly separated from those elsewhere in Europe or the world; in the domain of gender and family, these include long-term trends towards companionate marriage and nuclear households, and changing visions of parent-child relations. Yet the Revolution did fundamentally alter the frame for thinking about relationships between the individual, families, and the state. Here, as I have argued elsewhere, one can see a shift over the course of the Revolution, from a model of the family as the Nation to one of a Nation of families.[40] Revolutionaries challenged the idea of the family as a hierarchical unit that served to protect property and lineage, emphasizing instead individual liberty, the voluntary aspects of familial bonds, and the moral basis of the family. As Suzanne Desan has argued, there was a tension between seeing the family as a unifying social glue and emphasizing individual liberty within households: revolutionaries left unresolved the relationships between individuals, family, and society as a whole.[41]

The Revolution also transformed connections between masculinity and military service. Historians have argued about the extent to which the Revolution changed the fundamental nature of war, and others in this volume address that topic more systematically. But it is undoubtedly the case that the Revolution instituted military service as a duty for all citizens, and sought to turn the image of the soldier from one either of a swashbuckling aristocratic officer or a pathetic wretch into a universal cultural hero. Some historians identify the Revolution itself as a turning point in instituting a new model of militant virility, including a focus on stoic suffering and sacrifice.[42] Others, in another form of debate over what to identify as the direct legacy of the Revolution, have suggested that the Napoleonic wars changed this model in influential ways, instituting forms of martial masculinity that would be spread throughout much of Europe and the globe.[43]

While the Restoration government would briefly abolish conscription in 1814, it returned in a modified form in 1818 and registration for the draft became a rite of passage for young men throughout the nineteenth century.[44] The idea that men could be required to fight and die for the Nation—and women required to send off their sons and lovers—would, of course, be one of the defining features of the twentieth century. Yet it is worth noting the limits of equating masculinity with military service and soldiering with citizenship. Relatively few historians have explored these limits and their legacies, beyond the very real issues of draft dodging and desertion. During the Revolutionary and Napoleonic wars, wounded veterans embodied masculine heroism: their injuries served as proof of their patriotism and virility. But as mutilated, disfigured, and often impoverished figures, they could also appear as incapable of acting as attractive mates or independent heads of household. The status of veterans in the post-Revolutionary era would become even more complicated. Men and women during the Revolution sometimes debated whether military service was the best or the only appropriate means of serving the state; in the aftermath of the war, the question of whether soldiers should be considered an integral part of the Nation at all surfaced with particular acuity. At the same time, as my own work has shown, the experience of two decades of almost constant warfare, and the subsequent transition to peace, shaped women's experiences in ways that are still only poorly understood.[45]

More generally, one of the most powerful legacies of the Revolution is that of human rights and new models of citizenship. The specific articles of the 1789 Declaration of Man and Citizen served as a partial template for later declarations, most notably the Universal Declaration of Human Rights for the United Nations in 1948 and the European Convention of Human Rights of 1953. The more general concept of rights was applied to, and appropriated by, a vast range of individuals and groups, often in ways unimagined by those who first articulated new visions of citizenship and rights. In the Revolutionary context, this led to the consideration of rights for religious minorities, from Protestants to Jews, to the status of free people of colour and slaves, to women, and to the poor. In the longer term, it helped inspire claims to citizenship and rights across the globe.[46]

Yet not all versions of rights were compatible, nor were revolutionary ideas about rights necessarily stable or consistent. Resistance to oppression was not necessarily compatible with a right to security; rights to property and liberty were often in tension—most infamously for slaves and slaveholders. The French Revolution generated three different declarations: the 1789 version is the most iconic and influential, but revolutionaries experimented with alternatives in 1793—though that was never officially implemented—and in 1795. One of the biggest differences was their vision of economic justice. The 1789 declaration proclaimed that employment should be based on merit. The 1793 version made sweeping claims about the state's duty to provide education and employment or the means of existence to those unable to labour. It also called for maximum prices and limits to individual wealth. In contrast, the 1795 version sought to establish a property-owning political class. To some extent, these differences simply reflect competing stages and strands of the Revolution, but the articulation of these political and social visions as declarations of rights gave them potential force and relevance for future movements.

There were several other challenges entailed in the development of new ideas of rights. Some of these are common to parts of the world that experimented with new visions of equality. As Lynn Hunt has argued cogently, once the American and French Revolutions showed that equality could become a principle of government, inequality had to be formally justified.[47] In the wake of such transformations, new doctrines emerged in nineteenth and twentieth century contending that certain groups should be precluded or excluded from rights. These doctrines often attributed 'natural' differences to such groups, claiming that they were intrinsically and unchangeably inferior and thus incapable of acting as full citizens. Indeed, when combined with a new understanding of time and progress, such visions of difference potentially created not only justifications of inequality, but also new forms of it.

Another challenge is more specific to the ways in which rights were imagined and instituted within France and the French Empire. Revolutionaries were deeply wary of separate groups within the Nation. This was true from the inception of the Revolution; in 1788, the abbé Sieyes' *What is the Third Estate?* defined the Nation in terms of those who abided by common law in order to attack the privileges of the nobility. Revolutionaries distrusted 'corporate' bodies in all forms, from the nobility to workers' guilds to monasteries and nunneries and formal political parties. As Alyssa Sepinwall has shown, they championed a vision of 'universalism' that could be both liberating and constraining.[48] When members of previously disenfranchised groups were recognized as citizens, they also had to give up a separate communal identity. This is probably clearest in the case of Jewish emancipation in 1791. To be accepted as full French citizens, Jews had to both renounce laws that regulated them as a distinctive group and limit public displays of their religious identity.[49] While subsequent history—from colonialism to Vichy to modern immigration—reshaped how French authorities defined and treated groups, it is worth noting the lasting resonance of this vision. French law and culture has continued to regard collective identities with suspicion; the hyphenated identities common, for example, in America (e.g. Norwegian-American) are rare in France, and a variety of measures limit public expressions or acknowledgement of collective ethnic or religious identity separate from the Nation, particularly for non-Catholics.[50]

Indeed, one of the most powerful conceptual legacies of the Revolution may be the 'Nation' and its cognates of national identity and nationalism. As with any influential term, it is multivalent, ranging from a territorial identity to a political idea of people united against parasitic elites and tyrannical rulers; and from a legal community of citizens and their government to a more emotional vision of transcendent homeland commanding loyalty. Neither the 'Nation' nor 'nationalism', nor its conceptual cognates of 'national identity' or 'national citizenship' were invented with the French Revolution; theorists argue over whether nations should be seen as distinctly modern institutions, while historians have looked for the origins of nationalism in old regime France.[51] Conversely, regional identities remained strong and connections to the nation-state uneven well into the nineteenth and twentieth centuries. Yet the 'Nation' was an unquestionable touchstone of the Revolution, as a geographic, legal, political, and emotional entity.

It also shaped subsequent ideas and experiences. Mona Ozouf called attention to the 'transfer of sacrality' from the church to the nation-state; the development of nationalism as a kind of civic religion has had a long resonance.[52] The idea that French territory was uniform and citizens legally equal also made the distinction between 'French' and 'foreign' salient in unprecedented and often lasting ways. Here too the questions of timing and of both deliberate appropriation and structural change become important. The Revolution and the Napoleonic wars precipitated the rise of nationalism elsewhere, sometimes unintentionally, as those threatened by conquest sought to rally support against the French by cultivating competing national identities. At the same time, the Revolutionary experience provided models of nation-building, an idea of 'nation-forms' that has circulated around the world.[53] It also offered specific visions of national belonging, sometimes in contrast to models developed elsewhere; the French conception is often characterized as a 'voluntarist' or civic model in contrast to more ethnic or cultural criteria for belonging, although that distinction is also often murkier than it appears.

Finally, we turn to the bleakest legacy of the Revolution: violence. It is impossible— or at the very least, would be immoral—to assess the Revolution without acknowledging the Terror. Estimates vary, but about 17,000 men and women went to the guillotine in 1793–94. The total losses become larger if you take into consideration the roughly 10,000 deaths of those in prison awaiting trial, a similar number of summary executions of rebels in arms, and perhaps half a million casualties on both sides in the civil wars in western and southeastern France (counting in that total all the effects of both combat and disease on a dislocated population). Such numbers are still small compared to the horrific totals of twentieth-century violence, but they are particularly troubling precisely because men and women were killed in the name of rights and regeneration.

Assessing the legacy of the Terror depends in part both on how contemporaries understood its origins and how subsequent theorists explained its causality. As with the Revolution more generally, the process of defining the Terror began in its immediate aftermath. Men and women sought to assign responsibility for horror—often condemning Robespierre and specific individuals, and in the process, explicitly or implicitly, exculpating other actors and institutions that played a role in its institutionalization.[54] In the years that followed, the French struggled to come to terms with the consequences of mass violence. Ronen Steinberg has recently argued that even within the frameworks of partisan struggles, they engaged in serious debate about accountability, retribution, and reparatory measures.[55] Such debates were both shaped by, and helped shape, the extent to which people believed it was possible to preserve or reinstitute elements of the Revolution while separating them from the violence that had accompanied them.

At the same time, violence clearly did not end with Robespierre's execution. Particularly in southern France, the experience of these years transformed factional disputes into a cycle of vengeance and counter-vengeance.[56] While revolutionaries in the later 1790s and Napoleon's government dismantled some of the laws and institutions that had made the Terror possible, they also instituted less spectacular and more targeted forms of repression. This suggests more structural legacies in how violence was instituted and experienced, at least in the immediate wake of the Revolution. Howard Brown argued that the Terror changed the 'economy of violence,' separating it from rituals of collective legitimation, and turning into the first resort of personal or factional quarrels. Brown's immediate goal is to explain the rise of what he calls 'liberal authoritarianism' with Napoleon; his longer-term claim is that the period fostered a modern 'security state.'[57]

Historians have also engaged in passionate debate about the nature and causality of the Terror. The debate has often been framed in terms of 'circumstances' versus intrinsic violence; either the Terror was the product of the particular conditions of 1793–94—especially real or perceived threats to the Nation that led to violent action by those desperate to preserve their cause—or it was inherent either to the French Revolution in particular or revolution in general. To some extent, this is a false dichotomy; we can see aspects of the Revolution that made a descent into repression more likely without ascribing inevitability; conversely, the circumstances of 1793–94 help explain the path and the intensity of the Terror, even if they do not exonerate those responsible for it. Indeed, historians have increasingly emphasized the processes that led to the Terror, as well as its reverberations afterwards, focusing on issues including the experience of civil war, socio-economic challenges, emotional and intellectual frameworks, and regional differences.[58]

Assessing the conceptual legacies of the French Terror also depends in part on how distinctive one believes it to be. The repression in Revolutionary France has often been viewed in light of twentieth-century atrocities, particularly the Stalinist Terror in the Soviet Union and Eastern Europe. Some later actors did refer to Jacobin ideology as one justification for their policies; revisionists and theorists looking for the origins of totalitarianism have also retroactively insisted on connections and parallels.[59] Others, however, have challenged the 'national myth' of the French Revolution as a uniquely problematic episode of violence.[60] They call attention less to later revolutions than those that preceded or paralleled the French Revolution, especially the American and Dutch cases, noting that experiences of civil war, emergency measures in time of war, and attempts to control dissent and arrest suspects were far from specific to France.

One aspect of the Terror is ideological. As David Andress has noted, Jacobins were not seventeenth-century Puritans or Russian Bolsheviks, driven by an all-consuming and long-established ideology.[61] But there were distinctive conceptual aspects, including the attempts to 'regenerate' mankind through political education and terrorizing or killing those who disagreed, deemed incapable of regeneration and implicitly outside of humanity. Indeed, the dehumanization of enemies is the flip side of human rights, a grimmer conceptual legacy. This does not mean that the Revolution invented the treatment of individuals or groups as sub-human; the long history of slavery, con-quest, torture, massacres, and other horrors would quickly belie any such claim. Nor can we draw a direct line between the French Revolution and subsequent persecution or oppression: unlike later movements, revolutionaries never consistently branded an eth-nic group or collectivity as irredeemably inhuman, although they came close to doing so in the Vendée. Revolutionaries did create new categories of *hors de la loi*, those placed outside of law, society, and even humanity itself.[62] Such labels made it easier to reconcile the rights of man with state-sponsored violence. Even after the Terror, they served to justify and continue war against foreign enemies.

A related question for assessing the legacies of the Terror and of revolutionary vio-lence in France is that of who actually implemented it, how one moved from a con-ceptual framework that made the Terror imaginable to putting it in place. Many of the contributors to a recent volume edited by Michel Biard argue that reducing the Terror to state violence makes it hard to understand its contradictory effects at different levels and with different actors.[63] Here there is a substantial debate about how much the Terror should be defined as state-sponsored violence; some, like Patrick Gueniffey, emphasize state violence; conversely, Jean-Clément Martin has argued that violence was due less to ideology or the power of state than its weakness and inability to control competing forces. Such debates shape both the degree to which we see the growing power of the state as a legacy of the Revolution and the links between governments and violence.

More generally, it is not necessary to subscribe to a view that the Terror was preor-dained to note that brutality and liberty were intertwined throughout the Revolution. The same crowds that destroyed the Bastille prison in July 1789 also impaled the severed heads of officials on spikes and paraded them through the streets. Forms of violence changed throughout the Revolution—as did the degree to which it was tolerated or actively instituted by authorities—but violence itself was recurrent. Depending on one's perspective, the Revolutionary experience served to legitimate violence as a necessary and effective means for social transformation—or to discredit dramatic social change by linking it to danger and destruction.

Overall, the French Revolution did not change everything—or everyone—whatever awed or distressed commentators may have proclaimed. Many of its accomplishments were limited, or partially reversed, at different points during the Revolution itself or in the years that followed; so too were some of its more disturbing aspects. As we have seen, assessing its legacies depends on what aspects of the Revolution one emphasizes, and how one imagines the motors of history. Yet it is equally clear that its conceptual lega-cies, while complex, are real and powerful.

NOTES

1. My thanks to Brian Ogilvie, Judith Miller, Alyssa Sepinwall, Denise Davidson, and David Andress for their comments and suggestions.
2. Pierre Louis de Lacretelle, *De l'établissement des connoissances humaines* (Paris, 1791), 179.

3. Dominique Georges Fréderic De Pradt, *Les trois âges des colonies* (Paris, 1801), 3: 324.

4. Jean-Gabriel Peletier, *L'ambigu ou Variétés littéraires et politiques* (London, 1814), 47, 20.

5. Abbé Beauchamp, *Crimes de la révolution française: obligation de les réparer par la pénitence* (Paris, 1820), 253.

6. For some recent comparative approaches to the origins of the Revolution, see Peter R. Campbell (ed.), *Origins of the French Revolution* (Basingstoke, 2005); Thomas Kaiser and Dale Van Kley (eds), *From Deficit to Deluge: The Origins of the French Revolution* (Stanford, 2011); and Suzanne Desan, Lynn Hunt, and William Max Nelson (eds), *The French Revolution in Global Perspective* (Ithaca, 2013).

7. Paul Hanson, *Contesting the French Revolution* (Chichester, UK; Malden, MA, 2009).

8. See Furet's famous declaration that the 'French Revolution is Over', in *Interpreting the French Revolution* (Cambridge, 1981).

9. Steven Kaplan, *Farewell Revolution, Disputed Legacies. France, 1789/1989* (Ithaca, 1995).

10. William Sewell, *Logics of History: Social Theory and Social Transformation* (Chicago, 2005).

11. For a focus on structural changes, see Geneviève Fraisse, *Reason's Muse: Sexual Difference and the Birth of Democracy* (Chicago, 1994). For appropriations of Revolutionary examples and rhetoric, see Martin Johnson, 'Memory and the Cult of Revolution in the 1871 Paris Commune', *Journal of Women's History* 9, no. 1 (1997), 39–57, and Karen Offen, 'Women's Memory, Women's History, Women's Political Action: The French Revolution in Retrospect, 1789-1889-1989,' *Journal of Women's History* 1, no. 3 (1990), 211–30.

12. For one argument for the inspirational value of the Revolution, see E. J. Hobsbawm, *Echoes of the Marseillaise: Two centuries look back on the French Revolution* (New Brunswick, NJ, 1990).

13. Indeed, such references remained salient in the 2012 presidential elections.

14. Alice Conklin, 'Colonialism and Human Rights: A Contradiction in Terms? The Case of France and West Africa, 1895–1914,' *American Historical Review* 103, no. 2 (1998), 419–42.

15. Natalie Petiteau, *Ecrire la mémoire: Les mémorialistes de la Révolution et de l'Empire* (Paris, 2012); Mette Harder, 'Ex-conventionnels versus historians of the French Revolution', in Carolina Armenteros, Tim Blanning, Isabel DiVanna, and Dawn Dodds (eds), *Historicising the French Revolution* (Newcastle, 2008).

16. Pascal Dupuy, 'The Revolution in History, Commemoration, and Memory', in Peter McPhee (ed.), *A Companion to the French Revolution* (Chichester, UK, 2013), 486–502. See also Ann Rigney, *The Rhetoric of Historical Representation: Three Narrative Histories of the French Revolution* (Cambridge, 2003).

17. Guillaume Mazeau, *Le bain de l'histoire. Charlotte Corday et l'attentat contre Marat* (Seysesel, 2009).

18. Bettina Frederking, '"Il ne faut pas être le roi de deux peuples": Strategies of National Reconciliation in Restoration France', *French History* 22, no. 4 (2008), 446–68; Natalie Scholz, 'Past and Pathos: Symbolic Practices of Reconciliation during the French Restoration', *History & Memory* 22, no. 1 (2010), 48–80.

19. Ernst Renan, 'What is a Nation?', reprinted in Geoff Ely and Ronald Suny, *Becoming National: a Reader* (New York, 1986).

20. Offen, 'Women's Memory'.

21. Available at <http://www.fordham.edu/halsall/mod/1945vietnam.html>, accessed 7 June 2013.

22. Specifically, Clemenceau argued in 1891 that the Revolution had to be accepted or rejected as a whole.

23. Furet, *Interpreting the French Revolution*. Simon Schama, *Citizens* (New York, 1989).

24. Michael Fitzsimmons, *The Night the Old Regime Ended: August 4, 1789 and the French Revolution* (University Park, 2003); Timothy Tackett, 'The Flight to Varennes and the Coming of the Terror', *Historical Reflections* 29, no. 3 (2003), 469–93; David Andress, *Massacre at the Champ de Mars: Popular Dissent and Political Culture in the French Revolution* (Rochester, 2000).

25. William Sewell, 'Le citoyen/la citoyenne: Activity, Passivity, and the Revolutionary Concept of Citizenship', in *The French Revolution and the Creation of Modern Political Culture*, Colin Lucas (ed.), (Oxford, 1987), 105–23.

26. See Peter McPhee, *Living the French Revolution* (New York, 2006), and Peter McPhee, 'The Economy, Society, and the Environment', in McPhee, ed., *Companion to the French Revolution*, 454–69. Bernard Bodinier and Eric Teyssier, *L'événement le plus important de la révolution: la vente des biens nationaux (1789–1867) en France et dans les territoires annexés* (Paris, 2000); Rafe Blaufarb, *The Politics of Fiscal Privilege in Provence, 1530s to 1830s* (Washington, DC, 2012).

27. Rafe Blaufarb, *The Invention of Modern Property* (Oxford, forthcoming).

28. Denise Davidson, *France after Revolution: Urban Life, Gender, and the New Social Order* (Cambridge, MA, 2007).

29. For one version of these debates, see Sara Maza, *The Myth of the French Bourgeoisie: An Essay on the Social Imaginary, 1750–1850* (Cambridge, MA, 2003), and reactions to the book.

30. Lynn Hunt, 'The World We Have Gained: the Future of the French Revolution', *American Historical Review* 108, no. 1 (2003), xvi–19.

31. Mona Ozouf, 'Regeneration', in *A Critical Dictionary of the French Revolution*, ed. François Furet and Mona Ozouf (Cambridge, MA, 1989), 781–91.

32. William Reddy, 'Sentimentalism and its Erasure: The Role of the Emotions in the Era of the French Revolution', *Journal of Modern History* 72, no. 1 (2000), 109–52; William Reddy, *The Navigation of Feeling: A Framework for the History of Emotions* (Cambridge and New York, 2001).

33. See especially the forthcoming work by Judith Miller.

34. Jan Goldstein, *The Post-Revolutionary Self: Politics and Psyche in France, 1750–1850* (Cambridge, MA, 2005).

35. For an introduction, see Amanda Vickery, 'Golden Age to Separate Spheres? A Review of the Categories and Chronology of English Women's History', *The Historical Journal* 36, no. 2 (1993), 383–414; and Laura Lee Downs, *Writing Gender History* (London, 2002).

36. Jennifer J. Popiel, *Rousseau's Daughters: Domesticity, Education, and Autonomy in Modern France* (Durham, NH, 2008).

37. Such interpretations received particular attention in the late 1980s and early 1990s. Relevant works include Dominique Godineau, *The Women of Paris and their French Revolution*, trans. Katherine Streip (Berkeley, 1998); Joan Landes, *Women and the Public Sphere in the Age of the French Revolution* (Ithaca, 1988) and Olwen Hufton, *Women and the Limits of Citizenship in the French Revolution* (Toronto, 1992).

38. See especially Suzanne Desan, *The Family on Trial in Revolutionary France* (Berkeley, 2004).

39. For some explorations of these legacies, see Anne Verjus, *Le bon mari: Une histoire politique des hommes et des femmes à l'époque révolutionnaire* (Paris, 2010), and Anne Verjus and Denise Davidson, 'Generational Conflict in Revolutionary France: Widows, Inheritance Practices, and the "Victory" of Sons', *William and Mary Quarterly* 70, no. 2 (2013), 399–424.

40. Jennifer Heuer, *The Family and the Nation: Gender and Citizenship in Revolutionary France* (Ithaca, NY, 2005).

41. Suzanne Desan, 'The French Revolution and the Family', in McPhee, ed., *Companion to the French Revolution*, 470–83.

42. Alain Corbin (ed.), *Histoire de la virilité: Tome 2, Le triomphe de la virilité, le XIXe siècle* (Paris, 2011), especially Jean-Paul Bertaud, 'L'armée et le brevet de virilité', 63–82, and 'Virilité militaire', 157–202.

43. See especially Michael J. Hughes, *Forging Napoleon's Grande Armée: Motivation, Military Culture, and Masculinity in the French Army, 1800–1808* (New York, 2012).

44. Annie Crépin, *La conscription en débat, ou le triple apprentissage de la nation, de la citoyenneté, de la république* (Artois, 1998); Annie Crépin, *L'histoire de la conscription* (Paris, 2009); David M. Hopkin, 'Sons and lovers: popular images of the conscript, 1798–1870', *Modern & Contemporary France* 9, no. 1 (2001), 19-36.

45. See Jennifer Heuer, 'The Soldiers' Reward: Love and War in the Age of Napoleon', forthcoming.

46. Lynn Hunt (ed.), *The French Revolution and Human Rights: A Brief Documentary History* (New York, 1996) and Lynn Hunt, *Inventing Human Rights* (New York: W. W. Norton, 2007). See also Jennifer Heuer, 'The French Revolution and Human Rights', in David Forsythe (ed.), *The Human Rights Encyclopedia* (Oxford, 2009), 281–6.

47. Hunt, 'The World', 61.

48. Alyssa Sepinwall, *The Abbé Grégoire and the French Revolution: The Making of Modern Universalism* (Berkeley, 2005); Alyssa Sepinwall, 'Les paradoxes de la régénération révolutionnaire: Le cas de l'abbé Grégoire', *Annales historiques de la révolution française*, no. 321 (2000), 69–90.

49. Among others, see Frances Malino, *A Jew in The French Revolution: The Life of Zalkind Hourwitz* (Oxford, 1996) and Ronald Schechter, *Obstinate Hebrews: Representations of Jews in France, 1715–1815* (Berkeley, 2003).

50. Alyssa Sepinwall, 'Sexuality, Orthodoxy and Modernity in France: North African Jewish Immigrants in Karin Albou's *La Petite Jérusalem*', in Lawrence Baron, ed., *Modern Jewish Experiences in World Cinema* (Waltham, MA, 2011), 340–7.

51. Oliver Zimmer and Len Scales, *Power and the Nation in European History* (Cambridge, 2005); David Bell, *The Cult of the Nation in France: Inventing Nationalism, 1680–1800* (Cambridge, MA, 2001).

52. Mona Ozouf, *Festivals and the French Revolution* (Cambridge, Mass., 1988).

53. William Sewell, 'The French Revolution and the Emergence of the Nation Form', in *Revolutionary Currents: Transatlantic Ideology and Nationbuilding, 1688–1821*, (ed.) Michael Morrison and Melinda Zook (Lanham, 2004), 91–125; Chimene I. Keltner, *The Paradoxes of Nationalism: The French Revolution and its Meaning for Contemporary Nation Building* (Albany, 2007).

54. Bronislaw Baczko, *Ending the Terror: The French Revolution after Robespierre* (Cambridge, 1994).

55. Ronen Steinberg, 'The Afterlives of the Terror: Dealing with the Legacies of Violence in Post-revolutionary France, 1794-1830s,' Ph.D. Thesis, University of Chicago, 2010.

56. D. G. Sutherland, *Murder in the Aubagne: Lynching, Law, and Justice during the French Revolution* (Cambridge, 2009).

57. Howard G. Brown, *Ending the French Revolution: Violence, Justice, and Repression from the Terror to Napoleon* (Charlottesville, 2006).

58. David Andress, *The Terror: The Merciless War for Freedom in Revolutionary France* (New York, 2006).

59. J. L. Talmon, *The Origins of Totalitarian Democracy* (London, 1952).

60. Jean-Clément Martin, *Violence et Révolution—Essai sur la naissance d'un mythe national* (Paris, 2006). Annie Jourdan, 'Les discours de la terreur à l'époque révolutionnaire (1776–1798): Etude comparative sur une notion ambiguë', *French Historical Studies* 36, no. 1 (2013), 51–82.

61. David Andress, 'The Course of the Terror, 1793–1794', in Peter McPhee (ed.), *A Companion to the French Revolution* (Chichester, 2012), 293–310.

62. Anne Simonin, *Le déshonneur dans la République: une histoire de l'indignité, 1791–1958* (Paris, 2008).

63. Michel Biard (ed.), *Les politiques de la Terreur, 1793–1794* (Paris, 2008).

SELECTED READING

Armenteros, Carolina, Tim Blanning, Isabel DiVanna, and Dawn Dods, eds., *Historicising the French Revolution* (Cambridge, 2008).

Bell, David, *The First Total War: Napoleon's Europe and the Birth of Warfare as We Know It* (Boston, 2007).

Darnton, Robert, 'What was Revolutionary about the French Revolution?', in *The French Revolution in Social and Political Perspective*, ed. Peter Jones (London, 1989), 18–29.

Forrest, Alan, *The Legacy of the French Revolutionary Wars: The Nation-in-Arms in French Republican Memory* (Cambridge, 2009).

Hobsbawm, E. J., *Echoes of the Marseillaise: Two centuries look back on the French Revolution* (New Brunswick, N.J., 1990).

Hunt, Lynn. 'The World We Have Gained: The Future of the French Revolution', *American Historical Review* 108, no. 1 (2003), xvi–19.

Kaplan, Steven Laurence, *Farewell, Revolution. Disputed Legacies. France, 1789/1989* (Ithaca, 1995).

Klaits, Joseph and Michael H. Haltzel, eds., *The Global Ramifications of the French Revolution* (Cambridge, 1994).

Offen, Karen, 'Women's Memory, Women's History, Women's Political Action: The French Revolution in Retrospect, 1789-1889-1989', *Journal of Women's History* 1, no. 3 (1990), 211–30.

Petiteau, Natalie, *Ecrire La Mémoire: Les Mémorialistes de la Révolution et de l'Empire* (Paris, 2012).

Sepinwall, Alyssa, *The Abbé Grégoire and the French Revolution: The Making of Modern Universalism* (Berkeley, 2005).

Sewell, William, 'The French Revolution and the Emergence of the Nation Form', in *Revolutionary Currents: Transatlantic Ideology and Nationbuilding, 1688–1821*, eds. Michael Morrison and Melinda Zook (Lanham, 2004), 91–125.

Vovelle, Michel, *1789: L'héritage et la mémoire* (Privat, 2007).

Woloch, Isser, *The New Regime: Transformations of the French Civic Order, 1789–1820s* (New York, 1994).

CHAPTER 37

GLOBAL CONCEPTUAL LEGACIES

DAVID A. BELL

'I have begun', the Russian Socialist-Revolutionary Pitirim Sorokin confided to his diary in mid-1917, 'to study more intensively the great French Revolution. How history repeats itself. Who are we but Russian Girondins? What will be our fate?'[1] There was nothing particularly unusual about Sorokin's musings. Throughout the Russian Revolution, actors and observers alike repeatedly referred back to revolutionary France, seeing its history as a script Russia was fated to follow. France loomed as large in their imaginations as ancient Rome had done for the French revolutionaries themselves.

In recent decades, however, the French Revolution has ceased to have such bewitching effects in the world beyond the Hexagon. Occasionally, protestors or rebels will invoke a slogan or a symbol of 1789, as Chinese students did during the Tiananmen Square protests of 1989. But they very rarely cite it as a model or a script, or compare their ambitions to those of the Jacobins. Just as often, indeed, they will explicitly disavow the comparison. In the summer of 1989, writing in the French newspaper *Libération* in the midst of the Revolution's bicentennial, Polish dissident leader Jacek Kuroń explained that while the Polish people wanted a change in regime and an end to communism, they did not want a revolution on the French or Russian model. They considered it too violent and uncontrollable.[2] That same year, the British observer Timothy Garton Ash even tried to label events in the crumbling Soviet bloc a 'refolution'—a combination of 'revolution' and 'reform' (the neologism didn't take).[3] In the first thirteen years of the twenty-first century, upheavals in the former Soviet Union and the Arab world, while often described as 'revolutions', have generally seemed even more distant from the model of 1789. After initial successes—usually the toppling of a hated leader—they have mostly had confused and dispiriting aftermaths, characterized by the dissipation of revolutionary energy, not the coalescence of a steadily more radical revolutionary movement.[4]

If, then, we are to chart the global conceptual legacies of the French Revolution for the contemporary world, we cannot simply do so by looking for explicit references to 1789.

In that sense, the French Revolution is indeed 'over'. We face the far more difficult task of trying to locate, in present-day global politics and culture, lines of continuity that can be traced back to revolutionary events.

Of course, no such lines are ever entirely straight and clear, and genealogies can always be contested. For instance, did the French Revolution, and its Declaration of the Rights of Man and Citizen, play the critical role in shaping modern human rights politics? Perhaps they merely gave a new twist to far older ideas. Perhaps their importance pales before that of the American Revolution, and the American Bill of Rights? Or perhaps, by contrast, all these apparent continuities are deceptive, and the key elements of modern human rights politics are of far more recent vintage? Advocates are easily found for each of these positions.

Given such challenges, it makes little sense to offer inflated claims for the French Revolution as the *fons et origo* of all modern politics and culture. It is more useful to try to show how the Revolution contributed to them, sometimes as one factor among many, sometimes as something more. In what follows, I will look at six broad conceptual areas where the French Revolution's legacies have been particularly strong: nationalism, republicanism, human rights, war and peace, political ideology, and revolution itself. In each case, I hope to suggest something of the ways the French Revolution contributed to the making of present-day politics and culture around the globe.

NATIONALISM

The French Revolutionaries hardly invented nations, or the idea of the nation. They did, however, do more than any previous political figures to elevate 'the nation' to the status of highest possible political authority. 'The principle of all sovereignty', proclaimed Article 3 of the *Declaration of the Rights of Man*, 'resides essentially in the nation. No body and no individual may exercise any authority which does not proceed directly from it.'[5] The Revolutionaries thereby did much to associate the principle of *popular* sovereignty enunciated by Anglo-American predecessors with the idea of a specifically *national* community—one bound together by more than just a common territory and common political allegiances.[6]

The Revolutionaries also introduced something radically new into the history of nations, namely the idea of a nation as a political construction. Before 1789, Europeans commonly saw nations as essentially natural entities—families writ large that could grow in strength, or wither and die, in rhythms similar to those of biological organisms. But in the late eighteenth century, French writers began to use the word 'nation' in a different way, implying that such an entity needed a high degree of spiritual and political unity. These writers in fact often lamented that France, which had been unproblematically referred to as a 'nation' for centuries, was *not* one, and needed to *become* one.[7]

During the Revolution itself, a large proportion of the initiatives undertaken by the successive aAssemblies could be put into the category of 'nation-building'. The reorganization of French territory was seen not merely as administrative rationalization, but as a means of destroying old provincial identities and fostering national unity. The reorganization of the Church aimed at curbing the influence of a power that revolutionaries, following long Gallican tradition, stigmatized as 'foreign'. The programme of revolutionary festivals was meant to provide vivid, tangible evidence of the French nation coming together around a single purpose. A swathe of initiatives targeted distinct local customs and practices, aiming to replace them with 'national' ones. Most strikingly, from early on the revolutionaries identified the multiplicity of languages spoken in France, which the old regime had taken for granted as a fact of nature, as a source of discord and a problem to be solved. These initiatives, it can be argued, marked the appearance of nationalism, as opposed to national sentiment, in Western politics.[8]

These ideas—of national sovereignty and of nations as political constructions—spread rapidly in the Western world during the age of revolutions and the following decades. Ironically, they proved as useful to self-proclaimed counter-revolutionaries as to revolutionaries themselves. Against Napoleon's attempts to forge a European super-state, Spaniards and Germans resisted in the name of their nations, even borrowing the French Revolutionary concept of the 'nation in arms', while trumpeting their loyalty to thrones and altars. Nonetheless, in the decades that followed the end of the Napoleonic wars, emergent nationalist movements were again most generally associated with revolutionary causes—particularly those in Greece, Italy, Germany, and the emergent states of Latin America.[9]

Nationalist ideas, of course, underwent great transformations throughout the nineteenth and twentieth centuries. Most pointedly in central Europe, programmes of conscious nation-building came to focus not only in the transformation of attitudes and practices in a given territory through education, but in the alteration of borders and populations. Borders would be pushed outwards to envelop members of the 'national' language-group and 'historically national' territories, while national minorities within the borders would be segregated, or even expelled. Ideals of national sovereignty consistent with liberal democracy gave way to notions of 'national self-determination' which, in many cases, privileged collectivist group cohesion almost entirely over individual rights, despite the hopes of liberals such as Woodrow Wilson. This collectivism became a key feature of the nationalist ideas that circulated both on the European far right and in Communist movements in the early twentieth century (it should not be forgotten that Stalin wrote a book entitled *Marxism and the National Question*). These shifts provided the justification for bloody population transfers, such as the movement of nearly 1.5 million people between Greece and Turkey in the early 1920s.[10] By this point in history, few nationalist movements showed much consciousness of their debt to the French Revolutionaries (although triumphant Irish nationalists after the First World War did, like the Italians fifty years previously, adopt a tricolour flag).

Yet even at this late moment in the history of nationalism, some direct echoes of the French Revolutionary past still lingered. For instance, the Versailles Conference's endorsement of plebiscites as the means of measuring 'self-determination' had direct precedents in the plebiscites staged in the Revolution to justify the annexation of territories such as Avignon to France. And the notion of 'restoring' a set of borders supposedly justified by historical tradition had arisen in the Revolution as well, when French officials defended claims for extending France's borders to the 'natural frontiers' of the Rhine and the Alps with copious allusions to historical precedent.[11]

In the early twenty-first century, interestingly, the forms of nationalism and nation-building that flourished so virulently in the early twentieth have again faded from view. 'Historical' claims to territory have lost respectability (for instance, German claims to Silesia and East Prussia, or Romanian ones to Moldova), minority rights have become enshrined in constitutions, and collectivist notions of 'self-determination' are countered by assertions about the universality of human rights. Today, once again, the most prominent demands for 'nation-building'—not least of all in France itself—centre on the peaceful 'integration' of minority groups, usually from immigrant backgrounds, into national communities through an emphasis on a common language and shared values.[12] In this sense, the French Revolutionary legacy has again come to the fore.

REPUBLICANISM

Just as nearly all sovereign political units on the globe now identify themselves as 'nations', so a large majority of them have explicitly republican forms of government. Needless to say, the idea of the republic, like the idea of the nation, long antedated the French Revolution. Nonetheless, the Revolution contributed in striking ways to the development of republicanism as a global political phenomenon, and its legacies can still be traced in the forms that republics take today.

Republicanism came late to France. The 'classical republican' political language which, as John Pocock showed many years ago, had such a powerful influence in early modern Italy, Britain, and America, had relatively little influence in France before 1789 (its major old regime exponent, the *abbé* Mably, had more importance after this date than before; Montesquieu and Rousseau both had a far more conflicted relationship to republicanism). Even during the first two years of the Revolution, the idea of a 'French Republic' remained bizarre to most French citizens. When Louis XVI fell in August 1792, even some provincial Jacobins still found it difficult to imagine France without a monarch, and asked who would now take the throne.[13]

The classical republican thought traced by Pocock was not in fact easily compatible with French Revolutionary radicalism. Yes, it could generate radical critiques of existing power relations, because of its stress on civic virtue and independence, its potential egalitarianism, and its opposition to all forms of undue domination. But it also stressed the frailty of human virtue and the need for a mixed, balanced constitution, and some of its exponents believed it compatible with monarchy. Montesquieu is most responsible for the modern opposition of 'republic' to 'monarchy'. But forty years later, James Madison defined a republic rather as 'a Government in which the scheme of representation takes place', seeking to distinguish it principally from 'democracy'.[14]

The French Revolutionaries forever changed the way the world would imagine this form of government. By proclaiming a republic upon the fall of the monarchy in the summer of 1792, they ensured that Montesquieu's distinction, rather than Madison's, would henceforth dominate understandings of the term. Just as important was the association of France's First Republic with an overtly 'revolutionary' government that formally suspended its own constitution, accorded to itself exceptional central powers, and effectively placed the execution of those powers in the hands of a single elected Assembly. Thanks to these events, short-lived as they were, the association of 'republics' with 'mixed government' received a shock from which it could never fully recover. It hardly needs saying that the First Republic's experiments in radical utopianism, and its spiral into a politics of Terror, together destroyed any necessary association of republics with moderation. While classical republican thought hardly disappeared in the 1790s, Jacobin republicanism now overshadowed it.

The Revolutionaries also created a powerful new array of symbols around the concept of the republic. Earlier, classical republicans obsessed over the death of republics—the slide into corruption and decadence, the surrender to tyranny. They assumed that a society, once corrupted and spoiled, would find it almost impossible to resume a true republican life. The French Revolutionaries, however, created an enduring mythology about the *birth* of republics: the toppling of tyrants, the 'regeneration' of a population fallen into somnolence. Nothing more powerfully embodied this legend of birth than the 'Republican Calendar' which dated time itself from the foundation of the Republic in September of 1792.

Since 1795, countries around the world have, of course, experimented with an overwhelming variety of 'republican' forms of government, including federal democracies like the United States, the 'People's Republics' of the former Communist bloc, and the 'Islamic Republic' of Iran. Even Napoleon Bonaparte's authoritarian Empire remained, in theory, a republic: its founding document stated that 'the government of the Republic is confided to an Emperor'.[15] France's current Fifth Republic, with its powerful presidency, is widely considered a blending of republican and monarchical elements.

But amidst this chaos, the legacy of French Jacobin republicanism is clearly perceptible. Republics today are, by commonly accepted definition, not monarchies. They are not always mixed governments, and they do not have to be moderate. Indeed, they do not even necessarily have to have a 'scheme of representation'—following from the sans-culottes of the First Republic, it is possible to imagine forms of direct democracy existing in a 'republic'. Republics *do* have to recognize the principle of popular sovereignty. And so, not surprisingly, the distinction between 'republic' and 'democracy' which most early modern readers of political literature recognized very clearly, has today partially collapsed.[16] Most American university students, to judge from my own experience, cannot clearly distinguish the two. These definitional changes are due above all to the French Revolutionary experiment.

Furthermore, the powerful symbolism of the birth of republics—the republican flag flying over the palaces of tyrants—has resounded powerfully in modern history, thereby maintaining the close association of republics with revolutionary change. From France itself in 1848 and 1870, to China in 1911, Russia in 1917, and Germany in 1918, the proc-lamation of a republic has formed a basic part of what Keith Michael Baker and Dan Edelstein have labelled the modern revolutionary 'script'.[17] If, in the classical republican imagination, republics gave way to empires, today empires give way to republics.

What French writers today sometimes refer to as the French 'model' of republican-ism arguably owes more to the experience of the Third Republic (1870–1940) than to the First. This model is generally held to include such elements as a powerful, meritocratic public educational system; a brand of secularism (*laïcité*) that not only aims at the sepa-ration of church and state, but the exclusion of religion from the public sphere; and a strong emphasis on the rule of law.[18] Yet to the extent that the Third Republic consciously imagined itself the heir of the French Revolution, a revolutionary legacy remains vis-ible in this 'model' as well. And the model itself remains widely influential, especially in Europe, Latin America, and the countries of the former French Empire.

HUMAN RIGHTS

French people today often cite human rights as the Revolution's single most important legacy for the modern world. Scholars in the rest of the world do not always agree. The 1789 'Declaration of the Rights of Man and the Citizen', they point out, had predeces-sors elsewhere, especially in the Anglo-American world. And while the Declaration still necessarily occupies a large place in any global history of human rights, the always-contested concept has also undergone many changes since 1789. Notably, human rights are no longer primarily seen as depending, for their enjoyment and enforcement, on citizenship in a particular state. To the contrary, they are now often seen as a justifica-tion for imposing limits on a state's sovereign power, even over its own citizens.[19]

Historians generally agree that eighteenth-century concepts of the 'rights of man', a neologism of the period, differed in important respects from earlier concepts of 'nat-ural rights'. Rights bestowed by nature are not necessarily rights enjoyed in an organ-ized polity. Indeed, for social contract thinkers, most radically Thomas Hobbes, 'natural rights' were precisely what humans needed to *relinquish* so as to form a properly consti-tuted state. Other thinkers argued that some natural rights persisted even in the social state, and John Locke posited that states existed in the first place to protect the rights to 'life, liberty and estate'. But only in the Enlightenment did the idea become com-monly accepted that humans possessed certain rights simply as a condition of their humanity, and that no state had the authority to abrogate these rights. The American Revolutionaries first put this idea into formal declarations, in the Virginia Declaration of Rights of June 1776, and then in Jefferson's soaring phrases at the start of America's Declaration of Independence.

The originality of France's 1789 Declaration came less from its contents than from the political purpose it served. The actual list of rights, hastily cobbled together by a minor National Assembly committee, contained few major conceptual innovations.[20]

But whereas the American proclamations of rights justified seizures of power that had largely already taken place, the French Declaration justified a seizure of power that was still largely to come in the course of the Revolution. In fact, it was with the Declaration itself that the Assembly staked its claim to rule, as the agent of the sovereign nation, and to construct a new government committed to the rights it was enumerating.[21]

Despite the universalist promise implicit in the Declaration's title, its text nonetheless explicitly applied only to French citizens—'members of the social body'. Furthermore, the document itself cautioned that the rights it proclaimed could and would be limited by law. As historians have noted, these restrictions made it possible for the same Assembly that passed the Declaration soon to level criminal charges of '*lèse-nation*' against its own members for challenging its authority.[22] The Revolution's human rights politics, in other words, were strongly shaped by the new concepts of the nation that were emerging at the same time.

Early twenty-first-century conceptions of human rights differ in some important ways from those of the French Revolution. Most importantly, human rights are today commonly held to represent limits on the sovereign powers of states. Abuses of these rights may be held to justify armed international intervention, even the overthrow of the government in question (as elaborated in the so-called doctrine of 'responsibility to protect'). It has been argued that 'human rights politics' as we understand the phrase today, actually only dates from the 1960s and 1970s.[23] And to the extent that contemporary interventionist politics has a genealogy stretching back to the eighteenth century, it lies less in the French Declaration than in international efforts to end the slave trade. Even the French Revolutionary decree abolishing slavery, in 1794, explicitly limited its enforcement to French colonies. French soldiers in the Caribbean did *not* free slaves in occupied enemy territory.[24]

But when it comes to the Revolution's long-term legacies in the domain of human rights, just as in 1789, the larger political context matters more than the Declaration's precise contents. As Lynn Hunt has noted, the Declaration 'transformed everyone's language virtually overnight', and connected the cause of human rights more closely to the French Revolution than to any other event in world history.[25] In the United States, and the other new states of the Americas, the need to guarantee rights provided a justification for revolution, but the principal goal of revolution was independence. In France, rights were both justification *and* goal. The Declaration of 1789, quite simply, provided the French Revolution with its explicit purpose. Moreover the act of declaration itself, carried out in a dramatic and impressive manner, henceforth dominated worldwide discussion of revolutionary events (as Tom Paine soon confirmed by titling his great rejoinder to Edmund Burke *The Rights of Man*). The Declaration formed part of the first French Revolutionary constitution, and most subsequent French constitutions either contained their own declaration of rights, or made reference, as the current French constitution does, to the text of 1789.[26]

The establishment of human rights as the goal of revolutionary action also provided women and minority groups with an obvious means of holding the Revolution, and its successor movements, up to their own self-proclaimed standards. It only took two years for Olympe de Gouges to reply to the Declaration with her *Declaration of the Rights of Woman*, to be followed a year later by Mary Wollstonecraft's *A Vindication of the Rights of Woman*. Not a few Revolutionaries also quickly noted the monumental hypocrisy of declaring 'all men are created free and equal in rights' while allowing over 700,000 human beings to be held in bondage in French colonies (more than in the United States at the time). More successfully than these two groups, French Jews referred to the Declaration when making their claim to full civil rights, which the Assembly soon granted them. The Revolution, in short, stands as one of the most important sources and models for groups insisting that universal human rights apply to all humans.[27]

Meanwhile, if the establishment of new political structures remains symbiotically connected to the act of declaring rights, this connection is itself an important legacy of the French Revolution. It is no coincidence that the powers that came together in the aftermath of the Second World War immediately felt the need to incorporate into their enterprise a Universal Declaration of Human Rights, issued in 1948, whose rhetoric closely echoes the Declaration of 1789. The 1948 Declaration, in turn, has provided the touchstone of legitimation for the human rights politics that have emerged since the 1970s—both in questions of humanitarian intervention, and in the monitoring of human rights abuses by non-governmental organizations such as Human Rights Watch and Amnesty International. In this sense, the existence of a widely acknowledged standard against which to criticize human rights abuses still owes a great deal to the National Assembly's grand gesture of 1789.[28]

WAR AND PEACE

From some perspectives it might seem as if the French Revolutionary Wars, far from leaving lasting conceptual legacies, marked the last gasp of a pre-modern age of international relations. After all, the French armies of the 1790s fought with weapons that had evolved only incrementally since the seventeenth century, and that would soon be cast aside by the innovations of the Industrial Revolution. As Albert Sorel observed many years ago, the territorial goals they pursued followed quite directly from those of the French monarchy. It has even been argued that the Revolutionary and Napoleonic Wars, taken together, marked the last paroxysm in a period of anarchic, brutal European warfare, before the coming of a long peace, and more stable international order, with the Congress of Vienna.[29]

Yet in several crucial ways, the Revolution did in fact mark a break with earlier ways of thinking about war and peace, while presaging a modern age of ideological warfare, and even 'total war'. Making this point, of course, does not mean holding the Revolutionaries themselves responsible for the horrors of modern warfare. It means simply that they participated in a larger political and cultural shift which led, quite against their conscious intentions, in this direction.

The Revolution's first great innovation in the international realm came in May 1790, when the Assembly voted to incorporate into the constitution a resolution that became known as the 'Declaration of Peace to the World': 'The French nation renounces the undertaking of any wars aimed at conquest, and will never employ its forces against the liberty of any people.'[30] This marked the first official sanction given by any European state to what might be termed 'Enlightened pacifism'. Unlike earlier, predominantly religious varieties of pacifism, enlightened pacifism was grounded in secular theories of 'stadial' historical change. Its adherents held that once states had moved into modern, 'commercial' stages of history, peaceful values of politeness and sociability would replace older ones of martial valour. War would become both anachronistic and counter-productive, and so vanish from the earth. Within two years, France would seemingly violate this pledge by declaring war on Austria and Prussia. The mostly-Girondin advocates of war justified the move as a necessary, pre-emptive strike to protect against imminent attack.

Yet in the build-up to war, and still more after the actual start of hostilities, these advocates did not always come off as entirely reluctant warriors. To the contrary, they also sometimes presented the conflict as a welcome one that would rejuvenate the French nation, cleansing it of poisons. 'Peace', Madame Roland wrote to a friend in 1791, 'is taking us backwards. We will only be regenerated by blood.' Others saw an opportunity for waging a universal war of liberation. 'This expiatory war', declared the radical republican Charles-Philippe Ronsin in a popular 1791 stage play, 'will renew the face of the world, and plant the standard of liberty in the palaces of kings.' French war propaganda sometimes took on an decidedly apocalyptic tone. The war, as General Charles-François Dumouriez told the National Convention in October of 1792, would be 'the last war', a great, final spasm of bloodshed that would pave the way for perpetual peace.[31]

Given these attitudes, and the increasingly vast ideological gulf between revolutionary France and its adversaries, it is no surprise that the actual conflict soon took on a very different character from the so-called 'cabinet wars' of the old regime. This was a war in which both sides openly called, not merely for the defeat, but for the overthrow of the opposing governments. It was a war in which each side demonized the other as monstrous barbarians, to such an extreme degree that in the spring of 1794 the Convention ordered its forces to take no British or Hanoverian prisoners (French commanders, thankfully, failed to comply).[32] It was a war which would, very much like revolutionary politics itself, fall into a spiral of radicalization which could only end with the collapse of one side or the other.

Parts of this history remained influential for most of the modern period, but have largely disappeared today. A faith in the regenerative, cleansing powers of war, widely shared in the Western world on the eve of the First World War, was largely scourged out of Western culture by the carnage that followed (although the Nazis desperately tried to recover it). The development of nuclear weapons, and then the emergence of the United States as the predominant superpower after the Cold War, have removed the conditions under which a 'total war' similar to the two world wars could take place. The idea of a war for universal liberation, so present in Marxist rhetoric from the mid-nineteenth into the mid-twentieth century, largely evaporated with the collapse of Communism.

But the belief that the progress of civilization will eventually render war both anachronistic and counter-productive remains a widely accepted postulate of the human sciences. A steady stream of popularizing (and best-selling) books has predicted war's necessary and perhaps even imminent disappearance, from Norman Angell's colossal success *The Great Illusion* on the eve of the First World War, down to Steven Pinker's recent *The Better Angels of Our Nature*.[33] These attitudes have, ironically, made it increasingly difficult, in the modern period, to see warfare as an ordinary, unexceptional instrument of state policy, pursued for specific, limited ends. We have instead witnessed a tendency, frighteningly intensified in the age of nuclear weapons and terrorism, to see every episode of war portrayed by political leaders in apocalyptic terms as a crusade against ultimate evil. Hence the tendency of Western leaders, and especially American presidents to denounce their enemies as new 'Hitlers', and for supporters of war to damn their opponents as 'appeasers' willing to follow the path of Chamberlain and Daladier in 1938.

This contemporary culture of war reflects a history that extends well beyond the French Revolution itself, to the Enlightenment, and to the entire age of democratic revolutions. Nonetheless, it was the French Revolution in which these features of the culture first crystallized, and were first officially endorsed by a sovereign political regime. So in this sense, contemporary attitudes towards war and peace remain heavily marked by the French Revolutionary legacy.

Political Ideology

One of the most obvious lexical legacies of the French Revolution is 'ideology'. The word was coined by the prominent intellectual and liberal noble Antoine Destutt de Tracy (1754–1836), in a series of lectures delivered at the newly created National Institute between 1796 and 1798. A philosophical heir to Locke and Condillac, Destutt defined ideology as the science which traced how sense impressions of the external world, entering the human mind, led to the formation of ideas. He hoped it would become the basis for grammar, education, logic, and morality, and take its place at the heart of a new French school curriculum. Elaborated at great length in a work he called *Elements of Ideology*, it was ridiculed by Napoleon as an 'obscure metaphysics'. John Adams was even less impressed, when informed about it by Thomas Jefferson: 'What does it mean? [...] Does it mean Idiotism? The Science of Non compos Menticism? The Science of Lunacy?'[34]

Clearly, Destutt's concept bears only a very partial resemblance to the later, more familiar concept of 'ideology' as a system of ideas that links an analysis of social conditions to a programme of political action. It is just as far from Marx's notion of 'ideology' as a system of ideas that serves as a mask for particular social interests. In fact, it would be easy to conclude that the word's appearance during the Revolution was little more than a coincidence.

Yet in some important ways, the Revolutionaries created the conceptual elements out of which later generations would forge what we now think of as 'ideological politics'. I will here point to three. First was the habit, first adopted during the period of the National Assembly (1789–91) of seeing political life as a single spectrum of belief, stretching from 'left' (and indeed 'the extremity of the left') to 'right'.[35] More than the terms 'left' and 'right' themselves, this literally one-dimensional view of politics had a crucial effect in structuring modern ideological politics. It allows ideologues to cast themselves as 'correctly' placed on the spectrum while reducing disagreement with their views to simple 'deviation' in one direction or another. Robespierre demonstrated the utility of this approach with his constant positioning of himself between the 'twin shoals' of 'moderantism' and 'excess', personified by the *indulgents* and the *Hébertistes*.[36] Lenin and Stalin would follow the same path with their attacks on 'left deviationism' and 'right deviationism' in the early Soviet Union. Similarly, in 1953 Mao Zedong instructed the Chinese Communist Politburo: 'Do not depart from this general line, otherwise "Left" or Right mistakes will occur.' Just as easily and effectively, ideologues can pronounce the principle of 'no enemies to the right' (or left)—a strategy notably adopted in the early twenty-first century by the 'Tea Party' faction of the Republican Party in the United States.[37]

Second, the Revolution saw an efflorescence of clubs, lobbies, and pressure groups which emerged to advocate both for particular issues or for a more general set of political principles. Among the earliest of these were the anti-slavery Society of the Friends of the Blacks, and its opponent, the pro-slavery Colonial Committee of Saint-Domingue, both founded in 1788, which provided what Marcel Dorigny has called a new sort of 'political apprenticeship'.[38] These were both soon overshadowed, however, by the various incarnations of the Jacobin Club. It not only had at least 6,000 sister clubs in France itself, but also formally affiliated with hundreds of political clubs and societies in Western Europe, the Americas, and even India.[39] In this extraordinary reach, and the extraordinary effectiveness in the sphere of Revolutionary politics, the Jacobins created a model of extra-parliamentary—and indeed, extra-national—political action without precedent in world history. Whether or not the Jacobins constituted a modern 'political party', they served as a model that later revolutionary parties would build on. Lenin, let it be remembered famously defined a revolutionary Socialist as 'a Jacobin indissolubly connected with the organization of the proletariat'.[40]

Finally, it should be noted that from the very start, these new political forms in the Revolution engendered a reaction against politics itself—a desire to resolve all political differences in a single, consensual, 'pragmatic' or 'objective' programme and form of government. Pierre Serna has keenly characterized this reaction as a 'politics of the extreme center', and has traced its continuity through French history down to the present day.[41] One of its most systematic early manifestations, in fact, was Destutt de Tracy's programme of 'ideology', which, from a modern point of view, looks distinctly anti-ideological. But the quest for a 'pragmatic' politics that can enter into force once ideologies have exhausted themselves has spread far beyond France. It arguably reached its height in the decades after the Second World War, when Albert Camus advocated the 'end of ideologies', and liberals across the West attempted to instantiate a broad consensus around the institutions of free-market democracy and the welfare state.[42] In 1960, a prominent American social theorist could call ideology 'an irretrievably fallen word', and suggest that the great ideologies of the twentieth century had reached a point of 'exhaustion'.[43] Today, his judgements seem entirely vindicated. Around the globe, most prominent political thinkers and actors explicitly reject the label 'ideological' for themselves. Yet that very gesture is, in its way, a legacy of the French Revolution.

REVOLUTION

Of all the conceptual legacies of the French Revolution, however, the clearest, and arguably the most important is the modern concept of 'revolution' itself. As Keith Michael Baker has conclusively demonstrated, before the late eighteenth century, the word 'revolution', in Western political parlance, generally denoted a relatively sudden, unpredictable, and uncontrollable upheaval.[44] Most often, the word was used to describe a violent change of dynasty. Eighteenth-century historians commonly started book titles with the phrase 'The Revolutions of ... ' Revolutions were things that happened to people, not things that people themselves were seen as capable of consciously directing. The word does not appear in the American Declaration of Independence, and in 1777, John Adams could write to his son about 'the late Revolution in our government', implying that the event was already finished and in the past.[45]

As France's old regime began to crumble in 1789, observers immediately started to refer to what was going on as a 'revolution' in the traditional fashion. But within a matter of months, they began speaking of it less as a sudden and cataclysmic *event*, than as an ongoing *process*. And soon, they went even further, to present 'the' revolution as something that could be controlled and directed. Baker characterizes the shift as one from revolution as 'fact' to revolution as 'act'. It was at this moment that the noun and adjective 'revolutionary' came into being, referring to people or actions that actively drive revolutions forward. In 1792, Robespierre renamed the executive committee of Paris's municipal government the 'General Revolutionary Council', making it the first political institution in history to bear such a title.

Dan Edelstein has added a further fascinating wrinkle to the story, noting that by 1792–93, 'the revolution' seemed to be taking on a life of its own, becoming, in the eyes of its advocates, a quasi-mythic force, and a source of legitimacy. After the fall of Louis XVI in 1792, there were calls to put the king on trial. Louis-Antoine Saint-Just, however, insisted that the people had already delivered a verdict through their revolutionary action. Any procedure that might exonerate the king therefore amounted to putting the Revolution itself on trial. This proposal fell on deaf ears, but a year later, Saint-Just made a remarkable speech successfully demanding that the ruling National Convention formally suspend the new constitution it had just approved, and to declare the government 'revolutionary' until the end of hostilities.[46]

This new concept both reflected the volatile nature of events in France, and also helped drive them forward, by giving the political actors of the day a way to see 'revolutions' as exceptional historical moments in which ordinary practices and principles could be suspended. Robespierre developed an elaborate theory distinguishing between ordinary 'constitutional' government, whose role was to govern a republic, and 'revolutionary' government, whose role was to found it. In the latter, he argued, the state needed far greater leeway, both to protect its citizens and ensure that institutions would be given a durable form.[47] 'Revolution' was not just becoming a process, but a utopian one which might extend into the future, indefinitely. The concept could therefore provide a justification for everything from the Revolutionary calendar, to ambitious new programmes for universal education and charity, to the attempts to eradicate Christianity. It encouraged the revolutionaries to think that they might be able to remould human nature itself, creating what Robespierre called, in his final, chiliastic months in power, 'a new species' that had leapt 2,000 years ahead of the rest of the human race.

It is hard to exaggerate the hold which this new model of revolution exerted over imaginations throughout the world during the next two centuries. In country after country, generations of would-be revolutionaries plotted to take power and instigate upheavals of similar, or even greater ambition to what they had seen in France. Starting in the mid-nineteenth century, the model was potently combined with socialist visions of history as a story of class struggle, but the idea of revolution as an ongoing, consciously directed process with utopian goals remained much the same. In Russia, China, southeast Asia, Latin America, and the Middle East, self-proclaimed 'revolutionary' regimes took power with goals of nothing less than transforming human beings into something new and better. Such a goal might even entail what Leon Trotsky would call the 'permanent revolution'. To be sure, very few of these revolutionaries wanted to directly imitate events in France. Most of them saw the French Revolution itself as a failure, and only in France itself—especially at the time of the Paris Commune of 1871—did would-be revolutionaries dream of literally replaying the 'script' of 1789. But these other revolutionaries nonetheless remained deeply indebted to the concept of revolution, as the French experience had transformed it.[48]

Only in the late twentieth century, as I noted at the start of this chapter, did the idea of large-scale, radical revolution lose its allure across most of the globe. The failures and frustrations of the revolutionary regimes in the Soviet Union and China in particular, with their unfathomably vast death tolls, led to a moment in which Francis Fukuyama could plausibly claim that the Western model of free-market democracy had gained hegemony over all its ideological rivals (whether or not this triumph amounted to the 'end of history', as he also claimed, was another matter entirely).[49] While revolutions might still be considered necessary to topple tyrants and to implement major political reforms, the idea of a massive, ongoing, and perhaps utopian process that the radical French revolutionaries envisaged has largely lost its appeal. In this sense, the age of revolutions is over, and for the foreseeable future, at least, no new Pitirim Sorokin is likely to study the history of the Girondins and the Jacobins and muse about how 'history repeats itself'.

Yet if 'revolution' is disappearing from global politics, it remains a central concept of global culture, society, and economics. Indeed, in the early twenty-first century we speak of revolutions more than ever. We speak of scientific revolutions, of the digital revolution, of revolutions in bio-technology, and for that matter of the 'romance revolution', of a 'revolution in marketing', even an 'oat revolution' (the phrase is trademarked). There is a perfume called Revolution; also a cell phone.[50] One could look at this evidence and conclude that the word has lost its meaning almost entirely. Yet one can also conclude from it that revolution remains the world's single most important metaphor of modernity, the way that modern people express their experience of rapid, constant, barely controllable, exhilarating, but also terrifying change. And 'revolution' in this sense is very much the legacy of what transpired in France at the end of the eighteenth century, for this new experience of overpowering change was one of the things that participants in, and observers of the French Revolution found most remarkable about it. Frequently, they compared the experience to the compression of time itself. Just as Robespierre believed the French had squeezed two millennia of progress into five years, Chateaubriand, looking back on the events many years later, wrote that the fall of the Bastille was separated from Waterloo by many centuries.[51] To this day, when we seek to describe how it feels, and what it means to experience time in this way, we recognize the crucial ways in which what we call modernity did in fact begin with the French Revolution.

Notes

1. Quoted in Dimitry Shlapentokh, *The French Revolution and the Russian Anti-Democratic Tradition: A Case of False Consciousness* (New Brunswick, 1997), 234.
2. Jacek Kuroń, 'Une Révolution polonaise?' *Libération* (4 August 1989), 4.
3. Timothy Garton Ash, *The Magic Lantern: The Revolution of '89 Witnessed in Warsaw, Budapest, Berlin and Prague* (New York, 1993 [1990]), 14.
4. See David A. Bell, 'Inglorious Revolutions', *The National Interest* 129 (January–February, 2014), 31–8; Reinhard Schulze, 'Vom Anfang und Ende der Revolution—Fünf Bermerkungen mit Blick auf die arabische Welt', *Journal of Modern European History* 11, no. 2 (May, 2013), 220–42.
5. 'Déclaration des droits de l'homme et du citoyen de 1789', www.assemblee-nationale.fr/histoire/dudh/1789.asp (accessed 23 January 2014).
6. On the French Declaration, see Stéphane Rials, *La declaration des droits de l'homme et du citoyen de 1789* (Paris, 1989); more generally the essays in Dale Van Kley, *The French Idea of Freedom: The Old Regime and the Declaration of Rights of 1789* (Stanford, 1994). On these issues in general, see Lynn Hunt, *Inventing Human Rights: A History* (New York, 2007); Samuel Moyn, *The Last Utopia: Human Rights in History* (Cambridge, MA, 2010); Dan Edelstein, 'Enlightenment Rights Talk', *Journal of Modern History* (forthcoming); Kate Tunstall (ed.), *Self-Evident Truths?: Human Rights and the Enlightenment* (London, 2012).
7. See David A. Bell, *The Cult of the Nation in France: Inventing Nationalism, 1680–1800* (Cambridge, MA, 2001), esp. 1–21.
8. Bell, *Cult of the Nation*, 140–97; Marie-Vic Ozouf-Marignier, *La formation des départements. La représentation du territoire français à la fin du 18e siècle* (Paris, 1989); Mona Ozouf, *Festivals and the French Revolution*, trans. Alan Sheridan (Cambridge, MA, 1991).
9. See on these questions David A. Bell, *The First Total War: Napoleon's Europe and the Birth of Warfare As We Know It* (Boston, 2007), 263–301; more generally, the still useful survey

by Hugh Seton-Watson, *Nations and States: An Enquiry into the Origins of Nations and the Politics of Nationalism* (London, 1977).

10. See Eric D. Weitz, 'From the Vienna to the Paris System: International Politics and the Entangled Histories of Human Rights, Forced Deportations, and Civilizing Missions', *American Historical Review* 113, no. 5 (December 2008), 1313–43; Eric D. Weitz, 'Self-Determination: How a German Enlightenment Idea Became the Slogan of National Liberation and a Human Right', *American Historical Review* (forthcoming).

11. See Edward James Kolla, 'Legality, Legitimacy, and the Will of the People: The French Revolution and the Transformation of International Law, 1789–92', unpublished PhD dissertation (Johns Hopkins University, 2010); Peter Sahlins, 'Natural Frontiers Revisited: France's Boundaries since the Seventeenth Century', *American Historical Review* 95, no. 5 (December 1990), 1423–51.

12. See notably on this subject Patrick Weil, *How to be French. Nationality in the Making since 1789*, trans. Catherine Porter (Durham, 2008).

13. J. G. A. Pocock, *The Machiavellian Moment: Florentine Political Thought and the Atlantic Republican Tradition* (Princeton, 1975); Johnson Kent Wright, *A Classical Republican in Eighteenth-Century France: The Political Thought of Mably* (Stanford, 1997); Keith Michael Baker, 'Transformations of Classical Republicanism in Eighteenth-Century France', *Journal of Modern History* 73, no. 1 (March 2001), 32–53.

14. Montesquieu, *The Spirit of the Laws*, trans. and ed. Anne M. Cohler, Basia Carolyn Miller and Harold Samuel Stone (Cambridge, 1989), 21–30; James Madison, 'The Federalist No. 10' (1787), www.constitution.org/fed/federa10.htm (accessed 23 January 2014).

15. 'Constitution de l'An XII—Empire—28 floréal An XII', www.conseil-constitutionnel. fr/conseil-constitutionnel/francais/la-constitution/les-constitutions-de-la-france/ constitution-de-l-an-xii-empire-28-floreal-an-xii.5090.html (accessed 23 January 2014).

16. For a general survey, see John W. Maynor, *Republicanism in the Modern World* (Cambridge, 2003).

17. Keith Michael Baker and Dan Edelstein (eds), *Scripting Revolution* (Stanford, forthcoming).

18. See Claude Nicolet, *L'idée républicaine en France: Essai d'histoire critique* (Paris, 1982). For a brief exposition of the distinctiveness of the 'French model' see Régis Debray, *La République expliquée á ma fille* (Paris, 1998).

19. On these issues, see especially Hunt, *Inventing Human Rights*; Moyn, *The Last Utopia*; Edelstein, 'Enlightenment Rights Talk'.

20. Stéphane Rials, *La declaration des droits de l'homme et du citoyen de 1789* (Paris, 1989); more generally the essays in Van Kley, *The French Idea of Freedom*.

21. See Marcel Gauchet, *La Révolution des droits de l'homme* (Paris, 1989).

22. 'Déclaration des droits de l'homme et du citoyen', preamble; see Charles Walton, *Policing Public Opinion in the French Revolution: The Culture of Calumny and the Problem of Free Speech* (New York, 2009), esp. 97–136.

23. This is the argument of Moyn, in *The Last Utopia*.

24. See Jeremy D. Popkin, *You Are All Free: The Haitian Revolution and the Abolition of Slavery* (Cambridge, 2010).

25. Hunt, *Inventing Human Rights*, 133.

26. Thomas Paine, *Rights of Man, Being an Answer to Mr. Burke's Attack on the French Revolution* (London, 1791); 'Texte intégral de la Constitution du 4 octobre 1958 en vigueur', www.conseil-constitutionnel.fr/conseil-constitutionnel/francais/la-constitution/

la-constitution-du-4-octobre-1958/texte-integral-de-la-constitution-du-4-octobre-1958-en-vigueur.5074.html (accessed 23 January 2014).

27. Olympe de Gouges, *Déclaration des droits de la femme et de la citoyenne* (Paris, 1791); Mary Wollstonecraft, *A Vindication of the Rights of Woman: With Strictures on Political and Moral Subjects* (London, 1792) On these issues, see Shanti Marie Singham, 'Betwixt Cattle and Men: Jews, Blacks, and Women, and the Declaration of the Rights of Man', in Van Kley (ed.), *The French Idea of Freedom*, 114–53.

28. See Hunt, *Inventing Human Rights*, 174–214.

29. Albert Sorel, *L'Europe et la Révolution française*, 8 vols. (Paris, 1885–1904); Paul Schroeder, *The Transformation of European Politics, 1763–1848* (Oxford, 1996).

30. Quoted in Bell, *The First Total War*, 105. In general, on these debates and the intellectual background, see Bell, *The First Total War*, pp. 52–119.

31. Quotes from Bell, *The First Total War*, 117, 115, 1.

32. See Sophie Wahnich, *L'impossible citoyen: L'étranger dans le discours de la Révolution française* (Paris, 1997), 237–346.

33. Norman Angell, *The Great Illusion* (London, 1910); Steven Pinker, *The Better Angels of Our Nature: Why Violence has Declined* (New York, 2011). See also Bell, *The First Total War*, 302–17.

34. Antoine Destutt de Tracy, *Élémens d'idéologie*, 4 vols (Paris, 1817–18); Napoleon Bonaparte, quoted in Frederick Copleston, *Nineteenth and Twentieth Century French Philosophy* (London, 1975), 20; John Adams, quoted in Joseph J. Ellis, *Founding Brothers: The Revolutionary Generation* (New York, 2002), 238.

35. See notably Marcel Gauchet, 'La droite et la gauche', in Pierre Nora (ed.), *Les lieux de mémoire III: Les France*, 3 vols (Paris, 1992), I, 394–467.

36. Maximilien Robespierre, *Rapport sur les principes du gouvernement révolutionnaire* (Paris, 1794).

37. Mao Zedong, 'Refute Right Deviationist Views That Depart From the General Line' (1953), www.marxists.org/reference/archive/mao/selected-works/volume-5/mswv5_28.htm (accessed 23 January 2014). See, for instance, Ed Kilgore, 'No Enemies to the Right: The Defining Element of the GOP Primary', *The New Republic* (25 February 2012), www.newrepublic.com/article/101118/michigan-republican-primary (accessed 22 January 2014).

38. Marcel Dorigny, 'La Société des Amis des Noirs: Antiesclavagisme et lobby colonial á la fin du siécle des Lumières (1788–1792)', in Marcel Dorigny and Bernard Gainot (eds), *La Société des Amis des Noirs, 1788–1799* (Paris, 1998), 40.

39. Jean Boutrier and Philippe Boutry, *Atlas de la Révolution française 6: Les sociétés politiques* (Paris, 1992).

40. Vladimir Lenin, *One Step Forward, Two Steps Back* (1904), cited in Robert Mayer, 'Lenin and the Jacobin Identity in Russia', *Studies in East European Thought* 51 (1999), 127–54, at 127.

41. Pierre Serna, *La République des girouettes: 1789–1815 et au-delà. Une anomalie politique: La France de l'extrême centre* (Paris, 2005).

42. Albert Camus, 'Ni Victimes ni Bourreaux', in *Actuelles I: Ecrits politiques (Chroniques 1944–48)* (Paris, 1950), 127.

43. Daniel Bell, *The End of Ideology: On the Exhaustion of Political Ideas in the Fifties* (New York, 1988 [1960]), 406, 402. Bell was the father of the author of the present article.

44. Keith Michael Baker, 'Revolution 1.0', *Journal of Modern European History* 11, no. 2 (May 2013), 187–219; earlier findings appeared in Keith Michael Baker, 'Inventing the French

Revolution', in *Inventing the French Revolution: Essays on French Political Culture in the Eighteenth Century* (Cambridge, 1990), 203–23.

45. Quoted in Bell, 'Inglorious Revolutions', 32–3.
46. Dan Edelstein, 'Do We Want a Revolution without Revolution? Reflections on Political Authority', *French Historical Studies* 35, no. 2 (Spring 2012), 269–89.
47. Robespierre, *Rapport*.
48. This history is thoroughly analysed by the essays collected in Baker and Edelstein, *Scripting Revolution*.
49. Francis Fukuyama, 'The End of History?' *The National Interest* 16 (Summer 1989), 3–18.
50. Carol Thurston, *The Romance Revolution: Erotic Novels for Women and the Quest for a New Sexual Identity* (Champaign, 1987); Tom LaForge, 'Marketing revolution: the rise of the relationship economy', *The Guardian* (9 October 2013), www.theguardian.com/sustainable-business/social-impact-brand (accessed 22 January 2014); www.betteroats.com (accessed 22 January 2014).
51. Quoted in Antoine Casanova, *Napoléon et la pensée de son temps: Une histoire intellectuelle singulière* (Paris, 2000), 19.

Selected Reading

Baker, Keith Michael, 'Transformations of Classical Republicanism in Eighteenth-Century France', *Journal of Modern History* 73, no. 1 (March 2001), 32–53.

Baker, Keith Michael and Edelstein, Dan (eds), *Scripting Revolution* (Stanford, forthcoming).

Bell, David A., *The Cult of the Nation in France: Inventing Nationalism, 1680–1800* (Cambridge, MA, 2001).

Bell, David A., *The First Total War: Napoleon's Europe and the Birth of Warfare As We Know It* (Boston, 2007).

Bell, David A., 'Inglorious Revolutions', *The National Interest* 129 (January–February 2014), 31–8.

Best, Geoffrey (ed.), *The Permanent Revolution: The French Revolution and its Legacy, 1789–1989* (Chicago, 1988).

Edelstein, Dan, 'Do We Want a Revolution without Revolution? Reflections on Political Authority', *French Historical Studies* 35, no. 2 (Spring 2012), 269–89.

Fehér, Ferenc (ed.), *The French Revolution and the Birth of Modernity* (Berkeley, 1990).

Furet, François, *Marx et la Révolution française* (Paris, 1986).

Furet, François, *Le passé d'une illusion: Essai sur l'idée communiste au XXe siécle* (Paris, 1995).

Furet, François and Ozouf, Mona (eds), *The Transformation of Political Culture 1789–1848* (Oxford, 1989).

Hunt, Lynn, *Inventing Human Rights: A History* (New York, 2007).

Klaits, Joseph and Haltzel, Michael H. (eds), *The Global Ramifications of the French Revolution* (Cambridge, 1994).

Maynor, John W., *Republicanism in the Modern World* (Cambridge, 2003).

Moyn, Samuel, *The Last Utopia: Human Rights in History* (Cambridge, MA, 2010).

Shlapentokh, Dimitry, *The French Revolution and the Russian Anti-Democratic Tradition: A Case of False Consciousness* (New Brunswick, 1997).

INDEX

....

9 780198 845942